This new edition of *Global Politics* is cert[illegible] tudents. Edkins and Zefuss clearly know how to grab studen[illegible] them to think and then rethink. Every chapter here, I'n[illegible] onderful classroom discussions. *Global Politics* is sr[illegible], lively and gritty.

[illegible]a Enloe, author of Seri[illegible] Crashes

If you thought the first edition was amazing, wait until you read this! *Global Politics 2.0* is the most intellectually rewarding textbook in the field to-date. The revolutionary question-based approach now challenges, provokes, and inspires across an even wider range of issues in contemporary political life. This version of Edkins and Zehfuss, with its unrivalled line-up of world-leading scholars, sets the bar even higher—it is a must-read for students and lecturers alike.

Nick Vaughan-Williams, Reader in International Security,
University of Warwick, UK.

Unlike the majority of IR manuals, this book does not try to domesticate the ways we learn and teach global politics. Instead of spoon-feeding students with theories and concepts, it invites students to think about the international by focusing on the very questions that drive them to study world politics. I wish a manual like this had been available back when I was an undergraduate student.

Erica Simone A. Resende, Rio de Janeiro
State University, Brazil.

This engaging text treats readers as intelligent adults, inviting them to apply their own observations and experiences to the issues it addresses. Long case examples illustrating concepts like nationalism (China), and democracy (Argentina) let readers see how the moving parts of theories operate in practice. The chapter on the financial crisis is accessible, incorporates several tiny case examples from Iceland to Occupy, and carefully distinguishes among the contributions of states and other actors to what is happening. No text covers everything but what is examined here invites readers to continue their investigations, and provides tools to do just that.

Mary Ann Tetreault, Distinguished Professor Emerita,
Trinity University, San Antonio TX.

In my twelve years of teaching introduction-level courses in Globalization and IR, I have never seen a textbook come close to 'Global Politics'. The book brings an unprecedented degree of attention to the challenge of balancing theoretical rigor with facility of access. Many books will recite 'the theories' but none will get your students to think so deeply about the questions of our time. Power, subjectivity, sovereignty, security, neoliberalism, it's all here. This new edition adds fresh and relevant material addressing the Internet, global revolt, and the everyday politics of the *ongoing financial crisis.*

Nicholas Kiersey, Assistant Professor in Political Science,
Ohio University, USA.

Global Politics: A New Introduction makes international politics and theorising accessible and intelligible for students. It gives equal weight to theoretical approaches and case studies, and the centrality of questions as a basis for inquiry is both engaging and unique.

Christine Agius, Lecturer in Politics, Swinburne University of Technology, Australia.

Global Politics offers students analysis of the most pressing issues of today: climate change, migration, economic upheaval, resistance, inequality, and conflict – while also placing contemporary global politics in the context of histories of colonialism, nationalism, capitalism and statehood. It is an invaluable resource in helping students think through complex concepts in new and accessible ways, giving them illustrative examples about foundational topics in global politics, from democracy, ethics and human rights, to political economy, and war and peace. Moving beyond conventional stories about the nature of international relations, *Global Politics* captures the richness of the study and practice of international affairs today.

Alison Howell, Assistant Professor, Department of Political Science, Rutgers University (Newark), USA.

GLOBAL POLITICS

A NEW INTRODUCTION

The second edition of *Global Politics: A New Introduction* continues to provide a completely original way of teaching and learning about world politics. The book engages directly with the issues in global politics that students are most interested in, helping them to understand the key questions and theories and also to develop a critical and inquiring perspective.

Completely revised and updated throughout, the second edition also offers additional chapters on key issues such as environmental politics, nationalism, the internet, democratization, colonialism, the financial crisis, political violence and human rights.

Global Politics:

- examines the most significant issues in global politics – from war, peacebuilding, terrorism, security, violence, nationalism and authority to poverty, development, postcolonialism, human rights, gender, inequality, ethnicity and what we can do to change the world;
- offers chapters written to a common structure which is ideal for teaching and learning and features a key question, an illustrative example, general responses and broader issues;
- integrates theory and practice throughout the text, by presenting theoretical ideas and concepts in conjunction with a global range of historical and contemporary case studies.

Drawing on theoretical perspectives from a broad range of disciplines including international relations, political theory, postcolonial studies, sociology, geography, peace studies and development, this innovative textbook is essential reading for all students of global politics and international relations.

Jenny Edkins is Professor of International Politics at Aberystwyth University, UK.

Maja Zehfuss is Professor of International Politics and Associate Dean for Postgraduate Research in the Faculty of Humanities at the University of Manchester, UK.

There is a Companion Website at www.routledge.com/cw/edkins/ containing substantial additional material and resources for instructors and students.

Features include:

- **About the book**: More information about the book, editors, contributors and the table of contents.
- **Sample chapters**: Several complete chapters fully downloadable as PDFs.
- **Useful weblinks**: Related websites suggested by contributors and organised by chapter.
- **Maps and tables**: Fully downloadable maps and tables used within the book. Organised by chapter and ideal for use with PowerPoint slides.
- **Interactive library**: A library of additional audio-visual material online suggested by the Publisher and organised by chapter. Updated regularly.
- **Journal articles for further reading**: Links to further articles by the contributors on related issues.
- **Audio files**: Downloadable audio files of interviews by the book's editors with several of the contributors exploring the challenges and issues raised by the text.

GLOBAL POLITICS

A NEW INTRODUCTION

Second edition

Edited by

Jenny Edkins and Maja Zehfuss

Routledge
Taylor & Francis Group
LONDON AND NEW YORK

First published 2008

This edition published 2014
by Routledge
2 Park Square, Milton Park, Abingdon, Oxon OX14 4RN

Simultaneously published in the USA and Canada
by Routledge
711 Third Avenue, New York, NY 10017

Routledge is an imprint of the Taylor & Francis Group, an informa business

British Library Cataloguing in Publication Data
A catalogue record for this book is available from the British Library

Library of Congress Cataloging in Publication Data
Global politics: a new introduction/edited by Jenny Edkins &
Maja Zehfuss. – 2nd ed.
p. cm.
Includes bibliographical references and index.
Geopolitics. 2. World politics. I. Edkins, Jenny. II. Zehfuss, Maja.
JC319.G595 2013
327—dc23 2012024065

ISBN: 978–0-415–68482–8 (hbk)
ISBN: 978–0-415–68481–1 (pbk)
ISBN: 978–0-203–07689–7 (ebk)

Typeset in Galliard and Scala Sans
by Florence Production Ltd, Stoodleigh, Devon, UK
Printed by Bell & Bain Ltd, Glasgow

Contents

Contributors

Louise Amoore is Professor and Deputy Head of Department in Geography at Durham University. Her current research interests include the techniques and technologies through which security decisions are made. She has been working on the risk-based projections of subjects that become risk indicators for security interventions – recently completing a four-year ESRC/NWO project 'Data Wars' with Marieke de Goede. She is the author of *Globalisation Contested: An International Political Economy of Work* (Manchester University Press 2002), the editor of *The Global Resistance Reader* (Routledge 2005) and the co-editor, with Marieke de Goede, of *Risk and the War on Terror* (Routledge 2008). Her new book *The Politics of Possibility: Risk and Security beyond Probability*, is to be published by Duke University Press in 2013.

Elena Barabantseva is a Lecturer in Chinese International Relations at the University of Manchester. Her recent research has been informed by a scholarly curiosity in what the historical and current processes of human mobility and cultural diversity reveal about nation-state, international order, sovereignty, citizenship and identity. She is the author of *Overseas Chinese, Ethnic Minorities and Nationalism: De-Centering China* (Routledge 2010), co-editor (with Claire Sutherland) of *Citizenship and Diaspora* (Routledge 2011) and co-editor (with William A. Callahan) of and contributor to *China Orders the World: Normative Soft Power and Foreign Policy* (Woodrow Wilson Center Press with Johns Hopkins University Press 2012). She is a fellow of the Higher Education Academy.

Roland Bleiker is Professor of International Relations at the University of Queensland. From 1986 to 1988 he worked in the Korean Demilitarized Zone as Chief of Office of the Swiss Delegation to the Neutral Nations Supervisory Commission. His most recent books are *Divided Korea: Toward a Culture of Reconciliation* (University of Minnesota Press 2005/2008), *Aesthetics and World Politics* (Palgrave 2009/2012) and, as co-editor, *Mediating Across Difference: Pacific and Asian Approaches to Security and Conflict* (University of Hawai'i Press 2010). Bleiker is currently working on a collaborative project that examines how images – and the emotions they generate – shape responses to humanitarian crises.

Joanna Bourke is Professor of History at Birkbeck College, University of London. She has published books on Irish history, gender and 'the body', the history of psychological thought, modern warfare, the emotions, sexual violence and the human/animal divide. Her most recent books are *Fear: A Cultural History* (Virago 2005), *Rape: A History* *from the 1860s to the Present* (Virago 2007) and *What It Means To Be Human* (Virago 2011). Her books have been translated into Chinese, Italian, Portuguese, Spanish, Catalan, Russian, Greek, Finnish and Turkish. *An Intimate History of Killing: Face-to-Face Killing in Twentieth Century Warfare* (Granta 1999) won the Fraenkel Prize in Contemporary History for 1998 and the Wolfson History Prize for 2000.

Paul Cammack is Professor of Global Political Economy in the Department of Asian and International Studies at City University Hong Kong. His work explores the governance of global capitalism from a classical Marxist perspective, with particular reference to the relationship between states, international institutions, and the logic of global capital. The recent focus of his research and teaching is on the G20, and the politics of social protection. He is author of *Capitalism and Democracy in the Third World* (Continuum 1997) and most recently of articles in *Antipode*, *Third World Quarterly* and the *Journal of Contemporary Asia*.

Simon Dalby is CIGI Chair in the Political Economy of Climate Change at the Balsillie School of International Affairs, Waterloo, Ontario. He was formerly Professor of Geography, Environmental Studies and Political Economy at Carleton University in Ottawa. He is coeditor of *Rethinking Geopolitics* (Routledge 1998), *The Geopolitics Reader* (Routledge 1998, 2006), the journal *Geopolitics*, and author of *Creating the Second Cold War* (Pinter and Guilford 1990), *Environmental Security* (University of Minnesota Press 2002) and *Security and Environmental Change* (Polity 2009).

Matt Davies is Lecturer in the School of Geography, Politics and Sociology at Newcastle University. He has also held positions in the Political Science Department, of Pennsylvania State University–Erie, York University (Toronto), and Wabash College, Crawfordsville, Indiana. He teaches on international political economy, the politics of culture, and the politics of Latin America. His books include *Poverty and the Production of World Politics: Unprotected Workers in the Global Political Economy* (with Magnus Ryner, 2006) and *International Political Economy and Mass Communication in Chile: National Intellectuals and Transnational Hegemony* (1999).

Carl Death is Senior Lecturer in International Political Economy at the University of Manchester. He is the author of *Governing Sustainable Development: Partnerships, Protests and Power at the World Summit* (London: Routledge, 2010). His research is located at the intersection of African politics and development (particularly post-apartheid South Africa), environmental politics and sustainable development discourse, and Foucauldian governmentality analysis. He has focused particularly upon the constitutive role of dissent, protest and resistance, and as such his research has drawn upon social movement theory. He explores these issues through case studies, most notably the 2002 Johannesburg World Summit on Sustainable Development.

Michael Dillon is Emeritus Professor of Politics at the University of Lancaster. He has published widely in international politics and security as well as in cultural and political theory. He is the author of *Politics of Security* (Routledge 1996), co-author of *The Liberal Way of War* (Routledge 2008), co-editor of *Foucault on Politics, Security and War* (Palgrave Macmillan 2008) and author of *Deconstructing International Politics* (2012). He is working on *Biopolitics of Security in the 21stt Century* for Routledge. He also co-edits the *Journal of Cultural Research*.

Roxanne Lynn Doty is Associate Professor in the Department of Political Science at Arizona State University. She is the author of *Imperial Encounters: The Politics of Representation in North-South Relations* (University of Minnesota Press 1996) and *Anti-Immigrantism in Western Democracies: Statecraft, Desire, and the Politics of Exclusion* (Routledge 2003). Her most recent book, *The Law into Their Own Hands: Immigration and the Politics of Exceptionalism*, was published by University of Arizona Press in 2009. Her current research interests include critical international relations theory, various border issues, identity, and the politics of academic writing.

Jenny Edkins is Professor of International Politics at Aberystwyth University, and has also taught at the University of Manchester and the Open University. Her publications include *Missing: Persons and Politics* (Cornell University Press 2011), *Trauma and the Memory of Politics* (Cambridge University Press 2003) and *Whose Hunger? Concepts of Famine, Practices of Aid* (University of Minnesota Press 2000, 2008). She is co-editor (with Nick Vaughan-Williams) of the Routledge book series *Interventions*, and co-organiser of the Gregynog Ideas Lab Summer School in PostInternational Politics.

Stuart Elden is Professor of Political Theory and Geography at the University of Warwick and the editor of the journal *Society and Space* (*Environment and Planning D*). He is the author of five books, including *Terror and Territory: The Spatial Extent of Sovereignty* (University of Minnesota Press 2009) and *The Birth of Territory* (University of Chicago Press 2013). He is currently working on projects on Shakespeare, Foucault and concepts of the world. He blogs at www.progressivegeographies.com.

M. I. Franklin is Reader in Global Media and Transnational Communications at Goldsmiths. Previous books include *Postcolonial Politics, the Internet, and Everyday Life: Pacific Traversals Online* (Routledge 2004), *Resounding International Relations: On Music, Culture and Politics* (Palgrave Macmillan 2005), and *Understanding Research: Coping with the Quantitative–Qualitative Divide* (Routledge 2012). Her latest book is *Digital Dilemmas: Power, Resistance and the Internet* (Oxford University Press 2013). A former Chair of the Feminist Theory and Gender Studies Section of the International Studies Association, she is currently Co-Chair of the Internet Rights and Principles Coalition at the UN Internet Governance Forum.

Marieke de Goede is Professor of Politics at the University of Amsterdam, where she co-directs the MSc programme 'The European Union in a Global Order'. She is currently conducting a research project called European Security Culture that examines and assesses anticipatory and preemptive security measures in Europe and their political implications. She is author of *Speculative Security: The Politics of Pursuing Terrorist Monies* (University of Minnesota Press 2012) and co-editor, with Louise Amoore, of *Risk and the War on Terror* (Routledge 2008). De Goede is associate editor of the journal *Security Dialogue* and a member of the Peace and Security committee of the Dutch Advisory Council on International Affairs (AIV) that advises the Dutch government.

Naeem Inayatullah is Professor of Politics at Ithaca College. He is co-author (with David Blaney) of *International Relations and the Problem of Difference* (Routledge 2004) and *Savage Economics* (Routledge 2010). He is co-editor (with Robin Riley) of *Interrogating Imperialism* (Palgrave 2006) and editor of *Autobiographical International*

Relations (Routledge 2011). He was the President of the Global Development section of the International Studies Association 2007–08.

Sankaran Krishna is Professor in the Department of Political Science at the University of Hawai'i in Manoa and his work so far has centred on nationalism, ethnic identity and conflict, identity politics, and postcolonial studies, located primarily around India and Sri Lanka. He teaches courses on critical comparative politics; nation/ethnicity and insecurity; states, citizens and subjects; the material economies of globalization; and global and Asia-Pacific politics. He is author of *Globalization and Postcolonialism: Hegemony and Resistance in the 21st Century* (Rowman and Littlefield 2009) and *Postcolonial Insecurities: India, Sri Lanka and the Question of Nationhood* (University of Minnesota Press 1999).

Debbie Lisle is a Senior Lecturer in International Politics and Cultural Studies in the School of Politics, International Studies and Philosophy at Queen's University Belfast. She is the author of *The Global Politics of Contemporary Travel Writing* (Cambridge University Press 2006) and has also written on contemporary art, graffiti, museums, war films, tourism and travel. In general, her research explores how global politics is represented in the cultural realm, and how audiences come to understand certain accepted 'truths' about their world. Her current research re-imagines the relationship between tourism and war by demonstrating how both practices are intimately connected.

Peter Mandaville is Associate Professor of Government and Politics and Director of the Ali Vural Ak Center for Islamic Studies at George Mason University and a Nonresident Senior Fellow at the Brookings Institution in Washington DC. He is the author of *Global Political Islam* (Routledge 2007) and *Transnational Muslim Politics: Reimagining the Umma* (Routledge 2001), as well as co-editor of the volumes *The Zen of International Relations* (Palgrave 2001), *Meaning and International Relations* (Routledge 2003), *Globalizing Religions* (Sage 2008) and *Politics from Afar: Transnational Diasporas and Networks* (Columbia University Press 2012). Much of his recent work has focused on the comparative study of religious authority and social movements in the Muslim world. He has also served in government as a member of the US Secretary of State's Policy Planning Staff (2011–12).

Kate Manzo is Senior Lecturer in International Development in the School of Geography, Politics and Sociology at the University of Newcastle. She is author of *Domination, Resistance and Social Change in South Africa: The Local Effects of Global Power* (Praeger 1992) and *Creating Boundaries: The Politics of Race and Nation* (Lynne Rienner 1996). Her current research interests include Africa in the politics of development, images of Africa in western media, and the iconography of climate change.

Anne Orford is the Michael D. Kirby Professor of International Law and an Australian Research Council Future Fellow at Melbourne Law School. Her publications include *International Authority and the Responsibility to Protect* (Cambridge University Press 2011), the edited collection *International Law and Its Others* (Cambridge University Press 2006) and *Reading Humanitarian Intervention* (Cambridge University Press 2003). She has held visiting positions at the universities of Gothenburg, Lund, New York University, and Paris 1 (Panthéon Sorbonne), and was awarded the degree of

Doctor of Laws honoris causa by Lund University in 2012 and by the University of Gothenburg in 2012. Her current research explores the development of population control, humanitarian aid, and market-oriented agrarian reform as transnational responses to the food insecurity from the era of formal empire through to the twenty-first century.

Mustapha Kamal Pasha is Professor in the Department of International Politics at Aberystwyth University, UK. He specializes in International Relations theory, Political Economy, Human Security and Contemporary Islam. Currently, he is Vice President of the International Studies Association. Professor Pasha is the author/editor of several books, including recent articles in *International Politics*; *Critical Review of International Social and Political Philosophy*; *Global Society*; *Annals of the American Academy of Political and Social Science*; *Journal of Developing Societies*; *Alternatives*; and *Millennium: Journal of International Studies*. He also serves on the editorial boards of *Globalizations*, *International Political Sociology*, *Critical Asian Studies*, *Asian Ethnicity*, and *Critical Studies on Security*. Currently, he is completing a book on the confluence of Islam and International Relations.

V. Spike Peterson is Professor of International Relations in the School of Government and Public Policy at the University of Arizona, with courtesy appointments in the Department of Gender and Women's Studies and Institute for LGBT Studies. She is the author of *A Critical Rewriting of Global Political Economy: Integrating Reproductive, Productive, and Virtual Economies* (Routledge 2003), co-author of *Global Gender Issues in the New Millennium* (with Anne S. Runyan, Westview Press 2010) and editor of *Gendered States: Feminist (Re)Visions of International Relations Theory* (Lynne Rienner 1992). She has held Visiting Research Fellowships at Australian National University, University of Bristol, University of Göteborg and the London School of Economics. Her current research focuses on informalization, global householding, and global insecurities.

Véronique Pin-Fat is Senior Lecturer in International Politics at The University of Manchester. She received a Teaching Excellence Award from the University of Manchester in 2012 and was awarded the Bernard Crick Main Prize for Outstanding Teaching by the Political Studies Association in 2006. She has a particular interest in the relationship between language, ethics and global politics. She is the author of *Universality, Ethics and International Relations: A Grammatical Reading* (Routledge 2010), is co-editor with Jenny Edkins and Michael J. Shapiro of *Sovereign Lives: Power in Global Politics* (Routledge 2004) and with Jenny Edkins and Nalini Persram of *Sovereignty and Subjectivity* (Lynne Rienner 1999).

Giorgio Shani is Senior Associate Professor of International Development and Peacebuilding in the Department of Politics and International Relations at International Christian University, Tokyo. He is the author of *Sikh Nationalism and Identity in a Global Age* (Routledge 2007) and co-editor of *Protecting Human Security in a Post 9/11 World* (Palgrave 2007). His main research interests focus on reconceptualising 'identity' and 'security' in a 'post-western' world. He served as Chair of the Global Development Section of the International Studies Association in 2010–11 and is currently writing a book on *Religion, Identity and Human Security*.

Michael J. Shapiro is Professor of Political Science at the University of Hawai'i. He is the author of numerous books, including *Violent Cartographies: Mapping Cultures of War* (University of Minnesota Press 1997), *Methods and Nations: Cultural Governance and the Indigenous Subject* (Routledge 2004), *Deforming American Political Thought: Ethnicity, Facticity, and Genre* (University Press of Kentucky 2006), *Cinematic Geopolitics* (Routledge 2009), *The Time of the City: Politics, Philosophy and Genre* (Routledge 2010), *The New Violent Cartography*, co-edited with Sam Opondo (Routledge 2012), and *Studies in Trans-Disciplinary Method: After the Aesthetic Turn* (Routledge 2012).

Lucy Taylor teaches and researches at the Department of International Politics, Aberystwyth University. She works on Latin American politics – especially Argentina. She is currently exploring decolonial political strategies, inspired by the work of contemporary Latin American approaches to understanding world politics, especially the theoretical insights of Walter Mignolo and Nelson Maldonado Torres. Her work focuses on two aspects. First, she has opened a new approach to decolonizing International Relations by rethinking the USA from Latin America. Second, she explores the challenges and ambiguities of decolonizing Latin America's most Europeanized country, Argentina. Lucy is President of the Society for Latin American Studies (SLAS) and a co-editor of the *Bulletin of Latin American Research.*

Annick T. R. Wibben is Associate Professor of Politics and International Studies at the University of San Francisco. She teaches international politics and specialises in critical security studies, international theory and feminist international relations. She is the author of *Feminist Security Studies: A Narrative Approach* (Routledge 2011) and coordinates the Feminist Security Studies Network. Her current research project examines security narratives involving women in the US military. She has a keen interest in issues of methodology, representation and writing, which she also explores in her work on (feminist) pedagogy.

Maja Zehfuss is Professor of International Politics and Associate Dean for Postgraduate Research in the Faculty of Humanities at the University of Manchester. She is the author of *Constructivism in International Relations: The Politics of Reality* (Cambridge University Press 2002) and *Wounds of Memory: Politics of War in Germany* (Cambridge University Press 2007). Her current research examines the politics of ethics in the context of war. She is a member of the National Academy of Teaching.

Teaching with *Global Politics: A New Introduction*

Jenny Edkins and Maja Zehfuss

This textbook offers a different way of teaching global politics. Many of us have become dissatisfied with traditional introductions, which seem to fall into two camps – either starting with various 'theoretical approaches', or introducing global politics as a series of 'issues', or indeed offering some combination of the two. Beginning with contending approaches, while radical and inspiring when first introduced in the late 1980s, has become well-worn and somewhat formulaic. Beginning with issues as an alternative can be equally frustrating. Although this new book includes both approaches and issues, it does not prioritise either. Instead, it begins with questions.

People come to the study of world politics with a series of questions about how to conceptualise the world and their place within it, motivated often by a desire for change. To give an example, many of these questions concern how we live in a world where so many people are brought together in such proximity. Who are 'we' anyway? Are we individuals, first and foremost, or social beings? What forms of identity do we adopt and why? What happens when things go wrong and we end up with wars and conflicts or severe economic inequalities?

The approach that this book presents takes questions like these as its starting point. It uses them to draw out the concrete historical and geographical locations within which the questions are situated, examine the challenge and complexity of response, and emphasise the need to think carefully about the broader assumptions or theoretical

FIGURE 0.1
'Tiger Foood'. Calvin and Hobbes. Image ID: 16449. http://www.amureprints.com/img1/Calvin/1989/ch891110.gif

BOX 1 AIM OF THE BOOK

Rather than asking students to set their questions aside whilst they study 'theory' or 'issues', the book tackles the questions people bring with them head on.

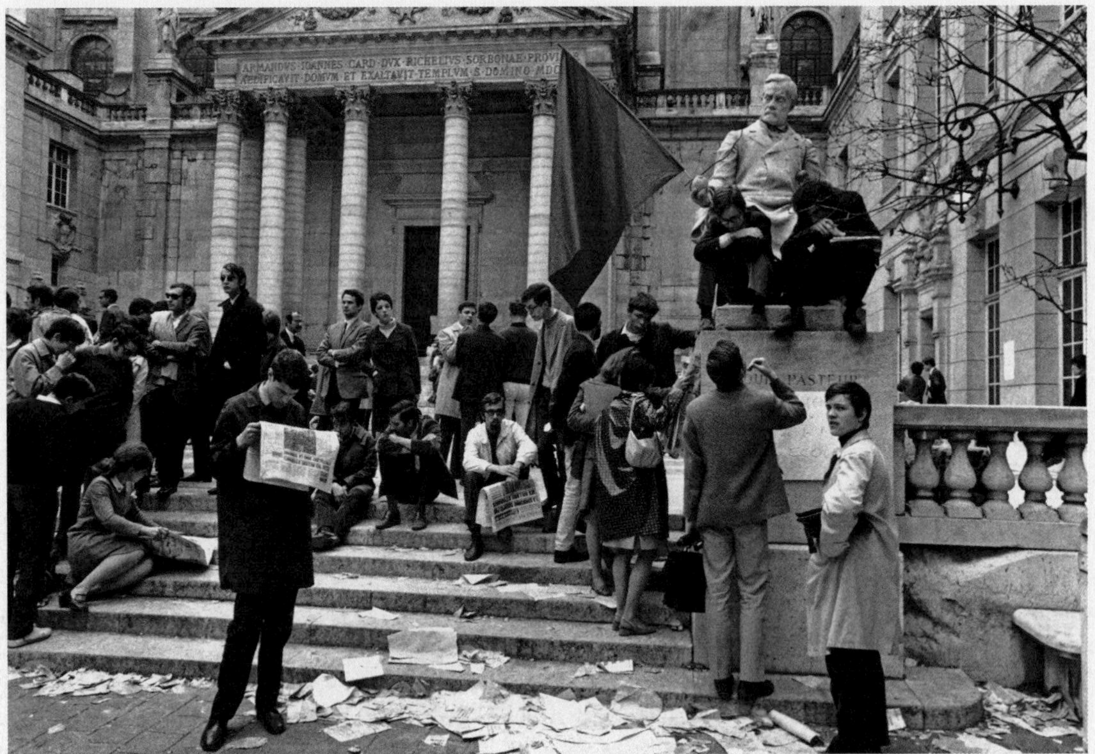

FIGURE 0.2
The Sorbonne University, Paris, occupied by students, 14 May 1968. Bruno Barbey/Magnum Photos

As we say in the introduction and explore again in the concluding chapter, this textbook, unlike Calvin's maths textbook in the cartoon below, doesn't give answers – magic or otherwise – to be learned and taken on faith. In our view, the questions that the various chapters pose can be addressed in different ways and from different perspectives, and there are no final answers to be had: only more questions. As we say at the end of the conclusion, the questions remain intractable, there for each new generation – from the generation of students of '68 to that of the occupy movement and beyond – to formulate and tackle anew.

Moreover, we would stress, following Jacques Rancière, that we all – students and professors alike – approach the questions as people of equal intelligence. As two people intrigued by many of the same puzzles that students bring to the study of international politics, our goal in this book is to treat their questions as important, show that other people agree and trace how some people have thought about them.

approaches that underlie the questions we ask as well as the responses we give. Each chapter thus follows the same structure, with sections examining the question, an example, what responses there might be and broader issues raised. Taking students' questions seriously in this way fosters engagement, empowers and inspires students, and provides a sound basis for further study.

Chapters have four sections: the question; illustrative example; general responses; broader issues.

The book employs a number of pedagogical tools to do its job. Although the book tackles profound questions, it addresses these in a clear and accessible way. The language used is straightforward; any terms that might be difficult are carefully explained, sometimes in brackets, sometimes in marginal comments. Because the different questions that the book examines are intertwined, there are links from chapter to chapter. Throughout the book, more information about particular thinkers, detailed explanations of issues referred to, and background about historical events is given in boxes that appear alongside the main discussion. The numerous illustrations aid understanding as well as emphasising the actual people and places involved in global politics. Cartoons provide pointed reflections and humorous asides.

Marginal comments are a feature of the book. They explain concepts, make links from one chapter to another, and raise questions to think about. Other pedagogical features include boxes, images, maps and cartoons.

In its illustrative examples, the book covers many parts of the world and is wide in its historical scope. A range of different issues and events are covered, and thinkers who have addressed global questions in a variety of ways discussed. An index of names lists thinkers and other people mentioned in the course of the text for ease of reference, alongside a general index that includes places, events and concepts, issues and topics, ideologies and theories introduced and indicates where each is covered in the book.

For a list of the thinkers and other people covered see the index of names.

There are many different ways of approaching the design of a course in global politics that uses this book – either the whole book or a selection of chapters. Some people have used the book with an existing course that approaches the subject through theoretical approaches or issues. The range of material presented in the book – much extended in this second edition – makes it possible to select material to fit an existing framework. However, many more people have taken the opportunity to teach and design courses in the entirely new way that the book proposes – focusing on questions – with all the advantages this allows.

The book is designed with newcomers to the field in mind, whether first- or second-year undergraduates, or, indeed, graduate students. It is equally suitable for private study. The text does not assume any previous knowledge, and carefully explains new concepts and events as and when they are encountered. It works well as the text for an introductory course, and in our experience those who have not encountered the area before find the style and approach both accessible and intellectually challenging. The book is accessible in the way it is presented, but it does not shy away from the difficult and complex questions of global politics. We have found that our students appreciate this approach and enjoy tackling the challenges that the difficult questions of contemporary political life pose to us all.

The text is suitable for introductory courses, but also works well at a higher level.

The chapters can be read in any order – we have grouped them in a certain way, but they can be read in a different order too. Each chapter stands on its own and does not assume knowledge of concepts explained in earlier chapters, though there will often be cross-references in the marginal comments to places in the book where additional discussion of concepts, places, events, or writers appear. And each chapter is written by

FIGURE 0.3
'A religion'. Calvin and Hobbes Image ID: 8643. http://www.amureprints.com/img1/Calvin/1991/ch910306.gif

a different author, giving the reader a series of distinct views, approaches and styles – within the overall framework of four sections in each chapter. We would suggest that it would be useful to read the introduction first, though, since it sets out in more detail the framework and ethos of the book and discusses reading strategies; and the concluding chapter draws out some important issues related to the book as a whole.

SECOND EDITION

The second edition includes eight completely new chapters examining recent events and covering even more areas of the world.

For the second edition, all the chapters have been updated and eight new chapters have been added. A variety of new questions are asked concerning, for example, saving the planet, how the internet is being used, how people come to identify with nations, the idea of democracy, and what human rights mean. We examine recent events such as the global financial crisis and the Arab Spring, and look in more detail at how colonialism works and what counts as violence. New examples used in the chapters range from drone attacks and financial targeting in Pakistan, through grassroots democracy in Argentina, the headscarf ban in France, and social movements and environmentalism in South Africa to the protests of the occupy movement.

As editors, we learnt a lot about global politics in putting the first edition of this book together. What is more, we really enjoyed reading the chapters, and seeing what this new way of approaching the subject made possible. We hoped that *Global Politics: A New Introduction* would enable students to think through the intriguing questions that they had, and we hoped that it would be enjoyable to teach with. All the feedback that we have had from the first edition suggests that this has been the case: the book has been widely adopted and positively received, and we hope that this second edition will prove as popular.

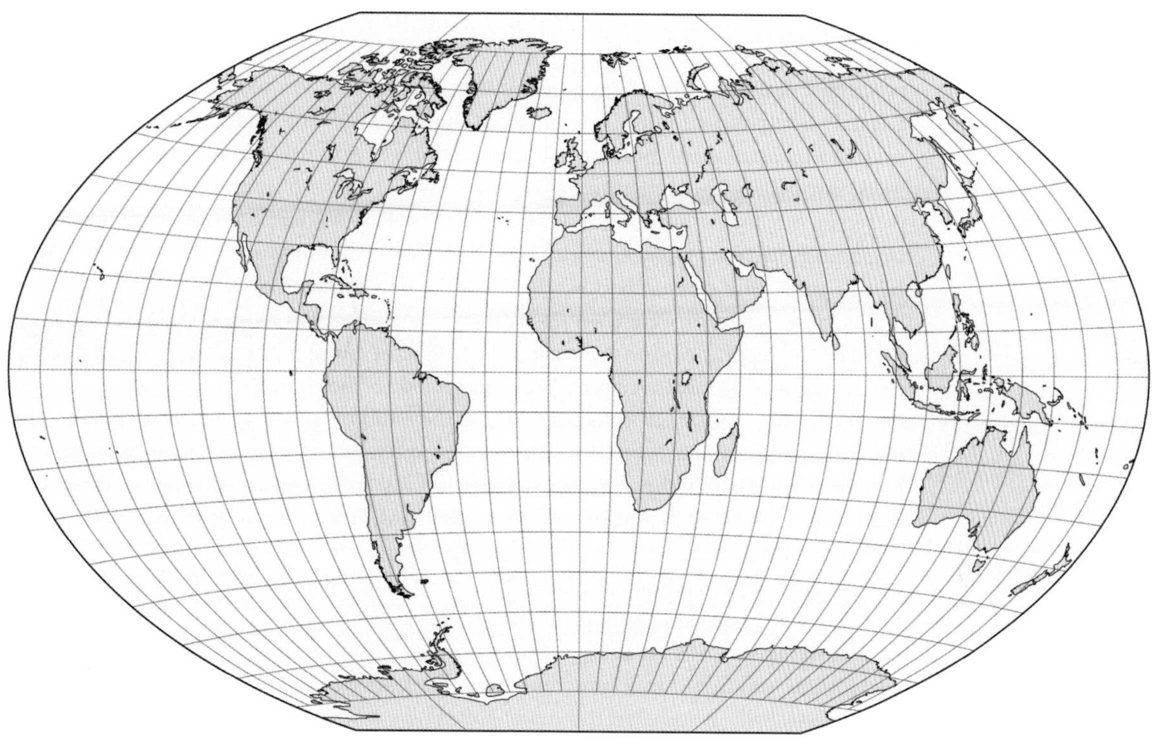

FIGURE 0.4
Map of the world: *Global Politics* covers so many countries that highlighting them all on this map would have been difficult.
http://www.progonos.com/furuti/MapProj/Normal/ProjMAz/Img/Z1/mp2_Winkel3-s75.png

ACKNOWLEDGEMENTS

Putting together the first edition was only possible because of the support and enthusiasm of numerous people all along the way, from first concept to finished book. First of all the many anonymous reviewers who looked at the proposal and responded with enthusiasm and support – sometimes qualified support, but support nonetheless – and the smaller group who read the initial manuscript in its entirety or in part and gave us detailed feedback. As well as this formal seal of approval, the excitement of numerous colleagues whom we bored with accounts of what we were up to sustained us along the way. The biggest thanks are of course owed to our initial band of contributors, who agreed readily to our requests for contributions, and put up with good grace with a pair of very intrusive editors and the demand for numerous revisions, expansions and explanations. That they remained nothing short of enthusiastic throughout all this was more than we were entitled to hope for. We were overwhelmed by the quality of the chapters – their content and their style – which in all cases not only met but exceeded our expectations of what we knew at the start was a very high-calibre bunch of authors. We would also like to thank our students: the initial idea for the book would not have taken shape without them, their engagement and disengagement during the courses we have taught provided the inspiration for a new approach.

Their detailed input in terms of identifying questions that they brought to the study of global politics provided the basis for the design of the book. Finally, the project would never have seen the light of day without the energetic support of the team at Routledge. Craig Fowlie believed in the project from the start, and this made us think that maybe we had a concept worth pursuing. Moira Taylor was unstinting in her support and hard work through all the difficulties along the way. Finally, although in the end his name is not in our list of authors, thanks are due to Rob Walker for his insistence at the beginning that we pursue our idea. He told us we should write it ourselves – I hope he will agree with us that had we done so, the end product would have been nothing like as strong as what we ended up with.

For the second edition we were able to call on another amazing group of authors for the eight additional chapters. We are obliged to them for their willingness to write for the book, and their tolerance when they discovered just what persistent and demanding editors we were. Once more the outstanding quality of the writing they produced has delighted us, and their work has vastly expanded the scope and reach of the book. Our original authors are due our thanks too, for the goodwill with which they approached the task of revising and updating their chapters. Craig Fowlie's team at Routledge, and in particular Nicola Parkin, who has taken charge of seeing the project through, have been unflagging in their enthusiasm. In the preparation of the second edition we have benefited again from formal and informal feedback from readers of the first edition, and from the comments of people who have used the book in their teaching. We are especially grateful to the many colleagues who have been generous enough to tell us how much they enjoy teaching with the book: it has been wonderful to know that the volume has been received as such a significant contribution to enabling a way of teaching that many were already moving towards. Particular mention needs to be made of Naeem Inayatullah's inspirational pedagogy, which one of us has been honoured to be able to observe at close quarters, and for his engagement with the project: his input has been invaluable. We are very grateful.

Eight new chapters and the complete revision of every existing chapter has been hard work, but again each time we have re-read the manuscript our enthusiasm has been redoubled. We noticed with the first edition that it seemed to be ahead of events in many ways – Obama had not been adopted as presidential candidate when we went to press with his image in the book – and it will be interesting to see whether the second is prescient too. Certainly, for us this new edition is both a reaffirmation of our initial approach and a chance to ask new questions and to highlight new illustrative examples. Thank you all.

CHAPTER 1

Introduction

Jenny Edkins and Maja Zehfuss

- *The question*
  WHAT DOES THIS INTRODUCTION TO GLOBAL POLITICS DO?
- *Illustrative example*
  HOW DO WE USE ILLUSTRATIVE EXAMPLES?
- *General responses*
  WHAT SORTS OF RESPONSES MIGHT THERE BE?
- *Broader issues*
  WHAT ASSUMPTIONS DO WE START FROM?
- CONCLUSION

THE QUESTION
WHAT DOES THIS INTRODUCTION TO GLOBAL POLITICS DO?

This is a textbook, but it is more than that. It is a guide for students to the questions about world politics that puzzle all of us. There are no easy answers to be had, and none of the chapters pretend that there are. There are only difficult and challenging questions – that lead to more difficult and more challenging questions. We think this is because the difficulties of global politics reflect the difficulties of 'life, the universe and everything'. This makes this book in some sense a sort of hitch-hiker's guide. We don't give you answers, not even Douglas Adams' (1979) answer – you will need to read his *Hitchhiker's Guide to the Galaxy* (if you haven't already) if you want to know his answer – but we do try to give you a guide to how other people have formulated questions and how they have attempted to respond to them. Many textbooks behave as if the 'great minds' have come up with the answers: they haven't. The questions remain open and intractable, there for each new generation to formulate and tackle for

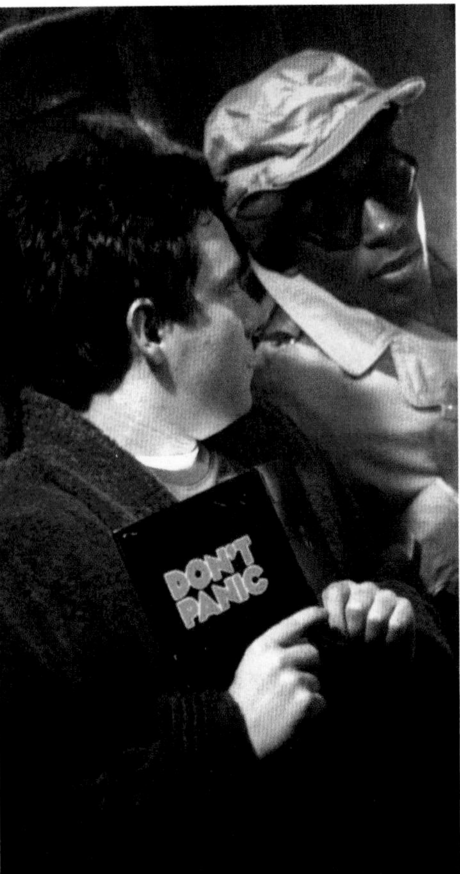

FIGURE 1.1
Martin Freeman as Arthur Dent and Mos Def as Ford Prefect in Touchstone Pictures' *The Hitchhiker's Guide to the Galaxy*. Ronald Grant Archive

themselves. This section of the introduction explores what questions we address, and discusses how the approach this book takes relates to that taken by other textbooks of world politics or international relations.

So, instead of starting from the sorts of explanations of global politics that 'great minds' have given (as those textbooks do that start from 'theories') or starting from some problem in global politics (as those textbooks do that start from 'issues'), in this book we start with questions. As we have been teaching global politics, our students have asked us very intriguing questions. Often we have found that our students' curiosity is motivated by the same sorts of questions that stimulate our own interest in global politics. In this book we have tried to put together a set of these questions. Each chapter starts by introducing its main question. So this book tackles twenty-seven main questions. But often when we start thinking about one particular question we realise that it raises a number of other questions. Each chapter therefore focuses on one main question – the one you see in the chapter heading – but it will also discuss related questions and make reference to other chapters and their questions. We sometimes use a feature called 'marginal comments' to alert you to how the discussion in one chapter links to the question or explanation in another. Let us briefly explain what we mean by questions being related in this way.

The way we plan to use comments in the margins of the textbook is explained here.

You might, for example, wonder why people can't freely decide where they want to live (Chapter 10). Some of you may indeed have encountered this problem when you applied to a university: you may have wished to go to a university that is not in the state of which you are a citizen and this might have set off a series of problems. You may have had to apply for a visa and pay higher tuition fees, and you may at the same time be ineligible for (some of the) available scholarships and find it difficult to acquire the right paperwork to be able to get a part-time job. Your citizenship has a material impact on how you can live your life.

So, in some way, you know the answer to the question: people can't move freely because states can decide who may and may not legally live within their borders. But how is it that states have this right? And why is the world divided into states in the first place? (Chapter 11). As you think about this you may notice that we often talk of this division in terms of 'nation-states'. But how and why have nations and states come to be related in this way? Does our allegiance to a particular nation overlap with our relation to a state? (Chapters 12 and 13). You have now started thinking about how we think about our identity. So now you need to figure out who we think we are (Chapter 5) and how we even begin to think about the world. For example, in determining how we behave towards others (say, whether we should give them financial assistance), does it matter whether these others belong to the same or another community? (Chapter 2). Or whether we think they are risky or dangerous? (Chapter 23). If how we think about the world has an impact, then what about particular ways of conceptualising the world and our place within it, such as religious beliefs. How do they affect politics? (Chapter 6). And how do we come to believe what we believe in the first place? In order to understand that, perhaps we need to know how we find out what's going on in the world (Chapter 8). And, come to think of it, did we start in the best place to think about global politics? We started with you: as good a place as any, you may think. But is there not more to the globe than the people that live on it? As we increasingly worry about climate change, we might wonder whether there is not more to existence than human concerns (Chapter 3).

So, you see, many of our questions are connected with each other. We invariably start with a particular question or concern, and often we may not even realise that it is

FIGURE 1.2
'Like all of us, he asked many different questions throughout his life.' Artist: Richard Jolley. CartoonStock ref.: rjo0698. www.CartoonStock.com

related to global politics. But as we pursue ways of thinking about and responding to the question we find that new questions are raised, often questions that concern global issues.

ILLUSTRATIVE EXAMPLE
HOW DO WE USE ILLUSTRATIVE EXAMPLES?

What you will find in this book are a lot of fascinating, and at times moving, accounts of what is going on or has gone on in particular places at specific historical points in global history. Sometimes these stories will be large-scale histories and at other times they will recount the experiences of maybe one person and their life. You will get to know a lot about many different places: this section of the introduction will map some of them for you.

The book contains many illustrative examples. We tell you here what we mean by that, and why we think they are important.

When we just explained why questions are often related to each other, we did not have space to say very much about why we are asking the question or who might be affected by it. We briefly showed you how you yourself might have been affected by citizenship regulations, but we did not go into any detail. In each of the chapters, however, the authors tell you at some length about a particular context in which the question they examine has arisen. We call this an illustrative example. It's an example because for each question there will be many other cases that one could look at in relation to the question and, of course, another case may highlight different issues. But the example chosen will illustrate what issues arise when we explore the question in a particular context. It will show you why the question is important, who is affected by it and what is at stake in responding to it one way or another. You will, of course, have

FIGURE 1.3
Tahrir Square, Cairo, during 8 February 2011, at the height of the protests in Egypt. http://en.wikipedia.org/wiki/File:Tahrir_Square_during_8_February_2011.jpg

realised that in order to cross a border legally you need the right documentation. And you probably know that many people in different regions of the world attempt to enter countries illegally and often they risk their lives in the process. But by looking at the particular example of the US–Mexico border, the author of Chapter 10, Roxanne Doty, is able to show how the US border enforcement policies of the 1990s led to a sharp increase of deaths along the border and how these policies were linked to larger developments in economics and security.

BOX 1.1 THE THIRD WORLD

The term 'third world' was first coined in 1952. At that time, during the Cold War, the world seemed to be made up of three groups of countries: the 'modern', liberal, industrialised countries of the 'West' (US, UK and other European states, Japan, Australia, Canada and so on), the communist states of the USSR or Soviet Union, and the 'underdeveloped' or non-industrialised states: states in Africa, Asia, South America. These groups were seen as making up the first, second and third 'worlds', respectively. The term 'third world' was problematic, not only because this picture of the world was oversimplified from the start and became increasingly so as countries in Asia for example began to industrialise rapidly, and later when the communist regimes of the Soviet Union collapsed, but also because of the implicit hierarchy of 'first', 'second' and 'third'. Alternative terminologies have been suggested: 'developing world', 'emerging countries' or the division North–South, for example, but none of these are satisfactory either and the term 'third world' remains in common use.

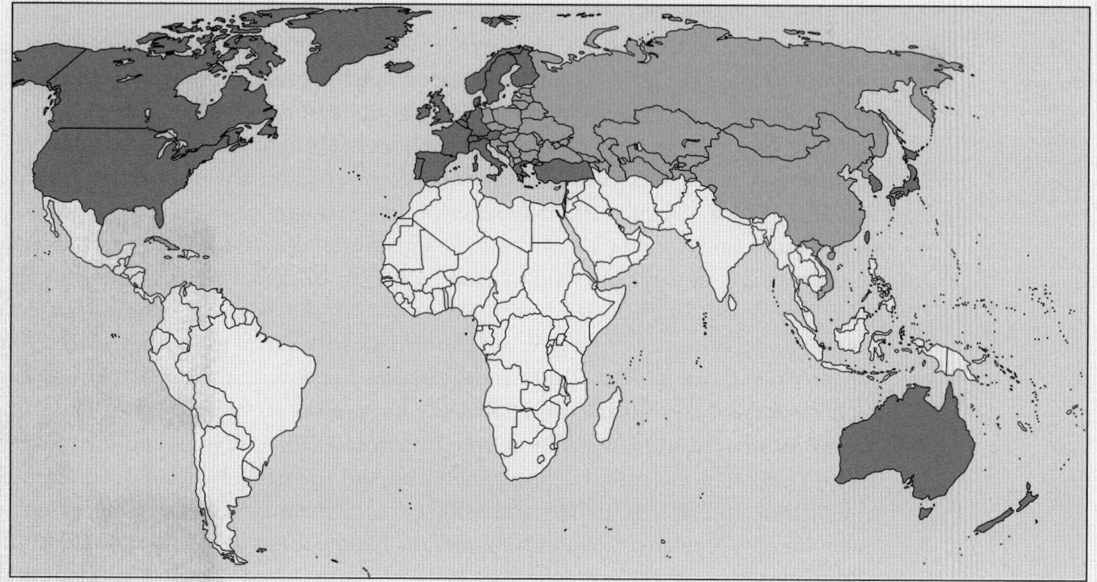

FIGURE 1.4
The three 'worlds'. Public domain

For many people the question of which country they are authorised to live in is one of life and death. We think it is important to acknowledge this when we ask why people cannot simply choose where they wish to live. This is also the case with the other questions explored in the book. When we ask what we can do to stop people harming others, we need to understand why people are harming each other in the first place (Chapter 25). The precise circumstances matter. And when we do decide that we want to do something, say to work for the overthrow of a regime we find oppressive, as people in Egypt did in 2011, or to get people not to waste resources, we need to think about how exactly we intend to go about it. Do we march and demonstrate or do we work through non-governmental organisations (NGOs) (Chapter 4)? How do we actually organise our activism (Chapter 9)? What you will come across in the chapters of this book is a series of detailed accounts, sometimes heart-rending, of things that have happened or are happening in particular places at particular times. This means that as you read the book, you will learn quite a bit about different places across the globe, the places where 'global politics' happen. We'll try to map some of these places in this section of the introduction.

What counts as a 'global' issue is not obvious, and people will have different views on this. And the terms people use are different too: some people talk of 'global politics', as this book does, and others of 'world politics'. The traditional term is 'international politics' or 'international relations' but we don't use either of these traditional terms here, since they seem to limit global politics to relations between states or nations.

Some chapters explore phenomena that are obviously global in scope, such as climate change (Chapter 3), but they might still affect people in different places differently. This is important in order to understand the politics: those people who are in danger of losing their livelihoods and homes because of the impact of hurricanes, for example, are likely to think that climate change is a very pressing issue, whereas people living in areas not so affected might not want to assign resources to avoiding environmental change. Similarly, while there is global inequality across the globe and within each country, what this means, and what it means to be poor, depends on where you live. Chapter 19 examines developed countries in Europe, North America and Japan, but also developing and emerging countries such as Brazil, Russia, India and China.

You will also learn about many other places and how they relate to each other, creating what we call global politics and responding to it. Asia, for example, is prominent in this book. Chapter 12 looks at Chinese identity and how the Chinese state regards so-called Overseas Chinese. Chapter 16 examines how colonialism worked in India. We have already noted that Chapter 19 gives you information about inequality in Japan, India and China. Chapter 20 examines responses to poverty in South Asia, Bangladesh in particular, and Chapter 23 looks at the Afghanistan–Pakistan border and the impact of the way it is thought of as a risky place. Chapter 26 takes you to a different part of Asia, North and South Korea, and looks at the difficult relations between these two countries and how they relate to wider issues in global politics, especially the Cold War. Chapter 25 looks at East Timor's development and recent attempts to constrain violence there. Like in many other cases, the question of independence for East Timor cannot be understood in separation from other countries or regions and their involvement, such as, in this case, Portugal, Indonesia and Australia. Nor can the question of colonialism in India be understood without a discussion of how Britain benefited economically. Similarly, Chapter 6 focuses on Islamic states in the Middle East, but it also discusses countries located in Asia and, of course, Africa. Chapter 4 examines the debate about sustainability that took place at the Earth Summit in South Africa: a powerful illustration of how a global event impacts on and is affected by its local context. Chapter 15 focuses on an African country, Ivory Coast, and its role in the cocoa trade.

This, again, only makes sense if we also look at the history of colonisation by France and the way in which the global economy impacts upon Ivory Coast. Chapter 14 examines what democracy might mean by looking closely at Argentina, but once more the colonial legacy and the links with other parts of the world are important.

It will come as no surprise to you that the United States often comes into the story of these examples. In a number of the chapters there is a clear focus on the United States (Chapters 5, 10, 13, 21, 24), but many of the others also make reference to this country. Europe is also significant. Chapter 11 focuses on Europe and in particular the state as we now understand it, Chapter 27 examines the headscarf ban in France, and Chapter 7 looks at the end of the Cold War in Europe, but many other chapters tell you something about Europe or particular European states.

So our 'illustrative examples' allow us to take you on something of a tour around the globe and let you learn something about places that you might not know that much about yet. But there is another reason why we examine such particular examples. In the last section, we showed you that often, when we try to respond to one question, we come across a lot of other questions. So, when we ask why people cannot simply choose where to live, we may say that this is because states can decide who may live within their borders. But this really is only a partial answer: we don't yet know why it is that states may do that. In other words, there are often many other things that we need to know in order to think through particular questions. Sometimes we actually don't really appreciate quite what it is we need to know unless we think a bit more about why we are actually asking the question, what it means for particular people, for example. In other words, the devil is often in the detail. Let us explain this in relation to a particular example.

When we think about a question in general terms, things can seem simpler than they are: the complexity of a question, and the way it is difficult to come to an abstract all-encompassing answer, often only becomes apparent when we examine a case in detail, which is one of the reasons for using illustrative examples in the book.

Why are there wars?

To illustrate how looking at the detail of what happens at particular points in time in specific places helps, this section of the introduction will do just that with respect to the question 'Why are there wars?' This is certainly a question that has intrigued and vexed many thinkers. You have probably asked yourself this very question at one point or another. Most likely you were prompted by a particular war. So you may have wondered, for example, about why a group of other countries led by the United States intervened militarily in Iraq in 2003. You may have seen pictures of the destruction caused on television or read about the deaths of service personnel and Iraqi civilians in the press. You may even know people who were involved in this war in some way, and you may have been concerned for their lives. So you would be asking the question 'Why are there wars?' very much with a sense of dissatisfaction in mind. What you really are asking might very well be: Why are there wars when they cause such destruction and misery, when they kill people? This is, incidentally, why you have quite possibly not asked yourself in the same sort of way why there is peace, for example. Intuitively, we would prefer peace over war. If there are wars nevertheless, we would like to have an explanation for that. We don't seem to require an explanation for peace – or peace, say, in Sweden – in the same way.

At least part of the reason why we want an explanation for war is that wars involve deliberate and significant destruction. Using military force means intentionally destroying things. Ideally, the destruction is aimed at and limited to military targets, that is, basically, enemy combatants and those things that enable them to act as combatants, such as, most obviously, their weaponry. Often other things and people get destroyed, too, however. If this was not the aim of the action that brought about the destruction, then this is called 'collateral damage' and is not illegal under international law, unless it is excessive. Nevertheless people are killed.

You probably don't much like the idea of killing people and, if so, you are likely to think that war is not such a good idea. But it's not that simple. First, sometimes people claim that, while wars do kill people, particular wars kill fewer people than the alternative. So, if Saddam Hussein's Iraq really had possessed weapons of mass destruction and had used them, many more deaths might have ensued. The argument therefore is that we must go to war in order to avoid deaths. But of course you can immediately see that this is a really problematic claim: you have to make all kinds of assumptions about what might happen in order to argue this. And as the case of Iraq shows, one can very easily be wrong about such things. Second, if you are really against war because war kills people, you should probably also be against cars. A total of 3,180 people were killed on the United Kingdom's roads, for example, in the 12 months ending in March 2006 (Wilkins 2006). That means almost nine people died as a result of road traffic accidents every day. This is a considerable number of deaths, and people certainly campaign to reduce the number of these deaths, but there is not the widespread condemnation of cars (as a cause of death) that there is of wars.

Chapter 28 engages further with the dilemmas that arise in considering war as a response to perceived wrong in the world.

Chapter 23 examines how things we often think of as non-violent – financial regulation designed to prevent people financing terrorism, for example – also kill people, if not perhaps as obviously.

Bombing of German cities in the Second World War

In order to think through why this might be the case it is helpful to think about a particular example. We could look at the war in Iraq, but we actually want to examine something different, an aspect of the larger set of events that is called the Second World War. You probably already know something about this war. You will be aware that the Allies won. When we say 'the Allies', we generally mean the United States, the Soviet Union, the United Kingdom and France, although it really is all a bit more complicated. Germany and Japan surrendered to the Allies in May and August 1945 respectively. This 'world' war was fought in a large number of places across the planet, but we want to only look at one aspect of it: the bombing of German cities.

For more on the Second World War see **Chapter 22**.

From 1940 onwards Britain's Royal Air Force bombed 131 towns and cities across Germany, some of them repeatedly (Sebald 2004: 3). From 1943 the United States Army Air Force was also involved in what was then called the combined strategic bombing offensive. It is often said that there was a significant difference between how the US and the UK went about the bombing. The US is said to have been involved in 'counterforce' targeting (that is, they aimed to attack militarily relevant sites only) whereas the UK engaged in 'countervalue' targeting (that is, they deliberately targeted cities and the people who lived within them). One strategy was meant to disable the Germans from continuing the war by taking away from them the means for conducting the war, the other to demoralise the population such that they would overthrow the government or in some other way give up the fight. Another way to put this is to say that the US was involved in 'precision' bombing of particular, militarily valuable targets whereas the UK was involved in what is variously called 'area bombing', 'carpet bombing' or 'obliteration bombing'. Of course, things were not that straightforward: there was considerable debate in both countries throughout the war about bombing strategies, and as a result approaches to bombing changed over time. And it was the Americans who actually built a replica of Berlin in the Utah desert in order to figure out how to destroy the city by setting off a fire storm through the bombing (Davis 2002).

The precise extent of the destruction caused by these operations is difficult to measure precisely, but it was certainly considerable. A. C. Grayling notes that '485,000 dwellings were completely destroyed and 415,000 severely damaged' (Grayling 2007: 103) and this constituted 20 per cent of Germany's housing stock at the time. W. G. Sebald uses slightly different figures. He speaks of 3.5 million homes destroyed and 7.5 million civilians rendered homeless. There were 31.1 cubic metres of rubble per inhabitant in Cologne and 42.8 in Dresden (Sebald 2004: 3).

We know that hundreds of thousands of people died in these raids, though there is no precise figure that is agreed. According to the US Strategic Bombing Survey of September 1945, 305,000 German civilians were killed by bombs and another 780,000 injured (Grayling 2007: 104). A figure of about 600,000 civilian deaths is also often cited. One of the problems in determining the death toll is that human remains could often not be recovered, in particular where bombing had led to a fire storm. There is a bit more clarity about the airmen who were killed. 55,000 members of RAF Bomber Command died – that is an astonishing 44 per cent of them, according to Jörg Friedrich (2002) – and 7,700 aircraft were lost (Grayling 2007: 104).

The bombing of Dresden is particularly infamous. This is in part because it happened so late in the war, on 13 February 1945, but also because the destruction caused was particularly devastating. Dresden, like Hamburg in 1943, was one of the cities where the bombing set off a fire storm. A variety of bombs was used on cities. Some were designed to create a shock wave that would reduce buildings to rubble or, at a greater distance, break windows and strip roofs. A much bigger effect could, however, be achieved by using incendiary bombs. These would start a fire, sometimes using phosphor which could not be put out with water. Other bombs, involving a timed

FIGURE 1.5
Dresden, 1945: Cremation on Altmarkt. Photo: Library of Congress. Digital ref.: 3b40632

delay mechanism, would stop firecrews from putting out the blazes. Eventually, the fire would start to create a wind that would fan the flames even more. The heat would become unbearable. The fire in Dresden was such that later waves of bombers had to fly at a higher altitude. No markers could be made out any more and in at least one instance an order was given to simply bomb 'the middle of the fires' (Taylor 2005: 320). The fires were visible for about 100 miles (Taylor 2005: 325).

In fire storms many died not from blasts, but from asphyxiation. They died because they stayed in the air raid shelters. In some shelters in Dresden, several thousand people were killed by lack of oxygen, smoke poisoning and carbon monoxide poisoning (Taylor 2005: 329). Others were buried alive underneath buildings that had collapsed (Taylor 2005: 330). Those who left the shelters had to contend with new waves of attack, time-delayed bombs that would continue to go off and, of course, the fire. The fire in Dresden was strong enough to suck people towards its core. They also had to attempt to escape the 'tornadoes of burning sparks and debris'. In the city centre, many were simply burnt to death (Taylor 2005: 331–2).

Frederick Taylor cites at length from a letter by one survivor, Hans Schröter, to a woman whose parents' deaths he had seen:

> We had got through both raids and thought we would now survive. This unfortunately was not to be the case. The door of the basement of No. 38 [Marienstrasse] was buried under rubble, so the only option was the emergency exit to No. 40 and 42. When we got through to No. 40, flames were already pouring down the steps, so that to save our lives we had to act with the utmost haste. [. . .] To push through the exit required enormous courage, and many could not summon it – including, perhaps, your beloved parents. They may have thought we'll be all right in the basement, but they had not reckoned with the oxygen shortage. As I emerged, I saw my wife and son standing by the security post on the *parterre* of No. 42. [. . .] When we got back [after two minutes], however, my loved ones had disappeared. I checked every shelter and basement on the street. Nowhere were they to be seen, everything wreathed in flame, no entry possible. Unable to find my family, I summoned my last instincts for survival, got as far as the Bismarck Memorial.
>
> (2005: 336)

The following day Schröter returned to his home.

> The sight that greeted my eyes was appalling. . . Everywhere charred corpses. I quickly headed home, hoping to find my loved ones alive, but unfortunately this was not so. They lay on the street in front of No. 38, as peacefully as if they were asleep. What I went through at that point you can easily imagine. Now I had to find out if my parents-in-law or other friends could be rescued from our basement alive. [. . .] As we opened up the emergency exit from No. 38, the heat that came out was so intense that we could not go down there. [. . .] The basement of No. 42 was full of bodies. I counted about fifty. Eulitz was among them. I could not see your parents, as everyone was piled on top of each other.
>
> (Taylor 2005: 337)

GENERAL RESPONSES
WHAT SORTS OF RESPONSES MIGHT THERE BE?

Reading these harrowing accounts, you may well be at a loss to know quite how to respond. No response seems adequate in view of the horrors described here. We find ourselves engaged and moved by such accounts in a way quite different from the way we might engage with an 'academic' argument. We wonder whether our emotional response is acceptable, or whether we are required to put this aside and take a dispassionate view – though whether or to what extent we may find that possible is questionable. Just for the sake of argument, let's differentiate between two sorts of responses as we think about this. On the one hand, you may think that it is extremely important to engage with what happened to individual people in this war, and with the horrific effects that the bombing had on people's lives, and deaths. These effects are likely to produce strong emotions in those who read about them. You may be appalled, for example, that people were burnt alive. You are prompted to imagine yourself or your family members in a similar situation, and think about how you would feel and react. You may then feel a strong desire to do something about it – a responsibility, if you like, to prevent others from having to suffer in this appalling way.

You might like to look at **Chapter 8**, where the author discusses her emotional response to a film about war.

On the other hand, you may think that these individual stories and hardships have to be put into some sort of context, and that thinking about them in that way is equally, or even more, central. You may consider that, whilst clearly you would not wish such suffering on anyone, there are other important issues to be considered here, and that we could lose sight of these if we were to allow ourselves to be overwhelmed by an emotional response. Some people want to respond in what they consider to be more rational, objective or abstract terms. Some might want to say that we should weigh up the pros and cons of the bombing campaigns which led to such horrendous suffering, rather than simply react to the suffering itself. The bombing of German cities was part of the Allies' larger fight against the Third Reich. It is often said to have been a response to the bombing of cities by the Nazis, in particular the bombing of Rotterdam in May 1940. The Second World War is often represented as a necessary or even 'good' war. Note that what is meant here is the war fought by the Allies, even if that is often not mentioned. People often assume that 'we' all look at this war from the perspective of the Allies, the victors. It was a good war because the Third Reich was such an appalling political system. Many people, it is argued, were saved from the murderous policies of the Third Reich by the victory of the Allies, and the death of several hundred thousand German civilians is not such a large price to pay in this context.

This is related to the idea of 'just war' discussed in **Chapter 21**.

Does it matter that this way of waging war killed many civilians? Does it matter how people died? Is there something particular about how people die in war? Usually we don't look at deaths in detail. But if we want to understand why there are wars, do we not need to grasp what wars are in this sort of way? Arguably, war is, precisely, about killing people (Bourke 1999). Some people might say that getting too involved with the deaths and their gruesomeness detracts from thinking about the 'real' issues. What they usually mean by this is that we need to focus on the need to fight the Third Reich.

Is there a difference between deaths in war and deaths in a car crash? Could this be why we might think differently about ending war than ending road accidents? Or is there no difference? **Chapter 22** discusses killing in war; **Chapter 23** discusses violence more broadly.

But now we are already talking about how people think about war, how they respond to the question of why there are wars. Responses to questions are what we look at in the second section of each chapter.

Each chapter begins by discussing detailed, grounded historical practices, such as the example that we set out in the last section, one situation within which the chapter question might have arisen. We have shown now how examining a particular example can affect how you might think about a question, what you might think is important, and can make it difficult to know how to respond.

In the section called 'General responses', each of the chapters therefore looks at how people have responded in general to the question at issue. When we say 'respond to a question', there seem to be three senses in which we might do this. First, there is an emotional response; second, looking for an answer to the question; and third, doing something about it or taking some action in response to the question. We have discussed the emotional response, and criticisms that could be made against it, just now. We might also think through the question, in the way in which scholars do, for example, looking for an answer. We mentioned earlier that some textbooks seem to suggest that the 'great minds' have come up with the answer to your questions, and this is the sort of thing that we will be exploring in this part of the chapters. You already know that we don't really believe that there are such answers that we can turn to. But it's still important to engage with such attempts at answers. Doing so not least helps us understand better why we might not be satisfied by such answers.

There are a number of ways of responding to questions. In this section we examine what we mean by 'responses' and what different types of responses there might be. We identify three: an emotional response, an academic response and a policy/activist response.

There is another way in which we might think about responses: we might look to act in response to the question by doing something about it. So, if we were to further explore the question of why there are wars, we could examine groups that have opposed war and try to understand how they have aimed to overcome the problem. Of course, these two senses of response – the academic and the activist response – are not separate. How you aim to get rid of war is likely to be informed by the way in which you think about the question of why there are wars. But some of our chapters stress one sense of 'responding' to the question, whilst others focus on another. Whichever way they interpret responses, these chapters always give you a range of different responses to think about and compare.

Let's first look at ways of thinking through the question as a form of response. One thing you will notice is that some of the ways of responding to different questions are actually similar to each other. Some ways of thinking – or what will be called pictures of the world in Chapter 2 – have a lot to say about a whole range of issues in global politics. A number of the chapters examine Marxism as a response to the chapter question (Chapters 8, 15, 17, 19 and, briefly, 11). Marxism takes economics to be fundamental to understanding politics, and so it's no surprise that the chapters that focus on obviously economic issues use this way of thinking about the world. But, of course, the point is that economics also matters when we might not notice it right away, for example when we try to understand the media (Chapter 8). A number of the responses explored in the different chapters highlight the significance of the history of colonisation and its effects in the present (Chapters 3, 15, 16 and 21), which is related to this way of thinking. Liberalism or neoliberalism also holds that economics is really important, but, as you will see, it has a rather different idea about how the economy 'works' and therefore a very different idea of how we should respond to particular questions (Chapters 17, 19 and 20). You will also notice that 'pluralism' (Chapter 8) is very similar to liberalism.

Other ways of thinking start in a different place. One important question in politics is often who you are or, put differently, what group you belong to. Chapter 5 examines different ways of thinking about this important issue of identity: it makes a difference whether we think identity is static or dynamic. Chapter 2 looks at different ways of conceptualising what we should do in the world and, again, this is related to who we think we are. The chapter compares and contrasts the cosmopolitanism of Charles Beitz and the communitarianism of Michael Walzer. The latter sees the community we belong to as significant in responding to the question, whereas the former sees individuals as the subjects of global politics. Chapter 12 examines how notions of national identity are produced and thought about, and Chapter 13 looks at a different set of thinkers and ways of thinking that tell us about why we might feel allegiance to a community, such as Thomas Hobbes, John Locke and Jean-Jacques Rousseau. Chapter 27 shows how our identity as human beings can be seen as part of particular ways of thinking.

Some chapters think of responses more in terms of actions in response to the question at issue. Chapter 10, for example, examines ways in which citizenship has been organised by states and the problems this creates. Chapter 21, which examines why some people think they know what is good for others, looks at two contemporary expressions of this attitude: the Euston Manifesto and the idea of benevolent imperialism. When there is conflict in the world, we often want to know how to move beyond it. Chapter 26 examines two different responses to this problem: confrontation or engagement.

But these two senses of 'response' are not as separate as they may appear. The examination of indigenous perspectives in Chapter 3, for example, represents not only a completely different way of thinking our place in the world, a different cosmology, if you will, but this directly implies a different way of relating to the natural world, that is, a different way of acting. Similarly, the idea that politics and religion are best kept separate, called secularism, has practical implications: politics is in many states organised in accordance with this belief (Chapters 6, 7 and 27). The potential tensions this separation produces are brought out clearly in Chapter 27. Different conceptions of the law favour different ways of responding to political problems (Chapter 25). Ideas about geopolitics or strategy (Chapters 3, 11, 22 and 24) also have an effect on how we think it is appropriate or profitable to act in the world. This interconnection is shown very clearly in Chapter 24. Changes in technology may in turn affect how we think and act (Chapters 9, 11, 18 and 24).

BROADER ISSUES
WHAT ASSUMPTIONS DO WE START FROM?

Looking at the general responses that people have come up with to the questions that our chapters address often leads to broader questions, questions that might need to be thought about before we can even begin to think about the particular question at issue in the chapter. Sometimes, the responses we examine will already have assumed certain answers to these broader questions. In other words, they will have taken certain things for granted, without even examining or thinking about them. This is often not deliberate. Sometimes it is very difficult to identify what has been taken for granted, precisely because it *is* 'taken for granted' and so widely assumed to be the case that it

Is it possible to manage without making assumptions? Is it possible to identify what our assumptions are?

is not subject to question. We don't even see that we have made certain assumptions before we start. It seems to be 'common sense': there seems to be no alternative way to think about it.

However, if we want to delve more into how we might respond to the questions that concern us, we need to try to identify some of the assumptions that ground our usual ways of thinking. Knowing (or, rather, trying to think about) what assumptions we start from is standard practice in much academic and scholarly reflection. If we don't do this, we may end up with answers to our questions that are limited in ways we can't recognise, and that don't enable us to think beyond (or even be aware of) the constraints that 'common sense' imposes, or come up with useful ways of addressing our concerns. Robert Cox (1981) has characterised two ways of thinking about global politics. One he calls 'problem-solving theory'; the other he calls 'critical theory'. Problem-solving thinking works *within* the assumptions of what counts as common sense at a particular point in time. It looks at the problem, or in our case the question, on its own terms, and seeks an answer within the same framework or set of assumptions that raised the question in the first place. Critical thinking seeks to *question* the problem itself, and the common sense it takes for granted. Our thinking is conditioned by social, cultural and ideological influences, and critical theory seeks to uncover this conditioning. A critical approach would seek to ask why a particular issue had been put forward as a problem to be solved in the first place: what were the common sense assumptions hidden behind thinking of that as a problem? Such an approach would also ask who would *benefit* from the problem being solved, if we were to solve it on the terms in which it is posed. In general, Cox argues, problem-solving theory works to reinforce what is called the status quo – it keeps in place accepted ways of thinking and the structures of political and economic power that go along with those ways of thinking. As he famously said 'Theory is always *for* someone and *for* some purpose' (Cox 1981: 128); his argument was that in order to think critically we had to make sure we examined the power relations in which our thinking was inevitably embedded. Critical thinking, in other words, 'stands apart from the prevailing order and asks how that order came about' (Cox 1981: 129) because, if we do want to change anything, we first have to understand the world as it is. Many of the chapters of this book attempt to think in this critical type of way when examining the general responses that have been given to the questions they address; often the general responses will have been in problem-solving mode, and thinking beyond this approach reveals the broader issues at stake.

Scholars sometimes distinguish between Robert Cox's 'critical theory' and the ideas of the Frankfurt School (people like Jürgen Habermas and Theodor Adorno), which are often called 'Critical Theory' in capital letters.

Chapter 28 further discusses the idea of change and the sorts of assumptions that are behind it.

Identifying the assumptions within which our thinking might be working is much more difficult and challenging than it might seem. However, it is also very rewarding: once we pinpoint our hidden assumptions, we open up the possibility of different ways of thinking about the world. These different ways of thinking are not, of course, ways that avoid making assumptions, but they are based on *different* assumptions. And, since theory and practice are not as separate as they seem, as we will discuss in a minute, this also opens up the possibility of *doing* things differently. It doesn't mean that we can change the world overnight, of course not, but it does open up ways of thinking about how we might work for the change we want, a question that we look at in more detail in the concluding chapter of the book. Perhaps just as importantly, it enables us to see how what we do has been constrained by the common sense within which we have been thinking.

BOX 1.2 ANTONIO GRAMSCI

FIGURE 1.6
Antonio Gramsci

Italian Marxist thinker Antonio Gramsci (1891–1937) was imprisoned by Mussolini's fascist regime in Italy between 1927 and 1935, and he wrote his most famous works during that period. As a result of these circumstances, they are written in the form of fragmentary notes, avoiding the use of words such as 'Marx' and 'class' (a key concept in Marxist thought as Chapter 14 explains). Gramsci's years in prison led to a complete breakdown of his already far from robust health. His thirty-three prison notebooks were smuggled out of his clinic room to safety by his sister-in-law Tatiana Schucht when he died in April 1937.

It is very important to ask how the common sense that limits our thinking is produced. Antonio Gramsci argues that 'in all periods there co-exist many systems and currents' of thought, which are first born and then spread or diffused in society; in this process of diffusion 'they fracture along certain lines and in certain directions' (1971: 327). We need to examine how these processes work. But these ways in which accepted ways of thinking are produced and circulated is not something that can be thought of as separate from academic enquiry itself. As students of global politics we are not outside common sense: it influences us too. We all have what Gramsci called a 'spontaneous philosophy', contained in language, common sense, and the collections of beliefs, religious or otherwise, that we hold (1971: 323). There is not just one common sense: common sense is a product of history and circumstance. We are each, Gramsci says, the 'product of the historical process to date which has deposited in [us] an infinity of traces, without leaving an inventory' (1971: 324).

Our task, then, if we want to think critically, is to make such an inventory, or, in other words, to attempt to figure out what those influences might be that have made us think and act the way we do. The job is to track down our assumptions, and to acknowledge what is unquestioned or taken for granted in our ways of thinking. Common sense needs to be replaced by criticism, or what we might call critical theory, in the sense that Cox used this term, as we discussed just now.

There is one further point that needs to be made about our ways of thinking – or what Gramsci calls our 'philosophies' and what we might here want to call, in our terminology, our 'theories'. Let's look at what Gramsci (writing at a time when it was common sense to assume that the pronoun 'he' could unproblematically be taken to refer to 'he or she', and 'man' to encompass 'woman') says in one of his *Prison Notebooks*:

> Philosophy in general does not in fact exist. Various philosophies or conceptions of the world exist, and one always makes a choice between them. How is this choice made? Is it merely an intellectual event or is it something more complex? . . . Which

> . . . would be the real conception of the world: that logically affirmed as an intellectual choice? Or that which emerges from the real activity of each man, which is implicit in his mode of action? And since all action is political, can one not say that the real philosophy of each man is contained in its entirety in his political action?
> (Gramsci 1971: 326)

How we think about the world and the impact this has is discussed in more detail in **Chapter 2**.

The important point that he is making here is that the way people choose to think about and explain the world is, after all, part of 'the world' and influences what happens. It cannot be separated from other things people do.

These two things, 'theory' and 'practice', if you like, are often kept separate by people who think about global politics. However, one of our starting points in this book is that the distinctions that are often made between the detailed, historical study of events and things people do in the world and the more general explanations that are put forward to help us account for these things we observe – the distinction between practice and theory, as it is often called – is in many senses artificial, as Gramsci argues.

Gramsci is by no means the only writer to have tackled the question of what role common sense or our conceptions of the world play in our thinking and our politics. Michel Foucault, whose work you will come across in Chapters 4, 5, 7, 11, 23 and 24, has also examined the intimate relation between theory and practice, or, in his terminology, knowledge and power (Foucault 1980). He argues that at any particular period in history there is a particular 'regime of truth' in place that validates what should count as true. Certain people are authorised to determine what is true, and there are specific ways of assessing truth. In the modern era, in the western world, it is predominately the scientific method that is assumed to be capable of guaranteeing truth. What we call knowledge for Foucault is not something that is independent but rather something that is always tied up with power structures. He offers us what he calls a toolbox which we can use to prise open these systems of truth and if we like destabilise them: demonstrate their contingent, historical character, or in other words the way in which they are not universally true or valid. His genealogical method uses a combination of detailed historical excavations and localised, specific knowledges. Ludwig Wittgenstein too has looked closely at the role language plays in limiting our thought. His work is explained in Chapter 2, so we won't say much about it here. Wittgenstein talks in terms of language games and pictures. He argues that when we think we are explaining the world we are only tracing again and again a picture of the world that frames our ideas of it. We are always operating within what he calls a 'language game' or a certain 'grammar'.

Do you think that the authors of the chapters in this book are authorised in this way? Is education a way of giving people authority?

We have seen here a number of different ways of thinking about how we might look at the relation between thinking about the world and doing things in the world, and we have found several different views on how to approach this. Gramsci, Foucault and Wittgenstein differ in the terminology they use and in the specific arguments they put forward, but they would all agree that direct access to 'the world' is not possible: we always think about the world and the questions of global politics starting from within a particular 'common sense' (Gramsci), 'regime of truth' (Foucault), or 'language game' (Wittgenstein).

Of course there is another group of views entirely, which we haven't discussed here. There are people who argue that there is no problem at all – or less strongly, no real problem – in separating theory and practice. For these people, it is possible to have an independent, neutral position (or one that is more or less independent or neutral) from which an objective view of the world can be formulated. Truth can be found, and our job as academics, for these people, is precisely to be seekers after truth. This is called a 'correspondence theory of truth', and it is discussed in Chapter 2.

Do you think an objective view of the world – sometimes also called 'scientific' – is possible? How would you find out whether your answer to this question was right or wrong?

CONCLUSION

The question of whether there is any possibility of objective knowledge of the world is one of the broader questions that many of the other chapters in this book raise, too. In our view the diversity of accounts and explanations of events in global politics demonstrates that there is no neutral view to be had. Different accounts of cosmology and what the world is, different common senses and different philosophies, lead to different approaches. And different political starting points are linked with different explanations. We would ask that you bear in mind as you read through this book that, while in the 'general responses' section they examine existing ways of approaching the question, what the authors of the various chapters give are their own arguments and their own interpretations. They are not in a position to give an unbiased, neutral view: no one is, as far as we are concerned. Try to think of them as individuals – check them out in the list of contributors to see where they come from, and refer to them by name when you are discussing their chapters.

In view of everything we have discussed in this introduction, we would encourage you, as you read the chapters, to practise a way of reading that is open and generous at the same time as being critical. As scholars we are accustomed to focus on critique, and moreover, apt to forget that any critique, like the writing we are critiquing, is the expression of a particular position: it comes from somewhere, it is not purely objective. There is no neutral, objective point for critique, any more than there is for writing. Naeem Inayatullah of Ithaca College in New York State (author of Chapter 21) offers some thoughts on ways of reading. He notes that writers write because they have a need to say something. Of course, in writing chapters of this textbook, the authors have very generously responded to invitations from us as the editors of the book. But what they choose to write and how can still be seen as reflecting a need to say something. When we read, Inayatullah suggests, a first step might be to ask 'What needs does the writer bring and how does the text reveal or conceal those needs?' However, he points out that already we have a problem:

> You might ask, as I did, 'Hey, I have my own needs; what do I care about the needs of the author?' The author expresses a need in the writing, but we as readers bring our own needs to the text. The problem is that the two needs mostly likely differ; what the author has to offer might not be what you or I need. So what do we do about this problem?
>
> (Inayatullah 2008)

There are two common ways of reading that he thinks are unproductive. The first is to focus 'almost exclusively on the authority of the text and the author' (Inayatullah

2008). You try to learn what the text says – you summarise it in your notes, ready to regurgitate in class, in essays or in exams. This is a way of learning that we are all used to – and indeed, on some occasions, like taking the 'theory' part of a driving test for example, it produces good results.

The second way of reading focuses just on the reader's own needs. You go through the text gutting it for the things that you are looking for – for things you can use for a particular purpose: an essay, for example. You skim read, looking at the headings, reading the odd word here or there, and assuming that you can guess what lies in between. But this is counterproductive too. You are so focused on your own needs that 'a sense of impatience with the text disallows a fruitful engagement . . . Because the response is not based on a careful or generous reading, it often misses the point and the spirit of the text' (Inayatullah 2008).

Inayatullah suggests that what we should aim for is a balance between these two approaches. He recommends that we try to be conscious of our own needs as we approach the text, but then 'suspend those needs, bracket them, and place them in the background' because 'to read the text with care and generosity we have to do our best to accept the author's assumptions' (Inayatullah 2008). Once we have read the text in this way, which is not easy, we should then un-bracket our own needs and be as critical as we possibly can be, whilst giving praise where praise is due. Finally, we should think about what the author's response to our criticisms might be.

It is crucial in all this to remember that the authors of what you are reading are not so very different from you: they are people who look around them and think about what they see; they explore what other people think, like you do, and they make their own judgements, just like you do. They are not some super-human breed of extraordinary intelligence (nor devious beings of great duplicity). They have thought carefully about what they are writing about and about how to write it. They probably have reasons for doing things you consider stupid – leaving out things you think should be there, for example – though they may not have: they may just have made a mistake. They make every effort to present to you arguments that they disagree with, and they indicate where those arguments can be found. We would encourage you to follow this up in the further reading that is given so that you can form your own views. And sometimes they make their own feelings about the material clear, and try to persuade you of their view. We encourage you to listen to their views carefully but then to form your own views and judgements about each of the chapters – and each of the questions in the book. You may well come to different conclusions. As we said at the start of this introductory chapter, there are no answers: the questions remain open and intractable, there for each new generation of scholars to formulate and tackle for themselves.

FURTHER READING

Cox, Robert W. (1981) 'Social forces, states and world orders', *Millennium: Journal of International Studies* 10, 2: 126–55.

This article sets out the difference between 'critical theory' and 'problem-solving theory' in thinking about global politics, and why this is important.

Donald, James and Stuart Hall (1986) *Politics and Ideology*, Milton Keynes: Open University Press; Beechey, Veronica and James Donald (1985) *Subjectivity and Social Relations*, Milton Keynes: Open University Press.

If you want to follow up on the relationship between politics and the way we think, these two readers extend the discussion in interesting ways.

Hall, Stuart (1996) 'Gramsci's relevance for the study of race and ethnicity', in David Morley and Kuan-Hsing Chen (eds) *Stuart Hall: Critical Dialogues in Cultural Studies*, London: Routledge.
In this chapter, Stuart Hall gives a very clear explanation of the main features of Gramsci's work and its contemporary importance.

Hollis, Martin and Steve Smith (1991) *Explaining and Understanding International Relations*, Oxford: Clarendon Press.
Hollis and Smith make a distinction between 'explaining' and 'understanding', which is similar to the distinction between critical and problem-solving theories discussed here.

Rancière, Jacques (1991) *The Ignorant Schoolmaster: Five Lessons in Intellectual Emancipation*. Translated by Kristin Ross, Stanford, CA: Stanford University Press.
This short text explores ways of teaching and argues that the master who explicates produces learning that stultifies.

REFERENCES

Adams, Douglas (1979) *The Hitchhiker's Guide to the Galaxy*, London: Pan Books.

Bourke, Joanna (1999) *An Intimate History of Killing: Face-to-Face Combat in Twentieth-Century Warfare*, London: Granta.

Cox, Robert W. (1981) 'Social forces, states and world orders', *Millennium: Journal of International Studies* 10, 2: 126–55.

Davis, Mike (2002) *Dead Cities*, New York: The New Press.

Foucault, Michel (1980) *Power/Knowledge: Selected Interviews and Other Writings 1972–1977*, trans. Colin Gordon, Brighton: Harvester Press.

Friedrich, Jörg (2002) *Der Brand: Deutschland im Bombenkrieg 1940–1945*, Munich: Propyläen Verlag.

Gramsci, Antonio (1971) *Selections from the Prison Notebooks*, London: Lawrence and Wishart.

Grayling, A. C. (2007) *Among the Dead Cities: Is the Targeting of Civilians in War Ever Justified?* London: Bloomsbury.

Inayatullah, Naeem (2008) *Classes: Reading, Writing and Grading*, Homepage: http://www.ithaca.edu/naeem/reading.shtml.

Sebald, W. G. (2004) *On the Natural History of Destruction*, trans. Anthea Bell, London: Penguin.

Taylor, Frederick (2005) *Dresden: Tuesday 13 February 1945*, London: Bloomsbury.

Wilkins, Lucy (2006) 'Are Britain's roads getting safer?', BBC News Online, 17 August, http://news.bbc.co.uk/1/hi/uk/5256506.stm.

For a range of further resources supporting this chapter, please visit the companion website for *Global Politics, 2nd Edition* at www.routledge.com/cw/edkins/

CHAPTER 2

How do we begin to think about the world?

Véronique Pin-Fat

THE QUESTION
THINKING AND LANGUAGE

How we think about the world matters in very important ways. It impacts on what we do from day to day, for a start. For example, if, as a student, you have a poor opinion of a particular lecturer at your university or college – if you have decided that he or she is boring or difficult to follow – you will be less likely to attend the lecture, unless of course you think there are strong conventions in place to compel you to go. If you think of the world as a dangerous place, this may impact on how you travel to the lecture: you may avoid public transport, for example, and decide to walk, because of the possibility of a terrorist attack. Such an attack may be statistically very unlikely, but the way you picture the world will affect how you interpret such 'evidence' and how you behave. Other students may see travelling on the bus or the train as a way of making a political statement, a way of 'defying' those who want to prevent life going on as usual.

This chapter explores the notion that how we think about the world affects how we live in it. It is of course not just a matter of how we live in it on our own, but how we live in it with others. You encounter lots of people in your life from the moment you wake up to the moment you go to bed. Some of them may be close to you and you may even love them. Some you don't know so well, but may see regularly like students and lecturers. Some you've never met but have heard or read about, like people all over the globe who appear in the news. And, of course, there may be some people you just do not like, find 'weird', or plain annoying. Either way, we don't live in the world on our own and somehow need to find ways of accommodating each other.

Living in the world with other people is the realm of politics and ethics. Broadly speaking ethics is about how we should live with other people in the world and politics is about what kinds of living and ways of thinking about who we are are made possible. So, for example, should someone whom you regard as 'weird' be treated any differently to someone you love? Furthermore, what counts as 'weird'? What does that tell us about 'normal'? Are people whose lives are different to ours, perhaps because they live in a different country to us or practice a different religion, 'weird'? Ethics and politics looks at both how we should regard and accommodate each other and what kinds of things make it possible to, for example, treat each other with respect and those which don't. That I might view you as 'weird' or even 'inhuman' (politics) may very much dictate how I then treat you (ethics). When we examine more closely how we think about the world, it turns out that ethics and politics are inseparable.

The significance of being treated as 'human' and the problem of who gets to count as such is explored in **Chapter 27**.

Is thinking about the world something that just happens in our heads? Perhaps, but our thinking about the world must in some way be public, or accessible to others. We formulate and communicate ideas and thoughts by means of language. Language is public. It consists of shared rules and vocabularies, for example. Language seems a strong candidate for giving us access to how we think about the world and, as such, the relationship of language to the world is a central theme of this chapter.

The thoughts we have about the world reveal a number of things: the types of things that we believe are in the world, the kinds of people that we think we live amongst, what we think is important, what we think is possible, and even how we believe we should think about the world. These thoughts are all attempts to make sense of the world and our place in it. So, the questions that we are going to look at here are:

These broad questions are examined in the context of thinking about danger in Section 3 of **Chapter 24**.

1 How do we begin to think about the world and make sense of it?
2 Does the world exist independently of any thoughts we might have about it?
3 Is the way we think about the world simply a representation of what it is?

This may seem a bit abstract, but let's look more closely now at the effects that our thinking has in the world.

Some people regard thinking and language as something that is separate from the world. They see the world as carrying on independently of what we think. According to this way of thinking, we produce various representations of the world, but the world continues regardless of our thoughts about it. However, as I mentioned above, what we are going to explore in this chapter is how what we think about the world actually impacts on the world: it changes the world and our relations with the people in it. We also examine how, if we ignore the impact our ways of thinking have on the world, we can find ourselves complicit in what happens in ways we might not wish to be. In other words, this chapter suggests that if we don't sometimes pause to think about how we think about the world we might find ourselves accepting and endorsing practices we might find immoral, wrong or unjust.

ILLUSTRATIVE EXAMPLE
THINKING ABOUT TORTURE: THE TICKING BOMB SCENARIO

We will begin by looking at an example of thinking. The form of thinking we will examine is the one most often used to think about torture. It is called 'the ticking bomb scenario'. Although we will be engaging with *thinking* about torture here, it is important to be clear that this does not necessarily mean we are engaging with the practices of torture and their justification or otherwise. In fact, as we shall see, sometimes our thinking about torture avoids engaging with it in important ways.

Can you think of other scenarios that you have come across? What is it that makes something a scenario? It might be helpful to think about this question as you read this section.

Torture obviously affects people's bodies and lives; it causes great physical suffering and pain and has profoundly negative emotional and psychological effects. Elaine Scarry, in her book *The Body in Pain* (1985), goes as far as to say that torture in a sense destroys, or in her words 'unmakes', the world: it destroys ideas of the world and our place in it that have been painstakingly put together. Some governments have condoned torture and created official policies around its use. The particular way of thinking about torture that I want to examine – the ticking bomb scenario – has been an important part of recent debates. Examining the use of the ticking bomb scenario to think about torture, and the practical implications of that way of thinking, provides an example of how ways of thinking about the world have very real effects.

An absolute prohibition against torture is embodied in a convention to which many states have agreed, the United Nations Convention Against Torture and Other Cruel, Inhuman or Degrading Treatment or Punishment. In the Convention Against Torture (CAT) (1984), torture is prohibited because it violates 'the inherent dignity of the human person' (Preamble). Torture is defined as:

> any act by which severe pain or suffering, whether physical or mental, is intentionally inflicted on a person for such purposes as obtaining from him or a third person information or a confession, punishing him for an act he or a third person has committed or is suspected of having committed, or intimidating or coercing him or a third person, or for any reason based on discrimination of any kind, when such pain or suffering is inflicted by or at the instigation of or with the consent or acquiescence of a public official or other person acting in an official capacity. It does not include pain or suffering arising only from, inherent in or incidental to lawful sanctions.
>
> (Article 1)

The Convention continues: 'No exceptional circumstances whatsoever, whether a state of war or a threat of war, internal political instability or any other public emergency, may be invoked as a justification of torture' (Article 2, section 2). The Convention Against Torture, therefore, prohibits any circumstances being used as a justification for torture. However, the argument has been made that there are circumstances when torture can be justified. This argument often begins with the positing of a particular scenario. Here is how the scenario goes:

> *Imagine this: There is a time-bomb planted in the centre of a large city somewhere in the United States or a European capital, in Washington, Paris, London, or Berlin, for example. It is armed, ticking and counting its way down towards detonation. You have the person who planted it in custody. He won't talk. Hundreds, if not thousands, will die if the information on the whereabouts of the bomb is not revealed. Should you torture the person that you are holding in custody in order to find out where the bomb is and stop it from exploding?*

This hypothetical situation is called the ticking bomb scenario. The scenario is often used as a starting point in thinking about whether torture can ever be justifiable. It is used to test the limits of the absolute prohibition against torture: the idea that we shouldn't use torture under any circumstances. The ticking bomb scenario challenges this prohibition by asking whether it can be displaced or disregarded in exceptional circumstances, even though the Convention Against Torture prohibits this explicitly as we have seen. Often, the answer that the scenario leads to is that it can. Let us examine how allowing an exception to the prohibition of torture comes about through the thinking that lies behind the scenario.

A scenario can mean an imagined or hypothetical sequence of events; the word also refers to the outline of the plot of a play or film.

How does a hypothetical scenario like the ticking bomb function to justify torture in practice? It does so by providing *only* the kind of information we need to conclude that we might be justified in torturing the person we have in custody.

Using this hypothetical scenario gives us certainty about a number of things:

When we buy into a scenario, we no longer have to worry about things that the scenario already tells us are one way rather than another – we put them to one side.

- We are certain that the person we have in custody is the person who planted the bomb and not someone who is lying about having planted it or an innocent person.
- We are certain that we know that the bomb has been planted in a large city and that it will kill lots of people rather than just one or two.
- We are certain that the bomb will go off, that is to say, we are confident that it won't just fizzle, splutter and fail to detonate.
- We are certain that if we torture the person in custody he or she will tell us the true location of the bomb and not lie.
- We are certain that it is possible to torture the person for the short period of time that the bomb is ticking and not a moment longer (weeks, months, years) in order to extract the information on the location of the bomb.
- We are also very confident that when we do torture that person, our torture methods won't kill him or her before he or she tells us where the bomb is planted.
- We assume then, that we (or our agents) are trained, effective torturers with a practical knowledge of torture techniques. We are certain that our torture methods work; torture will make the person in custody tell us where the bomb is and therefore, allow us to find it, disarm it, and save many valuable lives.
- We also know that saving lives is an appropriate justification.

The scenario is neat and tidy. It has been constructed very carefully to eliminate many difficult issues. This isn't deliberate deception particularly. Rather it is a function

BOX 2.1 TORTURE AFTER 9/11

The debate about possible justifications for the use of torture came to the fore, especially in the United States, after 11 September 2001 when the US president George W. Bush declared and pursued a 'war on terror'. During this 'war' the United States has detained people in prisons outside its own territory including Abu Ghraib prison in Iraq, the US airbase in Bagram, Afghanistan and most (in)famously the US naval base in Guantánamo Bay, Cuba.

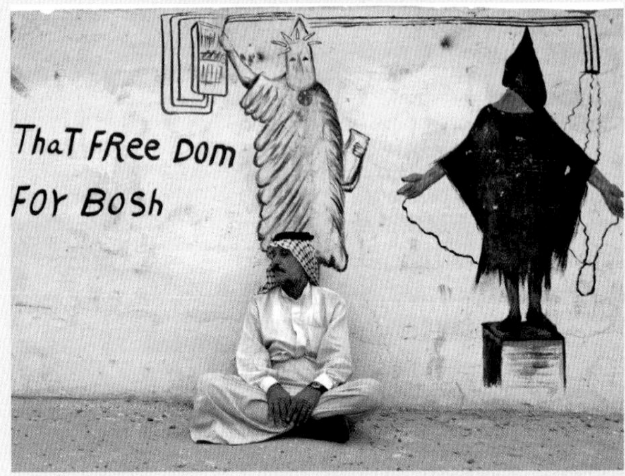

FIGURE 2.1
Iraqi Graffiti mural depicting prisoner abuse on wall in Sadr City, Baghdad. Photo: Ali Jasim/Reuters

FIGURE 2.2
Guantánamo Bay: A detainee is escorted for interrogation in 2002. Photo: Andres Leighton/AP

It was not until May 2004 that accounts and images of US military personnel torturing detainees in Abu Ghraib prison, Iraq, burst into public view although there had been secret US military investigations into allegations of torture, and reports of its use from organisations such as the International Committee of the Red Cross.

In particular, the Bush administration's use of Guantánamo as the central prison for 'unlawful enemy combatants' became subject to global condemnation because of its violation of the Geneva Conventions and the use of torture 'lite'; so-called 'harsh interrogation techniques'. Such was the negative symbolism of Guantánamo that two days after his inauguration President Obama signed executive orders to close the detention camp, stopping the Bush administration's use of the military commissions system for prosecuting detainees and ending the Central Intelligence Agency's secret interrogation programme. However, in March 2011 President Obama permitted military trials to resume, albeit with revamped procedures, and has all but admitted his failure to close the camp wherein 172 'high risk' detainees remain.

Unfortunately, allegations and the evidence for the use of torture extend further than the prisons with the use of extraordinary rendition or 'torture by proxy'. This policy is one where 'hundreds of people have been unlawfully transferred by the USA and its allies to countries such as Syria, Jordan and Egypt . . . [where] they risk enforced disappearance, torture and other ill-treatment' (Amnesty International 2007: 9). Evidence of the extent of the practice controversially entered the public domain through posts of secret and confidential American diplomatic cables on the website Wikileaks in November 2010.

of the hypothetical scenario. It deliberately eliminates specific aspects of a situation in order to focus solely on the core issue: whether the prohibition against torture is absolute. By abstracting the core issue in this way, the idea is that we can 'test' the limits of the prohibition.

The scenario works by providing compelling reasons for torture being justified under certain circumstances. However, it is a scenario set up in such a way that we *already* know that torturing the detainee is justifiable. Since the scenario tells us that saving lives is good and torture saves lives, it must be the case that torture can be justifiable. The scenario is a purely theoretical construct and deliberately so. In order to construct a hypothetical scenario such as this, one must believe that theory (thinking about the world) and practice (doing things in the world) can be separated. A separation is made and assumed to be possible.

You will often find that people simply assume that saving lives is a good thing. But we don't always act to save everyone's lives. In fact, we routinely endanger some people's lives, and not always in order to save others. Soldiers and enemy civilians are only the most obvious cases here; arguably, the global economy also relies on putting some lives at immediate risk.

When we read the ticking bomb scenario more closely, we notice that it does two other things, as well as separating theory and practice.

First, the scenario suggests that we need to employ our rationality and come to conclusions based on either certainty or, at a minimum, reasonable belief. There are certain things we need to know before we can make a decision and we need to balance them up rationally. Often what we are balancing are competing values. In the case of the ticking bomb it is the value of the strict prohibition of torture *versus* the value of saving a significant number of lives. As we have seen, the scenario suggests that abstraction is helpful. The ticking bomb scenario is deliberately and consciously designed to reduce the problem of torture to only two competing values and to compel us to choose which value is more significant. It is, necessarily, a simplification. But, in the view of those using this scenario, simplification can help us determine more accurately what we should do.

Rationality came to be seen as incredibly important in the period called the Enlightenment, but it was also a quality attributed to men in particular. See **Chapters 5 and 6**.

Second, although the scenario suggests that all human life has value – not only the lives that are at risk from the bomb's explosion, but also that of the person we have in custody – it is clear that 'we' are not the person who planted the bomb, nor are 'we' associated with them. The scenario is not constructed from the point of view of the person who is in custody. There is no mention of what justifications he or she may have, or what reasons there may be, for planting the bomb. Of course, this does not mean that there are any justifications, but the scenario does not explore whether there are any reasons for planting the bomb or not. For example, the ticking bomb scenario is not one where a person plants a bomb that threatens hundreds of lives in order to prevent others from taking hundreds of other, different, lives. The scenario is completely silent about the purported bomber's motivations other than the desire to kill people with the explosion of the device. This means that 'we' are the potential (albeit righteously reluctant yet well trained) torturers in the scenario. Furthermore, 'we', as potential torturers, feel more akin to those whose lives are at risk from the bomb than to the person we have in custody. Whoever he or she is, it seems that they are not 'us'. Whoever 'we' are, we are not in Kabul, Addis Ababa, or Shanghai, for example as the scenario, interestingly, always imagines that the bomb is planted in an advanced industrialised country.

As an abstraction then, the ticking bomb scenario shows much more than might be supposed at first glance about the way of thinking about the world that it involves. When we look at what the scenario leaves out, what it does not allow us to consider explicitly, we find that it ignores the question of how far our feelings and responsibilities

© Mike Baldwin / Cornered
"I found out what makes him tick, but he still won't tock."

FIGURE 2.3
'I found out what makes him tick. . .' Artist: Mike Baldwin. CartoonStock ref.: mba0459. www.CartoonStock.com

may stretch: should or do they include others who are not part of what 'we' think of as 'us'? Perhaps our obligations are limited to those who belong with us in a particular community or perhaps they stretch beyond nationality and extend to the whole of humanity.

A scenario could be said to be similar to a theoretical explanation, in that theories tend to leave things out, and to be abstract.

In practice, things are more complicated than the abstract scenario. The situation may not be one of choosing between the value of one life (the person in custody) and that of many others (the potential victims of the bomb). We cannot always be sure that we have the right person in custody. We are often uncertain. This implies that we may have to torture others as well, since they might equally know where the bomb is planted. We are more likely to be dealing with several (or even hundreds of) possible 'knowers' that would need to be tortured to reveal the location of the bomb *versus* hundreds of lives to save. Indeed, it is precisely the kind of logic employed in the ticking bomb scenario that leads to large numbers of people being detained in the 'war on terror': they may be 'knowers'. In practice, the logic of the ticking bomb scenario provides a justification for detaining people in great numbers. If so, the neatness of the scenario begins to break down, and with it its strict separation of theory and practice. The scenario no longer refers to an exception that applies to only one life (the bomber's) but begins to implicate many others.

The prohibition of torture, as set out in the Convention Against Torture (United Nations 1984), does not treat torture as an act that is perpetrated on only one individual either. The Convention Against Torture's references to 'a public official or other person acting in an official capacity' (Article 1) as perpetrators of torture make it clear that the Convention is concerned with prohibiting the institutionalisation and widespread political use of torture by states. The Convention Against Torture and the abundant evidence of torture being used globally show that, in practice, torture implicates many, many lives. In global politics then, what is at stake in the practices of torture is not a question of the justifiability of an isolated incidence of the action of one person (the torturer) on only one other (the person in custody). It is, more accurately, the actions of many ('us') on many ('them').

Our short study of the ticking bomb scenario has served as a way of introducing questions about a way of thinking about the world: one that employs an abstract rationality and separates thinking about the world, or theorising, from the world itself, or practice, and one that ducks the question of whether our obligations are limited to people who share the same community with us or whether they extend to the whole of humanity. We have seen that this way of looking at the world can provide a justification for actions that in practice can lead to the torturing of many people, not just one.

GENERAL RESPONSES
THINKING ABOUT ETHICS: TWO RESPONSES

The ticking bomb scenario implies that the decisions that we have to make about whether or not to use torture should be thought of as *moral* decisions. They are decisions about what we *ought* to do or what we *should* do. Very often, moral decisions are seen to be the result of applying some kind of rule governing our treatment of others and understanding exactly how the rule should apply. For example, the ticking bomb scenario rationally examined the limits of applying the rule 'torture is an absolute moral prohibition' and found that the rule was not absolute after all. We noted at the start of the chapter that, roughly speaking, *ethics* is about how we should live with other people in the world. Thinking about ethics means broadly thinking about moral rules and how they govern the ways in which we treat each other. Often such rules are phrased in terms of moral duties, moral obligations and/or moral responsibilities. When we come to explore how people have thought about the question of ethics in global politics, straight away we encounter discussions about the rules that should govern our duties and obligations and how far they should stretch: whether our duties and obligations should extend only to those within the political community or state in which we find ourselves, or whether they should extend to the whole of humanity. This question of how far our moral obligations extend is traditionally captured by the debate between cosmopolitans and communitarians. We have already encountered hidden aspects of this debate in our exploration of the ticking bomb scenario when it was noted that whoever the bomber is the bomber isn't one of 'us'. If the bomber's nationality seems to make a moral difference, or indeed none, to your conclusions about the ticking bomb scenario then the cosmopolitan–communitarian debate is deeply relevant. This is because the debate thinks through the moral implications of whether 'we' are best understood as members of the whole of humanity (cosmopolitanism) or as members of specific political communities (communitarianism).

Charles Beitz and Michael Walzer, from the cosmopolitan and communitarian traditions respectively, have sustained answers to how far our ethical obligations extend in global politics. I will look at the work of each thinker in turn. In order to begin to understand and unravel the implications of each set of answers, I will focus on the pictures or representations they use. I will say more about what we mean by pictures or representations in the next section, but for the time being it is sufficient to note that

The work of different thinkers is often grouped into different schools of thought, perspectives or approaches. While sometimes useful, 'boxing' people like this risks oversimplifying complicated questions.

thinking about the pictures they use is helpful in highlighting the way in which each answer is their attempt to provide an accurate and true representation of the realities of global politics.

- First, a focus on *pictures of reason* will serve to reveal traditional, differing, views on what an academic study of global politics is supposed to focus on as most relevant to ethics and how we should think about it.
- Second, *pictures of the subject* tell us what or who, supposedly, 'we' are and more particularly, what it is about 'us' as moral subjects that provides us with moral value or character. This is vitally important because such pictures not only tell us who or what has the highest moral value in global politics, but the moral subject towards which we are primarily ethically responsible in practice.
- Third, *pictures of ethico-political space* tell us where the possibility of ethical action in global politics is believed to take place. They seek to depict what the 'world' of global political reality is 'really' like and its hostility, or otherwise, to the accommodation of ethics in practice.

Communitarianism: Michael Walzer

For other views of what the state, or what is sometimes called the nation-state, is as a form of political community, and how it is held together, see **Chapters 11, 12 and 13**.

Of course, what counts as human and what doesn't is historically and culturally changeable. See **Chapters 5, 21 and 27**.

In the work of Michael Walzer we find a communitarian set of answers to questions of ethics in global politics. Communitarians focus on the state as a moral subject in global politics. As Walzer's picture of ethico-political space will reveal, the moral value of the state lies in its political community.

To understand the moral significance of the community we first need to examine Walzer's *picture of the subject*. According to Walzer, being human is about being complex: creating meaning and culture which 'we' both reflect and are reflected in (Walzer 1994: 85). Human beings have equal moral value because they are all culture- and meaning-producing creatures. Each subject participates in their own community. Globally, there is a vast plurality of differing social and cultural meanings because whilst 'we' all produce meanings and culture, 'we' do not all produce the same ones. Is it possible to talk of a common humanity since there will be differing opinions about what 'humanity' might mean? Yes, says Walzer, although 'our common humanity will never make us members of a single universal tribe. What members of the human race have in common is particularism (that is, attachment to particular groups over humanity as a whole): we participate, all of us, in thick cultures that are our own' (Walzer 1994: 83).

For Walzer being human is about creating meanings and therefore different cultures; unsurprisingly his *picture of reason* is a picture of shared understandings, which are radically particularistic. In contrast to the cosmopolitan thinker, Beitz, whose view we examine below, for Walzer reason is not separate from its social, historical and cultural contexts. What is rational depends on what those of us who share the same understandings mean by it. Applying this to ethics, Walzer's position is one that emphasises that standards of rightness and wrongness, justice and injustice, etc., depend on particular socio-cultural practices.

Having prepared the ground, we can now better appreciate Walzer's *picture of ethico-political space*. In the final analysis, he produces an international ethics that centres on states as the moral subjects (Walzer 1977). States, he argues, have moral value because they contain a political community. The community is the expression of a common life that its members have produced, sustained and participated in as meaning-producing human beings. A state, for Walzer, consists of a political community and its government (Walzer 1985 [1980]: 220, 235). The political community has rights to territorial integrity and sovereignty and these rights belong to the state through the consent of its members. Through consent, members form a metaphorical 'contract' with the state that it should protect the common life which they have shaped over a long period of time.

The state's claim to territorial integrity and political sovereignty is discussed in **Chapter 11**.

For Walzer, upholding the state rights of territorial integrity and sovereignty should form the basis of an international morality. However, only legitimate states' rights should be respected. He says that states are only legitimate if there is a fit between the government and community such that the former represents the peoples' political life in accordance with their own traditions and specific way of life. The problem, of course, is how can we judge fit when 'our' opinions about being governed according to 'our' traditions will be so different from others? For example, 'we' might think that only democratic forms of governance provide a fit and hence, provide legitimacy to governments. Well aware of this, Walzer says that in the majority of instances states should presume that other states are legitimate, and should not intervene in their affairs. Nevertheless, there may be very rare occasions when the principle of non-intervention can be overridden. For Walzer, these would be when the absence of fit is radically apparent, as in the case of either a struggle for national liberation, a civil war, or the massacre, enslavement or expulsion of a mass of people.

Changing attitudes to intervention are the subject of **Chapter 25**.

What does this add up to? It adds up to an approach to international ethics which says that, for the most part, we should leave states alone to live the historical and culturally specific lives they have created for themselves. We can't expect to understand other ways of living from our own specific perspectives and so not only do we have no right to intervene but we lack the capacity to understand the situation objectively. In short nationality and citizenship, as forms of belonging to political community, make a moral difference because they mark a difference in interpretations and understandings of the world.

Cosmopolitanism: Charles Beitz

The second answer to ethics in global politics is a cosmopolitan one, found in the work of Charles Beitz. In contrast to Walzer, Beitz considers individuals who are rational, free and equal to be the moral subject of global politics.

Chapter 13 examines ways of conceptualising the political community by looking at a number of novels. One of the characters is a committed cosmopolitan.

Beitz applies John Rawls' theory of justice to international politics (Beitz 1999 [1979]; Rawls 1971). He seeks to find out which principles of justice would be chosen to create a perfectly just world order (an 'ideal theory'). But how would such a principle, where 'social and economic inequalities are to be arranged . . . to the greatest benefit of the least advantaged', be chosen? To think about this, Beitz uses a hypothetical scenario called the global original position. He sees using this scenario as a purely theoretical exercise of moral reasoning – like the ticking bomb scenario – and one that is impartial. It requires that we suspend any bias and put to one side being a particular self with particular interests: according to his *picture of reason*, this is possible. In the

BOX 2.2 JOHN RAWLS

John Rawls (1921–2002) is widely regarded as the late twentieth-century's greatest liberal political philosopher. His major intellectual preoccupation was to defend the notion that civil and political rights are inviolable and that such rights were the first duty of a liberal state. His most important book, *A Theory of Justice*, was first published in 1971. In it he explores the contours of a just society with the argument that 'Each person possesses an inviolability founded on justice that even the welfare of society as a whole cannot override. Therefore, in a just society the rights secured by justice are not subject to political bargaining or to the calculus of social interests.'

FIGURE 2.4 John Rawls. Photo: Jane Reed, University of Harvard

scenario, state representatives would not know their nationality or whether their state had large natural resources, but they would know that resources are unevenly distributed globally and each state needs adequate resources for there to be a successful and just global society. Consequently, Beitz argues, the parties would rationally choose a global principle that redistributed natural resources justly, because no state representative would want to find that they had few or no natural resources.

For Beitz's cosmopolitan ethics to work, he needs to argue that principles of justice can apply to the non-ideal environment of global politics. Why? It all has to do with Rawls. Rawls thinks his principles can only be applied to domestic societies as 'cooperative ventures for mutual advantage' (Rawls 1971: 4). Beitz disagrees and argues that international politics is sufficiently similar to domestic politics to count as a cooperative scheme, even though international institutions and practices may not be genuinely cooperative. Beitz's point is that there is enough transnational activity – trade, international investment, aid and communications – to mean that burdens and/or benefits are produced which need to be justly distributed. Beitz offers us a *picture of ethico-political space*, then, that emphasises the similarity between domestic and international politics. Because of their similarity the principles of justice discovered by ideal theory and the hypothetical scenario apply.

The problem of the distribution of benefits across the globe is certainly a major issue in global politics today. See **Chapter 19**.

But who are 'we' according to Beitz? For whom are global burdens and benefits to be redistributed in the name of justice? Beitz's answer is the individual: persons who have rights and interests. Beitz rejects the view that non-person based interests are appropriate or relevant from the moral point of view. According to his *picture of the subject* it is persons, rather than states, nations or communities who should benefit. This is the badge of a cosmopolitan position. Furthermore, Beitz believes that persons have a natural duty to create and sustain just institutions. In other words, the principles of justice (which ideal theory locates using the hypothetical scenario of the global original position) can become part of the non-ideal world because it is a natural duty of moral subjects to secure justice *and* because the international context is sufficiently like the domestic to make acting on such a duty appropriate and realistic.

For the cosmopolitan then, international ethics is understood from an impartial perspective that any human being can take simply because they are a rational human being. Unlike Walzer, Beitz is arguing that we can understand other cultures and make moral judgements without worrying about mistranslation or misunderstanding. For Beitz, the important thing is to base our moral judgements and therefore, our international ethics on ideal principles of justice. As such, what morally matters the most is not our nationality nor our citizenship but rather, our humanity.

We summarise Walzer and Beitz's different pictures in Figure 2.5.

	Walzer (Communitarian)	*Beitz (Cosmopolitan)*
Reason	Reason cannot overcome interests, biases and socio-cultural meanings	Reason transcends our interests and biases
The subject	The state or the political community is the moral subject	The individual (as a member of humanity) is the moral subject
Ethico-political space	Ethics takes place within states; those outside are not our primary moral concern	Ethical responsibility extends to every person regardless of where they live

FIGURE 2.5
Table summary of Walzer and Beitz

BROADER ISSUES
THINKING ABOUT THINKING

Surveying the way two thinkers in global politics approach ethics gave us two sets of *pictures* of reason, the subject and ethico-political space. *Importantly, both approaches share the impulse to picture.* Regardless of the content of the pictures, each approach believes that theirs is an accurate and true representation of the *reality* of reason, the subject and ethico-political space.

Attempts to describe global political reality are forms of representation, or what I have called pictures. The assumption is that the truth or falsity of a picture or representation depends on how accurately it corresponds with reality. This depends on postulating what we call a *word–object relation*. The meaning of a word depends on it naming or accurately representing the corresponding object that exists independently in reality. So, for example, 'political community' refers to a common way of life; and so on. In this way of thinking, all the things referred to exist outside language and act as the foundation of the world. They exist in a reality that is independent of any thoughts or words we might have about it. Our words simply refer to the foundation or essence of such things as political community and principles of justice. This is what picturing

Holding a mirror up to reality and checking whether the image accurately reflects reality is another way of thinking of this: **Chapter 24**.

assumes. It is called a correspondence theory of truth. When a picture accurately portrays reality, or when our words name the correct 'thing' or object, then the picture is true. The picture is false if it is inaccurate.

But what happens if you begin to wonder about the whole endeavour of picturing and the pictures themselves? What happens if we shift our attention towards pictures as the problem rather than the answer to ethics? If we did make such a shift we would be involved in something different: another approach. This different approach questions whether pictures can fully capture reality at all. In other words, it questions how and where we draw the lines around what we think reality is and what impact these lines have on people's lives and the ways in which they are able and unable to live them with each other.

Pictures, framing and language games

Before we return to looking at torture and ticking time bombs as an example of how pictures impact on people's lives and our treatment of each other, we first need to ask why pictures might be problematic. The philosopher Ludwig Wittgenstein argued that when we provide answers they tend to be of the kind 'This is how things are.' However, as Wittgenstein says:

> one thinks that one is tracing the outline of the thing's nature over and over again, and one is merely tracing round the frame through which we look at it. A *picture* held us captive. And we could not get outside it, for it lay in our language and language seemed to repeat it to us inexorably.
>
> (Wittgenstein 1958: §§114–15)

You may have come across references to 'regimes of truth', 'ideologies', 'theoretical approaches': these often mean the same thing, or something very similar, to what is called 'language games' here.

Wittgenstein implies that pictures are part of the practice of language that he calls language games. Rather than picturing reality as though reality were outside our language, pictures constitute or create reality. This does not mean that there is no

BOX 2.3 LUDWIG WITTGENSTEIN

Ludwig Wittgenstein (1889–1951) is one of the most influential philosophers of the twentieth century. His major intellectual preoccupation was with the relationship between language and the world and how our misunderstandings of it lead to philosophical problems. In his lifetime he published only one work, the *Tractatus Logico-Philosophicus* (1922) perhaps most famous for its phrase 'Whereof one cannot speak one must remain silent.' His later philosophy was posthumously published as *Philosophical Investigations* (1958). His influence remains important outside philosophy, including in thinking about global politics.

FIGURE 2.6
Ludwig Wittgenstein. von Wright and Wittgenstein Archives, University of Helsinki

external reality. But it does mean that we are wholly dependent upon language to make sense of and understand the world we live in. And if this is so, then language tells us *what* to think about the world or what we call reality. The importance of this cannot be overstated. It means that how we think about the world is regulated by our language games or practices. In turn, if our thoughts are regulated by language, it means that our thoughts are practices: ways of being in the world. This is why pictures, as snapshots of what we think about things and people in the world, affect the world we live in. For example, naming a person who plants a ticking bomb a 'terrorist' or a 'freedom fighter' matters beyond the choice of mere vocabulary. Using the term 'freedom fighter' seems to suggest that the person may have a justifiable reason for their actions, whereas 'terrorist' does not. Another way of putting this important point would be to say that our language games constitute the limits of possibility: they tell us what it is possible to do and how it is possible to exist and act in the world.

Chapter 28 takes up the issue of language and our relation to what we call reality in a slightly different way.

In summary, thinking about language games emphasises how language makes a difference to how we live and act in the world with others. Pictures tell us what we think 'reality' is and therefore regulate how we act and live in it. Elaborating this further we can say that pictures are practices of telling us what shall count as 'true', 'false', 'humanity', 'political community': any 'thing' (object) or any 'body' (subject). Therefore, the pictures that relate to ethics are a set of practices that tell us what ethics is. Making pictures the problem rather than the answer makes the job of asking how we think about the world and ethics in global politics very different. Thinking about the world becomes a questioning of how thinking or picturing regulates the ways in which we act and the impact this has on people's lives.

Let's now return to thinking about torture and the ticking bomb scenario in order to illustrate the shift towards an approach that sees pictures of reason, the subject and ethico-political space as the problem, not the answer.

Pictures of reason, the subject and ethico-political space

The ticking bomb scenario is the practice of a specific kind of picture of reason: a particular idea of what we think 'thinking about' the world requires. In this case, we will see that Charles Beitz and the United States administration of George W. Bush deployed the same picture of reason as that underlying the ticking bomb scenario. There is a good chance that you are familiar with this picture. It is often associated with liberalism.

Liberalism is a pervasive ideology. Many of the chapters mention it, in particular those that explore the global political economy.

The ticking bomb scenario operates with a picture of reason as abstraction. It operates in three steps. *Step one* presents us with a dilemma; whether the value of the life of the bomber can be overridden in order to save other lives. However, this dilemma is not generated by the scenario. It is what the scenario *is* about and why it has been constructed. Having constructed it for this purpose, *step two* requires imagining or thinking hypothetically of anything that might be an exception to an absolute prohibition against torture. Obviously, the candidate for an exception is a ticking bomb. The scenario is asking us whether we think that a ticking bomb really is an exception. Once we've decided that, then *step three* in this picture of reason is to find 'real world' cases or practices where the justifications for torture appear. The shape of this picture of reason is one where there is a clear separation between theory and practice. How we are to act in the world is first determined by theory as the exercise of reason in the abstract. The next issue is then to apply theory to the world. These steps are also how Beitz generates his principles of justice. He identifies the issue, provides a hypothetical scenario (the global original position) and from that deduces global principles of justice that should be applied to the world.

How can we engage with this picture of reason differently? One way is to trace the effects of this picture rather than engage with its 'truth' or 'falsity'. There are many effects, but we can highlight an important one here. Separating theory and practice means just that: separating them. This then raises the obvious problem of how the two can be reunited, if at all, as the practice of theory. But more importantly, we might want to think about whether theory and practice can be separated in the first place. One way we could do this would be by asking what kind of people are included in this picture of reason. The scenario is not interested in, nor does it include, actual cases of torture: who was tortured, how, why and by whom. The only people that are in the picture are people using abstracted reasoning. They don't have feelings of guilt, humiliation, fear, enjoyment, or confusion nor do they feel pain or scream for example. The scenario also does not include any politics; why the 'bomber' might have planted the bomb, why he planted it where he did, who has captured him, who has labelled him as a 'terrorist' and why, etc. The scenario is deliberately designed to strip away all this information and ask us to make decisions in the absence of the much messier, complicated fabric of global politics.

This section has been arguing that pictures are practices even if, as in this case, they are conceived as purely theoretical. Examining the ticking bomb scenario's picture of reason as the problem involves exploring the possibility that, through its separation of theory and practice, it may be a practice that sanitises torture through its lack of reference to any specific people or political context. Arguably, this has the effect of making torture seem more rational, more palatable and less objectionable. If so, the creation of a scenario that allows for the possibility that torture *is* justified may well be implicated in the actual practice of torture. This would mean that the strict separation of theory and practice that the scenario depends on for making torture justifiable might not be possible in the first place.

So those talking about torture in this way are in some sense responsible for the actual torture that takes place: their talk has made that torture possible.

An example of this would be the Final Report of the Independent Panel To Review [US] Department of Defense Detention Operations, which was published in August 2004 as a response to accounts of the torture of prisoners in Abu Ghraib prison, Iraq, by US military personnel in late 2003. The Report was commissioned by the then US secretary of defense, Donald Rumsfeld, to provide independent advice on the abuse of detainees. The Report stated that 'For the US, most cases for permitting harsh treatment of detainees on moral grounds begin with variants of the "ticking time bomb" scenario' (Schlesinger *et al.* 2004: Appendix H, 2). Why does this matter? The point is that the Report clearly accepted that the ticking bomb scenario *justifies* torture and that this was the position shared by the Bush administration. Therefore, the picture of reason that underlies the ticking bomb scenario was part of a set of shared practices employed by the administration. Given this, for the US and the Report, the issue then became how 'harsh treatment' can be used, by whom and under which circumstances, but no longer *whether* it should be used. Indeed, what consequently emerged was a distinction between torture 'lite' and torture – the former being a justified form which is,

FIGURE 2.7 Samrong Military Hospital, Cambodia. Photo: Olivier Pin-Fat

purportedly, moderate and restrained (Wolfendale 2009). Bearing this in mind, we must ask whether the ticking bomb scenario is complicit in the use of torture because the use or practice of its picture of reason makes torture possible. Moreover, once thinking along these lines is made permissible it makes possible any further distinctions we might want to make about 'lite' forms of it and current debates on whether waterboarding, for example, is a form of torture or not. This is a very long way away from the original position of the CAT which says that there are no circumstances under which torture may be justified. I suggest it's the abstract thinking of the 'ticking bomb' scenario which leads us to these practices so horribly quickly.

Pictures of reason are also related to pictures of the subject. In the bomb scenario, it is clear that subjects are meant to come to their decisions rationally and this is what matters most. Our alternative approach would ask what kind of subject this is: what does it include and exclude? It is fascinating that the ticking bomb scenario does not mention pain, as pain is, perhaps, what we most associate torture with. The subjects in the scenario (the torturer and the tortured) are pictured as disembodied. That is to say, that they are viewed as people with reason but with no body that can feel pain. Nor are they pictured as having emotions. Not only does the bomber in the scenario not scream, he does not cry, he has no relationships of love and he holds no beliefs in his heart rather than his head. It is very difficult to explore how far our bodies and emotions matter in global politics and ethics, but the point is, we can ask whether this picture of the subject that excludes them seems to miss something important about being human. In so far as this picture of the subject is a practice, it has the effect of excluding emotions and embodiment from consideration. This is, furthermore, a political act since it is telling us what matters most about being human. So, for example, if the tortured bomber begins begging for the torture to stop should we listen to him? Or should we only listen if he

When we talk about other forms of violence – war for example – we also tend to talk as if there were no actual bodies involved. See **Chapters 1 and 22**.

is presenting us with rational reasons to stop? Is compassion, for example, irrelevant to global politics and ethics?

Apart from this picture of the subject as disembodied, without emotions and without emotional ties to others, the subject is neither social nor political. Again this is a picture most associated with liberalism and is also shared by Beitz. In the ticking bomb scenario the bomber and the potential torturer do not belong to any specified society or culture, have no specified citizenship, no specified notions of belonging or identity, and no political reasons for acting. In section 3, we traced how this is a picture of the subject that Beitz employs and we saw Walzer's objections to it. However, instead of asking which thinker has the 'true' picture, what we need to do using our alternative approach is trace the effects of the practice of each picture. As we have seen in the ticking bomb scenario, the picture of the subject is employed in a way that contributes to the separation of theory and practice by abstracting people from the context within which they are living and acting. Consequently, the ticking bomb scenario does not ask whether there might be any justifications for the bomber planting the bomb.

This leads us nicely into thinking about the relationship between pictures of reason and the subject and the picture of ethico-political space. *Where* does ethics or politics take place? Ironically, the pictures of reason and the subject in the ticking bomb scenario do not explicitly suggest a particular place because of their commitment to the absence of a specific society and a disembodied subject. Place lies in the background as a hidden assumption. However, it is clear from the practice of these pictures that the scenario is supposed to apply to the United States or a state much like it. The clues are in the setting up of the scenario. The bomb is planted in Washington, Paris or London for example. There are two things to notice about this. One, the potential victims of the bomb will be people living in the US or an advanced industrialised state. Two, therefore, the potential torturers will be the US or a liberal democratic, advanced industrialised state. This is the ethico-political space within which the ticking bomb scenario is set. We could see this as a problem and we could ask what happens to the scenario if it is set elsewhere. What if, for example, a ticking bomb is planted somewhere in Afghanistan and the bomber is a US soldier being held by the Taliban? Does this make a difference to how we would come to a decision about the justifiability of torture? And, if you feel that it does, why does it? Would you want to make a distinction between the Taliban practising torture 'lite' and torture? Regardless of your answers, in the ticking bomb scenario we have a picture of ethico-political space as one occupied by states; more specifically, liberal democratic states.

We might want to ask whether it is only liberal democratic states that can justifiably use torture. Moreover, we can go further by asking whether the spaces within which ethics and politics take place in global politics must be territorial spaces like states, nations or political communities. *Perhaps ethics is all around us and is unavoidable.* We live in a world of pictures, where what we think about the world matters. If, as this chapter has suggested, pictures are the problem, then ethico-political space, and the need and occasion to think about the problem of picturing, is everywhere: it is in the state, at home, in the lecture theatre, in this textbook, in abstract thoughts and hypothetical scenarios. If we fail to be aware of how we think about the world and its effects, we may find ourselves blindly complicit in a variety of practices, like torture. It should make us pause to think about how we think about the world.

CONCLUSION

This chapter has traced how and why what we think about the world matters. It began by posing questions about how the way we think about the world impacts on our treatment of others. In order to highlight how thinking affects the world, the chapter examined the abstracted way of thinking deployed by the ticking bomb scenario. The chapter showed that thinking about thinking very quickly led us to questions of ethics in global politics. Not only was the ethics of torture implicated but also the much broader question of whether our moral obligations extend primarily to 'us' as fellow citizens or 'us' as the whole of humanity. This apparent choice between an international ethic based on communities or on humanity was identified as the cosmopolitan–communitarian debate; a debate which provides well-established answers to what pictures of reason, the subject and ethico-political space consist of. Finally, the chapter examined a different approach: a way of thinking that sees pictures as the problem, not the answer, a way of thinking that can be seen as an ethico-political endeavour in itself. In the final analysis, the chapter is a plea for us, whoever 'we' may be, to be mindful of how we live in the world and our ethico-political relations with others.

FURTHER READING

Brecher, Bob (2007) *Torture and the ticking bomb*, Oxford: Wiley-Blackwell.

Fierke, K. M. (2002) 'Links Across the Abyss: Language and Logic in International Relations', *International Studies Quarterly* 46, 3: 331–54.
An introduction to the relevance of Wittgenstein for global politics.

Greenberg, Karen J. (ed.) (2006) *The Torture Debate in America*, New York: Cambridge University Press.
A detailed survey of aspects of the torture debate in the US.

Pin-Fat, Véronique (2010) *Universality, Ethics and International Relations: A Grammatical Reading*, Abingdon and New York: Routledge.

Walzer, Michael (2004) *Arguing About War*, New Haven, CT and London: Yale University Press.
A more recent meditation on war and intervention.

WEBSITES

Amnesty International, http://www.amnesty.org
A human rights non-governmental organisation that monitors human rights around the world.

United Nations, Committee Against Torture, part of the Office of the High Commissioner for Human Rights, http://www2.ohchr.org/english/bodies/cat/
This Committee is responsible for monitoring the prevention of torture.

Wikileaks, wikileaks.org
This site includes collections of leaked official documents, for example The Guantanamo Files, Iraq War Logs and Afghanistan War Logs.

REFERENCES

Amnesty International (2007) *Report 2007: The State of the World's Human Rights*, London: Amnesty International.

Beitz, Charles (1999 [1979]) *Political Theory and International Relations*, Princeton, NJ: Princeton University Press.

Rawls, John (1971) *A Theory of Justice*, Cambridge, MA: Harvard University Press.

Scarry, Elaine (1985) *The Body in Pain: The Making and Unmaking of the World*, New York and Oxford: Oxford University Press.

Schlesinger, James R., Harold Brown, Tillie K. Fowler and Charles A. Homer (2004) *Final Report of the Independent Panel to Review Department of Defense Detention Operations*, August.

United Nations (1984) *Convention Against Torture and Other Cruel, Inhuman or Degrading Treatment or Punishment*, December.

Walzer, Michael (1977) *Just and Unjust Wars: A Moral Argument with Historical Illustrations*, London: Allen Lane.

——(1985 [1980]) 'The Moral Standing of States: A Response to Four Critics', in Charles R. Beitz, Michael Cohen, Thomas Scanlon and A. John Simmons (eds) *International Ethics*, Princeton, NJ: Princeton University Press.

——(1994) *Thick and Thin: Moral Argument at Home and Abroad*, Notre Dame, IN: University of Notre Dame Press.

Wittgenstein, Ludwig (1922) *Tractatus Logico-Philosophicus*, trans. by C. K. Ogden, London: Routledge and Kegan Paul.

——(1958) *Philosophical Investigations*, trans. by G. E. M. Anscombe, ed. G. E. M. Anscombe and Rush Rhees, 3rd edn, Oxford: Basil Blackwell.

Wolfendale, Jessica (2009) 'The Myth of Torture "Lite"', *Ethics and International Affairs* 23, 1: 47–61.

For a range of further resources supporting this chapter, please visit the companion website for *Global Politics, 2nd Edition* at www.routledge.com/cw/edkins/

CHAPTER 3

What happens if we don't take nature for granted?

Simon Dalby

THE QUESTION
FROM ENVIRONMENT TO BIOSPHERE

We are part of a complicated biosphere: a thin layer of air, soil, ocean and life surrounding a small planet (Smil 2003). The food we eat, the water, and other things, we drink, the clothes we wear, the buildings we live in, the cars we drive, and yes, the sewage we flush away each day, are all essential to human life, and as such, matters that concern how we organise our lives and how we interact with each other. In other words they are very much a matter of politics even if they are frequently not thought about in quite this way.

Environment is technically a word that means what surrounds something else. Originally the word 'environs' usually meant the area around a town. Updated in the twentieth century it came to mean what surrounds humanity, the outside factors of air, land and water that provide the context for human living. Environmental discussion from the 1960s onwards focused in part on the human disruptions of parts of this

The changing use of terms such as 'environment' and 'nature' reflects changing language games, as discussed in **Chapter 2**. **Chapter 4** uses the rather different term 'ecology'.

HUMAN WATCH-CONFERENCE
"Everything is going according to plan. The ocean levels are rising faster than expected so world domination could be sooner than later. Our only fear is that these dumb beasts will destroy themselves before their work is done."

FIGURE 3.1 'Human Watch: conference'. Artist: Patrick Hickey. CartoonStock ref.: phin28. www.CartoonStock.com

environment. Oil spills and smoke, pesticide poisonings and chemical contamination combined with discussions of urban congestion and suburban sprawl to suggest that humanity was doing damage to the environment, and wasting resources in the process too (Ward and Dubos 1972). This concern about wasting, or running out of, key minerals, fuel supplies and even food added to the worries about pollution. Conservation of resources linked up with the pollution discussions in this discourse of environment which arrived on the political scene as a series of protest movements in developed countries in the late 1960s and 1970s (Sandbach 1980). Governments responded in various ways and most states now have environment departments; environmental movements became a new and powerful international political force (Wapner 1996).

See **Chapter 4** for further discussion of the political movements and parties that have arisen around this issue.

But while environmental thinking is understood to be essential to discussing the future intelligently, it is now complemented by a growing realisation of the need to think much more carefully about the whole biosphere. But when we try to do that, when we try to think about the planet as a whole, and start with the natural systems within which humanity exists, big important questions about how we got here and what kind of a planetary home we are making for future generations quickly get raised. In all the discussions about biodiversity, mad cows, genetically modified crops, ethical consumption, and above all climate change, how society is organised does get discussed, but frequently in terms of the appropriate role for experts and government regulations. But the categories we use in this discussion, and the term 'environment' itself, frequently

Is future human well-being the most important thing?

BOX 3.1 GROWTH AND THE ENVIRONMENT

In the early 1970s some thinkers revived concerns usually linked to the name of Thomas Malthus that resources would run out, stopping economic growth. In the much discussed report on the *Limits to Growth* early computer projections about when resources would run out were coupled to pessimistic concerns about pollution and the eventual collapse of industrial society was forecast (Meadows *et al.* 1974). The arguments about the limits to growth in the 1970s suggested that the planet was running out of essential resources so development would have to come to a halt one way or another. It also suggested that pollution would be a major cause of societal collapse. All of which suggested that economic growth couldn't go on indefinitely on a small planet. Vehement criticisms came from many who argued that the poor would be denied the benefits promised by economic development.

Thus to make environmental concerns palatable, discussions focused on a strategy to overcome the deleterious aspects of economic growth in terms of sustainable development. Designed to promote economic activity that would not deny future generations the necessities for their livelihood, sustainable development was the key theme in the widely cited final report of the World Commission on Environment and Development (1987) headed by Gro Harlem Brundtland, *Our Common Future*. The suggestion in its pages, that development had to continue to add to human wealth so as to deal with problems of poverty and all the social and health ills that came with it without destroying the global environment, became the core of the discussion about development and environment in the United Nations and provided the background for the huge Earth Summit in Rio de Janeiro in 1992. Sustainable development continues to be the framework for United Nations discussions of the future goals for humanity.

don't help in either describing our present predicament or in trying to work out how to proceed in particular circumstances. Mostly this is because in these present circumstances the distinctions between town and country, city and rural areas, are making less and less sense. Seeing environment as separate – a question of nature outside cities, a matter of rural affairs or a distant concern – has gradually given way to understandings, however vague and imprecise, that we all live in a single interconnected biosphere.

The Anthropocene is a new geological epoch, where 'humans have become a force of nature reshaping the planet on a geological scale' (*Economist*, 26 May 2011).

In the last few years this recognition has led to intense discussions about how we should understand our place in the world. The sheer scale of human activity means that we have effectively become a force of nature, changing the planet to such an extent that geologists are discussing what is now widely called a new period in earth's history, the Anthropocene (Steffen *et al.* 2007, Kolbert 2011). The implications of this are profound for thinking about world politics, because although we have been slow to realise it, humanity has taken its fate into its own hands. Indeed some of the earth system scientists who are thinking through how interconnected things are in the biosphere have suggested that we are living through a second Copernican revolution, one where once again our understanding of our place in the universe is being changed profoundly (Schellnhuber *et al.* 2005). Now we understand ourselves as nature, as part of the biosphere that we are rapidly changing. We aren't on earth; we literally are earth.

Copernicus argued that the earth was not the centre of the universe, with the sun moving round it, as had previously been thought. Do we still think 'man' is the centre of the universe, or is the planet as a whole indifferent to human survival?

Humanity is deciding what kind of a planet future generations will live in, and changing it in ways that are similar to some of the massive extinction events of the ancient

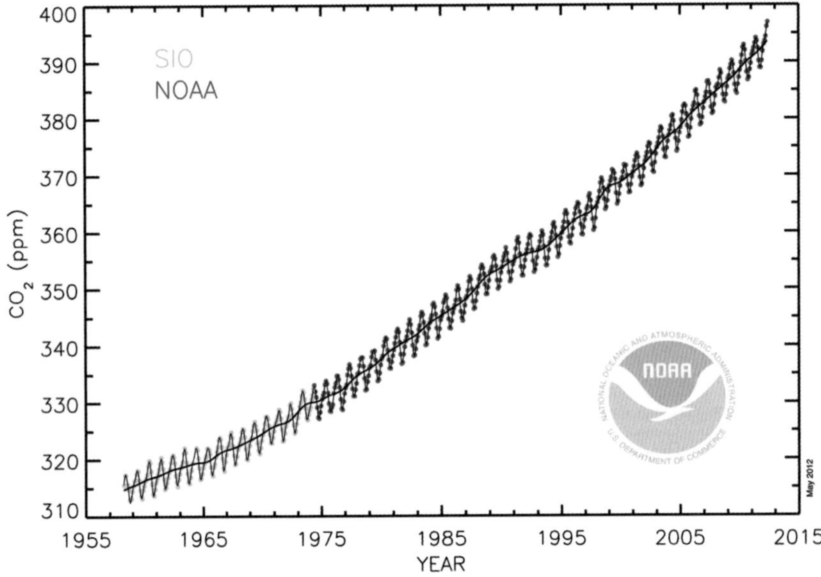

FIGURE 3.2 CO_2 concentrations from the Mauna Loa Observatory, Hawaii. Global Monitoring Division, Earth System Research Laboratory, National Oceanic and Atmospheric Administration

geological past. We are making decisions about which life forms will exist in the future; literally playing God. Nature is no longer 'out there', the given context for the human drama. We are remaking nature, and in the process making decisions about what kind of world future human generations will live in. We can no longer take nature for granted. This is profoundly political, a matter of world politics quite literally.

ILLUSTRATIVE EXAMPLE
CLIMATE CHANGE

The recognition that human actions are inadvertently causing huge changes to the planet has been emphasised recently by the discussion of climate change. Climate change is a complicated process, but one that is now partly driven by human actions. The complexity arises because the atmospheric system and its links to both land and ocean involve numerous flows of energy and matter that vary with seasons and from place to place. Human actions change the land fairly directly, and so may cause direct effects; a black asphalt car park radiates heat on a sunny day very differently from the hayfield that it replaced. But by far the greatest change that humanity is introducing into the climate system is the addition of carbon dioxide, methane and other so called greenhouse gasses that trap heat within the atmosphere.

Over long geological time scales of the past, forests and other life forms have absorbed carbon dioxide from the air. Some of them, when they died, have been covered with silt and buried. There over millions of years various chemical processes underground have turned the organic matter into coal, petroleum and natural gas. In the last few centuries humanity has been rapidly reversing this long term trend. Now by literally turning rocks into air, for that is what we are doing every time we burn coal to make electricity, drive a car or use fossil fuels in countless other ways, we are changing the makeup of the atmosphere and in the process changing the systems that drive the biosphere's climate and creating a new set of circumstances for humanity (Flannery 2006). Environment is no longer something 'out there', separate from humanity, but something we are increasingly remaking by our actions.

People often assume that culture is 'made' but nature is 'given': our impact on the environment suggests that it is much more complicated than that.

Capitalism and industrialisation

Climate change is especially important in any discussion of global politics both because it has global ramifications and because its causes stem from how we collectively organise our contemporary urban society. While coal and to a very small degree petroleum have been used by people for thousands of years, it is only since the beginning of what is called the Industrial Revolution late in the eighteenth century that using them has begun to have a noticeable effect on the earth's atmosphere. Once the steam engine was put in motion, first in railway engines, then as the power system for steamships, the global economy rapidly became connected: 'Suddenly the price of wheat in Liverpool and the rainfall in Madras were variables in the same vast equation of human survival' (Davis 2001: 12). The substitution of fossil fuels for labour both dramatically changed the structure of British, and subsequently other, societies and simultaneously set in motion the accumulation of carbon dioxide in the atmosphere.

Changes during industrialisation and the rise of capitalism are discussed in **Chapter 17**.

The impact of these changes in India are discussed in **Chapter 16**.

This whole process of what Lewis Mumford (1934) once called carboniferous capitalism – because the coal that powered industrial society came from the carboniferous period in geological history – was accelerated dramatically when petroleum was refined and oils and gases started being used for lighting, heating and then, crucially, in the internal combustion engines used to power cars and lorries. When one adds in the energy used in road, parking lot and bridge construction, a very substantial part of the energy used in contemporary society is directly related to automobiles and their

FIGURE 3.3
Traffic congestion

BOX 3.2 CLIMATE CHANGE CONTROVERSY

In the last few years the public discussion about climate change has been noteworthy for its rancour, and a very noisy and visible group of pundits and think tank experts who have persistently disputed the findings of climate science, attempting to ridicule the work of the Intergovernmental Panel on Climate Change, and reduce public confidence in other scientists who are raising the alarm about accelerating climate change.

Much of the controversy is driven by political concerns in the United States in particular to constrain the role of government in regulating businesses, and the oil industry in particular. Many of the books denying the reality of climate change can be directly connected to a network of conservative foundations and think tanks (Jacques *et al.* 2008). Part of the problem has been repeated media practices of providing 'balance' to a story by interviewing one or two scientists who dispute some aspects of climate science and suggesting that these views are equally important as those of the vast majority of scientists that are doing the science and have no doubts that the planet is warming and that human disruptions of many natural systems are the cause (Boykoff 2011).

Further difficulties come when media accounts simplify complicated scientific issues, arguing that science should provide certainties that it simply can't do (Hulme 2009). Holding science up against such unrealistic expectations frequently allows claims to be made that there is a debate about whether climate change is real. This despite the fact that the vast majority of scientists actually doing the research, rather than those making comments in the media, have been tracking the changes in environmental systems for decades. What is much less clear is how the changes already set in motion will play out in coming decades, and with what impacts on particular people in vulnerable places, like low lying cities close to shore. But this is very different from claiming that change isn't happening.

infrastructure. Cars have become status symbols, recreational toys, temporary offices, and much more than transportation in our lives. They are frequently advertised as instruments of the domination of nature and of freedom to go anywhere without consequences (Paterson 2007). They have become symbols of modernity.

But much more than just cars are involved in the use of carbon fuels. Power generating stations using coal are a substantial source of carbon emissions; at least part of the electricity used to power the computer used to write this chapter came from coal powered generation; very little came from solar or wind power. Many of the items of everyday life are made of plastics and petroleum, including the keyboard on which this chapter was typed. The container ship and the trucks that brought it round the world from the factory to my office were also powered by fossil fuels and have implications for far distant ecologies (Dauvergne 2008). These things are simply part of our everyday world, and the consequences of these modes of life have, until recently, rarely been considered as a matter of world politics.

Accelerating change and unpredictable effects

Climate has been relatively stable for the last 10,000 years or so since the end of the last ice age. There have been some dramatic short term disruptions, as when the Krakatoa volcano in Indonesia blew its top in 1883 and put huge quantities of material into the atmosphere which dimmed the sunlight for a couple of years (Winchester 2003). But mostly over this period of the planet's existence, climate has stayed within a fairly narrow range close to what we became familiar with before the 1980s. While some societies, perhaps most notably the Maya civilisation in the Americas, have possibly collapsed due to environmental change, this stable set of circumstances allowed for the emergence of agricultural societies and the beginnings of human civilisations (Diamond 2005). Now numerous indications of climate change are becoming obvious, not only to scientists and those who use satellites and weather stations to monitor change, but also to bird-watchers who pay attention to bird migrations, gardeners and farmers who have to plant and harvest according to the seasons, not to mention the people who plan such things as winter snow removal budgets in many cities of the Northern Hemisphere.

The processes changing the atmosphere, the phenomena of global warming, are fairly simple to outline. Increased burning of fossil fuels puts more carbon dioxide (CO_2) into the atmosphere. Plants and oceans can't absorb all this increased volume of gas so it starts to accumulate. Prior to the Industrial Revolution carbon dioxide was fairly stable at about 270 parts per million in the atmosphere. Now it's getting close to 400 parts per million and forecasts for the rest of this century suggest that it might get as high as 500 parts per million or close to double its pre-industrial levels. Because we know from the geological record that global climate varies very closely in line with CO_2 concentrations and there is no record in the last half a million years of CO_2 anywhere

BOX 3.3 GREENHOUSE GASES

Carbon dioxide is a relatively large molecule among atmospheric gases, and large molecules trap infrared radiation, keeping the heat that would otherwise escape back into space in the atmosphere. Methane is an even more potent greenhouse gas; human activities have so far caused nearly a doubling of methane in the atmosphere, but it stays in the atmosphere a much shorter time than carbon dioxide. The CFCs (chlorofluorocarbons) that are the cause of so much worry about ozone layer depletion are also very potent greenhouse gases. (The international agreement in the late 1980s to phase out the production of CFCs will also in the long run help reduce the amount of this greenhouse gas in the atmosphere (Soroos 1997).) Water vapour too is sometimes a powerful greenhouse gas. Cloudy nights in temperate climate zones are usually less likely to have frost than clear ones. But in daytime when those clouds reflect sunlight back into space they act to cool the surface. This makes water a very difficult gas to work into predictions of climate change. Other ironies of atmospheric change include the fact that while aeroplanes flying high in the atmosphere are pouring carbon dioxide into the air they are also emitting other polluting gases, or aerosols, that act to reflect sunlight and cool the earth's surface, which counteracts the warming of the carbon dioxide. This strange fact was confirmed by measurements over the United States in the few days after 11 September 2001 when air traffic was grounded. Likewise air pollution in Asia from fires and inefficient engine combustion is both a local health hazard and probably reducing the warming from the sun by its shading effects when it reflects sunlight, but ironically heating the air when the soot absorbs heat.

close to existing levels, there is great concern in the scientific community about what the future holds for the biosphere and for humanity (Flannery 2006).

While the details of how these changes in the atmosphere play out in the biosphere are complicated, some general trends are clear and some are very worrisome. Not least what worries scientists is that many of the likely responses to increased atmospheric temperatures will be neither gradual nor predictable. Feedback loops are already beginning to accelerate trends that speed up heating. Neither will changes be evenly spread geographically. Already it is clear that heating is having dramatic effects in the polar regions of the planet. Ice and snow reflect a lot of sunlight because they are white. Where ice and snow melt, and either ground or ocean is exposed, more sunlight is absorbed as heat because of the darker colour. This warms the area, encouraging further melting. While sea ice melting doesn't affect the level of oceans, both warming of the ocean water, and melting of ice on land, does raise sea levels.

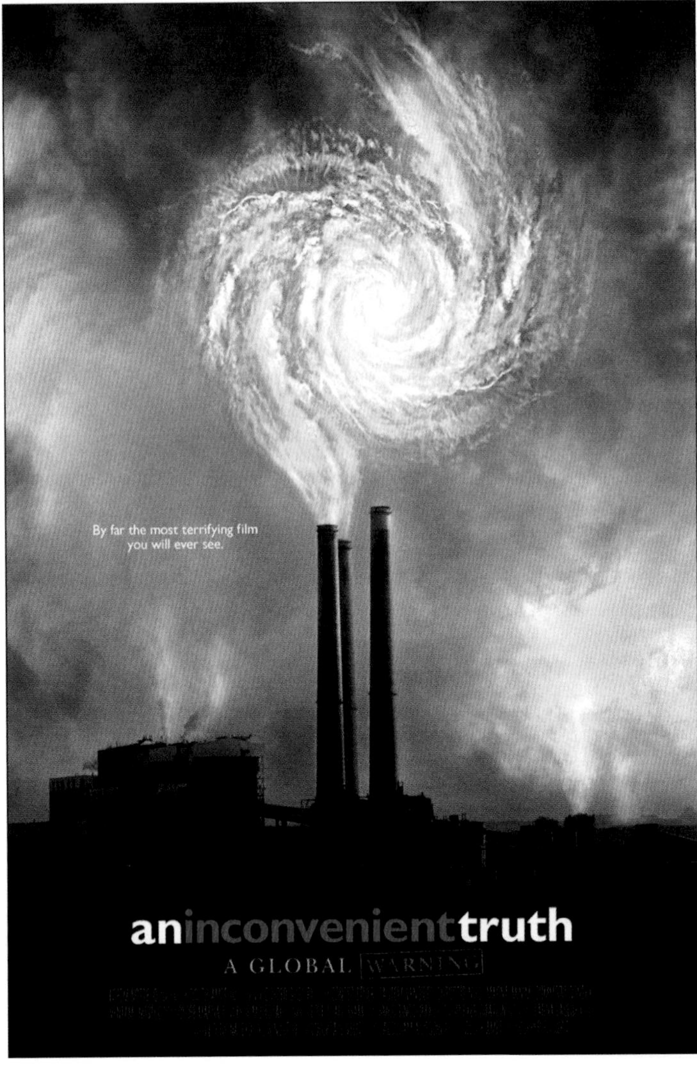

FIGURE 3.4
Image of smokestacks producing hurricanes from *An Inconvenient Truth*. Lawrence Bender Productions. Poster courtesy The Kobal Collection

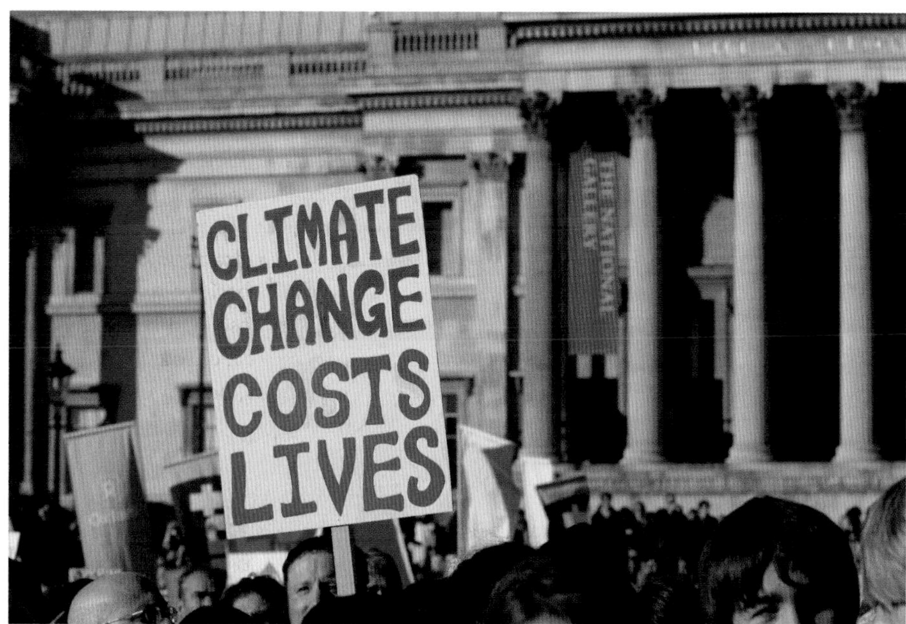

FIGURE 3.5 Demonstration on climate change, London November 2006. Photo: Dave Walsh, Greenpeace

One other possible effect of climate change is the increased severity of large storms. The 2005 hurricane season in the Caribbean, and the fact that hurricane Katrina devastated Louisiana and, due to a failure of the dyke system round New Orleans, flooded that city, focused attention on the vulnerability of populations to storms (Dalby 2009). In 2011 hurricane Irene moved north in the United States, and while it weakened and missed New York, it too caused extensive flooding damage. Hurricanes, or typhoons as they are called in the Pacific, are fed by warm ocean water, and as the oceans warm, it is likely but far from certain that more severe storms will occur (Shepherd and Knutson 2007). It might transpire that more frequent less severe storms happen, but the real danger comes with the possibility of bigger and more severe storms. Not least this is because so many people now live in harm's way. Many poor people have no choice but to live on marginal land in coastal areas, river valleys and hillsides vulnerable to flooding or landslides. If extreme weather events become more frequent people in these areas and in large low lying delta areas may be especially vulnerable. New Orleans will not be the last coastal city to suffer the consequences of storms and rising sea levels.

Although that said, it is also worth pausing to consider the simple fact that emergency measures, if taken in time, do frequently save lives and reduce the damage to property. The example of the Cuban system, where a complicated and flexible system of neighbourhood and community responsibility, and an effective shelter programme, works to protect people from the impacts of hurricanes that regularly hit the island, shows that much can be done to reduce vulnerabilities if appropriate preparations are made (Sims and Vogelmann 2002). And yet in numerous countries there has been a reluctance to tackle these issues. Activists attending the Earth Summit in Rio de Janeiro in 1992 sketched out some basic principles for acting as though we collectively live in a vulnerable biosphere, principles that subsequently became the 'Earth Charter', the

BOX 3.4 THE UN AND THE ENVIRONMENT

The Conference on the Human Environment held in Stockholm in 1972 marked the first attempt by the United Nations to discuss global environmental matters in a comprehensive manner (Ward and Dubos 1972). While the United Nations Environment Programme (UNEP) was established in the 1970s to deal with environmental matters, it was not a major United Nations priority in the years that followed. Nonetheless in the 1980s UNEP was involved in the discussions about the global atmosphere, stratospheric ozone depletion and the establishment of the Intergovernmental Panel on Climate Change (IPCC), the scientific body that evaluates and summarises climate change science for governments.

The early IPCC (see http://www.ipcc.ch/index.html) technical reports fed into the deliberations at the huge Earth Summit, the United Nations Conference on Environment and Development (UNCED), which was held in Rio de Janeiro in 1992 (Chatterjee and Finger 1994). Among the agreements that came from this conference attended by most of the heads of state on the planet was the Framework Agreement on Climate Change (Soroos 1997). This in turn produced the much more talked about Kyoto Protocol late in the 1990s, an agreement that entered into force on 16 February 2005 when Russia finally became part of the agreement. This protocol, and the numerous elaborations and modifications worked out at subsequent conferences of the parties, has become the key focal point of international efforts to limit greenhouse gas emissions.

But most of this remains a matter of regulating emissions, and frequently of intense arguments about how to allocate responsibilities, quotas and measurements. Neither the Kyoto Protocol nor the Framework Convention is a forum for planning global sustainable development or ensuring the rapid spread of technological innovations such as photo-voltaic cells, solar water heaters or green building designs. It remains mostly focused on environment, rather than on building a sustainable economy, although discussions of such programmes as clean development mechanisms at least suggest the possibility of the United Nations playing a more active role in building a green economy. The real test for the United Nations system and its ability to shape the future will be what comes after the Kyoto agreement when additional states are incorporated into more extensive climate change arrangements. But as exemplified by the weak agreement in Durban in December 2011, where states agreed to negotiate by 2015 a binding treaty that would take effect only in 2020, these institutions are at least so far, failing to come up with comprehensive enforceable rules to govern fossil fuel use and to ensure that ecosystems can effectively adapt to their new circumstances in the Anthropocene.

closest thing there is to an international manifesto for sustainable living. While the government delegations did enact some international agreements in Rio, notably the framework convention on climate change, progress on dealing with greenhouse gas emissions has been slow in most states.

Attempts to act on environmental concerns are often not helped by the way the world is divided into territorial units called states. See **Chapter 11**.

GENERAL RESPONSES
HOW DO WE FRAME THE ISSUE IN TERMS OF GLOBAL POLITICS?

But how are we to understand all this politically? What modes of thinking might we invoke to think through these new circumstances? In this section three different ways of thinking about this issue, drawing from environmental history, indigenous perspectives and geopolitics, address the question of whether human-centric, or perhaps more precisely modern urban human perspectives are all that are required. Looking back into history we can see how the current ecological circumstances came about and come to understand in what senses our climate change predicament is really new. Looking outside Western thinking to the sometimes very different views from indigenous peoples who were conquered by modern societies provides an interesting contrast with modern understandings of environment. Finally, by looking at where fuels come from and the consequences of the waste products from their combustion, we can see where the problem lies and how power at the largest scale matters.

Environmental history

The crux of recent environmental history is captured in the title of one of the key texts in the field, Alfred Crosby's (1986) *Ecological Imperialism*, where matters of imperialism are linked directly to the ecological consequences of European conquest. Although it is frequently not thought of in these terms, the history of imperialism is all about changing landscapes and ecologies. Much of this is not done deliberately, but the introduction of horses and cattle in the Americas, not to mention rabbits to Australia, has dramatically altered the environments of these continents. In addition, growing wheat and other crops, as well as clearing large forests to make agricultural fields, involves a complete change of the plants and animals in areas where colonisation occurs.

Processes of imperialism and colonial conquest are discussed in **Chapters 15, 16 and 21**.

Looking to the huge changes wrought on the landscapes of North America, in particular in the nineteenth century, as what quickly started to look like an American empire spread rapidly across the continent, suggests clearly that what we now take for granted as 'the environment' is much more of an artificial construction than a natural entity. Widespread slaughter of the buffalo herds, the eradication of many bird species, and the clearing of forests for cultivation of crops changed the ecology of the continent fundamentally. On the western frontier, beyond the area easily farmed, the 'wild west' became ranching country, the buffalo replaced by roaming cattle overseen by the ever-present 'cowboy'. This part of ecological imperialism has become part of popular American, and now global, culture where the Western has generated a genre of movies and books. The wilderness was enclosed, farmed, and above all rendered tame and safe for European settlement while Chicago grew into a city of stockyards and the centre of the meat industry (Cronon 1991).

Accounts by people whose ancestors were displaced by the changes in the United States are interesting. See **Chapter 13** where the writings of Sherman Alexie are discussed.

But this expansion of human control over environments, and the conversion of wilderness into tamed landscape, is a larger part of the human experience as agriculture has gradually eliminated or pushed hunter-gatherer peoples into marginal areas. It has been followed by the emergence of an urban civilisation, one that has expanded dramatically in the last century to appropriate minerals, fuel, and land from the distant corners of the planet to supply essential materials to the cities (Dauvergne 2008). The human species, this colonising medium-sized mammal, has expanded its range to the whole planet, and the consequences are so dramatic that we are now shaping the evolution of the biosphere in new ways. The total scale of this transformation has led to discussions of the novelty of this situation; to borrow the phrasing from another major book (McNeill 2000) in the field of environmental history, there now is *Something New Under the Sun*.

Indigenous perspectives

In the process not only have animals and plants, trees, fish and birds been displaced and frequently simply annihilated, but indigenous cultures have also perished. Much of the expansion of European power, and its appropriation of land and resources through direct colonisation in the Americas and Australia, was done at the expense of the indigenous cultures that were there before Europeans encountered them. Indigenous perspectives on history make this clear. Many cowboy movies are about fighting 'Indians' in the wild west, a theme that reflects the fact that the native societies were caught up in the conquest and frequently fought back in the face of invasion. The cavalry didn't always get there in time.

One of the key assumptions in the conquest of the Americas was that the land Europeans were entering was 'empty', at least in the sense that it wasn't being farmed and used 'productively'. If native peoples were using the land they weren't doing so in ways that the European conquerors thought were significant, so the removal of the natives wasn't seen as a problem. The legal doctrine of *terra nullius* literally specified the land as empty. Civilisation was about dominance and control over land and resources; the benefits of civilisation came only with the adoption of these modes of controlling the environment. The fact that indigenous peoples frequently had complicated and sophisticated understandings of their local ecosystems, and that they often harvested animals in ways that ensured their reproduction in the long term, was rarely understood by settlers.

See **Chapter 11** for a discussion of territoriality.

Native cosmologies in North America, and frequently in the case of indigenous peoples elsewhere, do not start with the assumptions of a humanity apart from nature. Living within ecosystems, native peoples frequently don't make that fundamental separation between people and everything else (LaDuke 1999). What 'modern' societies might designate as native religion, but what might be much better understood as an integral part of local cultures, frequently requires some notion of respect for the animals one captures and kills to eat. This is not a picture of an environment external to humanity to dominate and control, an external entity to mine and exploit for resources and commodities; it is seen as a place to inhabit, a home that provides the necessities of life and will continue to do so if cared for appropriately. Thus long term consequences,

For a discussion of the place of religion in global politics, see **Chapter 6**.

and the possibilities of ecological renewal, are integral to the political considerations of native cultures.

The connections between life and land are ignored by modern modes of thinking that reduce fecund ecologies to resources, and land to a commodity that should be exploited for short term commercial gain. None of this is to take a romantic view of traditional societies. The assumption that native societies and environments were a paradise prior to the disruptions of colonisation is neither historically accurate nor politically helpful, but the dramatic contrast in cosmologies is useful in thinking about the assumptions of an external nature that can be managed in present circumstances. Native cosmologies challenge the separation of nature and society that modernity is based upon.

Is the easy distinction between humans and other species a particular feature of modern thinking?

Geopolitics

Looked at in the largest scale, that of geopolitics and power at the global scale, the pattern of resource exploitation and disruption of local ways of living continues as ever larger appropriations of resources are made to feed and fuel consumption in the metropoles. Nowhere is this more evident than in the case of petroleum, the substance

FIGURE 3.6 Oil refinery. Lonely Planet Images

that is at the heart of the problem of climate change, and a matter once again of geopolitics (Klare 2009). Because it is used so widely in contemporary society, petroleum has become an essential commodity. Some of the oil wells in current use are in remote places where indigenous peoples live. These peoples have been involved in numerous struggles against the environmental despoliation caused by wells and pipelines, and also in attempts to gain some of the financial benefits of oil extraction. The pattern of colonisation and the displacement of indigenous peoples, and the story of their resistance, continues (Gedicks 2001).

Many of the oil production facilities on the planet are far from where the petroleum is refined and used. In the Persian Gulf region a struggle to control the oil trade has plunged local states and Western powers into conflict repeatedly. Violence comes with oil. It is valuable enough to fight over. Given its importance for the global economy, those who would control that economy are tied into struggles to control both the supplies directly and the profits that can be made from selling the products. American efforts in particular to control the petroleum supplies in the Gulf are tied directly into rivalries with Iran and formerly with Iraq (Bacevich 2005). But this is not a simple matter of the American government doing the bidding of the oil companies to protect their supplies. It's a much more complicated situation than that, not least because oil company profits go up when supplies are tight and prices rise.

Here the most obvious contradictions in the global politics of our times become very evident. The violence involved in trying to control the petroleum trade is in fact a violence to perpetuate the production of a substance that is a direct threat to the stability of the planet's climate. Thus America is at war in the Middle East in part to protect an unsustainable global society; it is fighting to maintain a way of life that is imperilling all our futures. In part it is doing so out of sheer inertia: things have long been done this way so they continue to be done this way. In part it is also a belief in technology and the power of the internal combustion engine and a globalised economy to provide wealth that ensures that the overall lot of humanity continues to improve. It's a mode of existence that simply doesn't think that environment matters that much. It perpetuates the assumption that environment is an externality to the important matters of human society, to the provision of commodities and status in particular.

There are many views as to what gives rise to violence as a method of action to solve problems. See **Chapter 22**. **Chapter 23** discusses the different forms violence can take.

BROADER ISSUES
CHALLENGING CARBONIFEROUS CAPITALISM

We now have to think about environment, social change and geopolitics simultaneously to try to see how political economy links all of them together, tying the fate of marginalised people into the economic and security priorities of political elites in the metropoles. But we also need to think about arguments that challenge the continued operation of carboniferous capitalism and about how social change might happen if environment and the consequences of imperial geopolitics for indigenous peoples were taken into account. We can no longer operate on the assumption that there is a separation between us and the planet; there is no external nature that we can manipulate without having to deal with the consequences. The changing composition of the air makes this fact unavoidable. There is no distant place we can safely put our waste,

To what extent does capitalist economics rely on growth? Is sustainable growth a contradiction in terms? The related notion of sustainable development is discussed in **Chapter 4**.

pollution or sewage. Neither can we ignore the consequences of our modes of consumption for the lives of marginalised people growing the crops we use or struggling with the disruptions caused by mines, oil wells and pipelines in many places (Sachs and Santarius 2007). Struggles over nature are human struggles.

Despite the growing recognition of this as the appropriate starting point, and all the discussions about the Kyoto protocol and subsequent climate change negotiations over the last decade, the growth in the use of fossil fuels has continued apace. Asian economies are booming and the large economies of India and China in particular seem determined to catch up with Western models of urban carboniferous capitalism (Worldwatch Institute 2006). Car ownership is rising rapidly; national pride is linked to the existence of national car production facilities in many states in Asia in particular. This economic growth is based on petroleum fuels, following on from American, Japanese and European practice rather than innovating with new fuels. Oil is still king. This is not surprising for developing economies where playing catch-up is the dominant mode of economic activity, but as oil becomes increasingly scarce and supplies are potentially disrupted by instabilities and wars in the Middle East, the wisdom of such a development strategy seems highly doubtful. If climate change is taken seriously this is doubly so.

Development strategies have a range of serious consequences for the people subject to them. See also **Chapters 15 and 20**.

While environmental change isn't new in the human experience, as environmental historians have made clear, the potential for rapid shifts in climate makes numerous people vulnerable now in ways that are perhaps similar to the late nineteenth century when famine swept through parts of the European empires, in part because of the economic disruptions caused by the globalisation of the grain trade and the effects this had on regional agriculture (Davis 2001). If all this happens while hurricanes and droughts become more severe, there is a potential for major human disasters. Beyond that the most worrisome dimension of environmental change is the potential for a dramatic flip in the climate system that radically changes the whole arrangement of climate zones (Alley 2004). While no one expects a series of changes on the scale of the plot of the 2004 Hollywood disaster movie *The Day After Tomorrow*, the possibility of a very nasty climate surprise is of great concern, especially because there is little evidence that, at least at the moment, international political institutions could deal effectively with such an event.

Mike Davies' study of what he calls *Late Victorian Holocausts* is discussed in **Chapter 16**.

In particular this is suggested by the pattern of thinking that appears in much of the negotiating about climate change, not least by the frequent assumption that Northern consumers can sink their carbon emissions in plantations in poor countries. Rather than dealing directly with reducing consumption, part of the strategy has been to export the pollution and plant trees where labour and land are relatively cheap in other states (Lohmann 2006). All of which reminds historians of the story of colonial plantations designed to supply commodities for markets in the metropoles. Poor peoples are once again displaced to grow tree crops that are at best a temporary way of soaking up some of the carbon emissions, but a way that gets Northern consumers off the hook for the moment and allows them to claim to be carbon neutral. This postpones dealing with the industrial and transportation systems that continue to turn rocks into air so we can all enjoy having cool toys, big and small. The costs are displaced on to poor people in the South and onto our grandchildren who will bear the brunt of what disruptions today's fuel use sets in motion in the future. Environmental justice for whom?

Some people might see carbon offsetting as an example of neo-colonialism. See **Chapter 15**.

"There is nobody else. I'm afraid we've wiped out all of the other species."

FIGURE 3.7
'There is nobody else'. Artist: Stan Eales. CartoonStock ref.: sea0186. www.CartoonStock.com

BOX 3.5 CARBON OFFSETS AND TRADING

If too many greenhouse gases are being produced by economic activities, is it possible to get them out of the air? If so, why not deal with the problem of greenhouse gases by offsetting production against activities that reduce gas production and remove gases from the atmosphere? If tropical trees grow quickly, and in the process absorb carbon from the atmosphere, then why not invest in plantations that can soak up emissions, and offset the use of fossil fuels against tree growth? This argument is the basis of a growing social movement and investment market in carbon offsets, as well as a part of the larger international markets for carbon dioxide credit trading designed to reduce the growth of greenhouse gases. In so far as it provides a constituency in business groups to promote action on climate change, and facilitates social movements who wish to offset consumer lifestyles and make them carbon neutral, carbon offsets may by useful.

But critics are quick to point out various flaws in offset thinking (Lohmann 2006; Monbiot 2006). Most obviously if industries are offsetting their emissions they may not have the same incentives to reduce greenhouse gases, which is what really needs to be done. If consumers offset their emissions, and hence stop feeling guilty about the ecological consequences of what they are doing, rather than changing how they live to actually reduce their emissions, then offsets aren't helpful. If quick growing but ecologically inappropriate trees, like the eucalyptus that needs lots of water, are grown they may badly affect water supplies and other aspects of the environment. Badly designed programmes of plantation farming may aggravate the problems faced by marginal farmers or indigenous peoples on whose lands the plantations are grown. Plantation agriculture was key to colonial development; calling the forests carbon offset trees and having local governments administer the forests doesn't change this old pattern.

Recently these questions of offsets and justice have been made even more pressing by the strategies of states and corporations to buy up land in Southern countries to provide food and in some cases plantation type agriculture to make biofuels, supposedly a more ecologically friendly way of getting fuels than using petroleum products. This strategy of what is now called 'land-grabbing' continues the practice of displacing marginal peoples, but does it frequently in terms justified by various 'green' or development arguments (Matondi *et al.* 2011). This may be a form of development that sustains Northern consumers, but at the cost of further disruptions to Southern peoples, in Africa in particular. This is part of a larger pattern of the spread of the economic logic known as neo-liberalism that has become a mode of governance in many places in the absence of effective state regulation or clear development strategies focused on making livelihoods sustainable. But, as critics have recently forcefully argued, it is precisely these economic forces that make people especially vulnerable in the face of climate change in the global South (Parenti 2011).

The World Summit on Sustainable Development took place in South Africa in 2002; see **Chapter 4**.

The political and economic arguments against tackling environmental change have usually asserted that change is simply too expensive. Only recently have economists and politicians begun to take seriously the opposite and altogether more compelling argument, that it will be a lot cheaper to act now to reduce the dangers, rather than paying potentially huge costs later. As the Stern Report on climate change, the British government document that investigates in detail the costs of climate change, put it: 'we have never seen a market failure like this' (United Kingdom Treasury Department 2006). Which brings the discussion back to politics, and who should do what to deal with the 'failure' of the existing mode of organising human affairs to consider the consequences of our modes of life for the future, or for marginalised native peoples struggling to adapt to the influx of modernity on their lands and cultures. In Al Gore's (2006) words we now simply have to deal with the *Inconvenient Truth* of climate change; but how to do so remains very difficult.

Al Gore was US vice president from 1993 to 2001. He was later noted for his campaign to promote environmental awareness, in particular his documentary film *An Inconvenient Truth*, which won him both an Oscar and a share of the Nobel Peace Prize in 2007.

There is currently no mechanism in human affairs to decide on what should be produced, or how and where to ensure that catastrophe is avoided. Global agreements on everything from ozone depletion through bans on the trade of endangered species to climate change are attempts to rectify this gap. But mostly they look to limit damage rather than change modes of living so as not to do damage in the first place. The focus is frequently on regulations and legislation driven by environmental groups, and in some states the presence of a green political party, to force business to stop emissions of pollution (Lipschutz 2004; Clapp and Dauvergne 2011). Many of these regulations are highly technical matters worked out by experts in the industries being regulated. Reducing politics to such technical negotiations suggests that what matters are fine details about chemical formulas, trading quotas and industrial standards. The big questions about what kind of a society is best, how we might live together and what needs to be done to ensure the safety and wellbeing of our children and those in distant places too, are frequently squeezed out of discussion. But the sheer scale of human induced change means that these questions keep coming back; the politics of climate change are now simply unavoidable (Boykoff 2009).

Liberals believe that there is an informal mechanism that determines what is produced and so on – what Adam Smith called the 'invisible hand'. See **Chapter 17**.

These questions have not been ignored by the business community or by regulators in Europe in particular, where numerous initiatives have been taken to try to use market mechanisms to change economies so that they use less fossil fuel. To do so the policy

BOX 3.6 THE STERN REPORT

The *Stern Review Report on the Economics of Climate Change* was released by the British government's Treasury Department in October 2006. In the 700-page report Sir Nicholas Stern makes the case that spending money now to head off the worst effects of climate change is much more sensible than waiting to deal with the consequences later. Whatever the finer points of the economic discussion, his case is simple and direct. If nothing is done the economic disruptions caused by climate change will be dramatic and painful to future generations. Relatively modest intelligent investments now can head off future economic disruptions and are hence good public policy designed to benefit economies in the future. Even if these investments slow economic growth slightly now, Stern argued, they are well worth it in terms of avoiding future losses. The Stern Report is noteworthy because it clearly focuses on the costs of doing nothing, whereas most of the economic arguments about climate change suggest that it is economically rational to do little or nothing because the costs of trying to change economic systems will be very considerable. By reversing this logic Stern has had a fairly immediate political effect on the larger debate about how to think about the future of the global environment. What the Stern Report also suggests clearly is that policy needs to deal with both adapting to climate change, some of which is already inevitable, and mitigating some of its worst effects by taking actions now to slow down the rate of increase of greenhouse gases concentrations in the air. Mitigation is needed not just to buy time for humans and their economies to adapt, but crucially to give natural ecosystems the time they need to adapt to the coming changes. In the words of the United Nations Development Programme (2007: vi) 'While we pursue adaptation we must start to reduce emissions and take other steps at mitigation so that the irreversible changes already underway are not further amplified over the next few decades. If mitigation does not start in earnest right now, the cost of adaptation twenty or thirty years from now will become prohibitive for the poorest countries.'

has been to put a price on carbon, cap the overall amount of fuel that various sectors of industry and business can use and regulate the overall use of carbon based fuels. Issuing carbon use permits, and allowing businesses to trade those that they don't use, should in theory encourage efficiency improvements, and allow efficient businesses to make extra money by selling their carbon credits on a market for such things. This 'climate capitalism' has begun to change how businesses in Europe in particular do things (Newell and Paterson 2010). There have been numerous attempts at extending these arrangements to the global scale, and while getting the pricing of carbon wrong in some cases hasn't generated the kind of fuel use reductions that advocates might have hoped for, clearly new forms of climate governance are emerging from these initiatives, ones that pose profound questions about politics in terms of where the sources of authority for making these kinds of decisions and regulations lie.

CONCLUSION

Facing major changes in the circumstances of human existence, which is what the climate change discussion is all about, demands that different questions be posed, and the big

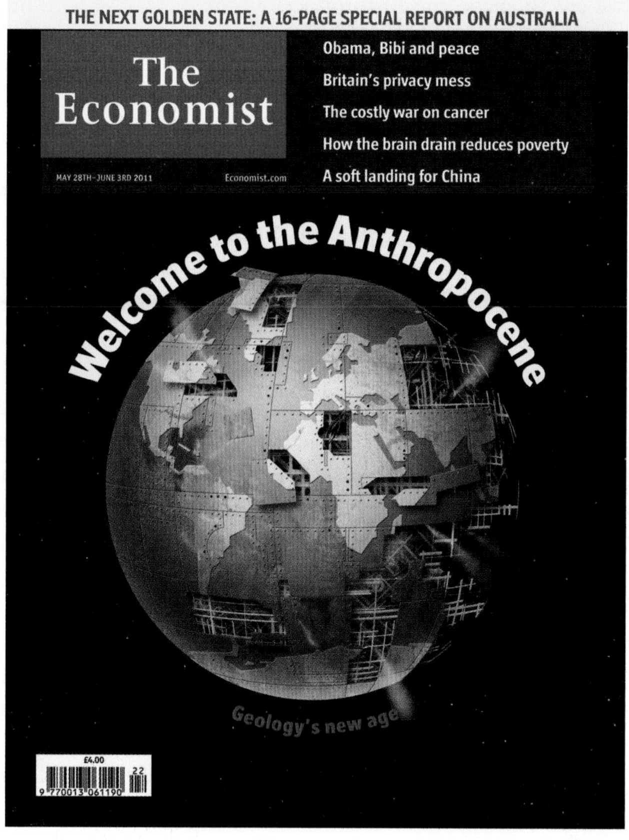

THE NEXT GOLDEN STATE: A 16-PAGE SPECIAL REPORT ON AUSTRALIA
The Economist
Obama, Bibi and peace
Britain's privacy mess
The costly war on cancer
How the brain drain reduces poverty
A soft landing for China
MAY 28TH–JUNE 3RD 2011
Economist.com
Welcome to the Anthropocene
Geology's new age
£4.00

FIGURE 3.8
'Welcome to the Anthropocene'. Cover illustration of *The Economist Magazine* on 26 May 2011. http://www.economist.com/node/18744401

issues of how to live collectively in a changing biosphere are discussed much more carefully. We clearly need institutions that arrange matters so that we produce the things we actually need to live well without completely disrupting natural cycles in the biosphere. Our existing political institutions have so far mostly failed to grapple effectively with the new circumstances of human existence. Native cosmologies, and their insistence that we are all part of the cycles of life, might have many lessons to teach about how we reconsider those institutions and think about how to live well within a small, vulnerable biosphere. Ecological science too shows us that we are part of the environment, not the masters of it. It's not out there in the wild spaces distant from civilised cities; it's part of the systems of life that we have dramatically changed by our industries and our profligate use of energy and materials.

Climate change challenges many of the modern assumptions about politics. The whole modern mode of thinking, of managing an external environment to maximise the production of things, rather than human wellbeing, has shaped public administration and regulation in national and international discussions. Assuming that a stable nature will always be there for us is no longer a sensible assumption for political discussion. Science has now made it abundantly clear that we are living in a biosphere that our actions are reshaping, and that now we need to rethink these modern assumptions if we are to shape the Anthropocene in ways that ensure human civilisation continues. Environment is no longer just a matter of pollution and resource constraints, parks and conservation. It is now a much more important matter, which enters directly into any discussion of how we should live. New institutions and new ways of making decisions about what we make, and hence what kind of world we produce for future generations, need a whole lot more attention from politicians and scholars.

But we can learn from history as well as from science. The indigenous focus on living within one's surroundings, inhabiting rather than controlling, is one valuable lesson. Another lesson is that distinctions between rural nature and urban civilisation are no longer useful when it comes to thinking about politics or public administration. A focus on the flows of material and energy in the biosphere becomes necessary; looking at the connections between things and people makes political responsibility for one's actions unavoidable in the Anthropocene. In short, starting from natural systems and thinking about the interconnections between our actions and distant places where the energy and commodities we use come from, rather than thinking from the viewpoint of modern consumers disconnected from the rest of the world where nature is taken for granted, makes life more complicated but in turn gives us a very useful perspective on global politics.

FURTHER READING

The best popular explanation of the science of global warming is probably Tim Flannery's (2006) *The Weather Makers.* Vaclav Smil's (2003) guide to *The Earth's Biosphere* is precisely what its title suggests and useful for the rest of the science that matters in discussing environmental politics. An overview of the current state of the world's natural environments and how all this relates to development is in the United Nations Environment Programme report *Geo5 Global Environmental Outlook: Environment for Development*, released in 2012. The Anthropocene has been discussed widely in the media in 2011, notably in the March 2011 issue of the *National Geographic*, and the 'Welcome to the Anthropocene' cover story of *The Economist*, 26 May 2011. Mike Hulme's book *Why We Disagree About Climate Change* (Cambridge University Press 2009) is the essential guide to why climate change has become so controversial.

Wolfgang Sachs and Tilman Santarius' (2007) book on a *Fair Future*, is excellent on the principles of thinking ecologically while seeing the interconnections between the South and North. Peter Dauvergne traces the global implications of consumption in his *Shadows of Consumption* (2008). The larger scholarly discussion of environment and global political economy is in Jennifer Clapp and Peter Dauvergne's (2011) *Paths to a Green World*, while journalist Christian Parenti discusses the convergence of neoliberalism and climate change in his *Tropic of Chaos* (2011). Peter Newell and Matthew Paterson's *Climate Capitalism* (2010) traces some of the complex new governance mechanisms of the emerging carbon economy. My own book *Security and Environmental Change* (2009) spells out the need for innovative thinking about politics and security in particular in the Anthropocene.

WEBSITES

The rapidly changing science of global change is summarised by the International Geosphere Biosphere Program (IGBP) at http://www.igbp.kva.se/. The 2007 Nobel prize-winning Intergovernmental Panel on Climate Change (IPCC) can be found at http://www.ipcc.ch/. The United Nations Environment Programme's Global Environmental Outlook programme is online at http://www.unep.org/geo/. Real Climate, at http://www.realclimate.org/, is where scientists keep the general public up to date with the science of climate change.

Background information on the writing of the text of the Earth Charter, and details about current campaigns based on it, including material related to the 2012 Rio de Janeiro conference, can be found at http://www.earthcharter.org/. The World Watch Institute at http://www.worldwatch.org/ publishes numerous well-researched articles and reports on many environmental matters including climate change. Greenpeace International's climate campaign is at http://www.greenpeace.org/international/campaigns/climate-change. The World Wildlife Fund publishes periodic useful summaries of the state of the world's ecosystems in its Living Planet Reports available at wwf.panda.org/.

REFERENCES

Alley, Richard B. (2004) 'Abrupt Climate Change', *Scientific American* 291, 5: 62–9.

Bacevich, Andrew (2005) *The New American Militarism: How Americans are Seduced by War*, New York: Oxford University Press.

Boykoff, Max (ed.) (2009) *The Politics of Climate Change*, New York: Routledge.

Boykoff, Max (2011) *Who Speaks for the Climate? Making Sense of Media Reporting of Climate Change*, Cambridge: Cambridge University Press.

Chatterjee, Partha and Matthias Finger (1994) *The Earth Brokers: Power, Politics, and World Development*, London: Routledge.

Clapp, Jennifer and Peter Dauvergne (2011) *Paths to a Green World: The Political Economy of the Global Environment*, Cambridge, MA: MIT Press.

Cronon, William (1991) *Nature's Metropolis: Chicago and the Great West*, New York: Norton.

Crosby, Alfred (1986) *Ecological Imperialism: The Biological Expansion of Europe 900–1900*, Cambridge: Cambridge University Press.

Dalby, Simon (2009) *Security and Environmental Change*, Cambridge: Polity.

Dauvergne, Peter (2008) *The Shadows of Consumption*, Cambridge, MA: MIT Press.

Davis, Mike (2001) *Late Victorian Holocausts: El Niño Famines and the Making of the Third World*, London: Verso.

Diamond, Jared (2005) *Collapse: How Societies Choose to Fail or Succeed*, New York: Viking.

Flannery, Tim (2006) *The Weather Makers: How We are Changing the Climate and What It Means for Life on Earth*, Toronto: HarperCollins.

Gedicks, Al (2001) *Resource Rebels: Native Challenges to Mining and Oil Corporations*, Boston: South End Press.

Gore, Al (2006) *An Inconvenient Truth*, New York: Rodale Books.

Hulme, Mike (2009) *Why We Disagree about Climate Change: Understanding Controversy, Inaction and Opportunity*, Cambridge: Cambridge University Press.

Jacques, Peter J., Riley Dunlap and Mark Freeman (2008) 'The Organisation of Denial: Conservative Thinktanks and Environmental Skepticism', *Environmental Politics* 17, 3: 349–85.

Klare, Michael (2009) *Rising Powers/Shrinking Planet*, New York: Metropolitan.

Kolbert, Elizabeth (2011) 'The Age of Man', *National Geographic*, March.

LaDuke, Winona (1999) *All Our Relations: Native Struggles for Land and Life*, Cambridge, MA: South End Press.

LeBillon, Philippe (2005) *Fuelling War: Natural Resources and Armed Conflict*, Adelphi Paper 373, Abingdon: Routledge.

Lipschutz, Ronnie D. (2004) *Global Environmental Politics: Power, Perspectives, and Practice*, Washington, DC: CQ Press.

Lohmann, Larry (ed.) (2006) *Carbon Trading: A Critical Conversation on Climate Change, Privatisation and Power*, Development Dialogue no. 48, http://www.dhf.uu.se/publications.html.

Matondi, Prosper B., Kjell Havnevik and Atakilte Beyene (eds) (2011) *Biofuels, Land Grabbing and Food Security in Africa*, London: Zed Books.

McNeill, J. R. (2000) *Something New Under the Sun: An Environmental History of the Twentieth-Century World*, New York: Norton.

Meadows, D. H., D. L. Meadows, J. Randers and W. W. Behrens III (1974) *The Limits to Growth*, London: Pan.

Monbiot, George (2006) *Heat: How to Stop the Planet from Burning*, London: Penguin.

Mumford, Lewis (1934) *Technics and Civilization*, New York: Harcourt.

Newell, Peter and Matthew Paterson (2010) *Climate Capitalism: Global Warming and the Transformation of the Global Economy*, Cambridge: Cambridge University Press.

Parenti, Christian (2011) *Tropic of Chaos: Climate Change and the New Geography of Violence*, New York: Nation Books.

Paterson, Matthew (2007) *Automobile Politics: Ecology and Cultural Political Economy*, Cambridge: Cambridge University Press.

Sachs, Wolfgang and Tilman Santarius (eds) (2007) *Fair Future: Resource Conflicts, Security and Global Justice*, London: Zed.

Sandbach, Francis (1980) *Environment, Ideology, Policy*, Oxford: Blackwell.

Schellnhuber, H. J., P. J. Crutzen, William C. Clark and J. Hunt (2005) 'Earth System Analysis for Sustainability', *Environment* 47, 8: 11–25.

Shepherd, J. Marshall and Thomas Knutson (2007) 'The Current Debate on the Linkage Between Global Warming and Hurricanes', *Geography Compass* 1, 1: 1–24.

Sims, Holly and Kevin Vogelmann (2002) 'Popular Mobilization and Disaster Management in Cuba', *Public Administration and Development* 22, 5: 389–400.

Smil, Vaclav (2003) *The Earth's Biosphere: Evolution, Dynamics and Change*, Cambridge, MA: MIT Press.

Soroos, Marvin (1997) *The Endangered Atmosphere*, Columbia: University of South Carolina Press.

Steffen, W., P. Crutzen and J. R. McNeill (2007) 'The Anthropocene: Are Humans Now Overwhelming the Great Forces of Nature?' *Ambio* 36: 614–21.

United Kingdom Treasury Department (2006) *Stern Review Report on the Economics of Climate Change*, London.

United Nations Development Programme (2007) *United Nations Development Report 2007–2008 – Fighting Climate Change: Human Solidarity in a Divided World*, New York: UNDP.

United Nations Environment Report (2012) *GEO5 Global Environmental Outlook: Environment for the future we want*, Nairobi, Kenya: UNEP.

Wapner, Paul (1996) *Environmental Activism and World Civic Politics*, Albany: State University of New York Press.

Ward, Barbara and Rene Dubos (1972) *Only One Earth: The Care and Maintenance of a Small Planet*, Harmondsworth: Penguin.

Winchester, Simon (2003) *Krakatoa: The Day the World Exploded, 27 August 1883*, New York: HarperCollins.

World Commission on Environment and Development (1987) *Our Common Future*, Oxford: Oxford University Press.

Worldwatch Institute (2006) *State of the World 2006*, New York: Norton.

For a range of further resources supporting this chapter, please visit the companion website for *Global Politics, 2nd Edition* at www.routledge.com/cw/edkins/

CHAPTER 4

Can we save the planet?

Carl Death

- *The question*
  ENVIRONMENTAL POLITICS AND SUSTAINABLE DEVELOPMENT
- *Illustrative example*
  THE WORLD SUMMIT IN 2002
- *General responses*
  EXISTING ANALYSES OF ENVIRONMENTAL GOVERNANCE
- *Broader issues*
  POST-ECOLOGISM AND ECO-GOVERNMENTALITY
- CONCLUSION

THE QUESTION
ENVIRONMENTAL POLITICS AND SUSTAINABLE DEVELOPMENT

A whole range of environmental issues – including global climate change, stresses on food and water supplies, urban hazards and pollution, the loss of biodiversity and the degradation of fragile ecosystems – seem to be increasing in scale and intensity. For some, these issues seem to threaten the survival of the planet itself, or at least the survival of many species, including our own. In many countries such concerns have become prominent political issues. In Europe, there have been Green political parties in government (*Die Grünen* in Germany), green members of legislative assemblies (Green Party MP Caroline Lucas was elected for Brighton Pavilion in the 2010 UK general election), and in North America there are government bodies tasked with protecting the environment (such as the Environmental Protection Authority in the USA).

Green parties are often identified with environmentalism, but they also have particular (and sometimes largely shared) approaches to economic policy and social issues.

Asking 'can we save the planet' raises many questions about whether we are still thinking in human terms – both in terms of the 'we' doing the saving, and what *we* are saving the planet for: our species, our society, all animal and plant species, or the lump of rock itself? See also **Chapter 3**.

Chapter 28 explores in more detail why changing things can be tricky.

Several chapters look at other social movements, such as feminism (**Chapter 5**), religious movements (**Chapter 6**), civil disobedience (**Chapter 7**), nationalism (**Chapter 12**), pro-democracy movements (**Chapter 14**), and how to change the world (**Chapter 28**).

In some other countries such issues are raised by relatively small numbers of dedicated environmental activists or grassroots community groups. Whatever the relative profile of environmental issues in different political contexts, however, it is hard to disagree with the observation that what might be called a 'global environmental movement' has become increasingly prominent. This chapter explores the politics and history of environmental movements and activists, each of which have asked themselves and their societies some version of a fundamental question: Can we save the planet?

In popular culture and mythology in many different societies saving the planet is a task for heroes. A popular American cartoon series in the early 1990s, *Captain Planet and the Planeteers*, epitomised this desire for an ecological hero. Five young 'Planeteers' were summoned from across the world by the spirit of Gaia (the spirit of the Earth), who was threatened by human pollution. These young activists could call upon Captain Planet when the crisis threatened to overwhelm them, and in every episode he would eventually prevail against the eco-villains.

Putting all of our faith in an imaginary cartoon hero is probably not the best way to save the planet, however, this chapter explores how a range of movements, organisations and individuals have taken action themselves. In it I will reflect on their actions and some of the debates these actions have raised, rather than try to tell you how to save the world. Indirectly, this might provide some ideas to help you develop your own answer to the chapter's question. Indeed, this has been one of the big hopes of the environmental movement over the past 50 years: that by encouraging more and more people to think about environmental issues, and raising awareness of environmental problems, perhaps we will be able to save our world. In a later section I question whether awareness-raising is enough to save the planet.

As even a brief history of the environmental movement shows, such social movements often begin as marginal, fringe, or radical alternatives, posing a fundamental challenge to society and its values. As movements grow and become more successful, they often become more professional, more mainstream, and have more impact. But this can sometimes mean that they become less radical.

FIGURE 4.1
Green Party MP Caroline Lucas was elected to Brighton Pavilion in the 2010 UK general election. Photo: Corbis

BOX 4.1 THE ENVIRONMENTAL MOVEMENT

The environmental movement is quite a misleading term. There is no one environmental movement. Rather there are a whole range of groups, movements, organisations and institutions that have campaigned on environmental issues, with very different ideas about how to save the planet.

One version of the story of modern environmentalism is that it arose as part of the counter-cultural youth movements of the 1960s in the USA and Western Europe, alongside feminism and the peace movement. At the height of flower-power culture and anti-Vietnam war protests in the USA, some 20 million Americans took part in massive rallies across the country for the first 'Earth Day' on 22 April 1970. This was regarded by many as the birth of the modern environmental movement, and has continued to colour perceptions of environmentalism. Indeed, the perception of environmentalists as white, middle-class 'hippies' continues to hold some sway nearly half a century later. This is despite the existence of many grassroots environmental movements in working-class communities, communities of colour, and the rest of the world outside North America and Europe.

Environmental movements in North America and Europe were strongly influenced by books like Rachel Carson's *Silent Spring* (1964), which observed how pesticide use was damaging bird populations. In the 1970s the idea of environmental limits – both limited natural resources and the limited capacity of ecosystems to absorb pollution – became widespread, reflected in the report of the Club of Rome, a global think-tank whose members are concerned with the future of humanity and the planet, called *Limits to Growth* (Meadows *et al.* 1974). Environmental disasters served to add credence to environmentalist warnings. As awareness of climate change became more widespread in the 2000s the environmental or green movement could be said to be stronger and larger than ever before.

This chapter explores the question of whether we can save the planet, as well as reflecting on the political consequences of our efforts to do so. My central point is that we need to be wary of uncritically accepting calls to put aside our differences and unite to save the planet. Rather, we need to ask what sort of planet we are trying to save, and what consequences our actions might have for future generations, people in different parts of the world, the weakest and least resilient, and on other species. And who are the 'we' that are tasked with deciding on these changes? The illustrative example focuses on the 2002 UN World Summit on Sustainable Development, which was held in Johannesburg, South Africa. Attempts to save the planet are found at different levels of global politics: international organisations and institutions like the United Nations and its programmes; transnational organisations and movements such as global NGOs, NGO-networks, and transnational social movements; and local grassroots environmental movements, which exist almost everywhere in the world in some form or another. Activity at all these three levels can be seen in relation to this mega-summit.

BOX 4.2 TIMELINE OF MODERN ENVIRONMENTALISM

April 1961	The World Wildlife Fund (WWF) founded in Switzerland, growing rapidly to become one of the first global environmental organisations.
March 1967	The *Torrey Canyon* super-tanker runs aground off the coast of Cornwall (UK), carrying a load of 120,000 tonnes of crude oil.
May 1969	Friends of the Earth founded in the USA.
April 1970	First Earth Day.
December 1970	US Environmental Protection Authority established over concerns about pollution.
September 1971	Greenpeace founded when activists set sail from Vancouver to Amchitka Island in Alaska to bear witness against US nuclear tests. The tests were halted the following year.
June 1972	Stockholm Conference on the Human Environment (UNCHE) attended by 113 governments.
March 1979	Central core meltdown at the Three Mile Island nuclear power plant in Pennsylvania (USA).
1983–1987	World Commission on Environment and Development (called the Brundtland Commission after its chair, Gro Harlem Brundtland) holds hearings; its report popularised the concept of sustainable development.
December 1984	Gas explosion at the Union Carbide pesticide plant in Bhopal (India) causes at least 3,387 deaths from gas leaks and injures hundreds of thousands.
April 1986	Chernobyl nuclear meltdown in the Ukraine (then part of the Soviet Union) leads to the evacuation of 350,400 people and the spread of radiation across Europe.
December 1988	International Panel on Climate Change (IPCC) established by the International Meteorological Organisation and the UN Environment Programme to review and assess scientific research on climate change.
June 1992	Rio Earth Summit (UNCED) in Brazil attended by 172 governments and almost 20,000 people.
August 2002	Rio+10 World Summit on Sustainable Development held in Johannesburg (South Africa), and attended by over 190 countries and 22,000 participants.
April–July 2010	Oil leaks from the BP *Deepwater Horizon* platform into the Gulf of Mexico for three months before it can be stopped.
March 2011	Fukushima Daiichi nuclear disaster in Japan following an earthquake and tsunami.

ILLUSTRATIVE EXAMPLE
THE WORLD SUMMIT IN 2002

Between 26 August and 4 September 2002 representatives of over 190 countries, 100 world leaders and over 22,000 other participants met in Johannesburg, South Africa, 'in the interests of all humanity and our common planet' (South African president Thabo Mbeki in UN 2002b: 155). The Johannesburg World Summit on Sustainable Development was one of the largest political meetings ever held, and it was intended to reinvigorate the global commitment to sustainable development. For many of the world leaders, diplomats, media reporters, NGOs and ordinary people who attended, it was a moment for heroes to step forward, to save the planet at the summit or pinnacle of global politics.

There is another account of the environmental movement in **Chapter 3**. Questions of development, economics and poverty are discussed in **Chapters 15, 17, 19 and 20**.

The 2002 Summit must be understood in the context of a longer history of global governance and UN conferences on environment and development, including Stockholm and Rio. The 2002 Johannesburg Summit was intended to review progress made in the 10 years since the 1992 Rio Conference on Environment and Development (UNCED), and identify new areas for action. Its focus was supposed to be on implementation, as it was felt that ecological and developmental problems were well-known and increasingly monitored and measured. What was needed was action. The Johannesburg Summit was supposed to promote solutions – to speed up efforts to save the world.

So what did the Johannesburg Summit achieve? Did it live up to its billing as an opportunity for political heroes to chart a path for sustainable development that would avoid crashing spaceship Earth into an environmental disaster?

FIGURE 4.2
South African president Thabo Mbeki signing the Political Declaration at the end of the summit negotiations, 4 September 2002. http://www.iisd.ca/2002/wssd/photoindex.html

BOX 4.3 SUSTAINABLE DEVELOPMENT

At the Stockholm Conference in 1972 debates centred on the apparently conflicting priorities of economic development and the protection of the environment. Whilst environmental activists from Europe and North America were trying to protect and conserve ecosystems, politicians from developing countries refused to accept environmental limits to their development. 'Poverty is the worst form of pollution', Indian Prime Minister Indira Gandhi famously told the conference (in Dresner 2002: 28).

The idea of sustainable development was an attempt to break out of this apparent conflict between environmental limits and development. Its most famous expression was in the Brundtland Report, which defined sustainable development as 'development which meets the needs of the present, without compromising the ability of future generations to meet their own needs' (World Commission on Environment and Development 1987: 43). It recognised that 'overriding priority' should be given to the needs of the world's poor, whilst also suggesting that there were environmental limits on the ability of technology and social organisation to meet current and future needs. This synthesis of environmental limits and development priorities was further enshrined in the Rio Conference in 1992 at which 8,000 delegates agreed on 27 principles for sustainable development, a road map for achieving sustainable development known as *Agenda 21*, two legally binding international conventions on biodiversity and climate change, and a declaration on forests (Adams 2009: 86–9).

For some commentators sustainable development has become 'the dominant global discourse of ecological concern' (Dryzek 2005: 145), whilst for others it is a vague statement of ideals that amount to little more than 'polite meaningless words' (Middleton and O'Keefe 2001: 31). In any case it has proved one of the most long-lasting and influential slogans or aspirations for the environmental movement.

Inter-governmental negotiated outcomes and bilateral partnerships

The verdict, as one might expect, was mixed. Few believed the Summit had fulfilled the pre-conference hype of the people of the world coming together to solve environment and development problems, but then, as many pointed out, such expectations were unrealistic anyway. The Johannesburg Summit was never about saving the planet in a heroic manner, but instead was intended to review progress and promote further action. On this score some participants were cautiously optimistic about some of the Summit outcomes, including an aspirational Johannesburg Declaration, a detailed Plan of Implementation, and an array of what were known as *type-II partnerships* (Chasek and Sherman 2004). Whereas the Declaration and Plan of Implementation were multilaterally negotiated texts agreed between state representatives (known in UN-speak as *type-I outcomes*), the partnerships were bilaterally agreed public-private partnerships between states, international organisations, private sector actors, NGOs, local governments and a whole range of other people, that were designed to achieve sustainable development in specific, concrete projects on-the-ground. As they were recognised by the official UN conference, but not negotiated by the government delegates, they were known as *type-II outcomes.*

The announcement of 251 such partnerships in Johannesburg, and the creation of an online database which continues to record and informally monitor the partnerships, was regarded by conference-watchers as a major success for the USA and its allies (Japan, Canada, Australia and New Zealand). They had sought to encourage a shift away from state-centric approaches to sustainable development, instead looking to the private sector and civil society – a term referring to non-state and (usually) non-profit groups and organisations like NGOs, community groups, and faith-based organisations. The prominence of the partnerships was seen as a vindication for those who had argued strongly that the world did not need countless new international legal agreements and treaties, targets and timeframes, but rather needed to harness the energy and vitality of the private sector and civil society to implement a multitude of specific projects.

This view of the Johannesburg Summit – as a signal of a new style of conference and a new flexibility in global governance – was summed up by the post-conference statement of Jonathan Lash from the World Resources Institute, a prominent environmental NGO:

> This Summit will be remembered not for the treaties, the commitments, or the declarations it produced, but for the first stirrings of a new way of governing the global commons – the beginnings of a shift from the stiff formal waltz of traditional diplomacy to the jazzier dance of improvisational solution-oriented partnerships that may include non-government organisations, willing governments and other stakeholders.
>
> (World Resources Institute 2002)

Examples of the sorts of projects listed as type-II partnerships include the 'Community Water Initiative', a $1.2 million project run by UNDP and other NGOs such as WaterAid together with a range of governmental agencies to improve community access and control over water resources; the 'Congo Basin Forest Partnership', a $230 million project to promote cooperation between all the partners in the sustainable management of the conflict-ridden Congo Forest; and the 'Renewable Energy and Energy Efficiency Partnership', which aims to accelerate a global market for renewable energy and energy efficiency, and as of July 2009 had supported 145 projects with a total investment of over €11 million (leveraging an extra €54 million through co-financing). The online database, run by the UN Commission for Sustainable Development, currently lists 348 partnerships (see http://webapps01.un.org/dsd/partnerships/public/welcome.do).

Others have been less optimistic about the new partnerships and their potential to save the planet. Many onlookers and activists believed the partnerships were included as a last minute face-saver when it became clear the summit would fail to agree on new international legal agreements and specific, binding treaties, targets and timeframes (Gutman 2003: 23). Many participants in Johannesburg – including the European Commission, the governments of South Africa and Denmark, and large NGOs like WWF – had demanded concrete commitments on issues like water and sanitation, corporate accountability, renewable energy, biodiversity, environmental health, chemicals, and the relationship between trade and environmental protection. Despite a few exceptions, these commitments were not forthcoming (Death 2010: 66–7).

If large global summits do not achieve much in terms of commitments for change, do you think they serve some other purpose?

Indeed, in the Summit aftermath many people questioned to what degree such mega-conferences were at all useful. They seemed to be just weeks of hot air from politicians and bureaucrats, which had little effect on real-life environmental or development problems. In the words of UK International Development Secretary Clare Short, 'we do not need more big multilateral agenda-setting conferences, we need a real period of intensive implementation' (in Lean 2002). In fact, many pointed out that such meetings might actually do more harm than good, considering the environmental costs of flying thousands of people to South Africa for two weeks. Others doubted the commitment of highly polluting transnational corporations and representatives of states like the USA (which in 2002 was at war in Afghanistan and on the verge of invading Iraq) to genuinely reform their behaviour and save the planet through non-binding partnerships.

Post-Johannesburg there was certainly an identifiable feeling of summit-fatigue. The enthusiasm that had marked the 1992 Rio Earth Summit had all but ebbed away, and in the cold light of Johannesburg it was clear that few environmental problems had improved since 1992, and many had worsened. In 2004 a UN report pronounced that 'the era of global conferences is largely over' (in Death 2010: 4).

Despite this fatigue, such summits have not gone away. Indeed, in June 2012 the UN held the Rio+20 Conference on Sustainable Development in Brazil. These meetings are simply too important for politicians who need to show they are doing something about environmental problems and who are tempted to try to play the role of planetary hero. They are also important for the development of a network of transnational environmental NGOs, and for grassroots movements.

Transnational NGO networks in Johannesburg

As environmentalism has moved from a fringe, radical, counter-cultural movement towards the centre of political debate and the peaks of summit governance, the visibility and prominence of large transnational NGOs has similarly increased. As Peter Willetts notes, 'NGOs have changed from being peripheral advisors of secondary status in the diplomatic system to being high status participants at the centre of policy-making' (2000: 193). Large international summits such as Rio in 1992 and Johannesburg in 2002 have played a crucial role in this transition (Chatterjee and Finger 1994; Wapner 2003).

Summits are important events for big environmental NGOs like WWF and Greenpeace for many different reasons. They provide a place to meet, exchange ideas, network, and promote their own ideas and projects. In Johannesburg in 2002 the Global Peoples' Forum was held in a massive exhibition hall where civil society groups had stalls, talks, and meetings. There was also a venue for water activists (called the WaterDome), a cultural and exhibition centre (called the Ubuntu Village), an Environment Centre at Nedcor Bank, as well as more radical gatherings at the Peoples' Earth Summit, the South–South Biopiracy Summit and environmental justice groups who met at Shaft 17, an old mine-turned conference centre. The Johannesburg Summit was therefore a 'summit of many summits', and extended far beyond the official negotiations (Chasek and Sherman 2004: 117).

How accountable are large transnational NGOs to their supporters? Where does most of their funding come from: individual supporters' donations, or governments?

More than simply a meeting place for fellow activists, however, the proliferation of global summits since Rio in 1992 has become something of a reason for existence for many transnational NGOs. NGO campaigns are often organised around the timetables of conferences like Johannesburg, and being seen and heard at such meetings

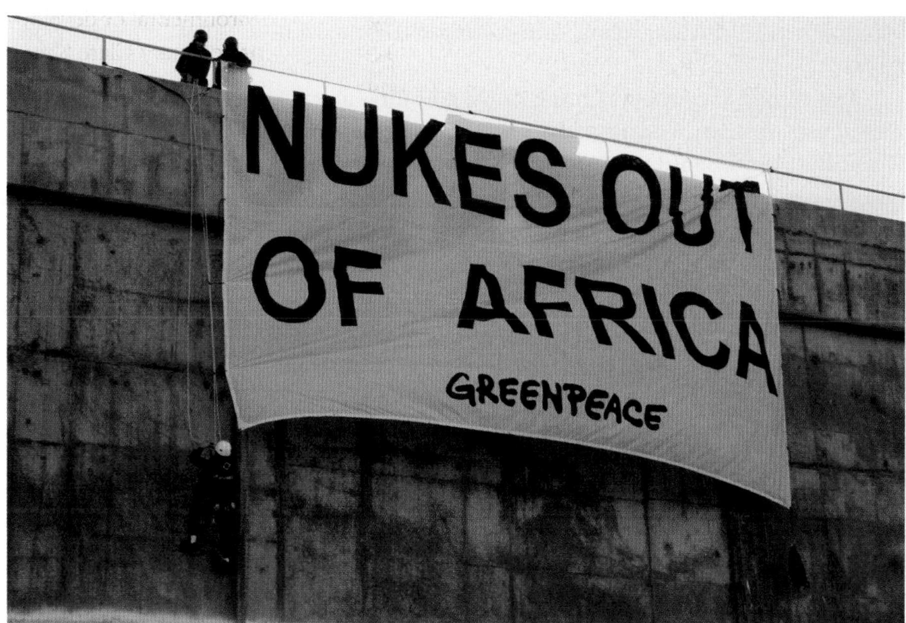

FIGURE 4.3
Greenpeace activists who scaled the Koeberg Nuclear Power Plant near Cape Town, during the World Summit on Sustainable Development in August 2002. http://www.greenpeace.org/africa/en/News/news/Nukes-not-the-answer-zuma/

demonstrates to their supporters and funders that they are hard at work. Many NGOs have also found themselves being co-opted onto governmental delegations because of their expert knowledge of specific issues, particularly by smaller states who often lack the resources or capacity to send a large team of experienced diplomats to every set of international negotiations. This presents both opportunities and dangers to NGOs, who can gain considerable power and influence through such access, but can face the danger of having their independence and legitimacy eroded.

The conduct of Greenpeace in Johannesburg in 2002 is an excellent example of the delicate balance between insider-access and outsider-credibility. Greenpeace have portrayed themselves since their creation in 1971 as a radical group of environmental crusaders, campaigning against governments and corporations who threaten the natural environment. Their campaigns against whaling and nuclear power have provided particularly vivid images of the David-against-Goliath struggles of committed environmentalists placing their own lives at risk to halt industrial whaling in the Pacific or nuclear tests in the Arctic – real-life Captain Planets.

Despite this heroic image, Greenpeace is a modern NGO with a thoroughly professional structure. It lobbies governments and corporations, and employs scientists, researchers, brand-managers and administrators as well as tree-climbing activists. In 2010 it received donations from 2.8 million individuals, giving a worldwide income of over €200 million (Greenpeace 2010).

This dual identity was illustrated by two incidents at the 2002 World Summit on Sustainable Development. The first was just prior to the opening of the Summit when Greenpeace activists hung a banner saying 'Nukes out of Africa' from the roof of the Koeberg Nuclear Power Plant near Cape Town. This was a carefully calculated act to gain attention in the global media, and it reinforced Greenpeace's traditional brand as heroic activists willing to risk danger to bear witness against environmental threats.

The second incident was more down-to-earth (literally and metaphorically). On 28 August Greenpeace held a joint press conference with the business lobby group, the World Business Council for Sustainable Development (WBCSD). Despite the historic hostility between environmentalists and the big multinational corporations the WBCSD represents, which include Shell, BP, Toyota, Eskom, Unilever, EXXON, Coca-Cola and Dow Chemicals, the two organisations used the conference to emphasise their shared views on the need for action on environmental issues. According to Björn Stigson, president of the WBCSD, 'this is a good example of where the need to save the planet is so important it transcends any other differences we may have' (in Brown 2002). They later clarified, however, that the meeting 'in no way should be seen as business endorsing the Kyoto principles' on climate change (in Rutherford 2003: 149). Such incidents show that Greenpeace is willing to make tactical alliances and forge cooperative partnerships, as well as headline-grabbing protests, and shows the degree to which the organisation has grown and changed in the last 40 years.

The relationship between environmental problems and the carboniferous capitalism that these big corporations arguably represent is discussed in **Chapter 3**, and the problems of capitalism in general are discussed in **Chapters 17 and 19**.

Grassroots environmental movements in Johannesburg

Although it was the government delegates and the big transnational NGOs that were most high-profile in 2002, the Johannesburg Summit also illustrates some of the political issues and divisions that affect local, community-based grassroots movements who campaign on environmental and development issues. It is such groups who are the bedrock of modern environmentalism. As Doyle and McEachern point out, it is important to remember that 'environmentalism, in all its forms, was born in environmental movements' (2008: 84).

FIGURE 4.4 Social movement protestors march from Alexandra township to the World Summit on Sustainable Development to protest against unsustainable development. 31 August 2002. http://www.iisd.ca/2002/wssd/31photos.html

From a grassroots perspective the 2002 Summit was fractious and confrontational, and came at a particularly tense time for South African politics. The so-called miracle transition from the racist apartheid state to the 'Rainbow Nation' of a democratic South Africa was almost a decade old, and whilst much progress had been made on a whole range of issues such as democracy, racial reconciliation and human rights, there was increasing frustration with continuing high levels of poverty and inequality. In 2002 groups like the Landless Peoples Movement were highlighting the lack of progress on land redistribution and rural dispossession, whilst the Anti-Privatisation Forum was campaigning against neo-liberal government economic policies which meant that poor urban communities were having their electricity supplies cut off, water supplies restricted, and were being evicted from their houses (Bond 2002). Local environmental NGOs like Earthlife Africa and GroundWork were drawing attention to South Africa's very high rates of greenhouse gas emissions per person, resulting from the country's reliance on coal-fired energy, as well as heavily polluted local environments in residential areas like South Durban which were still primarily occupied by poorer Black and Indian communities (McDonald 2002).

Poverty is not the same as inequality. **Chapter 19** discusses inequality and **Chapter 20** poverty.

Many of these tensions came to a head during the civil society preparations for the Johannesburg Summit. Fears that the governing African National Congress (ANC) was attempting to take control over civil society participation in the Summit resulted in a breakaway movement which decided to march against the ANC and the World Summit, proclaiming slogans like 'Our world is not for sale!' and declaring their opposition to 'the hoax of the W$$D' (Death 2010: 121). Delegates arriving in South Africa were therefore faced with the surprising image of over 20,000 protestors marching from the township of Alexandra to the conference venue in the well-off suburb of Sandton, apparently in opposition to the official UN summit and its promise to 'reinvigorate the global commitment to sustainable development' (UN 2000: 1). The marchers declared that:

> Alexandra represents a microcosm of everything that is wrong with the W$$D. The massive unemployment, lack of essential services, housing evictions, water and electricity cut-offs, environmental degradation, and generalised poverty that is present-day Alexandra sits cheek-by-jowl with the hideous wealth and extravagance of Sandton where the W$$D is taking place. While the fat cat bureaucrats and politicians will be hiding themselves away in luxurious Sandton and spewing out meaningless rhetoric and resolutions about the poor and sustainable development, the people of nearby Alexandra continue to live in dire poverty and to wage a daily struggle for survival. The tragic irony could not be more apparent.
>
> (in Death 2010: 131)

Whilst the mass march on Saturday 31 August was peaceful, other protests during the Johannesburg Summit were not. Riot police clashed with activists on a number of occasions, sometimes using firearms, and a total of 196 people were arrested. All were subsequently released without charge, leading to allegations that the South African government was criminalising political protest and undermining civil liberties in order to ensure a smooth, successful and peaceful international conference (Duncan 2003).

BOX 4.4 SOUTH AFRICA: FROM APARTHEID TO RAINBOW NATION

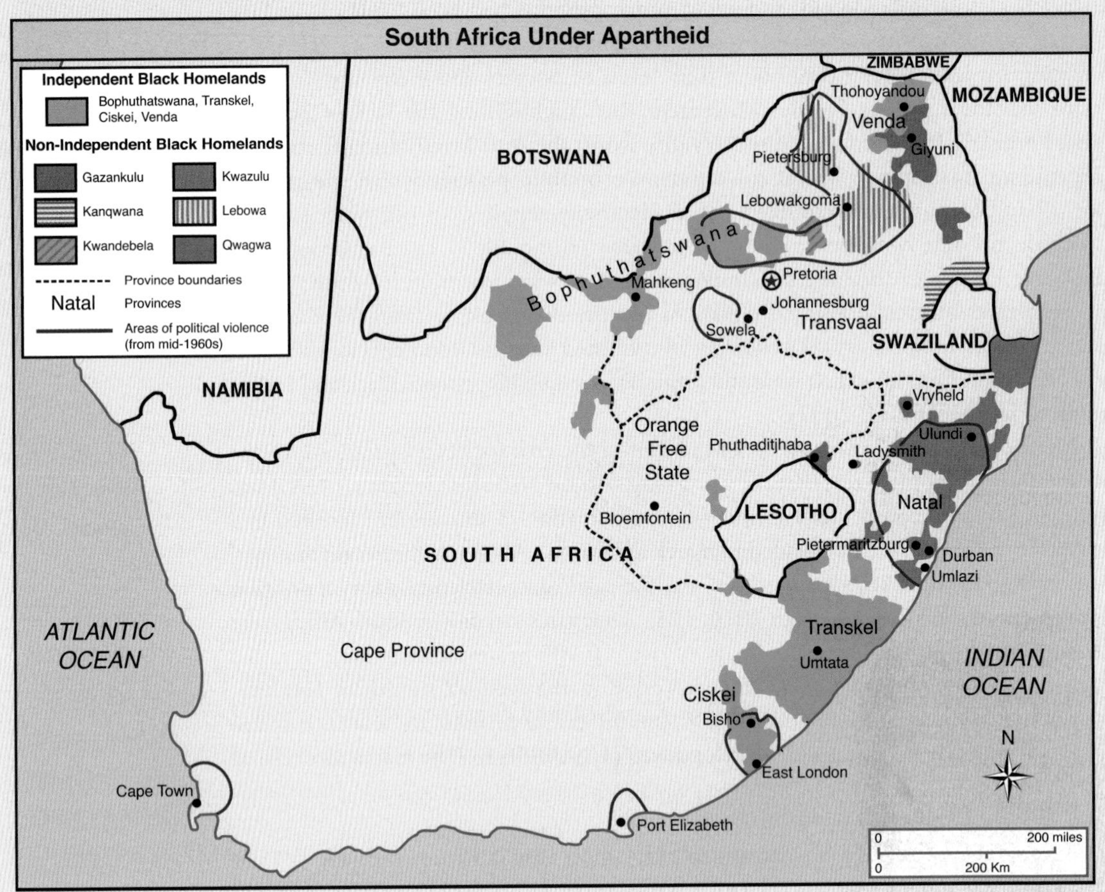

FIGURE 4.5
South Africa under apartheid. http://finalproject2009ec.wikispaces.com/file/view/HMOF7–27-c.gif/75456821/508x409/HMOF7–27-c.gif

For many South Africans the 2002 Summit was a national coming-of-age ceremony. Ten years previously South Africa had not even been represented at the Rio Conference, whereas in 2002 it was the proud host of the international community. This transition was made possible by the ending of apartheid in 1994.

Apartheid was a system of legal racial segregation enforced by the National Party government between 1948 and 1994, and which led to South Africa's increasing international isolation. Under apartheid (an Afrikaans word meaning 'apartness') the rights of the majority non-white inhabitants of South Africa were severely restricted, and the black population (almost 75 per cent of the country) was confined to ten homelands or 'Bantustans', comprising only 13 per cent of the land. This was ostensibly to pursue 'separate development', but was designed to protect and entrench minority white rule. Racial segregation in South Africa had begun in colonial times, but following the general election of 1948 new legislation classified inhabitants into distinct racial groups ('black', 'white', 'coloured' and 'Indian'). Residential areas were segregated, sometimes by means of forced removals. Under so-called 'petty apartheid', marriages between whites and other racial groups were banned, utilities and beaches were segregated, separate education and medical systems were created, and land and business ownership were restricted.

Apartheid was met with significant internal resistance and violence, in which Nelson Mandela and the African National Congress (ANC) became central. Mandela was imprisoned for 27 years and became the symbol of the anti-apartheid movement, but trade unions, the churches, civic movements and the Communist Party were also extremely important. The apartheid state responded with brutality, massacring schoolchildren as well as assassinating activists, and seeking to destabilise neighbouring states in Southern Africa.

Internal protests and external pressure eventually combined to force National Party politicians to the negotiating table, and in 1990 President Frederik Willem de Klerk unbanned the ANC and freed Nelson Mandela. After tense years of negotiations, multi-racial democratic elections were held in 1994, which were won resoundingly by the ANC. As the country's first black president, Mandela reassured whites that South Africa belonged to all those who lived in it, and leading anti-apartheid activist Archbishop Desmond Tutu proclaimed the country a 'rainbow nation', reflecting its many different cultures, ethnicities and languages.

FIGURE 4.6
Outgoing South African president F. W. De Klerk and Nelson Mandela in 1994.
http://www.blackpast.org/files/blackpast_images/Mandela_and_deKlerk_0.jpg

Hosting the UN Summit therefore brought to the foreground many of the tensions in contemporary South Africa: between the state and the social movements, between environmental activists and social justice activists, between the local and the global, and between neo-liberalism and sustainable development. Perhaps one of the most important things highlighted by these protests is that beneath the slogans of 'saving the planet' and 'implementing sustainable development' – with which few people could really disagree – there are considerable political differences over who is going to save what, how, and at what cost.

GENERAL RESPONSES
EXISTING ANALYSES OF GLOBAL ENVIRONMENTAL GOVERNANCE

Asking about how particular *representations* work – what ways of thinking they make possible – is like asking what *pictures* of the world do – how pictures frame the world and limit what we can say or do, as discussed in **Chapter 2**.

To think about these issues we need to move beyond straightforward calls to save the planet, and ask serious questions about the power relationships, values and consequences of global environmental governance. This section considers some of the most prominent ways of looking at environmental politics, and the differences between them, with a particular focus on how they represent the role of global environmental governance and/or environmental movements in saving the planet.

Tragedy of the commons

The views of scholars referred to as liberal institutionalists are discussed in **Chapter 19**. The term encapsulates an approach that is essentially liberal or neo-liberal, in that it starts with the rational individual and the free market, but also includes a belief in the value of international institutions.

There is more about the views of scholars from this so-called realist tradition in **Chapter 24**. Bear in mind that putting scholars into boxes in this way – categorising them as liberal institutionalists or realists – is rarely a neutral exercise and is generally an over-simplification of people's views.

A typical explanation of global environmental problems might run as follows: environmental resources, such as the atmosphere or the oceans, are common global goods from which everyone benefits but no one directly owns. Everyone thus seeks to maximise their own benefits from the shared resources and tries to avoid the costs of protecting them. This leads, so the argument goes, to what is known as the 'tragedy of the commons' (Dryzek 2005: 29). Much scholarship has focused on ways to resolve this apparent tragedy – to save the planet, if you like – and for those referred to as liberal institutionalists, the solution is to build systems of cooperative global governance. They are concerned with how best to design international institutions in order to encourage states to cooperate and protect their shared environment. Summits like Rio and Johannesburg are seen as important steps in this process, indeed they are often seen as benchmarks for gauging the character of world environmental affairs (Wapner 2003: 1). The work of Peter Haas is a good example of this approach, and in an influential article he argued that such summits are part and parcel of a 'broader process of multilateral governance and may contribute to stronger and more effective environmental governance by states' (2002: 74).

On the other hand, scholars from what is called the realist tradition tend to be more sceptical about our potential to overcome this underlying tragedy, particularly where valuable natural resources are at stake and when states claim a sovereign right to develop and grow their economy. Conferences and institutions, to these scholars, are sites of struggle for power politics and competing national interests. Everyone is trying to get an outcome that benefits their own state or nation – a result that is in their state's interest – and the one who is the most powerful is the one who wins, in this view.

BOX 4.5 TRAGEDY OF THE COMMONS

The idea of the tragedy of the commons was put forward in a 1968 article by Garrett Hardin. He explained it as follows:

> The tragedy of the commons develops in this way. Picture a pasture open to all. It is to be expected that each herdsman will try to keep as many cattle as possible on the commons. Such an arrangement may work reasonably satisfactorily for centuries because tribal wars, poaching, and disease keep the numbers of both man and beast well below the carrying capacity of the land. Finally, however, comes the day of reckoning, that is, the day when the long-desired goal of social stability becomes a reality. At this point, the inherent logic of the commons remorselessly generates tragedy.
>
> (Hardin 1968)

What happens then is that people still increase the number of cattle they keep on the commons, and it becomes overgrazed. Each cattle owner is acting in their own interest – as a rational actor, according to Hardin's idea of rationality – but the outcome is tragic.

Garrett Hardin was an American ecologist who was very concerned with the question of overpopulation. He also put forward the idea of lifeboat ethics – the argument that any lifeboat has a limited carrying capacity, and to exceed that – to try to help everyone – will mean the lifeboat sinking with all on board.

FIGURE 4.7
Garrett Hardin. Photo: Vic Cox

Typically, British ex-diplomat Tony Brenton argues that ultimately state interests will take precedence over international agreements, shared institutions, and non-state actors, and that the 'centres of decision [will] remain in national capitals' (1994: 8). Robert Putnam argues that these are 'two-level games' where diplomats and politicians have to keep in mind the demands of both opposing negotiators and their own domestic audiences (1988). From this perspective saving the planet is only possible when the most powerful states – or key actors within them – realise it is in their interest to ensure it. This may come only when their very survival is at stake.

Game theory is the study of how people – assumed to be rational actors – maximise their own well-being or profit in their dealings with others, or in other words in a game where there are other players.

A similar scepticism, and attention to the power relations at work in summits and conferences, is evident in the work of scholars in the critical and Marxist traditions. In this account, summits like Rio and Johannesburg usually end up only entrenching dominant political and economic interests, rather than actually helping to save the planet (Chatterjee and Finger 1994; Paterson 2000: 2). Patrick Bond concluded that the

Some of the basics of a Marxist position are summarised in **Chapter 19**.

Johannesburg Summit in 2002 'will be remembered, at best, as just another site for UN blahblah, and at worst, as the amplification of corporate control over both nature and everyday life' (2002: 382). From this perspective any realistic chance to save the planet will depend on the overthrow or significant reform of industrial capitalism, and perhaps a political, economic and social revolution.

Industrial capitalism is called 'carboniferous capitalism' in **Chapter 3**. Does the author of that chapter take a Marxist or critical approach? Is it worth trying to put writers into boxes in this way?

A green revolution?

What emerges from these approaches is some degree of pessimism about our potential to save the planet. Only the most optimistic liberal institutionalists would claim that existing governance structures, international institutions, and diplomatic efforts are doing enough to solve environmental problems. This was echoed by diplomats in Johannesburg in 2002:

> The global environment continues to suffer. Loss of biodiversity continues, fish stocks continue to be depleted, desertification claims more and more fertile land, the adverse effects of climate change are already evident, natural disasters are more frequent and more devastating, and developing countries more vulnerable, and air, water and marine pollution continue to rob millions of a decent life.
>
> (UN 2002a: 13)

If business-as-normal is failing to save the planet, then something drastic is clearly needed. For this, many environmental activists argue, we need to return to the radical challenge posed by the environmentalism of the 1960s and 1970s.

For this reason many scholars of environmental politics have focused their attention on understanding and explaining the successes and failures of environmental social movements, rather than state actors. Paul Wapner argues that the role of environmental movements in 'disseminating an ecological consciousness' and pushing broader cultural change is far more significant than the action of states and international institutions (1995: 320–2). Timothy Doyle and Brian Doherty divide contemporary environmentalism into emancipatory and governance movements; the former work 'to increase the power resources of the poor and environmentally degraded', and the latter 'seek to globalise environmentalism through disciplining the local into a carefully constructed and restricted version of the global' (2006: 883 and 891). Strengthening and linking up emancipatory social movements is required if we are to save the planet, according to Doyle and Doherty, whereas they suggest that many large transnational environmental groups – particularly conservation groups like WWF – have actually become too wealthy, too professionalised, and too comfortable within the existing system of power relations.

Such a commitment to local movements, grassroots struggles and community organisations has long been a feature of both the environmental movement and much scholarship on environmentalism. Environmental justice movements in the USA, for example, have sought to strengthen the capacity of local communities to have a say over the location and management of environmental hazards. Community-based natural resource management schemes operate on the premise that strengthening local involvement in conservation initiatives and biodiversity management will achieve both environmental and development goals. For many activist-academics like Vandana Shiva, 'the reversal of ecological decline involves strengthening local rights' (1993: 155).

BROADER ISSUES
POST-ECOLOGISM AND ECO-GOVERNMENTALITY

What many of these differences in responses seem to lead to, politically, is quite an old debate between reformists and revolutionaries. The former believe we can save the planet through reforming existing institutions (they include liberal institutionalists, most diplomats and politicians, and many of those within NGOs that participate in negotiations at conferences like Rio and Johannesburg), whereas the latter think some kind of revolution is necessary (they include many radical environmentalists and thinkers in the Marxist tradition). This split is perhaps best illustrated by the well-known divisions within the German Green Party (*Die Grünen*), a party historically committed to participative democracy and pacifism as well as its ecological principles, which traditionally had seen itself as a grassroots 'movement-party' very different to more mainstream political parties (Doyle and McEachern 2008: 174–77). During the 1980s and 1990s there were increasingly bitter splits within the party between factions known as the *Realos* and the *Fundis*. The *Realos* felt that deals should be made with other political parties to get into power, and that adopting modern, professional, hierarchical structures was the best way of achieving their environmental goals. The *Fundis*, on the other hand, felt that adhering to their principles was paramount, and that playing the same political games as other parties would fundamentally compromise those radical principles.

For people in the Marxist tradition, attempts to work for reform of the capitalist system – to improve wages or working conditions for example, or to provide welfare – merely reduce the chances of revolutionary change, and delay or impede the desired overthrow of the system.

Eventually the *Realos* won out, and *Die Grünen* entered coalition government with the Social Democratic Party in 1998. The more radical pacifist wings of the party were dismayed to see green ministers sanctioning the March 1999 bombing of Serbia and the invasion of Afghanistan in 2001. The sight of once-outsider movements and activists entering mainstream politics, lobbying at intergovernmental conferences, and holding joint press conferences with big business has led to considerable soul searching within the green movement and a broader sense of activist disillusionment.

Some academics have labelled such developments a symptom of an era of 'post-ecologism' and 'a politics of unsustainability' (Blühdorn and Welsh 2007). They argue that 'the historically radical and transformative elements of environmental movements and eco-political thought [have been] blunted through mainstreaming' (Blühdorn and Welsh 2007: 185). In effect, they argue, environmentalism has become too successful – it has made everyone aware of the importance of environmentalism – but it has had little or no observable effect on actual environmental issues. Species are still becoming extinct, climate change is accelerating, populations and economies are growing. Awareness has been raised, and we are all nominally environmentalists now – but we still all live unsustainable lives.

How can we explain this apparent paradox of increasing environmentalism but worsening environmental quality? Ingolfur Blühdorn argues that people join environmental movements, campaigns and protests not because they think they will succeed, but because that makes them feel better about themselves. In fact, according to

FIGURE 4.8
The German Green Party unveiling a campaigning slogan in 2009. http://www.wiwo.de/politik-weltwirtschaft/die-gruenen-entdecken-die-finanzkrise-403309/

Blühdorn, environmental activism 'can hardly be described as goal-oriented strategic action, but at best as the collective processing of helplessness' (2006: 27). This is a sobering thought, and initially seems quite pessimistic about our potential to save the world.

One of the ways to read this argument about post-ecologism, however, is that environmental activism is at least as much about saving ourselves as it is about saving the planet. Or, to put it differently, that the way in which we think about ourselves and our own identity and subjectivity is just as important for environmental activism as how we think about nature and the planet. As Captain Planet always reminded the Planeteers, and through them the youth of the world: 'the power is you!'

In exploring these final thoughts about government of the self and government of the environment, I want to turn to the literature on green or eco-governmentality, which draws on the work of Michel Foucault and applies it to the study of environmental politics.

Michel Foucault's view of power and resistance is discussed in **Chapter 7**. See also **Chapters 1, 5, 11, 23 and 25**.

The question of why we obey is discussed in **Chapter 7**.

The political thought of Michel Foucault is discussed in other chapters, but this section uses one of his ideas in particular: that of governmentality. Governmentality refers to rationalities or mentalities of government, and it is characterised by the study of how contemporary society works as much or more through multiple and fragmented networks of power and knowledge than through the centralised power of states or the law (Foucault 2007; Rose 1999). Instead of simply being told what we can or cannot do, we internalise certain norms, standards, and forms of conduct. This can be seen quite clearly in the case of environmentalism: in many societies all sorts of techniques are used to persuade us to recycle, or use public transport, or buy green products, or measure our carbon emissions. Matthew Paterson and Johannes Stripple have shown how initiatives like carbon footprinting (measuring your individual carbon dioxide emissions), offsetting (paying for projects to conserve carbon emissions elsewhere, such

FIGURE 4.9 'Environment policy'. Artist: Fran. CartoonStock ref.: forn88o. www.CartoonStock.com

as planting trees, to offset a flight or purchase), dieting, rationing and personal allowances (different ways of trying to get individuals to restrict their carbon emissions) have been promoted in various different ways, with various effects (2010). All sorts of social institutions – from schools, to businesses, to political parties, social organisations and NGOs, as well as the state – are involved in promoting sustainable lifestyles.

Applying an eco-governmentality perspective to questions of environmental politics implies that rather than trying to immediately tackle really big questions of principle, such as reform versus revolution, or environment versus development, we should begin by looking at the specific, concrete practices and technologies that already surround us. Of particular importance are the consequences of the ways in which people have gone about trying to save the planet. Carbon offsetting, for example, might be one way to try and save the planet from climate change, but it also risks putting the responsibility primarily on individual consumers, rather than our elected representatives; it implies that a flight can somehow be equalled out by a donation to a tree farm, perhaps discouraging more radical changes to our lifestyles; and it risks creating the impression that some countries (typically the less well-off and less powerful) exist as carbon reserves for balancing out the carboniferous capitalism of the Western world. Similarly, seeing environmental issues through the lens of Hardin's tragedy of the commons suggests that humans are always competitive, solely or primarily interested in maximising their wealth, and are unable to compromise or work together.

A governmentality approach is designed to shine a spotlight on the political implications of particular rationalities of government – ways of trying to govern the actions of others – and to make explicit some of the assumptions, values, and effects that often get obscured by the urgency of trying to save the planet. Who, for example, is being tasked with being heroic saviours of the planet? Is it scientists and engineers? Or international bureaucrats working for the UN? Politicians and the political elites?

CEOs in the private sector? Or unelected self-nominated grassroots activists and NGOs? If they are to work together in partnership, who sets the rules and monitors the power relationships? What forms of knowledge – science, economic efficiency, diplomatic realpolitik, social justice – are to be the criteria for how we judge their efforts?

One of the criticisms of some of the Foucauldian-inspired literature on governmentality, especially in the 1980s and 1990s, was that it seemed to direct attention to forms of governance, power and control, rather than forms of resistance and dissent. It is certainly true to say that many of the key studies of governmentality (Dean 1999; Rose 1999) pay little attention to social movements or activists. Similarly, there was little focus in the early eco-governmentality research on the sorts of environmental movements and grassroots activists that had inspired modern environmentalism in the first place (Darier 1996; Goldman 2001; Luke 1995). Some concluded from this that governmentality scholars were pessimistic about the ability of environmental movements and activists to change or save the world.

BOX 4.6 MITCHELL DEAN'S ANALYTICS OF GOVERNMENT

Mitchell Dean has developed Michel Foucault's work on governmentality into an analytical framework for studying mentalities or rationalities of rule, meaning any calculated or rationalised direction of human conduct (1999: 2). He focuses our attention on the fields of visibility created, the forms of knowledge produced, the techniques and technologies employed, and the forms of subjectivity performed.

Fields of visibility. All forms of government, according to Dean, employ certain pictures, diagrams, images or maps of what is to be governed. In the global governance of climate change, for example, the planetary carbon dioxide cycle is pictured as a suitable field for political interventions.

Forms of knowledge. All forms of government rely upon particular scientific or legitimate ways of discovering the truth. Foucault was particularly interested in how the eighteenth-century state relied upon the growing science of statistics to know more about economies and populations (Foucault 2007). In a similar way the government of climate change is only possible through the disciplines of environmental economics, biodiversity management, hydrology, agricultural science and so on.

Techniques and technologies. Government happens on the ground in concrete and specific ways, through the countless instruments and policies of planners, social workers, professionals and practitioners. Environmental governance relies upon a profusion of indicators produced by states, development institutions and NGOs to measure and manage carbon dioxide levels, species conservation, clean water and sanitation, energy consumption, and so on.

Production of subjectivities. Similarly, all forms of government imagine and produce particular types of individual or organisation. Modern environmentalism has sought to produce environmentally responsible citizens who recycle, walk or cycle to work or take public transport, and who measure their carbon footprint and offset their flights (Paterson and Stripple 2010). On the other hand, environmental activists who march against runway expansions or climb power plants are criminalised and portrayed as irresponsible.

Whilst this quite schematic way of studying and comparing various governmentalities is not the only way to use Foucault's work, it has been quite productive in the study of environmental governance. For a survey of some literature using this approach see Death (2010: 55–7) and Okereke *et al.* (2009: 71–2).

However, Foucault's own work was interested in forms of resistance and dissent. Indeed he devoted a lot of attention to the existence of what he called counter-conducts – 'struggle[s] against the processes implemented for conducting others' (Foucault 2007: 201) – and he stressed the close relationship between power and freedom. Modern environmental governance is simultaneously about the government of the self and others, rather than domination or control from afar. In this vein more recent research has sought to use some of Foucault's work to study social movements and environmental activism, showing how environmental movements have advanced alternative ways of framing environmental problems, new types of knowledge, and new ways of being responsible environmental subjects (Barry 2001; Death 2010). For example, environmental campaigners in South Africa have framed environmental issues as the result of over-affluent consumer lifestyles and global injustice, rather than the tragedy of the commons. Community groups in Durban have collected their own air samples, contesting the industrial control of scientific monitoring, and have linked up with similar campaigns in the USA, Ireland, Nigeria and elsewhere, providing a different image of responsible environmental citizenship from the consumer who buys green products and recycles (Barnett and Scott 2007; Death 2010). Whilst such movements are not free of power relations, their existence does mean there is more flexibility and responsiveness within contemporary forms of environmental governance than some more pessimistic analyses suggest.

An eco-governmentality perspective is not designed to provide easy answers to the question 'Can we save the planet?' Neither does it produce clear-cut principles for deciding whether particular governmental rationalities are good or bad. Rather it is intended to draw attention to some of the political opportunities, consequences and dangers produced, often indirectly, by the forms of governance adopted in the name of saving the planet. What is clear, however, is that dealing with environmental problems will require at least as much attention on ourselves, and the creation of new forms of sustainable and responsible individual subjects, as it will on the political and economic structures that have produced global environmental degradation.

The possibility that the more we try to protect ourselves, the more dangers we create, is one explored in **Chapter 25**.

CONCLUSION

If you wanted a definitive answer or clear set of instructions for how to save the planet you will by now be rather disappointed with this chapter. But hopefully it has managed to provide some ideas about how other people – often very committed and dedicated activists, academics and politicians – have tried to protect the environment in a variety of often quite heroic ways. Whether through large global conferences, or big transnational NGOs conducting high-profile campaigns, or local groups trying to protect a specific site or improve environmental conditions for their community, many people have devoted a lot of their time and energy, and made substantial personal sacrifices, in the name of the environment.

From a longer term perspective, humanity has proved very resilient and highly adaptable over the past few thousand years, and we have created complex societies and economies unlike anything else on the planet. It is true that these have had many negative environmental and social consequences. Foucault noted that 'modern man is an animal whose politics places his existence as a living being in question' (1998: 143). But our politics also gives us the potential to change the way societies and economies are organised. So, can we save the planet? The planet will almost certainly outlast us. However, as a species we have the capacity to do both wonderful *and* terrible things. The really important question is perhaps not whether the planet will survive, or whether we can conserve things as they are now, but rather: What sort of changes will we produce, and what sorts of effects will this have on future generations, on people in different parts of the world, on the weakest and least resilient, and on other species? And who are the 'we' that are tasked with deciding on these changes?

When people talk of saving the planet they actually seem to mean saving biodiversity or even the conditions for maintaining human existence exactly as it is. It is not clear that any of the global environmental problems – such as climate change – actually threaten the planet very much at all.

FURTHER READING

Adger, W. Neil and Andrew Jordan (eds) (2009) *Governing Sustainability*, Cambridge: Cambridge University Press.
A wide-ranging collection of essays by leading authorities on environmental governance, from both critical and more problem-solving perspectives. It begins with the assertion that the crisis of sustainability is primarily a crisis of governance.

Darier, Eric (ed.) (1999) *Discourses of the Environment*, Oxford: Blackwell.
A provocative and stimulating range of essays exploring the links between Michel Foucault's work and environmental politics, including eco-governmentality, bio-politics and population, gender and sexuality, nature, ethics and art.

Kütting, Gabriela (ed.) (2011) *Global Environmental Politics: Concepts, Theories and Case Studies*, Abingdon: Routledge.
An excellent introduction to key thinkers and actors, as well as case studies including forests, water, biodiversity and climate change, by a range of expert scholars.

Kütting, Gabriela and Ronnie Lipschutz (eds) (2009) *Environmental Governance: Power and Knowledge in a Local-Global World*, Abingdon: Routledge.
More critical research essays on environmental power relations in a range of contexts, including ecovillages, grassroots movements and global ecosystem monitoring.

Wissenburg, Marcel and Yoram Levy (eds) (2004) *Liberal Democracy and Environmentalism: The End of Environmentalism?* London: Routledge.
This collection poses the important and difficult question of whether environmentalists have any reason to carry on their struggles. Environmental concerns have been thoroughly 'mainstreamed' and integrated into liberal politics, so do we still need environmentalists?

WEBSITES

A range of environmental social movements, activists and grassroots movements can be found at:

http://www.ecoequity.org/
http://www.climatenetwork.org/
http://www.thecornerhouse.org.uk/
http://www.twnside.org.sg/
http://www.groundwork.org.za/
http://www.earthlife.org.za/

Some of the most influential large transnational environmental NGOs can be found at:

http://www.wri.org/
http://wwf.panda.org/
http://www.foei.org/
http://www.greenpeace.org/international/en/
http://www.iucn.org/
http://www.conservation.org

International institutions and UN bodies working on environmental issues can be found at:

http://www.unep.org/
http://www.un.org/esa/dsd/index.shtml
http://www.uncsd2012.org/rio20/
http://unfccc.int/2860.php
http://www.ipcc.ch/
http://www.iied.org/
http://www.iisd.org/

REFERENCES

Adams, W. M. (2009) *Green Development: Environment and Sustainability in a Developing World*, London: Routledge.

Barnett, Clive and Dianne Scott (2007) 'Spaces of Opposition: Activism and Deliberation in post-Apartheid Environmental Politics', *Environment and Planning A*, 39, 11: 2612–631.

Barry, Andrew (2001) *Political Machines*, London: Athlone Press.

Blühdorn, Ingolfur (2006) 'Self-Experience in the Theme Park of Radical Action? Social Movements and Political Articulation in the Late-Modern Condition', *European Journal of Social Theory*, 9, 1: 23–42.

Blühdorn, Ingolfur and Ian Welsh (2007) 'Eco-Politics Beyond the Paradigm of Sustainability: A Conceptual Framework and Research Agenda', *Environmental Politics*, 16, 2: 185–205.

Bond, Patrick (2002) *Unsustainable South Africa: Environment, Development and Social Protest*, London: Merlin Press.

Brenton, Tony (1994) *The Greening of Machiavelli: The Evolution of International Environmental Politics*, London: RIIA and Earthscan.

Brown, Paul (2002) 'Big business and Greenpeace Urge Action on Climate Change', *Guardian* (UK), 29 August.

Carson, Rachel (1964) *Silent Spring*, London: Hamish Hamilton.

Chasek, Pamela S. and Richard Sherman (2004) *Ten Days in Johannesburg: A Negotiation of Hope*, Pretoria: DEAT and UNDP.

Chatterjee, Pratap and Matthias Finger (1994) *The Earth Brokers: Power, Politics and World Development*, London: Routledge.

Darier, Eric (1996) 'Environmental Governmentality: The Case of Canada's Green Plan', *Environmental Politics*, 5, 4: 585–606.

Dean, Mitchell (1999) *Governmentality: Power and Rule in Modern Society*, London: Sage.

Death, Carl (2010) *Governing Sustainable Development: Partnerships, Protests and Power at the World Summit*, Abingdon: Routledge.

Doyle, Timothy and Brian Doherty (2006) 'Green Public Spheres and the Green Governance State: The Politics of Emancipation and Ecological Conditionality', *Environmental Politics*, 15, 5: 881–92.

Doyle, Timothy and Doug McEachern (2008) *Environment and Politics*, Abingdon: Routledge.

Dresner, Simon (2002) *The Principles of Sustainability*, London: Earthscan.

Dryzek, John S. (2005) *The Politics of the Earth: Environmental Discourses*, Oxford: Oxford University Press.

Duncan, Jane (2003) 'A Flash in the Pan? The Relevance of the WSSD for Freedom of Expression', in Simon Kimani Ndung'u (ed.) *The Right to Dissent: Freedom of Expression, Assembly and Demonstration in South Africa*, Johannesburg: Freedom of Expression Institute.

Foucault, Michel (1998) *The Will to Knowledge: The History of Sexuality, Volume I*, London: Penguin.

——(2007) *Security, Territory, Population: Lectures at the Collège de France 1977–1978*, Basingstoke: Palgrave Macmillan.

Goldman, Michael (2001) 'Constructing an Environmental State: Eco-governmentality and other Transnational Practices of a "Green" World Bank', *Social Problems*, 48, 4: 499–523.

Greenpeace International (2010) *Annual Report 2010*, Amsterdam: Greenpeace International.

Gutman, Pablo (2003) 'What did WSSD Accomplish? An NGO Perspective', *Environment*, 45, 2: 20–28.

Haas, Peter M. (2002) 'UN Conferences and Constructivist Governance of the Environment', *Global Governance*, 8, 1: 73–91.

Hardin, Garrett (1968) 'The Tragedy of the Commons', *Science*, 162, 3859: 1243–48.

Lean, Geoffrey (2002) 'UN Blocks Future Summits', *Independent* (UK), 8 September.

Luke, Timothy W. (1995) 'On Environmentality: Geo-Power and Eco-Knowledge in the Discourses of Contemporary Environmentalism', *Cultural Critique*, 31: 57–81.

McDonald, David A. (ed.) (2002) *Environmental Justice in South Africa*, Athens, OH: Ohio University Press.

Meadows, Donella H., Dennis L. Meadows, Jørgen Randers and William W. Behrens III (1974) *The Limits to Growth: A Report for the Club of Rome's Project on the Predicament of Mankind*, New York: New American Library.

Middleton, Neil and Phil O'Keefe (2001) *Redefining Sustainable Development*, London: Pluto Press.

Okereke, Chukwumerije, Harriet Bulkeley and Heike Schroeder (2009) 'Conceptualising Climate Governance beyond the International Regime', *Global Environmental Politics*, 9, 1: 58–78.

Paterson, Matthew (2000) *Understanding Global Environmental Politics: Domination, Accumulation, Resistance*, London: Macmillan.

Paterson, Matthew and Johannes Stripple (2010) 'My Space: Governing Individuals' Carbon Emissions', *Environment and Planning D: Society and Space*, 28, 2: 341–62.

Putnam, Robert D. (1988) 'Diplomacy and Domestic Politics: The Logic of Two-Level Games', *International Organization*, 42, 3: 427–60.

Rose, Nikolas (1999) *Powers of Freedom: Reframing Political Thought*, Cambridge: Cambridge University Press.

Rutherford, Paul (2003) '"Talking the Talk": Business Discourse at the World Summit on Sustainable Development', *Environmental Politics*, 12, 2: 145–50.

Shiva, Vandana (1993) 'The Greening of the Global Reach', in Wolfgang Sachs (ed.) *Global Ecology: A New Arena of Political Conflict*, London: Zed Books.

UN (2000) *Resolution 55/199: Ten-year review of progress achieved in the implementation of the outcome of the United Nations Conference on Environment and Development*, 20 December 2000, New York: United Nations.

——(2002a) The Johannesburg Declaration on Sustainable Development, adopted at the WSSD 17th plenary meeting on 4 September 2002, Johannesburg: United Nations.

——(2002b) *Report of the World Summit on Sustainable Development, Johannesburg, South Africa, 26 August–4 September 2002*, New York: United Nations.

Wapner, Paul (1995) 'Politics beyond the State: Environmental Activism and World Civic Politics', *World Politics*, 47, 3: 311–40.

——(2003) 'World Summit on Sustainable Development: Toward a Post-Jo'burg Environmentalism', *Global Environmental Politics*, 3, 1: 1–10.

Willetts, Peter (2000) 'From "Consultative Arrangements" to "Partnership": The Changing Status of NGOs in Diplomacy at the UN', *Global Governance*, 6, 2: 191–212.

World Commission on Environment and Development (1987) *Our Common Future: World Commission on Environment and Development*, Oxford: Oxford University Press.

World Resources Institute (2002) 'WRI Expresses Disappointment over Many WSSD Outcomes', press release, 4 September.

For a range of further resources supporting this chapter, please visit the companion website for *Global Politics, 2nd Edition* at www.routledge.com/cw/edkins/

CHAPTER 5

Who do we think we are?

Annick T. R. Wibben

- *The question*
  NARRATIVES AND POLITICS
- *Illustrative example*
  THE US FEMINIST MOVEMENT
- *General responses*
  HOW CAN WE CONCEPTUALIZE IDENTITY?
- *Broader issues*
  DO WE NEED TO IDENTIFY WITH A GROUP?
- **CONCLUSION**

THE QUESTION
NARRATIVES AND POLITICS

Our idea of who we think we are is often based on something called identity: national, ethnic, racial, gender, class, sexual or religious identity are among the categories that are used in discussions. To think about the question of identity, we need to do two things: (a) begin to see how we are always already subjected to identity politics, and (b) examine what some of the implications of being identified (or identifying) with a particular group can be in global politics.

Once we have come to understand why identity is such an important concept, we can take a closer look at how identity politics play out in the particular case of the women's movement in the United States and what the experiences of this movement can teach us about identity politics in other settings. Identity politics is inspired by the interests of, and intended to benefit, a particular group with a shared identity. It has been a key form of political activism, though one that is much criticized as we shall discover shortly.

As soon as a baby is born, people begin to identify this new person in various ways. Besides assuming the baby's ethnicity or nationality, this very often means identifying the baby's gender. Today, with the advent of new technologies, many people will seek to find out whether they are having a girl or a boy even before birth. The consequences of this early identification range from 'getting ready' by selecting a name and painting a nursery in the 'right' colour, to selective abortions in countries like India (where a preference for males is common) or China (where the preference for males is coupled with a one-birth policy). Thus, from an early age, before birth even, identity politics matter.

We tell stories about who we are, and these stories are closely related to the pictures we form of the world: see **Chapter 2**. The way our stories relate to belonging to a nation (or national identity) is discussed in **Chapter 13**.

Narrative theorists have pointed out that we are all *homo fabulans* – storytellers. Narratives are 'the primary way by which human experience is made meaningful' (Polkinghorne 1988: 1). Through narratives we make sense of the world, produce meaning, articulate intentions, and legitimize actions. While our lives begin with us being subject to the stories of our parents and others around us, we soon begin to tell our own stories about who we are and where we belong. As we grow, and as the stories of who we are change over time, we might be disappointed when we realize that how our family or community sees us does not match how we identify ourselves.

China's view of people of Chinese ancestry living outside China is discussed in **Chapter 12**.

As we enter new life situations the process of identification continues: We might be confronted with racism for the first time and begin to rethink our identity in terms of race (Winddance Twine's classic on 'Brown-skinned White Girls' (1996) discusses the case of girls who in college become identified as Black). We might realize that having children can mean not ever reaching a leadership position in the workplace. We might find that our religious heritage or nationality limits our movement, as in the case of Palestinians living under occupation in Gaza and the West Bank or of Mexican immigrants to the US. Our image of ourselves and what others see in us (and how they expect us to act) is always unfinished. And – there are always multiple stories of who we are intersecting at any one time. Most of these are beyond our control and many times they offer conflicting accounts.

Chapter 10 discusses Mexican immigration to the US in some detail.

As we identify ourselves through these stories, we draw on various markers of identity that have been passed down to us through the stories we were told. In this ongoing process we are constantly comparing our experiences with those of the rest of the group that we identify with. We discover a shared tradition, a feeling of belonging when our experiences match the standards of identification. We devise new stories, and challenge or reject those that others tell (about us or themselves), when they do not match our experience.

The markers of identity that are emphasized in these stories – whether they be national, ethnic, racial, gender, class, sexual or religious in kind – always signal the belonging to a particular group. In other words, they identify us as a member of a particular group and not of another in the same category (accordingly, when applied strictly as in the case of fundamentalist movements, one cannot be Hindu and Muslim at the same time and most countries in the world will still only allow their citizens to hold one passport). That is, at the same time as they place us *inside* this particular group, they also place us *outside* another group.

Of course, identities are often not mutually exclusive. Many people consider themselves to belong to two groups that others may consider to be separate. This is visible in the proliferation of hyphenated identities, such as Mexican-American.

What is more, by identifying certain traits of belonging to this particular group, they also tell us who the Other is. We cannot understand what it means to be inside,

BOX 5.1 THE BREAK-UP OF YUGOSLAVIA

During the break-up of the former Yugoslavia, ethnic and national identities were harnessed in an intense struggle over power and resources. For several decades, while the state known as Yugoslavia existed, the identities that were soon to become a source of intense and bloody conflict were fluid and not politically significant. Yugoslavs lived together in broad-based communities. During the early 1990s, at the end of the Cold War, different groups within Yugoslavia began to signal their belonging to a particular group (e.g. Serb). While doing so, they placed themselves outside another group (e.g. Bosnian) and began to also distinguish other traits that were reasons for being considered other (e.g. being Muslim in the case

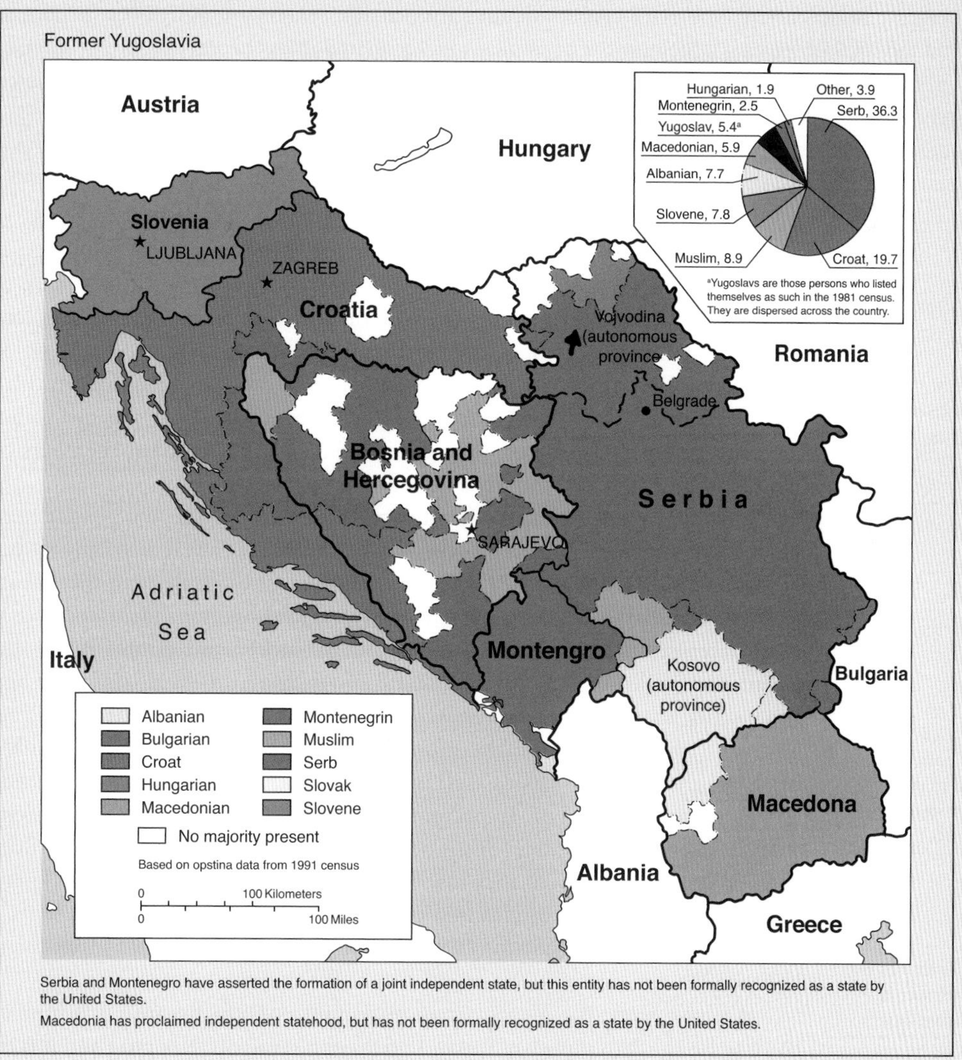

FIGURE 5.1
Former Yugoslavia, based on 1991 census

of many Bosnians). For many young Yugoslavs in particular this was the first time that their religion and heritage came to matter, since they had led a largely secular lifestyle before then.

As the politics of identity intensified, every Yugoslav had to identify with one of the emerging groups: Albanians, Bosnians, Croats, Macedonians, Montenegrins, Serbs and Slovenes. The leaders of these different groups began to claim a right to national self-determination (asking for the international community to recognize their group as independent). Some of them, especially Serbs but also Croats, began to 'purify' the regions that they identified as belonging to their group. This meant that those who were seen as others were subjected to increasing oppression and even armed violence (see Campbell 1998).

Whether woman or man, being identified as other (e.g. Bosnian) could lead to being held in concentration camps where rape, hard labour and random execution were common. What is more, age mattered too: In Srebrenica a large number of refugees had gathered under protection of the United Nations. In July 1995 the Serb military, in their efforts to 'cleanse' the area seen as belonging to Serbia, attacked the safe zone. While they allowed women and children to leave, men of fighting age were massacred. Three markers of identity – gender, age and nationality – came to matter greatly for these men (see Carpenter 2003).

without at the same time identifying who or what is outside. Without this 'constitutive outside', something seen as fundamentally different, identity would no longer be meaningful. Even the broad identifier 'human' relies on the juxtaposition with the 'non-human' (e.g. animals, plants or rocks). The latter tell us what it means to be 'human' (e.g. not an animal, not a plant, not a rock). As such, at its base, members of a group may have little more in common than not being 'them'.

What it might mean to question notions of the human as used in the term 'human rights' is discussed in **Chapter 27**.

In addition to marking this boundary, those on the inside are privileged over those on the outside in a number of ways: They can decide what it means to belong and consequently who does not. They often enforce purity inside with the threat of being outside, thus marking what is outside as inferior to those traits identified with the group (e.g. heterosexuality might be considered the norm and people with other sexual orientations will not only be excluded but considered deviant, sinful, or appalling in some other way). This holds true whether the group is in a hegemonic or a subjugated position (whether they are the group in charge or not). In a hegemonic position, however, the in-group has easy access to resources (economic, military, and cultural) as well as control thereof. Important institutions (e.g. the education system) will be shaped to conform to their needs and to transmit their values. Thus, 'although the boundaries are ideological, they involve material (biological, legal, social) practices and therefore have material origins and effects' (Yuval-Davis 1994: 410). At its extremes, being identified (or identifying) with one or another group could mean the difference between life and death.

The impact of colonialism on the identity of both the colonizer and the colonized is discussed in **Chapter 16**.

Chapter 6 examines the example of Islam as a source of identification.

We have seen that identity is an important concept because it is fundamental to the way we think of ourselves today: it gives us a sense of belonging and it is the marker of our tradition, history and heritage. Identity politics are comforting as they promise security and meaning: 'Stability lies in part in clearly defined sex roles, family life and religious orientation' (Moghadam 1994: 19).

We have also noted that identity politics is also a boundary politics that prescribes what is accepted and expected for members of the in-group, the 'good' people. As such, identification takes place by identifying against others, not just excluding but oppressing them and the traits associated with them. The result is that being identified (or identifying) with a particular group is always potentially dangerous.

How can we draw strength from identifying with a group and at the same time curtail the violence it so often entails? The next section looks at a specific example of identity politics – the case of the feminist movement in the United States in the second half of the twentieth century. By looking at the history of the movement and the challenges it has faced, we will be able to better understand the complexities of identity and how we may address identities in conflict without recourse to violence.

ILLUSTRATIVE EXAMPLE
THE US FEMINIST MOVEMENT

Feminist identity politics rely on the idea that some groups are oppressed because they are identified in a particular way: being identified as women, with the associated traits of femininity, leads women to have a shared experience of oppression. Some feminists have argued that this experience that *all* women share, and which is fundamentally different from that of *all* men, should be the basis for feminist politics. Feminists who

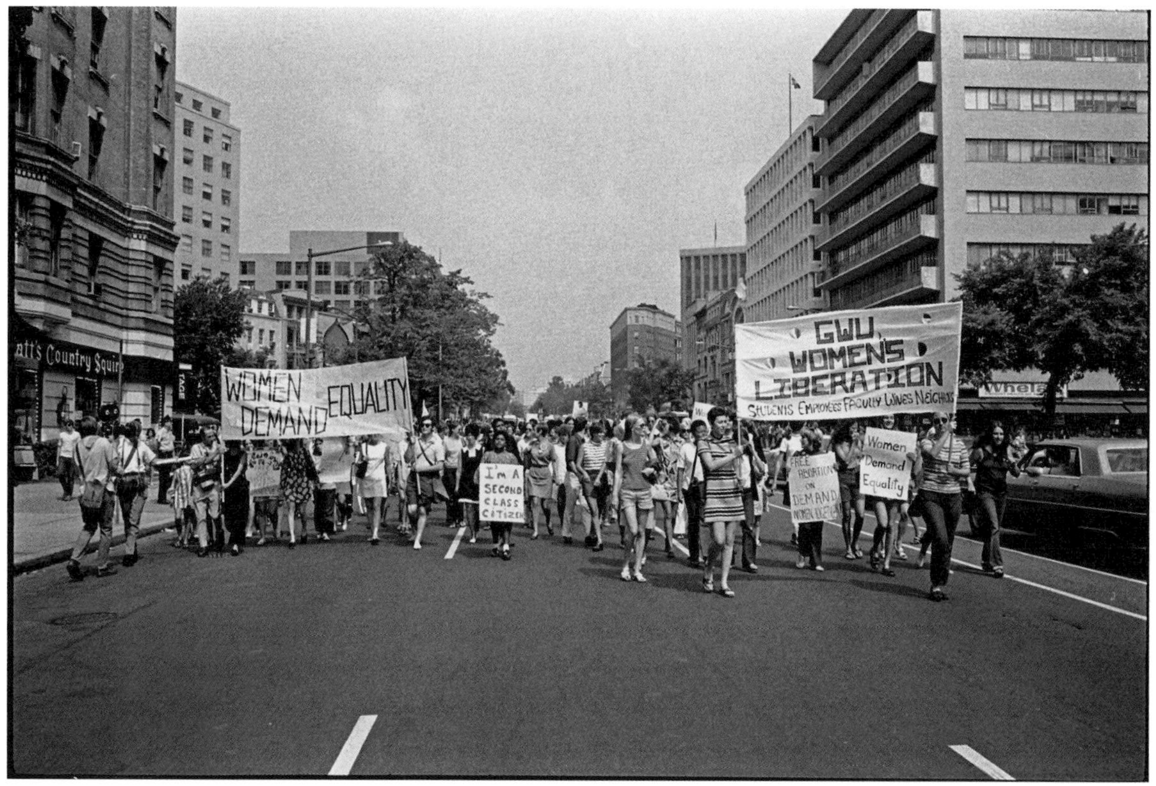

FIGURE 5.2 Women's liberation march. http://college.cengage.com/history/primary_sources/us/womens_liberation_march.htm

began thinking along these lines in the 1960s are called second-wave feminists (first wave feminism refers to feminist activism of the late nineteenth and early twentieth century, in particular that of the suffragettes who were fighting for a woman's right to vote and to hold public office). Most second-wave feminists, inspired by liberal political thought, sought to overcome oppression by working to achieve equality between women and men. Therefore they are also referred to as liberal or equality feminists.

Emergence of feminist activism

For other forms of activism see **Chapters 4 (environmentalism) and 14 (grassroots politics)**; contemporary activism is discussed in **Chapters 9 (the Arab Spring), 18 and 28 (the Occupy Movement)**.

Feminist activism and scholarly activity emerged in many locations and was inspired by a broad range of oppressive circumstances and disciplines (e.g. history, literature, philosophy, politics, psychoanalysis, sociology) and oppressive circumstances. The work of these women (and some men) produced some important insights that challenged the foundations of the social and political order as well as what is today considered worthwhile knowledge.

Asking the basic question, 'Where are the women?' feminists found that often no one had looked for them before.

Much of the knowledge that had been collected in massive volumes on library shelves, that was being taught in schools and universities, and that was being used to make important policy decisions, was based on the experiences of men. Even knowledge about women-centred processes like pregnancy, birthing, childrearing and other activities that involved women's bodies or activities largely assigned to women, was dominated by men.

MORRIS
"I heard they spent all day arguing whether to let women into the boardroom."

FIGURE 5.3
'I heard they spent all day arguing.' Artist: John Morris. CartoonStock ref.: jm01622. www.CartoonStock.com

BOX 5.2 CAROL GILLIGAN

Carol Gilligan, a feminist psychologist, wrote a well-known book called *In a Different Voice* (1982). In it she examines theories of childhood development to find that 'The disparity between women's experience and the representation of human development, noted throughout the psychological literature, has generally been seen to signify a problem in women's development' (Gilligan 1982: 1–2).

Her studies, however, led her to suggest that it is not that girls are failing to develop properly, but rather that the models used to assess development are based solely on the experiences of men. Reviewing studies of play, for example, she instead suggests that girls develop differently because they have a different value system. They tend to give preference to the continuation of relationships over the setting and following of rules.

FIGURE 5.4
Carol Gilligan, Photo: Nancy Palmieri

These types of observations led Gilligan to develop an ethics of care as an alternative moral framework, also for politics. While her work has been criticized by many feminists for essentializing women's voices and experiences – saying that she makes a virtue out of qualities that are the result of subordination – her work continues to resonate with many women. Joan Tronto, in *Moral Boundaries* (1993), Fiona Robinson, in *Globalizing Care* (1999) and Virginia Held, in *The Ethics of Care* (2006), have thought more about some of the implications of Gilligan's approach for global politics.

Feminists decided that the bias of science and policy could only be corrected by gathering knowledge about women. They argued that these new insights, based on women's experiences, would transform ways of thinking and cultural categories. A very important and innovative approach to examining and challenging patriarchy (structures of male domination) was feminist consciousness-raising. The premise of this approach was that 'through discussion women would begin to see what they had once been convinced were personal problems are actually political problems' (Kauffmann 1990: 28). Indeed, when women began to share their experiences in partnerships, friendships, the workforce, or the marketplace, they discovered systematic patterns of male domination in all of these areas.

This pervasiveness of patriarchy led feminists to question the entire setup of the private/public dichotomy and the assumptions underlying some of the primary categories of political thought. Jean Bethke Elshtain, in *Public Man, Private Woman* (1981), did a re-reading of canonical texts and rethinking of classic political concepts from a feminist perspective. Another effort focused on recovering women's writing (cf. Spender 1983) to see what historical trends could be uncovered and to develop a broader appreciation of women's experiences.

Traditionally, women and their concerns were seen to belong to the private sphere, whereas politics took place in the public sphere, to which only men were admitted.

In addition, some women began to write about their experiences of oppression due to their identification as women. Betty Friedan's *Feminine Mystique* (2001 [1963]) was one of the most influential books of this type.

FIGURE 5.5
Betty Friedan

Published in the early 1960s, many credit it with jumpstarting second-wave feminism. Friedan began writing the book after she attended her college reunion where she gave a questionnaire to 200 of her fellow female classmates asking them about their life expectations and experiences. The survey confirmed that many women were unhappy and did not know why – Friedan began calling this 'the problem which has no name'. She eloquently linked the symptoms to an idealized image of femininity – the 'feminine mystique' – which encourages women to confine themselves to the narrow roles of housewife and mother, forsaking education and career aspirations in the process. Her book is still an eye-opening read for many women, but its concerns and suggestions reveal her white, middle-class experience.

María C. Lugones and Elizabeth V. Spelman, while not addressing Friedan's work directly, worry about the consequences of extrapolating from specific women's experiences to arrive at an account of *the* woman's voice. They worry that changes perceived as making life better for some women might not at all be liberating for women:

> whose lives would be better if they could spend more time at home, whose identity is inseparable from their religious beliefs and cultural practices [. . .], who have ties to men – whether erotic or not – such that to have them severed in the name of some vision of what is 'better' is, at that time and for those women, absurd.
> (1983: 579)

The problem that speaking for a group implies that the group shares experiences is not, of course, unique to the women's movement, but rather an issue that all movements have to deal with.

While the situation might still *seem* oppressive, and even *be* oppressive, they argue that feminist theory should aim to be 'respectful, illuminating, and empowering' (1983: 580) to women in particular settings rather than true or false in an abstract sense. Feminisms should always remain contextual.

This exchange reveals a major problem with second-wave feminism: Many of the women who were part of the movement at the time assumed that their experiences were the same as those of *all* women. They assumed that the oppression they experienced was the same as that experienced by *all* women. They imagined their avenues for empowerment, such as equality with men, would free *all* women from oppression. Or maybe, they did not think about their bias because their identity as white, middle-class women had not been challenged.

FIGURE 5.6
bell hooks

bell hooks (she never writes her name with capitals) suggests that the very idea that the feminist movement aims for equality between women and men should raise a number of questions. 'Since men are not equals in white supremacist, capitalist, patriarchal class structures, which men do you want to be equal to?' (hooks 1984: 18). She argues that this very question reveals the bias in liberal, second-wave feminism. Marginalized and poor women, especially if they are not white, immediately recognize that this definition of feminism is flawed since the men in their communities are not in a powerful position. Being like them would not entail an end to oppression. Therefore, liberal (equality) feminism is revealed to be part of the problem, rather than the solution. The framing of the problem as one of equality with men illustrates an unwillingness of white, middle-class feminists to examine their own privilege and their complicity in the structures of oppression.

BOX 5.3 PRIVILEGE

Let us take a moment to examine privilege. Privilege is a structure of unearned assets that we take for granted and that are considered 'normal'. Peggy McIntosh, in 'White Privilege and Male Privilege' (1993 [1988]) argued that the privilege of some is always premised on the denial of advantages to others, but we are rarely encouraged to see this – after all few of us want to consider ourselves oppressors.

If we think about it, however, most of us will be able to identify some form of privilege we enjoy: white privilege, class privilege, male privilege, heterosexual privilege and more. Being privileged means that society reflects your worldview and that what you do goes uncensored. Think about it: As you go about your daily life, do people ever restrain your behaviour? When you turn on the media, do you hear about or see people with your lifestyle, your ethnicity, or your sexual orientation? Are your religious holidays and customs celebrated by the majority of people in your country? Do you ever limit your movement for fear of being attacked violently because of your gender, race or sexual orientation? Has someone questioned your affection for your partner or described your interaction with your children as unnatural? How many times have you been oblivious to the needs, language, and customs of others without being affected by this ignorance?

Unacknowledged privilege is dangerous both personally and politically because it means that we *are* oppressors without even realizing it. These unearned assets are valued in ways that provide advantages within particular social structures to some – and not others – but it can be hard to see this. 'Whites are taught to think of their lives as morally neutral, normative and average, and also ideal, so that when we work to benefit others, this is seen as work that will allow "them" to be more like "us"'(McIntosh 1993 [1988]: 32). If we want to change structures of domination, we have to first challenge our complicity in their perpetuation by addressing privilege.

Intensification of identity politics

The famous feminist slogan – 'the personal is political' – which is central to feminist consciousness-raising in second-wave feminism, takes on new meaning as Black, Chicana (that is, Mexican-American), Lesbian and Third World feminists begin to demand that their experiences and their voices be taken seriously:

> We want to express to all women – especially to white middle-class women – the experiences which divide us as feminists; we want to examine incidents of intolerance, prejudice and denial of difference within the feminist movement. We intend to explore the causes and sources of, and solutions to these divisions. We want to create a definition that expands what 'feminist' means to us.
>
> (Cherríe Moraga and Gloria Anzaldúa 1983 [1979]: xxiii)

As this excerpt from *This Bridge Called My Back* (1983 [1979]) shows, feminists can no longer assume that there is an experience that *all* women share and which can therefore be the basis of the women's movement.

A phase of intensified politics around identity, what Kauffmann has called the anti-politics of identity (1990), begins. Rather than basing political action on supposedly

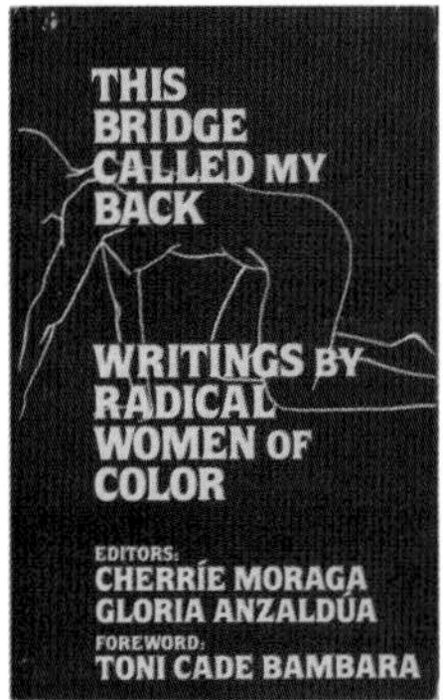

FIGURE 5.7
This Bridge Called My Back. Book cover

The complexities of identities produced as a result of colonialism are discussed in **Chapter 16**.

shared identities, identity itself becomes the subject of politics and the focus of examination. Consequently, various previously accepted elements of our life-stories become sites of political contestation. We might develop new ways of thinking and being, transform cultural categories to match new ideas, or even develop separate cultural programmes for each specific subcategory of identity. Hyphenated identities like 'black-lesbian-radical-feminist' or 'white-working-class-eco-feminist' are adopted to specify the belonging to a particular group.

An increasing number of feminists consequently begin to focus their attention on identity itself, even though many of the initial criticisms by Black, Chicana, Lesbian and Third World feminists of second-wave feminism specifically pointed to the material consequences of identity politics. This shift is evoked not just by the political critiques outlined above, but also by a philosophical shift that will be outlined in more detail in the next section. Suffice it to say that gender and sex came to be seen as socially constructed. This means, they are no longer thought to have a base in nature, anatomy or anthropological essence, but are seen to be constructed in a process of social, cultural and political struggles. This conceptual development allows us to examine the processes involved in identity formation more closely and to recognize the power struggles involved in identifying different markers and creating group hierarchies. It also alerts us to the fact that identity shifts both contextually (e.g. the same person might be identified as Ashanti in Ghana, Ghanaian in Africa, African in Europe) and over time (e.g. as we discover our sexuality, we might realize that we differ from the heterosexual norm).

Notwithstanding these advantages, the move toward examining identity without reference to the social, economic and political order within which it is embedded proved problematic for feminism for a number of reasons. First, the specificity that is sought by an ever-increasing number of hyphenations creates the illusion that people indeed possess a single, fixed identity (rather than one that is continually in flux). What is more, it also suggests that this identity can be captured if only we can dissect all its details (rather than accepting that it is impossible to portray all the facets of a person). An increasing fragmentation and a new wave of exclusions ensues as the sub-groupings become smaller and smaller. The focus on personal experience swiftly becomes an inward focus away from the commonalities that consciousness-raising sought to discover.

Instead, (trendy) subcultures and a politics of lifestyle evolve which closely resemble the logic of the marketplace. The outcome is a culture of political correctness and a focus on personal conduct, rather than revolutionary change. Identity politics in this vein are anti-politics (Kauffmann 1990), since the focus is on what people wear, eat, and say (individually) rather than what they are doing politically (as a social movement). Says Carmen Vasquez,

> We can't even agree on what a 'Feminist' is, never mind what she would believe in and how she defines the principles that constitute honour among us. In key with the American capitalist obsession for individualism and anything goes as long as it gets you what you want, feminism in America has come to mean anything you like, honey. There are as many definitions of Feminism as there are feminists, some of my sisters say with a chuckle. I don't think it's funny.
>
> (quoted in hooks 1984: 17)

Vasquez does not think it is funny because these practices lose sight of commonalities that, arguably, form the basis for collective struggles such as that of the women's movement. Preoccupied with their own micro-politics, this type of feminist identity politics neglects to analyse shared oppression and thus to build a basis for solidarity. As it assumes that a person's racial, religious, sexual or class identity and that person's political views are one and the same, it repeats the flaws of second-wave feminism: Where second-wave feminism unproblematically spoke for *all* women – these feminists no longer speak for anyone (but themselves). Either way, the structures of (male) oppression remain unchallenged. When feminists no longer communicate across the diverse groupings that make up the women's movement, they stop engaging in a shared political process.

The focus on individualism and the market in the context of modernization in South Asia also leads to the diversion of collective struggle for change: **Chapter 20**.

When seeking a unified feminist project, no homogeneous group of women can be assumed. To form a movement that accommodates all women, feminists need to engage in a politics of identity that examines privilege. When occupying a position of privilege, it is necessary to acknowledge one's complicity in upholding the structures of oppression (sexism, racism, homophobia, etc.). Only then can feminist and other activists strategically inhabit whatever privileged status they may enjoy to change the status quo.

This requires a reform of consciousness-raising as a feminist strategy. Whereas in the past, 'consciousness-raising techniques assume[d] as a basis for political action a reality that has to be discovered and then changed', Nira Yuval-Davis suggests thinking of it as 'a reality that is being created and re-created when practiced and discussed' (1994: 414). Consciousness-raising can no longer be a simple uncovering of experience but has to become a way to challenge representation and to confront privilege and power. Two separate questions need to be asked here: (1) 'How our identities are represented in and through the culture and assigned particular categories' and (2) 'Who or what politically represents us, speaks and acts on our behalf' (Brundt quoted in Yuval-Davis 1994: 415).

GENERAL RESPONSES
HOW CAN WE CONCEPTUALIZE IDENTITY?

The previous section examined the case of feminist struggles with identity politics in the United States. It is fair to say those struggles mirror as well as intersect with a wider debate about identity and questions of belonging. For example, while both sex and gender used to be seen as natural, we now think of them as broadly socially constructed. The same holds true for the way we understand identity more generally. This is a very recent phenomenon, however, since it was only during the twentieth century that scholars began to think in these terms. This section looks at these different ways of thinking about identity and the markers used to signify it – e.g. nation, ethnicity, race, gender, class, sex or religion – and what some of their limitations are.

Biology and natural history

Before discussing different ways of thinking (theories) that offer competing explanations today, it is important to examine their historical precursors. Understanding how ideas

Chapters 12 and 13 explore how nations are made and **Chapters 10 and 14** explore the significance of race in other contexts.

have developed over time helps to imagine them changing again. Take the example of female and male identity: Until quite recently, they used to be thought of as determined by biology and now are seen as socially constructed. However, the whole field of biology only developed about 200 years ago, so how did people think of this difference before then? What about other markers of identity, such as race or nation?

Biology developed out of a larger field of study called natural history. During the eighteenth century and beyond, natural history encompassed all descriptive aspects of the study of nature, including humans.

When describing what was later called race, for example, scholars of natural history included everything 'from the morphology of the skin, to the discussion of sexual desire, to music and poetry' (Appiah and Gutman 1996: 49). A person was perceived to possess an essence of some sort that gave rise to all of these traits. Only during the nineteenth century did fields like anatomy, physiology, anthropology, sociology and biology develop. With the emergence of these fields new concepts and frameworks were pioneered which broadened the horizons of scholars and lay people alike.

The work of Charles Darwin (1809–82) introduced new ways of thinking about inheritance and natural selection as well as new categories like species and race. Darwin used the term race to refer to animals and plants as well as to people. The increasing

FIGURE 5.8
The depiction of supposed essences, as imagined in natural history.
From S. Wells, *New Physiognomy or Signs of Character . . .*, New York, 1871

acceptance of Darwin's theories gave scientific support to the idea that different kinds of human groupings – races – could be clearly distinguished. The traits associated with different races would become the subject of studies, called race science or raciology (Gilroy 2000). From the association of facial features (e.g. nose, lips, shape of the eyes) to assumptions about intelligence and sexual inclination, we find raciology produced material that has been used time and time again to justify discriminatory policies at home and abroad. What is more, entire ideologies like orientalism (that is, the inevitably prejudiced representation of Eastern cultures and peoples by outsiders) and anti-semitism are based on raciology.

Orientalism is explained in **Chapter 6**.

Static and dynamic approaches to identity

Whereas identity used to be thought of as having its roots in nature or some sort of spiritual or anthropological essence, most scholars today subscribe to some form of the

BOX 5.4 HUTU AND TUTSI IN RWANDA

Through colonialism many of these European ideas spread throughout the world and with them assumptions about the superiority of European races. The Hamitic myth and its role in the 1994 genocide in Rwanda is a case in point. The Hamitic myth, whose origins can be traced to the Bible, originally provided justification for the enslavement of people of African descent. It was re-evaluated after the discovery of the achievements of ancient Egypt and from then on used to describe those peoples who appeared most 'European-like' in appearance and achievement.

During the colonization of Africa, the Tutsi of Rwanda were identified as Hamitic and therefore preferable to the Hutu, who were not considered worthy of cultural redemption. While these ideas were first introduced by German colonizers, the subsequent Belgian colonial administration perfected the idea of two distinct races by issuing identity cards which indicated racial belonging (in 1935). Prior to colonization the distinction between Tutsi and Hutu seems to have largely been one of caste (with the Tutsi being cattle keepers and the Hutu farmers, though movement between the two groups was common and the distinction largely associated with the type of work undertaken). What is more, they spoke the same language, shared similar customs and frequently intermarried.

The colonial authorities expanded existing hierarchies by using the Tutsi as a proxy government for Rwanda. The Belgians also supported the expansion of Tutsi power by providing the Tutsi with better education (with the help of Catholic missionaries). When the Tutsi demanded greater decision-making power and even independence, in 1959, the Belgians reversed the hierarchy and thereafter supported Hutu demands. Meanwhile, based on the same Hamitic myth used to justify colonial violence, anti-Tutsi propaganda like the *Hutu Manifesto* began to proclaim that if the Tutsi were indeed foreign invaders with European ancestry, the country should rightfully be governed by Hutu.

After achieving independence in 1961 and being governed by the Hutu majority, rumours of plots by Tutsis to resubjugate the Hutus marred Rwandan politics and were used to justify supposedly preventive killings of thousands of Tutsi. The erstwhile culmination of this 'Hutu power' movement was the 1994 Rwandan genocide, during which approximately 800,000 Tutsi and moderate Hutu were killed in a period of 100 days (see Gourevitch 1998 and Mamdani 2001).

idea that identity is socially constructed. As noted above, this implies that identities are seen to be constructed in a process of social, cultural and political struggle, rather than given by nature. That being said, there are some important differences in the manifold approaches to identity that are bundled under this label.

In the static approach we exist as individuals first, and then adopt or choose an identity; in this thinking, individuals 'have' an identity, as if it were something we could possess. This is often seen as common sense.

For the dynamic approach we don't 'exist' as individuals first – our coming into being as subjects already carries with it an identity or identities. This is more difficult to explain.

A stark contrast exists between those approaches that have a static conception of identity and those that take a dynamic approach to subjectivity. The static perspective presumes the existence of an individual and asks questions about that person's identity, whether this be their race, sexuality, gender, class, or some other marker of significance. Like someone taking or drawing a picture, it captures a particular point in time. The competing approach, what might be termed the dynamic perspective, does not assume subjectivity prior to its identification with these markers. The emphasis of this approach is on the processes through which we become identified and how they change (us) over time. To concretize these distinctions, we will discuss each perspective in turn.

R. W. Connell, in his book *Masculinities* (1995), provides some examples of ways of thinking about gender that follow the static perspective. A very common approach associated with this perspective is positivism (an approach based on the view that the scholar can take up a position outside the world that is being studied). Here the focus is on what we can observe in relation to a particular marker of identity – the way women or men actually are, for example. John Gray's self-help book *Men Are from Mars – Women Are from Venus* (2002) uses this type of approach to list characteristics that statistically seem to be more common to either gender's relationship behaviour. The picture that is painted as a result can only provide broad brushstrokes and, while claiming to be universal, will actually be quite specific and directly match only few people's experience.

A main criticism of this approach is that it is very conservative (in the sense of traditionalist) – it can only ever observe the current status quo and it does not lend itself well to imagining alternative options. What is more, often the variation among one group (e.g. in the relationship behaviour of different women) is greater than the differences that exist between different groups (that is, between the behaviours of women and men). As such, this approach easily becomes self-referential – it describes what it observes and then observes what it has previously described. In the case of *Men Are from Mars – Women Are from Venus* the author observes how women or men are more likely to behave and then writes a book about it. When people read the (self-help) book, they begin to behave according to these ideas and their actions then seem to support the initial observation. However, they could just as well be a consequence of having read the book.

Another way of thinking that matches the static perspective is a normative approach. While it is often contrasted with positivism because it may explicitly challenge the status quo, a normative approach is similar: from a position assumed to be outside the world that is being analysed, it describes how things ought to be (rather than how they are, as the positivist approach does) and then observes whether individuals comply with the norm. Yet, strong normative ideals often mean that few actually ever reach them.

For example, while a norm for masculinity is that everyone be as tough as a cowboy in a John Wayne film, we might find that many men never dream of riding a horse and 'roughing it'. What is more, some men might match the depiction of cowboys in *Brokeback Mountain* (a film that chronicles the complex 20-year love story of two cowboys) and not the heterosexual norm often associated with masculinity. This raises

BOX 5.5 JACQUES LACAN

FIGURE 5.9
Jacques Lacan. Photo: www.ildiogene.it/Ency/Pages/Immagini/Lacan

Psychoanalysis, a field that arose at the end of the nineteenth century as a result of the work of Sigmund Freud (1856–1939), is concerned with the role of the unconscious. Regarding the question of identity, the work of Jacques Lacan (1901–81) in particular is of interest. Lacan, himself trained in psychoanalysis, reviewed many of Freud's original ideas proposing that the unconscious should be understood as structured like language. Doing so, he linked psychoanalysis and semiotics (the study of signs).

Lacan introduced the idea of the 'mirror stage', which describes the formation of the conscious self via the process of identification. Simplified, for Lacan the act of identifying with one's own image in the mirror provides the illusion of wholeness. Yet, he also argues, the act creates a fundamental misunderstanding: The image is always partial. There is always a lack that we seek to compensate to become whole again. Or, conversely, there is an excess which cannot be captured no matter how hard we try to examine all details of who we are. An important element of the Lacanian mirror stage is also the caregiver (Lacan refers to the mother), who represents the Other to whom the child turns for recognition and who provides the first experience of being a subject – an I. (For a discussion of the relevance of Lacanian and other psychoanalytically inspired approaches for global politics, see Edkins 1999.)

some questions: How normative (widespread) is the norm? Can the description of some normative behaviour or appearance help us understand multiple masculine identities? Or is there just one norm and do men who do not meet the standards of heterosexuality or toughness become less manly?

To reiterate, what makes both of these approaches static approaches is that they rely on the observation of characteristics of already known entities (e.g. female and male individuals). That is, they list the characteristics that supposedly identify a person after having already decided that a certain sample of them belongs to one group (e.g. Asian Americans) and not to another (e.g. Native Americans). What is more, neither approach leaves much room for variations within the group, such as feminine men or masculine women. There is little or no room for greyscales here (e.g. what happens to people of mixed descent, that is, both Asian American and Native American?). As such, the world easily becomes black and white.

The dynamic approaches discussed here agree that a main mistake of static accounts of identity is that they assume a cohesive, fixed subject that can be identified (a subject which we can know). They suggest instead that subjectivity is always already a product of discourses – national, ethnic, racial, gender, class, sexual or religious – that circulate at any given time and place (some are local, some regional, and some global which also means they can be quite different and then conflict with each other). From this perspective the possibilities for who we can be are not up to the individual, but set out in advance and also limited by society. Identification (the creation of subjectivity), then, takes place in the process of articulating the relationship between subjects and discourses

What sort of a subject is at the heart of our thinking is also discussed in **Chapter 28**.

– between ourselves and the principles, expectations, and constraints of society. This means that who we are is always a matter of becoming rather than one of being: We should thus ask how we have become identified and who we can become, rather than who we are or have been.

Since these are the types of questions thinkers espousing dynamic approaches are interested in, they examine the processes through which the body is identified (or inscribed) to become a recognizable subject in a particular location (e.g. of a nation, a class, or a religious group). In addition, drawing on psychoanalytical insights, they consider difference a key to the development of identity – without an other that cannot be subsumed, there would be no distinctness to ourselves. This is also exemplified in many languages, e.g. in the dichotomies that are so prevalent in Western thought: weak/strong, female/male, black/white. It is possible to analyse this difference through a semiotic approach that contrasts the meanings assigned to different markers (or signifiers) in a particular symbolic structure.

Jacques Derrida was particularly interested in thinking through the impact of such dichotomies. Some of his ideas are discussed in **Chapter 28**.

Chapter 28 also explores the issue that we always confront language as already existing.

The dynamic conception of identity, particularly its constitutive relation to difference and its argument that subjects do not pre-exist discourse, has been criticized for lacking a conception of agency. Seyla Benhabib notes, 'if these agents retain capacities for resistance, resignification or for "subverting gender codes" in Butler's language, from where do they derive?' (1994). If who we are is determined by discourses that predate our existence, how can change occur that moves beyond these structures? We will look at some possible answers to this question in the next section when we turn again to looking at identity politics in a broader context.

BOX 5.6 JUDITH BUTLER AND PERFORMATIVITY

FIGURE 5.10 Judith Butler. Photo: Berkeley University

An influential application of psychoanalytical and other insights is Judith Butler's conception of identity as performance. She first introduced it in her book *Gender Trouble* and has refined it since. Her main argument is that 'gender is always a doing, though not a doing by a subject who might be said to pre-exist the deed' and therefore that 'identity is performatively constituted by the very "expressions" that are said to be its results' (1990: 33). In other words, by acting out what signifies being a certain kind of person, e.g. a white woman, one's subjectivity as a white woman is constituted and one is identified as such.

Butler uses the example of drag queens to make her point, arguing that drag performance enacts the way in which any (gender) identity is assumed. In his performance the drag queen also denaturalizes femininity by exaggerating its elements and by disturbing its coherence, since the performed gender does not match the expected behaviour for a man.

It is important to note that Butler does not consider gender performance a choice. Rather, drawing on the work of Michel Foucault (1926–84), she argues that the performance is disciplined by regulative discourses of gender. This means that we are made to conform and our performance is constrained by the repetition of certain expected standards of behaviour (norms), which consequently appear to constitute a core of identity.

Notwithstanding the discussion of these two approaches as though they are entirely separate frameworks, it should be noted that not all discussions of identity can be neatly separated this way. The distinction is useful, however, to tease out some broader conceptual issues that help us understand the variety of approaches: A main difference between the two approaches discussed here concerns their assumptions about what type of knowledge is possible (epistemology). Whereas the static approach believes that it is possible to clearly identify various markers that make up a person's identity, the dynamic approach is less certain about this possibility and sees different markers as together constituting, through processes of identification, a subject.

In addition, the two approaches conceptualize agency differently: The static approach often considers the possibility of multiple identities also suggesting the option of a choice between them (or at least of emphasizing different markers). Scholars associated with the dynamic approach, on the contrary, tend to spend considerable time focusing on identity politics as a disciplinary tool that limits who we can become. How these differences matter when we answer the question that guides this chapter is the topic we will turn to now.

BROADER ISSUES
DO WE NEED TO IDENTIFY WITH A GROUP?

So far we have discussed why we need to pay attention to identity at all, how identity politics have played out historically in the US feminist movement, and how identity has been conceptualized. What we have yet to address is the question posed at the outset of the chapter: If our identity is often linked to group identification, do we need to identify with a group? Thinking this through raises other questions.

To begin, whenever someone uses the term 'we' it is a good idea to ask who 'we' includes. In this case, who is the 'we' that is asked to identify with a group? The answer to the question whether 'we' have to identify with a group might depend on our position of privilege, for example. Few white people ever have discussions about how their whiteness affects their ability to go about their daily lives, get an education, or to be treated equally before the law. Black people who live in countries where they are not the majority, however, need to teach their children from an early age how to navigate everyday racism for their own survival. Thus, while they might not want to identify as Black so as not to be subject to the effects of racism, considering that they are always already identified as such, they might decide to claim a Black identity. Doing so can provide them with a support network and avenues to challenge discriminatory policies as a group – but it can also lock them into another cycle of identity politics.

We might further ask – and the formulation of this question depends on our theoretical orientation – whether it is even up to us to identify with a group or whether others identify us. The static approaches discussed in the previous section would contend that it is up to us to choose our identity (within limits) and that we are also identified by those around us according to the markers of each identity category. The dynamic approaches would likely argue that the question itself reveals a misunderstanding of the processes of identification. Instead of us being able to identify with a group, who we can be is limited by the parameters of belonging to a particular group and is constantly

When you are identified by someone else as 'a student', for example, do you feel that the category fits you perfectly? Or do you sometimes feel that you are *more* than just a student, and, at the same time, *less* than what a student is supposed to be?

BOX 5.7 BLACK POWER

The Black Power movement exemplifies this conundrum of identity politics: In an effort to reverse the script of racism, being Negro is reconstructed as being Black. This requires a refusal to assimilate to white norms of behaviour and the building of 'complex traditions of politics, ethics, identity and culture' (Gilroy 2000: 12). The goal is to be respected *as a black person*, not despite being a black person. Over time this movement has 'gone far beyond merely affording protection and reversed the polarities of insult, brutality and contempt, which are unexpectedly turned into important sources of solidarity, joy, and collective strength' (Gilroy 2000: 12).

Yet, like all identity politics this one too requires 'that there be some script that go with being [Black], there will be expectations to be met; demands will be made' (Appiah and Gutman 1996: 99). The question that arises is whether one tyranny is being replaced by another that still leaves too little room to diverge from the norm (it is just a different norm now). What is more, we might wonder, as Black-lesbian-feminist Audre Lorde famously did, whether the master's tools will ever dismantle the master's house. While rejecting all things associated with Whiteness might be a source of strength and even a necessary step in challenging racial hierarchies, ultimately it is only when the idea of race itself is abandoned that real change has occurred. However, as long as groups on either side of the divide hold onto the notion (usually those that benefit from its existence in some manner), this is unlikely.

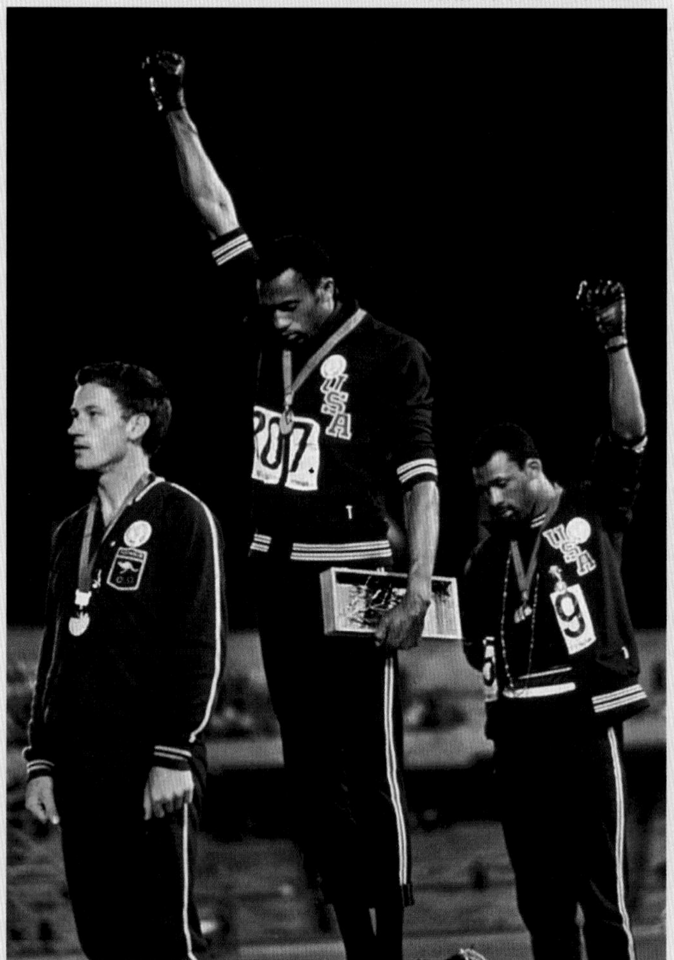

FIGURE 5.11
The Black Power salute in the 1968 Summer Olympics: Tommie Smith (centre) and John Carlos (right) salute while silver medallist Peter Norman (left) wears an Olympic Project for Human Rights badge to show his support for the two Americans. Photo: AP/PA Photos

in flux. Processes of identification are ambivalent from the start and there is no point at which a unified subject is possible: 'There is always "too much" or "too little" – an overdetermination or a lack, but never a proper fit, a totality' (Hall 1996: 3).

This conceptualization also suggests a response to the criticism that agency is impossible in a framework that stresses the constitutive role of discourse. Since identity never properly fits and is constantly challenged due to encounters with other people and varying discourses that increasingly circulate globally, there are continuous ruptures where identities can be negotiated. Where identity is already under revision, there is also room for agency. Besides, challenges arise in the name of anticipated or actual suffering – 'visions of what is better are always informed by our perception of what is bad about our present situation' (Lugones and Spelman 1983: 579).

BOX 5.8 PATRICIA HILL COLLINS: INTERSECTIONALITY

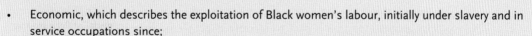

FIGURE 5.12 Patricia Hill Collins. Photo: University of Maryland, College Park

Patricia Hill Collins, pioneer of *Black Feminist Thought*, writes in the preface to the second edition of her book (2000 [1990]) about the importance of combining the work of revisioning individual black women's consciousness with challenges to larger structures of oppression and injustice. Failure to do so will only replace one form of domination with another. To do away with all forms of domination, she specifically locates her thinking in relation to other projects that share a concern for social justice and urges activists to recognize similarities among these varied projects. To this end, she further develops the idea of intersectionality to conceptualize the complexities of multiple and conflicting identities.

Intersectionality 'refers to particular forms of intersecting oppressions, for example, intersections of race and gender, or of sexuality and nation'. Collins further notes that thinking about identity in terms of intersectionality 'reminds us that oppression cannot be reduced to one fundamental type, and that they work together in producing injustice' (2000 [1990]: 18). She gives the example of African American women who are subject to three interdependent dimensions of oppression:

- Economic, which describes the exploitation of Black women's labour, initially under slavery and in service occupations since;
- Political, which refers to the routine denial of rights and privileges accorded to white male citizens, such as voting, holding public office, getting a good education, and being treated fairly in the justice system; and
- Ideological, which covers both controlling images and certain qualities attached to Black women (2000 [1990]: 4–5).

The dimensions of oppression are interdependent and can be located in a matrix of domination. Collins argues that 'regardless of the particular intersections involved, structural, disciplinary, hegemonic and interpersonal domains of power reappear across quite different forms of oppression' (2000 [1990]: 18). What they have in common, just like the intersections highlighted with regard to African American women's oppression, is that they constitute a highly effective system of social control to keep people in their assigned, subordinate place.

Finally, the question suggests that we have to identify with *one* group. Yet, none of us are *only* Asian or *only* Christian or *only* woman. Can we have multiple identities? What happens when they conflict? Does being a member of many oppressed groups (e.g. being Chicana and lesbian) imply that the oppression adds up? Or multiplies? What if one is part of both an oppressing (e.g. male) and an oppressed (e.g. working-class) group? Again, the way the questions are asked reveals some of the underlying assumptions behind them. For example, when people talk of having multiple identities, they often try to signal that identities need to be viewed in context and that some of them might be strategically more useful for the particular social, cultural and political struggle for hegemony (that is, the dominance of one group over other groups). All the while, such language also seems to suggest a maximum of autonomy – as though one has a closet full of identities that may be worn as one chooses. Most scholars will agree that such a conception, one that entirely disregards any structural limitations, is unhelpful and inaccurate. Instead, we are always already part of and contributing to particular structures.

Adopting Collins' framework of intersectionality to think of varied dimensions of identity, and the oppressive effects of identity politics, limits the ever-present tendency to think of identity in overly individualistic terms. When asking questions about domination and oppression, we always also have to look at the structures that facilitate and perpetuate them. We might then find that discourses of identity both enable and limit who we might become, how we have been represented, and how we might represent ourselves (Hall 1996). Our task is to recognize them as temporary resting points, to see in them the workings of power (and struggles for hegemony), and to challenge their effects.

CONCLUSION

In this chapter we have begun to develop some tools to understand different conceptions of identity and the complex consequences of identity politics. Yet, much of what this chapter focuses on relates to the negative, indeed deadly, effects of identity politics, and one might wonder: Why not do away with the concept once and for all? The simple answer is that it gives us a sense of belonging and a sense of direction. This might explain why greater attention is paid to identity as people become increasingly mobile and as ideas circulate ever widely in this globalized world such that we may now talk of an 'explosion of usage' (Hall 1996: 1).

What is more, it is particularly those approaches that question the idea of an essential, primary, and cohesive identity that have proliferated in recent years. What they suggest is that the way we have thought about identity, with a core self that may be adjusted slightly but remains largely stable through time and space, is no longer adequate. Yet, while these approaches are 'no longer serviceable – "good to think with" – in their originary and unreconstructed form' (Hall 1996: 1), they are still needed due to the centrality of questions of agency and politics. As Stuart Hall summarizes, it is 'an idea which cannot be thought in the old way, but without which certain key questions cannot be thought at all' (1996: 2).

Thus, even if we cannot agree on how identity should be conceptualized, which markers should triumph, or even whether the preoccupation with identity is only a symptom of late modernity – we can maybe ask better questions about the occurrence of identity politics and its material effects. And – we can begin to recognize how our own privilege oppresses others, but also how it gives us the power to promote change. Who do we think we are, indeed?

FURTHER READING

Campbell, David (1998) *National Deconstruction: Violence, Identity and Justice in Bosnia*. Minneapolis: University of Minnesota Press.
A detailed analysis of the identity politics at play during the break-up of the former Yugoslavia. In 1999, the book received a prize for being the best English-language publication on the topic.

Collins, Patricia Hill (2000 [1990]) *Black Feminist Thought: Knowledge, Consciousness, and the Politics of Empowerment*. Boston: Unwin Hyman.
For students who want to learn more about the intersections of gender and race (but also other forms of oppression), this is a 'must read'. It also provides some of the best ideas out there for moving beyond identity politics and toward justice.

Gourevitch, Phillip (1998) *We Wish to Inform You that Tomorrow We Will Be Killed with Our Families: Stories from Rwanda*, London: Picador.
Probably the best account of the Rwandan genocide, based on a series of interviews with Rwandans between 1995 and 1998. Not for the faint-hearted.

Hudson, Valerie M. and Andrea den Boer (2004) *Bare Branches: The Security Implications of Asia's Surplus Male Population*, Cambridge, MA: MIT Press.
Examines how global security might be affected by the preference for males in many Asian societies and thus offers a great case study of the importance of identity politics today.

Kaldor, Mary (2006) *New and Old Wars: Organized Violence in a Global Era*, 2nd edn, Cambridge: Polity Press.
A major work for those who want to understand the role of identity politics in today's wars. Kaldor locates the difference between old and new wars in the latter's distinctive war economies, their genocidal tendencies and the use of identity politics as a means to political power.

Ryan, Barbara (ed.) (2001) *Identity Politics in the Women's Movement*, New York: New York University Press.
This collection has most classic and recent statements on feminist identity politics (in the US) and offers a great overview for students interested in the subject.

Wibben, Annick T. R. (2011) *Feminist Security Studies: A Narrative Approach*, London: Routledge.
Presents a feminist reading of security studies, suggesting that identity politics and security politics implicate each other. It also suggests ways to learn to listen to each others' stories of who we are as a way forward.

WEBSITES

American Anthropological Association, *RACE: Are We So Different?*, http://www.understandingrace.org/home.html
An extensive website (and exhibition) that examines race through multiple lenses.

BBC World Service, *Yugoslavia History File*, http://news.bbc.co.uk/hi/english/static/map/yugoslavia/
A timeline with a series of maps and historical information on Yugoslavia (1900–2003).

Deutsch, Barry, *The Male Privilege Checklist: An Unabashed Imitation of an Article by Peggy McIntosh*, http://www.amptoons.com/blog/the-male-privilege-checklist/
A checklist and links to further privilege discussions.

Heyes, Crissida (2002) *Stanford Encyclopedia of Philosophy*: 'Identity Politics', http://plato.stanford.edu/entries/identity-politics/
Part of the extensive online *Stanford Encyclopedia of Philosophy*, this entry on identity politics explores many of the issues raised in this chapter from a philosophical perspective (in reference to many different markers of identity) and provides additional links.

Human Rights Watch (1999) *Leave None to Tell the Story: Genocide in Rwanda*, http://www.hrw.org/reports/1999/rwanda/
A detailed report on the genocide in Rwanda, with an update on the tenth anniversary in 2004.

Korenman, Joan, *Women of Color Websites*, http://research.umbc.edu/~korenman/wmst/links_wc.html
A regularly updated list of women of colour resource websites.

SSRC, *Is Race 'Real'?*, http://raceandgenomics.ssrc.org/
This forum, organized by the Social Science Research Council, discusses recent controversies surrounding race after recent advances in genetics.

The World Wide Web Virtual Library, *History: Yugoslavia (1918–1995)*, http://vlib.iue.it/history/europe/yugoslavia.html
An extensive website useful for further research on historical information (also has some maps).

REFERENCES

Appiah, K. Anthony and Amy Gutman (1996) *Color Conscious: The Political Morality of Race*, Princeton, NJ: Princeton University Press.

Benhabib, Seyla (1994) 'From Identity Politics to Social Feminism: A Plea for the Nineties', *Philosophy of Education Yearbook 1994.*

Butler, Judith (1990) *Gender Trouble: Feminism and The Subversion of Identity*, London: Routledge.

Campbell, David (1998) *National Deconstruction: Violence, Identity and Justice in Bosnia*, Minneapolis: University of Minnesota Press.

Carpenter, Charli (2003) 'Women and Children First: Gender Norms and Humanitarian Evacuation in the Balkans, 1991–1995', *International Organization* 57, 4: 661–94.

Collins, Patricia Hill (2000 [1990]) *Black Feminist Thought: Knowledge, Consciousness, and the Politics of Empowerment*, Boston: Unwin Hyman.

Connell, R. W. (1995) *Masculinities*, Berkeley: University of California Press.

Edkins, Jenny (1999) *Poststructuralism and International Relations: Bringing the Political Back In*, Boulder, CO: Lynne Rienner.

Elshtain, Jean Bethke (1981) *Public Man, Private Woman*, Princeton, NJ: Princeton University Press.

Friedan, Betty (2001 [1963]) *The Feminine Mystique*, New York: W.W. Norton & Company.

Gilligan, Carol (1982) *In a Different Voice: Psychological Theory and Women's Development*, Cambridge, MA: Harvard University Press.

Gilroy, Paul (2000) *Against Race: Imagining Political Culture Beyond the Color Line*, Cambridge, MA: Harvard University Press.

Gourevitch, Phillip (1998) *We Wish to Inform You that Tomorrow We Will Be Killed with Our Families: Stories from Rwanda*, London: Picador.

Gray, John (2002) *Men Are from Mars – Women Are from Venus*, London: HarperCollins.

Hall, Stuart (1996) 'Introduction: Who Needs "Identity"?', in Hall, Stuart and du Gay, Paul (eds) *Questions of Cultural Identity*, London: Sage Publications.

Held, Virginia (2006) *The Ethics of Care: Personal, Political, Global*, Oxford: Oxford University Press.

hooks, bell (1984) *Feminist Theory: From Margin to Center*, Cambridge, MA: South End Press.

Hudson, Valerie M. and Andrea den Boer (2004) *Bare Branches: The Security Implications of Asia's Surplus Male Population*, Cambridge, MA: MIT Press.

Kauffmann, L. A. (1990) 'The Anti-Politics of Identity', *Socialist Review* 90, 1: 67–80. Reprinted in Barbara Ryan (ed.) (2001) *Identity Politics in the Women's Movement*, New York: NYU Press.

Lugones, María C and Elisabeth V. Spelman (1983) 'Have We Got a Theory for You! Feminist Theory, Cultural Imperialism and the Demand for "The Woman's Voice"', *Women's Studies International Forum* 6, 6: 573–81.

Mamdani, Mahmood (2001) *When Victims Become Killers: Colonialism, Nativism, and the Genocide in Rwanda*, Princeton, NJ: Princeton University Press

McIntosh, Peggy (1993 [1988]) 'White Privilege and Male Privilege: A Personal Account of Coming To See Correspondences Through Work in Women's Studies', in Anne Minas (ed.) *Gender Basics: Feminist Perspectives on Women and Men*, Belmont, CA: Wadsworth.

Moghadam, Valentine M. (1994) 'Introduction: Women and Identity Politics in Theoretical and Comparative Perspective', in Valentine M. Moghadam (ed.), *Identity Politics and Women: Cultural Reassertions and Feminisms in International Perspective*, Boulder, CO: Westview Press.

Moraga, Cherríe and Anzaldúa, Gloria (1983 [1979]) *This Bridge Called My Back: Writings by Radical Women of Color*, New York: Kitchen Table, Women of Color Press.

Polkinghorne, Donald E. (1988) *Narrative Knowing and the Human Sciences*, Albany, NY: SUNY Press.

Robinson, Fiona (1999) *Globalizing Care: Ethics, Feminist Theory, and International Relations*, Boulder, CO: Westview Press.

Spender, Dale (1983) *Feminist Thinkers: Three Centuries of Women Thinkers*, New York: Random House.

Tronto, Joan C. (1993) *Moral Boundaries: A Political Argument for an Ethics of Care*, London: Routledge.

Winddance Twine, France (1996) 'Brown-skinned White Girls: Class, Culture and the Construction of White Identity in Suburban Communities', *Gender, Place, and Culture: A Journal of Feminist Geography* 3, 2: 205–24.

Yuval-Davis, Nira (1994) 'Identity Politics and Women's Ethnicity', in Valentine M. Moghadam (ed.), *Identity Politics and Women: Cultural Reassertions and Feminisms in International Perspective*, Boulder, CO: Westview Press.

For a range of further resources supporting this chapter, please visit the companion website for *Global Politics, 2nd Edition* at www.routledge.com/cw/edkins/

CHAPTER 6

How do religious beliefs affect politics?

Peter Mandaville

THE QUESTION
THE ROLE OF RELIGION TODAY

What do we mean when we talk about religion? Scholars have struggled and argued for many years about how to define religion. Some emphasize the idea that religion is concerned primarily with conceptions of God, divinity, and the meaning and order of human existence. Others have tended to emphasize the way religion serves to draw distinctions between *sacred* (that is, transcendent or other-worldly) forms of space and belief and more mundane, or *profane* domains of 'worldly' human endeavour. Some definitions, such as that of anthropologist Clifford Geertz (1973), focus on the symbolic power of religion and its ability to influence how people understand their place in the world and also to impart meaning to the actions they undertake. Other scholars have pointed out that the idea of religion as a distinct category or sphere of human activity reflects a specifically Western worldview and historical tradition. Talal Asad (1993) points out that in other cultural traditions it is not so easy to make a firm separation between religion and other spheres of life such as politics, culture, society, and economics.

This point will be important later when we discuss the meaning and nature of secularism, the belief that the state and morals should be independent of religion. Secularism, as we will see, is a vitally important concept because it leads us to ask questions about whether religion and politics are in fact separate categories and, if so, what the appropriate relationship between them should be. Religion and secularism are also implicated in important ways in broader debates about what it means to be 'modern'.

The question of secularism and the headscarf ban in France are topics of **Chapter 27**.

For now, however, let us assume that when we are talking about religion we are referring to individuals and groups who base their identities and ethics at least in part on a tradition and set of beliefs about the creation of the world and the order within it that locates the source of this creation and order outside purely human or natural agency.

Often whether we hold religious beliefs or not is central to our picture of the world, to use the terminology from **Chapter 2**.

BOX 6.1 DEFINITIONS OF RELIGION

Thinkers from different fields and disciplines have put forward varying definitions of religion. For **anthropologist** Clifford Geertz, religion is '(1) a system of symbols which acts to (2) establish powerful, pervasive, and long-lasting moods and motivations in men by (3) formulating conceptions of a general order of existence and (4) clothing these conceptions with such an aura of factuality that (5) the moods and motivations seem uniquely realistic' (Geertz 1973).

For **theologian** George Lindbeck, religion is 'a kind of cultural and/or linguistic framework or medium that . . . makes possible the description of realities, the formulation of beliefs, and the experiencing of inner attitudes, feelings, and sentiments' (Lindbeck 1984).

Marxist writers such as Louis Althusser tend to emphasize the idea that religion functions as a form of 'false consciousness' which socializes us into accepting as normal certain historically and materially contingent relations of social power (Althusser 2001).

So where do we see religion at work in global politics today? Many people if asked this question right now might think first and foremost of the Islamic world. Particularly since the events of 11 September 2001 – when hijackers associated with the terrorist group Al-Qaeda flew airliners into several targets in New York City and Washington DC – and subsequent attacks such as the London bombings of 7 July 2005, Islam has been a major subject of discussion. Much of this debate has been around questions of terrorism and support for violence. The United States, for example, declared militant Islamic extremism to be the major target of its new 'war on terror'. Considerable attention has also been paid to Islamic movements in other countries that have used violence in the pursuit of their political goals, such as HAMAS in the Palestinian territories and Hizbullah in Lebanon. Other examples

Chapters 2, 23 and 26 have more on the 'war on terror'.

where Islam or 'Islamic' groups have been seen to play a role in world politics include the period when Afghanistan was under the rule of a highly conservative movement known as the Taliban. Well before the United States accused and eventually overthrew their regime for supporting terrorism, the Taliban had attracted widespread criticism from the world community for violating human rights and for their harsh treatment of women. Finally, countries such as Iran, which regard themselves as Islamic states, are seen by some as a challenge when they assert that they are subject to divine authority. Within Europe, a number of recent incidents such as the Danish Cartoon Affair have fuelled debates about whether 'religious' Muslims and 'secular' Europeans can co-exist. Most recently, the phenomenal rise of Islamic political parties in elections following the revolutions that swept through parts of the Arab world in 2011 have prompted new questions about what happens when religion and politics mix.

Whether people who subscribe to fundamentally different values can live together and how has vexed many thinkers across the centuries. What do you think?

BOX 6.2 THE DANISH CARTOON AFFAIR

In September 2005, the Danish newspaper *Jyllands Posten* published a series of cartoon depictions of Muhammad, the Prophet of Islam. Most famous among them was an image depicting the turban on Muhammad's head as a bomb. Several months after the publication of the cartoons, protests broke out in a number of Muslim countries almost simultaneously (an interesting globalization story in itself, involving the Internet, satellite TV, and transnational activist networks). Angered by what they perceived as an attack on the Prophet and an insult to Islam at a time when global tensions were high in the aftermath of the 11 September 2001 attacks and the US invasion of Iraq, rioters attacked Danish embassies and several countries initiated an embargo on Danish goods. In Europe the Danish Cartoon Affair prompted a debate about how to strike a balance between freedom of speech and respect for cultural difference. It also further fuelled an ongoing debate about whether the values of Europe's rapidly growing Muslim community were compatible with Western norms.

Despite the current tendency to focus on the Islamic world, there are many other examples where religion seems to play a role in global politics. A number of recent conflicts have had strong religious dimensions. Think for example of Northern Ireland where the divisions between the two conflicting sides broke down along the Protestant and Catholic denominations of Christianity. For more than 20 years, Sri Lanka saw a civil war pitting Hindus and Buddhists against each other. In the former Yugoslavia, much of the bloodshed in the 1990s was explained in terms of ethnic rivalries between Catholic and Orthodox Christians as much as between Christians and Muslims. While many of the participants in these conflicts did not define their actions and motivations by direct reference to religion, the religious factor was important because it allowed the leadership of certain parties to raise the stakes by appealing to a greater cause. Religion is also present in world politics in ways far less dramatic and violent. For example, millions

The situation in Northern Ireland was long considered an intractable conflict but is now more stable: see **Chapter 26**.

Understanding these conflicts requires exploring the politics of identity: see **Chapter 5**.

FIGURE 6.1
'Do you believe in God?'
Artist: Bryan Bartholomew. CartoonStock ref.: bbrn51 www.CartoonStock.com

of Catholics around the world recognize the spiritual authority of the pope as the final arbiter, globally, of matters relating to church doctrine. We can also see today the role of various religious groups in seeking to build new bases of mass popular support, such as the recent upsurge in conversions to Pentecostal Christianity in Africa. The strength of the Christian Evangelical movement in the United States has been a major factor in the political success of that country's Republican party in recent years. The United States represents a very interesting case in which church and state are formally separated, but where religion features very heavily in political discourse. This has led some, such as the political theorist William Connolly (2005), to see in the United States a new form of theocracy (that is, government by religion) premised on affinities between belief in God and absolute faith in market capitalism. Religious institutions can sometimes also form alliances of the sort traditionally seen in global politics. For example, at the United Nations International Conference on Population and Development in 1994, the Vatican (the authority of the Catholic pope) sought to make common cause with a number of conservative Muslim states in opposing birth control and abortion. Globalization has also promoted the emergence of 'New Religious Movements' that combine aspects of various faith traditions while addressing concerns relating to environmentalism, social justice, and the search for meaning and spirituality in a complex world (Clarke 2006). Some of these groups, such as the Falung Gong movement in China, seek to challenge the political status quo.

Chapter 21 examines the approach of Christian thinking to the question of the treatment of conquered peoples.

For more on capitalism see **Chapters 17 and 19**.

ILLUSTRATIVE EXAMPLE
ISLAMIC STATES AND MOVEMENTS

Much of the discussion about religion in global politics today focuses on the Muslim world. This is not only because of the events of 11 September 2001 or the Danish Cartoon episode mentioned above. Even for some time before these events, it was not uncommon to find claims being made that Islam was problematic because in its belief system religion and politics could not be separated – meaning that the Muslim world was resistant to secularism and modernization (see below). Those advancing such ideas – many of whom are scholars associated with the Orientalist worldview discussed below – seemed to assume that Islam was something quite static and unchanging: a rigid set of beliefs impervious to change or progress. When we look at the evolving relationship between religion and politics throughout Islamic history, however, quite a different perspective emerges. We find not only that Islam has been remarkably dynamic and diverse as a belief system, but also that the motivations and patterns of political behaviour displayed by Muslims are wholly amenable to explanation through conventional themes and theories of political analysis.

History of the Islamic world

From humble beginnings in the western part of present day Saudi Arabia, the religion of Islam expanded rapidly in the second half of the seventh century and soon encompassed most of the Middle East, Persia, and North Africa. In subsequent eras, Islam spread further east to South Asia and eventually to the furthest southeastern reaches of the Asian continent into present day Malaysia and Indonesia. Various Islamic dynasties rose and fell during the Middle Ages, and at their height these empires represented the apex of human civilization, science and learning.

The most important Muslim power in the early modern period was the Ottoman Empire (ca. 1300–1922). The Ottomans were the first Muslim rulers to interact with European powers after the formation of the modern state system in the seventeenth century, and were well integrated into the structures and processes of global politics. In the late nineteenth century an anti-colonial movement known as Pan-Islam emerged. The Pan-Islamists argued that Muslims were facing a similar condition of imperial bondage at the hands of European colonial powers. Their solution was to encourage the political unity of Muslims, invoking the centuries-old religious idea of the *umma* – an Arabic term that refers to the world community of Muslim believers. The leaders of this movement did not advocate returning to a conservative, literalist interpretation of Islam, but rather emphasized the compatibility of Islam with modernity and science. For them, the imperative was to *reform* Islam.

The emergence of the state in Europe is traced in **Chapter 11**, and the formation and dissolution of empires in **Chapter 16**.

On the significance of territory see **Chapter 11**.

The Ottoman Empire found itself on the losing side of World War I and was dissolved in its aftermath, with Britain and France gaining control of many of the territories that had previously been under its control (such as Syria, Lebanon, Palestine, Iraq and Egypt). This war also effectively marked the beginning of the end for the various European empires, with some of them fragmenting into various new nation-states. In the Anatolian peninsula, heartland of the former Ottoman lands, a new country, the Turkish Republic, was founded in 1922 by Mustapha Kemal. 'Kemalism' – the ideology

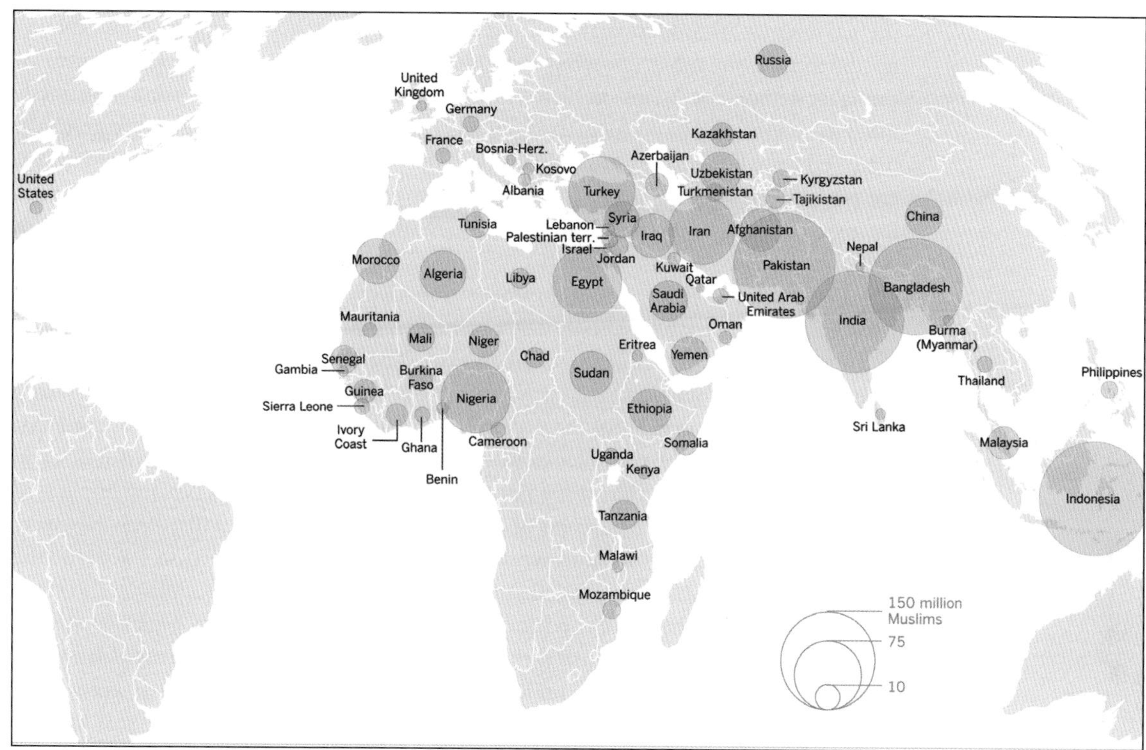

FIGURE 6.2 Distribution of Muslim population by country and territory (only countries with more than one million Muslims are shown). Pew Research Center's Forum on Religion & Public Life, 'Mapping the Global Muslim Population', October 2009.

deriving from the major project of sweeping political, economic, and cultural reform he initiated – emphasized the ideals of Europeanization and *secularism* as the proper way to 'be modern'. To this day, Turkey enforces a strict separation between religion and state; this is embodied in laws and policies that restrict the public role of religion more strongly than in many countries we usually think of as secular (not concerned with religion), such as France, the UK or the USA.

After World War II, many of the former Ottoman territories under British and French control became independent states. Many of these were led by governments that embraced various models of national secular politics – chief among them Egypt under Gamal Abdel Nasser (r. 1952–71) who became the iconic leader of a regional Arab Nationalist movement. This secular-nationalist model had quickly trumped the emerging project of Pan-Islamism early in the twentieth century, and as the modernizing drive of these new governments proceeded in countries such as Egypt, some sectors of Egyptian society began to feel that the country risked becoming corrupted by foreign ideologies.

For an examination of the implications of secularism as enshrined in the French Constitution see **Chapter 27**.

Islamism: Islamic political movements

The early postcolonial period in the Middle East saw the consolidation of a political ideology, commonly referred to as Islamism, that rejected the national-secular model in the name of a vision of social order deriving from the direct application of Islam to the governance of modern states. In its totalizing, systematic approach, Islamism was no different from other contemporary ideological counterparts such as socialism or capitalist democracy. Islamism hence needs to be understood as expressing a distinctly modernist approach to politics. Its supporters, known as Islamists – who were generally highly educated members of the Muslim world's new middle classes (doctors, engineers, etc.) – saw in Islamism a way to embrace new institutions and technologies without having to abandon their values and beliefs – in other words, it was a way to be modern without having to become Western.

The most important social movement embodying this new vision of political Islam was founded in Egypt by a schoolteacher named Hassan al-Banna. In 1928 he established a group known as the Muslim Brotherhood. The Brotherhood sought to ensure a continued role for religion in society and saw itself as an antidote to the Westernizing and secularizing tendencies of the political elite. Many Islamist leaders also argued that the doctrine of modern nationalism was incompatible with the teachings of Islam and the ideal of the *umma*. While not a political party, the Brotherhood became implicated in the evolving political landscape of Egypt in the 1930s and 1940s. Branches were established throughout the Arab world, and similar groups founded in Pakistan (the Jama'at-i Islami) and Turkey (the Refah Party). With its enormous popularity and rapid inroads into the country's new educated and middle classes, Nasser began to see the Muslim Brotherhood as a political threat. Banned and driven underground from the 1950s, the movement became radicalized. This phase of its existence is commonly associated with its chief thinker at the time, Sayyid Qutb. Qutb – whose ideas became very influential on successive generations of radical Islamists (including groups such as Al-Qaeda) – had become convinced, like a number of his contemporary Third World activists, that it had become impossible to work within the existing political system to ensure a political role for Islam. Revolutionary politics and armed struggle (*jihad* – from the Arabic word for 'strive'), in Qutb's teaching, were required to achieve social change in the Muslim world.

Other social movements are discussed in **Chapters 4, 14 and 18**.

Qutb's views appealed only to a fringe minority in the Muslim world and, in the successive generation, to only a small fraction of Islamists. His views on *jihad*, for example, were generally regarded as a highly unorthodox departure from traditional understandings that emphasized the defensive nature of jihad. In other Muslim-majority countries during this period, Islamist parties had evolved into opposition movements. Banned from formal politics in Egypt, the Muslim Brotherhood instead began to build a strong base of social support at the neighbourhood and municipal levels, establishing social service and charity networks, and gaining control of all leading professional associations and syndicates.

While these may seem to be highly localized developments, an important part of what allowed the Islamists to build up this kind of support within Egypt's civil societal spaces was what we refer to today as *globalization*. As Anwar Al Sadat (president of Egypt 1970–81) opened up Egypt's economy to world markets and the country undertook neoliberal economic reforms at the behest of institutions such as the International Monetary Fund (IMF), the scale of state welfare and employment provision was scaled back significantly. This created 'gaps' in the provision of basic services that the Islamists were able to fill, gaining widespread support and popular legitimacy in the process.

Globalization and its effects are discussed in **Chapter 17**.

Islamic states

In 1979, Iran experienced an 'Islamic revolution' led by religious scholars (chief among them the Grand Ayatollah Khomeini) but carried out by a combination of religious and secular social forces, including socialists and urban merchants. In its aftermath, the radical wing of the clergy purged all non-religious political elites to establish a new Islamic Republic of Iran and impose a conservative and literalist interpretation of Islamic law (*shari'ah*) on a largely unsuspecting population. Iran thus joined the ranks of the world's 'Islamic states', alongside two other countries, Saudi Arabia and Pakistan. Saudi Arabia was founded between the two world wars as a theocratic monarchy (that is, one governed by religious leaders) based on a political alliance between a princely family (the Sa'ud) and a religious establishment seeking to purvey an indigenous form of Islam – highly austere and puritanical – known as Wahhabism. With the discovery of vast oil wealth under its deserts, Saudi Arabia was catapulted to a position of geopolitical prominence, establishing a close alliance with the United States that has endured for many years. The second Islamic state already in existence was Pakistan, established in 1947 at the time of the post-colonial partition of India. Initially established as a homeland for the Muslims of the Indian subcontinent, the exact nature and meaning of Pakistan's status as an Islamic state has constituted a chief source of political debate in the country for decades. For some, Pakistan was an Islamic state in the same sense in which Israel is a Jewish state – that is, as a national homeland for the members of a given religion rather

Development and modernization in states in South Asia according to principles of Western modernity conflicts with ideas of Islamic modernity: **Chapter 20**.

FIGURE 6.3 Ayatollah Khomeini returns from exile on 1 February 1979. Photo: AP Photos

than a state whose political and legal systems are derived directly from religion. Others in Pakistan argued that the government of Pakistan should be actively working to extend the remit of *shari'ah* to all sectors of society.

Radical Islamist groups

The Cold War and its geopolitics are explained in **Chapter 26**.

The 1980s saw a significant increase in the global visibility of political Islam – the ideology of Islamism and its adherents, known as Islamists – as it became increasingly entwined with Cold War geopolitics. Several events and movements formed during this decade help us understand the contemporary interface between Islam and global politics. After the Soviet Union's invasion of Afghanistan in 1979, a number of volunteer fighters from the Arab world travelled to Afghanistan to assist in repelling what they interpreted as an atheist incursion into Muslim territories. These 'Arab-Afghans' were important insofar as their experience during these years (1980–88) helped to crystallize the ideological and geopolitical vision that would later define Al-Qaeda. Among this group of supporters from the Middle East was Usama Bin Laden, a member of the wealthiest commercial family in Saudi Arabia, who had renounced his family's business in the name of what he saw as a larger struggle against new forms of global, imperial atheism (disbelief in the existence of God). The eventual withdrawal of Soviet forces from Afghanistan was interpreted by Bin Laden as a victory and as evidence of Islam's ability to triumph over the world's superpowers (at that time the USSR and the USA).

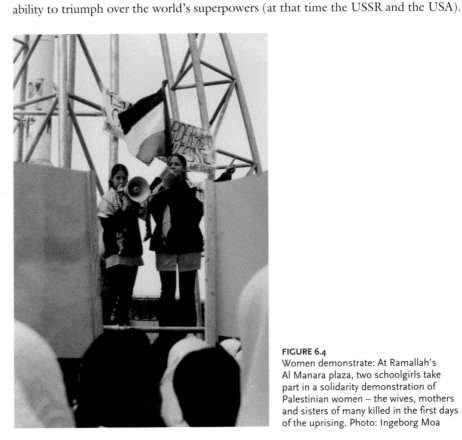

FIGURE 6.4
Women demonstrate: At Ramallah's Al Manara plaza, two schoolgirls take part in a solidarity demonstration of Palestinian women – the wives, mothers and sisters of many killed in the first days of the uprising. Photo: Ingeborg Moa

Out of this experience was hence born Bin Laden's vision, Al-Qaeda: an effort to globalize the Afghan experience.

Two other important Islamist groups active today were also established during this period. Although Hizbullah in Lebanon and HAMAS (an acronym for *Harakat al-Muqawwama al-Islamiyya* – the Islamic Resistance Movement; the word also means 'zeal' in Arabic) in the Palestinian territories have been linked to Al-Qaeda in contemporary discussions because of their militant tactics, such direct connections are inaccurate and mask the fact that Al-Qaeda and groups such as Hizbullah and HAMAS are motivated by and pursuing distinct political agendas. Chief among these differences is the fact that HAMAS and Hizbullah are primarily movements of religious nationalism. Hizbullah was established in the wake of the Israeli invasion of Lebanon in 1982 with an Islamist agenda limited to Lebanon. Likewise HAMAS, which emerged in the context of the first Palestinian *intifada* (uprising, or 'shaking off') in the late 1980s, has always defined its political agenda in terms of Palestinian national liberation from Israeli occupation and, subsequently, the establishment of an Islamic state in its territories.

While their political aims may be geared towards nationalist aspirations, both of these groups have received significant support from neighbouring states and various transnational fundraising networks. Hizbullah, for example, has strong ties to Iran and Syria, while HAMAS – as a branch of the Muslim Brotherhood – has been able to tap into that group's funding infrastructure in addition to receiving direct support from various states in the Middle East. In recent years, the nature and role of both organizations has become increasingly ambiguous. Hizbullah and HAMAS both have at least three dimensions to their activities:

1 They provide basic social services such as education and healthcare to the disenfranchised (that is, those deprived of the rights of citizenship) populations of Lebanon and the Palestinian territories, ensuring strong measures of grassroots support.
2 They have political bodies that compete in parliamentary elections alongside other parties. Hizbullah has enjoyed strong representation in the Lebanese legislature since the end of the civil war and HAMAS gained control of the Palestinian Authority in 2006.
3 They maintain armed wings that permit them to employ violence when they find it expedient to do so.

Why politics turns to violence is discussed in **Chapter 22**.

While not globally organized like Al-Qaeda, both HAMAS and Hizbullah factor heavily in the global politics surrounding the Israel/Palestine conflict and Lebanon. Hizbullah, for example, taps into the media infrastructure of contemporary globalization via its own satellite television station Al-Manar ('The Beacon').

On the media in general, see **Chapter 8**, and on the uses of the Internet, **Chapter 9**.

Thus, Al-Qaeda – for many, the group that most readily springs to mind today when speaking of Islam and global politics – needs to be situated within a diverse and multi-faceted ecology of world political Islam. Al-Qaeda was established in Afghanistan by Arab-Afghan fighters following the decision by the Soviet Union to withdraw its troops after a failed occupation effort. Emboldened by this seeming victory, Al-Qaeda sought to export the Afghan model to other countries in which Muslims were understood to be fighting foreign invasions or resisting imposed secularism. The move

BOX 6.3 SUNNI AND SHI'ITE ISLAM

The instability and violence experienced by Iraq in the years following the US invasion of 2003, much of which occurred along sectarian lines, prompted discussion about the difference between two major branches of Islam. The distinction between Sunnis and Shi'ites goes back to the time of the death of the Prophet Muhammad and a debate over who should succeed him as the leader of the Muslim community. One group argued that leadership should stay within the Prophet's family and rallied around the candidacy of Ali (hence *Shi'i* or 'Partisans' of Ali), Muhammad's cousin and son-in-law. Others favoured choosing a leader from among the Prophet's longest-serving and most trusted companions, and their view prevailed. A distinctive Shi'ite political identity, however, did not emerge until several decades later when Ali's family was killed by the army of a rival noble clan seeking to consolidate its ruling position. In the ensuing centuries, Shi'ites developed their own parallel institutions and schools of religious law. Indeed, in its conventional usage the term Sunni refers to the orthodox schools of religious jurisprudence. As Shi'ites faced persecution over the ensuing centuries, their identity came to be defined in part in terms of dispossession and disenfranchisement. That said, Shi'ite leaders eventually established a number of important empires, notably the Fatimids in Egypt (910–1171) and the Safavids in Persia (1501–1736). There are different denominations within Shi'ism, the largest group being the 'Twelvers' – so named because they recognize a line of twelve leaders in the *imamate*, a religio-political institution unique to Shi'ite Islam. Shi'ites today constitute approximately 10–15 per cent of the world's Muslim population, or 130–195 million. Over half are found in two countries, Iran (90 per cent of the population) and Iraq (around 60 per cent of the population). Some analysts see potential for increased sectarian tensions between Sunnis and Shi'ites in the wake of the political upheavals sweeping much of the Middle East (Nasr 2007).

to establish the group also represented a major shift away from the worldview of earlier radical Islamists such as Qutb and the groups he inspired. For them, the goal was to successfully attack and supplant the 'near enemy', that is the leaders of secular-national regimes in the Middle East and other Muslim majority countries who were perceived as the proxies of Western powers. Bin Laden and Al-Qaeda's new emphasis on the 'far enemy', inspired by the Afghan experience, emphasized instead the idea of directly attacking what they understood to be the source of global imperialism and atheism – namely, the United States. Al-Qaeda's goals are the liberation of Muslim territories from occupying infidel forces and the making of a world that is 'safe for Islam' – a world in which a social political order based on *shari'ah* can be realized. Some within this camp understand this to mean the re-establishment of centralized political authority in the Muslim world via a new Caliphate, an institution that had existed since the seventh century but had been abolished by Kemal at the end of the Ottoman Empire.

Al-Qaeda is sometimes seen as an entirely new terrorist threat because it is a network, but contemporary Western warfare also revolves around the idea of network: see **Chapter 24**.

Al-Qaeda today is better thought of as a discourse of resistance whose material reality is found in a transnational coordinating network highly skilled in forging temporary operational ties with local/regional movements or individuals in order to engage in violent activism. Far from representing a knee-jerk reaction to globalization, Al-Qaeda appropriates the logistical and communicative infrastructures of globalization to pursue the fulfilment of a narrative, a 'story', internalized by its leadership, about the necessity and inevitability of Islam's triumph over the infidel (unbelieving) forces of world power – particularly the United States and its allies in Europe and elsewhere. Al-Qaeda as a radical Islamist group is quite unorthodox even within the wider *jihadist* movement, many of whose members did not agree with Bin Laden's decision to carry out the September 2001 attacks. While Al-Qaeda's model of global Islamic politics has attracted only a few thousand of the world's 1.6 billion Muslims as actual members, some in the Muslim world are drawn to Bin Laden as a symbol of anti-Americanism (even while they usually disagree with the methods he employed). Many today question the future of Al-Qaeda as a terrorist organization, particularly in the wake of Bin Laden's death at the hands of the US military in 2011. Much of the current activity associated with Islamic radicalism is to be found in settings such as Somalia, Yemen and Nigeria, far divorced from Al-Qaeda's purported headquarters in South Asia. And even where the Al-Qaeda name continues to be used by some groups, it is not always clear that they have much direct connection with what remains of Al-Qaeda's core leadership.

The use of various forms of 'counter-terrorist' violence in the Afghanistan–Pakistan region is discussed in **Chapter 23**.

In the wake of the attacks of 11 September 2001 (and subsequent bombings in Europe and elsewhere attributed to Al-Qaeda and its affiliates), we have seen Muslim identity around the world being increasingly regarded as a political question – particularly among Muslim populations in Europe and North America. This has meant that debates around Islam and Muslims have come to take on wider significance beyond the question of terrorism and violence, reinvigorating discussions of whether 'Islam' and 'the West' are compatible in cultural or civilizational terms. We have seen aspects of this in events such as the 2006 Danish Cartoon Affair and the controversy surrounding the pope's speech later that same year, in which the head of the Catholic church seemed to imply that Islam was violent by nature and Muslims incapable of exercising reason.

Moderate Islamic politics

While much of the public debate and discussion of Islam is focused on Al-Qaeda and the minority of extremist groups in the Muslim world, there are a number of other important trends to recognize. Some scholars have claimed that the global jihad movement has essentially failed and become re-domesticated (Gerges 2005), while others argue that the Islamist movement as a whole has become so thoroughly integrated into the norms and structures of global modernity as to represent the onset of 'post-Islamism' (Roy 2004). Other analysts see in this something more akin to the normalization of Islamist politics, meaning that we are beginning to see signs that the old, rather constraining model of the Muslim Brotherhood no longer holds sway. Certain observers suggest that the inclusion of Islamist parties in the political systems of countries such as Jordan, Yemen, and Kuwait has had a moderating effect on the Islamist movement (Schwedler 2006). This trend toward Muslim Democracy, as it has been termed (Nasr 2005), can be seen in the victory of 'semi'-Islamist parties such as the Justice and Development Party in Turkey (commonly known by its Turkish acronym AKP). This is a new form of conservative politics comparable to the Christian Democratic parties of Europe in which religion functions primarily as a reference point for public morality rather than a direct source of legislation. In other words, these are Islamically-based political parties which accept the legitimacy of the formally secular state and which are willing to work pragmatically alongside other parties (secular liberals, socialists, etc.)

to pursue shared goals. It is too early to know whether or not such a trend is taking hold, but it is certainly noteworthy that 'new Islamists' (Baker 2006) of this sort have sprung up in countries as diverse as Morocco, Turkey, Egypt, Jordan, Pakistan and Indonesia in recent years.

These uprisings, which are often known as the Arab Spring, are discussed in **Chapter 9**.

In 2011, a set of popular uprisings across North Africa and elsewhere in the Arab world led to the downfall of several longstanding regimes, including those of the presidents of Tunisia and Egypt. These two countries are particularly noteworthy because of the intensity of the efforts undertaken by their previous governments to regulate and suppress religious forces aspiring to enter politics. In both countries, long oppressed Islamist movements – En-Nahda in Tunisia and the Muslim Brotherhood in Egypt – achieved great success at the ballot box in subsequent elections. In some settings, ultraconservative Islamic groups known as Salafis entered politics for the first time and enjoyed similar success. For some, this development represented evidence that Islamist parties had, by and large, become moderate and mainstream political forces ready and willing to accept the rules of democracy. Other observers – not to mention religious minorities and advocates of secularism in some of these countries – questioned whether the Islamists' conceptions of democracy and rights were compatible with universalist

FIGURE 6.5
A general view of the first Egyptian parliament session after the revolution that ousted former president Hosni Mubarak in Cairo, 23 January 2012. Asmaa Waguih/Reuters. http://photoblog.msnbc.msn.com/_news/2012/01/23/10216029-egypt-parliament-opens-for-the-first-time-following-the-fall-of-mubarak

understandings of, for example, international human rights. For their own part, these groups quickly began to struggle under the pressure of converting themselves from opposition movements into governing officials responsible for solving complex social and economic problems in their respective societies – all the while still trying to preserve some relationship to a religious framework.

For a discussion of human rights and the French headscarf ban, see **Chapter 27**.

So as we can see, it is impossible to provide a single, overall characterization of the role of Islam in global politics. As a community of faith encompassing over a billion people and spanning multiple continents, Islam is itself highly diverse, and so are the ways in which it impacts and interacts with global politics. Multiple streams of Muslim politics are clearly recognizable today, and one cannot easily determine which of them predominates. Indeed, in many cases the ebb and flow of various trends is a function of the prevailing global political climate. What has become clear, however, is that an overview of recent history of political Islam helps to lay bare a set of presumptions about both the relationship between religion and politics (i.e. the question of whether they should be kept separate in a properly 'modern' world), and also the extent to which religion helps us to understand the supposed motivation of political players.

GENERAL RESPONSES
DO RELIGION AND POLITICS MIX?

The idea of the interface or mixing of religion and politics being problematic and potentially dangerous is a byproduct of the rise of secularism, often regarded as one of the hallmarks of modern society. But where did the assumptions and expectations associated with secularism come from, and how have they come to play such an important role in mediating our understanding of how (and whether) religion matters in politics? There is an almost total absence of references to religion in books about global politics prior to the 1990s. It is as if scholars were blind to religion as a force in global affairs, or did not find it to be helpful in explaining international politics.

Secularism

In formal political terms, secularism refers to the idea of a separation between the institutions of church and state. Its origins are to be found in the rise of European modernity and the establishment of the sovereign state. Aspects of the discourse on secularism are, however, to be found throughout the historical record and within the core texts of world religions such as Christianity and Islam. In the Christian tradition, for example, the famous passage of the Bible about rendering 'unto God what is God's and unto Caesar that which belongs to Caesar' is generally regarded as acknowledging a categorical distinction between worldly, political power and the transcendental, other-worldly mandate of religious authority. In the Islamic tradition, while there is no formal theological division between religion and politics, Islamic history is replete with the rise and fall of empires whose day-to-day affairs seemed to reflect a similar distinction in the minds of rulers.

For a discussion of how the separation between religion and politics has played out historically in France, see **Chapter 27**.

The modern history of secularism is associated with two important developments in European intellectual and political history: the philosophical Enlightenment, and the birth of modern political sovereignty.

The Enlightenment was associated with a shift in how people thought about the origins and status of knowledge. Where truth was previously understood to derive from religion and faith, the Enlightenment – and modernity more generally – entailed a shift to the idea that truth and knowledge could be determined through the effort of human reason. Furthermore, the human condition was no longer seen as subject to divine providence. Rather, human beings were now understood to possess the capacity to change the world around them. One aspect of secularism, then, is a shift away from relying on religious belief to provide knowledge and understanding of the world, and the rise of a belief in the ability of the autonomous, rational, thinking subject to comprehend the world and to change it for the better.

This 'rational, thinking subject' is modelled on what is considered to be male, and therefore women and supposedly feminine qualities have often been considered less significant or even entirely excluded. See **Chapters 5 and 17**.

BOX 6.4 KEY ENLIGHTENMENT THINKERS

Voltaire (1694–1778): a leading French critic of organized religion who emphasized the power of human reason and agency in shaping society.

David Hume (1711–76): a Scottish philosopher who argued that knowledge and understanding of the world is something that derives from the human senses – an approach known as empiricism – rather than from divine sources.

Immanuel Kant (1724–1804): one of the leading German philosophers of the Enlightenment whose work remains highly influential today. Kant exhorted people to 'dare to know'. He used the Latin phrase for this: *sapere aude*.

John Locke (1632–1704): an English thinker whose ideas on liberty, the individual, and property were central to the development of political modernism.

Adam Smith (1723–90): a Scottish economist and moral philosopher generally regarded as the leading theorist – in his book *The Wealth of Nations* – of modern capitalism.

This new orientation gave rise to the attitudes and methods that underpin the modern natural sciences, many of which were later reproduced in an effort to create social science. Eventually, some scholars began to associate the advent of modernity with an evolutionary model of human development. According to this model, societies that have undergone modernization are further along in terms of developmental progress than those societies characterized by the persistence of traditional beliefs and practices, such as religion (Lerner 1958). Modernization is generally understood as a process whereby societies 'evolve' according to the trajectory of the Western political economy from about the sixteenth century – meaning that they adopt capitalism, industrialization, and, increasingly today, also political liberalism and democracy.

The use of statistics to analyse and explain the social world is one such phenomenon: see **Chapter 19** for some of the problems with this.

The political-institutional understanding of secularism is associated with the emergence of modern sovereign states in Europe, a development commonly dated to the Peace of Westphalia in 1648. After the Wars of Religion in the preceding century, it was agreed among rulers that religion should be kept separate from matters of state. This was to ensure that the legitimacy of the sovereign would remain free from attempts by church authorities to interfere in politics, and produced a situation in which many found themselves subject to official state religions. The rise of liberalism in political thought – in large measure a reaction against this idea – soon produced the form of government known as republicanism. In a modern republic, the location of sovereignty and the responsibility to govern are understood to shift from being the preserve of monarchs to being the right of the peoples so governed – hence *res* ('concern') *publicus* ('of the people'). In the republican model, public affairs are to be regulated by the rule of law, popularly legislated, rather than by the whim of monarchs or the faith-based 'irrationality' of religion. As part of this shift away from official religions of state, religion came to be seen as a private matter – that is, a sphere of activity belonging to the realm of the individual and whatever voluntary associations might arise between consenting individuals outside the influence and determination of the state. But we should also note that the supposedly 'secular' character of a given society does not always tell the whole story. Religion is a powerful social force and even many countries that formally practice secularism still bear strong traces of religion in their legal and ethical systems. One clear example of this can be seen in the laws that govern modern warfare. Contemporary notions of 'just war' in the West, for example, are strongly informed by early Christian discussions of morality and armed conflict.

The emergence of states in Europe is traced in **Chapter 11**, which also explains the Peace of Westphalia. **Chapter 7** discusses secular forms of authority. **Chapter 27** explores the implications of the inscription of a particular form of secularism known as *laicité* in the French Constitution.

Liberalism and republicanism are different 'pictures' of political space in the sense explained in **Chapter 2**.

Being confined to the private realm means to be excluded from the public sphere where decisions are made about who gets which resources. This is why feminists have challenged the boundary between private and public. See **Chapter 5**.

These early Christian discussions are covered in **Chapter 21**.

In recent years, a number of interventions by scholars coupled with political events in the world have led to a reconsideration of some of the conventional thinking about secularism and place of religion in the world today. Some sociologists of religion for whom a general trend towards greater secularization in the modern world was once taken for granted have since backed off from that position (Berger 1999). Others have argued that in fact we are seeing a greater public role for religion around the world (Casanova 1994), with some connecting this to an increased search for meaning and purpose in a highly complex, globalizing world (Laidi 1998). Some, such as William Connolly (1999), warn of the dangers associated with excluding religious sources of morality from public debate. Scholars of non-Western societies have also been critical of the secularization thesis, but in a different way. For them, it is not so much that the supposed trend towards secularism has been reversed, but that it was never an appropriate account of the world in the first place. Writers such as Talal Asad (1993) have argued that the very idea of religion and politics as wholly distinct and separate spheres is itself a Eurocentric proposition, reflecting the particular experience of modernity as it evolved in Europe and North America. For him, it is therefore inappropriate to try and apply this schema as a universal explanation of the relationship of religion and politics. Several Indian political theorists have argued along similar lines that the notion of secularism is inappropriate for understanding the relationship between religious communities and national society in that country (Chatterjee 1998; Nandy 1995).

For a discussion of British colonialism in India see **Chapter 16**.

Religion in the social sciences

One well-known social science account of international affairs is Samuel Huntington's 'Clash of Civilizations' thesis, in which 'civilizational' blocs pursue security and interests

BOX 6.5 HUNTINGTON'S 'CLASH OF CIVILIZATIONS'

Samuel Huntington's thesis first appeared in the influential policy journal *Foreign Affairs* in 1993, and several years later in book form as *The Clash of Civilizations and the Remaking of World Order* (1998). Huntington's book was about the role of culture and religion in world politics. He argues that in the post-Cold War world, cultural blocs – which he labels 'civilizations' – will become the major protagonists of global affairs. 'The fault lines of civilizations', he says, 'will be the battle lines of the future'. In Huntington's view, each civilization expresses a unique worldview and set of values. As contact between these cultural or symbolic systems intensifies in the face of global pressure to integrate economies, political communities, and cultures, the incompatibility of different civilizations leads to increased tension and eventually actual conflict between them. What are the civilizations he is talking about? For Huntington, many of the divisions between civilizations are religious in nature. His Western civilization is largely composed of the Protestant and Catholic Christian majority nations (except Latin America, a sort of Western sub-civilization according to Huntington). Others in his list include the Muslim world, the Orthodox Christian world, the Hindu world, and the Buddhist world. To these can be added three others, the Sinic world (covering China and areas of Southeast Asia), Japanese civilization and also Sub-Saharan Africa, whose status Huntington leaves unclear.

defined in terms of cultural values. Huntington also provides us with a rigid understanding of culture with little space to account for the considerable diversity and nuance that exists within and between his civilizations.

Huntington paints a picture of the world that seems to provide an easy explanation for recent terrorism and the responses to it. But, as **Chapter 2** shows, such pictures do not simply enable us to see what is already there: they make the world we see. They also make invisible what does not fit into the picture.

Claims about civilizations and religions as the new primary blocs in world politics have been subject to considerable critique (Hall and Jackson 2007; Huntington 1996) in recent years. Likewise the popularity of Huntington's thesis has ebbed and flowed, with the attacks of 11 September 2001 seeming for some to give credence to the idea of a civilizational struggle between Islam and the West. Numerous criticisms have been levelled against Huntington's thesis. His concept of civilization is so large and heavily abstracted that it is difficult to map it on to any kind of social reality – in other words, it is difficult to think of civilization in terms of lived experience. The blocs that Huntington identifies as civilizations are, in some cases, so enormously diverse that it becomes nearly impossible to treat them analytically as a single cultural unit. Furthermore, Huntington's thesis operates with a very static and stultifying conception of culture. In order to make the argument about civilizational difference as a source of conflict, he is forced to reduce highly complex and fluid belief systems to rather stagnant and essentialized ideal types that, again, bear little resemblance to social reality. It is difficult to see the dynamic and intersubjective qualities that define culture in Huntington's reified (that is, in a way that makes the abstract concept appear real) civilizations. In terms of our discussion so far, Huntington's argument is important to examine critically because of the way in which it ends up having to reduce complex, multifaceted human subjects to their religious identities in order to maintain its own logic.

BROADER ISSUES
CULTURE, FUNDAMENTALISM AND RELIGIOUS IDENTITIES

Before Huntington's analysis of clashing civilizations, other scholars of world politics were beginning to stress the importance of cultural and religious forces in world politics, but in considerably more subtle terms (Der Derian and Shapiro 1989). These writers asked us to consider the relevance of wider social theory for understanding some of the central problems in contemporary global politics. They argued, for example, that it is difficult to understand many of today's problems without recognizing the inherently postcolonial nature of global affairs (Darby 1998; Doty 1996).

The importance of colonial history in understanding the postcolonial present is discussed in **Chapters 15, 16, 20 and 21**.

Others have argued that culture is the very terrain upon which conceptions and practices of world order and power have played out throughout modern history. For these scholars, culture is crucially important because of its intimate relationship with processes of identity formation and the making of 'others' (see Chapter 5). The ideas of Edward Said are particularly relevant in this regard.

Edward Said's landmark text *Orientalism* (1978) made the argument that culture and power are closely related in the historical establishment of particular forms of world order. More specifically, Said delves into various domains of cultural production (literature, art, scholarship) in the European world during the colonial period in order to understand the relationship between *representation* and geopolitical power. His focus on representation was prompted by the fact that in reviewing depictions of various peoples the West seemed to regard as 'outside' or Other – particularly in the Islamic (or 'Oriental') world – Said found that the stories told about the non-Western world seemed to regularly and systematically associate these cultures with traits that were the opposite of Western values and that carried strongly negative connotations. For example,

Examining 'representation' is a different way of saying that you are interested in the 'picture' that a particular view generates. See **Chapter 2**.

FIGURE 6.6
An example of 'Orientalist' art in Edward Said's sense: *The Snake Charmer*, Jean-Léon Gérôme, 1870. © Sterling and Francine Clark Art Institute, Williamstown, Massachusetts, USA

Muslim peoples were often represented as exotic, overly-sensualized, lazy or violent as opposed to rational, orderly, and hard-working – all characteristics, supposedly, of Western modernity. Said argues that this is something more than just subjective bias, however. He suggests that this system of cultural representation, which he terms Orientalism, was a core component of the exercise of colonial power. In other words, Said argued that one of the ways in which the West constituted its own identity and legitimized its dominance was to construct the non-Western world – the object of its imperial geopolitics – as its absolute other. This helped to justify and naturalize the hierarchies of power between various (culturally-defined) world regions, and eventually to institutionalize the European sovereign state model as a global system.

These colonial hierarchies of power continue to have significant effects: see **Chapters 15, 16 and 20**.

For Said, culture is not simply one factor in understanding global politics, but a core terrain upon which it plays out: global politics, on this reading, *is* culture. Some scholars have argued that Said overstates his case and ignores reciprocal processes of Western objectification and representation by non-Western peoples (Buruma and Margalit 2004), while others suggest that Said's theory continues to hold some merit in terms of understanding the underlying logic not only of Huntington's neo-Orientalist vision, but also central thrust of US foreign policy in the aftermath of the Cold War (Ó Tuathail 1996).

Writers such as Tariq Ali have engaged this issue through the theme of fundamentalism. The term is important for us to consider since it is generally associated with religion, and particularly with Islam. A term that originally came into usage to describe certain forms of American Christianity in the nineteenth century, 'fundamentalism' emerged as a common designation of danger in reference to various Islamist movements from the 1980s. Some critics have dismissed its utility simply because it does not provide any analytical value (Pieterse 1994). They argue that by emphasizing one's adherence to the 'fundamentals' of a given religion does not tell us much about the nature and behaviours associated with a given religious identity. For example, one might easily follow the fundamental beliefs of Islam and never even consider becoming involved with political movements or violent groups. Ali's (2003) intervention in this debate is interesting because he seeks to decouple the term fundamentalism from an exclusively religious connotation and to associate it instead with any form of thought or ideology that is uncompromising in its worldview and which represents itself as the sole source of truth or the only solution to global problems. Viewed in this way it becomes possible to recognize today the existence in global politics of various kinds of fundamentalism, some of which are not religious in nature. For example, sometimes the assumptions and practices associated with the neoliberal economic policies that underpin organizations such as the International Monetary Fund and the World Trade Organization take on the aura of 'religion' when, in the absence of no strong proof of their remedy, global policymakers place considerable faith in these approaches as a route to salvation from global poverty.

There is evidence that neoliberal economic policies have changed the way we view poverty but are unable to end poverty as they claim to. See **Chapter 20**.

Ali's depiction of fundamentalism takes a different direction, however. He tries to show that in the wake of the attacks of 11 September 2001, there emerged a curious form of parallel fundamentalism that can been seen through a comparison of the discourses and worldviews contained in the rhetoric of US president George W. Bush and the statements of Al-Qaeda leader Usama Bin Laden. Each of these global political actors represented themselves as the guardians and purveyors of absolute moralities. Bin

Laden promised to work to establish a world system based on Islamic law, while the subsequent policy choices of the Bush administration seemed to suggest that it was driven by a worldview (commonly described as neo-conservative) that sought to remake the world in its image. In this sense, the 2003 war with Iraq can be interpreted as an effort by the United States to transplant its own model of good governance (liberal democratic, capitalist) to the heart of the Middle East. This way Bush and Bin Laden both revealed themselves to be pursuing projects of absolute and universalizing morality – much in the vein of religion even where religion was not explicitly invoked. Neo-conservatism is an example of ideology – that is, a template of meaning making with a singular horizon that allows people to understand the world in ways that lead to certain, unavoidable conclusions about what must be done in response to the circumstances of the world. Ideology not only mediates how we perceive the world around us, but also prescribes all-encompassing solutions for dealing with the world it hands us (Eagleton 1991). It hence becomes possible to draw strong parallels between religion and ideology, rather than treating religion as something entirely unique. Many, however, would reject this comparison on the grounds that religion deals with a fundamentally different and foundational order of questions about the very condition, sources and meaning of existence.

It is interesting to compare the discussion of the role of 'language games' in **Chapter 2** with the discussion of 'ideology' here.

This debate is all the more important to bear in mind due to the tendency on the part of some analysts of global politics to privilege religious affiliations as if they are forms of identity that trump all others. We see this in commonplace practices such as the use of the term 'Muslim world' or when writers refer to large categories such as 'Muslims in Europe'. While such terminology is often merely trying to be descriptive,

For a discussion of other sorts of identity and the complications involved in thinking about identity see **Chapters 5, 12 and 13**, and, for another discussion of religious identity, **Chapter 27**.

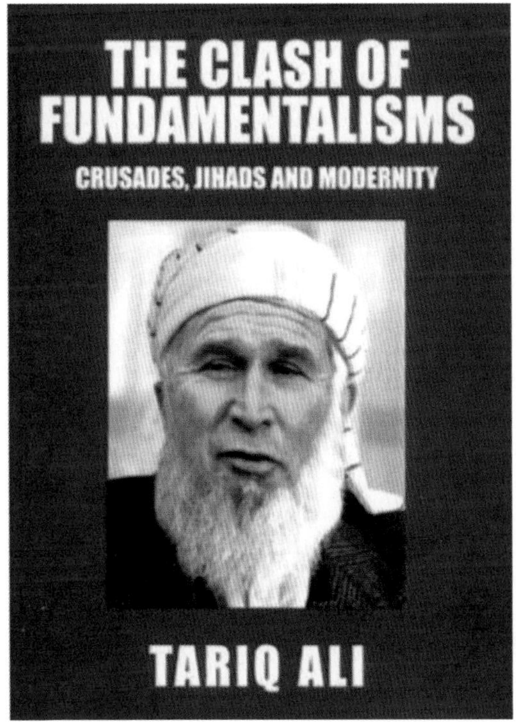

FIGURE 6.7
President Bush dressed as Bin Laden on the cover of Tariq Ali's *The Clash of Fundamentalisms*. Verso

it becomes problematic when it begins to ascribe behaviours to religion – that is, when we begin to make assumptions that because a country happens to be part of something called the Muslim world, or because someone happens to be Muslim, then they will necessarily think or act in a certain way. This is, in essence, a point about the danger of projecting religiousness onto people who hold multiple identities and whose considerations and decisions as regards their political behaviour cannot be reduced to religion. For example, it can be argued that in many cases the views and motivations of people in the so-called Muslim world can just as easily, if not more accurately, be understood in relation to the problems and concerns of Third World or developing world identities – that is, in relation to issues of global inequality in socioeconomic terms, and politically in terms of the asymmetry of power between countries in the global North and the global South. Further complicating the analysis is the fact that even where religious language is deployed to mobilize political identity, the root causes of the antagonism underpinning these claims are sometimes better found in other domains (e.g. the political disenfranchisement of a minority group). Projecting religious identities onto large groups can even mask the true sources of political discontent in some cases. For example, during the Paris riots of 2006, it was not uncommon to find the participants in these riots being described as 'Muslim protesters' even though none of their claims was couched in terms of Islam. It would have been more accurate in that case to approach the issue in terms of the mobilized discontent of unemployed immigrants.

See **Chapter 13** for a picture of the 2006 Paris riots and a discussion of how they related to the question of the nation; see **Chapter 27** for a discussions of Muslims in France.

Also of great importance is the need to recognize the inevitability of great diversity within the various traditions of world religion. Christianity, Judaism and Islam all contain within them multiple currents, denominations, and sects, and all of them vary considerably depending on where in geographical and cultural terms they are practised. In the Muslim world there is certainly a highly visible yet numerically very small radical fringe prepared to use violence to subvert the current world order. There are many more Muslims, global public opinion surveys suggest (Pew 2005), committed to an interpretation of Islam that is in harmony with values of tolerance, pluralism and democracy. A majority of the world's Muslims are not affiliated with any kind of political movement nor understand their religion as a system of beliefs that requires that one behave politically in any particular way. This fact strengthens the point made above about the need to look beyond religion to understand the political identities and worldviews of peoples that we often too easily categorize in terms of their religion.

Do you consider that your political worldview is informed by religion?

Finally, we need to resist the idea that religious identities or political claims framed in terms of religion are somehow beyond the comprehension of what we otherwise regard as political reason. Conflicting parties in Sri Lanka's armed dispute whose primary desires can be understood in relation to social stability and personal security, for example, may appeal to aspects of Hinduism and Buddhism that emphasize peace. In countries such as Turkey and Indonesia, parties whose political platform is defined in terms of eliminating government corruption, will often speak of Islam as the source of their public morality without having any interest in setting up Islamic states. Furthermore, we can even see evidence today of religious and secular parties forming coalitions in support of shared goals. For example, within the broad Global Justice and 'alter-mondialisation' movements today, one can find socialists, environmentalists, and religious parties of various denominations trying to achieve social justice (a key value in Islam and certain interpretations of Christianity) and preserve the planet. While their languages may differ – e.g. 'Mother Earth' vs. the human relationship with the planet as a sacred covenant – all of these people are committed to a common vision of participation and co-operation in world affairs. Viewing religion in this regard allows us to identify it as just one among many similar ideational sources at play in global politics. Rather than viewing and treating religion as a space of exception in global politics – as a unique force beyond reason and comprehension – we are better off treating it as one of many terrains and languages through which the global political is engaged. Islam, for example, needs always to be understood in relation to *Muslims* – that is, to the people who profess its belief and interpret its meaning in terms of their life experience and circumstances. Only by contextualizing religion in this way, in terms of lived experience, can we understand how and where it intersects with the global political.

Some forms of environmentalism are interesting here because they do not place the human at the centre: see **Chapters 3 and 4**.

CONCLUSION

The question of religion in global politics is nothing if not highly complex. In addressing the framing question with which we opened the discussion, 'Does religion matter in global politics?' it would seem that we need to answer this in the affirmative, but with certain very important qualifications. More specifically, three points bear drawing out by way of summary and conclusion: (1) the importance of understanding when and how to grant importance to religion in seeking to understand global politics – in other words, recognizing that religion is present in a given global political situation does not mean that that situation should be read exclusively or even primarily in terms of religion; (2) the importance of recognizing the presence of enormous diversity within world religions and the dangers entailed in treating them as monoliths; and (3) the fact that religious identities and world political claims framed in terms of religion are not necessarily categorically distinct or unconnected from other kinds of political and ideological claims. Indeed, as several examples today can show, these sorts of claims are often motivated by a desire on the part of both the 'religious' and the 'non-religious' to achieve similar goals even where the languages they use may differ.

FURTHER READING

Haynes, Jeff (1998) *Religion in Global Politics*, Harlow: Longman.

A survey of key religious trends in all major world regions with an emphasis on the dynamic and increasingly interdependent relationship between them.

Jenkins, Phil (2006) *The New Faces of Christianity: Believing the Bible in the Global South*, New York: Oxford University Press.

An analysis of the phenomenal growth of Pentecostal Christianity in Africa and other parts of the developing world in recent years.

Juergensmeyer, Mark (1994) *The New Cold War? Religious Nationalism Confronts the Secular State*, Berkeley: University of California Press; (2003) *Terror in the Mind of God: The Global Rise of Religious Violence*, Berkeley: University of California Press; and (2006) *The Oxford Handbook of Global Religions*, New York: Oxford University Press.

A leading sociologist reflects on the relationship between religion, conflict and nation-states in the global era across a broad range of faith traditions.

Kurtz, Lester (2006) *Gods in the Global Village*, 2nd edn, Thousand Oaks, CA: Sage.
Examines the impact of globalization on how people understand the role of religion and the structure of its organization.

Mandaville, Peter (2007) *Global Political Islam*, London: Routledge.
A broad overview of the history and evolution of Muslim politics with a particular focus on the interface between globalization and political Islam.

WEBSITES

BeliefNet, http://www.beliefnet.com
The leading website on global religions.

Islam Online, http://www.islamonline.net
A portal for Muslim issues and information. The site closely associated with Yusuf al-Qaradawi, a leading Islamic scholar-jurist with a global audience. Represents the perspective of mainstream conservative Islamic orthodoxy.

Muslim Wakeup! http://www.muslimwakeup.com
A self-described 'progressive' Muslim site, featuring articles dealing with various social issues such as the relationship between Islam and feminism. An interesting contrast to Islam Online.

The ISIM Review, http://www.isim.nl
A forum courtesy of the Institute for the Study of Islam in the Modern World in the Netherlands, this publication frequently features short articles on the Muslim world with a strong global politics focus.

IslamiCity, http://www.islamicity.com
One of the major Islamic portal websites, with a variety of articles on contemporary Muslim issues; search engines for Islamic textual sources; and information on Muslim media and local services (mainly in the USA).

REFERENCES

Ali, Tariq (2003) *The Clash of Fundamentalisms: Crusades, Jihads, and Modernity*, London: Verso.

Althusser, Louis (2001) *Lenin and Philosophy and Other Essays*, new edn, New York: Monthly Review Press.

Asad, Talal (1993) *Genealogies of Religion: Discipline and Reasons of Power in Christianity and Islam*, Baltimore, MD: Johns Hopkins University Press.

Baker, Raymond (2006) *Islam Without Fear: Egypt and the New Islamists*, Cambridge, MA: Harvard University Press.

Berger, Peter (ed.) (1999) *The Desecularization of the World: The Resurgence of Religion in World Politics*, Washington, DC: Ethics and Public Policy Center.

Buruma, Ian and Avishai Margalit (2004) *Occidentalism: The West in the Eyes of Its Enemies*, London: Penguin.

Casanova, Jose (1994) *Public Religions in the Modern World*, Chicago: University of Chicago Press.

Chatterjee, Partha (1998) 'Secularism and Toleration', in Rajeev Bhargav (ed.), *Secularism and Its Critics*, New Delhi: Oxford University Press.

Clarke, Peter (2006) *New Religious Movement in Global Perspective: A Study of Religious Change in the Modern World*, London: Routledge.

Connolly, William E. (1999) *Why I Am Not a Secularist*, Minneapolis: University of Minnesota Press.

——(2005) 'The Evangelical-Capitalist Resonance Machine', *Political Theory* 33, 6: 869–86.

Darby, Philip (1998) *The Fiction of Imperialism: Reading Between International Relations and Postcolonialism*, London: Cassell.

Der Derian, James and Michael Shapiro (eds) (1989) *International/Intertextual Relations: Postmodern Readings of World Politics*, Lexington, MA: Lexington Press.
Doty, Roxanne Lynn (1996) *Imperial Encounters: The Politics of Representation in North–South Relations*, Minneapolis: University of Minnesota Press.
Eagleton, Terry (1991) *Ideology: An Introduction*, London: Verso.
Geertz, Clifford (1973) *The Interpretation of Culture*, New York: Basic Books.
Gerges, Fawaz (2005) *The Far Enemy: Why Jihad Went Global*, Cambridge: Cambridge University Press.
Hall, Martin and Patrick Thaddeus Jackson (eds) (2007) *Civilizational Identity: The Production and Reproduction of 'Civilizations' in International Relations*, New York: Palgrave.
Huntington, Samuel (ed.) (1996) *The Clash of Civilizations? The Debate*, New York: Council on Foreign Relations.
——(1998) *The Clash of Civilizations and the Remaking of World Order*, New York: Simon and Schuster.
Laidi, Zaki (1998) *A World Without Meaning: The Crisis of Meaning in International Politics*, London: Routledge.
Lerner, Daniel (1958) *The Passing of Traditional Society: Modernizing the Middle East*, Glencoe, IL: The Free Press.
Lindbeck, George (1984) *The Nature of Doctrine*, Louisville, KY: Westminster John Knox Press.
Nandy, Ashis (1995) 'An Anti-Secularist Manifesto', *India International Quarterly* 22, 1: 35–64.
Nasr, Vali (2005) 'The Rise of Muslim Democracy', *Journal of Democracy* 16, 2: 13–27.
——(2007) *The Shia Revival*, New York: W. W. Norton.
Ó Tuathail, Geraóid (1996) *Critical Geopolitics: The Politics of Writing Global Space*, Minneapolis: University of Minnesota Press.
Pew Global Attitudes Project (2005) *Islamic Extremism: Common Concern for Muslim and Western Publics*, Washington, DC: Pew Research Center.
Pieterse, Jan Nederveen (1994) 'Fundamentalism Discourses: Enemy Images', *Women Against Fundamentalism Journal*, 5: 2–6.
Roy, Olivier (2004) *Globalized Islam: The Search for a New Ummah*, New York: Columbia University Press.
Said, Edward (1978) *Orientalism*, New York: Pantheon Books.
Schwedler, Jillian (2006) *Faith in Moderation: Islamist Parties in Jordan and Yemen*, Cambridge: Cambridge University Press.

For a range of further resources supporting this chapter, please visit the companion website for *Global Politics, 2nd Edition* at www.routledge.com/cw/edkins/

CHAPTER 7

Why do we obey?

Jenny Edkins

THE QUESTION
OBEDIENCE, RESISTANCE AND FORCE

On the whole we seem to be fairly obedient creatures. We go from day to day doing mostly – not always, of course – what is expected of us. We usually respect conventions about property and ownership, we are polite and well-mannered to our friends as a general rule, and we tend to do as we are told – by our boss, the traffic warden, the doctor, the tax inspector and so on. Why do we obey people like this? Is it because we have to? Well, clearly we risk losing our job or falling foul of the law if we don't. But do we make this calculation every time, or do we just do what is expected because that is easiest? Or are we obeying some internal voice – our conscience – or, if we are religious, the precepts of our faith?

What happens if we disagree with the way things are organised – if, for example, it has been decided that the government is going to build new nuclear power plants, and that part of the money we pay in taxes will go towards this? If we disagree with this decision, what do we do? Most of us accept that the government is entitled to make such decisions, even if we think they are doing something very unwise, even criminal, and we do nothing: we pay our taxes and let them get on with it. Some of us maybe don't: we organise a demonstration, we challenge the decision, we withhold our taxes. We are disobedient, usually in a non-violent sort of way, called 'civil disobedience' – we disobey, but we are civil about it. And usually, of course, our action makes no difference: the decision we disagree with doesn't change.

Chapter 28 discusses some of the problems with the idea of changing the world.

Of course, if we live in a democracy, we get the chance every so often to express our disagreement with the decisions of a particular government by voting them out of office. This really does not give us much of a voice in what goes on, but if we want to be more involved, we have various routes open to us. We could stand for election ourselves, become a political activist and help formulate party policy, lobby the government, perhaps through joining or working for a campaigning organisation. To take any of these routes, we would have to follow a series of conventions and jump a number of hurdles, all of which rely on us doing what's expected in a particular context. At this point it is beginning to seem as though the whole of social and political existence involves 'doing what's expected'. Even if we decide that the whole system of government that we live under is so appalling that we should work to change it, we still have to organise politically – even revolutions can demand some obedience along the way, although ultimately major *dis*-obedience, even violent disobedience, may be what is planned.

Ways in which people organise to campaign for change are discussed in many of the chapters of this book – for example **Chapters 4** (environmental movements), **5** (feminism); **6** (religious movements); **9** (web campaigns); **10** (immigration protests); **14** (direct democracy movements).

In many respects, it is good to be able to do what is expected – to know what that is without giving it too much thought, and to just do it. Fairly automatic obedience can be much easier than trying to work out what on earth we are supposed to do in a totally unfamiliar or chaotic situation. It is good to have a framework of conventions

A.BACALL
"I am going to close my eyes and cover my ears. I expect the student who took my chair, my desk, and my chalkboard to bring them back."

FIGURE 7.1
'I am going to close my eyes'. Artist: Aaron Bacall. CartoonStock ref.: aba0400. www.CartoonStock.com

and rules in place, even though some of them may not be ideal, and for there to be someone else, in a leadership position, who is responsible for dealing with any crises that may come along. We know where we are and who we are in such a case. When we come across a situation where there is nothing to guide us – when a major accident happens, when our life changes suddenly – we can find ourselves having to completely rethink what to do, from scratch.

What happens when we are asked to do something that we really think we shouldn't be doing – if we are asked to injure someone, for example. This isn't something that seems to happen under normal circumstances to most of us, but if, as we have seen, we are generally obedient creatures, we might want to think about what would happen if, for example, someone whose authority we respected, or someone who was in a position to enforce their authority, told us that it was necessary for us to injure someone. A famous experiment by Stanley Milgram seems to show that people in general are willing to cause fairly severe injuries to others if told to do so by someone in a position of authority – in Milgram's case, someone wearing a white coat. There are of course many examples where people are ordered to do something that normally they might consider they shouldn't do: soldiers who kill in combat, for example. There are cases that perhaps seem less extreme too, for example when civilians in Nazi Germany carried on with mundane administrative tasks even though they knew or suspected that what they were doing was part of the bureaucracy of killing (Baumann 1991; Lanzmann 1995).

Milgram's experiment is discussed in **Chapter 22**. Does this experiment show that there is something called 'human nature'? If we believe that it does, do the answers to political questions in fact lie in psychology? Or not? **Chapter 27** discusses the notion of 'human' implied in human rights.

BOX 7.1 HUMAN NATURE

Quite often in debates about global politics someone will claim that it all comes down to human nature: in other words that what we think will happen in a particular situation depends on what we think that humans are, essentially, quite apart from any social, political or cultural context. Those that claim this often suggest that we should look to psychology to provide the answer: for example, to experiments like the Milgram experiment, which seems to tell us that people are quite happy to obey an authority figure, whatever that figure asks them to do.

However, there are many people who would question the idea that there is something called human nature. They would point to the problems with the way using the idea of the essential nature of something acts as a trump card: it halts the argument. And it is almost impossible to prove or disprove. If someone acts in a way that seems contrary to an essential human nature their action can be discounted as an exception, or as caused by some intervening factor. And vice versa.

Another problem with the idea of human nature is that it assumes that we know what a human being is – we know who counts as human and who doesn't. However, this distinction is more problematic (and political) than it appears at first glance. Philosophers over the ages have tried to specify what distinguishes human beings from animals, for example, but there is no agreement to be found. And who counts as human changes over time. There was a time when women were not considered fully human. The difficulties become apparent when we think of contemporary limit cases – the foetus, for example, or a person who shows no evidence of brain activity. At what point does someone become or cease to be a human being?

How do those in authority enforce their demand that we obey? How do they make us obey if we don't want to? Usually, they persuade us that we should, first of all: if we are tempted to drink and drive, then they show us advertisements designed to bring home the damage we might do as a result, or impose a fine if they catch us. But if persuasion doesn't work, we move to the next stage: they will forcibly stop us from driving, ultimately by confining us behind prison bars. 'They', the agents of the government, are entitled to use force, in the form of the armed forces or the police, to guarantee obedience. Of course, this is not a *carte blanche*: when the Ohio National Guard shot dead four student demonstrators and injured others during an anti-Vietnam War protest at Kent State University in 1970, this was widely regarded as an unreasonable, and hence illegitimate, use of force by the state government. And in the Arab Spring in 2011, the actions of governments in North Africa and the Middle East who used force against their own citizens who were demonstrating for change were widely condemned.

Although shooting fellow citizens who are demonstrating peacefully is not something we would expect our armed forces to do, the fact that it could happen, and does occasionally, must be at the back of our minds when considering any action that challenges the government. If we are seriously intending to overthrow a government, then we need to think of the possibility that the government will use force to resist this challenge to its authority. Indeed, often a challenge to the government that seeks to replace it with another political order will take the form of an armed rebellion, in anticipation of the armed response.

ILLUSTRATIVE EXAMPLE
THE REVOLUTIONS OF 1989

To understand more about the questions of authority and obedience that we've raised, let's look at some instances where a political order was challenged, people were disobedient, and authority, at least temporarily, collapsed. It may seem strange to examine examples where people do not obey in order to address the question 'Why do we obey?', but sometimes, indeed quite often, looking at cases when something doesn't happen can help us understand what is going on when it does. We will not be looking here at violent revolutions, where guerrillas or insurgents (as armed resistance movements against the authorities tend to be called) confronted the armed forces of the state. Instead we focus on examples where the government was taken on or defied by its own unarmed citizens. What happens when a number of people stand up and refuse to obey? We will be exploring in some detail what people who were involved in one way or another in events of this type thought and did. Although the most well-known recent example is the Arab Spring, the successful outcomes of the demonstrations in some cases, and the violent repression that they provoked in others, are too recent to enable us to make a judgement, or to examine closely and in detail what happened. Another very recent example where civil disobedience and protest took new and interesting forms is the global Occupy movement. Both Occupy and the Arab Spring draw on older ideas of the occupation of public space with tents and the assembling or movement of large numbers of people, ideas which we will see in action in the two cases we examine below.

The events of the Arab Spring are discussed in **Chapter 9** and the Occupy movement in **Chapters 18 and 28**.

We will talk particularly about examples of acts of disobedience, performed in some cases by an individual person, and in others by large gatherings of people. In each case we need to think about why and to what extent these acts of disobedience succeeded, and whether, ultimately, they failed. Theda Skopol's work on social revolutions is interesting here (Skocpol 1979). She argues that although revolutions are often directed against the authority and power of the state, what happens in the end is not the reduction of state power but actually the reverse: its reinforcement. A different set of rulers, with perhaps different ideological commitments, take over the running of the state apparatus after a revolution, but the state itself, as an institution, is strengthened rather than weakened.

What exactly we mean by the state is discussed further in **Chapter 11**. A lot of thinking about politics forgets that the state is not a 'black box' but made up of various different people and organisations.

A number of events that could be described – indeed *were* described – as revolutions, took place in 1989, in different parts of the world, and with apparently vastly different outcomes. The 1989 democracy movement in China came to an abrupt end on 3 June 1989, when the armed forces of the state violently dispersed demonstrators who had camped in Tiananmen Square in the heart of Beijing. Their demands had been expressed through peaceful demonstrations throughout the city, where it seemed that students and workers – indeed the entire population of Beijing – had turned out in support. Some of the communist party leaders were also in support of the movement, but not those at the head of the then party leadership. Hunger strikes by students encamped on the square itself took place, and they constructed a huge 'goddess of democracy' from white plaster. There were attempts at negotiation, and calls for the students to return to their universities. After a lengthy period of demonstrations and many weeks of hunger strike, it became clear that the hard-line voices within the communist leadership had won out and that the order had been given for troops to enter the city and suppress the demonstrations. Despite this, for some time things continued as before: the troops of the 'People's Army' were persuaded by demonstrators who spoke to them face-to-face to turn back, and not to fire on their fellow citizens. However, in the end, on the night of 3 June 1989, the tanks moved into Tiananmen Square.

Chinese politics is discussed in **Chapter 12**.

These events in China were watched around the world, as were the events of the Arab Spring. Scenes of buses carrying flag waving and cheering supporters, small tents crowded into Tiananmen Square in which the hunger strikers lay, the square itself – vast, but looking more like a city within a city than the huge and daunting empty space of ceremonial and power that it was supposed to be – all these images were broadcast worldwide. Images of the violence in the square on the night of 3 June were also shown worldwide: students fleeing before the advancing soldiers, the injured being rushed away by friends, the tanks crushing everything in their path.

A very famous image from that time is the photograph of one man standing in front of a column of tanks advancing down Chang'an Avenue a few days later, on 4 June. This picture shows a lone person, carrying nothing but what looks like a shopping bag and a jacket and wearing a white shirt, who places himself in the roadway precisely in the path of an advancing column of tanks. People around the world watching the video images of this saw the tank-driver's several attempts to drive around the man, first to the right and then to the left – thwarted by the man determinedly repositioning himself in front of the tank, time and time again, eventually so close to it that the tank could not get around at all. The tank stopped – and the demonstrator climbed up onto the tank to speak to the driver or get inside the tank, before climbing down. The tank

FIGURE 7.2
Tiananmen Square, Beijing, China, 1989. Photo: Stuart Franklin, Magnum

then started up its engine again, and the whole incident repeated itself, before the tank once more came to a stop. Finally, the man disappeared, two other men hustling or helping him away, depending on how you see it – we don't know the outcome, and we don't know who the man was, or whether he is still alive (Thomas 2006).

This image of how one man, apparently fearless, could stop the advancing might of the state, embodied in the tank, was and remains, an iconic image. Later that year came the revolutions of 1989 in what was at that time called Eastern Europe. These upheavals formed part of the end of the Cold War and the eventual collapse of the Soviet Union. The people involved in the protests demanding change in Eastern Europe had seen what had happened in China. Although in East Germany, for example, the state had limited information to that according with the official Chinese line, people had been able to pick up broadcasts from West Germany (Prins 1990: 211). They knew what was at stake: the tanks could arrive. On 17 June 1953 Soviet tanks had been sent in as part of the violent suppression of strikes and demonstrations in Berlin which left at least fifty people dead. And in 1968 Soviet tanks had rolled into Czechoslovakia in response to the reform movement known as the Prague Spring. It could well happen again. Communist leaders, too, those who could call in the tanks, had seen what this had led to in China: a period of destabilisation.

For more about what the Cold War involved, see **Chapter 26**.

In East Germany that autumn, the situation was confused. There had been a series of major street demonstrations calling for change, in Leipzig, where the numbers of people demonstrating rose from 50,000 on 9 October 1989 to 100,000 on the 16th, 150,000 on the 23rd and 300,000 on the 30th, and in East Berlin, where 500,000 people marched on 4 November (Prins 1990: 81, 227–8). Soviet leader Mikhail Gorbachev had made statements to the effect that he would not intervene in the changes going on in the various states that at that time formed part of the Soviet bloc. The communist leadership in East Germany had changed – Erich Honecker had given way, to be replaced by Egon Krenz. In countries all around East Germany, in Hungary, Czechoslovakia, Romania, and Poland, as well as in places such as Ukraine and Estonia which at that time were part of the Soviet Union itself, similar unrest was being expressed. By the beginning of November it had become clear to the party leadership that changes would have to be made to travel restrictions on East German citizens – by then large numbers of East Germans had been leaving the country for the West via the newly-opened borders to the West, first in Hungary and later in Czechoslovakia – 50,000 had left between 3 and 8 November via the latter route (Prins 1990: 81, 228).

BOX 7.2 THE BERLIN WALL

At the end of the Second World War in 1945, Germany was divided, for administrative purposes, between the four allied powers: Britain, France, the US and the Soviet Union (the USSR, or Union of Soviet Socialist Republics). The sector allocated to the USSR became East Germany, or the Deutsche Demokratische Republik (DDR) and the remaining three sectors West Germany, the Federal Republic of Germany. The former capital city of Germany, Berlin, situated in the Soviet zone, was also divided, and in 1961 a wall was constructed around West Berlin, to prevent citizens from the communist zone crossing to the West. The wall embodied in concrete the 'Iron Curtain' that divided West and East during the Cold War.

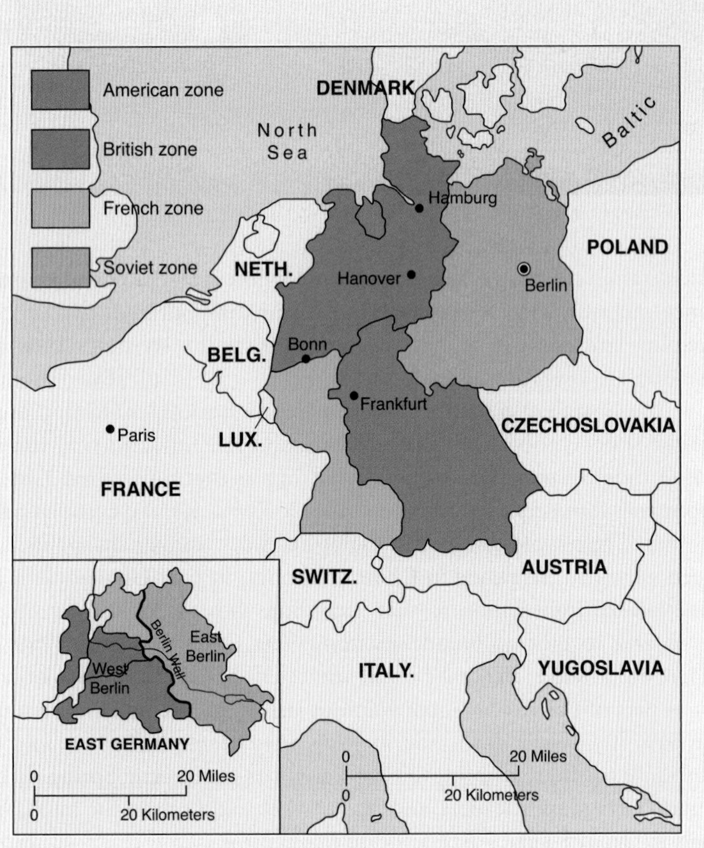

FIGURE 7.3
Berlin and the division of Germany at the end of the Second World War

Then, on 9 November at a press conference at about seven in the evening, the government Press Officer Günter Schabowski made a statement about new travel regulations that were to be established, permitting East Germans to travel to the West with appropriate visa documentation. Questioned repeatedly by the press as to when these new regulations were to come into effect, Schabowski eventually replied 'immediately': he had not been fully briefed – this was not the intention. To those listening to his announcement, the implications were unclear.

One of those who heard the announcement over the radio was Harald Jäger, on duty that evening at Bornholmer Strasse, one of the checkpoints between East and West Berlin, in his role as deputy director of the Passport Control Unit (PKA). This is his account of what happened as he was having dinner:

> I heard Schabowski's words that we had come to an arrangement whereby citizens of the GDR were permitted to travel to West Berlin or the FRG without any preconditions. In response to a question from a journalist when this would be valid the gist of Schabowski's response was: immediately. Upon this wording my dinner got stuck in my throat. I said: What is all this? What sort of intellectual diarrhoea is this? I left my dinner and immediately went into the pre-(passport) control area for leaving the country at Bornholmer Strasse in order to ring Colonel Ziegenhorn. Colonel Ziegenhorn was our superior at the time and director of the operational headquarters of the Main Division VI [Passport Control and Search] of the Ministry for State Security. The gist of Colonel Ziegenhorn's response was: 'Have you also heard the television broadcast of Schabowski'. I said: 'Yes. What should we do?'. Colonel Ziegenhorn said: 'Wait for now. There is no possibility of leaving the country under these conditions. Continue to monitor the situation at Bornholmer Strasse and call me regularly about the developing situation.'
>
> (Chronik der Mauer: no date a)

Within about half an hour, there were a large number of people – Jäger estimates around a hundred – at the checkpoint. They had heard Schabowski's statement, like Jäger, and were demanding to go through to the West. Over the next minutes and hours the crowd swelled from a few hundred to many thousands, as more people arrived to find out what was going on and to demand to be let through. Many ordinary East Berliners had heard the radio but decided at first that it was a meaningless announcement and carried on with what they were doing. Later, however, the mood changed, and people made their way to the checkpoints. This was an extremely risky thing to do: 'no East German without a visa on his passport – vetted by the secret police, the Stasi, and rarely granted – ventured near any of the city's checkpoints . . . It was a criminal offence – "unwarranted intrusion into a border area"' (Hilton 2001: 325), and there was a shoot-to-kill policy for anyone trying to climb the Wall. Many people had died in the attempt since it was built.

At Bornholmer Strasse checkpoint, Jäger called his superior again, several times, and eventually the colonel agreed that they should let a small number of people through, to ease the pressure. Those who were most pushy were to be let past, and their passports stamped on the photograph, such that they were effectively disbarred from returning. As well as the most 'provocative', others were to be let through as well, so that the crowd would not have the impression that to get through all that was needed was for them to be particularly aggressive. This was 'the bureaucracy of madness', but passport huts were opened and at around 9.20 p.m. the first people began to filter through, some with their passports stamped over the photo, some not (Hilton 2001: 331).

This action did not solve the problem for Jäger, but exacerbated it:

> The pressure increased even more. The citizens of the GDR now saw that we were letting some persons leave the country. The reason for this was not clear to them. They assumed that it would now start, that they would be permitted to leave. We had to continue to prevent them because we had the order to only let some persons leave the country and not all of them. The pressure continued to increase and the number of people at the checkpoint Bornholmer Strasse also continued to increase.
> (Chronik der Mauer: no date b).

It became clear to Jäger that something had to give. His guards were looking to him for solutions, but he was getting no help from his superiors. The crowd was waving and chanting; there was a risk, he thought, that people could panic and have been crushed, or that one of the guards might panic and fire a shot, despite the instructions they had not to use their pistols (Hilton 2001: 341–2). Jäger made up his mind:

> When I saw what could develop, that our members of staff had been driven into a corner and that the demand by the citizens of the GDR became stronger and stronger, I decided to open everything and to immediately stop passport controls.
> (Chronik der Mauer: no date c).

He was taking a great risk. 'Normally, you'd expect something to happen to you. I had refused to carry out – well, implement – the orders' (Hilton 2001: 343).

FIGURE 7.4 Berlin/Checkpoint Bornholmer Strasse, 10 November 1989. http://bobbysworld.tumblr.com/post/238267267 http://www.chronikderwende.de/bilder/704_Der_Tag_9_11_1989.jpeg

But although he didn't know it, Jäger was not alone. A similar situation was repeated at other checkpoints around the city: the pressure of ordinary East Berliners who had decided to test out the meaning of the announcement that evening for themselves, confused border guards without instructions as to what to do, and a general air of excitement and anticipation.

Once news that the Wall had been opened spread, people from all over Germany – and indeed from further afield – travelled to Berlin to see for themselves. Andreas Ramos, a Dane, writes of his visit:

> I stood with several East German guards, their rifles slung over their shoulders. I asked them if they had bullets in those things. They grinned and said no. From some houses, someone had set up loudspeakers and played Beethoven's ninth symphony: Alle Menschen werden Bruder. All people become brothers. On top of every building were thousands of people. Berlin was out of control. There was no more government, neither in East nor in West. The police and the army were helpless. The soldiers themselves were overwhelmed by the event. They were part of the crowd. Their uniforms meant nothing. The Wall was down.
>
> (Ramos 1995–2007)

GENERAL RESPONSES
AUTHORITY AND LEGITIMACY

There are a number of writers who have looked at how we should think about revolutions. We have already mentioned Theda Skocpol; others include, for example, Ted Gurr (1970), Charles Tilly (1993) and John Dunn (1989). You might be interested in following up this strand of the literature, but what we want to do here is not look at how people have thought about revolutions but rather examine a number of approaches to the question of social and political authority and community. The question that interests us in this chapter is 'Why do we obey?' and we want to turn now to focus not on revolutions but on the times in between, when we all do as we are told, or seem to.

Two thinkers who have explored the question of why we generally seem to obey sources of social and political authority, though in different ways, are Max Weber and Emile Durkheim. These two writers were part of the wave of intellectual effort that produced the disciplines of social and political theory and, more specifically, sociology, in the late nineteenth and early twentieth century. One of the inspirations behind this work was the notion that religious sources of authority – the belief in something or someone outside human society, something that transcends human experience, rather than something inside or immanent to it – were no longer what was most significant. As anthropologist Talal Asad puts it, in this period 'religion was considered to be an early human condition from which modern law, science and politics emerged and became detached' (Asad 1993: 27). Before the eighteenth century, religious sources of authority were deemed to provide the answers. A transcendent being or god was regarded as the source not only of creation but of the ethical rules and standards that we were to aspire to. Most often, punishment for disobedience to the commands of a deity was not to come in this life, but in the next. Rewards for obedience would come in heaven, not on earth. These religious views began to lose their hold with the rise of discourses of secularisation in Europe. The source of authority came to be seen as being in the individual person, or in the social and political order which individuals subscribed to. This led to the urgent need for accounts of those non-transcendent forms of authority: if what or whom we obeyed was not a transcendent godhead, what or who was it, and how were we to think through what was going on here? The social and political sciences both attempted to provide an answer and, in doing so, reinforced the move from religion to secularism that seemed to be taking place. The source of authority was relocated from a transcendent source to a source in the individual or in the society or the political order (Mavelli 2008). We return to this point when we discuss Hobbes and the English Civil War in the final part of this section.

For a discussion of the rise of secularism and the European Enlightenment, and the contrast between the religious and the secular, see **Chapter 6**. **Chapter 27** shows how the inscription of secularism in the French Constitution has practical political implications.

Alongside, and part of, the driving force of the discourse of secularism was the notion that the social sciences ought to be able to explain the social world in much the same way as the physical sciences had succeeded (as it seemed then) in explaining the natural world. In other words, it should be possible to discover the laws of social behaviour, just as scientists had discovered the laws of nature – like gravity, thermodynamics and so on. If we weren't to explain the natural world as God's creation but as the result of scientific laws, perhaps we should be able to explain the social world in the same way. However, although some later sociologists who draw on this work do see Weber and Durkheim as having striven for 'scientific' laws of society, or in other words, for generalisations that would enable us to predict and control social affairs, it is perhaps best to think of them rather differently.

Note here the link between sources of authority (what we obey, or what authorises what we do), and ideas of truth (how we know, or what authorises knowledge).

For Max Weber, the social world was a complicated affair. Although he was interested in the questions raised by Marx, concerning the interrelation of 'all institutional orders making up a social structure' (Gerth and Mills 2007: 49), he wanted to contest the Marxist view that in the end history could be accounted for by economic factors, as in historical materialism, which he saw as a monocausal account (Gerth and Mills 2007: 47). For Weber an account that tried to simplify everything down to a single over-riding cause would be misleading: in social life what happened had a multiplicity of causes. He was interested in how social structures of power worked through bureaucracy and discipline, for example, and how social differentiation in terms of economic class and social status were inter-related. He studied social structures and religion in India and in China where very different forms of differentiation – by caste, or by education – arose. He was fascinated by the way that capitalist industrialisation had happened in Europe but not in China or India. Perhaps his most famous book is *The Protestant Ethic and the Spirit of Capitalism* (1930) where he traces how the development of Calvinist religious practices of duty in a calling contributed to the conditions of possibility for the growth of capitalism in Europe. Of course, once capitalism had taken root and material goods had 'gained an increasing and finally inexorable power' over people's lives, it continued even when the practices associated with it had long ceased to have any religious meaning. As Weber so poignantly puts it 'the idea of duty in one's calling prowls about our lives like the ghost of dead religious beliefs' (Weber 1930: 182). In putting forward this argument, it was *not* his aim 'to substitute for a one-sided materialistic an equally one-sided spiritualistic causal

For more on historical materialism see **Chapter 19**.

Could Weber's work on the rise of capitalism be seen as Eurocentric or imperialist? See the discussion in **Chapter 16** of the relation between Europe's industrialisation and the impoverishment of the Indian subcontinent.

interpretation of culture and of history' (Weber 1930: 183) but rather to point to another possible starting point for further investigation, investigation which would always have to focus on the specifics of particular historical conjunctures.

One of the reasons that Weber has been misread as attempting a simple causal analysis might be his use – as an analytical tool – of what he called constructed or ideal 'types' (Gerth and Mills 2007: 294). These 'types' are an aid to thinking, and are consciously ahistorical: any real-life historical situation will, Weber insists, be much more complex. In his discussion of forms of authority he uses this method. He identifies three 'types' of authority:

> All ruling powers, profane and religious, political and apolitical, may be considered as variations of, or approximations to, certain pure types. These types are constructed by searching for the basis of *legitimacy*, which the ruling power claims. Our modern 'associations' are of the type of 'legal' authority. . . . The past has known other bases for authority, bases which, incidentally, extend as survivals into the present . . . 'charismatic authority' [and] 'traditional authority'.
>
> (Gerth and Mills 2007: 294–6)

In the modern form of legal-rational authority, 'the legitimacy of the power-holder to give commands rests upon rules that are rationally established by enactment, by agreement, or by imposition' (Gerth and Mills 2007: 294). This rests in turn on a constitution. Orders are based on these impersonal rules, not on the authority of the person giving the orders as a person. A hierarchical organisation of officials who wield power and the separation of public and private spheres go along with this form of authority. The other two 'types' of authority are different. The first of these, charismatic authority, is a form of rule to which those who obey submit because of 'their belief in the extraordinary quality of a specific person' (Gerth and Mills 2007: 295). Charismatic authority is legitimised through heroic feats, victories, miracles and the like, and disappears if these magical powers appear to vanish. The second, traditional authority, is based upon a belief in 'what actually, allegedly, or presumably has always existed' (Gerth and Mills 2007: 296). The most familiar types of traditional authority are the rule of father or husband over the household, the lord or master over the serf, the prince over officials, nobles, and vassals, and the sovereign prince over subjects. In particular historical situations, these last two forms of authority exist alongside each other, and both remain significant, even under legal-rational systems of authority.

For more on Max Weber, in particular his ideas about the state, see **Chapter 11**.

What is important here is that we have an analysis that sees power or authority as possessed by a specific and identifiable few in any society who can command the obedience of others. They are obeyed because their authority or power to command is deemed legitimate – because of either its legal-rational, charismatic or traditional basis.

For Emile Durkheim, the social realm is not just a collection of individuals, but something more, something unique and quite distinct: 'Society is a reality *sui generis*; it has its own characteristics' (Durkheim 1995: 15). This leads to certain implications:

> Precisely because society has its own specific nature that is different from our nature as individuals, it pursues ends that are also specifically its own; but because it can

> achieve those ends only by working through us, it categorically demands our cooperation. Society requires us to make ourselves its servants . . . It subjects us to all sorts of restraints, privations and sacrifices without which social life would be impossible. And so, at every instant, we must submit to rules of action and thought that we have neither made nor wanted and that sometimes are contrary to our inclinations and our most basic instincts.
>
> (Durkheim 1995: 209)

We obey these rules, not just because of any superior physical force that compels us to do so, says Durkheim, but because of the moral authority that society has: 'we defer to society's orders not simply because it is equipped to overcome our resistance but, first and foremost, because it is the object of genuine respect' (Durkheim 1995: 209). Indeed 'a society is to its members what a god is to its faithful' (Durkheim 1995: 208). In ordinary circumstances, the weight of the general view or shared convictions has enormous force; when people come together in a large gathering this is amplified and things happen and emotions are aroused that each person as an individual would be incapable of, and that all look back on afterwards with surprise (Durkheim 1995: 212). In revolutionary periods it is because of such heightened interaction and what that generates that 'people live differently and more intensely than in normal times'

BOX 7.3 THE REFORMATION IN EUROPE

The Reformation is located in what historians call the 'early-modern' period in Europe which runs from the late fifteenth to early eighteenth centuries (MacCulloch 2004). It took place in Western Christendom – an area 'almost equivalent to what would become "Europe"' (Collinson 2003: 1). According to *The Cambridge Modern History*, written in 1903,

> the Reformation of the sixteenth century had its birth and growth in a union of spiritual and secular forces such as the world has seldom seen at any other period of its history. On the secular side, the times were full of new movements, intellectual and moral, political, social, and economic; and spiritual forces were everywhere at work, which aimed at making religion the birthright and possession of the common man – whether king, noble, burgher, artisan, or peasant – as well as of the ecclesiastic, a possession which should directly promote a worthy life within the family and the State. These religious impulses had all a peculiar democratic element and were able to impregnate with passion and, for a time, to fuse together the secular forces of the period. Hence their importance historically.
>
> (Ward *et al.* 1903)

One of the best known figures is Martin Luther, born on 10 November 1483, at Eisleben. His Ninety-Five Theses, nailed to the door of the Castle Church at Wittenberg at noon on All Saint's Day, 1 November 1517, were a forthright critique of the practice of the Sale of Indulgences – for the forgiveness of sins – by the Catholic Church. His case was not just that this had become a corrupt practice, but that the Church could not in this way stand between the believer and their God. Forgiveness came from God alone, and could not be bought or sold.

(Durkheim 1995: 213). We depend on society in the way that we might depend on a religious figure, and we do what society expects us to because of that dependence.

So far then, we have looked at the way two leading figures in the new discipline of sociology – located specifically in the turn to secularism in Europe – thought about questions of power, authority and obedience. There is one further response to these questions that I want to examine, before we turn to what some of the broader questions these responses lead to might be. I want to examine the thought of Thomas Hobbes (1588–1679). His work was not part of the nineteenth-century movement towards a social science at all; he was a seventeenth-century political philosopher, concerned to rethink forms of authority in the absence of a divinity. Living in England at the time of the English Civil War, one of Hobbes' priorities was to find some arguments for stability and peace, rather than the chaos and instability into which the country had sunk. The Civil War had lasted from 1642 to 1651 and the questions at stake concerned whether the monarch should rule alone by divine right or only with the consent and under the authority of parliament – or indeed, whether parliament could rule without a sovereign.

What is the relationship between power and authority? Are they the same thing? Why do we talk of obedience to authority, but capitulation or resistance to power?

On the one hand, the authority of the pope as head of the Catholic Church had been challenged. In England the Reformation set in train a series of struggles that led

FIGURE 7.5
Title page from Thomas Hobbes' *Leviathan* (1651). http://cache.eb.com/eb/image?id=99235&rendTypeId=4

eventually to the developing view that religion should be regarded as a private affair, a matter for individual conscience, not an affair of state: different religious practices could be tolerated within one political community. The modern sovereign individual, conceived of as a separate, self-contained and self-accountable entity, was emerging. On the other hand, the authority of the monarch or sovereign was still seen as coming from God, and how this could be otherwise was yet to be thought through. Hobbes' contribution to the debates of his time did not please the royalists: he argued for a strong central authority, sovereign or commonwealth, to avoid the chaos of a war 'of every man against every man' (Hobbes 1651), but sovereign power or sovereignty – the supreme authority of the sovereign – came not from the divine right of kings but from the people, who, as sovereign individuals combining together, entered into a social contract to ensure their peace and security. In other words, sovereignty for Hobbes came not from above but from below, not from outside this world but from within it.

According to Hobbes, when individuals combine and enter into a social contract, their individual power or authority is added together to form a power greater than any of them (Hindess 1996: 24). He calls this the Leviathan: a giant man, made up of the bodies of small individual men and carrying a sceptre and a sword, as the famous illustration on his title page shows. This quantitative view of power – as something that can be added up – forms the basis of many understandings of power in social and political life. Power is seen as something that 'determines the capacity of actors to realize their will or to secure their interests' (Hindess 1996: 26). Alongside the capacity to act is the right to act: the question of the perceived *legitimacy* of the one who possesses power to exercise it. This of course, as we have seen, was the question that exercised Weber.

BROADER ISSUES
THINKING ABOUT POWER

We tend to talk about the state as if it were a person – we talk about what Britain or India does, for example, which makes it easy to talk of a state 'having power' too. Why might that be unhelpful?

To think of power in this simple, quantitative way, as some mysterious entity or substance that we can't see but that can be possessed and exercised, and which means that someone gets to do what they want to do, doesn't really help us very much. We can talk about how much power a particular person (or state) *has*, but when someone we think of as powerful – as *having* lots of power – doesn't get to do what they want, then we simply admit that maybe they had less power than we thought. In other words, this conception of power leads to some very circular arguments. On the one hand, people with power can do things, so we can tell who is powerful by looking at what people do. But on the other hand, those who look as though they do pretty much what they want we describe as powerful. This doesn't get us very far.

This argument that people might be more complex than is allowed in this notion of the sovereign individual is also explored in **Chapter 13**.

Even if we think of power like this though, there seems to be no way of telling in advance, who will turn out to have been the most 'powerful' in any particular situation. Nor, indeed is there any obvious way of knowing for certain who *has* got what they wanted: people are too complicated in terms of motivations and desires for that. And people tend not to behave all the time as the sovereign individuals they are deemed to be in modern liberal economic and political theory in any case: they may be more concerned to do what they think others want them to do than to satisfy their own wishes and desires.

For a discussion of Foucault's notion of governmentality, see **Chapter 4**.

A different way of thinking about questions of power, authority and obedience is found in the work of French political thinker Michel Foucault. He poses a basic challenge to the ways of thinking about power that we have encountered so far, ways of thinking that see a clear dividing line between those that have power or authority and those that obey, and thus see power as fundamentally repressive. In the thinking we have examined, power in someone else's hands is something that prevents us from doing what we want to do. Foucault finds this way of thinking curious:

> In defining the effects of power as repression, one adopts a purely juridical conception of power, one identifies power with a law that says no, power is taken above all as carrying the force of a prohibition. Now I believe that this is a wholly negative, narrow, skeletal conception of power, one which has been curiously widespread. If power were never anything but repressive, if it never did anything but to say no, do you really think one would be brought to obey it? What makes power hold good, what makes it accepted, is simply the fact that it doesn't only weigh on us as a force which says no, but that it traverses and produces things, it induces pleasure, forms of knowledge, produces discourse. It needs to be considered as a productive network which runs through the whole social body, much more than a negative instance whose function is repression.
>
> (Foucault 1980: 119)

In fact, Foucault argues, it is best not to talk of 'power' at all, but of 'power relations'. In all social interaction, relations of power are involved. When two people talk over coffee, when a group meets for a lecture in a university setting, when we take a walk along the beach or when we chat over the internet, in all these social relations, relations of power are involved. In some cases it might seem that power relations are all one way – for example, that your lecturer gets to do what they want, despite disruptive students such as those shown in the cartoon at the start of this chapter. And some people these days, influenced by Foucault's work in some way but not fully taking on board what he meant, talk continually of 'power relations' as if that meant the relations that people who 'have' power can exert over those that don't. In the student–supervisor relationship, when they say there are 'power relations' involved, in a dark tone of voice, these people tend to mean that one side is more power-full than the other. That is not what Foucault meant.

Foucault wanted to draw our attention to the way in which in any social relations there is a tension or a negotiation going on which traverses what is happening. Power, for Foucault, means nothing unless there is resistance. And in all social relations or interactions there are interactions of power and resistance. I will suggest the walk on the beach, perhaps, and when we get there, you might suggest which way we should go. Although you might have preferred a climb up the hillside to the beach in the first place, or I might have wanted to walk inland whereas you fancied taking a walk round the headland, we agreed on what to do and we do it. If we went our separate ways instead, we would no longer have enjoyed each other's company – which, presumably, we both wanted to do. There is clearly difference and deference – distinctions of age or gender, familiarity with the terrain, willingness to be led or to lead – which will come into play. And the interaction as we take our walk on the beach will reinforce or perhaps dislodge those differences. In other words, when we get back to the car, things will have changed: we won't be quite the people we were when we set out. Our relationship may be different; we may be different. This I think is something of what Foucault means when he says that power is a productive network that runs through all interaction, which 'traverses and produces things', 'induces pleasure, forms of knowledge, produces discourse' – and by 'discourse', he doesn't just mean the conversation we enjoyed on our walk.

What has all this talk of walks on the beach to do with the serious business of politics, authority and obedience? The point I think is that we can take this talk too seriously – by which I mean, we can believe too much in the fiction of an authority that we have to obey. It is useful to have such a fiction; as we have said before, it simplifies daily life. It also gives us something to believe in – some power above ourselves, something that will survive us, or that in the meantime, enables us to make sense of our lives. If we follow Foucault's suggestion and cut off the king's head, then there are other ways of thinking about politics.

Of course in the English Civil War, the king's head was literally cut off. What Foucault means here is somewhat different. He means that we should stop thinking in terms of some larger legitimate central authority or source of rules, which we just then have to work out how to obey. We need instead to rethink politics without the sovereign. To return to our walk – maybe our walk on the beach was not particularly significant in the grand scheme of things, but what of one man's walk along Chang'an Avenue in Beijing, or the walk thousands took to the checkpoint at Bornholmer Strasse? These were in many senses just walks too, with similar debates about whether to go, when to go, where to go and so on: in all these instances, what we are looking at is forms of social interrelations. Maybe the notion of power relations that Foucault is asking us to consider is more help here than notions of centralised, validated authority. Maybe that authority is constituted through numerous interactions and power relations. Maybe it doesn't have some sort of independent, separate existence before those interactions. Certainly, as we have seen, it is vulnerable to challenge by individuals or groups who are not what we could call 'powerful'.

Slavoj Žižek writes in 1993:

> The most sublime image that emerged in the political upheavals of the last years . . . was undoubtedly the unique picture from the violent overthrow of Ceauşescu in Romania [in December 1989]: the rebels waving the national flag with the red star, the Communist symbol, cut out, so that instead of the symbol standing for the organising principle of the national life, there was nothing but a hole in its centre.
>
> (1993: 1)

For further discussions of Slavoj Žižek and his Lacanian approach, see **Chapters 5 and 23**.

The communist authorities had been overthrown, but nothing had yet been put in place instead. Where there is no organising principle, nothing to tell us to obey, this makes a certain lack or gap in the social order visible. Žižek argues that the social order is always incomplete in this way, but that this incompleteness is generally hidden from sight by the symbol that we put at the centre of things (God, communism, the sovereign, the nation, the people). We think we are obeying an authority of some sort, one that has the force to make us comply, but what we are following is a symbol – and

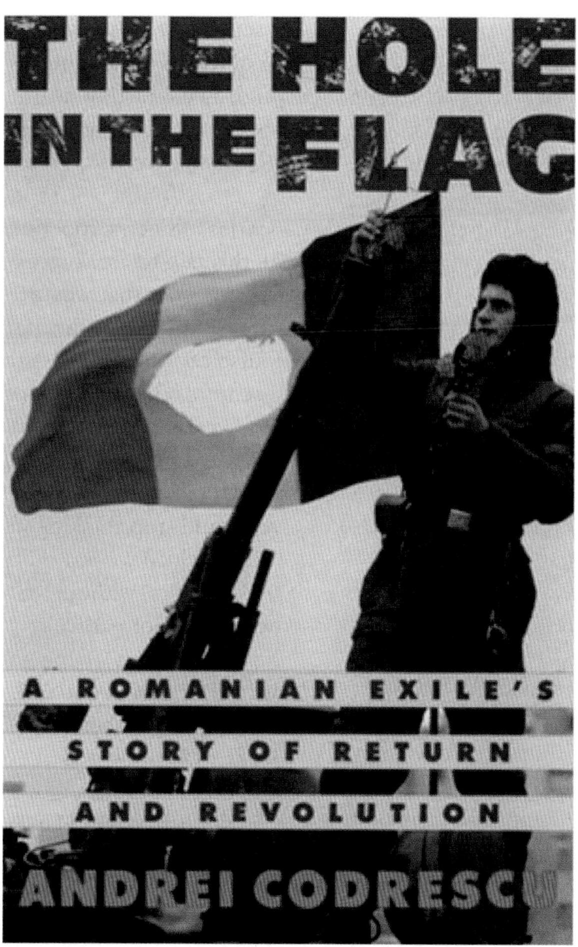

FIGURE 7.6
The hole in the Romanian Flag, 1989. Andrei Codrescu, *The Hole in the Flag: A Romanian Exile's Story of Return and Revolution*. William Morrow & Co., 1991

we need a symbol like this to conceal the emptiness, the meaninglessness, at the heart of social life.

Foucault complains that we still think of politics in terms of centralised power and the legitimation of particular forms of authority. We need, he says, to cut off the king's head – and here he means the head of the Leviathan as well. Foucauldian conceptions of power point to the need to 'think about politics in the absence of its defining constitutive fiction' (Hindess 1996: 158). This fiction is not just sovereignty, but the notion of political community – or 'society' in the Durkheimian sense.

When the revolutionaries of Eastern Europe cut the communist symbol from the centre of the flag, they did not just cut out sovereign power – the communist rule that had been overthrown – they highlighted the notion of what Žižek calls 'tarrying with the negative': the possibility of not replacing that sovereign with anything at all, not even with what we call, vaguely, political community, but rather tarrying with, or remaining in, a state of the absence of rule. Is there not perhaps always a certain absence or incompleteness to any social order or form of authority? Is it not always in some sense little more than a fiction?

Taking this sort of approach would lead us to think of *relations* as what we should be studying – relations of *power* in the Foucauldian sense among them of course – and how those relations produce the entities at their nodal points as well as the hub (community, society, etc.) that the relations appear to centre around. Note that we do not need to say *social* relations, or limit ourselves to relations between *people*. Bruno Latour is interested in exploring the role of things in the interrelationships that he studies. Things – materialities – he says, should be seen as part of the collectives we study – 'collective' being the word he chooses to replace the word 'society' (Latour 2005: 25). Think of the role of the Wall in the example we discussed in this chapter. Do materialities like these not form a vital part of the relations we want to think about? Doesn't limiting politics to people or human beings (however blatantly obvious and unquestionable it may seem to do so) already concede that the type of community or relation we are thinking of is one defined by exclusion – the exclusion of whatever, at that particular moment of history, counts as non-human, or imperfectly human: women, non-Whites, children and the poor are or were at one time regarded as insufficiently human to vote, and thus excluded from the political community, for example. Though it might seem ridiculous to take this as far as questioning the distinction between the animate and the inanimate, there is some sense in which all our distinctions are insecure and open to change.

The fence between Mexico and the US discussed in **Chapter 10** might be a similar example.

Chapters 5, 16, 21 and 27 discuss these types of exclusions.

In their study of Paris, Latour and photographer Emilie Hermant explore the networks of interactions that produce the city of Paris – the work of individuals and agencies that designate the streets with the names that then appear on the maps that visitors use to make their way around the city and on the walls of the buildings that line those streets, for example, or the way that the fabric of the city is continually built and rebuilt, and its changes and famous inhabitants charted in wall plaques and signs, by a network of engineers, surveyors and stone-masons (Latour and Hermant 1998). The body of the city, like a human body, 'resembles', according to Latour, 'a jet of water that maintains its shape through the swift movement of countless tiny drops, each adding its minute contribution to the slightly trembling form' (Latour and Hermant 1998: Plan 52). Both the body and the built fabric of the city can be rebuilt, stone by stone or cell by cell, and can remain the same and yet different. Stop the movement and there is nothing: 'a gurgling at the bottom of a greenish basin; a corpse; a crumbling ruin' (Latour and Hermant 1998: Plan 52). Latour argues that political bodies like the French state or the municipal council of Paris are similar, and neither more nor less durable.

At the end of their study, they return to the question of power. They argue that the networks that frame life occupy only a tiny space:

> The word 'power' changes meaning. It no longer denotes states of unquestionable things. . . . There is indeed power; that is, force, virtualities, empowerment, a dispersed plasma just waiting to take shape. . . . Yes, the power is invisible, but like the virtual, like the plasma, like the perpetual transformations of buildings and bodies.
>
> (Latour and Hermant 1998: Plan 53)

The power of the sovereign or the king or the state is no more fixed than is a human body or a building: like these, it is always in the process of transformation, always being rebuilt. Relations of power and their intricate movements are what matter, in other words, not the power-full and the power-less.

CONCLUSION

We have taken a journey in this chapter, a walk even, beginning with the question of why we obey, how we might think about what makes forms of power and authority in 'society' work, and what it might mean to disobey. We examined moments when it seemed that the authority of well established and repressive systems of government might be being challenged – in one case the challenge seemed to fail, whereas in the other it seemed, for a moment at least to succeed. We have not of course examined what happened next in East Germany or the rest of what was the Eastern European Communist bloc. Some commentators might argue that the hope for new possibilities – talk of a 'third way' between communism and capitalism, for example, was widespread in 1989 – did not materialise. After all, the former communist states became in short order obedient parts of the capitalist world. And, finally, we explored some other ways of thinking about the workings of relations – through notions of power relations and networks – in what we used to call social life.

FURTHER READING

Foucault, Michel (2000) 'The Subject and Power', in *Essential Works of Foucault 1954–1984*, ed. Paul Rabinow, New York: The New Press.
This short piece by Foucault, which first appeared in 1982, gives a good account of how he sees his work on power, including why we should study the 'subject' and how one should analyse power relations.

Hindess, Barry (1996) *Discourses of Power: from Hobbes to Foucault*, Oxford: Blackwell.
Useful discussion of power that distinguishes power as capacity and power as right, and contains chapters on notions of power in critical theory and John Locke, as well as Hobbes and Foucault.

Latour, Bruno (2005) *Reassembling the Social: An Introduction to Actor-Network-Theory*, Oxford: Oxford University Press.
Elaborates on Actor-Network-Theory and how it differs from other approaches to sociology; the website 'Paris: the invisible city' (listed below) does the same job in a different format.

Weber, Max (1930) *The Protestant Ethic and the Spirit of Capitalism*, trans. T. Parsons, London: Unwin.
A fascinating and classic account of the relation between the particular rationalism underlying industrial capitalism in the West and the ethics of certain Protestant sects.

WEBSITES

The Berlin Wall/Berliner Mauer 1961–1989, Senate Chancellery, Governing Mayor of Berlin, http://www.berlin.de/mauer/oeffnung/index.en.html
Gives full details, with maps, of remaining sections of the Wall, memorial sites and former border crossing points, as well as a section on the opening and fall of the Wall.

Chronik der Mauer (in German) Bundeszentrale für politische Bildung, Deutschlandradio, and Zentrum für Zeithistorische Forschung Potsdam e.V., http://www.chronik-der-mauer.de/index.php
Gives a day-by day account of events with links to video clips and broadcasts.

Foucault on Bachelard (in French), http://www.youtube.com/watch?v=kAwWwQZ_3FQ
A gem of a clip (2 min) of Foucault talking about the problem of obediently following prescribed reading lists or sticking to canonical texts.

Latour, Bruno and Emilie Hermant (1998) *Paris: Invisible City*. Available online at http://www.bruno-latour.fr/virtual/EN/index.html
In this online essay, Latour introduces Actor-Network-Theory (ANT) through a study of 'Paris' accompanied by Hermant's photographs.

Lutteroth, Jule (2004) 'Wir kommen jetzt öfter', 9 November, Spiegel Online, http://www.spiegel.de/panorama/zeitgeschichte/0,1518,326184,00.html

Thomas, Antony (2006) *Tiananmen Square: The Tank Man*, Cutting Edge Documentary, 90 mins. PBS Frontline, 11 April 2006, http://www.pbs.org/wgbh/pages/frontline/tankman/ or at http://video.google.com/videoplay?docid=4727787930108202470
Documentary about the man who stood in front of the tank, and the surrounding events during the Tiananmen Square protests in 1989 and since.

REFERENCES

Asad, Talal (1993) *Genealogies of Religion: Discipline and Reasons of Power in Christianity and Islam*, Baltimore, MD: Johns Hopkins University Press.

Bauman, Zygmunt (1991) *Modernity and the Holocaust*, Ithaca, NY: Cornell University Press.

Chronik der Mauer (no date a) http://www.chronik-der-mauer.de/index.php/de/Media/VideoPopup/day/9/field/audio_video/id/14521/month/November/oldAction/Detail/oldModule/Chronical/year/1989.

Chronik der Mauer (no date b) http://www.chronik-der-mauer.de/index.php/de/Media/VideoPopup/day/9/field/audio_video/id/14524/month/November/oldAction/Detail/oldModule/Chronical/year/1989.

Chronik der Mauer (no date c) http://www.chronik-der-mauer.de/index.php/de/Media/VideoPopup/day/9/field/audio_video/id/14538/month/November/oldAction/Detail/oldModule/Chronical/year/1989.

Collinson, Patrick (2003) *The Reformation*, London: Weidenfeld and Nicolson.

Dunn, John (1989) *Modern Revolutions: An Introduction to the Analysis of a Political Phenomenon*, 2nd edn, Cambridge: Cambridge University Press.

Durkheim, Emile (1995) *The Elementary Forms of the Religious Life*, trans. K. E. Fields, New York: The Free Press.

Foucault, Michel (1980) 'Truth and Power', in *Power/Knowledge: Selected Interviews and Other Writings 1972–1977 by Michel Foucault*, ed. Colin Gordon, Brighton: Harvester; also published as Michel Foucault (2000) 'Truth and Power', *Essential Works of Foucault 1954–1984*, ed. P. Rabinow, New York: The New Press.

Gerth, H. H. and C. Wright Mills (2007) *From Max Weber: Essays in Sociology*, London: Routledge.

Gurr, Ted R. (1970) *Why Men Rebel*, Princeton, NJ: Princeton University Press.

Hilton, Christopher (2001) *The Wall: The People's Story*, Stroud: Sutton Publishing.

Hindess, Barry (1996) *Discourses of Power: From Hobbes to Foucault*, Oxford: Blackwell.

Hobbes, Thomas (1651) *Leviathan*. Available in several editions, and online at, for example, http://oregonstate.edu/instruct/phl302/texts/hobbes/leviathan-contents.html.

Lanzmann, Claude (1995) *Shoah: The Complete Text of the Acclaimed Holocaust Film*, New York: Da Capo Press.

Latour, Bruno (2005) *Reassembling the Social: An Introduction to Actor-Network-Theory*, Oxford: Oxford University Press.

Latour, Bruno and Emilie Hermant (1998) *Paris: Invisible City*, http://www.bruno-latour.fr/virtual/EN/index.html.

MacCulloch, Diarmaid (2004) *Reformation: Europe's House Divided 1490–1700*, London: Penguin.
Mavelli, Luca (2008) 'Beyond Secularism: Immanence and Transcendence in the Political Thought of William E. Connolly', in Alan Finlayson and Samuel Chambers (eds), *Becoming Plural: The Political Thought of William E. Connolly*, London: Routledge.
Mommsen, Wolfgang J. (1990) *Max Weber and German Politics 1890–1920*, trans. M. S. Steinberg, Chicago: University of Chicago Press.
Prins, Gwyn (ed.) (1990) *Spring in Winter: The 1989 Revolutions*, Manchester: Manchester University Press.
Ramos, Andreas (1995–2007) *A Personal Account of The Fall of the Berlin Wall: The 11th and 12th of November, 1989*, http://www.andreas.com/berlin.html.
Skocpol, Theda (1979) *States and Social Revolutions: A Comparative Analysis of France, Russia and China*, Cambridge: Cambridge University Press.
Thomas, Antony (2006) *Tiananmen Square: The Tank Man*, Cutting Edge Documentary, 90 mins. PBS Frontline, 11 April 2006, http://www.pbs.org/wgbh/pages/frontline/tankman/.
Tilly, Charles (1993) *European Revolutions 1492–1992*, Oxford: Blackwell.
Ward, A. W., G. W. Prothero and Stanley Leathes (1903) *The Cambridge Modern History Vol. 2*. Cambridge: Cambridge University Press, http://www.questia.com/reader/.
Weber, Max (1930) *The Protestant Ethic and the Spirit of Capitalism*, trans. T. Parsons, London: Unwin.
Žižek, Slavoj (1993) *Tarrying with the Negative: Kant, Hegel and the Critique of Ideology*, Durham, NC: Duke University Press.

For a range of further resources supporting this chapter, please visit the companion website for *Global Politics, 2nd Edition* at www.routledge.com/cw/edkins/

CHAPTER 8

How do we find out what's going on in the world?

Debbie Lisle

THE QUESTION
THE MEDIATION OF INFORMATION

All of our questions about global politics – about war, famine, migration, protest, violence – assume that we *already know* what counts as a significant world event. It is as if we are all-knowing and God-like creatures – swirling around the heavens looking down on all sorts of important and fascinating activities. Much as we would like such omniscient powers, the reality is that we are all stuck here on earth, each of us rooted to a particular time and place, and each of us armed only with specific and partial knowledge about the world. So before we answer the question of finding out what's going on in the world, we have to recognize our own 'situated-ness'; that is, how our own particular time and place shapes the way we come to know the world. Recognizing our specific position means that nobody has first-hand access to activities and events going on outside of their specific and immediate context. That information must be gathered, constructed and sent to us through various forms of

Though we may think we have exclusive knowledge that we should convey to others: see **Chapter 21**.

Chapter 5 shows how we are situated before even being born.

technology (for example, television screens, internet connections, radio frequencies, mobile phones), and we must have the appropriate equipment and skills to receive and understand this information. This chapter explores this process of communication – how information from one context is delivered to another context – by looking at how global politics is shaped, constructed, represented and disseminated by mass media institutions and interpreted by mass audiences. In short, it looks at what happens to information as it moves through the media.

Some form of media – some technology of representation – is necessary in any form of communication. As Neil Postman argues, we couldn't know anything in the world without different forms of media to convey information:

The importance of language games and pictures of the world is discussed in **Chapter 2**.

> The information, the content, or, if you will, the 'stuff' that makes up 'the news of the day' did not exist – could not exist – in a world that lacked the media to give it expression. I do not mean things like fires, wars, murders and love affairs

BOX 8.1 NEIL POSTMAN

Postman was one of the pioneers of media and communication studies, and wrote a very important book entitled *Amusing Ourselves To Death* (1987). He was interested in how television, as a specific technology of communication, shapes the information we receive. Postman argues that American television privileges image over content, and therefore feeds the audience 'dumbed-down' entertainment rather than rational political argument. As an example, Postman offers the following:

> it is implausible to imagine that anyone like our twenty-seventh President, the multi-chinned, three-hundred pound William Howard Taft, could be put forward as a presidential candidate in today's world. The shape of a man's body is largely irrelevant to the shape of his ideas when he is addressing a public in writing or on the radio, or, for that matter, in smoke signals. But it is quite relevant on television. The grossness of a three-hundred-pound image, even a talking one, would overwhelm any logical or spiritual subtleties conveyed by speech . . . You cannot do political philosophy on television. Its form works against the content.
>
> (1987: 7)

Simply put, a fat person – no matter how persuasive their views – would never be elected president because he or she would not look good on television. Postman's argument is that we have allowed television to set the agenda for political debate, and because television favours image-friendly sound-bites, we ignore many sane and viable political ideas that may not be easily conveyed through such an image-conscious medium. For Postman, the *form* that this information passes through (that is, television) is shaping the *content* of political debate (that is, it only allows those arguments that can be made quickly by beautiful people relying on images and sound-bites). He contrasts the current situation of television with nineteenth-century public meetings when large audiences regularly gathered to listen to political debates that lasted up to 7 hours (1987: 45–50). Can you imagine that? *Seven* hours! Postman argues that television has shrunk our attention spans so much that we can barely focus on political issues for 7 minutes, let alone 7 hours.

> did not, ever and always, happen in places all over the world. I mean that lacking a technology to advertise them, people could not attend to them, could not include them, in their daily business.
>
> (1987: 7–8)

When Postman's argument is applied to the study of global politics, we see that the objects, issues and events we usually study (for example, wars, revolutions, invasions, treaties) do not even exist without the media – without the technologies of communication – to express them. So while it is certainly important to study objects, issues and events in global politics – the 'stuff' that makes up 'the news of the day' – it is also important to study the process by which that information is gathered, shaped, disseminated and received. Indeed, most of us do not form our opinions about global politics by going directly to Baghdad, or Kabul, or the Pentagon (the US Department of Defense). But we do form our opinions based on what we receive about these events from various media sources like television programmes, webpages, newspaper articles and Twitter feeds. Moreover, even those people who do travel directly to war zones – diplomats, soldiers, journalists, experts – form their opinions and create solutions based on information they receive from the media. Another way to say this is that all objects, issues and events in global politics are mediated. That is, we know about them, and formulate our opinions on them, by consuming and interpreting media representations (Debrix and Weber, 2003). Surely, then, it is important to explore how our opinions about global politics – about whether it was right to intervene in Iraq, about whether human rights should be universal, about the extent of American dominance – are shaped and influenced by the mass media.

Of course global politics is about many things as well as these, as the various chapters in the textbook show.

The way we access information has changed over recent years. **Chapter 9** discusses how the way we use the internet makes a difference.

In this chapter, we will be exploring the process of mediation in two registers. First, we will look at the news media which gathers and delivers information in an immediate and direct manner. This incorporates the journalists, cameramen/women and photojournalists who are 'on the ground' at specific events and whose information and images are delivered to mass audiences through, for example, television news channels, newspapers, radio stations, webpages and blogs. In the study of global politics, this is what most people think of when questions of the media arise. But there is a second and very important register that reflects on the 'news of the day' after the fact, and shapes it into a more coherent, convincing and long-lasting narrative. Here, I'm referring to films, documentaries, novels and television series that take the central issues of global politics (war, for example) as their subject matter. It is very important to address these reconstructed narratives of global politics for they often turn complex news stories with multiple viewpoints into a single, sanitized narrative that appears inevitable, natural and difficult to contest. Indeed, there is a great deal to think about regarding the differences between immediate representations of global politics (like television news) and belated reconstructions of those events (like war films). Which is more powerful, and why? Which is more moving, and why?

The importance of the stories we tell about who we are – our identity – is discussed in **Chapter 5**, and the political implications of ways whole regions of the world are represented in **Chapter 23**.

It is tempting to understand the process of media communication through a relatively simple 'transmission model'; that is, an unambiguous message is transmitted from a sender through the media to a receiver (Fiske, 1990: 6–23). However, this view is problematic because it assumes the media are a neutral conduit for relaying information when in fact all media expressions are inevitably biased; that is, they 'lean towards a particular view of a given issue (Burton, 1997: 226). Such a simplified model ignores the situated-ness of those people constructing media stories and the fact that their partial view of the world shapes the choice of issues and events to cover and the manner in which those choices are editorialized. More importantly, categorizing the media as a neutral vehicle for information delivery assumes that journalists and media producers have direct access to some clear, unmediated truth that they can faithfully record and transmit to audiences. But nobody – not even the most rigorous news reporter – enjoys such a privileged and omniscient access to reality. As Chapter 2 explained, that access is inevitably partial and biased not just because of our situated-ness, but also because we operate with already established pictures of the world which privilege some issues, groups and policies and exclude others. This goes for elite media producers just as much as it goes for millions of audience members. This problem of bias is especially important when it comes to the news media which purports to be simply conveying information in a neutral manner rather than actively constructing it according to an overarching agenda. In this sense, the news media are always pursuing an impossible goal: they strive for a neutral and objective reporting of events, knowing that such accuracy can never be achieved. Bias is not something the media can escape: there is no possibility of representing the world in a way that doesn't also advocate a particular – and necessarily biased – picture of the world. Once we recognize our own situated-ness, discount the neutrality of the media and acknowledge that all information is mediated, noble journalistic goals such as 'the pursuit of truth' become very complicated indeed.

Established pictures of the world tend to privilege Western approaches (see **Chapters 16 and 20**), assume a neo-liberal approach to economics (**Chapters 19 and 20**) and conceal women's perspectives (**Chapters 5 and 17**), for example.

With these insights about situated-ness and bias in mind, how do we even begin to answer the question of finding out what's going on in the world? This chapter offers three ways to begin. First, it explores the fundamental issue of bias with respect to news media representations of war and tracks the contradictory role of the news media as either a watchdog on government or a mouthpiece for its policies. Second, the chapter pulls back from these specific examples to examine wider questions about the media's role in democratic society. Does the media offer a genuine plurality of viewpoints, or does it pretend to do so while actually offering us a singular viewpoint that protects elite power? And finally, this chapter uses a reconstructed media representation – a popular Hollywood war film – to explore the different ways audience members interpret stories of war. By delivering the 'truth' about war through an unashamed mobilization of our emotions (for example, pride, empathy, fear), reconstructed mediations of war often have a much longer-lasting and widespread impact on audiences.

ILLUSTRATIVE EXAMPLE
MEDIA BIAS: NEWS REPRESENTATIONS OF WAR

In the UK, the media are understood as the 'Fourth Estate'; that is, the news media pride themselves on their independence from power, and their ability to advocate public interest by acting as a watchdog on the government. This ability to act as a check and balance on the government may be quite uncontentious in the normal course of events, but is seriously tested during times of war when the government puts pressure on the media to support its pro-war stance and help to mobilize public support in their readers,

Do the findings of the 2011–12 public enquiry under the chairmanship of Lord Justice Leveson in the UK, investigating alleged links between the news media, the police and politicians, throw any idea of the media as a watchdog into doubt?

viewers and listeners. In other words, the government wants to discourage the watchdog tendencies of the media during times of war so their decisions will be supported rather than questioned and critiqued. One way governments curb the intrusion of the media is by protecting and classifying information in the name of national security – in effect, they practise a form of official censorship. When the media fail to question such efforts by the government, a rather cosy pro-war consensus is established between government policy, media stories and public opinion. In this mode, the media do not act as a watchdog, but rather as a mouthpiece for the government. It is as if the government is willing to tolerate the pesky watchdog antics of the media during the normal course of events, but when we go to war the media must get in line, stop asking difficult questions and uncritically advocate the government's decisions.

These two positions are never as clear-cut as I suggest, and it is therefore helpful to think of the government and media in a constant tug-of-war: the government wants the news media to act as a mouthpiece to generate public consensus, and the news media want to act more like a watchdog by holding the government to account. Neither ever completely succeeds, and as these three examples illustrate, using reductive categories of 'watchdog' and 'mouthpiece' invokes a problematic causal relationship between the news media and public opinion (that is, the idea that the news media can single-handedly influence and change what we think) that effaces the way new media technologies shape the story.

The Vietnam War (1960–75)

This war has come to be understood as the most important lesson for any modern government trying to control the media during times of war. The historical context of the war is important: it was taking place at the same time as the mass media were developing with unprecedented speed in the Western world. Radio was still popular, but television was quickly becoming the medium of choice; indeed, Vietnam is often referred to as the first television war. As well, this was the era when photojournalism flourished, and many photographers such as Tim Page, Larry Burrows and Don McCullin became famous when their picture essays were published in broadsheet newspapers and Sunday supplements.

The Vietnam War is significant because Western journalists, photographers and cameramen had unprecedented access to the battlefield and tried to cover all aspects of the war. This proliferation of stories, photographs and newsreel coverage meant that Western audiences were confronted with increasingly graphic images of conflict every morning in their newspapers and every night on the television news. These graphic media stories were very different from the patriotic newsreels people remembered seeing at the cinema during World War II, and gradually audiences began to turn against the war. One of the most famous images that galvanized anti-war sentiment across the world was taken by Nick Ut in 1972. It shows a young girl named Phan Thi Kim Phuc running down the street fleeing a Napalm attack. Her clothes have been burned off, and her face conveys both shock and terror. It was images like this that prompted media theorist Marshall McLuhan to state that 'Television brought the brutality of the war into the comfort of the living room. Vietnam was lost in the living rooms of America – not on the battlefields of Vietnam' (1975).

Even though the patriotic newsreels did not show this, World War II was extremely violent: see **Chapter 22**.

BOX 8.2 DON MCCULLIN, WAR PHOTOGRAPHER

Don McCullin started his photography career on the streets of North London, but became famous for covering conflicts in Cyprus, Beirut and Vietnam. This image of a shell-shocked US Marine was taken in Vietnam during the Battle for Hue City in 1968. Like many photographers, McCullin started out by wanting to get close to the action: 'I don't believe you can see what's beyond the edge unless you put your head over it; I've many times been right up to the precipice, not even a foot or an inch away. That's the only place to be if you're going to see and show what suffering really means' (Bannon and Eastman House, 2003: 677). But after years of covering war-zones, McCullin became depressed about the morally ambiguous position of the war photographer: if you are a witness to such suffering, shouldn't you try and help instead of standing back and taking pictures? McCullin himself has done both – he has helped wounded soldiers, but he has also taken pictures where he could have intervened. This tricky position made McCullin seriously question the morality of his chosen profession, and he spent much of the 1990s taking pictures of the tranquil Somerset landscape. Recently, however, he has returned to photography by documenting the conflict in Syria, but also wider social issues such as AIDS in Africa.

FIGURE 8.1
Portrait of a shell-shocked marine, Hue, Vietnam, 1968. Photo: Don McCullin

This assertion – that media images caused Western audiences to turn against the war – assumes that the media started off in mouthpiece mode writing stories that generally aligned with military policy, but switched to watchdog mode as the prolonged horrors of the war became apparent (it is usually claimed that the My Lai massacre in 1968 in which American forces killed hundreds of innocent Vietnamese was the decisive turning point). Although media scholars have refuted this simplified claim by detailing a much more complex relationship between media images, public opinion and government policy during the Vietnam War (showing, for example how the Western media followed the political elite in Washington), 'the media lost us Vietnam' remains the dominant narrative of the war (Hallin, 1986; Williams, 1993). That simplified consensus taught the American government and military two valuable lessons: (a) never allow the media unrestricted access to the battlefield; and (b) always practise news management by controlling the stories that are given to the media, and by extension, to the public.

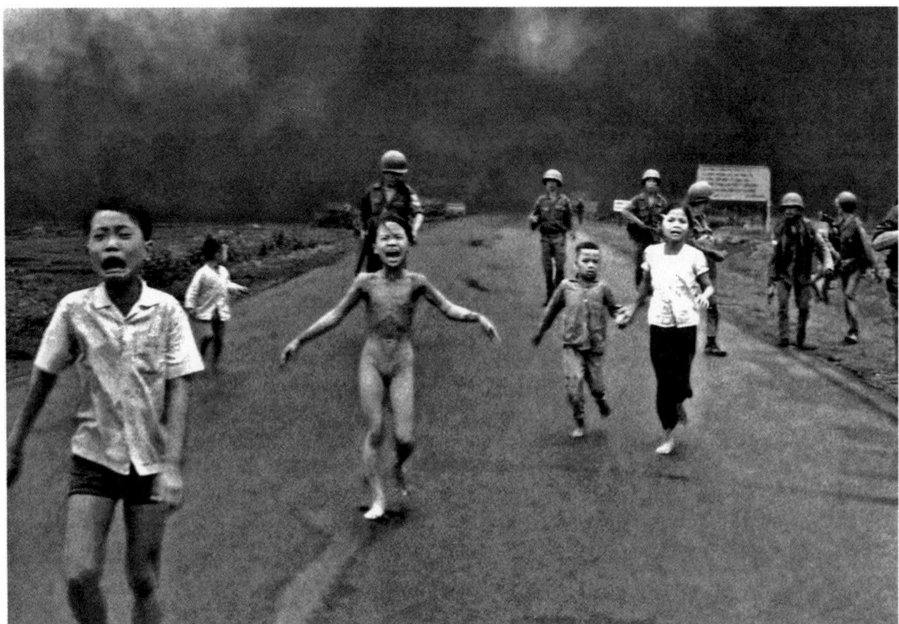

FIGURE 8.2
Napalm attack.
Photo: Nick Ut/AP

The Gulf War (1990–91)

By the time the Gulf War started in 1990, the American government and military had fully taken on board the simplified narrative that the media had lost them the Vietnam War. It created a new body – the Department of Defense News Media Pool (DoDNMP) – that was put in place to effectively control and manage the news media's access to the battlefield. Structurally, this involved organizing reporters into official pools with military escorts, giving official news briefings about military operations, restricting the travel and movement of journalists, and subjecting all copy written by journalists to a 'formal security review' (Tumber and Palmer, 2004: 3). Unsurprisingly, this situation was very unpopular with the news media who argued that they could not do their jobs properly – as watchdogs – if they were not given direct access to the battlefield. As war correspondent P. J. O'Rourke explained at the time:

> You may wonder what the job of being a Gulf War journalist is like. Well, we spend all day broadcasting on the radio and TV telling people back home what's happening over here. And we learn what's happening over here by spending all day monitoring the radio and TV broadcasts from back home. You may also wonder how any actual information ever gets into this loop. If you find out, please call.
>
> (1992: 196)

What is important to remember about the Gulf War is that the over-riding relationship between the media and the government was consensual. Either because the media were successfully managed – and even censored – by the military's news management practices, or because they reflected a general public support for the military intervention, the Western media generally supported this war.

BOX 8.3 THE CNN EFFECT

Piers Robinson defines the 'CNN effect' as 'the ability of real-time communications technology, via the news media, to provoke major responses from domestic audiences and political elites to both global and national events' (2002: 2). Certainly there are significant historical examples of media images shaping and even provoking public and government action, for example, television images of the Ethiopian famine in 1984 mobilized millions to donate money and put pressure on their governments to send aid (Philo, 1993). After the Gulf War however, the media seemed to have more power to shape foreign policy decisions about interventions in Bosnia, Somalia, Kosovo and Rwanda. The CNN effect continues to be debated by media analysts, military press officers and governments, especially the extent to which the news media can cause or provoke a policy response, and whether the media only speeds up foreign policy actions that were already in preparation.

But it is also important to remember that the changing media–military relationship in the Gulf War was developing in a new and different context. If Vietnam was the first television war, then this was the first information war where, for the first time, news was broadcast 24/7 all around the globe. This meant that news was conveyed in real-time on channels like CNN, and people could watch live footage of scud missiles being launched, bombs exploding, and troops firing weapons. Journalists, reporters, military press officers, editors and news producers were forced to adapt to a completely transformed news cycle in which they responded to 'live-feed' images without the usual context or background – and they did this around the clock. Such intense media saturation during the Gulf War intensified the idea that the news media can determine how governments respond to international crises. Indeed, throughout the 1990s people identified the 'CNN effect' in which the military no longer works in a *pre-emptive* mode (that is, controlling and censoring reporters during war), but now works in a *reactive* mode where it is forced to respond – sometimes militarily – to issues raised by the media.

The Iraq War (2003)

By the time the decision to invade Iraq was taken, the world was still recovering from one of the biggest media events in history: the attack on the Twin Towers on 11 September 2001. The intense media scrutiny that surrounded this event carried over into the reporting of the subsequent invasions of Afghanistan and Iraq. Once again, the US military sought to re-establish its control over the media – this time by implementing a system of embedding more than 600 US and international reporters who lived, worked and travelled with selected military units.

11 September 2001, was followed by what was called the war on terror, and the Iraq war was part of that: see **Chapters 2 and 26**.

By offering 'a first-hand, up-close view of combat missions', the military used the strategy of embedding to get the media back 'on side' after the contentious relationship that had developed between the two institutions during the 1990s (Pfau *et al.*, 2004: 75). But the strategy of embedded journalism actually allowed the military to exercise a new and more subtle form of information management. For example, all embedded journalists had to sign a lengthy contract which restricted what they were allowed to report (for example, nothing on future operations, no photographs of prisoners of war) and prevented them from carrying private mobile phones or satellite telephones, or travelling in their own vehicles (Tumber and Palmer, 2004: 16). Such strategies of information control seriously compromised the media's ability to act as a watchdog because each reporter effectively became a member of the military troop. Journalists bonded with soldiers (often using 'we' in their stories) and were entirely dependent on the military for transport, food and security. As a result, even the most experienced journalist became, in effect, a propaganda tool for the government (McLane, 2004: 82–3).

One of the things that distinguished the Iraq War from previous conflicts was the increasing use of internet news sources and blogs. For those fed up with the spin emanating from Western news agencies and looking for war coverage not compromised by embedded reporting or vetted by the Pentagon, it was possible to access news from independent media sites such as the *Independent Media Centre* (www.indymedia.org), or from Arab media sources such as *Al Jazeera* (http://english.aljazeera.net/News). Moreover, many people were taking control of this medium in an active way by posting ideas, images and commentary on web pages and blogs. Indeed, the Iraq war ushered in the era of the 'warblog' where established journalists (for example, Arianna Huffington on www.Huffingtonpost.com/theblog), soldiers stationed in Iraq (for example, 'My War: Killing Time in Iraq' at http://cbftw.blogspot.com) and concerned citizens offered personal interpretations and generated web-based discussion about the war. One of the most popular warblogs during the conflict – 'Where is Raed?' (http://dear_raed.blogspot.com/) – was run by Salam Pax, an ordinary Iraqi citizen who uploaded reports about daily life in a war zone. It was on these websites and warblogs that the information war charted a new course. The gathering and dissemination of news was no longer the province of established media institutions: the birth of citizen journalism meant that anyone with internet access and computer skills could contribute to the unfolding story. The power and reach of the internet for disseminating news became undeniable when infamous images from the war – digital photographs of American soldiers torturing Iraqis at the Abu Ghraib prison, video clips of Al Qaeda beheading one of its kidnap victims, and mobile phone shots of Saddam Hussein being hanged – were circulated globally and discussed widely. This is not to suggest that the internet is always truthful or accurate, but it is to recognize that during the Iraq War, the internet became a crucial forum where ordinary people could access both official and alternative news sources, participate in online discussions about the war, disseminate controversial links and images and actively shape this news story.

This active use of Web 2.0 technology has developed much further since then and has played a significant role in posting information about events – and especially the impact of violence on people – within the so-called Arab Spring: see **Chapter 9**.

For more on what happened at Abu Ghraib and how this became possible see **Chapter 2**.

As James Der Derian (2001) has argued, we can no longer understand the operation of modern war without examining its *virtual* character – how military organizations, diplomats and statesmen are making use of computer technology and virtual networks in order to better mobilize for combat. Equally, we need to pay careful attention to the increasing use of social media in political struggles, conflicts and revolutions. As academic and media commentator David Campbell argues regarding the political unrest in North Africa and the Middle East in 2011, claims that Twitter and Facebook caused the revolutions are misplaced and grossly oversimplified (Campbell, 2011). Certainly social networking is an important part of the new media landscape, but it is – like the telegraph and telephone before it – simply a technology of communication, and the

The use of new media in the Arab Spring, and questions concerning the governance and control of these new technologies, are discussed in **Chapter 9**.

BOX 8.4 JAMES DER DERIAN'S MIMENET

James Der Derian argues that we can no longer think of society as a simple military-industrial complex in which the government, business elites and the military run things in a cosy triad. Contemporary society must now be understood as a *military–industrial–media–entertainment–network* – or MIMENET – in which technologies such as computer simulations have erased the line between the virtual world and the real world. He explains, for example, how Hollywood has joined forces with the military to produce computer generated 'simulation-based training environments' in order to make combat *more real* for soldiers in training. Why practise killing 'fake' enemies when you can kill very realistic computer-generated ones? Such simulations are also shaping the thoroughly digitized battlefield as soldiers now rely on computer technologies to transform foreign territory into fully functional 3-D images that help them effectively track, expose and target their enemies. Der Derian is concerned with how all this computer technology effectively sanitizes the consequences of war: what happens when enemies are reduced to pixels on a screen – when war is effectively reduced to a video game? He argues that we are living in an age of '*virtuous war*' where violence is executed 'from a distance – *with no or minimal casualties*' (Der Derian, 2001: xv). This distance radically changes the soldier's moral proximity to the enemy who has now become thoroughly dehumanized and digitized. As Der Derian argues, 'virtuous war has an unsurpassed power to commute death, to keep it out of sight, out of mind. Herein lies its most morally dubious danger. In simulated preparations and virtual executions of war, there is a high risk that one learns how to kill but not to take responsibility for it' (Der Derian, 2001: xvi).

real questions we need to be asking are about who uses and controls it, how its bias operates, and whose interests it is serving.

These examples of the changing relationships between the news media/military/government/public during war are instructive, for they show us how information is transformed during the process of communication. Whether it is the government trying to control journalists' access to the battlefield, reporters trying to reveal the military's less palatable actions to audiences back home or audiences putting forward their own version of events, it is clear that nobody remains neutral in their efforts to use and abuse information during war. With the never-ending struggle between the media as either watchdog or mouthpiece, audiences must try to distinguish between truth, fact, spin, propaganda, rhetoric and analysis. No wonder that millions of us have taken matters into our own hands by tweeting, posting and blogging our own views about global politics!

GENERAL RESPONSES
THE MEDIA, POWER AND DEMOCRACY

These two primary roles of the media in society (as either watchdog or mouthpiece) are explained, analysed and developed by two contrasting schools of thought. It seems there is no way to resolve the contradictory position of the media in society: it will always be both watchdog and mouthpiece. At the heart of this debate is a fundamental disagreement over the extent to which the media can influence government actions – especially with respect to foreign policy. Those from the pluralist tradition argue that the media is only ever there to serve the public interest and keep democratic values alive. In this sense, the media is always in watchdog mode, keeping an eye on the government and making sure it doesn't get out of control and neglect what the electorate wants. Those from a more critical tradition argue that the media operates primarily as a mouthpiece for government interests. Because the media are beholden to those in power, they help persuade the masses that the government's decisions are the *right* decisions for everyone.

Pluralist perspective

The pluralist position is really an acceptance of, and a belief in, the values and realities of liberal-democratic societies. In essence, pluralists see the media as simply an extension of the public sphere in ancient Greece where people went to receive information and debate the issues of the day. For pluralists, the media performs two crucial democratic tasks: (a) it informs the public, and (b) it acts as a watchdog on those in power. What is interesting, of course, is that all governments, no matter what their ideological orientation, always accuse the media of exploiting their position as watchdogs and filing deliberately biased and critical reports against them. So, for example, while the Clinton administration claimed to be fighting a right-wing bias in the media throughout the 1990s, Figure 8.3 illustrates the Bush administration's belief that the media had a left-wing bias against its policies during the Iraq war.

The Greek city-state or *polis* was one of the earliest forms of political unit in Europe: see **Chapter 11**.

Bill Clinton was president of the United States from 1993 to 2001. Donald Rumsfeld's role in the US administration during the Bush presidency is discussed in **Chapter 24**.

FIGURE 8.3
At war: Rumsfeld and liberal media bias.
Cox & Forkum © 2004

For pluralists, such balanced accusations demonstrate that the media is getting it right: they should *always* keep the government on their toes, no matter what ideological principles that government espouses.

Along with the protection of free speech, the reduction of government interference in the media, and an increase in people's access to information, pluralists advocate the principle of consumer choice. For example, if a newspaper, news channel or webpage is too right-wing for you, then you can choose a more left-wing broadsheet, television station or policy blog. Pluralists always emphasize the range of media products available to the consumer – from small circulation newspapers like *Socialist Worker* to broadsheets like the *New York Times*. Pluralists accept that each different media outlet presents a partial and slanted view of the world, but argue that it is the consumer who ultimately decides which partial view prevails and becomes accepted by the mainstream. In this approach, a basic symmetry exists between media outlets and their audiences. If a marginalized viewpoint is unpopular, it is squeezed out and becomes commercially unviable. As O'Sullivan argues, such a variety of media outlets 'act as a barometer of changing tastes and preferences. Diverse audience interests are reflected in a diversity of media choice. If there is a demand, media corporations will respond' (O'Sullivan *et al.*, 2003: 146). In this sense, pluralism is founded on the notion of consensus: there is a consensus on the predominant social values in society, which is reflected in mainstream and popular media.

Media that promote different views arguably don't offer a simple choice, as we are not necessarily aware of the 'picture' of the world which informs what we can see and think: see **Chapter 2**.

Critical perspective

Those who approach the media from a critical perspective start from the assumption that we live in a hierarchical society where power is concentrated in the hands of only a few people at the top. This does not just mean those in government, but also those who control wealth (business leaders), and those who control information (media leaders). The basic assumption of a critical approach is that the media will work to secure the interests of this elite group. In effect, they operate as a mouthpiece for elite power by *encouraging* the idea that the hierarchical structure of society is beneficial for everyone (including those at the bottom), and *discouraging* the fact that the elite benefits disproportionately from such a social structure. For critical scholars, the elite uses the media as a tool of persuasion: they try and convince everyone that the hierarchical structure of society is serving *everyone's* interests, not just their own.

This does not mean that the media completely relinquishes its role as a watchdog. Indeed, the critical approach argues that the media are perfectly capable of attacking the occupants of political office; that is, whatever party and group of politicians happens to be in power at any particular time. However, this watchdog role is very limited. While the media *are* able to critique politicians, they are *not* able to critique the foundations and structures of political power itself. This is how the media works in tandem with elite power: it offers superficial critiques of particular parties and policies (for example, 'George Bush's foreign policy agenda is flawed'), but it never goes so far as to question the foundations of the system itself (for example, 'if we live in an egalitarian society, how come so many families still live in poverty?'). And this is why the hierarchical and unequal structure of the system – a structure which, remember, serves to protect the dominant position of the elite – continues to persist. Critical scholars argue that the

For a discussion of power and authority see **Chapter 7**.

Chapter 19 looks at inequality within the United States.

media gives the *impression* of being a check on governmental power and stimulating debate, but what it actually does is control and confine the terms of that debate so that the foundations of the system are never questioned. In effect, the media works to engineer consent from the public – it manages and controls public debate so that the fundamental structure of society is not disrupted (Chomsky and Herman, 2006; Wheeler, 1997: 19–26).

You'll come across Marx and his ideas in a number of chapters in this book: **Chapters 15, 17 and 19**, for example.

Given their view that the media are members of the elite, it is not surprising that critical scholars – especially those from a Marxist perspective – are very concerned with questions of media ownership and influence. If the media is effectively a mouthpiece for elite power, then any information that does not serve elite interests and values will be suppressed. This suppression can be active, direct and violent, for example, in totalitarian regimes press freedom is replaced by a system of propaganda. But, more often, it is more subtle and difficult to detect. We saw an example of this in the Gulf War when the close relationship between the media and the government resulted in a widely held pro-war consensus in which dissenting voices were silenced. Many critical scholars argued that the same kind of consensus was recently established between the Bush administration and powerful media conglomerates such as Rupert Murdoch's News Corporation. Indeed, Robert Greenwald's documentary *Outfoxed: Rupert Murdoch's*

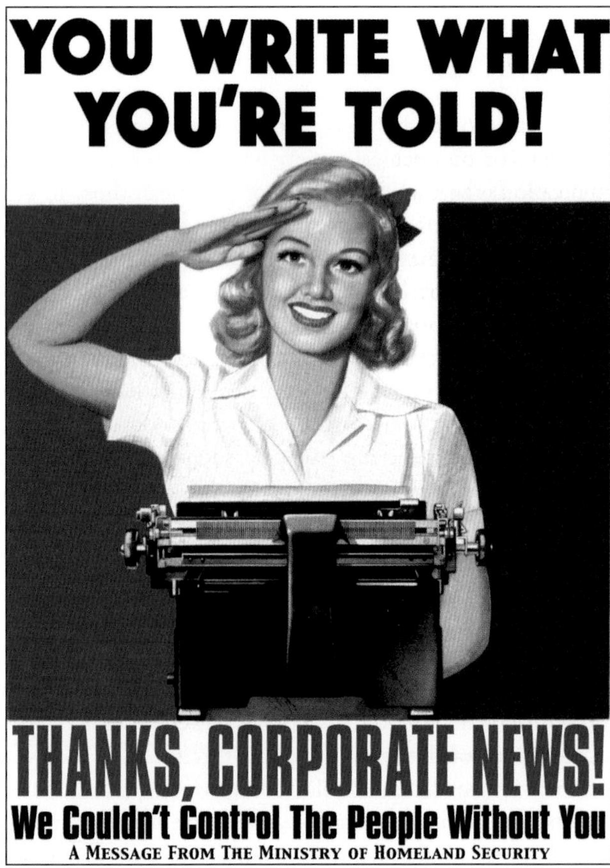

FIGURE 8.4
You write what you're told. Micah Wright poster from the Propaganda Re-Mix Project. Poster © 2008 by Micah Wright, courtesy of AntiWarPosters.com

War on Journalism provides a compelling argument about how News Corporation manipulated news content – especially about the War on Terror (www.outfoxed.org). When this kind of cosy relationship between elite groups is established, citizens are discouraged and actively prevented from asking difficult or subversive questions. Graphic artist Micah Wright's re-working of World War II iconography to comment on the American news media's complicity with Bush's interventions in Iraq and Afghanistan after 2001 (see his 'Propaganda Re-Mix Project' at http://homepage.mac.com/leperous/PhotoAlbum1.html) provides a useful reminder of what happens when the media act as an uncritical mouthpiece for government interests.

The power of the audience

While the pluralist vs. critical debate does analyse the media's wider role in society, it doesn't pay enough attention to the power of the audience. Pluralists assume that audiences interpret media products according to the same dominant values of consensus, whereas critical scholars believe that audiences are so pacified by media products that they have become too stupid to identify how the media reproduces elite power. Cultural theorist Stuart Hall (1993) offers a compelling alternative to this debate in his encoding/decoding model which foregrounds the power of the audience.

In a similar way to Stuart Hall, Jacques Rancière foregrounds what he calls *the emancipated spectator*. See **Chapter 18** for a discussion of Rancière's work.

Hall argues that any media message is made up of codes, or signs. During the process of communication, media producers arrange these codes so that they convey a preferred meaning, which is then sent through media channels and delivered to audiences. But Hall makes two important developments here. First, he suggests that all media texts are *polysemic*; that is, each document – a television show, a photograph, a blog – contains a number of possible interpretations. What happens in the process of communication is that all these different interpretations are gathered up and squashed into a preferred meaning that serves elite political agendas. Second, he suggests that there is no guarantee that the preferred meaning encoded into a media text will be read in the intended way by its consumers. Certainly many people will 'get the message', but many people will not – and some will deliberately refuse it. For Hall, this is because the audience can never be seen as a homogeneous group of passive citizens. When consuming the media, each audience member will take up a different position depending on their own context.

People who watch and read the media uncritically are in the dominant–hegemonic position: they decode and accept the preferred meaning because it accords with their own political values. People in this position do not question the motives or agendas behind a media product, but simply enjoy it as an innocent leisure practice. People who watch and read the media with some critical awareness are in the negotiated position: that is, they accept the basic message of a programme or story, but they may differ or disagree on certain specific points. These critical moments can arise when the reader has more personal knowledge or experience than is being expressed. So, for example, you may read a newspaper story about why Britain is being 'swamped' by refugees and asylum seekers, and while you may agree that this is a growing political issue, you may disagree with the racist overtones of the story. In this case, you may have written an essay on this subject for one of your classes, and you may have discovered a number of alternative reasons why refugees and asylum seekers are now a permanent feature in

You may in fact wonder why people cannot simply choose where they wish to live: see **Chapter 10**.

BOX 8.5 STUART HALL

FIGURE 8.5
Stuart Hall.
Photo: Stuart Hall

Stuart Hall is one of the most prominent cultural studies theorists of our time. His work analyses how cultural and media products are part of a struggle between elites who want to secure their hegemonic (or dominant) position in society, and those who want to stop them. The media, of course, is central to this struggle; indeed, this 'representational arena' is where the struggle for hegemony takes place. For example, the media bolsters the elite's position when it constructs 'moral panics', reproduces stereotypes and scapegoats non-mainstream identities, but it also challenges that elite position when it gives voice to marginalized groups and individuals (Hall *et al.*, 1978; Hall and Jefferson, 1993). For Hall, much depends on the audience, who *may* read cultural and media products in a passive and uncritical manner, or *may* actively construct alternative and oppositional meanings. While Hall's work is indebted to Marxism – indeed, he claims to always be 'within shouting distance of Marx' – he remains uncomfortable with how some Marxists privilege the category of class and neglect our complex identity negotiations of race, gender and sexuality. Much of his later work examines how these negotiations play themselves out in the 'circuit of culture' where representations are produced, disseminated and consumed (Hall, 1997: 15–63; Du Gay *et al.*, 1997). For example, newspaper representations of black British athletes reveal a much wider struggle over multiculturalism and national identity in Britain (Hall, 1997: 223–34). When these athletes are winning races, newspapers emphasize their British qualities – but when they are losing races (or worse, when they are failing drug tests), newspapers accentuate their identities as black men and women. Central to all of Hall's work is the idea that hegemonic elites intervene in the 'circuit of culture' to produce and stabilize dominant meanings. The job of any critical reader is to identify, analyse and resist those moments of domination by offering independent, critical and alternative readings.

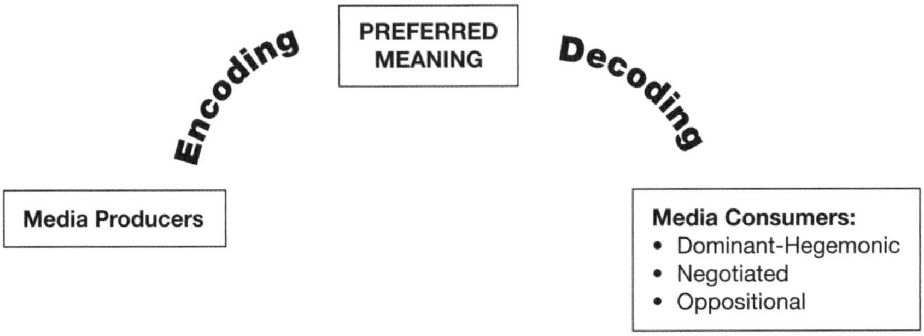

FIGURE 8.6
A simple formulation of Hall's model of encoding/decoding.
Stuart Hall

global politics. Hall argues that most audience members adopt this negotiated position with respect to the media. Finally, people who watch and read the media with a critical eye are in the oppositional position: they understand perfectly well what the preferred meaning of the story is, but they deliberately reject it and draw on alternative values. This last position is important for Hall, for it suggests that audiences are not the passive and duped creatures that some critical approaches would have us believe. Rather, audiences have the capacity to resist the preferred meanings in any media text, and therefore question any consensus that might develop between the media and the powers-that-be.

While Hall's model does simplify the process of media communication, its importance lies in the way it foregrounds the power of the audience and highlights critical reading strategies. It is only by identifying the dominant agendas being encouraged by the media – especially in the area of global politics – that we can challenge those moments when dominant agendas masquerade as 'the truth' in order to squeeze out more uncomfortable or unpalatable, diverse and complex accounts of global events.

Is it a bad thing that all media information advances someone's agenda? Is it a bad thing if they pretend not to have an 'agenda'?

BROADER ISSUES
HOW TO READ THE MEDIA

While Hall's model provides a useful account of audience power, it assumes that our responses to media representations are always rational, judicious and measured. This is, of course, seldom the case: we react to media representations instantaneously and emotionally. Think of the way avid sports fans watch their favourite teams compete live on television: they shout at their own players to do better (and they swear at the opposition for being terrible); they scream and whoop and jump and go crazy when victory is assured; they are outraged when 'unjust' refereeing decisions are awarded; and they sometimes weep with depression when their beloved team loses. It is almost as if they believe that if they shout loud enough at the television their favourite player will listen to their tactical suggestion (crafted carefully from the sofa), or the referee will reverse a penalty decision. This is not rational behaviour by any means. But it is one example of how *all* audience members – including you and me – become emotionally engaged in media representations. When media producers are trying to convince us of something – the *rightness* of a policy, the *hilarity* of a pratfall, the *guilt* of a prisoner, the *trauma* of a victim, the *joy* of a victory, the *pain* of a death – they don't do it by appealing to our rational natures. They do it by appealing to our emotions. And it works: we giggle, we scoff, we roll our eyes, we bury our head in our hands, we laugh out loud, we raise our eyebrows, we look away when it gets scary, we shout and cheer, and sometimes we cry.

The news media accounts of war that we have examined pride themselves on documenting the truth, evidence and proof about global politics. But if all media representations advocate a particular agenda (that is, they are biased), then it follows that media producers will use clever editing tricks, powerful imagery and moralizing rhetoric to get their point across. These efforts are intended to bypass our critical and intellectual faculties, inject themselves straight into our emotional conscience, and

The Glasgow Media Group has produced path-breaking and controversial empirical analyses of bias in the UK news media, beginning with studies of bias against unions in the 1970s.

How we should remember wars is itself a significant question: see **Chapter 22**.

create an intended effect (for example, supporting a war or opposing it). The institutional conventions, norms and practices of news production dictate that such emotional appeals are subtle, nuanced and not immediately apparent; indeed, the Glasgow Media Group has done excellent work over the years carefully showing us how these techniques are employed. However, to clearly illustrate the work of emotion in media representations of war, it is useful to examine a belated reconstruction of a battle, whose truth claims (for example, 'This is how it really was') are produced through the emotional registers of sentimentality melodrama and nostalgia. Film director Stephen Spielberg is a genius at securing consensus over historical truth claims by appealing to the audience's emotions. With that in mind, let's critically analyse his 1998 war film *Saving Private Ryan* through Hall's decoding model in order to identify a multiplicity of rational audience responses, but also to explore the work of emotion in audience interpretation.

The film depicts the famous Allied D-Day landings in Northern France during World War II. It follows a group of soldiers who have been assigned a special task: to locate and retrieve a Private Ryan, whose three brothers have been killed in action, and who is to be returned home to his mother. The preferred meaning of the film, encoded by Spielberg, is about the courage, bravery and heroism of ordinary American soldiers during World War II. Those who enacted a dominant–hegemonic reading of the film were swept away by Spielberg's narrative – not just the awesome and 'realistic' visuals of the opening D-Day landing scenes, but also by the touching moments of male camaraderie as a disparate group of soldiers banded together for a humanitarian mission. Viewers in this position were deeply moved by Spielberg's graphic depiction of the horrors of war and the many sacrifices made by American soldiers in the name of freedom. As one veteran of the D-Day landings explained, 'Spielberg has given us what we used to call an optimistic tragedy. We come away sobered but feeling better about the strength of our democracy' (Metcalf, 1999: 46). Those who enacted a negotiated reading were also moved by the narrative trajectory of the film, but were able to point out some inconsistencies in Spielberg's narrative. For example, the film makes it seem as if the Americans were the only forces involved in the D-Day landings, and ignores the participation of British, Canadian and other European troops. Indeed, French viewers reacted badly to the 'Americentric' portrayal of war, especially the patriotic flag waving at the beginning and end of the film (Hedetoft, 2000: 278–97). Those who enacted an oppositional reading of the film took issue with Spielberg's claim that the horrific and detailed opening landing sequence constituted an anti-war statement – the idea being that after seeing such horrors on screen, nobody would ever support war again. As World War II veteran Howard Zinn explains, the film does nothing but glorify and romanticize the myth of combat: 'I disliked the film intensely, indeed, was angry at it. Because I did not want the suffering of men in war to be used, yes, exploited, in such a way as to revive what should be buried along with all those bodies in Arlington cemetery – the glory of military heroism' (1998: 138). For critics like Zinn, *Saving Private Ryan*'s failure to live up to its anti-war credentials by critiquing the military establishment meant that it worked like all seductive Hollywood war films – as a recruitment tool for the military.

This example is particularly interesting because it demonstrates how two veterans of World War II – men who actually fought on the European battlefields – derived totally different meanings from the same film. This brings up the question of whether we *know* something better if we are there, experiencing an event first hand. But by the time both Metcalf and Zinn watched *Saving Private Ryan* in 1998, their 'first hand' experience of World War II had been filtered, refracted and shaped by over 50 years of media and cinematic representations of that event. Indeed, these representations helped them transform the incoherent, traumatic and terrifying experiences of battle into a clear and concise narrative of 'what happened'. For Metcalf – and for many people who live in Allied countries (including Steven Spielberg) – World War II is seen as a noble, heroic and just battle against an evil enemy. Indeed, this is the *preferred meaning* of the film. But Zinn rejects this message and takes a more *oppositional* stance: no war – not even World War II – is ever worth the sacrifice and loss of innocent life, and all patriotic and uncritical commemorations of such events should be resisted. Here we have two radically different interpretations of World War II – there is not just disagreement over 'what happened', but also disagreement over the meaning of such an event, and how that meaning is represented in a film like *Saving Private Ryan*. The problem, here, is that negotiated and oppositional readings require an analytical ability to indentify the preferred meaning and develop some form of logical counter-argument to it. Such readings ignore the ability of cinematic reconstructions to seduce viewers emotionally into a particular point of view that masquerades as a singular truth. While the dominant–hegemonic position might be frowned upon because it renders audience members passive, at least it acknowledges the way viewers are emotionally drawn into a film, and the pleasure they get from engaging at that level.

I remember being entirely moved by this film the first time I saw it on its release in 1998. I was pinned to my seat for the initial D-Day landing scene, I fell half in love with the wise but tough Captain Miller (played by Tom Hanks), I hated the Germans – especially the traitorous prisoner of war, I was full of admiration for a military that wanted to protect Mrs Ryan's only remaining son, and I wept buckets at the film's final

FIGURE 8.7 Tom Hanks, Matt Damon and Ed Burns in *Saving Private Ryan* (1998). Dir. Stephen Spielberg. Dreamworks SKG, Paramount Pictures and Amblin Entertainment. Ronald Grant Archive

Can you think of a film you've seen recently that has appealed to you emotionally in these sorts of ways?

rendering of heroic sacrifice. But I was very perplexed at this response: why was I so moved by this film? I wasn't alive during World War II, and I didn't personally know anyone who fought during that war. This was a different world to my own. And then I started thinking about how *Saving Private Ryan* related to the world I was living in – a decade in which violence was returning to the global stage with great force, but a decade in which the moral justifications for violence were, at best, hopelessly complex.

I realized that *Saving Private Ryan* is much more about conflict in the 1990s than it is about World War II: it encourages us to remember a 'good and just' war in order to *forget* the moral complexities of recent interventions (for example Bosnia, Kosovo, Somalia, Afghanistan, Iraq). In fact, my overblown emotional response was precisely what Spielberg ordered: his nostalgic commemoration created a 'comfortable surrogate' for the uncomfortable world I faced every day when I watched the television news or read the newspaper headlines (Kolker, 2000: 257). This is because stories about important historical events are directly shaped by the issues of *the present* rather than the past. Very simply, it is not some overarching, finally settled and uncontested notion of 'the truth' that dictates how we talk about the past – it is our *present* concerns and struggles that shape such discussions.

I was shocked, to say the least, at the way I had been so successfully manipulated by Spielberg's story. In every subsequent viewing, I discovered another layer to this deception: the rather obvious musical score, the cynically timed combat sequences punctuated by slower narrative elaboration, the faceless German enemy, the stereotypical troop of 'characters' (that is, the wise-ass from the Bronx, the innocent rookie, the thoughtful doctor), and the unabashed patriotism of the American flag. Every time I watched it I got angrier at Spielberg's ability to manipulate the audience. And yet despite all this 'rational' knowledge, I still could not help but be moved, somehow, by the larger themes of sacrifice, brotherhood and heroism. Going back to Hall's model, including this emotional register provides a much more comprehensive account of the negotiated viewing position most of us adopt when encountering representations of war. We still need to work out how such representations are manipulating us and trying to convince us of a dominant political agenda, but we also need to acknowledge how we are moved when we see images depicting the consequences of war – when people's cities are destroyed, when their loved ones are killed, and when their homelands implode in violence.

The emotions set off by witnessing others' suffering raise questions: What can we do to stop people harming others? And what issues arise when we believe that we know what is good for them? See **Chapters 25 and 21**.

My point is not to deny our emotional reactions; indeed, feelings like empathy, compassion and anger connect people across the world and inspire many common practices such as charity donations, aid packages, debt relief and humanitarian interventions. My point is simply that we must look carefully at how direct news media accounts and belated reconstructions of global politics mobilize both our reason *and* our passion in trying to put a particular point across. Too often, emotional appeals mask the dominant political agendas that are being served by the media. We've seen how Spielberg's narrative about sacrifice reproduces American patriotism and secures a consensus for contemporary foreign policy decisions. And while emotional appeals are more muted in the news media, they still underscore what purports to be a wholly 'factual' endeavour (think, for example, of how front line reports are often anchored with the story of an individual victim of war – a mother, a child, a shopkeeper, a teacher – so that audiences back home can feel a personal connection to someone in a conflict far away). By all means, we must maintain the capacity to be moved by powerful media representations – to be inspired into debate, discussion and action – but we must also leave ourselves room to experience the pleasures of emotional engagement (for example, laughter, sadness, shock, catharsis). The point is that we cannot exempt the media from critical examination. We must call attention to those moments when our emotions are deliberately manipulated in an effort to encourage a specific political position (e.g. going to war or *not* going to war).

CONCLUSION

There is, of course, an easy answer to the question 'How do we find out what's going on in the world?' Very simply, we ask questions. This is always the first step – be curious and take an active role in discovering the ins and outs of global politics. But this chapter has taken a further step by asking us to think about *where* we direct our questions, about the forum within which we discover, debate and discuss global politics. And this forum is undoubtedly the media in its broadest sense – newspapers, television, radio, film, magazines, blogs, podcasts, Twitter feeds, advertisements, etc. The main point of this chapter has been to demonstrate that the media is not a neutral space; rather, it plays an active role in shaping and influencing our opinions about global politics. The influential role of the media is nowhere more apparent than during times of war: indeed, there are many examples of the media acting as a mouthpiece for government during war, to the point of becoming a vehicle for propaganda. In this sense, we cannot leave it up to the media to provide a balanced view. We, as consumers of the media, need to develop critical reading skills so we can identify when and how the media tries to manipulate and shape our views about the world in order to serve a dominant political agenda.

It might be worth asking where the questions we ask come from. Are they neutral, or do they come from who we think we are, and what we think is important, before we start asking questions?

FURTHER READING

Lawrence Grossberg, Ellen Wartella and D. Charles Whitney (1998) *Mediamaking: Mass Media in a Popular Culture*, New York: Sage Publications, is the most comprehensive introduction to the overall relationship between the media and society. It develops a politically sophisticated account of the media, and provides good examples and illustrations of the main theoretical concepts.

John Fiske (1990) *Introduction to Communication Studies*, London: Routledge; and Dennis McQuail (2005) *McQuail's Mass Communication Theory*, London: Sage Publications, both give a more in-depth look at the theoretical framing of communication. They help to explain the complicated transfer of information from producers, through the media, to the consumer, and both books tackle the difficult question of how meaning is generated in this process. Within the study of global politics, Francois Debrix and Cynthia Weber (eds) (2003) *Rituals of Mediation: International Politics and Social Meaning*, Minneapolis: University of Minnesota Press, offer good examples of the contested space between events in global politics and their mediated representations.

Mark Wheeler (1997) *Politics and the Mass Media*, Oxford: Blackwell, chapter 1, provides a good review of the main debates between pluralist and critical (especially Marxist) approaches to the media, as does Georgia Chondroleou's (2002) article 'Studying the Media and Politics in Britain: A Tale of Two Literatures?', *British Journal of Politics and International Relations* 2, 2: 359–73.

Tim Allen and Jean Seaton (1999) *The Media of Conflict: War Reporting and Representations of Ethnic Violence*, London and New York: Zed Books; Susan Carruthers (2000) *The Media at War: Communication and Conflict in the Twentieth Century*, London: Palgrave; and Andrew Hoskins and Ben O'Loughlin (2010) *War and Media: The Emergence of Diffused War*, Cambridge: Polity, are good starting points that provide general accounts of the relationship between the media and war. The work of the Glasgow Media Group provides good in-depth analysis of bias in war reporting, see especially (1995) *Industry, Economy, War and Politics: Glasgow University Media Reader, Vol. 2*, London: Routledge; and (2004) *Bad News From Israel*, London: Pluto. There are numerous books recently published about the media's role in specific conflicts, especially the 'war on terror'; see for example Francois Debrix (2007) *Tabloid Terror: War, Culture and Geopolitics*, London: Routledge; and Andrew Hoskins and Ben O'Loughlin (2009) *Television and Terror: Conflicting Times and the Crisis of News Discourse*, Basingstoke: Palgrave.

WEBSITES

Communication, Culture and Media Studies Infobase, http://www.cultsock.ndirect.co.uk/MUHome/cshtml; also known as 'Cultsock'. Media Communication Studies site at the University of Aberystwyth, http://www.aber.ac.uk/media

These two sites provide a comprehensive introduction to the theories, debates and methods of media studies.

Indymedia, http://www.indymedia.org; a collection of independent media resources. Fairness and Accuracy in Reporting, http://www.fair.org/index.php; a media watch group.

There are a variety of websites dedicated to independent media reporting of which these two are among the best.

The War and Media Network, http://www.warandmedia.org; The Global Media Project at The Watson Institute for International Studies at Brown University, http://watsoninstitute.org/globalmedia

Interdisciplinary research into the role of the media during war is developing rapidly, and these two websites in particular help to navigate, foster and promote this work.

The Iraq War Archive, http://www.iraqwararchive.org

More specifically, a useful website about media coverage of the Iraq war.

David Campbell's website and blog *Photography, Multimedia, Politics,* http://www.david-campbell.org offers in-depth analysis and reflection on the role of visual documents in the media.

OTHER RESOURCES

Outfoxed: Rupert Murdoch's War on Journalism, Documentary by Robert Greenwald (www.outfoxed.org).

REFERENCES

Bannon, Anthony and George Eastman House (2003) *1000 Photo Icons*, Cologne: Taschen.

Burton, Graeme (1997) *More than Meets the Eye: An Introduction to Media Studies*, 2nd edn, London: Arnold.

Campbell, David (2011) 'Thinking Images v.9: Egypt, Revolution and the Internet', 8 February, *Photography, Multimedia, Politics*, available at http://www.david-campbell.org/2011/02/08/thinking-images-v-9-egypt/ (accessed 19 July 2011).

Chomsky, Noam and Edward Herman (2006) *Manufacturing Consent: The Political Economy of the Mass Media*, London: Vintage.

Debrix, Francois and Cynthia Weber (eds)(2003) *Rituals of Mediation: International Politics and Social Meaning*, Minneapolis: University of Minnesota Press.

Der Derian, James (2001) *Virtuous War: Mapping the Military-Industrial-Media-Entertainment Network*, Boulder, CO: Westview Press.

Du Gay, Paul, Stuart Hall, Linda Janes, Hugh Mackay and Keith Negus (1997) *Doing Cultural Studies: The Story of the Sony Walkman*, London: Sage Publishers and The Open University.

Fiske, John (1990) *Introduction to Communication Studies*, London: Routledge.

Hall, Stuart (1993) 'Encoding/Decoding', in Simon During (ed.), *The Cultural Studies Reader*, London: Routledge.

——(1997) *Representation: Cultural Representations and Signifying Practices*, London: Sage Publishers and The Open University.

Hall, Stuart, Charles Critcher, Tony Jefferson, John Clarke and Brian Robert (1978) *Policing the Crisis: Mugging, the State and Law and Order*, London: Palgrave Macmillan.

Hall, Stuart and Tony Jefferson (eds) (1993) *Resistance Through Rituals: Youth Subcultures in Post-war Britain*, London: Routledge.

Hallin, Daniel C. (1986) *The 'Uncensored War': The Media and Vietnam*, Oxford: Oxford University Press.

Hedetoft, Ulf (2000) 'Contemporary Cinema: Between Cultural Globalization and National Interpretation', in Mette Hjort and Scott MacKenzie (eds), *Cinema and Nation*, London: Routledge.

Kolker, Robert Phillip (2000) *A Cinema of Loneliness*, 3rd edn, Oxford: Oxford University Press.

McLane, Brendan R. (2004) 'Reporting from the Sandstorm: An Appraisal of Embedding', *Parameters*, 34, 1: 77–88.

McLuhan, Marshall (1975) *Montreal Gazette*, 16 May.

Metcalf, Roy (1999) 'So Costly a Sacrifice: Saving Private Ryan', *Social Policy*, 29, 4: 44–7.

O'Rourke, P. J. (1992) *Give War a Chance*, London: Picador.

O'Sullivan, Tim, Brian Dutton and Philip Rayner (2003) *Studying the Media: An Introduction*, 3rd edn, London: Hodder and Arnold.

Pfau, Michael, Michel Haigh, Mitchell Gettle, Michael Donnelly, Gregory Scott, Dana Warr and Elaine Wittenberg (2004) 'Embedding Journalists in Military Combat Units: Impact on Story Frames and Tone', *Journalism and Mass Communication Quarterly*, 81, 1: 74–88.

Philo, Greg (1993) 'From Buerk to Band Aid: The Media and the 1984 Ethiopian Famine', in John Eldridge (ed.), *Getting the Message: News, Truth and Power*, London: Routledge.

Postman, Neil (1987) *Amusing Ourselves to Death: Public Discourse in the Age of Show Business*, London: Methuen.

Robinson, Piers (2002) *The CNN Effect: The Myth of News, Foreign Policy and Intervention*, London: Routledge.

Tumber, Howard and Jerry Palmer (2004) *Media at War: The Iraq Crisis*, London: Sage.

Wheeler, Mark (1997) *Politics and the Mass Media*, Oxford: Blackwell.

Williams, Kevin (1993) 'The Light at the End of the Tunnel: The Mass Media, Public Opinion and the Vietnam War', in John Eldridge (ed.), *Getting the Message: News, Truth and Power*, London: Routledge.

Zinn, Howard (1998) 'Saving Private Ryan', *Social Justice*, 25, 3: 138–43.

For a range of further resources supporting this chapter, please visit the companion website for *Global Politics, 2nd Edition* at www.routledge.com/cw/edkins/

CHAPTER 9

How does the way we use the Internet make a difference?

M. I. Franklin

THE QUESTION
WHAT IS THE INTERNET?

The Internet has already made an indelible mark on many facets of human endeavour, at least in those parts of the world with access to its web-based news and entertainment, information exchange and networking opportunities, pay-for or 'free' consumer products and services, community and creative spaces. It makes a difference precisely because of how ubiquitous this supraterritorial computer-mediated network of real-time communications has become in the Global North. Whilst new users are coming online at an increasing pace in the Global South, two-thirds of the world's population are not yet online. UN agencies and private-sector partners aim to 'connect the next billion' under the auspices of the Millennium Development Goals and other UN covenants (IGF 2008; United Nations General Assembly 2000; La Rue 2011). Despite this united front, however, differences in how individuals, communities, businesses and governments use the Internet, to what ends and on whose terms and conditions raise questions that go to the heart of social, political and economic life in coming years, as do its misuses and non-uses.

The predominant uses of the Internet are for news, entertainment and keeping in touch with friends or work-colleagues, but political and economic applications have also been intrinsic to its short history. In the 1990s the Internet was used to generate global awareness of the Zapatista Movement's cause in Mexico and used to good effect in the anti-globalization protests of the late 1990s and early 2000s, heralding the arrival of web-based Indymedia, citizen journalism and the blogosphere's influence on public opinion and policy-making. Global financial markets' refinements of Internet capabilities were instrumental in the 1980s. The Internet itself was the driving force behind the dot-com boom and bust – the spectacular rise and fall of IT companies – at the turn of the twenty-first century and its instantaneous, 24/7 global flows remain indispensable to the global political economy.

How we find out about the world is the subject of **Chapter 8**; of course, today many of us get much of our information about what goes on from the Internet.

The financial crisis of 2008 is discussed in **Chapter 18**.

Attention has now turned to the role the new generation of the Internet, known as Web 2.0, plays in the rapid spread of social unrest in Europe (from student demonstrations in Athens 2008 to riots in London 2011), in political revolutions in the Middle East and North Africa (from Egypt to Tunisia to Libya), and in sociopolitical mobilization elsewhere (from anti-government demonstrations in Teheran and Rangoon to the Occupy movement in New York and London). The Internet itself is increasingly a focus for local and international mobilization against the ways governments and corporations use it against their own citizens and customers, for example, by impeding access to information online, eroding freedom of expression by censoring or filtering web-content, compromising people's privacy through unreasonable personal data collection and retention, or monitoring online behaviour in ways that undermine human, civil and economic rights (Jørgensen 2006; La Rue 2011).

The Occupy movement is discussed in **Chapters 18 and 28**.

BOX 9.1 ZAPATISTAS

The Zapistas, or, in full, the Zapatista Army of National Liberation (*Ejército Zapatista de Liberación Nacional*, EZLN), are a group based in Chiapas, a state of Mexico. They are of interest to scholars and students of global politics because of their very distinctive style of opposition to the contemporary global order, and although they are a relatively small group engaged in local struggles, their ideology and the writings of their leader, Subcommandante Marcos, have influenced resistance groups elsewhere, in part due to their Internet presence.

FIGURE 9.1
Subcommandante Marcos on twitter, http://twitter.com/#!/Sub_Marcos

BOX 9.2 WHAT IS WEB 2.0?

When we speak of 'social media' we are also referring to a particular generation of commercial products and services that integrate once separate uses into one package, or platform. Email, web-browser, photo archives, live-chat, and web-links are now bundled together to make it easier for us to contact friends and family in real-time, create links to others by 'friending' someone, and share information. *Social Networking Sites* like the current market-leader Facebook (based in the USA), RenRen (based in China), and micro-blogging services like Twitter epitomize this Web 2.0 generation of software applications. Their runaway success and push to further integrate media, electronics, and Internet uses belies the fact that Web 2.0 has not replaced what came before. The Internet is comprised of overlapping layers of software applications and users from different periods in its short history.

In short, the Internet has become not only a critical means and medium for everyday life, economic power, and sociopolitical dissent but also integral to the exercise of power: an object for struggles over its ownership, control, and design (Mueller 2002; Clinton 2010; Nye 2002; Giacomello *et al.* 2009). States, corporations and civil society groups are staking their claims on the Internet's future as an affordable, socially just, profitable means of communication and information exchange. These conflicting priorities are putting pressure on traditional decision-making bodies as everyday realities of Internet use float out of reach of national legislatures and jurisdictions. Classical notions of national sovereignty and its territorially bounded understandings of accountability, legality and legitimacy are no longer sufficient. The working principle that the Internet is, by definition and design, a quintessentially global and open medium that nonetheless needs to be brought more or less under control is currently hotly contested.

Chapter 11 traces how these ideas of territoriality and sovereignty came into existence in the first place.

But what do we mean when we talk about the Internet? In practice, this term encompasses information and communication technologies based on connecting up computers and telecommunications systems in such a way that they can communicate with one another by way of systems of interoperating Internet protocols: software codes govern the way these interoperable systems function (Lessig 2006; Holmes 2007; Cerf 2012). The world-wide web and latest generation of social media that enable us to search the web, generate our own content, get in touch with others in a few seconds, overlays the Internet's underlying 'network of networks' architecture (see Mueller 2002). These all follow the pathways laid out by imperial and post-imperial telecommunications submarine and satellite connections from the previous century. In this sense critical hubs and functions of the Internet's telegeography, like the telegraph and telephone before it, reside in and fan out from the USA, UK and Western Europe.

For a discussion of imperial expansion see **Chapter 16**.

Nonetheless, as the latest chapter in this larger history of telecommunications, the Internet and its uses are no longer the preserve of its Anglo-Euro-American founding fathers; computer geeks-cum-millionaires, national and regional defence establishments, state-owned or private corporations. We need to think of the Internet as more than a

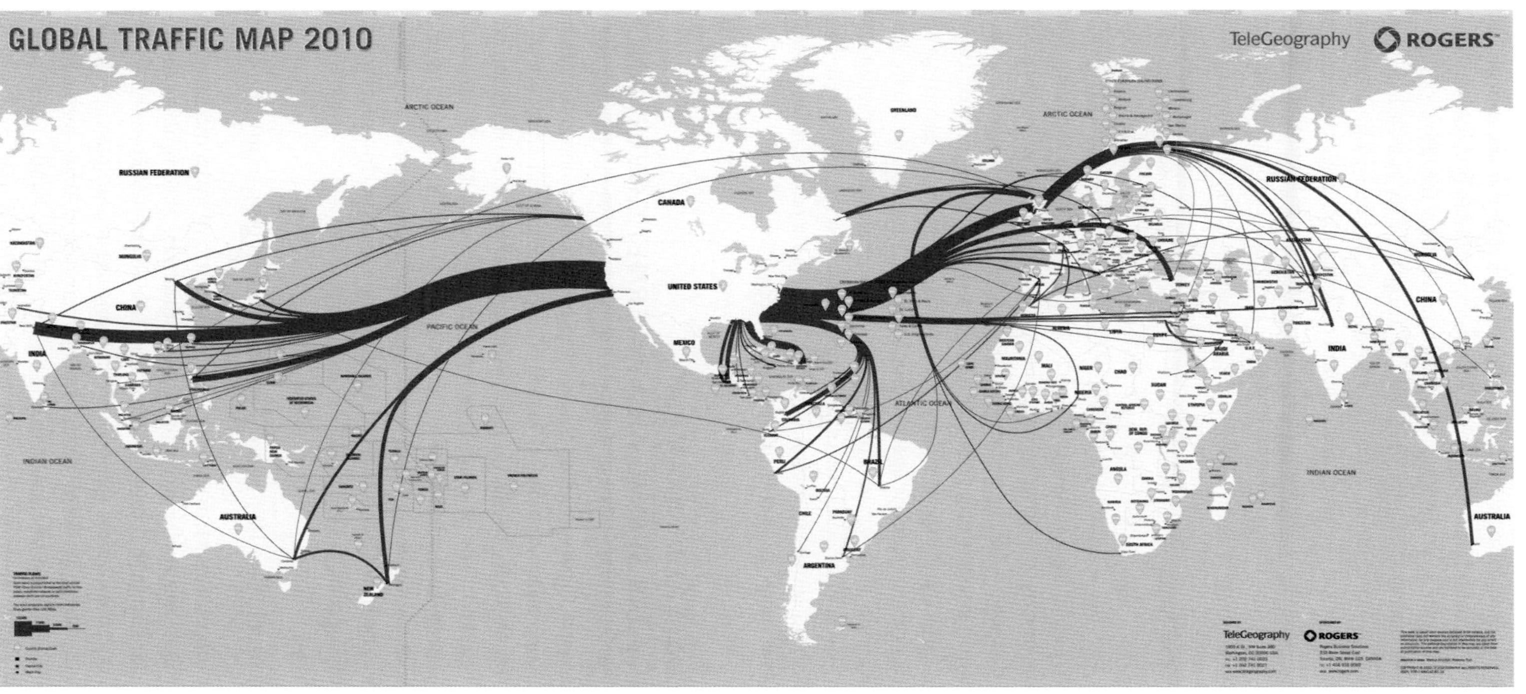

FIGURE 9.2
TeleGeography: map 2010, http://www.telegeography. com/telecom-resources/map-gallery/global-traffic-map-2010/index.html

tool or piece of engineering that has made local–global connections and instantaneous communications around the world not only possible but fashionable. Like its precedents, the Internet is embedded in the modernization narrative of the rise of the modern nation-state and empire. As such the Internet – its constituent parts and as a whole – is also a sociocultural artefact, a historically located form of material and symbolic – 'hard' and 'soft' – power that engenders repression, expression, and opposition (Haraway 1990; Nye 2002; Holmes 2007). Moreover there is currently more than one Internet in use, if not in the planning stages. Here too corporate and state actors have overlapping and conflicting plans for the future (Giacomello *et al.* 2009; Deibert and Rohozinski 2010; Goldsmith and Wu 2006).

What is meant by modernization, and the various changes linked with this term, is discussed in many places in this book. See **Chapters 6 and 17**, for example.

The Internet has also become indispensable in making war and peace, embedded in power hierarchies, a focal point for terrorist and counter-terrorist communication and activities, a lightning rod for political movements and social revolution. For ordinary users, the benefits of having access to the web outweigh the risks: 'transparency is good', being overly concerned about being tracked online is 'old school'. But what if this entitlement of life in the developed world was no longer a given? What if a whole network, say that of a country, neighbourhood, or institution came under a sustained cyber-attack by an external agent, infecting a website, accessing encrypted communications of government agencies, our bank accounts? To whom are these transgressors answerable if they are working outside a national jurisdiction? Are there limits to transparency, freedom of information, and free speech in cyberspace in light of new security dilemmas in digital settings? If so, is there one rule for ordinary users and one for governments or corporations in cyberspace?

It has been argued that the US, China and Europe are developing very different Internets with different deep architectures (Goldsmith and Wu 2006: 184). Security and financial organizations already operate their own private networks.

ILLUSTRATIVE EXAMPLE
THE ARAB SPRING AND INTERNET GOVERNANCE

To unpack these questions this section focuses on an illustrative example of distinct but interconnected domains of action in which different ideas about Internet uses are a central concern. The first is power struggles *through* the Internet: struggles taking place via the web. The second is power struggles *over* the Internet: struggles contesting ownership and control of its critical resources, services, transmission, and design. Various responses common to both these domains provide some focal points for further exploring how the ways we – and others – use the Internet make a difference in the following section.

The revolution has been 'Tweeted': struggles using the Internet

The Internet, in particular the latest generation of social media, was deployed in political uprisings and the overturning of authoritarian governments in North Africa and the Middle East in the spring of 2011. Because of the way mobile phones, instant messaging and micro-blogging services can send messages and images quickly over the web, and the way these are then picked up by mainstream news media, the success and global media coverage of these uprisings went hand in hand. These power struggles on the streets and transmitted through the Internet in Tunisia and Egypt that toppled the Ben

BOX 9.3 THE ARAB SPRING

In December 2010 a man set himself on fire on the street in Tunisia in protest, and that event sparked a series of protests and movements that spread across the Middle East and North Africa. Revolutions in Tunisia, Egypt and Libya led to the ousting of authoritarian regimes that had been in place for decades, and violent repression by forces loyal to the state took place in Bahrain, Syria, and elsewhere. The revolutionary movements were notable for their occupation of public spaces, such as Tahrir Square in Cairo, and for the involvement of young people across the region. These protests inspired the Occupy movement in the US, Europe and elsewhere. For an interactive timeline of events, see http://www.guardian.co.uk/world/interactive/2011/mar/22/middle-east-protest-interactive-timeline.

FIGURE 9.3
Arab Spring – Yemen: a girl raises her hand with her fingers painted with flags of Yemen, Egypt, Syria, Tunisia and Libya as she marches during a demonstration to demand the ousting of Yemen's President Ali Abdullah Saleh in the southern city of Taiz, 22 June 2011. Photo: Khaled Abdullah/Reuters. http://www.takepart.com/photos/year-end-arab-spring

FIGURE 9.4
Map of Middle East and North Africa, http://familysecuritymatters.org/imgLib/20110220_MidEastMap6.jpg

Ali and Mubarak regimes respectively were the crest of a wave of uprisings known as the Arab Spring. Whilst the causes for uprisings and uses of the Internet differ from place to place (e.g. the way events unfolded and were conveyed to the world in Libya differed from those in Saudi Arabia, Bahrain, the Gaza Strip, and Yemen in the same period), these events and their precursors in Iran and Burma, the Green and Saffron movements respectively, have come to represent how the Internet, social media, and revolution work together. Like previous partnerships between grassroots uses of media to mobilize and challenge incumbent powers, this wave of 'Facebook' or 'Twitter' revolutions shows powerful uses of these technologies by citizens to overthrow repressive governments.

Television viewers and Internet users in the West, whether unconnected to the events or friends and family of the protesters, were treated to unedited, live streamed coverage of events shot from the hip by participants. Professional bloggers and others, dubbed 'citizen journalists' edited and re-circulated or retweeted these images around the world, through personal and group-based social networks. And all in the space of seconds, minutes, and hours. In stark contrast to conventional media coverage – when in war the first victim is the truth as media images and messages are tightly controlled by incumbents – these images spilled out and generated momentum before news and security services could edit them for wider consumption.

Traditional methods of controlling the media in wartime are discussed in **Chapter 8**.

The unremitting flow of tweets and mobile phone footage not only conveyed a more compelling sense of what was going on; this surfeit of images and analyses from non-professionals overwhelmed news-desks. Using a mobile phone to record events was no longer for private purposes. The whole world, watching online, could witness the events too. Immediately, journalists' use of images without verifying the source raised criticism of non-impartiality, created openings for disinformation if not a distortion of the size and significance of the events flying across the web.

FIGURE 9.5
Protestors use mobile phones in Tunisia. Photo: Fred Dufour/ AFP/Getty Images

More importantly, countermanding applications, or use of the same media by authorities, played their role in complicating the legitimacy of the media. Incumbents immediately swung into action to stem the tide. In 2011 during the height of the Egyptian uprisings and occupation of central Cairo, the beleaguered Mubarak government, in partnership with Vodafone, cut off telecommunications, depriving demonstrators in Tahrir Square from using their mobile phones and Twitter services in particular. Overnight this revolution could no longer be tweeted. The response from media and civil rights activists in the West was swift. Vodafone was widely condemned for its collusion with the Mubarak regime, and protesters' access to services was restored, though Vodafone's standing in some quarters was compromised. This incident encapsulates the tensions between different uses of the same technology for different ends; here the former authoritarian regime and a transnational corporation were seen to join forces against the will of the Egyptian people. In a previous case – a less successful revolution in terms of regime change – violent clashes between anti-government protesters and Iranian government forces in 2009 were widely disseminated by mobile phones, on YouTube, via Twitter and on Iranian-based and Western blogs. These messages and media uses were systematically countered by an array of government-backed systems to filter, redirect and censor the content generated by dissidents (Sreberny and Khiabany 2010). These struggles unfurled not only in the streets but also in cyberspace.

The stakes have been raised, and not only on the ground, where it takes more than a Twitter account or black-out of a mobile phone image to make or break a revolution. Governments around the world have mobilized to protect but also monitor citizens for any number of reasons. Control of media messages in periods of civil unrest and war has been the concern of governments throughout history, intensifying with the arrival of television and now the Internet. Moves to control or repress undesirable uses of the Internet have exercised regulators, autocrats and political representatives since it took off; examples include EU member-states collaborating to counter online pornography flows, and the UK government's attempt to curtail the use of mobile phones after the 2011 London riots.

The use of media in war, and how it has developed over time, is the subject of **Chapter 8**.

More worryingly for (new) media watchers in some quarters is the way global corporate actors are making unilateral decisions that effectively restrict access and unmitigated uses of the Internet in parts of the world where users have little say. Internet service providers Yahoo! and Google have also come under fire for complying with the Chinese authorities' request for personal data and preventing access to offending websites respectively (Franklin 2010; Goldsmith and Wu 2006). In early 2012, Twitter announced that it was now company policy to remove tweets from users on the instructions of countries not happy with what their tweeting citizens are saying. This action would be taken on a case by case basis and Twitter would make it clear that the tweet has been censored. The company was accused of bowing to pressure from repressive regimes in areas with potentially huge market-share, but calls to boycott the service received mixed responses from local dissidents and activists. The high-profile Chinese artist and government critic Ai Weiwei was cited as tweeting 'If Twitter starts censoring. I'll stop tweeting.' At the same time, activists in parts of the Arab world noted the importance of uses of Twitter during the demonstrations that eventually overturned the Tunisian and Egyptian regimes; during the height of the protests, the

Twitter, the market-leader in 'micro-blogging' services, describes itself as 'a real-time information network' containing 'small bursts of information' called tweets; limited to 140 characters, users use the hash symbol to mark keywords – and for other purposes: see http://www.newyorker.com/online/blogs/susanorlean/2010/06/hash.html.

majority of hash tags were in Arabic. What counts for these users is that in these circumstances 'Twitter . . . proved to be one of the most activist-friendly of social networks' (El Dahshan 2012).

Large Internet service providers are aware of these contradictory claims on their services. In the case of Twitter, the company insisted that it would only take down posts, on request, within any specific country's jurisdiction. It would keep the offending tweets accessible to the rest of the world, notify the user, and send withheld tweets to the 'Chilling Effects' website, maintained by the Electronic Frontier Foundation. From a legal and commercial perspective, companies hosting user-generated content find themselves offending repressive regimes, users and a range of media watchers simultaneously. The bottom-line is that non-compliance with a government request to take down content carries the threat of services being blocked anyway. Being seen to 'do evil' (Google's informal company slogan is 'don't do evil') by onlookers and paying customers damages the corporate brand. For those who argue that states ultimately hold the reins over how the Internet can or should be used, this is a powerful argument for their case.

As with Vodafone in Egypt and Google in China, states do not act alone either. When sued in France for hosting a sale of Nazi memorabilia, Yahoo! eventually blocked the sale even though as a US-based company they were not liable under French law. Internet companies already have or are developing the means to control content at certain times and in certain places: Google bans content in China but it also filters searches in Germany and France; Facebook can restrict access to content based on who is viewing and whether the content is legal in a particular country.

However, for every service that is blocked locally – or on a national level – on the web, an alternative route is found by users themselves or through a range of services providing proxies and other ways of masking a tweet, online posting or text message.

Internet governance: struggles for control of the Internet

These recent waves of social and political struggles, transmitted through the Internet's social media services despite attempts to block their global spread, highlight ongoing struggles over control of the Internet. In the wake of these events, a series of policy-priorities have been put on the UN agenda about whether access to the Internet is a means to an end, that of combating global poverty, injustice and socioeconomic inequality, or an end in itself, a development goal.

'No single actor controls every single hub of cyberspace' (Giacomello *et al.* 2009: 206).

According to the United Nations General Assembly and participating agencies, the Internet is both in effect, in that the uses to which it can be put and the conditions of those uses require a fresh approach. State-centred and piecemeal solutions to harnessing information and communications technologies for the purposes of development had to be replaced. To this end, the UN General Assembly set up a series of 'high-level summits' in 2003 in order to 'build a global consensus' on the best way to govern the Internet (United Nations General Assembly 2000; WSIS Civil Society Caucus 2003, 2005). The Internet Governance Forum is the latest in UN consultations about the policy implications of media and communications at an international level. The first meetings in the 1970s were hosted by UNESCO (MacBride 1980; Jørgensen 2006), the second set of meetings, the World Summit on the Information Society (2003–2005), was hosted by the International Telecommunications Union. The Internet Governance Forum as an autonomous organization, began in 2006. What sets the WSIS and IGF consultations apart is the way they are premised on a 'multistakeholder participatory model' that includes representatives from civil society, corporate and government sectors.

Whilst to its critics largely a talk-shop, and to its supporters an indispensable advocacy platform in a longer reformist project, the objective of the UN Internet Governance Forum is to bring these three sectors of society to the table in order to discuss often controversial issues around how the Internet functions, is accessed, financed, and monitored as a supraterritorial means of communication. Rights-based discourses framing the Internet as a sociocultural artefact and global public good challenge, in the politest possible way, commercial strategies and foreign policy objectives; official declarations of principles and plans of action are compiled alongside civil society declarations, insider and outsider actions, workshops, and plenary sessions.

The World Summit on the Information Society began with great hopes on the part of civil society participants in Geneva in 2003. Expectations and ambitions had been markedly tempered by the last summit in 2005 in Tunis and establishment of the Internet Governance Forum the following year. Given the events that unfolded barely 5 years later in this city, the rumblings of political dissent and alternative summits held in central Tunis by disgruntled civil society participants allied to Tunisian women's rights and human rights activists in pre-Twitter days take on an even larger significance with the benefit of hindsight.

The function of summits as part of global governance is discussed in the context of another World Summit – on sustainable development – in **Chapter 4**.

Whilst not yet in the headlines of the global media, the imprisonment and harassment of Tunisian citizens accessing the web in ways deemed unacceptable by the government at the time paved the way in many respects for a series of concerted mobilizations by coalitions within subsequent UN Internet Governance Forum meetings around the Internet and human rights, and a wave of international struggles against attempts to curtail the open and global premises of Internet use by repressive regimes and comparable legislative measures in the USA, the EU, Australasia and South America.

But have the agenda-points and arcane discussions that characterize these UN-brokered consultations on the Internet and society at the highest political level had any bearing on events on the ground in the Arab Spring? Protesters and their opponents have used the Internet and other media without recourse to the slow grinding of well-oiled diplomatic and institution building wheels. By the same token, these events have directly influenced if not coloured these meetings: the World Summit on the Information Society meetings in Tunisia were constantly dealing with government intervention and human rights issues; the 2009 Internet Governance Forum meeting in Sharm El-Sheikh took place in the last year of the Mubarak regime; and China's objection to any global agenda-setting about the Internet's underlying functionality was patently clear in official and unofficial actions.

GENERAL RESPONSES
REGULATION, CENSORSHIP AND RIGHTS

When considering the Internet's influence on politics, culture and society, responses range from the highly specialized techno-legal point (technical standards for instance), to the normative and sociocultural (digital rights, gender or race inclusion). In political terms responses take the form of organized advocacy, direct action online and off, legislation, behind the screens lobbying and commercial strategies. This section looks at three interconnected responses to the growth of Internet use: attempts to regulate the digital commons; tracking, monitoring and censoring content use; and the development of a charter of human rights and principles for the Internet.

For another discussion of the implication of regulation and its absence see **Chapter 17** on the 'informal' economy.

Regulating the digital commons

In late 2011 and early 2012, a broad US-based and international mobilization gathered momentum around two bills put forward to the US Congress: the Protect IP Act (Preventing Real Online Threats to Economic Creativity and Theft of Intellectual Property Act, or PIPA) and the Stop Online Piracy Act or SOPA. Activism online and on the ground contributed to these two bills being withdrawn, although many commentators believe this was a respite only. Prior to these events, international mobilization had already been focusing on the latest in a long line of international trade agreements: the Anti-Counterfeiting Trade Agreement, ACTA. Currently signed by many Organisation for Economic Co-operation and Development (OECD) members yet opposed vehemently by grassroots groups and NGOs within signatory countries, this agreement is seen as the precursor of the Protect IP Act and the Stop Online Piracy Act. All three initiatives target applications that emerge from the Internet's capabilities to help create and disseminate knowledge, products, and services outside intellectual property and copyright regimes.

For more on the OECD see **Chapter 23**.

The main bone of contention is that these moves, made in the name of protecting copyright, create a precedent for government-directed forms of Internet censorship. Protesters see Western governments in partnership with corporate interests producing a situation whereby freedom of information and freedom of expression are sacrificed. More to the point, the techniques and technologies put in place to track and prosecute transgressors under these laws could then be put to use by repressive regimes.

The Internet to date has been the home for interlocking peer-to-peer or P2P networks that facilitate exchanges of music, films and other cultural products, which some call piracy. And the existence of non-proprietary (that is, where use is not restricted by trademark, patent or copyright laws) software constitutes a formidable counter-cultural impetus against attempts by vested interests to regulate in punitive, non-transparent ways. The success of P2P networks and free and open-source software advocates in carving a niche in the user-habits of successive generations of digital natives has been a bone of contention for the largely American music and film companies and software manufacturers since the early years of the web. These alternative communities and their open-access, lateral ethos continue to flourish despite concerted attempts to isolate, locate and then prosecute transgressors. One reason is that, if successful, the 'implementation of these blunt policy instruments will require more and more public-funded surveillance and censorship' of the Internet and its corollary media and communications devices and networks (Abraham 2012).

For discussions of the global economy and its impact in the Global South, see **Chapters 15, 17 and 20**.

The online actions and offline lobbying focused on a seemingly neutral response to a seemingly technical and legal problem: use of the Internet to bypass having to pay for something. But the use of the Internet by economies in the Global South to generate

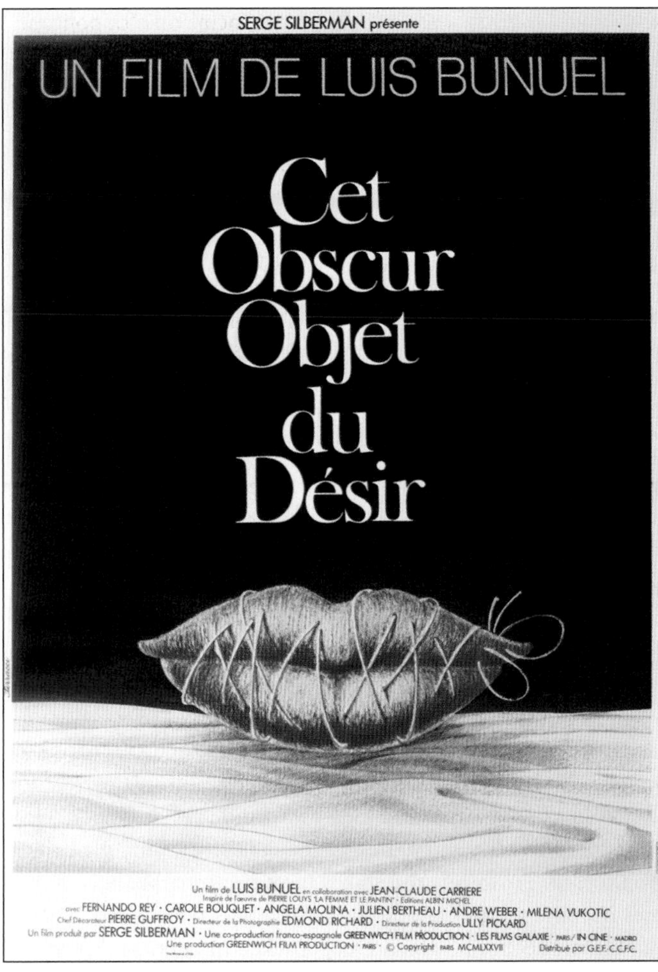

FIGURE 9.6
From poster for *Cet obscur objet du désir*, Luis Buñuel, http://www.movieposterdb.com/poster/23a329c7

income by developing viable alternatives to pricey Western goods and services is a broader question (Abraham 2012).

Filtering and censorship

The ability to navigate the web in a relatively open way is possible because the Internet's transmission infrastructure and accompanying protocols are not encrypted. We can traverse the web with relative impunity on an everyday level. But these practices, and the digital footprint we leave when opening a web-page, doing a Google search, or registering for a service, leaves traces that others can follow if they choose to do so (Latour 2007). Conversely, agencies such as schools, libraries and universities, and parents for that matter, have an interest in keeping material considered harmful or inappropriate from younger or vulnerable users. Increasingly sophisticated filtering software blocks access or censors content called up by a user, from sexually explicit or exploitative images of children to politically or religiously sensitive material. Since the 1990s, it has been possible to block web access and content. In addition, web activities

Has the media always involved censorship or bias? See **Chapter 8**.

FIGURE 9.7
'Cyberpolice!' By Chappatte, www.globalcartoons.com http://www.globecartoon.com/Contact.html email: Chappatte@globecartoons.com

of users can be monitored for reasons of state and for market research. Facebook or Google users take as a given that their searches and activities generate advertising revenue and produce targeted advertising based on their digital footprints.

Debates about accountability, legality and redress rage over these seemingly benign forms of filtering and monitoring. However, the stakes have risen markedly in recent years, both as technologies become smarter and in the light of less benevolent applications of these same tools. One innovation, called Deep Packet Inspection, lies at the intersection of these responses to over-zealous forms of Internet control and wider questions about who the Internet is ultimately for. Deep Packet Inspection is a much more subtle form of control precisely because it is deep within the transmission infrastructure; once deployed users are not even aware that it is affecting what they access and what they eventually see. This application basically performs a form of triage on the substance of the traffic being carried by the service provider; the undesired content or that which a provider wants to charge the user for is then ordered accordingly. Desirable, that is, paid for or politically correct content, gets the green light. The rest has to wait. Whilst this sifting process is automated and performed in seconds, it amounts to censorship by other means. It effectively undercuts the intrinsic neutrality of Internet transmission, the essential condition of the Internet as a global open medium.

Whilst commercial interests and efficiency arguments make a strong case for Deep Packet Inspection as Internet uses grow and capacity comes under pressure, opponents note that Western-owned filtering tools are complicit in their use by repressive governments: the Syrian authorities, Gaddafi's Libya and Chinese government all make or have made use of Euro-American expertise and tools to filter and block Internet traffic (Deibert 2008; Holmes 2007). For example, freedom of expression watchers note that the Boeing-owned tool, Echelon, was deployed by the Mubarak regime to track protester messages; other Deep Packet Inspection tools were used in Ben-Ali's Tunisia, and by the military junta in Burma.

Human Rights and Principles for the Internet

At recent intergovernmental forums setting Internet governance agendas, a number of NGO-led initiatives came together to advocate putting human rights right at the centre of deliberations. Approaching access and the conditions of Internet use as a right rather than a privilege shifts the terms of debate away from market-based or state-centric problem solving.

At the UN Internet Governance Forum meeting in Hyderabad in 2008, a loose coalition of NGOs, grassroots groups, government representatives, private sector companies and academic participants set to work under the auspices of what is called the Internet Rights and Principles (IRP) Coalition on the process of drafting an overarching charter of human rights and principles for the online environment. Participants consulted online, through email and listserv, web-based, and social media facilitated discussions and drafting, and offline, in related meetings around the world. The aim was to bring the Universal Declaration of Human Rights and other civil, social, and economic rights covenants into the digital era. After a year of drafting, 'collabowriting' and consultations, the first version of the Charter of Internet Rights and Principles for the Internet was launched in 2011.

Note that human rights and their value are contested, as **Chapter 27** points out.

Emerging out of the UN Internet Governance Forum meetings, with roots in the preceding World Summit on the Information Society meetings, these initiatives also reach further back, to calls for a New World Information and Communications Order in the 1970s (MacBride 1980). In those pre-Internet days freedom of expression and free press advocates had a comparable role to the digital activists today. Whilst many onlookers, governments, legal practitioners, and members of the international human rights community have been circumspect in their assessment of the point of this exercise, the IRP Charter has managed to bring a number of issues into one frame. These discussions were taking place as the Arab Spring uprisings were gathering momentum and the safety of Tunisian and Egyptian bloggers, Tweeters and old school activists was in the spotlight. The IRP Charter makes visible all these contradictory forces. Those drafting, commenting, and disseminating the eventual Charter represented the range of stakes in the future of the Internet in so far as their particular affiliation, political ideology and technical expertise allowed. The IRP Coalition is in short a child of the Internet era, even though the document on which the Charter is based is one of the foundation documents of the United Nations, the Universal Declaration of Human Rights.

All participating parties in the Charter drafting and launch concur that the Internet is as much a product of its times as it is a driver of change. The Internet in this respect is not only the point of this thought experiment but also the means by which the Charter project emerged. Participants consider the future of the Internet as a 'people-centred medium' to be a matter of concern and a reason to mobilize around, as others use it to reach into our inner lives or suppress and control populations. Whilst differing intensely on the implications of considering the Internet in rights-based terms, coalition

BOX 9.4 TEN PUNCHY PRINCIPLES

Charter of Human Rights and Principles for the Internet

1 **Universality**: All humans are born free and equal in dignity and rights, which must be respected, protected and fulfilled in the online environment.
2 **Accessibility**: Everyone has an equal right to access and use a secure and open Internet.
3 **Neutrality**: Everyone must have uniform access to the Internet's content, free from prioritization, discrimination, censorship, filtering or traffic control.
4 **Rights**: The Internet is a space for the promotion, protection and fulfillment of human rights. Everyone has the duty to respect the rights of all others in the online environment.
5 **Expression**: Everyone has the right to hold and express opinions, and to seek, receive, and impart information on the Internet without arbitrary interference or surveillance. Everyone has the right to communicate anonymously online.
6 **Life, liberty and security**: The rights to life, liberty, and security must be respected, protected and fulfilled online. These rights must not be infringed upon, or used to infringe other rights, in the online environment.
7 **Privacy**: Everyone has the right to privacy online free from surveillance, including the right to control how their personal data is collected, used, disclosed, retained and disposed.
8 **Diversity**: Cultural and linguistic diversity on the Internet must be promoted, and technical and policy innovation should be encouraged to facilitate diversity of expression.
9 **Standards and regulation**: The Internet's architecture shall be based on open standards that facilitate interoperability and inclusion of all for all.
10 **Governance**: Rights must form the legal and normative foundations upon which the Internet operates and is governed. . . . in a transparent and multilateral manner, based on principles of openness, inclusive participation and accountability as prescribed by law.

(IRP Coalition 2011; see CGR.br 2009)

members also concurred that it is now the medium of choice for people to meet, organize, do business, make mischief, generate community. As the **Charter's** 'About the Charter' web-page points out:

> This Charter interprets and explains universal human rights standards in a new context – the Internet. The Charter re-emphasizes that human rights apply online as they do offline. . . . The Charter also identifies Internet policy principles which are necessary to fulfil human rights in the Internet age – to support and expand the capacity of the Internet as a medium for civil, political, economic, social and cultural development.
>
> (IRP Coalition 2011)

As individual governments incorporate rights to access the Internet into their constitutions or debate national digital rights bills, the terms and conditions of these moves remain problematic. Whilst the use of the Internet to undermine or enhance existing human rights has entered national, regional and international policy-making debates, questions about a rights-based as opposed to a problem-solving approach remain contentious. In the meantime as debates about the pros and cons of the Internet as a right gain traction in the blogosphere and online media outlets (Cerf 2012; Bernal 2012; Jørgensen 2006), the United Nations Human Rights Council has embraced the principle underlying the IRP Charter (La Rue 2011).

BROADER ISSUES
INTERNET FUTURES

The Internet is all about interconnectedness, a particular understanding of communications no longer premised on face-to-face or physical proximity. We use the Internet to connect with others in non-embodied, supraterritorial, instantaneous and multiplex interrelationships which operate in ways that see computer programs, machines and humans intimately connected. Changes in the way we use these technologies are co-defined by ways in which they use us. These 'couplings' between humans and machines (Haraway 1990; Franklin 2009) are where Internet politics and the politics of the Internet cut right across conventional frameworks and objects of analysis and action, such as the *a priori* distinction between mind and body; modernist cartographic conquests of space, time, and territory; organic understandings of embodiment; and experience around power hierarchies of gender, race and class.

The jury is still out as to whether all the changes the Internet is bringing are a good or bad thing, and whether it really marks a break in the history of humankind, as significant as the invention of the wheel or the printing press. It facilitates multilateral connections across time-zones and geographical borders and has gained a leading role in longstanding narratives of progress and development through science and technology, and their contestation.

Several broader issues emerge from this selective account.

Futures and pasts

First there are historical issues. As a telecommunications architecture, information resource and way to communicate, the Internet has been up and running for about 40 years. It is only in the last 25 years that it took off in popular terms around the world. Since 2004, with the development of commercial services that combine once separate uses such as email, instant messaging, web-pages and blogs into one package, social media uses of the Internet – or Web 2.0 – have changed the way Internet users see and experience their world. Together with the integration of powerful tools that navigate and search the web for us, this generation of social media affects the way the Internet now looks and feels, co-creating the sort of material we access online. User-generated content, peer-to-peer networking, and speedy ways to locate information from anywhere now characterize the Internet as we know it.

This relatively short history – the modern printing press dates from the mid-fifteenth century, the telephone from the late nineteenth century – is also one that is still being written. In this chapter we are not talking about a set of media and technologies past. We are looking at something that is still under construction, in constant flux and with noticeably faster waves of innovation and obsolescence. By the time this book goes to print a number of the events and tools mentioned may well already be yesterday's news, and back catalogue.

Various forms of activism are discussed in this book: environmentalism (**Chapter 4**); feminist movements (**Chapter 5**); religious movements (**Chapter 6**); grassroots democracy (**Chapter 14**); anti-capitalist movements (**Chapter 18**); and anti-war movements (**Chapter 28**), for example.

For activists and advocacy networks working towards a variety of social justice goals the Internet has become an indispensable tool for mobilization, networking and fund-raising. More than that however, it has become an advocacy goal in itself as these groups start forming alliances with others advocating a more socially-embedded, human rights based approach to the design and policy priorities of all aspects of the current and future Internet architecture, both as a global overarching information infrastructure and a local, culturally specific one.

These platforms and their various political and social contours are challenging the local–national–international matrix by which scholars have studied global politics. They organize trans-locally across various borders and are taking up successive generations of new media without dispensing with face-to-face or local understandings of sociopolitical organization and mobilization. The Internet represents both costs and opportunities in terms of national and multilateral authority and accountability. Those with the money, resources and time make full use of all that today's Internet media has to offer; they employ micro-blogging, blogs, websites, and standard email formats to further their cause. Corporations, governments, and activists are becoming increasingly cyber-savvy. In this sense the Internet is not just a network of things, it is also a cultural practice, part of, not outside, the media and society.

Rethinking world order in a digital age

As user-generated content straddles parochial, personal and global domains of action and reflection, jurisdiction over the practices and content of online users at home and abroad does too. The Internet, however defined, is not a single determinant of these effects. This technology of technologies comprises more than one way of being online; successive generations of software systems overlay one another.

When considering the broader implications of how we use the Internet we need to beware of reiterating instrumentalist or determinist understandings of the interplay between politics, society and technology (Benjamin 1973; Haraway 1990). The Internet is more than one thing in material terms, and it means more than one thing in cultural and symbolic terms. Its systems and ways of doing things are the outcome of accident and design, investment and luck, state intervention and market forces. As noted by Donna Haraway in the late 1980s, we get the Internet we deserve in so far as it is a critical factor in:

For a discussion of technology and the division of the world into territorial states see **Chapter 11**.

> an emerging system of world order analogous in its novelty and scope to that created by industrial capitalism: we are living through a movement from an organic, industrial society to a polymorphous, information system . . . from the comfortable old hierarchical dominations to the scary new networks . . . called the informatics of domination.
>
> (Haraway 1990: 203)

BOX 9.5 DONNA HARAWAY

FIGURE 9.8
Donna Haraway with Cayenne, 2006. Photograph by Rusten Hogness. Wikipedia commons: en.wikipedia.org/wiki/File:Donna_Haraway_and_Cayenne.jpg

In the late 1980s, the radical biologist, feminist and social activist Donna Haraway published her *Cyborg Manifesto* (1990), an essay in which she presented an alternative vision of future 'fruitful couplings' between humans and machines that would transcend conventional, embodied experiences and power hierarchies along gender, race, and class lines of privilege and exclusion. The essay's combination of futurist thinking, feminist science fiction, and Marxian critique came as neoliberal thinking and its accompanying belief in market-based globalization reached a peak in the 1980s. Haraway notes that the promises of liberation, permissiveness, and freedom offered by technological progress come with a price if they are taken on board uncritically by ordinary people and policy-makers. Like other thinkers before and since, Haraway notes that human beings and society have been increasingly dependent on automated machines and systems for centuries (see Franklin 2009; Holmes 2007; Latour 2007). Haraway's work has set the benchmark in the way disciplines as disparate as primatology, feminism, biotechnology and computing regard the intersection of power relations around gender, race and class.

The Internet is also a vision of the future based on struggles over its development to date in the parts of the world from which it has emerged. Hence the Internet represents a resolutely hi-tech, Western understanding of the world. Yet as non-Western parts of the world come online, non-Western users in the Internet's heartlands leave their digital footprint in cyberspace as well, and emerging powers (India, China and Brazil for instance) take a proactive stance to rolling out Internet access on their own terms, we can see competing visions of the future Internet coming into force.

Who 'we' are influences how we use the Internet

The way different actors use the Internet – spontaneously or more strategically – makes a difference to the sorts of stakes they have in its future. States have always been active on the web, using the Internet if not in projects of E-Government or E-Commerce then to roll out a variety of cyber-security programs that target not only citizens but also potential terrorist threats. By some accounts, states have always controlled the Internet and should continue to do so (Goldsmith and Wu 2006; Giacomello *et al.* 2009); Secretary of State Hillary Clinton's Digital Diplomacy is a US foreign policy position paper on the matter (Clinton 2010). It is also hard to overlook the formative role played by the US military defence establishment in financing the Internet's core architecture, from its prototype, the ARPAnet, to ownership and control of its underlying functionality, the domain name system (Mueller 2002). In short, the architecture, freely available and pay-for products and services that make up the Internet have always had a double life, useful for both civil and military purposes (Holmes 2007; Deibert 2008).

For more on the role of corporations in the global economy, see **Chapters 15, 16 and 17**, for example.

Corporations are intrinsic to the form and substance of today's Internet. Once small start-up companies in people's garages have become powerful transnational corporations who own and control much of what we do online: Microsoft, Google, Wikipedia, Facebook and Amazon. These large corporations and smaller commercially oriented users see the Internet as an indispensable part of their daily business; indeed their business is made from our downloads, the advertising revenue generated by our web-searches, and the merchandising that can be generated by the integration of online and offline public relations and advertising.

At the same time, however, civilian uses and applications in the USA and elsewhere played a major role in the development of the web as a social, egalitarian and open-ended space to communicate and exchange ideas. Part of the West-Coast counterculture in the USA during its early years, much of its later applications and architectural development have emerged from software designers and computer engineers looking to connect up people and places with compatible and easy-to-use systems and applications. More affordable and adaptable operating systems now run and facilitate user-generated and institutional uses of the Internet in parts of Western Europe and the Global South such as India.

Pitted against this free and open-source ethos is a more commercial one that now dominates our desktops, smart-phones and operating systems. The Internet we use is currently owned and controlled by powerful corporations: Microsoft, Apple, Google, Wikipedia, Amazon, Facebook, Skype and Twitter. The Google generation and the next

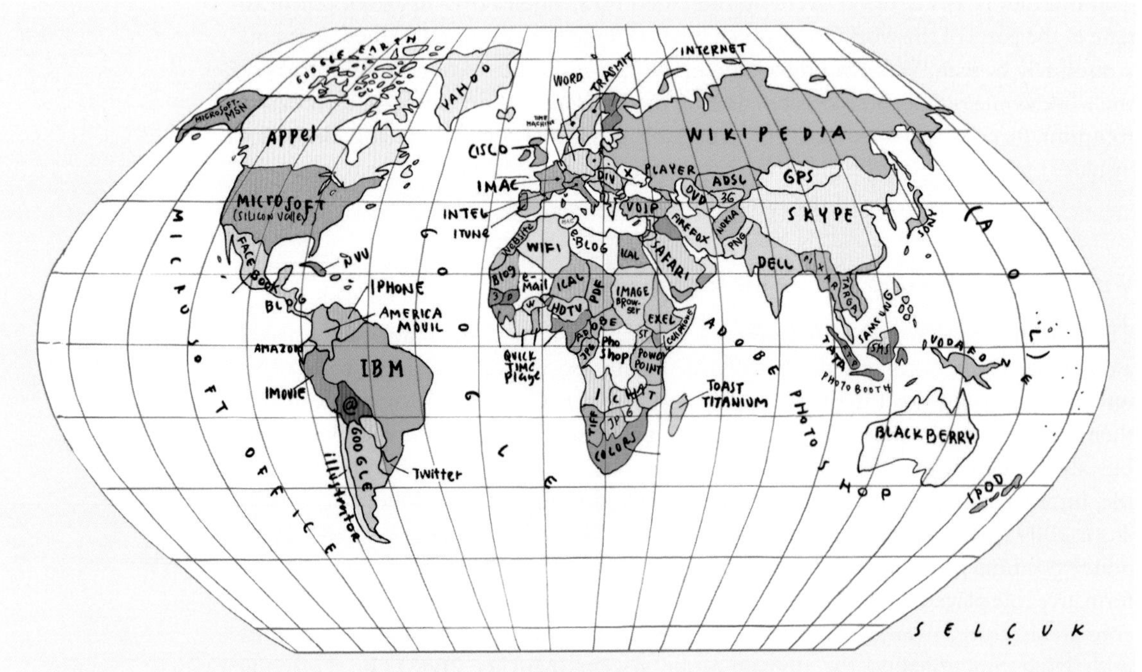

FIGURE 9.9
Selçuk, *Le Monde diplomatique* (2010). selcuk.demirel @wanadoo.fr

BOX 9.6 WHAT IF THE INTERNET GROUND TO A HALT?

Imagine if the Internet ground to a complete halt across the world, denying access to the world's population currently able to access the web. What would happen to our social life, the way we work, what we do in our free time? How would local councils, government departments, banks, and stock markets operate? At the institutional level, how would the United Nations, universities, schools, libraries, hospitals, transnational corporations, small and medium-sized businesses function?

What if we were to discover that the content of our messages to friends, family, or work colleagues were being monitored without our knowledge? What if our personal data was being used by a social networking site not just for market research but to generate advertising revenue without our consent? What if we were imprisoned or threatened with deportation for sedition or participation in activities deemed illegal in another country? What if we found out that the Internet we use is a far more limited one in terms of the sort of things we can do online than the one other people use abroad? What if those products and services we currently use became illegal (music downloads), no longer fully accessible (YouTube), or too expensive (subscriptions to our social network service)?

If we experienced an injustice online where could we turn for help or redress? If this agent is a corporation, for example, a computer game manufacturer or social networking site, we may then discover that on ticking the terms and conditions of use we actually gave tacit permission for our personal data, our digital footprint to be tracked for market research purposes; it is up to us to activate our privacy settings ourselves. Even if this (ad-tracking and filtering harmful content) watchful eye is benign then what sorts of watchdogs are in place to ensure that these practices are within the law? What if it were not so benign, say our own government? Who do we turn to then? Stronger still, what if unwittingly we bring ourselves and others under scrutiny, in danger of being denied access, being prosecuted or even deported?

Finally, what if we were to decide that we no longer wanted to use the Internet, to decide to un-subscribe ourselves – pull our photos and postings off the web? Who do we contact, under whose jurisdiction does our life online and our profile/s fall anyway? Do we own the rights to our own photos? How do we track down those tagged photos out there on the web – should we try? Do we have a right to forget and be forgotten? Is non-connectedness an option?

generation of digital natives still have relatively unimpeded access to a variety of commercial and non-commercial uses of the Internet. But for how long?

I will end this section by way of one final example; one whose outcome stems from and affects how we use the Internet: the privacy policies of Internet service providers who effectively use the Internet on our behalf.

Public privacy matters

Visible on the right-hand side of millions of screens, the following phrase announced a change in Google's privacy policy effective from 1 March 2012:

> We're changing our privacy policy and terms. This stuff matters.
>
> (Google Banner 2012)

On clicking the 'find out more' link, at the end of the presentation of what was or was not changing to the way this corporation tracks, stacks, and stores data based on millions of people's individual web-searching activities, the reader would come upon the following legal stipulation:

> Notice of change: 1 March 2012 is when the new Privacy Policy and Google Terms of Service will come into effect. If you *choose* to keep using Google once the change occurs, you will be doing so under the new Privacy Policy and Terms of Service.
> (Google Banner 2012, emphasis added)

'Beware: your digital imagination leaves traces' (Latour, 2007).

Many media and Internet rights activists and advocacy groups in the Global South as well as Washington DC regard the ability that Internet service providers, in this case the world's largest one, have to dictate the terms of use troubling. The implications of Google's decision to integrate millions of people's personal data for personal privacy and corporate accountability in the future is a contentious point. For considering how the way we use the Internet and how those uses are governed, overtly and covertly, with or without our active or tacit consent, the issue for many is that 'we cannot depend on the private sector alone to defend our constitutional rights. . . . Private intermediaries only bother with defending freedom of expression when it undermines their business interests' (Abraham 2012).

CONCLUSION

'The computer is not only a machine or tool: it is also a medium that determines *how* we perceive just as much as *what* we perceive' (Deuber-Mankowsky 2008: 993).

We take the Internet so much for granted nowadays that we overlook how socioculturally embedded it is in everyday life for the 30 per cent of the world that still currently controls its strategic infrastructure. We overlook how new users are mainly in the Global South or emerging economies in Brazil, India and China. Even without considering how these more recent users might use the Internet in ways other than those we are used to, the way in which the Internet mediates and co-constitutes contemporary political life cannot be grasped in an instrumental way of thinking about technology and society.

How we use the Internet and the way these uses impact on the Internet's past and future functioning emerge from contradictory impulses, including spontaneous practices, long-term research and development investment strategies, and conscious deployments that are always contestable even if they are presented as self-explanatory to everyday users.

The Internet, however defined, and as it morphs into the succeeding generation from the Web 2.0 of the social media we all have come to rely on or resent in varying measures, has already made a difference, based on the way we and others have been using it, or not. As this chapter has shown, when we gauge the difference Internet use makes, vantage points and the politics of access matter. A person in the US, whether an activist, lobbyist or congress-person, accesses and uses their Internet in different ways from those doing so from a European, Chinese or Indian vantage point. Digital and embodied activists, terrorists, digerati and those who want to log-off and unplug for ever, all have different stakes in the battle shaping up over who gets to set the agenda for how the Internet will be used, and on whose terms it will be used in the future.

FURTHER READING

Internet studies is a broad and multidisciplinary literature and one that is booming. It is also one where the products and services covered have a short shelf-life. To get a sense of this fast-moving terrain, the following books provide key anchor points in disciplinary and historical terms: Neil Spiller's *Cyber_Reader* (2002) provides access to landmark texts from precursor and contemporary thinkers. *The Social Media Reader* edited by Michael Mandiberg (2012) brings us into the Web 2.0 era. *The Routledge Handbook of Internet Politics* edited by Andrew Chadwick and Phillip Howard (2009) provides a good entry for mainstream approaches in politics. Jørgensen (2006) engages with human rights activism related to UN consultations, whilst Napoli and Aslama (2010) cover a range issues at the intersection of policy-making, political activism and media advocacy in the USA. Lessig (2006) and Mueller (2002) are landmark texts dealing with the inner workings of the Internet behind the screen. Donna Haraway's *Cyborg Manifesto* (1990) and Brian Holmes' essay, 'Future Map' (2007) are radical interventions on alternative ways of thinking about the interconnection of information and communications technologies, culture and society.

WEBSITES

The list of useful websites below covers intergovernmental organizations, advocacy and activist networks active in the crisscrossing domains of Internet and media policy-making, direct action, and alternative media and information.

Intergovernmental, activist, advocacy networks

International Telecommunications Union – World Summit on the Information Society: http://www.itu.int/wsis/index.html
Internet Governance Forum: http://www.intgovforum.org/cms/
Association For Progressive Communications (APC): http://www.apc.org/en/projects/Internet-rights-are-human-rights
Avaaz: http://www.avaaz.org/en/index.php
Accessnow: https://www.accessnow.org/
Global Voices: http://globalvoicesonline.org/
Anonymous: http://anonnews.org/; http://twitter.com/anonymousirc
Chilling Effects: http://chillingeffects.org/

Blogs

Whilst the first three bloggers are all US-based, they have been regularly monitoring and commenting on the Internet's use, misuse, and changing contours of its institutional and infrastructural landscapes for some time. The last three are NGOs with a comparably long-standing and clear view of the issues at stake from a Global South perspective.

Internet Governance Project: http://blog.Internetgovernance.org/
Rebecca MacKinnon: RConversation at http://rconversation.blogs.com/
Douglas Rushkoff: Homepage and Blog: http://www.rushkoff.com/
IT4Change: http://www.itforchange.net/
Centre for Internet and Society: http://cis-india.org/
Association for Progressive Communications – Women's Networking Support Program (APC-WNSP): http://www.apcwomen.org/

REFERENCES

Abraham, Sunil (2012) 'Sense and Censorship', Centre for Internet and Society, 31 January, http://cis-india.org/Internet-governance/sense-and-censorship.

Benjamin, Walter (1973) 'The Work of Art in the Age of Mechanical Reproduction', in Hannah Arendt (ed.), *Walter Benjamin, Illuminations*, London: Fontana Press.

Bernal, Paul (2012) The Internet IS a (Human) Right, Symbiotic Web Blog, 11 January, http://symbioticweb.blogspot.com/2012/01/Internet-is-human-right.html.

Cerf, Vint (2012) 'Internet Access is not a Human Right', *New York Times*, 4 January, http://www.nytimes.com/2012/01/05/opinion/Internet-access-is-not-a-human-right.html?_r=1.

CGR.br (2009) Brazilian Internet Steering Committee Principles, http://www.cgi.br/english/regulations/resolution2009–003.htm.

Chadwick, Andrew and Phillip N. Howard (eds) (2009) *The Routledge Handbook of Internet Politics*, London and New York: Routledge.

Clinton, Hillary Rodham (2010) *Internet Freedom*, speech delivered at the Newseum in Washington, DC, 21 January, http://www.foreignpolicy.com/articles/2010/01/21/Internet_freedom?page=full.

Deibert, Ronald J. (2008) 'Black Code Redux: Censorship, Surveillance, and the Militarization of Cyberspace', in Megan Boler (ed.), *Digital Media and Democracy: Tactics in Hard Times*, Cambridge, MA and London: MIT Press.

Deibert, Ronald J. and Rafal Rohozinski (2010) 'Risking Security: Policies and Paradoxes of Cyberspace Security', *International Political Sociology* 4, 1: 15–32.

Deuber-Mankowsky, Astrid (2008) 'The Phenomenon of Lara Croft', in Michael Ryan (ed.), *Cultural Studies: An Anthology*, Malden, MA and Oxford: Blackwell Publishers.

El Dahshan, Mohamed (2012) 'Quit Twitter? No. Let's Trust It', *Guardian*, 28 January: 18.

Franklin, M. I. (2009) 'Sex, Gender and Cyberspace', in Laura Shepherd (ed.), *Gender Matters in Global Politics: A Feminist Introduction to International Relations*, London and New York: Routledge.

——(2010) 'Digital Dilemmas: Transnational Politics in the 21st Century', *Brown Journal of World Affairs*, 16, 11: 67–85.

Giacomello, Giampiero, Johan Ericksson, Mahmoud Sahli, Miriam Dunn-Cavelty, J. P. Singh and M. I. Franklin (2009) 'Who Controls the Internet? Beyond the Obstinacy or Obsoleteness of the State', *International Studies Review* 11, 1: 205–26.

Goldsmith, Jack and Tim Wu (2006) *Who Controls the Internet? Illusions of a Borderless World*, New York: Oxford University Press.

Google Banner (2012) http://www.google.co.uk/, 9 February.

Haraway, D. J. (1990) 'A Cyborg Manifesto: Science, Technology, and Socialist Feminism in the 1980s', in Linda Nicholson (ed.), *Feminism/Postmodernism*, New York and London: Routledge.

Holmes, Brian (2007) 'Future Map or How the Cyborgs Learned to Stop Worrying and Learned to Love Surveillance', http://brianholmes.wordpress.com/2007/09/09/future-map/.

Internet Governance Forum (IGF) (2008) *Workshop #52: ICTs and an Environmentally Sustainable Internet: Another Challenge of Connecting the Next Billion Internet Users*, http://www.intgovforum.org/cms/2008-igf-hyderabad.

IRP Coalition (2011) Charter of Human Rights and Principles for the Internet: Beta Version 1.1, http://Internetrightsandprinciples.org/node/367.

Jørgensen, Rikke F. (ed.) (2006) *Human Rights in the Global Information Society*, Cambridge, MA: MIT Press.

La Rue, Frank (2011) *Report of the Special Rapporteur on the Promotion and Protection of the Right to Freedom of Opinion and Expression.* Human Rights Council, UN General Assembly, A/HRC/17/27, 16 May.

Latour, Bruno (2007) 'Beware, Your Imagination Leaves Digital Traces', *Times Higher Education Supplement*, 6 April, http://docs.google.com/View?docid=ad6vvc428w8_103gzv2fdgf.

Lessig, Lawrence (2006) *Code Version 2.0*, New York: Basic Books.

MacBride, Sean (ed.) (1980) *Many Voices, One World: Towards a New More Just and More Efficient World Information and Communication Order*, report by the International Commission for the Study of Communication Problems, Paris/London/New York: Unesco/Kogan Page/Unipub.

Mandiberg, Michael (2012) *The Social Media Reader*, New York and London: New York University Press.

Mueller, Milton (2002) *Ruling the Root: Internet Governance and the Taming of Cyberspace*, Cambridge, MA: MIT Press.

Napoli, Philip M. and Minna, Aslama (eds) (2010) *Communications Research in Action: Scholar–Activist Collaborations for a Democratic Public Sphere*, New York: Fordham University Press.

Nye, Joseph S. Jnr (2002) 'The Information Revolution and American Soft Power', *Asia Pacific Review* 9, 1: 60–76.

Spiller, N. (2002) *Cyber_Reader: Critical Writings for the Digital Era*. London and New York: Phaidon Press.

Sreberny, Annabelle and Gholam Khiabany (2010) *Blogistan: The Internet and Politics in Iran*, London and New York: I. B. Tauris.

United Nations General Assembly (2000) *Millennium Development Goals*, http://www.un.org/millenniumgoals/.

WSIS Civil Society Caucus (2003) *Shaping Information Societies for Human Needs: Civil Society Declaration to the World Summit on the Information Society*, 8 December, http://www.itu.int/wsis/docs/geneva/civil-society-declaration.pdf.

——(2005) *Civil Society Declaration: Much More Could Have Been Achieved*, document WSIS-05/TUNIS/CONTR/13-E, 23 December, http://www.worldsummit2003.de/download_en/WSIS-CS-summit-statement-rev1-23-12-2005-en.pdf.

For a range of further resources supporting this chapter, please visit the companion website for *Global Politics, 2nd Edition* at www.routledge.com/cw/edkins/

CHAPTER 10

Why is people's movement restricted?

Roxanne Lynn Doty

THE QUESTION
BORDER CROSSINGS

On 22 February 2006 US Border Patrol agents found the body of the first undocumented border crosser to die in Cochise County, Arizona for that year (*Arizona Daily Star* 2006). The man's name was Antonio Dominguez Callejas, from Vera Cruz, Mexico. He was 47 years old and had died of exposure and dehydration approximately 35 hours before he was found. Antonio's death was just one of over 400 undocumented border crossers who would die in 2006 and one of the 3,600–4,000 who have died in the past 10–12 years (Rubio-Goldsmith *et al.* 2006; US Government Accounting Office 2006). Approximately 20 per cent of these deaths have been women and children. The situation on the US–Mexico border is not unique. According to the United Nations Economic and Social Council, over 3,000 migrants died between 1997 and 2000 attempting to reach Europe, most of these while attempting to cross the Straits of Gibraltar (United Nations Economic and Social Council E/CN.4/2002/NGO/45). These deaths painfully illustrate that while it is undoubtedly true that advances in transportation and communication have facilitated the relatively easy movement of some people across the globe, some movements entail unspeakable tragedy.

Globalization has been accompanied by increasing numbers of people moving across borders for various reasons. Many forms of border crossing are wholeheartedly welcomed by governments. For example, almost all governments encourage and actively seek to promote the movement of peoples across their borders in the form of international tourism, which is the world's largest export earner as well as one of the most important sources of employment. In many countries it is the number one industry. In January 2007, the secretary-general of the World Tourism Organization reported that world tourism had entered a historically new phase of growth which began in 2004. In 2005, there were 800 million international arrivals. In 2006 international arrivals surpassed 840 million, representing over 20 per cent growth in the span of 3 years (United Nations World Tourism Organization 2007). Another form of movement across borders that is increasing and that is encouraged by governments involves education. In 2004, approximately 2 million students were enrolled in institutes of higher education outside their country or origin (Freeman 2006; Thorn 2005). Indeed the movement of people across borders for the purpose of higher education is not only encouraged by governments, but has also become part of the global marketplace, with the World Trade Organization taking it on as an area of concern (Altbach 2001).

Changes in the global political economy are discussed in **Chapter 17**.

Other forms of movement across borders such as international business travel, overseas employment, and some types of immigration are also welcomed and facilitated by governments. Economically motivated migration is described by immigration scholars in terms of 'push' and 'pull' factors. The lack of job opportunities, low wages, and poverty 'push' people to leave a country. They are 'pulled' to those places where employment opportunities exist and/or where they can earn higher salaries (Isbister 1996: 95–8; Hollifield 2000). As the world continues to become increasingly interconnected in numerous ways, so too does the movement of people across borders accelerate. A couple of examples illustrate this. In the United States, the number of persons granted permanent legal residency in 1986 was 601,708 (Migration Policy Institute 2004). By the year 2006 this figure was 1,266,264 (Migration Policy Institute 2007). The inflow of people from other countries to the United Kingdom for 1991 was 53,900. By 2006 this number had increased to 143,205 (Migration Policy Institute 2007). Clearly these various realms of movement are part and parcel of the phenomenon of globalization. However, not all movement is welcomed and often encounters strong and at times ugly opposition. This is most obviously the case when it comes to the movement of peoples who, for various reasons, do not have the proper authorization. Many human beings who have crossed sovereign, national borders without the proper documentation have met with a similar fate to Antonio. Those who do make it often encounter intense, passionate, and sometimes violent opposition in most of the Western industrialized countries. Almost all Western industrialized countries have enacted increasingly restrictive immigration policies over the past decade. This has been the case especially when it comes to unskilled immigrants.

The term 'globalization' is a contested one. Some people argue that changes are exaggerated; others see globalization as a key change in the contemporary world.

Why is this the case? Why is it that some can move relatively freely across borders, but many others face often insurmountable hurdles? Why are people free to move within national borders, but not across them? At one level there are obvious answers to these questions. People can generally move freely *within* national borders if they are citizens

Of course, we need to ask why national borders exist in the first place. Why is the world divided in this way? See **Chapter 11**.

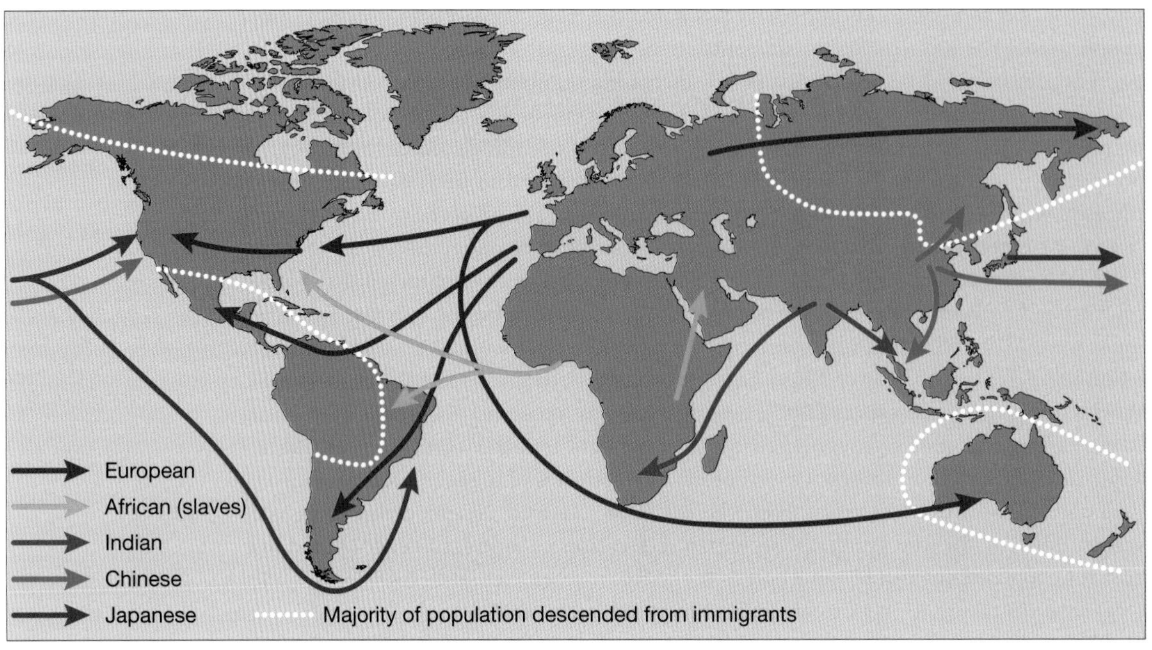

FIGURE 10.1
Map of world migration routes since 1700. After A. Getis (1991) *Introduction to Geography*, 3rd edn, Dubuque: W.C. Brown Publishers

Struggles over what constitutes Chinese national identity and citizenship are discussed in **Chapter 12**, and identity in general in **Chapter 5**.

Chapter 13 examines another aspect of citizenship: the life stories of those who are exiled from their 'home' and those who are uneasy in their allegiance to the nation-state in which they live. **Chapter 12** explores how China treats people of Chinese ancestry now living outside China.

or if they are in the country legally. People can move freely *across* national borders if they have legal authorization to do so. However, these simple, straightforward answers are not entirely adequate to this extraordinarily complex issue. Both citizenship and legality are complex concepts and practices. The ways in which citizenship has been granted as well as the ways in which it has been denied have been linked to social and political phenomena that involve power and struggles over meaning and identity. The same is true for the realm of legality and illegality. For example, it is important to remember that at various times in the history of the United States some practices were legal that would be considered totally unacceptable today, e.g. the enslavement of African-Americans, the internment of Japanese-Americans, and the denial of voting rights to Native Americans and women. Those practices created severe constraints on what citizenship could mean and who could possess it. If the human beings who fell into these categories attempted to exercise the rights that were granted to others it was considered illegal. However, laws change as a result of peoples' fights for rights. Both citizenship and legality are dynamic rather than static. They are undergoing continual change. So, pointing to citizenship and legality as reasons why people's movements are restricted provides us with only partial answers. We still must ask *why* movement should be restricted based on these two things. The term 'illegal' conveys a black and white world in which those who cross without the proper authorization are considered criminals regardless of the circumstances that led them to cross. If we are satisfied with citizenship and legality as reasons why people's movements are restricted, our analysis stops and we go no further. We do not explore the meaning of these concepts themselves and the contexts within which they become significant. We do not examine the powerful forces underlying official policies that pertain to citizenship or the right to move across borders legally. We do not ask *why* they should be accepted as valid reasons for immigration policy.

To understand why people cross borders and why movements are often restricted it is important to explore the contradictory forces that are at work in the world. If we dig deeper we may rethink our preconceptions about citizenship and legality. A more in-depth, critical exploration is essential if we are to understand why, despite the absence of citizenship and the absence of proper authorization, people still move across borders in very large numbers and often at very great risk. A more in-depth analysis is also important if we are to begin to explore the possibilities for change in how we think of borders. In light of the immense consequences restrictions on free movement have for human beings and the society they create, it is necessary for us to engage in a more critical examination as to why and how peoples' movement is restricted and what the outcomes of such restrictions have been.

The UN secretary general Ban Ki-moon has suggested that the free migration of peoples should be welcomed as a way to tackle problems such as poverty (*Guardian* (London), 10 July 2007).

ILLUSTRATIVE EXAMPLE
THE US–MEXICO BORDER AND THE IMMIGRATION CRISIS

La linea, as the line separating Mexico from the United States is sometimes referred to, extends 1,951 miles (3,141 km) from the Pacific Ocean in the west to Brownsville,

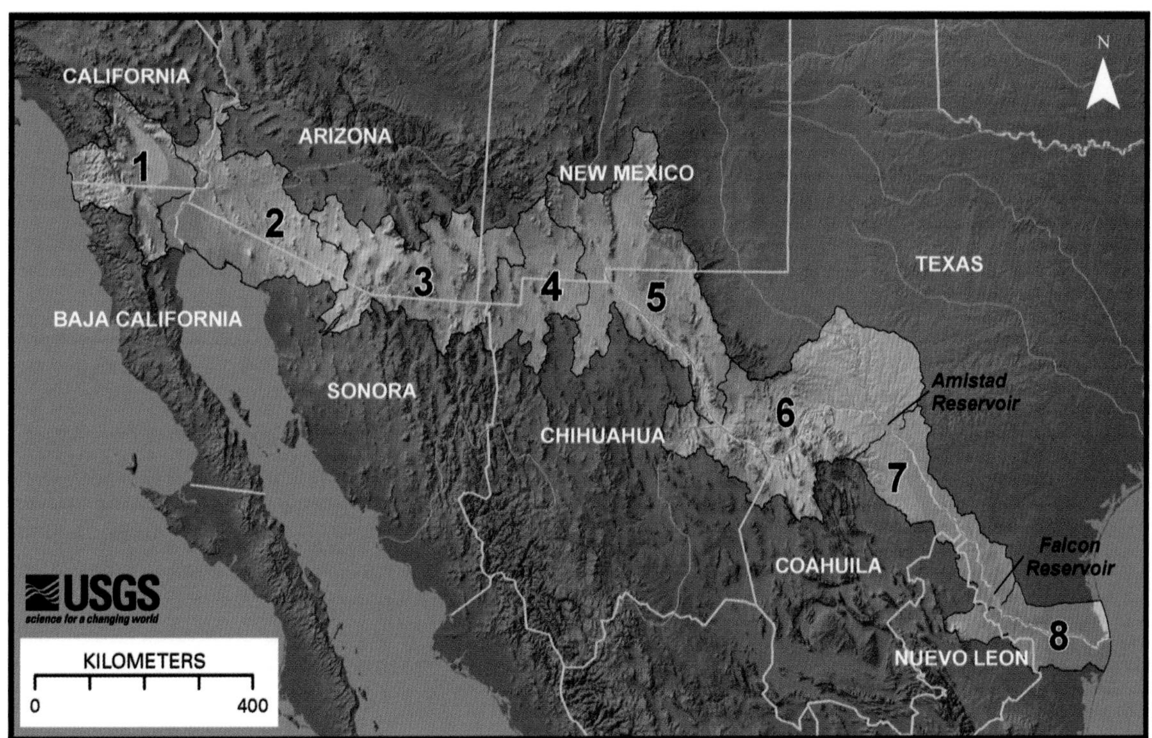

FIGURE 10.2
Aerial photo-map of US–Mexico border. Public domain. USGS

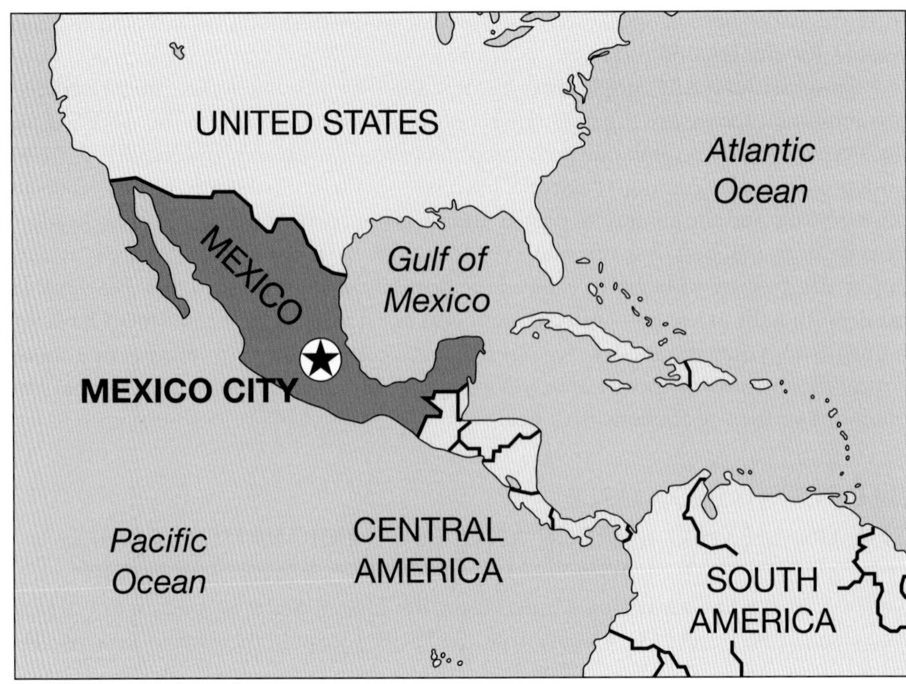

FIGURE 10.3
Map showing US and Mexico in context

Texas and Matamoros, Tamaulipas in the east. It is the longest contiguous border (shared physical boundary) in the world between a first world country and a third world country. It is also the most frequently crossed international border in the world. This border over which many peoples' movement is restricted is a place where, in the words of one writer, 'the Third World grates against the first and bleeds' (Anzaldua 1987). While there are many unique aspects of the current US immigration crises revolving around this particular border, it speaks to and exemplifies the more general phenomenon that the entire world is experiencing. The movement of peoples across national borders without authorization is truly a global phenomenon. This section presents the background to the contemporary issue of undocumented immigration from Mexico into the United States, detailing the border enforcement policies of the 1990s that gave rise to skyrocketing numbers of deaths of migrants as they attempted to cross through dangerous terrain. It also discusses the consequences in terms of the increased use of human smugglers, the efforts of citizen border patrol groups who have taken it upon themselves to guard the US–Mexico border, the formation of migrant rights groups and an anti-immigrant movement. This section concludes with a review of policies that have been proposed and some that have been adopted.

Chapter 18 talks about what it means to think in terms of the idea of 'crisis'.

The contemporary immigration crisis can be traced to several events far removed from the US–Mexico border. In 1993 New York's World Trade Center was bombed by suspected unauthorized immigrants. In the same year two Central Intelligence Agency employees in Virginia were assassinated by an unauthorized immigrant from Pakistan. These two events as well as the economic recession that persisted in the United States at the time, helped to fuel anti-immigrant sentiment (Nevins 2002). They also contributed to the framing of undocumented immigration as a national security issue. Against this background, in the early morning hours of 6 June 1993 a ship carrying 286 human beings without authorization to enter the United States ran aground on Rockaway Beach in Queens, New York. The name of the ship was the *Golden Venture* and the unauthorized passengers were from China, mostly from the province of Fujan. Ninety of the passengers had boarded that ship in February off the coast of Thailand. Another 200 boarded in March off Mombasa, Kenya, having been stranded there for a year after the other smuggling ship they were on, *Najd II*, broke down. Ten passengers drowned and the others were immediately detained by the US Immigration and Naturalization Service (INS) and jailed. While this had little to do with the southern border of the United States it brought the issue of undocumented immigration to the forefront of national attention. It also contributed to notions of the US being 'invaded' by 'illegal aliens'.

Border control strategies

Around the same time, Silvestre Reyes, then border patrol chief in El Paso, Texas, launched a border operation called *Operation Blockade*, later renamed *Operation Hold the Line* because the first name was considered offensive. On 19 September 1993 he deployed 400 agents and their vehicles in a highly visible show of force along a 20-mile section of border between El Paso, Texas and Ciudad Juarez, Mexico. This marked a departure from the previous strategy of pursuit and apprehension *after* the border had been crossed. Almost immediately apprehensions fell dramatically. Reyes and *Operation Hold the Line* thus received a great deal of favourable national publicity.

Why might people find the name 'Operation Blockade' offensive? Is the changed name any better? Why?

Based on the 'success' of *Operation Hold the Line,* in 1994 the US Immigration and Naturalization Service, in consultation with the US Defense Department's Center for Low Intensity Conflict, developed a new comprehensive border strategy, 'prevention through deterrence'. This became and continues to be the official border enforcement strategy of the United States (US Government Accounting Office 2001). The logic of this strategy was to deter migrants from crossing in the more populated areas. *Operation Hold the Line* in El Paso, Texas was joined by *Operation Gatekeeper* in San Diego, California. The strategy initially targeted these two border areas because at the time they accounted for approximately two thirds of all undocumented entries into the United States. *Operation Gatekeeper* entailed the installation of high-intensity floodlights to illuminate the border day and night as well as eight-foot steel fencing along 14 miles of the border beginning at the Pacific Ocean. Border Patrol agents were stationed every few hundred feet behind this wall (Dunn 1996; Andreas 2000; Nevins 2002).

As had been the case in El Paso, this strategy drastically reduced the number of undocumented crossings and the San Diego area went from being the busiest port on the entire border to a relatively quiet area. 'Prevention through deterrence' was deemed a success and these two operations were joined by *Operation Safeguard* in Nogales, Arizona in 1995. This operation was extended to the cities of Douglas and Naco in 1999. Attention was also heavily focused on deterrence with the passage of the 'Illegal Immigration Reform and Immigrant Responsibility Act' in 1996. Funds were authorized for the construction of additional layers of fencing in San Diego, for the purchase of new military technology, and for the hiring of 1,000 border patrol agents a year through

What do the names 'Operation Gatekeeper' and 'Operation Safeguard' suggest?

FIGURE 10.4 Martin Margas Posadas, 18, from Puebla, Mexico, right, and another man wait in the US Border Patrol holding cell in Campo near California's border with Mexico. Photo: Marc Campos, *Inland Valley Daily Bulletin* staff photographer

the year 2001. In 1997 *Operation Rio Grande*, was put into effect in South East Texas, 60 additional miles of fencing were added to *Gatekeeper* and 10 additional miles to *Hold the Line*. The overall effect of these border enforcement policies has been to push migrants to increasingly remote and dangerous crossing routes and to engage the services of human smugglers or *coyotes*. While crossings decreased in certain areas the overall numbers of undocumented border crossers continued to rise. The 'Binational Migration Institute' (BMI) at the University of Arizona in Tucson recently reported that the 'funnel effect' created by the US border policies of 'prevention through deterrence' is the 'primary structural cause of death of thousands of North American, Central American, and South American unauthorized men, women, and children who have died while trying to enter the US' (Rubio-Goldsmith *et al.* 2006).

Interestingly, and important to note especially in terms of locating this issue in the context of globalization, is the fact that the North American Free Trade Agreement (NAFTA) was being negotiated during the same period of time that the new border enforcement strategies were being put into place. Significantly NAFTA sought to promote the free movement of goods and capital, but not people. Virtually no attention was given to the movement of people for jobs or any other reasons. Efforts to increase border enforcement intensified around the time that NAFTA took effect in 1994. *Operation Gatekeeper* and the other border operations can be seen as efforts to appease those who held the view that NAFTA would increase immigration. It contained no provisions for labour and thus ignored any effects it would have on workers. More recently there has been a sharp drop in reported undocumented border crossings. According to the Pew Hispanic Center, a Washington-based research group, the number of migrants entering the United States without legal authorization during the

BOX 10.1 NORTH AMERICAN FREE TRADE AGREEMENT (NAFTA)

NAFTA is a trade agreement between the United States, Canada and Mexico. NAFTA eliminated all non-tariff trade barriers to agricultural trade between the US and Mexico. Many other tariffs were also eliminated immediately, with others being phased out over a 5–15-year period. Some experts argued that NAFTA would lead to more economic development in Mexico and thus reduce the incentive for undocumented migration to the US. Others said it would increase migration. Both of these seemingly opposed viewpoints were supported by The US Commission for the Study of International Migration and Cooperative Economic Development in 1990. This commission argued that free trade and economic integration was the best long term remedy for unwanted immigration, but that in the short to medium term immigration would likely increase. This has been referred to as the 'migration hump' (Martin 2003). NAFTA was expected to displace millions of Mexican corn farmers (Martin 1993). In an important sense, NAFTA exemplifies the more general contradiction of a world characterized on the one hand by the increased desirability and ease of movement across borders for commodities, services, and some people; and on the other hand by severe restrictions placed on others who are nonetheless compelled to move across those very same borders.

period 2007–9 was about 300,000 which was down significantly from the 850,000 who entered during the 2000–5 time period. The economic recession in the United States is the major reason for this decline and some experts expect the downward trend to end once the economy rebounds (Tran 2010).

Anti-immigration legislation

The contemporary immigration crisis in the United States has met with various proposals, bills, and new laws especially at the local level of cities and towns. The state of Arizona passed Proposition 200 in November 2004, which denies undocumented migrants access to jobs, healthcare, and legal protection. This was a catalyst for a rash of nationwide measures. As of August 2006 more than half of the states in the United States had passed anti-immigrant measures. The city of Hazelton, Pennsylvania passed one of the nation's harshest laws, approving $1,000 fines for landlords who rent to undocumented migrants. In August 2006 landlords in Valley Park, Missouri began evicting tenants who were not in the United States with the proper documents. In September 2006, US Immigration and Customs Enforce (ICE) agents fanned across three counties in the state of Georgia in raids targeting undocumented migrants. Citizens and non-citizens alike were rounded up because of physical appearance. These are just a few of the many examples of local responses to undocumented migration. At the national level, in December 2005 the US House of Representatives passed House Bill 4437, 'Border Protection, Anti-Terrorism, and Illegal Immigration Control Act of 2005', commonly referred to as the Sensenbrenner Bill after its sponsor Representative James Sensenbrenner. This bill is considered by migrant rights groups and many others

The European Union is an example of an area of free movement of goods like NAFTA, though in the EU movement across internal borders between states is normally free for people as well. In the EU too there has been concern about the effect of the ensuing internal labour migration.

to be one of the most draconian in recent history. It would require all employers to use an electronic data base to verify an employee's eligibility to be in the US, authorizes a high-tech fence along sections of the US border, and makes it a criminal offence to come to the aid of migrants in distress. Many humanitarian, religious and medical workers would immediately become criminals. The House bill would have also required immediate detention and deportation of any undocumented person. In response to this bill, the US Senate introduced a compromise bill that proposed a guest worker programme and created paths to citizenship for *some* of the estimated 12 million undocumented migrants who currently live and work in the United States. National level immigration legislation is currently stalled, but continues to be one of the country's most important and divisive issues. As a consequence of the lack of federal immigration legislation, states have begun to pass laws at the local level. On 23 April 2010 Arizona governor Jan Brewer signed SB1070, the Safe Neighborhoods, Immigration, and Law Enforcement Act. The law creates several new misdemeanours, including working or seeking to work without legal status. During any stop, police must ask about one's immigration status if their suspicions are aroused. While the law prohibits racial profilng, what constitutes reasonable suspicion of illegal status is not clear (Aguila 2010; Provine 2010). SB1070 caught the attention of local politicians throughout the United States who expressed interest in similar legislation. In June 2011 the state of Alabama passed HB56, which required publicly funded schools to check students' immigration status and criminalized giving an undocumented migrant a ride. The state of Georgia has taken steps in the same direction (Hogue 2011).

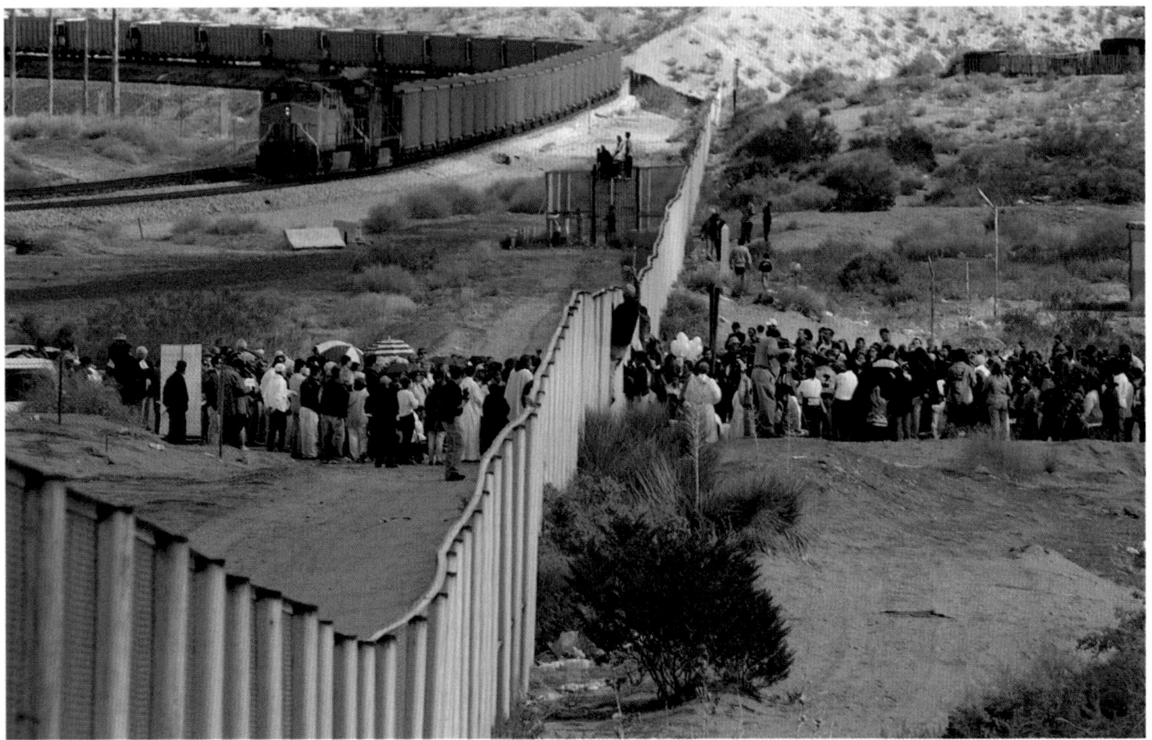

FIGURE 10.5 Day of the Dead, 2 November 2004, Anapra, Mexico. Mass celebrated at the border in memory of undocumented migrants who died while crossing the US–Mexico border. AP/PA Photos

Another proposed piece of legislation that seeks to reinforce a different kind of border is the current effort in the United States to deny birthright citizenship to babies born to undocumented parents. Almost every anti-immigrant organization as well as some policy makers are in favour of revoking this long standing right that is guaranteed in the 14th amendment to the US Constitution. House Bill 698, which was sponsored by 49 members of the US House of Representatives in 2006, would have eliminated this right. The Bill was defeated in December 2006 but it is predicted that it will continue to resurface.

In many parts of the world there is no right to citizenship of a country as a result of birth within its borders alone; often one's parents' citizenship counts too.

Vigilante groups

Some individuals and groups have responded to unauthorized immigration into the United States by taking it upon themselves to engage in the unofficial and unauthorized, though not necessarily illegal, patrolling of the US–Mexico border regions. This phenomenon received much national and international attention with the April 2005 Minuteman Project in southeastern Arizona. By the autumn of 2005 over forty other anti-immigrant border vigilante groups had formed in the United States. These groups not only engage in the physical patrolling of the border, but also often hold rallies at day labour sites where migrant workers gather waiting for work, and at state capitals and Mexican consulates. Despite these responses people continue to cross without the proper documents and border crossing continues to be a dangerous undertaking. Every year with the approach of spring and summer, as the temperatures begin to rise in the Southwestern United States another season of death begins.

GENERAL RESPONSES
IDEAS OF STATES AND CITIZENSHIP

US immigration laws and border enforcement strategies implicitly and explicitly make many assumptions about nations, states, territorial borders, citizenship, and identity that underlie efforts to restrict the movement of peoples. The assumptions that make US border policies possible are mirrored in academic literature that describes a world where the insides of societies are clearly distinguished from the outside. Such a view presents a world that is neatly divided into nation-states separated legally by sovereign territorial borders that are mutually recognized and respected by other states. People living within states' sovereign territorial borders share certain legal, political, social, and cultural marks of identity whose ultimate expression is that of citizenship. On such a view, even though there is much movement across borders, ultimately there exists a link that is impossible to disentangle between the sovereign legal territorial state and its inhabitants, its citizens. These are 'givens', and if they seem to be under threat they must be protected. The nation consisting of citizens who share a national identity is generally assumed to be naturally connected to the state.

There are other ways the world could be ordered. For a discussion of how the world of sovereign states with territorial borders came into being and is sustained, see **Chapter 11**.

Such a view is also inherent in other concepts such as sovereignty, national identity and national security. These concepts which we draw upon to understand the world and which inform policy makers contain within them the notion of a unitary identity for both individuals and collectives. Such an understanding of the world is also ingrained

The problems with this view of the nation-state and citizens sharing a national identity are discussed in **Chapter 13**. Many of the inhabitants of a nation-state do not identify with it in any straightforward way. **Chapter 12** examines how we come to think in terms of nations in the first place.

The way idealized pictures of the world help us begin to think about the world is discussed in **Chapter 2**, and the question of common sense in **Chapter 1**.

in our ways of being and acting in the world. When it comes to unauthorized movements of people, this view presumes that it is natural for the world to be disturbed by people who move across sovereign borders without authorization because some people belong in some places and other people belong in other places. Given sufficient money, enough border patrol agents, military troops, high enough walls, sophisticated enough technology and the political will of leaders, territorial borders can be fortified and secured. The safety and sanctity of the citizen can thus be ensured. The world can be restored to its 'natural' state.

The way of thinking described above is very powerful today. One of the reasons for this may be the fact that it contains a certain commonsensical element. On first glance, it may seem to us simply an accurate description of 'how the world is'. Our lives contain many things that contribute to this sense of 'naturalness', e.g. flags, national anthems, passports, and so on. However, if we pause to critically reflect upon the situations described above, we come away with a much different picture that suggests the 'givens' that we begin with are outdated. We can ask if the 'givens' contained in conventional ideas are sustainable, and at what cost. A great deal of effort is required to maintain the 'truth' of idealized pictures of the world and the conventional view of states, nations, citizens, and identity is increasingly one that does not match the way the world actually is. When such idealized views are called into question by what is happening on the ground, in peoples' everyday lives, and when conventional ideas seem to be becoming unravelled, these efforts generally intensify. We see this happening today in the United States with calls to 'close our borders' and 'protect our sovereignty' on the part of segments of the general populace. We also see it in the various laws and proposals dealing with undocumented immigration discussed above. We must ask though, what is sacrificed in such efforts to sustain these ideas and categories that may no longer suit the world? Crossing borders without the proper documentation obviously entails many sacrifices that stem from restrictive policies that prevent migrants from obtaining the proper documentation; leaving home and family, paying huge sums of money to smugglers, and often paying with their lives. We also need to ask what society as a whole sacrifices when restrictive immigration laws are put into place and when laws aimed at those who already live here without the proper documents are enacted. Further, we need to question the very meaning of society and the values and ideals that have generally been associated with it. We need to rethink our understanding of citizenship and the identities it encompasses and those that it excludes.

Currently, about 12 million undocumented immigrants reside in the United States, although we should remember that it is very difficult to obtain a completely accurate count simply because these people are undocumented. The most widely used method of calculating the undocumented population in the United States is referred to as the 'residual method'. This method estimates the unauthorized population by subtracting the legally resident foreign population from the total number of foreign-born counted in a census (Migration Policy Institute 2004). Some have been here most of their lives, some arrived yesterday. Some live next door to 'us' and send their children to 'our' schools, and pay taxes to 'our' government. Some even fight in 'our' wars. Some live in shacks in the canyons and hills around 'our' most upscale housing developments. Some own their own businesses. Others are 'day labourers' who stand on street corners waiting for work. 'They' reflect the diversity that defines what the United States is today.

Still, none of 'them' have very many rights because their identities are primarily defined by the absence of citizenship. This privileged status is currently out of reach for most of these people. They are therefore subject to arrest and deportation at any time. In the United States the number of undocumented migrants detained jumped to 28,000 during fiscal year 2007, up from 19,700 the previous year (*Arizona Republic* 2007). Undocumented migrants are held in city and county jails as well as detention facilities all over the country, some of which are privately run. Whole families are often detained. An example is the T. Don Hutto Family Residential Detention Center in Taylor, Texas which is owned and operated by the privately run Corrections Corporation of America. This centre, which was opened in May 2006, has come under fire from civil liberties and immigrant rights groups who accuse it of being run like a prison (Rutland 2007). The Center has now been converted into a women's detention facility. Immigration raids at work and other places are also on the increase. It is not uncommon for routine traffic stops to result in deportation for those who are undocumented. In March 2007, three high school students in the Phoenix, Arizona area were deported to Mexico after being stopped for drag racing. An honours student in the justice studies

FIGURE 10.6
Los Angeles immigration demonstration, 25 March 2006.
Photo: Lucas Jackson, Reuters

programme at Arizona State University who has lived in the United States since he was a toddler faced deportation proceedings after being stopped in March 2007 for making an improper right turn (Nanez 2007).

Such a situation makes a statement about the limitations of citizenship as it is currently understood. Citizenship, as a legal category and a category of identity that is attached to a piece of geographical territory is extremely problematic today. Globalization presents challenges to this concept and raises serious questions as to whether the conventional concept of the citizen in political and legal practices which function to exclude and deny rights to those who are not citizens can ultimately survive. The human beings who contribute to society, but live in fear because of their undocumented status, make a silent statement about the limitations of current understandings of 'the citizen'. Recently, this contestation has taken a more visible and openly articulated form, as illustrated in the massive migrant rights demonstrations that took place throughout the US in the spring of 2006.

Citizenship has always contained an exclusionary element. Inherent in the concept of citizenship is the notion of an insider, which necessarily implies an outsider. For example, for Aristotle, one of the most influential of the ancient Greek philosophers, women, foreigners, and slaves were outsiders.

For more on how we imagine what it means to be a citizen and why this matters see **Chapter 14**.

What has been touted as 'universal' citizenship in the United States has, at various moments in history, excluded women, African-Americans and others. It currently excludes millions of people who are physically present inside US territory, but are officially deemed outsiders. This situation has led many to call for immigration reform that grants 'amnesty' to some undocumented migrants who have lived in the United States for various lengths of time. Anti-immigrant activists and policy-makers have been quite vocal in opposing any pathway to future citizenship for any migrants who are in the United States without authorization. Granting legal status and the opportunity for citizenship to unauthorized migrants is not a new idea. The ***Immigration Reform and Control Act of 1986 (IRCA)*** created a process whereby more than 2.7 million authorized migrants gained lawful permanent residence in the United States (Papademetriou 2005). France undertook a similar policy in 1966 with 'regularization', which allowed migrants who had entered without authorization or overstayed their visas to receive legal working papers (Freeman 1979). More recently, in 2005, Spain launched a programme that granted 'amnesty' to undocumented migrants who had entered the country prior to August 2005, had a job contract, and no criminal record (BBC News 2005).

As the above examples show, it is possible to find instances in which unauthorized immigrants have been granted the opportunity for citizenship. Still, such programmes generally encounter widespread opposition. Currently, in the United States such opposition has prevented any policy solutions. To understand such opposition it is useful to examine some of the issues raised by citizenship itself. While the notion of citizenship is extremely complex in itself, we need to probe even further. The following section discusses the issues of race and culture that have historically been linked in various ways to citizenship.

BROADER ISSUES
CULTURAL RACISM

'The border' is a multifaceted phenomenon, and while there are many forces at work today that seem to make borders increasingly irrelevant and that facilitate the movement of people, there are also numerous attempts to prevent such movement. The territorial line that slices through the ocean, mountains, desert, rivers, and canyons of the United States is an aspect of a much larger phenomenon that artificially divides human beings from one another. There are many borders in the world that create a self and an other, a subject who belongs and one who does not, a subject who can be called 'citizen' and one whose very existence in a particular place is deemed illegal. The movement of peoples without the proper authorization is a 'site' where many manifestations of various understandings of borders come together and where issues of identity and belonging are brought to the fore. The ways in which a society responds to the human beings who enter its sovereign territory without proper authorization says much about how it conceives of itself and 'others'. It also says much about how the issue of identity intersects with notions of justice, fairness and equality. Particularly pertinent to identity within the context of the movement of peoples are the issues of race and culture. Race and culture often do not enter debates over people's movements in an obvious way. Race and culture are both extremely complex and slippery concepts whose meanings have been intertwined.

Identity can take many forms, and national identity is only one of them. **Chapter 5** discusses the process of identification in general, and gender and racialized identities in particular; **Chapter 14** also looks at race, **Chapter 6** examines religion, and **Chapter 21** the distinction between 'civilized' and 'barbarian'.

BOX 10.2 RACE AND CULTURE

Balibar and Wallerstein (1991) have observed that national identity and citizenship have a long history of being linked with racial categories of identity, and racial identity has often been linked to culture. Race and culture are impossible to define in a 'scientific' way that would permit one to proclaim with certainty that current immigration policies in the United States are racist or that anti-immigrant positions are racist. Like the concept of identity discussed below, race and culture are not static phenomena. It is notoriously difficult to say with absolute certainty what elements make up a culture. Ironically this is one of the reasons this term is so powerful. Vagueness and ambiguity are often what make concepts powerful. For example, political leaders use the term 'national interest' quite frequently and never say with any degree of precision what it means exactly. Nonetheless, it often functions to arouse much passion and support amongst the populace. Similarly, when political leaders and scholars express the concern that immigration, and especially undocumented immigration, poses a threat to a nation's culture they very rarely say precisely what they mean. Furthermore, when one begins to examine the things they could possibly mean, we are often left with very little that is concrete. Some thinkers have suggested that culture can function as a smokescreen for race. Biological notions of race have been thoroughly debunked and yet race as a category of identity lingers, and it retains quite a bit of power despite the illusiveness of what it 'is'. Culture is equally slippery. While some markers of culture, such as language, seem relatively straightforward, it remains a notoriously 'slippery' and contested concept.

Australian citizenship test...
ESKY
...the practical section.

FIGURE 10.7
Australian citizenship test.
Artist: John Ditchburn 1/05 2006–240.
© John Ditchburn

How then does one begin to think of the relevance of race and culture when it comes to the issue of restricting the movement of peoples? One way to approach this very difficult issue is to consider our understanding of identity itself. If we understand identity as stable and fixed, as something that defines the essence of individuals and groups and differentiates them from other individuals and groups, we are likely to come away with an essentialist understanding of humanity. Such an understanding suggests that we can determine essential characteristics of peoples that define who they are and that differentiate them from others. However, if we question this view and think of identity as inherently unstable, multiple, and often full of tension, we will be less quick and less certain about categorizing people, defining them by the colour of their skin, the places they come from, their ancestors, and so on. In other words we can think of identity in a more complex way as a phenomenon that is socially constructed. We can think of identity as something that does not necessarily come before political and social practices, but rather is constructed by these things.

Chapter 5 distinguished between two views of identity, both of which see it as socially constructed, not essentialist. The first, called there the static view, sees a pre-existing individual who then adopts an identity. The second, the dynamic view, sees subject and identity as being produced at the same time.

These two understandings of identity are relevant when it comes to the issues of race and culture. Race and culture throughout history have often been thought of as stable markers of identity that define a group of people. The consequences of this when it comes to race have been particularly odious, for example slavery, lynching, the Holocaust, colonialism. Historically, race has also been an important element in US immigration policy. The US Immigration Act of 1924 was praised by Adolf Hitler:

> Compared to the old Europe, which has lost an infinite amount of its best blood through war and emigration, the American nation appears as a young and racially select people. The American union itself, motivated by the theories of its own racial researchers, [has] established specific racial criteria for immigration.
>
> (quoted in Romo 2005)

As part of the general 1924 restrictions, the Oriental Exclusion Act banned all immigration from Asia (Reimers 1992). Such blatant forms of racism are easy to recognize. In contemporary times, thinking of race as a fixed, genetic marker (phenotype) has been thoroughly debunked. Studies indicate that there really is no such thing as race in any biological, genetic sense.

Chapters 5 and 14 also explore the issue of race.

Today, it is a great deal more difficult to justify political and social practices that are blatantly racist. Still, it would be a gross and dangerous mistake to claim that racism no longer exists. If this is the case, then perhaps the term race is not only linked to one's skin colour or any other biological or genetic indicator. Even in earlier times, the concept of race extended beyond blood or genetics and was often linked to other factors such as nationality, tradition, geography and culture (Doty 2003). All of these factors have come into play in constructing identities for peoples. What this suggests then, is that it is possible to have a kind of racism that draws upon something other than skin colour. This is what the concept of cultural racism, or what some have referred to as neo-racism, is meant to convey (Barker 1981; Balibar and Wallerstein 1991; Doty 2003; Taguieff 1990). Neo-racism suggests that it is natural for antagonisms [hostilities] to develop between members of a bounded community, i.e. a nation, and 'outsiders' (Barker 1981: 21).

See **Chapter 5** for a discussion of early biological views of difference.

The notion of cultural racism has been applied to immigration issues in Britain and Europe, and is also a useful way to understand at least a portion of the immigration 'crisis' in the United States today. This is clear in popular notions that immigrants, especially those from Mexico, pose a threat to the cultural integrity of the United States, to 'our way of life' and to the very definition of who 'we' are. Over the past 10 years or so we have witnessed a proliferation of writings that expound upon the presumed dangers that immigrants pose to the cultural integrity of the United States. These range from extremist internet blogs to highly respected academics. Samuel Huntington's *Foreign Policy* article 'The Hispanic Challenge' (2004a) and his subsequent book, *Who Are We?* (2004b) are highly controversial and much criticized but they resonate with other popular publications. The most recent of these is Pat Buchanan's *State of Emergency: The Third World Invasion and Conquest of America* (2006). These are all examples of precisely what the term neo-racism is meant to capture. They create the notion of 'others' whose 'assimilability' is questionable and who therefore threaten 'our' very existence. This way of thinking about peoples and cultures and borders provides a simplified and dangerous way of interpreting the consequences of the movement of human beings, with or without the proper authorization. This is not to suggest that the 'old-fashioned' racism does not still exist. A recent study of traffic stops in the state of Arizona, found that Highway Patrol officers were more than twice as likely to search vehicles driven by Hispanics and Blacks than those operated by Anglos (Wagner 2007). The recent racial profiling lawsuit against Arizona's sheriff Joe Arpaio, in which his office is charged with basing traffic stops to ask for immigration status on race, also attests to the continuance of 'old-fashioned' racism (Billeaud 2011).

How is this different from or similar to the ways in which China manages its population? See **Chapter 12**.

For more on how such discourses of danger work and affect politics see **Chapter 24**.

CONCLUSION

The immigration 'crisis' in the United States today raises questions that are pertinent to most other advanced industrialized democracies which have experienced and continue to experience immigration from countries deemed 'third world' and who find themselves with a substantial number of human beings who have arrived without the proper legal documents. The European Union is often cited as an example of a case in which freedom of movement has triumphed over sovereign national borders. When the provisions of the Schengen Agreement came into force in 1995, travellers between member states were no longer required to show passports (Gelatt 2005). However, the existence of the European Union has not eliminated undocumented migration, and freedom of movement is only granted to citizens of member states. It has not eliminated exclusionary practices (Balibar 2004). In an important sense the question raised by Samuel Huntington, i.e. *Who Are We?* is a pertinent one, but not necessarily in the sense in which he poses it. Constructing categories of human beings who are defined in large part by their lack of documents raises important questions about the values that have traditionally been attached to 'us'. The restriction of peoples' free movement raises important questions about what values such as democracy and human rights can mean in an age of globalization when borders mean very little and very much at the same time.

These questions about democracy and human rights are also taken up in **Chapters 14 and 27**.

In our contemporary world borders are easy and difficult to cross at the same time. Exclusion is increasing and decreasing at the same time. From a critical perspective there are very few satisfactory responses to the question of why people's movement is restricted. Restrictive legislation on the part of the United States as well as many European countries has for the most part failed in terms of reducing immigration. Efforts to limit and/or prevent people from moving across sovereign territorial borders without the proper documentation have given rise to numerous other problems such as the increase in human smuggling, deaths of migrants in their dangerous journeys, and an underground world of human beings who live amongst us but do not enjoy the same privileges as citizens.

FURTHER READING

Andreas, Peter (2000) *Border Games: Policing the US–Mexico Divide*, Ithaca, NY: Cornell University Press.
Useful for background to recent US policies pertaining its southern border.

Balibar, Etienne (2004) *We the People of Europe? Reflections on Transnational Citizenship*, Princeton, NJ and Oxford: Princeton University Press.
This book reflects upon the ways of understanding what citizenship means and this may be changing due in part to migration.

Brian Barry, and Robert E. Goodin (eds) (1992) *Free Movement: Ethical Issues in the Transnational Migration of People and Money*, University Park, PA: Pennsylvania State University Press.
This book presents several essays addressing the movement of goods, services and people across borders and the ethical questions raised by these movements.

Brubaker, Rogers (ed.) (1989) *Immigration and the Politics of Citizenship in Europe and North America*, Lanham, MD: University Press of America.
Addresses the issue of citizenship in the context of immigration.

Cornelius, Wayne, Philip Martin and James F. Hollifield (eds) (1994) *Controlling Immigration: A Global Perspective*, Stanford, CA: Stanford University Press.
Good general overview of immigration from a global perspective.

Massey, Douglas S., Jorge Durand and Nolan J. Malone (2002) *Beyond Smoke and Mirrors: Mexican Migration in an Era of Economic Integration*, New York: Russell Sage.
Essays on Mexican migration into the United States.

Massey, Douglas S., Joaquin Arango, Graeme Hugo, Ali Kouaouci, J. Edward Taylor and Adela Pellegrino (2005) *Worlds in Motion: Understanding Immigration at the End of the Millennium*, Oxford: Oxford University Press.
Good general overview of contemporary immigration issues from a global perspective.

Reimers, David M. (1998) *Unwelcome Strangers: American Identity and the Turn Against Immigration*, New York: Columbia University Press.
History of anti-immigrant groups and activities in the United States.

Sassen, Saskia (1996) *Losing Control? Sovereignty in an Age of Globalization*, New York: Columbia University Press.
Focuses on governance in an age of globalization in which immigration is a major issue.

WEBSITES

Congressional Research Service (CRS) (http://www.opencrs.com) is the public policy research arm of the US Congress. It issues about 3,000 briefs, reports and issue papers per year, including papers on immigration issues.

Immigration Policy Center (IPC) (http://www.ailf.org/ipc) is part of The American Immigration Law Foundation (AILF) was established in 1987 as a tax-exempt, not-for-profit educational, charitable organization. The Foundation is dedicated to increasing public understanding of immigration law and policy and the value of immigration to American society, and to advancing fundamental fairness and due process under the law for immigrants.

Migration Policy Institute (MPI) (http://www.migrationinformation.org): MPI is an independent non-partisan, non-profit think tank in Washington DC that provides analysis, development and evaluation of immigration policies at the local, national and international levels. It was founded in 2001 by Demetrios G. Papademetriou and Kathleen Newland, and grew out of the International Migration Policy Program at the Carnegie Endowment for International Peace (http://www.carnegieendowment.org/).

The Southern Poverty Law Center (http://www.splcenter.org) was founded in 1971 as a small civil rights law firm. Today, SPLC is internationally known for its tolerance education programmes, its legal victories against white supremacists and its tracking of hate groups. Located in Montgomery, Alabama – the birthplace of the US Civil Rights Movement – the Southern Poverty Law Center was founded by Morris Dees and Joe Levin, two local lawyers who shared a commitment to racial equality. Its first president was Julian Bond. This organization publishes news items and reports on hate groups, including border vigilantes.

More information about the European Union (EU) can be found on the website Europa: The European Union at a Glance: http://europa.eu/abc/index_en.htm. The reasons why the EU was founded are detailed and the history of its most recent expansions is charted. The rules for the movement of workers are given on another part of this site: http://ec.europa.eu/youreurope/nav/en/citizens/index.html#.

REFERENCES

Aguila, Jaime R. (2010) 'The Immigration Debate about Mexicans', *Voices of Mexico*, issue 88, CISAN-UNAM, 2011, 82–86.

Altbach, Philip G. (2001) 'Higher Education and the WTO: Globalization Run Amok', *International Higher Education*, Center for International Higher Education, Boston College, www.bc.edu/bc_org/avp/soe/cihe/newsletter/News23/text001.htm.

Andreas, Peter (2000) *Border Games: Policing the US–Mexico Divide*, Ithaca, NY: Cornell University Press.

Anzaldua, Gloria (1987) *Borderlands: La Frontera*, San Francisco: Spinsters/Aunt Lute Book Company.

Arizona Daily Star (2006) 'Cochise Reports 1st Death of Illegal Entrant in '06', 22 February, http://www.azstarnet.com/SN/printDS/117018, accessed 24/02/06.

Arizona Republic (2007) 'Number of Immigrants Detained in the US Increases', 5 November.

Balibar, Etienne (2004) *We the People of Europe? Reflections on Transnational Citizenship*, Princeton, NJ and Oxford: Princeton University Press.

Balibar, Etienne and Immanuel Wallerstein (1991) *Race, Nation, Class*. London: Verso.

Barker, Martin (1981) *The New Racism*, London: Routledge.

BBC News (2005) 'Spain Launches Immigrant Amnesty', September. Online http://newsvote.bbc.co.uk/mpapps/pagetools/print/news.bbc.co.uk/1/hi/world/europe/4242411.

Billeaud, Jacques (2011) 'Arizona Judge Hears Latino Racial Profiling Case', MSNBC News, 22 December, http://www.msnbc.msn.com/id/45765678/ns/us_news-crime.

Buchanan, Patrick J. (2006) *State of Emergency: The Third World Invasion and Conquest of America*, New York: Thomas Dunne Books, St. Martins Press.

Doty, Roxanne Lynn (2003) *Anti-Immigrantism in Western Democracies*, London and New York: Routledge.

Dunn, Timothy J. (1996) *The Militarization of the US–Mexico Border 1978–1982*, Center for Mexican American Studies, Austin, TX: University of Texas at Austin.

Freeman, Gary P. (1979) *Immigrant Labor and Racial Conflict in Industrial Societies: The French and British Experiences*, Princeton, NJ: Princeton University Press.

Freeman, Richard B. (2006) 'People Flows in Globalization', National Bureau of Economic Research, Working Paper 12315.

Gelatt, Julia (2005) 'Schengen and the Free Movement of People Across Europe', *Migration Information Source*, 1 October, Migration Policy Institute.

Hogue, Ilyse (2011) 'Alabama's HB56 and the Dark Side of Fake Economic Fixes', *The Nation*, 17 October, http://www.thenation.com.

Hollifield, James F. (2000) 'The Politics of International Migration', in Caroline B. Brettell and James F. Hollifield (eds) *Migration Theory: Talking Across Disciplines*, New York: Routledge.

Huntington, Samuel P. (2004a) 'The Hispanic Challenge', *Foreign Policy* 141: 30–45

——(2004b) *Who Are We? The Challenge to America's National Identity*, New York: Simon and Schuster.

Isbister, John (1996) *The Immigration Debate*, West Hartford, CT: Kumarian Press.

Martin, Philip (1993) 'Trade and Migration: NAFTA and Agriculture', Washington, DC: Institute for International Economics, www.iie.com.

——(2003) 'Immigration: Shaping and Reshaping America', 10 October, Monograph, University of Michigan, http://ww.npc.umich.edu/news/events/PRB-Monograph-Final.pdf.

Migration Policy Institute (2004) 'Where the Numbers Come From', http://www.migrationinformation.org/feature/062005_explan.cfm, accessed 01/09/2005.

——(2007) 'MPI Data Hub – Migration Facts, Stats, and Maps', http://www.migrationinformation.org/DataHub/countrydata/data.cfm, accessed 05/11/07.

Nanez, Dianna M. (2007) 'Don't Ask, Don't Tell: Immigration Era Ending', *Arizona Republic*, 24 April.

Nevins, Joseph (2002) *Operation Gatekeeper: The Rise of the 'Illegal Alien' and the Making of the US–Mexico Boundary*, New York and London: Routledge.

Papademetriou, Demetrios G. (2005) 'Reflections on Restoring Integrity to the United States Immigration System: A Personal Vision', *Migration Policy Institute Insight*, no. 5, September.

Provine, Doris Marie (2010) 'Arizona's New Anti-Immigrant Law and Federal Immigration Reform', *Voices of Mexico*, issue 88, CISAN-UNAM, 98–102.

Reimers, David. M. (1992) *Still the Golden Door: The Third World Come to America*, New York: Columbia University Press.

Romo, David Dorado (2005) *Ringside Seat to a Revolution*, El Paso, TX: Cinco Puntos Press.

Rubio-Goldsmith, Raquel, M. Melissa McCormick, Daniel Martinez and Inez Magdalena Duarte (2006) 'The "Funnel Effect" and Recovered Bodies of Unauthorized Migrants Processed by the Pima County Office of the Medical Examiner, 1990–2005', Report submitted to the Pima County Board of Supervisors by the Binational Migration Institute, Mexican American Studies and Research Center at the University of Arizona, Tucson, Arizona, October 2006; Latin America Working Group, www.lawg.org/countries/mexico/death-stats.htm.

Rutland, Patricia J. (2007) 'T. Don Hutto: Homeland Security Bars U.N. Inspector', *The Austin Chronicle*, May 11.

Taguieff, Pierre-Andre (1990) 'The New Cultural Racism in France', *Telos* 38: 109–22.

Thorn, William (2005) 'Regulation of the Cross-border Supply of Higher Education Services – an Australian Perspective', Paper presented at the World Trade Organization Symposium on Cross-Border Supply of Services, Geneva, 28–29 April 2005, www.wto.org/English/tratop_e/serv_e/sym_april05_e/thorn_e.doc.

Tran, My-Thuan (2010) 'A Sharp Drop in Illegal Border Crossings Reported', *Los Angeles Times*, 1 September, http://articles.latimes.com/print/2010/sep/01/nation/la-na-immigration.

United Nations Economic and Social Council (2002) E/CN.4/2002/NGO/45, http://daccessdds.un.org/doc/UNDOC/GEN/G02/103/78/PDF/G0210378.pdf.

United States Government Accounting Office (2001) 'INS Southwest Border Strategy: Resource and Impact Issues Remain After Seven Years', Report to Congressional Committees, August, GAO-01–842.

——(2006) 'Border-Crossing Deaths Have Doubled Since 1995; Border Patrol's Efforts to Prevent Deaths Have Not Been Fully Evaluated', Report to Bill Frist, Majority Leader, US Senate, August, GAO-06–770.

United Nations World Tourism Organization (2007) 'UNWTO Secretary-General Opens FITUR 2007', News Release of the World Tourism Organization, www.world-tourism.org/newsroom/Releases/2007/january/opensfitur.htm.

Wagner, Dennis (2007) 'Racial Trends Found in DPS Traffic Stops', *Arizona Republic*, 7 November, http://www.azcentral.com/news/articles/1107dps1107.html.

For a range of further resources supporting this chapter, please visit the companion website for *Global Politics, 2nd Edition* at www.routledge.com/cw/edkins/

CHAPTER **11**

Why is the world divided territorially?

Stuart Elden

THE QUESTION
FORMS OF POLITICAL AND GEOGRAPHICAL ORGANISATION

If we look at an atlas, we find that it often begins with two maps of the world. One of these is physical, the other political. The first shows relief, depicting mountain ranges and plains, significant rivers, land masses and oceans. The second shows the same land and water, but this time the earth is brightly coloured, divided up and with clear lines separating out states from each other, and capital or other major cities marked as signs of human impact. We find the same divide when we move to maps of the continents later in the atlas.

The physical maps show a world that has barely changed in human history, although our knowledge of it certainly has. The political maps though bear almost no relation to the situation a few hundred years ago, let alone a few thousand. Territorial changes were common until the 1940s, many new states emerged from the process of decolonisation after World War II, and certain areas – notably eastern Europe and central Asia – will have dramatically changed in the lifetime of readers of this book. The final settlement of some areas remains an issue today.

Taking this kind of perspective shows us that the division of the world into separate territorial units, called states, is both artificial and arbitrary. Today it is generally accepted as the norm for political and geographical organisation. Yet this has not always been the case. Looking at older maps shows a very different perspective. Until relatively recently, large parts of the world were either unknown entirely (such as desert, mountain or polar regions), unknown to people in other parts, or known to them only in the vaguest of ways. Land masses and key rivers appeared on maps of the world drawn in Europe, but the inland areas of islands or continents were largely undiscovered by Europeans and unmapped by them.

Although this division of the world into states is accepted as the norm, it does create problems in terms of tackling important issues, such as climate change: see **Chapter 3**. This division also means that not everyone is authorised to live where they choose, creating many serious difficulties: see **Chapter 10**. And it is arguably being challenged by the spread of the internet (**Chapter 9**) and a globalised economy and global financial institutions (**Chapters 17 and 18**).

Maps of Europe in the Middle Ages show a jumble of political allegiances, with different rulers having control over a patchwork of land (Figure 11.1). Take a map of the situation in the fourteenth century, for instance.

There are lands owned by the Church in Rome, lands within the Kingdom of France that owe allegiance to German princes, and the reverse. England has areas of strategic control on the continent, while the houses of Austria and Luxembourg have power far beyond their nominal location. The rulers of contemporary cities or regions such as Naples or Burgundy control vast swathes of land. Focusing in on a smaller area would show more complications. And, as noted above, at this time large parts of the rest of the world were either unknown in whole or part to European cartographers.

Much later, Africa's land was divided by European powers in the late nineteenth century into 'spheres of influence', which only later evolved into definite control on the ground (Figure 11.2).

The division of the world into territorial units called states reflects a particular relation to space. Yet, just as not all human communities have been the same as modern states, so too with their relation to the land they inhabit. Hunter-gatherer communities have a very different relation to space than those societies that cultivate land and domesticate animals. They tend not to have fixed dwellings and may move with the seasons in search of water and food. A recent legal case may help to illustrate this.

The modern state of Botswana includes large parts of the Kalahari desert (Figure 11.3). The indigenous San or Basarwa people of this area, often known as the 'Bushmen', are looked at as one of the oldest peoples in the world. The Central Kalahari Game Reserve in Botswana was created by the British as colonisers in 1961 to allow them to remain in their ancestral lands. On independence in 1966 the government of Botswana proposed that they move into new settlements outside of this area, in which hospitals and other social services were provided. One of the reasons given was for the protection of the wildlife in the Reserve. The discovery of diamonds in the 1980s meant that this movement took on a new urgency for the government, despite the resistance of the San people. In 2002 this eviction was facilitated by violence, the refusal of hunting licences and the ceasing of food rations. In late 2006 a Botswana court ruled that the eviction was illegal and that the people could return.

The history of colonialism in India is discussed in **Chapter 16**; colonialism continues to have an impact in a range of ways: see also **Chapters 15, 20 and 21**.

This idea that we must protect the environment is one that has historically emerged and changed: see **Chapters 3 and 4**.

In this example we can see the clash between a modern state and its territorial claims, including the desire to exploit its natural resources, and a different understanding of space of a nomadic people who live from and on the land, rather than cultivate it

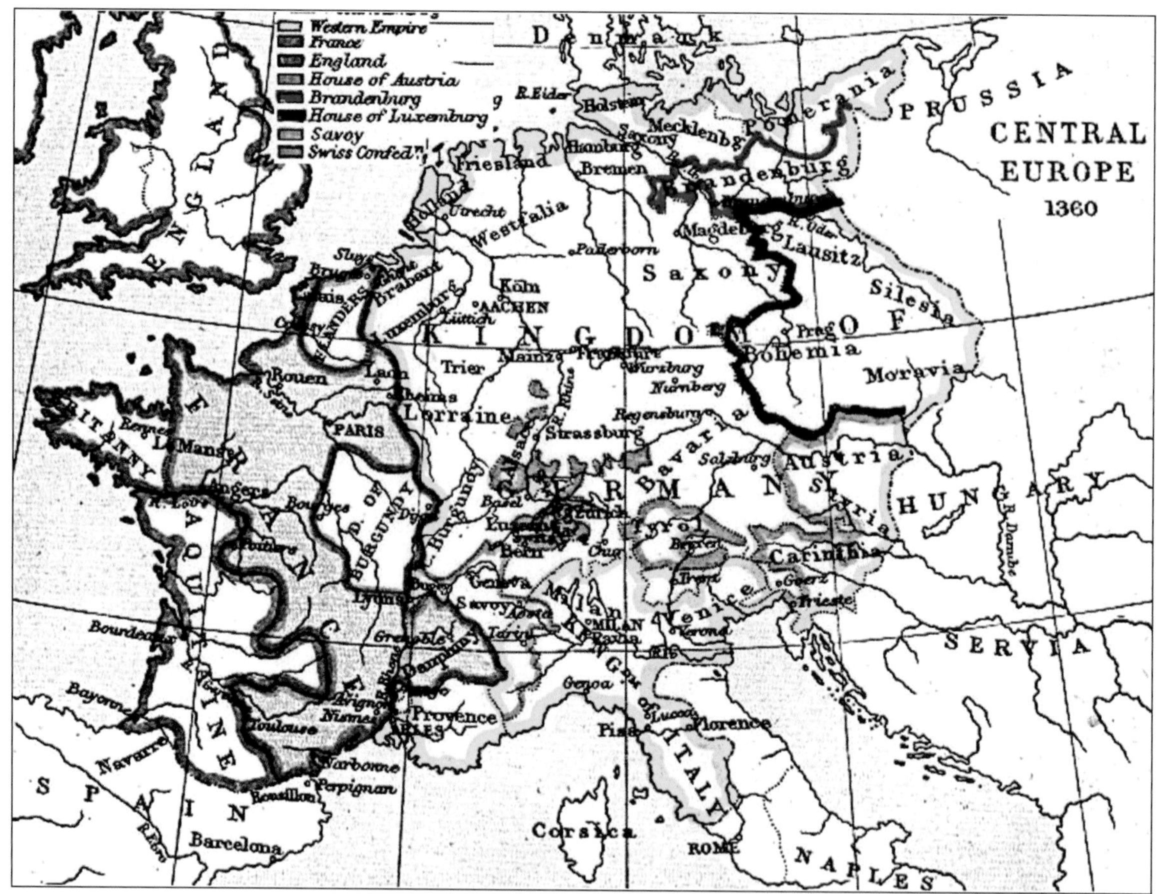

FIGURE 11.1
Map of Central Europe in 1360. From *Atlas to Freeman's Historical Geography*, edited by J. B. Bury, Longmans Green and Co. Third Edition 1903

The desire to exploit natural resources is often a source of conflict: see **Chapter 3**.

(see Townsend 2004). Even looking at the geometric boundaries of the Reserve and the western border of the state imposed over a physical and human landscape shows two very different spatial logics.

Standard definitions of territory suggest that it is an area of space under the control or jurisdiction of a group of people, which might be a state, but which might potentially be other types of political organisation. Jean Gottmann notes that

> Although its Latin root, *terra*, means 'land or 'earth', the word territory conveys the notion of an area around a place; it connotes an organisation with an element of centrality, which ought to be the authority exercising sovereignty over the people occupying or using that place and the space around it.
>
> (1973: 5)

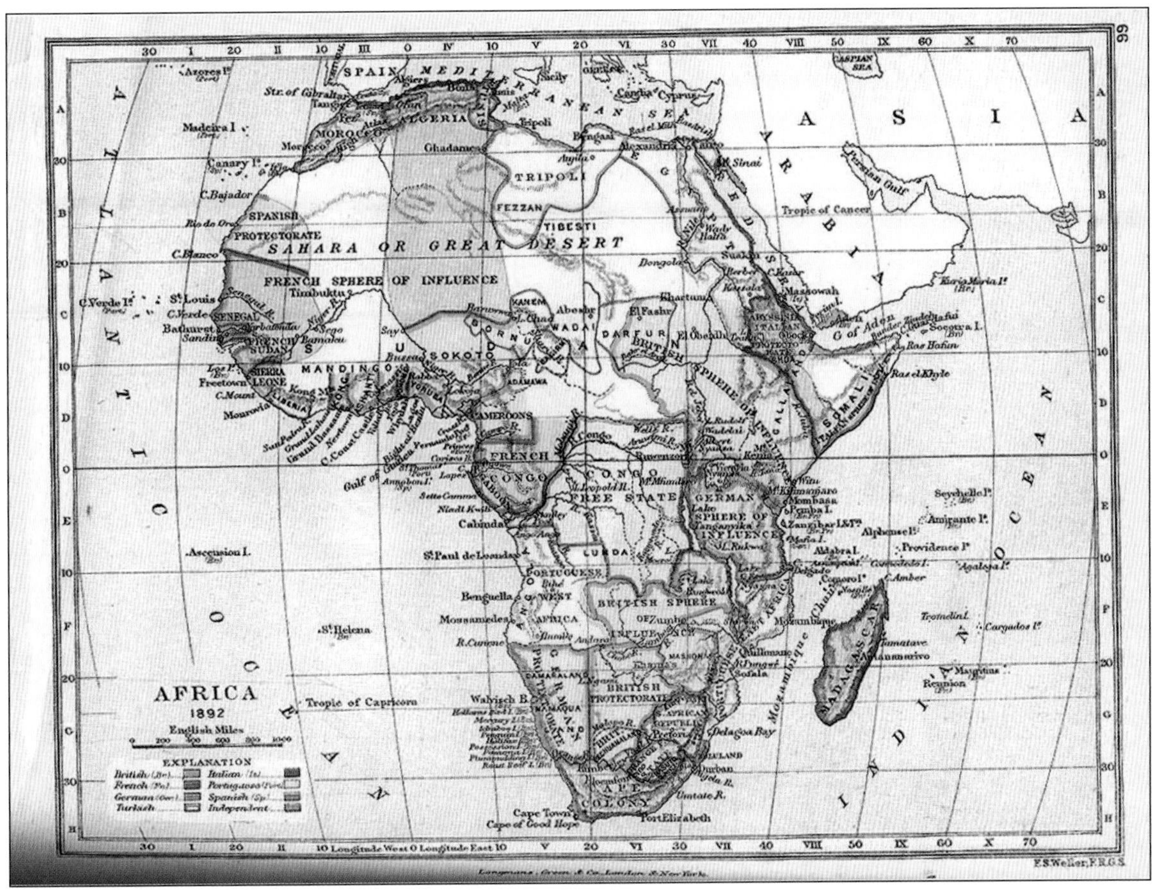

FIGURE 11.2
Map of Africa in 1892. From *A School Atlas of English History*, edited by Samuel Rawson Gardiner, London: Longmans, Green, and Co., 1892

The geographer David Storey suggests that

> The term 'territory' is most usually used in reference to the area of land claimed by a country. However territories exist at a variety of spatial scales from the global down to the local. Territory refers to a portion of geographic space which is claimed or occupied by a person or group of persons or by an institution. It is, thus, an area of 'bounded space'.
>
> (2001: 1)

The claim that a territory is a bounded space leads to the idea of a state as what the sociologist Anthony Giddens called 'a bordered power container' (1985; see Taylor 1994, 1995). The notion of a bounded space is important not just as one of the key ways in which territories are defined, but because it brings us to the notion of a boundary or border.

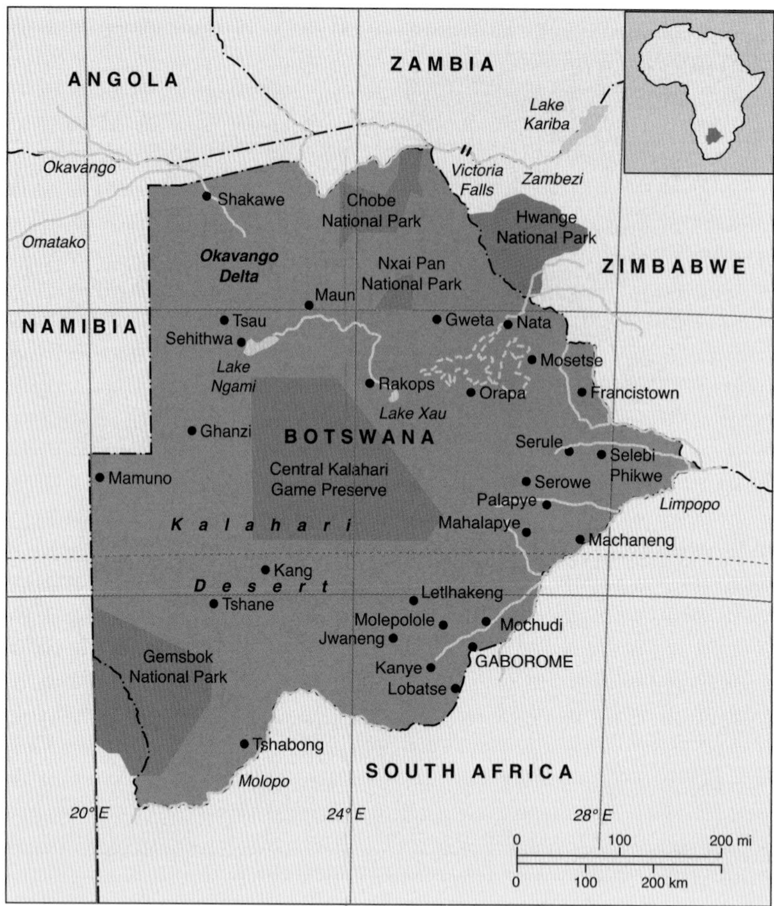

FIGURE 11.3 Map of Botswana and Central Kalahari Game Reserve

The relation between the state and its territory is therefore crucial to understanding both terms. The German sociologist Max Weber famously declared that 'a state is that human community which (successfully) lays claim to the monopoly of legitimate physical violence within a certain territory, this "territory" being another of the defining characteristics of the state' (1994: 310–11).

Weber therefore stresses four key things: community; legitimacy; violence; and territory. The state is a particularly human grouping, within a discrete area, and within that area it makes a claim to complete control. He is suggesting that this type of political rule is inherently tied to a particular place, and the people within it. The state is able to command absolute authority within that discrete area, without the involvement of other forces – be they other states or political groupings. Its authority is absolute because it is both undivided (no other body has that power) and unlimited (the state can do what it wants, without reference to other bodies). Other political groups, such as private armies or rebel forces, or independence movements are, by their nature, illegitimate, that is, without moral or legal justification. This is the notion of sovereignty – the power to command and rule, which is rendered legitimate through a claim to authority. The international political system, such as that set out in the United Nations Charter, largely

For more on Weber's work on power and authority see **Chapter 7**.

BOX 11.1 MAX WEBER

Max Weber (1864–1920) was a German historian and political economist. He is seen as one of the founders of sociology, and is known for his writings on the city, religion and the historical development of the state. He was involved in the negotiations for the Treaty of Versailles (1919) and helped to draft Germany's Weimar Constitution which came into force in 1919. His most famous works are *The Protestant Ethic and the Spirit of Capitalism* (1958, written 1904–5), *Economy and Society* (1968, written 1914) and the essay 'Politics as a Vocation', from which the quotation in this chapter is taken.

FIGURE 11.4
Max Weber. Deutsches Historisches Museum, Berlin. Ref. F52/2693

subscribes to this view of the relation between politics and place. States are held to have exclusive internal sovereignty (jurisdiction within their own borders) and equal external sovereignty. Equal external sovereignty, or equal jurisdiction, means that no state should be a puppet of another, and that there should be no hierarchy of states. In practice there are many instances where this is clearly not the case, but these assumptions function as an important legal and political fiction that structures the world and helps to maintain the international order. Today, though, international agreements increasingly do put limitations on state sovereignty, including on actions that impact on the environment, the use of nuclear power and treatment of refugees.

For some of these agreements regarding the environment see **Chapter 3**, and concerning the internet, **Chapter 9**.

Why, then, is the world divided territorially? Why are borders drawn where they are? Has the world always been divided in this kind of way? Why do some rivers and mountain ranges form borders, yet others do not? Why do some lines of division take on such importance, while other lines drawn on maps or on the ground do not? Contrast, for example, the difference between the heavily militarised line of control between India and Pakistan in the mountains of Kashmir, with the largely uncontrolled border region between Pakistan and Afghanistan. Why have the borders of Germany, for example, moved so dramatically over the twentieth century? Why are the borders in Africa drawn in such a way, with so many straight lines cutting through the landscape? Why, with the notable exception of Antarctica, where territorial claims are suspended, is almost every piece of land on the planet under the control of a single state, which claims exclusive rights to what happens in this area? This is not to say that there are no disputed territories – examples would include Kashmir, the 'occupied territories' of the Palestinian West Bank and the Gaza Strip, and many others in the Middle East – but rather that the norm is that they are 'owned' by a state. Why, increasingly, are the oceans being similarly divided? Why should geographical location dictate citizenship, rights and responsibilities? The place where you are born, or where your parents are from, determines many of the conditions that will affect the rest of your life.

Although some people are able to change where they live, taking on citizenship of or permanent residence in another state, this is not an option for many people. Questions of immigration and the status of refugees show the close relation between geography and rights. Many indigenous peoples find themselves excluded from their historical lands, either entirely, or because modern borders cut across them. Many states treat those who live within their territory in terrible ways, but what possibility do these people have to leave; and what rights or responsibilities do regional or international organisations have to protect them? This question has been especially raised in the last few years with the examples of Rwanda, East Timor, Kosovo and Sudan, but the international community does not yet seem to have come up with a satisfactory answer.

For more on the complex relationship between citizenship, geography and rights see **Chapters 10, 12 and 27**.

Chapter 25 examines in detail whether we are able to stop people from being harmed and in particular the case of East Timor. **Chapter 25** also talks about what it means to look to the 'international community' for answers.

ILLUSTRATIVE EXAMPLE
THE DEVELOPMENT OF THE EUROPEAN TERRITORIAL STATE

In order to get some sense of how territory emerged, and why this model of ordering political space spread across the world, I will outline the history of the European state, with an emphasis on its geographical aspects. This allows us to see how not all political organisations have the same relation to space.

Ancient Greece, the Roman Empire and the Middle Ages

The ancient Greek city-state, known as a *polis*, was one of the earliest forms of political unit in Europe. It dominated Greek political culture between the eighth and third centuries before the common era (the period before the birth of Jesus Christ) and is discussed in writers such as the philosophers Plato and Aristotle and the historians Thucydides and Herodotus. Although it had an urban centre, this human community spread into the neighbouring countryside and cultivated land in this region. It thus had a centralised source of power, and a broader extent where it reached out to neighbouring land. Although there were wars between *poleis*, there was often lots of unclaimed land between them. Unlike modern states they did not take over all of the land in the broader region, and some rural shrines, for example were shared between neighbours. We therefore have a model of political rule that is strongly centralised, with power being less strong as we move away from the centre.

The *polis* and political thought related to it has had a lasting impact on the political imagination: see **Chapters 5, 10 and 27**.

Rome began as something similar to a Greek city-state, but as it waged wars against its neighbours in the region it began to accumulate more and more land. By the time the republic fell and it became an empire, it had expanded further and further away from the Italian peninsula. Roman political geography is complicated, with different parts of the empire ruled in different ways, either through allegiance, paying tribute (goods, slaves or money) or incorporation into Roman systems (see Nicolet 1991). Rome did not recognise other political units as being on the same level as itself – unlike the way neighbouring states do today. Land was, effectively, part of the Roman Empire, or it could become so at some point in the future. This is the idea of *terra nullius* – empty or no-man's land. This meant that they did not accord other groups the same rights of possession that they gave themselves, something that European powers later used to justify colonisation of large parts of the rest of the world. While Rome sometimes built walls or barriers, such as Hadrian's Wall in northern England or the fortifications on the Rhine River in modern day Germany, these were more for defensive purposes than to mark the final borders of Roman expansion. Land both sides of Hadrian's Wall was cultivated, for example, and another wall was built further north (the Antonine Wall) as Rome expanded its reach. At this time the idea of a frontier – as an area of land between different political rulers – predominated over a boundary as a single line of control. While today a boundary is, nominally, a line with zero width between two political units such as states, at this time the idea of a frontier as a zone, or something having width, was much more common. What is important about this is that a frontier zone will usually have people living in it, as well as resources within it. A border can be either a line or a zone, but today most are lines, even though there is a lot of discussion of border regions looking at areas across these lines.

The idea of *terra nullius* was also used by the European conquerors in relation to the American continent: **Chapter 3**. For more about the growth and contraction of empires, see **Chapter 16**.

With the collapse of the Western Roman Empire in the fifth century of the common era, Europe became a much more jumbled and complicated political unit. Various kings, tribes and other political groupings, including the church, had power over land. This was often at a very small scale, and there were frequent invasions and transfers of authority. Large parts of Western Europe were unified under the Carolingian Empire, and the king of the Franks, Charlemagne, was crowned Holy Roman Emperor by the Pope on Christmas Day, 800. Three centuries after the fall of the Western Roman Empire, therefore, an attempt was made to re-establish it as the Holy Roman Empire. Despite the French author Voltaire's joke that this was neither holy, Roman nor an empire, this was a way for the Church in Rome to exercise political power across much of Europe for several hundred years.

Religious wars and the rise of the state

With the fractures in religion around the Reformation – a period of conflict over the trajectory of the Catholic Church, particularly over corruption and the power of the priesthood – there arose a particular kind of political problem. If the prince or king of a region within the Empire converted to Calvinism or Lutherism, which religion would be dominant in their lands? Would it be the religion of the local ruler or that of the Church in Rome? This caused a great deal of conflict in the sixteenth and seventeenth centuries, leading to various agreements between the units within the empire. The two most famous are the Diet of Augsburg in 1555, which laid down the principle of *cuius regio, eius religio* – to whom the rule, or region, his religion – and the Treaties of Westphalia in 1648. Augsburg's settlement, which allowed for Lutheran princes or free cities to have this as the official religion, was effectively extended to Calvinists in 1648.

For more on how the relationship between religion and politics is understood and organised see **Chapters 6, 7 and 27**.

Chapter 6 tells you more about the Reformation and Martin Luther in particular.

While Westphalia brought to an end most of the fighting in the Thirty Years War, France and Spain continued fighting until the Treaty of the Pyrenees in 1659. This is in some senses even more important, as it led to a joint commission for setting the exact border between Spain and France, and can be said to have created the first modern boundary from what had previously been more of a frontier (see Sahlins 1989).

BOX 11.2 THE PEACE OF WESTPHALIA

The Peace of Westphalia (1648) comprised two treaties negotiated in the northwest of modern Germany, at the towns of Münster and Osnabrück. The treaties brought to an end the Thirty Years War (1618–48). The Osnabrück Treaty was between Sweden and the emperor of the Holy Roman Empire, the one at Münster between France and the emperor. There were a number of things at stake in the negotiations, including religion and political power. The Westphalian treaties are often used to mark the beginning of the modern era of politics, with the idea of absolute state sovereignty, sometimes known as the Westphalian System. While the dating is misleading (see Teschke 2003), a range of characteristics we would associate with modern states are indeed given to political units within the Empire by the treaties. For example, they are given the right to declare war and peace, and have the entitlement to make laws, raise taxes, keep a standing (permanent) army, and to make new fortifications and alliances without prior consent of the Emperor.

The treaties importantly stress the 'free exercise of territorial right' (Treaty of Münster, Article 64; Treaty of Osnabrück, Article VIIII, 1) or the 'territorial right and superiority' (Osnabrück, Article V, 30) that the princes have, thus linking political rule, or sovereignty, to land, to territory.

FIGURE 11.5
The Swearing of the Oath of Ratification of the Treaty of Westphalia at Munster, 24th October 1648 by Gerard Ter Borch (1648).

From this period on, the state model began to become the standard form of political organisation in Europe. This was not entirely a result of the Peace of Westphalia, since many states – such as England, France and Sweden – existed before this time. The emergence of city-states in northern Italy during the Renaissance is also important, as they began to develop more modern forms of political rule, developing from classical ideas (see Larkins 2010). Equally, many of the features of the modern system of states – such as equal sovereignty, and the presumption against non-interference in domestic affairs – clearly did not become norms until much later. Yet around this time states or individual rulers began to pay much more attention to the importance of clearly demarcating where their rule extended to.

Note that the presumption against non-interference is ignored in various ways. **Chapters 15 and 20** highlight the interference of global financial institutions in the domestic policies of 'developing' states and **Chapter 21** examines why some people sometimes think it's good to interfere in other states.

It is worth noting that the state predates the nation. The nation is often taken to have developed in the late eighteenth century. The development of the nation, and ideas of national identity and nationalism, is a similarly contested and historical development. Today people often talk about the nation-state. This is problematic for at least two reasons. First, it assumes that the two are the same thing, when one is a grouping of people and the other a political unit. The borders of each *can* coincide, but most states include people of different nationalities, and at times the same nationality has been found in more than one state, such as North and South Korea today, or East and West Germany in the late twentieth century. Second, a straightforward equation of the nation with the state generally fails to note the historical and contingent development of each term.

Chapter 12 examines how nations have to be made and **Chapter 13** how such constructions are always challenged by alternative stories of community.

The situation in North and South Korea is examined in **Chapter 26** and the end of the division between East and West Germany is explored in **Chapter 7**.

Imperialism and empire

The European model for dividing states was gradually spread across the world between the fifteenth and twentieth centuries (see Badie 2000). These European empires differed from many earlier empires, such as the Roman Empire, in their spatial extent. Whereas the Roman Empire had expanded contiguously – that is, to land immediately bordering its existing possessions – European empires occupied land at a distance. Other parts of the world became the location for inter-European rivalries. These included French and English competition in North America, and Spanish/Portuguese claims for different parts of the world. Later these took on a particularly concentrated form in the late nineteenth century with the 'scramble for Africa'. This was a process by which European powers carved up Africa for their own purposes.

There were of course also non-European empires: see **Chapters 12, 16 and 21**.

Thus the Western European model of territorial division between states was exported to much of the rest of the world. Initially this was as colonial possessions, but as these places gained independence they largely inherited the boundaries of colonial division. In South America, for instance, the division between Spanish and Portuguese possessions, and internal divisions between parts of the Spanish Empire became the boundaries of the newly independent states. This became known as the doctrine of *uti possidetis*, a Latin phrase meaning that what you will have is 'what you possess'. In 1964 the Organisation of African Unity passed a motion that suggested that this should be the principle of decolonisation for that continent too. While this had the benefit of preventing a territorial free-for-all, it has meant that the largely arbitrary boundaries of Africa remain, creating many ongoing problems (see Lalonde 2002).

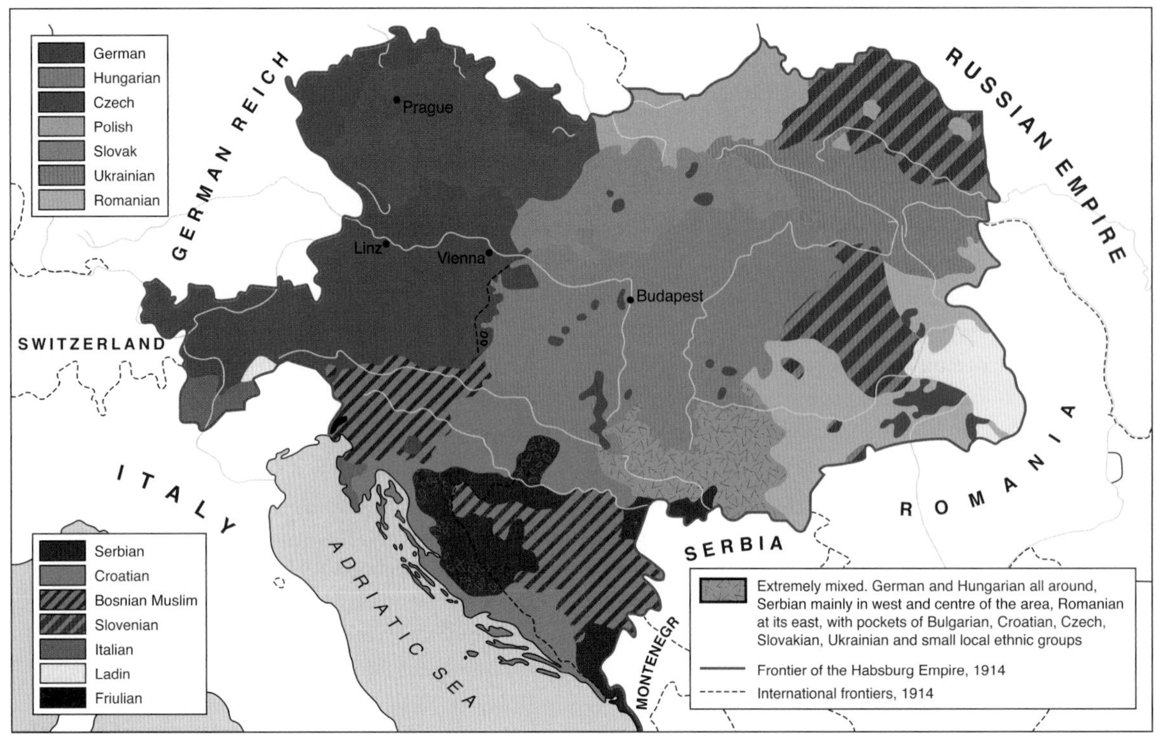

FIGURE 11.6 Map of ethnic distribution of the Habsburg Empire, 1914. http://www.historyonmaps.com/BWSamples/HabsburgEthnic.html

Within Europe the break-up of empires has led to the emergence of a number of new states. After the First World War the defeated powers of Germany, Austria-Hungary and the Ottoman Empire were either broken up or had territory removed as part of a punitive settlement. In the various treaties of the Peace of Paris, which included the Treaty of Versailles, the victorious powers sought to rebuild the map of Europe. Germany lost territory to many of its neighbours including Belgium and Poland. The Habsburg Empire was fragmented into a number of smaller states, including Austria, Hungary and a number of states in central Europe and the Balkans.

To avoid lots of small states, some rather artificial ones were created such as Czechoslovakia, which included Czechs and Slovaks, and Yugoslavia. Yugoslavia meant the federation of the Southern Slavs, and was effectively a line drawn around a large number of different peoples – Slovenes, Serbs, Croats, Albanians, Montenegrins and Macedonians. From the Ottoman Empire modern Turkey was created – still a multi-ethnic state – and a number of new states in the near and Middle East. Many of the world's most insuperable territorial problems – such as Iraq and Israel/Palestine – date from this time.

At the end of the Cold War many of these states fragmented into smaller entities. Some of these were along broadly nationalist lines, though there is much debate as to whether these pre-existed the division or were in some way produced by that process. Self-determination – the idea that a group of people in a discrete area should be able to govern themselves – again became very popular. Earlier uses of this ideal, such as those that shaped the Peace of Paris, had been tempered by recognition of considerations concerning the viability of new states. Equally, as can be seen from the map above, it is rare for national groups to neatly fit into discrete geographical areas, with the situation on the ground often far more complicated, with a mosaic of different identities. In addition, some people do not identify in this way. The compromise that the international community fell upon was that republics within federal states could become independent states. This meant that Czechoslovakia was able to split into the Czech Republic and Slovakia in a largely peaceful way. This is known as the Velvet Divorce, a reference to the Velvet Revolution in 1989 which had overthrown communist rule without much bloodshed. The Soviet Union similarly broke up along republic lines – its full title was the Union of Soviet Socialist Republics (USSR) – into fifteen separate states. This led to independence for the European states of Ukraine, Belarus, Moldova and the Baltic States of Estonia, Latvia and Lithuania, the states of the Caucasus (Georgia, Armenia and Azerbaijan) as well as a number of new states in Central Asia such as Uzbekistan and Kazakhstan. Many of these states, especially those in Central Asia, had no experience of independence before and were often unable to deal with some of its implications. In addition, many of the republics' boundaries were poorly specified.

For a description of how the British state came into being as an amalgamation of different national groups over a period of several hundred years, and how Ireland seceded from the UK in the 1920s, see **Chapter 16**.

The break-up of Yugoslavia is extremely complicated, but again largely occurred along the lines of the former republic of that federal state. Bosnia did not work on this basis, since its multi-ethnic nature and the interests of its neighbours led to prolonged civil war, and the forcible movement or destruction of populations, known as 'ethnic cleansing'. These problems were solved to some extent by a complicated cartography of division and incorporation at the Dayton conference of 1995. Yet this did not end the problems in Yugoslavia, with Kosovo, an autonomous province of Serbia, seeking independence. NATO went to war in 1999, ostensibly to protect the civilian population of Kosovo from Serbia. While the aerial bombardment produced the desired outcome of a Serbian withdrawal, it also produced problems of a different nature. This was the status of Kosovo itself, which caused much discussion concerning its future either within Yugoslavia or Serbia, as an international protectorate, or as an independent state. While Russia objected because of its support from Serbia, even states that supported Kosovo's declaration of independence in 2008 feared it would create a precedent for other states to break up. The republics within the Yugoslav federation, or those within the Soviet Union (the Union of Soviet Socialist Republics), were able to gain recognition for their independence and take on the boundaries of internal division. Kosovo, though, was a province within a republic, and so was not of the same constitutional standing. Among other examples, this is the same kind of distinction that Chechnya has within Russia or Abkhazia within Georgia. These complications will be returned to below.

Yugoslavia broke apart in the 1990s amidst violent conflict. For more on this and a map of the region see **Chapter 5**. This break-up involved a particular kind of identity politics, as discussed in the same chapter.

NATO's Kosovo operation and its legality were controversial: see **Chapter 25**.

GENERAL RESPONSES
THE EMERGENCE OF TERRITORY

There are many explanations for the emergence of territory as a particular way of ordering the relation between political rule and space.

Some writers use the idea of territoriality to understand territory. These accounts suggest that human relations to space can be understood through modes of behaviour.

Chapter 5 notes such biological perspectives in relation to the way we think about gender and race.

Some valuable studies have been made of 'human territoriality', looking at how humans, both individually and collectively, encounter, work and change the spaces around them. Some of this work begins from a biological perspective, deriving insights from comparing human behaviour to that of animals (see Malmberg 1980). While this way of approaching the topic can produce some valuable insights, its problem is that human social organisation has changed more rapidly than our biological drives, and so a biological approach is of limited historical use.

Some work on territoriality does not suggest such a purely biological approach, but incorporates a more social angle (Sack 1986). For Sack territoriality is a geo-political strategy, not a basic vital instinct. Territory is a social construct – produced through interaction and struggle – and therefore thoroughly permeated by social relations. To analyse the territory as a mere container of social action is to miss a vital part of the picture. Sack's analysis, as well as that of a number of other writers, incorporates elements of a range of approaches to understanding territory.

Political-economic approach

Chapter 19 introduces Marx and Engels's work.

Chapter 17 shows the impact of industrialisation upon people and their work situation.

Some accounts see territory as a form of property. Marxist accounts particularly suggest that developments in economics are important. In *The German Ideology*, Karl Marx and Friedrich Engels suggest that antiquity is tied to the city-state and its 'little territory', and the Middle Ages to the country (1970: 45). Though the economic system of the Middle Ages, feudalism, thus put a great deal of focus on land, it was only with capitalism and the emergence of the modern state that there was a real emphasis on people and land as significant taxable assets. To have land under a system of centralised control, and to remove overlapping jurisdiction, became an imperative. This was tied to the emerging focus on the importance of private property, the growth of new towns and cities and a shift of power toward the middle classes with increased industrialisation. This led to a stress on the importance of national markets rather than local ones, and a widespread centralisation of the state, and therefore a control of its land, as territory.

One of the best examples of this argument is found in the work of the Marxist theorist Perry Anderson, particularly in his books *Passages from Antiquity to Feudalism* and *Lineages of the Absolutist State* (1974a, 1974b). Anderson offers a broad analysis of the material forces shaping the development of successive historical periods, suggesting that this is a Marxist account. However his account goes broader than the merely economic.

> The typical medium of inter-feudal rivalry, by contrast, was military and its structure was always potentially the zero-sum conflict of the battlefield, by which fixed quantities of ground were won or lost. For land is a natural monopoly: it cannot be indefinitely extended, only redivided. The categorical object of noble rule was territory, regardless of the community inhabiting it. Land as such, not language, defined the natural perimeters of its power.
>
> (Anderson 1974b: 31)

This is a complicated series of claims. Anderson is suggesting that feudal power structures revolved around possession of land, often fought over. If one feudal lord gained land, another would have lost it. Land is a scarce resource, and cannot be produced, only redistributed. Given that political control revolved around possession of land, people were much less important. Changes in economic structures produced a different social structure.

Political-strategic approach

Hinted at in Anderson's quotation above, and more explicitly stressed in other accounts, is that territory emerges as important for more strategic reasons. States wanted to ensure that their land was practically manageable, and so were concerned with issues around security. France, for example, following the Treaty of the Pyrenees, began a process of mapping and surveying its land, moving towards what it called its 'natural frontiers'. These were the Alps and the Pyrenees, the English Channel, the Atlantic and Mediterranean, and the Rhine River. This gives rise to the roughly hexagonal shape of modern France. To ensure this, France exchanged some land to the northeast to even up its boundary with the Netherlands, and employed technical specialists to map and reinforce its borders more generally. The unification of Germany and Italy in the nineteenth century shows a national project that included the bringing together of disparate political entities in a unified territory.

Some people might claim that territory is now much less central to thinking about security: see **Chapter 24**.

These accounts stress the importance of power relations in understanding control of space, either explicitly, as in some work by and influenced by Michel Foucault, or through other terms such as 'sovereignty' or 'authority'. Weber's analysis of the historical development of the state would fit in this category. The sociologist Michael Mann has provided a very detailed account from this broad perspective (1986, 1993),

Foucault's work is also discussed in **Chapters 4, 7 and 23**.

BOX 11.3 MICHEL FOUCAULT

Michel Foucault (1926–1984) was a French historian and philosopher. His studies of madness, medicine, punishment and sexuality have had a significant impact in a range of disciplines. His work on power and its relation to knowledge has been particularly important. Foucault argues that power flows throughout society rather than from a central source, and that it is best analysed through a series of relations. Power is *exercised*, which means we should study how it is used, rather than nominal possession of power. Especially in his later works he is interested in how power can be creative, rather than simply repressive, and how both forms of power are important in understanding the modern human subject. His most influential work for those interested in politics is *Discipline and Punish* (1976), but the ongoing publication of his lecture courses, such as *Society Must Be Defended* (2003, from 1975–76) and *Security, Territory, Population* (2007, from 1977–78) are beginning to have an important impact.

FIGURE 11.7
Paris. 1973. Demonstration in support of immigrant workers. In the foreground: the French philosopher Michel Foucault.
Photo: Gilles Peress. Magnum

stressing the changing dynamics of power and in particular military and strategic interests in the development of the state, though, like Anderson he only tangentially discusses territory.

The political-economic and political-strategic models for understanding territory have much merit, and it is undoubtedly the case that there were a number of interlinked changes that impacted on political rule over space. Both types of analysis are vital to understanding how territory emerged as an organising category (see Elden 2010; 2013). However, elements of both ways of understanding territory can be found in earlier political systems. The first, of land as a form of property, can be found in ancient Greek texts such as Plato's *Laws*, and was clearly a crucial factor throughout the Middle Ages. The Domesday Book, from 1086, was a survey of the lands in England for the knowledge of William the Conqueror, who had invaded 20 years before. The second is closer to a sense of land as terrain, and in this sense can be found in any number of ancient texts such as Thucydides' *History of the Peloponnesian War* or Julius Caesar's accounts of the *Gallic War* or the *Civil War*. Some aspects of the particularity of modern understandings of territory are discussed in the Broader Issues section.

Changing importance of the territorial state

Chapter 25 examines in more detail how sovereignty is significant in the context of conflict and possible resolutions.

Thinking territorially is a powerful way of operating, for among other things it enables states to claim exclusive internal jurisdiction – the right to do anything they want within their boundaries. States are unlikely to give up this control without a struggle. Nonetheless, several challenges to this way of working have occurred over the last few decades.

One of these is the rise of supra-national organisations, such as the European Union. This is taking over key aspects of the role of states, such as making laws and monetary policy, and the rejected European Constitution pushed for moves toward a common defence and foreign policy. With the weakening of internal borders to allow the free movement of goods and people, the European Union has challenged a number of the territorial aspects of the states which have joined as members (see J. Anderson 1996; Bialasiewicz *et al.* 2005).

Globalisation has also challenged the idea of self-contained territorial states, with suggestions that flows of information, goods and energy around the world now transcend state boundaries. This has led some to suggest that globalisation can be understood as deterritorialisation or supra-territorialisation. Deterritorialisation means that territory is no longer fixed, and supra-territorialisation that spaces of interaction can no longer be contained with the borders of states (see Scholte 2005).

The movement of people around the world, and in particular wide-scale economic migration, has also produced a series of challenges to the exclusive territorial power of the state. Andrew Linklater has suggested that these broad processes require us to rethink notions of identity, national ties, rights and belonging. This will open up 'new forms of political community which sever the links between sovereignty, territory, citizenship and nationalism' (Linklater 1998: 213). Yet while in the 1990s a series of suggestions were made about the decreasing power and importance of state borders, a number of more recent changes, notably following the attacks of 11 September 2001, have produced a movement in the opposite direction. The building of the security wall in

See **Chapter 10** for a map of migration flows.

BOX 11.4 THE EUROPEAN UNION

The basis for the EU was set up in the aftermath of the Second World War to bring peace, stability and prosperity to Europe. From the Schuman Declaration and the six-nation Common Market of the 1950s the EU has grown and after its 2007 enlargement includes twenty-seven countries. The three main decision-making bodies in the EU are: the Parliament, the Council of Ministers of the EU, and the European Commission. Its annual budget is over €120 billion [$190 billion] in fields like regional and social development, agriculture, research and energy. Citizenship of the EU brings with it a series of fundamental and political rights, including the right to travel, live and work anywhere in the EU. Countries of the EU work closely together on trade issues and development policy, and the EU is developing a common foreign and defence policy.

(From Pascal Fontaine (2006), 'Europe in 12 Lessons', http://europa.eu/abc/12lessons/index_en.htm)

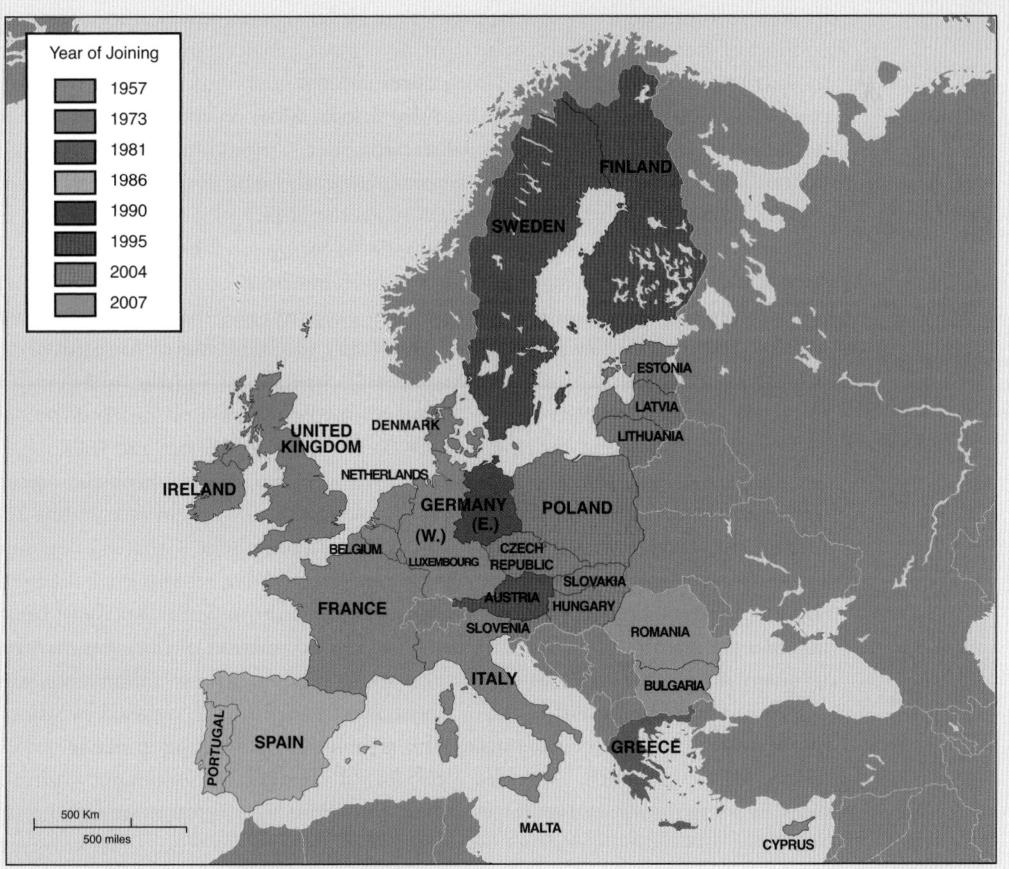

FIGURE 11.8
Member states of the European Union 2007

the Palestinian occupied territories by Israel and the reinforcing of the USA's borders, especially with Mexico, are two of the most obvious examples of this trend.

Other challenges, notably those of an environmental nature, produce problems and require solutions that transcend the territorial nation-state. Pollution, infectious diseases such as HIV/AIDS, SARS and avian flu, nuclear proliferation, poverty and global climate change all show the limitations of individual countries trying to resolve problems, and have led to a number of supranational and therefore supraterritorial initiatives. For many analysts, these show the broader context we need to understand contemporary politics within.

The environment and the challenges it poses are discussed in **Chapters 3 and 4**.

The involvement of the international community in the internal affairs of states has developed over the post-Cold War era. As well as the debate over the war in Iraq, there have been a number of other instances. International intervention, albeit belatedly, in Bosnia and later in Kosovo was framed as protecting civilian populations. US assistant secretary of state Richard Holbrooke famously described the former as 'bombing for peace'. In the latter case it effectively gave autonomy to Kosovo from Serbia, leading to its later recognition as an independent state. International intervention was not forthcoming in Rwanda in 1994, when the two main ethnic groups in the country were massacring each other. In East Timor, international intervention helped to protect that country's claim for independence from Indonesia. Most recently, the war in Libya was begun with the aim of protecting civilian populations, though regime change was clearly the goal of Western powers. Similar issues are currently being discussed in relation to Syria.

The international interventions in East Timor and Kosovo are further discussed in **Chapter 25**. Aspects of the case of Libya remain controversial. Was there a civil war in any case before the intervention? Was regime change the aim?

All of these can be seen as limitations to the ability of a state to do as it chooses within its own boundaries (see Yamashita 2004; McQueen 2005). In the context of the 'global war on terror' this logic of intervention has been extended to states that allow terrorist groups to operate from within their territory, and those that pursue weapons of mass destruction. The first was used to justify the bombing of Afghanistan and the overthrow of the Taliban, as well as attacks on Lebanon and Somalia by America's allies; the second was the primary reason advanced for the invasion of Iraq and the deposing of Saddam Hussein, and the ongoing tensions over North Korea and Iran.

North Korea and the invasion of Iraq are both discussed in **Chapter 26**.

In international law, the idea of territorial integrity requires both the preservation of existing boundaries and the sovereignty of states within them (see Elden 2009). If the second, *territorial sovereignty*, is held to be contingent – that is, dependent on particular behaviour – can the first, *territorial preservation*, remain unchallenged? Why should a state be limited by what it can do within its boundaries but those boundaries not be open to question? The length of the US occupation of Iraq was, in large part, to maintain it as a unified state when it descended into sectarian civil war. The uncomfortable situation of Kosovo, whose independence is recognised by some but by no means all states, demonstrates the problems of creating precedent. Will the independence of South Sudan be a model for changes to boundaries within Africa? Russia's war with separatists in Chechnya, and China's conquest of neighbouring lands like Tibet and its independence movements in Xinjiang province (also known as East Turkistan) help to explain why some powerful countries are wary of further opening up this question. Yet Russia fought the 2008 war in Georgia on the basis of separatism for Russian-speaking people in the republics of South Ossetia and Abkhazia.

It is therefore clear that the question of territorial division is at the very heart of contemporary debates about global politics. It is interesting to consider what specific types of space and place are implied by political practice, which of course extends to scales below that of nation-states and the world as a whole. Contemporary political changes, particularly in relation to globalisation, are producing profound changes in the constitution of the state, but the developments in terms of political geography, namely territory, are much less certain. Territorial issues, especially when thought through the notion of territoriality, can say much about the spatial organisation of regions, towns, rural development and other forms of the relation between people and place.

BROADER ISSUES
TECHNIQUES AND THE FUTURE OF THE TERRITORIAL STATE

States have not always existed, and territorial division is neither fixed nor the only way in which humans have encountered and organised space. One thing that is significantly different in the period when territory, at least in its modern sense, emerged was the availability of a number of techniques. The mapping and control of territory is, in large part, dependent on them. The emergence of certain techniques, dependent in part on changes in scientific and philosophical ways of viewing the world, shows that this is a historical development.

They include advances in geometry, such as the coordinate or analytic geometry pioneered by René Descartes (a form of geometry that uses algebra, coordinates and equations); developments in cartography and land surveying; and improvements in the accurate measurement of time through more advanced clocks. Knowing the exact time both in your current location and at another known point was essential to getting an accurate measurement of longitude. This is because the sun circles the earth in 24 hours and there are 360 degrees of longitude. Therefore 1 hour time difference from your starting point is 15°; 4 minutes is 1°. In order to accurately measure distances, and especially to know where ships were at sea, this was of enormous importance. Latitude is easier to measure, as it can be obtained from the angle of the sun or known stars to the horizon, though this too requires a certain calculative ability and the right instruments. Only with these kinds of facilities could modern boundaries be established as more than a line staked out on the ground. For mountainous regions, for deserts or tundra, or particularly for the abstract division of unknown places in the colonised world, such techniques were crucial.

The development of new forms of technology often has an impact on how our lives are organised and how we relate to the world: see **Chapters 8, 9, 17, 18 and 24**. It is debatable, though, which comes first: a new technology or a change in social and political conditions.

Just as Mann stresses the development of certain military techniques, so too does the geographer Edward Soja suggest the importance of cartographic ones alongside purely economic factors:

> Conventional Western perspectives on spatial organisation are powerfully shaped by the concept of property, in which pieces of territory are viewed as 'commodities' capable of being bought, sold, or exchanged at the market place. Space is viewed as being subdivided into components whose boundaries are 'objectively' determined through the mathematical and astronomically based techniques of surveying and cartography.
>
> (Soja 1971: 9)

BOX 11.5 GEOMETRIC TERRITORIAL DIVISION

Examples of these kinds of geometric territorial division include

- The western boundary between the USA and Canada, which runs along the 49th parallel of latitude. Compare this to the eastern boundary between the states, established much earlier between colonial possessions of the British.
- The surveying of the Mason–Dixon line in the 1760s, which was to settle a boundary dispute between Maryland and Pennsylvania when they were both British colonies. The line runs at approximately 39° 43′ 20″.
- The rectangular land survey of the lands of the United States west of the Mississippi in the late eighteenth and nineteenth centuries, leading to the geometric shape of many of the western states. There is a town called Four Corners which is the only place in the USA where four states (Utah, New Mexico, Arizona and Colorado) meet at a single point.
- The straight line boundaries of the states within Australia.
- The division of Africa between colonial powers at the 1884–85 Berlin Congress.
- Some of the borders in the Middle East and in the Arabian peninsula, many of which were set after the break up of the Ottoman Empire following the First World War.

One of the key techniques is in the practice of actually making boundaries, and the process of taking this from the map to the land. In political geography there is usually a three-stage process of boundary making outlined

- *Allocation*, which sets the general shape, making use of straight lines, coordinates of latitude/longitude, and depiction on a map.
- *Delimitation*, which involves the selection of specific boundary sites on the ground.
- *Demarcation*, where the boundary is marked by pillars, cleared vistas, fences, etc. (Jones 1945).

It is clear that the first stage, and even elements of the second, can be done without any detailed knowledge of the land itself, whereas the third necessarily requires presence on the ground. Many colonial boundaries were only allocated or loosely delimited, leading to many subsequent problems. Today, maintenance and management of previously demarcated boundaries and the effective demarcation of those that were merely allocated or delimited is an ongoing concern. Poorly maintained borders often lead to conflict, such as the war between Ethiopia and Eritrea in 1998–2000.

This attitude towards colonial borders was due to a range of reasons, including a lack of interest; technical difficulties were often overcome when resources were at stake.

Recognising this historical aspect of territorial division is important, because it allows us to see that the modern way of ordering the world is not the only possible system. It allows us to escape what the geographer John Agnew has called the territorial trap. Agnew suggests that this is a threefold assumption: that modern state sovereignty is a given that requires clearly bounded territories; that there is a necessary opposition between foreign and domestic affairs; and that the territorial state is the geographical

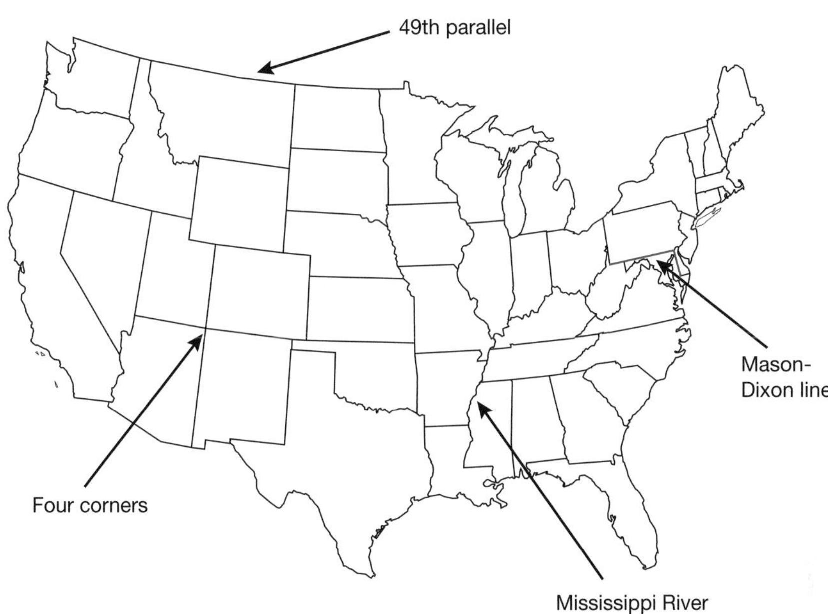

FIGURE 11.9
Map of mainland USA

'container' of modern society (1994). Similarly, for Gottmann, it is all too easy to uncritically assume the modern, or legal sense of territory as a 'portion of geographical space under the jurisdiction of certain people' (1973: 5).

The kinds of techniques that allowed states to map and control their own territory and to abstractly divide up other places are not isolated. Rather they are part of a much wider range of developments in the natural and human sciences around that time. This was a historical period that included the Renaissance, literally a *rebirth* of interest in the literature, science and politics of classical Greece and Rome. Many modern inventions emerged at this time, and scientists, writers and philosophers discussed a whole range of ideas. The beginning of modern political theory in writers such as Niccolò Machiavelli, Jean Bodin and Thomas Hobbes, modern philosophy (René Descartes, John Locke, Baruch Spinoza and Gottfried Leibniz), and modern science (Galileo, Isaac Newton) are all closely related. There is a concentration on reason – both in terms of abstract science and thought, but also in terms of political practice. The emergence of a number of mathematical and calculative techniques, such as land surveying, triangulation and geometry, are closely linked to state practices, with many of the sponsors of cartographers being states or other rulers. In addition, the development of political arithmetic, which later became known as statistics – literally the knowledge of states – began at this time (Elden 2007).

Chapters 7 and 13 note Thomas Hobbes's influence, too.

Chapter 6 explains how this concentration on reason is related to the Enlightenment.

Recent innovations in technology have led to developments in how boundaries are discussed at peace conferences and put into practice on the ground. Some of the more technologically inspired methods were used at the Dayton peace conference to set the boundaries of Bosnia. These included digitised maps that could be redrawn and calculated far more quickly than by hand, allowing the cartographers to work at the same speed as the negotiations; statistical analyses that would quickly compute what percentage of territory different political groups would get depending on the placing

Statistics are extremely important to how we understand and govern the world: see especially **Chapter 19**. See also the discussion of governmentality in **Chapter 4**.

of lines; and visualisations. These last were perhaps the most stunning innovation, allowing the negotiations to see the terrain they were dividing as if they were flying over it (Johnson 1999). For political leaders unable to read maps, such as Slobodan Milosevic, these were a powerful technique. Since Dayton, techniques have further evolved, and GIS (Geographical Information Systems) software is extensively used in boundary making, as it has been for the Ethiopia–Eritrea border, maritime boundaries, and as a tool of the discussions in the Israel/Palestine 'peace process'.

The emergence of a particular model of the state and its control of territory emerged, this chapter has argued, at a particular historical juncture and in a specific geographical context. This was then spread to most other parts of the world through colonisation. Recognising that the territorial state is a historical development shows both that it has not always existed, and that there is no essential reason why it always should. This leads to the question of whether this particular model of the state will endure, and whether territory is as important in the twenty-first century as it has been for the past few centuries.

Some writers suggest that globalisation is productive of new ways of understanding space, suggesting that new techniques have emerged. Manuel Castells, for example, has suggested that we have moved from a 'space of places' to a 'space of flows' (Castells 1989; 1996: 405–59). His suggestion is that location is no longer as important as it once was, but connection, through networks, has superseded it.

> Our societies are constructed around flows: flows of capital, flows of information, flows of technology, flows of organizational interactions, flows of images, sounds and symbols. Flows are not just one element of social organization: they are the expression of the processes dominating our economic, political, and symbolic life. . . . Thus, I propose the idea that there is a new spatial form characteristic of social practices that dominate and shape the network society: the space of flows. The space of flows is the material organization of time-sharing social practices that work through flows. By flows I understand purposeful, repetitive, programmable sequences of exchange and interaction between physically disjointed positions held by social actors.
>
> (Castells 1996: 412)

Technologies of communication are discussed in **Chapters 8 and 9**.

There is undoubtedly much to be said in favour of this analysis. New forms of technology, particularly in terms of communication and the passage of information, have transformed social relations. In this interlinked and interdependent world we are now often supposed to be closer – in a sense of our concern and interaction – to people many miles away than to our nearest neighbours. Proximity is not the same as distance. And yet, attachment to particular places, and willingness to fight, die and kill for land and the placing of boundaries continues.

Discussion of supraterritorialisation or deterritorialisation ultimately requires a more detailed analysis of territory itself, in order that we can see what we are supposedly moving beyond. Given these changes, surely the stress should be on understanding the remaking of spatial relations (reterritorialisation) in this new configuration of power, rather than simply assuming their superseding (see Elden 2005; Sassen 2006). In addition, while the techniques deployed today in terms of control of territory and its division are different in degree from those of several centuries before, they still rest on essentially the same calculative understanding of space. The network society is still a connection of mathematically determined locations. In these terms globalisation is an extension of the idea of territory as calculative space to the world, the globe, as a whole. Just as territory is not simply land or terrain, the globe is more than merely the earth. It is a geometric and political category, increasingly owned, distributed, mapped, calculated, bordered, and ordered or controlled.

CONCLUSION

This chapter has attempted to show how the modern territorial division of the world is both contingent in its specifics and in its general ordering. The relation between territorial issues and contemporary politics works in a number of ways, from issues concerning national identity, war, globalisation and rights. The history of the concept of territory helps us to understand how some of these issues came to be decided in the way that they are. Yet while there are numerous territorial disputes current in the world, and widespread debate about the relation between territory and sovereignty in the era of 'globalisation', there seem to be no generally agreed principles for changing the way in which the world is divided territorially.

FURTHER READING

There is extensive literature on topics relating to territory, especially the state, and on specific territorial issues, but relatively little on the idea of territory itself. Storey (2001, 2011) and Delaney (2005) provide accessible introductions to the topic, along with a range of examples, as does Malcolm Anderson (1996) although this is now a little out-of-date. Jones (2007) is good on the British case, and Jönsson *et al.* (2000) provide some useful historical detail in the European context, which Badie (2000) and some of the chapters in Cowen and Gilbert (2008) usefully expand. Ruggie (1993) and Taylor (1994 and 1995) provide a survey of work in the field, continued and supplemented by Paasi (2003) and the two chapters on 'Territory' in Agnew and Duncan (2011). Jones (1945) is still unparalled as a technical guide; and Anderson (2003) is useful for information. Huth and Allee (2002) is rather technical, but the appendices are very useful. Kolers (2009) takes a liberal theory of justice and applies it to territorial issues, especially in Israel/Palestine, but the conceptual understanding of territory is limited. Black (1997) and Pickles (2004) are very readable and provide lots of good examples of the relation between politics and cartography. Soja (1971) and Gottmann's accounts (1973) are still useful, and, for the most comprehensive analysis of territory from the perspective of territoriality, see Sack (1986).

WEBSITES

Borderbase, http://www.nicolette.dk/borderbase/index.php
Site with lots of information. Choose a country at top left to see a map and often a photo of its borders.

Borders and Territory, http://www.paulhensel.org/territory.html
Site maintained by Paul R. Hensel, University of North Texas, with a large range of useful information, particularly concerning territorial claims.

Centre for International Borders Research, http://www.qub.ac.uk/cibr/
Research centre at Queen's University, Belfast.

CIA World Factbook, https://www.cia.gov/library/publications/the-world-factbook/
Information on boundaries and territorial disputes.

Exploring Geopolitics, http://www.exploringgeopolitics.org/
Interviews with academics on a range of topics, including territory and boundaries.

Google Earth, http://earth.google.com/
Not always accurate, but lots of fun.

International Boundaries Research Unit (IBRU), http://www.dur.ac.uk/ibru/
Research Centre based at Durham University. Website contains lots of information on boundaries, including a news archive, links and newsletters. Many of IBRU's publications are available for free download.

International Crisis Group, http://www.crisisgroup.org/home/index.cfm
NGO which provides regular reports and updates on geopolitical issues, including those with a boundary or territorial element.

Nijmegen Centre for Border Research, http://www.ru.nl/ncbr/
Go to the 'Border Portal' for a list of relevant literature and links.

Perry-Castañeda Library Map Collection, http://www.lib.utexas.edu/maps/index.html
An excellent collection of contemporary and historical maps housed at the University of Texas at Austin.

REFERENCES

Agnew, John (1994) 'The Territorial Trap: The Geographical Assumptions of International Relations Theory', *Review of International Political Economy* 1, 1: 53–80. Reprinted in John Agnew and Stuart Corbridge (1995) *Mastering Space: Hegemony, Territory and International Political Economy*, London: Routledge.

Agnew, John and James Agnew Duncan (eds) (2011) *The Wiley-Blackwell Companion to Human Geography*, Oxford: Wiley-Blackwell.

Anderson, Ewan (2003) *International Boundaries: Geopolitical Atlas*, Chicago: Fitzroy Dearborn.

Anderson, James (1996) 'The Shifting Stage of Politics: New Medieval and Postmodern Territorialities?' *Society and Space* 14, 2: 133–53.

Anderson, Malcolm (1996) *Frontiers: Territory and State Formation in the Modern World*, Oxford: Polity.

Anderson, Perry (1974a) *Passages from Antiquity to Feudalism*, London: NLB.

——(1974b) *Lineages of the Absolutist State*, London: NLB.

Badie, Bertrand (2000) *The Imported State: The Westernization of the Political Order*, translated by Claudia Royal, Stanford, CA: Stanford University Press.

Bialasiewicz, Luiza, Stuart Elden and Joe Painter (2005) 'The Constitution of EU Territory', *Comparative European Politics* 3, 3: 333–63.

Black, Jeremy (1997) *Maps and Politics*, London: Reaktion.

Castells, Manuel (1989) *The Informational City: Information Technology, Economic Restructuring and the Urban-Regional Process*, Oxford: Blackwell.

——(1996) *The Rise of the Network Society, The Information Age: Economy, Society and Culture*, Oxford: Blackwell.

Cowen, Deborah and Emily Gilbert (eds) (2008) *War, Citizenship, Territory*, New York: Routledge.

Delaney, David (2005) *Territory: A Short Introduction*, Oxford: Blackwell.

Elden, Stuart (2005) 'Missing the Point: Globalisation, Deterritorialisation and the Space of the World', *Transactions of the Institute of British Geographers* 30, 1: 8–19.

——(2007) 'Governmentality, Calculation, Territory', *Environment and Planning D: Society and Space* 25, 3: 562–80.

——(2009) *Terror and Territory: The Spatial Extent of Sovereignty*, Minneapolis: University of Minnesota Press.

——(2010) 'Land, Terrain, Territory', *Progress in Human Geography* 34, 6: 799–817.

——(2013) *The Birth of Territory*, Chicago: University of Chicago Press.

Foucault, Michel (1976) *Discipline and Punish: The Birth of the Prison*, trans. Alan Sheridan, Harmondsworth: Penguin.

——(2003) *Society Must Be Defended*, trans. David Macey, London: Allen Lane.

——(2007) *Security, Territory, Population*, trans. Graham Burchell, London: Palgrave.

Giddens, Anthony (1985) *The Nation-State and Violence*, Cambridge: Polity Press.

Gottmann, Jean (1973) *The Significance of Territory*, Charlottesville: University Press of Virginia.

Huth, Paul K. and Todd Allee (2002) *The Democratic Peace and Territorial Conflict in the Twentieth Century*, Cambridge: Cambridge University Press

Johnson, Richard G. (1999) 'Negotiating the Dayton Peace Accords Through Digital Maps', United States Institute of Peace, www.usip.org/virtualdiplomacy/publications/reports/rjohnsonISA99.html.

Jones, Rhys (2007) *Peoples/States/Territories: The Political Geographies of British State Formation*, Oxford: Wiley Blackwell.

Jones, Stephen B. (1945) *Boundary-making: A Handbook for Statesmen, Treaty Editors, and Boundary Commissioners*. Washington, DC: Carnegie Endowment for International Peace, Division of International Law.

Jönsson, Christer, Sven Tägil and Gunnar Törnqvist (2000) *Organizing European Space*, London: Sage.

Kolers, Avery (2009) *Land, Conflict and Justice: A Political Theory of Territory*, Cambridge: Cambridge University Press.

Lalonde, Suzanne (2002). *Determining Boundaries in a Conflicted World: The Role of Uti Possidetis*, Montreal and Kingston: McGill's-Queen's University Press.

Larkins, Jeremy (2010) *From Hierarchy to Anarchy: Territory and Politics Before Westphalia*, London, Palgrave.

Linklater, Andrew (1998) *The Transformation of Political Community: Ethical Foundations of the Post-Westphalian Era*, Cambridge: Polity Press.

Malmberg, Torsten (1980) *Human Territoriality: Survey of Behavioural Territories in Man with Preliminary Analysis and Discussion of Meaning*, The Hague: Mouton Publishers.

Mann, Michael (1986) *The Sources of Social Power: Volume 1, A History of Power from the Beginning to AD 1760*, Cambridge: Cambridge University Press.

——(1993) *The Sources of Social Power: Volume 2, The Rise of Classes and Nation States 1760–1914*, Cambridge: Cambridge University Press.

Marx, Karl and Friedrich Engels (1970) *The German Ideology*, edited by C. J. Arthur, London: Lawrence & Wishart.

McQueen, Carol (2005) *Humanitarian Intervention and Safety Zones: Iraq, Bosnia and Rwanda*, Basingstoke: Palgrave Macmillan.

Nicolet, Claude (1991) *Space, Geography, and Politics in the Early Roman Empire*, translated by Hélène Leclerc, Ann Arbor: University of Michigan Press.

Paasi, Anssi (2003) 'Territory', in John Agnew, Katharyne Mitchell and Gerald Toal (eds) *A Companion to Political Geography*, Oxford: Blackwell.

Pickles, John (2004) *A History of Spaces: Cartographic Reason, Mapping and the Geo-coded World*, London: Routledge.

Ruggie, John (1993) 'Territoriality and Beyond: Problematizing Modernity in International Relations', *International Organization* 47, 1: 139–74.

Sack, Robert David (1986) *Human Territoriality: Its Theory and History*, Cambridge: Cambridge University Press.

Sahlins, Peter (1989) *Boundaries: The Making of France and Spain in the Pyrenees*, Berkeley: University of California Press.

Sassen, Saskia (2006) *Territory, Authority, Rights: From Medieval to Global Assemblages*, Princeton, NJ: Princeton University Press.

Scholte, Jan Aart (2005) *Globalisation: A Critical Introduction*, 2nd edn, Basingstoke: Palgrave Macmillan.

Soja, Edward (1971) *The Political Organisation of Space*, Commission on College Geography Resource Paper no. 8, Washington, DC: Association of American Geographers.

Storey, David (2001) *Territory: The Claiming of Space*, London: Prentice Hall.

——(2011) *Territories: The Claiming of Space*, London: Routledge.

Taylor, Peter J. (1994) 'The State as Container: Territoriality in the Modern World-System', *Progress in Human Geography* 18, 2: 151–62.

——(1995) 'Beyond Containers: Internationality, Interstateness, Interterritoriality', *Progress in Human Geography* 19, 1: 1–15.

Teschke, Benno (2003) *The Myth of 1648: Class, Geopolitics and the Making of Modern International Relations*, New York: Verso.

Townsend, Jeff (2004) 'Botswana: The San (Bushmen) Rights Case', CRS Report for Congress, http://www.botsblog.com/pdf/crs_botswana_101904.pdf.

Weber, Max (1958) *The Protestant Ethic and the Spirit of Capitalism*, New York: Scribner's Press.

——(1968) *Economy and Society*, edited by Guenther Roth and Claus Wittich, New York: Bedminister Press.

——(1994) *Political Writings*, edited by Peter Lassman and Ronald Spiers, Cambridge: Cambridge University Press.

Yamashita, Hikaru (2004) *Humanitarian Space and International Politics: The Creation of Safe Areas*, Aldershot: Ashgate.

For a range of further resources supporting this chapter, please visit the companion website for *Global Politics, 2nd Edition* at www.routledge.com/cw/edkins/

CHAPTER 12

How do people come to identify with nations?

Elena Barabantseva

THE QUESTION NATIONAL AFFILIATIONS

When we are asked where we are from, we rarely have second thoughts about our national affiliations. We readily come to identify ourselves as English, Irish, Algerian, Kurdish, German or perhaps highlight our mixed background as Turkish-German, American-Chinese, and so forth. What is it that prompts us to associate with a particular national community? What factors drive and influence this identification process?

The question of how we come to identify with a nation is central to politics. Ethnic and national differences and particularly their mobilization for political ends have been at the core of many violent conflicts and political campaigns in distant and recent history. We recurrently see the destructive power of ethnic tensions in the world, be it on the streets of Sarajevo during the Bosnian war's deliberate bombings of the central market in 1994 or of Bradford during the ethnic riots between Asian and white residents in July 2001. The markers of distinction, such as language, religion, or descent lie at the crux of identity politics and ethnic conflicts, yet it is not obvious why in certain

Chapter 5 discusses identity politics, and mentions violent conflict in the former Yugoslavia; **Chapter 13** discusses instances when markers of national identity do not work.

situations these markers create boundaries of separation and spark conflicts and in other cases they do not.

The nation is, to say the least, a concept fraught with tensions. For some it is the product of natural and objective allegiances, and for others it is a modern construct attributed to the growth of modern technology and ideologies. Although it is common in political discourse to refer to a nation-state as a basic unit of analysis, it is useful for the purposes of analysis to keep the nation distinct from the state, as the majority of states present themselves as multiethnic or multinational. The discursive practices of nationalism serve to maintain, sustain, and normalize the socio-cultural boundaries of the society. Politicians often resort to national sentiments to achieve political ends, such as independence, greater autonomy, or anti-immigration legislation. Even if most of us have not witnessed violent forms of nationalism, we certainly have come across or even taken part in its everyday expressions. Hoisting a national flag, celebration of national holidays, supporting a national team during international sport events, singing the national anthem, and voting in televised competitions like the annual Eurovision Song Contest are all examples of moments when people express their national loyalties.

Chapter 11 discusses territorial boundaries and why they arose.

I suggest in this chapter that how we come to identify with nations is most prominently expressed in marginal spaces, boundaries or limits of what is assumed to be a national community. At their margins concepts, like a nation, become frayed, revealing the complexity of assumptions that at the centre appear a seamless whole. Examining the relational position of marginal groups in nationalist discourses offers a perspective highlighting the contested and complex nature of the nation. The analysis of how marginal groups figure in the dominant national narratives sheds light on how the nation takes shape against the backdrop of human diversity found within and outside of its assumed boundaries. The focus on the margins also illuminates where and how the lines of inclusion and exclusion in the national project are drawn.

Chapter 13 focuses also on such marginal groups within the nation, and also examines stories of exile.

The marginal spaces of the nation could take different expressions depending on which of the analytical categories are considered. In this chapter I consider the role of ethnic factors and territoriality in constructing a nation. Marginality here denotes the position of groups on territorial and cultural edges of what is assumed to be the national core. Although the margins of any nation would be worth analysing, the chapter takes a closer look at the configurations of the Chinese nation.

ILLUSTRATIVE EXAMPLE
THE MARGINS OF THE CHINESE NATION

To have a better idea of how Chinese rulers have viewed and treated people at its ethnic and territorial margins, we should briefly dwell on the history of Chinese rulers' interactions with both culturally different people and so-called overseas Chinese – Chinese people living outside their place of birth or origin in China.

From empire to nation

Since the first unified Chinese state (221 BCE) Chinese emperors referred to their domains as the central state (*zhongguo*) and distinguished between people who inhabited the central state's territories and those who lived outside them. The core of Chinese civilization lay within the central state, while the populations outside it were barbarians. The Empire significantly enlarged when the nomadic Manchus overthrew the Ming dynasty in 1644 and expanded the expanses of the Empire through the conquest of Xinjiang, southwest China, Tibet, Mongolia, and Taiwan. The Manchu court had to tackle the dual problem of establishing their legitimate authority in the Empire and guaranteeing the unity of the growing multiethnic political entity. They popularized the idea that 'the Center and the Outer are one family' to emphasize the universalism and multiethnic character of their empire (Zhao 2006: 6–7; Leibold 2007: 10–11). The

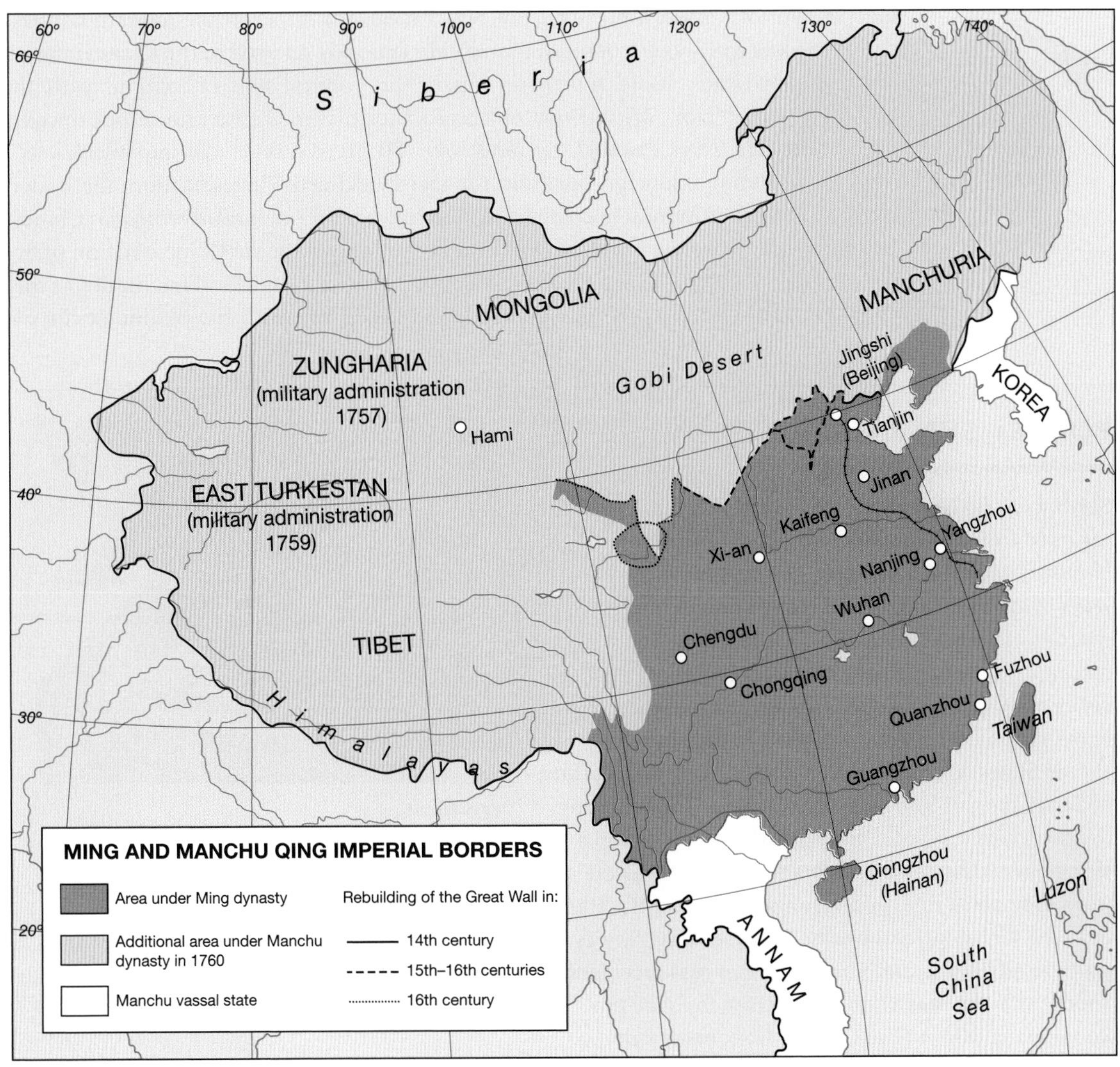

FIGURE 12.1
Imperial China: Ming and Manchu dynasties. http://warandgame.files.wordpress.com/2010/03/chin2.jpg

formulation of new national concepts and categories of distinction were integral to the transformation of Chinese imperial structure into the modern state. New administrative divisions, ethnographic categorization, and the promotion of the idea of a multiethnic entity were all used to help to transform imperial subjects into national citizens. This suggests that the processes associated with nation-crafting were already part of the Chinese imperial governing structure.

Categorization on the basis of ethnicity or indeed race can be seen in many parts of the world. **Chapter 5** touches on the examples of Yugoslavia and Rwanda.

In the late nineteenth century the new political term had entered the Chinese political vocabulary. Competing political groups employed the notion *minzu* or nation to propagate new kinds of political allegiances among the Chinese. At the time China was subjected to the status of a semi-colonial state by European and Japanese powers, and the term *minzu* signalled the emergence of the idea of a new Chinese nation independent of foreign influences. For Sun Yatsen, the father of the modern Chinese nation, *minzu* was about 'common blood'. He famously referred to the Chinese nation as the Yellow Race, using *minzu* to equate the political unit of 'nation' with the biological unit of 'race'. *Minzuzhuyi*, or 'the doctrine of *minzu*', was one of the principles of Sun Yatsen's *Three Principles of the People.* To prevent separatist implications as a result of excluding ethnic groups from the racially defined Chinese nation, the leaders of the republican government coined a new inclusive term – *zhonghua mingguo* (Chinese Republic) – to make the new Chinese state coterminous with the Chinese nation of five nationalities (*minzu*): Han, Manchus, Mongols, Tibetans, and Muslims. In doing this, they equated boundaries of the new Chinese nation-state with the outline of the old

BOX 12.1 SUN YATSEN

FIGURE 12.2
Sun Yatsen on the balcony of his house in Guangzhou, China, 1923. © Bettmann/Corbis Photograph. *Encyclopædia Britannica Online.* Web. 3 Jan. 2012. http://www.britannica.com/EBchecked/media/122949/Sun-Yat-sen-on-the-balcony-of-his-home-in; http://media-3.web.britannica.com/eb-media/98/91198-004-50309F8B.jpg

Sun Yatsen (12 November 1866–12 March 1925) is widely regarded to be the founder of modern China. Born into a farming family in Guangdong, he spent his formative years studying in Hawaii and Hong Kong. A medical doctor by training, Sun quit his medical practice to dedicate his life to Chinese revolution. After organizing a series of unsuccessful uprisings against the imperial rule in the 1890s, Sun spent many years in exile in Japan, the United States, Europe and Canada soliciting political and financial support from overseas Chinese. The Wuchang uprising, where Sun did not play a direct role, led to a string of developments bringing to an end the 2,000 years of imperial rule. As a result of these events, referred to as the Xinhai Revolution, the Chinese Republic was proclaimed in 1912, and Sun became its first president. Shortly after the revolution, Sun Yatsen founded the Kuomintang (KMT) (The Chinese Nationalist Party), which to the present day remains one of the two main parties in Taiwan. The goals and ideals of the Kuomintang partly informed the establishment of the Chinese Communist Party in 1921.

BOX 12.2 CHINESE CIVIL WAR AND COMMUNIST REVOLUTION

The Chinese Civil War was a series of wars resulting from the struggle for power between the KMT and the CCP, who both fought for the control of China. The conflict sparked off in 1927 and lasted until 1949. The crucial turning point in the civil war was the CCP Red Army's Long March (1934–35) during which Mao Zedong confirmed his role as leader of the Chinese communists, and gained popularity and support in western and northern China. Despite major ideological and strategic disagreements, the KMT and the CCP tried to jointly fight against the Japanese aggression during the 1937–1945 Sino–Japanese war. However, the cooperation between the two parties was not successful. The civil war went on until the communist victory on the Chinese mainland in 1949, leading to the division of China into the People's Republic of China (PRC) governed by the CCP, and the Republic of China established by the KMT in Taiwan.

FIGURE 12.3
Chinese Civil War: South Park philosophy. http://fc04.deviantart.net/fs42/i/2010/290/d/b/south_park_chinese_civil_war_by_southpark philosopher-d1yynjd.jpg

Qing Empire. The stripes of red, yellow, blue, white and black on the five-colour national flag symbolized the 'harmonious cohabitation of five ethnic tribes' (*wuzu gonghe*) in one single nation.

In a parallel development, Sun Yatsen and his followers resorted to the discourse of common descent and culture to encourage overseas Chinese to contribute to the cause of the Chinese Republic. Although banned for a long time during the dynastic rule, overseas migration was popular among Chinese in the coastal areas, and by the mid-nineteenth century hundreds of thousands of overseas Chinese became wealthy merchants in Southeast Asia. Late-Qing officials and the leaders of Republican China realized the potential significance of overseas Chinese for the Chinese nation-building project, and they made extensive efforts to raise contributions and investments from overseas Chinese for development projects in China. The term *huaqiao* (Chinese sojourner) became a popular term to refer to overseas Chinese. This term was intended to appeal to the national sentiments of overseas Chinese in the hope that they would invest their wealth and energy into modernizing the Chinese Republic. It emphasized overseas Chinese's symbolic 'biological' attachment to a 'native home' and played to the common ancestral and cultural roots of all Chinese:

> Whoever is a descendant of the Yellow Emperor, no matter whether resident in the Chinese mainland or in Hong Kong, Macao, Taiwan or another part of the world, proudly recognizes that the dragon is the symbol of China, that China is the land of the dragon and the Chinese people are the descendants of the dragon.
>
> (Zhang Ke quoted in Sautman 1997: 82)

An adoption of the *jus sanguinis* principle confirmed in the Nationality Law of 1909 granted citizenship to all Chinese overseas, and allowed a 'dual citizenship' for Chinese nationals living in other countries. This constructed a new sense of Chinese national identity that narrowly focused on common race descending from a mythological ancestor, the Yellow Emperor. Thus, for China's republican leaders Chinese culture, nation, and race became coterminous. These early-twentieth century nationalist discourses highlight the power and centrality, as well as the ambiguity, of the ideas of common blood and descent in determining the limits of the Chinese nation.

The *jus sanguinis* principle is the principle that a child's citizenship or nationality is the same as that of its parents, as opposed to the *jus soli* principle, where a child's nationality is that of the territory on which they are born.

Chinese communist nationalism

When the Chinese communists came into power in 1949, they extensively used nationalist rhetoric and were preoccupied with socialist nation-building, but their nationalist discourse was of a different kind. The Chinese Communist Party's (CCP) analysis of China's national situation and its formulation of the national question were influenced by the interpretation of the 'class struggle' and 'peasant revolution'. Communists believed that national distinctions and borders will come to an end as a result of successful class struggle: 'First the dying out of classes, then the state, finally the nation – that is true of the whole world' (Mao Zedong quoted in Fei Xiaotong 1981: 85). Instead of the 'nation', the CCP's discourse centered on the concept of 'the People' (*renmin*) which characterized the CCP's categorization of who belonged and who was excluded from the Chinese revolutionary stock:

> We must first be clear on what is meant by 'the people' and what is meant by the 'enemy'. The concept of the 'people' varies in content in different countries and in different periods of history in a given country . . . At the present stage, the period of building socialism, the classes, strata and social groups which favour, support and work for the cause of socialist construction all come within the category of the people, while the social forces and groups which resist the socialist revolution and are hostile to or sabotage socialist construction are all enemies of the people.
>
> (Mao Zedong 1957)

The formulation of new socialist style nation-building produced a new notion of 'the people' which was made ideologically contingent on the category of class and encompassed only the revolutionary masses while dismissing the rest of the population as enemies or non-people. The notion of 'the people' was at the heart of the United Front of revolutionary struggle, another key term in communist China. The United Front was built around the focal role of the CCP, and Mao Zedong frequently mentioned overseas Chinese and ethnic minorities among other United Front participants as the central forces in the revolutionary struggle. For example, in Mao's declaration at the First Plenary Session of the Chinese People's Political Consultative Conference, overseas Chinese and ethnic minorities were among the representatives of the 'will of the people' (Mao Zedong 1949). In its designation of who belonged to the overseas Chinese, the CCP used the *jus sanguinis* principle assuming a common bond among all Chinese in China and abroad. The only criterion which was supposed to make this group homogeneous was to be patriotic towards the New (communist) China.

BOX 12.3 MAO ZEDONG AND COMMUNISM IN CHINA

The establishment of Communist China in 1949 was predicated on the idea of building a class-free society. After the communist victory, the new government initiated a series of socio-economic reforms and campaigns aimed at achieving this goal and radically transforming Chinese society in accordance with the teachings of Mao Zedong. One of such campaigns, the Great Leap Forward (1958–1961), aimed at the fast transformation of Chinese agrarian society into an industrial communist country. The government's blind diversion of resources into the production of steel and iron resulted in China's worst famine of the twentieth century. Another infamous socio-political movement, the Cultural Revolution, lasted for a decade from 1966 to 1976. One of its main goals was to combat the 'four olds' of China: old customs, old culture, old habits and old ideas. As a result of the Cultural Revolution, an uncountable number of cultural relics was destroyed and numerous people tortured and killed by Red Guards, the young revolutionary followers of Mao. After the death of Mao Zedong in 1976, the new leader of the CCP, Deng Xiaoping, initiated a series of pro-market economic reforms and the opening of the country to outside investments. Although there were continuous calls for similar reforms in the political sphere, the CCP reinstated its unshakeable one-party rule over the country during the mass crackdown of the student-led pro-democracy movement in Tiananmen Square in 1989.

FIGURE 12.4
Mao Zedong announcing the foundation of the PRC in 1949.
http://www.chinadaily.com.cn/china/images/cpc2011/attachement/jpg/site1/20110701/002170196e1c0f775a2112.jpg; http://www.chinadaily.com.cn/china/cpc2011/2011-07/01/content_12814296.htm

According to the Chinese leaders, 'all patriots belong to one big family' (Zhou Enlai quoted in Lien Kuan 1978: 15).

The first national census after the establishment of the PRC in 1953 included information on ethnic minorities and listed some 11.7 million overseas Chinese as part of the Chinese population (Cressey 1955: 388). While ties of blood were used as a defining criterion for overseas Chinese, the implementation of the 1954 national minority identification project (*minzu shibie*) was aimed at identifying ethnic groups in China and followed Chinese interpretations of the nation defined by Joseph Stalin in the Soviet Union. Language, territory, economy, and psychological mindset became

Joseph Stalin was leader of the USSR until his death in 1953. His role in the Second World War is discussed in **Chapter 22**.

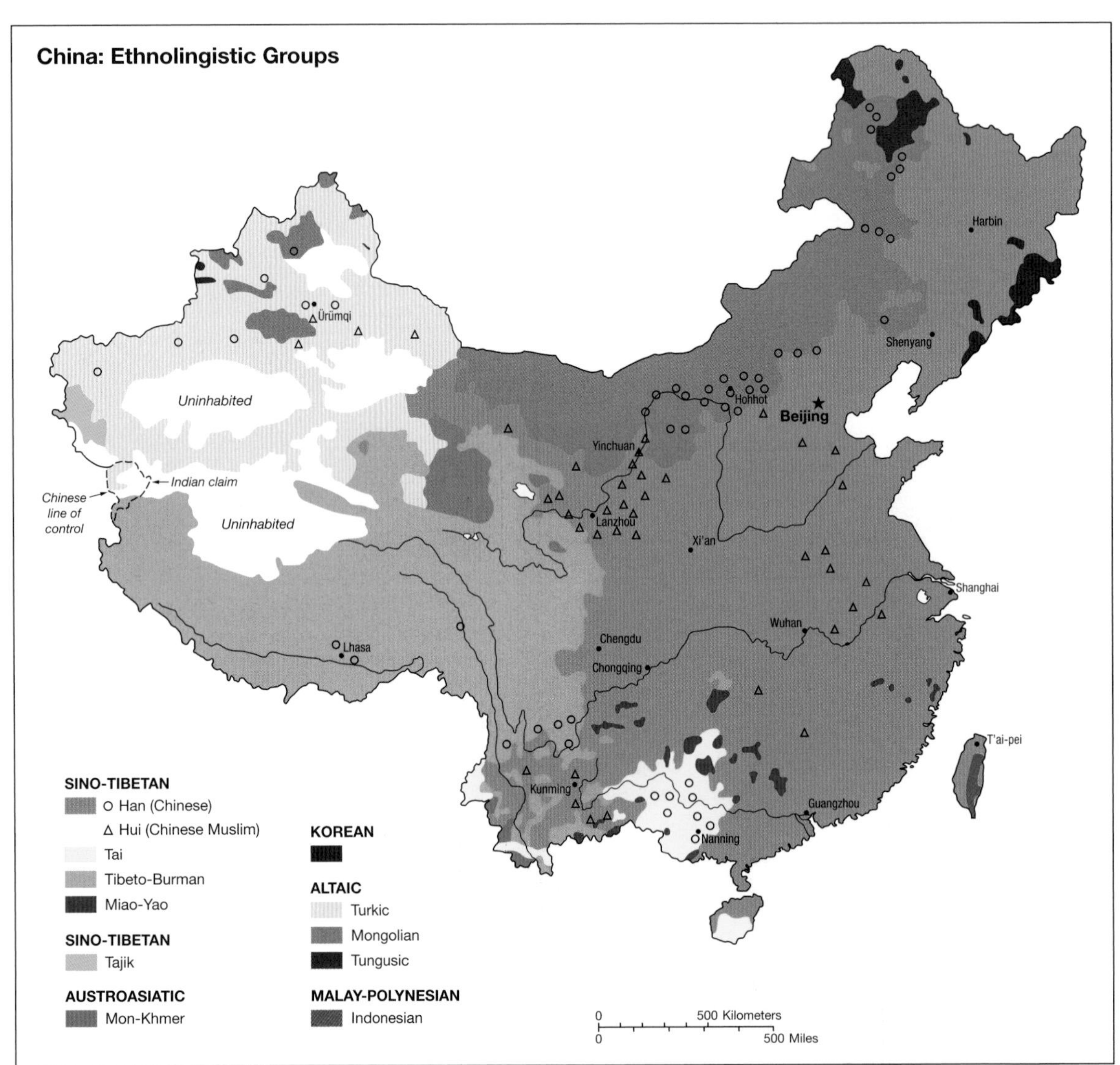

FIGURE 12.5
Ethnolinguistic map of China 1983. http://upload.wikimedia.org/wikipedia/commons/thumb/9/95/Ethnolinguistic_map_of_China_1983.png/640px-Ethnolinguistic_map_of_China_1983.png

the markers of distinct ethnicity within the PRC. Throughout the identification project, China's ethnic minorities were identified and categorized into fixed ethnic groups with special needs and characteristics. Special ministry-level institutions – the Overseas Chinese Affairs Department and the Ethnic Affairs Commission – were established with the intention of formulating and implementing government policies towards overseas Chinese and identified ethnic groups. While the categorization into ethnic groups (56 by 1979) brought to light the diversity of Chinese society, policies towards overseas Chinese, on the other hand, relied on the assumption of the centrality of blood ties in how the Chinese state saw its people identify with it. By the mid-1950s, the Chinese communist leadership realized that they were failing to solicit contributions from the overseas Chinese, and that they faced the danger of upsetting their amicable relations with Southeast Asian states. These states were suspicious of the connections the overseas Chinese in their countries had to communist China. At this point, the PRC took the step of withdrawing the right to dual nationality, which has been prohibited in China up to the present day.

Post-Mao nation-building

Since the start of the economic reforms and opening-up of China to the rest of the world in 1978, economic development has overwhelmingly been presented in Chinese official discourse as a solution to China's national problems, an all-encompassing answer to the problems of regional and social inequality, ethnic cohesion, cultural development and potential ethnic strife. Overseas Chinese and ethnic minorities remain central in this nation-building discourse. Ethnic minorities have been presented as in need of economic development, while China's majority Han population, and particularly successful overseas Han Chinese, have been increasingly seen as an extension of the Chinese nation united under the goal of 'rejuvenating the nation'. After the period of isolation from the rest of the world during the ten years of the Cultural Revolution (1966–76), China has re-established and reinforced its links with overseas Chinese (Zhuang 2001; Thunø 2001; Xiang 2003). In recent years scholars have observed a growing 're-Sinicization' of overseas Chinese communities worldwide, which is attributed to the active role of the Chinese state in promoting its presence among overseas Chinese (Ong 2006; Liu 2010). The Chinese government's network of institutions for overseas Chinese is one of the largest and most comprehensive in the world, working with what one Chinese scholar described as 'the previous three generations and the coming three generations' (Cheng 2007: 47).

In contrast to the way overseas Chinese are viewed and treated as an extension of the Chinese territorial nation, the role of ethnic minorities during the reform period has been to enable China to be presented as a multiethnic, diverse and 'colourful' society. The post-Mao era in China was marked by a 'cultural fever' (*wenhua re*): a valorizing of ethnic minority cultures, which suddenly flourished after years of suppression during the Cultural Revolution. Ethnic minorities have become an imperative feature in national holiday celebrations, such as the annual spring festival TV gala, and other nationally important events such as the opening ceremony of the Beijing Olympics (Leibold 2008). The ethnically diverse and harmonious image of the Chinese state is a preferred portrait projected to the outside world through global celebrations. However, certain ethnic

How is this different from or similar to the idea of the 'melting pot' in the United States?

FIGURE 12.6
Children representing all of China's ethnic groups, dressed in regional costume, march with the national flag at the Beijing Olympics. Almost immediately after the Olympics opening ceremony it emerged that most of the children who took part in the event were of the Han nationality. Photo: AFP. http://olympics.scmp.com/Article.aspx?id=2672§ion=latestnews

groups in China are widely perceived as troublemakers, violent, and untrustworthy. This in particular concerns Uyghurs and Tibetans, but also affects other groups like Huis and Mongols. Uyghurs and Tibetans have been targets of the 'three evils' campaign against 'separatism, terrorism and religious extremism' since the mid-1990s, but in particular after 9/11 and recent ethnic clashes in Tibet in 2008, Xinjiang in 2009, and Mongolia in 2011. These developments have affected most representatives of these groups, irrespective of their political views. For example, the whole of Xinjiang was cut off from the internet after the clashes in Xinjiang, and Uyghurs travelling outside of the region could not make use of internet cafes. They were seen as a potential threat and a source of danger simply because of their ethnic group affiliation and religion.

Contemporary official formulations of the Chinese nation echo the interpretations put forward by the nationalist government in the early twentieth century and the Maoist government in the mid-twentieth century. The Chinese nation is framed around the image of an active Han majority and passive ethnic minorities, who have to be led to achieve better living standards. Ethnic minorities are on the receiving end of development practices, and the possibility of a perspective of equality or an appreciation of diversity as a constituent quality of the Chinese national project is inhibited. The current national discourses are rooted in the history of Chinese imperial rulers' encounter with ethnic difference, long prior to China's encounter with Western modernity in the nineteenth century.

The statuses of ethnic minorities and overseas Chinese in the Chinese nation reflect the long process of negotiating what constitutes China and who the Chinese people are. The binary opposition of the Han versus China's ethnic minorities lies at the core of how the Chinese nation has been formulated by the state. The juxtapositions between the Han and ethnic minorities, advanced and backward, civilized and barbarian, modern and traditional, have characterized the dynamics of Chinese national identity. The Chinese nation could perhaps be seen as taking shape somewhere in-between, at the meeting points, often coincidental ones, of these dialogical processes. The dichotomous relationship between the Han Chinese and China's ethnic minorities does not mean that processes bringing these groups together are mutually exclusive and run in opposition to each other. The dialogical aspect of this relationship stresses that the role of these groups is complementary and equally influential in how Chinese identity takes shape.

GENERAL RESPONSES
NATIONALISM STUDIES

China's engagement with populations within and outside its immediate territorial boundaries suggests that the study of nationalism and how people come to identify with particular nations cannot be restricted to examining the processes within the state. Yet, the vast majority of nationalism studies takes the state as a reference point for the study of nationalism. Explaining the link between state, as a territorial political unit, and nation, as an ethno-cultural collectivity of people, has been the main focus of analysis in nationalism studies. The two dominant approaches to the study of nationalism and nations in this respect are primordialist and modernist accounts of nations.

Primordialism

The primordialist perspective emphasizes the importance of objective factors in the formation of ethnic groups, such as language, common ancestry, religion, and so forth. The main representatives of this view are Geertz (1963), Horowitz (1985), Van den Berghe (1987), Smith (1996), Hastings (1997) and Hutchinson (2000). Differing in their research methodologies and foci, these scholars share three elements in their interpretations of the nation. First, they agree that the organization of an ethnic group is driven by the idea of common descent and common cultural features of the community. That is, an ethnic group comes into being where a group of people share blood allegiances, kinship and cultural attributes. Second, these factors, on which ethnic ties are premised, are rooted in the nature of human beings. In other words, ethnic identity is seen as a fundamental sentiment because of its psychological significance for a human being. Third, primordial ties become more significant through recurrent reference to them in symbolic and cultural attributes of the community: myths, traditions, and heritage. Although the primordial perspective is well equipped to explain the persistence and power of ethnic categories in the contemporary world, it does not take into account the fluid and variable character of ethnicity. It emphasizes the natural origins of national belonging rather than seeing it as being a result of social interaction.

What does it mean to think that there is such a thing as 'human nature'? See the box on this in **Chapter 7**. **Chapter 5** questions the way there was once thought to be a 'male' nature and a 'female' nature. Is thinking that there is a 'human' nature very different?

According to the primordialist reading of a nation, a nation-state is a product of a historical process whereby ethnicities turn into political units, and where the ethnic allegiances and cultural origins of nations are the central and most durable axes of alignment within a nation-state. In his study of the origins of nations, Anthony Smith (1983, 1996) refers to the *ethnie* (pre-modern ethnic community) as a human organization which characterizes much of the world even today. Although rejecting the idea of the continuous character of ethnicity, Smith contends that it remains a socio-cultural 'model' for human organization and communication, which grants 'an underlying sense of historical and cultural community' (Smith 1996: 111). Smith argues that objective cultural material is a basis for the construction of ethnicity, which is then re-invented in the process of nation-making in order to foster the creation and maintenance of solidarity networks underpinning the nation-state. As a result, for Smith nations are influenced and partly constructed by objective elements, which stem from the historical roots, myths, symbols, memories, and values which originate in pre-modern *ethnies*.

These so-called 'solidarity networks' are what Shapiro calls 'centripetal forces' in **Chapter 13**. The focus in **Chapter 13** is on the 'centrifugal' forces which tend to pull a nation apart.

It is problematic for primordialism to take into account historical-political factors influencing the evolving character of nation-building processes. By treating proto-nations or *ethnies* as objective communities, the primordial perspective ignores the power relations shaping the emergence, maintenance, and persistence of ethnicities and nations. Seeing the emergence of nation-states as a natural process, primordialism underplays the role of power in shaping the nation-building process. Furthermore, the assumption of ethnicities being predetermined and fixed presupposes a certain degree of pessimism

feggo
"We can't stay here, and your father has connections in China."

FIGURE 12.7
'We can't stay here, and your father has connections in China.' Artist: Feggo. CartoonStock ref.: fgan136. www.CartoonStock.com

as to the future of multiethnic states: 'clearly, multiethnic states face a problem of legitimacy that is incommensurable with that of nation-state' (Van den Berghe 1987: 75). For primordialists, ethnic conflict is an endemic and unavoidable characteristic of multiethnic societies, which not only puts the nation-building process under question, but also destabilizes and challenges the state's cohesion.

Modernism

The modernist perspective links the emergence of nations to the modern period in history, which is associated with the changes brought about by industrialization and modernization (Gellner 1983; Hobsbawm 1990; Anderson 1991; Breuilly 1996). These approaches locate the emergence of a nation within the framework of modern state. The two most influential studies which stress this link are those by Ernest Gellner (1964, 1983) and Benedict Anderson (1991). Gellner attributes the beginning of nation-building to a variety of factors associated with the period of modernization and establishes that the pre-existence of common culture is not vital for initiating the process of nation-building. For Gellner 'nationalism is not awakening of nations to self-consciousness: it invents nations where they do not exist' (Gellner 1964: 169). Gellner underscores the distinctive feature of nationalism as a theory of political legitimacy in guaranteeing a correspondence of political and cultural principles within the boundaries of a political community (Gellner 1983: 1). The change in the mode of production and transformation of communication prompts a need for a culturally homogeneous community of centrally-educated people. Gellner binds nationalism to states, arguing that only taken-for-granted politically and morally centralized units can provide a necessary though not a sufficient environment for nationalism. Hence, nationalism in Gellner's account is limited to already existent states and is largely a state-driven phenomenon aimed at exercising moral legitimacy over the members of a political community which finds its expression in the promotion of nationalism, because nations and states 'were destined for each other; . . . either without the other is incomplete, and constitutes a tragedy' (1983: 6). A standardized culture shared by all members and promoted by means of education plays a crucial role in this process. Controlled by the state, the spread of culture is closely linked to power, which is concentrated in the hands of the state elite.

Chapter 11 discusses the formation of the territorial state in a similar way: as part of a process of modernization beginning in Western Europe and spreading to the rest of the world. How does this account square with the account of the rise of the Chinese nation-state given in this chapter?

For Anderson (1991), capitalism with its growing print technology, paralleled by the growing usage of vernacular languages, precipitated the creation of a prototype of a modern nation. He argues that only under the conditions of print-capitalism and growing usage of vernacular languages can people be mobilized in their ethnic and national self-identification into a nation, which he terms as a form of 'imagined political community'. Print-capitalism as a co-process provides grounds for people to think about themselves, and to relate to others in profoundly new ways (Anderson 1991: 36). Perception of a nation as a horizontal brotherhood conceals its internal disparities and inequalities. The fear of oblivion and an ability to control 'homogeneous, empty time' transform the perception of community as a social landscape with past and future, and reinforces popular imagination of an attachment to a territorially fixed, immutable, and eternal community which becomes a defining element of nationalism. In contrast to Gellner, who points to the essentially 'fabricated' character of a nation, Anderson

How does this argument about print technology link with other arguments about technology – for example, the role of technology in delineating territorial boundaries in **Chapter 11** or the idea that the technology of Web 2.0 has created different ways to connect politically, as discussed in **Chapter 9**? Is technology autonomous?

FIGURE 12.8
Table of accounts of nationalism

	Primordialist	**Modernist**
Origins of nations	Archaic, deeply rooted in human evolution	Modern, with the emergence of capitalism and printed technologies
Character of nations	Objective and natural, attributable to common language, religion, descent, or other similar factors	Political, formulated and manipulated by the political and intellectual elite for political ends
The role of national territory	Essential	Essential

attributes its emergence to imagination based on certain pre-existing cultural grounds which gained their significance in people's minds with the changes brought about by print-capitalism.

Modernist interpretations of the idea of a nation, including Gellner's and Anderson's, often underscore the political character of nationalism. They emphasize the status position of those who articulate nationalism, arguing that nationalism is one of the manifestations of the exercise of state power (Breuilly 1996; Brown 2000; Hobsbawm 1990). By reinforcing 'populist consciousness' among its subjects by different means of communication and mass-education in a standardized language, political elites take the lead in the creation and transformation of ethnic identities in a culturally diverse society into a unified community under legitimate control or a ruling leadership. The leading role of intellectuals in mobilizing a community around a unified 'high culture' for modelling and advancing a strong, bureaucratic, and centralized state is also recognized in this literature (Gellner 1983; Anderson 1991; Greenfeld 1992). Those who underline a political role for nationalism tend to promote the nation-state as the most important model for political community, and a basic political unit in modern societies. In fact, Hobsbawm (1990: 9–10), one of the prominent proponents of the modernist interpretation of nationalism, argues that a nation 'is a social entity only insofar as it relates to a certain kind of modern territorial state, the "nation-state"'.

The rise of notions of bounded territory is discussed in **Chapter 11**.

Both primordialist and modernist accounts of the origins of nations, maintain that territorial boundedness of a political community is one of the essential preconditions for the formation and successful functioning of the state as a nation-state. They stipulate that common territory is a crucial marker of a people's unity and group identity, and it contributes to the perception of a group as something naturally bounded by shared beliefs and myths and a common destiny (Anderson 1991: 2). These scholars underline how common territory promotes a sense of group distinctiveness and separateness, and draws a defined inner/outer borderline between the members of the political community and outsiders that raises crucial questions concerning nationality and citizenship, exclusion and inclusion and the goals of the state (Anderson 1991: 19; Hastings 1997: 30). Even when territory does not play a crucial role in defining a nation, they argue, most nationalist ideas are played out around the idea of their own 'physical space' where they can 'act out their dreams and fulfil aspiration' (Smith 1983: 19; Oomen 1994: 45). The authors adhering to this point of view assert that territory plays the role of an historical home, a 'homeland', which is endowed with the romantic and poetic role of a 'nation cradle', and is also a driving force of progress and the destiny of a nation:

> '[T]he external frontiers' of the state have to become 'internal frontiers' or – which amounts to the same thing – external frontiers have to be imagined constantly as a projection and protection of an internal collective personality, which each of us carries within ourselves and enables us to inhabit the space of the state as a place where we have always been – and always will be – 'at home'.
>
> (Balibar 1991: 95)

Thus, in both approaches clear territorial boundaries are a primary condition for a cultural community to develop nationalism and a must for formulating national identity. A 'territorial trap', identified by John Agnew as a common way of thinking about international politics, has been characteristic of nationalism studies too (Agnew 1994). The equation of nations with states, or what other scholars have called the 'methodological nationalism' of nationalism studies, has restricted discussions on important contemporary phenomena, including increased and accelerated human mobility, hybridization of human identities, and the profound effects of digital technologies. A close link between population and state territory in the academic discussions on nationalism has reified the widely held perception of a state's unified and homogeneous national population. How the significance of territoriality changes with time, and how it influences the boundaries of inclusion and exclusion in the particular historical and political context of the nation, is not illuminated in this body of literature. While national boundaries of exclusion and inclusion are constantly redrawn, the role of territoriality in erecting national distinctions is more ambiguous, with different meanings at different points in history.

For more on the territorial trap see **Chapter 11**.

BROADER ISSUES
TRANSNATIONALISM AND HYBRIDITY

Primordial and modernist approaches to nationalism, albeit differently, emphasize the importance of territorial and ethnic factors in the construction of the nation. These studies do not highlight how the contours of the nation might be influenced by the ongoing effects of globalization and state practices exceeding state territorial limits. Yet the scope and content of a national project does not always correspond with the territorial confines of the state. A fast growing body of literature points to the multifarious character of nationalism, which can be subnational, national, transnational, or virtual in nature. When the focus is on the nation-state or a particular ethnic group as a main source of nationalism, the role of territory is presumed and taken for granted. This focus does not take into account how territoriality intersects with other markers of identity, such as class, race, religion, language, gender, or sub-national ethnicity in delineating where the limits of national identity are to be drawn. For example, primordial and modernist accounts of nationalism stress the relevance of population as a whole and focus on the people who are already to be found within the physical boundaries of the state. They pay far less attention to how nation-building is affected by the processes of emigration from the state's territory, or to the way that people can have multiple

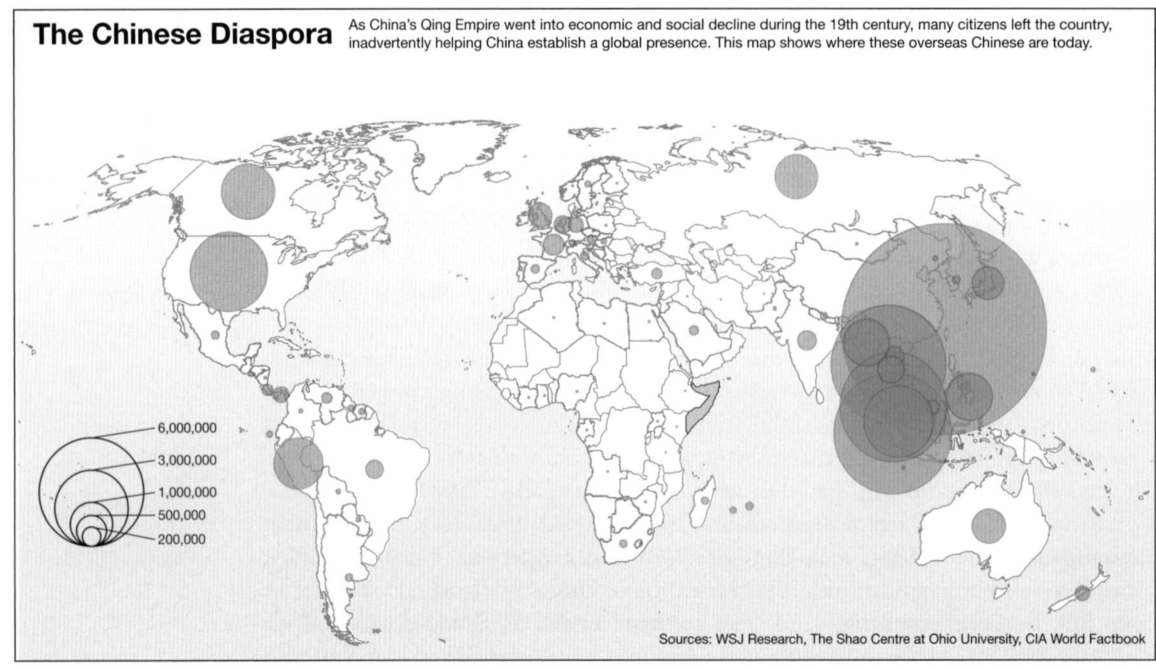
The Chinese Diaspora
As China's Qing Empire went into economic and social decline during the 19th century, many citizens left the country, inadvertently helping China establish a global presence. This map shows where these overseas Chinese are today.
6,000,000
3,000,000
1,000,000
500,000
200,000
Sources: WSJ Research, The Shao Centre at Ohio University, CIA World Factbook

FIGURE 12.9
Chinese Diaspora map. http://2.bp.blogspot.com/_leoGYAeiH44/TEyjGz_oTNI/AAAAAAAAKro/biY4v5nWBoA/s640/chinese+diaspora.jpg; http://online.wsj.com/article/SB10001424052748704682604575369390660095122.html#articleTabs%3Dinteractive%26project%3DCHINAMAP_1007

The existence of multiple allegiances within the nation-state is discussed in depth in **Chapter 13**; **Chapter 10** examines the status of immigrant communities. **Chapter 14** looks at minority groups in Argentina.

national allegiances. The issues of immigration and the status of migrant communities in the host societies have traditionally been seen as the platform for analysing the questions of national identity. Yet, the position of the state towards outgoing migrants and migrant communities abroad, or diasporas as they are often referred to in scholarly literature, is significantly less studied. The focus on state territory as a primary source and scope of nation-building in primordial and modernist studies does not capture how national identity takes shape in between domestic and international realms. Nor does it stress that national territory itself is a product of particular historical developments, and should not be seen as fixed and immutable.

Transnational politics of the state

This chapter's illustrative example shows the pertinence of transnational aspects in Chinese nation-building through the Chinese state's links to overseas Chinese. This issue relates to the effects of transnationalism on nation-building as a state-driven process. The term transnationalism was introduced in the early 1990s by a group of American anthropologists to characterize the emergence of new social spaces produced by migrant communities through their links to their country of origin and their host society. Cross-border solidarities of transnational migrants have been portrayed in this scholarship as a challenge to national projects of states (Glick Schiller *et al.* 1992: 1) and sometimes as an alternative to the project of building and sustaining nation-states (Appadurai 1997;

Guarnizo and Smith 1998; Meyer and Geschiere 1999). The prevalent argument expressed across this literature holds that transnational subjects participate in practices which benefit from the processes associated with the phenomenon of globalization – flexible production, consumption, mobility, etc. – while escaping the attachment to a particular territory and the hierarchical structures and processes dictated by the state. Migrants are presented as those who act beyond state control, shift social bases and subjectivities, and question the meaning of national citizenship. Arjun Appadurai, for example, introduced the concept of 'global ethnoscapes' to refer to the transnational identities which are transformed and shaped by the transnational spaces they enter (Appadurai 1990). These transnational identities in the view of Appadurai shattered 'the monopoly of autonomous nation-state' (Appadurai 1997: 10). Yet, the state as an important factor conditioning and even benefiting from transnational processes falls out of this analysis.

The mobility of capital – the ready movement of money as opposed to people – is important. See **Chapters 15 and 17** for example.

The increasing effects of global mobility and fluidity do not leave the structure of the state unaffected. Although the deterritorialized patterns of production, consumption, and identity politics restrain a totalizing hegemony of the state – the state no longer seems quite so all-powerful – they are not necessarily eroding the power of the state in drawing the contours of the nation associated with it. In the conditions of increased human mobility, the state does not relax its powers over the imaginaries of its transnational subjects, but extends its control over them. Chinese nation-building processes taking place outside the boundaries of the state through overseas Chinese policies, as discussed above, are an example of such transnational practices.

Territory is not necessarily an obsolete feature in nationalist discourses, but we need to stress the complex interplay between territorial and non-territorial factors in shaping the nation. For example, our illustrative case on the Chinese state's engagement with overseas Chinese and ethnically diverse people in China shows how the Chinese leadership has been equally preoccupied with incorporating ethnic minorities *and* reaching out to overseas Chinese in its nation-building efforts. This suggests that the Chinese state's formulation of who belongs to the Chinese nation is not strictly dictated by where China's territorial borders lie. Nation-building practices often extend far beyond national territory, as the next section shows.

China in Africa and novel nation-building

In recent years China's aid and development projects overseas, in particular in Africa, have attracted a lot of public and scholarly attention. While Western commentators have been preoccupied with assessing the role of China's involvement abroad, the Chinese state has been formulating new interpretations of China's long and positive engagement with Africa. In this regard it is interesting to note how the figure of Muslim Chinese Admiral Zheng He and his travels around the world during the Ming Dynasty (1368–1644) are now used in Chinese official discourse as a 'proof' of China's long engagement with and presence in Africa. Since the early 2000s a considerable amount of 'scientific work' by Chinese scholars established a long Chinese presence in Africa. According to one scholarly account, during one of the expeditions to Africa led by Admiral Zheng a trade vessel sank and survivors settled in Kenya and married local Kenyan women. In 2005, Chinese scholars 'confirmed' one Kenyan girl's Chinese ancestry and granted her a scholarship to study in China (Kahn 2005). The new 'discoveries' of China's long engagement with Africa have been used by the Chinese state as evidence of normality and as a historical precedent for China's re-emergence as a major economic and development actor on the continent, and of the long presence of Chinese people there. China's active economic and development engagements with Africa thus have translated into a novel nation-building project disturbing the geopolitical, cultural, and racial boundaries of the Chinese nation.

As I argued earlier in this chapter, the official formulations of the Chinese nation have hinged on racial assumptions claiming that all Chinese, including overseas Chinese, are descendants of the Yellow Emperor, the progenitor of all Chinese. Would the Kenyan girl of Chinese ancestry be considered an overseas Chinese, and therefore part of the Chinese nation? There is no clear answer to this question, but probably not since her Chinese ancestry goes beyond 'three generations'. Since the start of China's economic reforms in 1978 the official usage of the overseas Chinese concept (*huaqiao huaren*) has expanded to encompass not only all those who emigrated from China a long time ago, but also new migrants, and Chinese students studying abroad. In July 2010 Chinese vice-president Xi Jinping in his address to the participants of the sixth 'Root-seeking' tour, which brought together 6,000 overseas Chinese participants from fifty-one countries, underlined that young people taking part in this event were brought together by their common 'sense of closeness', and that because 'their blood is Chinese' they would be 'willing to carry on the Chinese culture that has lasted thousands of years' (*People's Daily Online*, 2010). The open use of racial arguments in

For more on how the imaginary of race and citizenship often intertwine see **Chapter 10**.

FIGURE 12.10
Overseas Chinese youth learn Chinese calligraphy during the Chinese Root Seeking Tour Summer Camp in Hangzhou, capital of east China's Zhejiang Province, July 19, 2012. (Xinhua/Li Zhong)

FIGURE 12.11 Lou Jing. Bi yueping/Imaginechina

outlining who belongs to the Chinese nation by one of China's top politicians calls into question the alleged multiethnic character of the Chinese state supposedly encompassing fifty-six ethnic groups.

The other side of China's engagement with Africa is a growing number of Africans in China. According to some estimates there are anywhere between 20,000 and 100,000 African traders and entrepreneurs, mostly Nigerians, in Guangzhou, which is sometimes called a 'chocolate city'. In 2008, the issue of mixed-race Chinese was caught in the national and global limelight, when Lou Jing, a Shanghaiese, made it to the last thirty in the Chinese version of *Pop Idol*. She is a child of a black father and a Chinese mother. Following her success on the TV show, there was a lot of heated discussion and soul-searching on the Chinese internet about what it meant to be half-black half-Chinese. It is likely that with the growing role of China in the world, and its attractiveness as a destination for work, study, property investment, travel, and life in general, the number of mixed marriages will go up, and the boundaries of Chinese identity will be further questioned and destabilized. The dominant state narrative of the Chinese presence in Africa re-writes the history of Chinese migration to suit its national and development agenda. The question which remains open is how the Chinese state might reconcile its often racist interpretations of the Chinese national boundaries with the accelerated diversification and problematization of Chinese identities within and outside its national boundaries. With the hybridization of Chinese identities due to China's globalization and complex migration dynamics, the boundaries of the Chinese nation are increasingly in flux, and the ambiguities and limits of the Chinese nation will be pushed further.

Contemporary discussions on how people come to identify with nations need to account for increasing levels of diversity within societies across the globe. While immigration was until recently seen as a phenomenon characteristic of Western societies, the levels of human mobility and diversity are changing most countries. In these circumstances it will be increasingly difficult to assign one category of national belonging to one person. Hyphenated ethnic affiliations along the lines of African-Chinese, Russian-Japanese, Morrocan-French, Turkish-German, Chinese-Italian, African-Caribbean-English are becoming increasingly widespread. But how often do we think of ourselves in national terms? Does the Kenyan girl identify herself as Kenyan and Chinese since the Chinese state recognized that some Chinese blood runs through her body?

Hyphenated identities are also discussed in **Chapter 5**.

Postcolonial cultural theorist Homi Bhabha proposes that national identities, like other kinds of identity, are daily 'performed', reflecting our subjective perceptions of national past, present, and future. For Bhabha we can speak of the nation only as a fragmented and hybridized construct, temporally inscribed through a series of performative acts (Bhabha 1990: 160). In other words, we come to articulate our national belonging at particular moments when we are prompted to do so by the circumstances we find ourselves in. Most frequently it happens when we apply for a national passport or visa to visit another country, are suddenly stopped at the port of entry for additional questioning or security check, have to fill in a census form and decide what category of ethnicity we would ascribe ourselves to, have to pick a national team to support during international competitions, or when somebody else, like the Chinese scholars in the case of the Kenyan girl, tells us that we fall under a particular national category. These moments of encounter trigger how we come to identify with nations.

Homi Bhabha's work is also discussed in **Chapter 16**.

BOX 12.4 HOMI BHABHA AND HYBRIDITY

Homi Bhabha (born 1949) is an influential post-colonial scholar, whose writings have been concerned with examining the legacies of imperialism and colonialism in the contemporary world. His work on hybridity is particularly influential and has found wide application beyond cultural studies, including in the studies of politics. By hybridity he refers to new cultural forms taking shape as a result of interaction and flow of different cultures. The notion of hybridity questions the hierarchical relationship and immutability of cultures presupposed in colonial relations. Hybridity challenges once powerful essentialist understandings of culture and identity.

FIGURE 12.12 Homi Bhabha. Photo: Stephanie Mitchell, Harvard University

Through this recurrent reminding of the need to belong to a particular nation, national identity is routinized as 'a form of life' (Ozkirimli 2000: 195). Although traditionally nationalism was understood as bound to the territorial confines of the state, with the expanding effects of globalization forcing the economic, social and political dimensions of life to escape the constraints of time and space, the meaning of nation and territory has been undergoing an uninterrupted transformation.

Therefore, rather than understanding how people come to identify with nations through drawing clear-cut distinctions between domestic/international, inside/outside, us/them, we might find it more productive to examine how national identities take shape at the meeting points of these distinctions, or 'in the boundaries in-between nations and peoples' (Bhabha 1990: 4). Rather than asking what nation we belong to, we might find it more helpful to ask how we become subjects of a particular nation. Michel Foucault's concept of subjectification is very relevant in this regard. Subjectification defines how we become subjects with particular identities through either the exertion of control and dependence or through identity and conscience (Foucault 2002: 331). It refers to a complex interaction between people and their surroundings shaping individual identity. In this sense subjectification corresponds to the idea of an individual as a product of both dialogical and self-reflective processes where the individual's production of meaning intersects with the influences of power. Subjectification helps to capture, for example, how certain people relate to the Chinese nation though the de-territorialized identity politics of the state. It also highlights the way that the nation cannot be perceived as a conglomeration of people sharing common history, language, beliefs, customs, and living on the same territory, but rather how particular markers of distinction are employed by the sovereign power to construct the illusion of a common people and a common national identity.

CONCLUSION

We have considered the ways in which people come to identify with nations by looking at how nationalist discourses in China address questions of cultural difference and common origins. While traditional approaches to nationalism emphasize unity, cohesiveness, and the commonality of the people within a particular territory brought together under the rubric of the nation, I proposed that we should consider nationalist discourses at the conceptual margins of the nation to appreciate how these discourses work and what they include and exclude. It is in these marginal spaces that the problematic, contested, contingent, and ambivalent nature of the nation is most apparent. Chinese nation-building policies towards overseas Chinese and ethnic minorities illustrate how nationalism is not delimited by the territorial sovereign boundaries of the state, but works in conjunction with other non-territorial markers of distinction, such as race. The process of subjectification of the fragmented body of 'relevant people' is an alternative way of thinking about how people come to identify with nations. When we consider the dynamics of the state-led nationalist project, which expands state sovereignty to include people far away from its territory, the role of state territoriality as a primary feature of a nationalist project becomes more ambiguous.

FURTHER READING

Barabantseva, Elena (2010) *Overseas Chinese, Ethnic Minorities, and Nationalism: De-Centering China*, London: Routledge.
On the role of overseas Chinese and ethnic minorities in Chinese state nationalism.

Bhabha, Homi (1990) *Nation and Narration*, London: Routledge.
A postcolonial critique of nationalism studies.

Callahan, William A. (2010) *China: the Pessoptimist Nation*, Oxford: Oxford University Press.
On the interplay of security/identity dynamics in Chinese nationalism.

Callahan, William A. and Barabantseva, Elena (eds) (2012) *China Orders the World: Normative Soft Power and Foreign Policy*, Baltimore, MD: Woodrow Wilson Center Press and the Johns Hopkins University Press.
On how Chinese traditional ideas inform contemporary discourses and policies.

Dikötter, Frank (1992) *The Discourse of Race in Modern China*, London: C. Hurst & Co.
On the history of racial discourses in China.

Duara, Prasenjit (2009) *The Global and Regional in China's Nation-formation*, Abingdon: Routledge.
Stresses the interplay of global and regional factors in Chinese nation-building.

Gladney, Dru C. (2004) *Dislocating China: Reflections on Muslims, Minorities, and Other Subaltern Subjects*, London: Hurst and Company.
On the complex character of Chinese nationalism.

Shirk, Susan (2007) *China: Fragile Superpower*, New York: Oxford University Press.
On the fragility of China's rise.

WEBSITES

H-Nationalism: http://www.h-net.org/~national/
An academic forum on nationalism, including reviews of recent publications on nationalism.

http://www.ethnic-china.com/index.htm
Chinese scholars' resource on Chinese ethnic minority cultures.

Ohio University Library database on overseas Chinese resources: http://www.library.ohiou.edu/subjects/shao/main.html.

REFERENCES

Agnew, John (1994) 'The territorial trap: the geographical assumptions of international relations theory', *Review of International Political Economy* 1, 1: 53–80.

Anderson, Benedict (1991) *Imagined Communities: Reflections on the Origin and Spread of Nationalism*, London: Verso.

Appadurai, Arjun (1990) 'Disjuncture and difference in the global cultural economy', *Public Culture* 2, 2: 1–24.

——(1997) *Modernity at Large: Cultural Dimensions of Globalisation*, Minneapolis: University of Minnesota Press.

Balibar, Etienne (1991) 'Racism and nationalism', in Etienne Balibar and Immanuel Wallerstein, *Race, Nation, Class: Ambiguous Identities*, London: Verso.

Bhabha, Homi K. (ed.) (1990) *Nation and Narration*, London: Routledge.

Breuilly, John (1996) *Nationalism and the State*, Chicago: University of Chicago Press.

Brown, David (2000) *Contemporary Nationalism*, London: Routledge.

Cheng Xi (2007) 'The "distinctiveness" of the overseas Chinese as perceived in the People's Republic of China', in Mette Thunø (ed.), *Beyond Chinatown: The New Chinese Migration and Expansion of China*, Copenhagen: Nordic Institute of Asian Studies (NIAS Press).

Cressey, George B. (1955) 'The 1953 census of China', *The Far Eastern Quarterly* 14, 3: 388.

Fei Xiaotong (1981) 'Modernisation and national minorities in China', in Fei Xiaotong, *Toward a People's Anthropology*, Beijing: New World Press.

Foucault, Michel (2002) 'Subject and power', in James D. Faubion (ed.) *Power: Essential Works of Foucault 1954–1984*, London: Penguin.

Geertz, Clifford (1963) 'Primordial sentiments and civil politics in the new states', in Clifford Geertz (ed.), *Old Societies and New States*, London: The Free Press of Glencoe.

Gellner, Ernest (1964) *Thought and Change*, London: Weidenfeld and Nicolson.

——(1983) *Nations and Nationalism*, Oxford: Basil Blackwell.

Glick Schiller, Nina, Linda Basch, and Cristina Blanc-Szanton (1992) 'Transnationalism: a new analytic framework for understanding migration', *Annals of the New York Academy of Sciences* 645: 1–24.

Greenfeld, Liah (1992) *Nationalism: Five Roads to Modernity*, Cambridge, MA: Harvard University Press.

Guarnizo, Luis E. and Michael P. Smith (eds) (1998) *Transnationalism from Below*, New Brunswick, NJ: Transaction Publishers.

Hastings, Adrian (1997) *The Construction of Nationhood: Ethnicity, Religion and Nationalism*, Cambridge: Cambridge University Press.

Hobsbawm, Eric J. (1990) *Nations and Nationalism Since 1780*, Cambridge: Cambridge University Press.

Horowitz, Donald L. (1985) *Ethnic Groups in Conflict*, Berkeley: University of California Press.

Hutchison, John (2000) 'Ethnicity and modern nations', *Ethnic and Racial Studies* 23, 4: 651–69.

Kahn, Joseph (2005) 'China has an ancient mariner to tell you about', *New York Times*, 20 July, http://www.nytimes.com/2005/07/20/international/asia/20letter.html?pagewanted=print.

Leibold, James (2007) *Reconfiguring Chinese Nationalism: How the Qing Frontier and Its Indigenes Became Chinese*, New York: Palgrave Macmillan.

——(2008) 'Whose people's games?: Ethnic identity and the 2008 Beijing Olympics', *China Beat*, http://www.thechinabeat.org/?p=299.

Lien Kuan (1978) 'History of overseas Chinese and their glorious tradition', *Peking Review* 21: 15.

Liu Hong (2010) 'Overseas Chinese and a rising China: The limits of a diplomatic "diaspora option"', in Yongnian Zheng (ed.), *China and International Relations: Chinese Views and the Contribution of Wang Gungwu*, London: Routledge.

Mao Zedong (1949) 'Long live the great unity of the Chinese People', declaration of the First Plenary Session of the Chinese People's Political Consultative Conference, 30 September, *Selected Works of Mao Tse-tung*, http://www.marxists.org/reference/archive/mao/selected-works/volume-5/mswv5_02.htm.

——(1957) 'On the correct handling of contradictions among the People', Speech delivered at the Eleventh Session (Enlarged) of the Supreme State Conference. *Selected Works of Mao Tse-tung*, http://www.marxists.org/reference/archive/mao/selected-works/volume-5/mswv5_58.htm.

Meyer, Birgit and Peter Geschiere (eds) (1999) *Globalization and Identity: Dialectics of Flow and Closure*, London: Blackwell.

Ong, Aihwa (2006) *Neoliberalism as Exception: Mutations in Citizenship and Sovereignty*, Durham, NC: Duke University Press.

Oomen, Thom K. (1994) 'State, nation, ethnie: the processual linkages', in Peter Ratcliffe (ed.), *Race, Ethnicity and Nation: International Perspectives on Social Conflicts*, London: UCL Press.

Ozkirimli, Umut (2000) *Theories of Nationalism: A Critical Introduction*, London: Macmillan.

People's Daily Online (2010) 'Overseas Chinese youths urged to serve as communicators between cultures', 26 July, http://english.people.com.cn/90001/90776/90883/7079580.html.

Sautman, Barry (1997) 'Myths of descent, racial nationalism and ethnic minorities in the People's Republic of China', in Frank Dikötter (ed.), *The Construction of Racial Identities in China and Japan: Historical and Contemporary Perspectives*, London: Hurst and Co.

Smith, Anthony D. (1983) *Theories of Nationalism*, 2nd edn, London: Duckworth.

——(1996) 'The origins of nations', in Geoff Eley and Ronald Grigor Suny (eds), *Becoming National: A Reader*, New York: Oxford University Press.

Thunø, Mette (2001) 'Reaching out and incorporating Chinese overseas: The trans-territorial scope of the PRC by the end of the 20th Century', *The China Quarterly* 168: 910–29.

Van den Berghe, Pierre L. (1987) *The Ethnic Phenomenon*, New York: Praeger.

Xiang Biao (2003) 'Emigration from China: A sending country perspective', *International Migration* 41, 3: 21–48.

Zhao Gang (2006) 'Reinventing China: imperial Qing ideology and the rise of modern Chinese national identity in the early twentieth century', *Modern China* 32, 3: 3–30.

Zhuang Guotu (2001) *Huaqiao Huaren yu Zhongguo de Guanxi* (Overseas Chinese Relations with China), Shenzhen: Guangdong gaoji jiayu chubanshe.

For a range of further resources supporting this chapter, please visit the companion website for *Global Politics, 2nd Edition* at www.routledge.com/cw/edkins/

CHAPTER 13

Does the nation-state work?

Michael J. Shapiro

THE QUESTION
STATES, NATIONS AND ALLEGIANCE

Modern political thinking tends to be absorbed in, if not wholly exhausted by, two closely interrelated historical trajectories. One is the process of state formation, the other that of nation-building. As a result, modern political discourse is usually understood on the basis of the geopolitical world of nation-states.

With respect to the state part of the hyphenated term 'nation-state', scholars have focused on the process by which states were formed by monopolizing violence within a bounded territory. As a variety of historical accounts have put it, the monopolizing of violence required disarming diverse sub-state affiliated groupings, asserting fiscal control over the population, and establishing recruitment procedures for armies and bureaucracies. All of these moves were aimed at securing territorial boundaries and centralizing and governmentally controlling all aspects of the population, in order to become a separately governed entity with centralized control. As a result, states are understood primarily as territorial entities with exclusive, coercively and legally supported sovereignty.

In contrast, the nation part of the hyphenated expression takes on its meaning with respect to time inasmuch as nations are understood as peoples who belong to a shared cultural community with a historical trajectory. As a result citizen-subjects receive what Jürgen Habermas calls a 'double coding'. They have both territorial and historical identities. But it is controversial as to how the second coding, the one involving historical time, is to be understood. To avoid the assumption that members of a nation-state derive their coherence on the basis of a myth of a 'prepolitical fact of a quasi-natural people', Habermas (1998) suggests that the communal attachment of nation-state members should be regarded as civic rather than organic, i.e. based on political and legal entitlement rather than hereditary belonging. However, contrary to Habermas' attempt to avoid naturalistic identity politics, the state's legitimation of its control over a population frequently involves the pseudo histories, which Eric Hobsbawm and Terence Ranger have famously referred to as the 'invention of tradition' (1992).

The way identities have been thought about is also discussed in **Chapter 5**. The question of identity politics is examined there in relation to the feminist movement. Certain ways of thinking of gender and sexuality play a role in nation-building as we see in this Chapter. The process of producing a national identity is examined in more detail in **Chapter 12**.

At the level of the individual citizen-subject, such inventions operate as a basis for allegiance. As I have noted elsewhere, that allegiance is best understood as allegiance to a story:

> Given the complex sets of forces that have been responsible both for assembling as a 'people' those groupings identified as 'nations' and the ambiguities and contentiousness associated with the ways that such assemblages claim territories, their primary national stories must bear considerable weight. Indeed, there are nothing other than commitments to stories for a national people to give themselves a historical trajectory that testifies to their collective coherence.
>
> (Shapiro 1999: 47)

The emergence of the state as the seemingly obvious form of political organization and its relation with territory and sovereignty is discussed in **Chapter 11**, and **Chapter 12** looks at how China employs centripetal force to produce a nation.

The weight that the stories must bear takes on its significance in the face of competing allegiances which apply especially to those who reside in a single nation-state but understand their self-fashioning and hence loci of allegiance as either split or as existing elsewhere. While the nation-state deploys various forms of cultural governance to apply centripetal force to national coherence – ceremonies, national holidays, national museum displays, and so on – other genres or forms reflect the centrifugal forces that apply to those who exist in different imaginaries or different identity narratives.

An ethnoscape is a landscape of diverse ethnic subjects, usually binational.

For example, the Hanif Kureishi and Stephen Frears film *Sammy and Rosie Get Laid* (1987) provides an exemplary moment of difference from national allegiance in the UK. At one point in the film, Sammy, a Pakistani immigrant, says to his wife Rosie, a native Englishwoman, 'We are not British, we're Londoners.' And the film as a whole challenges traditional geopolitical presumptions. London, like most cosmopolitan cities, contains an ethnoscape with the kinds of differing experiences and thus multiple allegiances that disrupt the traditional statist political discourse. As Gayatri Spivak puts it in her reading of the film, London contains a variety of types who constitute a 'challenge to the idea of the nation' – for example the 'homeworker' exists along with other 'super exploited women in export processing zones' and thus represents a perspective on connections with nationhood that conflict with that of the traditionally scripted citizen-subject (Spivak 1993: 252).

The significance of homeworkers and the feminization of labour in the contemporary global economy is discussed in **Chapter 17**. Spivak's work is discussed again in **Chapter 27**.

Heeding Spivak's example, I want to identify one such homeworker (who ultimately became a writer), Jamaica Kincaid. She is a naturalized American who provides an alternative perspective to the mythology of the nation-building project of the US 'Founding fathers'. A descendant of the coerced labour force in the Caribbean (she is from Antigua), where slaves with no control over the conditions or pace of the work produced both cotton and sugar, the latter a product that by the mid-seventeenth century (and for one and one half centuries thereafter) was 'by far the most valuable product exported from the Americas' (Eltis 2002: 40), Kincaid became a writer after initially arriving in the US as a servant (an *au pair*). Now someone with divided national and cultural experiences, she is one who has, in her terms, her 'feet . . . in two worlds' (2000: 123). Given her heritage of coerced labour and her experience as a bonded servant, Kincaid has a different basis for perception of the American founding experience from those who unambivalently celebrate the creation of America's founding documents. For example, while looking at the famous portrait in Philadelphia's Liberty Hall of the signers of the Declaration of Independence, Kincaid ponders the occupational infrastructure of their studied ease and suggests we imagine those not in the picture, those whose labour has assisted in the enactment of the European thought-world in America's founding:

FIGURE 13.1 *Congress adopting the Declaration of Independence* by John Trumbull (1756–1843). US engraving after John Trumbull's 1816 version painted for the US Capitol Building Rotunda. The Art Archive. ref.: AA401943

Questions of gender, race and sexuality arise in **Chapters 5, 10, 14 and 17** particularly. The modern nation-state relies on a particular picture of the family.

> America begins with the Declaration of Independence . . . but who really needs this document. . . . There is a painting in Philadelphia of the men who signed it. These men looked relaxed; they are enjoying the activity of thinking, the luxury of it. They have time to examine this thing called their conscience and to act on it . . . some keep their hair in an unkempt style (Jefferson, Washington), and others keep their hair well groomed (Franklin), their clothes pressed . . .
>
> (1997: 70)

She continues with a speculation about those who have worked to prepare the men for the occasion:

> the people who made their beds and made their clothes nicely pressed and their hair well groomed or in a state of studied dishevelment.

Kincaid shares her ambivalent allegiance with other writers who have articulated their unease in their nation-state loci of residence.

ILLUSTRATIVE EXAMPLE
WORLDS OF UNEASE WITHIN THE NATION-STATE

French sociologist Pierre Bourdieu pointed to the difficulty of thinking outside of the reasons of state that promote national allegiance with his remark, 'To endeavour to think the state is to take the risk of taking over (or being taken over by) a thought of the state' (1998: 35). He recommends a method of hyperbolic doubt, which he attributes to Thomas Bernhard's novel *Alte Meister Komödie* (1985). Bourdieu's notion of the 'genesis and structure of social space' in which creativity is possible is useful because it implies, at a minimum, that we should look at how a writer who resists or at least complicates nation-state allegiance is socially situated. Bourdieu provides a path to the resistance of state-dominated political thinking by displacing the biographical causation model associated with mainstream literary analysis with attention to the spatio-temporality of the field within which a writer either recycles or challenges the dominant orders of intelligibility. However, if instead of seeing the existing social order as a hierarchical system of social 'fractions', as Bourdieu does, we view it as a fractal field, a historically produced amalgam or blend of diverse life worlds that have been assembled by a history of state directed 'nation-building' and its forms of political economy, we can identify counter-hegemonic personae whose writing challenges the myth of national coherence.

FIGURE 13.2 Pierre Bourdieu

Specifically, much of the politics of contemporary writing reflects the counter-memories of those groups that have been territorially displaced by a history of political economy that is associated with the formation of the European-oriented model of political order. Global and local economic management by powerful states is responsible for depositing the diverse bodies that inhabit the social fields within the modern nation-state. For example, in the US case, many African American, Native American and exiled writers do not (as Bourdieu would have us believe) select from existing idioms within the hierarchy of available styles that have congealed within state-dominated social orders.

Memories and counter-memories – alternative ways of remembering – arise in **Chapters 22 and 26** where memories of violent conflict are discussed.

Rather, their writing expresses profound ambivalence toward the literary field within which their work is deployed, precisely because of the tendency of that field to be complicit with the state's presumption (its primary mode of 'thought') that it governs a unitary and coherent national culture.

The state's way of thinking here could perhaps be described, in the terms used in **Chapter 2**, as its picture of political space.

The examples of structures of feeling and identity commitments that are in tension with national allegiance are legion, but given the space available, I look at three cases, reviewing briefly some of the writing of Toni Morrison, an African American, Sherman Alexie, a Native American, and Michelle Cliff, a diasporic Jamaican. All of their texts constitute modes of thought generated from outside the spaces authorized by the conventional nation-building narrative, within which every individual is an undifferentiated sovereign citizen-subject and the social order is merely an ahistorical class structure.

Michelle Cliff

I begin with Michelle Cliff because her observation on languages, expressed by one of her fictional characters, serves to characterize the agenda for writers who recognize the traps lurking in familiar systems of intelligibility. The narrator in her novel *Free Enterprise* reflects on the historical role of each language's participation in the imperial domination of her homeland. 'English', she says, 'was the tongue of commerce' . . . 'Spanish was the language of categories', by which she means the creation of a biopolitical matrix of economically and politically ineligible, miscegenated (mixed) blood types, and Latin was the language of Christian spiritual hegemony. 'Against these tongues', she adds 'African of every stripe collided' (1993: 7).

The familiar 'language games' in the terms used in **Chapter 2**.

FIGURE 13.3 Michelle Cliff

Although Cliff writes in English, because of her diasporic experience, which leaves her outside of ordinary national attachments, she sees the nation-state as an ontological as well as a territorial actor (one concerned as much with identity coherence as with territorial control) and, accordingly, she sees nation-state governance as symbolic as well as territorial. For example, her novel *No Telephone to Heaven* (1987) focuses on transnational lives that constitute or produce oppositional imaginaries (alternative ways of imagining the emergence and existence of the life world) opposed to those of conventional national subjects. The diasporic perspective in the novel is realized both geopolitically and linguistically – geopolitically by the back and forth movement of her main character, Kitty Savage, between the US and Jamaica (as well as back and forth from England) and linguistically in the collision of idioms, standard English and Jamaican patois, and in the anti-narrative structure, a set of dissociated narrative fragments.

It is important to note the form as well as the content of Cliff's writing. She uses the genre or form of the novel, which in the nineteenth and early twentieth centuries displaced other narrative forms in the third world. Although, as Franco Moretti has pointed out, the nineteenth-century novel often functioned as a nation-building genre, especially in the case of the historical novel; subsequently Cliff and many other third world writers have made the novel a site of resistance to the national and global imaginaries of the 'first world'. Yet Cliff shows a profound ambivalence toward writing in general because she recognizes the difficulty of extracting a thought from the outside whilst working within languages that encode structures of domination or control over others. As she has noted, her primary linguistic imaginary is silence, a form of resistant aphasia, which she sees as the ultimate location for one who would wholly resist the colonizing forces within language. Cliff's political inflection of silence is manifested in her *No Telephone to Heaven* when her character, Kitty Savage, is described as breaking her silence when she discovers a shop with Jamaican foods in New York. Ultimately, although Cliff's 'attempt to bound off a space of silence via the symptom of aphasia' (Aguiar 2001: 70) is never consummated – Cliff continues to write – it reflects her suspicion that however hybrid and resistant her cacophony of voices and assemblage of narrative fragments in her novels are to the dominant idioms and historical memories of the state, she can never be wholly present to herself as a resisting body in her writing.

If the language we speak contains structures of domination we inhabit in coded form, then sometimes the only way out is to refuse to speak altogether: to pretend to be aphasic as a form of resistance. In her book *This Sex Which Is Not One*, feminist Luce Irigaray says that faced with the patriarchy embedded in language, 'Women among themselves begin by laughing.' (1985: 163)

Sherman Alexie

Sherman Alexie shares Michelle Cliff's ambivalence toward writing and also embodies the split consciousness of one who exists in two different life worlds. For Alexie, the contemporary Indian presence in the US, which occupies his attention, is both geographically and ethnologically ambiguous. Accordingly, his main character, Low Man Smith in his story, 'Indian Country' (2000), is a writer and doubtless his literary stand in. Low Man describes himself in one of the story's conversations as one who is 'not supposed to be anywhere'. Moreover, Low Man's Indianness, along with that of other Native American characters in the story, is highly diluted. He is a 'Spokane', but he speaks and understands no tribal languages, was born and raised in Seattle, and has visited his own reservation only six times.

FIGURE 13.4 Sherman Alexie. Photo: Jérôme de Perlinghi/Corbis

The 'Indian country' for which Alexie's story provides a fragmentary mapping has resonances with a prophetic remark by the Oglala, Black Elk roughly 70 years earlier. Noting what was left of his Indian country after a century in which the political economy of Euroamerica pushed a white cultural nation westward, he remarked, '[t]hey have made little islands for us . . . and always, these islands are becoming smaller' (Neihardt 1932: 12). Similarly, if viewed pictorially, the 'Indian country' that emerges in Alexie's literary landscape would have to be a few faintly visible colour flecks on a map of the US's western states. And, tellingly, the precarious and obscure visibility of that country is reinforced throughout the story's dialogues by continual challenges to traditional Indian practices of intelligibility. For example, when Low Man asks an older Indian, Raymond, if he is an elder, Raymond shifts to a non-Indian idiom: 'elder than some, not as elder as others', he replies. Given his awareness of the ways in which Native American sense-making is always already colonized by a Euroamerican idiom, Alexie has his alter ego Low Man Smith articulate a profound ambivalence toward being immersed in the US literary field. Low Man refers to the chain bookstores that carry his books as 'colonial clipper ships', and in the process of moving about an urban venue in search of a non-chain bookstore, he tries to divest himself of his laptop, first trying to trade it in a Seven Eleven store and then handing it to a clerk in a Barnes & Noble chain bookstore, pretending he found it.

The encounters of colonizers with those they colonized are discussed in **Chapters 16 and 21**.

Toni Morrison

Finally, Toni Morrison articulates the same ambivalence toward her participation in US literary culture as Cliff and Alexie. She makes her political challenge to literary culture explicit by referring to the paradox inherent in her participation as a novelist in a culture of literacy. She admits that she 'participates in the public sphere constituted by print literacy [but] . . . her fiction strains to constitute itself as anti-literature and to address a type of racial community that she herself recognizes to be unavailable to the novelist' (Dubey 1999: 188). Morrison's audience or constituency takes on its coherence as a transnational black culture of great diversity, forged as much through structures of exclusion and episodes of displacement as through practices of solidarity. And much of the cultural imaginary that forms the implied readership of her novels is preliterate. Yet, like Cliff and Alexie, Morrison continues to write. And, most significantly, her novel *Paradise* (1999), which addresses itself to a historical episode of racial exclusion, effectively enacts the critical posture that Bourdieu has identified as the antidote to 'state thinking', the necessity of creating a 'rupture' that challenges the state's '*symbolic* violence', its mobilization of and control over the mental structures that make its institutions appear '*natural*'. The conceptual strategy or 'tool for rupture' is, according to Bourdieu, 'the reconstruction of genesis', which brings 'back into view the conflicts and confrontations of the early beginnings and therefore all the discarded possibilities'.

Race and its perceived significance for community are also discussed in **Chapters 5, 10 and 14**.

FIGURE 13.5
Toni Morrison.
Photo by Kate Kunz from cover of *Paradise*, publisher Alfred A. Knopf, New York, 1998

The 'genesis' to which Morrison's novel is addressed is the ideology and story of American exceptionalism that fuelled a major aspect of the Euroamerican nationhood project. Initially, the religious, patriarchal leaders of the early New England settlers strove to inculcate the presumption that America was to be a new Jerusalem, 'a site specifically favoured by God – perhaps the very place that he had chosen to initiate the millennial Kingdom of Christ' (Kammen 1997: 175). Subsequently, from the early nineteenth century on, a secularized or non-religious version of American exceptionalism has held sway among many American historians who have been vehicles of 'the assumption that the United States, unlike European nations, has a covenant that makes Americans a chosen people who have escaped from the terror of historical change to live in timeless harmony with nature' (Noble 1968: ix).

The role of religion in America today is briefly discussed in **Chapter 6**.

The idea of the covenant and the imperatives that flow from it – the need to resist change and the need to maintain the purity of the lineage that is charged with the special mission – produce the woeful consequences described at the beginning and end of Morrison's novel. The novel suggests that at best the exceptionalist narrative stifles politics and at worst it leads to violence. In addition to the closure of the political, the other consequence (violence) provides the chilling opening to the novel, whose first line is, '[t]hey kill the white girl first'. Thereafter, an understanding of this opening event requires that the reader follow a complex and shifting narrative that eventually explains a deadly attack by a group of men from a covenanted, all-black community in Oklahoma on the women in a nearby convent that has served as a women's shelter.

Chapter 21 discusses how we might think about the way in which those with 'exclusive knowledge' attempt to enlighten others, a version of the 'exceptionalism' or 'special mission' mentioned here.

The attackers are from Ruby, a small western all-black community in which the older members situate themselves in a historical narrative that celebrates the perseverance of their ancestors in the face of rejection and their subsequent redemption through adherence to the codes of a special mission. Descended from former slaves, the town's ancestors left discrimination in the late nineteenth-century American South only to be denied entry into both white and black communities in Oklahoma, which, as Morrison had learned, had twenty-six all-black towns at the turn of the twentieth century (Hitchens 1998: 450). The Rubyites' special mission, an African American version of American exceptionalism, is engendered by their rejections, to which they refer in their narrative as the 'disallowing'. Having walked from Mississippi to Oklahoma, attracted by an advertisement about an all-black town, they discovered that their blackness was a threat to the lighter-skinned 'Negroes' who shunned them: 'The sign of racial purity they had taken for granted had become a stain' (Morrison 1999: 194).

Coping with the shock of a rejection (which they had expected only from whites), they founded their own all-black community of Haven in Oklahoma and subsequently moved even farther into western Oklahoma to found Ruby, which they regarded as the fulfilment of their ancestors' intention to construct an Eden, a paradise on earth run by a group of racially pure blacks. The town chronicler, Patricia, summarizes the '8-rock's' (descendants from the original founders) model for maintaining purity: 'Unadulterated and unadulteried 8-rock blood held its magic as long as it resided in Ruby. That was their recipe. That was their deal. For immortality' (Morrison 1999: 217). But while 'Ruby' ('who can find a virtuous woman? For her price is far above Rubies', Proverbs xxxxi 10) contains signs of paradise – for example the soil seems almost miraculously fertile, so that while Haven had only barren muddy ground, Ruby has flourishing gardens – it also turns out to be a stiflingly conservative, patriarchal and even misogynist community. And rather than turning inward to confront divisive issues, when the younger Ruby generation departs from the original covenant, the patriarchs of Ruby displace their problems on a nearby community functioning with a different covenant. The assault with which the novel begins is on a shelter for women, whose inhabitants have had connections with some of the town's men. The shelter is in a former convent (in a mansion that had once served as a 'cathouse') outside the town.

Morrison's novel enacts Bourdieu's suggestion about the necessity of creating a rupture by returning to the founding myths that sustain violence, actual or symbolic. While identifying a racially fractured America, she contests both the Puritan reading of American exceptionalism and the African American attempt to simulate that exceptionalism while accepting it as a dogma and thus attempting to preserve or freeze the meanings generated in founding acts. In accord with Bourdieu's methodological injunction, she subjects founding myths (of both Euro and African America) to hyperbolic doubt.

GENERAL RESPONSES
STORIES OF COHERENT NATIONHOOD

Nation-building

In contrast to the writers I treat in the preceding section, much of the history of artistic production has been complicit with the cultural governance policies of states seeking to fashion a coherent and unitary national culture. For example, the development of French Grand Opera during the nineteenth century was structured to invite the people

FIGURE 13.6
Paris Opera, architect Charles Garnier, 1857–1874. Photo by Flickr member Peter Rivera, Creative Commons attribution 2.0 generic. http://o.tqn.com/d/architecture/1/0/G/y/Paris-Opera-House.jpg

into the nation, various national theatre initiatives were similarly aimed at the fashioning of national culture, and without state prompting, the nineteenth-century historical novels – for example those of Sir Walter Scott – articulated a geographical dynamic that reflects a process of the cultural integration necessary for the state to claim a coherent cultural nation. His novels typically involve a process of border attenuation.

The French headscarf ban, discussed in **Chapter 27**, is an example of an attempt to produce a unitary national secularism.

This nation-building orientation of the arts, especially in the nineteenth century, has been echoed by the dominant approaches to nationalism in the twentieth. The best known scholars of nationalism – Benedict Anderson, Ernest Gellner, Anthony Giddens, Charles Tilly and countless others have emphasized the centripetal forces of national allegiance, primarily by focusing on mainstream media and state-run agencies and institutions. In particular, Benedict Anderson's well known mantra that nations, as 'imagined communities' (1991), became objects of widespread symbolic allegiance through the operation of mediating genres (for example newspapers) is widely accepted by practitioners of comparative politics and international studies.

For more on these scholars' work on nation-building see **Chapter 12**. For Tilly's work on violence see **Chapter 23**.

Traditional theorists of nationalism focus on two very different kinds of issues. The first and perhaps most pervasive in the literatures is the problem of allegiance, where 'nationalism' becomes a problem of the process through which citizens become identified with their nation-state. To treat that problem theorists turn to various media. In Anderson's case (1991), the primary medium is the daily newspaper. Other thinkers have looked at the roles of national cultural institutions, for example, national theatres (Kruger 1992), music (Attali 1985), landscape painting (Bermingham 1986; Miller 1993; Daniels 1993), film (Burgoyne 1997; Hjort and MacKenzie 2000) and novels (Moretti 1998). In the case of each medium, idioms are adduced by the theorist to

Chapter 8 has a discussion of the importance of media representations in the context of war.

FIGURE 13.7 Shakespeare's Globe Theatre in London. Photo: © Laura Porter (2007) licensed to About.com, Inc. http://golondon.about.com/od/londonpictures/ig/South-Bank/Globe-Theater.htm

identify the way the medium encourages people to imagine the nation, for example to 'picture' it in the case of landscape painting, to identify its process of attenuating internal borders in the case of the historical novel, in the case of music, the collectivizing sentiments that harmony creates, in the case of film, the way founding myths are transmitted, and the way national theatres invited people into the nation by emphasizing what is distinctive about Englishness or Irishness or Frenchness, etc.

For more on Partha Chatterjee see **Chapter 16**.

It should be noted, however, that the emphasis in the writings of third world scholars has been very different. For example, looking at the results of the nationalist imagination in Asia and Africa, Partha Chatterjee (1993) focuses not on the centripetal aspect of identity formation but on a significant difference from the way that nationalism has been produced in the west. For Chatterjee, anti-colonialist nationalisms involved a struggle with imperialist powers and depended very much on spiritual media.

Citizens' rights

Chapter 10 looks at some of the implications of not being a citizen of the country you want to live in and **Chapter 27** explores the link between citizenship and rights.

The second and increasingly important issue has been a treatment of the process by which citizens have extracted rights. Within this perspective, citizenship is treated as a result of enactments, a form of 'transactional citizenship', where national affiliation is 'the outcome of historically specific processes of claim-making and bargaining between state and societal actors' (Tilly 1996). However, if we recognize that nation-states contain groups that exist outside of the boundaries of society, for example indigenous peoples, 'claim-making' can be seen as a luxury of peoples who already enjoy some form of social recognition. To theorize nationalism in such cases is to develop a frame for treating the resistances of those groups who are 'ungrammatical' within the primary discourses of the nation-state (Shapiro 2004). A focus on national allegiance tends to render invisible those peoples who have not been clearly welcomed into the nation.

The mythic social contract

However misleading the assumptions of the scholarly writers who focus on the dynamics of national allegiance may be, at least their conclusions are based on analyses of concrete institutions – for example the history of the press in the case of Anderson, and the monopolization of coercion in the case of Giddens and Tilly. The dominant trend in political theory has been less attentive to actual historically developing institutions and mediating agencies. Drawing on approaches to the social contract emerging from the political theory canon, especially from the writings of Thomas Hobbes, John Locke and Jean-Jacques Rousseau, a nation-friendly model of the social order has held centre stage in the social sciences. It has been assumed that a unitary social order has developed on the basis of an implicit contract by which each citizen agrees to forego coercive means in return for the protection offered by centralized coercion.

In what way is the social contract 'mythic'? How has the idea that it is a real contract become part of our common sense? What does that do to the way we think about politics?

Thinkers who have told this mythic story base it on a model of egoism. They argue that the primary urge is toward a self-interestedness that would naturally provoke a 'war of all against all' (Hobbes 1981). What induces the social contract for Hobbes is a rational approach to one's interests, based on the recognition that only a strong centralized state can offer one protection against the predatory designs of others. Locke offers a similar view – that everyone is inclined to want to have complete autonomy over their persons and possessions. Rationality prevails and they effectively agree to give up the right to punish transgressions against their person and property to a centralized

For a discussion of Hobbes' claims about authority and the sovereign see **Chapter 7**.

FIGURE 13.8
Youths in Paris suburb, Le Blanc Mesnil, 3 November 2005.
Photo: AP/PA Photos

state. And among thinkers of the social contract, Rousseau is another who assumed that the 'natural' state is one in which everyone provides for their own self-preservation and would rather resist any form of collective mastery but is forced to recognize that it is necessary to yield to certain collective conventions.

We thus have, famously, three versions of a mythic social contract that the thinkers presume to be the basis of the collective coherence that became the condition of possibility for the control necessary to govern the modern nation-state. If we heed the dynamic situation of most social orders, created as the flows of immigrant and refugee bodies that introduce ideational and practical schisms, the idea of a social contract becomes increasingly unwarranted.

In **Chapter 10** you can find more on flows of immigrants.

Nevertheless, it is an idea that persists. While everywhere one can witness the absence of an operating social contract, evident for example in the periodic riots in the immigrant-filled suburbs of Paris, the *banlieue parisienne*, in the clan antagonisms in various African countries, in the immiseration and exclusion of *los Indios* in various Latin American countries, and in the 'prison industrial complex' disproportionately targeted at (what are constructed as) 'ethnic minorities' in the US, the existence of a coherent and consensual society remains the legitimating alibi for most political theorists.

BROADER ISSUES
AN ALTERNATIVE POLITICAL IMAGINARY

In order to provide a counter-model to the mythic consensuality that has been the basis of the presumption that states contain a unitary and coherent national society, we need an alternative image of the political. The French philosopher Jacques Rancière, writing on the politics of aesthetics, sees a politically acute version of aesthetics as a window into the existence of many worlds, each of which is lived differently (2004).

Jacques Rancière's work, and his ideas of politics and the distribution of the sensible, are discussed in some detail in **Chapter 18**.

In order to pursue this insight and suggest an alternative political imaginary from the mainstream social contract notion, I turn here to a piece of literature, Milan Kundera's novel *Ignorance* (2002), which is based on the ambiguous national experience of exiles who share Kundera's own experience.

The novel begins with an alienating remark delivered to Irena, a Czech ex-patriot living in Paris, by her friend, Sylvie: 'What are you still doing here?' When Irena asks in response, 'Where should I be?', Sylvie's rejoinder is 'home'. It is 1991, and Sylvie has the expectation that Irena, despite having lived in Paris for 20 years, still thinks of Czechoslovakia as home and will want to return to participate as a citizen in the new independence, after the dissolution of the former Soviet bloc (Kundera 2002: 3). The intermittently contentious dialogue continues briefly until Irena breaks off into a book- and film-influenced fantasy about emotional returns.

Irena's silent meditation about emotional returns triggers Kundera's break from his characters to a richly annotated philosophical discussion of nostalgia, with references to a range of fictional and actual émigrés who either returned or resisted returning (for example Odysseus who returned to Ithaca and Schoenberg who did not return to Austria, respectively). Apart from the specifics of the particular fictional and historical characters he treats, Kundera constructs a global cartography. The novel provides a mapping not only of the post-Soviet geopolitical world but also of the way geopolitics and passion are linked. To assess the thinking that the mapping enacts, we are in need of a philosophical perspective that can address the overlay of passion on political territoriality that frames Kundera's narrative.

Many of Kundera's philosophico-literary excursions in his novels are inspired by Friedrich Nietzsche's philosophy, most famously his *The Unbearable Lightness of Being* (1984), which shares Nietzsche's sentiment that the possibility of an eternal return renders Being heavy. The thought of an eternal return gives 'to acts and events the moral import they would lack in a godless universe wherein every act or event occurred only once' (White 1990: 66). Ever since that novel, Kundera has pondered the problem of moral and emotional weight as he has connected Nietzsche's version of a mythological return with the problem of the émigré's actual or potential return. Because for Kundera, emotional and moral registers are intimately connected, it is not surprising that toward the end of his meditation on nostalgia in *Ignorance*, he refers to the way Homer sets out a 'moral hierarchy of emotions', which provides the basis for Odysseus' abandonment of Calypso, whose 'tears' are represented as less worthy than 'Penelope's pain' (2002: 9). From Kundera's Nietzschean perspective, moral hierarchies are oppressive. Hence we are able to understand the demoralized Odysseus, who suffers from the terrible bargain he has made by giving up an intense passion for the weaker emotion of nostalgia and the self-applied pressure from his expected responsibilities as a husband and patriarch. He has become the forlorn Odysseus, the Ulysses so well described in Tennyson's famous poem (1842), the Ulysses who laments:

Chapter 26 explains more about Nietzsche.

> Match'd with an aged wife, I mete and dole
> Unequal laws unto a savage race,
> That hoard, and sleep, and feed, and know not me.

Most significantly, for what Kundera sees this lending to his story of contemporary émigrés and returnees, Odysseus discovers that while 'for twenty years he thought about nothing but his return . . . the very essence of his life, its centre, its treasure, lay outside Ithaca', and, further, while he had enjoyed a receptive audience while in exile (for example 'the dazzled Phaeacians' who listened to his adventures 'for four long books'), in Ithaca, 'he was one of their own, so it never occurred to anyone to say, "tell us"' (Kundera 2002: 34–35).

Similarly, when Irena returns to Prague, her old acquaintances show little interest in her 20 years of life outside Prague. It was one thing for her former friends to ignore the French wine she brought and instead persist in drinking beer but quite another to ignore her words: 'They can drink beer if they insist, that doesn't faze her; what matters to her is choosing the topic of conversation herself and being heard' (Kundera 2002: 37). Inasmuch as the identity of an individual, like the collective identity of a nation, requires recognition, the inattentiveness of her Prague acquaintances to Irena's Paris life deprives her of confidence in the identity narrative she has adopted.

On the other side of the self–other relationship to identity, what the women's disinterest in Irena's other life reflects is their unwillingness to extend sympathy across national boundaries. When we consider the identity issue at stake in Irena's encounter with her former acquaintances, we have to appreciate the politics of the history–memory disjuncture that Kundera is addressing through the fates of his characters.

'History', as Pierre Nora points out, is produced by the way 'our hopelessly forgetful modern societies, propelled by change, organize their past' (Nora 1989: 8). In the process of that organizing, memory tends to be eradicated: 'Memory and history, far from being synonymous appear now to be in fundamental opposition.' While memory is 'a perpetually active phenomenon' reflective of the sense-making of people coping with their life worlds, 'history is the reconstruction, always problematic and incomplete, of what is no longer' (Nora 1989: 8).

Chapter 22 shows how memories affect politics and make wars possible.

Nora's distinction is effectively enacted in Kundera's narrative of the experience of *Ignorance's* émigrés. While others try to impose a geopolitical allegiance on them, predicated on the way the former compatriots want to organize history, the émigrés try to maintain an intimacy with their memories, their lived temporalities. To the extent that the novel lends its characters an ethico-political outcome, it is the achievement of a refusal to give in to the identities, resident in an imposed history, which are thrown at them by their non-listening families, friends and acquaintances.

BOX 13.1 GILLES DELEUZE AND FELIX GUATTARI

Deleuze and Guattari collaborated on two volumes of a study of what they called *Capitalism and Schizophrenia*. The second volume (1987) provides a radical challenge to identity politics in general and to the codes within which state allegiance is promoted. For them, the state is a 'machine of capture'. In response to such capture, they elaborate what they call 'lines of flight', ways of eluding state capture.

FIGURE 13.9
Gilles Deleuze and Felix Guattari. Photo courtesy of Charles J. Stivale

Hence, applying Nora's distinction to the historical moment of Kundera's novel, 'history' imposes allegiance, while memory, the 'perpetually active phenomenon' that ties people to an 'eternal present' is the condition of possibility for intimacy. To put it another way (in the language of the philosophers Deleuze and Guattari), 'history' involves the imposition of officially inscribed molar codes, the collective identity spaces tied to the macropolitical world of states, while memory is what contains the molecular level, the multiple layers of individual micropolitical potential for becoming, experiencing and associating (1987).

To be allied to the codes associated with history, which are geopolitically oriented temporalities that Irena's friends and husband impose on her, Irena must ignore her life. As Deleuze puts it, 'the sensuous signs of memory are signs of life' (2000: 65).

Thus when Irena sees Josef in Prague (she recalls him from a brief romantic liaison), her memory of a sensuous past is activated, and, crucially, she is encouraged to think. As Deleuze notes, for Proust 'truth depends on an encounter with something that forces us to think'. And here that thinking helps Irena to distance herself from the expectations of others and allow intimacy (with herself as well as with an other) to trump geopolitical allegiance. Intimacy challenges what Lauren Berlant refers to as 'the normative practices, fantasies, institutions and ideologies that organize people's worlds' (2000: 2).

Irena's experience of a return is similar to that of the man she encounters romantically in Prague. Josef is an émigré living in Denmark, whose wife, now dead, had urged him to visit his old homeland, once the Soviets had departed ('"Not going would be unnatural of you, unjustifiable, even foul," she said' – Kundera 2002: 139). When Josef visits his former friend N in Prague, whom he had not seen for 20 years, N and his wife ask nothing about his Danish life:

> There was a long silence and Josef expected questions: If Denmark really is your home, what's your life like there? And with whom? Tell about it! Tell us! Describe your house! Who's your wife? Are you happy? Tell us! Tell us! But neither N nor his wife asked any such question.
>
> (Kundera 2002: 159)

Before following Irena and Josef, who meet and have an affair during their brief return, we need to appreciate Kundera's approach to the politics of the identity struggle they undergo.

Kundera's attachment to Nietzschean philosophy, which he deployed in his *The Unbearable Lightness of Being* (1984) notwithstanding, I want to discuss his *Ignorance* with reference to David Hume's philosophical inquiries into the passions. While his *The Unbearable Lightness of Being* thinks in a Nietzschean way, Kundera's *Ignorance* thinks in a Humean way. The overlay of passions on the novel's literary geography complicates mappings that focus exclusively on national allegiances and summons the Humean argument that passions direct ideas.

To capture the kind of network that Kundera's novel proposes, we can extrapolate from an insight that Gilles Deleuze derives from his reading of Hume on human nature. In contrast with much of the political theory canon (often drawn, for example, from the writings of John Locke) in which the social bond within the socio-political order is ascribed to a contract between ruler and the ruled, Hume's philosophy offers 'a radical change in the practical way the problem of society is posed' (2005: 46). Given the Humean insistence that it is 'affective circumstances' that guide people's ideas (because the 'principles of passion' control ideational inclinations), association within the social domain becomes a matter of modes of partiality (Deleuze 2005: 45). Accordingly, the problem of the social is to be understood not through the concept of the contract, which implies that the main political problem is one of translating egotism into sociality, but in terms of partialities, which makes the problem one of how to stretch the passions into commitments that extend beyond them, how, as Deleuze puts it, 'to pass from a "limited sympathy" to an "extended generosity"' (2005: 46), for as Hume insists, 'the qualities of the mind are *selfishness* and *limited generosity*' (Hume 1978: 494). To the extent that the extended generosity that justice represents is to develop, 'it takes its rise

BOX 13.2 DAVID HUME

David Hume (1711–76) is recalled as a philosopher, historian and economist and is best known for his affiliation with British empiricism. However Hume's version of empiricism is a radical version. Rather than basing his empiricism on a simple and direct relationship between sensations and intelligibility, Hume analysed the principles of human nature – the passions and associations – that create the conditions of possibility for a relationship between what is sensible and what is intelligible. In so doing, Hume initiated what would later be the Kantian revolution in philosophy and its post-Kantian revisions, which directed attention away from things (the object world) and to the conditions (formal and historical) of the subject.

FIGURE 13.10
David Hume, by and published by David Martin, after portrait by Allan Ramsay, 1766, National Portrait Gallery

from human conventions', that are necessitated by the '*confin'd generosity of men, along with the scanty provision nature has made for his wants*' (Hume 1978: 494–95).

The extrapolation I want to apply to Kundera's narrative locates the problem in a global rather than merely social space. In this expanded spatial context, the issue becomes not one of a person's moderating her/his partialities in relationships with the consociates of a national society but with potential consociates within alternative national spaces. Hume did contemplate the problem of extending sympathy across national boundaries, noting that 'we sympathize more with persons contiguous to us, than with persons remote from us. . . . With our countrymen, than with strangers . . .' (1978: 581). However, to appreciate Kundera's overlay of sensibilities on the dynamic mapping that exiles have created, we have to recognize a complication that Hume's notion of 'selfishness' fails adequately to register.

Such broader issues about our changing allegiances are also considered in **Chapters 11 and 12. Chapter 16** considers the similar complexities of the identities and allegiances of colonizer and colonized.

The self-consciousness required to be selfish – to be in touch with one's passions – is difficult to achieve in a world in which others impose regulative ideals with respect to what those passions are supposed to be. The disruption to Irena's hard-won sense of self as a French citizen with a French 'structure of feeling' is a result not of the newly won Czech independence, which would not by itself have summoned an ambivalence, but of having to deal not only with a French friend who pressures her to reassume a former feeling and its attendant national commitment but also of pressure from a husband of Swedish origin who, ironically, has no such feeling for his 'native' country. Her husband, Gustaf, a committed cosmopolitan, argues that although he has no nostalgia for *his* country of birth, she should have some for hers. Similarly, Josef must deal with his wife's expectation about how he should feel and behave and, subsequently, the censorious feelings of his brother and sister-in-law, who had remained during the Soviet occupation. Certainly there are those who possess what Pico Ayer calls 'a global soul' (2000) or, who, like Salman Rushdie, detest the 'narrowly defined cultural frontiers' implied in the very idea of a 'homeland' (1991: 19). But however passionate cosmopolitans may be about their attachments to multi-cultural urban settings and their commitment to resist narrow geopolitical allegiance, the emotionally charged cartography they define looms less large, in terms of both space and affective intensity, than the one defined by exiles.

Chapter 2 has more to say about cosmopolitanism.

CONCLUSION

I began by noting that while the hyphenated term, nation-state, has been the primary referent of modern political discourse, the focus it attracts leaves many political subjects in the shadows. It is possible to provide a counter-history – based on particular counter-memories – to the nation-state oriented story of political modernity. Because the state sovereignty story, which is the dominant within academic approaches, fails to register much of the experiences of both citizen subjects and those without recognized political qualification, I turn primarily to literatures in which those subjects' experiences are articulated. Two dimensions of that turn are important. First, the personae whose writings are selected are drawn from those whose movements inscribe an experiential story that challenges the narratives within which the nation-state version of political subjectivity is developed. Second, the form of the writing, which among other things registers the identity ambiguities of the authors and their characters, provides a contrast with the certainties manifested in the identity discourses of the nation-state.

In order to locate the personae who challenge the nation-state story of political modernity, one must focus on the process by which bodies enter the national societies that have been mythically represented as formed by a consensual social contract. For example, émigrés whose territorial statuses have arisen from coercive forces rather than relatively free choices have different political narratives to offer. In particular, as I point out in my treatment of Milan Kundera's novel *Ignorance*, the struggle of exiles to achieve self-mastery in the face of conflicting identity pressures provides an exemplary counter-memory to the abstract narratives of entrenched or immobile citizen-subjects with unambiguous national allegiances. To place their stories within a socio-political frame, one must abandon the social contract version of national societies and turn to a version that can register the situations in which territorial allegiances are in flux, ambiguated, and productive of changing sentiments toward self and other.

To recover the centrifugal political forces that undermine the mythologies of nation-state consolidation, one needs to contrast the academic and artistic texts that serve to reinscribe and/or consolidate nation-state political imaginaries with those writing events that provide challenges and alternatives, that counter the totalizing story of political modernity and that have exposed as an illusion the conceit that the nation-state is unproblematically consolidated.

FURTHER READING

Balibar, Etienne and Immanuel Wallerstein (1991) *Race, Nation, Class: Ambiguous Identities*, London: Verso.

This collection provides a critical approach to racism, which, influenced by the writings of the philosopher Louis Althusser and the historian Fernand Braudel, locates the phenomenon not merely in attitudes but in social relations and structures.

Bhabha, Homi (ed.) (1990) *Nation and Narration*, New York: Routledge.

This collection on nations and nationalism applies literary tropes in order to show how nations generate paradoxical allegiances through the narratives within which they locate themselves.

Campbell, David (1998) *National Deconstruction*, Minneapolis: University of Minnesota Press.

This study of the violence in Bosnia refigures and extends Jacques Derrida's concept of deconstruction, turning literary tropes into political and ethical critique.

Corrigan, Philip and Derek Sayer (1985) *The Great Arch*, Oxford: Basil Blackwell.

This investigation of English state formation locates the emergence of national allegiance within a long historical trajectory.

Edkins, Jenny, Véronique Pin-Fat and Michael J. Shapiro (eds) (2004) *Sovereign Lives*, New York: Routledge.

This collection treats the geo- and biopolitical aspects of sovereignty at the level of the lives impacted by sovereign prerogatives and practices.

Giddens, Anthony (1983) *The Nation State and Violence*, Cambridge: Basil Blackwell.

This is a sociological treatment of the articulation between the development of the nation-state and the violence of its self-creation.

Lloyd, David and Paul Thomas (1998) *Culture and the State*, New York: Routledge.

This is a neglected but excellent treatment of the cultural governance perspectives and practices that have accompanied state formation.

Shapiro, Michael J. (1994) *Methods and Nations: Cultural Governance and the Indigenous Subject*, New York: Routledge.

This investigation of cultural governance and the neglect of the indigenous subject in the discourses of the social sciences on nation-building applies aesthetic theory, as it is articulated in film, music and landscape painting.

Tilly, Charles (1990) *Coercion, Capital and European States, AD 990–1990*, Cambridge, MA: Basil Blackwell.

Tilly provides a historical narrative of the role of coercion in state formation.

Walker, R. B. J. and Saul H. Mendlovitz (eds) (1990) *Contending Sovereignties*, Boulder, CO: Lynne Rienner.

This collection provides critical, interdisciplinary approaches to sovereignty.

REFERENCES

Aguiar, Marian (2001) 'Decolonizing the Tongue: Reading Speech and Aphasia in the work of Michelle Cliff', *Literature and Psychology* 47, 1–2: 94–108.

Alexie, Sherman (2000) 'Indian Country', *The New Yorker*, March 13.

Anderson, Benedict (1991) *Imagined Communities: Reflections on the Origins and Spread of Nationalism*, London: Verso.

Attali, Jacques (1985) *Noise: The Political Economy of Music*, trans. Brian Massumi, Minneapolis: University of Minnesota Press.

Ayer, Pico (2000) *The Global Soul: Jet Lag, Shopping Malls, and the Search for Home*, New York: Vintage Books.

Berlant, Lauren (2000) 'Intimacy: A Special Issue', in Lauren Berlant (ed.) *Intimacy*, Chicago: University of Chicago Press.
Bermingham, Ann (1986) *Landscape and Ideology*, Berkeley: University of California Press.
Bernhard, Thomas (1985) *Alte Meister Komödie*, Frankfurt am Main: Suhrkamp.
Bourdieu, Pierre (1998) 'Rethinking the State: Genesis and Structure of the Bureaucratic Field', in Pierre Bourdieu, *Practical Reason: On the Theory of Action*, Stanford, CA: Stanford University Press.
Burgoyne, Robert (1997) *Film Nation*, Minneapolis: University of Minnesota Press.
Chatterjee, Partha (1993) *The Nation and its Fragments*, Princeton, NJ: Princeton University Press.
Cliff, Michelle (1987) *No Telephone to Heaven*, New York: Dutton.
——(1993) *Free Enterprise*, New York: Dutton.
Daniels, Stephen (1993) *Fields of Vision: Landscape Imagery and National Identity in England and the United States*, New York: Polity.
Deleuze, Gilles (2000) *Proust and Signs*, trans. Richard Howard, Minneapolis: University of Minnesota Press.
——(2005) *Pure Immanence*, trans. Anne Boyman, New York: Zone Books.
Deleuze, Gilles and Felix Guattari (1987) *A Thousand Plateaus: Capitalism and Schizophrenia*, trans. Brian Massumi, Minneapolis: University of Minnesota Press.
Dubey, Madhu (1999) 'The Politics of Genre in *Beloved*', *Novel: A Forum on Fiction* 32, 2: 186–94.
Eltis, David (2002) 'Introduction', in David Eltis (ed.) *Coerced and Free Migration: Global Perspectives*, Stanford, CA: Stanford University Press.
Habermas, Jürgen (1998) 'The European Nation-State: On the Past and Future of Sovereignty and Citizenship', translated by Ciaran Cronin, *Public Culture* 10, 2: 397–416.
Hitchens, Christopher (1998) 'Morrison's West', *Vanity Fair* 450, February.
Hjort, Mette and Scott MacKenzie (2000) *Cinema and Nation*, New York: Routledge.
Hobbes, Thomas (1981) *Leviathan*, New York: Penguin.
Hobsbawm, Eric J. and Terence O. Ranger (1992) *The Invention of Tradition*, Cambridge: Cambridge University Press.
Hume, David (1978) *A Treatise of Human Nature*, 2nd edn, Oxford: Oxford University Press.
Irigary, Luce (1985) *This Sex which is Not One*, Ithaca: Cornell University Press.
Kammen, Michael (1997) *In the Past Lane: Historical Perspective on American Culture*, New York: Oxford University Press.
Kincaid, Jamaica (1997) 'The Little Revenge from the Periphery', *Transition* 73: 68–73.
——(2000) *My Garden Book*, New York: Vintage.
Kruger, Loren (1992) *The National Stage: Theater and Cultural Legitimation in England, France, and America*, Chicago: University of Chicago Press.
Kundera, Milan (1984) *The Unbearable Lightness of Being*, trans. Michael Henry Heim, London: Faber and Faber.
——(2002) *Ignorance*, trans. Linda Asher, London: Faber and Faber.
Miller, Angela (1993) *The Empire of the Eye: Landscape Representation and American Cultural Politics 1825–1875*, Ithaca, NY: Cornell University Press.
Moretti, Franco (1998) *Atlas of the European Novel: 1800–1900*, New York: Verso.
Morrison, Toni (1999) *Paradise*, New York: Plume.
Neihardt, John G. (1932) *Black Elk Speaks*, New York: Morrow.
Noble, David (1968) *The Eternal Adam and the New World Garden*, New York: George Braziller.
Nora, Pierre (1989) 'Between Memory and History: *Les Lieux de Memoire*', *Representations* 26: 7–24.
Rancière, Jacques (1999) *Disagreement: Politics and Philosophy*, trans Julie Rose, Minneapolis: University of Minnesota Press.
——(2004) *The Politics of Aesthetics: The Distribution of the Sensible*, trans. Gabriel Rockhill, New York: Continuum.
Rushdie, Salman (1991) *Imaginary Homelands*, London: Granta.

Shapiro, Michael J. (1999) 'Narrating the Nation, Unwelcoming the Stranger', in Michael J. Shapiro, *Cinematic Political Thought: Narrating Race, Nation and Gender*, New York: New York University Press.

——(2004) *Methods and Nations: Cultural Governance and the Indigenous Subject*, New York: Routledge.

Spivak, Gayatri Chakravorty (1993) *Outside in the Teaching Machine*, New York: Routledge.

Tilly, Charles (ed.) (1996) *Citizenship, Identity and Social History*, New York: Cambridge University Press.

White, Alan (1990) *Within Nietzsche's Labyrinth*, New York: Routledge.

For a range of further resources supporting this chapter, please visit the companion website for *Global Politics, 2nd Edition* at www.routledge.com/cw/edkins/

CHAPTER 14

Is democracy a good idea?

Lucy Taylor

THE QUESTION
DEMOCRACY

I am sure that for most of you this seems to be a crazy question – of course democracy is a good idea! Democracy stands for freedom, equality, fairness and holding political leaders to account, doesn't it? Well, you're right, it does, and these ideals are upheld as central aspirations by ordinary people right across the world who struggle against authoritarianism or dictatorships, violence and powerlessness. My aim in this chapter is not to argue against democracy either, but rather to invite you to think a little more deeply and critically about what lies behind the idea 'democracy'. What kind of political system do we see in our mind's eye when we say 'democracy'? Who do we imagine to be a citizen? Which countries do we think can teach the world about democracy and which ones need to learn? As you can tell already, there are a lot of questions to ask and I can't provide answers for them all. However, learning to ask deeper or different questions of the world is the purpose of studying in the university and elsewhere, and of this book. In this spirit, I hope by the end of this chapter to convince you not to be an anti-democrat but to be a critical democrat.

Not only is democracy a very common political system across the globe, it is the system which is most emphatically encouraged by a whole range of international institutions (such as the United Nations, the World Bank, the International Monetary Fund (IMF)), key countries (the USA, European countries, Brazil, India) and many international NGOs (such as Transparency International, Amnesty International, Oxfam) (Grugel 2002). Official world opinion is very much in favour of democracy, which it sees as being not only an *effective* way to govern but a *virtuous* way to govern (Crick 2002; Held 2006). That is, the label 'democracy' is underpinned by what people call a normative claim (an ethical or moral claim). This notion of moral goodness is closely connected to the idea that democracy is the political system which best defends human rights – in which individual humans are most likely to be treated with equality, respect and care by the state.

These global institutions are discussed in many places in the book, but see particularly **Chapter 25** (United Nations), and **Chapters 15 and 19** (World Bank and IMF).

Chapter 27 covers the relationship between human rights and democracy.

Many ordinary people concur with this idea that democracy is a morally better way to be governed. The words on the banners in Tahrir Square, Egypt or on the placards outside Aung San Suu Kyi's house in Burma, or indeed on the Plazas of Buenos Aires were: Liberty! Human Rights! Justice! Freedom! Equality! Elections Now! Here, ordinary people are expressing their desire to be treated with fairness, respect, equality and care by those who make decisions about society (Grugel 2002). They assert the power of people in society to have a say in their country's future – and their own. For many people, democracy is not just about a series of elections, institutions and rules, it is a way of life based on mutual respect and the capacity to be a political agent (not a powerless subject). This democratic idealism is a potent political force – but to what

The terms 'agent' and 'subject' are used very differently in different chapters of the book. Sometimes the word 'subject' indicates something positive, as in **Chapter 18** for example. So, approach these terms with care.

FIGURE 14.1
US secretary of state Hillary Clinton (left) holds hands with Burma's pro-democracy leader Aung San Suu Kyi as they meet at Suu Kyi's house in Yangon, 2 December 2011. Reuters/Soe Zeya Tun. http://static.lifeislocal.com.au/multimedia/images/full/1580389.jpg

extent can the liberal democracy advocated by the USA and the World Bank really channel those ideals? Are there other models for a democratic society? Looking behind the glossy assumptions of liberal democracy, and thinking about different perspectives on democracy is one of the key aims of this chapter.

We are going to explore democracy through the example of Argentina. I am not going to explain the institutional set up there – the electoral system, the relationship between president, congress and the judiciary, the Constitution, etc. There are plenty of excellent books which explore these issues more generally and others which explore Argentina's political institutions (O'Toole 2007; Foweraker *et al.* 2003). Rather, I want to focus on two aspects. First, I will show through the example of Argentina some of the ways in which electoral democracy is embedded in society – its inequalities, norms and cultural expectations. Second, I want to illustrate the importance of democratic dynamics outside the electoral sphere, and particularly in social movements and community organizations. I will draw on three examples in order to make my points. These are: Peronism (a study of populism and emotion in politics), the Mothers of the

The role of social movements or grass-roots organizing is discussed in many other places in the book, for example **Chapter 4** (environmental movements); **Chapters 18 and 28** (the Occupy movement); and **Chapter 9** (the Arab Spring).

FIGURE 14.2
Latin America. http://ec.europa.eu/europeaid/images/maps/latin-america_continent_en.png

BOX 14.1 DEMOCRACY IN LATIN AMERICA TIMELINE

1492	*Colonialism*: Conquest of the Americas, native peoples subjected to slavery and violent oppression; population also decimated by disease. Native peoples rebel repeatedly. Africans abducted and forcibly transported to work in all aspects of the economy, including plantations. Europeans (mostly men at first) arrive to hunt for gold, settle land and work in the colonial bureaucracy.
1810–1820	*Nation-building*: Wars of independence, borders established and constitutions devised setting out the relationship between central and provincial government, the balance of power between presidency, congress and judiciary, and the mechanisms for election of political leaderships. Limited franchise (eligibility to vote), military involvement in politics, the importance of popular acclaim.
1850s–1900	*Limited inclusion*: Liberals and conservatives. Political battles between modernizing, urban-looking liberals inspired by European models and traditional, rural elites who aimed to conserve power and peonage. Slavery abolished in Brazil 1888.
1900s–1930s	*Inclusion*: Economic development, urbanization, industrialization, European migration. Development of socialist, communist and anarchist politics plus trade unionism, anti-poverty movements and early feminism. Mexican Revolution (1910); rebellions in Nicaragua (1932); communist military uprising in Brazil (1930); socialist government in Chile (1932); pro-indigenous socialism in Peru.
1930s–1940s	*Backlash*: Violent suppression of popular movements; military governments and dictatorships in Central America.
1940s–1950s	*Populism*: Accommodation of popular demands and expansion of the nation-state. Economic boom, rapid urbanization. Getúlio Vargas as president in Brazil; Hugo Banzer in Bolivia; Jacobo Árbenz Guzmán in Guatemala.
1960s–1970s	*Rise of communism and socialism*: Cuban Revolution 1959; Colombia 1965 Revolutionary Armed Forces of Colombia (Fuerzas Armadas Revolucionarias de Colombia (FARC)); rise of Salvador Allende Gossens in Chile; rebellions in Central America (Nicaragua, El Salvador, Guatemala).
1965–1975	*Military dictatorships*: Some new (Brazil, Uruguay, Chile, Peru) some old (Anastasio Somoza Debayle in Nicaragua, Alfredo Stroessner in Paraguay). Democracy suspended, human rights violated.
1983–1990	*Democratization*: Return to civilian rule and electoral politics, human rights issues. Alternation of power via political parties, anti-corruption drives.
1992–today	*Indigenous social movements protest* against 500 years of colonial oppression.

Plaza de Mayo (exploring the role of social movements and the issue of human rights) and the crisis of representation in 2001 (examining the rejection of representative democracy and grassroots organizing).

I will look at some of the general responses to the question of democracy in the second section of the chapter, which examines and questions the way elections are seen as central and equality assumed. I will then go on to ask deeper, broader questions about the nature of 'actually existing' democracy, asking where the idea came from in time (history) and space (geography) and what impact the history of thinking about democracy has on the way that we study democracies today. I will end by returning to the question of democracy's 'goodness', setting out some ways to start thinking differently that might help you to ask more critical questions of the democracies which you study.

ILLUSTRATIVE EXAMPLE
DEMOCRACY IN ARGENTINA

The story of institutional democracy in Latin America falls into two stages. Following independence in the 1810s and 1820s, the nineteenth century was characterized by processes of nation-building which involved wars to demarcate territory, the establishment of political institutions and the generation of national identities (Vanden and Prevost 2002). This was a struggle about how power was to be organized. The twentieth century was then characterized by political conflict over popular inclusion and socio-economic equality – a struggle over who could wield power, and whether popular or elite interests would be served (Hellinger 2011). For most of the period, democracy was understood through class politics but from the 1970s feminist demands also challenged the concentration of power in male hands, and from the 1990s indigenous and Afro-Latin American demands began to contest dynamics of racialized discrimination and exclusion. This struggle for inclusion, which sometimes took the form of armed rebellion, has met with significant resistance, and the history of most countries is peppered with uprisings, military dictatorships, violence and intense suffering. The democracies which rule the continent today, incomplete and troubled as they are, are nevertheless a source of pride for most Latin Americans and have certainly been hard won (Hellinger 2011).

The question of the division of the world into territorial entities is discussed in **Chapter 11**, and the question of national identities, and the problems with this idea, in **Chapters 12 and 13**.

Questions of race and gender are discussed in **Chapter 5** and racialized exclusion in **Chapter 10**. The way in which racialized exclusion is rooted in the experience of colonialism in India is discussed in **Chapter 16**.

The story of democracy in Argentina during the twentieth century is similarly tumultuous, alternating between periods of repression and exclusion – there were no fewer than five military coups, in 1930, 1943, 1955, 1966, 1976 – and periods of elections (Rock 1985). Since 1943, electoral politics has pivoted around the Peronist party, the vehicle for the political ambitions of Juan Perón and, of course, his wife Evita (Lewis 2001; Romero 2002). Even when the Peronist party was barred from electoral politics, between 1955 and 1962 and between 1963 and 1972, and Perón was exiled in Spain from 1955 to 1973, Peronism continued to dictate the terms of political life through its vast and highly organized trade union movement which disrupted the efforts of its opposition, the Unión Cívica Radical (UCR), to govern effectively. The activities of a youthful revolutionary Peronist group, the Montoneros, in the 1960s and 1970s, and the implosion of the last elected Peronist government from 1973, led the military

FIGURE 14.3
Juan and Evita Perón, shown in 1950 (Associated Press). http://isurvived.org/Pictures_iSurvived-2/Peron_Juan-Evita_BIG-FLIP.GIF#

to intervene decisively in 1976, determined to eradicate the Peronist menace which had, as they saw it, plagued Argentina since 1943 (Romero 2002).

This last military government was extremely repressive and violent, and banned all political organizations and parties, dissolved Congress, stripped the universities and stacked the judiciary with supporters. For the military, democracy had brought political chaos, economic incompetence and a loosening of social morals. For them, the armed forces were the only agency capable of defending *la patria* (the motherland). The return to democracy in 1983 was precipitated by the military's loss of the Falklands/Malvinas War in 1982, but was framed by the issue of human rights violations, a perspective which brought a strong moral agenda to democratization, urging in the words of The National Commission on the Disappeared (CONADEP) human rights report that 'never again' would democracy be usurped in Argentina (Lewis 2001).

Following this brief context, I now want to focus on three elements of Argentine democracy which help me to illustrate key aspects of democracy as it is lived out and practised. These are: Peronist populism; human rights and the Madres de la Plaza de Mayo; and the 2001 crisis of representation and radical alternative forms of democracy. These will help to demonstrate the importance of the social realm for politics, both as a political context and as an alternative arena for political activism.

How Peronism works: populism

Peronism is a political movement named after Juan Perón, and sure enough the figure of Perón and his wife Evita remain the ideological and emotional centre of the party. The party is a clear example of populism. This is a form of government that combines electoral democracy – and democratic rhetoric – with a cult of personality (Levitsky 2003).

Up until the 1940s, Argentina's large working class had been vociferous and demanding but, influenced by a strong anarchist movement, it focused on denouncing the 'fat-cat' elite (the 'oligarchy') and demanding wage rises, rather than mobilizing for state power. Perón captured this constituency in the 1940s (James 2000). Using his charismatic personality, he made them feel important and strong. He lauded the working class as the true creators of Argentine wealth and denounced the idle upper classes who lived from the workers' sweat even while they looked down their noses at the working man. Once in power in 1943, Perón also won people's support by improving their lives (James 2000). He supported higher wages for workers, invested heavily in housing, hospitals and schools, and built holiday resorts for the working class.

Chapter 7 discusses Max Weber's notion of charismatic authority.

The relationship between Perón and the masses was developed especially via Evita, who was an equally charismatic speaker. Eva Perón came from a humble background herself and used her position of power to berate the bone-idle oligarchs in speeches to millions of workers who felt that she understood their pain – she could represent them because she *was* them (Fraser and Navarro 1996). As a woman, Eva Perón also represented a model for female political action, one which gave women a central place in politics, but which confirmed traditional gender roles. Juan Perón portrayed himself as a super-human leader with the vision and understanding to take Argentina to its rightful position in the global elite (Auyero 2000; James 2000). This built a masculine image in which a macho capacity to get things done was matched with fatherly wisdom. Evita, the dutiful wife, declared her unconditional support for him and urged the subordinated working class to trust in Perón as she did. She pledged, like the mother of the people, to work tirelessly and selflessly to help the poor and unfortunate in Argentina. Indeed she championed the building of orphanages, shelters for single mothers and housing projects, and she distributed thousands of sewing machines and toys, furniture, houses and money to the poor who flocked to see her (Fraser and Navarro 1996). By playing up to these idealized gender roles, Juan and Eva Perón legitimized their powerfulness and won the hearts of the people, as well as appealing to their rational interests by raising wages and building houses.

Perón democratized Argentina in two ways: first, he gave ordinary people a sense of inclusion and importance in the country; second, he distributed national wealth more evenly, raising people's standard of living. Politically, however, his legacy is more ambiguous. On the one hand he drew thousands of ordinary people into political activity through rallies and local-level party organization. He took seriously their concerns and dreams, and made them his priority. He also gave women the right to vote in 1953 and presented an appealing model of female activism, which drew thousands of women into party politics. On the other hand, the relationship between Juan Perón and the masses under charismatic populism was characterized more by a beneficent, fatherly authoritarianism than democratic equality. Perón asserted that he knew best what the workers needed, he would provide for them, and all he asked for in return was loyalty. What's more important, the workers agreed, worshipping Juan Perón and especially Evita. Moreover, Evita Perón's model of female political action confined women's activism to supportive tasks at the grassroots – supporting male candidates by organizing events or leafleting – and did not translate into a feminist politics. Indeed it served to confirm unequal gender roles, not challenge them. Thus, while Peronist policies were *socially* democratizing, the *political* relationship was based on a willing subordination and inequality.

Compare Max Weber's idea of charismatic authority as opposed to legal-rational authority, which is discussed in **Chapter 7**.

What would it take to challenge gender roles? Gender roles in the global economy are discussed in **Chapter 17** and feminist politics in **Chapter 5**.

FIGURE 14.4
The Mothers of the Plaza de Mayo. http://wikis.lib.ncsu.edu/images/b/bf/MothersofPdM.jpg; http://wikis.lib.ncsu.edu/index.php/Las_Madres_de_la_Plaza_de_Mayo_and_Other_Reactions

Madres de la Plaza de Mayo: social movements and human rights

The military dictatorship of 1976–83 was one of the most brutal in Latin America, ordering the abduction, murder and disappearance of around 30,000 people whom it understood to be enemies of the Argentine nation. The climate of fear was so intense that very few spoke out against the dictatorship, but the most vocal of those were the human rights groups, especially the Madres [Mothers] de la Plaza de Mayo (Fisher 1989).

The Madres are the mothers of the young people who were 'disappeared' by the military government. They met, and indeed continue to meet, once a week in Buenos Aires' central square to walk around its central obelisk in quiet condemnation of the military government. They also mobilized Argentine and international opinion against human rights abuses and the military dictatorship (Bosco 2006). They captured the world's attention by protesting during the 1978 World Cup and took their international campaigns to the UN. Indeed, their plight helped to establish human rights at the centre of the global agenda and they remain an influential force, both in Argentina and the world. They have an unassailable position of political power, backed by the moral strength of their identity as mothers, the unspeakable suffering of their children, and their status as defenders of democracy in Argentina.

Do the Madres confirm or challenge gender roles?

The Madres' campaign is linked to the mother/child relationship and draws on idealized notions of motherhood, known as *Marianismo*, which is inspired by the Virgin Mary's example. This was a powerful moral tool in their armoury and a vital contribution to the new democracy in Argentina (Navarro 2001). The Madres argued for the moral strength of democracy by anchoring it in their demand for the right to life, for truth about what happened to their children and justice: that the rule of law be applied to the perpetrators of state crimes, those who organized the disappearances. That is, they set a tone for understanding democracy to be not only a series of elections and institutional mechanisms, but a 'good' society – a moral way of life based on equality and respect.

Their second significant contribution was to reveal the capacity of social organizations – groups of ordinary people – to change political life. While political parties were banned and repressed, social movements – especially the human rights movement – were the beacon around which ordinary people could mobilize, take to the streets and demand the return to democracy (Eckstein 2001). Paradoxically, the banning of political parties actually freed up space to allow people to imagine and enact different ways of organizing, pressing for demands and creating solutions to problems. It was no coincidence that the feminist movement, indigenous groups, community organizations, and early gay and environmental movements all contributed to the anti-military campaigns in Argentina and across Latin America. In doing so, they brought new issues and concerns to a political agenda that had been dominated by class politics, as well as fresh ways of organizing and new political actors. Social movements politicized ordinary people at the grassroots of politics, giving them a sense of political agency – a sense that they could do things politically – training them in political skills such as organization, public speaking, publicity and negotiation, as well as generating new approaches to understanding the world. The social movements therefore helped to democratize the political agenda of the new democracies, opening up the realm of formal politics to encompass women's equality, indigenous thinking, green issues and gay rights (Hellinger 2011). In turn, many of these social organizations framed their campaigns in terms of human rights, a move which deepened and widened the human rights campaigns themselves.

Social movements – a term used by scholars who study organizations which people form to take political action – are important in environmental politics: see **Chapter 4**.

The Madres themselves were women, mostly housewives, with little political experience, but they became the emblems and leaders of the anti-military movement. Once democratization occurred, their insistence that truth and justice be served pushed the Argentine government to open prosecutions against the junta leaders, urging the newly elected president Alfonsín to not go back on his word that justice for human rights would be a priority. This was their third major contribution to democracy: holding the government and their representatives to account (Navarro 2001). In doing so, they established the idea and practice that civil society organizations had a vital 'watchdog' role to play in democracy, an idea that is now well established in Argentina and across the region.

The example of the Madres allows us to see that democratic action is not just the preserve of political parties. Democracy is also served in myriad ways by the development of social movements. These groups of ordinary people acting as political agents in the social realm can introduce new ideas, broaden the range of voices heard and hold politicians to account, not via elections but through on-going protest.

The term 'civil society' is used to refer to a part of society that is separate from 'the state' or explicitly 'political' organizations. Is this idea of 'civil society' as watchdog similar to the idea in **Chapter 8** of 'the media' as watchdog? Is it a pluralist view? What criticisms might be raised here? Is the media part of civil society? Does it make sense to think of state and civil society as separate?

2001: the crisis of representation

The period following the transition to democracy since 1983 has seen plenty of ups and downs in Argentina's democratic fortunes, but none has shaken the country so much as the social explosions of 2001–2. Thousands of people took to the streets of the cities in protest about the political elites who had led them since 1983 through periods of hyper-inflation in 1988, a paper-thin, credit-backed boom from 1991 to 1998, and then crashing impoverishment which saw the middle classes enveloped by a rising tide of poverty (López Levy 2004).

Periods of so-called financial crisis, and terms such as inflation and credit boom, are discussed in **Chapter 18**.

The key slogan to emerge on the protest banners was 'que se vayan todos! [get rid of them all!]'. People felt deceived by their politicians and cut off from the political debate, unable to raise their concerns and horrified by a political class who seemed indifferent to their struggles and concerned only with lining their own pockets (Levitsky and Murillo 2005). The importance of this assessment was not whether it was true, but that people perceived politicians to be distant, uncaring and self-serving. While everything has since gone back to normal, it is important to remember that this was a crisis in which the established systems of capitalism and representative, liberal democracy very nearly imploded. This was not only because Argentina's currency was in free fall and three presidents were rejected in one week, but also because ordinary people found new ways to 'do' the economy, to 'do' politics, to 'do' democracy.

People created new ways to exchange goods and labour. At first this took the form of bartering – swapping clothes for surplus food grown in the garden, or plumbing skills for computer work. As time went on, and especially once the government froze people's bank accounts, communities began to invent their own currencies, which could be used to trade in local shops (López Levy 2004). Another very common response to the lack of work was for employees to simply take over businesses that had been abandoned in the crisis to reopen them as cooperatives. In this way, everything from a large ceramics factory to medical clinics, a sugar refinery and a Buenos Aires hotel were taken over as workers' cooperatives (Sitrin 2006). Such economic initiatives involved significant democratization too. It was common in the workplaces and communities to develop large, open discussions that used direct democratic decision-making procedures. People would cram into a community centre or factory floor and debate long and hard about how to organize their initiative, who should be the leader, how the money should be divided, how the work should be organized, etc. The same kind of mechanisms were developed in the many soup kitchens, neighbourhood assemblies, media collectives and unemployed workers' movements in which people of all sorts got together to organize themselves (Sitrin 2006; López Levy 2004). While these organizations were far from ideally democratic – they featured power struggles, discrimination, political party take-overs and apathy – they did offer a significant alternative to institutionalized liberal democracy and shook up – at least for the time – politicians' complacency about their role in democracy and decision-making.

The crisis of democracy in 2001 reveals several key points about democracy in Argentina. First, even though the political and economic system seemed to be imploding, there was no hint that the military would step in to restore order, as it had done so many times previously. This signified that the military had been definitively stripped of their political role, and that, while the political class was vilified and loathed, democracy as an ideal remained strong. This tendency – loving democracy, hating politicians – is a consistent trend in post-transition public opinion polling across the continent, as well as in Argentina. Second, moments of systemic crisis, when the deep structures of daily life suddenly become unstable, can create conditions in which ordinary people generate creative solutions to everyday problems. The state seemed about to fall to pieces, the economy to be crumbling before their eyes, so people found new ways – and enacted them – of sustaining their lives. More than that, the way in which people organized their communities afresh, by-passing the network of state institutions altogether, was not only effective but also explicitly and fiercely democratic. The open meetings practised direct democracy, while the cooperative businesses were run by collectives. This direct democracy was very hard work, not only because it took a lot of time and thinking, but because people had to unlearn and reinvent the way that their society worked. It was not surprising, then, that, when the state regained control and capitalism was reasserted through the free-flow of money, people returned to the familiar way of life. While a pessimist might see this as a defeat for alternative forms of democracy, this episode in Argentine history indicates that democracy *as a way of life* is highly prized in Argentina and that different ways to *do* democracy are not only imaginable but workable too.

Chapter 18 argues the opposite, namely that when we identify something as a crisis we are likely to call in 'experts' to sort it out. Why do you think the idea of crisis could generate such different responses in different contexts? Or are they less different than it seems?

Is this what British prime minister David Cameron meant when he talked about the 'Big Society' in the 2010 UK General Election?

GENERAL RESPONSES
ELECTIONS AND EQUALITY

I have approached this discussion of democracy in Argentina by focusing on the relationship between citizens and decision-makers. This perspective takes seriously the impact of ordinary people's political activism and is interested in alternatives to the conventional institutions and processes of representative democracy. My approach contrasts to approaches that study its most obvious mechanisms and actors. Textbooks start with the public face and legal structure of democracy, analysing constitutions, how elections are organized, and the relationship between the president, the executive (government), the parliamentarians (usually Congress and Senate) and the judiciary (courts and judges) (see Held 2006; Inglehart 2009; O'Toole 2007). The way that these rules of the game are configured significantly influences how it is played, so comparing the systems is important when deciding which is the most fair.

However, these kinds of approaches look at objective factors – they deal with legal statutes and the database of votes cast – without worrying about some of the assumptions that are built into their approach to democracy. Two of the most common assumptions are: that representative democracy is primarily a question of voting for representatives following rational deliberation – so social movements and emotions are largely irrelevant; that all citizens are basically equal – so social inequalities make no difference to your ability to act politically. As you can see, these assumptions are powerful because they appeal to our common sense of what democracy is about: choosing leaders, based on the equality of all. Let's take them one at a time in this section, which examines the general responses to the question of democracy. In the next section, on broader issues raised by this question, I tackle another, more deeply buried assumption: that the best democracies are to be found in the West – so countries elsewhere should take note of how things are done there and apply the lessons learned.

Democracy is primarily about elections following rational reflection

Elections are a very important part of organizing a representative liberal democracy, but as we have seen from our analysis of democracy in Argentina, there are much broader ways to think about democratic political practice. Moreover, the electorate is swayed not only by logical interest maximization – working out by a process of logical rational reasoning how to get the best deal – but also emotional appeals.

As we have seen, social movements, such as the Madres de la Plaza de Mayo, have been pivotal in Argentine democratic life. Similarly, the new forms of community and workplace organizing in the wake of the crisis of 2001 demonstrate that democratic politics can take place not only at the national level and through political parties but also at the community level and through direct democratic debate. Without the Madres, the transition to democracy in Argentina would have been far less certain and the military would have been in a far more powerful position, able to compromise the new democracy (Bosco 2006). A crucial role for social organizations is to hold governments, both democratic and authoritarian, to account on behalf of the wider society. In that sense, the Madres exercised their democratic rights by condemning the military regime – even when elections were cancelled and political parties were banned – through social mobilization at home and campaigns in the international realm.

It is through social organizations, moreover, that ideas about democracy have been expanded to include serious consideration of new rights such as those of women or native peoples. Such claims build on the idea that democracy is a way of life, not just a way to make decisions. The Madres understood democracy in the broad sense to be an ethical way of living which involved respect for others, equality and fairness. The grassroots democracy initiatives of 2001 went further. They argued that an idea of representative democracy based just on voting was the problem, not the solution. They pointed to the lack of accountability between elections and the enormous gulf between politicians and those they supposedly served, which allowed them to be corrupt and to act without the agreement of the people. Moreover, when they began organizing for local currencies or workplace cooperatives, questions of democracy, transparency and accountability were absolutely central to their endeavours (Sitrin 2006). How they made the decisions was just as important as what they were. In that sense they too were profoundly interested in creating institutions and mechanisms that were fair and promoted equality, and their aspirations have a lot in common with scholars who want to create the best electoral system. However, those involved in the cooperatives and community groups went beyond rules to try to democratize the workplace and its practices, the community and its bonds, as well as the personal relationships that knit these political sites together.

How do you feel about a notion of democracy that is limited to casting your vote every few years? Do you think someone in Egypt who had waited 35 years before casting their vote in the presidential elections of 2012 (see **Chapter 6**) would feel differently?

The Peronist party sought to gain power through elections, so of course voting is highly relevant. However, I showed how the votes cast were motivated not only by the rational deduction that a vote for Perón meant higher wages and a welfare state. It was also motivated by powerful emotions – the sense of belonging in one's political entity, the sense of affinity with Evita, the sense of belief in the father-figure of Juan Perón (Fraser and Navarro 1996). It is about feeling happy with the gendered model of society being portrayed – a model which makes sense with the daily relationships between man and wife embedded in the cultural norms of a Catholic country.

BOX 14.2 HOW POLITICS WORKS AT THE PERONIST GRASSROOTS

The following are quotes drawn from a fascinating study of clientelism (a system of relations of mutual obligation between client and patron, where the patron is very much in charge) amongst political activists and their clients who receive material benefits – mostly food, medicine and jobs – from their patrons.

> *Clientelism*: Children's day . . . is celebrated every year on the first Sunday in August. This year Councilwoman Matilde [a Peronist municipal representative] and her followers are organizing three different public gatherings. . . . Adolfo came in the municipal station wagon together with . . . Patón. Patón is a public employee [who] . . . usually drives the truck that brings drinking water to the Fifth Road on a daily basis . . . they unload milk bottles, bags full of toys, and two brand new bicycles. The milk comes from Plan Vida [a government programme]. It is not supposed to be used for political purposes . . . yet preparing hot chocolate for the children of Paraíso on 'their day' is a 'good cause' – as Matilde tells me – noble enough to divert public resources to political use. It is 2.00 p.m. when we return to Matilde's house after an exhausting day. I am just about to leave when she tells me 'You see? After what you just saw . . . votes will come. I don't have to go and look for them . . . votes will come anyway'
>
> (Auyero 2000: 80–82)

> *Emotion*: the political activists. 'My passion is the people' Matilde told me on a hot afternoon . . . 'I take care of them as if they were my own children' . . . Both [Matilde and Susana] were precocious children: early in their lives they were extirpating 'lice from the hair of the poor'. Both have been Peronists since birth. Both have known the mayor since birth. Both wear a wristwatch adorned with the image of Eva Perón.
>
> (Auyero 2000: 120)

> *Emotion*: the recipients of favours. Rosa points out what an 'excellent person' Juancito Pisuti [another local Party worker] is: 'The way he takes care of people, he is an exceptional human being . . . he suffers . . . he has a solution for everyone . . . he willingly advises everyone. Many people ask him for money . . . and he gives them his own money. . . . He is keen to serve. He likes to help people' (p. 164). . . . 'I always show up at Matilde's UB [grassroots party office] out of gratitude or because of our friendship, they always call me and I go' Adela says. Her daughter got her a job as a public employee with the municipality through Matilde. Her husband got his as a garbage collector with the municipality through a letter of recommendation from Angel, Matilde's husband.
>
> (Auyero 2000: 152)

Peronism has always relied on distributing state goods (like jobs, food or medicines) downwards to its supporters who in return continue to support the party. This is known as clientelism or patronage politics. People's support for the party is in some ways rational (they value privileged access to medicine, for example) but Javier Auyero's study of a poor community – Villa 21 in Buenos Aires Province – demonstrates that feelings of affection, trust, dependency, gratitude and a sincere desire to help can infuse this goods-for-votes transaction (Auyero 2000). It is through social bonds that votes come, rather

FIGURE 14.5
Children pass a community centre painted with images of Eva and Juan Domingo Perón, in Buenos Aires. Photo: Victor R. Caivano/Associated Press. http://www.washingtonpost.com/world/argentina-heading-to-polls/2011/10/21/gIQAAyGd3L_gallery.html#photo=6

than rational calculation. The party's grassroots offices (called Unidades Básicas) play just as much of a social role as a political one, hosting mother and toddler groups, pensioners' lunches and weekend barbecue parties as well as party meetings. These are all activities that happen between elections and do not have an explicit political message. However, they do have a significant political impact, building support, trust, political belonging and obligation.

The social realm is absolutely vital for understanding why people vote Peronist, then, and for exploring the quality of democracy. It helps us to see the role of emotions as well as interests and to reveal the way that inequality works through the political system. Those scholars who focus on elections have the benefit of working with an element which seems to fulfil the democratic desire for equality – every vote counts the same as others. However, because democracy is more than voting – and because politics is unavoidably embedded in the social realm – this ideal of equality falls apart as soon as we step out of the voting booth. The next key point discusses this.

All citizens are equal

One of the reasons why the idea of democracy carries such moral power is because it aspires to treat all citizens equally. It is this radical principle which underpins a rule of law which applies equally to everyone, a political principle which states that anyone can be president, and that everyone's vote has the same power. However, equality in practice very seldom lives up to its ideal on paper.

It can be argued that the emphasis on equality produces a neglect of difference: see **Chapter 27**.

Unsurprisingly, then, Argentine democracy's record on equality is mixed. On the one hand, significant advances towards formal equality have been made. The political franchise was extended to women in 1953, for example, and all citizens over 18 years of age may vote and stand for election. However, Argentine politics, in common with the vast majority across the globe, is dominated by powerful men, often from political dynasties, who are usually white and upper-middle class (Levitsky and Murillo 2005). The party of the working class – Peronism – has built its identity around their political inclusion and key concerns like shorter working hours, higher wages, better hospitals. However, while poorer people have become integrated within the party system at the local level, the higher up the party hierarchy one goes, the more likely it is that representatives will be drawn from the elite. Moreover, while women play an integral role at the party's grassroots, they become increasingly scarce the higher up the ladder one ascends. This is partly because the example of Evita solidified women's role as participating yet subordinate political actors in relation to the natural strength of their men. Peronists who are both working-class and women therefore experience two dimensions of discrimination – class and gender – which combine to contain their political activism to the fascinating, but much less powerful, grassroots politics.

One of the issues that emerged in the community and workplace organizations that sprang up during the crisis of 2001 was the way that some people's voices were not heard in the direct democracy discussions that took place on the factory floors or at community centres. Those who were lower status tended to speak less or their ideas were more likely to be ignored. Gender hierarchies not only allow men to take control of the democratic arena; many women defer to them because they associate politics and authority with masculinity. These social inequalities – embedded in families, partnerships,

BOX 14.3 GENDER TENSIONS IN THE DIRECT DEMOCRACY

Two informants discuss the dynamics of gender discrimination in direct democratic scenarios.

> 'Most of the popular kitchens were started by a few women who did everything. Eventually they brought their husbands in to work, since the men were at home all day not doing anything. You know what happened though? As soon as the men showed a little interest in what was happening in the popular kitchens, the women instantly shut their mouths and let the men take charge. So we have a lot of work to do to break with all of this. . . . In some meetings there are more women than men, but it's always the men who speak more. . . . There are *compañeros* [comrades] who've fought next to you on the streets for years, but sometimes they'll tell you to go wash the dishes. It's typical. It's a joke.'
>
> (Sitrin 2006: 211)

> 'The issue of machismo is deeply embedded in everything, and that makes it hard to deal with . . . We never discussed it before, but now we've entered a time when we're talking about a lot of things that used to be taboo. I think that one of the things that happens is that we prioritize, and machismo is low on the list.'
>
> (Sitrin 2006: 214)

communities – can significantly compromise the equality of voice, and therefore of action and ideas, which are essential to an ideal democratic scenario.

Questions of race are also considered in **Chapter 5** in relation to feminist identity politics, and **Chapter 10** in relation to immigration and citizenship.

A third dynamic of exclusion that we have yet to touch on is race. Race is complex in Argentina because a reality of racial diversity is hidden behind a myth of whiteness (Andrews 2004). That is, Argentina portrays itself to the outside world and, importantly, to itself, as being a European outpost in Latin America. When we look at the country's tourist websites we see images of tango and mountains and football, maybe wine and polo and a capital city that looks like Paris or New York. We do not imagine Argentina to have African roots, and we do not associate it with indigenous people.

The exclusion of people of African descent from China's national story is examined in **Chapter 12**. For more on how colonialism produced and continues to produce such exclusions see **Chapter 16**.

Contrary to established images, Argentina is actually home to a significant number of indigenous people (Ray 2007; Gordillo and Hirsch 2008). It also has a considerable Afro-Argentine community, most of whom are descendants of slaves brought to Argentina in the eighteenth century, and who accounted for a third of Argentina's population in 1800 (Andrews 2004). However, nineteenth-century elites promoted the idea of Argentina as a European place. They encouraged mass immigration from Europe, especially Spain, Italy and Jews escaping the pogroms of Russia and Eastern Europe, and wrote out indigenous and Afro-Argentines from their nation's story. This myth of whiteness has a palpable effect because it makes people with non-European heritage invisible in the image and practices of the state and on the political stage.

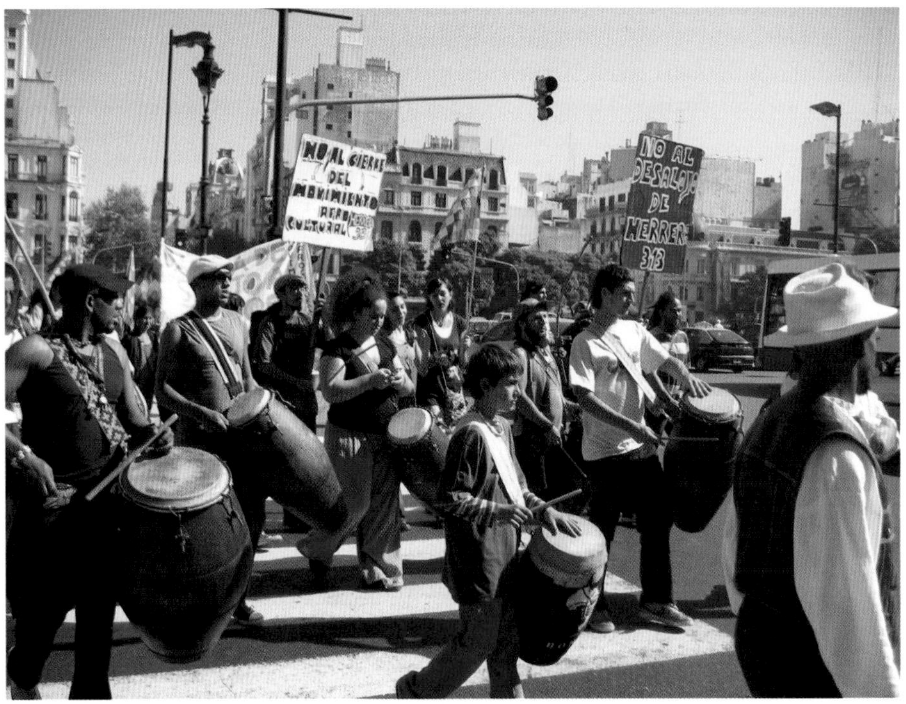

FIGURE 14.6
Afro-Cultural Movement protesters march to the beats of candombé drumming, a quintessential Afro-Argentine musical form. Many supporters of Afro-Argentine culture these days appear to be white, although some of them self-identify as Afro-descendants. (Anil Mundra/GlobalPost.) http://www.globalpost.com/dispatch/argentina/090810/afro-argentines-assert-identity-culture?page=4

This is why we haven't touched on race before – because it has been invisible to the democratic scene of discussion and struggle. Peronism does not recognize race as an issue for democracy and race was invisible to the original human rights campaigns. Moreover, the revival of indigenous organizing prior to and during the crisis of 2001 was understood to address different issues, concerning the right to land and environmental degradation, rather than the crisis of capitalism or liberal democracy. In Argentina, race cannot be imagined as an issue for democracy, because it is politically invisible. This is exactly why it is a serious problem for democratic equality because race is made invisible, and a society cannot confront or discuss racism if racial difference doesn't appear to exist.

The absence of explicitly Afro-Argentine or indigenous Argentine politicians in Argentina's parliament should cause us to ask how racial discrimination works through the political system. Is it because there are statutes that preclude black participation, as there were in South Africa during apartheid, for example? No, on paper the rules do not discriminate against the poor, against women or against indigenous people or Afro-Argentines. However, those rules are enacted by people operating in a society that is infused and structured by dynamics of class, gender and race discrimination. Discrimination means that the de facto exercise of power in a democracy is systematically skewed against certain sorts of people. Combating that discrimination requires not only that we have fair and equal legislation, then, but also that we look at how ideas such as sexism and racism work through society. For me, democratization is not just about living under an elected government that enacts a non-discriminatory rule of law. It means attempting to create a democratic society in which the principles of equality and fairness are enacted not only through the law but also in our human relationships.

BROADER ISSUES
WHOSE DEMOCRACY?

Here I want to explore a key assumption buried deep within conventional understandings of democracy – that the best democracies are in the West. To do so, I will ask where democracy came from and what implications this has for its expansion across the globe. Again, my aim is not to say that actually-existing democracy is a bad thing, but rather that democracy comes from a certain place in history (time) and geography (space). It is not surprising, therefore, that polities (political entities) with different histories or located in different places might think about or implement democracy differently (Shapiro and Hacker-Cordón 1999).

Chapter 27 makes a similar argument about how a particular notion of human rights comes from a certain place and time.

Most analyses of democracy start with an assessment of political systems in the USA, the UK and other European countries. It is through these cases that students are introduced to parliamentary versus presidential systems, and the importance of the rule of law, separation of powers and elections for democracy. Because students learn about Britain, France and the USA first, and because we already assume that these places are the heartland of democracy, this generates the idea that Western democracies are what is normal. It is against the yard-stick of Western democratic experience that non-Western countries are typically measured. This creates two difficulties.

First, if we take political model 'W' as our starting point for assessing how democratic political models are, then model 'non-W' is always going to fall short.

FIGURE 14.7
In 2010 demonstrations against austerity measures and calling for democracy were taking place in Greece, the so-called home of European democracy. http://1.bp.blogspot.com/_AkJIk-OYfMQ/TNj4z_6LyBI/AAAAAAAABEE/LzolPYn5fDU/s400/mn-greece18_ph_0499569781.jpg; http://marxistupdate.blogspot.com/2010/11/reclaiming-europe-that-gave-birth-to.html

The distinction between Western and non-Western is a binary opposition. The exclusion of the non-West is necessary to produce the idea of the West, and the binary is not neutral: one of the pair (Western) is valued more highly than the other. There is a hierarchy involved. Other examples of binary oppositions are discussed in other chapters, for example, man/woman (**Chapter 5**); rich/poor (**Chapter 20**); donor/recipient (**Chapter 21**).

That is, non-Western polities are systematically disadvantaged by this approach because being 'non-W' is already automatically not-as-good-as-'W' and it is defined as lacking something. Second, this comparison is not value neutral, that is, the label 'democratic' has a silent tag 'good' attached to it, and the label 'non-democratic' is silently tagged with the word 'bad'. We say that 'democracy' is not just a descriptive word but is infused with normative content (norms are moral rules). The danger of starting with Western models as our way of judging democracies is that countries that are not Western are set up to fail at the task of democracy by a skewed way of thinking. Moreover, they are judged harshly for it. It becomes logical and clear, then, which countries are understood to be more advanced, and which need to learn democratic lessons, and from whom.

One of the reasons why this has come about is because democracy as it appears in textbooks has been devised and written about by scholars in the West – especially Europe and the USA. It is almost always traced to the Greek city states and their use of direct democratic methods – open discussion and voting in the market square – to make decisions about the community (see Crick 2002). This example is certainly inspirational, but why focus on Ancient Greece? Is this because every other political community at the time was living under violent despotism? Is there no democratic inspiration that could be drawn from Amazonia? Or China? Or Mecca?

There are many complex reasons why it is a European model for a fair and equal society that has emerged as the foundation stone of what we might call 'actually existing democracy' today. One of the most important is that the academic world developed in such a way during the eighteenth and nineteenth centuries that Western universities came to dominate the production of philosophical and political ideas, right up until the present time (Mignolo 2005). This was caused not only by the explosion of Renaissance ideas followed by the intellectual revolutions of the Reformation and Enlightenment but also by the rapid expansion of capitalism which provided the money to found universities and fund scholars, students and the printing, and purchase, of books. This capitalism was driven not only by the agrarian and industrial revolutions inside countries but also by the pursuit of international economic opportunities driven by colonial exploitation and imperial trade.

This form of capitalism has been termed print capitalism; see **Chapter 18**.

The conquest of the Americas, the setting up of trading companies reaching into the East, the development of the transatlantic slave trade and the eventual colonization of Africa, Australasia and the East Indies generated extraordinary riches, which fuelled European development. More than that, colonialism brought Europe into contact with very different kinds of societies. This provoked people who were trying to make sense of the world – philosophers and political thinkers – to generate a wealth of new ideas, as conventional thinking was shaken up by their encounter with the unknown and, to their eyes, the strange (Mignolo 2005). For example, it was after reflecting on the European encounter with Native Americans that Hobbes began to understand the nature and desirability of the state in which he lived, famously characterizing the Native American 'state of nature' as 'nasty, brutish and short'.

For more on the particular example of the British East India Company see **Chapter 16**.

This encounter between colonizer and colonized was, moreover, unequal. The colonizer took power and asserted his dominance over the colonized territories and peoples. This military and political conquest over others seemed to confirm the superiority of the colonizer. It was a short step to go from a reality of superior force to a supposed superiority of intellect, of culture, of ideas and ways of living. This generated an extreme confidence amongst Europeans, and their descendants in the colonies, who came to see the world and its peoples as a resource that they, equipped with their superior technology, spirituality and organization, could justifiably exploit.

The intellectual debates that took place at the time about whether the Spaniards arriving in Latin America in the sixteenth century had the right to rule over the indigenous people that lived there are discussed in **Chapter 21**.

This global patterning of superiority and inferiority was colour-coded. The racialized hierarchies separated out white Europeans from Africans or indigenous peoples, using visual markers on people's bodies – skin colour, hair, eye shape, etc. – as a way to make assumptions about people (Mignolo 2005). These assumptions linked biological facts (black/white skin) to assumptions about intelligence, people's capacity for moral thought and the value of their cultural philosophies (their world-view) and practices (how they organized their societies). In this way, global hierarchies between peoples which emerged alongside colonialism were explained not by history or the force of arms but in terms of inherent, naturalized, biological differences.

The supposed link between biological appearance and personality or other characteristics is examined in **Chapter 5**. Race is further explored in **Chapter 10**.

Although colonialism seems to be over and racist ideas are no longer permissible, the global hierarchies that were established during the colonial period continue to influence our thinking about who is more advanced than whom, and who should do the teaching, and who the learning. It is this certainty that the West has got it right which motivates the desire to export Western models of democracy and capitalism, particularly through Western-dominated agencies such as the United Nations or the World Bank (Grugel 2002). The UN has promoted its vision of democracy through its system of Human Rights Resolutions, which seek to define the rights of disadvantaged groups such as women, children and indigenous people. The World Bank furthers its democratic priorities by linking favourable economic treatment on global credit and loans to good governance and anti-corruption initiatives, both of which focus on the institutions of democracy. We should not judge the World Bank's concern with public transparency too hastily – after all, those who suffer most from high-level corruption are ordinary people. However, its assumption that corruption is a problem in Africa or Latin America, *but not in the USA or UK*, perpetuates a portrayal of Third World countries as being not only badly run (untrustworthy) and less democratic (morally bad) but also inferior. Importantly, these hierarchies not only serve to maintain Third World countries in a low global position, but also serve to keep First World countries in a high global position from where they can continue to set the agenda and form the rules.

The export of European ideas of human rights via the UN is discussed in **Chapter 27**, and of neo-liberal economics and a good governance agenda via the World Bank in **Chapters 15, 17 and 20**.

The coining of the term 'Third World' is discussed in **Chapter 1**.

Let me return now to think about the way that 'actually existing democracy' is configured. We saw how contemporary democracy emerged from the cradle of European thinking and its emerging political systems. This means that when we say 'democracy', actually we are often saying 'liberal democracy' (Shapiro and Hacker-Cordón 1999). Liberal democracy is culturally particular to the history (time) of Europe (space). It has been devised by people – mostly white, European men from privileged backgrounds – who have had certain sorts of experiences and lived in certain sorts of societies with certain sorts of religions, ideas about men and women, notions of race and colonial power relationships.

Compare the way in which human rights are institutionalized in a particular form – a form that derives from Western images of what it might mean to be human – but then that form is exported to the rest of the world: it is universalized (**Chapter 27**).

I do not mean that we should ignore what they have to say – indeed what they say isn't the problem. The problem is that Western academia, which arguably dominates global thinking, tends to universalize what they say. That is, they hold up a particular understanding of democracy and say that it is universal. In this way, ideas and suggestions that came out of a liberal and Western experience of democracy are applied to all kinds of societies with different cultural beliefs, different priorities, and historical experiences. Can liberal assumptions make sense for a black woman in Uganda, or a Muslim in Pakistan, or a shaman in Amazonia?

Do liberal assumptions even make sense for everyone in so-called Western countries such as Europe or the USA?

Let's think about a few problems that universalizing liberal democracy might cause. First, if non-liberal political communities try to enact ideas which were developed by other people first, and in a very different society, then they are: (a) trying to impose alien ideas which are going to be difficult to reproduce, given that people elsewhere are different; and, (b) drawn into playing catch up all the time. In this way they are set up to fail because; as we saw earlier, the yardstick of success against which they are measured was devised by those who invented the system in the first place (and is always being refined – just out of their reach). Second, it means that different interpretations of the same ideal, such as equality or freedom, are seen as inferior, and different ways of imagining or enacting social relationships are lost. For example, one of liberalism's key ideas is that people are primarily individuals, and that freedom means the freedom to do what one wants without impinging on the same freedom for others. However, communitarian ways of looking at freedom, such as Confucianism or Native American understandings, see freedom as deriving from the well-being of the community. Third, there are some things which liberal approaches hardly recognize but that are a top priority for non-liberal polities. For example, Western democratic models typically reject the idea that religious teachings are compatible with institutional democracy: religion and politics should be kept separate. However, many Muslim societies see this connection as natural, and see moral teachings as contributing towards building a good, equal and fair society or a good rule of law.

Buddhist, Sikh and Hindu ideas of community and freedom are in many ways similar, as discussed in **Chapter 27**, and Christian beliefs could sit uncomfortably alongside the secular liberal idea of individualism. Muslim thinking about the connection between religion and politics is discussed in **Chapter 6**.

In Latin America, indigenous peoples have mounted the biggest challenge to the operation of Europeanized liberal democracy (Hellinger 2011). They begin by pointing out that the basic foundations of countries – the constitutions, the language, the religion, the party systems – were devised by the white settler elites who traced their ancestry to Europe. The political systems of these countries were designed by and for the dominant – the colonizer – and indeed settlers and their descendants have exclusively occupied the presidency and dominated political decision-making. For indigenous peoples, then, democracy has not meant freedom, equality and political agency but exclusion and inequality (Gordillo and Hirsch 2008). In the last 20 years or so indigenous organizations have begun to challenge the assumptions and practices of liberal democracy. The first indigenous person to hold high office after 500 years of European rule is Evo Morales from the Aymara ethnic group, who attained the Bolivian presidency in 2005. While many

FIGURE 14.8
The president of Bolivia, Evo Morales, with indigenous priests during a ritual at the pyramid of Akapana. Efe Agencia. http://www.eforobolivia.org/blog.php/?p=1473

indigenous people argue that he has not gone far enough, Morales has devolved significant power to the *ayllu* or traditional community councils and has often promoted the native view that places the environment (Pachamama, mother earth) at the centre of human society and political thinking (Hellinger 2011). In this way, Morales is not only changing the institutional set up of Bolivia's democracy, he is also attempting to change its moral compass by situating policy making within a different set of cultural norms. That is, he is altering not only the structures of democracy but its underlying philosophy. However, even though these changes better reflect the outlook of the indigenous population, which accounts for 65 per cent of the population, the settler minority, which has ruled Bolivia until now, claims that Morales is jeopardizing Bolivia's democracy precisely because his reform interprets democracy from a non-liberal perspective.

Indigenous thinking about the environment is discussed in **Chapter 3**.

Not all contributions to rethinking democracy are so fundamental, and Latin Americans have also found ways to enhance democracy within the liberal worldview. Ideas that have taken off in Latin America – and have spread across the world – include creating parliamentary quotas for women. Begun in Argentina in 1994, this institutional mechanism places the country high in the world rankings for gender equality in parliament, especially in comparison to the UK and USA. Another initiative from Latin America, begun in Brazil in 1989, is participatory budgeting (Hellinger 2011). Here, ordinary people in a community get together to decide how to spend their community's budget for the year through debate, deliberation and voting. Latin Americans value democracy as an ideal very highly. Perhaps it was (and is) the very experience of inequality, violence and injustice which makes Latin Americans such strong advocates of democracy's ideals like freedom of speech and thought, fair-dealing from the state, peaceful social relationships or equality. In my view, if we imagine that people who have lived through violent authoritarianism have nothing to contribute to devising better, fairer political systems, then we are overlooking a resource of experience and ideas that could enrich democracy for all. Moreover, imagining that liberalism is the only way to enact democracy restricts our understanding of democracy's ideals and limits our political imagination and the possibility of generating fairer ways of organizing society.

CONCLUSION

Is democracy a good idea, then? In the end, for me, the answer to the question is yes. I think that democracy seeks to enact political ideals that I find crucial and that are shared by a wide range of cultures and societies. However, I think that we need to democratize our understanding of democracy.

I have argued that one of the key problems with what we call democracy is the way that it has been hitched to the political systems of powerful countries, wrapped up in a moral lesson about the way that societies ought to be. This way of thinking links a descriptive term to a hidden value judgement (democracy = good, non-democracy = bad). These value judgements are all the more powerful because they are naturalized and invisible. *One of the things that we can do when we are thinking about democracy, then, is to make these value judgements visible and problematize them.* This helps to unsettle our easy assumptions and urges us to look afresh at the situation. We might ask ourselves: what is undemocratic about the UK or the UN? What is democratic about Cuba or the Arab League? That doesn't mean that we have to turn around and reject liberal democracy or embrace one-party states – far from it. What it might do, though, is reveal different priorities. We might not agree with the Cuban government that free access to healthcare is more important than political pluralism, but stopping to consider the options might make us think again about the importance of health in a very poor society.

Another important issue to emerge, especially from the illustrative example of Argentina, is the importance of the social realm. The discussion of Peronism showed how important the social realm was for the generation of political loyalties, obligations and emotional attachments. In addition, the subtle yet effective working of discrimination within a supposedly democratic context was revealed. *One of the things that we can ask, then, is not only how fair and equal are the democracy's rules but also, how democratic are the political relationships that happen below, around and alongside these mechanisms?* In order to do this, we need to anchor our analysis of democracy in real places, taking into consideration the historical, economic and cultural context in which the ideals of equality, fairness and freedom are understood. This means not only asking 'How does democracy work in the everyday world?' but also recognizing that 'freedom' in one place might have very different meanings than 'freedom' in another.

Chapter 6 shows this generation of loyalties in relation to religious movement.

More than that, though, the Argentine case revealed that it is the social realm that has been the cradle of democracy, not the formal political realm. It was social mobilization that pushed for the return to democracy and developed the human rights agenda. It was social organizations that brought new issues – gender, race – and new voices to the political agenda, and developed new ways of doing democracy or imagining the economy. *If we want to look for ways to broaden or deepen democracy, then, we should look to the social realm and imagine democracy as not just a way to choose decision-makers but a way of life.*

I have tried to demonstrate that the answer to the question 'Is democracy a good idea?' is not straightforward – indeed that it is a highly politicized question. There is no one way to be democratic, and in my view a plurality of ideas, voices and cultural understandings can enrich all our democracies, even those that are longest established. For me, asking deeper and different questions about the way in which we organize our lives, our democracies, and our global relationships is a vital task for all students and scholars, and promoting democracy in thought is a vital task for us all.

FURTHER READING

If you want to do some reading on democracy and its different variations, then David Held's *Models of Democracy* (2006) is a great place to start – it is clear and demonstrates the different ways that Western political philosophy theorizes democracy. However, like very many other democratic theorists, Held writes from a Western-centric perspective. To raise some critical ideas, have a look at Ian Shapiro and Casiano Hacker-Cordón's edited collection *Democracy's Values* (1999) as well as Jean Grugel's book *Democratization* (2002) which places a key emphasis on social movements and citizen participation. David Potter, David Goldblatt, Margaret Kiloh and and Paul Lewis' edited textbook *Democratization* (1997) offers insights on democracy from around the world. If you are interested in exploring contemporary democracy in Latin America, have a look at Hellinger's new textbook *Comparative Politics of Latin America* (2011) – a comprehensive and accessible text which reads Latin American politics through the struggle for democracy. Another excellent textbook is Vanden and Prevost's *Politics of Latin America: the Power Game* which has very useful country case-study chapters. Finally, if you are interested in Argentine politics, then there are two good histories by Lewis (2001) and Romero (2002). For a riveting insight into Evita Perón, see Fraser and Navarro's biography (1996), while López Levy's short yet fact-filled and inspiring book *We Are Millions* (2004) charts the events of the 2001 crisis. The Mothers of the Plaza de Mayo have attracted a lot of academic attention over the years, but Navarro's chapter (2001) is an insightful analysis of their politicization of motherhood. Little as yet has been written (in English) about indigenous or Afro-Argentine experience. However, Gordillo and Hirsch's journal article (2008) is a useful overview of indigenous exclusion in Argentina and introduces a special issue of the journal on Native Argentines; and Andrews' book *Afro-Latin America* (2004) draws often and particularly on the Argentine experience.

WEBSITES

http://www.buenosairesherald.com/
Buenos Aires Herald: this daily newspaper has been publishing in English since 1876 and is a fantastic resource for news, politics, economy, sport, etc. The major Spanish language newspapers are *La Nación* (http://www.lanacion.com.ar/) and *Clarín* (http://www.clarin.com/).

http://www.evitaperon.org/
Evita Perón Foundation: a very pro-Evita website but nevertheless filled with fascinating photos, histories and insights.

http://www.iwgia.org/regions/latin-america/argentina
IWGIA, International Work Group for Indigenous Affairs: founded in 1968 by academics, this is an international human rights organization which supports indigenous peoples' struggle for human rights, self-determination, right to territory, control of land and resources, cultural integrity, and the right to development.

http://www.quotaproject.org/
International IDEA Quota Project: electoral gender quotas, which are widespread in Latin America and were developed first in Argentina in 1994, are the focus of this project. Check out which countries have the most women parliamentarians and which the least – you might be surprised! How do you think the UK or USA fare?

http://lanic.utexas.edu/la/argentina/
LANIC (Latin American Network Information Center): a fantastic portal for sources of information on Latin American politics, culture economy, etc. Some links are in Spanish.

http://www.latinobarometro.org/latino/latinobarometro.jsp
Latinobarómetro: an ongoing and highly respected public opinion survey which involves some 19,000 interviews in eighteen Latin American countries. It is particularly focused on issues of democracy and grew out of the democratization process in Chile. A fantastic resource, some of which is free.

http://www.opendemocracy.net/
This on-line news magazine presents news analysis, debates and blogs about the world. It aims to be serious, but accessible and original, and publishes thought-provoking pieces by journalists, academics and experts on the topic of democracy.

http://www.wola.org/
WOLA (Washington Office on Latin America): an organization that promotes human rights, democracy, and social justice by working with partners in Latin America and the Caribbean to shape policies in the United States and abroad: includes reports, podcasts and interviews with Latin American pro-democracy activists.

REFERENCES

Andrews, George Reid (2004) *Afro-Latin America, 1800–2000*, Oxford: Oxford University Press.

Auyero, Javier (2000) *Poor People's Politics: Peronist Survival Networks and the Legacy of Evita*, Durham, NC: Duke University Press.

Bosco, Fernando J. (2006) 'The Madres de Plaza de Mayo and Three Decades of Human Rights' Activism: Embeddedness, Emotions, and Social Movements', *Annals of the Association of American Geographers*, 96, 2: 342–65.

Crick, Bernard (2002) *Democracy: A Very Short Introduction*, Oxford: Oxford University Press.

Eckstein, Susan (2001) *Power and Popular Protest: Latin American Social Movements*, Berkeley: University of California Press.

Fisher, Jo (1989) *Mothers of the Disappeared*, London: South End Press.

Foweraker, Joe, Landman, Todd and Harvey, Neil (2003) *Governing Latin America*, Oxford: Polity Press.

Fraser, Nicholas and Navarro, Marysa (1996) *Evita: The Real Life of Eva Perón*, New York: W. W. Norton.

Gordillo, Gastón and Hirsch, Silvia (2008) 'Indigenous Struggles and Contested Identities in Argentina Histories of Invisibilization and Reemergence', *Journal of Latin American and Caribbean Anthropology*, 8, 3: 4–30.

Grugel, Jean (2002) *Democratization: a Critical Introduction*, Houndmills: Palgrave Press.

Held, David (2006) *Models of Democracy*, Oxford: Polity Press.

Hellinger, Daniel (2011) *Comparative Politics of Latin America: Democracy at Last?*, New York: Routledge.

Inglehart, Ronald (2009) *Democratization*, Oxford: Open University Press.

James, Daniel (2000) *Doña Maria's Story: Life, History, Memory and Political Identity*, Durham, NC: Duke University Press.

Levitsky, Steven (2003) *Transforming Labor-Based Parties in Latin America: Argentine Peronism in Comparative Perspective*, Cambridge: Cambridge University Press.

Levitsky Steven and Murillo, María Victoria (2005) *Argentine Democracy: The Politics of Institutional Weakness*, Pennsylvania: Penn State University Press.

Lewis, Daniel K. (2001) *The History of Argentina*, Houndmills: Palgrave Press.

López Levy, Marcela (2004) *We Are Millions: Neo-liberalism and New Forms of Political Action in Argentina*, London: Latin America Bureau.

O'Toole, Gavin (2007) *Politics Latin America*, Harlow: Pearson.

Mignolo, Walter (2005) *The Idea of Latin America*, Oxford: Blackwell.

Navarro, Marysa (2001) 'The Personal Is Political: Las Madres de la Plaza de Mayo', in Susan Eckstein (ed.) *Power and Popular Protest: Latin American Social Movements*, Berkeley: University of California Press.

Potter, David, Goldblatt, David, Kiloh, Margaret and Lewis, Paul (1997) *Democratization*, Polity.

Ray, Leslie (2007) *Language of the Land: The Mapuche in Argentina and Chile*, Copenhagen: IWGIA.

Rock, David (1985) *Argentina, 1516–1987: From Spanish Colonization to the Falklands War and Alfonsín*, London: I. B. Tauris.

Romero, Luis Alberto (2002) *A History of Argentina in the Twentieth Century*, Pennsylvania: Penn State Press.

Shapiro, Ian and Hacker-Cordón, Casiano (1999) *Democracy's Values*, Cambridge: Cambridge University Press.

Sitrin, Marina (2006) *Horizontalism: Voices of Popular Power in Argentina*, Edinburgh: A. K. Press.

Vanden, Harry and Prevost, Gary (2002) *Politics of Latin America: The Power Game*, Oxford: Oxford University Press.

For a range of further resources supporting this chapter, please visit the companion website for *Global Politics, 2nd Edition* at www.routledge.com/cw/edkins/

Chapter 15

Do colonialism and slavery belong to the past?

Kate Manzo

THE QUESTION
SLAVERY: ABOLITION AND CONTINUATION

To what extent does the global politics of development remain influenced by colonial practices and power relations? Colonialism has been defined as 'the direct political control of a people by a foreign state' (Bernstein *et al.* 1992: 168), as 'the control by one group over another inhabiting a separate territory' (De Alva 1995: 262), and as 'an empire that was developed for settlement by individual communities or for commercial purposes' (Young 2001: 16). Colonialism therefore implies some degree of foreign command and political control, whether or not settlers are present. Two significant aspects of the colonialism of old were slavery in Africa and the establishment of a global trading network controlled by European powers and their various agents. The official worldwide demise

How colonialism works in practice is explained in **Chapter 16**.

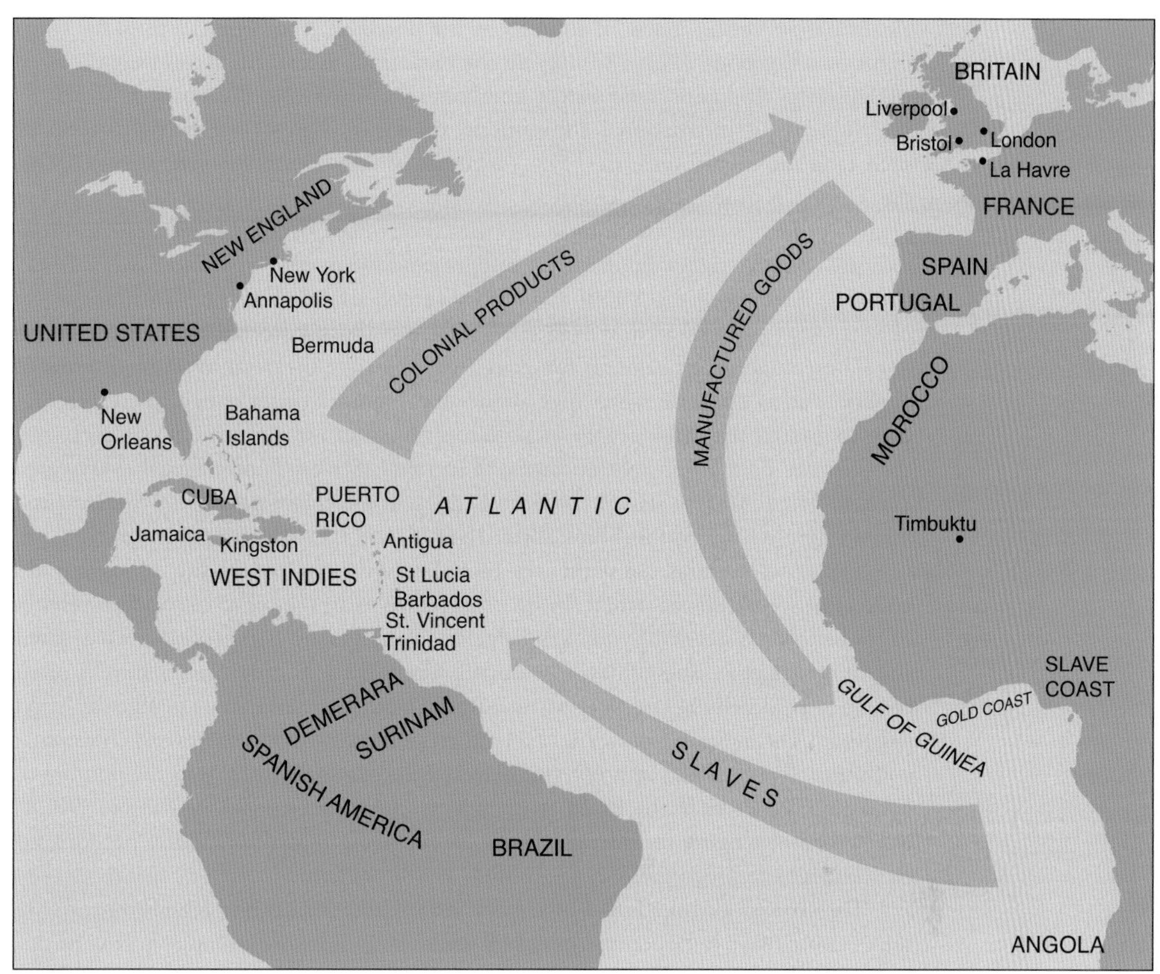

FIGURE 15.1
The global trade in slaves. http://oregonstate.edu/instruct/phl302/distance_arc/images/triangular.jpg; http://oregonstate.edu/instruct/phl302/distance_arc/locke/locke-slavery-lec.html

of both these aspects is signalled rhetorically by two key concepts, namely abolition and national development. But the reality behind the rhetoric in contemporary West Africa suggests that today's world is *not* postcolonial in any meaningful sense.

Considering slavery first, the British Parliament's ratification of the Act for the Abolition of the Slave Trade in March 1807 marked the beginning of the end of the transatlantic trade in slaves from Africa to the British colonies. Some years were to pass before official recognition that – in the words of then home secretary Sir Robert Peel – 'the abominations of the slave system could not be tolerated much longer' (Peel 1833: 1). The Slavery Abolition Act of May 1833 brought an immediate end to the legal principle of property in man but it did not (as Peel himself noted in an article in *The Times*) immediately eliminate slave labour. In an effort to reconcile the competing interests of slaveholders and abolitionists, the Act made provision for the slave's eventual emancipation 'in the course of 12 years by the purchase of his freedom from the fruits of his own exertions' (Peel 1833: 2). In the meantime, all existing slaves were required to register as 'apprenticed labourers' and continue to work for their masters.

Subsequent international conventions are a sure sign of the partial success of such early abolitionist measures. The League of Nations' Slavery Convention of 1926; the United Nations' 1948 Universal Declaration of Human Rights; and the Rome Final Act of 1998 represent notable efforts to both define slavery and eradicate it. More recently, human rights campaigners and organisations (such as Anti-Slavery International) have taken the 200th anniversary of the abolition of the slave trade as an opportunity to raise awareness of all forms of slavery, both historical and contemporary.

These ongoing movements for change demonstrate the need to think in terms of abolitionism as a process rather than abolition as a finished achievement. Furthermore, they show that the major legacy of abolitionism is not the elimination of slavery but the illegality of the principle of 'property in man'. Slavery is now illegal everywhere because 'freedom from slavery has been defined in international law as a fundamental human right' (Bales and Robbins 2001: 18).

The most obvious consequences of the international outlawing of slavery are concealment and official denial. In his classic analysis of the 'new' or modern version of slavery that is defined by its very illegality, Bales (1999: 8) notes that 'even when shown photographs and affidavits, nations' officials deny its existence'. Slavery is often redefined as something else, such as 'indentured labour' or (even more benign) as 'child fostering'. The inevitable outcome of all this is uncertainty over numbers and conceptual confusion. For example, whereas Anti-Slavery International (2007) puts the number of contemporary slaves in the world at 12 million, the 'best estimate' of Bales (1999: 8) is 27 million – a figure considerably lower, he suggests, 'than the estimates put forward by some activists, who give a range as high as 200 million'.

For a discussion of the relation between law and politics see **Chapter 25**.

The current global context of secrecy, denial, uncertainty and confusion compels the question of what the concept of slavery means if not legal ownership of human beings or 'property in man.' A useful starting point is the book *Disposable People*, which defines slavery as 'the total control of one person by another for the purpose of economic exploitation' (Bales 1999: 6). In this and other writings, Bales consistently argues that while slavery has changed in form over time it has clearly not disappeared. Its defining characteristics – and the keys to understanding such contemporary forms of the phenomenon as debt bondage and enforced prostitution – are still violence, control and economic exploitation (Bales and Robbins 2001).

As useful as it is in distinguishing the 'old' from the 'new' slavery, Bales' work does not highlight key distinctions between *slavery* as a type of forced labour and *trafficking* (by agents, recruiters and transporters) as a means to that end (Manzo 2005). Nor does Bales address the differences between slavery and other forms of labour exploitation. Varying systems of production and labour regimes clearly co-exist now, just as they did in the colonies of old. If all forms of violence, control and economic exploitation are labelled as slavery then the millions of illegal and badly-paid migrant workers in the world necessarily belong in that category. They don't, however, if we maintain a definition of slavery as unpaid forced labour. This definition is a useful synthesis of insights drawn from two bodies of work. One is Marxist theory, notably its important distinction

See the discussion of forms of labour in the global political economy in **Chapter 17**.

FIGURE 15.2
Children in a police vehicle after being apprehended at the border on their way out of Nigeria to the Republic of Benin. Photograph: STR/AFP/Getty Images. http://static.guim.co.uk/sys-images/Environment/Pix/columnists/2010/12/3/1291380806013/MDG-International-Day-for-007.jpg; http://www.guardian.co.uk/global-development/poverty-matters+technology/apple

between slavery as a mode of labour exploitation typified by unpaid work and proletarianisation as a system of labour exploitation typified by wage labour. The other is theories of slavery, which generally emphasise forced labour (through violence and coercion) as the basis of the master–slave relationship.

Chapter 19 examines the expansion of the global proletariat.

Even if slavery is defined relatively narrowly as unpaid forced labour, it is still possible to find evidence of its existence. A case in point is the former French colony of Côte d'Ivoire (known also by its English name of Ivory Coast). Thanks to the efforts of investigative journalism in Britain and the United States, the West African country found itself at the turn of the twenty-first century (along with multinational corporations such as Cadbury and Mars) at the centre of the so-called chocolate slavery debate.

There may be millions of slaves globally, but it was the widespread references to 15,000 trafficked children from Mali working without payment on Ivorian cocoa farms that helped turn a regional African phenomenon into a matter of international concern.

Migration across borders can be forced, like child trafficking, or voluntary. For a discussion of movements of people across the US–Mexico border see **Chapter 10**.

That is because the enslavement of trafficked *children* (who are defined in international law as persons under the age of 18 years) constitutes a triple abuse of international human rights conventions and protocols. Violated along with the fundamental human right to freedom from enslavement are the human right to freedom from trafficking and the child's right to freedom from labour.

In West Africa as elsewhere, legal enforcement of prohibition is the other side of the coin of official ignorance and denial of contemporary slavery. Chronicles of the experiences of emancipated young people exist thanks to the efforts of the Malian government (among others) to liberate and repatriate child slaves. The oral testimonies of those typically enticed away with false promises and then held in place by violence and threats will not settle the question of exact numbers. But these stories of entrapment into unpaid forced labour are nonetheless important in offering compelling evidence that slavery (as I've defined it) actually exists in Ivory Coast.

ILLUSTRATIVE EXAMPLE
COLONIALISM AND CAPITALIST DEVELOPMENT IN IVORY COAST

Child slavery in Ivory Coast is best understood in a wider context – in relation to the effects of global capitalist development on the West African region.

The story of modern slavery in Ivory Coast (which became a colony of France in 1893) must begin in the early twentieth century – with an understanding of what Amin (1973) calls the outward-directed economic development of French West Africa. That term captures in shorthand the three key features of the colonial political economy that still epitomise the region today:

1 an economic growth pattern marked by heavy dependence on the export of a handful of primary products;
2 a forced labour system for the production of agricultural commodities; and last but not least,
3 a global supply chain controlled all the way along by colonial companies, traders, intermediaries and middlemen.

Colonial production and unequal exchange

The name Ivory Coast derives from a profitable international trade in ivory during the seventeenth century. That trade was virtually over by the beginning of the subsequent century, however, thanks to the resulting decimation of the elephant population. It therefore wasn't until after the subsequent push inland in the mid-nineteenth century that France began to establish a firm foothold in the West African colony.

Here as elsewhere, the driving force behind colonial settlement was the desire for economic exploitation, notably the promise of fertile environments for cash crop production (i.e. production of agricultural commodities for sale rather than consumption or use). By the early twentieth century, the principal cash crops in the southern forest zones of Ivory Coast were coffee and cocoa, whereas in the northern savannas the main cash crop was cotton.

For a detailed discussion of the economic impact of colonialism on India, and indeed on Britain, and a discussion of various forms of colonialism, see **Chapter 16**.

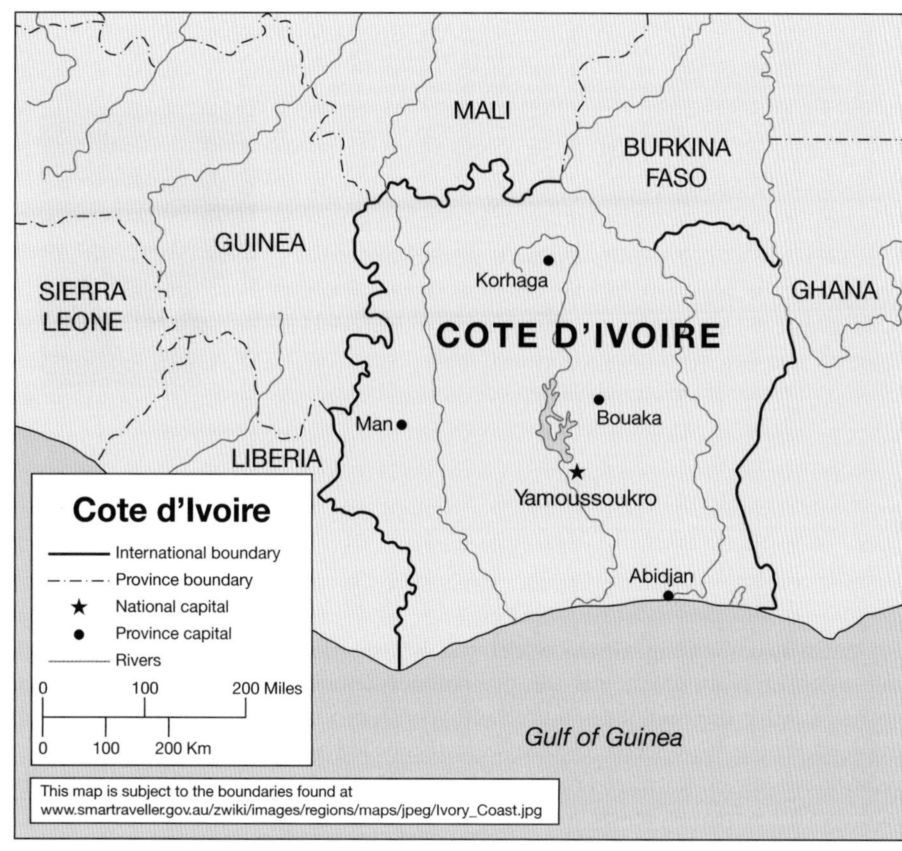

FIGURE 15.3
Map of Côte d'Ivoire

Cotton was already in production for sale to local artisans before the arrival of colonial powers (Bassett 2001). However, the intervention of the French Textile Development Company (Compagnie Française de Developpement des Textiles – CFDT) marked the onset of a classically colonial pattern of unequal and uneven exchange. A raw material of relatively low value produced in the colonies was exchanged for finished manufactures (in this case textile goods) produced in the metropolis. Furthermore, the entire international supply chain was controlled by an integrated network of colonial operators:

> The terms on which this cotton was exchanged reflected the manner in which production was organised: the private company [i.e. CFDT] responsible for cotton production in the colonies was a subsidiary of the sole metropolitan buyer of French West African cotton. At the same time, the sale of manufactured textile goods to the colonies was the responsibility of large trading companies affiliated to the metropolitan textile industry. These companies enjoyed exclusive rights to the French West African market, protected by trade restrictions debarring all but French textile products.
>
> (Campbell 1975: 37)

BOX 15.1 FELIX HOUPHOUET-BOIGNY

Among those leading the fight for the abolition of forced labour and the rights of African planters was Felix Houphouet-Boigny. A qualified physician from a wealthy family of planters, Houphouet-Boigny held political posts in French ministries prior to Ivorian independence. An ardent anti-communist, he was commonly known in the West as the 'Sage of Africa' or the 'Grand Old Man of Africa'. He was the country's president from independence in 1960 until his death in 1993.

FIGURE 15.4 Felix Houphouet-Boigny. Courtesy of Célestin Mbenti Nkoudou

Compare this to the changes in Indian manufacturing under British rule described in the next chapter.

As in neighbouring Ghana under the British, the basic structure of colonial cultivation in Ivory Coast was the plantation economy. From 1912 (when cocoa became a cash crop) until the end of World War II, production by Africans was doubly enforced. Those with access to land were compelled to cultivate cocoa by colonial authorities while, at the same time, French planters were guaranteed a steady supply of workers via a system of labour conscription.

The French abolition of the forced labour system in 1945 marked the onset of a series of changes. That system was abolished thanks to the collective efforts of the 20,000 indigenous planters who came together in 1944 to form the African Agricultural Union.

Post-independence economic development

Ivory Coast was one of many African states to achieve formal political independence in 1960. According to Amin (1973: 50), the abolition of forced labour was a catalyst for the plantation-based agricultural development to follow. Agriculture was not the only aspect of post-independence development, however. Infrastructure (roads, railways and ports) and import substitution industrialisation (i.e. the government policy of replacing imports with domestically-produced goods) to support the development of national manufacturing (such as textile mills and food-processing plants) were also central to the new government's strategy for national development. But with formal political power in the hands of the landed plantation-based class, post-independence development not surprisingly entailed a focus on agricultural growth (Campbell 1975: 37).

Ivorian economic growth was successfully achieved in the first decade after independence via policies of agricultural expansion and diversification. Production rose for all crops – everything from domestically-consumed yams, plantains and manioc to the exported commodities of coffee, cocoa, bananas and pineapples. Another significant earner was wood, exports of which 'rose from a 1950 figure of 90,000 tons to 1,250,000 tons in 1965' (Amin 1973: 52).

Despite (or indeed because of) such changes, economic development remained outward-directed. Increases in food production failed to achieve self-sufficiency. The food deficit actually worsened, leading to greater dependence on grain and rice imports (Amin 1973: 52). Added to that, the development of Ivory Coast was still based mainly on agricultural exports, with expansion and diversification relying heavily on external factors of production in the form of foreign investment, imported technology, and an inflow of immigrant labour from the West African region (Amin 1973: 44; Crook 1990: 651).

Last but not least, the guiding official principle of cooperation with France in all fields only cemented the pre-existing power of French companies, managers, advisers and traders. To return to the cotton example, those who had once produced and marketed raw cotton continue to do so: 'the large export-import houses affiliated with French industry maintained sole access to the Ivorian market by virtue of a quota system, in force until February 1969, which required special licenses for any textile products from sources other than France' (Campbell 1975: 38). In sum, the entire supply chain of unequal and uneven exchange remained immediately after independence in the hands of the same controlling interests as before.

It is interesting to read this account of economic development alongside the account of changes in the global political economy in **Chapter 17**. See also discussions of global inequality and poverty in **Chapters 19 and 20**.

The politics of last resort: development crises and structural adjustment

Before turning to the specific factors responsible for the appearance of modern slavery in Ivory Coast, it's necessary to consider the internal benefits of outward-directed economic development. Which domestic forces within Ivory Coast, in other words, might have profited from the pattern of development described in the previous section?

At least until 1981, when the first crisis of development became impossible to ignore, the internal benefits to growth went disproportionately to 'the original power elite' in control of the Ivorian state (Crook 1990: 651). It wasn't only that a development model founded on agricultural growth was bound to generate capital for landowners. It was also that the wealth generated from state-led industrial development, i.e. the combination of import-substitution policy and direct public investment in domestic manufacturing, enabled the new ruling elite to consolidate its political position. The key institutions, in this regard, were not only the government and civil service but also an expanding machinery of economic administration and control, notably the agricultural extension agency, the Ministry of Agriculture and the crop-marketing board (Crook 1990).

What does the use of the term 'crisis' do? Often it signals or legitimises the use of emergency measures, decided not democratically but by so-called experts. This is discussed in **Chapter 18**.

The Ivorian economy grew at an average rate of 7.2 per cent a year from independence in 1960 to 1981 (Ridler 1993: 301). For the Houphouet-Boigny regime, those decades of spectacular economic growth no doubt served the dual purpose of political and economic stability. But the limits of the Ivorian economic 'miracle' were already apparent to some well before the combined effects of a series of pressures 'finally delivered Côte d'Ivoire into the hands of the international bailiffs or, as they are quaintly called in development jargon, the "donor community"' (Crook 1990: 649).

Note that economic growth does not necessarily improve everyone's wealth: see **Chapters 19 and 20**.

Samir Amin argued in the early 1970s that the writing was already on the wall for an economic development model based on three limiting factors. One was the dual dependence of export-oriented agriculture on paid foreign labour (for production) and foreign markets for cash crops. A second was the dependence of import-substitution industries on domestic consumption – the growth of which was severely limited by restrictions in income. And last but not least – most damaging of all – was the method of financing development through foreign capital and investment. Thanks to high rates of investment return (a pattern of capital repatriation reminiscent of the colonial period), Ivory Coast had already passed 'from the stage of development, characterised by a net inflow of foreign capital, to that of exploitation, characterised by a reversal in the balance of flows and an increasing preponderance of re-exported profits' (Amin 1973: 56).

Note that this argument shows a liberal mindset: according to liberal thought if only markets operated freely, development would automatically occur. See **Chapter 20**.

The subsequent crisis of development has been blamed in part on political interference in markets, notably the channelling of payments to farmers for cash crops through the *Caisse de stabilisation* or crop marketing board (see Crook 1990: 659; also Ridler 1993: 302). As implied by its French name, the basic purpose of the *Caisse* was price stabilisation. Instead of exposing traders and farmers to free market forces, the Ivorian government operated a national system of guaranteed purchase and fixed producer prices. This system was a double-edged sword, for while it safeguarded livelihoods in periods of slump, it paid sub-market prices in periods of boom. The system was thus paradoxical for farmers and traders, as it benefited them most when market prices were low. The government, on the other hand, clearly benefited from the 'good years', when 'important elements of the nation's budget for expansion and investment were funded by the *Caisse* surpluses' (Crook 1990: 659).

What finally brought matters to a head was not development policy as such but a series of external 'shocks'. The most damaging single factor was the international drop in commodity prices that followed the short-lived boom of the mid-1970s. Despite the efforts to diversify agriculture, Ivory Coast still depended for the bulk of its export earnings on cocoa and coffee. The loss of foreign exchange earnings meant that terms

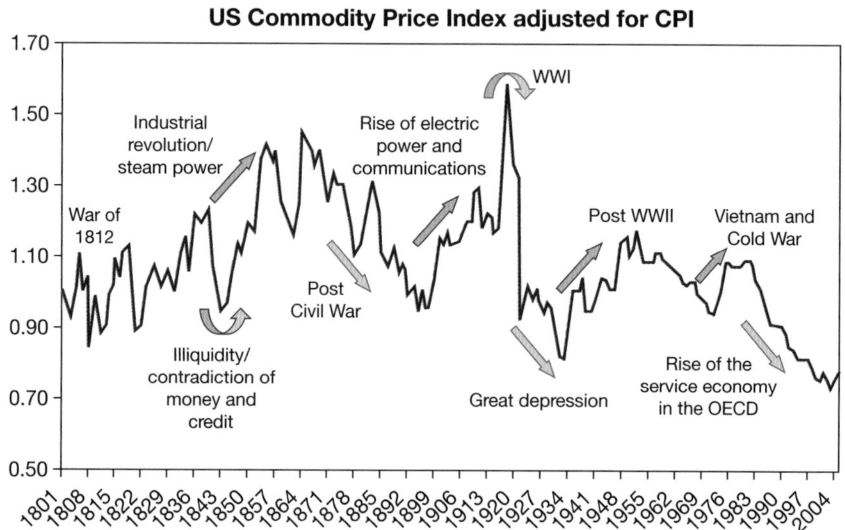

FIGURE 15.5 US Commodity Price Index adjusted for consumer price inflation. Mineweb.com. With permission

BOX 15.2 STRUCTURAL ADJUSTMENT

The term 'structural adjustment' is shorthand for 'the process by which the IMF and the World Bank base their lending to underdeveloped economies on certain conditions, pre-determined by these institutions' (Milward 2000: 25). Sometimes known as the 'Bretton Woods twins' or International Financial Institutions (IFIs), the IMF and World Bank are the product of formal negotiations that took place at Bretton Woods, New Hampshire, USA, in 1944. The aim of the Bretton Woods conference, which was orchestrated by Britain and the United States, was to initiate a post-war international economic order based on fiscal discipline, exchange rate stability, free markets, and growth in international trade. The empowerment of the IFIs to oversee and manage this new order was a key consequence of Bretton Woods. All adjustment programmes reflect this background, and what I have elsewhere called 'the twin pillars of the neo-liberal (essentially capitalist) development agenda, namely market-based economic arrangements and minimalist states' (Manzo 2003: 438).

of trade inevitably declined, i.e. Ivory Coast was forced to pay relatively more for imports thanks to the declining value of its exports.

Matters were only made worse by the wider context in which commodity prices dropped. They fell at a time of continued foreign borrowing to sustain public expenditures; of decline in the value of the US dollar (the currency in which commercial loans were denominated); and of rising prices for imported oil. The cumulative effect was a dramatic increase in national indebtedness. By 1981, Ivory Coast's external debt was ten times higher than it had been only three years earlier, 'and debt-service costs had increased even faster' (Ridler 1993: 303).

That combination of factors explains why the Ivory Coast government initially turned (like so many in Africa) to the International Monetary Fund (IMF) for financial assistance.

The first structural adjustment programme (SAP) for Ivory Coast was introduced in 1981 and updated periodically throughout the decade. The changes demanded were a 'one size fits all' programme of currency devaluation, liberalisation of prices and interest rates, fiscal restraint and austerity (i.e. cuts in state expenditure), and trade liberalisation (Ridler 1993: 303).

Once seemingly confined to the 'third world', talk of financial crises and austerity programmes spread to other parts of the world – for example, to Europe in 2012. See **Chapter 18**.

As with so many African countries, negative economic growth and an increasingly unsustainable debt burden were for Ivory Coast the dark at the end of the adjustment tunnel. The Ivorian government has been doubly blamed for the new 'manifestly impossible austerity programme' demanded by the IMF and World Bank in February 1990 (Crook 1990: 669). The regime of Houphouet-Boigny has been faulted, first of all, for maintaining an agricultural policy of cocoa expansion – apparently with World Bank support – until April 1988 (Crook 1990: 662–3). In this way it failed to foresee the consequences of further declines in international commodity prices.

Second, the regime in power failed to fully implement its SAPs – refusing, for example, to cut the salaries of public sector employees as demanded by fiscal austerity (Ridler 1993: 304–5).

And yet, even its critics acknowledge the limited room for manoeuvre of a state such as Ivory Coast, where 'the survival of a regime often depends on the degree to which lenders restrain their demands' (Crook 1990: 650). Throughout post-independence Africa, political legitimacy has depended on economic performance and delivery. An obvious factor in this regard has been high rates of growth, which have helped to paper over the contradictions of outward-oriented development. Contradictions are more easily exposed in periods of downturn and reversal – which are inevitable for cash crop exporters in particular. Thanks to the price volatility of international commodities, declining terms of trade can be unpredictably sudden and sharp. This happened to Ivory Coast, for example, between 1985 and 1990 when the world prices of cocoa more than halved (Ridler 1993: 304).

Again, compare this account of economic development to the changes in the global political economy described in **Chapter 17**.

Equally significant is the state's capacity to regulate and administer the national economy. As argued by Mbembe (2001: 76), the post-independence African state's 'credit with the public' stems from a combination of financial means, administrative power, and distribution of goods. In this light, the determination of the Ivorian government to keep the cocoa trade going and maintain a large civil service makes political sense. Enabling farmers to be paid (through the *Caisse*) while guaranteeing public sector employment was perceived as key to the legitimacy of 'Houphouet and his cronies' (Crook 1990: 669).

Some Islamic movements also acquire 'credit with the public' through the provision of services: see **Chapter 6**.

What changes were attributable to the heightened influence of the IMF in Ivory Coast in the 1990s? The basic argument of the next section is that structural adjustment has been responsible for a redistribution of benefits. Far from undermining existing patterns of inequality, however, structural adjustment has only made matters worse.

GENERAL RESPONSES

THE EFFECTS OF ADJUSTMENT: DEPROLETARIANISATION AND MODERN SLAVERY

Colonial political economy was typified by cash crop dependence, enforced production of cash crops, and supply chain control. It is against each of these criteria that the effects of structural adjustment – and its redistribution of benefits – are therefore to be assessed.

Compare this to India, where colonisation went hand in hand with industrialisation in Britain and de-industrialisation in India. **Chapter 16** discusses how the economy in the metropole and the colony are interlinked – to the benefit of the colonisers.

Cash crop dependence has only intensified under the IMF's generalised framework of export promotion and market-led growth. Following the death of Houphouet-Boigny in 1993 and his replacement by his constitutional successor, National Assembly president Henri Konan Bedie, the Ivorian government entered into a concessional loan agreement through the IMF's Enhanced Structural Adjustment Facility (ESAF) for low income countries. In return for a low interest loan of 0.5 per cent (to be repaid over 5–10 years), the 'international bailiffs' demanded a standard policy package of currency devaluation, cuts in government spending, and (most tellingly) the liberalisation of banking and trade.

In regard to export agriculture, specifically, the donor community echoed the old 'apologists for colonialism' who argued that African farmers would derive positive benefits from the opportunity to produce coffee, cocoa and palm oil (Rodney 1982: 154). Contemporary donors insisted that a flourishing free market would benefit Ivorian farmers by freeing them from government interference and allowing them access to the true price of their commodities on the world market.

This insistence on the free market is informed by neo-liberal ideas: see **Chapter 20**.

The Bedie government responded by capitulating to the long-standing demand for devaluation of the Ivorian Franc. The national currency was devalued by 50 per cent in 1994 at the same time as export taxes were eliminated. These measures have been thanked for a subsequent economic comeback marked by a jump in growth rates and a drop in inflation. But fortuitous timing was equally significant. The donor-mandated reforms coincided with improved international prices for cocoa and coffee.

The combined effect of externally-imposed policies and world market forces was an immediate explosion of cocoa production (up 44 per cent from 1994 to 1996) and Ivory Coast's movement to the top of the ranks of world cocoa producers. The country now accounts for 40 per cent of global supply.

So who or what might have benefited, at this stage, from structural adjustment? Certainly not Ivory Coast's forest zone – the historical site of cocoa production. The country's protected tropical forests have become increasingly vulnerable to illegal logging and cocoa expansion. As for the Ivorian government, structural adjustment initially was a double-edged sword. While it brought the traditional benefits of growth (as described earlier) it also undermined state capacity for economic administration and control at a delicate time of political transition. In this context, the Bedie government trod the familiar African path described by Mbembe (2001: 76). It became increasingly repressive and reliant on control of the forces of coercion to try to stifle dissent.

Who else might have benefited from these policies of structural adjustment, if not the agricultural producers nor the government?

Farmers and planters would have to be the clear beneficiaries of a programme of reforms designed to limit state power and expose them more fully to world market forces – but only as long as the price of their commodities remains high and (equally importantly) buyers pay producers the true market rate.

Unfortunately for agricultural producers, basic economic logic of supply and demand dictates that prices must inevitably fall. Cocoa (like other exportable cash crops) 'is characterised by boom and bust cycle – as global production/supply rise, price of cocoa beans fall and vice versa' (International Labor Rights Fund, undated: 4).

An apt illustration of the consequences of 'boom and bust' economics (i.e. a period of economic expansion followed inevitably by a period of recession) is what happened when world cocoa prices plummeted in 1999. Ivorian farmers were particularly hard hit because the drop coincided with the final abandonment of the *Caisse* system of guaranteed prices. Ivorian cocoa production is labour-intensive and historically reliant on workers from the West African region. With the donor-enforced completion of the process of trade liberalisation, both the migrant workforce and the 70 per cent of the Ivorian population engaged in agricultural activity were therefore negatively exposed to the full force of structural adjustment.

In response to increased rural poverty and government repression, military forces under the leadership of General Guei overthrew the Bedie administration on 24 December 1999 and replaced it with the so-called National Council for Public Salvation (Country Watch, undated: 4). After a disputed election in October 2000, General

Guei was replaced as president by Laurent Gbagbo. Following an unsuccessful coup attempt by Guei's supporters in 2002, army rebels seized control of the northern regions of the country and plunged Ivory Coast into civil war. France (the former colonial power) soon dispatched military forces to the country to police a dividing line between the north and the south. The French military was still there nine years later – along with reinforcements from the United Nations (UN) – as the international community (in the guise of France, the UN and the African Union) attempted to broker a power-sharing agreement and presidential elections. Another disputed election in December 2010 sparked fresh violence when Gbagbo refused to cede power to rival candidate Alassane Ouattara – himself a former deputy managing director of the IMF. Gbagbo was finally removed from power following his arrest in April 2011 by a combination of Ouattara's forces, UN peacekeepers and French troops (Talbot 2004; Rice and Watt 2011). After his subsequent inauguration as president, Ouattara wasted little time in predicting a rise in national cocoa output – up to 50 per cent of the world's total (Charbonneau and Bases 2011).

The Marxist concept of deproletarianisation helps explain why, in a neo-liberal context of shrinking state capacity, trade liberalisation and associated political unrest, Ivorian farmers 'have been pushed to use their own children or those supplied by traffickers' in efforts to sustain rural livelihoods (International Labour Rights Fund, undated: 6). At the root of this concept is the proletarian – a person who survives by selling their labour power and working for wages. The corresponding term proletarianisation has been mentioned already. Unlike slavery – which was defined earlier as unpaid forced labour – proletarianisation refers to a crucial aspect of capitalist development, namely the process whereby large numbers of people who once owned the means to produce goods and services for sale become employed solely as wage labourers.

How does 'deproletarianisation' compare with the 'informalisation' of labour discussed in **Chapter 17** and the expansion of the global proletariat discussed in **Chapter 19**?

Deproletarianisation is shorthand for a Marxist view of regression or reversal, whereby forced labour is reintroduced as a method of worker discipline and a way to cut costs under capitalism.

The deproletarianisation thesis calls into question the standard explanation for the rise of modern slavery that's offered by Bales (1999: 12–13). There the emphasis is on two key contributing factors within a wider context of economic globalisation and population growth. One is socio-economic modernisation. The other is labour *supply* – the basic notion being that a ready availability of willing young workers necessarily drives labour costs down.

The problem with the 'over-supply' thesis is that it doesn't really explain why slaveholders should need to drive labour costs down beyond the point of paying a pittance to paying nothing at all. Deproletarianisation helps to answer that question, even if it is a framework for understanding all forms of agrarian forced labour and not an explanation for modern slavery per se.

The underlying premise is that agricultural producers will protect their economic interests by switching labour regimes for the same reasons that Britain switched from 'informal empire' to formal colonialism. Producers of commodities will resort to forced labour when they *must* and not simply because they *can*.

The value of that suggestion is twofold. On the one hand, it would seem to make logical sense given the global illegality of slavery (and attendant risk of prosecution) discussed in the introduction. Even if the outlawing of slavery doesn't eradicate the practice it still alters the calculus of slaveholders, turning what was once an accepted convention and best possible option into a final resort.

On the other hand, deproletarianisation reflects the actual behaviour of Ivorian farmers. Modern slavery in Ivory Coast is more of a variable than a constant, ebbing and flowing with changes in commodity prices. Farmers, furthermore, have readily turned to more conventional methods of protecting their livelihoods. They took to the streets in 2004, for example, in protest at the changes introduced since the abolition of the *Caisse* and the abandonment of the system of minimum pricing. Uncertain of market prices and distrustful of the trio of semi-private agencies set up after 2000 to oversee the cocoa trade, growers complained of their diminished capacity to withstand economic shock. They argued that the sliding levy scale introduced to compensate for heavy losses in global markets offered far less protection than the old guaranteed minimum price (BBC News 2004: 1).

To connect deproletarianisation to structural adjustment in this way is not to excuse the behaviour of slaveholders. The point is to demonstrate the political consequences of neo-liberal development. The argument thus far clearly reinforces the conventional message sent by human rights activists (such as the International Labour Rights Fund) that structural adjustment hits hardest at the poor.

It is necessary to conclude now by considering the other side of the neo-liberal coin. If farmers and planters are only the winners in theory of neo-liberal development, then who or what are the beneficiaries in practice?

That question returns the analysis to the issue of supply chain control. In Britain's 'informal empire', free trade agreements were a means to protect dominant commercial interests while exploiting relatively weak states. They were thus implicitly hierarchical, in both an economic and political sense. At the top (as the following quote from Rodney implies) were the 'white colonialists' who exercised political control and profited most economically from the status quo; at the bottom was the economically exploited and politically disempowered African peasantry.

So was it the large corporations who benefited? How is this linked back to colonialism?

Current global food chains are remarkably similar to the colonial division of labour, as the following exposition of coffee markets demonstrates.

BOX 15.3 COLONIALISM'S DIVISION OF LABOUR

A peasant growing a cash crop or collecting produce had his labour exploited by a long chain of individuals, starting with local businessmen. Sometimes, those local businessmen were Europeans. Very rarely were they Africans, and more usually they were a minority group brought in from outside and serving as intermediaries between the white colonialists and the exploited African peasant . . . The share of profits which went to middlemen was insignificant in comparison to those profits reaped by big European business interests and by the European governments themselves.

(Rodney 1982: 154–5)

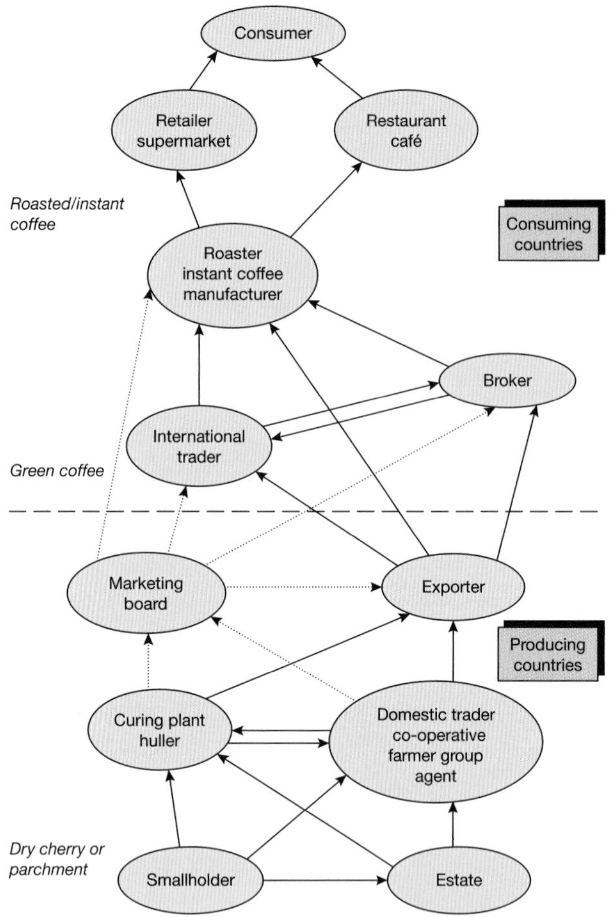

FIGURE 15.6
General structure of the global coffee-marketing chain. Stefano Ponte (2002) 'The "Latte Revolution"? Regulation, Markets and Consumption in the Global Coffee Chain', *World Development*, 30, 7: 1099–1122

With regard to Ivorian cocoa, next in line to individual farmers and co-operatives are the farmgate buyers and exporters, who are now (thanks to trade liberalisation) in a better position to haggle with farmers over prices. These 'local' businessmen and companies (the largest of which are actually subsidiaries of foreign corporations) have been accused of short-changing producers by 'buying their beans cheaply and selling at big profits in the rising market' (Cowell 2002: 1; see also Global Witness 2007: 18). As the London-based International Cocoa Organisation (ICA) noted in a 2000 report, 'Ivory Coast's mostly illiterate farmers are ill-equipped to negotiate with [the] hard-bargaining commodity buyers' who systematically underpay (quoted in Cowell 2002: 2). For farmers then, the consequence of the abandonment of fixed prices is only the privatisation of their exploitation and not (as promised) their payment at true market rates.

Further along the supply chain are London-based brokerage firms such as Armajaro, a company headed by the trader Anthony Ward (the man nicknamed 'Chocolate Finger' by business associates). Serving as brokers between African exporters and Western cocoa processors, these companies stand to make fortunes in commodities futures markets from speculative buying and selling.

Beyond the brokers are the cocoa grinders and processors who buy raw beans to turn into semi-finished products such as cocoa powder and butter. This group suffers from commodity price rises if they cannot pass on the rising costs to their own buyers. These, in turn, are food companies in general and chocolate and confectionary manufacturers in particular (Cowell 2002: 4).

Dominant brand-owners such as Cadbury and Mars are the 'big business interests' that arguably dominate the entire cocoa supply chain (Tiffen 2002). Their relative commercial dominance, rather than proximity to any actual slaves, placed them at the centre of the 'chocolate slavery debate' mentioned earlier. But the multinationals are not the end of the chain. Beyond them are two other links. One is the retail outlets that may squeeze manufacturers by refusing to countenance price increases on the finished products they sell (Cowell 2002: 4). The other is assorted consumers like us, who contribute directly to global demand. Furthermore, if cocoa is indeed a 'conflict resource' that has 'contributed to funding armed conflict' (Global Witness 2007: 3) then consumers of chocolate containing cocoa from the Ivory Coast have helped indirectly to sustain situations of 'divided leadership and associated human rights abuses' (Furman 2010: 2).

Are you eating a bar of chocolate as you read this? Which company made it? Do they tell you where they source their cocoa from?

As consumers, we are all implicated, then, in child slavery. What should we do about it? Is consumer action enough?

Overseeing the whole commodity chain are the new agents of 'informal empire' – the IMF and World Bank and, arguably, the World Trade Organization. From their command centres in Washington DC, this 'unholy trinity' of multilateral institutions governs a world economy 'that their neoliberal ideology insists is best left institutionally ungoverned' (Peet 2003: 23). This inherent contradiction exposes the triumvirate to powerful dissent and may well undermine it eventually. No empire lasts forever, not even the most powerful.

In the meantime, all three institutions are sustained by a combination of institutional learning and powerful support. They 'have learned that a little spin and some confessions of partial failure . . . excuse many abuses in the exercise of power' (Peet 2003: 24). Even more importantly, the 'unholy trinity' represents a conglomerate of economic and political interests. At its economic heart are the major beneficiaries of neo-liberalism – multinational corporations in general and, according to Peet (2003: 202), investment banking in particular. At its political heart are the governments of the leading capitalist countries. Counted among their ranks are the former colonial powers. They (like France in the Ivory Coast) may still turn to military means to protect their vital interests – but only when informal strategies fall short of the mark or misfire.

BROADER ISSUES
IS TODAY'S WORLD POSTCOLONIAL OR NEO-COLONIAL?

Answers to questions are never simply a matter of either common sense or empirical fact. They inevitably depend on two inter-related factors. One is meaning – the issue of how key concepts in the question are understood and defined in their own terms as well as differentiated from other similar concepts. The second is perspective – how those

Think about the notion of pictures of the world presented in **Chapter 2**. Are the concepts we use and the perspective we adopt part of our picture of the world?

same key concepts are interpreted from within a particular theoretical framework. Concepts and theory together determine intellectual focus and approach – the ways in which arguments are presented and evidence marshalled.

With the above points in mind, this final section, which raises the larger question of whether today's world is postcolonial or neo-colonial, begins with a critical interrogation of the meaning of the key concepts 'postcolonial', 'colonial' and 'neo-colonial'.

Postcolonialism

The fundamental issue with the term 'postcolonial' is whether the *post* in the term signals *after*. The perspective from which this issue is considered is 'postcolonial theory' – a term that is itself open to interpretation thanks to the diversity of self-consciously postcolonial scholarship. Postcolonialism is best seen as a 'site of critical inquiry' (Slater 1998: 655) or a set of shared ideas rather than a single theory or unified body of thought (Abrahamsen 2003: 191).

Postcolonial theory, first of all, refuses to treat 'postcolonial' as a synonym for 'European decolonisation'. The world can only be considered 'postcolonial' if we assume that historic patterns of economic control and command necessarily ended with formal

BOX 15.4 DEFINITIONS OF POSTCOLONIALISM

The postcolonial does not privilege the colonial. It is concerned with colonial history only to the extent that that history has determined the configurations and power structures of the present.

(Young 2001: 4)

Postcolonial theory involves discussion about experiences of various kinds: migration, slavery, suppression, resistance, representation, difference, race, gender and place (among others).

(Power 2003: 123)

The post-colonial . . . can be defined in relation to a period of time that is marked by the power of the colonizing process.

(Slater 1998: 653)

Colonialism, as conventionally defined in terms of formal settlement and control of other people's land and goods, is in the main over, but many of its structures and relations of power are still in place.

(Abrahamsen 2003: 195)

Postcoloniality . . . is a salutary reminder of the persistent 'neo-colonial' relations within the 'new' world order and the multi-national division of labour.

(Bhabha 1994: 6)

colonial rule. Patterns of continuity amid change mean that international power relations have moved beyond colonialism in some ways while remaining thoroughly colonial in others. There is thus still some utility (despite the criticisms levelled against it) in the Marxist concept of neo-colonialism considered later in this section.

Second, postcolonial theory is fundamentally concerned with topical issues and themes and not with colonial history per se. It is interested in contemporary manifestations of historic aspects of European colonialism, such as slavery in Africa. As the discussion so far has argued, while slavery per se is an institution defined by unpaid forced labour, the defining feature of *modern* slavery is the shift in the master–slave relation from the legal ownership that obtained in the colonial era to illegal control. The trafficking of children from countries like Mali to work on cocoa plantations in the Ivory Coast exposes the covert character of modern slavery while situating its patterns of economic domination, violence and resistance in global economic context. This focus consciously integrates the economic concerns of traditional Marxism with the politics of international human rights, thus offering an example of what Young (2001: 7) calls 'postcolonial cultural critique'.

In explaining slavery's persistence, the issue once again is continuity amid change; specifically, the issue of how child enslavement can exist (if not positively flourish) in a world of international human rights law, formal decolonisation and capitalist development. The answer suggested here embeds the problematic of modern slavery firmly within the workings of the world economy as well as the frameworks and strategies designed to promote capitalist development. Attention to two key processes, namely deproletarianisation and structural adjustment, shows how the fundamentally uneven and hierarchical character of colonial power relations remains invested in contemporary theories and practices of development.

Colonialism

Before we return to the question of whether today's world is postcolonial in any meaningful sense, or more properly neo-colonial, we need to ask what colonialism entailed. As David Slater has noted, there are crucial distinctions between the Iberian colonisation of Latin America by Spain and Portugal, on the one hand, and the pan-European colonisation of Africa and Asia on the other (Slater 1998: 653). Both colonisation and decolonisation began and ended much sooner in the American continent than they did in the other two. All of Latin America except for Cuba and Puerto Rico were formally independent by 1825, whereas the process of Asian decolonisation only began with the independence of India from Britain in 1947. At that time, the only two African countries not under colonial rule were Ethiopia and Liberia. The decolonisation of Libya in 1951 marked the onset of decolonisation in North Africa while the trailblazer in sub-Saharan Africa was Sudan in 1956.

Early colonisation in the Americas is discussed in **Chapter 21** and contemporary politics in Argentina are the subject of **Chapter 14**. The colonial period with its enduring effects in India is explained in **Chapter 16**.

So, it is safe to say (as scholars generally do) that European decolonisation has largely run its course. But by the same token, it would be dangerous to assume that all aspects of colonialism have reached an unequivocal end, for two reasons. First, the geography of independence remains spatially uneven. Many islands as opposed to continents in the world (such as French Martinique and the Dutch Antilles) continue to fly European flags and are effectively still colonies. Meanwhile, as Young (2001: 3) points out, more recent invasions (such as that of Tibet by China and Kashmir by India) signal the arrival of a new generation of colonial rulers.

Second, there was always more to colonialism than what Potter (1992) calls its 'international political dimension', i.e. the direct control and formal political rule of a subject population by a foreign power. On the one hand, colonialism in practice was arguably marked by six other features, namely:

- bureaucratic elitism and authoritarianism;
- statism (i.e. comprehensive political control of the economy);
- use of 'traditional' authority figures;
- use of force;
- technological advantage; and a
- hegemonic ideology designed to legitimate and perpetuate the existing regime.

(Potter 1992)

According to Potter (1992: 219), it was only the international political dimension of colonial rule that was 'snapped at independence'.

On the other hand, colonialism needs to be understood in relation to motives as well as features. As the Ivory Coast case demonstrates, European colonialism was driven by economic as well as territorial interests in land. For Britain at least in the mid-Victorian period (roughly the 1850s to the 1870s or slightly later), 'informal empire' was the preferred means of extending supremacy. 'Refusals to annex are no proof of reluctance to control', as Gallagher and Robinson (1953: 3) have memorably said. But Victorian policy makers viewed annexation only as a method of 'last resort' to secure British interests. Formal political rule was not considered as long as commercial penetration, political influence and economic command could be achieved by other means. First among these were free trade agreements and treaties of friendship 'made with or imposed upon a weaker state' (Gallagher and Robinson 1953: 11–12).

There is a discussion of the European territorial state and its imperial expansion in **Chapter 11**.

Young (2001: 19) suggests that different motivations (for commercial exploitation and settlement) gave rise to 'two distinct kinds of colonies' within European empires – 'the settled and the exploited, the white and the black, which would be treated very differently'. Colonies varied as well in terms of their systems of production and labour regimes. Bernstein *et al.* (1992: 186) identify four broad types of colonial labour regime, namely: forced labour (of which slavery is a notorious exemplar); semi-proletarianisation; petty commodity production; and proletarianisation. Slavery was only ever a feature of plantation economies or 'colonies of domination' (Young 2001: 23). It did not typify colonialism per se.

Different forms of colonialism are discussed in **Chapter 16**.

What *did* come to typify all European colonies was their insertion into trade on the world market. Whether it was the primary motivation for it or not, the establishment of a global trading network controlled by European powers and their various agents was a significant aspect of the colonialism of old.

Neo-colonialism

The conviction that nothing much has changed in the world economic order since independence, in that patterns of economic power and unequal exchange remain more

BOX 15.5 DEFINITIONS OF NEO-COLONIALISM

Following World War II decolonization quickly accelerated and colonialism shifted in meaning once more as the Left – now fully committed to the use of 'colonialism' to describe an economically or politically dependent condition – rechristened the predicament of the newly liberated but economically devastated nations as 'neocolonialism'.

(De Alva 1995: 267)

The imposition of the international division of labour under formal colonialism had the indirect effect of laying the foundations for the continued economic control and domination over colonial resources even in the absence of direct political overlordship and administration.

(Hoogvelt 1997: 30)

Neocolonialism denotes a continuing economic hegemony that means that the postcolonial state remains in a situation of dependence on its former masters, and that the former masters continue to act in a colonialist manner toward formerly colonized states.

(Young 2001: 45)

or less exactly as they were, is at the heart of the neo-Marxist concept of neo-colonialism. A term first coined by Kwame Nkrumah – 'the man who had been able to transform the politics of Ghana and pressurise the British into leaving without a single shot being fired' (Young 2001: 45) – is most obviously neo-Marxist in the sense that the framework of analysis was inspired by the writings of Russian Marxist Vladimir Lenin. The title of Nkrumah's 1965 book – *Neo-colonialism: The Last Stage of Imperialism* – is a clear echo of Lenin's earlier analysis of colonialism as a system of economic exploitation in *Imperialism: The Highest Stage of Capitalism* (Nkrumah 1965; Lenin 1939).

FIGURE 15.7
Kwame Nkrumah

Nkrumah's basic argument was that a resource-rich country such as Ghana could not develop autonomously thanks to its insertion within an international division of labour centred on capitalist exploitation and external control of markets. This analysis not only inspired a more general neo-Marxist framework for the analysis of underdevelopment in West Africa (see Amin 1973). It also played well among many other leaders of newly-independent states – especially those elsewhere in Africa confronted with the same 'harsh reality' of economic dependence on exports of primary commodities (Young 2001: 45).

The charge that those same new rulers were metaphorically in bed with the enemy and thus part of the problem was captured in the development of underdevelopment thesis of Andre Gunder Frank, which emphasised the

FIGURE 15.9
Andre Gunder Frank.
http://wsarch.ucr.edu/archive/gunder97cd.html

In other words, is it really helpful to try to decide whether one approach or the other is 'better'? How would we ever be able to decide this once and for all? And in any case, aren't there many different approaches subsumed under each of these labels?

complicity of the post-independence ruling class or 'comprador bourgeoisie' with the interests of international capital (see Frank 1967). Frank's analysis of capitalism and underdevelopment in Latin America exposed the internal benefits as well as costs of outward-directed development while enfolding the problem of underdevelopment within a broader analysis and critique of the expansion of capitalism into a world system.

As Slater (1998) points out, a degree of intellectual mud-slinging can give the impression that neo-colonialism and postcolonialism are incompatible terms. The former stands accused of over-emphasising the continuity of colonialism and the power of the West while the latter has been charged with a seeming 'avoidance of political economy and in particular class politics, and more pointedly an implicit acceptance of global capitalism' (Slater 1998: 655). This whole debate raises much bigger and troubling questions (which have been explored in more depth elsewhere) about the utility of simple binary distinctions between postcolonial theory and area studies (Abrahamsen 2003) and between culture and political economy (Manzo 2005).

Suffice it to say here that the field of postcolonial studies is expansive enough to embrace a variety of theoretical persuasions. The concept of neo-colonialism (like other Marxist concepts) is not foreign to postcolonial theory. There is no necessary contradiction in terms between neo-colonialism and postcolonialism and, more generally, between neo-Marxist thought and postcolonial theory. Their common frame of reference is the contemporary effects of colonial power relations over time.

CONCLUSION

The end of formal colonial rule has not ended historic patterns of economic control and exploitation any more than the abolition of slavery has eradicated enslavement. Slavery – like colonialism itself – persists despite its official demise. While both have changed in form they are sustained in a variety of ways by economic and political interests.

Although the geographic focus of the chapter is Africa (West Africa in particular), the issues raised are global in scope and broader in character. It is necessary to think about the wider relationship between capitalism and slavery; the uneven and unequal consequences of development in theory and practice; and the prospects of meaningful change.

A general lesson to draw from this analysis is that neither colonialism nor slavery is antithetical to capitalist development. Capitalism may well benefit more in theory from the invisible hand of the free market than from mechanisms of force (be it forced labour regimes or the enforced subjugation of formal political rule). But as the history of Ivory Coast's agricultural commodities trade demonstrates, capitalism in practice has always relied for its trans-national expansion on unequal relations of power. Inequalities may be inherent in the international division of labour and global supply chain. But labour exploitation and unequal exchange are not naturally occurring phenomena. They are political outcomes and the effects of global relations of power involving states and, increasingly, the agents of 'informal empire'. As such, they are always (like colonialism and slavery) subject to change.

FURTHER READING

Archer, Leonie (ed.) (1988) *Slavery and Other Forms of Unfree Labour*, London and New York: Routledge.
An edited overview of theories of slavery.

Coote, Belinda (1996) *The Trade Trap: Poverty and the Global Commodity Markets*, Oxford: Oxfam.
A critical analysis for Oxfam of the relationship between poverty and global commodity markets.

Laycock, Henry (1999) 'Exploitation via Labour Power in Marx', *The Journal of Ethics* 3, 2: 121–31.
An exploration of the Marxist distinction between slavery and other forms of labour exploitation.

Manzo, Kate (2005a) 'Modern Slavery, Global Capitalism and Deproletarianisation in West Africa', *Review of African Political Economy* 32, 106: 521–34.
An exploration of the relationship between capitalism and modern slavery in Africa, using Ivory Coast as a case study.

Memmi, Albert (2006) *Decolonisation and the Decolonised*, Minneapolis and London: University of Minnesota Press.
A portrait of the contemporary situation of formerly colonised areas and peoples.

Mohan, Giles, Ed Brown, Bob Milward and Alfred B. Zack-Williams (2000) *Structural Adjustment: Theory, Practice and Impacts*, London and New York: Routledge.
A detailed exploration of all aspects of structural adjustment, including consideration of alternatives.

Mshomba, Richard E. (2000) *Africa in the Global Economy*, Boulder, CO and London: Lynne Rienner.
An exploration of how Africa has been affected by trade-related policies and agreements, including international commodity agreements.

WEBSITES

Anti-Slavery International, http://www.antislavery.org
The world's oldest international rights organisation.

Free the Slaves, http://www.freetheslaves.net
A non-profit organisation dedicated to ending slavery worldwide.

Stop Chocolate Slavery, http://vision.ucsd.edu/~kbranson/stopchocolateslavery
A website dedicated to raising awareness of slavery and other labour abuses in the production of chocolate.

World Rain Forest Movement, http://www.wrm.org.uy
Some useful information on the environmental consequences of commodity production.

REFERENCES

Abrahamsen, Rita (2003) 'African Studies and the Postcolonial Challenge', *African Affairs* 102, 407: 189–210.

Amin, Samir (1973) *Neo-colonialism in West Africa*, Harmondsworth: Penguin.

Anti-Slavery International (2007) 'About 1807–2007', http://www.antislavery.org/2007/about.html (accessed 12/03/2007).

Bales, Kevin (1999) *Disposable People: New Slavery in the Global Economy*, Berkeley, Los Angeles and London: University of California Press.

Bales, Kevin and Peter T. Robbins (2001) '"No One Shall Be Held in Slavery or Servitude": A Critical Analysis of International Slavery Agreements and Concepts of Slavery', *Human Rights Review* 2, 2: 18–45.

Bassett, Thomas J. (2001) *Peasant Cotton Revolution in West Africa: Côte d'Ivoire, 1880–1995*, Cambridge: Cambridge University Press.

BBC News (2004) 'Cocoa Delays Hitting Ivory Coast', 1 October: 1–2, http://news.bbc.co.uk/1/hi/business/3706952.stm (accessed 03/04/07).

Bernstein, Henry, Hazel Johnson and Alan Thomas (1992) 'Labour Regimes and Social Change under Colonialism', in Tim Allen and Alan Thomas (eds) *Poverty and Development in the 1990s*, Oxford and New York: Oxford University Press.

Bernstein, Henry, Tom Hewitt and Alan Thomas (1992) 'Capitalism and the Expansion of Europe', in Tim Allen and Alan Thomas (eds) *Poverty and Development in the 1990s*, Oxford and New York: Oxford University Press.

Bhabha, Homi K. (1994) *The Location of Culture*, London and New York: Routledge.

Campbell, Bonnie (1975) 'Neo-colonialism, Economic Dependence and Political Change: A Case Study of Cotton and Textile Production in the Ivory Coast 1960 to 1970', *Review of African Political Economy* 2, 2: 36–53.

Charbonneau, Louis and Daniel Bases (2011) 'Ivory Coast May Produce Half of World Cocoa', Reuters, 25 September: 1–2, http://af.reuters.com/article/investingNews/idAFJOE78002B20110925?sp=true.

Country Watch (undated) 'Overview – (Côte d'Ivoire) Ivory Coast', http://countrywatch.altavista.com (accessed 29/03/07).

Cowell, Alan (2002) 'War Inflates Cocoa Prices but Leaves Africans Poor', *New York Times*, 30 October, http://www.globalpolicy.org/socecon/develop/africa/2002/1030cocoa.htm (accessed 25/03/03).

Crook, Richard C. (1990) 'Politics, the Cocoa Crisis, and Administration in Côte d'Ivoire', *The Journal of Modern African Studies* 28, 4: 649–69.

De Alva, Jorge K. (1995) 'The Postcolonization of the (Latin) American Experience: A Reconsideration of "Colonialism", "Postcolonialism", and "Mestizaje"', in Gyan Prakash (ed.) *After Colonialism: Imperial Histories and Postcolonial Displacements*, Princeton, NJ: Princeton University Press.

Frank, Andre G. (1967) *Capitalism and Underdevelopment in Latin America: Historical Studies of Chile and Brazil*, New York: Monthly Review Press.

Furman, Katherine (2010) 'Conflict Chocolate: Your Role in Côte d'Ivoire's War', 02 September, http://www.consultancyafrica.com/index.php?option=com_content%view=article&id.

Gallagher, John and Ronald Robinson (1953) 'The Imperialism of Free Trade', *The Economic History Review* 6, 1: 1–15.

Global Witness (2007) *Hot Chocolate: How Cocoa Fuelled the Conflict in Côte d'Ivoire*, June, http://www.globalwitness.org.

Hoogvelt, Ankie (1997) *Globalisation and the Postcolonial World: The New Political Economy of Development*, London: Macmillan.

International Labor Rights Fund (undated) 'The World Bank and IMF Policies in Côte d'Ivoire: Impact on Child Labor in the Cocoa Industry', http://www.laborrights.org/projects/childlab/WBIMFcocoa.pdf.

Lenin, Vladimir I. (1939) *Imperialism: The Highest Stage of Capitalism. A Popular Outline*, New York: International Publishers.

Manzo, Kate (2003) 'Africa in the Rise of Rights-based Development', *Geoforum* 34, 4: 437–56.

——(2005) 'Exploiting West Africa's Children: Trafficking, Slavery and Uneven Development', *Area* 37, 4: 393–401.

Mbembe, Achille (2001) *On the Postcolony*, Berkeley and Los Angeles: University of California Press.

Milward, Bob (2000) 'What Is Structural Adjustment?', in Giles Mohan, Ed Brown, Bob Milward and Alfred B. Zack-Williams (eds) *Structural Adjustment: Theory, Practice and Impacts*, London and New York: Routledge.

Nkrumah, Kwame (1965) *Neo-colonialism: The Last Stage of Imperialism*, London: Heinemann.

Peel, Sir Robert (1833) 'Abolition of Slavery in the British Colonies', *The Times*, 14 May, http://dspace.dial.pipex.com/town/terrace/adw03/peel/economic/abolition.htm (accessed 12/03/2007).

Peet, Richard (2003) *Unholy Trinity: The IMF, World Bank and WTO*, London: Zed Books.

Ponte, Stefano (2002) 'The "Latte Revolution"? Regulation, Markets and Consumption in the Global Coffee Chain', *World Development* 30, 7: 1099–1122.

Potter, David (1992) 'Colonial Rule', in Tim Allen and Alan Thomas (eds) *Poverty and Development in the 1990s*, Oxford and New York: Oxford University Press.

Power, Marcus (2003) *Rethinking Development Geographies*, London and New York: Routledge.

Rice, Xan and Nicholas Watt (2011) 'Ivory Coast's Laurent Gbagbo Arrested – Four Months On', *Guardian*, 11 April: 1–2, http://www.guardian.co.uk/world/2011/apr/11/ivory-coast-former-leader-arrested.

Ridler, Neil B. (1993) 'Fixed Exchange Rates and Structural Adjustment Programmes: Côte d'Ivoire', *The Journal of Modern African Studies* 31, 2: 301–8.

Rodney, Walter (1982) *How Europe Underdeveloped Africa*, Washington, DC: Howard University Press.

Slater, David (1998) 'Post-colonial Questions for Global Times', *Review of International Political Economy* 5, 4: 647–78.

Talbot, Chris (2004) 'Ivory Coast: Two Years of French and United Nations Occupation', *World Socialist Web Site*, 14 August: 1–4, http://www.wsws.org/articles/2004/aug2004/ivry-al4.shtml.

Tiffen, Pauline (2002) 'A Chocolate-coated Case for Alternative International Business Models', *Development in Practice* 12, 3/4: 383–97.

Young, Robert (2001) *Postcolonialism: An Historical Introduction*, Oxford: Blackwell.

For a range of further resources supporting this chapter, please visit the companion website for *Global Politics, 2nd Edition* at www.routledge.com/cw/edkins/

CHAPTER 16

How does colonialism work?

Sankaran Krishna

THE QUESTION
COLONIALISM AND UNDERDEVELOPMENT

How is it that in 1492 what were then called the East Indies were lands of such fabled wealth and riches that they could lure Christopher Columbus and his intrepid crew to embark on a dangerous and uncertain voyage to find them, and yet, by 1992, the same Indies – now known as South and Southeast Asia – could be synonymous with poverty and squalor? How did they go in just five centuries – the blink of an eye in terms of human time on this planet – from spaces of wealth and desire in the western imagination to a benighted third world? Why, when historical evidence shows various parts and regions of the known world were relatively equal in terms of standards of living for a long period of time, do we today inhabit a planet sharply bifurcated in terms of the quality of life?

Columbus thought a shorter and safer route to the East Indies was to be found by sailing westward.

There are many answers proffered to such questions. One common answer is that Western Europe experienced certain startling developments from about the mid-fifteenth century in science, astronomy, the reform of religion, commerce, industry, and an efflorescence of intellectual and artistic achievement that enabled it to progress rapidly in comparison to other parts of the world. Terms and concepts such as the Renaissance, Reformation, Enlightenment, scientific and industrial revolutions are seen as signposts on a journey towards modernity that Europe uniquely undertook earlier than all others and an explanation for its success and their failure. A second answer, albeit one less commonly expressed aloud today, is that lighter-skinned races are more intelligent and hard-working than peoples with darker skins: the division of the world in terms of a largely white, developed, and affluent first world and a poor, dark, and underdeveloped third world is said to be a consequence of this fact. A third common explanation is that richer countries seem to have milder climates and more abundant natural resources while poorer countries seem to have very hot and arid climates along with barren lands. Yet another explanation offered is that for whatever reason people in western countries have smaller families and consequently there's more for everyone to share whereas there are just too many people in third world countries fighting over scarce resources making each of them poorer.

For more about ideas of Renaissance, Reformation and Enlightenment see **Chapters 6, 7, 11 and 17**.

Racism is discussed in **Chapters 5, 12 and 14**.

This chapter focuses on the history and impact of colonialism as the main reason for the contemporary divide between first and third worlds – and suggests that many of the proposed explanations are underlain by this more fundamental cause. In the sections that follow, we look at an illustrative example to understand how colonialism

BOX 16.1 COLONIZER AND COLONIZED

> The conquest of the earth, which mostly means the taking it away from those who have a different complexion or slightly flatter noses than ourselves, is not a pretty thing when you look into it too much. What redeems it is the idea only. An idea at the back of it; not a sentimental pretence but an idea; and an unselfish belief in the idea – something you set up, and bow down before, and offer a sacrifice to.
>
> (Joseph Conrad, *Heart of Darkness*)

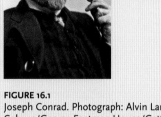

FIGURE 16.1
Joseph Conrad. Photograph: Alvin Langdon Coburn/George Eastman House/Getty Images. http://www.guardian.co.uk/books/2008/jul/05/saturdayreviewsfeatres.guardianreview25

FIGURE 16.2
Ashis Nandy. http://westheavens.net/en/ashis-nandy/

> At least six generations of the Third World have learnt to view [colonialism] as a prerequisite for their liberation. This colonialism colonizes minds in addition to bodies and it releases forces within the colonized societies to alter their cultural priorities once and for all. In the process, it helps generalize the concept of the modern West from a geographical and temporal entity to a psychological category. The West is now everywhere, within the West and outside; in structures and in minds.
>
> (Ashis Nandy, *The Intimate Enemy*)

For a discussion of colonialism in Ivory Coast see **Chapter 15**.

works – that of British India. To consider general responses we first define what we mean by colonialism, modern colonialism and its different forms. To examine broader issues raised, we look at the psychological aspects of how colonialism works. Colonialism, far from being over and in the past, continues to hold us and our futures in its thrall to this day.

ILLUSTRATIVE EXAMPLE
INDIA AND BRITAIN

While a short chapter cannot offer a full picture how colonialism works in different historical contexts, we may get a better understanding through a detailed study of one example. For this, we turn to the Indian experience with British colonialism, tracing it from its beginnings in the seventeenth century with the activities of the British East India Company.

From its creation in 1600 by a charter of Queen Elizabeth I of England, the British East India Company strove for the right to trade with India. In 1614, the company sent a representative, Sir Thomas Roe, to the Mughal Emperor Jahangir, father of Shah Jahan who built the Taj Mahal. Sir Thomas appeared as a supplicant at the court of the great Moghul, entreating him for the right to trade with India along the western coastline. At this point, the Mughal Empire was at its zenith and its sovereignty extended over nearly the entire subcontinent. Over subsequent decades, the East India Company expanded its toe-hold on the western coastline of India into a series of warehouses or factories in the southern and eastern parts of India as well. It primarily bought cheap in India – cotton textiles, silks, spices, ivory, handicrafts, and other exotic goods – and sold dear in Europe.

The East India Company's monopoly over the lucrative trade with India made it a growing power within England. Yet it was kept in restraint for at least two reasons. First, strange as it may sound to a reader in today's world, back then there was little that England produced that found a ready market in India – so the company had to pay for its purchases with gold and silver. This leak of bullion made its trade less appealing for many who entertained a mercantilist view of national wealth and power. Under mercantilism, the power of a state was seen as arising from the amount of gold and silver retained within its borders, and foreign trade was seen as a zero-sum game. So every country tried to maximize exports while keeping imports to a minimum. Second, given the enormous strength of the Mughal Empire, the company had to behave itself if its right to trade in India were to be renewed periodically.

For a discussion of the rise and decline of other empires, see **Chapters 11 and 12**.

The Mughal Empire underwent a slow decline from the 1730s on and wars of succession had further weakened it by the middle of the eighteenth century. As the power of the imperial throne in Delhi eroded, various princes, nawabs, rajahs, and other regional satraps asserted their autonomy and were soon embroiled in internecine wars over tribute and land. The East India Company, which had a well-trained military, recruited largely from the local populace, to protect its warehouses, agents and trading routes, as well as to do battle with other European rival companies in India such as the French and Portuguese, entered into these conflicts and began to play on the rivalries for its own profit. A major turning point occurred when, in the aftermath of the Battle

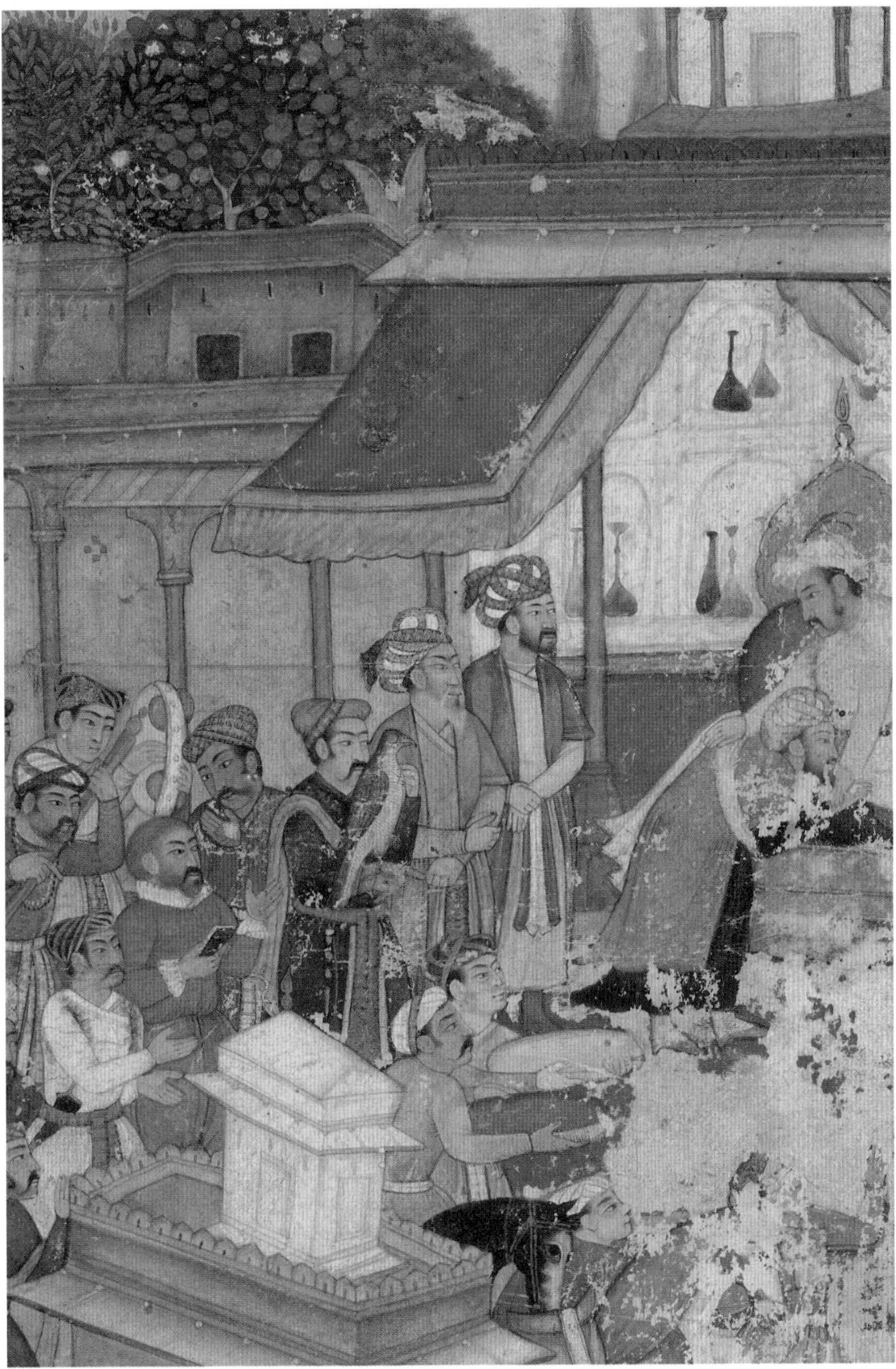

FIGURE 16.3
Jahangir investing a courtier with a robe of honour watched by Sir Thomas Roe, English ambassador to the court of Jahangir at Agra from 1615 to 1618, and others. On paper. Colophon on verso gives calligrapher's name, As`af `Ibadallah al-Rahim, and date 23 Ramadan 985/4 December 1577. http://en.wikipedia.org/wiki/Thomas_Roe

of Plassey in 1757, the East India Company acquired for itself the right to collect land revenue – as if it were a domestic political power – in the province of Bengal.

In its opportunist entry into politics, the East India Company was acting neither on behalf of nor at the behest of the British crown but incrementally and in its own short-term interests as they evolved. With the Industrial Revolution gaining momentum back in Britain, the company's army equipped itself with the latest technologies in armaments and organized itself along superior lines. Over the next hundred years, from 1757 to 1857, the company became the de facto power over an ever-widening swath of the Indian subcontinent. It used rivalries as well as instances where there was no clear heir to the throne to scheme its way to power. Its economic and political clout grew apace as it filled the vacuum left by the Mughal Empire. The viceroy of Britain's Indian colony ruled from Kolkata and outfitted himself with all the regalia and splendour of an Indian maharajah. He was assisted by an ever-expanding military of local soldiers in the British Indian army and by a fabled civil service recruited in England that rapidly became a byword for corruption and excess. Through these decades, the company raj was frequently wracked by scandal over the fortunes amassed by its officers in India. The company was especially efficient in its collection of land revenue from the Indian peasant, and the absence of close oversight from London made it accountable only to itself. In 1857 East India Company rule in India teetered on the brink of collapse as a revolt that began within the British Indian army spread through much of northern India. After months of bitter fighting across the subcontinent, company rule prevailed – but only just. In the aftermath of the revolt, formal sovereignty was handed over from the East India Company to Queen Victoria and India now became an official Crown colony.

The nearly two centuries of colonial rule in India from 1757 to 1947 saw the decisive rise of Britain to the world's leading industrial and political power, the factory of the world, and the Empire on which the sun never set – while India spiralled downwards into underdevelopment. The Indian economy was steadily extraverted – that is, transformed into a source of raw materials, agricultural commodities and minerals for the burgeoning factories of Britain, and a market for Britain's finished industrial exports. This was most dramatically seen in the textiles sector as India went from being one of the world's leading producers and exporters of cotton textiles and finished goods to being an importer of finished textiles and an exporter of raw cotton. The precise opposite occurred in Britain where many of the key inventions in the Industrial Revolution had been in the domain of spinning and weaving. Britain rapidly became a major exporter of textiles and finished goods while importing raw materials from places like India.

Capitalist industrialization in Europe is discussed in **Chapter 17**.

See the outline of Adam Smith's work in **Chapter 17**.

During the nineteenth century, Britain used its political power to impose free trade on its colonies: the very same policies that had led the thirteen American colonies to secede in 1789. Free trade had received a powerful impetus through the writings of Adam Smith and the idea of comparative advantage as argued by David Ricardo. The 'imposition of free trade' (an oxymoron or contradiction in terms if ever there was one) ensured India could not protect its domestic industries, which were being wiped out by the onslaught of cheap imports of manufactured goods from Britain. Nor could Indians establish new factories based on the import of the emerging technologies of the Industrial Revolution as the restrictions imposed by free trade meant they could not take advantage of tariffs to protect their nascent industry. The contrast with Japan,

Why might 'free trade' be a contradiction in terms? The impact of free trade policies in Ivory Coast are discussed in **Chapter 15**.

BOX 16.2 BRITAIN

In 1600, when Elizabeth I granted the charter to the East India Company, she was queen of England. Wales had been annexed to England during the reign of her father Henry VIII, who came from the Welsh Tudor dynasty. Scotland at that time was a separate kingdom, but on Elizabeth's death in 1601 her crown was inherited by James VI of Scotland, who became James I of England, bringing under one ruler the three kingdoms of England, Scotland and Ireland. Formal union of Scotland and England, and the creation of the new kingdom of Great Britain, did not take place, however, until the Acts of Union in 1707. It was not until 1801 that England, Scotland and Ireland were brought together as the United Kingdom of Great Britain and Ireland, through another act of union. In 1921, the major part of Ireland became a separate state, and the title of the British state changed in 1927 to the United Kingdom of Great Britain and Northern Ireland. A series of measures in the twentieth century and since have devolved certain regulatory and legislative powers back to the various parts of the United Kingdom, but the state remains the same, under its short title of the UK, or Britain. England, Scotland, Wales and Northern Ireland are part of the UK and not, at present, separate states.

FIGURE 16.4
Head office of the East India Company, Leadenhall Street, London, about 1800. Engraving by William Watts. Metropolitan Toronto Reference Library Board. http://www.creationism.org/books/TaylorInMindsMen/TaylorIMMa01.htm

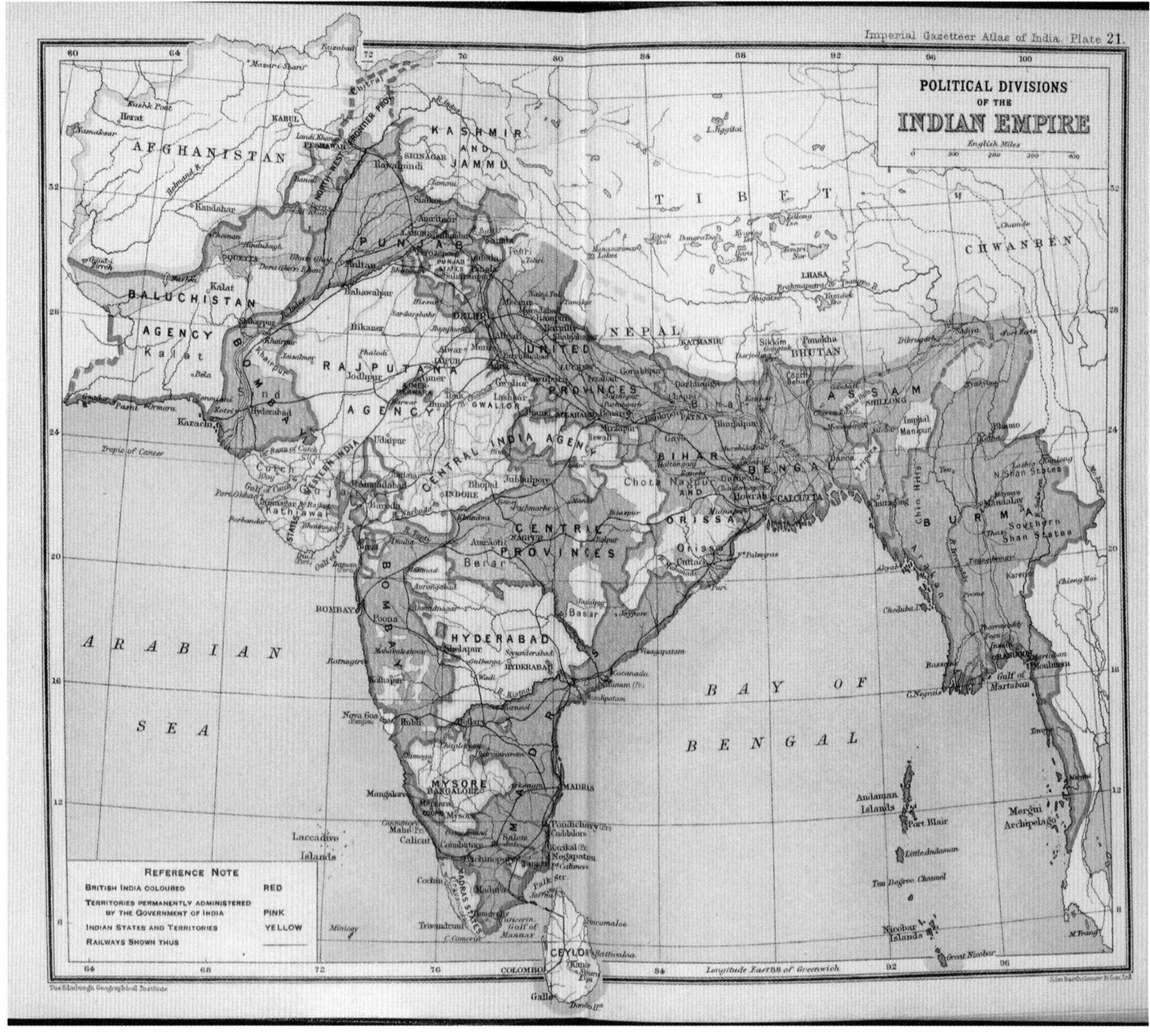

FIGURE 16.5
Map of India in 1937. British Library. http://portico.bl.uk/reshelp/images/apacfamhist/india2.jpg; http://portico.bl.uk/reshelp/images/apacfamhist/large14923.html

which successfully resisted colonialism in the nineteenth century, is arresting here. Japan protected its infant industries and imported the new technologies, rather than the products, of industrializing Europe. To many, it is no coincidence that Japan, which escaped colonialism, was also the only instance of successful economic development in the non-western world by the early twentieth century.

Fabled manufacturing towns in India like Dacca and Murshidabad went into sharp decline and the millions employed in the textiles and handicrafts industry were now out of work. Unlike England, and to some extent the rest of Britain, where those forced off the land were absorbed by factories emerging in the towns, in India, the displaced workers, artisans and craftsmen moved in the opposite direction – from towns to villages

– swelling the numbers eking a living off the land. In other words, English urbanization was paralleled by Indian ruralization. In England, the rapidly declining rural population energized the invention of technologies to make agriculture more mechanized and high-yielding. In India, the swelling population in the rural sector meant smaller holdings, more labour-intensive methods of cultivation and less inclination to innovate and use technology in agriculture. In England, urbanization and rising affluence eventually made it logical to have smaller families, whilst in India endemic poverty and ruralization made it paradoxically rational to hedge your bets on an uncertain future by having more children. Successful British economic development and Indian underdevelopment were two sides of the same coin – an interlinked process resulting in affluence on one side and poverty on the other.

Processes of urbanization and ruralization worked differently in different parts of the British Isles itself, of course. In Ireland, for example, there were parallels to what happened in India: the subdivision of rural holdings meant unsustainable subsistence agriculture and widespread famine in the mid-nineteenth century.

Colonial rule in India, intent as it was on simplifying and increasing the collection of land revenue, had instituted private property in land. It made land alienable (that is, it could be bought and sold) and replaced previously existing communal rights of access to land (a process of destroying the commons that occurred in varying ways with depressingly similar results in every part of the planet touched by capitalism and/or colonialism). It was also far more efficient in its collection of ever-increasing amounts of land revenue, irrespective of the vagaries of weather and yields, to finance a growing bureaucracy. The East India Company's increasing military adventurism all across the subcontinent and elsewhere in the British Empire further contributed to an ever-increasing demand for revenue from the Indian peasant. For instance, the British used their Indian army thrice in China between 1829 and 1856, in Persia in 1856, Singapore and Ethiopia in 1867, Hong Kong in 1868, Afghanistan in 1878, Burma in 1885, Egypt in 1882, and Uganda and the Sudan in 1896. The costs of all these expansions of empire were charged to the Indians, as were the entire costs of maintaining the Indian colonial edifice. Meanwhile, large tracts of land were converted into plantations producing tea, coffee, indigo (used as a dye for textiles), poppy (for producing opium) and other cash-crops for export – and labour conditions on the plantations, all owned by Europeans, were no better than slavery. The result was a mass of impoverished landless and small peasants on the brink of starvation, above it a narrow elite of absentee landlords, mostly native, that was the bulwark of colonial rule in the country, and at the apex an alien regime living in high style and siphoning huge amounts of wealth back to the home country.

The Occupy movement (discussed in **Chapter 18**) aims to reclaim the notion of the commons.

Contemporary slavery and its relationship to colonial practices is discussed in **Chapter 15**.

The devastation these developments caused across the Indian countryside is not as well known as it should be. In his *Late Victorian Holocausts*, Mike Davis outlines the impact in stunning detail. The collapse of the commons and notions of community due to the introduction of private property in land, climatic variations in monsoon rains due to El Niño currents, and the hegemony of ideas such as laissez-faire or free market economics with its hostility to state intervention, interacted to produce famines on an unprecedented scale in the second half of the nineteenth century. In India, China, northern Africa and Brazil mainly, Davis estimates that anywhere between 31 million and 61 million landless labourers, small farmers and their families died due to starvation. In India, these were deaths that could have been prevented: the colonial regime continued to levy high taxes on farmers, continued to export food grains out of the country rather than move them to areas of deficit, and refused to help by distributing grain because they considered that would constitute political interference in the domain of the economy.

BOX 16.3 OPIUM WARS AND THE IMPACT OF COLONIALISM ON CHINA

Ever since the inception of European trade with Asia (following the discovery of the sea-route to India by the Portuguese explorer Vasco da Gama in 1498), western powers coveted trading relations with China. Yet, through the seventeenth and eighteenth centuries, Chinese commodities such as tea, porcelain and silk were much sought after in Europe without there being any comparable demand for European goods in China. The emperors of the Ming and Qing dynasties were hostile towards international trade – they imposed heavy tariffs on European goods and severely restricted the activities of European merchants to just four ports along the southeastern flank of their empire. They were also wary of the implications of powerful trading companies for their own sovereignty. Such trade led to a drain of silver from Europe to China, something that went against mercantilist tenets. Using arguments drawn from emergent theories of free trade and Smithian liberalism, the western powers sought to break the Chinese restrictions over trade through all means legal and illegal.

One crucial way of minimizing the drain of silver on account of the China trade was for trading companies such as the East India Company to illegally export opium (grown in the Bengal Presidency after the Battle of Plassey in 1757 gave the Company control over that region) into China. Company vessels would transport the opium from Indian ports (especially Kolkata) to the southeastern Chinese coastal cities from where Chinese smugglers would take over. Opium addiction spread across southeastern China and soon the profits from this trade were reflected in the diminution of the drain of silver from England to China. By the 1820s opium (now smuggled in to the extent of close to 1,000 tons a year) threatened the Qing dynasty itself as it was riven by factions, some of whom profited greatly from the profits of the illegal

FIGURE 16.6
Lin Zexu supervising the destruction of 2.6 million tons of opium in 1839 over 26 days (3–29 June 1839) in the sea off Humen town. Destroy_opium_2.jpg_ (400 × 239 pixels, file size: 17 kb, MIME type: image/jpeg), Wikipedia commons

drug and others who saw it as the entering wedge of a western plot to destroy Chinese sovereignty. The First Opium War (1839–42) was fought after the dynamic governor-general of Hunan and Hubei, Lin Zexu, confiscated a huge cache of the illegal opium and had it destroyed; put a number of Chinese smugglers to death; and quarantined many British merchants in the port cities. The war ended with the British decisively winning, forcing the Chinese to cede Hong Kong to them under the Treaty of Nanking for a period of 150 years, and greatly 'liberalizing' Chinese trade with the west. These victories were further cemented after the Second Opium War was fought over similar issues between 1856 and 1860.

While it's obvious that British inability to penetrate Chinese markets with goods that attracted buyers, and the consequent drain of silver from Britain, were the main reasons for the Company going to war with China, such reasons were drowned in the moralistic claims of the superiority of free trade. Drug addiction was foisted upon the Chinese, and drug production forced upon the regions of Bengal and Bihar in India – all in the name of liberal economics and the common sense of laissez-faire. Few examples better illustrate the ways in which ideologies like free trade were used as instruments of colonial domination and exploitation than the Opium Wars. To the Chinese, the Treaty of Nanking and the cession of Hong Kong inaugurated what they saw as a hundred years of humiliation – ended only with the victory of the communists under Mao a century later in 1949, and today completed with China's rise to world power status.

FIGURE 16.7
Villagers in Rajputana in 1899. From the book by Mike Davies, *Late Victorian Holocausts*, Verso. http://www.fathom.com/course/10701057/139_famine.jpg; http://www.fathom.com/course/10701057/session3.html

Though such famines were routinely portrayed by colonial administrators, economists and the media as natural disasters or acts of God or nature, such claims are belied by a simple fact: neither the pre- nor post-colonial history of India show any evidence of mass deaths due to famines. They were unique to the colonial era. Davis powerfully connects all these themes together as he notes:

> We are not dealing . . . with 'lands of famine' becalmed in stagnant backwaters of world history, but with the fate of tropical humanity at the precise moment (1870–1914) when its labor and products were being dynamically conscripted into a London-centered world economy. Millions died, not outside the 'modern world system' but in the very process of being forcibly incorporated into its economic and political structures. They died in the golden age of Liberal Capitalism; indeed, many were murdered . . . by the theological application of the sacred principles of Smith, Bentham and Mill . . . Although crop failures and water shortages were of epic proportions – often the worst in centuries – there were almost always grain surpluses elsewhere in the nation or empire that could have potentially rescued drought victims. Absolute scarcity, except perhaps in Ethiopia in 1889, was never the issue. Standing between life and death instead were new-fangled commodity markets and price speculation, on one side, and the will of the state . . . on the other.
>
> (Davis 2002: 9–11)

Even against this macabre background, the Great Bengal famine of 1943–44 stands out as the definitive instance of the horrors of colonial rule in India. As three million perished to starvation in eastern India in those two years, Britain continued to export food from India to sustain her war effort against the Axis powers in the Second World War, and refused to either move food grains from surplus districts to deficit ones within India or use the state apparatus for relief. The three million who died during the Bengal famine represent about half the number of European Jews killed in the Nazi Holocaust. The latter event justly receives an enormous degree of attention in the writing of history. Yet the Bengal famine is relegated to a forgotten footnote, if mentioned at all. Recent work by historians demonstrates that the prime minister of Britain at the time, Winston Churchill, was fully aware of the scale of the Indian famine, was presented with policy actions to avert or mitigate it, and consciously chose to let it happen (Mukherjee 2011). Churchill is widely regarded as not merely an inspirational war-time leader for Britain and the Allies, but celebrated as a statesman for his defence of freedom and democracy against totalitarianism. From the perspective of Indians then and now, he should have been tried for genocide and crimes against humanity.

The oft-celebrated achievements of colonial rule turned out to be mixed blessings to put it mildly. For instance, the railways that knitted colonial India together were, mile for mile, the most expensive built anywhere in the world. They were overwhelmingly financed by revenue raised within India and the investors (all in Britain and the west) were guaranteed a minimum return on their principal, irrespective of costs, delays, profitability or problems. All the steel, locomotives, carriages, machinery and raw material were sourced in England rather than locally, as were the engineers and skilled manpower. They were built to move agricultural goods and raw materials from the interior of India to the port cities for export, and for the dissemination of English imports into the interior. The other impetus for the railway was the rapid movement of troops for the internal security of the colonizers and an expanding frontier. Both these requirements meant they did a poor job of linking the different parts of India to each other. In Britain, the construction of the railways had what economists describe as powerful forward and backward linkages to the rest of the economy: steel mills, coal mines, technical schools, engineers and craftsmen, upholsterers and carpenters, scientists and machinists, a whole ensemble of men and skills flourished in its wake. In India, the railways had no such transformative impact – the forward and backward linkages were all elsewhere.

The English language is often considered another beneficial colonial legacy and obviously it was that in many ways. But in a poor and unequal society, learning English was inevitably monopolized by a narrow elite. Wittingly or otherwise this equation of education with facility in the language of the conqueror and his culture meant the Indian elite grew alienated from its own land and people. Education itself came to be reduced to instrumental and careerist concerns, and a vehicle for the colonization of Indian minds. Similar patterns ensued on other fronts: the civil service, the Westminster-style parliamentary system, institutions such as the census, and sundry other inheritances.

FIGURE 16.8
Free India, 20 May 1947. *Daily Mail*, Leslie Gilbert Illingworth. Gandhi, and a group of protesters, including a US sympathiser, are holding placards demanding that the British get out of India. All around them are the bodies of those who have died of hunger or civil war. http://sites.google.com/site/cabinetmissionplan/illingworth-cartoons-on-india-daily-mail-uk-1942–194

Without being churlish, one could argue that every supposedly beneficial colonial inheritance had an obverse that deepened India's divisions and alienated Indians from each other and themselves.

The cumulative effect of British colonialism in India, which officially ended with independence and the partition of the subcontinent into India and Pakistan on 14–15 August 1947, was a textbook case of underdevelopment. India had been transformed from the fabled land of Columbus' imagination to a society marked by an over-populated, under-employed and technologically stagnant agrarian sector, little domestically owned industry (though some enclaves did emerge in the first half of the twentieth century), one of the lowest per capita incomes, literacy levels and life expectancy in the world, a large malnourished and physically weak population – one moreover deeply divided amongst itself on grounds of caste, class, region, language and religion, and an overall economy that was an appendage to the requirements of Britain rather than operating for the benefit of its own population. Over the same period, Britain had moved from a relatively obscure island society on the northwest shoulder of Europe to the world's hegemonic power, its greatest empire and the industrial and financial capital of the world, with one of the highest per capita incomes and standards of living. The two historical processes – Indian underdevelopment and British ascent – were inextricably interwoven. While India's experience with colonialism and underdevelopment may have been longer and more saturating than many others, in its essence this model was replicated with some variations all across the modern third world.

GENERAL RESPONSES
WHAT IS MODERN COLONIALISM?

As with many concepts in global politics, the term colonialism is defined in different and not always compatible ways by various scholars. For the purpose of this chapter, a working definition is: *Colonialism refers to the combination of economic, social, political, cultural and other policies by which an external power dominates and exploits the people, ideas and resources of an area.*

The Roman Empire is briefly discussed in **Chapter 11**, the Chinese Empire in **Chapter 12** and Spanish colonialism in **Chapters 14 and 21**.

From this definition, it is apparent that colonialism has been a part of global politics for a very long time. For example, we know that at its zenith the ancient Roman Empire extended as far as the coastline of contemporary France on the west, well into today's Britain in the north and to Persia (Iran) on its eastern flank. Other examples – the Moors (whose ambit extended from Vienna to Spain and flanked the northern and southern coastlines of the Mediterranean), the Chinese and Indian empires – show a similar geographical spread. Yet the colonialism that occurred after the discovery of the New World in 1492 by Christopher Columbus and his band of explorers funded by Spanish royalty was peculiarly devastating, incredibly thoroughgoing, and cleft the world in unprecedented and lasting ways. This post-Columbian era, that is, after 1492, will be referred to as *modern colonialism* and is the focus of this chapter.

Modern colonialism differs from previous forms of colonialism in many ways. First, all previous instances of colonial empire were invariably across the same land-mass, even if they stretched for thousands of miles. Modern colonialism hinged on advances in seafaring technology – lighter and more reliable ships and navigational techniques –

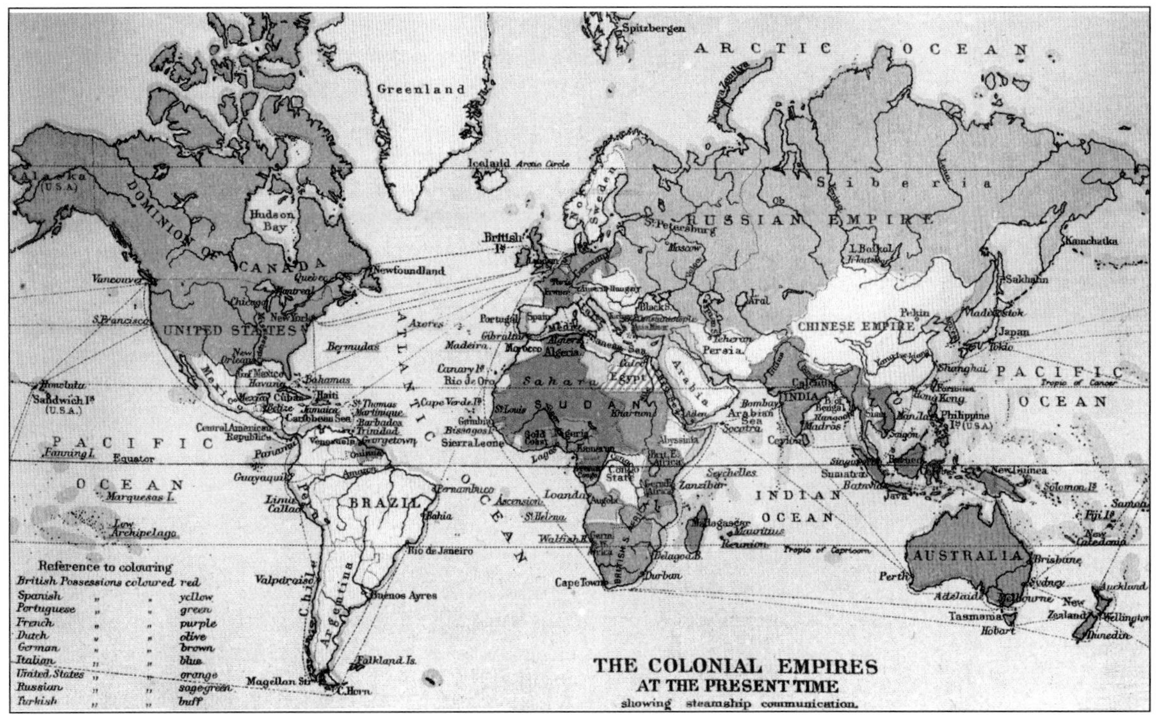

which enabled the conquest of peoples much further away. In terms of time, the very duration and saturation of modern colonialism often distinguished it from earlier epochs where colonial settlement ebbed and flowed with the strength of an individual sovereign in a distant capital ruling largely through local intermediaries. Whereas, prior to 1492, a relatively small portion of the world could be termed as being under foreign rule, on the eve of what came to be known as the First World War in 1914 as much as 90 per cent of the world's territory was under the political and economic control of a handful of European powers, Japan and the United States. Britain alone ruled as much as 20 per cent of the world's territory at this point.

FIGURE 16.9
Map of the Colonial Empires 1907. http://www.probertencyclopaedia.com/photolib/maps/Map%20of%20The%20Colonial%20Empires%201907.htm

Second, the discovery of the New World, Australia and Oceania unleashed a degree of intended and unintended violence that was unprecedented. The genocide of indigenous populations of the Americas, Australia and the Pacific islands; the depopulation of those regions due to diseases against which they had no immunity; and the forced movement of millions of Africans as slaves to the plantations and mines of the New World (the first Africans were transported across the Atlantic as early as 1498) and the enslavement of the surviving indigenes meant colonialism in the post-Columbian era was of a very different order from any that preceded it. To give two examples of the impact: the indigenous population of pre-contact Brazil was estimated at about five million, while today they number only about 330,000 (Young 2001: 1). Similarly, the native population of the Hawaiian islands, which had been somewhere between 800,000 and 1,000,000 in 1778 when Captain James Cook arrived, had declined to as few as 50,000 a century later (Stannard 1993).

Third, the advent of capitalism as a mode of production and the Industrial Revolution, both of which began in the late eighteenth to early nineteenth centuries in Britain and the northwestern shelf of the European continent and spread to other western countries and the United States in turn, was of enormous consequence. Capitalism and the Industrial Revolution meant earlier, small or quantitative differences in technological and agrarian productivity, armaments and economic efficiency between Europe and the rest of the world now exploded into a qualitative difference that fractured the planet as a whole. Pre-Columbian forms of colonialism could be charged at best with xenophobia or ethnocentrism, and violence necessitated by the dictates of conquest. Modern colonialism, intertwined as it was with that most dynamic and exploitative system of economic organization – capitalism – justified itself on the basis of a total racial, economic, cultural, religious and political superiority of the west over the rest of the world. This notion of an enduring and divinely ordained civilizational destiny for the west energized and justified genocide, racism, economic exploitation and cultural contempt on a scale hitherto unseen. Two macro-historical works that depict the inter-related emergence of capitalism and colonialism on a world scale are Frank (1978) and Stavrianos (1981).

For a discussion of how capitalism produces and sustains inequality, see **Chapter 19**.

The fact that modern colonialism was inextricable from capitalism and the Industrial Revolution meant western ethnocentrism could now parade successfully as universalism. Europe, and fragments of it in settler colonies such as the United States, arrogated to itself the right to interpret the world for everyone everywhere and for all time – past, present and future. In essence, this meant today's Europe was the ideal tomorrow for the rest of the world and the future of the planet was for Europe to determine. European concepts and categories were the means by which everyone everywhere could and did understand themselves and their likely futures. Eurocentrism is ethnocentrism on the steroids of capitalism and industrialism (for more on this, see Chakrabarty 2000).

Chapter 20 talks about the way European forms of modernity are presented as the only ones.

While the histories of British, French, German, Dutch, Belgian, Spanish, Portuguese and American (not to mention Russian or Japanese) colonialisms were enormously diverse in both time and space, one can for reasons of simplicity distinguish between two main forms: settler colonies and domination or exploitation colonies. The main examples of settler colonies would be the United States, Canada, Australia, New Zealand, Rhodesia (today's Zimbabwe), apartheid South Africa, Algeria and a few others. These were territories annexed by Europeans with a view to settling a part of the home country's own population there in a permanent fashion. Settler colonies dispossessed the natives of their lands through extermination of the natives; treaties of dubious legality; the idea of private property and cultivation as the only proper legal form of land ownership; economic deprivation; military conquest and forced internment on reservations; and disease.

The concept of a settler colony radically revises our understanding of the United States, Canada or Australia. For example, far from being a bastion of freedom, democracy, individual rights and anti-colonialism, whose founding is dated to 1776 with the Declaration of Independence penned by Thomas Jefferson, the US, from this perspective, remains a settler colony whose ongoing history is that of an occupier of native American land. As historians like Howard Zinn and authors like Toni Morrison emphasize, the story of the United States properly begins not in 1776 or 1789 at the conclusion of its 'family squabble' (Byrd 2011: 2) with King George's Britain, but rather in 1492 with the extermination of the native American and the enslavement of the black in the new world. By the same logic, the future history of the United States could conceivably move in the direction of the freedom of its indigenous peoples – the native Americans – and others, such as the Hawaiians – as they liberate themselves from colonialism. From this same perspective, Israel would be seen as an example of settler colonialism inaugurated in 1948 with the dispossession of the indigenous Palestinian people and the establishment of a Jewish state dominated by those of European descent.

The implications and continuing impact of this history in the contemporary US are discussed in **Chapter 13**.

Domination or exploitation colonies are territories that were annexed for trade and commercial activities but with no intent of settling there permanently. Such colonies were often no less violent or racist in terms of their treatment of the indigenous populations. For instance, though Belgium ruled the Congo for barely a few decades, historians estimate the death toll of Africans during that interlude to exceed eight million (Hochschild 1999). But for climatic and other reasons these colonies were not regarded as worthy of long-term settlement for Europeans. The British in South Asia (India, Pakistan, Bangladesh and Sri Lanka), Southeast Asia (Burma, Malaysia and Singapore), East Africa (Kenya, Uganda), the Caribbean (Barbados, Trinidad, Guyana, Jamaica) and the Pacific (Fiji); the Dutch in Indonesia; the French in the Middle East, North Africa (Algeria) and Southeast Asia (Vietnam); the Belgians in Central Africa (Congo); the Spanish and the Portuguese in the southern cone of Africa or the Philippines; the Japanese in Korea and Manchuria; and Germany and Italy in parts of Africa are all examples of domination colonies.

For a discussion of the continuing impact of French colonialism in Côte d'Ivoire, see **Chapter 15**.

One provocative way of explaining the difference between settler colonies, such as the United States and Australia on the one hand, and domination colonies, such as British India or Dutch Indonesia on the other, would be to say that in the former the indigenous populations were largely ethnically cleansed by genocide and the rest forced onto reservations, leaving the country free for white occupation, while in the latter, since there were too many of the locals to begin with, colonialism contented itself with political, economic and cultural domination without permanent settlement or mass emigration.

As with any typology that attempts to capture a complex global history, these definitions are imperfect. For example, nineteenth-century China was colonized in the sense that western powers signed a series of treaties with various port cities that enabled them to establish a colonial pattern of economic and other relations. Yet the Chinese emperor retained political sovereignty in Beijing into the early decades of the twentieth century and no one country managed to colonize China in the way India was colonized by Britain. The length and depth of the colonial experience also varied greatly across these examples, and our typology does not quite capture other instances such as colonies that were exclusively plantations or islands that were trading platforms.

The distinction also does not fully capture the Latin American experience, which was in some ways a combination of settler and exploitation colonialism. It was settler colonialism in the sense that large numbers of Spanish and Portuguese emigrants colonized the continent beginning in 1492 and were followed by tens of thousands of other Europeans in the centuries after that lived there permanently. Millions of indigenous Latin American Indians were exterminated and the countries were exploited economically for the benefit of Spain and Portugal. Gradually, these settlers of European/Iberian origin gained political independence from Spain and Portugal, as the

For more on Latin America, see **Chapter 14**.

thirteen colonies of the United States did from Britain, but, for a variety of reasons, the comprador elites of Latin America were unable to successfully develop as independent economies the way the United States did through its more nationalist elite.

Latin America became part of the third world and was a colony as far as its relations with Europe and the United States were concerned. In this sense, it was an exploitation colony at the mercy of more powerful western nations. However, the settler colonial legacy is evident in the fact that, to this day, the political, economic, social and cultural elite of Latin America are overwhelmingly of Iberian/European ancestry while the bulk of the population is a mixture of native peoples, black Africans, and other racial groups such as the Chinese, Japanese and East Indians who were brought there to work on plantations. To put it crudely, the higher one moves up the class ladder in Latin America, the whiter the population and the lower one moves down that same ladder, the darker the people.

The way this legacy affects the various racial groups in Argentina is discussed in **Chapter 14**.

BROADER ISSUES
THE PSYCHOLOGY OF COLONIALISM

So far the chapter has concentrated on the economic dimensions of colonialism, and used India as an illustration. However, the colonial encounter had an impact on the psyche of both colonizer and colonized: neither came to the encounter already made or constituted, as it were. Internal colonialism is at least as dangerous as external colonialism, and colonial ways of thinking have consequences for humanity and our planet as a whole.

For a discussion of the dynamic constitution of identity, see **Chapter 5**.

Given the scale of devastation caused by colonialism, it may be counter-intuitive to suggest colonialism was more damaging to the colonizer than to the colonized. Yet that radical thought constitutes our point of departure in this section. Colonialism demanded of the colonizer an immense effort to repress thoughts contrary to the enterprise of domination. It required unremitting faith in one's own racial superiority, masculinity and civilizing mission. Yet the inescapable fact was that it was fellow human beings who were victims of this violence – and doubt always crept through the defences. Observers as varied as Joseph Conrad, Mahatma Gandhi, Aime Césaire, Hannah Arendt, Frantz Fanon, Albert Camus, Ashis Nandy and Martin Luther King Jr have noted that colonial violence invariably came back to haunt the colonizer and their society in deep and fundamental ways. Césaire argues that what was distinctive about the Holocaust and the violence of the Second World War was neither its scale nor barbarity but merely that Europeans were doing to each other what they had been doing to non-whites in the colonies for centuries.

Ambivalence and mimicry

The ambivalence at the core of the colonial project can be understood by a foray into science. An important aspect of western domination and self-confidence arose from its evident mastery over nature through science and the scientific method (Adas 1990; Prakash 1999). In India, for example, the British justified their rule at least in part by their claim to a superior scientific rationality. Their successes were presented to the

BOX 16.4 'SHOOTING AN ELEPHANT', BY GEORGE ORWELL

In his book *Burmese Days*, George Orwell writes of his time as a young police officer in an isolated village in colonial Burma. One day an elephant ran amok, destroying property and trampling a villager. As the sole possessor of a rifle in the village, and the embodiment of order, Orwell was expected to shoot the beast. Yet, this was hardly the right thing to do, as elephants routinely have such bouts of '*mast*' and return to normality shortly thereafter. Here is Orwell's account:

FIGURE 16.10
George Orwell. Photo: Bettmann/Corbis

> But at that moment I glanced round at the crowd that had followed me. It was an immense crowd, two thousand at the least and growing every minute. It blocked the road for a long distance on either side. I looked at the sea of yellow faces above the garish clothes-faces all happy and excited over this bit of fun, all certain that the elephant was going to be shot. They were watching me as they would watch a conjurer about to perform a trick. They did not like me, but with the magical rifle in my hands I was momentarily worth watching. And suddenly I realized that I should have to shoot the elephant after all. The people expected it of me and I had got to do it; I could feel their two thousand wills pressing me forward, irresistibly. And it was at this moment, as I stood there with the rifle in my hands, that I first grasped the hollowness, the futility of the white man's dominion in the East. Here was I, the white man with his gun, standing in front of the unarmed native crowd – seemingly the leading actor of the piece; but in reality I was only an absurd puppet pushed to and fro by the will of those yellow faces behind. I perceived in this moment that when the white man turns tyrant it is his own freedom that he destroys. He becomes a sort of hollow, posing dummy, the conventionalized figure of a sahib. For it is the condition of his rule that he shall spend his life in trying to impress the 'natives,' and so in every crisis he has got to do what the 'natives' expect of him. He wears a mask, and his face grows to fit it. I had got to shoot the elephant. I had committed myself to doing it when I sent for the rifle. A sahib has got to act like a sahib; he has got to appear resolute, to know his own mind and do definite things. To come all that way, rifle in hand, with two thousand people marching at my heels, and then to trail feebly away, having done nothing – no, that was impossible. The crowd would laugh at me. And my whole life, every white man's life in the East, was one long struggle not to be laughed at.
>
> (George Orwell, *Burmese Days*. Available at http://www.online-literature.com/orwell/887/)

Orwell's predicament is emblematic of colonialism: it traduces the humanity of the colonizer, brings out some of the worst qualities of his society, represses his ethical and humane instincts, and alienates him from his fellow beings – all in the name of doing the right thing.

awestruck natives as spectacle: electricity, railways, dams, bridges that spanned giant rivers, the radio, vaccination and so on. Yet underlying this was a vexing contradiction: in order for these achievements to be appreciated as science, the native had to be regarded as a rational, logical and intelligent discerning human being capable of such genuine comprehension. On the other hand, if the native really could appreciate western science, then the entire set of beliefs that marked the native out as irremediably inferior and irrational had to be questioned, and with that the colonial project as a whole. Colonialism was steeped in an ambivalence that sought recognition of western superiority in the eyes of the colonized, and yet was incapable of being satisfied by such recognition, because the native was seen as unreliable, sly and a liar to begin with. This tight triangle – of wanting to be appreciated by the native for one's dexterity with science, but being unable to secure such appreciation because the very structure of colonial rule pre-empted it – followed by the self-hatred that comes from wanting such appreciation in the first place – is a recipe for paranoia on the part of the colonizer, and its frequent culmination in violence is depressingly predictable. The postcolonial theorist Homi Bhabha renders this triangle succinctly:

This idea of the human being as rational is also noted in **Chapter 6**.

> The frustrated wish 'I want him to love me,' turns into its opposite 'I hate him' and thence, through projection and exclusion of the first person, 'He hates me'.
> (Bhabha 1994: 100)

Caught in a game impossible to win, the natives develop their own strategies for surviving colonialism. Amongst them is what Bhabha insightfully analyses as mimicry. The native's excessive submissiveness, exaggerated forms of deference and overenthusiastic appreciation of the colonizer in the course of this mimicry continually threaten to slip into mockery and parody. It turns menacing to the colonizer as colonial rule had always hinged on the seriousness with which colonizer and colonized play their respective roles. Mimicry is a strategy of survival, a weapon of the weak, and is in that sense an ethically justifiable response by the native to a situation in which one is structurally disadvantaged. This means the native can be at peace with themselves – unlike the colonizer, to whom mimicry is a constant reminder of the fragility of their rule despite all their military, economic, political and cultural superiority.

Orwell's insight is that the ultimate fear of every colonizer is the fear of being laughed at or mocked.

Hybridity

Colonialism was ultimately an enterprise that sought to render the native and his society transparent and comprehensible. And on this count, it was always doomed to failure. Consider the predicament of Alexander Duff, a Christian missionary in nineteenth-century India. Despite decades of effort, Duff was constantly besieged by doubts about the efficacy or even the possibility of converting Hindus and others to Christianity. Translating the gospel into a domestic idiom always seemed to imperil the text and its intent. For example, when Duff expressed the idea that conversion to Christianity was a form of rebirth for the native, this was immediately decoded by the latter as a variation on Hindu ideas of reincarnation. Every idea or concept that Duff could put forward as Christian found an analogue in the infinite corpus of Indian religions that threatened to envelop it, alter its meaning and translate it beyond recognition.

The very possibility of conversion was derailed by the fact that Duff was not preaching or inscribing on a 'tabula rasa' or blank sheet but on native terrain that was preoccupied. It was preoccupied in at least two senses of that word: (a) the attention of the native was elsewhere – he was perhaps instrumentally calculating that appearing to convert to Christianity might net him some tangible benefits in the here and now; and (b) his mind was already thoroughly inscribed with the religious beliefs of his own traditions and every new and incoming idea from Duff could do no more than commingle with them, but could never replace them.

Colonialism therefore does not produce clones of the colonizer among the colonized, which would in any case destabilize the identity of the colonizer in unacceptable ways, nor does it leave the native untouched by its impact. Rather, it produces a hybrid space that is neither one nor the other (Bhabha 1994). Hybridity refers to this third space that is not an anodyne synthesis of the ideas and beliefs of the colonizer and the colonized but is something qualitatively different from either – a productive and aesthetic space, a new cultural formation replete with all the doubt, ambivalence, split-selves and alienated beings that comprise the colonial interface. Neither the culture of the colonizer nor colonized can be spoken of in some pristine form prior to their engagement with each other, but rather both emerge from it.

An ambivalence of a different yet similar sort is discussed in the account of exile given in **Chapter 13**.

Two examples help to illustrate this idea of colonialism as a joint social formation. The first is the way some of the earliest syllabuses on English literature emerged not at Oxford or Cambridge, the quintessential English universities, but rather in colonial universities and schools and in institutions set up to train English civil servants to represent the country abroad (Viswanathan 1989). Until the advent of modern colonialism, when Britain was called upon to represent itself as a civilized society with an ancient lineage, there had been no need to define its literature in terms of a heritage or canon. It was the colonial encounter that constituted the provocation to define what it meant to be essentially English: it was colonialism that produced the content of what it means to be literate in English literature today.

In similar vein, British policy against the practice of widow self-immolation (sati) in India was an act of British self-fashioning as civilized against Indians as barbaric and worthy of colonization (Mani 1998). Understandings of the practice of sati emerged out of interactions between colonial officials and Indian Brahmins or pundits, who now became the authoritative interpreters of something called Hindu tradition and scripture. As a result, there occurred a freezing and codification of the practice of sati itself, and of a diverse and subcontinent-wide set of practices into a unity called 'Hindu religion', which established the hegemony of Brahmins to speak for this Hinduism at all times and places. We actually know little about sati in pre-colonial times and it may have varied enormously across the space we now know as India. Once again, it was colonialism that was producing the content of categories – India, England, Hindu – that are seen nowadays as concepts or entities that predated colonialism.

What is also striking is that women had hardly any voice in the contentious debate over sati in colonial India. Instead, they were spoken *for* by various men: white colonial officials on a civilizing mission; Hindu priests (all or mostly Brahmin); Indian nationalists (upper caste and speaking for all of India), each with their own agenda. The widow becomes a site for the production of English civilization, Hindu tradition, independent India, and a variety of other projects, but her own voice is left out of the picture. Yet claims about the indigeneity of sati and its iconic role as a signifier of India become dubious given that we have little or no ability to recover an Indian past outside the lenses of colonialism.

Colonialism is best regarded as a joint social formation that produces the identity and content of both colonizer and colonized, rather than the domination of one already constituted entity over another. The work of Indian social theorist Ashis Nandy is especially insightful in this regard. Nandy points out that colonialism often seemed to be a pact between certain sections of both colonizer and colonized societies at the expense of others in them (Nandy 1983). In both societies, colonialism emphasized hyper-masculine, hetero-normative, and rationalist acquisitive values at the expense of the feminine, spiritual, queer and subaltern groups. This emphasis was portrayed as necessary to succeed and modernize in a competitive and social Darwinist world. The colonized middle classes embarked on modernizing their societies and becoming the new colonial masters. Decades of so-called independent economic development in societies such as India and elsewhere in the third world have been extraordinarily violent in their treatment of indigenous peoples, tribals, the poor and the environment as postcolonial elites have pursued industrialization, national security and modernity with all the zealousness of a recent convert.

For more on sustainable development and its critics, see **Chapter 4**.

In speaking of colonialism as something that is no longer a western malady but a planetary affliction, Nandy's work dovetails with critics of mega-development and proponents of sustainable development and deep ecology. He argues that it may be the so-called defeated subcultures and civilizations of this world that have managed to retain the values, skills and worldviews necessary for the survival of our planet and species. These subcultures are not burdened with the Orwellian civilizational responsibility and have retained a humility that may yet save us. Decolonization is not so much a political project as it is a slow and multifaceted unlearning of industrial, capitalist modernization itself (see Krishna 2009).

CONCLUSION

After a brief period during the heyday of decolonization from 1945 to 1970 in which colonialism was regarded as a sorry chapter in the history of the world, it has now become fashionable again to express nostalgia for the supposed stability and progress made under its aegis. The developmental failures, military dictatorships and failed states that litter Africa are particularly favoured as reasons for a new spell of enlightened western despotism. The *Washington Post*'s Sebastian Mallaby and Harvard historian Niall Ferguson are only two of many distinguished commentators who have explicitly favoured some western nations agreeing once again to shoulder the white man's burden in parts of the benighted third world.

Why some people think they know what is good for others is the subject of **Chapter 21**.

Chapter 28 explores the idea that western lives are represented as 'grievable', whereas non-Western lives are not.

What such misplaced nostalgia forgets, or perhaps never knew, is the incredible violence and destruction of humans that accompanied colonialism. The amnesia about the colossal scale of killings is matched today by the relative inattention to the Iraqi and Afghani war dead in the conflicts since the early 1990s. The first Gulf War in 1992 resulted in the deaths of between 100,000 to 200,000 Iraqi soldiers and civilians. This was in comparison to the 400 casualties suffered by the US-led Allied forces, mostly on

BOX 16.5 RESURRECTING EMPIRE

In his recent book of this title, Rashid Khalidi begins a chapter on contemporary US military intervention into Iraq and the Middle East with three epigraphs: one from the Napoleonic invasion of Egypt in 1798, the second from the British invasion of Iraq in 1917, and the third from Donald Rumsfeld, US secretary of defense, during the Second Gulf War of 2003 (Khalidi 2004: 37):

> Oh ye Egyptians, they may say to you that I have not made an expedition hither for any other object than that of abolishing your religion . . . but tell the slanderers that I have not come to you except for the purpose of restoring your rights from the hands of the oppressors.
>
> (Napoleon Bonaparte, Alexandria, 2 July 1798)

> Our armies do not come into your cities and lands as conquerors or enemies, but as liberators . . . it is the hope and desire of the British people and the nations in alliance with them that the Arab race may rise once more to greatness and renown among the peoples of the earth.
>
> (General F. S. Maude, commander of British forces, Baghdad, 19 March 1917)

> Unlike many armies in the world, you came not to conquer, not to occupy, but to liberate, and the Iraqi people know this.
>
> (Donald Rumsfeld, US secretary of defense, Baghdad, 29 April 2003)

All three quotes are eerily similar, essentially saying the same thing, namely: the west is intervening in the Middle East out of benevolence, not out of greed; they do not covet their riches but are there to help the people of these regions overcome autocrats; and they will flourish under the benevolent guidance of the west.

The durability and ethnocentrism of the idea that some people know what is good for others in these quotes separated by 200 years should tell us that colonialism and its mindset are alive and well.

account of friendly fire. This was not so much a war as a massacre, especially since it is now evident that many Iraqi soldiers were killed as they were trying to surrender. The death toll in the second Gulf War initiated by George W. Bush to overthrow the Saddam regime and establish an enduring set of US military bases in that country has exceeded 110,000.

Even these tens of thousands of deaths pale in comparison with what ensued during the interregnum between the two Gulf wars, a period when so-called liberal globalists such as Bill Clinton in the US and Tony Blair in the UK were heads of state. The embargo on Iraq, enacted with the support of the United Nations, is estimated

Chapter 23 discusses the impact of attempts to control terrorist financing in Pakistan on relief efforts during the floods in 2010.

to have caused the deaths of anywhere between half a million and one million Iraqis. The majority of these preventable deaths were those of infants, affected disproportionately by the absence of drugs and medicines under the embargo. The US repeatedly used its veto in the UN Security Council whenever any attempt was made to either lift the embargo or exclude such items as medical supplies. Three successive UN administrators in charge of the Iraqi embargo resigned, with one of them saying 'We are in the process of destroying an entire society. It is as simple and terrifying as that. It is illegal and immoral' (Mamdani 2004: 192).

As we conclude this chapter on how colonialism works, it would be wise to ask a simple question: why is it that violent death and destruction on such a scale continue to occur, and why is it that all too many of us seem to regard these as little more than aberrations in an otherwise normal world? In some part, the answer to that question lies in the history of modern colonialism. A legacy of this history has been to render the mass slaughter of people in places like Iraq and Afghanistan inconsequential. A variety of explicit and implicit pieties are invoked as we turn our eyes away: it's a small price to pay for the maintenance of global order; there are far too many of them for such deaths to matter in the first place; they would have slaughtered each other in such numbers whether or not we had intervened because war is all they know; force is the only language they understand and regrettable though it may be, war is a means of keeping them in line; and so on. Decades after the official decolonization of much of the world, it is depressingly evident that colonialism continues to work all too well in our world. However, it may be wise to remember that modern colonialism was also resisted at every point – from the very first encounters in the New World until the present moment. In the struggles for sustainable development, for the rights of the indigenous peoples all across the world, and in the movements to resist the power of corporate capitalism, we can discern the anticolonial impulse that has always been the tethered shadow of domination.

FURTHER READING

Hamza Alavi and Teodor Shanin (eds) (1982) *Introduction to the Sociology of 'Developing Societies'*, London: Macmillan.

This edited volume contains many of the classic essays that define colonialism, underdevelopment, imperialism, etc.

Samir Amin (1988) *Eurocentrism*, London: Zed Books.

A neo-Marxist work that embeds the emergence and rise of Eurocentrism in the history of capitalism and the rise of Europe to material dominance in the world.

Partha Chatterjee (reissued 1993) *Nationalist Thought and the Colonial World: A Derivative Discourse?* London: Zed Books.

This book demonstrates the degree to which anti-colonial nationalism in third world countries such as India remained trapped within the narrative of a European idea of modernization.

Frantz Fanon (1986) *Black Skin, White Masks*, trans. Charles Lam Markmann, London: Pluto (Original 1952).

A work that interweaves colonialism and racism, and is a brutally frank depiction on how both reduce us as human beings.

Andre Gunder Frank (1969) *Capitalism and Underdevelopment in Latin America: A Historical Survey of Chile and Brazil*, New York: Monthly Review Press.
Frank was one of the earliest and most forceful exponents of dependency theory. In this book he shows how Latin American economies prospered whenever their linkages to the Euro-American world were severed – and conversely were exploited and under-developed whenever those linkages were close and strong.

Mohandas Gandhi (1997) *Hind Swaraj and Other Writings*, Anthony Parel (ed.), Cambridge: Cambridge University Press (Original 1909).
A brilliant and prescient work that argued that industrial civilization and modernity, far from being desirable futures, were destroying the world. Many contemporary ideas such as sustainability are cogently presented by Gandhi in this work.

C. L. R. James (1980) *The Black Jacobins: Toussaint L'Ouverture and the San Domingo Revolution*, London: Allison and Busby (Original 1938).
Centred on the Haitian Revolution (1791–1804), James shows how L'Ouverture was in every way truer to the ideals of the French Revolution than were the French themselves.

Karl Marx and Friedrich Engels (1968) *On Colonialism*, 4th edition, Moscow: Progress Publishers.
For all the brilliance and verve of his analysis of capitalism, Marx was in many ways unremittingly orientalist and Eurocentric when it came to colonialism. In these essays, Marx describes British colonialism as the violent and unwitting instrument of history that would drag 'backward' societies such as India and China into the modern, capitalist world and hence liberate them from oriental despotisms.

Uday Singh Mehta (1999) *Liberalism and Empire: A Study in British Thought*, Chicago: University of Chicago Press.
This nuanced study shows how liberal ideas, far from contradicting imperialism and conquest, in fact enabled them in late eighteenth and nineteenth-century Britain.

Walter Rodney (1972) *How Europe Underdeveloped Africa*, Nairobi: Heinemann.
A Marxist analysis that shows the long-term effects of the slave trade, predatory capitalism and racism on African poverty and European wealth.

Edward Said (1978) *Orientalism*, New York: Vintage.
This work demonstrates how European perceptions of the Middle East – and of Islam – are inseparable from the history of western colonialism in this region. It further demonstrates the continuing legacy of this mode of thinking in contemporary US and western policy towards the Middle East.

Mrinalini Sinha (1995) *Colonial Masculinity: The 'Manly Englishman' and the 'Effeminate Bengali' in the Late Nineteenth Century*, Manchester: Manchester University Press.
Analysing imperialism and colonialism as a joint social formation, Sinha argues that much of what we think of today as quintessentially 'English' or 'Indian' actually emerged during the colonial encounter rather than pre-dating it.

Immanuel Wallerstein (1974–1989) *The Modern World System*, 3 volumes, New York: Academic Press.
These works consistently and robustly argue that capitalism can be understood only as a world-systemic or global phenomenon over the *longue durée*, and that the nation-state distorts or fractures our understanding in important ways.

WEBSITE

http://ipcs.org.au/
According to their website, the Institute of Postcolonial Studies 'is an independent organization located in Melbourne, Australia. It is committed to advancing the recognition of cultural difference, and encouraging mutual engagement and reconciliation.'

REFERENCES

Adas, Michael (1990) *Machines as the Measure of Men: Science, Technology and Ideologies of Western Dominance*, Ithaca, NY: Cornell University Press.

Bhabha, Homi (1994) *The Location of Culture*, London: Routledge.

Byrd, Jodi (2011) *The Transit of Empire: Indigenous Critiques of Colonialism*, Minneapolis: University of Minnesota Press.

Chakrabarty, Dipesh (2000) *Provincializing Europe: Postcolonial Thought and Historical Difference*, Princeton, NJ: Princeton University Press.

Conrad, Joseph (2012) *Heart of Darkness*, London: Penguin Classics.

Davis, Mike (2002) *Late Victorian Holocausts: El Niño Famines and the Making of the Third World*, London: Verso.

Frank, Andre Gunder (1978) *World Accumulation, 1492–1789*, London: Macmillan.

Hochschild, Adam (1999) *King Leopold's Ghost: A Story of Greed, Terror, and Heroism in Colonial Africa*, Boston: Mariner Books.

Khalidi, Rashid (2004) *Resurrecting Empire: Western Footprints and America's Perilous Path in the Middle East*, Boston: Beacon Press.

Krishna, Sankaran (2009) *Globalization and Postcolonialism: Hegemony and Resistance in the 21st Century*, Lanham, MD: Rowman and Littlefield.

Mamdani, Mahmood (2004) *Good Muslim, Bad Muslim: America, the Cold War and the Roots of Terror*, New York: Doubleday.

Mani, Lata (1998) *Contentious Traditions: The Debate on Sati in Colonial India*, Berkeley: University of California Press.

Mukherjee, Madhusree (2011) *Churchill's Secret War: The British Empire and the Ravaging of India during World War II*, New York: Basic Books.

Nandy, Ashis (1983) *The Intimate Enemy: Loss and Recovery of Self Under Colonialism*, New Delhi: Oxford University Press.

Prakash, Gyan (1999) *Another Reason: Science and the Imagination of Modern India*, Princeton, NJ: Princeton University Press.

Stannard, David (1993) *American Holocaust: The Conquest of the New World*, New York: Oxford University Press.

Stavrianos, L. S. (1981) *Global Rift: The Third World Comes of Age*, New York: William Morrow.

Viswanathan, Gauri (1989) *Masks of Conquest: Literary Study and British Rule in India*, New York: Columbia University Press.

Young, Robert (2001) *Postcolonialism: An Historical Introduction*, Oxford: Blackwell.

For a range of further resources supporting this chapter, please visit the companion website for *Global Politics, 2nd Edition* at www.routledge.com/cw/edkins/

CHAPTER 17

How is the world organized economically?

V. Spike Peterson

THE QUESTION
FROM LOCAL MARKETS TO GLOBAL POLITICAL ECONOMY

We begin with the apparently easy question: What is economics? A simple answer is that economics is the study of the production and distribution of goods and wealth. Like most dictionary definitions, this gets us started – but what do the additional words in the definition mean? They look reasonably familiar: production is about 'making' things, distribution is about 'dividing things up', and goods are various sorts of things, usually the kinds we can see or use (plates, watches, trucks). Wealth is a bit trickier: it may refer to 'money' generally, or more specifically to 'financial investments' – like stocks and bonds. Or it may refer to 'riches' in the broadest possible sense.

People have been making and exchanging goods for at least several thousand years, but they did not think about this in terms of the whole world. Indeed, *they did not think about this as 'economics'*. The earliest markets were areas where people came together to simply exchange one good – primarily food or functional items – for another.

Because transportation was difficult, only goods considered very valuable were worth carrying long distances. For most of human history then, markets were quite small, goods were primarily local, and exchanges in the market were simply part of reproducing everyday life. In other words, exchange activities were embedded in social relations more generally; like growing food or preparing meals, there was no reason to think about 'economics' separately.

As long as belief in and practices of subsistence agriculture prevailed, the scale and effects of markets were limited. During the Middle Ages in Europe such feudal conditions involved a complex web of kingdoms and other sites of power. Monarchs granted noblemen rights to land in return for loyalty and military services. Noblemen could in turn grant land to those who served them. The vast majority of people, called peasants, lived on and worked the land owned by others. Reciprocity was the norm: estate-owners granted access to land-based resources in return for military services and agricultural labour and products. Goods produced through agriculture and market activities in towns were important for funding military exploits, but cultural norms and aristocratic expropriation of wealth made the pursuit of profit for private gain quite difficult. An additional site of power was the Christian Church, with the pope at its head; this provided over-arching moral authority and constituted perhaps the most significant unifying cultural force.

For a map that shows what Europe looked like in the Middle Ages see **Chapter 11**.

From roughly the fifteenth century, Europeans built upon inventions and developments elsewhere to move from this decentralized system of agricultural production to state-centric and technologically enhanced forms of capitalist industrialization. The shift involved profound changes in people's identities, ways of thinking, and ways of structuring human behaviour. Centralizing European states promoted capitalist arrangements that favoured the accumulation of wealth by a minority, whose decision-making power shaped the choices of and resources available to the majority. Eventually, capitalist markets extended worldwide. To answer our chapter's question we must therefore familiarize ourselves with this transition. The following highly simplified account emphasizes changes that are especially important for understanding *today's* global political economy:

- the role of states in creating capitalist markets,
- how technologies matter,
- how work is organized, and
- whose work is valued.

For a discussion of states and nations and how we come to think of them as inextricably linked into 'nation-states' see **Chapters 11 and 12**.

Increasing consolidation of power in nation-states altered loyalties as well as 'economics'. Church-based authority declined due to religious debates, the development of rationalist thinking, and a new sense of human control over social and physical forces. From roughly the sixteenth century, centralized states adopted mercantilist policies to enhance their wealth through foreign exploration, trade, appropriation, slavery, plantation economies, and military conquest. Internally, mercantilism promoted positive trade balances (more exports than imports) and protection of domestic production; externally, it increased aggressive exploitation of 'new' lands and prompted conflicts as European powers fought over control of markets.

Rationalist thinking has been extremely important since the Enlightenment, which is discussed in **Chapter 6**. The decline in the significance of church-based authority is also explored in **Chapter 7**.

The effects of these developments on countries colonized by European powers are discussed in **Chapters 15 and 16**.

After the eighteenth century, capitalist industrialization consolidated and extended European power. As long as animals, humans, wind and flowing water were the only sources of energy, forms of power and production remained limited. The industrializing transition to making machines and harnessing steam power had vast consequences. The power of merchants who traded goods faded in favour of industrial capitalists who invested in machines and factory production that enabled greater productivity. Lives and landscapes were forever changed. Labour was increasingly commodified: peasants were driven off of or drawn from the land by new policies enforced by states; without access to land, they were compelled to become wage workers (referred to as members of the proletariat in Chapter 19) – selling their labour power to factory owners – for survival. Industrial capitalism transformed the scale of production, who produced what goods, by what means and with what value. The site of 'work' shifted away from households to workshops and factories where it was paid in wages, considered (economically) 'productive' and associated with 'breadwinning' men. These profound changes, and the emergence of liberalism, were a turning point in organizing economic activities, assigning value, and institutionalizing power (Rupert and Solomon 2006).

The effects these changes have had on the environment are discussed in **Chapter 3**.

Liberalism marked a decisive shift in thinking about reason, rights, individuals and power-wielding institutions. Its eighteenth-century form rejected arbitrary power in favour of rights to private property, religious choice, and individual freedom. These rights were the cornerstone of Europe's 'democratic' 'revolutions'. At the same time, liberalism

FIGURE 17.1
Textile mill in Lancashire, England. Photo: Getty Images

BOX 17.1 ADAM SMITH AND POLITICAL ECONOMY

FIGURE 17.2
Portrait of Adam Smith. Photo: Vanderblue Collection

In the late eighteenth century, Adam Smith produced the first systematic analysis of 'political economy'. He wrote about the state's essential role in managing flows of goods, facilitating exchange between nations, and ensuring that the state's wealth be used for the benefit of its population. He did not separate economics from politics, nor did he write about the whole 'world'. He criticized mercantilism and its promotion of state interference, arguing instead for a liberal 'free market' model of *laissez faire* ('let it be') policies. He believed that these would permit the 'invisible hand' of the market to operate and enable nations to prosper through pursuing their comparative advantage. Smith also cultivated a distinction between public and private and initiated a devaluation of household labour as not 'productive'.

produced an unstable tension: between freedom expressed in economic terms (through private property and unconstrained market arrangements) and equality expressed in socio-political terms (through democratic processes and requisite constraints to ensure equality of access, opportunity and participation).

Capitalist industrialization generated an unprecedented abundance of goods, but at considerable costs. It was especially devastating for all who lost access to land-based subsistence and were forced to earn wages – in typically harsh conditions – as the only way to survive. Moreover, the expansion of European wealth and power depended on the disruption of societies far from its shores: colonial practices cost Africa approximately 14 million people to slavery, destroyed India's flourishing cotton industry in favour of British exports, forcefully exploited the Chinese market, and directly and indirectly killed innumerable indigenous peoples of Oceania and the Americas. Early liberalism extended political equality to propertied males only. European claims to scientific progress and rational superiority were used to position 'whites' at the top of emerging racialized hierarchies and lent legitimacy to colonizing practices. And in spite of romanticism, the work of social reproduction in the 'domestic' sphere of the household lost value and status to the masculinized public sphere of politics and 'real' (waged) production.

Slavery persists today: see **Chapter 15**. Colonialism and developments in India specifically are discussed in **Chapter 16**; developments in Latin America are reviewed in **Chapter 14**.

Although they faced various forms of resistance, Europeans continued to consolidate their cultural, economic, political and military power (Held *et al.* 1999). They moved massive resources of raw materials and foodstuffs from non-industrialized areas to Europe, and ensured – through loans and precluding other options – that developing countries purchased Europe's manufactured goods. These processes generated prosperity in advanced industrialized countries (AICs), where union organizing benefited many waged workers and political movements secured 'welfare state' arrangements. During the twentieth century, improved transportation networks and new information and communication technologies extended the reach of capitalist markets, eventually encompassing the world (Peterson 2003).

Economics is inextricable from power operating in social systems more generally. This occurs through the interaction of various agents (individuals, corporations, states and international organizations) exercising various forms of power (purchasing and investing, job creation and termination, taxation and welfare, trade policies). This short history reveals both the changing role of markets and how, at every step, capitalist markets depended on the political power of states. Because economics is inseparable from power and politics, rather than 'world economics' we refer to *global political economy*. We now have a 'picture' of how the global political economy was created historically. But how is it organized *today*?

The importance of 'pictures' is discussed in **Chapter 2**.

ILLUSTRATIVE EXAMPLE
FORMAL AND INFORMAL WORK

When economists and the media talk about 'economics' they usually mean *formal* (contractual, regulated, legal) exchanges, where wages and salaries are negotiated, commodified goods and services are exchanged, and some degree of profit-seeking is assumed. One of the most puzzling and problematic developments in today's global political economy is the volume, value, extent, and socio-political significance of *informal* work activities (Kudva and Beneria 2006; Peterson 2010a). The latter refers to work that is not recorded or regulated (hence, informal) and ranges from socially necessary labour and volunteer activities, where cash is rarely exchanged and regulatory authorities are absent (e.g. household child and eldercare, domestic labour, community projects) to secondary, shadow and irregular activities, where some form of enterprise and payment is expected but legal regulation is either difficult to enforce or intentionally evaded (e.g. street vending, petty trade, home-based industries, sex work, drug dealing, arms trading).

Because it occurs 'outside' of the formal sector, informal work is rarely 'counted' in economic studies or analyses. Yet informal work was the rule prior to industrialization, and today researchers estimate that informal activities constitute more than one-half of *all* economic output, and equal 75 per cent of the gross domestic product of some countries. If we count work in domestic, caring and reproductive labour, subsistence agriculture, and the shadow economy, the time spent in informal activities today exceeds that of formal market exchanges. What are the implications of ignoring this enormous volume of work?

While size alone suggests that informalization (the process of increasing informal work) matters, its invisible, irregular and often illegal aspects pose additional challenges – illustrated starkly by criminal networks and the disorder they constitute for the global political economy. We lack adequate analyses of informalization partly because how to document and measure it is controversial (*Journal of International Affairs* 2000; Bajada and Schneider 2005) and partly because it was of little interest to economists until neoliberal restructuring spurred its growth. Economists have been narrowly focused on formal market activities, and also expected informal activities to wane as industrialization proceeded worldwide (Tabak and Crichlow 2000). In the context of neoliberal globalization, however, informal activities have continued and even increased.

Reliable data is a problem in general for analysing the global economy: see **Chapter 19**.

FIGURE 17.3
Gender segmentation of the informal economy. http://web.idrc.ca/es/ev-83646–201-1-DO_TOPIC.html

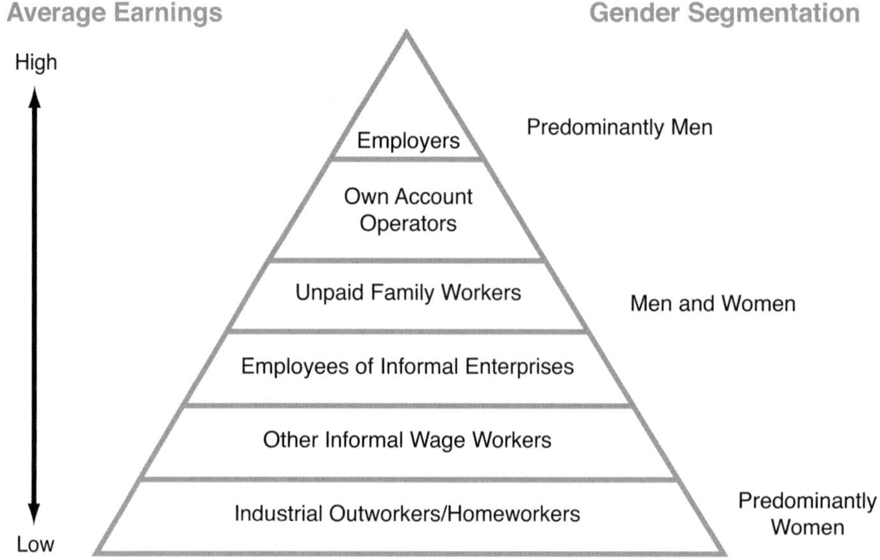

One source of this growth is flexibilization. Mass production of consumer goods in the twentieth century involved large and integrated factory work sites where workers gradually unionized, often gaining relatively secure, well paying jobs with good benefits. Neoliberal restructuring has transformed these arrangements, and flexibilization is the buzzword that characterizes the changes: production processes shift to spatially dispersed networks (the global assembly line; subcontracting; smaller enterprises); increasingly casualized (non-permanent, part-time) and informalized (unregulated, non-contractual) jobs; small batch, 'just in time' (short-term rather than long-term) production planning; and avoidance of organized labour (Cerny 1995).

Chapter 5 discusses feminist activism and the problems it has encountered.

Flexibilization feminizes the workforce: an increasing proportion of jobs require few skills and the most desirable workers are those who are perceived to be unorganized (undemanding), docile but reliable, available for part-time and temporary work, and willing to accept low wages (Beneria 2003; Barker and Feiner 2010). Prevailing stereotypes depict women as more attractive candidates for these jobs. Prevailing realities are that women – in spite of decades of activism and legal advances – continue to earn 30–50 per cent less than men worldwide. And in spite of heading almost one-third of the world's households, women are still thought of as secondary earners, not primary (that is, male) breadwinners. This assumption is used to 'justify' lower wages for women, as if their earnings were marginal to family well being and the 'real' economy of men's work (Chang 2000; Parreñas 2008). Feminization then refers to how flexibilization is simultaneously a material, embodied transformation of labour markets (more women workers) and a conceptual characterization of *devalorized* labour conditions (poorer pay and less secure work arrangements).

The terms 'liberal globalism' in **Chapter 19** and 'neoliberal globalization' in **Chapter 20** are roughly equivalent to the term 'neoliberalism' in this Chapter.

In general, flexibilization increases the power of management and decreases the choices available to most workers. The rhetoric of neoliberalism invokes flexibility as essential for competitive success and as an inherently positive policy. As this rhetoric becomes common sense it obscures how these policies are in fact politically and

BOX 17.2 GENDER AND FEMINIZATION

Gender is related to, but more complicated than, the conventional distinction between females and males. It refers to socially learned identities and ways of thinking and acting that are characterized as masculine or feminine. For example, 'reason' and assertiveness, appearing unemotional and 'in control', and being the 'breadwinner' are masculinized (associated with masculine characteristics). In contrast, 'emotion' and 'dependence', appearing uncertain and submissive, and being the 'homemaker' are feminized. The key pattern to recognize is that, in general and with powerful consequences, qualities associated with masculinity are valorized over, and at the expense of, those associated with femininity. This translates *economically* into devalorized (low status, poorly paid, insecure, etc.) feminized work – whether being done by males or females.

economically motivated; they benefit some at the expense of others. In the absence of regulatory frameworks that protect workers' rights and generate living wages (adequate for sustaining households), flexibilization translates into greater insecurity of employment, income, and benefits for the majority of the world's workers.

As the subcontracting, homework and casualization of labour associated with flexibilization become normal, so do the less formal and regulated work conditions of informalization. Insofar as flexibilization erodes labour's organizing power, protection of workers' rights, and wage expectations, it exacerbates the decline in family income that pushes more people to generate income in whatever way they can; they often do so by engaging in informal sector activities. Finally, because flexibilization translates into avoidance of taxes, it exacerbates the declining resources devoted to public welfare provisioning and spurs participation in informal activities to compensate in part for this loss.

We know then that informalization matters economically. The sheer size of it has tremendous implications for everyday lives, livelihoods and sites of power (Sassen 1998). Informalization matters because it undercuts some legitimate businesses and enables others. Its avoidance of taxes alone decreases public revenues, with far-reaching economic effects, especially on the most vulnerable groups. Perhaps most significant structurally, by avoiding indirect wages and regulation of labour relations and worksite conditions, informalization enhances the power of capital at the expense of labour. That is, it places downward pressure on wages more generally, which both decreases employed labour's earnings and power and has a disciplining effect on all workers.

Moreover, and inextricably, informalization matters politically. Informalization poses quandaries of documentation and measurement; policies may be misconceived and inappropriate if they are based on faulty estimates of national output, income distribution, or unemployment. Societies lose when informal activities evade tax collection, decrease public revenues and enable corruption. Recent scandals regarding insider trading and fraudulent accounting practices reveal how extensive the damage can be. Similarly, the reduction in tax revenues due to informalization has political effects in terms of who wins and loses as a consequence of selective public expenditures. Societies also lose when unregulated work practices pose safety, health, and environmental risks, when criminal activities thwart collective interests in law and order, and when illicit gains

FIGURE 17.4
Injusticia Global. Artist: Sergio Langer, *El Clarin*, Argentina

are used to fund conflicts. Critics of informalization hence argue that avoidance of regulations is directly and indirectly bad for wages, workers, the environment, and long-term prospects for societal well-being.

Like flexibilization, *some* individuals prosper by engaging in entrepreneurial activities – legal and illegal – made possible by a less regulated environment. This is especially evident in microenterprises favoured by neoliberals, in developing countries where informal activities are crucial for income generation, and in clandestine activities that are increasing worldwide (Friman and Andreas 1999; Naylor 2002). And like flexibilization, this work is polarized between a small, privileged group able to take advantage of and prosper from deregulation and flexibilization, and the *majority* of the world's informal workers – women, migrants, and the poor – who participate less out of choice than necessity due to economic *and* ideological devalorization (Hoskyns and Rai 2007; Peterson 2010a). Mainstream accounts emphasize elites and entrepreneurs, but most flexible and informal workers have few choices about the work that they do. And they do a great deal of it.

Compare the discussion of contemporary slavery in **Chapter 15**.

In short, informal activities are growing. They span a wide range of activities and crucial to their significance is how they *blur* conventional boundaries separating public and private, legal and illegal, production and reproduction, national and international. The majority of informal activities are also feminized – involving devalued identities, statuses, working conditions and forms of compensation (Chant and Pedwell 2008). Informalization thus poses fundamental questions about global political economy in relation to family livelihoods, conditions of employment, what counts as economic activity, and how activities are valued.

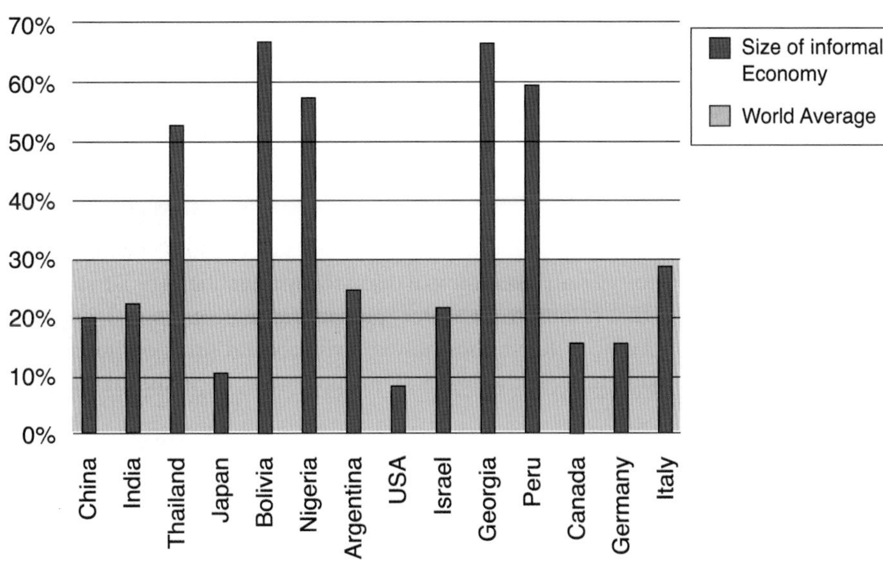

FIGURE 17.5
Average size of informal economy around the world measured as a percentage of GDP. http://www.atmmarketplace.com/article/129691/Another-100-years-of-cash; *also at* http://www.greensheet.com/emagazine.php?story_id=745

GENERAL RESPONSES
EXPLAINING THE POLITICS OF ECONOMICS

We know that neoliberal globalization is powerfully affecting how life is lived and work is done throughout the world. We also know that the recent growth in informal activities was unanticipated and that its effects are economically and politically important. Those who study global politics debate how and why these changes are occurring, and who the winners and losers are. What are the most familiar approaches, what do they include, what do they omit?

The imposition of policies of structural adjustment in developing countries such as Ivory Coast is part of neoliberalism and has had a huge impact: **Chapter 15**.

The disciplinary separation of economics from politics (and from sociology, anthropology, communications, and psychology) works against understanding the overlapping and interdependent dimensions of these disciplines. When Adam Smith initiated the study of political economy in the eighteenth century, he focused on market activities. He did so because the forces of industrial capitalism were dramatically altering conditions of social life and posed the most challenging problems. But he understood markets as inextricable from other social, institutional, and political dynamics. How then did the study of political economy become fragmented into economics and politics?

After the eighteenth century, forms of social organization based on state-driven market exchanges were intensified. Western-centric ideologies of progress, nationalism, secularism, science (as well as Christianity), and liberal capitalism were spread around the world, with extensive, though not homogeneous, effects. Advanced industrial countries dominated the world order and cultivated economic development models that sustained western supremacy. In these countries, mass production, collective bargaining, and the liberal-capitalist welfare state fostered the growth of a middle class. These cumulative developments had diverse effects. On the one hand, successful industrialization was associated with enhanced productivity, a proliferation of goods, greater

Rising inequality is the subject of **Chapter 19**.

consumer pleasures, and new identities. On the other hand, unemployment, harsh work conditions, and relentless competition meant new miseries, labour migrations, and increasing disparities between 'haves' and 'have nots' within and among nations.

As universities became central to the production of knowledge, studies of social life fragmented into disciplinary specializations. The study of political economy was divided into economics and politics, and the lure of scientific methods encouraged those who identified as economists to narrow and formalize their analyses. By the twentieth century, neoclassical economics became the predominant school of economic theory, and is subscribed to by most economists who advocate today's neoliberal re-structuring. This school presupposes that resources are scarce, human wants are unlimited, and that rational ordering of preferences determines how individuals and firms optimize their self-interests. Formal mathematical models and manipulation of statistical data are preferred methods.

In effect, this orientation focuses on objective phenomena and excludes from analyses that which is not quantifiable or not valued enough to be counted. Until recently, the study of global politics tended to marginalize consideration of race, gender, and even class. Related to this is a tendency to neglect how emotional investments and social identities – 'who we are' – have tremendous importance. They shape our desires, expectations, self-esteem, attitudes, values and how we act – especially toward 'others'. These subjective factors are difficult to measure but they matter to politics. Neglect of identities and subjective factors is in turn related to an avoidance of cultural phenomena, for example, popular music, television programmes, videos, films, YouTube, gaming and other forms of leisure (Best and Paterson 2010). Information and communication technologies expand the global reach of these media and powerfully shape what information people have access to and what ideological assumptions they then internalize. In sum, disciplinary boundaries and an emphasis on objective phenomena shape what we know about global politics, and especially the global political economy.

Chapter 5 discusses who we think we are, and how gender and race are significant. **Chapter 14** addressed these same themes in the context of politics in Argentina.

The question of how we know what is going on in the world and the way this influences how we think is the subject of **Chapter 8**. **Chapter 9** engages with the changes brought by the development of technologies often referred to as Web 2.0.

Liberal and neoliberal approaches

Conventional – and hence the most familiar – accounts of global political economy are associated with the liberal tradition and its promotion by neoclassical economists of free market policies (Chwieroth 2010; Peck 2010). Basic assumptions of this position include: markets are efficient and morally desirable; the unfettered movement of trade and capital will result in optimal investment flows; countries benefit by emphasizing their comparative advantage; growth is imperative and will 'trickle down' to the benefit of all; open borders ensure the most efficient and equitable distributions of goods worldwide. The role of governments is to facilitate the operation of markets but otherwise not intervene in decision-making.

Chapter 19 discusses how the free market in fact leads to global inequality.

The policies of neoliberalism clearly emerge from this liberal tradition. The restructuring they entail is new because it is elevated to the global level. At the same time, it penetrates to the individual level: as public services and welfare supports decline, individuals alone are expected to ensure their well-being through smart consumerism and investing wisely for their retirement. 'Market fundamentalism' aptly conveys the meaning of neoliberalism: to promote the power of market-based decision-makers over that of public or government-based decision-makers. The over-riding objective of private

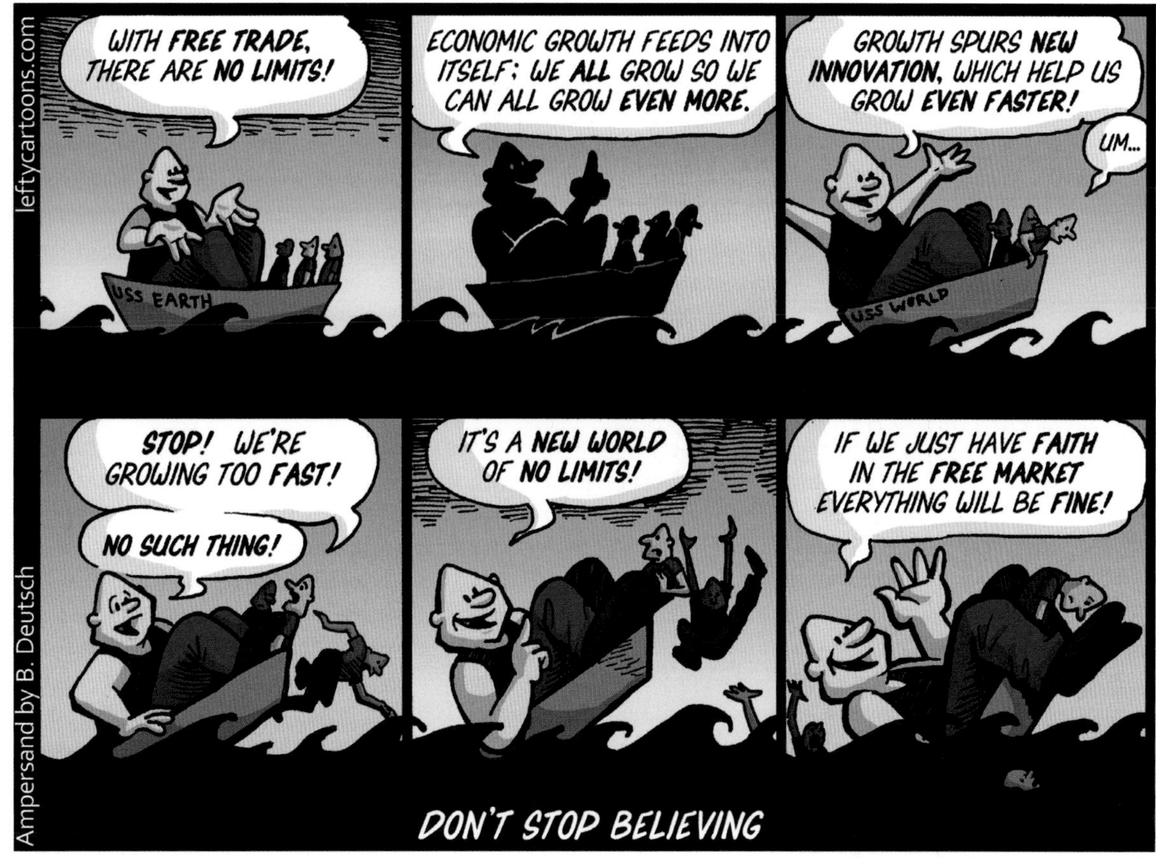

FIGURE 17.6 'Don't stop believing'. Artist: Barry Deutsch

and corporate capital (market forces) is to make profits for owners and shareholders. Unlike governments, the well-being of ordinary workers and citizens is not the primary concern. In the absence of government regulation, market forces are not accountable to workers or citizens and tend to undercut collective (democratic) efforts to direct production processes and determine how society's goods are distributed. In this sense, neoliberal policies of deregulation and privatization subject workers and citizens to regulation primarily by market forces, where the motivation is pursuit of profits rather than provision of public goods. The tension between promoting private gains and improving public welfare complicates both how we theorize global political economy and how we evaluate neoliberal capitalism.

The pursuit of profit has impacts on the environment, arguably a public good: **Chapter 3**.

If we liken restructuring to a global 'game' of neoliberal capitalism, its enthusiasts fundamentally believe in the game at play. That is, they subscribe to the model of human nature attributed to the players (atomistic, competitive, and rational individuals or states), to the expectations that flow from this model when no additional constraints are imposed ('each-to-his-own', winner-takes-all strategies), and to the projected long-term, system-wide benefits from playing what they understand anyway as the 'only game in town' ('there is no alternative'). In an important sense, these accounts render structural hierarchies invisible, either by being depoliticized (as 'the way things are' due

For a discussion of the idea that there is something called 'human nature' see **Chapter 7**.

to nature or ineluctable globalization) or marginalized (as perhaps regrettable but nonetheless subordinated to, or a distraction from, more pressing analytical concerns). This theoretical perspective dominates in economic analyses and mainstream media. Because most people hear little other than this account, they tend to believe it is the only one.

Liberal and neoliberal economists have focused on formal market activities, where commodified goods and services are exchanged and some degree of profit-seeking is presupposed. Those who study the global economy have focused on the role of large corporate firms and advanced industrial economies; both were considered historically the most successful choices and developmentally the most probable. For example, modernization theory assumed that 'the rest would follow the west' in terms of how they developed economically. It was assumed that informal activities would be displaced by industrialization, which involved the expansion of waged labour and increasing forms of regulation. Little theoretical attention was paid to activities that did not conform to these assumptions and expectations. As a result, economic theory ignored informal activities in favour of more familiar market processes that predominated in advanced industrial economies. From a critical vantage point, this silence reflected a relative lack of interest in issues of greater importance to poor and developing countries, and of greater consequence for vulnerable (feminized) populations.

Theoretical reassessment was spurred by growth in informal activities worldwide and, especially, as a prominent feature of economies in transition from centralized state-planning regimes toward neoliberal ones. For the most part, informalization that does not involve criminal activity tends to be interpreted positively by liberal economists. It is seen as a breeding ground for microenterprise or a creative and flexible response to inefficient or excessive regulation. Some argue that informally earned income has a stimulating effect on the formal economy. But there are different reasons for participating in the informal sector. The tendency to focus on the positive effects of entrepreneurial activities, undertaken primarily by middle- and upper-income groups, leads to a neglect of informalization among lower-income groups. The latter participate more for sheer survival and have too few resources to be engaged in activities that 'stimulate the economy'.

The idea that microenterprise has positive effects is behind the promotion of microfinance discussed in **Chapter 20**.

At the same time, there are growing networks of organized crime (Naylor 2002). These engage in illegal activities – drug smuggling, sex trafficking, arms trading – that are often very lucrative. The implications are especially disturbing when we consider how semi-clandestine and illegal operations are shaping the conduct of twenty-first-century militarized conflicts (Ballentine and Sherman 2003). The deleterious effects of illicit activities have prompted closer attention to informal activities that affect global finances and geopolitics. But the vast amount of informal work associated with households and caring labour – which increases during financial crises and wars – remains invisible in mainstream accounts (Seguino 2010). Also neglected are the effects of historical and growing inequalities worldwide and how these both reflect and are exacerbated by informalization (Tabak and Crichlow 2000; Berik *et al.* 2009).

Financial crises and their relation to people's everyday lives are the subject of **Chapter 18**.

Liberal and neoliberal analyses tend to dominate in economic theory, media accounts, and public consciousness. But there are dissenting voices, too, as some economists are uncomfortable with how neoliberal restructuring has been imposed, noting especially its tendency toward destabiliization of social conditions and the larger problems this can create. Given recurring financial crises and corporate accounting scandals, concerns are also raised regarding deregulation of financial arrangements and the difficulties of ensuring transparency and accountability (Best 2005).

To stay with the global game metaphor, these players subscribe to the assumptions and objectives of neoliberalism, but are more attentive to the dangers of applying them so rapidly and indiscriminately. Responses focus on 'adjusting' the implementation of policies, especially to ameliorate their most deleterious effects. In this sense, the rules of the game are not fundamentally challenged but the major players are encouraged to take a longer and broader view, to ease up on the immediately devastating practices so that the game itself proceeds with less conflict and loss, and fewer crises.

Marxist approaches

The most widely recognized alternative to liberal and neoliberal approaches emerges from the Marxist tradition. This includes a variety of perspectives and important distinctions, but what they share are critiques of capitalism (Rupert and Solomon 2006). The basic argument is that capitalism promotes the concentration of resources and power in a minority, *at the expense of the majority*. Marxist global political economy attempts to develop more holistic or structural explanations of how markets, firms, and governments interact. This approach takes institutions seriously and analyses them in relation to power differentials. For example, institutions may serve as mechanisms for establishing and maintaining class-based inequalities, and the state may be dominated by elites but also have a remedial role in alleviating class hierarchies. Another increasingly influential variant of Marxism features the insights of Antonio Gramsci. This approach pays particular attention to issues of culture and illuminates how hegemonic rule occurs through ideological consent. For example, the ideology of neoliberalism is promoted through multiple media, which cultivates an acceptance of capitalism as both desirable and inevitable ('there is no alternative').

See the discussion of historical materialism in **Chapter 19**.

Gramsci's work is also discussed in **Chapter 1**.

Marxist-oriented approaches offer critical vantage points and extensive research on changes in the organization of production, global divisions of labour, accumulation and regulation dynamics, and class and geopolitical hierarchies. Their emphasis on historical

BOX 17.3 KARL MARX

Karl Marx (1818–83) is best known for his analysis of the workings of capitalism as a mode of production, and its exploitation and commodification of workers and their labour. He argued that changes in the social *practices* of production, from slavery through feudalism to capitalism, changed the ways in which we *picture* the world. He was an active campaigner and his writings formed the inspiration for communist and socialist political programmes that placed the well-being of the collectivity above the rights of private property. He was clear that while 'the philosophers have only interpreted the world, in various ways; the point is to change it' (*Theses on Feuerbach*, XI; see McLellan 1977).

FIGURE 17.7
Karl Marx

developments is important for illuminating how systems are made and hence can be changed. Like liberal economists, they tend to focus on the formal sector but have also made significant contributions to theorizing informalization.

Proletarianization means an increasing number of workers engaged in and dependent on waged labour: see **Chapter 15**.

Marxism is associated with the view that formalization or proletarianization would replace other forms of labour as capitalism developed. At the same time, Marxists more indebted to historical materialism have long understood that full proletarianization is a structural contradiction for capitalism. Briefly, they argue that capital accumulation depends not only on profits gained through formal mechanisms of production and exchange but also, and continuously, on accumulation of profits through non-capitalist, nonwaged, casual, and/or informal economic activities that are not proletarianized.

A dimension of this thesis is that capital's pursuit of the highest profit entails *maintaining* a surplus ('reserve army') of labour that is not currently – or formally – employed but potentially employable. This surplus both enhances profits through maintaining downward pressure on wages, and disciplines employed workers through the threat of being replaced from these reserves. In other words, the availability of surplus labour compels workers to compete with each other; this competition enhances the bargaining advantage of employers by decreasing what they need to offer in terms of wages and benefits. The informal sector constitutes some of this labour surplus and tends to lower wages. First, avoidance of regulated work conditions avoids a variety of costs to firms and decreases average labour costs. Second, direct competition from informalized workers tends to decrease the number of higher-paid (formal) workers, and sometimes decreases how much they are paid. Given these dynamics, the wage contract underpinning formal work arrangements is only part and not the whole of economic activities; full proletarianization would undercut the expansionary capitalist pursuit of only the *highest* realizable profit rates.

Compare the discussion of deproletarianization in **Chapter 15**.

Moreover, Marxist analysts recognize that informalization is not a passing phenomenon. Rather, it is a structural feature of capitalist relations and plays a role in the periodic restructuring associated with capitalism's boom-and-bust cycles. During economic downturns, informal activities increase as formal employment opportunities diminish and people struggle to generate whatever income they can in whatever way possible. Similarly, the apparent newness of informal growth in advanced economies is due to conceptual selectivity (a focus on industrialized production, formal activities, etc.) and relegating informal activities to theories of development (focused on poor, 'third world' rather than industrialized economies).

In sum, Marxist approaches help us understand informalization as both a structural feature of capitalism (linking the informal to the formal economy through downward pressure on wages) and a long-term cyclical process (linking the expansion of informal activities to accumulation cycles). It broadens our focus to include informal activities as integral to formal waged production relations and all labour force formation. These are important advances in thinking about informalization. They remain limited, however, in two related ways. First, these analysts rarely extend their critique of structural hierarchies beyond economic indicators. Rather, they focus on class (within nations) and developed versus developing countries (between nations). Second, they continually neglect social reproduction, domestic labour, and intra-household dynamics.

BROADER ISSUES
THE HIDDEN COSTS OF NEOLIBERALISM

We have seen how liberal and neoliberal economists theorize global political economy, offer limited accounts of informalization, and tend to ignore structural hierarchies. Analysts drawing on the Marxist tradition expand our knowledge of informal–formal linkages and improve our understanding of historical patterns and *global* dynamics. They also provide illuminating critiques of economic hierarchies.

What continues to be left out of this picture and hence weakens our understanding of how the world economy is organized? What larger questions remain unexamined? In particular, who are the actual winners and losers in this game? And what are the long-term consequences? The puzzle of informalization offers a useful vantage point for considering these questions, exploring how value is assigned, and revealing the hidden costs of neoliberalism.

What does it mean to think of the global economy as a 'game' in the first place?

We know that work outside of the formal economy is not diminishing, as expected, but increasing with globalization and during economic downturns. Increasing unemployment, flexibilization, and erosion or prohibition of union power have meant declining real incomes and decreased job security for most workers worldwide. Deregulation and privatization undercut welfare provisioning, state employment, and collective supports for family well-being. As economic conditions deteriorate, individuals and households are thus pushed to engage in informal activities as a strategy for securing income however they can. The majority of informal workers are women, migrants, and the urban poor. The income they generate often enables families to survive but rarely enables them to prosper. For the most part, these vulnerable (feminized) populations

FIGURE 17.8
Informal economic activity. http://wiego.org/wiego/core-programmes/urban-policies

Chapter 19 examines the 'losers' of the global economic 'game' in some detail and **Chapter 16** argues that which countries do well in this game is rooted in the history of colonialism and the exploitation of other countries that it entailed.

remain excluded from the purported benefits of neoliberalism. In this sense, informalization takes advantage of, and exacerbates, inequalities based on gender, race and economic hierarchies. In effect, the majority of the global population loses in the game of neoliberalism.

A significant component of informalization involves activities undertaken to ensure social reproduction – the labour that is characterized as women's work. These activities are rarely analysed in mainstream accounts because they are not valued or easily quantified and hence not counted. This neglect is due in part to conceptual habits: locating men in the public sphere of power and real – that is, paid – work, and women in the household sphere of emotional maintenance, leisure, and caring – that is, unpaid – labour. It is also due to institutionalized practices: for example, academic disciplines that study social life as separate (psychological, social, economic, political) spheres of inquiry. Critics argue, in contrast, that what is regarded as women's work and informal activities are crucial for analysing the global political economy.

There is a discussion of feminist activism, and of racism, in **Chapter 5**. The distinction between public and private spheres is also discussed in that chapter.

In short, a more adequate understanding of global politics requires including the role of informalization, examining who the winners and losers are, and considering the consequences of excluding so many from neoliberalism's purported benefits. Analysts who are most attentive to these issues and combine a variety of theoretical approaches are feminists – especially those who are critical of colonialism and racism. They provide the most inclusive accounts of social reproduction, gendered work, and informalization. Their research is especially rich in providing empirical data and case studies; they enable us to theorize how work is assigned value; and they variously engage in theorizing *multiple* hierarchies.

The gendered division of labour

Feminism has no single meaning and there are many ways of thinking about how patriarchy operates. Differences shaped by history, culture, location, disciplinary interests, and theoretical orientations generate a wide range of approaches (Peterson and Runyan 2010). In general, feminist economists analyse the relationship between women's reproductive labour, the formal economy, and surplus accumulation. Research includes adding women's labour in social reproduction (care of children and elders, housework, etc.) to existing theoretical models, examining gender differences in labour markets and work conditions, and developing policy recommendations. Feminist international development economists concentrate on industrializing countries. They study not only how social reproduction and informal activities affect women's empowerment, but also how gendered values and strategies affect national development more generally.

Feminist economists who identify with Marxism theorize capitalism's relationship to women's work. They argue that bearing, raising, and appropriately socializing future workers *produces* labour power (workers) for the formal economy. The economic benefits of this unpaid labour accrue to employers who are thereby spared the full costs of producing the labour force. That is, employers do not have to pay for the work of social reproduction that is necessary for infants to become adults who are available for work. They argue that economic theory should address how workers themselves are produced before their labour is made available for either informal or formal deployment.

BOX 17.4 WORLD-SYSTEMS ANALYSIS

Proposed by Immanuel Wallerstein in the 1970s, world-systems analysis treats the present-day capitalist global economy as a modern world-system, which, to put it very simply, is made up of countries in the core (the rich, developed nations of the North), the periphery (so-called underdeveloped countries of the third world or global South) and the semi-periphery. When the theory was first proposed, the countries of the Soviet bloc formed the semi-periphery. The idea was that the semi-periphery provided a sort of buffer zone between the developed and underdeveloped world, and that while countries could move from one part of the world-system to another, the structure of the world-system was what was important. For more detail see for example: http://www.sociology.emory.edu/globalization/theories01.html.

Feminists also expand world systems analyses that focus on households as basic units of analysis (Smith and Wallerstein 1992). Although households vary, two key points emerge from this research. One is that informal labour associated with the household (e.g. subsistence, home-based production) underpins capitalist dynamics and profit-making, yet is neglected in mainstream economic theory. A second point is that – except for a small elite – wages alone are inadequate for sustaining households. To survive, most of the world's families combine available wage income with informal activities, public welfare support, and/or self-provisioning (do-it-yourself) labour. Also neglected is the expansion of 'global householding', as individuals increasingly cross national boundaries as part of sustaining the social and economic reproduction of households (Douglas 2006; Peterson 2010b).

What links these various observations is a gendered division of labour that was historically produced, extends worldwide, and assigns women and men different responsibilities. This division relegates to women the primary role in sustaining family and household well-being and depoliticizes the socially necessary work that women do and the disproportionate burden of responsibility placed on them when economic conditions degenerate. The processes involve gendered identities (breadwinner, home-maker) and ideologies (masculine work is for cash, feminized work is for love). Here the empirical studies of structural adjustment policies, flexibilization, and informalization merge in exposing how women are expected to 'take up the slack' when male wage-earning and public services decline. For many women, this increasingly means working a 'triple shift' – of reproductive labour, informal work, and formal employment.

Chapter 6 has more to say about ideology.

It is not simply women who suffer the costs of neoliberal globalization. As noted above, informalized workers and those with the fewest choices about how to survive include the majority of people – women *and* men – worldwide. These vulnerable populations are losers in the game of neoliberal capitalism, and their exclusion from its purported benefits has implications for all of us.

The costs of exclusions

The game metaphor enables us to see the 'whole' world through various lenses. From the vantage point of liberal and neoliberal economists, growth is the answer and

© Mike Baldwin / Cornered
BALDWIN
"Car stereo, forty bucks. Make it fifty and I'll throw in the car."

FIGURE 17.9
'The wider informal economy.' http://www.cartoonstock.com/directory/i/informal_market.asp

unfettered capitalism is the preferred and inevitable way to achieve it. From a similar starting point, but with increasing attention to global inequalities and the dangers these pose, more cautious voices are urging reforms. They advocate corrective policies in the hope of softening the costs of restructuring and dampening its most devastating effects. Less familiar are a number of explicitly critical perspectives. These include a range of Marxist approaches, some versions of institutionalism, many environmentalists, and a variety of feminist critiques.

Because they start from different positions, their criticisms are wide-ranging. Different players among them argue that neoliberal globalization: increases class inequalities, enhances the wealth and power of elites, fails to lift the poorest out of poverty, erodes the gains and prospects of organized labour, worsens un- and underemployment, displaces subsistence agriculture and local craft production, increases the unpaid work of women, fuels licit and illicit informalization, lowers standards in advanced economies, increases surveillance and discipline of workers, weakens worker demands through the threat of job losses and capital flight, reduces the state's capacity – or commitment – to prioritize domestic welfare, promotes environmental damage and toxic dumping on poor countries, fuels speculative and volatile financial markets, and poses systemic risks due to the integration of financial markets.

Corrective and transformative recommendations are equally wide-ranging and depend on particular issues and the perspective of the critic. In general however, these 'players' argue that the problems of the global economy are too deep for cosmetic fixes. Adjustments to soften the negative effects, or a slower pace to ameliorate damage, may afford important and even life-saving temporary relief but are simply not enough. The costs of neoliberalism for most people and the planet are simply too great. Hence, these players argue variously for different premises, different rules, and even a fundamentally different game.

This summary of positions reveals a singularly important factor in shaping one's assessment of neoliberalism. That factor is whether and to what extent the rules of the game and its premises are taken for granted as common sense. This common sense includes first, believing that 'there is no alternative' to capitalism. Adherents argue that this claim is supported by the historical, cumulative success of capitalist development and the displacement or collapse of all alternatives. The second and related belief is that neoliberalism is (ultimately) good for everyone: providing efficiency, creativity, growth, and even security.

Common sense is discussed in **Chapter 1**.

What are the consequences of accepting this 'common sense' and the particular game of capitalism that it perpetuates? In the short term, marginalized populations face daunting challenges: how to secure immediate resources for family survival and well-being, and how to maintain self-esteem and optimism under stressful conditions and unpromising futures. In the long term, growing inequalities drain people's sense of inclusion in a global community; increase feelings of frustration, despair and resentment; reduce the likelihood of people working together for common goals; and undermine democratic principles, which require inclusiveness (Uvin 2003). In combination, these conditions increase the impoverishment of the majority and the probability of conflicts.

Illuminating the social exclusions of neoliberalism shifts attention to the *costs* of perpetuating it as 'common sense'. Failure to count these costs is due in part to theoretical biases and disciplinary boundaries, and resistance to critical thinking. It is also due to the 'top down' vantage point of elite decision-makers, western states, and corporate executives. In spite of advocating 'global' processes and democratic ideals, those who promote neoliberalism pay little heed to voices and viewpoints outside of rich, powerful states, indeed outside of elite sites of power and authority within those states. Through their selective lenses the 'reality' in developing countries, the 'discarded fourth world', urban ghettos, and overburdened families is rendered invisible and hence simply not 'counted'.

What is being suggested here is that neo-liberalism is a 'problem-solving theory' in the terms discussed in **Chapter 1** and that what is needed instead is a critical theory.

CONCLUSION

Inequalities do not originate with neoliberalism, nor do its proponents claim to intentionally exacerbate them. Even the brief history summarized above reveals long and entwined histories of colonialism, racism, patriarchy, and economic inequality within and among nations. These hierarchies of difference were already internalized and institutionalized and could be used in support of neoliberal objectives, for example, by devaluing the informal work done by women, the poor and migrants. What distinguishes contemporary capitalism is its unprecedented global reach, and its ability to shape how 'all' of us think. Corporations control most of the world's media, and their primary objective is the pursuit of profit for private shareholders. Hence, the dominant media promote neoliberalism. But the narrow vantage point thereby broadcast to 'the world' effectively undermines critical thinking and democratic processes. People who are told only one story cannot help but believe 'there is no alternative'. Critical perspectives, lived realities, and alternative visions are simply 'not counted'.

For a discussion of corporations' control of and exposure to the internet see **Chapter 9**.

FURTHER READING

Bakker, Isabella and Stephen Gill (eds) (2003) *Power, Production and Social Reproduction: Human In/security in the Global Political Economy*, Basingstoke: Palgrave Macmillan.
Comprehensive discussion of the importance of social reproduction to economics and security.

Dickinson, Torry D. and Robert K. Schaeffer (2001) *Fast Forward: Work, Gender, and Protest in a Changing World*, Lanham, MD: Rowman and Littlefield.
Student-friendly account of global political economy that identifies key patterns and how people are organizing for better conditions.

Kofman, Eleonore and Gillian Youngs (eds) (2008) *Globalization: Theory and Practice*, 3rd edn, London and New York: Continuum.
Interesting and instructive collection providing diverse disciplinary treatments of globalization.

Marchand, Marianne H. and Anne Sisson Runyan (eds) (2011) *Gender and Global Restructuring: Sightings, Sites and Resistances*, 2nd edn, London: Routledge.
This volume integrates analyses of neoliberal globalization and post-9/11 neo-imperialism.

Miller, Raymond C. (2008) *International Political Economy: Contrasting World Views*, London: Routledge.
Accessible overview of the field that combines theoretical perspectives, empirical studies and comparative policy analysis.

Scholte, Jan Aart (2005) *Globalization: A Critical Introduction*, 2nd edn, Basingstoke: Palgrave Macmillan.
Especially accessible and comprehensive overview of globalization, including definitions, history, data, controversies, and policy implications.

WEBSITES

The UC Atlas of Global Inequality, http://ucatlas.ucsc.edu/index.php
Explores the interaction between global integration (globalization) and inequality, and provides maps, graphics and data.

Institute for Policy Studies, http://www.ips-dc.org/
A multi-issue think tank offering a cross-cutting analysis with a historical perspective; committed to strengthening and linking social movements.

Institute of Development Studies, http://www.ids.ac.uk/ids/
A leading global organization for research, teaching and communications on international development.

United Nations Development Programme, http://www.undp.org/
The UN's global development network, an organization advocating for change and facilitating exchange of knowledge, experience and resources.

United Nations Development Fund for Women, http://www.unifem.org/
The women's fund at the United Nations, providing financial and technical assistance to innovative programmes and strategies to foster women's empowerment and gender equality.

International Labour Organization, http://www.ilo.org/
UN specialized agency, promoting social justice and labour rights; research reports on informal and formal work.

REFERENCES

Bajada, Christopher and Friedrich Schneider (2005) *Size, Causes and Consequences of the Underground Economy: An International Perspective*, London: Ashgate.

Ballentine, K. and J. Sherman (eds) (2003) *The Political Economy of Armed Conflict: Beyond Greed and Grievance*, Boulder, CO: Lynne Rienner.

Barker, Drucilla and Susan F. Feiner (2010) 'As the World Turns: Globalization, Consumption and the Feminization of Work', *Rethinking Marxism* 22, 2: 246–52.

Beneria, Lourdes (2003) *Gender, Development and Globalization: Economics as if People Mattered*, New York: Routledge.

Berik, Günseli, Yana van der Meulen Rodgers and Stephanie Seguino (2009) 'Feminist Economics of Inequality, Development, and Growth', *Feminist Economics* 15, 3 (July): 1–33.

Best, Jacqueline (2005) *The Limits of Transparency: Ambiguity and the History of International Finance*, Ithaca, NY and London: Cornell University Press.

Best, Jacqueline and Matthew Paterson (eds) (2010) *Cultural Political Economy*, London: Routledge.

Cerny, Philip G. (1995) 'Globalization and the Changing Logic of Collective Action', *International Organization* 49, 4: 595–625.

Chang, Grace (2000) *Disposable Domestics: Immigrant Workers in the Global Economy*, Cambridge, MA: South End Press.

Chant, Sylvia and Carolyn Pedwell (2008) *Women, Gender and the Informal Economy*, Geneva: ILO.

Chwieroth, Jeffrey M. (2010) *Capital Ideas: The IMF and the Rise of Financial Liberalization*, Princeton, NJ: Princeton University Press.

Douglas, Mike (2006) 'Global Householding in Pacific Asia', *International Development Planning Review* 28, 4: 421–45.

Friman, H. Richard and Peter Andreas (eds) (1999) *The Illicit Global Economy and State Power*, Lanham, MD: Rowman and Littlefield.

Held, David, Anthony G. McGrew, David Goldblatt and Jonathan Perraton (1999) *Global Transformations: Politics, Economics, and Culture*, Stanford, CA: Stanford University Press.

Hoskyns, Catherine and Shirin M. Rai (2007) 'Recasting the Global Political Economy: Counting Women's Unpaid Work', *New Political Economy* 12, 3: 297–317.

Journal of International Affairs (2000) Special Issue: 'The Shadow Economy', 53, 2.

Kudva, Neema and Lourdes Beneria (eds) (2006) *Rethinking Informalization: Poverty, Precarious Jobs and Social Protection*, Cornell University Open Access Repository, http://hdl.handle.net/1813/3716 (accessed 11 November 2007).

McLellan, David (1977) *Karl Marx: Selected Writings*, Oxford: Oxford University Press.

Naylor, R. T. (2002) *Wages of Crime: Black Markets, Illegal Finance, and the Underground Economy*, Ithaca, NY: Cornell University Press.

Parreñas, Rhacel Salazar (2008) *The Force of Domesticity: Filipina Migrants and Globalization*, New York: New York University Press.

Peck, Jamie (2010) *Constructions of Neoliberal Reason*, Oxford: Oxford University Press.

Peterson, V. Spike (2003) *A Critical Rewriting of Global Political Economy: Integrating Reproductive, Productive, and Virtual Economies*, London and New York: Routledge.

——(2010a) 'Informalization, Inequalities and Global Insecurities', *International Studies Review* 12: 244–70.

——(ed.) (2010b) Critical Perspectives section: 'Gender and Global Householding', *Politics and Gender* 6: 271–304.

Peterson, V. Spike and Anne Sisson Runyan (2010) *Global Gender Issues in the New Millennium*, 3rd edn, Boulder, CO: Westview Press.

Rupert, Mark and M. Scott Solomon (2006) *Globalization and International Political Economy: The Politics of Alternative Futures*, Lanham, MD: Rowman and Littlefield.

Sassen, Saskia (1998) *Globalization and Its Discontents*, New York: New Press.

Schneider, Friedrich and Dominick H. Enste (2005) *Shadow Economies: Theoretical Approaches, Empirical Studies, and Political Implications*, Cambridge: Cambridge University Press.

Seguino, Stephanie (2010) 'The Global Economic Crisis, Its Gender and Ethnic Implications, and Policy Responses', *Gender and Development* 18, 2: 179–99.

Smith, Joan and Immanuel Wallerstein (eds) (1992) *In Creating and Transforming Households: The Constraints of the World-Economy*, Cambridge: Cambridge University Press.

Tabak, Faruk and Michaeline A. Crichlow (eds) (2000) *Informalization*, Baltimore, MD: Johns Hopkins University Press.

Uvin, Peter (2003) 'Global Dreams and Local Anger: From Structural to Acute Violence in a Globalizing World', in Mary Ann Tetreault, Robert A. Denemark, Kenneth P. Thomas and Kurt Burch (eds) *Rethinking Global Political Economy: Emerging Issues, Unfolding Odysseys*, London and New York: Routledge.

For a range of further resources supporting this chapter, please visit the companion website for *Global Politics, 2nd Edition* at www.routledge.com/cw/edkins/

CHAPTER 18

Is the financial crisis part of everyday life?

Matt Davies

THE QUESTION
POLITICS AND EVERYDAY LIFE

What is everyday life? Every day you get up, eat something, brush your teeth, go to the toilet, travel to school or work, see friends, work, study, go home, eat some more, spend time with your partner or maybe watch some television, go to sleep, and then do it all over again. These are just the ordinary, banal rhythms of your life: rhythms determined by your body, by the buildings you occupy and the arteries that connect them, and by the plans and obligations you encounter in the context of these daily activities. You will probably do these things, or similar things, for the rest of your life and you probably won't have to stop and think about them very much. You might save your thoughts and feelings and plans and hopes for 'higher' things. Everyday life is where we live, where we produce our experience, and also *not* where we live because it doesn't really occupy our attention – except, of course, when it is disrupted.

These sorts of activities are also mentioned at the start of **Chapter 3**, where it is suggested that they are part of the politics of the environment.

FIGURE 18.1
Henri Lefebvre. Photo: Sophie Bassouls/Sygma/Corbis

This means that there is an important sense in which our everyday lives exclude politics. Being political presumes that you are making some kind of claim, a claim for recognition as an equal subject that disrupts your positioning as unequal, voiceless, not a subject. How can you make a political claim in the part of your life that you perform routinely, without being obligated to stop and think about it?

This 'unreflected upon' character of everyday life preoccupied Henri Lefebvre, one of the foremost theorists of everyday life. For Lefebvre, the everyday was precisely what is left when the 'higher' activities of reflection, philosophy, planning and such are separated out from our daily lives. For example, our productive lives – our work – become means to satisfy 'higher' ends through consumption: people give up parts of their lives for a paycheque because the money they earn allows them to satisfy their wants and needs. Because these 'higher' activities can appear to us as the subjective part of our lives, everyday life comes to appear as an object from which our capacity for reflection has been abstracted. Indeed, because everyday life is so important for the reproduction of our social relations and for sustaining the 'higher' activities, it becomes an object *for* planning and programming. If we consider the purpose of advertising, for example, to be to produce new needs so new products can be sold, then we can see how advertisers make plans to intervene in the organization and practice of everyday life. In one of his more pessimistic descriptions of this relationship, in the mid-1960s, Lefebvre referred to everyday life in the modern Western world as having entered a phase he called the 'bureaucratic society of controlled consumption' (Lefebvre 1984 [1968]: 68–109).

At the same time, however, it's in the performance of these banal rituals that we enable ourselves to become subjects. This can create the possibility of politics as something 'outside' of our everyday lives, a 'higher' activity cultivated by our freedom to reflect and to think, enabled by the security of the satisfaction of daily rhythms. But – and this is why the 'at the same time' bit matters – we actually have to perform these rituals for everyday life to take place. They do not just enable 'higher activities' for ourselves or for others, they are the decisions and actions that we take, they are how we make ourselves subjects on an ongoing basis. So while politics is an exceptional, disruptive, 'higher' activity, it is also, *at the same time* an unexceptional, banal, everyday activity. It is this 'both . . . and . . .' character that makes the *location* of global politics such a complicated matter.

ILLUSTRATIVE EXAMPLE
FINANCE AND THE FINANCIAL CRISIS

The question of money and wealth, and how wealth is measured, are discussed in **Chapter 19**. The meaning of poverty is examined in **Chapter 20**.

We can see how this problem comes up by looking a bit more closely at finance and the financial crisis. How does the financial crisis affect our everyday lives? What is finance? In the first instance, finance is not the same thing as money. Money does several things for us: it makes it easy to exchange things in a market because it gives us a standard measure of values; money is also a store of value, so we get a sense of how wealthy a person or a corporation or a nation is by how much money they have; but crucially, money is also a commodity and as such, it is *scarce*: there is no guarantee that the right quantities of money will be in the right places to enable all the necessary exchanges to take place.

One way of trying to get money to the right places is for someone who owns money to lend it. This is where finance comes in. In the first place, if you are going to lend money to someone, you have to believe that they will be able to pay it back. This belief is called credit; we measure our confidence in someone's ability to pay by saying how much credit we are willing to extend to them. In addition to the extending of credit, finance is also about distributing risk. Someone who needs money but has little credit is a higher risk but they still need money, so finance puts them together with someone a little more willing to take the risk that they won't pay. The speculative lender will likely be prepared to take this risk because the person with less credit will pay more to borrow the money than a person with more credit. This points to the third important quality of finance, the way that money is a commodity: finance is a way that people make money from money, rather than from producing a 'real' good to be exchanged in the market.

Chapter 20 discusses some alternative schemes for providing finance: to what extent are these able to make a difference to the underlying issues addressed here?

'Financialization' refers to the progressive insertion of this logic of finance (extending credit, distributing risk, and making money from money) into more and more areas of social and economic life. You can imagine a life where finance plays a fairly restricted role. If there are no tuition fees for universities and your government provides you with maintenance grants, then you probably won't have to borrow money to pay for your higher education. If your wages increase roughly in correlation with the productivity of your labour – as they did during the post-Second World War boom until about 1975 in the United States – then you will probably be able to pay for most of the items you want to consume out of your earnings, the exceptions being only those extraordinarily expensive items, like housing, that you might pay for over long periods of time. You probably don't have to imagine a life where finance plays a fairly unrestricted role because that's the life you live now if you live in the US or the UK: student loans, car loans, credit cards, mortgages, daily stock market averages reported in the news, credit scores, online purchasing, pension planning, insurance. The bureaucratic society of controlled consumption that Henri Lefebvre described in 1967 has asserted itself with a vengeance as financial calculations regulate more and more areas of our everyday lives.

This situation – where finance plays a limited role – is described when the author of **Chapter 19** describes his experience as a British citizen born in the early 1950s.

Consider how tuition fees for university education mean that people are drawn into a system of loans and credit.

This art of calculation is increasingly inserted into everyday life. To manage all of the financial decisions and actions that affect your life, you have to decide how much risk you are willing to take on and how you might set out to increase your personal wealth through beating the average (or paying someone to beat the average for you) in the returns on your investments. Do you put your savings in the stock market? In real estate? In gold? How do you manage your credit score and credit history? There are video clips on YouTube (we examine these in more detail later in the chapter) which are all intended to be able to communicate explanations of finance with a non-specialist, everyday, audience. Say It Visually's (2008) video is for 'kids and grownups' literally: personal finance or 'financial literacy' has become a core element in primary and secondary education.

a.bacall
"Do we want to apply for a credit card that plays the song 'Money Makes The World Go Around' every time it is swiped?"

FIGURE 18.2
'Do we want to apply for a credit card . . .' Artist: A. Bacall. CartoonStock ref.: aban1188. www.CartoonStock.com

Because these are calculations, it is possible to get them wrong: you might lend money that can't be repaid, or borrow money you cannot pay back. The art of calculating credit and risk has become quite arcane and credit rating agencies exert the power they do because of the technical expertise for making financial calculations at their disposal. This is part of how financialization is linked to depoliticization. Financialization leads to a kind of technocracy because it shifts the responsibility for decisions away from people and to the algorithms and calculations. Furthermore, as these calculations are proprietary, financialization shifts the accountability for these decisions out of the public arena where they might be contested and into the private sector, where they are judged only on the basis of what they are worth in terms of their instrumental effectiveness.

Thus when someone defaults on their mortgage or when Lehman Brothers goes bankrupt, we tend not to see these as political acts. They just got their calculations wrong. But there are political consequences. The free-market system that was supposed to work without intervention or regulation seized up on the back of the collapse of the sub-prime bubble and of the major investment houses that were exposed. We called it a financial *crisis* because external intervention appeared to be required. And, as we will see below, the form this intervention took gives us a good look at where the global politics of the financial crisis was initially located: in equally technocratic institutions such as central banks, ministries of finance, treasuries, and international financial institutions involved in global governance, such as the International Monetary Fund.

The policies these agencies prescribed have not varied much over the last 30 years: austerity, privatization, liberalization. These policies are presented as medicine to ailing economies. But even as economic experts have devised these policies in accordance with technically sophisticated analyses, the implementation of these measures has never been a strictly technical matter. A political excess makes itself evident as austerity disrupts people's everyday lives. The current anti-austerity demonstrations in the UK, Greece, and Spain or the #occupy movements in the USA and elsewhere in 2011 share a common history with the anti-IMF riots in Africa when structural adjustment programmes were imposed in the 1980s in response to sovereign debts, and with the widespread demonstrations against cuts in Asia in the 1990s and the uprisings in Argentina in the 2000s. As much as such demonstrations appear to be local in their enactments, they are also an assertion of a global politics located much closer to everyday life.

The impact of the crisis in Argentina and how people altered their everyday lives in response is described in **Chapter 14**, and the results of structural adjustment programmes in Ivory Coast in **Chapter 15**.

This global political excess, the part of life that cannot be reduced to financial calculation, for example, would be important but rather meagre if it only mattered when everyday life is disrupted by economic austerity measures or anti-austerity demonstrations. It is hard to perceive the political in the everyday but as we saw above, the everyday is also always already political, even as it precludes politics. Financialization plays a role in creating this distribution of the sensible – the ways that politics is hard to perceive in everyday rhythms and is located remotely, at the 'level' of the international.

Has this financial crisis had an equal impact on people throughout the world?

You probably already have a pretty good idea of how the financial crisis that began to unfold in the autumn of 2007 has affected your everyday life. If you are reading this book as part of a university course, you may have to borrow money to pay for your fees

FIGURE 18.3
'Crisis? What crisis?' http://t2.gstatic.com/images?q=tbn:ANd9GcQF5Gs_EpFKC3fRD7Dqut6xptf9iKCwXZs3nMmuMczTH4oWmcbb; http://www.valuewalk.com/2011/12/when-finance-hijacked-our-economy/financial-crisis-cartoon/#.TwiTpCNlWQk

or for housing and maintenance; you might have a credit card (or several) that you use to buy essentials and other things; you might be casting a nervous eye towards the job market when you graduate; you may hope someday to be able to take out a mortgage and buy a home. Each of these depends on access to credit, and credit became much scarcer as the big investment banks and institutions in Europe and the US either failed or were bailed out while the financial markets crashed.

Of course, as well as economic crises, we also think of many other things as crises: the environmental crisis (**Chapter 3**), and humanitarian crises (**Chapter 25**) are two examples. What impact does thinking of these examples as crises have?

But why did we call it a crisis in the first place? 'Crisis' suggests (among other things) an emergency: in medical terms, a crisis is an extreme situation, a particular moment in which external medical intervention is needed to keep a patient alive. Given the continuity of financial crises over the last 30 years, you might be forgiven for wondering why we call them 'crises' and not just 'business as usual'. There is an effect that comes from thinking about these financial processes in terms of crisis, an effect that tells us something important about how we think about politics at the global scale. If a crisis is an emergency that requires intervention by a specialist, such as a skilled surgeon, then

BOX 18.1 POLITICS AND AESTHETICS: JACQUES RANCIÈRE

FIGURE 18.4
Jacques Rancière.
http://en.wikipedia.org/wiki/Jacques_Ranci%C3%A8re; http://en.wikipedia.org/wiki/File:Jacques_Ranciere.jpg

Jacques Rancière is a philosopher who has made a signal contribution to contemporary debates about politics and democracy as well as aesthetics. His work is very relevant to our discussion because of the ways that he links politics and aesthetics.

Democracy, for Rancière, is above all a practice of equality. Equality is not the same as equivalence, it doesn't mean we're all the same. What it does mean is that we are all equally capable of asserting ourselves in the realm of politics. Politics refers to the moment in which our habits and dispositions are disrupted and our perceptions change. The 'way things are' and are governed is held in place by what various other political philosophers call politics – this is the art and science of government – but Rancière refers to this practice of governing with the related term, 'police'. You can see the difference if you think of 'politics' as the practices and outcomes of disagreement and disputation, which changes how we perceive each other and our relations as we recognize each other as equal. Women's movements, for example, accomplished a change in people's perceptions through their political activities. Even people who disagree with their claims had to be able to recognize them as political claims if they intended to refute them. We can think of government, policy, law, and such in terms of how they 'police' existing arrangements. One of the intriguing implications of Rancière's formulation is that democracy, as a practice of equality, is not so much a kind of politics as it is the *precondition* for politics.

How we act and how we think about our acts – how we are subjects – in the context of 'police' depends strongly on how we can perceive the world. Aesthetics is not just a theory of beauty or art, then, but a theoretical account of the organization of our perceptions. This is how aesthetics and politics are tied together: both involve a *partage du sensible*, which we can translate variously as the *partition*, *separation*, *distribution*, and *sharing of the world* that is available to our senses. Art can change the way we can see the world by giving us new abilities to perceive it.

the input of the patient is really beside the point. Specialists take technical decisions and the patient's subjectivity – our sense of self, of being a centre of decision or action – is put on hold. Financial crises are examples of the way that when we think of politics at the global scale, or at the level of the international, politics is suspended at the scale or level of our everyday lives: decisions and actions are taken by technically skilled specialists who can operate at the international level while our everyday lives are restricted ('austerity') as we wait for the technically skilled experts to fix the problems.

Chapter 24 looks at how identifying certain things as dangerous can suspend politics.

Questioning whether financial crises are 'crises' does not demean the very real suffering of people. Financial crises lead to the suspension of democratic government by authoritarian rulers, the imposition of economic austerity measures, the privatization of public assets and shredding of social safety nets, all of which have been prescribed by economics specialists for economically technical reasons. Raising the question of what results from thinking of the financial crisis as a crisis, rather, is a means of investigating the politics behind the organization of how we not only make sense of but also manage to perceive the things we want to make sense of. Thinking of questions concerning the economy as technical matters, and of economic problems as requiring technical solutions, depends not only on how we think about the economy but also on what we can perceive an economy to be. Disrupting these sensibilities – these perceptions and understandings – is *both* aesthetic ***and*** political. And this disruption is important if we are to think of another politics in the face of perpetual financial crisis.

GENERAL RESPONSES
THE POLITICS OF THE FINANCIAL CRISIS

So far, the illustrative example in this chapter has examined finance and the financial crisis as a way of looking at the relation between everyday life and politics. And we've seen that, to the extent that the financial crisis is a technically complex problem beyond the comprehension of ordinary people in their everyday lives, 'global politics' feels like a remote, 'higher' level for the 'art and science of government' to take place, while everyday life appears as the space where unanticipated disruptions to the smooth operations of finance occurred and not as a space for politics.

In this section I want to examine two kinds of policy and political responses to the financial crisis – first, how international organizations and governments have responded, and second how ordinary people and citizens have responded.

A significant amount of the debate on the financial crisis centres on the actions of large financial institutions, such as savings and investment banks or stock and bond markets, or on governments, or on international institutions. As the housing market in the United States turned downward and institutional investors began to see both their gains and their equity in investments in housing disappear, the global financial system came under severe pressure. Grossly simplifying a complex sequence of events, when Lehman Brothers declared bankruptcy in September 2008, a number of serious economic and financial effects were felt right away. The Dow Jones – an index of aggregated stock market prices in the USA – lost over 4 per cent of its value on the day Lehman filed for bankruptcy and another 7 per cent two weeks later as investors sought safer refuges. Lehman's holdings of mortgage-backed securities were sold, putting

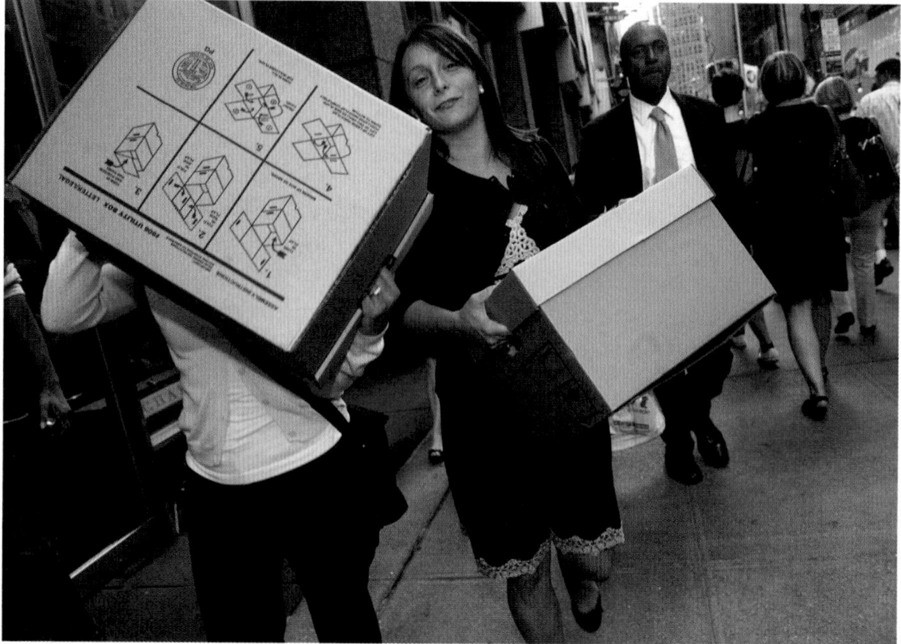

FIGURE 18.5 Women carrying boxes leave the Lehman Brothers HQ in 2008. Photo: Louis Lanzano/AP/Press Association Images

further downward pressure on commercial and other real estate. Lehman had loaned and borrowed a vast amount of investment capital as it brokered hedge funds (investments that are permitted to use highly aggressive or risky strategies) or borrowed and loaned on money markets, and these exposures to risky investments included other banks (such as Wachovia), mortgage financiers (such as Freddie Mac) and other government chartered corporations (such as Farmer Mac), subsidiary companies, and crucially, as a transnational corporation, it also exposed investors in Europe, London, Tokyo, Canada, and so on. The effects of the failure of Lehman put the global financial system at risk as credit began to disappear because investors feared exposure to failing institutions.

Thus was born the expression 'too big to fail'. Prior to the current financial crisis, many economists worried that bailing out failing investments skews the markets because if you know you won't lose your money, you don't need to worry about how much risk is involved in an investment. Economists call this problem 'moral hazard'. But the bankruptcy of Lehman posed another hazard, that of a deflationary spiral where falling wages, high unemployment, and low interest rates provoke a recession that reinforces the conditions that brought the recession about in the first place. To return to the idea that 'crisis' could refer to a medical condition, governments and international financial institutions clearly felt the need to stop the bleeding, and how this should be done was (and is) the subject of much debate.

Rather than wading into these debates, however, it is interesting to notice how states, corporations and banks, and international organizations have defined the problem denoted by 'financial crisis' and how this way of seeing the problem has shaped the kinds of solutions that they consider. It's not necessarily that economists and government officials are insensitive to the suffering of other people. However, because they have tended to see the economy as a sphere of circulation, they have tended to see the threat to the economy in the banks' inability or unwillingness to provide the credit needed to keep the circulation of goods, services, and money going. Or they have turned the financial crisis into a sovereign debt crisis, as responsibility for the financial instability has been shifted from banks and financial institutions to governments having trouble making payments on their foreign debts, such as Greece, or with growing fiscal deficits, such as the UK. Never mind that these deficits have been exacerbated by the recession and by providing public or state guarantees for private investors in failed banks. The point is that as the problems of financial crisis are defined in terms of the liquidity needed for sustaining the circulation of commodities, the solutions focus on the institutions such as banks and governments that affect that liquidity. Thus the arena for political disputation is circumscribed by the debates about the effectiveness of these policies. Other discourses, indeed other voices, simply cannot be heard in these circles.

The way a problem is framed is very important in determining how it is responded to. Certain framings demand certain responses.

But this doesn't mean other voices aren't speaking and disputing this way of framing the problems of financial crisis. As our short discussion of the Royal Society for the Encouragement of Arts, Manufactures, and Commerce's (RSA) animation of David Harvey's explanation in the next section will show even more clearly, disagreement and disputations that perceive the problems differently can come from unexpected directions. The actions of people not in these 'higher' circles of action and decision, which are focused on restoring liquidity as a solution to the crisis, appear as efforts to politicize finance. A few notable examples illustrate this.

FIGURE 18.6
Icelanders voting in referendum in Reykjavik, Iceland, on Saturday 6 March 2010, on approving the use of taxpayers' money to repay international debts. Photo: AP/Brynjar Gauti. http://media.washtimes.com/media/image/2010/03/06/ICELAND_FINANCIAL_CRI_Stai_s640x415.jpg?f36e0f9cc85cad0edd3739c1d7f3d763895e87a6

FIGURE 18.7
A woman shouts while taking part in an anti-austerity rally in Athens' Syntagma Square, 18 October 2011. Photo: Reuters. http://212.31.2.101/n.php?n=nationwide-strike-and-demonstrations-shut-down-greece-before-austerity-vote-2011–10–19

In 2010, after the collapse of three major banks in Iceland, the Icelandic Parliament, known as the Althing, passed a bill that would have provided state-backed guarantees to the deposit insurance corporation that was supposed to repay depositors who had savings in these banks. In particular, the retail bank Landsbanki had significant exposure to UK and Dutch depositors, so there was significant international pressure on Iceland to bail these banks out. The Althing passed a bill that reflected negotiated compromises with the UK and Dutch governments, but Iceland's president refused to sign the bill into law. Thus the bill went to a referendum. The first referendum to guarantee the funds for the bailout was held on 6 March 2010, and it was rejected by over 93 per cent of the voters. A second referendum was held on 9 April 2011, after the Althing had once again passed a bill that the president refused to sign – this time, the referendum failed by almost 60 per cent. Though people may have voted against these measures for diverse reasons, it was clear that using public funds to settle the obligations of failed private banks was deeply unpopular and rejected when voters were given the chance.

Popular anger at the public bailouts of banks and financial institutions and at the austerity measures imposed by various governments, often under pressure from the International Monetary Fund, can also be seen as efforts to politicize financial issues. Also in 2010 and 2011, often citing as examples the Arab Spring movements in North Africa and the Middle East, people began protesting and occupying public spaces in many parts of the world. Though again, the causes underlying these movements and the demands they make are complex and cannot be reduced to a single issue, they all tend to make evident popular anger at the 'need to resume business as usual' approach to the financial crisis – that is, 'restore order' or 'police' the crisis – adopted by their governments and their banks. Anti-austerity campaigns in Greece have resulted in several general strikes in the country, making it increasingly difficult for Eurozone bankers and heads of state to ignore popular anger at the terms in which the Greek public is expected to pay for Greece's debt. Similar protests have also rocked Italy and Portugal. In Spain, a country that prior to the financial crisis showed remarkably high growth rates and now shows remarkably high levels of unemployment, the movement for 'real democracy' is often referred to as 'los indignados' – the indignant people. By October 2011, the protests that began on Wall Street in New York City under the hashtag #occupy – the use of social media to mobilize has again been reminiscent of the Arab Spring movements – had spread not only to other US cities but to cities around the world, again with complex causes but focused on the perceived injustice of public protection for the wealth, privilege, and business practices of banks and finance in the face of recession, austerity, and unemployment for everyone else.

The actions of social movements in financial crises are also discussed in **Chapter 14**. There is more about Occupy in **Chapter 28**, and the Arab Spring is discussed in **Chapter 9**.

Again, and of course, the ends and the tactics of these political movements are debatable but it is clear that they are attempting to answer back to the efforts to remove the discussion of the financial crisis to the boardrooms and summits where the intricacies of technical disputes about economic policy limit the possibilities for discourse. Indeed, it is because the protests are debatable, because disagreement takes place amongst citizens and others demanding an equal voice, that they politicize the issues they address. The voters in the referenda in Iceland and demonstrators in Greece – and Italy, and Portugal, and Spain, and Korea, and the UK, and the USA, and Hong Kong, and Chile, and so on – create a global space that is not removed and insulated from everyday spaces in workplaces and universities, streets and squares. The people participating in these acts become specifically political subjects because they assert their voices against their exclusion from the policies and decisions imposed on them from the global space of heads of state and bankers, bureaucrats and technocrats.

FIGURE 18.8
The Occupy London Stock Exchange protesters at St Paul's. Photo: Carl Court/ AFP/Getty. http://www.guardian.co.uk/uk/2011/oct/19/occupy-london-st-pauls-protesters-leave

However, are such protest movements parts of everyday life? Or do they only occur as disruptions of, or in response to disrupting everyday life? To answer these questions, we must return yet again to the original question this chapter set out to address: Has politics been removed from everyday life?

BROADER ISSUES
RE-POLITICIZING FINANCE, RE-POLITICIZING EVERYDAY LIFE

Let's look at some examples of how the organization of our perceptions of the financial crisis tends to locate the space for politics beyond the spaces of our everyday lives – how it removes politics from our everyday life. What if you had to prepare a presentation on the financial crisis without having much background in finance or the international economy? Where would you start? Perhaps you would start with Wikipedia – as it happens, Wikipedia does have some good background information about the timelines of the financial crisis and some of the concepts and arguments that have been made to try to explain it. But maybe you would prefer to do a presentation that had helpful visual supports, something interesting to look at. A video hosting service such as YouTube would be a likely place to look for both explanations and visual representations of the crisis.

New media and the internet are discussed in **Chapter 9**.

The discussions in this part of the chapter will make more sense if you watch the YouTube clips as you go along.

And there is indeed a fair amount of material available on YouTube. A lot of clips have an authoritative look to them: talking heads in newsrooms or studios or lecture halls, speaking at length using technical, authoritative language. These films may (or may not) be informative. Visually, they are usually not very interesting. If you have 82 minutes to spare, you can watch a good example of a 'talking heads' (and PowerPoint presentation) video clip, a film of a panel of Yale University academic staff, titled 'Understanding the Financial Crisis' (2009). It was produced by Yale University and it is available at http://youtu.be/ScMLpqOvyVQ. It had 22,443 views as of 21 October 2011; comments were disabled.

Short, animated clips can be somewhat more accessible and visually interesting. If you wanted to make a short presentation with good visuals, you might turn to these instead. We will discuss four short animations here, each produced by an organization or individual that uses visualizations to explain complex issues like the financial crisis. Say It Visually's 2008 video clip, 'Understanding the Financial Crisis – For Kids and Grownups', had 205,357 views and 356 comments as of 9 October 2011. It is available at http://youtu.be/h4Ns4ltUvfw; see also http://www.sayitvisually.com/.

Also from 2008 was Enspire Learning's 'Understanding the Financial Crisis', which had 46,940 views and 37 comments as of 9 October 2011. This one is available at http://youtu.be/gF6LbFDjvW0; again, see also http://www.enspire.com/.

Jonathan Jarvis posted a clip in 2009 titled, 'The Crisis of Credit Visualized'. It appears in several different places on YouTube but an early version, part one of the full clip, had 1,145,448 views and 1,150 comments as of 9 October 2011. See Jonathan Jarvis (2009a) 'The Crisis of Credit Visualized', http://youtu.be/Q0zEXdDO5JU for Part One of an early version, with these hits and comments. A full version is at http://youtu.be/bx_LWm6_6tA; see also http://jonathanjarvis.com/.

And in 2010, as part of an ongoing series of animations of talks given at their institute, the Royal Society for the Encouragement of Arts, Manufactures, and Commerce (The RSA) posted a clip of a talk given by David Harvey on 'The Crises of Capitalism', which had 1,282,640 views and 5,420 comments as of 9 October 2011. It is at http://www.youtube.com/watch?v=qOP2V_np2c0. See http://www.thersa.org/ for more on the RSA, and see http://www.cognitivemedia.co.uk/ for information on the animation studio.

Each of the first three video clips that we will discuss – Say It Visually (2008), Enspire Learning (2008), and Jarvis (2009a and b) – tells a story that by now may be familiar. They focus on how credit expanded as investors sought new places to invest the savings that had accumulated through pension funds, savings, sovereign investment funds, and the like. They all begin, helpfully, by looking at the obscure financial instruments that were devised to make high risk investments attractive to investors and that expanded the market for credit, especially in housing and real estate in the United States. The videos illustrate and explain concepts like 'credit default swaps' and 'collateralized debt obligations' and 'mortgage backed securities' and show how, as financial capital swelled the markets for such instruments, intermediaries like banks made credit more widely available to increasingly high risk borrowers. Each also explains a little bit about the changing regulatory environment, such as the repeal of the Glass-Steagall Act of 1934. Glass-Steagall had separated retail banking – the banking ordinary customers use – from investment banking in the United States with a view to protecting ordinary depositors' money from more high risk speculation. In the story that each of these videos tells, the entrance into the financial system of high-risk borrowers – what Jarvis (2009a) calls 'less responsible' sub-prime borrowers – introduced a new element of risk into the financial system that increased returns for speculators willing to take on higher risks while spreading the risk more widely across the system. Thus when the high-risk investments went bad, such as when people could not make payments on their sub-prime mortgages, the whole financial system was compromised.

In his clip, David Harvey (2010) takes a different approach. Harvey starts by acknowledging that what we see are *stories* about the credit crunch, or as he puts it, *genres* of explanations. His account of the crisis is somewhat more sophisticated than the others, though no less clear, because he summarizes five such types of story and acknowledges that each has an element of truth to it: so there is a genre of explanation that looks at 'human frailty' or the predatory instincts of investors; one that looks at institutional failures; one that suggests that everyone has been obsessed with a false theory, which has made previously unfashionable theorists such as John Maynard Keynes and Hyman Minsky fashionable again; one that suggests that the crisis has cultural origins, such as the national character of the Greeks or the US preference for privately owning homes; and finally one that says that the crisis is the result of policy, especially too much regulation. Harvey, as a Marxist and a geographer, asks himself what kind of story he could tell that would be different to these, and he focuses his explanation on the contradictions that underlie capital accumulation. As with the previous video clips he simplifies his explanation to keep it short. He notes that where a company that produces items for the market tries to keep its costs down by keeping its wage bill down, it then finds a market where consumers have less to spend: consumers are just workers on the other side of the ledger. One way to solve this problem is to

The importance of examining narratives or stories is mentioned in **Chapter 5**; **Chapter 13** looks at stories told in novels and **Chapter 8** at media representations and film.

Marxist or historical materialist explanations of capitalism are examined in **Chapters 15, 17 and 19**.

provide consumers with credit. Finance, in Harvey's story, is one way of making sure that money gets to the place it needs to be to facilitate capital accumulation but it does so by enriching financiers at the expense of the rest of the economy. For Harvey, crisis, not stability, is the defining characteristic of capitalism.

We could go into greater detail with these explanations. Each is controversial, both from a technical, economic theory perspective and from a political perspective – as you might notice if you read some of the comments under the clips. But one interesting idea in the video clips is where they locate the dynamics of the system that goes into crisis. Remember that for Harvey, the crisis results from inherent tendencies in capitalism, what he calls 'internal contradictions of capital accumulation'. For Say It Visually (2008), Enspire Learning (2008), and Jonathan Jarvis (2009a and b), the financial crisis stems from some deal going bad, such as a mortgage default, that interrupts the otherwise smooth flows of money and promises-to-pay that define the economy. For these explanations, the economy is a sphere of *circulation*. For circulation to take place, exchanges must be enabled – for example, by providing credit to a purchaser. In a market, the things that get exchanged are equivalents, despite whatever might be different about them. Part of what money does is to measure or express the value of things in terms that enables them to be exchanged – so many hours of work I do for which I receive a wage are thus equal to a week's worth of groceries or a visit to the pub: x hours = y money = z pints of beer. In the sphere of circulation, *differences* are suppressed. In contrast, difference is crucial to the sphere of *production*: I have a different set of skills to yours; when we work, we exercise those skills by changing the materials we work on, adding value to those materials. As workers, we are different and we make differences in the world by working.

The centrality of the market to how the global economy works, and its uneven impact on everyday lives, is examined in **Chapter 17**.

Translating things like hours of work to money equivalents is called the commodification of labour: people's capacity to work is treated as something that can be bought and sold. At one time people themselves were bought and sold – slavery is discussed in **Chapter 15**.

We will return to the difference that difference makes in a moment but our project here is not to try to find out the 'correct' explanation of the financial crisis, it is to try to think about how these explanations *locate* politics. If the economy is identified as the sphere of circulation and in this sphere differences are suppressed, then it is hard to imagine a place for politics in the economy. Is the politics of the financial crisis properly conducted at the level of international agreements and banking practices? Is it a matter of national policy making and regulation? Or is there some way to think about the *politics* of the financial crisis in our everyday lives?

While the debates surrounding the meanings of these concepts and the dynamics that drive the systems do provide clues to this process of locating politics, what is also striking is the ways in which we *imagine* these concepts and dynamics locate politics. To unpack our imagining of the financial crisis will require some visual analysis, too.

The analysis of the way images work – as much by what they leave out as by what they show and how they show it – is an often neglected area of political analysis. For other examples, see the discussion of John Trumbull's painting of the US Declaration of Independence in **Chapter 13**, and of images of war in **Chapter 8**.

The kinds of economic activities that these clips make visible are purchasing, borrowing and lending. In other words, just as with the ways in which they explain the financial crisis by identifying the economy with the sphere of circulation, they also present and make visible the economy as a sphere of circulation. In the Enspire Learning (2008) clip, people and houses appear as stick figures, with nothing to distinguish one from the other. Say It Visually (2008) uses figures that are similar to 'clip art', figures with no facial features or other distinguishing characteristics. Just as money and promises to pay pass effortlessly from side to side, so also are the people completely interchangeable. Jarvis handles the presentation of the agents of these transactions a little differently, but no less generically: bankers can be distinguished from borrowers by their hats and rotund

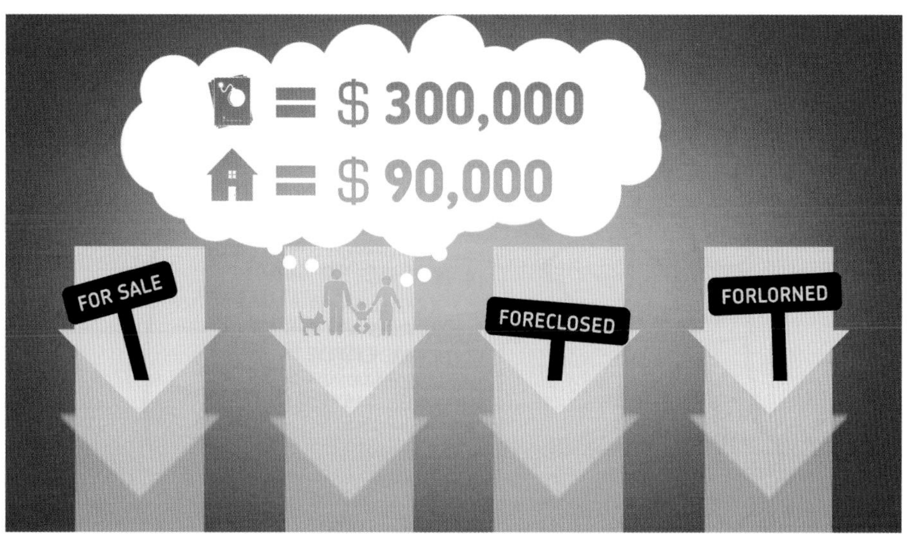

FIGURE 18.9 Jonathan Jarvis clip from YouTube. http://youtube/QozEXdDO5JU

bodies, for example. But the figures that stand in for the family of responsible borrowers are very similar to the generic figures representing people on road signs or toilet doors: the woman is distinguished from the man by a skirt, the baby by a nappy. When Jarvis does introduce some distinguishing characteristics, he refers to the 'well, less responsible' borrowers and he alters this road sign family by giving the adults bottles and cigarettes and replacing the family dog with more babies. Playing on our class prejudices, this clip places the blame for the failure of the financial system on less generic figures, with whom well educated middle-class people then no longer identify. The system of perfect equivalences and exchangeability was soured by irresponsible borrowers – with no further consideration as to why they did not have sufficient income or why they might fail to make their payments. The visual field produced in these three animations reinforces the explanations they give.

With regard to its visual field, Harvey's video clip again stands in stark contrast to the approach taken in the other clips. In the first place, the various figures are typically not generic but specific: you see former chairman of the US Federal Reserve Alan Greenspan, political commentator Glenn Beck, the former president of Brazil Lula da Silva, the economists Keynes and Minsky; Greece (represented by an urn and a statue) is different from Brazil (represented by a man playing a guitar) or the USA (represented by Uncle Sam).

But, in the second place and even more importantly, consider what is animated in the animations. The first three clips follow film conventions for movement and action: people move around, the banks and investors and the toxic assets are animated, words move into and out of the screen recalling the stock animations of a PowerPoint slide, giving a dynamic feel to the concepts they represent. The borrowers, the lenders, and the concepts that explain the crisis make the action in these clips. In contrast, in the animations produced by Cognitive Media for the RSA, the action presented is an artist's hand, drawing on a whiteboard. Throughout Harvey's talk, the drawings are made to comment on what he is saying, sometimes humorously, sometimes critically. The

FIGURE 18.10
David Harvey clip from YouTube. http://www.youtube.com/watch?v=qOP2V_np2co

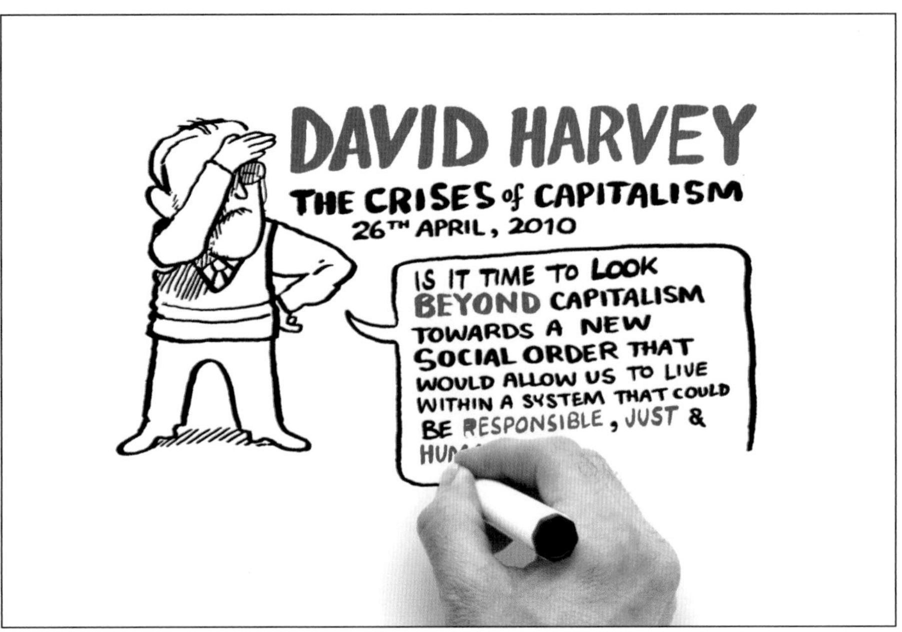

What do you make of the use of cartoons in this textbook? Are they just light relief, or do they have a political purpose?

cartoons stand in a relationship of *dialogue* with the voice of Harvey as an authority. They are *contesting* his explanations, even as they support what he says. And the *subject* of this film, the centre for action and decisions, is the artist's hand itself. Here we have expanded our explanation from the sphere of circulation to include the sphere of production – and difference – not by virtue of the particular explanation that Harvey makes: indeed, even though he emphasizes wage stagnation and the weakness of the labour movement since the 1970s as motivating the expansion of credit and of the power of finance, he is still referring to the ability of people to enter into purchases, he is still explaining the financial crisis in terms of finance and equivalence. Rather, the video expands the explanation in its visual field, by making the *making* visible.

What are the *political* consequences of the theoretical positions and aesthetic choices made in these clips? The representation of financialization in the films by Say It Visually (2008), Enspire Learning (2008), and Jonathan Jarvis (2009a and b), is supported by concepts that take on the air of technical, scientific knowledge to be conveyed to an uninformed audience. As animations, they do not rely on a 'reality effect' to assert their authority. However, while the drawings and animations do foreground the artificiality of the representations, they nevertheless rely on generic figures and mimic authoritative forms of addressing an audience. The economic theories in their explanations point to technical problems requiring expert solutions; they locate the economy in the sphere of the circulation of money, goods, and services, in which differences between things are ignored or suppressed to enable exchange to take place. The aesthetics of these films – what and how they make perceivable – replicates this erasure of difference and thus indicates no particular role to play in addressing financial crises on the part of the viewer they have just informed. Their distribution via YouTube mitigates this somewhat, by inviting comments and video responses, but the *politics* they invite seems to be located elsewhere: in the technical management of the economy of universal equivalence, not in the narrative or images of authoritative explanations and not in the everyday lives of consumers, borrowers, or viewers of clips on YouTube.

The theory, the aesthetics, and therefore the politics at work in David Harvey's short film are all different. For Harvey's economic theory, financialization is a political response to a political and economic problem. Harvey's explanation of his theory gestures towards the importance of the sphere of production for the economy but even more compellingly, the film makes its own production not only evident but also the very subject of the film. In doing so, the aesthetics also make the possibilities for contesting, challenging, commenting on, and even laughing at the various figures – including Harvey himself – involved in producing, explaining, or solving the financial crisis. In this way, the theoretical, economic, and aesthetic issues addressed in the film are all treated as political, and politics is located in the here-and-now of watching the clip. This may partly explain why Harvey's clip has generated almost five times as many comments as Jarvis's, the next most commented clip.

The answer we get looking at David Harvey's video clip gives us a hint about the ways that global politics and everyday life might be intertwined. If we 'get' the financial crisis well enough to be able to laugh at, respond to, and answer back to the claims about the necessary steps for solving the crisis, even if we are mistaken in our replies, then the politics is part of everyday life – and it produces a kind of global space in that everyday life.

CONCLUSION

So what is it that disrupts this distribution of the sensible, the distribution of what we can perceive that locates the global politics of the financial crisis so remotely from our everyday lives? Certainly, a part of the answer is itself political. People protest. They get angry, they share different experiences or stories, the safety of their own routines is broken by austerity and crisis, and they make their anger present by demanding to be recognized and heard.

But what happens to politics in everyday life itself? If financialization programmes act in such a way to keep global politics in the boardrooms and negotiating tables, then where do we see the possibilities for politics *in* everyday life? We have seen how financialization and the financial crisis present us with a view of the economy as the circulation of goods, money, and credit. And we have seen how in order to circulate, things have to be equivalent: difference disappears in the sphere of circulation. But the part of the economy that has no part in this view is production. The practice of production depends on difference as people bring different needs and different skills to work and as work transforms – makes different – the material we work on. And as the animation of David Harvey's talk so eloquently shows, making the making visible is also political: it brings that excluded part into the conversation as an equally apt voice.

The significance of production is explained further in **Chapter 19**.

Money abstracts from our differences and finance formalizes those abstractions. Everyday life is where we produce and reproduce ourselves and our social relations. This doesn't happen abstractly. Everyday life is our bodies – working bodies, parenting bodies, relaxing bodies – occupying and producing the spaces we live in. Geographers have shown how these spaces are multi-scalar: they are (simultaneously) intimate, local, regional, and global. Just as production is the part of the economy that has no part in the financialized economy, everyday life is the part of global space that has no part in the globalized economy. If we approach aesthetics as a pathway and practice to make this part perceivable, we are disrupting this distribution of the sensible and finding the global *politics* of everyday life.

FURTHER READING

One of the best, and angriest, introductions to the contemporary financial crisis is Matt Taibbi's 2010 book *Griftopia: Bubble Machines, Vampire Squids, and the Long Con That Is Breaking America*. Taibbi is a political journalist and contributor to *Rolling Stone* magazine. *Griftopia* not only provides a good description of the events and characters behind the crisis but he also provides clear and lucid explanations of the obscure and technical terms, such as credit default swaps, that have kept the discourse about finance technical and obscure, and not everyday.

Susan Strange was one of the earliest figures in international political economy to draw attention to the particular way the finance exercises power in the global system. See, for example, Susan Strange (1997/1986) *Casino Capitalism*. Gerald Epstein (2005) collected a series of important essays that tried to conceptualize financialization in his book *Financialization and the World Economy*.

However, as important as these contributions are as starting points, there is a great deal of research and theory that has gone much more deeply into the question of finance and financialization that is strongly relevant to understanding the financial crisis as a political moment. There is too much to present here but the following are some of the best examples and you can find further references in the bibliographies in these books. Adam Harmes' (2001) *Unseen Power: How Mutual Funds Threaten the Political and Economic Wealth of Nations* shows how financial instruments regulate policy and political options. Marieke de Goede's (2005) *Virtue, Fortune, and Faith: A Genealogy of Finance* is a groundbreaking theoretical and historical critique of finance and the forms of power/knowledge that underpin it. The most systematic and penetrating analysis of finance, international political economy, and everyday life can be found in Paul Langley's (2009) *The Everyday Life of Global Finance: Saving and Borrowing in Anglo-America*. Finally, a good introduction to money and finance in social context is Costas Lapavitsas' (2003) *Social Foundations of Markets, Money, and Credit.* I have elaborated some of the themes in the chapter in a recent article titled, 'The Aesthetics of the Financial Crisis: Work, Culture, and Politics' (2012). Of course, each of these approaches the issues from different theoretical perspectives and reading them will give you as much a sense of how deep the arguments go as of how things are supposed to work.

The analytical framework used in this chapter draws on the contributions of three of the most important figures in contemporary social and political theory. Henri Lefebvre's career spanned the twentieth century and he wrote over sixty books. His *Critique of Everyday Life* appeared in three volumes, published first in 1947 (revised in 1958 and appearing in English in 1991), second in 1962 (2006 in English), and the third volume appeared in 1981 (2008 in English). An overview of his theoretical work can be found in the collection edited by Stuart Elden, Elizabeth Lebas and Eleanore Kofman (2003) *Henri Lefebvre: Key Writings*. Jacques Rancière has also been extremely prolific. His political philosophy is presented succinctly in (1999) *Disagreement: Politics and Philosophy*. A good introduction to his approach to aesthetics is Jacques Rancière (2009) *Aesthetics and its Discontents*.

WEBSITES

In addition to the websites discussed in the text, these may also be helpful.

An excellent explanation of the financial forces behind the sub-prime crisis appeared on National Public Radio's and WBEZ's radio programme, *This American Life*. The episode is titled 'The Giant Pool of Money' and it can be heard at http://www.thisamericanlife.org/radio-archives/episode/355/the-giant-pool-of-money

Debtocracy is a documentary film about the crisis in Greece: http://youtu.be/qKpxPo-lInk

Mark Blyth, a professor at the Watson Institute for International Studies at Brown University, on what's wrong with austerity: http://youtu.be/FmsjGys-VqA

The UK newspaper the *Guardian* published a series of photos of the 'occupy everywhere' events of 18 October 2011: http://www.guardian.co.uk/world/gallery/2011/oct/18/occupy-movement-protest

Quantitative easing explained: http://www.bankofengland.co.uk/monetarypolicy/Pages/qe/default.aspx

Steve Keen's blog Debtwatch is an excellent source of heterodox economic analysis: http://www.debtdeflation.com/blogs/

REFERENCES

de Goede, Marieke (2005) *Virtue, Fortune, and Faith: A Genealogy of Finance*, Minneapolis: University of Minnesota Press.

Elden, Stuart, Elizabeth Lebas and Eleanore Kofman (eds) (2003) *Henri Lefebvre: Key Writings*, New York and London: Continuum.

Enspire Learning (2008) 'Understanding the Financial Crisis', video, http://youtu.be/gF6LbFDjvW0.

Epstein, Gerald (ed.) (2005) *Financialization and the World Economy*, Cheltenham, UK and Northampton, MA: Edward Elgar.

Harmes, Adam (2001) *Unseen Power: How Mutual Funds Threaten the Political and Economic Wealth of Nations*, Toronto: Stoddart.

Harvey, David (2010) 'RSA Animate – Crises of Capitalism', video, http://youtu.be/qOP2V_np2c0.

Jarvis, Jonathan (2009a) 'The Crisis of Credit Visualized – part 1', video, http://youtu.be/Q0zEXdDO5JU.

——(2009b) 'The Crisis of Credit Visualized – part 2', video, http://youtu.be/iYhDkZjKBEw.

Langley, Paul (2009) *The Everyday Life of Global Finance: Saving and Borrowing in Anglo-America*, Oxford: Oxford University Press.

Lapavitsas, Costas (2003) *Social Foundations of Markets, Money, and Credit*, London: Routledge.

Lefebvre, Henri (1984 [1968]) *Everyday Life in the Modern World*, New Brunswick, NJ and London: Transaction Publishers.

——(1991 [1958]) *Critique of Everyday Life vol. 1*, London: Verso.

——(2006 [1962]) *Critique of Everyday Life, vol. 2*, London: Verso.

——(2008 [1981]) *Critique of Everyday Life, vol. 3*, London: Verso.

Rancière, Jacques (1999) *Disagreement: Politics and Philosophy*, Minneapolis: University of Minnesota Press.

——(2009) *Aesthetics and Its Discontents*, Cambridge: Polity Press.

Say It Visually (2008) 'Understanding the Financial Crisis – For Kids and Grownups', video, http://youtu.be/h4Ns4ltUvfw.

Strange, Susan (1997/1986) *Casino Capitalism*, Manchester: Manchester University Press.

Taibbi, Matt (2010) *Griftopia: Bubble Machines, Vampire Squids, and the Long Con That Is Breaking America*, New York: Random House.

Yale University (2009) 'Understanding the Financial Crisis: The Stimulus, Bailouts, and other Solutions', video, http://youtu.be/ScMLpqOvyVQ.

For a range of further resources supporting this chapter, please visit the companion website for *Global Politics, 2nd Edition* at www.routledge.com/cw/edkins/

CHAPTER 19

Why are some people better off than others?

Paul Cammack

THE QUESTION
SOURCES OF INEQUALITY

Just by virtue of the fact that you are reading this book, you are likely to be among the better off people in the world – among those in a better economic or financial position; or in more advantageous circumstances. For a start, you are not among the estimated 17 per cent of the world's adult population classified as functionally illiterate (nearly two thirds of them women, by the way, although this is changing steadily). More than half the teenagers in the world get to stay on at school after 15 (55 per cent in 2008, and almost as many girls as boys); but if, as I expect, you have gone on to tertiary education (college or university), you are in the top 27 per cent, and now marginally more likely to be female than male (UNESCO 2011: 280, 325; UNESCO Statistical Database, table 9, accessed 24 January 2012). This doesn't guarantee that you are in a better economic or financial position than most, but it makes it very likely, as it puts you, relatively speaking, in very advantageous circumstances. Around 70 per cent of students in developed countries go into tertiary education, but only one in five (20 per cent) in developing countries, so your chance of having a college or university education is much higher if you grew up in a developed country. But wherever you grow up, your chance of making it to college or university is always better, the better off financially you are. And if you did, you'll be pleased to know that the longer you stay in education, the more you are likely to earn: in the United States, for example, male and female high school graduates in full-time work were averaging $43,140 and $32,227 per year respectively in 2009, while those with bachelor's degrees or better averaged $92,815 and $62,198 (US Census Bureau 2012, table 703). As you will quickly work out for yourself, the higher the level of education, the greater the relative disadvantage to women workers.

A thought experiment

Chapters 5 and 14 also examine how gender and race matter to people's lives.

Now, imagine that you could be someone else, and you could choose your gender and ethnicity, and when and where to live. Assuming you wanted the best chance of being economically well off, what would you choose?

If you chose now, rather than some time in the past, you would be sensible, for the richer developed countries at least. In the United States, again, average per capita GDP (the gross domestic product or total output of the country, measured in constant dollars, divided by the total population) was just under 60 per cent higher in 2010 than in 1979 (though, to be precise, it peaked in 2007–8). Second, you would be wise to choose to be male, as the figures in the previous section show. And if you did choose to be born in the US, you certainly shouldn't opt to be Hispanic. If you did, you would find yourself on the *lowest* average earnings, at $535 a week – less than if you were black ($611 per week), and much less than if you were white ($765 per week). In fact, you would do best if you chose to be Asian – the average salary of Asians in the US was $855 per week in 2010, perhaps because over half had a bachelor's degree or better, compared to 30 per cent of the white population, just under 20 per cent of the black population, and only 14 per cent of the Hispanic population. And over 10 million of the 14 million classified as Asian in 2009 were immigrants, a reminder that many people migrate in search of a better living – a poor one still, in the case of many migrants from Mexico and Central America, a much better one for most of the principally Chinese, Filipino, Indian, Vietnamese and Korean groups who make up the bulk of the Asian population (US Census Bureau 2012, tables 10, 229, 648, 681).

Despite this inequality within the United States and other rich nations, many people try to enter these countries in search for a better living and indeed take considerable risks to do so. **Chapter 10** examines the example of migration from Mexico to the United States.

Having said all that, if you did choose the US, you would be taking a risk. It is the richest of the large industrialized nations (the tiny Grand Duchy of Luxembourg, with a population under 500,000, is the richest state in the world by far), but it also has the highest and fastest rising income inequality in the rich world (Smeeding 2005: 968). If you were lucky, you might end up among the top 10 per cent, with an income around $100,000 a year; if you were very lucky indeed you might be among the one in ten thousand who take home over $14 million a year. Even this would be twenty times less than top CEO (Chief Executive Officer), Richard D. Fairbank of Capital One Financial, who took home $280 million in stock option gains in 2005. But as you can see from Figure 19.1, your chances of ending up with a high income would not actually have been good. Although *average* incomes were among the highest in the world, wealth

Income group	Number	Average income
All population	145,881,000	$46,806
Bottom 90%	131,292,900	$28,980
Top 91–95%	7,294,050	$110,424
Top 96–99%	5,835,240	$176,925
Top 99–99.5%	729,405	$370,887
Top 99.5–99.9%	583,524	$695,764
Top 99.9–99.99%	131,293	$2,316,353
Top 0.01%	14,588	$14,027,614
Top 100 CEOs	100	$34,479,120
Top 10 CEOs	10	$68,955,000
Top CEO	1	$249,420,000

FIGURE 19.1
Table of US average incomes, 2005. Emmanuel Saez, Updated Tables and Figures for 2005, at http://elsa.berkeley.edu/~saez/, accessed 29 July 2007

was actually heavily concentrated among the top 10 per cent of the population, and extremely concentrated towards the very top – the bottom 90 per cent averaged less than $29,000 per year. And incomes grew much more quickly for the rich than for the poor between 1979 and 2000. The poorest 10 per cent saw their incomes grow by only 8 per cent in total over those years, while the richest *doubled* their income (Smeeding 2005).

In the United States, then, inequality is dramatic, and far worse than it was 40 years ago. It has created the 'separate country' of Richistan, inhabited by just 1 per cent of the population (Frank 2007). In October 2007, just prior to the impact of the financial crisis, the US Inland Revenue Service calculated that income distribution had reached a new post-war peak of inequality in 2005, with the top 1 per cent of the population receiving 21.2 per cent of income (Ip 2007). This fell back somewhat after the crisis, but without raising expectations of a reversal in the long-term trend. The following section looks at the comparative picture, bringing in other rich industrial countries, and the 'emerging markets' of Brazil, Russia, India and China (sometimes referred to as the 'BRIC' countries because of their initials). As we shall see, although the US is an extreme case, the overwhelming majority of the world's population lives in societies that are becoming significantly more unequal. The third and fourth sections will explore some of the different explanations for and attitudes towards this growing global inequality, and the larger questions it provokes.

ILLUSTRATIVE EXAMPLE
INEQUALITY IN THE AGE OF NEOLIBERAL REFORM

There is nothing new about inequality between societies and individuals. It is and always has been a defining feature of global politics. Historically, such things as unequal ownership of land, rent from property and exploitation of political and military power have been important means of accumulation of personal and national wealth. In the nineteenth and twentieth centuries unequal access to education and policies that favoured urban rather than rural development also contributed to inequality between individuals and regions. But important as these issues still are, they do not explain contemporary patterns of inequality.

Changes in the global economy in the late twentieth century

Three changes that took place in the late twentieth century are shaping current patterns of global inequality. The first is the reversal of the significant post-Second World War shift towards greater equality in the advanced industrial economies, initiated by neoliberal reform in the UK and the US from the 1970s onwards. The second is the creation of a genuinely *global* capitalist economy over the same period, particularly as a consequence of the rise of the Asian economies (successively, Japan, Taiwan, Korea, China and India), and the re-establishment of market economies in the former Soviet Union and in Eastern Europe after 1989. The third is the concurrent promotion by leading governments and international institutions of greater openness and competitiveness in the emerging global capitalist economy. Current sources and patterns of inequality are not the result of chance, or of some mysterious force called 'globalization', but the product of a deliberate shift in policy, increasingly coordinated on a global scale. By the early years of the twenty-first century this had created a completely new set of global circumstances. As a result, the character and dynamics of inequality today are very different than in the past. The dynamic global expansion of capitalism has raised income levels in some of the poorest and most populous countries (such as China and India), so that if you compare average incomes across countries it looks as if global inequality has been reduced. But it has also made those countries much more unequal internally – so that the benefits of rising wealth are going disproportionately to a few. It is already possible to discern the outlines of the new pattern of inequality that will dominate in the future – the global ascendancy of capital over labour, the universal shift of income from workers to owners of capital, and the concentration of global income and wealth among a new class of global capitalists. Global capitalism may in the long run reduce inequalities between *countries*, but on present evidence it sharply increases inequalities between *individuals*. And increasingly, poverty comes not from exclusion from paid work, but from labour income inequality (poverty *in* work) (OECD 2012: ch. 5), especially in the UK and the US.

Chapter 17 examines some of the implications of this globalizing economy, in particular the phenomenon of informalization.

Chapter 16 shows how colonialism impoverished India.

A dramatic indication of this is given by the changing share of national income earned by the top 0.1 per cent of the population – the top one in a thousand in other words – up to the year 2000: in the US, the UK and Canada from 1913 to 2000, and for France and Japan from 1885 to 2000 (Figure 19.2). In the first three countries there was a sharp decline from the early twentieth century to around 1945 – the end

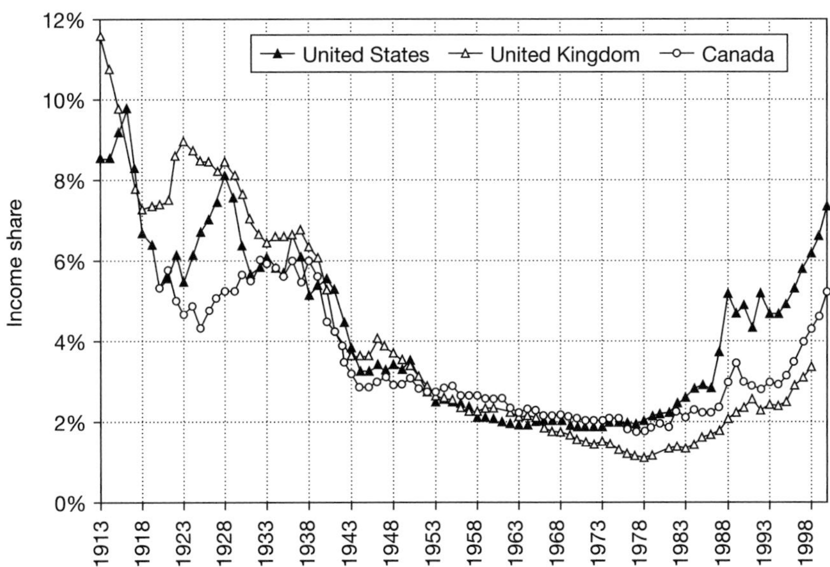

A. Top 0.1 per cent income share in English speaking countries

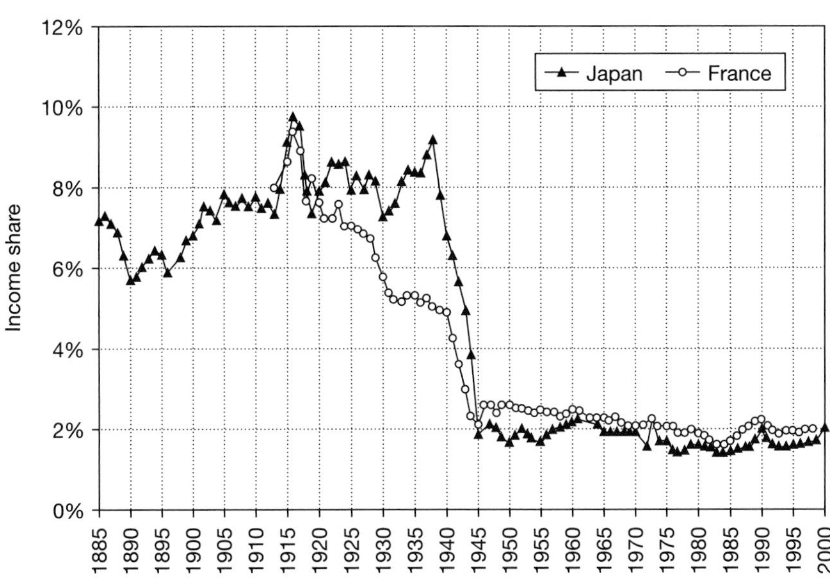

B. Top 0.1 per cent income share in France and Japan

FIGURE 19.2
Top 0.1 per cent income shares across countries. Piketty and Saez 2006: Figure 3, p. 203

Note that these graphs do not tell us who the top earners are, whether – for example – this group is predominantly white, predominantly male, predominantly from a privileged educational and/or socio-economic background.

of World War II, then a slight recovery, followed by a steady decline through to the late 1970s. But from the late 1970s onwards the share of income going to this tiny proportion of the population rose dramatically, back to where it was more than 60 years earlier (or 80 years ago in the case of the US), and continued to rise sharply. In France and Japan, too, the share of income going to the top 0.1 per cent of the population was relatively low and stable between 1945 and 1975. But while the share in France fell between the two world wars, as in the first three cases, in Japan it didn't fall at all until the Second World War. Second, in neither case did the share *rise* again from the early 1980s (Piketty and Saez 2006: 203). In the mid-1960s, the top thousandth of income earners were taking home about 2 per cent of national income in all five cases – two hundred times more than what an equal share would have been, but still very roughly a quarter of the share they had enjoyed 50 years earlier. Forty years later, the very rich in the US had practically gained back all they had lost, with the UK and Canada following the same path, but no such change had taken place in either France or Japan.

We are looking here only at the changing share of income of a tiny fraction of the population of just five countries. But the data tell us quite a lot about changing patterns of income distribution (how income is shared, or distributed, across different groups of the population) over the last century. First, they suggest that a substantial *redistribution* of income (a significant *change* in the way income was shared across the population) took place around the time of the Second World War, and was sustained thereafter. Second, though, it shows that to the extent that this was a global phenomenon (remember, we are looking only at five of the G7 countries – along with Germany and Italy, the seven leading developed economies in the world) it was unusual and relatively short-lived. Third, it suggests at least three different patterns: a Japanese (possibly East Asian) pattern, with 1939–45 a key turning point, and a stable distribution of income thereafter, and *two* 'Western' patterns – the first an 'Anglo-North American' pattern in which redistribution after the Second World War is rapidly reversed from the early 1980s, the second a French (possibly continental European) pattern in which it is not. A focus on the Nordic countries would reveal a third European pattern, accentuated more towards relative equality though recently under threat (OECD 2012).

The G7 countries are Canada, France, Germany, Italy, Japan, the UK and the US.

Measuring and comparing inequality

Measuring and comparing inequality in and between countries over time is complicated. As Box 19.1 explains, it cannot be done without good basic data (national statistics) and ways of comparing them; and the various ways of doing it have advantages and disadvantages. Figure 19.3 shows the measures of inequality discussed in Box 19.1 for ten countries around 2000 and around 2010 – three Scandinavian democracies known for their relative equality, and the seven leading developed nations known as the G7. The first column gives average levels of income (in terms of purchasing power), showing the US and Norway comfortably ahead of the rest. The remaining columns show different measures of inequality, and suggest that in every case except Norway they rose between 2000 and 2010. On every measure, the three Scandinavian democracies are the most equal. They have the lowest Gini coefficient (led by Denmark), and the poor receive well over half (57 per cent) of the median income (P10/P50), while the rich receive from around one-and-a-half to one-and-two thirds the median income

(P90/P50). In contrast, in the most extreme case among the developed states, that of the United States, the poor receive only 37 per cent of the median income, while the rich receive more than twice as much. As a result, the gap between the rich and poor (P90/P10) is twice as much in the United States as it is in Denmark and Norway, with the other developed G7 countries in between. So although the *average income* in the United States is almost the highest among these countries, if we look at the real incomes of the poor (P10 real income rank) the poor are better off in Canada, Denmark, Germany and Norway – as they are in Austria, Belgium, Luxembourg, the Netherlands, Switzerland and Taiwan (Brandolini and Smeeding 2007, fig. 3: 33). The *poor* in the United States, in other words, do not even make it into the top ten in global terms. As the authors point out, this is a consequence of a period of 'unrelenting increases in income inequality' from the 1970s on.

Paralleling the sudden surge in the incomes of the very rich (Figure 19.2 above), the Gini coefficient in the United States has risen steadily over the last 40 years, from a situation where it was already the highest in the developed world. The United Kingdom, the original home of the welfare state, and among the more equal of the developed

Income inequality in ten developed countries, 2000 (Japan 1992)–2010

	1	2	3	4	5	6	7			
Country	*GDP per capita (PPP) 2009*	*Rank*	*Gini circa 2000*	*Rank*	*Gini circa 2010*	*Rank*	*Comparing the poor and the rich*			
							P10/P50 (Poor)	*P90/P50 (Rich)*	*P90/P10 (Ratio)*	*P10 real income rank*
Denmark	37,720	4	0.225	1	0.248	1	0.57	1.55	2.8	2
Norway	56,214	1	0.251	2	0.250	2	0.57	1.59	2.8	1
Sweden	37,377	5	0.252	3	0.259	3	0.57	1.68	3.0	6
France	33,674	8	0.278	5	0.293	4	0.55	1.88	3.4	6
Germany	36,338	6	0.275	4	0.295	5	0.54	1.80	3.4	3
Canada	37,808	3	0.302	6	0.324	6	0.48	1.88	3.9	3
Japan	32,418	10	0.315	7	0.329	7	0.46	1.92	4.2	n.a.
Italy	32,430	9	0.333	8	0.337	8	0.45	1.99	4.5	9
UK	35,155	7	0.343	9	0.345	9	0.47	2.15	4.6	8
US	45,989	2	0.370	10	0.378	10	0.37	2.12	5.7	5

FIGURE 19.3
Income inequality in ten developed countries, 2000 (Japan 1992) –2010. Columns 1–2: UNDP, *Human Development Report 2011*, Table 10; Columns 3–6: OECD Stat Database, data extracted 24 January 2012; Column 7: Brandolini and Smeeding 2007, Figures 1 and 3

BOX 19.1 MEASURING AND COMPARING INEQUALITY

Measuring and comparing income

All measures of inequality within and across countries must be treated with caution. They are the results of very complex procedures, which have been refined in recent years, but remain fairly crude in many respects. For a start, for any one individual country it is hard to calculate real personal disposable income – the ideal common measure of the value of the income attributable to a single individual. In many countries a proportion of income for many comes from non-cash sources (such as food grown on family plots); the size of households and the number of people who depend on a particular income varies widely across the world; and while there are a wide range of sources of income that might be taken into account – wages and salaries, income from rent or investments, government transfers (such as welfare payments) – relatively few countries have good records of these, particularly for comparisons over extended periods of time. Second, it is impossible to compare incomes directly between countries. Comparisons based on exchange rates (usually made by converting local currencies into US dollars at the current rate of exchange) are very misleading – as anyone who has travelled knows, a dollar buys a lot more in China or India than in the US (and a lot less in Switzerland or Japan). This problem is overcome by calculating purchasing power parity or PPP – turning national currencies not into the equivalent in US dollars at the current rate of exchange, but into the equivalent in US dollars that you would need to buy a 'typical' basket of goods. This is a much better measure, but it is still complicated and rather rough and ready, especially as 'typical' purchases vary widely, and particularly between the rich and the poor.

Measuring and comparing income inequality

These difficulties associated with measuring incomes with and across countries are carried over into measures of inequality within and between countries.

The Gini coefficient

The commonest measure used is the Gini coefficient, which is a cumulative measure of overall inequality on a scale of 0 (perfect equality) to 1 (perfect inequality, or all wealth held by one person). On this measure, the lower the number the greater the equality. You will find varying calculations for each country, depending on the income sources included, and the degree of sensitivity of the analysis (i.e. whether it just divides the population into five broad bands with 20 per cent of the population in each, or say 100 bands, with 1 per cent of the population in each). The problem with the Gini coefficient is that it doesn't tell you how inequality is distributed. A given level of inequality might reflect serious absolute poverty along with modest prosperity for the rest, or very low levels of poverty combined with a small minority of very rich individuals, or extreme polarization – serious poverty for a minority, extreme wealth for a minority, and relatively equal incomes in between. These situations would have different explanations, and would perhaps evoke different responses.

Quintiles and deciles

An alternative method is to divide the total number of incomes into bands of five (quintiles, each including 20 per cent of the population) or ten (deciles, each including 10 per cent of the population), and to calculate the share of income going to each band, and the ratio between different bands. The World Bank uses quintiles, and we look at some of their measures in the third section below. It is more illuminating to use deciles, but even this is fairly crude, as we saw in our US example in the first section – there was a huge variation in income *within* the top decile.

Percentiles: P10, P50, P90

Finally, a method based on the same principle uses percentiles (dividing the population into 100 bands), and compares selected bands. The bands usually selected are P10 (the tenth percentile, or the top of the bottom 10 per cent), P50 (the fiftieth, or the top of the bottom half), and P90 (the ninetieth, immediately below the top 10 per cent). The very poor and very rich are excluded, but we can compare poor (P10), middle (P50) and rich (P90), and the ratios between them.

BOX 19.2 WEALTH AND INEQUALITY IN THE US

> The claim that the United States enjoys the world's highest living standard must be evaluated alongside the equally valid claim that the United States enjoys the greatest absolute inequality between the rich and the poor among developed countries. While the rich in America are truly well off by any measure of living standards, many poor Americans at the same time have living standards below those of other nations which are not as rich as the United States.
>
> (Brandolini and Smeeding 2007: 11)

countries in the post-war period, experienced a sharp increase in inequality between 1979 and 1990, the years in which Margaret Thatcher was prime minister. As Figure 19.3 shows, it remained in 2010 the most unequal of the developed European countries on all measures. For the UK and the US then (though not for Canada, whose *overall* level of inequality has not risen in the same way), the data considered here confirm the impression given by the evolution of the incomes of the very rich – a shift towards much greater inequality, rapidly from a low base in the case of the UK, and steadily from an already high base in the case of the US.

Developing and emerging economies

At the same time that the UK and the US have become so much more markedly unequal, the structure of the global economy as a whole has been changing in the same direction. Although the developed countries still dominate, newly emerging economies are taking a steadily growing share of foreign investment and world trade. The so-called BRIC countries (Brazil, Russia, India and China), together accounting for approaching 40 per cent of the global population, have been highlighted in recent years because they have been the favoured new destinations for, and increasingly the source of, foreign direct investment (UNCTAD 2011: ch. 2). They were only the most prominent examples of a host of emerging economies, concentrated in Asia but also including Mexico and Argentina in Latin America, and South Africa, by far the most industrialized economy in Sub-Saharan Africa.

Inequality and dynamic growth in Russia, Brazil, China and India

	1	2		3	4	5		6		7	
Country	*Population (millions) (2011)*	*GDP per capita ($PPP)*		*Gini circa 2000–11*	*Average annual growth of exports 2000-10*	*Share of World Exports (%)*		*Share of Inward World FDI (%)*		*Share of Outward World FDI (%)*	
		2000	2009			1990	2010	1990	2010	1990	2010
China	1,347,600	4,002	6,828	0.42	13.5%	1.8	10.4	1.7	8.5	0.4	5.1
India	1,241,500	2,644	3,296	0.37	15.9%	0.5	1.5	0.1	2.0	-	1.1
Brazil	197	7,194	10,367	0.54	15.5%	0.9	1.3	0.5	3.9	0.3	0.9
Russia	143	9,263	18,932	0.42	8.2%	1.6	2.6	-	3.3	-	3.9
Total						4.8	15.8	2.3	17.7	0.7	11.0

FIGURE 19.4
Inequality and dynamic growth in Russia, Brazil, China, and India. Columns 1–3: UNDP, *Human Development Report*, 2011; Columns 4–7: UNCTAD, *Handbook of Statistics*, 2011, Tables 1.1.1, 1.2.1 and (author's calculation from) 7.2.1

FIGURE 19.5
Chinese workers labour on the construction of the Shanghai World Financial Centre, 2006. Photo: AP

Among all of these China is easily the most significant. As Figure 19.4 shows, although its impact on global production and trade is as yet limited, its vast reserve of labour and its growth rate of near enough 10 per cent per year (compared to around 2 per cent for the developed countries as a whole) underpin a massive expansion in both exports and inward foreign direct investment (FDI) since 1990; and FDI outwards from China is growing fast, albeit from lower levels. India, almost equally populous, is only beginning to register on the same indicators, but is projected to advance rapidly. Brazil, a focus of much attention in the late twentieth century, has actually fallen back in comparative terms, while Russia, in its emergence since 1990, is representative of a much larger set of emerging economies in Central Asia, the former Soviet Union and Eastern Europe. Beyond the interest they have attracted in the global economy, these four countries have one thing in common – high or rapidly rising inequality. As Brazil's exceptionally high Gini coefficient shows, it is among the most unequal societies in the world. China and Russia (emerging from decades of socialist rule) and India (with its own post-independence history of broad egalitarianism) share a history of much greater equality. But since the inauguration of pro-capitalist reforms in China in 1978, and in Russia in the 1980s, this is changing rapidly, while in India inequality is rising sharply since neoliberal reforms were launched in the early 1990s – top incomes, for example, show the same trajectory as in the UK and the US (Banerjee and Piketty 2005). In none of these cases is increased integration into the global economy reducing inequality.

GENERAL RESPONSES
LIBERAL AND DEVELOPMENTAL PERSPECTIVES ON INEQUALITY

The information provided above tells us about emerging patterns of inequality, but it doesn't tell us *why* some people are better off than others. We might imagine that the sharp changes that coincided with the two world wars and the depression were unintended consequences of those larger events while the more equal distribution maintained after 1945 was a consequence of conscious policy choice. Policy choices might also explain rising inequality in the UK, the US, China and Russia under the impact of subsequent pro-market reform. If so, we would like to know, for example, why France and Japan share a different pattern, to what extent national cases reflect *regional* variations, and whether the trend towards greater inequality is likely to continue and to spread.

In other words, the information provided so far has identified a *research agenda* (questions we would like to be able to answer), but we haven't found any answers yet. In order to begin to do so, and to address the broader question of *global* patterns of inequality, we need to explore some current approaches to growth and inequality, and the extent to which they are reflected in the policies promoted by governments and international institutions around the world. We begin with liberal globalism, the dominant approach in both academic and policy-making circles, and we contrast it with the global developmentalism that is its principal interlocutor. The following section will question the adequacy of either of these approaches.

Liberal globalism

Liberal globalists advocate a world of liberal democratic states integrated through the market (Box 19.3), on the grounds that 'growth is good for the poor' (Dollar and Kraay 2002). For Martin Wolf, associate editor and chief economics commentator of the London-based *Financial Times*, governments should support markets in their own country, and co-operate to make markets work on a global scale – this is not just the best but the only way to raise living standards around the world.

BOX 19.3 LIBERAL GLOBALISM

A world integrated through the market should be highly beneficial to the vast majority of the world's inhabitants. The market is the most powerful institution for raising living standards ever invented: indeed there are no rivals. But markets need states, just as states need markets. In a proper marriage between the two, one has contemporary liberal democracy, incomparably the best way to manage a society. Its blessing needs to be spread more widely. The problem today is not that there is too much globalization, but that there is far too little. We can do better with the right mix of more liberal markets and more co-operative global governance.

(Wolf 2004: xvii)

David Dollar, head of the Macroeconomics and Growth Group in the Research Department of the World Bank, agrees: the answer to global poverty and inequality is more integration, not less. Liberal globalists tend to take an optimistic view of the impact of growth on poverty reduction, and to argue for example that if everyone benefits from growth it doesn't matter if the rich benefit most (Wolf 2004: 139), and that increasing inequality in Russia and China is an inevitable consequence of the abandonment of failed egalitarian policies (Wolf 2004: 167). Above all, they argue that a degree of inequality is inevitable, as economic growth depends upon private enterprise, and it is therefore essential for states to encourage economic activity across borders, and reward entrepreneurs. As the comments above suggest, liberal globalists are not hostile to the state. Rather, they are hostile to state intervention that inhibits the market, but strongly in favour of state support for markets, which they regard as essential at both national and global levels. Finally, liberal globalists are not unconditional defenders of the rich countries, or of the status quo. On the contrary, they condemn the protectionism of the European Union, the United States and Japan, and argue that it is hypocritical for countries that advocate commitment to liberal principles to refuse to practise it themselves. So for David Dollar: 'After all the rhetoric about globalization is stripped away, many of the practical policy questions come down to whether rich countries are going to make it easy or difficult for poor communities that want to integrate with the world economy' (Dollar 2007: 100). They call, therefore, for *more* liberal reforms, and their extension to *all* countries in the world.

Chapter 20 looks in more detail at how and why the liberal approach to poverty reduction has failed.

The European Union is explained in **Chapter 11**.

Global developmentalism

Global developmentalists share the commitment of liberal globalists to co-operation between states and the participation of all states in global markets, but they reject the liberal approach on the grounds that it overlooks the privileged position of the rich countries in the global economy as currently constituted, and the tendency for the benefits of growth to be unequally distributed. So Robert Wade argues that the liberalizing

BOX 19.4 GLOBAL DEVELOPMENTALISM

The 'development space' for diversification and upgrading policies in developing countries is being shrunk behind the rhetorical commitment to universal liberalization and privatization. The rules being written into multilateral and bilateral agreements actively prevent developing countries from pursuing the kinds of industrial and technology policies adopted by the newly developed countries of East Asia, and by the older developed countries when they were developing, policies aimed at accelerating the 'internal' articulation of the economy. . . . All this constitutes a shrinkage not only of development space, but also of 'self-determination' space. It ties the hands of developing country governments 'forever' to *the North's interpretation* of a market opening agenda ('you open your markets and remove restrictions on incoming investment, in return for [promises of] improved access to our markets').

(Wade 2003: 622)

measures pushed for by the US, the UK and the European Union in relation to global product and financial markets are shrinking the 'developmental space' open to developing economies.

The enforced liberalization of global markets rules out such things as industrial development strategies that rely for a period on selective protectionism – the very policies that brought about successful development not only in contemporary East Asia, but also in the United States in the past. Linda Weiss similarly argues that 'the rich nations as a group . . . have carved out a multilateral order which best suits their current developmental trajectory' (Weiss 2005: 724), and concludes that global rules support the upgrading of rich country economies while 'kicking away the ladder' (cf. Chang 2002) from under developing countries. Global developmentalists reject the idea that the first requirement of development policy is that it should promote global liberalism; they place greater stress on the continuing relevance of developmental strategy than on the prioritization of further liberal integration. They also tend to be more critical of emerging patterns of inequality. Wade, for example, has maintained that Wolf and others give a misleading account of the potential for liberal reform to address *either* poverty *or* inequality. Dismissing the liberal approach as 'faith-based social science' (Wade 2007: 107), he points to the overall drop in global rates of growth since neoliberal policies were introduced in the 1970s, the extent to which the argument for falling poverty and

FIGURE 19.6
Zuccotti Park in Manhattan's financial district during the Occupy Wall Street protests in 2011. http://farm7.static.flickr.com/6174/6224227970_46c9d42acf_b.jpg; http://synccity.blogspot.co.uk/2011/10/zuccotti-park.html

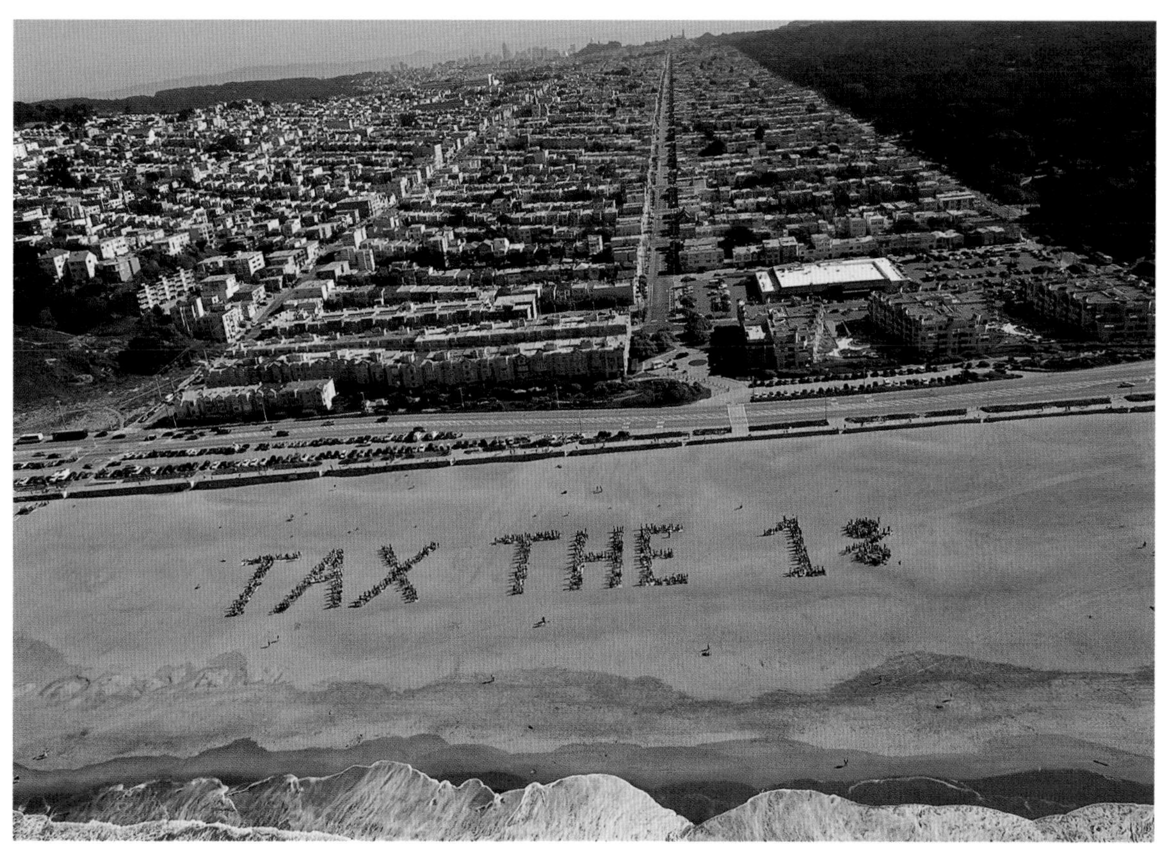

FIGURE 19.7 Protestors on a San Francisco beach. HumanBannersf.com, http://www.humanbannersf.com/

inequality depends upon the case of China (which has not followed liberal policies), and the widespread evidence (some of it reviewed above) that the benefits of growth have been very poorly distributed – the principal beneficiaries being the top half of the population of the rich countries, and China's middle classes (Wade 2007: 110–11).

Liberalism, developmentalism and the international institutions

International institutions over the last two decades, led by the World Bank, have been determined proponents of liberal globalism, unfailingly promoting liberal policies centred on further integration of the global economy. They have argued for greater openness in the global economy, and at national level they have favoured sound macroeconomic policy and a 'market-friendly' orientation on the part of governments. They have made the alleviation or elimination of poverty their major goal, but insisted that it is to be achieved by liberal means. While they have maintained the focus on privatization and reduced state intervention that was prevalent in the early 1990s (and particularly associated with the IMF), they have tended to place greater emphasis on institutional reforms that will underpin a liberal order at national and global levels – the *good governance* agenda. A liberal policy framework, according to these institutions, is still the best hope for the poor.

Chapter 15 explains how international financial institutions such as the World Bank came to be set up, and the impact their structural adjustment policies had in Ivory Coast. Much the same policies in the 2010s in the wake of the financial crisis (**Chapter 18**) have led to protests like Occupy Wall Street.

The World Bank's liberal globalism was best captured in the title of its 2005 World Development Report, *A Better Investment Climate for Everyone* (World Bank 2004), which urged all governments around the world to pursue liberal reforms in order to promote opportunity and entrepreneurship among their citizens. There were two significant features to this approach. The first was that it embraced many aspects of domestic policy, in particular in relation to the reform of tax and welfare regimes and labour markets. In other words, far from concerning themselves with matters of global regulation and integration, the international institutions became increasingly interventionist with regard to domestic policy. The World Bank's Comprehensive Development Framework and the HIPC (Heavily Indebted Poor Countries) and PRSP (Poverty Reduction Strategy Papers) initiatives developed and jointly operated by the IMF and the World Bank reflected this heavy emphasis upon domestic policy in developing countries (Cammack 2002). The second was that over the last two decades international institutions that were once strongly committed to global developmentalism embraced the agenda of global liberalism. The UNDP (United Nations Development Programme), along with UNCTAD (United Nations Conference on Trade and Development) and ECLAC (UN Economic Commission for Latin America and the Caribbean), once the strongest advocates of state intervention in support of national developmentalism, all followed this trend (Cammack 2006).

Chapter 20 raises questions about how we may understand and tackle poverty.

For more on the OECD see **Chapter 23**.

In all of these cases, the focus has been much more on poverty than on inequality, and where inequality is recognized as an issue (World Bank 2004: 32), the approach advocated is the increased access for the poor (whether as workers, consumers or entrepreneurs) to the principal elements of a liberal global economy – work, credit, and investment opportunity. In the early years of the twenty-first century there was a consensus, extending beyond the international organizations considered here to the European Union and the OECD, that the route to prosperity for developing countries lay not only in liberal reform, but in domestic economic and social reform. What is more, this consensus survived the 'global' (Atlantic) financial crisis of 2007–8. As was to be expected, the focus on economic inequality intensified. But in the UK and in the continental European countries afflicted by indebtedness, governments and international organizations alike advocated austerity and open markets as the cure. And as the balance of power shifted towards the emerging economies (prominent in the G20, the larger grouping of countries including India and China that played an increasingly prominent global role in the wake of the crisis), they worked increasingly closely with the IMF and the World Bank, while steering them towards a mix of 'global developmental liberalism' (Cammack 2012) and competitive global markets.

BROADER ISSUES
HISTORICAL MATERIALISM AND THE EXPANSION OF THE GLOBAL WORKING CLASS

Fifty years ago there was something approaching a global consensus that governments had a duty to act alongside or against market forces in order to address inequality. In Western Europe, with the UK as a leading example, governments owned and managed key national industries, and maintained tax regimes that were intended to bring about a redistribution of national income through high taxes on the rich, and substantial investment in a wide range of welfare programmes. My own experience, as a British citizen born at the beginning of the 1950s, is typical of many. I was born into a working-class family (my father a bus conductor, my mother a nursing auxiliary in a small local 'cottage' hospital), and moved into a newly-built council house in the mid-1950s. Through my childhood and into early adulthood I received free medical and dental care, free education, and a grant when I went to university that covered all my expenses and left me free of debt on graduation (at the same time, most of my friends, like most working-class children, left school at 15 – only in 1972 was the school-leaving age raised to 16). School-leavers and university graduates were as likely to work for the state in one way or another (in the police, the armed forces, government offices, education or the health service, or in a nationalized industry) as for the private sector. In world politics, the Soviet Union (along with the People's Republic of China) loomed large, not only as a possible enemy, but also as an alternative social and economic system. Between the capitalist and socialist camps, in what was becoming known as the Third World, there was little faith in the market as a solution to the problems of development. On the contrary, there was a consensus that governments (many of them newly established in the wake of decolonization) had a duty to mobilize resources through the state in order to force the pace of change. The dominant model, typified by the case of India under Nehru, was national developmentalism, centred on state ownership, the protection of industry, the active management of exchange rates, interest rates, and the money supply, and a broad commitment to egalitarianism. To the extent that there was an alternative, it was not 'reliance on the market', but social revolution – Ernesto 'Che' Guevara's call in 1967 for the creation of 'one, two, three, many Vietnams' captured what turned out to be the high point of revolutionary politics in the Third World.

The period when the Soviet Union and its allies were seen as the enemies of 'the West' was known as the Cold War: see **Chapter 26**. The term Third World is also from that time: see **Chapter 1**.

Jawaharlal Nehru was the first prime minister of independent India. He was in office from 1947 to 1964.

There is no doubt, then, that the world has changed. The previous sections of this chapter reflect a fundamental shift, the key to which has been a global neoliberal revolution, focused as much on domestic as on international policy. However, the liberal globalist and global developmentalist approaches reviewed above capture only a part of this shift, and in particular they touch very lightly on the question of why, in the contemporary world, some people are better off than others. This is because while

FIGURE 19.8
Alberto Korda's famous photograph of Che Guevara, 'Guerrillero Heroico'. 1960. © ADAGP, Banque d'images, Paris 2008

the first promotes global capitalism and the second gives it a developmental twist, neither looks critically at the way in which capitalism generates inequality, especially in the forms in which it is currently pursued around the world.

We can best focus on this question by going back 160 years, to the *Manifesto of the Communist Party* written by Karl Marx and Friedrich Engels in 1847–48, and more generally to the analysis of capitalist production offered by historical materialism (Box 19.5).

Karl Marx is introduced in **Chapter 17**.

The starting point for historical materialism is neither the market (as it is for liberal globalism) nor the developmental state (as it is for global developmentalism), but the social relations through which the material production on which social life depends take place; and in this context the relations between the bourgeoisie and the proletariat in the capitalist system, or the capital relation. As capitalism comes to dominate, society is increasingly shaped by the class struggle between the bourgeoisie (owners of the means of production) on the one hand and the proletariat (the majority forced to sell their ability to work in order to live) on the other, and Marx and Engels see this as the driving force behind social change.

The extended analysis of capitalist production that Marx eventually produced was spread across three volumes of *Capital* (1976 [1867]) (with a further three left unwritten), and several thousand further pages of published and unpublished material. Five key concepts extracted from this immense body of work suggest its relevance to understanding contemporary patterns of inequality:

1. Primitive (or better, original) accumulation: the process by which the bourgeoisie and the proletariat are initially constituted through the twin process of the expropriation (taking property from) of the peasantry and the accumulation of resources in the hands of a minority.
2. The exploitation of labour: Marx's claim that the source of profit is the capacity of the capitalist to pay workers for only a part of the surplus their labour creates, and to expropriate the rest for themselves.
3. The profit motive: the orientation of the capitalist towards the accumulation of capital, rather than any broader social purpose.

BOX 19.5 HISTORICAL MATERIALISM

The history of all hitherto-existing society is the history of class struggles. . . . The modern bourgeois society that has sprouted from the ruins of feudal society has not done away with class antagonisms. It has established new classes, new conditions of oppression, new forms of struggle in place of the old ones. Our epoch, the epoch of the bourgeoisie, possesses, however, this distinctive feature: it has simplified the class antagonisms. Society as a whole is more and more splitting up into two great hostile camps, into two great classes directly facing each other: Bourgeoisie and Proletariat.

(Marx and Engels 1973 [1848]: 67–8)

4 The constant revolution of production: the pressure on capitalists to compete with each other to reduce the price of production in order sell their goods in the market, either by obliging workers to accept lower pay or work longer hours, or by innovation and investment that increases the productivity of the worker.
5 Competition on a global scale: the resulting tendency for the production process to spill out beyond national borders and operate on a global scale.

Marx and Engels did not *predict* that capitalism would become global. First, because its development depended on class struggles within and across numerous different societies, the outcome of which could not be known in advance; and second because it was inherently subject to periodic crises, with similarly indeterminate outcomes. But they did expect that if it became global it would be through an uneven process of development, the key feature of which would be that the conflict between the bourgeoisie on the one hand and the proletariat on the other would increasingly shape political and social change.

Following this logic, we can see the neoliberal revolution as a victory (perhaps temporary) for capital over labour on a global scale, and we can interpret developments since the 1970s in the light of it. It is not just a question of opening up of new markets, as liberal globalists argue, but of the drafting in of millions of individuals into a vast new workforce – a global proletariat. This enormously enhances the power of capital by creating new opportunities both for new markets and for new sites of production. What is more, it obliges capitalist enterprises around the world to compete or go under, because of the new intensity of competition on a global scale. Governments committed to continued capitalist development have to respond by maintaining as competitive an environment as possible. In other words, they are driven by increasingly intense global competition to create 'a better climate for investment' in their own countries. And a key element of this is the provision of a workforce able to meet the needs of capitalists – in other words, a workforce available at a competitive price, and equipped to respond effectively to the rapidly changing needs of domestic and foreign enterprises.

This perspective immediately illuminates features of contemporary global development noticed by Wade and Dollar respectively. Wade notes that for the OECD countries (then 30 of the most developed economies in the world, now 34) as a group, there has been a sharp shift of income from labour (the proletariat) to capital (the bourgeoisie): the share of labour remuneration in business revenue fell back from a peak of 72 per cent in 1980 to 64 per cent in the early twenty-first century, while the share going to capital rose from 28 to 36 per cent. A more recent analysis suggests that

> In Western Europe, East Asia, North America and the Middle East and North Africa (MENA) region, labour shares have either remained stagnant or declined during the 1980s and 1990s after rising from 1960 to 1980. In Latin America and Sub-Saharan Africa, negative time trends have persisted through the entire period.
>
> (Jayadev 2007: 5)

Dollar, otherwise upbeat about the prospects for global growth, notes that 'wage inequality is rising worldwide' (Dollar 2007: 74) – in other words, middle and higher wage earners are tending to move away from low wage earners, with negative consequences for the distribution of income among wage earners as a class. Other sources confirm that this is a powerful contemporary trend (OECD 2007: 12–13).

Chapter 15 argues that in some cases it is useful to think in terms of deproletarianization, that is, a reversion to forced labour or slavery where the workers are not paid anything at all.

Workers in the informal economy often have no protection against exploitation by employers at all. See **Chapter 17**.

On this evidence, workers as a whole are losing out to owners of capital, and poor workers are falling back in relation to a minority of favoured top earners. There are three related considerations here. First, the expansion of the global proletariat is the objective both of international organizations and national governments around the world. The logic of the policies of the World Bank and other international organizations is to increase as much as possible both the size of the global workforce and its utility to, or exploitability by capital. This logic is reflected, for example, in the promotion of active labour market policy in developed and developing countries alike, where the emphasis is on ensuring that pension and welfare rights do not limit entry to the labour market, that workers can be 'hired and fired' with ease, and that groups under-represented in the labour market – lone parents, the disabled, and the elderly – are 'encouraged', principally by the removal of benefits, to find work. It is reflected, too, in more 'progressive' aspects of World Bank policy, such, for example, as its genuine commitment to the equal provision of education and work opportunities for girls and boys – progressive in gender terms, but *explained* by the broader goal of building a global proletariat. These policies are promoted with equal enthusiasm by governments from the UK and the US (principal exponents of welfare-to-work or 'active labour market' policies) to India and China. Second, the combination of globally integrated markets and the huge labour reserves in the developing world suggests that this is a fundamental structural feature of the global economy for the foreseeable future: according to the OECD, 22 million new jobs were created in the BRIC economies in 2000–2005, and there may be as many as 300 million surplus workers in China and India alone (OECD 2007: 26). Compare this with the total workforce of 358 million in all the G7 countries put together (OECD 2007, table 1.2: 21), and it is clear that the expansion of the global proletariat is neither fortuitous nor temporary, but a likely structural feature of the global economy for the foreseeable future, driven forward deliberately by the policies of governments and international institutions.

FIGURE 19.9
'We are the 99%'. Image widely circulated on the internet, copied from http://www.quickmeme.com/meme/356ml1/, 25 January 2012

CONCLUSION

The OECD expressed concern in 2007 that despite the consensus among economists that globalization is a 'win-win process', public opinion is largely hostile towards it. Its attempt to explain this 'paradox' confirmed the analysis offered in this chapter. First, globalization is taking place on an unprecedented scale, in terms of the number of countries involved, and its extension beyond industry to labour intensive services. As a result, 'most firms and workers are directly or indirectly competing in today's world economy'. Second, though, 'economic integration is occurring in the context of wider earnings inequality and perceptions of job insecurity' (OECD 2007: 12).

It is no accident, then, that practically every society in the world is becoming more unequal. Inequality within states is growing faster across the whole of the world at present than at any time in the past. The global explosion of inequality over the last 30 years or so, and the accumulating evidence of its shameful character and extent have made it a focus of increasing attention in the present century. It is a key feature, and perhaps *the* key feature of global society today. The managers of the global capitalist economy are well aware that sharply rising global inequality represents a threat to the system, especially in the wake of a crisis that has revealed the extreme instability and fragility of the global financial order as much as the shameless greed of its leaders. They have responded, not surprisingly, by arguing for broadly liberal policies: in 2012 the OECD addressed the issue of inequality directly, as it had repeatedly since the crisis, but still advocated the mix outlined above: investment in education, labour market reforms, and the removal of product market regulations that stifle competition, and of barriers to mobility across borders for workers (economic migration) – along with the removal of tax relief for the rich (OECD 2012: ch. 5). The latter point was a clear indication that it saw the legitimacy of the global capitalist order was under threat, a point that could hardly be missed as protests, typified by the 'Occupy Movement', gathered pace around the world, and the '99 per cent' mobilized against the 1 per cent who dominate.

Economic migration is often seen as a threat to be countered rather than something that should be facilitated: see **Chapter 10**.

The Occupy Movement is discussed in **Chapters 18 and 28**.

In the contemporary world, the reasons why some people are better off than others relate increasingly to policy choices *within* individual countries and across international organizations that favour not only open markets, but also owners of capital. As we have seen, domestic polices are strongly influenced and promoted by international institutions whose principal objective is to increase to the maximum the size of the global workforce and its availability to domestic and foreign capital alike. It follows that the OECD and other international institutions such as the IMF and the World Bank are probably right to suggest that the continuation of the same policies will produce further growth, though it will be interspersed with periodic crashes and crises. But it is a form of growth that also tends to generate inequality, because its commitment to competitiveness on a global scale eventually obliges propertyless workers across the whole of the world to compete with each other. Set against the optimism of governments and international institutions today that the benefits of growth will outweigh the costs of inequality is Marx's suggestion that 'the general tendency of capitalist production is not to raise, but to sink the average standard of wages' (Marx 1951 [1865]: 405). The material presented here suggests that the twenty-first century will see an experiment on a global scale in which these contrasting views will be tested.

Chapter 18 reflects on what it means to think of the global economy in terms of crises.

FURTHER READING

This chapter has argued that inequality is on a rising trend within practically every country in the world, and that there is nothing either accidental or inevitable about it. On the contrary, it is a consequence of the widespread adoption of neoliberal policies in what has become a genuinely global capitalist economy. Although it was written in 1847–8, the *Communist Manifesto* (Marx and Engels 1973) remains an essential starting point. Callinicos (1996), especially chapter 6, provides an excellent introduction to Marx's analysis of capitalism. Glyn (2006) explains beautifully, from a similar perspective, how the global political economy has evolved over the last 40 years. New sources of contemporary data and debate are appearing all the time. Recent concern about inequality on the part of international institutions is reflected in OECD (2012), UNDP (2013), and World Bank (2012), along with their predilection for market-friendly solutions. Reddy and Pogge (2009) offer an indispensable critique of the data on which poverty figures are based, and Rodriguez and Jayadev (2010) expand upon the information in Jayadev (2007). Hacker and Pierson (2010) show conclusively how what they rightly call 'winner-take-all' politics in the United States reflects deliberate policy choices on the part of *both* leading parties. Arnold and Pickles (2011) and Hewison and Kalleberg (2013) chart the changing character of the new global work force through the rise of 'precarious labour' in South and Southeast Asia. My own perspective is developed in Cammack (2012). Along with the websites listed below, you should search regularly (on Scopus, Web of Science or Google Scholar for example) for more recent work by the various contributors identified here.

WEBSITES

Centre for Global Development/Inequality, http://www.cgdev.org/section/topics/inequality
Current research on global inequality.

Inequality.org, http://www.demos.org/inequality/
Current research on poverty and inequality in the US.

International Poverty Centre, http://www.undp-povertycentre.org/
A joint UNDP/Brazilian government project with a wide range of publications, notably *Poverty in Focus*, and more advanced policy research briefs and working papers.

Joseph Rowntree Foundation, http://www.jrf.org.uk/
Current research on poverty and inequality in the UK.

Politics of Global Competitiveness, http://www.politicsofglobalcompetitiveness.net
Working papers from a Marxist-oriented research group of which the author is a member, reflecting and extending the arguments presented in this chapter.

UC Atlas of Global Inequality, http://ucatlas.ucsc.edu/home.html
Excellent interactive resource, with the capacity to generate global, regional and country maps on a range of topics related to global inequality and good links to other related sites.

REFERENCES

Arnold, Dennis, and John Pickles (2011) 'Global Work, Surplus Labor, and the Precarious Economies of the Border', *Antipode*, 43, 5: 1598–1624.

Banerjee, Abhijit and Thomas Piketty (2005) 'Top Indian Incomes, 1922–2000', *World Bank Economic Review* 19, 1: 1–20.

Brandolini, Andrea and Timothy M. Smeeding (2007) *Inequality Patterns in Western-Type Democracies: Cross-Country Differences and Time Changes*, Luxembourg Income Study Working Papers series, no. 458.

Callinicos, Alex (1996) *The Revolutionary Ideas of Karl Marx*, 2nd corrected edn, London and Sydney: Bookmarks. Online at http://www.istendency.net/pdf/revideas.pdf.

Cammack, Paul (2002) 'The Mother of All Governments: The World Bank's Matrix for Global Governance', in Rorden Wilkinson and Steve Hughes (eds), *Global Governance: Critical Perspectives*, London: Routledge.

——(2003) 'The Governance of Global Capitalism: A New Materialist Perspective', *Historical Materialism* 11, 2: 37–59.

——(2004) 'What the World Bank Means by Poverty Reduction and Why It Matters', *New Political Economy* 9, 2: 189–211.

——(2006) 'UN Imperialism: Unleashing Entrepreneurship in the Developing World', in Colin Mooers (ed.) *The New Imperialists: Ideologies of Empire*, Oxford: Oneworld Publications.

——(2012) 'The G20, the Crisis, and the Rise of Global Developmental Liberalism', *Third World Quarterly* 33, 1: 1–16.

Chang, Ha-Joon (2002) *Kicking Away the Ladder*, London: Anthem Press.

Dollar, David (2007) 'Globalization, Poverty and Inequality since 1980', in David Held and Ayse Kaya (eds) *Global Inequality*, Cambridge: Polity.

Dollar, David and Art Kraay (2002) 'Growth Is Good for the Poor', *Journal of Economic Growth* 7, 3: 195–225.

Frank, Robert (2007) *Richistan: A Journey through the American Wealth Boom and the Lives of the New Rich*, New York: Crown Publishers.

Glyn, Andrew (2006) *Capitalism Unleashed: Finance, Globalization, and Welfare*, Oxford: Oxford University Press.

Hacker, Jacob S. and Paul Pierson (2010) *Winner-Take-All Politics: How Washington Made the Rich Richer – and Turned Its Back on the Middle Class*, New York: Simon and Schuster.

Hewison, Kevin, and Arne L. Kalleberg, eds (2013) 'Precarious Work in South and Southeast Asia', Special Issue, *American Behavioral Scientist*, 57, 4, April.

International Poverty Centre (2007) *Poverty in Focus 11: The Challenge of Inequality*, International Poverty Centre, June, http://www.undp-povertycentre.org/site/PublicationShow.do.

Ip, Greg (2007) 'Income-Inequality Gap Widens', *Wall Street Journal*, 12 October: A2.

Jayadev, Arjun (2007) 'Capital Account Openness and the Labour Share of Income', *Cambridge Journal of Economics* 31, 3: 423–43.

Malone, Nolan, Kaari F. Baluja, Joseph M. Costanzo and Cynthia J. Davis (2003) *The Foreign-Born Population: 2000*, Census 2000 Brief C2KBR-34, Washington, DC: US Census Bureau, US Dept of Commerce.

Marx, Karl (1951 [1865]) *Wages, Price and Profit*, in Karl Marx and Friedrich Engels, *Selected Works*, vol. 1, Moscow: Foreign Languages Publishing House.

——(1976 [1867]) *Capital*, vol. 1, London: Pelican/New Left Review.

Marx, Karl and Friedrich Engels (1973 [1848]) 'Manifesto of the Communist Party', in Karl Marx, *The Revolutions of 1848*, edited by David Fernbach, London: Pelican/New Left Review.

OECD (2007) *OECD Employment Outlook 2007*, Paris: OECD.

——(2012) *Going for Growth 2012*, Paris: OECD.

——(2012) *Looking to 2060: Long-term global growth prospects*, OECD Economic Policy Paper No. 3. November.

Piketty, Thomas and Emmanuel Saez (2006) 'The Evolution of Top Incomes: A Historical and International Perspective', *American Economic Review, Papers and Proceedings* 96, 2: 200–5.

Smeeding, Timothy M. (2005) 'Public Policy, Economic Inequality, and Poverty: The United States in Comparative Perspective', *Social Science Quarterly*, Supplement to volume 86: 955–83.

Rodriguez, Francisco and Arjun Jayadev (2010) 'The Declining Labor Share of Income', *Human Development Research Paper*, 2010/36, UNDP.

UNCTAD (2007) *Handbook of Statistics*, Geneva: UNCTAD.

——(2011) *World Investment Report 2011: Non-Equity Modes of International Production and Development* (Geneva: UNCTAD).

UNDP (2011) *Human Development Report*, Geneva: UNDP.

——(2013) *The Rise of the South: Human Progress in a Diverse World*, Human Development Report 2013, New York: UNDP.

UNESCO (2011) *The Hidden Crisis: Armed Conflict and Education: Education for All Global Monitoring Report 2011*, Paris: UNESCO.

United States Census Bureau (2012) *Statistical Abstract of the United States* (online), at http://www.census.gov/prod/www/abs/statab2011_2015.html (consulted January 2012).

Wade, Robert H. (2003) 'What Strategies are Viable for Developing Countries Today? The WTO and the Shrinking of "development space"', *Review of International Political Economy* 10, 4: 621–44.

——(2007) 'Should We Worry about Income Inequality?', in David Held and Ayse Kaya (eds) *Global Inequality*, Cambridge: Polity.

Weinberg, Daniel H. (2004) *Evidence from Census 2000 about Earnings by Detailed Occupation for Men and Women*, Census 2000 Special Reports CENSR-15, Washington, DC: US Census Bureau, US Dept of Commerce.

Weiss, Linda (2005) 'Global Governance, National Strategies: How Industrialized States Make Room to Move Under the WTO', *Review of International Political Economy* 12, 5: 723–49.

Wolf, Martin (2004) *Why Globalization Works*, New Haven, CT and London: Yale University Press.

World Bank (2004) *World Development Report 2005: A Better Investment Climate for Everyone*, Washington, DC: World Bank.

——(2005) *World Development Report 2006: Equity and Development*, Washington, DC: World Bank.

——(2012) *World Development Report 2013: Jobs*, Washington: World Bank.

For a range of further resources supporting this chapter, please visit the companion website for *Global Politics, 2nd Edition* at www.routledge.com/cw/edkins/

CHAPTER **20**

How can we end poverty?

Mustapha Kamal Pasha

THE QUESTION
THE GLOBAL POOR AND CAMPAIGNS TO END POVERTY

Poverty is a durable face of global politics, one that invades our global public space and imagination with sustained vitality, a face we wish would disappear the moment we see it. We seem to know the poor even though we have not met them. They are an abstraction we embrace, a concrete part in ourselves we deny. Poverty is one of the most visible signs of otherness. It is *the* face of difference, of those who are removed from our space and experience, a connection to others not like us. Poverty consolidates the material divide between us and them, an ideational divide (that is, a divide in terms of how we understand the world). Something tells us that the poor are in a way like us, something we fear the most. Perhaps the anxiety that we could become like them gives us the inspiration to think about helping them, reaching out to them, without becoming like them.

Of course, some of 'us' are poor too. At least we live in relative poverty (as defined in Box 20.2 below) even though we live on far more in real terms than many of the global poor. See **Chapter 19**.

FIGURE 20.1
A visualization of global income distribution. Photomontage by Dr. Kurt Källblad, Malmö, Sweden. The Challenge of Inequality, *Poverty in Focus*, International Poverty Centre, June 2007, cover, www.undp.org/povertycentre

For more detail on global inequality and how it is measured see **Chapter 19**.

The poor seem to be everywhere, over half of the world's population according to United Nations reports (UNDP 2006), but often in far flung places removed from our everyday lives. Their existence is a distant presence that does not disrupt the functioning of *our* modern life. Perhaps, their being makes a particular form of life possible for us. We have a name for the place of the poor: the Third World, Bangladesh, Haiti, Africa. The match between the name and the place is not important. It is where poor people live. Faces of malnourished children, squalor, overcrowded slums and waste contrast sharply with our world of affluence, conspicuous **consumption**, **technological** advance and the promise of comfort. We are connected to the poor in episodic embrace on the evening telecast or a YouTube clip. Many feelings and emotions spring to life when we see the face of poverty – pity, sympathy, sorrow, pain, **alienation**, superiority, disgust.

It is interesting to think about the ways in which the lifeboat scenario works like the ticking bomb scenario discussed in **Chapter 2**. It tells us what the problem is in such a way that we have no room for manoeuvre.

In the fast age of digital communication and connectivity (Appadurai 2001), the end of poverty has become *the* truly 'global' public policy issue of our times, eclipsing global warming, human trafficking or illegal drugs. It is a campaign with very few sceptics and critics. A case against helping the poor was widely featured in public consciousness over three decades ago under the rubric of Lifeboat Ethics. It would be virtually impossible to endorse views of this nature now, although in terms of actual policy, lifeboat ethics is not much different from the logic of neoliberalism.

The poor tend to be differentiated based on particular distinctions and classification: we have 'extreme poverty', 'moderate poverty', and 'relative poverty'. On a global scale,

BOX 20.1 LIFEBOAT ETHICS

According to Garrett Hardin,

> If we divide the world crudely into rich nations and poor nations, two thirds of them are desperately poor, and only one-third comparatively rich, with the United States the wealthiest of all. Metaphorically each rich nation can be seen as a lifeboat full of comparatively rich people. In the ocean outside each lifeboat swim the poor of the world, who would like to get in, or at least to share some of the wealth. What should the lifeboat passengers do? First, we must recognize the limited capacity of any lifeboat.
>
> (Hardin 1974)

Hardin's argument is that taking everyone into the lifeboat would swamp the boat and everyone would drown – and thus that we cannot or should not help the poor.

FIGURE 20.2
Structural adjustment. Artist: Kirk Anderson

BOX 20.2 CLASSIFICATION OF POVERTY

> Extreme poverty means that households cannot meet basic needs for survival. They are chronically hungry, unable to access health care, lack the amenities of safe drinking water and sanitation, cannot afford education for some or all the children, and perhaps lack rudimentary shelter – a roof to keep the rain out of the hut, a chimney to remove the smoke from the cook stove – and basic articles of clothing, such as shoes. Unlike moderate and relative poverty, extreme poverty occurs only in developing countries. Moderate poverty generally refers to conditions of life in which basic needs are met, but just barely. Relative poverty is generally construed as a household income level below a certain level of average national income. The relatively poor, in high-income countries, lack access to cultural goods, entertainment, recreation, and to quality health care, education, and other prerequisites for upward social mobility.
>
> (Sachs 2005: 20)

the dividing line typically runs between north and south, between the advanced industrial nations and the developing world, but under conditions of global linkage there may be new lines of material discrimination between prosperity and wretchedness. Nevertheless, the prevailing view suggests that outside the Western Hemisphere, barring a few exceptions in Asia and parts of Latin America, vast populations endure poverty as a regular feature of daily lived reality in their cultural zones.

The recognition of poverty as a social problem has been based on different understandings of the factors that cause it. Natural explanations have highlighted geography, climate or population growth as the principal culprits. Some have spoken of cultural factors, including the prevalence of discrimination against women, the lack of an achievement drive or work ethic, even a 'culture of poverty' (Banfield 1958) that keeps poor people trapped in an unchanging stable symbolic world. Others have linked poverty to unequal economic and social structures, the working of a capitalist economy; others to 'entitlement failures' or a case where people lack rights to resources. 'Starvation', Amartya Sen notes, 'is the characteristic of some people not *having* enough food to eat. It is not a characteristic of there *being* not enough food to eat' (Sen 1981). From the perspective of the poorer regions of the global political economy, the colonial experience is *the* major structuring cause of poverty. The working of the current global economic order continues to replicate colonial governmentality.

Chapter 15 shows that neocolonial structures still prevail in global politics and **Chapter 16** discusses how colonialism works.

However, despite decades of international social policy, awareness campaigns, and noble intentions, poverty has not disappeared. On the contrary, the greater the effort to end poverty, the more palpable is the failure of imagined solutions.

ILLUSTRATIVE EXAMPLE
MODERNIZATION AND MICROFINANCE IN SOUTH ASIA

In recent years, many grand schemes have been advanced to remove the blot of poverty on human conscience. One of the predominant forms that attempts to end poverty has taken is neoliberal globalization, economic liberalization or market fundamentalism.

To understand how the neoliberal project works, this section looks at the particular context of recent experience in South Asia, a region where nearly half of the world's poor live.

Modernization and the rise of the middle class

Neoliberal modernization and the emphasis on growth can seem to be helpful in ending poverty, but this section argues that it is not. What reasons are advanced for this argument?

In the initial postcolonial decades in South Asia, the idea of modernization (for an excellent critique see Banuri 1990) captured the imagination of both state and society. Top-down development (development enforced by the state on people and often without their input) was promoted as the panacea to eradicate underdevelopment and cut poverty down to size. For a variety of reasons, including the failure of the state to deliver on its promise for sustainable economic growth within a globalizing world economy and the collapse of the socialist model of planned economics in the Soviet Union and Eastern Europe, the climate drastically shifted to promote market solutions for what are basically social problems.

FIGURE 20.3
Map of South Asia (India, Pakistan, Bangladesh, Sri Lanka, the Maldives, Bengal, Bhutan and Nepal) and neighbouring regions

The intensification of market relations and a market sensibility in South Asia has produced massive changes in the material and symbolic universe of populations. What is remarkable about the recent shift is the relative ease with which national elites have embraced the neoliberal project. The rise of a new middle class has been heralded as the singular achievement of countries like India in successfully negotiating globalization. This phenomenon is said to confirm the old adage that economic growth is the only cure for poverty, a key plank of anti-welfare thinking. The shift from the state to the market is accompanied by a culture of competition which is not merely confined to the business elites but has percolated down to the less well off. A great transformation appears to be underway in India, and in neighbouring countries.

A direct effect of growing neoliberal consciousness in India, and to comparable and varied degrees in the adjacent countries, is a rethinking of the discourse on ending poverty. Economic growth, *not* redistribution, is now considered the answer. While economic growth was always regarded as a necessary condition to alleviate poverty, it was subordinated to a wider commitment to development. The latter took the form of welfare, attention to a social wage, food subsidies, but also macro-economic targeting of poor regions for special treatment in the areas of education, infrastructural development and emergency relief. In public consciousness, the legitimacy of the state was interwoven with poverty alleviation.

The present constellation draws many elements from past imaginings and practice. However, the commitment of national elites to globalization has shifted the centre of gravity for poverty alleviation schemes. The poor have new uses in the neoliberal vision. The rise of the new middle classes in India, those with access to global culture and the means to reproduce its translocal variants, is inconceivable without the swelling ranks of the poor. The latter, the poor, provide the labouring capacity that enables the rich to live forms of life more attentive to the compulsions of cultural globalization. Increasingly, the fate of the poor rests on consolidation of middle-class privilege in an already polarized and polarizing social universe, similar to the uses of the poor in Western development experience. The more secure the middle class becomes, the more rigid the structures of poverty.

What we mean by privilege is discussed in **Chapter 5**.

The retreat of the state from development, in public consciousness and policy (Kothari 1993) in favour of non-governmental organisations (NGOs) leaves the question of growing inequality untouched. A second aspect of the deepening of neoliberal consciousness is the emergence of a culture of indifference in South Asia, a region known for its moral economy. The breakdown of the tacit social compact between the rich and the poor against the tide of a lifeboat ethics leaves the fate of the poor to the voluntary sector, a relatively powerless social force without the capacity to challenge the market and the forces of capital behind it.

Finally, the regime of neoliberal globalization extends beyond what is regarded as a self-defeating moral regard for the poor. India is the destination of global pharmaceutical giants testing new drugs on the millions of sickly poor with scant protections of law or their state. Excluded from the legally barred zones of scientific testing in the economically developed world, these companies have targeted the poorest populations of India (and elsewhere), where protections are in short supply and vulnerability high, in the quest for profits and profitability. The 'bare life' of the poor has entered the global sphere of accumulation in unanticipated ways, not merely providing labouring capacity. Superfluous humanity no more, but a valuable resource for enhancing global capital, the poor are a productive resource. This is a sharp break from the uses of the poor in the moral economy.

Giorgio Agamben's term bare life refers to the form of life that in sovereign Western forms of politics is produced as distinct from politically qualified life. Treating a person as 'bare life' is to disregard their moral or political standing, and merely ensure their survival. The idea of 'bare life' is discussed further in **Chapter 27**.

BOX 20.3 MORAL ECONOMY

The concept of a 'moral economy' is said to have originated with E. P. Thompson. He used it to mean 'a consistent traditional view of social norms and obligations, of the proper economic functions of several parties within the community, which, taken together, can be said to constitute the moral economy of the poor'.

(*Source*: James Kelly, University College Cork Multitext Project in Irish History, http://multitext.ucc.ie/d/Moral_Economy. See also E. P. Thompson (1971) 'The Moral Economy of the English Crowd in the 18th Century', *Past and Present* 50, 76–136)

Microfinance and emancipation from poverty

An altogether different example from South Asia illustrates the convergence of emancipatory notions of poverty alleviation and the pervasiveness of neoliberal consciousness. The case of microfinance in Bangladesh may not appear as an illustration of neoliberal consciousness. However, upon closer scrutiny, it reveals some curious features of the intrusion of neoliberal ideas into both the social and the individual worlds of the poor who have come to rely on microfinance to undo the effects of poverty. The irony lies in the perception of success and its illusory promise of ending poverty.

The argument here is that although the Grameen Bank seems a good thing, there are problems with it.

A brainchild of Nobel laureate Muhammad Yunus, the idea of microfinance is a far-reaching departure from standard conceptions of banking. As an ethically charged project to emancipate women from poverty, Grameen Bank has come to play a conspicuous role in alleviating poverty. Although the scale of its achievements are fairly modest given the scope of extreme poverty in Bangladesh, it has acquired a mythical status as a standard bearer for both market-based solutions to ending poverty and the uplifting of rural women in the poorer quarters of the global economy. Notwithstanding the recent controversy that some microcredit commercial lenders were allegedly taking advantage of borrowers, Grameen has continued to enjoy considerable appeal in poverty alleviation strategies. Since its inception as a formal bank in 1983 from a small project born in the village of Jobra in 1976, Grameen Bank has lent money to over seven million people, 97 percent of them women. The Grameen idea reverses the logic of banking to offer the least privileged access to finance.

The Grameen project takes as its point of departure the idea that the rural poor can manage money but also manage it well. Without collateral or legal guarantees, credit is advanced to the poor against the guarantee of a five-member group to which the borrower must belong. Although the group is not responsible for any repayment, there is unspoken moral pressure which ensures that the individual is responsible for the debt. Above all, presently 94 per cent of the equity of the Bank is owned by borrowers with only 6 per cent owned by the government. Against the 'poverty' of received poverty alleviation measures, the Grameen project clearly is a fresh intervention.

FIGURE 20.4
Muhammad Yunus visits Grameen Bank centres and loan holders, who are mostly women. Copyright © Grameen Bank Audio Visual Unit, 2006

BOX 20.4 THE GRAMEEN BANK

Grameen Bank methodology is almost the reverse of the conventional banking methodology. Conventional banking is based on the principle that the more you have, the more you can get. In other words, if you have little or nothing, you get nothing. As a result, more than half the population of the world is deprived of the financial services of the conventional banks. Conventional banking is based on collateral [property used as security against the loan and forfeited if the loan is not repaid]. Grameen Bank is collateral-free. Grameen Bank starts with the belief that credit should be accepted as a human right, and builds a system where one who does not possess anything gets the highest priority in getting a loan. Grameen methodology is not based on assessing the material possessions of a person; it is based on the potential of a person. Grameen believes that all human beings, including the poorest, are endowed with endless potential. Conventional banks look at what has already been acquired by a person. Grameen looks at the potential that is waiting to be unleashed in a person. Conventional banks are owned by the rich, generally men. Grameen Bank is owned by poor women. The overarching objective of the conventional banks is to maximize profits. Grameen Bank's objective is to bring financial services to the poor, particularly women and the poorest, to help them fight poverty, stay profitable and financially sound. It is a composite objective, coming out of social and economic visions.

(Yunus 2007)

The success story of the Grameen Bank has been an example in the development industry, and others elsewhere have tried to emulate the model, including sponsors from international inter-governmental agencies like the World Bank. Despite its laudable achievement in helping poor rural women in Bangladesh, a critical assessment presents a sobering qualification to the glow of the Grameen experience. Less apparent in usual celebrations of microfinance is the deepening of the incapacity to reverse the status of the Third World as such by allowing the poor the mere ability to avoid destitution. Microfinance shifts the focus of attention away from inequality to reducing poverty; it merely deflects deeper questions about the growing wedge between the very rich and those who can barely survive.

Increasing inequality between rich and poor is the subject of **Chapter 19**.

The effects of such finance on the situation of rural women, for example in Bangladesh, have also not received closer examination in accounts of the Grameen story. Microfinance rests on the idea of inculcating habits of competitiveness in local, global or translocal contexts among the poor without necessarily creating the conditions to produce alternative futures. The Grameen example suggests that competitiveness, and therefore neoliberal ideology, plays a significant role in claims about survivability with respect to poverty alleviation schemes. This implicates the non-governmental sector in other parts of the Third World, notably Africa. We now have a socialization process of not mere modernization, but imparting skills to understand the market and embrace efficiency, productivity, and cost-reduction. More significantly, the retreat of the state from concerns of development on the promises of empowering civil society and the voluntary sector in virtually all parts of South Asia in effect reproduces lifeboat ethics. Only those who can must survive.

How would you summarize the criticisms made here of the Grameen Bank? Do you agree that despite being seen by many as a success story, it is problematic in these ways?

GENERAL RESPONSES
THE NEOLIBERAL PROJECT AND THE EXPORT OF AN IDEOLOGY

Campaigns to end poverty

In recent years, many ambitious projects to change the fate of the poor have been the staple of highly publicized worldwide campaigns by international development agencies, governments, global rock stars, movie actors, and non-governmental relief agencies. At the G8 summit or World Economic Forum (an annual gathering of leaders from the rich industrialized countries) in 2005, poverty was recognized as a major concern. This recognition followed the unanimous signing of the United Nations Millennium Declaration by all 191 UN member states in 2002 to achieve eight Millennium Development Goals. Reduction of poverty was the first such goal, with the aim specifically of halving extreme poverty between 1990 and 2015 for the proportion of people whose income is less than a dollar a day and halving between 1990 and 2015 the proportion of people who suffer from hunger. Hardly a day goes by without public discussion of ending poverty. From schemes of debt forgiveness, through fair trade, to development aid, poverty alleviation now has given way to the 'end of poverty' discourse. It is no longer respectable to merely reduce poverty, we have to eliminate it. But from its earliest discovery as a social problem, endless talk and thinking has been devoted to trying to end poverty.

The G8 means the G7 countries – Canada, France, Germany, Italy, Japan, the UK and the US – plus Russia. The G7/G8 holds an annual summit and Russia was first included in 1997.

The neoliberal project has shifted the terrain of poverty alleviation in distinctive ways by decoupling the question of poverty from redistribution. In this revised framework of global governance, the embrace of NGOs and celebrities by state managers and the G8 elites is not coincidental. A voyeuristic culture of celebrity worship has displaced politics, shifting responsibility away from those with actual authority to a nebulous global sphere of liberal good heartedness and feel-good solidarity with 'the poor'. This sentiment is discernible in recent worldwide campaigns under the Millennium Development Goals umbrella to end poverty. The British Make Poverty History Movement, the Live8 rock concerts to raise public awareness of global poverty, and the Johannesburg-based Global Call to Action against Poverty, provide good examples of the shifting meaning and space of politics. Paradoxically, however, publicity also allows an occasional probe into uneasy aspects of the workings of the global economy, including inequality and the gulf between rhetoric and state practice.

FIGURE 20.5
Make Poverty History wristbands.
Photo: Global Call to Action Against Poverty (GCAP)

BOX 20.5 STRUCTURAL ADJUSTMENT PROGRAMMES

A key component of neoliberal globalization is a reliance on Structural Adjustment Programmes, the package of economic measures sponsored by the International Monetary Fund (IMF) and the World Bank to tackle the problem of poverty and underdevelopment in debt-stricken countries. Typically, these measures consist of fiscal discipline and the tightening of monetary policy, combined with an expansion of trade liberalization and privatization of the domestic economy. Within the neoliberal framework, debt-relief is linked to Structural Adjustment Programmes: the greater the compliance, the greater the support from the international donor community. In practice, Structural Adjustment Programmes have invariably hurt the more vulnerable sections of society as they reward those who have better capability to profit from opportunities presented by the market. The poor are on a weaker footing to compete, and hence more likely to suffer from welfare retrenchment, which is often the operational effect of Structural Adjustment Programmes.

The neoliberal solution

Chapter 17 also explains the idea of the market and where it comes from. Structural Adjustment Programmes and some of these negative implications for the poor are further discussed in **Chapter 15**. Austerity programmes implemented in parts of Europe in the early 2010s are similar: see **Chapter 18**.

The neoliberal project suggests leaving the problem of poverty to the functioning of the market by removing obstacles to its smooth operation. The market, the argument goes, is a social institution designed with human ingenuity to assemble people in a common quest to serve their individual self-interest. Unleashed from the fetters either of tradition or political authority, the market allows people with varied skills, crafts, or labours to come together and mutually profit by exchanging what they produce. The idea is not new. What distinguishes its contemporary version from views expressed over 200 years ago is the conviction that *society comes into being primarily through exchange and is held together by exchange*. Without the market, society does not exist. This is a fairly radical idea with the obvious implication that non-market sociability is either 'primitive' in relation to our modern present or a serious impediment to economic advance. Other socially produced institutions – state, family, community, and the cultural trappings in which these institutions come into being and persist – ought to be subordinated to the neutrality of the market. Non-market claims must be treated with circumspection to the degree that they get in the way of the market. The reduction of society to the market or the market principle redirects social life in pursuit of goals produced either within the market or induced by its ever-expanding horizons. From the perspective of this sensibility, the poor are not merely a nuisance or an unintended consequence of the drive to universalize the market, but those who lack the desire, talent or aspiration to compete.

The rupture of the market from other societal norms is a notable feature of the neoliberal project. Once norms intrinsic to the market spread across vast social spaces with ease and without effective resistance, the question of poverty cannot be thought of as having solutions that do not arise within the market. Despite the vagaries of the recent financial crisis in the rich countries, market-driven growth is seen as the true engine for eradicating poverty.

In a neoliberal universe, the problem of poverty is basically one of a lack of effective market-driven capacity. Once that capacity is created, poverty can become a thing of the past. The enemy for neoliberals is any agency that treats the poor as anything other than potentially rational maximizers. Empowerment lies in providing resources or skills to realize the natural trait to maximize.

The question of treating people as rational subjects arises in the context of strategic thinking in **Chapter 24**.

A second feature of the neoliberal solution to poverty is in the ability of the poor to effectively negotiate globalization. This suggests building a social world that no longer takes the local and its cultural boundaries as the zone of meaningful sustenance. To discard the local in favour of the global is a confirmation of the evolutionary promise of growth and development.

The neoliberal project is both a belief system and practice that has come to dominate the management of the global economy. As a belief system, it rests on the notion that development (which is an indispensable condition to eradicate poverty) should occur as an unintended feature of the market rather than planning. The prior assumption that buttresses this notion is that wo/man is primarily a *homo economicus*, a calculating animal seeking to satisfy endless private wants through exchange with other like-minded economic individuals. If governments get out of the way and do not stifle the natural propensity for each individual to participate in the sphere of exchange (or the market) in search of self-interest, all can prosper. The market is the ideal institution to produce wealth, to reward people for their labours, and as a consequence creates social harmony and prosperity. Neoliberals suggest that the primary needs of human beings are material, or their materiality takes precedence over other social, cultural or psychological considerations. If the task of producing wealth is left to the individuals themselves and governments are expected only to guarantee the social conditions for the functioning of the market, there is no reason to expect that poverty cannot be eventually eradicated.

Chapter 2 looks at thinking and practice. A 'belief system' is similar to what was discussed as a 'language game' there.

Critiques of the neoliberal project

Critiques of the neoliberal project have been fairly extensive and far-reaching, questioning both the grounds on which a disembedded economy (Polanyi 1944) can offer social cohesion or meaning as well as its endeavour to universalize a specific form of Western development experience to humanity. On the one hand, these critiques address the limiting vision that informs that project, and on the other, they challenge its export in the non-Western cultural zones.

Exporting Western individualism

In the first instance, the neoliberal project takes the cultural apparatus of (post)industrial Western capitalism as a model abstracted from history. The experience of one particular zone of humanity (northern Europe and later the United States of America) becomes the universal standard to idealize a success story worthy of global emulation. Absence of significant likeness to the experience of the West serves as the definitive story of poverty in the non-West. The heightened individualism captured in notions of economic rationality, efficiency, or performance as normative values superior to those generated in alternative societal or cultural arrangements has become global currency.

Embedded social practices appear deficient on this canvas of calculability. The atomistic proclivities of neoliberal subjectivity stand in sharp contrast to systems of generalized reciprocity, redistribution and social responsibility. In consuming the neoliberal project in societal and cultural zones less enamoured by its lure, serious obstacles appear on the ground. Without a deepened liberal subjectivity, neoliberalism takes on a coercive character, an imposition by the state to align society to assumed pressures of globalization. The latter dictate rationalization not merely of the economy, but of social relations in their entirety.

On a structural reading of the neoliberal project, the latter development is inevitable. Once human beings are reduced to becoming merely owners of a marketable labouring capacity, their relation to the social world is radically altered: relations with others, division between work and leisure, work and procreation all undergo a great transformation. So long as labouring capacity serves embedded social goals, work and purpose can appear as meaningful activity. The neoliberal project detaches social purpose from labouring capacity, assigning the atomistic individual a fictitious sovereign status. Under these conditions, social meaning takes on the character of individual self-seeking primarily in consumption. To consume means to realize subjectivity.

Problems with the idea of a sovereign subject in control of the world are discussed in **Chapters 7 and 28**.

Despite the realization that the neoliberal project may not serve either deeper social purpose or individual selfhood, globalization has facilitated its reach in uncharted zones. Virtually everywhere, communities, polities, and people, live, work, and think in words and worlds produced by the expansion of the project, not only the most ardent proponents in the geographically dispersed zones of economic, political, and cultural power, but also its alleged detractors. The attraction of neoliberalism lies in its promise to deliver individual happiness in material goods, tangible and within reach. Paradoxically, its hold on the imagination is most pervasive not only in the cultural West, but outside, in the minds of state elites and managers in the non-Western cultural zones, often inspiring mega-projects with unpleasant social and environmental effects, as we have seen in the second section of this chapter. Virtually on a global scale, the zealous commitment to the modernist vision has marginalized real alternatives or radically reshaped them.

Conceptualizing 'the poor'

In large measure, the success or failure of 'end of poverty' schemes depends upon how poverty is conceived and operationalized. Is it possible that the visibility of the poor may in some manner make them invisible? Once we see the poor in particular ways, are we concealing what is the most important feature of poverty?

Common understandings of poverty stress physical needs and their deprivation as the essential ingredient of what it means to be poor. Hence, poverty is said to have a 'vital core' tied to material sustenance. Human beings on this account are intrinsically biological beings. The failure to satisfy those needs qualifies them as the poor.

This idea, however, is not as simple as it seems. The poor are not merely those who lack the means for material sustenance. They are also those whose biological existence is an object of social policy (Dean 1992). In this sense, the poor become 'the poor'

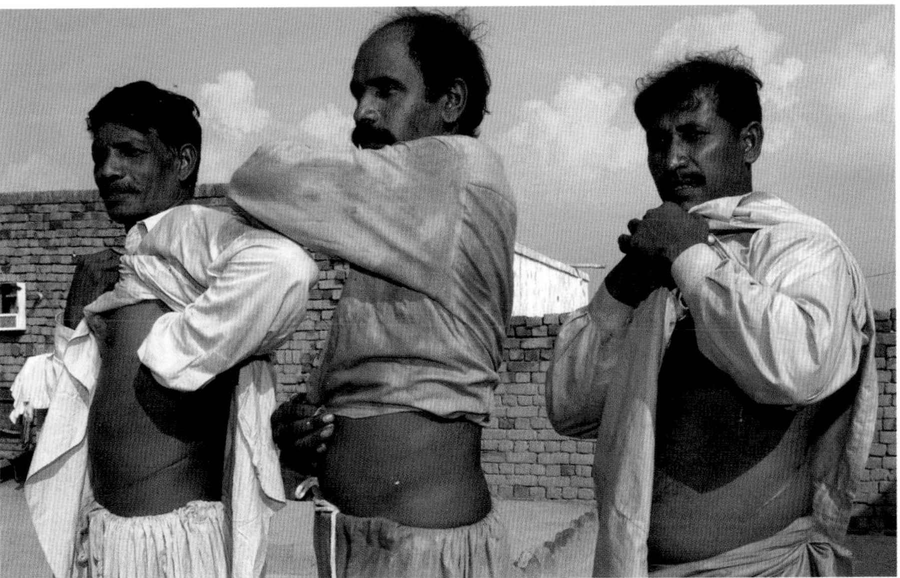

FIGURE 20.6
Price of poverty: Pakistani farmers in Jandala, near Multan, show the scars left after operations to remove their kidneys for cash. Photo: AP

only in the process of being classified as such. They have no existence separate from the classification by those who have the authority to classify them. Outside the sphere of classification, poverty is not a problem. It may be a problem of destitution (Nandy 2002). Although poverty has existed for centuries, it is only under modern social conditions that it assumes a particular form of visibility. Modernity engenders particular forms of classifications and distinctions that allow populations to be divided in specific ways that are coterminous with readily perceived 'objective' indices. These indices are highly mobile and can be deployed to advance grand claims. For instance, in the global war on terror, poverty increasingly appears as a matter of security, a cause of terror, a source of militancy (Belaala 2004; Willet 2005). Once the poor can be recognized within particular classificatory schemes, they can be linked to danger.

Compare this idea that poverty comes to be problematic by virtue of its classification to the discussion in **Chapter 24** of how particular events or people come to be seen as dangers.

The reduction of life to the satisfaction of physical needs is only one aspect of the problem of conceptualizing the poor. From the perspective of those regarded as 'the poor' there is also the question of the subjective state of the poor that is not easily captured in dominant accounting procedures. As Kirsten Hastrup (1993: 727) writes in the context of hunger, 'one of the hardest facts of life is that living is so painful to large numbers of people'. Extending her analysis, sharing the experience of the poor is virtually impossible if suffering takes only the form of visual and numerical representation. Suffering is usually experienced in silence, when speech becomes entirely inadequate. The experience of suffering is severed from the apparatus of meaning-making. Numbers also have the distinctive ability to sanitize the subjective side of human misery.

Chapter 19 explains how statistics are used and indeed needed in order to understand and analyse global inequality. But do these statistics allow us to comprehend the suffering involved?

In public consciousness, poverty does not produce the same heightened anxieties reserved for global terrorism and the latter's potential and real menace to humanity. However, it is also no longer a peripheral global concern buried in stories of modernization and progress and the promises of trickle-down growth. The notion that poverty would eventually disappear with the evolutionary processes of economic development and modernization is not very popular. Yet, public consciousness and

BOX 20.6 GIORGIO AGAMBEN

FIGURE 20.7
Giorgio Agamben

Contemporary Italian philosopher Giorgio Agamben argues that 'sovereign power' – the type of authority most commonly associated with the state – relies on the production of two forms of life as separate (1998). He calls these 'politically qualified life' (the citizen) and 'bare life' (the outlaw, the outsider, or the stateless person, for example). He claims that this separation has now been blurred, and that it no longer holds. Initially, there were certain places, which Agamben describes as 'zones of indistinction', where this blurring could be seen. His first example is the Nazi concentration camp. Here inhabitants no longer had any political or legal status and were subject to the whims of the camp guards. They could be killed without any justification having to be offered: their deaths did not count as murder. More recently, Agamben argues, in our culture of administration, management and capitalist consumerism, we have all potentially become something close to bare life, with no genuine political voice.

conscience do not mean that schemes to end poverty are effective. The gulf between the two lies, in part, in particular conceptualizations that detach the poor from their cultural universe or fail to see progress itself as the condition for poverty.

Uncoupling the poor from their cultural universe, and reducing them to data tends to produce the illusion that mere decreases in numbers would connote a process of ending poverty. What gets silenced in this conceptualization of poverty is that the aim of merely securing survival or bare life does serious violence to the poor in the act of salvaging them.

BROADER ISSUES
ALTERNATIVE VISIONS OF MODERNITY

Chapter 19 explains how such statistics work.

Dominant conceptions typically take a statistical threshold to define poverty. Behind that threshold lies a notion of material deficiency or the absence of goods that allow people to survive. What is missing in these understandings is the indivisibility of cultural forms of life and the material universe of people. It is not merely a question of survival, or even culturally ensured form of life, but the ability to be subjects or authors of their own lives rather than subjects or *dramatis personae* in an externally created production. The poor are those that not only lack material capacity to satisfy culturally informed needs, but the ability to live meaningful lives.

Hence, the notion that the poor are simply those who lack money or property misrecognizes the centrality of the idea of poverty. While money or property allows people to pursue goals outside bare survival, unless the idea of self-determination is brought to bear on the analysis, the poor remain trapped in other people's worlds as objects. This is not surprising as the neoliberal idea of finding the solution to poverty in the informal sector (de Soto 2000) and giving entitlement to either a bundle of goods (Sen 1981) or legally recognized token of owning capital (de Soto 2000) ultimately takes the poor as the receiving end of policy or ethically inspired aid. The historical link between foreign aid and religiously inspired charity may not be so remote. In both instances, the poor are cast as victims, although in some versions of Christian charity, the poor are singularly blessed with godly favour against the corruptibility of the rich who cannot enter paradise. Proximity to material goods in the contemporary sense is framed as a solution to make the poor vanish, but the historical evidence has not been very promising in this regard.

See **Chapter 21** for a discussion of the issues that arise when people think that they know what is good for others.

The lack of the capacity to produce not simply a particular form of cultural life but the ability to creatively redesign their social and life-worlds, that is, to modify their world, not simply adapt to it (Freire 1996 [1970]) does more violence than is apparent in neoliberal imaginaries. On the other hand, the seduction of statistics that rests on the reducibility of human experience to quantifiable data makes social relations opaque. Hence, the Millennium Development Goal of halving the proportion of the extreme poor appears an achievable and worthy mission. The comforting logic that statistical decline in the number of the extreme poor justifies international aid as one of the effective ways to end poverty rationalizes the status quo. Without redesigning the architecture of global political economy and infusing a redistributive principle at its centre, aid camouflages the inherent properties of global capitalism, which rests on the stubborn logic of leaving sizeable populations without the capacity to live meaningful lives. In a capitalist universe, the prison-house of poverty offers few escape routes unless people acquire access to the means that allow them to productively enter the world of exchange, not merely the guarantee of subsistence which some poverty alleviation strategies promote.

For Charles Beitz's view of global justice, which revolves around distribution, see **Chapter 2**.

The question of poverty cannot be posed with any meaningful determinacy outside modernity. No doubt, the poor have had their uses in pre-modern contexts, as moral brokers in the Manichean world of sin and redemption. Helping the poor may open up pathways to heaven. Traces of this role can be found in pleas for foreign aid, charity, and help. Acts of kindness and comfort to the poor have intertwined histories. The moral worth of humanity has rested on the capacity to extend succour and support to the needy, those with the least material possessions. Escape from the enticing world of riches has often been recognized as an essential pathway for spiritual progress and the experience of the sacred. Those who *voluntarily* elected to live in poverty demonstrated their closeness to the deeper wellsprings of life's mysterious purposes. The poor have not been without a productive function after all.

Western conception of modernity

With modernity, the poor tend to lose their cultural meaning, assuming the figure of bare life. Now objects of classification and study, the poor bid farewell to a morally configured world and enter the zone of politics and political economy. In the first instance, the poor are serialized, they become objectified as numbers. They no longer inhabit ethically complex structures of meaning. Within the strict world of modern state practice, the poor are merely objects with potential risks to the polity. Similarly, political economy ruptures the poor from a moral economy, pushing them into the world of labouring. Those outside the modern economy are simply a *social* problem.

The neoliberal project redesigns the problem of the poor. To alleviate poverty is to bring the poor into the world of exchange, and failing that, to supply them as matériel for profit (as the pharmaceutical example suggests). Those who cannot be brought in can be abandoned. However, the attempt to strip the poor from their moral universe is a failed enterprise. The ambivalence towards the poor lies precisely in the difficulty of severing the poor from an ethical world of meaning and judgement. In this context, the conceptualization of the poor as data serves as a surreptitious attempt to represent the poor in ethically neutral terms. The poor continue to enjoy a symbolic quality, and hence they cannot exist outside judgement. Yet, the breach with morality and ethics can allow vast expenditures of liberal guilt without disturbing the status quo. This would entail the unwanted question of whether the world in which the poor live is a world ethically constituted. Poverty alleviation is situated at the fault line of morality and ethics.

In alternative worlds, ethically constituted and culturally embedded, the poor cannot exist as mere data, objects of policy, or matériel. They are an intrinsic part of a cultural universe. Embedded economies, that is, economies limited in scope and purpose by ethical considerations not merely the self-serving impulses, recognize the violence entailed in severing people from their cultural contexts.

The rapid spread of the neoliberal project globally has curtailed the possibility to envision alternative worlds. In different cultural zones, with the notable exception of Latin America, a convergence appears to be building to address the problem of poverty, relying on market-based solutions. Those zones that apparently reject modernity reveal a curious mix of delinking the cultural accoutrements of West-centred modernity while embracing its technical rationality. The story of the Islamic Cultural Zones can be read on those lines.

For more on Islam in global politics see **Chapter 6**.

Islamic conception of modernity

A distinctive feature of any alternative construction of the poor would entail a modified understanding of modernity, one that recognizes the need to harness the pursuit of wealth within a wider framework of cultural and spiritual life. Unlike the hegemonic narrative of Western modernity which accords accumulation a privileged status in the larger scheme of things, an Islamic conception of modernity works with the notion of overlapping sovereignties in which human purpose and intentionality are embedded in concentric spiritual and secular pursuits: in family, community, the state, the *ummah* (community of believers). Humanity might flourish and both vertical and horizontal attachments bear moral and ethical content, not swallowed up by the pursuit of happiness or reasons of state.

An appreciation of a distinctively Islamic conception of modernity (as well as other non-Western modalities of embeddedness) allows a remapping of the place of the economy in society. The pursuit of happiness acquires an expansive, non-economistic, character linking other-worldly awareness with material reproduction. The individual makes concessions to societal interests and the well-being of the community, not as residual effects of political economy, but as normative principles for the Good Life. Embeddedness also means making human dignity the foundation of the social order.

FIGURE 20.8
Islamic banking today in the Gulf States and in Malaysia, where Islamic and 'conventional' banks compete freely.
Photo: AP

A key feature of the modern poor is their disconnection from any notion of dignity. Material dispossession means redundancy, unless the poor return to the social order in the shape of matériel to service the economy.

The notion of overlapping sovereignties is not cartographical, but a recognition of multiple commitments to tame the insatiable quest for self-aggrandizement and to prevent state idolatry. An ideal-typical Western conception of sovereignty is a compromise between state idolatry and self-interest, the former allowing the latter. Either the state, or the individual serves as the foundation for the social order. An Islamic social order shuns these distinctively secular constructions.

The Western conception of sovereignty and its history is explained in **Chapter 11**.

Difficulties of adopting alternative visions: Islamic Cultural Zones

Alternative visions to Western modernity, however, confront a social universe deeply scared by the unstoppable march of neoliberal globalization, but also the deepening of modernist traits of social organization, thinking, and practice. The colonial legacy has ensured that the derivative discourses of state practice would outlive the formal end of colonial rule. Sovereignty follows a modernist script throughout most of the Islamic Cultural Zones. In turn, the process of cultural disembeddedness shows no signs of abatement. Other-worldly concerns have moved to new sites of enunciation, as moral critique of the prevailing social order or as a regressive idiom to avoid objectionable cultural features of neoliberal globalization. In both instances, the institutional form of protest and resistance has taken a modernist turn.

Chapter 15 shows how the colonial legacy still seriously affects people's lives in formerly colonized states.

Within the shrinking spaces of neoliberalism, however, Islamic civil society has become the mainstay of solace and support to the poor throughout most of the Islamic

BOX 20.7 MURABAHA

An instance of an Islamic alternative to microfinance is the concept of *murabaha*, originally derived from Islamic jurisprudence, in which it refers simply to a sale (the exchange of a thing of value by another thing of value with mutual agreement). In the contemporary context it has become an integral part of 'interest-free' Islamic banking. In its original formulation, *murabaha* is a transaction which honours transparency: the seller divulges the real cost of the commodity, then adds some additional amount or a percentage as profit. Strict rules of compliance that preserve the transparency of the sale must be observed for a *murabaha* transaction, including the ascertainment of the actual cost of the product. The interesting aspect of *murabaha* lies in the aspiration to disrupt the autonomy of exchange in favour of a desire to recast the notion of profit and embed it in an economy of trust. By contrast, microfinance remains ensconced within a strictly market preserve and the compulsions of opaqueness that characterize the actual workings of a capitalist economy.

Cultural Zones. The evacuation of the state from its historic commitment to development or welfare is both a cause and effect of a broadening neoliberal governmentality. Often, the lines between political protest and Islamic variants of social welfare can get blurred, but from the perspective of the poor with nothing to lose, a rediscovery of their faith and sustenance are on a single register. Islamic civil society provides a small semblance of integration in a world falling apart. The promise of an integrated life may be illusory, but it becomes the proxy for thinking in an alternative medium.

For more on how Islamic movements are involved in welfare provision see **Chapter 6**.

The fate of the poor in the Islamic Cultural Zones, as elsewhere, rests on the fate of the hegemonic modern project for organizing social and life-worlds. While resistance to that project may be fragile, disorganized, and sporadic, it is not completely devoid of capacities to slow down the processes of cultural dispossession. An Islamic vision to reclaim aspects of humanity acquires greater salience in this context.

Discussions of poverty open up wider queries about the nature of the world order, relations between hegemonic and subaltern forces, normative questions of redistribution, and above all, about the neoliberal trajectory of globalization. The poor have generally avoided the more harmful features of cultural dispossession in the Islamic Cultural Zones. As the neoliberal project has expanded, Islamic civil society has also grown. Can this experience provide an alternative model to alleviate poverty, if not ending it?

The inclination to romanticize the poor must be resisted. Equally so, alternatives themselves must be embedded and sustainable, not mere reactions to more powerful tendencies. While the visible salience of Islamic civil society as an alternate site to address poverty can be received with greater openness, the bigger issue of neoliberal globalization cannot be left out of sight. Attempts to end poverty often fall into the trap of detaching understanding of the big picture from encouraging symptoms of change and transformation.

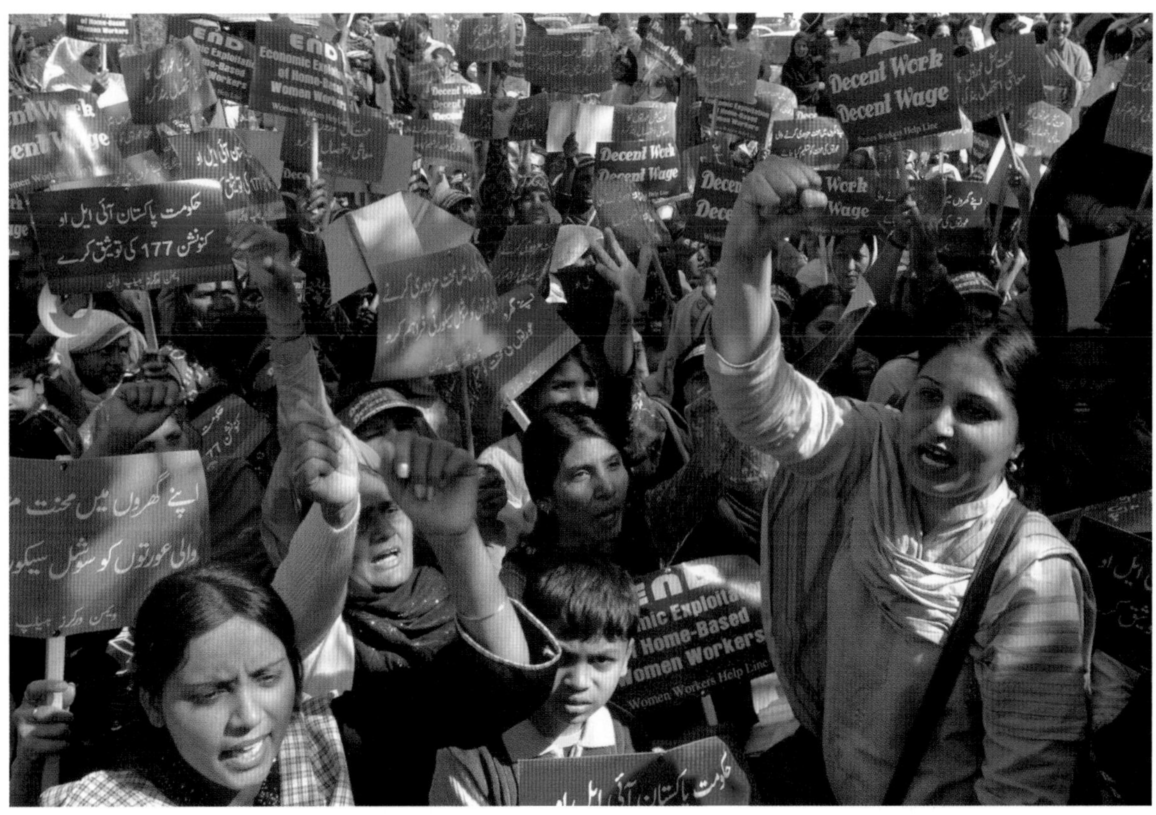

FIGURE 20.9
Activists of Workers Women's Association chant slogans during a rally to mark International Women's Day, Thursday 8 March 2007, in Lahore, Pakistan. Thousands of women demonstrated in nationwide rallies on International Women's Day, demanding freedom, equal rights and an end to discriminatory laws in this Muslim nation. Photo: K. M. Chaudary, AP

CONCLUSION

Poverty remains a durable feature of international relations. Despite many grand attempts to end poverty, the poor refuse to disappear from the global scene. The basic problem lies in neoliberal prescriptions that rest on economism. Some major shortcomings of neoliberal solutions to ending poverty become apparent in South Asia, including the failings of some innovative schemes like microfinance. The neoliberal project fails to accord the poor any notion of dignity or personhood. Ending poverty may not be possible in the foreseeable future, but an appreciation of cultural embeddedness in other formulations of modernity can restore the poor some measure of their self-worth. The quest of ending poverty may be better served if the process to transform the poor into 'bare life' can be averted, if not reversed.

FURTHER READING

Banerjee, Abhijit V. and Esther Duflo (2011) *Poor Economics: A Radical Rethinking of the Way to Fight Global Poverty.* New York: PublicAffairs.
Winner of several awards, this book offers a radical rethinking of the economics of poverty through numerous empirical examples, including hundreds of randomized control trials to establish why the poor live different lives despite similar abilities and desires enjoyed by those who are not poor.

Davies, Matt and Magnus Ryner (eds) (2006) *Poverty and the Production of World Politics*, Basingstoke: Palgrave.
An exciting collection relocating poverty within structures of global political economy.

Davis, Mike (2006) *Planet of Slums*, London: Verso.
A breathtaking account of new forms of poverty produced by runaway urbanization.

Dreze, Jean and Amartya Sen (1989) *Hunger and Public Action*, Oxford: Clarendon Press.
One of the major statements by two leading economists on the need for rethinking public policy to eliminate hunger.

Dreze, Jean and Amartya Sen (1991) *The Political Economy of Hunger*, vols I–III, Oxford: Clarendon Press.
Perhaps the most important studies of hunger and the complexity of understanding it.

Edkins, Jenny (2000) *Whose Hunger? Concepts of Famine, Practices of Aid*, Minneapolis: University of Minnesota Press.
A highly original book on the limits of received conceptions of eradicating famine.

Escobar, Arturo (1994) *Encountering Development: The Making and Unmaking of the Third World*, Princeton, NJ: Princeton University Press.
One of the most important post-structuralist critiques of modernization and development.

George, Susan (1976) *How the Other Half Dies*, Harmondsworth: Penguin.
A classic statement on global inequality and its effects.

Goulet, Denis (1971) *The Cruel Choice: A New Concept in the Theory of Development*, New York: Atheneum.
A key ethical critique of conventional theories of development.

Levine, David P. and S. Abu Turab Rizvi (2005) *Poverty, Work, and Freedom: Political Economy and the Moral Order*, Cambridge: Cambridge University Press.
One of the most compelling challenges to mainstream wisdom on poverty.

Mahbub ul Haq (1976) *The Poverty Curtain: Choices for the Third World*, New York: Columbia University Press.
One of the classics in the field of development economics and global inequality.

Schumacher, E. F. (1973) *Small Is Beautiful: A Study of Economics as if People Mattered*, London: Blond and Briggs.
One of the first books on environmentalism and sustainable development.

South Commission (1990) *The Challenge to the South: The Report of the South Commission*, Oxford: Oxford University Press.
An important report on Third World development from its perspective.

Yunus, Muhammad and Alan Jolis (2010) *Banker to the Poor: Micro-Lending and the Battle Against World Poverty*, US: ReadHowYouWant.com.
This autobiographical account of the founder of Grameen Bank, Muhammad Yunus, presents an incisive window into the genealogy of micro-finance and its socio-historical context.

UNDP (2003) *Human Development Report 2003: Millennium Development Goals: A Compact Among Nations to End Human Poverty*, http://hdr.undp.org/reports/global/2003/.
A very useful report on recent thinking on eliminating global poverty.

REFERENCES

Agamben, Giorgio (1998) *Homo Sacer: Sovereign Power and Bare Life*, trans. Daniel Heller-Roazen, Stanford, CA: Stanford University Press.

Appadurai, Arjun (2001) *Globalization*, Durham, NC: Duke University Press.

Banfield, Edward C. (1958) *The Moral Basis of a Backward Society*, Glencoe, IL: The Free Press.

Banuri, Tariq (1990) 'Modernization and Its Discontents: A Cultural Perspective on the Theories of Development', in Frederique Apffel Marglin and Stephen A. Marglin (eds) *Dominating Knowledge*, Oxford: Clarendon Press.

Belaala, Selma (2004) 'Morocco: Slums Breed Jihad', *Le Monde Diplomatique (English Language Edition)*, November: 4–5, http://mondediplo.com/2004/11/04/11/04moroccoislamists?var%20recherche=Belaala.

De Soto, Hernando (2000) *The Mystery of Capital: Why Capitalism Triumphs in the West and Fails Everywhere Else*, New York: Basic Books.

Dean, Mitchell (1992) 'A Genealogy of the Government of Poverty', *Economy and Society* 21, 3: 215–51.

Freire, Paulo (1996 [1970]) *Pedagogy of the Oppressed*, translated by Myra Bergman Ramos, London: Penguin.

Hardin, Garrett (1974) 'Lifeboat Ethics: The Case against Helping the Poor', *Psychology Today* 8: 38, 43: 123–26.

Hastrup, Kirsten (1993) 'Hunger and the Hardness of Facts', *Man*, New Series, 28, 4: 717–39.

Kothari, Rajni (1993) *Poverty: Human Consciousness and the Amnesia of Development*, London: Zed Books.

Nandy, Ashis (2002) 'The Beautiful, Expanding Future of Poverty: Popular Economics as a Psychological Defense', in Mustapha Kamal Pasha and Craig N. Murphy (eds) *International Relations and the New Inequality*, Oxford: Blackwell.

Polanyi, Karl (1944) *The Great Transformation: The Political and Economic Origins of Our Time*, Boston: Beacon Press.

Sachs, Jeffrey (2005) *The End of Poverty: How We Can Make It Happen in Our Lifetime*, Foreword by Bono, London: Penguin Books.

Sen, Amartya (1981) *Poverty and Famines: An Essay on Entitlement and Deprivation*, Oxford: Oxford University Press.

UNDP (2006) *Human Development Report 2006: Beyond Scarcity: Power, Poverty and the Global Water Crisis*, New York: UNDP.

Willet, Susan (2005) 'New Barbarians at the Gate: Losing the Liberal Peace in Africa', *Review of African Political Economy* 106: 569–94.

Yunus, Muhammad (2007) 'Is Grameen Bank Different from Conventional Banks?', June, http://www.grameen-info.org/bank/GBdifferent.htm.

For a range of further resources supporting this chapter, please visit the companion website for *Global Politics, 2nd Edition* at www.routledge.com/cw/edkins/

CHAPTER **21**

Why do some people think they know what is good for others?

Naeem Inayatullah

THE QUESTION
GIVING AND RECEIVING

Some people think they know what is good for others because they believe they know something crucial denied to others. For example, a society that believes it has mastered democracy may notice that other societies have authoritarian and dictatorial political institutions that leave people without a voice. In offering to help create democratic procedures, the 'democratic' society may wish to increase the freedom of others. The George W. Bush and Tony Blair administrations used this motive to justify their occupation of Afghanistan and Iraq. Or, a society with abundant wealth and food supplies might notice the beginning of famine in another part of the world. They might decide to feed those suffering from famine. Policy makers from wealthy societies might also feel compelled to teach others how to manage their agriculture and reorganize their economy so as to avert future catastrophes. International aid agencies and the World Bank offer such lessons to those who undergo periodic famines. Finally, scientists, social theorists, and policy makers in 'democratic' and 'wealthy' societies might believe that the absence of proper political and economic institutions result from a larger and deeper problem with other societies. They may deduce that such societies need a better understanding of the proper relations between humans and humans, between humans and nature, and between humans and the larger cosmos – the universe thought of as an ordered and integrated whole. They may believe that such societies lack the right kind of order and their thinking as a whole needs to be reorganized. Europeans have held this posture in their encounters with others for the last 500 years or so. In each case, those with true knowledge believe that they have a responsibility to share their knowledge and thereby improve others' lives.

We can react in two opposite ways to such claims. On one hand, we honour the belief that providing goods for others is an essential part of human responsibility. If we know how to sustain freedom; if we know how to reshape nature so that we can produce great wealth; or if we have learned how to create a social order that produces a vibrant democratic society with abundant wealth, then we must do our utmost to provide such goods for others. Not doing so would be selfish, irresponsible, and wasteful. When we accept the role of doing good for others we assume the indispensable value of our knowledge, the inherent sincerity of our motives, and the urgency of the recipient's need. As donors we assume our virtue and delight in our goodness.

Some will of course always dispute that we know how to sustain freedom, reshape nature or produce great wealth in the first place. For example, we may live in a wealthy country but that does not necessarily mean that wealth is abundant for everyone. See **Chapter 19**.

On the other hand, if someone targets us as a recipient of goodness we can become guarded. Perhaps an example will help us understand this wariness. Often parents dutifully try to prepare and guide their young towards future employment. They regard their life experience as a store of knowledge that should help their children replicate their successes and avoid their mistakes. Despite our parents' best intentions, however, we are uneasy and sometimes unwilling recipients of their advice and effort. A part of us questions the relevance of their experience to our current and future plans. Their concern for our career may feel like an intrusion. We may wonder if their worry results from a lack faith in our judgment. When others suggest that they know what is good for us, we imagine that they are actually pointing to our inadequacy. In response, we tend to stress our independence and defend our integrity. We may bristle at the donor's presumption that we are missing a vital perspective. We may even suspect the donor hides self-serving motives in the guise of helping.

Our defensiveness may be hasty and reactive but it may also emerge from deeper issues. How did the donor surmise that the recipient lacks something? Does the donor know the recipient well enough to formulate the recipient's lack? Is the donor's knowledge as vital and necessary to the recipient as the donor believes? Is the donor's duty driven by the desire to reorganize the world according to the donor's self-interested and limited vision? Don't conquerors and imperialists hide their baser motives by clothing them in the good?

Remember too that when we think about ethics and politics we draw on our pictures of the world, as discussed in **Chapter 2**. You might like to think about the pictures of reason, the subject and political space entailed in this discussion here.

On the one side, if we ignore the needs of others we deny our full humanity. On the other side, doing good for others can be intrusive, coercive, and detrimental to others' sense of autonomy and freedom. We seem split; stuck in the ethical and political tension between wanting to eradicate ignorance and suspecting that our pursuit of duty endangers others.

Can we find a way to move beyond the split? We can. Notice that we usually jump from one posture to the other without experiencing the tension that lies between them. We skip over the following kinds of questions: Can we act responsibly towards others

Discussions of colonialism in **Chapters 15 and 16** and contemporary interventions in **Chapter 25** are relevant here. **Chapter 14** asks whether democracy is a good idea.

The tricky issue of responsibility towards others is also discussed in **Chapter 28**.

Some of the problems with interventions by international institutions or states acting with their authorization are discussed in **Chapters 15 and 25**.

without undercutting their autonomy and freedom? Can we offer them democracy, wealth, and an alternative social order without colonizing them? From the other side we can ask these questions: how can we receive the 'gifts' and knowledge of donors and nevertheless sustain our political, economic, and cultural identity? What can we offer in return? Such questions emerge when we acknowledge the plausibility of both positions – the actual *responsibilities* of the donor and the legitimate *suspicions* of the recipient. When we can feel this tension we can begin to stretch.

Moving past this split requires us to search for the difference between proposing and imposing. Sincere intentions can still be impositions. The more genuinely I believe that I am providing you with a necessary good, the less I am likely to worry about *how* I provide that good and whether you experience it as an imposition. Proposing the good, in contrast, requires that donors re-examine their motivation. Donors may need to motivate their giving not by locating the receiver's deficiency, but paradoxically, by grasping their own lack. When parties seek to overcome their own lack by engaging in cooperative searches for mutual enrichment, then sustainable goods may emerge. Despite this note of hope, we want to bear in mind that even when humans understand how to move beyond this split, they mostly do not do so. The problem of producing the good for others has a long and deep tension that is wrecked with human intransigence. We make a mistake, therefore, if in grasping for a 'solution' to this problem we bypass its complexity and intractability.

To illustrate the concerns of this chapter, I might have turned to contemporary events. Interventions by institutions such as the United Nations, NATO, the World Bank, the International Monetary Fund, and various inter-state alliances provide familiar examples. Such ready examples, however, are unlikely to help us understand this problem's deep historical roots. My illustrations take us instead to the thirteenth and sixteenth centuries. These mostly unfamiliar times present some advantages: they state the issues in clear terms, they show how little the problem has changed over 700 years, and they demonstrate the enormous difficulty of our problem. Our challenge remains creating mutually enriching forms of interaction that do not diminish either party. We turn first to Francisco de Vitoria and sixteenth-century Europe.

ILLUSTRATIVE EXAMPLE
GOD'S PURPOSE: EARLY CHRISTIAN INCURSIONS

Spain in the Americas: Francisco de Vitoria's outrage

Catholics and Protestants were waging religious battles against each other in sixteenth-century Europe. Simultaneously, in the early part of that century, Spanish conquistadors were destroying and pillaging the strongest and wealthiest civilizations in the Americas. Francisco de Vitoria, who was among the most influential political theorists and theologians in sixteenth-century Catholic Europe, thought deeply about these two vital issues of the day. On one of these issues his position is clear-cut. He opposed Protestantism. His allegiance was to Catholicism, the emperor, and the pope. On the subject of Spanish treatment of Indians, he was shocked and embarrassed by the massacre and

BOX 21.1 FRANCISCO DE VITORIA

Francisco de Vitoria (1485–1546) is considered a canonical figure in international law. He was a Dominican theologian and founder of the Salamanca or Spanish school of jurisprudence. He and his students influenced and restructured the theological thinking of Europe. He was a central figure in the debate of the nature of the Indians in the sixteenth century, especially in his 1539 lectures, *De Indis* (*On the American Indians*, published in 1557, after his death). Charles V, emperor and king of Spain, was among those who consulted Vitoria.

FIGURE 21.1
Francisco de Vitoria.
http://en.wikipedia.org/wiki/images:Francesco_vitoria.jpg

looting of Indians. In a 1534 letter, he writes that merely thinking about the conquistadors 'freezes the blood' in his veins (Vitoria 1991: 331). Vitoria tried to curtail Spain's invading armies by rejecting their justifications for waging war against the Indians. However, he was not wholehearted in his defence of Indians because he was perplexed and troubled by their deficiencies. These include human sacrifice, cannibalism, a low-level civilization, the absence of Christianity, and violations of God's natural order. While Vitoria rebuked the conquistadors he did not believe that the Spaniards should evacuate Indian territories or abandon the natives. His arguments restrained Spanish violence while also providing correctives for Indian deficiencies. Vitoria believed he knew what was good for Indians.

Spanish imperialism in South America is also discussed in the context of a general discussion of colonization in **Chapter 16**, and specifically in relation to Argentina in **Chapter 14**.

The 'discovery' of the Americas posed a problem for all European thinkers. Were the Indians human? If so, what was their place in the cosmological order (the whole comprising the natural, the social, and the spiritual order)? The cosmological problem was also a specific legal concern: was the Spanish conquest and enslavement of Indians legitimate? Pope Alexander VI's 1493 bull, *Inter Caetera*, permitted Spanish and Portuguese evangelization and territorial acquisition but denied enslavement. In line with this reasoning, Vitoria rejected the view that the Indians were natural slaves – a popular position inspired by Greek philosopher Aristotle's views of slavery (see Chapter 10). Vitoria accepted Indians as human beings capable of understanding God's laws.

Like most Europeans however, Vitoria, did not *fully* embrace the Indians' humanity. 'Aberrant' and 'unnatural' Indian behaviour indicated that Indians were not sufficiently human (Pagden 1982: 64). Spanish thinkers found themselves in a paradox: if the Indians were irrational and thereby considered natural slaves, it becomes difficult to account for reports of their technological mastery, their cities and imperial political institutions, and their sophisticated (if satanic) religious practices. Yet, if the Indians were deemed rational human beings then explaining their human sacrifices, their

FIGURE 21.2 The Mexica (Aztec) peoples, followers of Moctezuma, face a powerful Spanish force under Hernando Cortés in the 1519–21 campaigns. Fray Diego Durán. *La Historia antigua de la Nueva España*, 1585. Manuscript facsimile, Peter Force Collection, Library of Congress

relatively primitive agricultural techniques and arts, and especially their acts of cannibalism became complicated. This was no small matter since the legitimacy of Spanish intervention in the Americas rested on the appraisal of Indian culture.

When Vitoria evaluates the reasons for the Spanish conquest of America he considers four oft-cited reasons for depriving the Indians of their rights to self-rule, territorial control, and property. The Indians are said to forfeit their rights because they are

1 sinners,
2 infidels,
3 mentally subnormal, or
4 intrinsically irrational beings (Vitoria 1991: 233).

He easily dismisses the first two reasons (Vitoria 1991: 240–6). Depriving sinners of their natural rights is based on the false belief – attributed to anti-Catholic radicals such as Wycliffe, Hus, and various Lutherans – that authority is based on the ruler's purity of faith. Vitoria understood the dangers to the Church if legitimacy of rule is tied to the quality of a ruler's faith. First, because no ruler is without sin. And, because someone can always use the claim of greater piety as a means to overthrow the established order. Vitoria refused the belief that sinners lost their rights as a result of their sins. He stood with a long line of thinkers going back hundreds of years who championed the security of the Christian Church against radical reformers.

The link between religion and political authority is explored in **Chapters 7 and 27**. **Chapter 6** examines this issue in a contemporary context.

Nor can the Indians be infidels, Vitoria argued, because infidelity requires prior knowledge of the rejected faith. Indians were ignorant of Christianity. And, if they were originally Christian, as some supposed, then they had degenerated too far from their Christian beliefs to be accountable for their false ideas.

In considering the Indian's deficient mental capacity and their lack of rationality, the third and fourth reasons, Vitoria first weighs the evidence from the Americas and then resists these claims as well. Although, as we shall see, he retains something of

FIGURE 21.3
'Oh let them go.'
Artist: Viv Quillin

their rationale, indicating that his opposition is not steadfast. The Indians, he writes, 'have judgment like other men'. They 'have some order in their affairs'. This order is expressed through 'properly organized cities, proper marriages, magistrates and overlords, laws, industries, and commerce, all of which require the use of reason'. They 'likewise have a form of religion' (Vitoria 1991: 250).

It is interesting to think of the picture of reason used here. How does it differ from the picture of reason employed by the thinkers about global ethics explored in **Chapter 2**?

On the other side of the ledger allegations of Indian cannibalism and human sacrifice weigh heavily on Vitoria. He allows the accusation 'that these barbarians are . . . foolish and slow-witted' and further acknowledges their 'sins against the law of nature' (Vitoria: 1991: 251, 273). Though he believes that such offences cannot cancel rights, they do indicate intellectual and social chaos in Indian life (Vitoria 1991: 272–5).

Vitoria finds human sacrifice more comprehensible than cannibalism (Vitoria 1991: 212–17). He acknowledges that sacrifice plays a part in Christianity, as in Abraham's willingness to kill his son and, of course, in Christ's own sacrifice on the cross. Despite this sympathy, Vitoria condemns Indian practices. He emphasizes the Indians' confusion about the proper cosmological order, not the similarities between the two systems of religion. He believes that Indians fail to apprehend the most important precepts of God's order. He concludes that they have a distorted vision of reality and that their mental capacity is deficient. Their disorder and deficiency are further expressed in various cultural and technological inadequacies: the Indians possess only a rudimentary knowledge of agriculture, they lack the ability to work iron and other metals, and they are unlettered.

In the end, Vitoria concludes that the Indians are unable to adequately govern their own domains. The following passage summarizes Vitoria's position, though he carefully distances himself from it by insisting that he offers it only for expository reasons:

> these barbarians, though not totally mad, as explained before, are nevertheless so close to being mad, that they are unsuited to setting up or administrating a commonwealth both legitimate and ordered in human and civil terms. Hence they have neither appropriate laws nor magistrates fitted to the task. Indeed, they are

> unsuited even to governing their own households; hence their lack of letters, of arts and crafts (not merely liberal, but even mechanical), of systematic agriculture, of manufacture, and of many other things . . . indispensable for human use.
>
> (Vitoria 1991: 290)

Are there some people we today consider 'human but inadequately so'?

For Vitoria, the Indians are human but inadequately so.

Having diagnosed Indian deficiency, Vitoria moves to the cure. Indians are not permanently foolish or irrational. On the contrary, as human beings they possess reason. The real problem is that they have not activated their dormant reasoning capacity (Vitoria 1991: 250). This failure is due to poor teaching. Vitoria assures us that the fault lies not in their nature, but 'mainly due to their evil and barbarous education' for 'they were so many thousands of years outside the state of salvation' (Vitoria 1991: 250). Notice that Vitoria shifts the status of Indians from slaves to children. Europeans thereby change from being lords and masters to becoming parents and teachers.

Vitoria then provides what today we would call his policy recommendation:

> It might therefore be argued that for [the Indians'] own benefit the princes of Spain might take over their administration, and set up urban officers and governors on their behalf, or even give them new masters, so long as this could be proved in their interest. . . . and not merely for the profit of the Spaniards.
>
> (Vitoria 1991: 290, 291)

European tutelage will bring enlightenment and order; this is what is good for Indians.

We might sympathize with Vitoria's struggle to reconcile Indian beliefs and practices with his own theological convictions. His Christian beliefs convince him that the Indians are God's children but these beliefs also require him to prescribe Christian instruction. In sum, Vitoria reins in the cruelty of the conquistadors, he refuses to make Indians slaves, and he recommends that the civilized world incorporate the Indians.

Certainty plays a role in the justifications for torture explored in **Chapter 2**.

If we leave aside the discussion of whether Vitoria is foolish or wise in his beliefs, we can pursue larger questions: Why is he so confident in his own faith? Why doesn't an encounter with the Indians raise doubts for him about his own worldview? Before we can turn to these questions, I first want to show that Vitoria's position on the Indians is part of a larger pattern of Christian relations with non-Christian societies, and more generally of relations between self and other.

Relations between self and other are an important part of global politics and are discussed in many chapters in this book. See particularly **Chapters 2 and 5**.

Today, even though contemporary world politics retains much of Vitoria's overall vision, we may regard his views on Indians as ethnocentric. Was Vitoria aware that his worldview was tainted by European and Christian partiality? Unlikely. The deeper source of his certainty derives from what I call exclusive knowledge.

Christian and infidel: Pope Innocent IV

Sinibaldo Fieschi was a leading canon lawyer before he became Pope Innocent IV (1243–54). As pope and lawyer, Innocent synthesized judgments about how Christians should treat non-Christians and he bound these ideas into a legal doctrine. His views illuminated Church thinking for more than 300 years and directly influenced Vitoria's fifteenth-century analysis of Spanish dealings with American Indians (Muldoon 1979:

BOX 21.2 EXCLUSIVE KNOWLEDGE

Exclusive knowledge is the idea that some group, usually 'our' group, has unique and superior knowledge about how the world works. It contains three specific assumptions:

1 one's own group has special access to knowledge about the order and the workings of natural and social life;
2 there is something superior and final about such knowledge; and
3 others' knowledge claims are inadequate or defective compared to ours.

Later we will discuss how these assumptions work against the great enemy of exclusive knowledge – doubt.

vii–viii, 140–47; Williams 1990: 13, 44). Our examination of Innocent IV's claims to exclusive knowledge remains relevant because we can hear the echoes of his voice in current theory and policy.

Innocent IV raised the following question: 'is it licit to invade the lands that infidels posses, and if it is licit, why is it licit?' (Muldoon 1979: 191–2). ('Licit' means allowed by law.) Innocent was asking if Christians had a right to dispossess non-believers. By contemporary standards, Innocent's question is surprisingly forthright. Nevertheless, despite several hundred years of work by canonists, he was wading into a disputed area. At the time, non-believers included Christian schismatics and heretics, Jews and Muslims living within Christian realms, and Muslims and Mongols beyond the frontiers of Christendom. Though he recognized differences between these groups, he collapsed them into a single category, non-Christian, in order to create a more uniform response to infidels (Muldoon 1979: 3).

FIGURE 21.4
Innocent IV. Library of Congress, ref. 3644545r

Innocent disallows dispossession of infidels simply because they are non-believers. He argues that *dominium* – the basic faculties and rights necessary to human functioning and self-rule, including the right to property and the offices of legitimate authority – rests in the hand of society's rulers regardless of their beliefs. While unpossessed or unruled territories are free for the taking, lands already occupied and ruled are considered the legitimate possessions of their holders. Innocent IV establishes that all peoples, regardless of their faith, have the right to property and self-government.

In which contemporary debates can you find similar considerations and arguments to the ones we are examining here?

We may be surprised that Innocent allows infidels a right to property given that he starts from the premise of exclusive knowledge of Christian truths. His generosity seems all the more astonishing given that, as pope, Innocent considers himself God's vicar. As God's vicar, he can claim universal *dominium* over the planet. Accepting others' right of *dominium* did not mean, however, that Innocent gave up *his* responsibility for *their* souls. He believes that the Church's responsibility for all human souls requires Christians to convert non-believers. However strong or weak the papacy's earthly political power, Innocent retains the pope's ultimate spiritual authority over all peoples, including infidels. He allowed arguments for dispossessing infidels through this belief.

On the assumption that God's law was evident to all, Innocent argued that infidel rulers forfeited *dominium* when they failed to punish their subjects' violations of natural law. In this circumstance, the pope could mete out justice by authorizing Christian military interventions in infidel societies (Muldoon 1979: 10–11). Innocent leaves unspecified what counts as a violation of natural law, though he mentions sexual perversion and idolatry as particularly serious violations. Such sins, if left unchecked, obligate the pope to summon Christian armies for the purposes of righting the natural order. His armies must withdraw, however, once the mission is concluded.

As long as Christian armies occupy infidel territory why not use them, we may ask, to convert the infidels to Christianity? Christian doctrine disallowed such force because meaningful conversion had to be voluntary. Infidel acquiescence to the sword was no vindication of the true faith. Nevertheless, Innocent recognizes that instructing infidels on proper worship, if not also manners and customs, requires missionary work. Of course, Innocent expects that infidels will resist Christian instruction and block missionary activity. Such resistance, however, amounts to impeding God's way. It justifies the suspension of infidel rights to *dominium* and authorizes Christian invasion. Similarly, the pope may intervene if infidels persecute Christians living under their rule. He may even move to create 'regime change' by replacing noncompliant infidel rulers (Muldoon 1979: 11–12).

Innocent disallows wars of dispossession but retains the claim of exclusive knowledge. On the basis of this knowledge, he then argues that certain kinds of intervention in infidel society are just and necessary. Innocent IV uses the same intellectual apparatus – the same combination of Biblical references, Roman law sources, and humanist thinking – to establish infidel rights *and* to legitimate dispossession of infidels.

We may ask if Innocent's arguments are tied to Christianity's exclusive knowledge or are they general principles available to all faiths and cultures? Can other faiths marshal these claims and proselytize in Christian society? 'No' replies Innocent. Christians alone have the right to proselytize, to convert others, and to intervene militarily for religious purposes. Christian knowledge excludes and exceeds other perspectives on ultimate truth. Innocent bluntly and unashamedly tells us why he authorizes Christian missions while blocking all other proselytizers: because 'they are in error and we are on the righteous path' (Muldoon 1979: 14).

For a discussion of sovereignty, see **Chapter 7**.

In sum, Innocent IV argues *for* the rights of infidels to property and self-government and thereby rejects claims that they can be dispossessed simply because they are not Christians. However, Innocent's defence of infidel *dominium* or, in modern terms, their 'sovereignty', is porous. He offers a justification that legitimates both military intervention and political/spiritual regime change. Further, consistent with the claim to exclusive knowledge, intervention is a distinctly one-way Christian prerogative. Like Vitoria, Innocent knows what is good for others. He knows that others lack the knowledge to which he, as a Christian, has full access. Exclusive knowledge and his duty to

BOX 21.3 THE JUST WAR TRADITION

The 'just war' tradition is a way of thinking that is prominent in contemporary politics and academic discussions. It is concerned, at least in part, with doing good for others. Vitoria's work, including his reflections on the legitimacy of the Spanish intervention in the Americas, is seen to have contributed to the development of this tradition and of international law (Bellamy 2006).

The just war tradition is concerned with when it is permissible to fight (this is called *ius ad bellum*) and how it is permissible to fight (*ius in bello*). The precise criteria listed under each heading vary for different just war thinkers. Roughly, the first category requires that a war is fought only

- with the right sorts of aims in mind, such as upholding the law or re-establishing peace (right intention);
- for the right sorts of reasons, such as self-defence against aggression (just cause);
- by the right sorts of political entity, typically now identified as states (right authority);
- for causes that are significant enough (proportionality of ends);
- and when no other means are available (last resort).

The second category requires that the means used in the war remain proportional to the particular objectives (that is, for example, that the least destructive weapon is used to accomplish a particular goal) and that civilians are not targeted (this is called discrimination or non-combatant immunity).

Just war thinkers see this tradition as limiting the ways in which military violence can be used (Coates 1997; Walzer 1992) but they have also justified recent wars. This often takes the form of arguing that we have to do some good for others (such as liberate Afghans from the Taliban or Iraqis from Saddam Hussein) and that we can only do so through war (Elshtain 2003; Walzer 2004).

retrieve the lost souls of non-believers, obligates him to endorse Christian work done for the good of others.

By using the examples of Vitoria and Innocent IV, I am not suggesting that either exclusive knowledge or the belief that one can do good for others is peculiar to Christianity or to Europe. On the contrary, exclusive knowledge seems a common characteristic of many cultures. We can appreciate its pervasiveness by examining an exchange between Christians and Mongols.

Christian and Mongol: the encounter with Güyük Khan

In the summer of 1244, Innocent IV moved the papacy from Rome to Lyons to escape the excommunicated emperor Frederick II's attack on Italy. At stake within western

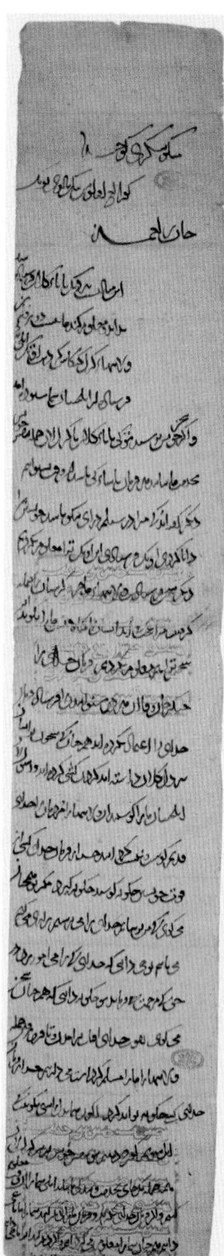

FIGURE 21.5
Letter of Güyük Khan to Pope Innocent IV. http://en.wikipedia.org/wiki/G%C3%BCy%C3%BCk_Khan

BOX 21.4 GÜYÜK KHAN

Güyük (c. 1206–1248) was the son of Ogedei Khan, and grandson of Genghis Khan. He reigned from 1246 to 1248 and was the first khagan, or great khan of the Mongols. Innocent IV hoped to form an alliance with Güyük Khan in order to defeat the Muslims. Güyük Khan's correspondence with Innocent IV reveals how both of them believed the other as the leader of a relatively inferior people.

Christendom was the power of the pope versus the emperor. Fear of the powerful Mongols and Muslims multiplied the internal hazards. While both the Muslims and Mongols posed military threats, the Mongols were less known. Innocent IV sent two groups of friars to establish contact and to learn more about the Mongols. He wanted to determine Mongol intentions, ascertain their capabilities, and establish an alliance with them against the Muslims. He also hoped to convert the Great Khan and his people to Christianity (Muldoon 1979: 42; Williams 1990: 4). The friars carried two letters from Innocent IV to Güyük Khan of the Mongols. These letters and the khan's response provide us with a sense of the encounter.

Innocent explains the central tenets of the Christian view and openly declares his responsibility for the khan's soul:

> Wherefore we, though unworthy, having become, by the Lord's disposition, the successor of this vicar, do turn our keen attention, before all else is incumbent on us in virtue of our office, to *your* salvation and that of *other* men . . . so that we may be able, with the help of God's grace . . . [to] lead those in error into the way of truth and gain all men for Him.
>
> (Dawson 1955: 74; emphasis added)

Güyük Khan's response, dated 1246, asks the pertinent question: how does Innocent know he speaks for God?

> Though thou likewise sayest that I should become a trembling . . . Christian, worship God and be an ascetic, how knowest thou whom God absolves, in truth to whom he shows mercy? How dost thou know that such words as thou speakest are with God's sanction?
>
> (Dawson 1955: 85–6)

How indeed? Güyük poses the question not as way of opening the debate, but instead to counter-assert his own exclusive intimacy with God: 'From the rising of the sun to its setting, all the lands have been made subject to me. Who could do this contrary to the commands of God?' (Dawson 1955: 86). His exceptionalism is nearly symmetrical to Innocent's:

> The eternal God has slain and annihilated these lands and peoples, because they have neither adhered to Chingis Khan, nor to the Khagan [khan of khans], both of whom have been sent to make known God's command . . .
>
> (Dawson 1955: 85)

The pope's rightful station, therefore, is not as God's vicar but as Güyük's subordinate:

> Now you should say with a sincere heart: 'I will submit and serve you'. Thou thyself, at the head of all the [Christian] princes, come at once to serve and wait upon us. At that time I shall recognize your submission.
>
> (Dawson 1955: 86)

Does the khan assume that the pope's submission to him will be good for Innocent and for Christians? Perhaps only in the sense that it would be good for Christians to have their lives spared. Regardless, Güyük Khan believes, much like Innocent and Vitoria, that his knowledge about the world and its workings is absolutely superior. All three assume a form of exclusive knowledge that permits them to suppose they know what is good for others.

GENERAL RESPONSES
HISTORY'S PROGRESS: CONTEMPORARY INTERVENTIONS

How have we in the twenty-first century responded to the question of 'why some people think they know what is good for others?' Have we moved away from the responsibility that comes from believing we have exclusive knowledge? As we shift from the fourteenth to the twenty-first century, can we assume that such claims to exclusive knowledge are relegated to the past? No. It is a mistake to believe that we have moved beyond the powerful pull of exclusive knowledge in contemporary life. Two examples display the strength of that pull. From the left we examine the Euston Manifesto and from the right the work of British diplomat Robert Cooper. I have selected these examples for two reasons. Both argue with bold fervour and with little regard for upsetting our usual sensibilities. They provide thereby a clarity that helps us to get to the heart of the issue. Second, juxtaposing the similarities of the left and right demonstrates that the pull of exclusive knowledge reaches not only across centuries but also across ideological divides.

Reform of the British left: the Euston Manifesto

The authors of the Euston Manifesto seek to reform the left. Specifically, they wish to 'draw a line between the forces of the left who remain true to its authentic values' and those who have been 'too flexible' in the face of the forces of cultural relativism (that is, in the face of those who claim that truth or values are not universal but rather differ between cultures). Their supreme belief in modernity is evident in a first principle: 'We reject fear of modernity.' They are for democracy – the liberal pluralist variety. They 'decline to make excuses' for tyranny and they promote universal human rights for all:

The terms 'left' and 'right' in politics refer to a group's position on a spectrum that ranges from socialist, egalitarian, democratic policies on the left to conservative, republican or libertarian policies on the right.

BOX 21.5 EXCLUSIVE KNOWLEDGE AT DIFFERENT POINTS IN HISTORY

Keep in mind that as we move from the thirteenth and sixteenth century to the present some things have changed. We can think of this change in two ways.

First, European concern shifts from a social order dominated by religious and theological matters to a secular worldview. Second, history is seen as produced by human action rather than being regarded as the result of God's will.

These shifts nevertheless retain something of the prior vision. History continues to be seen as moving towards an ever more perfect future. Most significant, the certainty that we know God's will shifts to the certainty that the modern period is the apex of progressive human history. Doubts about whether history really contains a progressive purpose or whether it has led humans inevitably towards perfection are hardly taken seriously.

Exclusive knowledge based on Christian beliefs now becomes exclusive knowledge based on European understanding of secular history. In the shift from a Christian to a secular European social order, the hold of exclusive knowledge remains firm across the centuries. Indeed, the attractions of exclusive knowledge may have become all the more powerful in their secular guise.

> We hold the fundamental human rights codified in the Universal Declaration to be precisely universal, and binding on all states and political movements, indeed on everyone. Violations of these rights are equally to be condemned whoever is responsible for them and *regardless of cultural context.*
>
> (Euston Manifesto, undated, emphasis added)

For more on the declaration and human rights more generally see **Chapter 27**.

Unlike Vitoria and Innocent, the Euston Manifesto does not spell out how such rights are derived. But they are universally binding, regardless of their origins. Presumably the presence of cultural variation means either that some societies have failed to learn the lessons of modern life or that they have simply rejected what is right and good.

Unlike Vitoria and Innocent, the Manifesto writers show little concern for how the powerful can use ideals as masks in order to dispossess the less powerful. This nonchalance comes through forcefully in principle 6, titled 'Opposing anti-Americanism'. They 'reject *without qualification* the anti-Americanism now infecting so much left-liberal (and some conservative) thinking' (Euston Manifesto, undated, emphasis added).

Just war thinker Michael Walzer was one of the signatories of the Euston Manifesto, but he was not in favour of the war against Iraq, which he argued was unjust.

The authors of the Manifesto admit to internal disagreement on one issue – the military intervention in Iraq. They diverge on the intervention's justification, its planning and execution, and the prospects for creating a democracy in Iraq. Nevertheless, they are unified in their view over the

> reactionary, semi-fascist and murderous character of the Baathist regime in Iraq, and *we recognize its overthrow as a liberation of the Iraqi people.* We are also united in the view that, since the day on which this occurred, the proper concern of

BOX 21.6 EUSTON MANIFESTO

This British-based group dates back to May 2005 after the general election when more than twenty met at a London pub to discuss how to differentiate their own left politics from the anti-war movement and the general state of left politics in the UK. A more formal meeting at a branch of the O'Neill's Irish-themed pub chain on London's Euston Road led to the document's first draft. The Manifesto was first published in the *New Statesman* on 7 April 2006. The first four signers of the manifesto – Norman Geras, Damian Counsell, Alan Johnson and Shalom Lappin – are believed to be the primary theorists of the manifesto.

The Euston Manifesto (http://eustonmanifesto.org)

> genuine liberals and members of the Left should have been the battle to put in place in Iraq a democratic political order and to rebuild the country's infrastructure, to create after decades of the most brutal oppression a life for Iraqis which those living in democratic countries take for granted – *rather than picking through the rubble* of the arguments over intervention.
>
> (Euston Manifesto, undated, emphasis added)

In contrast to Vitoria's caution about turning Indian life over to Spanish administrators, these writers express no hesitation in speaking for the Iraqi people and share no misgivings about delineating Iraqi liberation. They are unconcerned about overturning the principle of sovereignty. On the contrary, despite their initial differences, they appear unified in vigorously supporting intervention as a means of promoting modernity in Iraq and elsewhere. In removing significant doubts and arguments against intervention, the Euston Manifesto goes well beyond Vitoria and Innocent IV. The authors of the Euston Manifesto somehow 'know' that modernity and liberal democracy is good for all peoples in all contexts. They 'know', therefore, what is good for the Iraqi people and for all peoples of the Third World.

The authors of the Euston Manifesto might well strongly disagree with the interpretation offered here. We encourage readers to visit their site (http://eustonmanifesto.org) to formulate their own impression.

Benevolent imperialism and the British right: Robert Cooper

If we move from the liberal left to the right, we find in Robert F. Cooper's 'The Post-Modern State' (2002) a parallel claim about doing good for others. Cooper is a British diplomat with experience in Kenya and diplomatic posts in Japan, Germany and Afghanistan. Currently he serves as a counsellor in the European External Action Service, which serves as a foreign ministry and diplomatic corps of the EU and is a member of European Council on Foreign Relations – a pan-European think-tank. His arguments revive imperialism and colonialism. Though Cooper is not well published, his ideas have attracted the attention of academics and policy makers on both sides of the Atlantic.

For a detailed account of how colonialism works see **Chapter 16**.

Cooper's use of the term 'post-modern' flouts the usual academic convention wherein 'postmodern' is understood to query if not undermine the assumptions and certainties of modernity. Instead, Cooper treats post-modernity as the last and most

BOX 21.7 IMPERIALISM AND COLONIALISM

There is much debate about the terms colonialism and imperialism. Some use the two terms interchangeably, others want to differentiate between them. Both refer to forms of domination of one group of people, or one state, over others, whether economic, military or cultural, or a combination of all three. Distinctions are sometimes drawn depending on what forms of control are in place. For example, if settlers from one country establish a base in another, that is usually referred to as a colony. Imperialism can be distant control, without settlement but including, for example, the extraction of resources and tribute or taxation. However, this distinction does not avoid overlap: for example, the British Empire, when British subjects lived in and governed vast tracts of the world – or colonized these areas – was referred to as both British imperialism and as a colonial period. The period that followed was a period of de-colonization – or a period where those who had been colonized sought a return of self-determination and independence. It is useful to remember that various forms of empire predate or exist alongside the modern European state system – the Ottoman Empire, for example, began in 1300 and was at its height in 1683 – and that in the contemporary world some writers refer to US dominance as 'imperialism' or a form of empire. It is interesting to note that 'empires' are sometimes described as 'civilizations', and that the imperial power often sees itself as spreading 'civilization' to 'barbarians'.

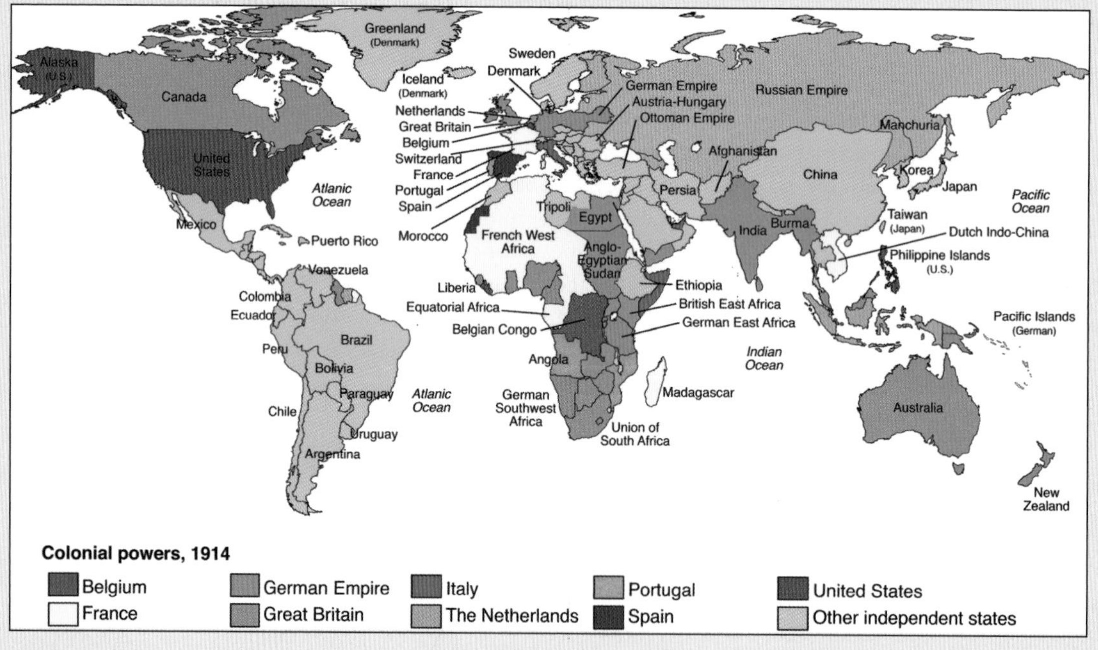

FIGURE 21.6
Map of colonial powers, 1914. Peter Mandaville, *Global Political Islam* (Routledge 2007)

advanced of three civilizational stages: premodern, modern, and postmodern. Cooper holds that the post-modern is the final and full realization of modernity. The European Union, Canada, and Japan (and with some ambiguity, the US) have overcome their 'imperial urge' and reached postmodern statehood (Cooper 2002: 12).

Much like Vitoria's Indian problem, Cooper's concern is that premodern states lack civilization. The less civilized premodern states threaten the emerging postmodern order by following the 'laws of the jungle'. His solution to this problem is that the postmodern state must practice a double standard. Inside their boundaries they can 'keep the law' of civilized society but outside they must operate according to the laws of the jungle:

> Among ourselves, we operate on the basis of laws and open cooperative security. But when dealing with more old-fashioned kinds of states outside the postmodern continent of Europe, we need to revert to the rougher methods of an earlier era – force, pre-emptive attack, deception, whatever is necessary to deal with those who still live in the nineteenth-century world of 'every state for itself'.
>
> (Cooper 2002: 16)

As with Vitoria, Innocent IV, Güyük Khan, and the Manifesto writers, knowledge of the absolute truth eclipses concern for the claims of others. Instead, Cooper advocates a return to colonialism and imperialism: 'The most logical way to deal with chaos [caused by the less civilized] . . . is colonization' (Cooper 2002: 17). Civilized states, however, will find returning to an old-fashioned colonialism contrary to their values. For this reason, says Cooper, what the world needs is a benevolent imperialism 'acceptable to the world of human rights and cosmopolitan values' (Cooper 2002: 17).

Faced with a world of infidels, of non-believers in modernity, Cooper follows the tradition of the true believer. He knows that modernity is the highest stage of civilization. He knows that others do not have it and may not like it. He knows that non-believers must be forced to accept modernity for their own good and for the good of all. Nor is Cooper's an isolated argument. The tone and substance of his presentation is widespread in our time. We can find it in the work, for example, of Max Boot (2002), Eliot Cohen (2001), Niall Ferguson (2003), Michael Ignatieff (2003), Robert Kagan (2002) and Robert D. Kaplan (2003). The ideology of these mostly academic writers ranges from liberal to conservative, but they all implore the United States to bear responsibility to do good for others by means of creating a benevolent imperialism. We can also perceive the theme of benevolent imperialism in the writing and policy prescriptions of the 'neo-conservatives' involved in the Project for the New American Century (www.newamericancentury.org/) and in the highest levels of the current US and UK administrations.

In summary: We can recognize two changes from Innocent's and Vitoria's time to ours. First, there is a shift in the features of the knowledge over which there is certainty. We move from theological convictions about God's purpose to secularized convictions about history's purpose. Second, Cooper and the Euston Manifesto writers show *less* concern for the claims of those outside the faith than did Vitoria and Innocent. Nevertheless, each of the thinkers we have examined assumes exclusive knowledge. They believe their exclusive knowledge permits them to know what is good for others.

BROADER ISSUES
DIAGNOSING THE NEED FOR EXCLUSIVE KNOWLEDGE

Recall the tension and the stretch with which we started. On the one side, we feel compelled to shoulder the duty of doing good. On the other side we feel our resistance when we are made good's recipient. I said that we usually jump from one position to the other without considering these two positions simultaneously. What might we learn if we accept the responsibility of doing good for others while also retaining our suspicions? Let us tentatively accept that all humans, cultures, and societies have some exclusive knowledge of the world. We may even accept that our desire to share the benefits of such knowledge need not always contain sinister motivations. For these reasons, however, we can imagine that others, whom we picture as recipients of our wisdom, may regard themselves as knowledge givers in their own right. As we envision giving them our gifts, they envision providing us with their gifts. Likewise, as we resist their generosity, they resist ours.

So far, we have assumed that we are either donors or receivers. What we have not done is consider that we are both. Are we not concurrently donors and receivers? Does not a holistic identity require that we acknowledge ourselves as both 'giver' and 'receiver'?

What picture of the subject is being suggested here? See **Chapter 2**.

Vitoria, Innocent, Güyük, the Euston Manifesto, and Cooper split this whole (Benjamin 1988). They take the whole that is 'giver *and* receiver of knowledge' and split them into two separate entities. They then apportion the role of 'giver' to themselves and 'receiver' to others. Further, by assuming that they have exclusive knowledge, they place the 'giver' on top as the superior being. The tragic result is that as they discharge their responsibility for giving to others, they weave into it their need to feel superior. Superiority turns responsibility towards others into charitable condescension. The tendency to claim exclusive knowledge comes, I think, from a need to claim such superiority.

But why do they and we need this sense of superiority? One answer is that we need this superiority in order to overcome the hidden doubts about the very same exclusive knowledge we espouse. Consider the proposition that no belief can be held without doubt. Doubt is belief's other and its foundation. Doubt is the dock from which the ship of belief sails. Doubt and belief are opposites but they also define each other. Exclusive knowledge – the belief that we have exclusive access to superior knowledge – goes hand in hand with the anxiety that our belief is common and ordinary. The need for superiority emerges from the doubt that perhaps we are ordinary or inferior.

Is such doubt impossible to face? Is that why claims to exclusive knowledge are so pervasive? While we may know people who are able to incorporate the hard kernel of doubt into their beliefs, nevertheless, as we saw in the examples above, holding beliefs and doubts together is difficult. Why? In harbouring doubt, we often begin to contemplate exactly what we want to avoid – our own lack (Fink 1993; Žižek 1993). We avoid that dreaded sense of incompleteness in our knowing and being. In claiming exclusive knowledge our logical rhythm goes something like this: our lack is the source of our doubt; that doubt creates within us a sense of insufficiency; to compensate for that insufficiency we project our superiority both to others and to ourselves; projecting and sustaining superiority requires us to trumpet our exclusive knowledge; this trumpeting cannot be convincing, especially to ourselves, unless others validate our claim; therefore we formulate a mission to convert others to our beliefs. Converting others must not be seen as a way of affirming our superiority but rather as a way of sharing our unique access to the good.

Just like we split knowledge from doubt, we split donor from receiver. A healthy self, however, may require a balanced combination of belief and doubt as well as a sensible mix of giving and receiving knowledge. An insecure self, on the other hand, holds fast to belief and casts doubt adrift. Similarly, an insecure self valorizes the donor while diminishing and cutting loose the receiver.

Remarkably, an insecure self's offerings may still produce something good. Despite the taint of superiority, those who believe that they know what is good for others may nevertheless have something good to give. The Spaniards might have had something worthy for the Indians, Innocent may have offered something of value to non-Christians, and contemporary purveyors of regime change and intervention may identify ways to improve Third World conditions.

If this is true, then why do we find ourselves resisting when others cast us in the role of good receiver? Why don't we simply accept the good they offer? We resist because we sense that the donor needs us to confirm his superiority. Receiving such goods confirms the donor's superiority and affirms our inferiority. Accepting this hierarchy is the real cost of receiving the donor's 'gift' and the crux of the problem (Mauss 2006; Sahlins 2003). From the receiver's perspective, the donor's actions seem far from a faithfully discharged duty. Instead, they seem like an offence against the integrity, self-sufficiency, and freedom of the receiver. Receivers resist and rebuke donors as long as the donor's motives are tainted by claims of exclusive knowledge. In response, and compounding the tragedy, donors regard this rejection of their gift as the irrationality of lesser people. Donors seem incapable of perceiving their need for superiority, nor do they search for the deeper reasons for the receiver's rejection. The tragedy plays out in three parts: the receiver's rejection of a potential good, the donor's inability to recognize that donor motivations are tainted, and the donor's misunderstanding of the receiver's rejection. Is it any wonder then why doing good for others has been so difficult?

Our most difficult and most important step in addressing this difficulty is recognizing the full scope of the tragedy. Can we do more? Let us return to the question raised by this chapter's title: Why do some people think they know what is good for others? My answer: we emphasize what is good for others in order to avoid the pain of facing our own lack. If so, what happens if we start facing this lack?

If all of us have some unique knowledge of the world, we also suspect that our knowledge is incomplete. We can give and we need to receive; we are both donor and receiver. Recognizing that we are incomplete and that we need others' goods, we can change our posture towards giving. Claiming exclusive knowledge can be replaced by a stance that seeks what we may call knowledge encounters (Bitterli 1993; Geertz 1986; Greenblatt 1976, 1991; Nandy 1983, 1987; Todorov 1984; Verma 1990). The rhythm of this sequence might go like this: our lack is the source of our doubt; that doubt creates within us a sense of insufficiency; to overcome that insufficiency we announce our need to others and to ourselves; we de-emphasize the good we can offer and instead highlight our lack and need; and we search for others who present the same posture, avoiding those projecting missionary values. In sum, we search for opportunities and partners that allow mutual sharing. In this way, we can have access to others' unique knowledge and they to ours.

I am not suggesting that we can easily realign the world so that everyone participates in knowledge encounters. Just one 'exclusive knower' with a powerful mission can disrupt a formative society of 'knowledge encounterers'. Rather, I merely contrast a logical sequence that produces the tragedy of 'exclusive knowing' with a sequence that might produce 'knowledge encounters'.

At a particular moment, others may know what is best for us. However, we may justly reject such knowledge if the donor's delivery is mixed with condescension. They might indeed know what is best for us but only we can decide to receive that knowledge and integrate it into our actions. Thinking in this way allows us to change the question. We can move from 'why do some people think they know what is best for others?' to 'how can we recognize that we are all a mix of donor and receiver?' And, to 'how do we create social institutions that help us to overcome our incompleteness?'

Ashis Nandy is discussed further in **Chapters 16 and 20** and George Orwell in **Chapter 16**.

Are there examples of those who have moved from a posture of 'exclusive knowledge' to that of 'knowledge encounter'? Todorov discusses the case of Las Casas, in his *Conquest of America* (1984), and Ashis Nandy contrasts the examples of Rudyard Kipling, George Orwell, and Mohandas Gandhi to similar effect in *Intimate Enemy* (1983).

Like Vitoria, Las Casas was outraged that the American Indians were being exterminated. And like Vitoria, he wanted to save the Amerindians from the conquistadors in order to convert them to Christianity. Only later in his life did Las Casas regard the Indians' religiosity as similar to his own belief in Christianity. He defended Indian religious practices by appealing to principles he took to be universal – a desire to worship and serve God. Even 'offensive' Indian religious practices became expressions of principles that underlie all religious practice. In this way, Las Casas moved away from 'exclusive knowledge'. He was unable, however, to use the religious knowledge of the Indians to inform and critique Christian conceptions. Had he done so, he would have moved to a more robust understanding of 'knowledge encounter'. Nandy's examples move us in this direction.

Nandy believes that 'exclusive knowledge' victimizes giver and receiver, both colonizer and colonized. Thus for Nandy, even though Kipling and Orwell support British imperialism they are also its victims. Both were born in India, influenced by their early years there, and sent to boarding school in England where they were bullied into manhood. Kipling's and Orwell's responses to colonialism, however, differ somewhat. Kipling identifies with the colonizer by denying those parts of him that appreciate India. As an adult writer, he demonstrates precise and intimate knowledge of India but uses that knowledge to legitimate colonization. Orwell also knows India well. He does not identify with the bully and thereby does not celebrate India's victimization. Nor, however, does he identify with the colonized. Orwell remains a divided figure who denies the posture of exclusive knowledge but does not quite know what to do with the partial knowledge offered by his various selves.

Is it significant that three of these four people are women?

Nandy then presents a small but important group – Sister Nivedita, Anne Besant, Mira Behn, and C. F. Andrews – who are able to transform their critical knowledge into practical convictions. Andrews finds alternatives within his society's dominant knowledge in order to fight alongside others while also fighting for himself. According to Nandy, the most creative response to colonialism, however, comes from the colonized. Through his strategy of non-violence Gandhi negotiates two traditions of knowledge: by appealing to the Christian idea of turning the other cheek, he re-presents Western knowledge in terms the West can accept. This method of resisting colonialism minimizes the colonist's strong suit, namely force and domination. Gandhi also reinterprets Indian knowledge so that his appeal to non-violence appears authentically Indian. Andrews and Gandhi encounter and negotiate knowledge that aims to produce cultural transformation in both the British and the Indians. Gandhi reinterprets knowledge so that fighting for India's liberation is simultaneously fighting for Britain's liberation.

CONCLUSION

Those who believe they have exclusive knowledge also tend to believe they know what is good for others. Wishing to share their knowledge and its benefits they devise projects that fulfil their responsibility to others. The problem is that receivers of such missions tend to resist donor plans. Recipients experience such assistance as an intrusion on their self-determination and an imposition on their freedom. As important, they suspect that the donor's claim of exclusive knowledge taints donor efforts. They believe that the donor's ultimate goal is to produce a hierarchy that elevates the donor and diminishes the receiver. Meanwhile, donors perceive receiver resistance as irrational ingratitude. For receivers, in turn, donor condescension confirms that donors are threatening their dignity and equality.

Our challenge is to undo this cycle of mutual incrimination and replace it with a cycle of mutual enrichment. This becomes possible when we move from a posture of possessing 'exclusive knowledge' to a circumstance where parties who regard themselves as both donors and receivers negotiate partial knowledge.

FURTHER READING

On 'splitting' see Benjamin's *The Bonds of Love* (1988). For more on Vitoria, see Pagden's *The Fall of Natural Man* (1982). Muldoon's *Popes, Lawyers and Infidels* (1979) provides context for Innocent IV's ideas. Dawson's *The Mongol Mission* frames the exchange between Innocent IV and Güyük Khan. Are there examples of those who have moved from a posture of 'exclusive knowledge' to that of 'knowledge negotiating'? Todorov discusses one such case, Las Casas, in his *Conquest of America* (1984). And Ashis Nandy contrasts the examples of Rudyard Kipling, George Orwell, and Mohandas Gandhi to similar effect in *Intimate Enemy* (1983). On the broader context for how the idea of 'doing good for others' shapes the history and theory of international relations, see Inayatullah and Blaney's *International Relations and the Problem of Difference* (2004).

WEBSITES

The Difference Site: http://www.dif-ferance.org/index2.html

Doing good for others requires we understand how others differ from us. This site is dedicated to understanding how and why difference is crucial to all aspects of life.

Project for a New American Century: www.newamericancentury.org/

Perhaps the most powerful force on the planet dedicated to doing good for others is this neo-conservative project. This site presents their arguments and the scope of their ambitions.

Charter of the United Nations: http://www.un.org/aboutun/charter/index.html
The Charter, like Vitoria and Innocent IV, provides arguments against intervention (chapter I), and arguments for when it is acceptable to intervene in order to do good (chapters VI and VII).

Euston Manifesto: http://eustonmanifesto.org
Go to this site if you want clear and concise arguments for intervening in order to promote the good.

Global Policy Forum <Empire> Humanitarian Intervention: http://www.globalpolicy.org/empire/humanint/index.htm
This site provides documents, articles, and speeches on the debate over humanitarian interventions.

REFERENCES

Bellamy, Alex J. (2006) *Just Wars: From Cicero to Iraq*, Cambridge: Polity.

Benjamin, Jessica (1988) *The Bonds of Love: Psychoanalysis, Feminism, and the Problem of Domination*, New York: Pantheon.

Bitterli, Urs (1993) *Cultures in Conflict: Encounters Between European and Non-European Cultures, 1492–1800*, Stanford, CA: Stanford University Press.

Boot, Max (2002) *Savage Wars of Peace: Small Wars and the Rise of American Power*, New York: Basic Books.

Coates, A. J. (1997) *The Ethics of War*, Manchester: Manchester University Press.

Cohen, Eliot A. (2001) 'World War IV', *Wall Street Journal*, November 20: A18.

Cooper, Robert F. (2002) 'The Post-Modern State', in Mark Leonard (ed.) *Re-Ordering the World*, London: Foreign Policy Centre.

Dawson, Christopher (1955) *The Mongol Mission: Narratives and Letters of the Franciscan Missionaries in Mongolia and China in the Thirteenth and Fourteenth Centuries*, New York: Sheed and Ward.

Elshtain, Jean Bethke (2003) *Just War Against Terror: The Burden of American Power in a Violent World*, New York: Basic Books.

Euston Manifesto (undated) http://eustonmanifesto.org.

Ferguson, Niall (2003) 'America as Empire, Now and in the Future', *The National Interest* 2, 29: 23 July, http://www.inthenationalinterest.com/Articles/Vol2Issue29/Vol2Issue29 Ferguson.html.

Fink, Bruce (1993) *The Lacanian Subject: Between Language and Jouissance*, Princeton, NJ: Princeton University Press.

Geertz, Clifford (1986) 'The Uses of Diversity', *Michigan Quarterly Review* 21, 1: 105–23.

Greenblatt, Stephen J. (1976) 'Learning to Curse: Aspects of Linguistic Colonialism in the Sixteenth Century', in Fredi Chiappelli (ed.) *First Images of America: The Impact of New World on the Old, Volume 2*, Berkeley: University of California Press.

——(1991) *Marvelous Possessions: The Wonder of the New World*, Chicago: University of Chicago Press.

Ignatieff, Michael (2003) 'The Challenge of American Imperial Power', *Naval War College Review* 56, 2: 53–63.

Inayatullah, Naeem and David Blaney (2004) *International Relations and the Problem of Difference*, New York: Routledge.

Kagan, Robert (2002) 'Power and Weakness', *Policy Review* June/July: 3–28.

Kaplan, Robert (2003) 'Supremacy by Stealth: Ten Rules for Managing the World', *Atlantic Monthly* 292, 1: 66–83.

Mauss, Marcel (2006) *The Gift: The Form and Reason for Exchange in Archaic Societies*, London: Routledge.

Muldoon, James (1979) *Popes, Lawyers, and Infidels: The Church and the Non-Christian World 1250–1550*, Philadelphia: University of Pennsylvania Press.

Nandy, Ashis (1983) *The Intimate Enemy: Loss and Recovery of Self under Colonialism*, Delhi: Oxford University Press.

——(1987) *Traditions, Tyranny and Utopias: Essays in the Politics of Awareness*, Delhi: Oxford University Press.

Pagden, A. R. (1982) *The Fall of Natural Man: The American Indian and the Origins of Comparative Ethnology*, Cambridge: Cambridge University Press.

Sahlins, Marshall (2003) *Stone Age Economics*, London: Routledge.

Todorov, Tzvetan (1984) *The Conquest of America: The Question of the Other*, New York: Harper and Row.

Verma, Nirmal (1990) 'India and Europe: Some Observations on Self and Other', *Kavita Asia* 1, 1: 114–44.

Vitoria, Francisco de (1991) *Political Writings*, ed. A. R. Pagden and Jeremy Lawrance, Cambridge: Cambridge University Press.

Walzer, Michael (1992) *Just and Unjust Wars: A Moral Argument With Historical Illustrations*, 2nd edn, New York: Basic Books.

——(2004) *Arguing about War*, New Haven, CT: Yale University Press.

Williams, Robert A. (1990) *The American Indian in Western Legal Thought: The Discourses of Conquest*, New York: Oxford University Press.

Žižek, Slavoj (1993) *Tarrying with the Negative: Hegel, Kant, and the Critique of Ideology*, Durham, NC: Duke University Press.

For a range of further resources supporting this chapter, please visit the companion website for *Global Politics, 2nd Edition* at www.routledge.com/cw/edkins/

CHAPTER **22**

Why does politics turn to violence?

Joanna Bourke

THE QUESTION
MASS KILLING AS A CULTURAL PHENOMENON

Mass slaughter at the command of the state was characteristic of the twentieth century. In the second decade of the twenty-first century, it shows no signs of abating. Now is the time to remind ourselves that war is not a metaphor for social crisis (the 'war on drugs') or an excuse for apocalyptic fantasies (the 'war on terror'). War is also much more than the enactment of international 'politics by other means', as the Prussian military theorist Carl von Clausewitz famously put it, through the purposeful destruction of another nation's infrastructure. Rather, war is the deliberate infliction of suffering and death on other people.

Violence is a complex and highly diverse phenomenon, including the corporal punishment of children, cruelty to animals, boxing, rape, and individual acts of indiscriminative mass murder. What is labelled 'violence' is itself highly normative: it has changed over time and the definition that becomes dominant is often the one favoured by powerful institutions and elites. There is also the risk that an act of violence is seen as a rupture in an otherwise violent-free context: clearly, this ignores the fact

BOX 22.1 CARL VON CLAUSEWITZ

Carl von Clausewitz (1780–1831) is still regarded as a major strategic and military theorist, and his ideas continue to be both controversial and influential. His dictum that war is merely an extension of politics by other means, elaborated in his famous book *On War* (1976) has had a significant impact on thinking about war. For a discussion of his reception over the years since he wrote, see Bassford (1994) and Heuser (2002). Also see the new edition of *On War*, published by Folio Books in 2011, including the useful introductory essays.

FIGURE 22.1
Carl von Clausewitz. Lithograph by Franz Michaelis after a missing painting by Karl Wilhelm Wach. Bildarchiv Preußischer Kulturbesitz

that those processes that enable outbursts have a long, and often deeply embedded history. Furthermore, to fully understand violence, each type of aggression requires a different analysis. For the sake of this chapter, then, violence will be defined as state-legitimated killing in wartime. This is the form of violence that politics regularly 'turns to' with particularly devastating effect.

It is easy to forget that the question, 'why does politics turn to violence?' cannot solely be addressed through explorations of statecraft and political failings. Too often, military history reads as though combatants were only on the battlefields to die for their country and its ideologies, rather than to attempt to kill as well. One of the reasons why politics and military conflict are so interconnected is because human beings seem remarkably prone to acts of extreme aggression against politically and culturally designated enemies. It is important, then to explore what enabled (and still enables) ordinary men, and sometimes women, to kill others in military conflict. This question becomes even more urgent once we recognise that most of those combatants were not 'socialised warriors', steeped in a military ethos indoctrinated through years of study and service in professional military organisations. Rather, in the major wars of the twentieth century, most combatants were short-term volunteers or conscripts, more comfortable on the shop floor or slumped over their office desks than at the rifle range or on the battlefield. Nevertheless, killing proved remarkably easy.

According to the most conservative estimate, in the last 100 years, 60 million men, women, and children were gratuitously slaughtered in wars legitimately by the state. The perpetrators were not obviously evil; they purported to be rational people engaged in mass killing for particular ends. But their actions cast a pall over that century's history. Two forms of politically-authorised slaughter can be distinguished. The first type involved the large-scale slaughter of service-personnel – an occurrence greatly facilitated by modernity's uncompromising application of aircraft, artillery, and explosives. The second type was the slaughter of civilians. It was only from the 1930s that the slaughter of non-combatants surpassed that of combatants in wartime. Indeed, from 1939, civilians were the victims of choice. While only 5 per cent of deaths in the 1914–18 war

Chapter 23 agrees that it is important to examine processes that enable outbreaks of violence. It looks at what takes place in the so-called war on terror – drone attacks on suspected terrorists and attempts to control terrorist financing – and asks what counts as violence.

If ordinary men and women refused to kill others, would it still be possible for states to go to war, or in other words, for politics to turn to violence?

Warfare in the twenty-first century is discussed in **Chapter 24**, and the question of death in war in **Chapters 1 and 28**.

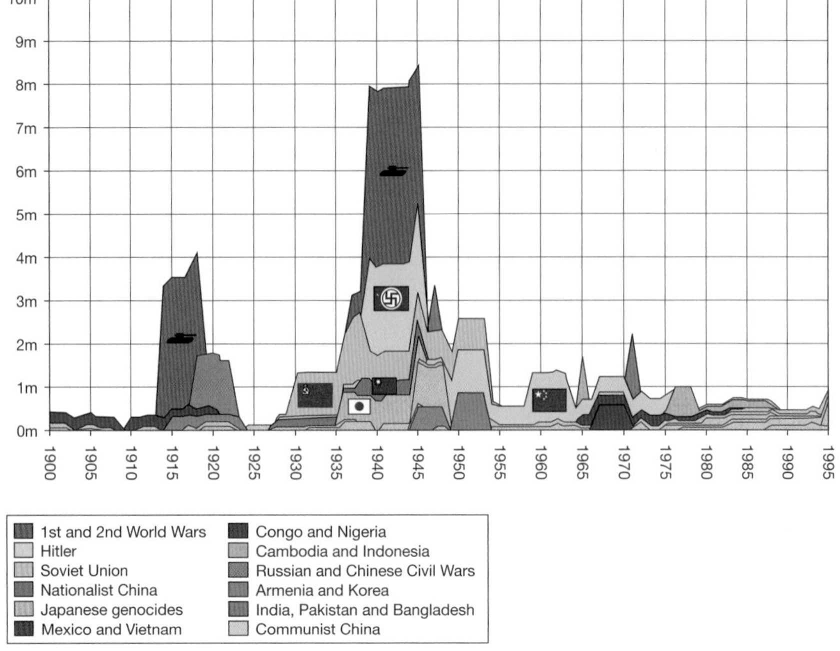

FIGURE 22.2 Wars, massacres and atrocities of the twentieth century: year by year death toll. Graphic and data: Matthew White, 1998

were civilian deaths, 66 per cent of deaths in the 1939–45 war were of civilians. In the 1939–45 war, considerably more civilians than military personnel were killed in Belgium, China, France, Greece, Hungary, the Netherlands, Norway, Poland, the Soviet Union, and Yugoslavia. The Holocaust is the pre-eminent instance of the wanton slaughter of non-combatants.

Approximately six million Jews were killed, including around two million children. As Hitler admitted in relation to Poland (where one-third of those killed by the Germans were children), destruction was 'our primary task. The aim is not the arrival at a certain line but the annihilation of living forces.' He advised his men to 'Be merciless. Be brutal. It is necessary to proceed with maximum severity. The war is to be a war of annihilation' (Lukas 1990: 89). Although the havoc wrought by Hitler's forces was unprecedented, the Axis powers (a coalition headed by Germany, Italy, and Japan that opposed the Allied powers – France, Britain, the USSR, China and the USA – in the Second World War) were not the only ones who targeted civilians. In the European theatre, one-quarter of American bombs were dropped on the residential or commercial sectors of German cities; according to the United States Strategic Bombing Survey, this was 'almost twice the weight of bombs launched against all manufacturing targets together' (US Strategic Bombing Survey 1945: 71). Most of the victims were women. For every 100 male casualties, there were 181 female casualties in Darmstadt, 160 in Hamburg, 136 in Kassel, and 122 in Nuremberg. Around one-fifth of those killed were children under the age of sixteen years and another one-fifth were over the age of 60 (Rumpf 1963: 160–1). In the Asian-Pacific theatre, the American's unilateral atomic bombing of Japan specifically targeted cities. Today, 90 per cent of victims of war are civilians. It has become impossible to understand modern culture without directing ones' gaze into the

For more on the bombing of German cities see **Chapter 1**.

FIGURE 22.3 Colour photograph showing damage in Hiroshima in March 1946 (US National Archives)

abyss of mass murder. Governmentally-authorised killing and gratuitous violence are no grotesque accidents – they are a cultural phenomenon, deliberately enacted.

What enabled the perpetrators to carry out these gross acts? Evil is not banal. Quite the contrary: violence has infused even the most subtle social and political nuances of the country from which it was born. This is why mass killings could take place with remarkably little psychological trauma for the perpetrators. Afterwards, most perpetrators denied feeling responsible or guilty. This is true even in cases of atrocity and genocide. For instance, many Turks continue to deny that the Armenian genocide of 1915 took place and many Vietnam veterans remain wedded to the defence of 'it was him or me' when justifying the slaughter of unarmed women and children. Prisoners accused of war crimes or crimes against humanity often protest their innocence. This disturbing fact was noted by visitors to refugee camps set up to harbour Hutus after the 1994 genocidal war in Rwanda. In the words of one journalist who described visiting a refugee camp in Goma:

> Perhaps the most disheartening of all is that most of the Hutus – despite their agony – still do not recognise that what happened to the Tutsis was a crime of enormous proportions. There is a state of collective denial by almost everyone you meet in the camps. People do not see their ordeal as self-imposed but as the fault of the Tutsis and the RPF [Rwandan Patriotic Front]: 'We are dying here because of the Tutsis and the cockroaches of the RPF who want to rule over us', said one woman, who was absolutely convinced of the correctness of killing Tutsis.
>
> (Black 1994)

Because it targets civilians, terrorism is seen as a particularly objectionable form of violence, but many more civilians are killed in warfare.

Hannah Arendt spoke of the 'banality of evil' in her analysis of the trial of Adolf Eichmann, a central figure in organising the Nazi genocides: see **Chapter 23**.

Have a look at the picture of children fleeing a napalm attack in **Chapter 8**.

History textbooks have also been influential in denying or, at the very least, understating levels of murderous belligerence. In Japan, for instance, school history textbooks seriously distort Japan's role in the war. In the resulting scandal in the early 1980s, some newspapers drew attention to the way certain phrases had been changed in the revised textbooks. For instance, the phrase 'aggression in North China' had become 'advance into North China'. A similar trend has been observed in Israeli textbooks.

Indeed, the striking thing about mass killing is that it involves almost unimaginable levels of complicity. The Turkish attack on the Armenians was planned at the highest governmental levels, as was the German management of the Holocaust. In Vietnam, official acceptance of the killing of civilians was encapsulated in such terms as 'free fire zones' and 'collateral damage'. In Rwanda, the Hutus were fairly confident of the support of their allies in France, Zaïre, and Egypt. Hutu perpetrators insisted that they were 'only obeying orders' when they killed. For instance, Robert Kajuga – president of the Interahamwe militia, the group responsible for a large proportion of the murders – claimed that Hutus acted in self-defence. In his words:

'Collateral damage' is still used to describe killing that goes beyond what is intended.

> The government authorises us. We go in behind the army. We watch them and learn. . . . We have to defend our country. The government authorises us to defend ourselves by taking up clubs, machetes and whatever guns we could find.
>
> (Hilsum 1994)

Atrocious acts are nourished within political, military, and civilian communities; people from all walks of life proved themselves capable of mass killing.

ILLUSTRATIVE EXAMPLE
KILLING IN WARTIME

Most accounts of killing in wartime highlight the aggression of whoever counts as enemies: 'they' killed 'us'. There is a vast literature on the violent behaviour of German and Japanese soldiers during the two world wars in English language writings, for instance. In contrast, British and American historians have been queasy about dealing with the way those they call 'our men' slaughtered men (uniformed and not), women, and children of enemy nations. What enabled British and American servicemen in the years 1914–18 and 1939–45 to kill?

Although accounts of the causes of war, or why politics turns to violence, often focus on the sorts of reasons given in the next section, this chapter argues that it is equally important to look at why people are willing to obey orders to kill. Do you find that argument convincing?

It should not surprise us that their languages of mass killing were drawn from the everyday clichés of life. In the diaries and letters of British and American combatants who committed acts of mass killing, there were three excuses that appeared most frequently: retribution, obedience, and parallel response.

No prisoners

The first excuse was the language of retribution. In the words of Sergeant John Henry Ewen in Bougainville: 'Our fellows wont [sic] take prisoners. I've seen them kill two or three now in cold-blood. I took a dim view of it the first time, but when you see your mates go, well I'd do it myself now' (Ewen 1944: 60). Or, as a Marine put it:

FIGURE 22.4
Supporting infantry walk forward up the slope into the bombardment during the First World War, the Battle of Ginchy, 9 September 1916.
Photo: (Lt) Ernest Brooks. Imperial War Museum

> Nobody wanted to take prisoners to begin with – nobody who had had a buddy killed, which was almost everybody. And nobody wanted to go somewhere to do it – leave his living buddies to walk the prisoners back behind the lines. Why take the risk? When they first started surrendering, we shot as many as we took.

Allied soldiers had to be bribed with promises of ice-cream and time behind the lines before they could be persuaded to capture more prisoners, as opposed to immediately slaughtering everyone who tried to surrender.

We were only obeying orders

The second excuse was the language of obedience: 'We were only obeying orders.' In the words of psychologist J. F. Brown writing in 1942, 'the guilt connected with the individual's aggressions in war are projected onto the enemy, and the responsibility for his aggression onto the officers' (Brown 1942: 378). The efficacy of 'obeying orders' as a way of minimising emotional conflict and therefore generating the 'appropriate' response in combatants (that is, murderous aggression) was widely recognised by military instructors who laboriously insisted upon instantaneous obedience to orders so that each man might be able to 'sleep like a child and awaken refreshed – to kill and fear not'

(Graham 1919: 3). The unfortunate consequence – that officers would experience more 'collective guilt' about the war than privates – was only rarely commented upon. By 'obeying orders', killing could be re-conceptualised as something other than murder.

Thus, one of the more notorious examples of the dilemma of 'only obeying orders' took place at a time when combatants *were* under order to obey orders: the July 1943 massacre in Biscari when American troops of the 45th Infantry Division's 180th Infantry Regiment slaughtered around seventy Italian and German prisoners of war. Captain John C. Compton was one of the men eventually charged with this war crime, but he based his defence on the grounds that Lieutenant General George S. Patton had ordered them to kill prisoners. Evidence was presented, showing that prior to battle, Patton had addressed the officers in the following way:

> When we land against the enemy, don't forget to hit him and hit him hard. We will bring the fight home to him. When we meet the enemy, we will kill him. We will show him no mercy. He has killed thousands of your comrades, and he must die. If you company officers in leading your men against the enemy find him shouting at you and, when you get within two-hundred yards of him, and he wishes to surrender, oh no! That bastard will die! You will kill him. Stick him between the third and fourth ribs. You will tell your men that. You must have the killer instinct. Tell them to stick him. He can do no good then. Stick them in the liver. We will get the name of killers and killers are immortal.
>
> (Weingartner 1989: 37)

The court accepted Captain Compton's defence and he was acquitted. His co-defendant was less fortunate. Instead of basing his defence on 'obeying orders', he claimed temporary insanity, tiredness, and stress. He was sentenced to life imprisonment, and was eventually released after six months imprisonment only on condition that he never spoke about the incident.

US and UK forces have been accused of abusing Iraqi prisoners, in particular at Abu Ghraib prison (see **Chapter 2**). Some of them have argued at their courts martial that they were only following orders.

What is crucial to understand is that the defence of 'obeying orders' is widely accepted, and not just by serving military personnel in wartime. In particular, this has been demonstrated in two specific contexts: one, a controlled experiment carried out by social psychologist Stanley Milgram about how much pain people would be willing to inflict if ordered to do so by a recognised authority (see Box 22.2) and, two, through questioning people about what they believed was **acceptable** in the stress of battle.

Psychologists Herbert C. Kelman and Lee H. Lawrence were impressed by Milgram's research, but their investigations into **aggression** were based on a more straightforward methodology. They simply asked people how they *imagined* they would behave under certain wartime circumstances. To make the question clearer, they presented their subjects with a hypothetical situation in which soldiers in Vietnam were asked to shoot all the inhabitants of a village, including old men, women, and children. Sixty-seven per cent of the respondents said that most people would follow orders and shoot, while only 19 per cent said that most people would refuse to shoot. When they were asked 'What would *you* do in this situation', slightly more than half said that they would shoot and one-third said that they would refuse to shoot. The researchers were particularly struck by this latter response:

BOX 22.2 MILGRAM EXPERIMENT

Milgram, a young and ambitious social psychologist at Yale University in the 1960s, was able to show how aggression could be induced in humans. Participants were told that his experiment was to observe the effect of punishment on memory, but actually Milgram wanted to discover what level of electric shock people would be willing to administer to another person when ordered to do so by the experimenter. The male subjects were given the task of teaching another person (who was, unknown to them, an actor) a list of paired associations. They were told to administer an electric shock when an incorrect answer was given. On each error, they were to increase the intensity of electric shock. To Milgram's amazement, some experimenters continued administering the strongest electric shocks, despite being able to hear the intense pain they were causing. Importantly, the men were much more willing to obey the order to hurt the other person when an authority figure (particularly from the prestigious Yale University) was in the room than when he was not present (Milgram 1974). Hiding behind the notion that they were 'only obeying orders', inhibitions to causing pain petered out.

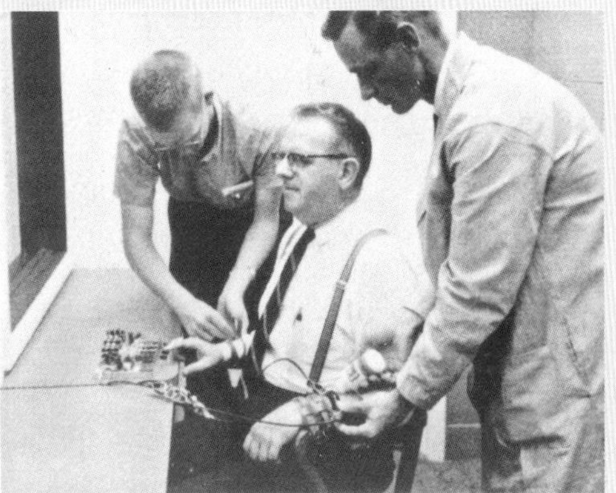

FIGURE 22.5
Milgram experiment. The four images depict: the shock generation showing the switches ranging from 15 to 400 volts; the teacher helps strap the learner into the chair and helps place the electrodes; the teacher is shown how to use the electronic shock apparatus; the teacher settles down to begin the experiment; calm and relaxed. From the film *Obedience* © 1968 by Stanley Milgram, © renewed 1993 by Alexandra Milgram and distributed by Alexander Street Press

> Since it was a hypothetical question, it would have been easy enough for respondents to give themselves the benefit of the doubt and to say that they would refuse to shoot. But the important point . . . is that for many people it is not at all clear that this is the socially desirable response.

Do psychological explanations imply that killing might be part of human nature? Is human nature an adequate explanation? See **Chapter 7**.

In other words, a majority of respondents felt that the desirable response was to follow orders. These respondents were 'not necessarily admitting to moral weakness; for many of them, in fact, this response represent[ed] what they would view as their moral obligation' (Kelman and Lawrence 1972: 177–212).

It was either him or me

The third rationale for mass killing (parallel response) was even more prevalent than 'just obeying orders'. If there was one persistent explanation for killing in wartime it was the notion that 'it was either him or me'. War was about 'kill or be killed'. As sociologist Neil J. Smelser pointed out in his study of the determinants of destructive behaviour, 'one of the most profound aspects of evil is that he who does the evil is typically convinced that evil is about to be done to him' (Smelser 1971: 17). Repeatedly, men reiterated that their choice was to slay or be slain. As the dedicated killer Sydney Lockwood dryly commented after knocking a German's head off: it 'was not nice but one of us had to die that night' (Lockwood, no date: 10). The sniper, Victor Ricketts, agreed, admitting that

> It's not too pleasant to have a fellow human in one's sights, with such clarity as to be almost able to see the colour of his eyes, and to have the knowledge that in a matter of seconds, another life has met an untimely end. However, one had to be callous, after all it was, an eye for an eye, a tooth for a tooth.

He then added, 'anyway, it could very well have been in reverse' (Ricketts, no date: 34). Like the other two rationalisations, this one is also entirely unconvincing: long-distance artillery, aerial bombardment, sniping, orders not to take prisoners, and unequal opponents were the norm, not the exception, in modern warfare.

Chapter 8 discusses war films and their impact on how we imagine war.

Of course, men and women in wartime were able to glibly recite these rationalisations for wartime killing because they are firmly embedded within a political and cultural milieu infused with martial images and values. Long before any declaration of war, combat art and literature, battle films, and war games attracted people to the killing fields. It is not difficult to see the attraction of such representations of war. Everything, and everyone, appeared as nobler and more exotic than everyday environments and encounters. Propaganda depicted the glorious flesh of the imagination: the stoic face of the soldier, the chiselled features of airmen, the muscular bulk of sailors, and the fertile curves of mothers, creators of life in the midst of terrible carnage. These representations of gender at war inspired military fervour. Despite the understandable emphasis that many historians have placed on the literature of disillusionment arising out of the ashes of war (see Fussell 1975), the heroic mode has never disappeared. Once our gaze is turned from a narrow canon represented by writers such as Wilfred Owen, Siegfried Sassoon and Edmund Blunden, stock phrases in a glamorous 'high diction'

FIGURE 22.6
US Army trainees practise hand-to-hand combat using pugil sticks during basic combat training at Fort Jackson, South Carolina. Photo: Air Force Staff Sgt. Stacy Pearsall. Courtesy of US Army

(baptisms of fire, transfigured youth, and gallant warriors) emerge as the dominant grammar of war (Bogacz 1986: 643–68). Although such narratives might not directly stimulate enaction, they generate an imaginary arena crowded with murderous potential and provide a linguistic structure or language within which aggressive behaviour might legitimately be fantasised.

Indeed, emotional and psychological survival in modern warfare depended upon combatants being able to justify their actions to their consciences. The difficulties many combatants experienced in coming to terms with the fact of having killed another human being led some influential officers – including one of the most influential military commentators, S. L. A. Marshall, author of *Men Against Fire* (1947) – to argue that 'fear of killing' was actually a more common cause of battle fatigue than 'fear of dying' (Marshall 1947: 78). Men grieved for the men they killed as well as for those they fought alongside. After all, they not only *took* souvenirs from their dead victims, they *placed* their own symbols (such as photographs or handkerchiefs) on them (Bourke 1999a).

Can you imagine killing in war?

Eagerness to kill

It could be argued that survival depended upon more than simply 'making sense' of violence or a blunt resilience of imagination – it also relied upon the ability of combatants to forge some degree of pleasure from the world around them. In the field, many ordinary service personnel found that they could enjoy acts of extreme violence against other people. Combatants were often unabashed about their eagerness to kill. Without the threat of *being* killed, killing was even more fun. The Australian, William Nagle, described killing German paratroopers who were trapped inside their planes on Crete.

'Not one man jumped from any of the planes that I fired at', he observed, admitting that he

> had a feeling of complete exhilaration, full of the hate to kill. I wanted to go on and on. I used up all twenty-four magazines quickly and the rest of the section were filling the empty ones as fast as I emptied them. I could have kissed the bren [light machine gun] with sheer delight but it was too dammed hot to touch.
>
> (Nagle, no date: 7)

Although these days we think of pilots as distanced from those they kill, the fighter pilots being discussed here were very close to the enemy fighter pilots they were aiming at.

Do you think it matters for these responses that fighter pilots were largely men?

Under what circumstances could men like Nagle feel that killing was exciting, exhilarating even? Clearly the 'outcome' was important. In the aftermath of battle, men were less liable to recall their sense of glee if it was clear that they were on the losing side. Unquestionably, the ultimate failure to protect one's comrades placed a powerful dampener on celebrations and giddy bragging. Even amongst the victors, however, excitement varied according to the branch of service. Airforce personnel were most liable to express pleasure in combat. According to one American survey conducted during the Second World War, three-quarters of combat aircrew expressed a willingness to perform further combat duty, compared with only two-fifths of combat infantrymen. The more 'personal' the fight, the more combat air crew enjoyed their job. Thus, when American aerial combat personnel were asked during the Second World War: 'if you were doing it over again, do you think you would choose to sign up for combat flying', 93 per cent of fighter pilots, 91 per cent of pilots of light bombers, 81 per cent of pilots of medium bombers, and 70 per cent of heavy bomber pilots replied 'yes' (Stouffer 1949: 333–35). Roderick Chrisholm flew a night fighter in the Royal Air Force during the Second World War. On 13 March 1941 he destroyed two enemy aircraft. The experience, he wrote, could 'never be equalled':

> For the rest of that night it was impossible to sleep; there was nothing else I could talk about for days after; there was nothing else I could think about for weeks after. . . . it was sweet and very intoxicating.
>
> (Chrisholm 1953: 71)

Equally, the Spitfire pilot, Flight-Lieutenant D. M. Crook, described the 'moments just before the clash' as 'the most gloriously exciting moments of life'. He was 'absolutely fascinated' by the sight of a plane going down and could not pull his eyes away from the sight. The day after shooting down his first plane, he bragged about it to his wife (readers are told that 'she was delighted') and 'with considerable pride' also informed his family of his success (Crook 1942: 28–31 and 75). The fact that the slaughter of fellow human beings could elicit feelings of satisfaction and pleasure was the dirty secret that dared not be uttered if combatants were to settle back to their calm civilian lives, after the war.

This is not to deny widespread disillusionment in war – simply to note that, by the time disillusionment came, it was already too late: the slaughter had already begun. Men who failed to translate their battle experiences into a positive narrative of personal transformation or rite of passage simply went mad. Time and again, we hear the broken voices of combatants who could not 'take it' any more. These were men whose starkly emotional sentences attested to how 'the sights cannot cannot be explained in writing. Writing is not my line. No fighting either For them that wants to let them fight Because I will never like it no no never', as one stammered from his hospital bed (Unnamed soldier in Scholes, no date). There are many such accounts, including more poignant descriptions of fear like the one a private sent to his mother after the Battle of the Somme, simply saying that 'It makes my head jump to think about it' (Hubbard 1916). The Second World War combatant and poet Shawn O'Leary, put it best in his poem of 1941 when he wrote:

> And I –
> I mow and gibber like an ape.
> But what can I say, what do? –
> There is no saying and no doing
> (O'Leary 1941: 20)

Or, as another terrorised private who spent time in a military mental hospital put it, 'I admit I am a coward. A bloody, bleeding coward, and I want to be a live Coward than a dead blasted Hero' (Bourke 1999b: 32).

GENERAL RESPONSES
BELLIGERENT STATES

In direct contradiction to the thrust of the chapter thus far, wartime violence is frequently abstracted from the people on the battlefield, centring instead upon the nation-state. Any analysis of wartime violence must acknowledge that war is not declared by citizens or soldiers, but by politicians. War only takes place if a nation's leaders decide either that there will be significant benefits accruing to victory over a (real or imagined) rival or if they see themselves (in reality or potentially) as threatened by an already antagonistic foe.

Do you find the state-based explanations in this section convincing?

Of course, this is too simplistic. Experts proffer a vast array of reasons why states become belligerent. Competing explanations can be illustrated by examining the most momentous war of the twentieth century: the Second World War. More has been written about this war than any conflict before or since, yet no one agrees on its origins.

For more on explanations of war that revolve around states and their interests see **Chapter 24**.

Economics

When examining the European dimension to that war, many historians trace its origins to 1914–18, implying that there was a 'Thirty Years War' of the twentieth century. In particular, imposing the humiliating Treaty of Versailles on Germany in 1919, which forced it to admit war guilt and stripped the country of territory and forced it to mortgage its economy with an outlandish reparations bill, set up a marker for another major conflict. As A. J. P. Taylor famously phrased it in his *Origins of the Second World War*, 'Powers will be Powers' (Taylor 1974: 278–9). In other words, it was inevitable that Germany would seek to regain what it regarded as its rightful place in the world.

There was an economic imperative for war, as well. In Germany, the Treaty of Versailles had been followed by rampant inflation and then, after a brief breathing space, by a severe economic depression. By 1938, however, under the Nazis, the economic outlook in Germany had changed. The economic recovery fuelled the sense of injustice that had arisen in the aftermath of the First World War. The strength of the German economy had resulted in a balance of payments crisis caused largely by the need to pay for the dramatic increase in imports of food and raw material. Industry and rearmament required ever more resources – and Hitler's regime was increasingly looking outside Germany to meet these needs.

Territorial ambitions

Furthermore, defeat in the First World War had failed to remove Germany's eastward ambitions. Adolf Hitler successfully played upon this national obsession. In this sense, Hitler's policy was fundamentally one of continuity with German politicians prior to 1918 and during the Weimar period of 1919–33. When Hitler came to power in 1933, National Socialism seemed to hold out the promise of a revived Germanic nation. Hitler did not invent many of the ideas that led to war. His promotion of the supposed need for *Lebensraum* (or 'living space') can be traced back to the nineteenth century, and his racist Social Darwinism was widely accepted in Germany by the early twentieth century. Finally, although Hitler's pathological hatred of the Jews is unquestioned (in his book *Mein Kampf*, he called them sub-humans, a cancer that had to be removed), the belief that Jews were responsible for all of Germany's ills – and particularly its fate during the First World War – was widely held by many Germans, on the hard and soft right, and originated in the rise of racial antisemitism.

Beliefs that the distinctions between different 'races' were biological were widely held at one time: see **Chapter 5**.

An evil leader

This emphasis on the ways Hitler epitomised wider concerns within German society in the 1930s can easily lead to a crude reductionism that employs a very simple equation: No Hitler, no war. It cannot be disputed that Hitler was a domineering political personality in Germany. It is difficult to imagine the Third Reich without him. He possessed a fanatical will and was at the same time an unprincipled opportunist. His desire to gain *Lebensraum* for his 'Aryan race' in Eastern Europe was wholehearted. The borders of 1914 were no longer enough, as he wrote in *Mein Kampf*:

> To demand the borders of 1914 is political nonsense of such a degree and consequence that it appears a crime. . . . The borders of 1914 meant nothing to the German nation. . . . We National Socialists, by contrast, must without wavering keep to our foreign policy aim, which is to secure to the German nation the soil and space to which it is entitled on this earth.
>
> (Remak 1976: 23)

Nor is there disagreement about his willingness to impose his will upon all his subordinates. When any of his subordinates, like his first foreign minister, Konstantin von Neurath, seemed reluctant to follow his lead into war, they were replaced.

However, it is far too easy to be carried away by this image of the ultimate in human evil. Indeed, this image of Hitler is largely a construction of Nazi as well as Allied propaganda. It is misleading to place too much emphasis upon Hitler as a cause of the war – whether as a personality in his own right or as someone who managed to epitomise wider and more entrenched national desires and ideologies. Much evidence suggests that Hitler had no coherent plan. Certainly, he was willing to risk millions of his own people in the pursuit of a racially 'pure', rejuvenated, Greater Germany. But he was more likely to simply take advantage of things as they happened, rather than working to a pre-planned strategy. Too much of the explanation for the origins of war has been placed on Hitler's lust for domination, and not enough on the expansionist ideology of Nazism.

Competing political ideologies

However, if focusing on Hitler is a form of reductionism, so too is an excessive emphasis on ideology. Some historians want to claim that the war grew out of a conflict of competing ideologies. Totalitarianism in Germany, Italy, and Japan faced up to the liberal democracies of Britain, France, and the United States. According to this argument, the Axis countries – and Germany in particular – failed to develop a strong liberal-democratic tradition. In other words, the problem was not Hitler but Germany. Hitler's antisemitism, virulent nationalism, and anti-socialism were simply more extreme than those shared by earlier German leaders and 'ordinary Germans'. This explanation is also unsatisfactory. The problem with blaming 'fascism' is that it fails to differentiate between the very different forms of this political ideology. Italian fascism was very distinctive from National Socialism, and neither resemble Japanese totalitarianism.

Chapter 6 has more on ideologies.

Strategic concerns

Finally, the origins of the war may also be traced to strategic concerns. War was inevitable if the territorial ambitions of certain nations were to have any hope of being achieved. Germany and Italy believed that they had something to gain from war. Hitler's plan vastly to expand the amount of land available for exploitation by the Aryan race in Eastern Europe has already been mentioned. The Italian dictator, Benito Mussolini, also pursued a foreign policy that was concerned with the supposed need for *spazio vitale* (again, 'living space') for Italians in North Africa and the Middle East. Mussolini's willingness to act upon this need was clearly signalled in October 1935, when Italian troops from neighbouring Italian Somiland and Eritrea invaded Abyssinia (modern-day Ethiopia). A year later, Italy and Germany militarily supported General Francisco Franco, the fascist dictator in Spain. Franco's victory in 1939 was a major economic as well as political coup for both powers. Spain's iron ore, tin, copper, zinc, and mercury were henceforth at their service. Mussolini also had ambitions to establish Italy as one of the Great Powers. Thus, when Mussolini signed the Pact of Steel with Hitler in May 1939 (which committed Germany and Italy to support each other with 'all its military forces on land, sea, and in the air'), he signalled his desire dramatically to extend Italy's 'Roman' empire.

Strategically, the origin of the war was more complex for the Soviet Union. At first, Joseph Stalin pursued a defensive foreign policy. The Soviet–Nazi Non-Aggression Pact of August 1939 decreed that Russia would remain neutral should Germany attack Poland. For Stalin, it was an attempt to protect the Soviet Union from German aggression. Stalin signed the Pact only after his attempts to find agreement with Britain and France were rebuffed. The Pact came as a surprise to the other Great Powers. After all, Hitler regarded the Russians as the 'scum of the earth' while Stalin viewed Hitler as the 'bloody assassin of the workers'. Whatever Stalin's long-term plans involved, it is clear that Hitler always intended the Pact to be a short-term strategy. In the words of the German ambassador to Italy, Ulrich von Hassell, in his diary of 29 August 1939:

> About the Russian pact Hitler said that he was in no wise altering his fundamental anti-bolshevist policies; one had to use Beelzebub to drive away the devil; all means were justified in dealing with the Soviets, even such a pact as this. This was a typical example of his conception of 'Realpolitik'.
>
> (Schweller 1998: 139)

FIGURE 22.7
Soviet soldiers raise the red flag over the Reichstag in Berlin on 2 May 1945. AP Photo/ ITAR-TASS, Yevgeny Khaldei

However, in the short term at least, the Pact proffered a great prize to the Soviet Union. The Pact had a secret clause dividing Poland between Germany and the Soviet Union. Stalin clearly understood that the Soviet Union needed to protect itself – and one way Stalin conceived of doing this was by creating a buffer zone. Until Hitler turned on him, Stalin also believed that the USSR had something to gain by belligerence.

As this brief summary suggests, therefore, historians and political scientists have given a number of strategic, economic, and defensive reasons for why political leaders committed modern nations to war, including national pride, the need for economic growth, territorial ambitions, bellicose leaders, and warlike ideologies. The relative weight given to each of these factors depends on the ideological stance of the analyst as much as any objective reality. The larger question embracing these, though, is straightforward: how, not why, is violence made possible by social context?

Are the explanations of economic reasons, territorial ambitions, evil leaders, competing political ideologies and strategic concerns still used to make sense of contemporary wars? Which of these, if any, persuade you most? Or are you more persuaded by the idea that it is important to look at other explanations, not abstracted from what happens on the ground? Does it depend which war you are thinking of?

BROADER ISSUES
LANGUAGE AND MEMORY

Whatever perspective is adopted, wartime killing can never be separated from social relations more broadly. As we have seen, state authorities initiate processes which lead to declarations of war. For those doing the fighting, emotions such as fear, rage, and exhilaration, as well as the belief in the need to 'obey orders', were some of the factors that enabled them to be converted into 'effective military personnel' after only perfunctory military training. We have also addressed to some extent the ways language has been used to prepare, facilitate, and then rationalise murderous violence in wartime. Some commentators have taken this point further, observing that, in the face of mass killing, language itself was perverted. Words no longer served as bridges, but as bombs. Terror became possible, not through mechanisms of mass organisation but through the *prevention* of affiliations, including linguistic ones. Syntax, grammar, and figures of speech were distorted and ritualised. The distinction between 'what is' and 'what ought to be' fractured. With mass killing, language became divorced from experience. A separation of 'act' from 'idea' took place.

Chapters 1 and 8 discuss emotional reactions to accounts of wartime deaths.

Chapter 2 argues that certain ways of using language can help enable torture, and **Chapter 23** looks at the way the presentation of the Afghanistan/Pakistan border as 'risky' makes forms of violence possible.

Language of technology

One example might be found by exploring the way technology not only increased the distance between perpetrator and victim, thus bringing into play psychological mechanisms of dehumanisation, but also provided a substitute language with which death could be spoken about. In 1945, sociologist Edward McDonald admitted as much when he witnessed that 'keen discussions' developed between servicemen about the 'rival merits of particular weapons'. These discussions

Chapter 24 explores how technological developments have changed warfare.

> become so involved with physics and ballistics that the participants neglect to realize that the weapon is used to facilitate death. A discussion on the most efficient ways of killing the enemy is not pleasant; however, a technological debate on the range and characteristics of a certain calibre rifle can be challenging and impersonal.
>
> (McDonald 1945: 445–50)

Or, as an American bomb technician admitted in the context of the Vietnam War, 'I don't *feel* like a war criminal. What I was doing is just like screwing fuses into sockets' (Lifton 1974: 347).

Euphemism

Technological languages were only one aspect of the way language was perverted in wartimes. Even more frequently, euphemistic languages were used to deny the experience of meting out death. Thus, for the Turks in 1915, the Armenians were 'suspects' who needed 'resettlement'. The 'deportation' of women, children, and the elderly was necessary for 'the restoration of order in the war zone by military measures, rendered necessary by the connivance of the inhabitants with the enemy, treachery and armed support' (Mazian 1990: 78). In other contexts, killing was re-conceptualised as 'action', 'severe measures', 'reprisal action', 'rendering harmless', 'evacuating', or 'giving special treatment'. 'Our' boys fought an honourable war 'against fascism' (as opposed to against other humans, many of whom – children, for instance – had an only tenuous attachment to fascism). Even the slaughter of prisoners of war or the wounded – illegal according to military regulation as well as international law – was not 'really' a crime. In the words of one officer commenting on the widespread killing of wounded Japanese, there were 'many grey areas around the Geneva Convention, I suppose' (Fraser 1992: 118). In other words, in the heat of battle, atrocious behaviour easily became an integral part of warfare.

Racist language

For more on racism and its impact on global politics see **Chapters 5, 10, 14 and 16**.

In the modern period, the most trenchant language employed in the task of mass murder was racism. Again, the terrifying application of racist languages occurred long before any killing machines were mobilised. In his classic *War Without Mercy* (1986), historian John W. Dower exposed the extent to which linguistic characterisations of the enemy as the ultimate racial 'other' enabled British and American servicemen to act with unsurpassed violence against their Japanese foe. For many British, American, and Australian servicemen and women, the Japanese were a brutish population and Allied troops were engaged in exterminating 'slant-eyed gophers' (in Admiral William F. Halsey's words) (Cameron 1994: 1). Equally, in Japan, long-standing derogatory caricatures of the enemy had a similar effect (Dower 1986). Anglo-Americans were described as demons (*oni*), devils (*kichiku*), fiends (*akki* and *akuma*), and monsters (*kaibutsu*). They also expressed virulent hatred of the Chinese. Shirō Azuma, for instance, was a Japanese soldier who participated in the murders and rapes in Nanjing (China) in 1937. He recalled:

> While the women were fucked, they were considered human, but when we killed them, they were just pigs. We felt no shame about it. No guilt. If we had, we couldn't have done it. When we entered a village, the first thing we'd do was steal food, then we'd take the women and rape them, and finally we'd kill all the men, women, and children to make sure they couldn't slip away and tell the Chinese troops where we were. Otherwise, we wouldn't have been able to sleep at night.
>
> (Schmidt 2000: 87)

In every war, it was important to encourage the fiction that the people being killed were not 'really' human. The Turks had a word for the Armenians: 'dog-food'. Dr Mehmed Resid, Governor of Diyarbekir in 1915 and nicknamed the 'Executioner Governor' in honour of the numerous tortures and murders he oversaw, said:

> Even though I am a physician, I cannot ignore my nationhood. I came into this world a Turk. . . . Armenian traitors had found a niche for themselves in the bosom of the fatherland; they were dangerous microbes. Isn't it the duty of a doctor to destroy these microbes?
>
> (Dadrian 1986: 175)

Nearly 80 years later, in Rwanda, Tutsis were described as 'cockroaches', with the Hutus simply engaged in 'bush-clearing'. Hutus were ordered to 'remove tall weeds' (adults) as well as the 'shoots' (children). Today, in the war in Iraq and Afghanistan, dehumanisation is equally important. As Abu Ghraib prisoner, Nori Samir Gunbar Al-Yasseri put it, the American guards

Chapter 23 discusses the war in Afghanistan, and **Chapters 5 and 21** examine how others sometimes come to be considered not fully human.

> stripped us naked as a newborn baby. Then they ordered us to hold our penises and stroke it. . . . They started to take photographs as if it was a porn movie. And they treated us like animals not humans. . . . No one showed us mercy. Nothing but cursing and beating. Then they started to write words on our buttocks, which we didn't know what it means. After that they left us for the next two days naked with no clothes, with no mattress, as if we were dogs.
>
> (Danner 2005: 228)

In war, the threshold of the human soars. Large groups of humans are relegated to the level of beasts.

For more on Abu Ghraib see **Chapter 2**.

Collective memories

Finally, the link between politics and murderous violence in wartime is generally swept under the carpet after the conflict. War does not begin with the declaration of hostilities, nor does it end with the signing of treaties. In the aftermath of conflict, there is an

BOX 22.3 WAR AND COLLECTIVE MEMORY

Maurice Halbwachs in *Collective Memory* (1980) and Frances Amelia Yates in *The Art of Memory* (1966) remind historians that it is crucial to examine the ways in which war is 'remembered' by groups, even nations. As historians Jay Winter and Emmanuel Sivan insist, memory is the 'socially-framed property of individuals (or groups of individuals) coming together to share memories of particular events, of time past'. Collective memory is 'the process by which individuals interact socially to articulate their memories' (Winter and Sivan 1999: 6).

attempt by political actors on all sides to shape the story of violence to conform to post-war needs, desires, and fears.

Chapter 13 examines counter-memories: in this case stories that challenge dominant narratives of national identity.

The emphasis on the politics of remembrance is crucial: memory itself is a battlefield. Once peace was declared, politics needed a public turning away from collective violence, typically through selective history-making. After all, national identity and honour depended upon the recitation of selective histories. At times, it required outright denial. This was never more the case than in the context of the Holocaust. As Heinrich Himmler vowed in October 1943, the destruction of the Jews was to be 'an unwritten and never to be written page of glory in our history'. This was one of the reasons why the Nazis built most of the camps in isolated areas and when faced with discovery attempted to hide the evidence by ploughing over Treblinka and destroying the gas chambers at Auschwitz, for instance.

Blatant denial of violence was a blunt instrument of power, however. More effectively, social and political elites espoused alternative recitals of the past. Accounts of Germans who fought in the International Brigades in Spain between 1936 and 1939, for instance, were employed within East Germany to forge a myth of national identity that could be distinguished from that of the West. According to the GDR, their state was portrayed as the heir to the democratic tradition of active resistance as represented by the Brigade. In contrast, West Germany was the heir to Hitler's reactionary Condor

BOX 22.4 THE BRONZE SOLDIER

The 'Bronze Soldier', a monument depicting 'a Red Army fighter lowering his head in honour of comrades who had fallen during the liberation of Tallinn from Nazi occupation in 1944' (Pettai 2007: 947), has proved a controversial 'site of memory'. 'For years, the memorial had served as a gathering place for mostly Russian Red Army veterans on 9 May (or "Victory Day", as it was known in the Soviet Union). For many Estonians, however, the statue was seen as a hurtful symbol of the Soviet occupation of Estonia and they wanted it removed' (Pettai 2007: 947). After serious protests and counter-protests, 'two special laws were passed [which allowed the government] to remove the monument amid large-scale Russian protests and street violence' (Pettai 2007: 947–48) in April 2007. The statue was moved from its town-centre location to a military cemetery.

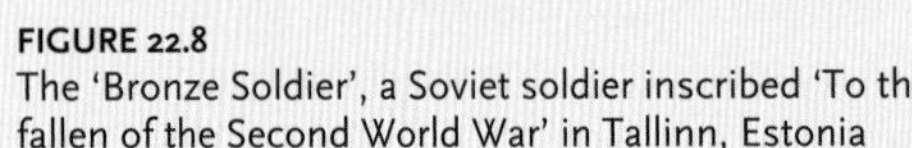

FIGURE 22.8
The 'Bronze Soldier', a Soviet soldier inscribed 'To the fallen of the Second World War' in Tallinn, Estonia

Legion. This process of creating a socialist, anti-fascist 'memory' of nationhood was not a benign exercise. After all, it meant sidelining Jewish victims of the Holocaust in the interest of glorifying the active resistance of the Brigadiers and the valour of Soviet soldiers and Communist resisters.

In West Germany too, a collective memory of the Second World War was developed that entailed the creation of a new hierarchy of victims and heroes. Nazi crimes were created 'in the name of' the Germans, as opposed to 'by' Germans. War memorials were built, but sometimes existed alongside Nazi monuments and museums. Nazis who were released after serving their prison terms portrayed themselves as victims of 'victors' justice'. More generally, many Germans promoted an image of themselves as hapless victims. Instead of focusing on German crimes, emphasis was placed on the expulsion of 11 million Germans from eastern and central Europe and the many thousands of German POWs who died in Soviet hands or who remained in captivity well into the 1950s. Political complicity in such denial was high. Thus, in 1949, the West German Federal Parliament passed legislation that effectively protected from prosecution 800,000 people who had participated in war crimes. Two years later, former civil servants of the Third Reich who had been barred from state service were readmitted. Politically, 'forgetfulness' was pursued. Chillingly, in 1949, nearly 60 per cent of Germans subscribed to the view that National Socialism had been 'a good idea badly carried out' while over 40 per cent still insisted that there was 'more good than evil in Nazism'. It was to be some decades before this national script changed.

Other participating countries were even more reluctant to face their past. In Italy, the fascist past was put to one side and the emphasis placed instead on the role of Italian partisans in resisting the German occupiers from September 1943. Although the myth of resistance was particularly strong on the political left, it was also embraced by the political right (after all, it was King Victor Emmanuel who dismissed Mussolini and declared war on Germany). Dates were equally important in the Soviet Union, where memorials were generally dedicated to the 1941–45 period, denying the Soviet–Nazi Non-Aggression Pact of 1939, the invasion of Finland, and the brutal occupation of Poland. War memory in the Soviet Union remains masculine, martial, and Russian, leaving little room for women, Jews, or other nationalities. Similarly, in Finland, attention was focused on the Winter War of 1939–40 rather than the Continuation War of 1941–44 when the Finns were allies of the Germans. In France, too, it took many decades before the role of French people in persecuting the Jews was recognised. In a typical act of denial, a 1956 documentary called *Night and Fog*, directed by Alain Resnais, was censored by the French to cut a scene showing French police collaborating with the deportations of the Jews. In other words, France reinvented itself: the Vichy regime was cordoned off in a space set unambiguously in the past while the resistance was elevated into a central place in everyday conceptions of national identity. It was not until 1994 that a monument to the Jewish victims of Vichy was built and 16 July became a 'day of remembrance'. Memory is as much about forgetting as remembering.

What events in the past are particularly important to your political community? Is there debate over how to remember them? Who gets to decide how memory is represented for the community?

Axis powers and the conquered territories were not the only ones keen to manipulate the story of war. War crimes and other atrocities carried out by British and American service-personnel were also written out of the grand narrative of war. In particular, the debate about the legality and morality of the aerial bombing campaign continues to excite furious debate. The mass rapes of French and Japanese women by American, British, and Australian soldiers during the Second World War are also rarely discussed. In the words of one American intelligence officer who witnessed the occupation of the German city of Krefeld:

> The behaviour of our troops, I regret to say, was nothing to brag about, particularly after they came upon cases of cognac and barrels of wine. . . . There is a tendency among the naïve or the malicious to think that only Russians loot and rape. After battle, soldiers of every country are pretty much the same, and the warriors of Democracy were no more virtuous than the troops of Communism were reported to be.
>
> (Costello 1985: 144)

As this intelligence officer was aware, euphemistic languages (such as 'warriors of Democracy') were just as crucial in the formation of a collective memory as they had been in enabling men to kill in the first place. We have already noted how professional historians play a large part in the creation of collective narratives of the past. Greek goddess Mnemosyne was not only the goddess of memory, but the mother of history as well. As historian Alon Confino dryly observed: 'The often-made contention that the past is constructed not as fact but as myth to serve the interest of a particular community may still sound radical to some, but it cannot (and should not) stupefy most historians' (Confino 1997: 1387). In such a way, historians are complicit in constructing a collective memory of war that elides or leaves out 'our' violence.

In *Les formes de l'oubli* (1998), French ethnographer Marc Augé reminds us that 'forgetting is an integral part of memory itself'. Memories are 'shaped by forgetting, like the contours of the shore by the sea' (Augé 1998: 21). However, the politics of forgetting can be as morally skewed as those of remembering. In 1998, the former Chilean dictator Pinochet urged that it is 'best to remain silent and to forget. It is the only thing to do' (*Observer* 1998). When perpetrators of violence call for the need to 'forget', we are right to be wary. As the Polish poet Zbigniew Herbert expressed it,

> Do not forget truly it is not in your power
> to forgive in the name of those betrayed at dawn
>
> (Herbert 1977: 79)

CONCLUSION

Do you agree that war is a result of specific cultures, rather than the product of something called human nature? Do you think there is such a thing as 'human nature'? For more on arguments based on human nature see **Chapter 7**.

Should we be pessimistic about a future in which violence is placed outside the realm of possibility? The frustrations resulting from imbalances of power and perceived injustices, the bellicose personalities of politicians and other leading state officials, ideological imperatives, and the territorial ambitions will always be with us. Fantasies associated with war remain deeply embedded within our society. A substantial majority of people agree with the statement that 'human nature being what it is, there will always be war and conflict' (Robertson 1980: 55). They are wrong. For long periods of history, wars have been absent. Some societies are more peace-loving than others. One-half of the world's population (that is, women) have been distinctly less keen on battle than the other half.

The anxiety evoked by uncovering the past is not only inevitable, it is also essential in the process of reconciliation. The duty to remember remains strong, particularly if a nation is to move towards a better future. In this way, South Africa's Truth and Reconciliation Commission (for all its faults) has been particularly innovative because its aim was not 'forgetting' but disclosure. Because amnesty for perpetrators of atrocity was predicated upon that person providing a detailed account of their actions, it enabled full public acknowledgement of the harms done to individuals and groups within society. 'Never Forget' is the phrase that has reverberated since the Holocaust. It is at the heart of both individual and collective ways of coming to terms with violent pasts. In the words of Polish writer Czeslaw Milosz, 'those who are alive receive a mandate from those who are dead and silent forever: to preserve the truth about the past' (Milosz 1991: 281). The choice between forgetfulness and remembrance is ours.

Chapter 26 examines how we may move beyond conflict and the role that memory plays in this process.

FURTHER READING

Bartov, Omer (1996) *Murder in Our Midst: The Holocaust, Industrial Killing, and Representation*, Oxford: Oxford University Press.
Bartov reflects on the holocaust and modernity.

Bourke, Joanna (1999a) *An Intimate History of Killing: Face to Face Killing in Twentieth Century History*, London: Granta.
The book gives an overview of the ways in which British, American, and Australian soldiers experienced combat.

Braudy, Leo (2003) *From Chivalry to Terrorism. War and the Changing Nature of Masculinity*, New York: Alfred A. Knopf.
Beginning in the Middle Ages and ending with twenty-first-century global terrorism, this book explores the ways in which European and American cultures have established the military ethos. Masculinity is at the heart of his explanations.

Dower, John W. (1986) *War Without Mercy: Race and Power in the Pacific War*, New York: Faber and Faber.
This is the best book comparing the experiences of American and Japanese servicemen in combat.

Fussell, Paul (1990) *Wartime. Understanding and Behaviour in the Second World War*, Oxford: Oxford University Press.
This is an analysis of war psychology in the Second World War.

Hughes, Matthew and William J. Philpott (eds) (2006) *Modern Military History*, London: Palgrave Macmillan.
This is the clearest textbook-introduction to modern military history.

Keegan, John (2004 [1978]) *The Face of Battle: A Study of Agincourt, Waterloo and the Somme*, London: Pimlico.
This is the classic study in battle psychology and the changing experience of combat over time.

Merridale, Catherine (2000) *Night of Stone: Death and Memory in Russia*, London: Granta Books.
This is an indispensable study of Russia experiences of war.

Overy, Richard (1999) *The Road to War*, London: Penguin Books.
This books provides a clear summary of the main arguments about the political and diplomatic origins of modern war.

REFERENCES

Augé, Marc (1998) *Les formes de l'oubli*, Paris: Payot & Rivages.

Bassford, Christopher (1994) *Clausewitz in English: The Reception of Clausewitz in Britain and America, 1815–1945*, New York: Oxford University Press, http://www.clausewitz.com/CWZHOME/Bassford/TOC.htm.

Black, Robert (1994) 'A Week in Goma', *Independent on Sunday* 31 July.

Bogacz, Ted (1986) '"A Tyranny of Words": Language, Poetry, and Antimodernism in the First World War', *Journal of Modern History* 58, 3: 643–68.

Bourke, Joanna (1999a) *An Intimate History of Killing: Face to Face Killing in Twentieth Century History*, London: Granta.

Bourke, Joanna (ed.) (1999b) *The Misfit Soldier*, Cork, Ireland: Cork University Press.

Brown, J. F. (1942) 'The Theory of the Aggressive Urges and War-Time Behavior', *The Journal of Social Psychology* 15: 355–80.

Cameron, Craig M. (1994) *American Samurai: Myth, Imagination and the Conduct of Battle in the First Marine Division, 1941–1951*, Cambridge: Cambridge University Press.

Chrisholm, Roderick (1953) *Cover of Darkness*, London: Chatto and Windus.

Clausewitz, Carl von (1st 1976, 2011) *On War*, ed. Michael Howard and Peter Paret, New York: Folio Books.

Confino, Alon (1997) 'Collective Memory and Cultural History: Problems of Method', *The American Historical Review* 102, 5: 1386–403.

Costello, John (1985) *Love, Sex and War: Changing Values 1939–45*, London: Collins.

Crook, David M. (1942) *Spitfire Pilot*, London: Faber and Faber.

Dadrian, Vahakn N. (1986) *The Role of Turkish Physicians in the World War I Genocide of Ottoman Armenians*, Oxford: Pergamon Press.

Danner, Mark (2005) *Torture and Truth: America, Abu Ghraib and the War on Terror*, London: Granta Books.

Dower, John W. (1986) *War Without Mercy: Race and Power in the Pacific War*, New York: Faber and Faber.

Ewen, John Henry (1944) *Bougainville Campaign*, Canberra: Australian War Memorial archives.

Fraser, George MacDonald (1992) *Quartered Safe Out Here: A Recollection of the War in Burma*, London: Harvill.

Fussell, Paul (1975) *The Great War and Modern Memory*, London: Oxford University Press.

Graham, Stephen (1919) *A Private in the Guards*, London: Macmillan.

Halbwachs, Maurice (1980) *Collective Memory*, New York: Harper and Row.

Herbert, Zbigniew (1977) *Selected Poems*, Oxford: Oxford University Press.

Heuser, Beatrice (2002) *Reading Clausewitz*, London: Pimlico.

Hilsum, Lindsey (1994) 'Hutu Warlord Defends Child Murder', *Observer*, 3 July.

Hubbard, Arthur H. (1916) 'Letters Written May–November 1916', London: Imperial War Museum Archives.

Kelman, Herbert C. and Lawrence, Lee H. (1972) 'Assignment of Responsibility in the Case of Lt. Calley: Preliminary Report on a National Survey', *Journal of Social Issues* 28, 1: 177–212.

Lifton, Robert Jay (1974) *Home from the War. Vietnam Veterans: Neither Victims nor Executioners*, London: Wildwood House.

Lockwood, Sydney W. D. (no date) 'No Man's Land', London: Imperial War Museum archives.

Lukas, Richard C. (1990) 'The Polish Experience During the Holocaust', in Michael Berenbaum (ed.) *A Mosaic of Victims: Non-Jews Persecuted and Murdered by the Nazis*, New York: New York University Press.

McDonald, Edward C. (1945) 'Social Adjustment to Militarism', *Sociology and Social Research* 29, 6: 449–57.

Marshall, Samuel Lyman Atwood (1947), *Men Against Fire. The Problem of Battle Command in Future War*, Washington, DC: William Morrow and Co.

Mazian, Florence (1990) *Why Genocide? The Armenian and Jewish Experiences in Perspective*, Ames: Iowa State University Press.
Milgram, Stanley (1974) *Obedience to Authority: An Experimental View*, London: Tavistock Publications.
Milosz, Czeslaw (1991) *Beginning with My Streets*, New York: Farrar, Straus, and Giroux.
Nagle, William (no date) 'Do You Remember When?' Canberra: Australian War Memorial archives.
Observer (1998) 29 November.
O'Leary, Shawn (1941) 'Shell Shock', in Shawn O'Leary, *Spikenard and Bayonet: Verse of the Front Line*, Melbourne: The Author.
Pettai, Vello (2007) 'Estonia', *European Journal of Political Research* 46, 7–8: 943–8.
Remak, Joachim (1976) *The Origins of the Second World War*, Englewood Cliffs, NJ: Prentice-Hall.
Ricketts, Victor G. (no date) Account of His Service, London: Imperial War Museum archives.
Robertson, Ian (1980) *Sociology*, New York: Worth.
Rumpf, Hans (1963) *The Bombing of Germany*, translated by Edward Fitzgerald, London: Frederick Muller.
Schmidt, David Andrew (2000) *Ianfu: The Comfort Women of the Japanese Imperial Army of the Pacific War. Broken Silence*, Lewiston, NY: Edwin Mellen Press.
Scholes, Dorothy (no date) Papers of Miss Dorothy Scholes, Wigan Archives Service.
Schweller, Randall L. (1998) *Deadly Imbalances. Tripolarity and Hitler's Strategy of World Conquest*, New York: Columbia University Press.
Smelser, Neil J. (1971) 'Some Determinants of Destructive Behavior', in Nevitt Sanford and Craig Comstock (eds) *Sanctions for Evil*, San Francisco, CA: Jossey-Bass.
Stouffer, Samuel A. (1949) *The American Soldier: Combat and Its Aftermath*, vol. II, Princeton, NJ: Princeton University Press.
Taylor, A. J. P. (1974) *Origins of the Second World War*, London: Penguin.
US Strategic Bombing Survey (1945) *Overall Report (European War)*, Washington, DC: US Government Printing Office.
Weingartner, James J. (1989) 'Massacre at Biscari: Patton and an American War Crime', *The Historian* 52, 1: 24–39.
Winter, Jay and Sivan, Emmanuel (1999) 'Setting the Framework', in Jay Winter and Emmanuel Sivan (eds) *War and Remembrance in the Twentieth Century*, Cambridge: Cambridge University Press.
Yates, Frances Amelia (1966) *The Art of Memory*, London: Routledge and Kegan Paul.

For a range of further resources supporting this chapter, please visit the companion website for *Global Politics, 2nd Edition* at www.routledge.com/cw/edkins/

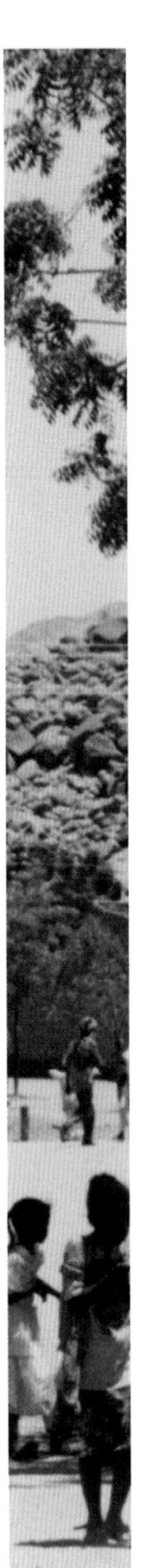

CHAPTER 23

What counts as violence?

Louise Amoore and Marieke de Goede

- *The question*
  WHAT IS VIOLENCE?
- *Illustrative example*
  VIOLENCE AND TARGETING IN THE WAR ON TERROR
- *General responses*
  THE RELATIONSHIP BETWEEN VIOLENCE AND POWER
- *Broader issues*
  VISIBLE AND INVISIBLE VIOLENCE
- **CONCLUSION**

THE QUESTION
WHAT IS VIOLENCE?

In our daily lives, we often think of violence as an aberration – as the moment when the usual order of things breaks down, when the political and legal institutions that protect us recede or fail. When we read media reports of a senseless knife attack in a city street, for example, the violence appears as a rupture in the recognisable order of daily life. And yet, we are also aware of violence as an instrument of politics, we know that sometimes violent acts are carried out in the name of a cause or to achieve a political objective. When a decision is made to go to war, for example, the case is often made in terms of political objectives. So, why is it that some acts are considered to be senseless violence that is beyond comprehension, while others are treated as necessary and legitimate acts in the pursuit of a better, more secure, more just world? How do we distinguish between politics and violence, and what are the political implications of such distinctions? What counts as violence?

War and the various arguments used to explain why it is necessary are examined in **Chapter 22**.

Even within the political realm, the distinction between apparently senseless violence and violence with a political objective persists. Consider, for example, the testimony that the former UK prime minister Tony Blair presented before the Iraq Inquiry in January 2010, when he contrasted the acts of terrorism perpetrated by the Irish Republican Army (IRA) with those witnessed in the events of 11 September 2001:

> For those of us who dealt with terrorism from the IRA, and, incidentally, I don't want to minimise the impacts of that terrorism; each act of terrorism is wicked and wrong and to be deplored. But the terrorism that an organisation like the IRA were engaged in was terrorism directed towards a political purpose, maybe unjustified, but it was within a certain framework that you could understand. The point about this act in New York was that, had they been able to kill even more people than those 3,000 they would have, and so, after that time, my view was that you could not take risks with this issue at all.
>
> (Tony Blair 2010: 11)

In his testimony, Blair sought to explain why it was that the violence witnessed on 9/11 so changed the world that even the decision on military intervention had to be made on the basis of new criteria. Though European states had become accustomed to the acts of terrorism of groups such as the Basque separatist organisation ETA in Spain, or the IRA in the UK, explained Blair, these were organisations whose violence was 'directed towards a political purpose', acting within a 'framework that you could understand'. By contrast, Al-Qaeda is understood to take on a new and networked organisational form, to substitute violent extremism for political purpose, and to be beyond the framework of understanding. Faced with such incomprehensible violence, Blair testified before the Iraq Inquiry, military action could be justified. So, for example, the hijackers of the aircraft on 9/11 have been called nihilists, whose acts of violence and wanton destruction are thought to be irreconcilable with political agendas and beyond the reach of established juridical or ethical codes (Walzer 2004).

The way in which a problem, danger or threat is represented has a real and material effect on what can be done, and what kind of response can be formulated. When violence is posed as an intrinsic part of a political campaign, for example, perhaps the cessation of violence can begin a process of negotiation and accommodation, as happened with the IRA. If an act of violence is considered to be beyond the scope of political response, what kinds of state acts and interventions become sanctioned? Was Tony Blair correct to say that new forms of terrorism justify revised thresholds of the legality of war, what Michael Walzer calls emergency ethics?

To begin to address the question of violence, it is useful to begin by reflecting on the relation between power and violence. Is violence an expression of power or powerlessness? What *is* violence? We think we know it when we see it, but how can it be defined and demarcated? How can we distinguish and study the differences between individual and collective violence; what distinguishes political violence from other kinds of aggression? Are there different types of violence, of which some can be considered a legitimate continuation of politics, while others are to be considered illegitimate and nihilist? What is the relationship between politics, power and violence? How can we distinguish political violence or terrorism, war, violent revolutionary movements or anticolonial struggles on the one hand, and non-violent protest or resistance, sanctions and non-military humanitarian intervention on the other?

The radical Islamist group Al-Qaeda is discussed in more depth in **Chapter 6**.

A nihilist is someone who believes life has no meaning or purpose, and, because of this, nihilism is often associated with destructiveness, though this is by no means necessarily a part of nihilism.

The effects of how we think about the world are the subject of **Chapter 2**, which also discusses Michael Walzer, and the way in which it is our thinking that makes the world appear dangerous is discussed in **Chapter 24**.

BOX 23.1 THE EVENTS OF 11 SEPTEMBER 2001

In the early morning of 11 September 2001, four aircraft were hijacked as they took off from airports in the eastern United States, loaded with sufficient fuel for flights to the western seaboard and carrying their usual number of passengers. The hijackers, four or five on each flight, and armed only with paper cutter knives, took control of the planes, killing the pilots and members of the crew. They turned the planes around towards cities on the East coast. Two were redirected towards New York, and flown directly into the twin towers of the World Trade Center, two iconic 100-storey office blocks situated in the financial district of Lower Manhattan. One was flown to Washington DC and hit the Pentagon, the headquarters of the US military. The fourth, thought perhaps to have been destined for the US Capitol building or the White House, was brought down in a field in Shanksville, Pennsylvania, allegedly by passengers on the plane. This fourth flight had been delayed, and passengers had heard on their mobile phones that other hijacked planes had by then hit buildings in New York.

The impact of the two planes flown into the towers of the World Trade Center caused massive fireballs, and cut off means of escape for those trapped in the buildings. Firefighters rushed to help, as people fell from the upper floors to their deaths. Just over an hour after the initial impact, to the horror of people watching events unfold from the streets of Manhattan or on their television screens around the world, both towers collapsed, disappearing into a cloud of dust. Nearly 3,000 people were killed, including those trying to rescue the office workers; the remains of over 1,000 have not yet been identified. The death toll was initially thought to be potentially around 40,000, but because the incident happened early in the morning, many office workers had not yet arrived at their desks, and others managed to evacuate safely.

The events of that day came to be known as 9/11; whether or not they represented a turning point in global politics is contentious.

ILLUSTRATIVE EXAMPLE
VIOLENCE AND TARGETING IN THE WAR ON TERROR

To map out a context for our discussion of the complex question of violence, and the difficulties of distinguishing between types of violence, we will explore here two intertwined forms of violence present in one geographical region of our world: the overt and visible drone attacks on the Afghanistan–Pakistan border; and the much less readily visible violence of targeting the financial transactions of aid agencies, such that the West failed to deliver sufficient aid to those affected by the severe flooding in that same region in 2010.

'The West' is often used to refer to a group of mostly Northern industrialised countries, suggesting that they share a culture, have common political interests and generally act together. Of course, it is not quite so simple, and **Chapter 6** talks more about this.

Drone targeting in Pakistan

In contemporary global politics, the borderlands between Afghanistan and Pakistan are cast as a particularly dangerous and unruly geographical space (Mohammad 2008; Elden 2009). This area, frequently also called AfPak, is imagined as a dangerous and cavernous borderland from which much of the contemporary terrorist threat emerges (Mohammad and Sidaway 2010). But AfPak is more than a dangerous territory: it is

FIGURE 23.1
Afghanistan–Pakistan borderlands: A US Government map from the 1980s now in the public domain showing the Afghanistan–Pakistan frontier (Durand Line area) and seeming to indicate Pashtun areas. http://independentindian.com/category/afghanistan/ http://drsubrotoroy.files.wordpress.com/2009/10/afghan1.jpg?w=780

Who is doing the imagining here? Who is it that casts these borderlands as dangerous?

considered to be spatially networked to cells and suspect groups in the West, radiating danger and the threat of violence into the heart of Western societies. 'From the streets of Western cities to the mountains of Afghanistan, to the tribal regions of Pakistan, to the islands of South East Asia, to the Horn of Africa' is how US president George W. Bush invoked the networked global imaginary of the terrorist threat (cited in Elden 2009: 81). Around Christmas 2010 for example, alarmist but unspecified terror warnings were issued in Germany, where authorities stated that they had concrete information that signalled a real terrorist threat. These warnings were partly traced to Indian criminal and fugitive Dawood Ibrahim, who was believed to be hiding in Pakistan. The threat remained unspecified in terms of timing and possible targets however, and led mostly to an intensified policing at airports, train stations and at the picturesque German Christmas markets. What Pakistani novelist Moshin Hamid (2010) calls the AfPak mindset, then, can be understood to entail a dispersed geo-political network that connects the Pakistan borderlands with real but unspecified threats in the urban centres of Europe.

Amid widespread political consensus that the Afghanistan–Pakistan borderlands represent the spatial origins of future terrorist violence in the West, the US began to develop its own specific form of response – the targeted killing of militants in the AfPak region using unmanned aerial vehicles (UAVs) or 'drones'. In the period from 2004 to 2010, the United Nations reports that drone strikes have killed 1,458 militants and 531 civilians. The use of unmanned drones, armed with Hellfire missiles, has increased dramatically over that time. In fact, since the coming into power of the Obama administration in the US, the number of these strikes has doubled, with 2010 witnessing over 210 strikes (United Nations 2010). This happened during the same period as the withdrawal of conventional military forces from Iraq.

For the state to exercise what sociologist Max Weber termed 'the monopoly of the legitimate use of physical violence' (Weber 2004: 33) but to do this not with armies and troops, but rather with remotely controlled missiles, the future terrorist violence of northern Pakistan has to be understood in a particular way. An unconventional violence, one that is beyond prevailing frameworks of political objectives, one might suggest, could only be met with a non-standard response. Certainly, it is UN special rapporteur on extrajudicial killing Phillip Alston's view that the drone strikes stretch the right of a state to exercise legitimate violence in self-defence. Though 'there are indeed circumstances in which targeted killings are permitted in armed conflict situations when used against combatants or fighters', concludes Alston's report, 'they are increasingly being used far from any battle zone. This expansive and open-ended interpretation of the right to self-defence goes a long way towards destroying the prohibition on the use of armed force contained in the UN Charter' (United Nations 2010). The representation of a world under threat of violence from a nebulous and networked source has been a necessary precondition for a violent state response that is arguably beyond the conventional limits of legitimate force. Put simply, the geographical spaces in which the US considers it legitimate to intervene with the help of drone strikes is expanding far beyond officially declared battle zones.

The rise of network warfare is discussed in **Chapter 24**.

BOX 23.2 UNMANNED AERIAL VEHICLES (UAVS) OR DRONES

What is an UAV or drone? An UAV is a powered aerial vehicle that does not carry a pilot or crew, but is controlled remotely by a pilot equipped with a video screen of live images taken from the drone. In contemporary military operations the UAV is armed with Hellfire missiles.

FIGURE 23.2
A drone. Photo: DoD/Corbis

Are they a new form of warfare? UAVs have been used for military reconnaissance and surveillance for some 30 years. However, under the Obama administration (and in the context of pressure to withdraw ground troops from Afghanistan), the number of drone missile strikes on the Afghanistan–Pakistan borderlands has doubled.

When were drones first used in attacks? The first test of an armed drone was in 2001 by the CIA (Central Intelligence Agency), when Hellfire missiles were launched from a Predator drone.

When was the drone first used on a real military target? The first deployment was in Yemen in 2002, again by the CIA. They used it to target a sports utility vehicle in the middle of the desert. It was claimed that the strike killed an al-Qaeda member, and five of his associates.

Who flies them? In 2010/11 the drones in Afghanistan were controlled from Creech air force base in the Nevada desert. In the US it is possible to take a course to learn how to control these aircraft, while at the moment the British stipulate that you must have been a combat pilot to control them.

How are they controlled? Somewhat like a console games controller, the pilots sit in front of a screen. The systems have high-resolution cameras and sensors to see things on the ground, as well as heat sensors to establish the presence of people within buildings and so on.

Who makes the decision to fire the missiles, the drone or the human? The pilot does, although in a lot of instances they won't have that much time – the drone will identify a target and ask them whether to shoot: yes or no? A lot of the time the pilot is vetoing targets rather than finding them.

Are other countries developing these armed drones? Yes, at the moment there are forty-three countries developing these programmes. It is difficult to put a precise figure on how many countries currently operate armed drones because there are many other unarmed uses for the drone, such as mapping, remote sensing, and surveillance. Russia alone has eighteen programmes, while the Chinese have a drone known as the Invisible Sword.

(*Source*: Adapted from *Channel 4 News*, 'Drones: The Secret War', screened 22 December 2010, synopsis available at http://www.channel4.com/news/pakistan-drone-strikes-the-cias-secret-war)

Financial targeting in Pakistan

The so-called war on terror is discussed in **Chapter 26**. This term, which came into use shortly after 9/11, more or less fell out of use in the period after Barack Obama took office as US president in 2008.

It is not only in the overt and visible violences of targeted killing that the people of the Afghanistan–Pakistan border find themselves vulnerable to the new interventions of the continuing war on terror. For a number of years, global financial authorities have expressed increasing concern over Pakistan's position in the global fight against money laundering and terrorism financing. In the context of this global pursuit of dirty monies, states have to adhere by a set of rules and recommendations developed by the Paris-based Financial Action Task Force (FATF), an OECD (Organisation for Economic Co-operation and Development) platform erected in 1989 to foster international cooperation against money laundering.

The FATF has been increasingly important since the attacks of 9/11, because it became charged with an agenda designed to cut off terrorists' access to financial resources and global banking systems. In this context, the FATF released in 2001 eight Special Recommendations on Terrorist Financing; later, a ninth recommendation was added. These recommendations include the criminalisation in national law of the financing of terrorism; the identification, freezing and confiscation of monies thought to belong to terrorists or potential terrorists; strict regulation of banks, which have to check the identities of their clients and examine their transactions for markers of suspicion; and the prohibition of informal money service providers. The demands that the FATF places on countries are far-reaching, especially if those countries have an underdeveloped banking sector that relies partly on informal money transfer networks. However, countries which do not adhere to these recommendations may receive criticism and negative evaluations in the regular country reports that the FATF produces. This may affect a country's credit rating and access to international capital markets.

For more about the global economy and neoliberalism, see **Chapters 15, 17 and 19**.

In 2009, the FATF reported that they were very 'concerned about the money laundering and terrorism financing risks posed by Pakistan' (FATF 2009). By June 2010,

BOX 23.3 ORGANISATION FOR ECONOMIC CO-OPERATION AND DEVELOPMENT

The Organisation for Economic Co-operation and Development (OECD), which has its headquarters in Paris, describes itself as 'an international organisation helping governments tackle the economic, social and governance challenges of a globalised economy' (http://www.oecd.org). Founded in 1961, when eighteen European countries plus the United States and Canada joined forces to create an organisation dedicated to global development, it currently comprises thirty-four member countries.

A recent study by Rianne Mahon and Stephen McBride (2009) says that 'the OECD deserves more attention than it normally receives. . . . In contrast with the International Monetary Fund (IMF), the World Trade Organization (WTO), and the World Bank, the OECD lacks the power to enforce compliance with its decisions. Yet, it is much less concerned with establishing binding obligations than it is with influencing the direction of policy, in ways that may in the future become binding on states'. According to Mahon and McBride, it is a 'rich nations' club' and may propagate values reflecting neoliberalism.

The Financial Action Task Force (FATF) was set up as an OECD body by the G7 in 1989 in order to develop and promote policies against money laundering. FATF issued forty recommendations against money laundering in 1990, and regularly reviews and evaluates member state progress in implementing these measures. FATF currently has thirty-six members, but has expanded its geographical scope since it works with associate members and regional bodies, such as the Caribbean Financial Action Task Force (CFATF). Although membership is voluntary and its recommendations are not binding, FATF country reports can be influential and countries work hard to receive good evaluations (Hülsse and Kerwer 2007). The importance of FATF as an international body increased significantly when after 9/11 it became charged with developing policies to fight terrorism financing.

BOX 23.4 FATF'S NINE SPECIAL RECOMMENDATIONS ON TERRORIST FINANCING

1 Ratification and implementations of UN instruments.
2 Criminalising the financing of terrorism and associated money laundering.
3 Freezing and confiscating terrorist assets.
4 Reporting suspicious transactions relating to terrorism.
5 International cooperation.
6 Registering and regulating alternative remittance [payments sent home by migrant workers] and informal money transfers systems.
7 Regulating wire transfers and ensuring that these contain all sender and receiver information.
8 Regulating non-profit organisations and ensuring that they cannot be misused.
9 Putting in place measures to detect cash couriers and the physical cross-border transportation of currency.

(FATF 2001)

FIGURE 23.3 Reporting suspicions. http://graphicwitness.org/ineye/beal.htm

FATF had identified Pakistan as a jurisdiction with 'strategic deficiencies' in its anti-money laundering and anti-terrorism financing regulatory structures. FATF elicited from Pakistan a 'high level political commitment' to cooperate more closely on improving its regulatory efforts in this area, by implementing better the nine recommendations, and by being more active in identifying, freezing and confiscating the monies thought to belong to potential terrorists, including a number of suspect charities.

The total amount of remittances sent by migrants in the West to their countries of origin annually is now far larger than all development aid taken together.

The global community, then, did not only target Pakistani territory militarily through drone strikes, but also in another way; namely, by demanding banking reform and changes in national policing practice against suspect monies. Specifically, Pakistani police action against a number of suspect charities was demanded by the international community. In short, Pakistan was put under pressure to step up its efforts against alleged terrorism in a dual way: through the military targeting of the drone strikes, and through the financial targeting of the FATF.

Twin targetings in Pakistan

At first glance, the military targeting of the drone strikes and the financial targeting of the FATF seem to be at opposite ends of the violence spectrum in terms of means and effects. If drone targeting leads to visible violence, death and collateral damage, financial targeting seems completely different: it works through high-level diplomacy, legal reform and the proscription or outlawing of certain organisations. Indeed, monetary targeting is more generally seen as an important, more effective and less violent alternative way to pursue terrorists than the visibly violent spaces of the war on terror like Guantanamo Bay, extraordinary rendition and drone strikes. However, if we look a little closer, we can discern more parallels between drone strikes and financial targeting than we might see at first glance. It is important to understand that the financial targeting of the FATF can also have violent (side) effects. In particular, they may have implications for the ways in which charities are able to operate and their effectiveness in getting the right aid to the right people at the right time in a case of humanitarian emergency. Let us discuss in turn the ways in which drone strikes and financial targeting may both have violent effects, and how they are interwoven in their political logics.

Guantanamo Bay and extraordinary rendition are discussed in **Chapter 2**.

First, it is important to understand the way in which financial sanctions work and the effects that they may have. In the first instance, new financial regulation and the criminalisation of terrorism financing has made the work of humanitarian and aid charities much more difficult. Charitable organisations have to demonstrate that they do not work together or otherwise associate with organisations that are suspected of supporting terrorists. In Pakistan, for example, it has become forbidden to cooperate with the organisations Lashkar-e-Taiba and Jawad-ud-Dawa, which are accused of supporting terrorists and of being involved in the planning of attacks such as those in Mumbai in 2008. Faith-based Muslim organisations, in particular, are now in a situation in which it is ceaselessly demanded that they demonstrate they are not implicated in funding what are regarded as dubious local organisations or associating with suspect entities. In order to give guidance to charities in the global fight against terrorism financing, the UK Charity Commission, for example, has issued stringent new anti-terrorism guidelines. These guidelines include the obligation for charities to 'take all necessary steps to ensure that their activities could not reasonably be misinterpreted' and to guard against 'any association with terrorist or inappropriate political activities' (Charity Commission UK 2009: 23 and 2).

But these guidelines raise a number of questions concerning the legitimacy of charitable work. How can one reasonably prevent one's activities from being misinterpreted? How can one avoid being involved in or associated with inappropriate political activity, and who decides on the appropriateness or otherwise of an organisation's political or charitable work? In order to navigate these requirements, charities have to develop a paper trail, in which they account for their charitable decisions, local employees, investments, accounts, transfers and transactions. Charities have to keep detailed records of their employees and beneficiaries, which requires, for example, the collection and storage of local personnel's CVs, birth certificates and other official documents, and explaining gaps in their CVs. The levels of scrutiny and record-keeping demanded under the new guidelines of the UK Charity Commission are, according to one faith-based charity, 'very extensive to the point of being unrealistic'. This charity struggles with comprehending the limits of what needs to be recorded, for example whether it would include maintaining CV-files and references of support staff such as cleaners in field offices. This problem is even more acute in territories where formal paperwork such as birth certificates, diplomas and other records, are badly maintained or difficult to acquire (Islamic Relief 2009).

To what extent do you think these difficulties are related to the idea that certain religious movements are involved in politics? See **Chapter 6**.

These seemingly less violent practices make it more difficult in cases of humanitarian emergency to deliver aid on the ground. Charities, especially if Islamic faith-based, face an impossible terrain of operation and have genuine difficulty doing their work. This was starkly illustrated through the contradictions that emerged over aid to Pakistani flood victims in 2010. On the one hand, the UN urgently appealed for help in August 2010 in the face of unprecedented suffering and damage caused by severe floods in large parts of Pakistan. The UN called the floods a 'disaster of almost unprecedented magnitude', and said that $460 million would be needed to provide food, shelter and basic medical services to the nearly 15 million people affected (MacFarquhar 2010). However, these public calls for action and donations obscured the political contestations over how aid was to be delivered to the people on the ground. One of the key questions in this respect was formulated in terms of how to prevent 'militant Muslim groups in the fragile northwest, where the worst flooding has occurred' from 'distributing their

'More people were affected by the flooding than the combined total of the Boxing Day Indian Ocean tsunami, 2005 Pakistan earthquake, Haiti earthquake and Hurricane Katrina'. John Barrett, head of the UK's Flood Response Team, DFID Pakistan.

Hizbullah and HAMAS, which are discussed in **Chapter 6**, are other examples of organisations commonly labelled terrorist that provide basic social services in their areas.

While Madrassah literally means any type of school, in English it is used to refer to an Islamic institution.

own aid and using the crisis to turn traumatized refugees against the government and the US' (Christian Science Monitor 2010). In this context, it is important to recognise that organisations like Jawad-ud-Dawa are not simply terrorist fronts, but illustrate the complex dividing line between aid, politics and religion in ungoverned territories. In areas where states largely fail to provide schools, hospitals and security, these organisations run Madrassahs and provide social support networks. Reportedly, Jawad-ud-Dawa was one of the first and few organisations to help victims of the 2008 earthquake on the Pakistani-controlled side of Kashmir, where it was 'welcomed by people in the area for stepping in where the Pakistani government had failed' (Filkins and Mekhennet 2006).

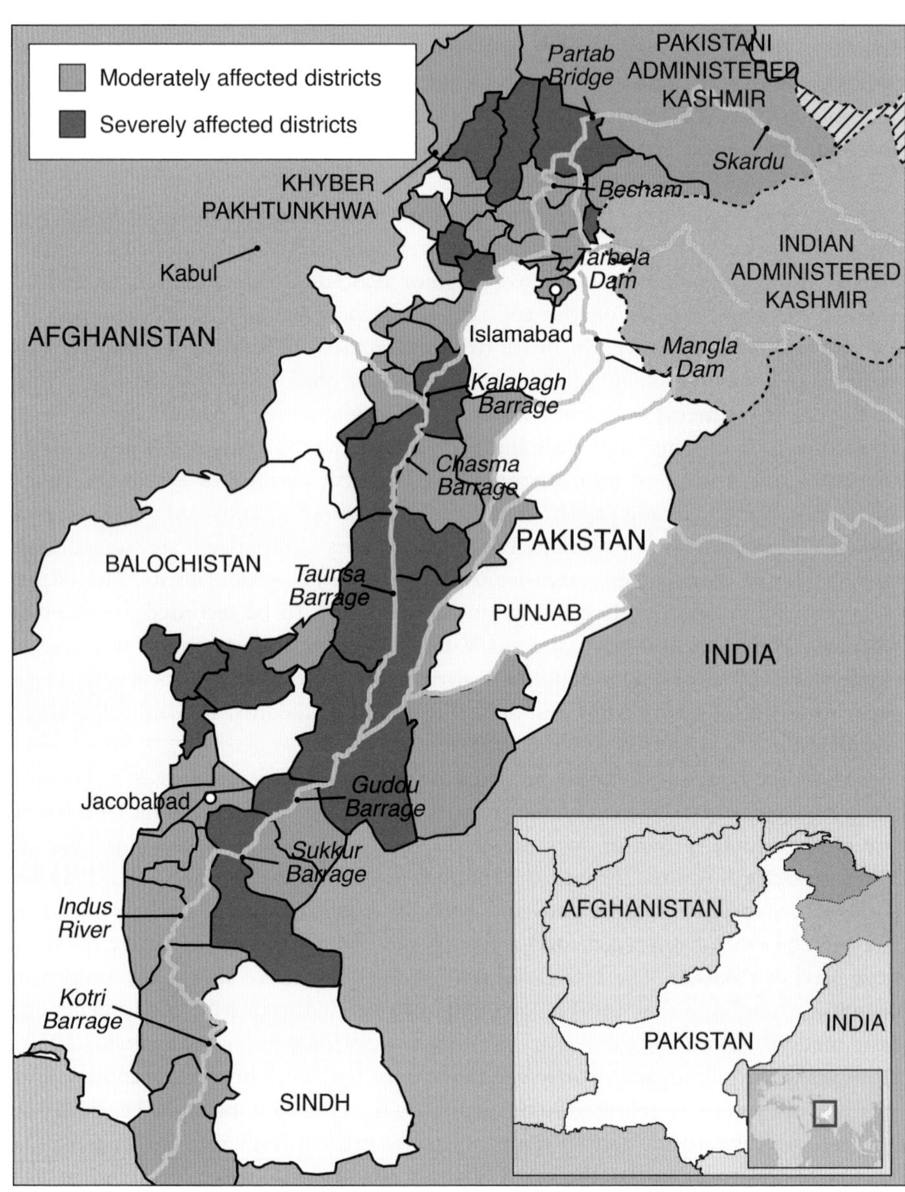

FIGURE 23.4
Areas affected by 2010 floods in Pakistan. http://www.dfid.gov.uk/Images/pakistan_affected_areas.jpg; http://www.dfid.gov.uk/pakistanfloodsmonitor2010

In this sense, the West's hesitant reaction to the floods in Pakistan in 2010 lays bare the profoundly conflicting ways of thinking about areas regarded as sources of danger in the continuing war on terror. Let us think about what can happen when a particular place becomes understood as a source of risk and danger, a terrorist threat, but then also becomes a place at risk of catastrophic flood. The representation of Pakistan as a place both risky and at risk has important and constraining effects on the response of the rest of the world. While the UN laments the lack of response in terms of aid flows, the responders with the infrastructure and capacity to deliver aid on the ground – charities such as Islamic Relief – are themselves subject to suspicion and time-consuming regulation that severely restricts their ability to respond effectively. Thus it is that the media can, on the same pages, lament the relative lack of donations to Pakistani victims, just as they simultaneously warn against potentially disastrous terrorist attacks emanating from 'mountainous' and 'cavernous' Pakistani border areas. The same international institutions who proudly announce millions to be donated in humanitarian aid can be, in the name of the war on terrorism financing, at the forefront of attacking and restricting the channels that are probably most capable of delivering such aid

FIGURE 23.5
Floods in Pakistan in 2010. Photo: Adrees Latif. http://www.treebadger.co.uk/wp-content/uploads/2010/08/Pakistan-Floods.jpg; http://www.treebadger.co.uk/worst-monsoon-floods-for-80-years-hit-pakistan/

effectively. The question of the blowback and increased impoverishment in the wake of these financial targetings is acute (Howell and Lind 2009). As one representative from British charitable organisation Islamic Relief puts it, if aid is disabled to orphanages or disaster victims in disputed and fragile territories, 'Who do they blame for their predicament? Is the world a safer place?' (Islamic Relief 2009).

So, it is possible that both drone strikes and financial targeting in the case of contemporary Pakistan may have violent effects on populations. If the effects of drone strikes are visible and immediate, those of financial targeting are less immediate and less visible but equally important if they work to disable vital charitable work and the provision of welfare and education. There is another reason why drone strikes and financial targeting may be more similar than it seems at first glance: they both operate through logics of precision targeting and new ways of governing in the so-called unruly spaces that have come to typify contemporary warfare. These logics of precision-targeting support specific interventions inside the sovereign space of another country *without* a formal declaration of war (Zehfuss 2011). Now that danger and enmity are perceived to be no longer contained in clearly demarcated geographical areas, but as dispersed and distributed from the mountains in Pakistan to Western-based sleeper cells, risk-based targeted governing becomes the new face of contemporary conflict. The violences of the drone attacks and financial targeting and freezing are not alternatives in a world after the war on terror, but are parallels in terms of their objectives as well as their logic. Both practices offer a dream of side effects-free precision targeting in an otherwise unruly territory (Valverde and Mopas 2004). Underlying this vision of painless targeting is an understanding of the Afpak borderlands as unruly territories, from whence the current global terrorist threat emanates. From this point of view, the Pakistani floods, however awful from the standpoint of human suffering, have provided an opportunity to intensify the targeted governing of this dangerous territory. The *less overt and scarcely visible violence* of stopping money and blacklisting a country is making its people more vulnerable to the *more overt forms of visible violence* manifested in drone attacks.

Chapter 24 talks about changes in contemporary ways of waging war that reflect many of these ideas; it notes that present-day military thinking sees the enemy not only as not contained geographically, but as always in a state of becoming-dangerous.

GENERAL RESPONSES
THE RELATIONSHIP BETWEEN VIOLENCE AND POWER

The example of the twin targeting of drone attacks and financial measures in Pakistan shows two things that are of more general importance for the study of violence and modern warfare. First, it shows how difficult it is to distinguish between war and non-war, combatant and non-combatant, particularly when modern wars are fought not against clearly locatable and identifiable enemies, but against dispersed enemy networks, which are intermingled with normal populations and urban environments (Duffield 2007; Kaldor 2007). Second, it shows that it is not always easy to recognise violence: although we think we know it when we see it, political measures that are pursued through diplomacy and international dialogue can still have violent implications and effects on the ground. In this sense, rules, negotiations and political relations may have violent presuppositions or violent effects.

Let us try to make sense of these points, and the complex relations between violence and power more generally, by examining what some of the experts have said about these issues. There are a number of theorists who have contributed to our understandings of the form and nature of violence.

Chapter 22 asks why politics turns to violence: why do soldiers kill, and why are wars fought?

War as an instrument of politics

One of the most important thinkers on war in the modern age was Prussian military theorist Carl von Clausewitz. Although first published in 1832, von Clausewitz's book *On War* (*Vom Kriege* in the German original) is still today considered to be one of the most important books on war and military strategy ever written. The book is especially famous for its argument that war is 'the mere continuation of politics by other means' (1873 [1832]: ch. 1, § 24). In other words, war is considered to be a political instrument involving the military engagement of strategic aims otherwise pursued through political processes and institutions. According to Clausewitz, the form of war needs to be tailored to the specific political aims that are being pursued, making war 'a true chameleon' (1873 [1832]: ch. 1, § 28). Although celebrated for being a first analysis of modern war, Clausewitz's book is also critiqued for offering a rationalisation of violence. Others have argued that Clausewitz is less relevant for understanding so-called new wars, because he focuses mainly on inter-state conflicts and his analysis is therefore less applicable to the geographically dispersed and intra-state conflicts that mark the early twenty-first century (Kaldor 2010).

For more on Clausewitz's thinking on war see **Chapter 22**.

Collective violence

The question of violence and violent politics is much broader than the question of war, especially in modern conflicts where the battlefield is not clearly demarcated or entrenched, as in our illustrative example (Coward 2009; Graham 2010). This has been recognised by political theorist Charles Tilly in his 2003 book *The Politics of Collective Violence*. Tilly seeks to understand the nature of collective violence, be it looting and rioting, violent resistance movements, or genocide. Despite the substantial differences between these phenomena, Tilly argues that they have common characteristics that go to the heart of the nature of violence as an 'episodic social interaction'. These shared characteristics, according to Tilly, are threefold: First, they inflict 'physical damage on persons and/or objects'; second, they involve 'at least two perpetrators'; and third, they result at least to some extent from 'coordination among persons who perform the damaging acts' (Tilly 2003: 3).

Based on the identification of these elements, Tilly proposes a comprehensive typology of interpersonal violence, in which the extent of coordination among perpetrators, coupled with the salience of damage, lead to a distinction of 'brawls' from 'broken negotiations' from 'violent rituals'. Tilly's aim with this typology is to help students of conflict explain variations in violence and differentiations in violent episodes. Tilly emphasises the increasingly irregular and differentiated nature of modern warfare, marked not by clearly demarcated battles between states, but by violent (terrorist) resistance, civil war and civilian involvement. For Tilly the war on terror is exemplary of the 'sea change in the nature of collective violence' that has taken place during the second half of the twentieth century. This 'sea change' involves the increasing importance of civil war, the participation of 'irregular forces' such as militias and mercenaries, the increase of the level of attacks on civilian targets, and the relation between violence and traditional political struggle (Tilly 2002).

Violence as indistinct

Although Tilly emphasises the socially embedded nature of any violence, his typology still demarcates violence as a very distinct form of social interaction. Put differently, Tilly suggests that there is a specific logic of violence that is clearly recognisable, and that connects episodes as widely different as a brawl and genocide. Anthropologist Paul Richards takes a different view. Richards objects to the notion that violence is a distinct and different form of social interaction that can be clearly demarcated from other kinds. In fact, he argues that it is precisely the assumption of the specificity of violence that leads students of war and violence to 'take it out of its social context' (2005: 3). Instead, Richards argues that war and peace, violence and non-violence are profoundly intertwined and not even clearly recognisable as distinct social states. He writes: 'war is often . . . a state of mind shared among participants [and] "peace" can often be more violent and dangerous than "war"' (2005: 5). The agenda fostered by Richards' problematisation of the line demarcating peace from war, is to encourage students and researchers *not* to leave the study of violence to security experts. Instead, Richards wants to foster a research agenda which re-embeds violence into its social contexts, and asks detailed questions about when, how and why violence manifests itself as a social relation among other possible manifestations. What we learn from Richards, then, is the profoundly social nature of violent interaction and the difficulty of clearly locating the point at which politics becomes violence.

Joanna Bourke's argument in **Chapter 22** stresses the importance of examining violence as a cultural phenomenon. How similar is her position to that of Richards?

When politics becomes violent

If Richards is right and there is no clear turning point at which violence starts, how then should we think of the beginnings of war or violent conflict, and how do we conceptualise the moment at which violence becomes possible? If it sounds a little far-fetched to understand war – partly – as a state of mind, let's consider an analysis of the war that took place in Bosnia at the beginning of the 1990s. In his detailed reading of how it was possible for this scale of death and destruction to occur unexpectedly in Europe, David Campbell shows that dehumanisation discourses played a key role. The violence was rendered possible, in this analysis, when political discourses in Yugoslavia – at the end of decades of communist rule – started to identify different categories of citizen on the basis of ethnic and religious divides. Campbell (1998) shows that these ethnic and religious identities are not eternal or inherent characteristics of population groups, but are actively appealed, constructed and contested in specific social and historical contexts. The violent conflicts in Bosnia, then, were based on powerful political representations that cast particular social groups as inferior, unreliable and other. 'I understand now that nothing but "otherness" killed Jews, and it began by naming them, by reducing them to the other', as Campbell (1994: 455) quotes Croatian author Slavenka Drakulic, 'Then everything became possible. Even the worst atrocities like concentration camps or the slaughtering of civilians in Croatia or Bosnia.'

What happens to this question of a turning point if we challenge the notion that violence is fundamentally different from other types of social relations?

The way that identifying with – or being identified with – a particular group can lead to violence is examined in **Chapter 5**, and the violence in the former Yugoslavia is briefly discussed. **Chapter 22** shows how dehumanising the enemy makes it possible for soldiers to kill.

BOX 23.5 HANNAH ARENDT

FIGURE 23.6
Hannah Arendt. Photo: Tyrone Dukes/*New York Times* (1972).

Hannah Arendt (1906–1975) is one of the most influential political philosophers of the twentieth century. She was born in Hanover in Germany in 1906. Being of Jewish descent, she was forced to flee Germany in 1933 and moved to Paris. In 1941, after Paris had been captured by the Nazis, she moved to New York, where she became closely associated with the New School for Social Research (now part of the New School). She was active in various magazines and aid organisations throughout her life. In New York, she hosted philosophical discussion and became a public intellectual. A key theme in Arendt's philosophical work concerns the causes, histories and operating modes of totalitarian regimes. In the *Origins of Totalitarianism*, published in 1951, she analyses the histories of Nazi Germany and Stalinist Russia, and seeks to explore their governmental logics and popular appeal. In 1961, Arendt attended the trial of Nazi war criminal Albert Eichmann in Jerusalem, to report on it for the American magazine *The New Yorker*. In her reports of this trial, she sketched Eichmann not as a monstrous war criminal, but as an uninspiring bureaucrat who claimed just to be following orders. Arendt coined the phrase 'the banality of evil' to describe the technocratic rationality and bureaucratic procedures with which the evil of the Third Reich was executed. Eichmann became an example of this banality of evil. However, Arendt's book was very controversial, especially among some Jewish communities, where the argument was seen to distract from the horrors of the Nazi regime and the individual responsibility of the perpetrators.

Understood in this way, particular representational practices and social discourses are themselves violent. Violence is not defined only through physical force or injury, but through the power that renders othering possible and that creates the conditions of possibility for war or torture. Through his work, Campbell encourages students of violence to analyse the processes of political representation and dehumanisation that render violence possible and politically acceptable. At the basis of Campbell's research agenda is an ethical stance that challenges scholars to remain aware of their own responsiveness and responsibilities toward the other in their work.

Hannah Arendt has also analysed the complex question of violence. For Arendt, power is too often equated with force and violence, when in fact it is a completely different phenomenon, relying on different social processes. Arendt concluded from her studies that violence is not the *continuation* of politics (albeit by other means), as Clausewitz would have it, but the *opposite* of politics. In other words, violence occurs when political regimes lose their legitimacy and credibility. Only a regime that has lost all social support needs brute force to enforce its will. Despite the brutal display of violence, however, such a regime is politically weak, because it does not succeed in

Would Arendt's analysis provide an account of the events of the Arab Spring in 2011 or in Syria in 2013?

For a discussion of why we obey, see **Chapter 7**.

enforcing its will by law or persuasion. Violence is an expression of powerlessness, rather than power. She writes: 'Power and violence are opposites; where the one rules absolutely, the other is absent. Violence appears when power is in jeopardy' (1970: 155). There are two key aspects to Arendt's argument here. First, only a weak power needs to use a gun or cannon to enforce its will. A strong power, in contrast, would rule through authority and consensus building. Second, such a turn to violence can ultimately do nothing other than destroy the very regime that uses it, because it exposes that the power behind the violence has crumbled. The gun or cannon work only as long as the state is able to command them. 'When commands are no longer obeyed, the means of violence are of no use', writes Arendt (1970: 148), 'Everything depends on the power behind the violence.'

To summarise, this section has examined how different scholars understand the question of violence. For Clausewitz, violence is a continuation of politics by other means. Violence, in this understanding, represents the *means* toward political *ends*. This holds true in Tilly's analysis; Tilly nevertheless draws attention to the radically transformed global landscape of violence in the twentieth and early twenty-first centuries, where intra-state conflict, terrorism and civilian participation have become more common. As in our illustrative example, the difference between violence and non-violence, combatant and non-combatant, has become more difficult to draw. However, rather than reifying violence as a special category of human interaction, authors like Richards and Campbell alert us to the social, cultural and historical embeddedness of the conditions of possibility of violence. They urge us to study the political and discursive developments that render violence acceptable and attractive. For Arendt, on the other hand, violence occurs when power structures break down, and in fact only serves to expose the weakness of the regime that deploys it. Thus, Arendt argues that violence is not the continuation, but the very opposite of power.

BROADER ISSUES
VISIBLE AND INVISIBLE VIOLENCE

Foucault's work on power is discussed in **Chapters 7 and 11**, and his notion of problematisation in **Chapter 24**.

As we can see, both in thinking about violence and in the practical issues of how violent effects are produced, it is not at all easy to draw a clear line between violent and non-violent action – between violence and politics – nor between the apparently legitimate monopoly of violence of the state and the illegitimate violences of terrorism or insurgency. For Michel Foucault, it is not the case that war begins at the point where politics reaches its limit, but precisely that politics itself is deeply inscribed with the techniques and violences of war. In his famous 1976 lectures at the Collège de France, like Arendt turning Clausewitz's dictum on its head, Foucault argues that 'politics is the continuation of war by other means' (2003: 48). Over the historical period that saw the 'state acquire a monopoly on war', when the practices and institutions of war existed 'only as a violent relationship between states', a new and curious 'battlefront' opens up within society (Foucault 2003: 51). The appearance of the institutions, codes and rules of peace and security does not mean that 'war has been averted', for 'war continues to rage in all the mechanisms of power, even in the most regular. In the smallest of its cogs, peace is waging a secret war' (Foucault 2003: 50). Even where overt and visible warfare appears to be averted, and where the liberal institutions of the rule of law seem to prevail, Foucault reminds his audience, there is 'blood dried in the codes' in which 'we must hear the rumble of battle' (2003: 15; see also Lobo-Guerrero 2012; Neal 2004).

Why might Foucault's analysis matter for our understanding of problems such as the intertwined violences of targeted killing and targeted sanctions in the Afghanistan–Pakistan borderlands? In part, because it draws our attention to the everyday forms of violence that become the preconditions for bombing and killing. The recognition of friend from foe, safe from dangerous, us from them, ally from enemy that structures the power relations of war, understood through Foucault's approach, is present even in the smallest cogs of everyday experience. Alongside the visceral violences of the theatre of war, then, we would need to attend to the more ordinary ways in which the war-like dividing lines are drawn. How does the entire population of a region become understood as potentially harbouring terrorists? What kinds of processes of othering have to take place for the world to target a people, be it militarily or financially?

So, for example, the Foucauldian attention to the presence of violence in 'the smallest of cogs' can be seen in the work of Judith Butler, who has commented on how lives come to count, or not, as grievable lives whose loss might be registered on the visible surface of global politics:

Butler is well known for her influential work on gender and performativity, which is examined in **Chapter 5**. Her work on the grievability of lives is discussed further in **Chapter 28**.

> The question that preoccupies me in the light of recent global violence is, Who counts as human? Whose lives count as lives? And, finally, What makes a life grievable?
>
> (Butler 2004: 20)

From the photographic images of abuse in the Abu Ghraib prison in Iraq, to the Guantanamo detainees, Butler is concerned with the forms of violence that are intrinsic to the way that human subjects are dehumanised, such that multiple other violences can be acted upon them with impunity (see also Butler 2010). Similarly, and writing on the act of suicide bombing, the geographer Nigel Thrift extends the act of violence itself beyond the identification of a clear agent, a perpetrator and a victim, to consider violence as a set of relations that multiply, change and transform:

> I want to blur the edges of violence, by arguing that violence is not just the physical trauma of bullet penetrating body or fist impacting jaw or knife rending flesh or, indeed, bomb cutting a swathe through an unsuspecting street. Rather, it is a line of flight which is expanding its grip through the invention of new kinds of affective performance.
>
> (Thrift 2007: 276)

In these formulations violence does not end with destruction or death, or even with the end of a war, but instead it circulates and moves, produces new things, generates new affects and emotions.

And so, the less immediately visible violences that see war spilling over into the spaces of everyday life matter greatly to what is possible in global politics, to what can be said and done, and to what kind of response can be formulated. As we saw in the example of Pakistan, it is not only the visible and overt violence of the drone strikes that impede the capacity for a response to disaster, but the less visible violence of the stopping of money and financial blacklisting, that place limits on the world's response to suffering.

The philosopher Slavoj Žižek makes a distinction between what he calls the 'subjective violence' that appears as the 'violent perturbation of the normal state of things', and a more 'objective violence' that is the less visible systemic violence 'inherent to the normal state of things' (2008: 2). What does Žižek mean? For him, what comes to count as violence in global politics is that which makes a visible tear in the fabric of daily life – the act of terrorism, the loss of life on the city street – the subjective violence with its identifiable subjects and human agents, its 'evil individuals' (2008: 10). 'At the forefront of our minds', he writes, are 'the obvious signals of violence, acts of crime and terror'. However, we should 'disentangle ourselves' from these signals, in order to see better how violence pervades normality itself, and how everyday life contains within it objective violence. To attend to Žižek's forms of objective violence, then, we would

Slavoj Žižek's work is also discussed in **Chapter 7**.

BOX 23.6 SLAVOJ ŽIŽEK AND 9/11

FIGURE 23.7
Slavoj Žižek: Still from the movie *Žižek!*, directed by Astra Taylor, 71 mins, USA 2005. http://www.zizekthemovie.com/press/zizek_pointing_full.jpg

Contemporary Slovenian philosopher Slavoj Žižek has a distinctive approach to the question of violence, drawing on the influences of Marx, Hegel, and the psychoanalytical work of Jacques Lacan. Combining philosophical thought with commentary on popular culture and cinema, Žižek is interested in how it is that the world comes to be seen in a particular way, what is visible, what is invisible, what it is possible to say, and what is left unsayable. In the immediate aftermath of the events of 11 September 2001, Žižek's essay 'Welcome to the Desert of the Real' was circulated via the internet. Drawing on a famous line from the 1999 blockbuster film *The Matrix*, Žižek urged contemporaries to reflect on the political meaning of the attacks and the way in which this scale of destruction was – oddly – both completely unexpected and already pre-visioned many times in Hollywood movies and sensational news stories. In the essay, Žižek cautioned that instantaneous reactions and reprisals would only 'serve to avoid confronting the true dimension of what occurred on 11 September', urging a pause, a time for thinking. For Žižek such thought must avoid seeking an enemy outside of ourselves, looking instead for how we are implicated in that which we are against. As he concluded: 'Therein resides the true lesson of the bombings: the only way to ensure that it will not happen HERE again is to prevent it going on ANYWHERE ELSE' (Žižek 2001, available at http://www.theglobalsite.ac.uk/times/109zizek.htm).

need to consider how it is that a population becomes designated as 'risky or dangerous', how people come to represent threats to society. Representing a population as risky or dangerous is violent in itself.

How certain things or people come to be seen as dangerous is discussed further in **Chapter 24**.

In Kathryn Bigelow's 2009 film *The Hurt Locker* a US Army explosive ordnance disposal team confront the daily violences of the Iraq war. Sergeant First Class Will James leads his bomb disposal unit into an abandoned warehouse, where they find a body bomb in the corpse of a young boy. James' team, Sanborne and Eldridge, wait for him to detonate the charge on the body, making safe the stored explosives. But, when James sees the boy's body, he pauses, looks again more carefully at the face. 'I know this boy', he says, 'his name is Beckham, he sells DVDs'. For an instant, the lines that separate the bomb disposal team from the people of Iraq is breached – the body bomber has a name, a set of relationships with the soldiers to whom he sold DVDs. James changes his mind – he removes the explosives from the boy's body, closes his eyes, covers him with a cloth, and carries him from the building. Sanborne and Eldridge are concerned, asking 'do you think it really is the boy? James has been acting a little weird lately', and concluding that it could be anyone: 'they all look the same don't they'. For them the distance between them and the boy is not breached, he remains irrevocably other. But for James, the objective violences of 'us' and 'them' that made his war possible has shifted, he is shaken by the encounter.

It might be interesting to compare this discussion with the discussion of *Saving Private Ryan* in **Chapter 8**.

Bigelow's film illustrates vividly the ways in which violence is located not only in the visceral acts of the theatre of war, but also within the very conditions that make it possible. In fact, for Bigelow's protagonist James, in the absence of being closed off from the enemy, and without what Judith Butler calls dehumanisation, his task is no longer possible. As we have described in this chapter, the different approaches to understanding violence and politics have quite distinctive effects in terms of what kind of response can be formulated. Just as the people of the Afghanistan–Pakistan borderlands find themselves targeted as a risky and dangerous population, so Will James' team make clear that their war can only be fought against a distanced and dehumanised enemy. When contemporary violence is divided so starkly between the smart weaponry of the automated drone and the terrorism that is somehow beyond comprehension, it is perhaps more important than ever to consider the close proximity between these forms of violence.

Attempts to memorialise those killed in war are often also seen as resisting dehumanisation: see **Chapter 28**.

CONCLUSION

In this chapter we have explored the question of what counts as violence and whether it is possible to distinguish forms of violence from non-violence or from political violence. There is, of course, a straightforward response to the question, one that says 'well, yes, forms of violence are differentiated everywhere and all of the time'. Just as we showed in the example of the Iraq Inquiry and the justification for war, the capacity to distinguish a legitimate sphere of legal geopolitical decision from the apparently incomprehensible acts of terrorist violence is an ever present aspect of our world. But in this chapter we have encouraged you to think about what happens when such distinctions are made. In the examples we have discussed of the double targeting of the Afghanistan–Pakistan borderlands – as a site of drone strikes but also as a population whose links to the world's flows of money and aid are to be monitored – the political measures of FATF or of military strikes may not be possible without the representation of a place and a population who pose risks to the rest of the world. In this way, in response to the question of whether we can distinguish between different types of violence, we might conclude that there is no natural or pre-given distinction. Instead, the lines that are drawn in given situations are deeply political – they shape the world in which we live, having effects on lives and livelihoods, provoking some responses whilst quietly preventing other action from being taken.

FURTHER READING

American Civil Liberties Union (2009) *Blocking Faith, Freezing Charity: Chilling Muslim Charitable Giving in the 'War on Terrorism Financing'*, New York: ACLU.

This detailed report by the ACLU examines the war on terror's effects on charitable giving in the US, and documents the ways in which fundamental freedoms are being undermined by these developments.

Louise Amoore and Marieke de Goede (eds) (2008) *Risk and the War on Terror*, London: Routledge.

This edited collection brings together different authors who have examined the way in which new risk management techniques are used in the wake of 9/11, for example to sort and classify airport travellers according to scores of 'riskiness' in advance of their arrival at the border. In this way, the book analyses a lesser known face of the war on terror.

Hannah Arendt (1970) *On Violence*, New York: Harcourt Brace.

Arendt's discussion of the relationship between power, politics and violence is accessibly written and thought provoking.

David Campbell (1998) *National Deconstruction: Violence, Identity and Justice in Bosnia*, Minnesota: University of Minneapolis Press.

One of the most detailed studies of the Bosnian war available, this book offers new perspectives on violence and ethics.

Michel Foucault (1979) *Discipline and Punish: The Birth of the Prison*, New York: Vintage.

Foucault's work on the birth of the modern prison is accessibly written and reorients not just our understanding of crime and punishment, but the ways in which we understand power more broadly.

Moshin Hamid (2007) *The Reluctant Fundamentalist*, London: Hamish Hamilton.

This novel was shortlisted for the Booker Prize, and tells the story of a Pakistani student who studies and works in the US, but who starts to question his world in the wake of 9/11. It is a wonderful read that leaves the reader to question the intentions of the narrator, the values of the West, the place of violence and the meaning of fundamentalism.

Achille Mbembe (2003) 'Necropolitics', *Public Culture* 15, 1: 11–41.

In this essay Mbembe proposes the notion of necropolitics to refer to the many ways in which weapons are deployed in order to destroy people and populations, at the same time as peoples are subjected to conditions of life that are akin to what he calls 'death worlds'. He offers an important critique of Foucault's concept of biopower.

Michael J. Shapiro (2004) 'The Nation State and Violence', in Jenny Edkins, Veronique Pin-Fat and Michael Shapiro (eds) *Sovereign Lives: Power in Global Politics*, London: Routledge.

One of a compelling collection of essays on the specific forms taken by contemporary sovereign power, Shapiro's contribution cites a line from Wim Wenders' film *The End of Violence*: 'Define violence. You're making a movie about it. Shouldn't you know what it is?'

WEBSITES

http://dronewarsuk.wordpress.com/

Dronewars aims to be a key information resource on the use of drones. The site also has the transcripts of lectures on the subject, for example by Professor Richard Falk, an international relations scholar at Princeton for over 40 years.

http://www.fatf-gafi.org/

The website of the Financial Action Task Force (FATF) provides background details on why the tracking of financial transactions has become a key element of counter-terror. Perhaps most interesting are the pages on 'high risk' jurisdictions.

http://www.iraqinquiry.org.uk/

Available on this site are the full transcripts of the UK's Chilcot Inquiry on the Iraq war.

http://www.charityandsecurity.org/

This network offers information and campaigns on the ways in which financial regulations and the pursuit of terrorism financing affects charitable work around the world.

REFERENCES

Arendt, Hannah (1970) 'On Violence', in *Crises of the Republic*, New York: Harcourt Brace & Company.

Arendt, Hannah (2004) *Origins of Totalitarianism*, revised edition, New York: Schocken.

Blair, Tony (2010) Transcript of Evidence, 29 January, http://www.iraqinquiry.org.uk/media/45139/20100129-blair-final.pdf.

Butler, Judith (2004) *Precarious Life: The Powers of Mourning and Violence*, London: Verso.

——(2010) *Frames of War: When Is Life Grievable?* London: Verso.

Campbell, David (1994) 'The Deterritorialization of Responsibility: Levinas, Derrida, and Ethics After the End of Philosophy', *Alternatives* 19, 4: 455–83.

——(1998) *National Deconstruction: Violence, Identity and Justice in Bosnia*, Minnesota: University of Minneapolis Press.

Charity Commission UK (2009) *Inquiry Report: Palestinians Relief and Development Fund (Interpal)*, registered charity number 1040094, 27 February.

Christian Science Monitor (2010) 'US and UN Aid to Pakistan floods,' 11 August, http://www.csmonitor.com/Commentary/the-monitors-view/2010/0811/US-and-UN-aid-for-Pakistan-floods-It-helps-fight-Taliban-effects-of-global-warming.

Coward, Martin (2009) *Urbicide: The Politics of Urban Destruction*, London: Routledge.

Duffield, Mark (2007) *Development, Security and Unending War: Governing the World of Peoples*, Oxford: Polity Press.

Elden, Stuart (2009) *Terror and Territory: The Spatial Extent of Sovereignty*, Minneapolis: University of Minnesota Press.

FATF (2001) 'FATF Nine Special Recommendations', October, http://www.fatf-gafi.org/document/9/0,3746,en_32250379_32236920_34032073_1_1_1_1,00.html.

——(2009) Chairman's Summary, Paris Plenary, 14–16 October, http://www.fatf-gafi.org/document/11/0,3343,en_32250379_32236836_43898507_1_1_1_1,00.html.

Filkins, Dexter and Souad Mekhennet (2006) 'The Money Trail: Pakistani Charity under Scrutiny', *New York Times*, 14 August, http://www.nytimes.com/2006/08/14/world/europe/14plot.html.

Foucault, Michel (2003) *Society Must be Defended: Lectures at the Collège de France 1975–76*, London: Penguin.

Graham, Stephen (2010) *Cities Under Siege: The New Military Urbanism*, London: Verso.

Hamid, Mohsin (2010) 'The Real Problem in the Afghan War Is India, Pakistan and Kashmir', *Washington Post*, 8 August, http://www.washingtonpost.com/wp-dyn/content/article/2010/08/06/AR2010080602658.html.

Howell, Jude and Jeremy Lind (2009) *Counter-Terrorism, Aid and Civil Society: Before and After the War on Terror*, Basingstoke: Palgrave.

Hülsse, Rainer and Dieter Kerwer (2007) 'Global Standards in Action: Insights from Anti-Money Laundering Regulation', *Organization* 14, 5: 625–42.

Islamic Relief (2009) interview with representatives, Birmingham, May 2009.

Kaldor, Mary (2007) *Old and New Wars*, Stanford, CA: Stanford University Press.

——(2010) 'Inconclusive Wars: Is Clausewitz Still Relevant in these Global Times?' *Global Policy* 1, 3: 271–81.

Lobo-Guerrero, Luis (2012) *Insuring War: Sovereignty, Security and Risk*, London: Routledge.

MacFarquhar, Neil (2010) 'Aid for Pakistan Lags, UN Warns', *New York Times*, 18 August.

Mahon, Rianne and Stephen McBride (2009) 'Standardising and Disseminating Knowledge: The Role of the OECD in Global Governance,' *European Political Science Review* 1, 1: 83–101.

Mohammad, Robina (2008) 'Pakistan – An Ungovernable Space?' *Environment and Planning D: Society and Space* 26: 571–81.

Mohammad, Robina and James Sidaway (2010) 'Stalingrad in the Hindu Kush? AFPAK, Crucibles and Chains of Terror', *Antipode* 43: 199–204.

Neal, Andrew (2004) 'Cutting Off the King's head: Foucault's Society Must Be Defended and the Problem of Sovereignty', *Alternatives: Global, Local, Political* 29, 4: 373–98.

Richards, Paul (2005) 'New War: An Ethnographic Approach', in Paul Richards (ed.) *No Peace, No War: An Anthropology of Contemporary Armed Conflicts*, Oxford: James Currey.

Thrift, Nigel (2007) 'Immaculate Warfare? The Spatial Politics of Extreme Violence', in Derek Gregory and Alan Pred (eds) *Violent Geographies: Fear, Terror and Political Violence*, London: Routledge.

Tilly, Charles (2002) 'Violence, Terror, and Politics as Usual', *Boston Review*, Summer Issue, http://bostonreview.net/BR27.3/tilly.html.

——(2003) *The Politics of Collective Violence*, Cambridge: Cambridge University Press.

United Nations (2010) *Report of the Special Rapporteur on Extrajudicial, Summary or Arbitrary Executions, Philip Alston*, http://www2.ohchr.org/english/bodies/hrcouncil/docs/14session/A.HRC.14.24.Add6.pdf.

Valverde, Mariana and Michael Mopas (2004) 'Insecurity and the Dream of Targeted Governance', in Wendy Larner and William Walters (eds) *Global Governmentality: Governing International Spaces*, London: Routledge.

von Clausewitz, Carl (1873 [1832]) *On War*, London: N. Trübner.

Walzer, Michael (2004) *Arguing About War*, New Haven, CT: Yale University Press.

Weber, Max (2004) 'Politics as Vocation', in David Owen and Tracy Strong (eds) *The Vocation Lectures*, Indianapolis: Hackett.

Zehfuss, Maja (2011) 'Targeting: Precision and the Production of Ethics', *European Journal of International Relations* 17, 3: 543–66.

Žižek, Slavoj (2008) *Violence*, London: Profile Books.

For a range of further resources supporting this chapter, please visit the companion website for *Global Politics, 2nd Edition* at www.routledge.com/cw/edkins/

CHAPTER 24

What makes the world dangerous?

Michael Dillon

THE QUESTION LIVING DANGEROUSLY?

Let's begin by breaking up this question into its two constituent questions. We can ask: '*Why* are things dangerous?' But we can also ask: '*How* do things become dangerous?'

Every time you ask a *why* question you run the danger of ending up lost in a kind of essentialism. What that means is that you become committed to a process of regressing backwards to the foundation or origin of things in the hope of finding a point beyond which you need regress no further. Asking questions of the world in this way – the world of politics especially – launches you on a kind of quest; the quest to get to the essence of things. Once you have found the holy grail (of the essence of things), the quest resolves itself into a mere technical business of showing how, because the essence of things is essentially like this (whatever that might be), then life is the way that it is: in this instance dangerous. Asking why is a time honoured way of proceeding. But I think there is a better one. The better one is to ask the *how* question.

This problem is discussed in **Chapter 2**. An example of this type of thinking is the way people put things down to 'human nature'. See also **Chapters 5 and 7**.

In this instance, the *how* question asks, how does the world become dangerous? Asking the *how* question does not mean that you do not address essential questions to do with the nature of things. You can and you do. But you approach them from a different direction. Things always become dangerous in specific historical ways. The *how* question focuses on how they do so. That is why I think that it is a better way of proceeding. You start with the specificity of things, first, and this allows you to put essentialist arguments in their place: which is always a historical place.

In the process of asking and answering the *how* question in respect of danger, you will also discover that part of the answer to how things become dangerous is because people insist on a certain essential commitment to, or express a faith in, the essence of things. Within every process of becoming dangerous, historically, certain essentialist beliefs will be operating. But so also will many other local, historical, technical, scientific matters as well as the accidents of pure contingency; events that have nothing, it seems, to do with the security and defence policy making that are privileged areas of dealing with danger in global politics, but nonetheless impact upon them just the same.

Chapter 18 shows how construing the financial crisis in a particular way silences other ways of thinking, **Chapter 23** argues that identifying the Afghanistan–Pakistan border area as 'risky' enables certain types of violence, and **Chapter 2** discusses the effect ways of thinking have on our actions in the world in broader terms.

This chapter therefore proceeds by foregrounding 'how' things become dangerous, but it also directs attention to the background of essentialist beliefs – known as ontologies – that are always already also present in all the different ways of construing the world as a dangerous place and talking about what makes the world a dangerous place and what ought to be done about it.

One final introductory point is necessary. The chapter takes the transformation of US strategic policy that occurred during the 1990s and first decade of the new century as its example. It does so for several reasons. First, this new military strategic discourse was part of the US response to the end of the Cold War. It transformed military strategic perceptions of global danger. Second, the example is a good one because it concerns how a whole new military strategic architecture of perceiving and acting upon danger was fashioned in the US during the course of the last 20 years. Finally, network-centric warfare provides a good illustration because while it appeared to be driven by the techno-scientific transformation known as the information revolution that took place during the course of the same period, this revolution itself was a vehicle for transforming essential beliefs about the very nature of material reality. Material reality came to be described in both informational and biological terms precisely because all life was said to be, 'essentially', a matter of information. Networking not only became a new, or newly emphasised, technique, it also became an ontology. If you see the world comprised of networks operating as a network you will see danger differently, and act accordingly.

The Cold War is discussed in **Chapter 26**.

Other instances where changes in technology seemed to be driving what happens are discussed in **Chapters 9, 11 and 23**. But do changes in technology come first, or is technological change itself the result of social change?

In providing an interrogation of how we become what we are taught to fear, what follows reinforces the point by showing how, in the specific instance of network-centric warfare, the US military was taught to fear dangers in global politics differently so that it could fight global wars differently. After 9/11 this transformation of security and war policymaking impacted as much on the civil and domestic structures of the countries of the entire North Atlantic rim as it did on their global military adventures.

What happened on 9/11 is described in **Chapter 23**.

One way or another, whether in fact you begin by asking why or by asking how, danger goes to the heart of what we essentially think we are, how we are historically shaped into what we are, and what we want to become. The politics of global danger is both a politics of truth as well as a politics of identity.

ILLUSTRATIVE EXAMPLE
NETWORK-CENTRIC WARFARE

In the twenty-first century, those calling for peace in the name of the radical interdependence of humankind find themselves making very similar arguments about the networked character of our civilisation to those made by new military strategic theorists in the United States who, after the collapse of the Cold War, invented a new form of war called network-centric warfare (Cebrowski and Garstka 1998; Alberts *et al.* 1999). What they share is recognition of the networked character of our global civilisation and the ways in which that networking has become central to our economic and social well-being and to questions of peace and security.

Danger both civil and military is now widely conceived in networked terms. One good, militarised example of this is the network-centric warfare that came out of the US led Revolution in Military Affairs (RMA) of the 1990s. In the process of summarising it, I will also say something about contemporary problematisations of networked danger in terms of terror and the threat posed by other civil contingencies such as social breakdown or the disruption of critical national infrastructures like power, finance, information, transportation, water, food and health systems. The information and biological revolutions problematised danger differently and changed the how as well as the what of global danger.

When something is *thought of* as a problem, it is 'problematised': it *becomes* a problem. The chapter returns to the notion of problematisation later.

Revolution in military affairs

From the 1980s onwards military equipment and military strategic thinking alike began to respond to the information and communication revolution that was revolutionising industrial production and social and cultural life in the western world (Mathews and Treddenick 2001). The claim was made that the impact of the information and communication revolution on military affairs has brought about what was first called a Military Technical Revolution (MTR), now more popularly referred to as a Revolution in Military Affairs (RMA). This RMA referred to two things: equipment and thinking. The second of these is I think even more important than the first.

FIGURE 24.1
A reflective view of the Blue Force Tracker (BFT) networking tool. Northrop Grumman Corp

Equipment

Informationalisation of weapon systems

The RMA referred to the very many ways in which the information and communication revolution has transformed military equipment. In popular terms we have become familiar with guided missiles, smart bombs that find their own ways to the target, and the ability to fight 24/7 irrespective of weather and daylight. We now know also that to light-up the enemy in electronic terms means you can destroy the enemy with near certainty. Just as weapons were revolutionised through the information revolution, so also were military communication systems. These are now global and local. They critically depend upon what the US military calls the global information grid which, with the

Chapter 23 talks about drone warfare.

Note that the suggestion that you can destroy the enemy with near certainty says nothing about whom else you might kill in the process.

FIGURE 24.2
Airmen with the 67th Network Warfare Wing monitor internet activity to maintain security of Air Force computer networks at Lackland Air Force Base, Texas. Photo: Master Sgt Jack Braden Courtesy of US Air Force

aid of communication satellites, now covers the world with a fine information net or mesh through which the coordination of large- and small-scale military operations now depends (Libicki 2000).

We can summarise the impact of the information and communication revolution on military equipment in terms of what I want to call 'the informationalisation of weapon and communication systems'. The counterpart of the informationalisation of weapons has, however, also been 'the weaponisation of communication and information'.

Weaponisation of communication and information

Just as information has become critical to the performance of weapon systems and their allied command, control and communication systems, so also therefore has information become a new domain of war. Precisely because military and other systems are themselves so dependent upon information, information itself has become weaponised. Here we are not simply referring to the traditional use of information for the purposes of political and military propaganda. We are referring instead to the ways in which information systems themselves are used against other information systems, for example, in that new form of war called 'cyberwar'. Informationalising weapons impacted also on the exercise of military command. To explore this and related changes such as those affecting operational military concepts and doctrines, as well as the training of military personnel, we have to move to the second most important feature of the RMA: changes in how the military think about the world.

Military thinking

In many respects we can say that these changes were concerned with the impact of information and communication on military equipment. The second and perhaps even more profound impact of the revolution in information and communications on the military has been a change not only in equipment but also in cognition. By that I simply mean that it has changed the military view of the world. It is the job of militaries to view the world in terms of danger. The question, once more, is to begin by asking, how do they now view the world in terms of danger? The answer is that they do so comprehensively now in network terms and, increasingly, also through concepts and metaphors which they take from the life sciences, such as biology. Here is how.

What has changed is the military's picture of the world, in the terms used in **Chapter 2**.

Network thinking

Network-centric thinking is consciously modelled on fundamental changes that have taken place in the American and in the global capitalist economy. These draw their inspiration not simply from the revolution in information and communication technology, but also from the molecular revolution in biology. What the revolution in

For more on the changes in communication technology see **Chapter 9**.

BOX 24.1 NETWORK-CENTRIC WARFARE

The single most important architect of this transformation of military cognition was an American, Admiral Arthur Cebrowski. It was Cebrowski who virtually invented the term network-centric warfare (NCW) in a leading article published in the 1990s in the *United States Naval Institute Proceedings*. NCW became the official military doctrine of the US in 2002. Almost all the basic ideas are contained in Cebrowski's essay. Cebrowski then went on to head a new Pentagon Office of Force Transformation (OFT), tasked with carrying this revolution in cognition throughout the American military. Championed by the then secretary of state for defense, Donald Rumsfeld, the RMA suffered a setback with the political and military reversals of the Iraq War. However much these may have arrested the ideological fervour with which the RMA and NCW were subsequently promoted, they have not materially affected the reorganisation of military training deployment, war-fighting and war-thinking that was inaugurated through NCW by the RMA.

FIGURE 24.3 Admiral Arthur Cebrowski

information and communication technology shares with the revolution in molecular biology is a reduction of material reality to 'code': information code for ICT (Information and Communications Technology) and genetic code for molecular biology (Dillon 2002 and 2004). Here a convergence of thinking based on the overarching idea of code fuels new ways of doing business and of construing danger in organic or biological ways. Network has become a key term of art for both business and the military since it is also a key term of art in the communication and information as well as in the life sciences.

Traditional geo-political thinking begins with bodies – like states – and then moves to how relations are transacted between these bodies. Network thinking reverses the flow. It thinks first in terms of relations and then about how relations shape the nature of bodies. It therefore emphasises interconnectedness, the means by which interconnectedness is formed, what travels down the channels of interconnection, the speed of interconnection and, more generally the new creative opportunities associated with exploiting interconnectedness.

There is a corresponding emphasis on the dangers that interconnectedness may also create; metaphors of disease and contagion, and of security in terms of immunity and resilience, also abound. Danger is seen in viral terms as something that is able to work on the body because of the ways in which it is also part of the body, whether the body is seen as the biological body or the corporate, social or military body. Security and war in the information age thus came to be thought in ways more akin to epidemiology, the science of pathology and disease management, or of surgical intervention. Threats arising within the system, in consequence of the very network character of the system, rather than merely posed from outside the system, came to prominence. Just as the individual biological body came to be understood in terms of complex adaptive networks of informational exchange governed in molecular terms by genetic code, then, so also did the (US) military body increasingly understand itself in terms of complex adaptive informational exchange networks as well.

What is a threat to some, may be an opportunity to someone else. Note how the networked character of information technology is thought to have enabled the protests collectively known as the Arab Spring: see **Chapter 9**.

Network operations were thereby claimed to deliver the same powerful advantages to the US military that they produced for American businesses, and global capital more generally. In network-centric warfare doctrine, information, speed, self-synchronisation and flexibility were said to be at a premium just as they remain so in the management ideology of global capitalism.

This elevation of information did not simply open up new enterprises for the military as it did for business – information warfare and digitised battlespaces for the military, e-commerce and so on for business. Neither did it mean that information was only a force multiplier, as the military say, increasing the fire-power and effectiveness of traditional weapon systems. Information was embraced as the new principle of formation – the 'prime mover' was the expression used by two of the RAND Corporation's most prolific information and network-centric warfare theorists (Arquilla and Ronfeldt 1997; Dillon and Reid 2009). No longer were military formations conceived as rallying around the flag. They rallied around – they were rallied through – information networks.

The strategic debate

Network-centric warfare became official US military strategic doctrine in May 2000 with the publication of the Pentagon's 'Joint Vision 2020'. Joint Vision 2020 committed

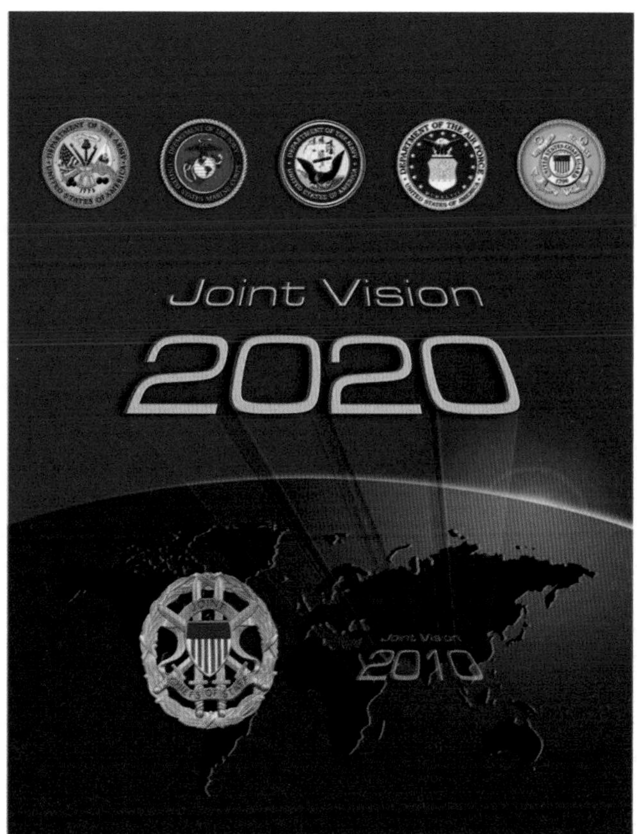

FIGURE 24.4
Joint Vision 2020 from http://www.dtic.mil/future jointwarfare/. Public domain

the US to what the document called 'Full Spectrum Dominance'. Claiming to look ahead to 2020, the document was clearly also aspiring to a military capable of 'perfect vision' and 'real-time' control to achieve what the document called 'Information Superiority' and 'Full Spectrum Dominance'. Joint Vision 2020 expressed a radically new military imperial vision. Empires are, however, also built on fear as much as they are on lust for control. They are about danger as much as they are about power. Even prior to 9/11 and because of the new military strategic logic that it had adopted, fearing every virtuality as well as every actuality, US military doctrine came to seek a form of global control through forces capable of continuous adaptation and transformation according to changing global threats.

There has been no revolution in military affairs alone. The RMA was the military face of the revolution in global affairs brought about in particular by the coincidence of the fall of the Soviet Union and the revolutionary digitalisation of information and communication technology. Thus the RMA was only as much an American way of war, as capitalism is an American way of making a living. Everybody got in on the act. Not least terrorist networks. For nothing was better designed to send such a powerful, threatening and radically disruptive message around the world's political and military communications networks than the bloody spectacle they engineered on 11 September 2001.

In colloquial terms '20/20 vision' refers to perfect vision: at 20 feet from the optician's chart, a person is able to read the lowest line of letters. The metric equivalent is 6/6 vision

For more on the problem of imperialism see **Chapters 16 and 21**.

The fall of the Soviet Union meant the end of the Cold War: see **Chapter 26**.

For a discussion of capitalism in the global political economy see **Chapter 17**.

Changing conceptions of the battlespace

For a discussion of the importance of territory see **Chapter 11**.

Traditional forms of conquest, as well as traditional measures of national capability, land or raw materials, for example, receded in significance under the logics and rationales of network-centric warfare. They did not disappear. But they became complexly related with these new discourses of threat, danger and war to form an ever more challenging global landscape of civil–military power relations.

Network forces are not designed to mobilise, march to the front or conduct mass frontal assaults or landings. Galvanised by information and intelligence garnered through the critical global infrastructures of surveillance and communication systems, employing informationalised weapon systems and weaponised information systems, network forces are supposed to swarm in combined arms and, together with hired locals, gather and disperse in different volumes and formations, combinations and directions. Consider, for example, the assassination of Osama Bin Laden. The duration of hostilities threatens to be just as indeterminate as the new battlespace.

War – the war on terror in particular – thus threatens to become infinite, while danger is seen in every aspect of our networked world (Reid 2007; Dillon and Reid 2009). It has also become big business since much of the military and security business that it has created is privately conducted. Danger is of course always big business; all our most powerful truth telling institutions – churches, states, media and corporations – claim a part of it and live well off it (Shearer 1998).

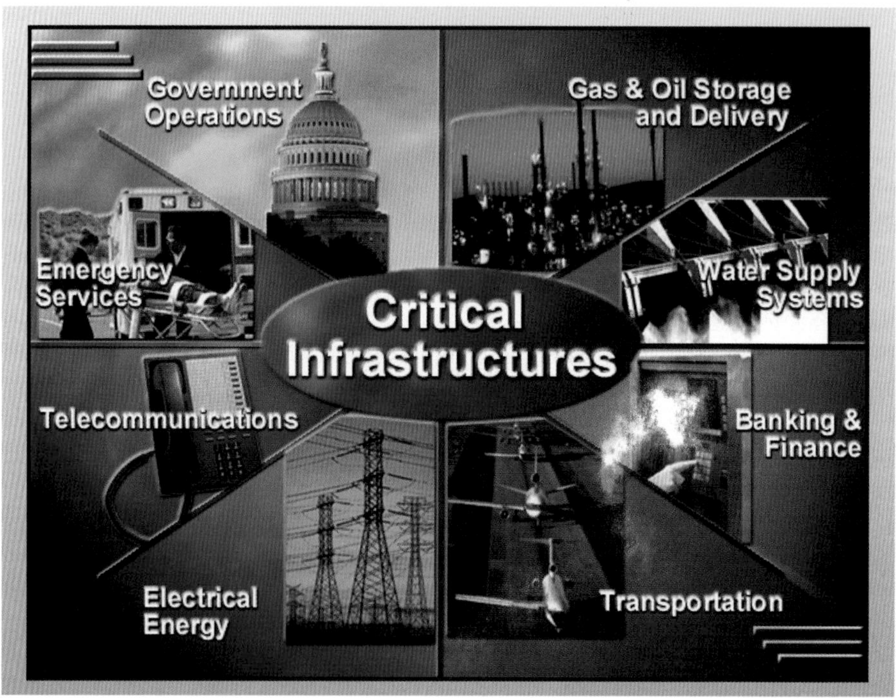

FIGURE 24.5
Critical Infrastructures. From 'Information Technology Research for Critical Infrastructure Protection', Shankar Sastry *et al.*, Summary of NSF/OSTP workshop, 19–20 September 2002

Most interesting and disturbing of all, however, is how the question of who or what is the enemy has been re-problematised. For in a networked world of danger everyone and everything is potentially dangerous and potentially therefore also the enemy. Distinguishing friend from enemy becomes a permanent full time occupation and it is moreover conducted within radical uncertainty of detecting who is friend and who is foe. Who looks to be friendly now, and who may turn into an enemy at some future date. From the perspective of network-centric warfare, particularly that practised now in the war on terror, it is no longer simply a matter of what makes the world dangerous, it is a matter of everything being in a virtual state of becoming-dangerous (Dillon 2007).

GENERAL RESPONSES
THINKING IN TERMS OF STRATEGY AND SECURITY

Defence, security and strategic studies

Global questions concerning danger and defence were once the preserve of the disciplines of security and strategic studies. These told us where danger lay, what things we should be frightened of, and where the solution to dealing with those fears could be found. They were able to do this because they once championed a very clear and relatively unopposed interpretation of global politics. In particular they claimed to understand political reality and they called themselves Realists (Molloy 2006). There are, however, different ways of interpreting reality, just as there are different ways of problematising danger. People inhabit different realities and so they also fear different things. Problematisations of the real are intimately related to problematisations of danger. Tell me what you think is real and I will tell you what you fear.

People operating within different language games inhabit different realities. See **Chapter 2**.

Realists said that the world was inhabited by agents. This agent, or subject, could be a collective or an individual human entity. It could be you or me or it could be a state or a nation. It didn't much matter because the subject was said to operate in more or less the same rationally self-interested way whether or not it was conceived as an individual or collective entity. Global politics was said to consist in such rationally self-interested behaviour. This did not prevent cooperation and collaboration. It simply meant that such collaboration was said to be goal-centred and self-interested as well. If it did not work out then resort to war was ultimately legitimate.

At least in international law, this right of states to make war was progressively restricted in the twentieth century. Massification, industrialisation and nuclearisation of war had raised the cost of war. Liberal thinking designed to bring war under the rule of law also became more influential. These developments did not end war. They merely changed the ways in which states legitimated their resort to war. Consider for example the odium that still surrounds the way in which US president George W. Bush and British prime minister Tony Blair resorted to war against Iraq without the sanction of the United Nations. Note also that lack of international legitimation that they insisted upon for everyone else did not prevent them from waging war without international legal sanction themselves.

For a description of how this works in liberal economics and the thinking of Adam Smith see **Chapter 17**.

Since Einstein's work on relativity and the ideas of quantum mechanics, physicists no longer think of time and space in the Newtonian way they used to. Time does not run at the same rate everywhere, for example, and the world is ultimately unpredictable: general laws no longer apply, and experimental observations change the thing they try to observe.

Environmental thinking sometimes retains this focus on human futures and human needs: **Chapter 3**.

Strategy is the study of the way subjects were said to calculate their goal driven behaviour. It had a lot of affinity with other disciplines like economics, which also presumed that the world was populated by such rationally calculating subjects. The strategist's subject of choice was the state rather than the corporation or firm. What these and other disciplines also shared was a way of understanding the structure of the real (ontology) and acquiring knowledge about it (epistemology).

Ontologically, the real, was said to be out there, existing independently of us. Epistemologically it was also said, however, that the real was comprised of intelligible laws that were accessible, in addition, to certain scientific ways of accessing them. The real was in short readable. Realists and strategists were preoccupied with telling us how to read it, especially where questions of global danger were concerned. This was a Newtonian universe in which there was one reality governed by one set of laws irrespective of time and place.

Hence what traditional security and strategic studies taught about the fear, danger and politics which motivated their so-called rational subject reflected this view of the world. Note incidentally how anthropocentric (human-centred) these concerns were. The planet didn't figure. Neither did other species. They only figure now in as much as they add additional issues to the strategic agendas of rationally calculating subjects. The world remains for them a space for rational subjects to use and abuse in pursuit of their interests. Since the essential nature of state behaviour globally was said to be as fixed as the laws of motion, the issue for such Realists was reduced to polishing up the mirror they held to reality so as to get as clear a reflection as they thought possible. States would be endangered if they forgot or operated in ignorance of the laws reflected back in this representation of the real.

This view of the real and of the world of global danger associated with it – of goal driven states pursuing conflicting ambitions up to the point of war if necessary – suffuses our entire culture because it is based upon a widely shared view of human beings as more or less rationally calculating subjects. Traditional security studies taught this modern way of understanding the real and its dangers; such as those of not calculating your self-interests wisely. In doing so they also claimed to be able to better educate subjects because these generally seemed to be incompetent at being rational and in need therefore of such education.

But even as it attained its apogee, this account of the real was being undermined from within the very establishments which had encouraged and propagated it – the United States Department of Defense, the US armed forces and their teaching and training establishments. That challenge came in the form not simply of network-centric warfare but through the wider philosophy which underpinned this form of warfare. That philosophy was the philosophy of 'transformation' enshrined in the Pentagon's Office of Force Transformation (OFT); established in 2001 but broken up in 2006 with the fall of its patron Donald Rumsfeld.

Part of the venom which surrounds the debate about network-centric warfare, and which once surrounded Rumsfeld and the OFT, is precisely the fact that network-centric warriors were propagating a different understanding of the real. They precipitated an internecine fight about the nature of the real as such. On the one side were the old geo-political warriors, schooled in Newtonian physics, Realism and the official history of peoples, states and fear proclaiming universal laws going back to the ancient Greeks

FIGURE 24.6
Donald Rumsfeld as US Defense Secretary.
AP Photo/Evan Vucci

and Romans. On the other side were those schooled in cybernetics, information systems, communications theory and molecular biology. These proclaimed a more bio-political reality comprised of complex adaptive systems which change their very nature as they behave in co-evolutionary ways with other systems. On the one hand, then, were the old geo-politicians for whom someone or some body – a sovereign of some description – had to be in charge of things. On the other were the newer, let's call them bio-philosophers relying on the idea of the evolution and co-evolution of complex adaptive systems capable of ordering themselves without anyone being in charge, or being sovereign: capitalism was a prime example.

For more on the problems with the idea of someone being sovereign or 'in charge' see **Chapters 7 and 28**.

Critical security thinking

If, however, the world does operate according to simple universal laws irrespective of time and place, laws that people had to learn and obey, how come people required so much Realist education to understand this? The answer could not simply be that people are ignorant and stupid. They have been around for a long time and, if the rules of 'the real' were that simple, word would have got around. A seed of doubt arises here. Perhaps the world is not merely how Realists describe it. Perhaps the real that the Realists proclaimed was just that: something that Realists proclaimed. Perhaps the real which Realists claimed to understand was not only different from the way they understood it, but perhaps it also required different means of understanding to appreciate what 'the real' was like in ways that the Realists could not understand given their ways of looking at the world. What was at issue, in other words, was not simply the material nature of reality but the means of apprehending that reality: truth and knowledge.

However much 'the real' stands obdurately outside and independent of us, and it does, it is not possible to escape the fact that our experience of the world is necessarily always mediated through the means we have of understanding, interpreting and communicating our different accounts of what the world is like. Even Realists sometimes admitted this. Where they refused to do so, their network-centric warfare counterparts had already sold the pass on them 'ontologically' and 'epistemologically'. By that I mean network-centric thinking understands the nature of reality (ontology) to be different, just as it deals with different ways of knowing that reality (epistemology). Realism's credentials were undermined from within where they had once been so powerfully accredited. The game of Realism began to die where it had once been so alive, at the centre of the US military machine.

If all this was so – and it was – then perhaps the reality which the Realists proclaimed was not as universal and uniform as they said that it was. If there are different ways of accessing the real, and of course there are as the examples of physics and biology indicate, then perhaps there are different experiences of the real as well. And if there are different experiences of the real then it follows that there are necessarily also different experiences of danger than those taught us through the (un)truth-telling practices of the Realists.

Here, then, was the Achilles heel of traditional security and strategic studies. It was a fundamental weakness which many critical security studies students began to probe (Booth 2005). There are different schools of critical security studies but they shared at least these three basic positions.

First they challenged the role which the goal-driven subject played in traditional strategic and security studies. There the subject was supposed to come pre-formed unaffected by its terms and conditions of life, just expressing a universal commitment to goal-driven self-interested behaviour. Critical security studies did not deny that humans can be self-interested or goal-driven and so on. They did, however, point out how much this behaviour had to be learnt, how much it was conditioned. In other words they argued that the goal driven subject did not pre-exist the power relations, historical conditioning and learnt behaviour that made the subject of security and strategic studies the subject it was said to be. In other words the 'Realist' nation or state seeking security was very much itself a function or outcome of traditional defence and security practices (Campbell 1998).

Second, they observed that there was more than one way of accessing the real. Knowledge is plural, not single. It is itself also a form of critical practice in which knowledge changes over time.

Third, they maintained that an intimate relation exists between knowledge and power. Realists too understood that knowledge could be a form of power. But they denied that their own truth-telling knowledge was a form of power, and appealed to the idea instead that their knowledge was a disinterested representation of the real. Critical analysts pointed out that wherever there was knowledge a form of power was also at work. Michel Foucault coined the term power/knowledge to make this point. In other words they introduced a note of suspicion into the very idea of disinterested knowledge because it was perfectly evident that truth-telling practices, better to use the ambivalent expression (un)truth-telling practices, are one of the single most important instruments of power. Equally, it was perfectly evident also that that truth-telling practices represent an enormously powerful force in how we live our lives, and even in how we imagine life to be. All knowledge is interested: it is invested with perspective. That does not disqualify it as knowledge. It just teaches us to be more circumspect about knowledge-claims, and always to ask who makes them, who gains and who loses in the advance of certain knowledge-claims and so on. We have, in particular, to get savvy about the power/knowledge games – the truth and un-truth telling practices – that teach us how to secure ourselves and what we ought to fear.

For more about Foucault see **Chapters 4, 7, 11 and 23**.

Robert Cox also argues that theories always imply a perspective: see **Chapter 1**.

There are always power and political implications to the pursuit of knowledge. Equally, however, there is always some kind of knowledge at stake in the practices of power and politics as well. Whatever claims are therefore made about the nature of the real, those claims may be made in the language of truth but they will always cash out also in the language of politics and power as well. There are different kinds of truths, different kinds of truth-telling practices and different kinds of truth-tellers.

BROADER ISSUES
UNKNOWN UNKNOWNS

Donald Rumsfeld was appointed US Secretary of State for Defense in January 2001. The White House announced his resignation immediately after the Republican Party losses in the Congressional Elections of November 2006. Rumsfeld was the great political patron of the RMA, proponent of network-centric warfare and ideologue of the doctrine of transformation. Despite his fall from grace, US military strategic discourse and posture had been changed irreversibly in the previous ten years.

Rumsfeld was also widely reviled and parodied for his use of the jargon of network-centric warfare and of force transformation. Apart from justified political opposition to the decisions he was making while defense secretary, such as the invasion of Iraq, the way he expressed himself provoked outrage and laughter because his language expressed a different understanding of the real. Incidentally it was still spoken on behalf of a traditional understanding of the real as well; that of US geopolitical imperial interests. In consequence it contained many contradictions. But contradiction is characteristic of politics, especially security politics. It is often the fuel that drives it. Seeking security,

There is more about the Iraq war in **Chapters 8 and 28**.

BOX 24.2 THE RUMSFELD DOCTRINE

THE UNKNOWN

As we know,
There are known knowns.
There are things we know we know.
We also know
There are known unknowns.
That is to say
We know there are some things
We do not know.
But there are also unknown unknowns,
The ones we don't know
We don't know.

(Donald Rumsfeld, 12 February 2002, Department of Defense news briefing)

Mutual Assured Destruction – or MAD – was the name given to the nuclear posture during the Cold War in which the United States threatened to annihilate the Soviet Union in the event that it should use nuclear weapons against it, even though this would have meant that the Soviet Union would have responded by annihilating the US in turn.

for example, we very often increase the dangers to which we are exposed (consider the case of the balance of terror struck by the nuclear doctrine of Mutual Assured Destruction). Contradictions also afford the gap, however, through which critique enters.

Rumsfeld's reflections, in news briefings especially, spoke of a world of understanding that was relatively novel to defence and security specialists; as well as to America's and the world's press corps. It was an understanding of the real that has in fact, however, been around for a long time. It, too, goes back to the Greeks, but its teaching had long fallen out of use, especially in the study of international relations and strategy. It has been resurrected and refurbished (given modern expression) in the new language of military strategic transformation and change. Rumsfeld's most notorious reflections on it, repeated here, had an almost poetic quality, which is why I record them as a poem.

They nonetheless contain some profound insights, especially about how we moderns problematise danger. I want to end this chapter by drawing out those insights. I especially want to draw attention to three closely related points. First, what Rumsfeld's 'poetry' teaches us about the modern reliance upon knowledge to problematise and deal with danger. Second, what his reflections teach us about the intimate modern alliance of power and knowledge (power/knowledge) when problematising danger. Third, what Rumsfeld's insistence on the significance of 'unknown unknowns' teaches us about how 'uncertainty' has drifted back into the very epicentre of our problematisation of fear and danger (Cilliers 1998). It is this in particular which calls into question knowledge's capacity to deal with the 'unknown unknowns' which now dominate our global/local landscapes of fear and danger: the unintended consequences, the strategic surprises, the bolts from the blue, the things perhaps to which the very light of our techno-scientific knowledge actually blinds us. In short all that 'shit' which we are unable to see but which Forrest Gump in the 1994 movie says happens and with whose often terrible consequences we are always going to have to deal.

Perfect vision

Recall that the document which authorised network-centric warfare as the military strategic doctrine of the US Armed Forces was, however, entitled 'Joint Vision 2020'. Titles like this should always be taken seriously. Experts spend a lot of time crafting them, and they always give away more than they intend. The 'Joint' in the title obviously refers to the interdependence of land, sea, air and other forces in the US military – joint commands, combined operations and so on. But it was also very clearly meant to invoke connectedness in general – the doctrine of networks as such. Equally, Joint Vision 2020 was not only looking forward 20 years to the year 2020. Again it was clearly invoking another idea; that which opticians refer to as 20/20 vision by which they mean 'perfect vision'.

Perfect vision is ordinarily associated politically only with hindsight. Only by looking back, it is said, can we see clearly how things really were. But what network-centric warriors are clearly also aspiring to is 20/20 vision in two other respects. The first of these is 20/20 vision in real time so that they can comprehend instantly all that is going on in the 'global battlespace'. Second, is 20/20 vision as foresight. They do not want to be caught out by what is coming down the road, because in the end you

FIGURE 24.7
Still from Steven Spielberg's science fiction film *Minority Report*. 20th Century Fox/Dreamworks/The Kobal Collection

can only fully escape danger and make everything secure if you can pre-empt the nasty surprises which time itself has in store for us. Think or watch *Minority Report*, Steven Spielberg's 2002 science fiction film set in the year 2054 AD, where crime is virtually eliminated from Washington DC thanks to an elite law enforcing squad, 'Precrime' (Weber 2006).

Ultimately, perfect vision expresses the desire for perfect security. But, perfect security – an end to danger – requires bringing an end to time. Were it possible, 20/20 vision would do just that. The continuous transformation to which network-centric warfare appeals is revealed here in its own terms as the primordial organising dream of political modernity; to bring an end to time here and now in this world through the perfection of our knowledge as the perfect vision of real time, fully transparent and communicable, information and foresight. In net war terms this is called 'shared situation awareness'.

The more we seek to secure, however, the more danger we seem to bring into the world. Spielberg explored these and other themes in his film. There is then a profound paradox at work in this military ideology. It wills the end to the change which the operation of time itself entails. But an end to time would simultaneously also mean the end of us; because we are time's creatures. No time. No us. The will to perfect security expresses the will to bring an end to ourselves. Fortunately, life is not so easily secured. The object of security (life) keeps objecting to the ways in which security seeks to secure it. It escapes being secured, and this introduces a point to which I will return in my conclusion. Paradoxical as it may sound, in order to survive we may have to become less obsessed with securing ourselves, recognising that there is more to life, and therefore more to politics, than politics of security which continuously also endanger us.

Recall, as well, the emphasis on continuous adaptability, transformation and change to which the US military now aspires, embracing the idea of co-evolution with the battlespace in order always to prevail over the enemy, whoever and whatever the enemy might be. Transformation is a military strategic vision of permanent revolution. A never ending event. But what this itself threatens is no profound emancipatory change in the human condition, just permanent revolution of the same, a sameness that escapes time itself.

And yet Rumsfeld also teaches us a further paradox: that there are unknown unknowns out there which our knowledge cannot reach and which our 20/20 vision will never attain. Note the profound shift that this records in the truth-telling practices of twenty-first-century security. They are founded now in uncertainty. Uncertainty is no mere ignorance which knowledge will eventually overcome. 'Unknown unknowns' have become the basis of its truth-telling practices now. Indeed, everything that we are now taught by western political, military and police authorities in their war on terror, especially, teaches us that we do not know when the strike will come, we do not know where the strike will come, and we cannot estimate how devastating the strike may be. But they are certain of this uncertainty. Uncertainty or radical contingency – not knowing and not being able to know – has paradoxically now, at the very height of our techno-scientific civilisation and its dream of 20/20 vision, become the very principle of formation around which military strategic and policing powers of the west revolve in their response to the dangers which our globally networked world now presents to us.

Being-in-formation

Excuse the awful pun. But here at the beginning of the twenty-first century, the modern vision which Donald Rumsfeld unwittingly poeticised has become one in which every thing is said to be information and everything is said to be continuously in-formation. Things which are continuously undergoing transformation and change are not fixed. They are always on their way to becoming something else. Our military, political and economic leaders, and even some of our teachers, insistently tell us that we have to be skilled at managing our own continuous transformation and change if we are to survive the dangers of the battlespace or the market place, and the danger ultimately of becoming outdated. Becoming outdated threatens unemployment, impoverishment, famine, defeat and despoilation. These days becoming outdated spells death. That is the fear we now teach ourselves. And yet that fear breeds another.

Becoming-dangerous

If no body, no thing is fixed, if every body is continuously in-formation, then it becomes difficult to secure any body at all since we can never be quite sure what the body is that we set out to secure. While our leaders simultaneous enjoin us to embrace transformation

FIGURE 24.8
'Well . . . at least we don't have to worry about anarchy any more.' Artist: Ron Cobb, 1968

and change, they are simultaneously also terrified by the fact that if we are continuously in-formation in the ways that they recommend we may also be continuously becoming-dangerous in ways that simply cannot be anticipated. No body is able to predict in precisely what ways we are transforming ourselves. Daft as it sounded to the press corps at the briefing in which he made these statements, this was the fear to which Rumsfeld was giving expression. It is the fear of all rulers who rule through the prioritisation of fear and danger. They do not know and cannot know what we are becoming and therefore they do not know and cannot know what dangers we will present to ourselves as well as to others. This recalls us back to that other time in American history and that other president, Franklin Roosevelt. Remember it was Roosevelt who said we had nothing to fear but fear itself. In another time confronted with other dangers we might do well to recall those words and reflect on how rule through fear and danger continuously also endangers itself.

CONCLUSION

For more on Foucault's thinking see **Chapters 4, 7, 11 and 23**. Compare this discussion of problematisation with the discussion of language games in **Chapter 2**.

A neat way of summarising the points made so far is to say, in the words of Michel Foucault, that what makes the world dangerous is a matter of problematisation (Foucault 2001). By that Foucault meant the many ways in which a crude state of affairs is translated into a specific problem or field of problems – he calls them fields of intervention – demanding action and calling for certain solutions. We could therefore say, in answer to the question, that what makes the world dangerous critically depends upon how danger comes to be problematised in specific ways by the truth-telling institutions and relations of power which constitute our societies.

Much greater emphasis has, however, been given in the twenty-first century to how human beings become a danger to themselves (Perrow 1999). Among many other factors the massification, industrialisation and nuclearisation of warfare, together with the recognition of environmental catastrophe, drove that point home to many states and societies during the course of the twentieth century. But there is an argument that goes beyond the environmentalist argument that we endanger ourselves because we endanger the environment. An argument is now regularly made instead – or in addition – that it is the very networked ways in which our civilisation now functions that circulates, intensifies and precipitates all sorts of new ways in which we endanger ourselves (Barabasi 2003). To the degree that we have become networked societies (Castells 2000), then what makes the world dangerous for us are the very close-coupled networks of global-local interchange – illustrated, for example, by the spread of disease and viruses through food chains and transportation networks as well as by network-centric warfare – which make our societies the societies that they are. The dangers to which we are subject come packaged with our forms of life.

FURTHER READING

Reid, Julian (2006) *Biopolitics of the War on Terror: Life Struggles, Liberal Modernity, and the Defence of Logistical Societies*, Manchester and New York: Manchester University Press.

An application of Foucault and other critical theorists, illustrating how biopolitics makes war on life, explicitly so in the war on terror.

Dillon, Michael and Julian, Reid (2009) *The Liberal Way of War: Killing to Make Life Live*, London: Routledge.

Tracking the relationship between liberalism, biopolitics and war, this book also explains how the RMA and network-centric warfare arose and how network thinking came to permeate security thinking throughout liberal states and societies at the beginning of the twenty-first century.

Dillon, Michael and Luis Lobo-Guerrero (2008) 'Biopolitics of Security in the Twenty-First Century: An Introduction', *Review of International Studies* 34, 2.

Provides a general introduction to what happens to security technologies when they take life as their referent object; also touches on the question of what happens to life when it becomes a security object.

Campbell, David (1998) *Writing Security*, Minneapolis: Minnesota University Press.

A pioneering work that deftly counteracted the politics of identity and subjectivity that had dominated international relations and security studies throughout the Cold War period and beyond.

Dillon, Michael (2008) 'Underwriting Security', *Security Dialogue* 39, 2–3.

Seeks an additional shift in our analytical focus, and empirical field of observation, to the biopolitics of security, which take 'life' rather than identity as their referent object, and especially to the ways in which the biopoliticisation of security installs 'risk' as one of its single most important devices.

Castells, Manuel (2000) *The Rise of the Network Society*, Oxford: Blackwell.
Explains the rise of globally networked societies and forms a background for understanding the radical interconnectedness of the world today.

Cebrowski, Vice Admiral Arthur and John Garstka (1998) 'Network Centric Warfare: Its Origin and Future', *US Naval Institute Proceedings* 124, January: 28–35.
The classic account of network-centric thinking and network-centric warfare. Get your minds around this text and you will understand what is going on, thus equipping yourselves to start posing other questions about how our contemporary discourses of danger unite military strategic and other discourses of security.

Foucault, Michel (2001) *Fearless Speech*, New York: Semiotext(e).
Start your adventure thinking about contemporary problematisations of security with the aid of Foucault here; specifically the last lecture which explains what problematisation means.

WEBSITES

Official website of the Foucault Society, http://www.foucaultsociety.org/
Rich source further references by Foucault and on Foucault.

Biopolitics of Security Network, http://www.keele.ac.uk/research/lpj/bos/
Website specifically devoted to the application of Foucault to questions of security and war.

Office of the now disbanded US Office of Force Transformation, http://www.oft.osd.mil/
Rich source of material on the relation of transformation to contemporary US military strategic doctrine.

RAND Corporation website on national security, http://www.rand.org/research_areas/national_security/
Source of military strategic classics on network-centric warfare, information warfare and the war on terror. Paradigmatic of contemporary military strategic discourse and the ways in which it colonises hitherto civil issues.

Home page of the UK Civil Contingencies Secretariat and the strategy of national resilience, http://www.ukresilience.info/ccs/aims.aspx
Use as a resource to track how security as resilience differs from simple military security and is disseminated throughout UK civil society.

Home page of the UK Ministry of Defence, http://www.mod.uk/defenceinternet/home
Use as a device to track how the UK mimics US military strategic discourse.

US Department of Defense website, http://www.defenselink.mil/
Use for direct illustration of themes made in the chapter.

ACKNOWLEDGEMENT

I want to record my thanks to Manav Guha. Without him I would not have the understanding of network-centric warfare which I have, or be as concerned about it as I am. What I know I have learnt through continuous question and answer with him.

REFERENCES

Alberts, David S., John J. Garstka and Frederick P. Stein (1999) *Network Centric Warfare: Developing and Leveraging Information Superiority*, 2nd edn, Washington, DC: US Department of Defense, Command and Control Research Program (CCRP).

Arquilla, John and David Ronfeldt (1997) 'Information Power and Grand Strategy: In Athena's Camp', in John Arquilla and David Ronfeldt, *In Athena's Camp: Preparing for Conflict in the Information Age*, Santa Monica, CA: RAND Corporation.

Barabasi, Albert-Laszlo (2003) *Linked: How Everything Is Connected to Everything Else and What It Means*, London: Penguin Books.
Booth, Ken (2005) *Critical Security Studies and World Politics*, Boulder, CO: Lynne Rienner.
Campbell, David (1998) *Writing Security*, Minneapolis: Minnesota University Press.
Castells, Manuel (2000) *The Rise of the Network Society*, Oxford: Blackwell.
Cebrowski, Arthur and John Garstka (1998) 'Network Centric Warfare: Its Origin and Future', *US Naval Institute Proceedings* 124, January: 28–35.
Cebrowski, Vice Admiral (Retd) Arthur K., Director, Office of Force Transformation (2002) Prepared Statement for the US House Appropriations Committee, 13 March.
Cilliers, Paul (1998) *Complexity and Postmodernism*, London: Routledge.
Dalby, Simon (2002) *Environmental Security*, Minneapolis: University of Minnesota Press.
Der Derian, James (2001) *Virtuous War: Mapping the Military-Industrial-Media-Entertainment Network*, Boulder, CO: Westview Press.
Dillon, Michael (2002) 'Network Society, Network-Centric Warfare and the State of Emergency', *Theory, Culture and Society* 19, 4: 71–9.
——(2004) 'Virtual Security. A New Science of (Dis)order', *Millennium: Journal of International Studies* 32, 3: 531–58.
——(2007) 'Governing Terror', *International Political Sociology* 1, 1: 7–28.
Dillon, Michael and Julian Reid (2001) 'Global Liberal Governance: Biopolitics, Security and War', *Millennium: Journal of International Studies* 30 1: 1–26.
——(2009) *The Liberal Way of War: Killing to Make Life Live*, London: Routledge.
Farrell, Theo and Tim Bird (2008) 'The Transformation of the British Armed Forces', in Terry Terriff, Theo Farrell and Frans Osinga (eds) *The Dynamics of Military Transformation in NATO*, Stanford, CA: Stanford University Press.
Foucault, Michel (1988) 'Truth and Power', ed. Colin Gordon, trans. C. Gordon, L. Marshal, J. Mepham and K. Sober, *Power/Knowledge*, Brighton: Harvester Press.
——(2001) *Fearless Speech*, New York: Semiotext(e).
Libicki, Martin (2000) *Who Runs What in the Global Information Grid?*, Santa Monica, CA: RAND.
Mathews, Ron and Jack Treddenick (eds) (2001) *Managing the Revolution in Military Affairs*, London: Palgrave.
McLuhan, Marshall (2001) *Understanding Media*, London: Routledge
Molloy, Sean (2006) *The Hidden History of Realism: A Genealogy of Power*, New York: Palgrave Macmillan.
Office of Force Transformation (2004) *Elements of Defense Transformation*, Washington, DC: US Department of Defense, http://www.oft.osd.mil/library/library_files/document_383_ElementsOfTransformation_LR.pdf.
Perrow, Charles (1999) *Normal Accidents: Living with High Risk Technologies*, Princeton, NJ: Princeton University Press.
Reid, Julian (2007) *The Biopolitics of the War on Terror: Life Struggles, Liberal Modernity and the Defence of Logistical Societies*, Manchester and New York: Manchester University Press.
Rumsfeld, Donald (2002) Department of Defense news briefing, 12 February.
Shapiro, Michael J. (2007) 'The New Violent Cartography', *Security Dialogue* 38, 3: 291–313.
Shearer, David (1998) *Private Military Armies*, Adelphi Paper 316, London: IISS.
UK Ministry of Defence (2005) *Network Enabled Capability*, JSP 777, London: Ministry of Defence.
Weber, Cynthia (2006) *Imagining America at War: Morality, Politics and Film*, London: Routledge.

For a range of further resources supporting this chapter, please visit the companion website for *Global Politics, 2nd Edition* at www.routledge.com/cw/edkins/

CHAPTER 25

What can we do to stop people harming others?

Anne Orford

THE QUESTION
INTERVENING FOR HUMANITY?

The question of 'what can we do to stop people harming others?' has animated much public engagement with international politics since the end of the Cold War. During the 1990s, this question was discussed in terms of the legitimacy of humanitarian intervention. The resort to force in international relations began to achieve a new respectability, not least because for many it seemed to offer a means for the international community, or at least a liberal alliance of democratic states, to bring human rights and democracy to protect people suffering in situations of genocide, civil war or large-scale human rights violations. In 2001, a significant shift in this debate was signalled with the publication of a report by the International Commission on Intervention and State Sovereignty (or ICISS) entitled *The Responsibility to Protect* (ICISS 2001). ICISS was an initiative, sponsored by the Canadian government, undertaken in response to serious concerns about the legality and legitimacy of the 1999 NATO action in Kosovo. The responsibility to protect concept is premised upon the notion, to quote former secretary-general Kofi Annan, that 'the primary raison d'être and duty' of every state is to protect its population (United Nations Secretary-General 2005: para. 135). If a state manifestly fails to protect its population, the responsibility to do so shifts to the international community. The responsibility to protect concept has since colonized internationalist debates about conflict prevention, humanitarian action, peacekeeping and territorial administration, and has garnered the support of a strikingly diverse range of states, international and regional organizations and civil society groups.

The idea that force should be used to relieve the suffering of others of course predates the 1990s. Christian Europe was for many centuries inspired to take action by the idea of saving the souls or rescuing the bodies of people elsewhere, and the self-appointed civilizing mission of European empire was premised upon the idea that benevolent tutelage in the art of European civilization was the answer to the suffering of those outside the community of faith. Even in the modern age of the United Nations (UN) Charter, in which states have theoretically renounced recourse to war as an instrument of foreign policy, there are many doctrinal and practical precursors to the concept of humanitarian intervention. Peacekeeping, for example, does not appear in the UN Charter as one of the grounds upon which recourse to force may be authorized. It emerged in the early 1950s, alongside the process of decolonization, as a means of responding to conflict over territory, threats to the sanctity of former colonial investments and civil war in post-colonial states. The use of force against states in Africa, the Middle East and Latin America was also justified during the Cold War on the basis that intervention was necessary to defend citizens of the home state who were abroad. Such doctrines served to justify armed intervention against Third World states, in the name of defending individuals at risk of harm. Nonetheless, during the Cold War period, the notion that a powerful state or a coalition of allies might intervene to rescue or protect the people of another state could not easily be represented as an apolitical action. The Brezhnev doctrine of intervention to protect the self-determination of socialist countries in the face of capitalist threats, and the Reagan doctrine advocating the legitimacy of pro-democratic invasion, were met with protest and derision. It was the institutional and ideological conditions of the post-Cold War period which led to the growth of support, amongst policy makers and academics, for the idea that force can legitimately be used as a response to humanitarian challenges.

The thinking that took place around Spanish colonization is discussed in **Chapter 21**. That chapter also considers the tensions inherent in 'helping others'.

See **Chapter 1** for more on the term 'Third World'.

Leonid Brezhnev was leader of the Soviet Union from 1964 to 1982. Ronald Reagan was president of the United States from 1981 to 1989.

The institutional conditions which made possible the shift in support for the notion of humanitarian intervention included the post-Cold War revitalization of the Security Council and the corresponding expansion of its role in maintaining international peace and security. For many years the coercive powers vested by the UN Charter in the Security Council seemed irrelevant. During the Cold War, the Security Council was paralysed by reciprocal use of the veto exercisable by the five permanent members (the P5) – China, France, the United Kingdom, the United States and what was then the Soviet Union. Under Article 27(3) of the Charter, decisions of the Security Council require the affirmative vote of nine members, and the concurring votes of the permanent members. The P5 regularly made use of that veto power during the Cold War to protect against international interference in their spheres of interest. The ending of the Cold War meant an end to that automatic use of the veto power. The range and nature of resolutions passed by the Security Council in the decade following the end of the Cold War suggested that the Council was willing to treat the failure to guarantee democracy

The Cold War is also discussed in **Chapter 26**.

BOX 25.1 THE UN AND USE OF FORCE

The UN Charter was adopted by the fifty founding member states of the new organization at San Francisco in June 1945. Under Article 24 of the UN Charter, the Security Council is the organ charged with the primary responsibility for maintaining international peace and security. Under Chapters VI and VII of the UN Charter, the Security Council is granted powers to facilitate the pacific settlement of disputes, and to decide what measures, including the use of armed force, should be taken to maintain or restore international peace and security. UN member states renounce the use of force as a tool of foreign policy, except in self-defence or where such action is authorized by the Security Council. The jurisdiction of the Security Council under Chapter VII is triggered by the existence of a threat to the peace, a breach of the peace or an act of aggression. Since 1989, the Security Council has proved itself willing to interpret the phrase 'threats to the peace' broadly, to include situations of civil war or humanitarian crises.

FIGURE 25.1
The UN Security Council, United Nations, New York. Photo: Eskinder Debebe

or human rights, or to protect against humanitarian abuses, as a threat to peace and security. The enthusiastic embrace of multilateral intervention (interventions involving more than one intervening country) extended to support for military action undertaken by regional organizations without Security Council authorization, most notably in the case of the 1999 intervention in Kosovo by NATO (the North Atlantic Treaty Organization), but also the intervention by the Economic Community of West African States in Sierra Leone.

The Cold War was seen as a struggle not only between different states but the ideologies that they subscribed to. **Chapter 26** looks at the role of ideology in conflict, and **Chapter 22** discusses competing ideologies as an explanation for war.

The ideological climate of the 1990s contributed to the plausibility of the notion that military intervention might be benevolent and disinterested – that powerful states might really come to liberate and not to occupy. A new kind of international law and internationalist spirit seemed to have been made possible in the changed conditions of a world no longer structured around the struggle between communism and capitalism. During the 1990s, many international lawyers suggested that the process of globalization was contributing to the emergence of an international community by creating the conditions for an increasingly interdependent world, linked by new technologies and the movement of goods, capital and people. In addition, globalization was thought to promise a degree of integration into a common or harmonized legal system, an increased move towards institutionalization, and a commitment to shared values of free trade, security, human rights and democracy. While international legal texts still invoke interdependence as a fact and the coming community of shared values as a destination, interdependence post-September 11 is more likely to be figured in terms of a shared vulnerability, and the coming community in terms of the fragility of faith and belief. In this context, the idea that military intervention might be a means of responding to the suffering of others has not disappeared, but it has shifted form, as we shall see. In order to try to think about the stakes of different approaches to the question of 'What can we do to stop people harming others?' I turn to look at an example of humanitarian intervention in action – the case of Timor-Leste.

For what happened on 11 September 2001, see **Chapter 23**; for its impact on security policy see **Chapter 24**; for its impact on immigration policy in the US, see **Chapter 10**; and for changes in perceptions of the place of religion in global politics after September 11 see **Chapter 6**.

ILLUSTRATIVE EXAMPLE
SAVING TIMOR-LESTE

Timor was colonized by Portugal in the sixteenth century, and remained under Portuguese occupation until 1942, when it was invaded by Japan. At the end of World War II, the Portuguese resumed control over the territory. In 1960, the UN General Assembly placed Timor on its list of non-self-governing territories, with Portugal as the administering power. Following the leftist overthrow of Portugal's authoritarian government in 1974, the new social democratic government in Lisbon reacted favourably to the call by Timorese nationalist movements for independence, but did little to oversee or facilitate the process of Timorese self-determination. The Timorese were left to resolve the difficulties that arose in the preparation for independence, in particular the contest between rival groups advocating independence on the one hand and integration with Indonesia on the other. The most popular among these groups was the pro-independence FRETILIN (Frente Revolucionária do Timor-Leste Independente or Revolutionary Front for an Independent East Timor), which Indonesian

Colonialism and its continuing impact today are examined in **Chapters 15 and 16**.

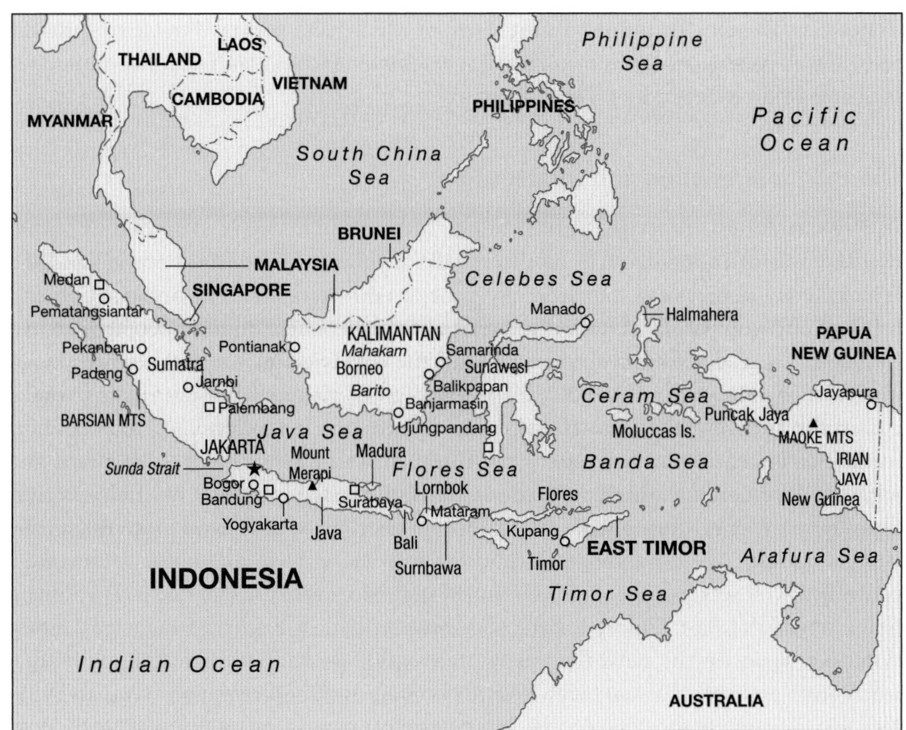

FIGURE 25.2 Map of Timor-Leste in context of Asia and Australia

President Suharto was to characterize in conversation with US president Gerald Ford as 'communist-influenced'.

On 28 November 1975, in the context of repeated cross-border attacks by Indonesian special forces seeking to provoke civil war and thus provide an alibi for intervention, FRETILIN declared Timor's independence. A little over a week later, on 7 December 1975, Indonesia launched a general invasion of Timor, carried out with the knowledge and tacit support of the US, UK and Australian governments. This support was motivated by issues of regional security, concern that an independent Timor might align itself with China and, in the case of Australia, the desire to secure access to Timor Sea oil and gas. Indonesia was to remain in military occupation of Timor for the next 25 years. During that period, an estimated 200,000 Timorese people were killed, and human rights violations were widespread and brutal. Resistance to Indonesian occupation was sustained throughout this period, perhaps most dramatically through the activities of FALANTIL (Forças Armadas de Libertação Nacional de Timor-Leste or Armed Forces for the National Liberation of East Timor) guerrillas based in the mountains, but also through diplomatic activity by the Timorese diaspora, widespread non-cooperation with Indonesian officials and clandestine resistance activities throughout Timor. The UN condemned Indonesia's aggression and continued to recognize Portugal as the administering authority over the territory. Australia, however, recognized de facto (factual) Indonesian occupation of Timor in 1978, and through the commencement of negotiations over maritime delimitation in the Timor Sea gave de jure (legal) recognition to the occupation. The result was the 1989 conclusion of the

Timor Gap Treaty with Indonesia, the terms of which were very favourable to Australia and allowed Australian access to oil and gas fields which would later become the subject of claims by an independent Timor-Leste.

The 1999 intervention and trusteeship

In 1998, Indonesia proposed that Timor be granted limited special autonomy within the Republic of Indonesia. The resulting talks involving Indonesia, Portugal and the UN secretary-general saw the secretary-general entrusted with the organization and conduct of a popular consultation to ascertain whether the Timorese people accepted Indonesia's special autonomy proposal. When the vote rejecting the autonomy proposal in favour of independence resulted in a campaign of violence and destruction waged against the Timorese, the international community responded by sending a multinational force (the International Force for East Timor or INTERFET) to restore peace and security. International financial institutions also exerted pressure on Indonesia by freezing payments during the post-ballot period. In the following months, the Indonesian armed forces and police withdrew from the territory and militia attacks were controlled. UN secretary-general Kofi Annan saw these events as significant. For Annan, '[t]he tragedy of East Timor, coming so soon after that of Kosovo, has focused attention once again on the need for timely intervention by the international community when death and suffering are being inflicted on large numbers of people' (Annan 1999: 49). He welcomed the 'developing international norm in favour of intervention to protect civilians from wholesale slaughter' (Annan 1999: 50). Richard Holbrooke, then US permanent representative to the UN, described it as 'the textbook realization of Churchill and Roosevelt's dream when they laid out the principles of the UN' (Traub 2000: 80). Australia's foreign minister Alexander Downer also lauded the role played by Australian troops as part of INTERFET in supporting self-determination and relieving suffering in the territory.

Chapter 15 explains how international financial institutions came to be set up.

> We saw an opportunity to allow East Timorese to decide their own future, and we helped them realize that chance. And when those who lost the ballot sought to overturn it through violence and intimidation, we put Australian lives on the line to end that suffering.
>
> (Downer 1999)

When we say 'international community' we sometimes mean all the states in the world, sometimes a group of rich and powerful states, sometimes the UN Security Council or – sometimes – the UN General Assembly. We imply that members of the international community share values and obligations. This can ignore or gloss over strong divisions and disagreements, and create legitimacy for a particular view that is not in fact shared by everyone.

Following the intervention, the UN and the World Bank adopted a major trusteeship role, taking over responsibility for administration in Timor during the period of transition to independence. The idea that the international community has a legitimate role as administrator of post-conflict territories and manager of the reconstruction process gained increasing acceptance at the international level during the 1990s. These developments in international relations flowed from a new faith in the international community as a benign, even civilizing, administrator. On 25 October 1999, Security Council Resolution 1272 established the UN Transitional Administration in East Timor (UNTAET) as a peacekeeping operation 'endowed with overall responsibility for the administration of East Timor and . . . empowered to exercise all legislative and executive authority, including the administration of justice'. The UN's view of its

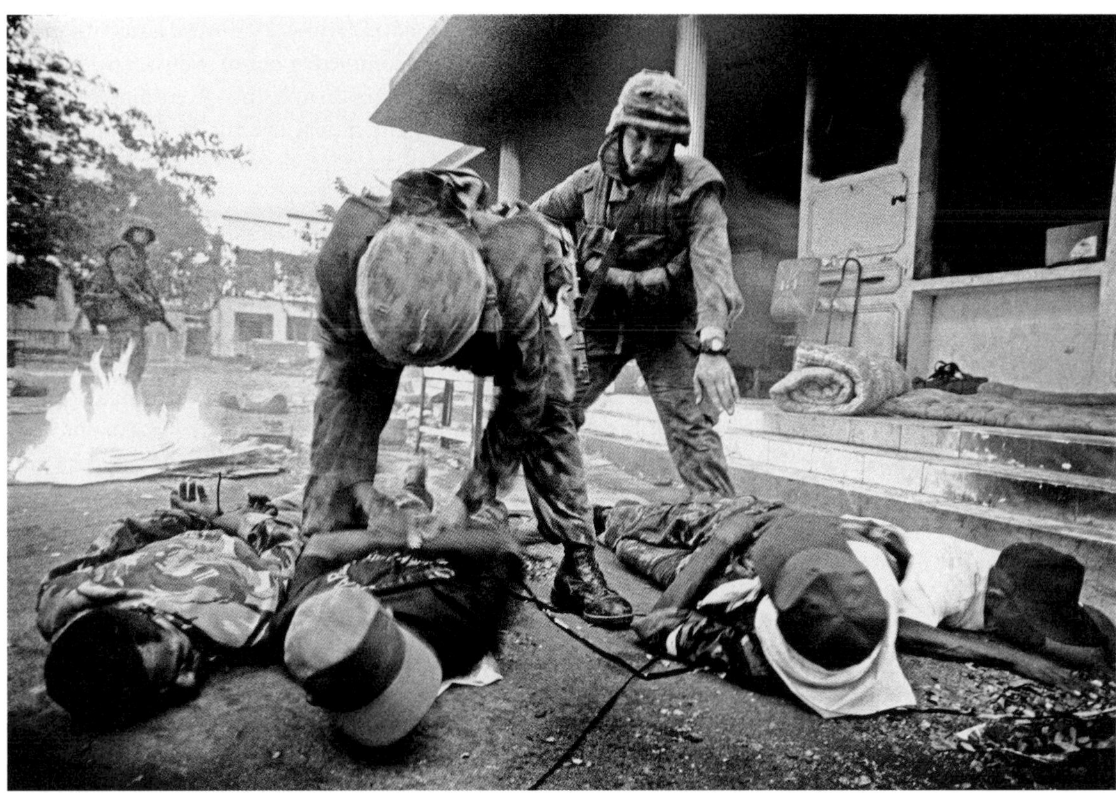

FIGURE 25.3 Australian troops, members of INTERFET, disarm and arrest members of the Aitarak Militia. Dili, East Timor, 21 September 1999. Photo: David Dare Parker

role in East Timor was well illustrated by Jean-Christian Cady, the Deputy Transitional Administrator of East Timor. Cady commented that the UN had to 'create a State, with a constitution, administrative, judicial and financial institutions, and a Public Service' and train police, 'not only on police methods and techniques but also on the ethics of a democratic police and respect for human rights, which is of course a new idea in East Timor'. Creating a bureaucracy was portrayed as equally difficult: 'What UNTAET wants to achieve is a Civil Service independent from political affiliations and cronyism, competent and not corrupt. These are ambitious goals anywhere but perhaps more so in this part of the world' (Cady 2000). Hans Strohmeyer, counsel to the transitional administrator, understood it as his job to 'invent a Timorese legal system' (Traub 2000: 82). These officials saw Timor as a blank slate in terms of existing knowledge and experience, marked by cronyism, incompetence and corruption. The UN's role was understood in the pedagogical terms that marked colonial discourse – the international community was to bring its tutees in East Timor to political and economic maturity through the creation and transfer of the bureaucratic machinery of the modern nation-state, and the training of the functionaries required to operate that machinery.

The World Bank also played a major role in the administration of East Timor, administering a multilateral trust fund to finance reconstruction and working with Timorese and UNTAET representatives to facilitate economic development. The Bank made clear that certain familiar Bank programmes and priorities were to be implemented

For a discussion of profiteering and the ambiguities of development under structural adjustment regimes put in place by the World Bank in Côte d'Ivoire, see **Chapter 15**.

in the management of East Timor. It determined as early as 1999 that East Timor was to have a small public sector, with a concomitant contracting out of many areas of service provision to the private sector, and particularly to foreign investors. According to critics, East Timor under UN and World Bank management was overrun by foreign, mainly Australian, companies making large profits out of contracts negotiated with INTERFET or UNTAET (Aditjondro 2000). NGOs such as East Timor's La'o Hamutuk argued that the combination of UN paternalism, World Bank development models and unrestrained foreign investment was creating a new form of colonialism, and deepening divisions within the East Timorese community (La'o Hamutuk 2000).

Independence

In August 2001, during the period of UN administration, democratic elections for a Constituent Assembly were held. FRETILIN won 57 per cent of the vote, and its secretary-general Mari Alkatiri became chief minister. On 20 May 2002, Timor-Leste formally gained its independence and Alkatiri became prime minister of the new state. Much of the period following independence was spent in difficult and protracted negotiations with Australia over maritime delimitation in the Timor Sea. Australia was reluctant to lose the access to resources it had secured in negotiations with Indonesia during its occupation of the territory. Two months before Timor-Leste became independent, Australia withdrew from the jurisdiction of the International Court of Justice on maritime issues and the International Tribunal for the Law of the Sea (Downer 2002). The Australian government continued to issue licenses for fields in disputed territories where Australian and Timorese claims overlapped (see Figure 25.4). The Australian government also refused to put revenues estimated at $1 million a day from these fields into a trust account pending resolution of the disputed claims to the territory. According to international lawyers from the Australian Attorney-General's department, Australia had no obligation to negotiate claims to these disputed territories, as Australia had exercised 'active jurisdiction' over them while Timor-Leste was occupied (Cleary 2007: 124). After four years of negotiations, the Treaty on Certain Maritime Arrangements in the Timor Sea (CMATS) between Australia and Timor-Leste was signed on 12 January 2006.

Eruption of violence and the 2006 intervention

In April 2006, violence between military factions, the police and militias broke out in Timor-Leste. The immediate trigger to this unrest was the dismissal of a group of personnel from within the Timorese defence force or FALINTIL – Forças Armadas de Defesa de Timor-Leste (F-FDTL). Most of those dismissed were soldiers who were on strike claiming that they had been discriminated against in favour of former members of FALINTIL. Prime Minister Alkatiri characterized the violence in Dili (capital of Timor-Leste) as an attempted coup and stated that the attacks were directed at 'blocking the democratic institutions' and preventing them from functioning, so that 'the only solution would be for national parliament to be dissolved by the President . . . which would provoke the fall of the Government' (ABC News Online 2006a). On 12 May, the prime minister of Australia announced that Australia was deploying two warships

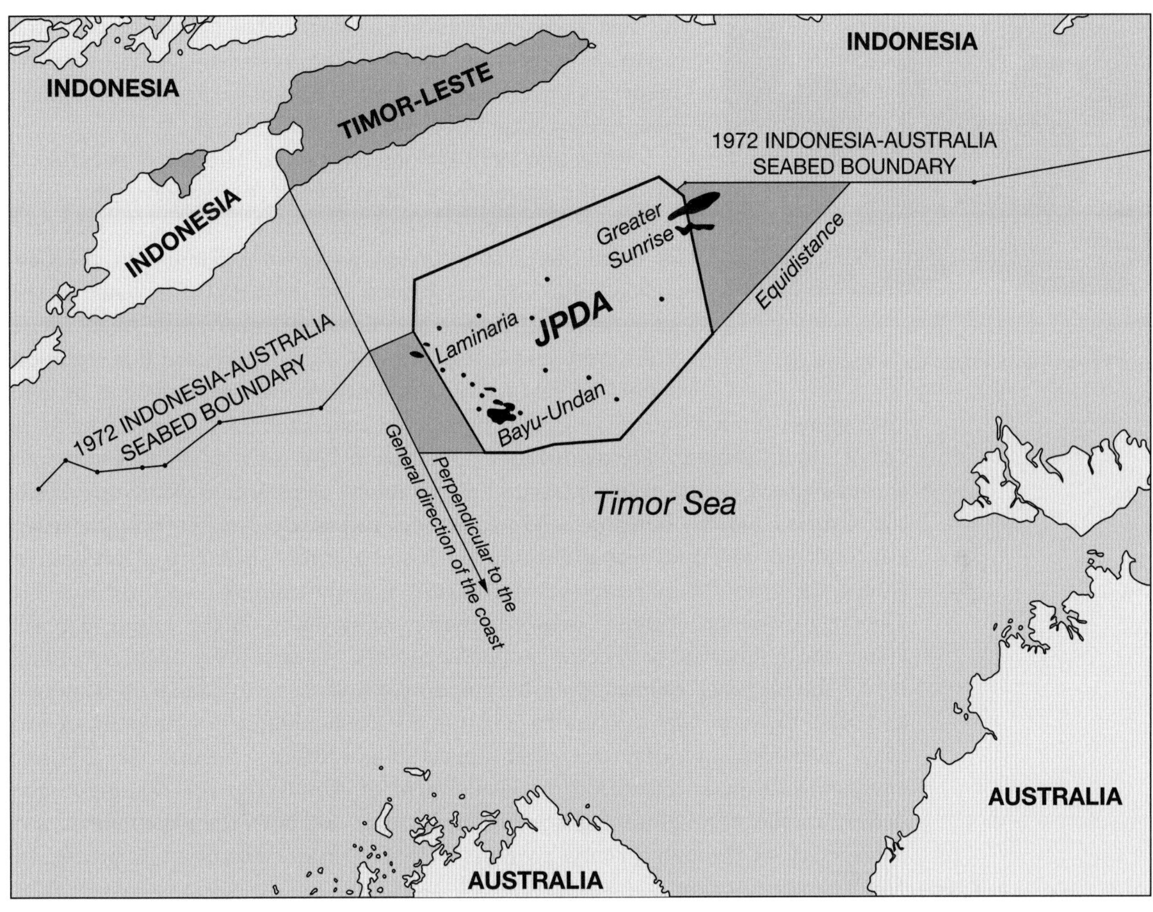

FIGURE 25.4
Map of the Timor Sea. Shaded sections of the map represent the areas of overlapping claims, in which Timor-Leste has asked that Australia exercise restraint in exploiting resources in accordance with its obligations under international law. Timor Sea Office, Office of the Prime Minister, Government of Timor-Leste

to Australia's northern waters 'in case East Timor requested international troops' (ABC News Online 2006b), a move protested by the Timorese government. However, on 24 May, in the context of escalating violence, Timor-Leste sent an official request for military assistance to Australia, Malaysia, New Zealand and Portugal, with the first international forces arriving in response the next day. A new UN peacekeeping force, the United Nations Integrated Mission in Timor-Leste (UNMIT), was created by Security Council Resolution 1704 in August 2006, to operate under Australian command. The renewed unrest and subsequent military intervention had a significant impact on Timorese and Australian politics. Prime Minister Mari Alkatiri resigned on 26 June 2006, as a result of claims aired on Australian media that he had been involved in distributing guns to militias. In February 2007, the Timorese prosecutor-general announced that he and international advisors had found no evidence in support of these claims, and that the investigation into this matter was closed (Cleary 2007: 255). José Ramos Horta was appointed by President Gusmão as the new prime minister on 8 July 2006, and in

FIGURE 25.5
José Ramos Horta. Photo: Glenn Campbell

his first press conference announced that he would ratify the CMATS treaty with Australia. The Australian Defence Department has since announced plans to build a permanent military base in the centre of Dili (Cleary 2007: 258).

While the 1999 UN intervention in Timor was understood within the narrative of humanitarian intervention, the 2006 intervention was quickly characterized in terms of the language of failed states and corrupt governance familiar to the new millennium. The UN treated the outbreak of violence as the expression of 'deep-rooted problems inherent in fragile State institutions and a weak rule of law', and proposed that attention should be paid to 'capacity-building and strengthening of state institutions' (United Nations Independent Special Commission of Inquiry, 2006: paras 221–2). In his August 2006 report on the situation in Timor-Leste, the UN secretary-general focused on the need for 'security sector reform', promotion of the rule of law and increased 'capacity-building' as responses to the civil unrest. The Timorese leadership was condemned by Australian prime minister John Howard: 'There is no point beating around the bush. The country has not been well-governed and I do hope that the sobering experience for those in elected positions of having to call for outside help will induce the appropriate behaviours inside the country' (Cleary 2007: 256). According to such international commentators, the eruption of violence revealed that the Timorese leadership had either failed to understand how a state should function properly, or had failed to implement certain technical aspects of governance. Neither the UN nor international experts considered the involvement of outsiders in contributing to the unrest, whether through taking sides in the factional disputes within the military and bureaucracy, or through draining government resources and attention into protracted Timor Sea negotiations.

The 2006 military revolt in Timor-Leste has been interpreted as simply a technical matter – a sign that yet another group of post-colonial tutees require further training

FIGURE 25.6
East Timor gas, Bush oil. Cartoon by Nicholson from *The Australian*. www.nicholson.com.au

in how a state should function and in tenets of the rule of law. For example, the *Economist* describes the situation in May 2006 as resulting from an 'incompetent and faction-ridden government' which 'led to chaos and the dispatch of fresh peace-keepers (*Economist* 2007). Such analyses strip this situation of any political content and represent Timor-Leste as an inadequate version of a European state, one that 'will need years more babysitting from the UN'. It is as if there is only one form of the state, such that we can no longer remember that this uniform model of political order might itself be subject to challenge (see Box 25.2). Yet this armed struggle could also be interpreted as a political event – as part of a conflict over the theory of the state which was involved in turning a revolutionary front into the Timor defence force. FALANTIL was initially created in August 1975 as the military arm of FRETILIN. With the creation of the independent state of Timor-Leste, the armed forces were named the F-FDTL (FALINTIL – Força Defensa Timor-Leste). As this name suggests, the military were envisaged as inheriting the political mantle of the revolutionary defenders of an independent Timor-Leste (La'o Hamutuk 2005). The dispute in 2006 resulted from tensions within the military between those soldiers from the western part of the country who claimed they were being discriminated against in favour of soldiers from the eastern part of the country who were active in FALINTIL and the resistance movement.

For a discussion of the problems with the idea that democracy is the right way of organizing politics and that the West knows best how to do this see **Chapter 14**.

Chapter 11 examines how the state emerged in Europe.

BOX 25.2 THE STATE AND REVOLUTION

In the months prior to the October revolution of 1917, from his exile in Helsinki, Vladimir Lenin finished work on an extraordinary manifesto entitled *The State and Revolution* (Lenin 1951). In this book, Lenin broke dramatically with the long tradition of European political thought and practice concerning the relation between church, state and individual (Harding 1996; Žižek 2002). *The State and Revolution*, and the Bolshevik seizure of power which this text anticipates, challenged existing conceptual frameworks for thinking about the proper form of the state and its relation to law.

FIGURE 25.7 Lenin disguised as 'Vilén', wearing a wig and with his beard shaved off. Finland, 11 August 1917

Lenin argued, following Friedrich Engels, that the state is a form of power which 'arose from society, but places itself above it and alienates itself more and more from it' (Lenin 1951: 17). The chief instruments of this state power are a standing army, a police force and a bureaucracy, all separate from the people. The state requires such special bodies of armed men because if the population were armed under conditions of irreconcilable class division and antagonism, armed struggle would result. Lenin argued that in the early twentieth century, these aspects of executive power – the military and the bureaucracy – had been strengthened enormously and that repressive measures against the proletariat had intensified. In response, Lenin called for this state machinery to be 'smashed' (Lenin 1951: 53). *The State and Revolution* offers a challenge to the conceptualization of the form of the state as a technical rather than a political question – a conceptualization underpinning the international project of state-building in Timor-Leste and elsewhere. Lenin's tract serves as a reminder that the relation between the military, the bureaucracy and the people themselves is not a technical question, but one which is at the heart of politics.

In addition, tension between the military and the police force was fuelled by the ties between the police force and former members of the Indonesian military. Thus the stakes of the unrest in 2006 were in part about a theory of the state which did not treat military power as somehow technical or neutral, and which resisted a vision of the military as somehow above or separate from the people.

GENERAL RESPONSES
LAW AND THE EXCEPTIONAL

For a discussion of why politics turns to violence in the first place, see **Chapter 22**, which discusses war in Europe. See also **Chapter 26** for the argument that moving on after conflict is a difficult and long-term process.

The question – what can we do to stop people harming others – can be approached as both a political and a legal question. In political terms, we might want to ask – what can we realistically or legitimately do to force or persuade people to stop hurting each other? What is the most effective form of action to achieve this end? What kind of political organization or world order would best ensure that people are protected from harm? We might also consider this to raise matters of law – what *can* we do, what are we permitted or authorized or obliged to do, to stop people hurting each other? This is a question about the scope and limits of lawful authority in times of emergency or states of exception. In this section, I will introduce a series of ways of thinking about the relation between legality and legitimacy, or norm and exception, which have informed the theory and practice of humanitarian intervention.

Metaphysical account of law

The first such theory of the relation between legality and legitimacy involves a metaphysical account of law. It is well illustrated by the dominant legal and political response to the NATO intervention in Kosovo in 1999. Commentators such as Bruno Simma and Antonio Cassese argued that the Kosovo intervention was illegal but legitimate (Simma 1999; Cassese 1999). For Simma, Cassese and many others at the time, the question of the legality of the Kosovo intervention was quickly answered – it was illegal as it did not conform to any of the authorized grounds upon which states could have recourse to force under the UN Charter. However, they felt that a commitment to justice required the international community to support the NATO intervention in Kosovo, despite its illegality. Determining whether the intervention was legitimate involved asking whether it was in conformity with universal values which transcended any given legal order.

These interpretations of the legitimacy of the NATO intervention underpinned the position put by then British prime minister Tony Blair. Blair portrayed the NATO intervention in Kosovo as a 'just war, based not on territorial ambitions, but on values' (Blair 1999a).

Chapter 21 explains what is meant by a 'just war'.

> This war was not fought for Albanians against Serbs. It was not fought for territory. Still less for NATO aggrandisement. It was fought for a fundamental principle necessary for humanity's progress: that every human being, regardless of race, religion or birth, has the inalienable right to live free from persecution.
>
> (Blair 1999b)

Such accounts are based upon the appeal to a universal law which transcends the rules of any existing legal system. It is reference to this universal law which gives legitimacy to the act of intervention. In such formulations, we see played out what Jennifer Beard has characterized as the metaphysics of modern Western identity (Beard 2006). Such a conception of humanitarian intervention is metaphysical in that it is based on notions of universal values and ideal forms, of which actually existing political communities represent only imperfect copies. Beard has argued compellingly that the impetus for the development of this metaphysics has been the encounters between the Old World and the New, or in contemporary language, the developed and the developing worlds. The developed world is represented as the embodiment on earth of 'an infinitely distant reality' and a 'potential state of fulfilment', the promise of which will be fulfilled once the peoples of the New World are redeemed (Beard 2006: 3, 4, 11).

Compare the account of the ticking-bomb scenario in **Chapter 2**.

See the discussion of colonial encounters in **Chapter 21**.

Realist account of law

A second account of the role of law in the global politics of intervention is not concerned with universal norms (as in the metaphysical account) and resists 'any assertion of a place for legitimate authority in the international order' (Carty 2006). This realist approach understands international law purely as an expression of the interests and will of sovereign states. In this familiar vision, global politics is portrayed as anarchic (that is, lacking an over-arching authority), and individual entities such as states are left 'to act instrumentally and calculate power in relative rather than absolute terms' (Huysmans 2006: 154). While norms may be generated by agreement between sovereigns, such norms are not the expression of moral values or of an objectified legal system, but rather of 'an existing historical political order' (Huysmans 2006: 155). Such an account, which finds support from both the left and the right of politics in debates over intervention, dismisses any portrayal of the systematic nature of the international order or any suggestion that international law may bring into being a political community. Instead, the realist approach privileges bilateral relations as at the heart of the existing international order. The international realm in this view is by definition exceptional – the lack of a legal system or a guarantor of law leaves only alienated entities engaged in functional encounters. International lawyers fulfil their tasks when they find ways for these entities to express their national interests or their instrumental objectives in the law they bring into being. In the case of Timor-Leste, this law might include the resolutions of the Security Council authorizing intervention in 1999, but the series of treaties that enabled the exploitation of maritime resources in an area subject to conflicting territorial claims would be seen as equally legitimate and valid expressions of national interest and sovereign will.

Decisionist account of law

A third account of the relation between legality and legitimacy is the decisionist account. Key to this account are the claims that the primary role of the state is to protect its citizens, and that the state depends for its survival upon the existence of a sovereign who can guarantee the values and law of the state. In order to begin to analyse the effects of this account of law, I want to turn to the writings of Carl Schmitt.

BOX 25.3 CARL SCHMITT

Carl Schmitt (1888–1985) was a German jurist and political theorist whose anti-liberal and anti-parliamentary views provided ideological support for the totalitarian state of Nazi Germany. Schmitt argued that the state has a responsibility to protect its citizens.

> [I]t must be taken into consideration that the totality of this kind of state power always accords with the total responsibility for protecting and securing the safety of citizens and that obedience as well as the renunciation of every right of resistance that can be demanded by this god is only the correlate of the true protection that he guarantees.
>
> (Schmitt 1996: 96)

However, for Schmitt, the state could not – and indeed should not – retain authority if it had no claims to legitimacy other than its capacity to provide protection. Civil society would continually regroup to challenge a state imagined as a kind of soulless, security machine. Schmitt sought to develop a theory of legality and legitimacy which would ground the political authority of the state.

FIGURE 25.8
Carl Schmitt

Two aspects of Schmitt's solution are relevant to contemporary debates about humanitarian intervention.

First, Schmitt argued that for the law and governance of a democratic state to be effective, that state must represent a homogeneous and unified nation. In order for the state to survive, there must exist a sovereign capable of properly distinguishing between friend and enemy and thus preserving the national homogeneity that was for Schmitt the necessary condition of effective government. The state must be willing to defend the values that bound together the members of a given political community of 'friends'. It was the defence of these particular values, and not some set of universal values that could be determined in advance, that gave legitimacy to the state. In order to protect the state against those who did not share such values, the qualitatively total state must control all aspects of the life of those within it. Thus Schmitt argued, pace Hobbes, that the state could not afford to respect individual freedoms such as freedoms of thought or conscience.

Chapters 12 and 13 raise questions about the view of a state as populated by a homogeneous group of people forming a nation.

Thomas Hobbes is discussed in **Chapter 7**.

Second, Schmitt developed the related argument that an individual could only submit to the law where certain political conditions were in place (Schmitt 2004 [1932]: 20). In particular, there must be only one lawmaker, and that lawmaker must be 'the final guardian of all law, ultimate guarantor of the existing order, conclusive source of all legality, and the last security and protection against injustice' (Schmitt 2004 [1932]:

19). In addition, for a '"formal" concept of law' to be 'conceivable and acceptable', there must be 'congruence between the parliamentary majority and the will of the homogeneous people' (Schmitt 2004 [1932]: 24). Underpinning this conception was the assumption that 'every democracy rests on the presupposition of the indivisibly similar, entire, unified people' (Schmitt 2004 [1932]: 28). If parliament did not represent the will of a unified people, respect for legislation would descend into sterile proceduralism. Schmitt argued that it made no sense to obey statutes passed by a (socialist) parliament simply on the grounds that as a matter of formal process they had been passed by a representative assembly. If the parliament had ceased to represent the will of an 'indivisibly similar, entire, unified people', then the sovereign law-maker who could act as guarantor of the legal order would have to be found elsewhere.

It is in this context that Schmitt wrote perhaps his most famous sentence: 'Sovereign is he who decides on the exception' (Schmitt 2005 [1934]: 5). For Schmitt, the essence of the legal form 'lies in the concrete decision, one that emanates from a particular authority' (Schmitt 2005 [1934]: 34). And every decision in turn 'contains a constitutive element' (Schmitt 2005 [1934]: 26). The law 'cannot realize itself', this realization occurs through the decision, and yet the law does not prescribe 'who should decide' (Schmitt 2005 [1934]: 33). This is the constitutive element contained within each decision, and indeed secreted within every legal order. According to this conception of law, whenever 'the legally highest authority does not have the actual capacity to make a decision and impose it according to the established procedures', the legal order comes under pressure (Huysmans 2006: 148). The problem of who can and should guarantee that a decision is made, and thus 'rescue the essence of the legal form', is central to Schmitt's theory of legality and legitimacy (Huysmans 2006: 149). Schmitt argued that in times of emergency, such as is experienced by people caught up in civil war, the preservation of the legal and political order depends upon the existence of a sovereign who can restore the legal form. The essence of the legal form in this conception is the decision. For a legal system to remain legitimate, it must allow for this sovereign decision to be taken if the existing order is under threat. A legal system needs a guarantor of its fundamental values to make such decisions in times of emergency. As we will see in the next section, this decisionist conception of the relation between law and sovereignty emerges in many contemporary arguments about the legitimacy of humanitarian intervention.

Democratic account of law

The fourth and final account of law which is relevant to understanding the debates about humanitarian intervention we might call democratic. This account of law was developed explicitly in response to Schmitt's constitutional theorizing in 1930s Germany. In particular, David Dyzenhaus has argued that the political theory of law developed in the work of Hermann Heller during this period offers a major challenge to Schmittian decisionism (Dyzenhaus 1997). Heller accepted that the question of whether law is valid is a political – rather than a technical or a metaphysical – question. He agreed with Schmitt that the question of the legitimacy of a constitutive law 'cannot, of course, be answered by referring to its coming into existence in accordance with some previously valid positive propositions' (Heller 2002 [1934]: 278). Rather, the determination of the legitimacy and thus the validity of a law requires a justification from principles that are immanent to the law itself. For Dyzenhaus, Heller's account of law requires that the determination of validity involve a consideration of whether any particular law 'is the product of a properly functioning democratic legal order' (Dyzenhaus 1997: 254). Law is understood to constitute and be itself constituted by the (idealized) commitment to understanding relations between individuals (or states) in terms of a political community of equals. In this account of law, all claims to authority or truth, even those made on behalf of law, must remain visible and contestable. Power cannot and should not be made to disappear 'into rational and logical relationships of legality' – rather, there is no outside to politics, including the politics of law (Dyzenhaus 1997: 256–7).

BROADER ISSUES
LEGALITY, LEGITIMACY AND THE POLITICS OF INTERVENTION

How do these different accounts of the relation between legitimacy and legality, or norm and exception, help us to think about what can be done – effectively, responsibly, lawfully – to stop people hurting each other? During the 1990s, a metaphysical account of law often underpinned the answer to this question. From this perspective, the way to stop people harming others is to bring into being a new global community capable of fully representing universal values of justice, peace, human rights and development. Those advocating increased intervention in the name of human rights often sought to elevate certain priorities, decisions or values above political debate. In this new age of wars on terror and in the context of the rise of competing forms of religious militancy, those advocating the use of force are far less likely to make use of universalist claims to be acting in the name of universal values or a common humanity. It is difficult to argue convincingly in such a climate that there exists a stable set of common values animating all states and peoples, or that coalitions of the willing might intervene in the name of defending such values.

For more on how religion and politics mix see **Chapter 6**. For an account of how the suspicion of religious militancy can hamper humanitarian assistance see **Chapter 23**.

In many ways, this is not a bad thing. Metaphysical accounts of humanitarian intervention as illegal but legitimate make it difficult to take responsibility for the practices that are authorized by the claim that one is acting on behalf of universal values to bring into being a global civil society. Where action is understood to be motivated by the need to redeem the lack of law, rights or development in another society, the measure of whether the action is proper will not be its immediate effects upon that society. Rather, the gaze will be upon the coming community which the action is designed to bring into being.

Let me give one example of the way in which this focus upon the future creates problems in the present. The international human rights tradition is committed to constraining executive government, regulating and confining the exercise of emergency or discretionary powers. And yet the approach taken by human rights activists in the debate about humanitarian intervention has been to call for military action to be taken in extreme circumstances to redeem universal values that may transcend particular legal orders. This call for increased intervention by powerful states necessarily relies upon executive governments, militaries and multinational corporations as its agents. While

The idea of human rights is also more contentious than is often admitted: see **Chapter 27**.

BOX 25.4 HABERMAS AND COSMOPOLITANISM

A focus on the coming cosmopolitan community is illustrated well by the work of Jürgen Habermas. Habermas endorsed the Kosovo intervention on the basis that it was understood by Continental European states 'as an "anticipation" of an effective law of world citizenship – as a step along the path from classical international law to what German philosopher Immanuel Kant (1724–1804) envisioned as the "status of world citizen" which would afford legal protection to citizens against their own criminal regimes' (Habermas 2004). The measurement of the propriety of this action is then in terms of the extent to which it represents a further step along the path to world citizenship and the coming cosmopolitan order.

Habermas has spelt out his vision of the Kantian project of international law in a series of essays published as *The Divided West* (Habermas 2006).

FIGURE 25.9
Jürgen Habermas

much of the human rights movement has been properly appalled by the abuses carried out by US military and security forces in the war on terror, advocates of humanitarian intervention do not ask whether increased intervention by the US military under its current rules of engagement offers the best strategy for the protection of individuals in Third World states. While much human rights activism has focused on the exploitative practices of multinational corporations in their operations in the Third World, advocates of humanitarian intervention do not ask whether enabling an increased presence by foreign contractors in the post-conflict period offers the best strategy for ending suffering in the Third World. These concerns are forgotten in the support for increased resort to military action and increased multinational corporate presence implicit in the call for greater international intervention. The metaphysical question – how can we bring into being a civil society to ensure that universal values are guaranteed to all of humanity? – provides an inadequate grounding for analysing whether humanitarian intervention is in fact a good thing for the people it is designed to serve.

For a discussion of torture and detention see **Chapter 2**.

This approach to intervention also makes it difficult to take responsibility for the violence of practices authorized by the international community in the name of ending suffering. The desire to 'do something' to save those at risk of harm in far off places is often a response to viewing televised images of suffering in the Third World. Images of suffering functioned throughout the 1990s to explain the need for institutional intervention, and in so doing operated also as forms of entertainment and spiritual enrichment for their audiences. The publics of militarily powerful states watched nameless starving, weeping, mourning strangers who appeared as part of a narrative in which the audience was persuaded of the superiority of its nation-state and its capacity to rescue and redeem these others. In contrast, the military actions undertaken by

Media representations of wars impact on how we see the world: **Chapter 8**. The problem of doing something about what is wrong in the world is explored in **Chapter 28**.

Chapter 20 examines our emotional response to the poor who are also imagined as living in far away places.

FIGURE 25.10
This photograph appears on many UN and national government websites. The image is of a United Nations peacekeeping soldier, a member of UNTAET's Portuguese contingent, accompanied by a group of local children as he conducts a security patrol in the Becora district of Dili, East Timor.

powerful states in the name of humanitarian intervention, such as that undertaken by NATO in response to the Kosovo crisis in 1999, are represented as bloodless. Body counts by intervening forces are often not made available, and the high-tech violence involved in bombing is portrayed in televised reports as spectacular rather than brutal. Images of peacekeepers often portray them as fatherly figures – talking to children, building schools or fixing roads.

For more on the problem of counting the dead see **Chapter 28**.

People who talk in terms of the national interest imagine that courses of action that are good for the state are also good for the people within it.

And yet, having pointed to the problems associated with the metaphysical account of law, the sceptical climate of the new millennium has its own dangers. The first of these is that the tendency to dismiss claims to universalism strengthens a national-interest based approach to foreign policy and a realist account of law. If all law is merely a reflection of the interests of powerful states, there is no reason to hope that anything can or will be done to ensure that the international order is premised upon a commitment to justice, human rights or equality. In this vision, law offers no constraint or limit to guide our thinking about what we *can* do in the world – according to this realist account, we can do whatever we have the military and economic power to do in situations where this will further our national interest. To the extent that law ceases to provide an expression of our national interest, we will withdraw from it, just as Australia withdrew from the jurisdiction of international tribunals in the context of the Timor Gap negotiations discussed above. Where such a vision of international law prevails, humanitarian intervention may serve merely to militarize relations between powerful and less powerful states. Law may offer some resources for stopping people harming each other, but only where this end is an expression of the interests of the entities who make up the existing order.

The sceptical environment also fuels the decisionist account of law. Indeed, this approach to law underpins much of the discussion of the emerging notion of the responsibility to protect, which has gradually colonized legal and political debate about intervention since its development by the International Commission on Intervention and State Sovereignty (ICISS), in 2001. ICISS was an international initiative designed to respond to the perceived tension between state sovereignty and humanitarian intervention in the aftermath of the NATO action. Its report proposed a re-characterization of the humanitarian intervention debate, 'not as an argument about any right at all but rather about a responsibility – one to protect people at grave risk' (Evans 2006: 708). According to ICISS, thinking of sovereignty in those terms enabled a clearer focus upon the 'functions' of 'state authorities'. Sovereignty as responsibility 'implies that the state authorities are responsible for the functions of protecting the safety and lives of citizens and promotion of their welfare' (ICISS 2001: 13). In circumstances where the state does not have the power, the capacity or the will to perform those functions, a 'fallback' responsibility to protect on the part of the 'broader community of states' is activated (ICISS 2001: 17). The ICISS report thus offered a theory of authority to justify the exercise of governmental functions by international actors (Orford 2011a). ICISS set out three responsibilities incorporated by the responsibility to protect, namely the responsibility to *prevent* conflict or risk to populations; the responsibility to *react*, including in extreme cases with military intervention; and the responsibility to *rebuild*, particularly after military intervention.

Our responsibilities to those beyond our own political community are discussed in **Chapter 2**. **Chapters 21 and 28** also explore responsibility.

The concept of the responsibility to protect was taken up in the report of the UN High-Level Panel on Threats, Challenges and Change. The Panel argued that what is needed today is a new security consensus.

FIGURE 25.11
Kosovars returning from the forced expulsions of 1999. Photo: Gilles Peress

> The essence of that consensus is simple: we all share responsibility for each other's security. And the test of that consensus will be action.
>
> (United Nations High-Level Panel 2004: 16)

Like ICISS, the Panel developed this notion of a shared responsibility by reference to notions of protection. The Panel endorsed what it referred to as 'the emerging norm that there is a collective international responsibility to protect, exercisable by the Security Council authorizing military intervention as a last resort'. The primacy of protection to the purpose of the state was taken up in the report of the UN secretary-general to the 2005 World Summit session of the General Assembly. The secretary-general there stated: 'I believe that we must embrace the responsibility to protect, and, when necessary, we must act on it' (United Nations Secretary-General 2005: para. 135). He continued: 'This responsibility lies, first and foremost, with each individual State, whose primary raison d'être [or reason for being] and duty is to protect its population'. According to the secretary-general, if 'national authorities' are not able to 'protect their citizens', this responsibility 'shifts to the international community'. The responsibility to protect was enshrined in the World Summit Outcome unanimously adopted by the General Assembly in September 2005, and has since been reaffirmed by the Security Council in resolutions dealing with the protection of civilians in armed conflict, the deployment of peacekeepers in Darfur, and the authorization of intervention against Libya (Orford 2011c).

How does the idea of 'responsibility to protect' work in practice? Can you think of a recent case where there might have been a 'responsibility to protect' but where nothing was done? Or one where something was done but it turned out to bring more harm to the people involved?

A decisionist conception of the need for a sovereign guarantor of law emerges in much of the responsibility to protect literature. This literature assumes that where existing order threatens to break down, a sovereign must be found who can in fact take the decision that a state of emergency exists. Advocates of humanitarian intervention in these terms focus much of their attention on calling for a decision to be made in times of emergency. So Thomas Weiss, a strong supporter of the notion of humanitarian intervention, comments that 'even if none of the choices are ideal, victims still require decisions about outside help' (Weiss 1999: 2). And the ICISS report states:

> The most compelling task now is to work to ensure that when the call goes out to the community of states for action, that call will be answered.
>
> (International Commission on Intervention on State Sovereignty 2001: 70)

To this degree, the responsibility to protect literature adopts Schmitt's solution to the dilemmas of legitimacy – the need for there to be a guarantor of the values of the legal order. The one who decides on the exception – the Security Council, the United States, the coalition of the willing – is the sovereign guarantor in this sense. This prioritizing of the role of the executive as guarantor of the legal order also manifests itself in the post-conflict phase. Intervention is often followed by the creation and legitimization of strong authoritarian administrations in which executive power is almost unrestrained. Here again we see an echo of 1930s Europe. As Alexander Somek suggests, the effect of authoritarian state theory was to diminish the space for parliamentary participation and expand the space for executive governance in the name of achieving social and economic integration (Somek 2003). This is precisely the nature and effect of post-

Is this transfer of a form of sovereignty to the Security Council, the United States of America or a random grouping of concerned states a new form of world government? Or merely a new imperial power? In whose interests is it likely to operate? To whom is it accountable?

conflict governance in the aftermath of international interventions in places such as Timor-Leste, where international administrators suspend democratic participation until political order and economic integration are secured.

At times, the responsibility to protect literature also draws on a more democratic politics of law. This account of the politics of international law treats issues of participation, representation and accountability as essential to establishing the legitimacy of particular forms of authority or of particular decisions. Attention to such questions of political practice have already emerged as a feature of institutional discussion of the responsibility to protect and collective security since 2001. For example, while the High-Level Panel endorsed the responsibility to protect, it spelt out that it is for the Security Council to decide whether or not resort to force is justified. It then stated that such decisions must not only be legal, but there must also be 'the common perception of their legitimacy – their being made on solid evidentiary grounds, and for the right reasons, morally as well as legally' (United Nations High Level Panel 2004). In its discussion of the question of legitimacy of the global collective security system, the High-Level Panel notes:

For a more extensive view of how democracy might work, other than through the standard institutional arrangements, see **Chapter 14**.

> If the Security Council is to win the respect it must have as the primary body in the collective security system, it is critical that the most important and influential decisions, those with large-scale life-and-death impact, be better made, better substantiated and better communicated.
>
> (United Nations High Level Panel 2004)

The High-Level Panel here seeks to expand the justificatory obligations of the Security Council. It assumes that the Security Council as a political organ representing the otherwise secretive security interests of powerful states is nonetheless part of a political community, to which it must account publicly for the bases of its decisions to authorize (or refuse to authorize) the use of force against Third World states. Arguments about the need for the international community to exercise responsibility while protecting were made strongly by states such as Brazil in the aftermath of the NATO intervention against Libya (Government of Brazil 2011).

As noted above, the responsibility to protect concept also directs attention to decisions other than those involved in the resort to force. According to the ICISS report, decisions about protection now involve not simply the decision about whether to use force, but the myriad decisions authorized by the notion that the responsibility to protect involves not just a responsibility to react, but also a responsibility to prevent and to rebuild. Although the scope of the responsibility to protect concept as endorsed in the World Summit Outcome is narrow, being limited to the responsibility to protect populations against genocide, ethnic cleansing, war crimes and crimes against humanity, the practices envisaged for the implementation of the concept are broad. According to Secretary-General Ban Ki-moon, implementation will involve 'utilizing the whole prevention and protection tool kit available to the United Nations system', with the aim of 'integrating the system's multiple channels of information and assessment' (United Nations Press Release 2008), adopting a 'unifying perspective' and facilitating 'system-wide coherence' (United Nations Secretary-General 2009). This will require an expansion and refocusing of the UN's 'early warning and assessment capacities', to

This shift is reflected in the existence of a new literature on state-building, as opposed to peace-building or peace-keeping. This again raises the question of how we know what is good for others (**Chapter 21**).

ensure that the UN 'acts as one in the flow and assessment of information' (United Nations Secretary-General 2010).

The responsibility to protect concept it thus being used to consolidate established practices of international executive rule, such as surveillance, peacekeeping, and civilian administration, and to provide a coherent normative framework for those practices (Orford 2011a, 2011b). The effects of the responsibility to protect will depend on the actions taken in relation to these other aspects of protection. Who will decide what protection will mean in a particular time and place, how it can be realized and which claimant to authority is able to provide it? What laws will govern questions of resource ownership, contract allocation and economic restructuring in post-conflict states? How will the powers and responsibilities of the (international) executive and the (local) parliamentary government be determined? Such issues will shape the political orders – both national and international – brought into being through these ongoing acts of intervention.

Does the doctrine of responsibility to protect have overtones of neo-colonialism? **Chapters 15 and 16** discuss similar questions.

CONCLUSION

The question – What can we do to stop people harming others? – registers the demand for justice in an age dominated by internationalist narratives, whether of globalization and harmonization, or of high-tech wars on terror and for humanity. In this chapter, I have suggested that there is both a political and a legal aspect to this question.

In political terms, the question of what we can *effectively* do to stop people harming others asks us to reflect upon what measures or actions are demanded of the international community in the name of humanitarian action in the post-Cold War era. This chapter has been critical of the tendency to answer this question by advocating resort to force as the means of protecting people in the Third World. Despite the prohibition against the use of force enshrined in the UN Charter, there has been a persistent trend to militarize the relationship between First and Third worlds, usually on the basis that an emergency exists justifying, if not requiring, resort to force. The focus on military action as the means for protecting those at risk of direct violence at the hands of the state, militias or insurgents detracts attention from the ways in which our world order is built upon other policies and practices which harm people – severe restrictions on asylum, strict controls over immigration, ruthless economic exploitation and an unjust international division of labour. Whether we 'can' change these policies raises questions of our own political capacity to participate in shaping the conditions of our lives and those whose lives we touch.

Examples of restrictions on movement are discussed in **Chapter 10** and economic exploitation in **Chapter 15**.

In legal terms, the question of what we can *lawfully* do to stop people harming others raises issues of the legal authority to take action and the protocols or procedures for making decisions about matters that affect the lives of others. It also raises questions about who has the name to speak in the name of law in a particular territory, and how different laws should encounter each other (McVeigh 2007; Orford 2007). In this sense, what 'we' can do is not something that can lawfully be determined only by 'us'. Rather than seeing politics as somehow separate from legality, decision-making about protection must be informed by a concept of law that is itself strongly political. Such a concept of law would assume that in order to be valid, law must be the product of a particular kind of political order and must in turn place obligations upon the members of the community it constitutes. At the least, these obligations would include a commitment to equal participation in the making of law as essential to establishing the legitimacy of particular forms of authority. Bringing decisions about what 'we' can do to help others within a fully political, and thus contestable, account of international law, offers some possibility of justice for those the international community claims to protect.

FURTHER READING

Critical legal readings of humanitarian intervention in the 1990s can be found in Orford (1999, 2003), Koskenniemi (2002) and Charlesworth (2002). Analyses of the significance of the responsibility to protect concept include Thakur (2011), Orford (2011a) and Evans (2008). A key text on the legacy of the civilizing mission for international law is Anghie (2004). Beard (2006) develops a rich account of international law as metaphysics, while Dyzenhaus (1997) provides a detailed analysis of the major constitutionalist theories of law that emerged in Weimar Germany. An analysis of the relationship between these constitutional accounts and the framing of contemporary global politics can be found in Huysmans (2006). Cleary (2007) is a revealing insider's account of the negotiations between Australia and Timor-Leste concerning the Timor Sea oil and gas fields.

WEBSITES

International Centre for Trade and Sustainable Development, http://www.ictsd.org/
News and information relating to trade and development issues and place to subscribe to the excellent Bridges Weekly Trade News Digest email service.

International Coalition for the Responsibility to Protect, http://www.responsibilitytoprotect.org/
Website of a coalition of non-governmental organizations that support the strengthening of the responsibility to protect concept.

La'o Hamatuk, www.laohamutuk.org
The website of a Timorese NGO, offering incisive analysis of the politics of contemporary international engagement with Timor-Leste.

National Security Archive, http://www.gwu.edu/~nsarchiv/
The website of a non-governmental research institute which collects and publishes declassified US government documents, particularly relating to US security and economic policies.

Timor-Leste official government site, http://www.timor-leste.gov.tl/
Official website of the Timorese government, providing historical material about Timor-Leste and covering all areas of governmental responsibility.

United Nations Peace and Security website, http://www.un.org/peace/
UN website providing access to material relating to peace and security.

REFERENCES

ABC News Online (2006a) 'E. Timor Unrest an Attempted Coup: PM', 9 May, http://www.abc.net.au/news/newsitems/200605/s1634598.htm.

——(2006b) 'East Timor Rejects Need for Peacekeepers', 12 May, http://www.abc.net.au/news/newsitems/200605/s1637481.htm.

Aditjondro, George (2000) 'From Colony to Global Prize', *Arena Magazine* 47, June: 22–32.

Anghie, Antony (2004) *Imperialism, Sovereignty and the Making of International Law*, Cambridge: Cambridge University Press.

Annan, Kofi (1999) 'Two Concepts of Sovereignty', *Economist*, 18 September: 49–50.

Beard, Jennifer L. (2006) *The Political Economy of Desire: International Law, Development and the Nation State*, London: Cavendish–Routledge.

Blair, Tony (1999a) 'Doctrine of the International Community', speech given to the Economic Club of Chicago, Chicago, 22 April, http://www.fco.gov.uk/news/speechtext.asp?2316.

——(1999b) 'Statement on the Suspension of NATO Air Strikes against Yugoslavia', London, 10 June, http://www.fco.gov.uk/news/newstext.asp?2536.

Cady, Jean-Christian (2000) 'Building the New State of East Timor', lecture given at the Centre for International and Public Law, Australian National University, 18 May.

Carty, Antony (2006) 'Visions of the Past of International Society: Law, History or Politics?', *Modern Law Review* 69, 4: 644–60.

Cassese, Antonio (1999) '*Ex Iniuria Ius Oritur:* Are We Moving towards International Legitimation of Forcible Humanitarian Countermeasures in the World Community?', *European Journal of International Law* 10, 1: 23–30.

Charlesworth, Hilary (2002) 'International Law: A Discipline of Crisis', *Modern Law Review* 65, 3: 377–92.

Cleary, Paul (2007) *Shakedown: Australia's Grab for Timor Oil*, New South Wales: Allen & Unwin.

Downer, Alexander (Australian Minister for Foreign Affairs) (1999) 'East Timor: The Way Ahead', speech given to the Rotary Club of Sydney, 30 November.

——(2002) 'Changes to International Dispute Resolution', media release, Canberra, 25 March.

Dyzenhaus, David (1997) *Legality and Legitimacy: Carl Schmitt, Hans Kelsen and Hermann Heller in Weimar*, Oxford: Oxford University Press.

Economist (2007) 'Timor-Leste', *Economist Backgrounders*, www.economist.com/research/backgrounders.

Evans, Gareth (2006) 'From Humanitarian Intervention to the Responsibility to Protect', *Wisconsin International Law Journal* 24, 3: 703–22.

——(2008) *The Responsibility to Protect: Ending Mass Atrocity Crimes Once and For All*, Washington, DC: Brookings Institution Press.

Government of Brazil (2011) Concept note on 'Responsibility While Protecting', annexed to the 'Letter dated 9 November 2011 from the Permanent Representative of Brazil to the United Nations addressed to the Secretary-General', UN Doc A/66/551-S/2011/701, 11 November.

Habermas, Jürgen (2004) 'America and the World', *Logos: A Journal of Modern Society and Culture* 3, 3: 101–22.

——(2006) *The Divided West*, trans. Ciaran Cronin, Cambridge: Polity Press.

Harding, Neil (1996) *Leninism*, Basingstoke: Macmillan.

Heller, Hermann (2002 [1934]) 'The Essence and Structure of the State', in Arthur J. Jacobson and Bernhard Schlink (eds) *Weimar: A Jurisprudence of Crisis*, Berkeley: University of California Press.

Huysmans, Jef (2006) 'International Politics of Exception: Competing Visions of International Political Order Between Law and Politics', *Alternatives* 31, 2: 135–65.

ICISS (International Commission on Intervention and State Sovereignty) (2001) *The Responsibility to Protect*, http://www.iciss.ca/report-en.asp.

Koskenniemi, Martti (2002) '"The Lady Doth Protest Too Much": Kosovo and the Turn to Ethics in International Law', *Modern Law Review* 65, 2: 159–75.

La'o Hamutuk (2000) 'The World Bank in East Timor', *Bulletin La'o Hamutuk* 1, 4: 1, http://www.laohamutuk.org/Bulletin/2000/Dec/lhbul4en.pdf.

——(2005) 'An Overview of FALINTIL's Transformation to FDTL and Its Implications', *Bulletin La'o Hamutuk* 6, 1–2: 1–5, http://www.laohamutuk.org/Bulletin/2005/Apr/lhbl6n1e.pdf.

Lenin, Vladimir (1951) *The State and Revolution*, Moscow: Foreign Languages Publishing House.

McVeigh, Shaun (ed.) (2007) *Jurisprudence of Jurisdiction*, Abingdon: Routledge-Cavendish.

Orford, Anne (1999) 'Muscular Humanitarianism: Reading the Narratives of the New Interventionism', *European Journal of International Law* 10: 679–711.

——(2003) *Reading Humanitarian Intervention: Human Rights and the Use of Force in International Law*, Cambridge: Cambridge University Press.

——(2007) 'Ritual, Mediation and the International Laws of the South', *Griffith Law Review* 16: 353–74.

——(2011a) *International Authority and the Responsibility to Protect*, Cambridge: Cambridge University Press.

——(2011b) 'From Promise to Practice? The Legal Significance of the Responsibility to Protect Concept', *Global Responsibility to Protect* 3: 400–24.

——(2011c) 'What Kind of Law Is This?', *London Review of Books Blog*, 29 March.

Schmitt, Carl (1996) *The Leviathan in the State Theory of Thomas Hobbes: Meaning and Failure of a Political Symbol*, Westport, CT: Greenwood Press.

——(2003 [1950]) *The* Nomos *of the Earth in the International Law of the* Jus Publicum Europaeum, trans. G. L. Ulmen, New York: Telos Press.

——(2004 [1932]) *Legality and Legitimacy*, trans. and ed. Jeffrey Seitzer, Durham, NC: Duke University Press.

——(2005 [1934]) *Political Theology: Four Chapters on the Concept of Sovereignty*, 2nd edn, trans. George Schwab, Chicago: University of Chicago Press.

Simma, Bruno (1999) 'NATO, the UN and the Use of Force: Legal Aspects', *European Journal of International Law* 10, 1: 1–22.

Somek, Alexander (2003) 'Austrian Constitutional Doctrine 1933 to 1938', in Christian Joerges and Navraj Singh Ghaleigh (eds) *Darker Legacies of Law in Europe*, Oxford: Hart Publishing.

Thakur, Ramesh (2011) *The Responsibility to Protect: Norms, Laws and the Use of Force in International Politics*, London: Routledge

Traub, James (2000) 'Inventing East Timor', *Foreign Affairs* 79, 4: 74–89.

United Nations High-Level Panel on Threats, Challenges and Change (2004) *A More Secure World: Our Shared Responsibility*, UN Doc A59/565, http://www.un.org/secureworld/.

United Nations Independent Special Commission of Inquiry for Timor-Leste (2006) Report, 2 October, Geneva, http://www.ohchr.org/Documents/Countries/COITimorLeste.pdf.

United Nations Press Release (2008) *Secretary-General Defends, Clarifies 'Responsibility to Protect' at Berlin Event on 'Responsibility to Protect: International Cooperation for a Changed World'*, UN press release SG/SM/11701, 15 July 2008.

United Nations Secretary-General (2005) *In Larger Freedom: Towards Development, Security and Human Rights for All*, report delivered to the General Assembly, UN Doc A/59/2005, 21 March.

——(2009) *Implementing the Responsibility to Protect: Report of the Secretary-General*, A/63/677, 12 January.

——(2010) *Early Warning, Assessment and the Responsibility to Protect: Report of the Secretary-General*, A/64/864, 14 July.

Weiss, Thomas (1999) 'Principles, Politics, and Humanitarian Action', *Ethics and International Affairs* 13: 1–22.

Žižek, Slavoj (ed.) (2002) *Revolution at the Gates: Žižek on Lenin – the 1917 Writings*, London: Verso.

For a range of further resources supporting this chapter, please visit the companion website for *Global Politics, 2nd Edition* at www.routledge.com/cw/edkins/

CHAPTER 26

Can we move beyond conflict?

Roland Bleiker

THE QUESTION
DEALING WITH SEEMINGLY INTRACTABLE CONFLICTS

This chapter examines one of the oldest and most difficult political problems: how to deal with conflicts that are so deeply entrenched that they seem virtually inevitable. Prospects for peace are particularly slim in societies that have experienced a major trauma, such as genocide or a war. From the Middle East to Afghanistan, from Sri Lanka to Somalia, from Iraq to East Timor and from Rwanda to Kashmir, years and often decades of conflict have left societies deeply divided and traumatized. New forms of violence constantly emerge, generating yet more hatred. Commentators speak of so-called intractable conflicts: situations where antagonisms have persisted for so long that they have created a vicious cycle of violence. A particularly influential example of such a position is Robert Kaplan's (2005) analysis of the ethnic conflict that devastated the Balkan region during the first part of the 1990s. Kaplan believes that the political volatility that followed the break-up of Yugoslavia was linked to old ethnic and religious hatreds between Croats, Serbs and Muslims. These deeply seated antagonisms, he stresses, go back hundreds of years to the clash between the Ancient Roman and Byzantine empires, between a Christian European West and a Muslim Ottoman East.

There is another discussion of the break-up of Yugoslavia in **Chapter 5**.

How can societies that have been torn apart by war and trauma ever become peaceful again? Politicians and scholars are deeply divided about how to answer this question. Numerous commentators strongly oppose the very notion of intractable conflicts. They locate the roots of violence not in ancient hatreds, but in much more recent political manipulations (see Naimark 2002). David Campbell, for instance, provides an interpretation of the conflict in the Balkans that differs fundamentally from Kaplan's. For Campbell (1998: xi) the problem did not lie in ancient ethnic hatreds. The conflict, he believes, was linked to the recent actions of political elites. They opposed multiculturalism and actively generated fear in an attempt to gain and retain power. Ethnicity then became politicized in a way that turned once peaceful neighbours into enemies.

David Campbell's understanding of violence is explored in **Chapter 23**.

Chapter 27 explains what multiculturalism is and why it has become controversial recently in some Western states.

The examples shown here are brief and necessarily incomplete. But they reveal an important point: each conflict is situated in a unique political, social and historical setting. The nature of a conflict can only be understood in the context of its unique environment. No general theory can ever do justice to these complexities. Violence and hatred do not appear without a reason. They emerge as a result of specific grievances and historical struggles. As a result there are no ready-made solutions that can restore order and stability.

Although each conflict is unique, one can still learn from how particular societies have dealt with their political challenges. There are, indeed, numerous cases where seemingly intractable conflicts have eventually given way to more peaceful or at least more stable situations. For instance, many conflicts linked to racial segregation, from the United States to South Africa, have meanwhile been replaced by political orders that promote racial equality, at least at the formal, institutional level. Or look at the situation in Northern Ireland. After several decades of violence and terror the situation today is more stable than it has been for a long time. Another example is the Cold War. After half a century of intense and global confrontations between a communist East and a capitalist West we now live in a world no longer dominated by the competition between two ideologically motivated superpowers.

Chapter 22 considers the opposite question: What brings about the move from politics to violence in the first place? How does armed conflict or organized violence come about?

What, then, can one learn from these positive and negative examples? Why can some conflicts be solved or at least managed while others generate ever more hatred and violence? Expressed in other words: what is the key to moving beyond conflict? Given the uniqueness of each conflict, this chapter examines the issues at stake not in an abstract manner, but in a concrete political setting: the deeply entrenched conflict on the divided Korean peninsula, where hatred and constant tension continue to dominate politics even half a century after the Korean War. But there is progress too. There are occasional breakthroughs: diplomatic agreements, cross-border visits, gestures of goodwill. And there are setbacks. Again and again. But hope emerges precisely from a more thorough understanding of what actually drives these patterns of progress and regress, conflict and co-operation, hatred and empathy.

Although the chapter illustrates the issues at stake through a case study on Korea it does not seek to provide an update on the most recent events. Doing so would be impossible, particularly in Korea, where politics is rapidly changing all the time. New events keep happening and the various actors involved regularly reposition themselves. Policy makers in North and South Korea, for instance, often alter their diplomatic attitudes depending either on strategic choices or domestic political struggles. Or look at how the stance of the United States, which plays a key role in Korea, has gone back and forth between an uncompromising confrontational position and a more tolerant attitude, reflecting respective policy debates in Washington. Rather than seeking to capture the latest stage of these ever changing political struggles, the purpose of this chapter is to illuminate the underlying dynamics that have shaped conflict in Korea for decades.

ILLUSTRATIVE EXAMPLE
THE CONFLICT IN KOREA

For the last half a century the Korean peninsula has been divided between a communist North and a capitalist South, each viewing the other as its ideological arch-rival. Over the years these antagonisms have become so deeply entrenched in societal consciousness that hatred and tension are seen as an inevitable aspect of politics. The reasons for this seemingly intractable conflict are located in particular historical events.

Historical background

Japan occupied Korea in the 1890s and formally annexed the country in 1910. At the end of the Second World War the two dominant victorious countries, the United States and the Soviet Union, dismantled the defeated Japanese colonial empire. In this context they divided the Korean peninsula into two parts along the 38th parallel. The US occupied the southern part and the Soviets the northern one. Separate political regimes were established on each side, reflecting the ideological standpoints of the two superpowers. In the south the Republic of Korea was formed in August 1948. The new country, led by its first president, the Korean expatriate Syngman Rhee, became a close ally of the US. The northern part of the peninsula then became the Democratic People's Republic of Korea. Its first head of state was Kim Il Sung, an anti-Japanese guerrilla fighter. The country adopted a unique nationalist form of communist ideology and became a close ally of both the Soviet Union and China.

The roots of the ongoing conflict in Korea are located not only in the division of the country but also, and above all, in the three-year war that devastated the peninsula from 1950 to 1953. More than a million people died as a result of the conflict that saw the North and the South confronting each other. The war also involved several external powers. China intervened on behalf of the North while the South was supported by a United Nations Command, led by the US. The trauma and hatred that the war generated continues to dominate virtually all aspects of politics today. Feelings of anger and revenge remain deep-seated.

These 'ideological visions' are like the language games that were discussed in **Chapter 2**. They influence people's thinking about the world. The Cold War was often seen as based on competing ideologies. Compare this with the view of contemporary conflicts as a 'clash of civilizations' or as derived from different religious views: **Chapter 6**.

On each side, an unusually strong state emerged and was able to promote a particular ideological vision of politics and society: a vision that constructs the other side of the dividing line as an enemy and a source of fear and instability. A passionate anti-capitalist attitude dominates the reclusive North while a more moderate but still pronounced anti-communist orientation prevails in the South (see Grinker 1998; Hart 1999; Cumings 1997).

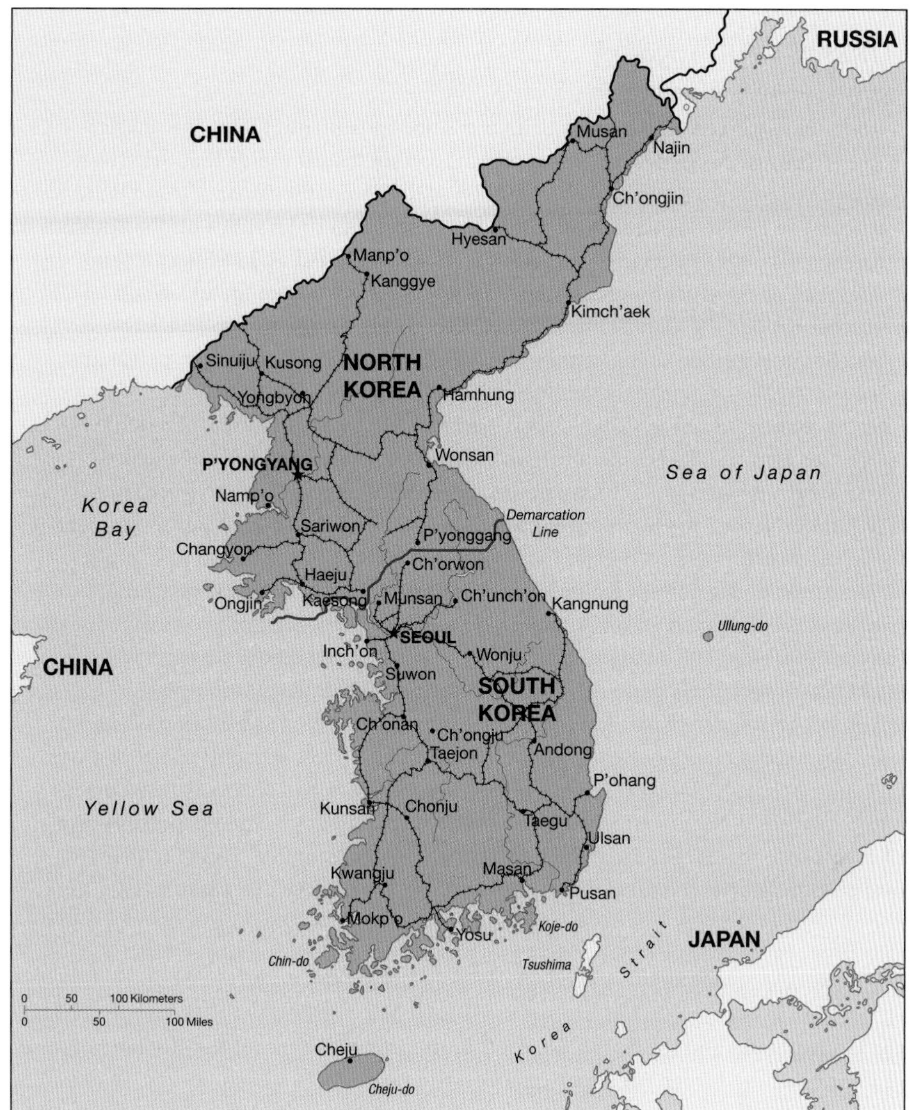

FIGURE 26.1 Map of the Korean Peninsula

Geographical context

The conflict scenario in Korea has been fuelled even more by the unusually important geographical location of the peninsula. Constituting a natural link between the Asian mainland and Japan, Korea has always been an important factor in the security policy of the surrounding powers. In the nineteenth century, two major wars were fought for control of the peninsula, one between Japan and China (1894/5), the other between Japan and Russia (1904/5). With the development of military technology in the twentieth century, the geographical importance of Korea has increased further. The division of the peninsula must to a substantial part be attributed to the strategic and symbolic importance of Korea in the emerging Cold War power struggle between

BOX 26.1 THE KOREAN WAR, 1950–53

The Korean War lasted from June 1950 until the signing of an armistice agreement in July 1953. It killed more than a million people. The most commonly accepted explanation for the war holds that there were constant political tensions on the peninsula ever since its division at the end of the Second World War. Then, in June 1950, a full-scale war broke out when North Korea launched a surprise attack on the South, trying to bring the entire peninsula under its control. Although the conflict started as a civil war it soon involved, on opposing sides, two of the great powers of the Cold War: first the United States, which intervened, together with other nations through a United Nations mandate designed to roll back the Northern occupation of the South; and then China, whose involvement saved the North from defeat and secured a military stalemate along the original dividing line at the 38th parallel.

The Korean Armistice Agreement of July 1953, which was never signed by South Korea, constitutes only a cease fire. A clause called for a political conference, on the basis of which the terms of a peace treaty were supposed to have been discussed. This conference, which took place in Geneva in 1954, failed in its prime task. In juridical terms, the two Koreas have thus remained in a state of war ever since. Half a century after the events, an estimated 10 million individuals are still separated from their families.

The wounds of the Korean War have dominated politics on the peninsula for half a century now. The two opposed Korean states have sponsored black-and-white accounts of the war: accounts that put all blame for the conflict on the other side. The antagonistic historical narratives then became essential elements in the creation of two diametrically opposed notions of nationhood, thus contributing substantially to fuelling conflict on the peninsula. An increasing number of revisionist historians have recently been trying to see beyond the black and white images that make up most accounts of conflict on the peninsula. Bruce Cumings (1997), for instance, stresses that intense fighting had already taken place for the 9 months prior to June 1950. Without denying North Korea's responsibility, Cumings presents the war as a complex set of events with multiple causes. Such revisionist positions on the origins of the war are controversial but also constitute an essential element in coming to terms with such a traumatic event.

Chapter 12 explains political developments in China.

the United States and the Soviet Union. But the competition over the Korean peninsula did not remain a Soviet-American affair. In the early 1960s China became increasingly independent of its communist ally, the Soviet Union. As a result, both of these important powers started to compete for influence over North Korea. Add to this that Japan's post-war reconstruction was so successful that it developed into an important economic force. The political situation in Korea thus became directly linked to the security and economic interests of four great powers, the United States, the Soviet Union, China and Japan.

Developments since the end of the Cold War

Much has changed over the last decades. The Soviet-led global alliance system fell apart in the early 1990s and the Cold War gave way to a new form of international politics. But in Korea strikingly much remains the same. The peninsula is still divided between a communist North and a capitalist South.

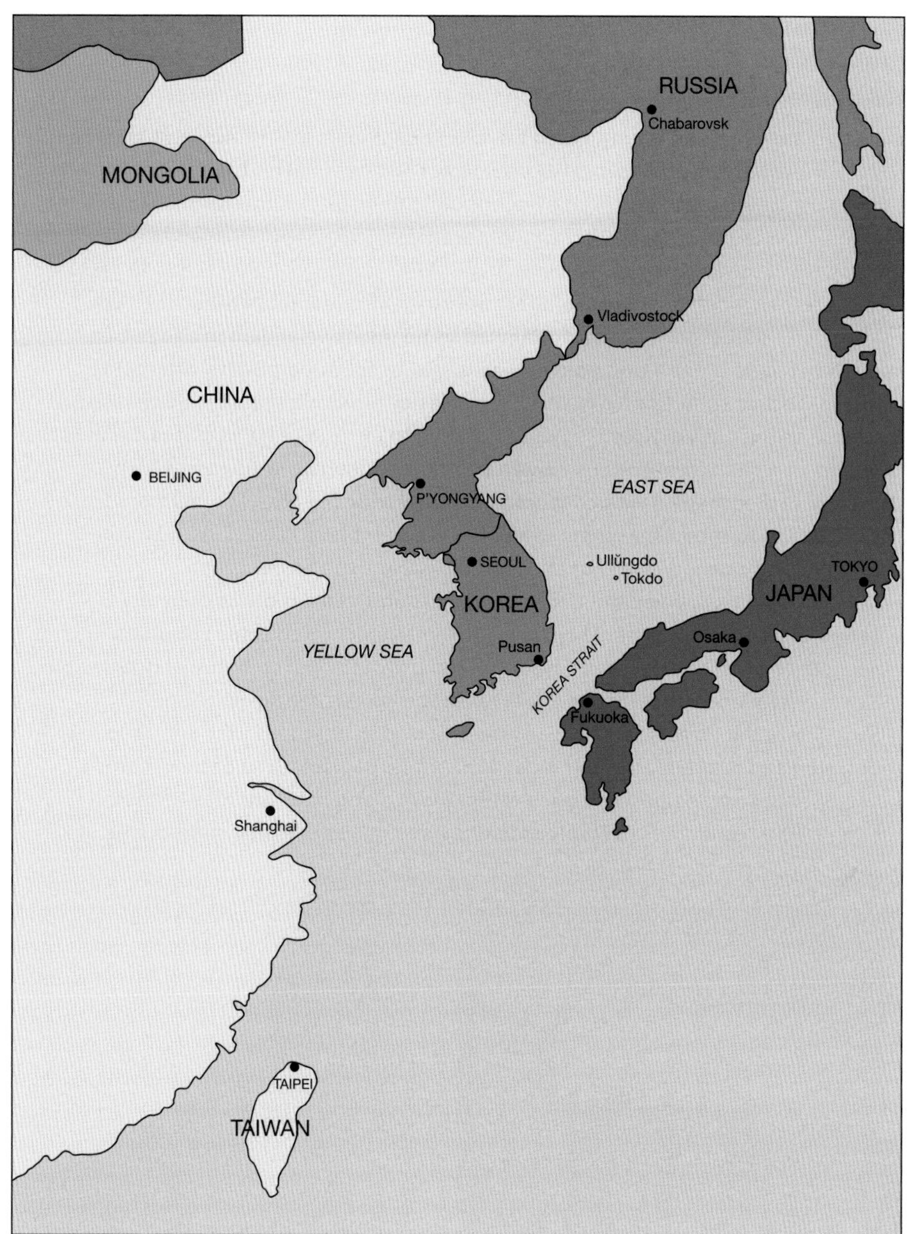

FIGURE 26.2
Map of the geographical location of the Korean Peninsula

The North remains an authoritarian communist regime. It is perhaps the world's most reclusive country. Travel to and from North Korea is severely restricted. The country's population has no access to foreign information sources and the government controlled media network is tightly censored. More information has recently become available about life within North Korea (Demick 2009; Hassig and Oh 2009; Myers 2010). But this does not change the country's seclusion and the highly secretive nature of its political power structure and decision making process. Add to this a set of

BOX 26.2 THE COLD WAR, 1947–1989

During the Cold War global politics was largely dominated by the competition between two rival alliance systems. One was led by the United States and advocated democracy and free-market capitalism. The other revolved around the Soviet Union and was driven by communist principles. Although the US and the Soviet Union were allies during the Second World War, an intense ideological rivalry emerged between these two so-called superpowers in the late 1940s.

The Cold War was cold because it did not involve a direct military confrontation between the two superpowers. But for four decades global politics was dominated by an intensive and often dangerous stand-off between them. In most parts of the world politics was driven by the superpowers' attempt to increase and maintain their respective spheres of influence (the areas of the world that they dominated). Numerous regional wars, such as the ones in Korea (1950–53) and Vietnam (1964–75), opposed capitalist and communist alliance partners. Equally problematic was an increasingly intense arms race, which developed because each side was preoccupied with containing and deterring the other. On numerous occasions the arms race threatened to provoke a global conflict. A key event here is the Cuban Missile Crisis of 1962, which nearly led to an open nuclear war between the US and the Soviet Union.

There were moments, as in the 1970s, when the two superpowers adopted a more conciliatory approach. This led to a period of so-called détente. There were also moments when some countries refused to submit to the dictate of either superpower. China, for instance, retained communist policies but started to distance itself increasingly from its communist ally and superpower, the Soviet Union.

The Cold War only ended once the Soviet-led alliance system started to crumble in the late 1980s. By the early 1990s the Soviet Union had disintegrated and most of its allies, particularly in Eastern Europe, abandoned their communist policies and embarked on moves to adopt democratic and free-market oriented forms of government. As a result, the US emerged as the most powerful global state, a type of sole superpower.

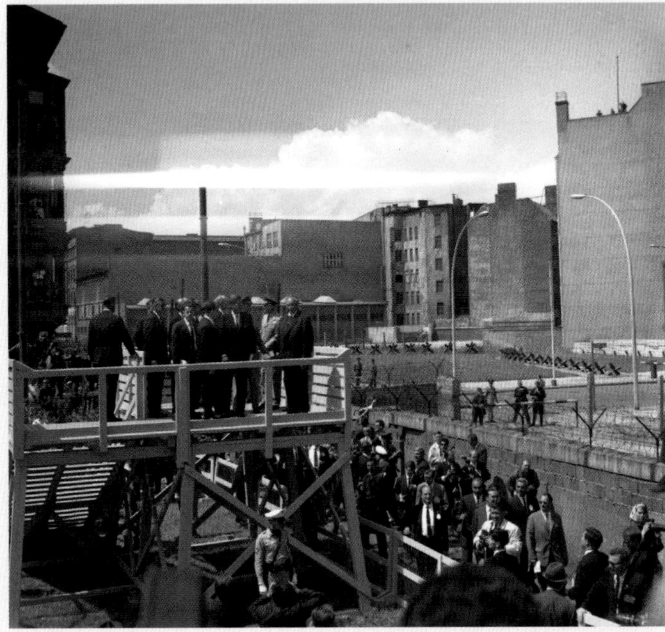

FIGURE 26.3
President John F. Kennedy at the Berlin Wall, Germany, June 1963. Photo: Robert Knudsen, White House. Courtesy of the John F. Kennedy Library, Boston

unimaginable daily challenges for the population. Having been devastated by several years of famine and economic mismanagement, North Korea is also one of the world's poorest countries.

Economic problems like these are not restricted to communist regimes. Compare the account of strategic adjustment and development in the Ivory Coast in **Chapter 15**.

The South, by contrast, has embarked on a successful path of democratization and economic development. Here too, the geographical situation has accentuated differences. With the collapse of the Soviet-led alliance system the communist regime in the North became even more isolated. It lost one of its strongest allies and trading partners, the Soviet Union. Even China, which intervened in the Korean War on behalf of the North and has remained a strong supporter ever since, is now distancing itself increasingly from the regime in Pyongyang, North Korea's capital. Add to this that the US, as the sole remaining superpower, has meanwhile become the single most influential external actor on the peninsula, substantially shaping the security issues at stake.

Neither the collapse of the global Cold-War system nor North Korea's increasingly isolated position have eased tension on the peninsula. Quite the contrary, the situation is as volatile as ever. At regular intervals tensions risk escalating into a more direct confrontation.

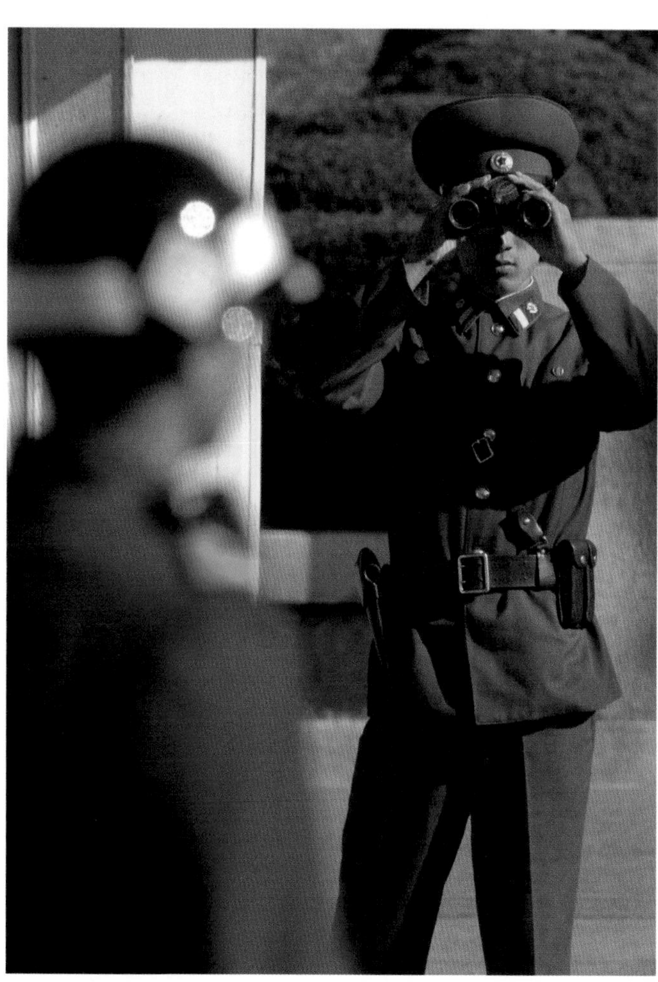

FIGURE 26.4
A North Korean soldier looks through a pair of binoculars as a South Korean solider stands guard in the demilitarized zone dividing the two Koreas, in the village of Panmunjom, on the North–South border, 2007. Photo: Jung Yeon-Je/AFP/Getty Images

These 'crises' are perhaps not as serious as the crises that occurred during the Cold War – the Cuban Missile Crisis which occurred when the Soviet Union stationed nuclear warheads in Cuba, within easy range of the US, could have led to a nuclear war between the two superpowers. For a discussion of what it means to think in terms of crises in the first place see **Chapter 18**.

Of particular importance are the various so-called nuclear crises that have haunted the peninsula during the last two decades. The first crisis emerged in the early 1990s. Although Pyongyang had signed the Nuclear Non-Proliferation Treaty in 1985, it retained its ambition to develop a nuclear weapons programme. US intelligence reports drew attention to a plutonium processing plant in Yongbyon. Various negotiation rounds followed. In 1992 North Korea agreed to have its nuclear facility inspected by the International Atomic Energy Agency. But only a few months later disagreements over inspections increased and in March 1993 North Korea declared its intention to withdraw from the Non-Proliferation Treaty. William Perry (2000: 121), then US secretary of defense, considered the subsequent crisis the only time during his tenure when he 'believed that the US was in serious danger of a major war'. An agreement signed in October 1994 managed to avert an open conflict. Pyongyang consented to freeze its nuclear programme in return for a number of US, South Korean and Japanese promises, including aid, heating oil and the eventual construction of two light-water nuclear reactors that would provide North Korea with energy sources.

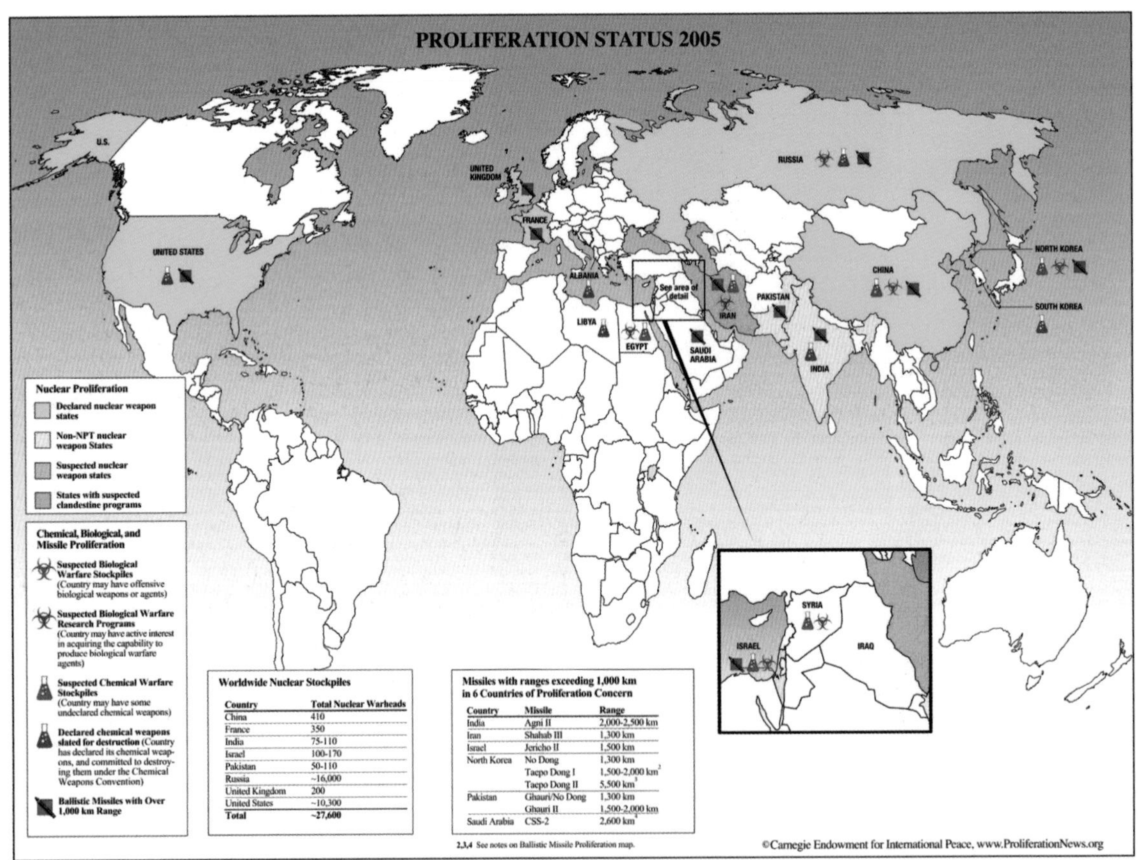

Worldwide Nuclear Stockpiles

Country	Total Nuclear Warheads
China	410
France	350
India	75-110
Israel	100-170
Pakistan	50-110
Russia	~16,000
United Kingdom	200
United States	~10,300
Total	**~27,600**

Missiles with ranges exceeding 1,000 km in 6 Countries of Proliferation Concern

Country	Missile	Range
India	Agni II	2,000-2,500 km
Iran	Shahab III	1,300 km
Israel	Jericho II	1,500 km
North Korea	No Dong	1,300 km
	Taepo Dong I	1,500-2,000 km[2]
	Taepo Dong II	5,500 km[3]
Pakistan	Ghauri/No Dong	1,300 km
	Ghauri II	1,500-2,000 km
Saudi Arabia	CSS-2	2,600 km[4]

FIGURE 26.5
Nuclear, chemical and biological weapons proliferation status in 2005. © Carnegie Endowment for International Peace, www.ProliferationNews.org

BOX 26.3 NUCLEAR NON-PROLIFERATION TREATY

The Nuclear Non-Proliferation Treaty, often referred to as the NPT, emerged in the late 1960s and entered into force in 1970. It was designed to stop the spread of nuclear weapons in an effort to reach a more stable and peaceful world. The treaty acknowledges that the five permanent members of the United Nations Security Council are so-called nuclear weapons states, because they had tested nuclear devices prior to 1967. These are the United States, the Soviet Union (now in the form of Russia), France, China and the United Kingdom. These five states sought to prevent all other states from acquiring nuclear weapons. In return for agreeing not to develop nuclear weapons, the states that signed up to the NPT were promised assistance from the nuclear weapons states to develop nuclear technology for energy, medical and other peaceful purposes. The nuclear weapons states also promised, under Article VI, to eliminate their nuclear weapons. As this has not happened, the discriminatory nature of the treaty, whereby five states continue to possess nuclear weapons, while others are prevented from doing so, has made the NPT controversial. The treaty was extended indefinitely in a landmark review conference in 1995.

A total of 189 countries have ratified the Non-Proliferation Treaty. India, Pakistan and Israel have not signed the treaty. The former two are confirmed nuclear powers while the latter is known to possess nuclear weapons but has not officially confirmed their existence. At numerous points during the last decades smaller states sought to develop nuclear weapons. These included Libya, which has subsequently renounced its programme, and North Korea, which withdrew from the NPT in 2003 and tested its first nuclear device in 2006. Iran's covert uranium enrichment programme has also caused controversy and political tension, so much so that, in November 2011, the International Atomic Energy Agency expressed 'increasing concern' about the programme and its destabilizing influence on the regional security situation.

The International Atomic Energy Agency is the recognized authority that deals with such disputes. As a UN agency based in Vienna, its mission is to ensure that non-nuclear weapons states do not develop nuclear weapons, and to promote the peaceful use of nuclear technology. More specifically, it foresees that all non-nuclear states that want to develop nuclear technology need to put in place certain safeguards. The respective procedures include opening up nuclear facilities for regular inspections by the International Atomic Energy Agency. These inspections are designed to make sure that the state in question is not diverting its nuclear technology programme to weapons purposes.

FIGURE 26.6
Non-proliferation Treaty signing ceremony, July 1968, Moscow. US Ambassador Llewellyn E. Thompson, left, signs the treaty with Soviet Foreign Minister Andrei A. Gromyko. Among US embassy and Soviet government officials witnessing the ceremony is Soviet Premier Alexei N. Kosygin, standing third from right. Photo: AP Wide World Photos

Once the nuclear crisis of 1994 was solved all parties concerned embarked on a more co-operative route. The inauguration of Kim Dae-jung (2000) as South Korea's president in early 1998 signalled the advent of a policy that was more conciliatory, or at least more willing to engage the arch-enemy across the dividing line. The US administration under President Clinton was strongly supportive of this approach. Of particular significance here is an official policy review, conducted by former defense secretary William Perry. This report located the main threat in North Korea's ambition to acquire nuclear weapons or to develop, test and deploy long-range missiles. At the same time, though, the Perry Report called for a fundamental review of US policy towards Pyongyang, advocating a position that rests not only on military deterrence, but also on a 'new, comprehensive and integrated approach' to negotiations with North Korea (Perry 1999: 8).

The new policy attitudes in Washington and Seoul, capital of South Korea, soon led to several breakthroughs, including the lifting of restrictions on trade with, investment in and travel to North Korea. Pyongyang responded in turn with a variety of gestures, such as a gradual (although still very timid) opening of its borders, agreements on family exchanges with the South and a tuning down of its hostile rhetoric. The process of détente culminated in June 2000 with a historic summit meeting between the two Korean heads of state, Kim Jong-il and Kim Dae-jung. But détente in Korea did not last long.

By early 2002 the fragile security arrangement started to break down. The new US president, George W. Bush, adopted a more confrontational policy, which sharply reversed the conciliatory approach pursued during the Clinton administration. In his first State of the Union Address, Bush singled out North Korea, together with Iraq and Iran, as one of three nations belonging to an axis of evil. He cited as evidence Pyongyang's export of ballistic missile technology and its lingering ambition to become a nuclear power. Soon afterwards, the Defense Department, in a report to Congress, included North Korea in a group of seven nations that were potential targets of pre-emptive nuclear strikes. Pyongyang reacted in an angry manner, warning that it would abandon the agreed freeze of its nuclear weapons programme, which it subsequently did. The situation then rapidly deteriorated. North Korea officially announced that it would restart its nuclear reactor at Yongbyon. It withdrew from the Nuclear Non-Proliferation Treaty and forced inspectors of the International Atomic Energy Agency to leave the country. In October 2006 the world community reacted with strong and unanimous protest against Pyongyang's announcement that it had successfully completed a nuclear test.

Tensions were partly diffused in 2007, when North Korea agreed to dismantle its nuclear programme. But by mid-2009 the situation was as dangerous as ever after North Korea conduced several new nuclear and missile tests and announced, yet again, that it would renege on its commitment to nuclear disarmament. The crisis reached an unprecedented level in 2010: a North Korean torpedo attack killed forty-six South Korean sailors, and the shelling of the island of Yeonpyeong killed four people and wounded twenty. Even moderate commentators now feared that 'for the fist time in decades, a new war on the Korean peninsula appears to be a distinct probability' (Lankov, 2010).

The most recent turn of events has only increased the unpredictable and potentially destabilizing situation in Northeast Asia. On 17 December 2011 the North Korean leader, Kim Jong-il, died of a heart attack. Just as he had assumed power after his father's death in 1994, Kim Jong-il was succeeded by his third son, Kim Jong-un. Thought to be in his late twenties, Kim Jong-un looks likely to continue his father's policies: embarking on occasional provocations designed to coerce the international community into providing North Korea with desperately needed aid. Given that Kim Jong-un still has to consolidate his power base, the chance of miscalculations and corresponding escalations is unusually high.

GENERAL RESPONSES

CONFRONTATION AND ENGAGEMENT: TWO APPROACHES TO CONFLICT

How is it possible to find a way out of the seemingly intractable conflict in Korea? Have decades of antagonisms and hatred created a pattern of conflict that can no longer be overcome? There are, certainly, no easy solutions.

One of the most difficult – and important – tasks is figuring out how to deal with North Korea. Totalitarian and reclusive, ideologically isolated and economically ruined, it is a very unusual country in today's liberal world order. But North Korea manages to survive, not least because its leaders periodically rely on threats, such as nuclear blackmail, to gain concessions from the international community. The dangers of these policies are evident and much discussed. Miscalculations or a sudden escalation could precipitate a human disaster at any moment.

Equally dangerous, although much less evident, are some of the attitudes with which key regional and global countries, such as the United States, seek to contain the volatile situation. Debates about how to deal with North Korea – and the Korean conflict in general – can be located at two ends of opposing poles. The prevailing approach advocates a confrontational attitude. It relies on economic sanctions and the projection of military threats in an attempt to contain the situation and bring about change within North Korea (Cha 2002; Eberstadt 1997; Rice 2000). Advocates of confrontation felt vindicated by the most recent crises, noting, as Edward Luttwak (2010) did, that 'it's time South Korea started shooting back'. The second approach favours engaging North Korea in political, economic and cultural interactions. It assumes that a peaceful solution emerges not from forcing North Korea into submission, but from integrating it into the world community (Harrison 1997; Dujarric 2001; Moon 2001). Advocates of engagement too believe that the most recent crises have only underlined the primacy of their position (Lankov 2010).

When we say 'international community' we sometimes mean all the states in the world, sometimes a group of rich and powerful states, sometimes the UN Security Council or – sometimes – the UN General Assembly. The term 'international community' is used frequently in **Chapter 25**.

Confrontation

First to the most commonly practised stance, which seeks to confront and undermine North Korea through a mixture of military threats and economic sanctions. 'If the North Korean regime is irredeemable', Marcus Noland (2000: 8) asks, 'should not the rest of the world act to hasten its demise?' Withdrawing support would, undoubtedly, worsen the economic situation in the North and precipitate yet another famine. But is this not the price to pay for bringing about necessary change? Providing Pyongyang with trade

FIGURE 26.7
The British nuclear test code-named Hurricane. Photo: The National Archives, Kew, Richmond, Surrey. ref.: ADM280/966

The question 'Why do some people think they know what is good for others?' which is dealt with in **Chapter 21**, is interesting here.

possibilities and humanitarian aid would, according to this logic, not only sustain a dictatorial and dangerous regime but also prolong the suffering of the North Korean people. Several non-governmental organizations (NGOs for short) that provided humanitarian aid, such as Oxfam and Médecins sans Frontières, left North Korea because they were prevented from adequately monitoring and evaluating the impact of their aid, which they feared did not reach the most vulnerable part of the population.

It is important to consider who and what comes to be seen as dangerous and why: see **Chapter 24**.

In the realm of security policy the confrontational approach is exemplified by the foreign policy of the United States under the administration of President George W. Bush. In his first State of the Union Address, Bush identified Pyongyang as one of several 'evil' rogue states. With the transition to a post-Cold War order, so-called rogue states replaced the Soviet Union as the main threat. North Korea, together with Iraq and Iran, were seen as the most dangerous of these rogues: totalitarian states that disrespected human rights and aspired to posses weapons of mass destruction. As had already been the case during the Cold War, military means are considered the key methods through which the threat of rogue states is to be opposed. Illustrative here is a US *Nuclear Posture Review* which became public in June 2002. It stipulated that the new US strategic doctrine relied on the possibility of employing pre-emptive nuclear strikes against terrorists and rogue states. North Korea was explicitly cited with regard to two possible scenarios: countering an attack on the South and halting the proliferation of weapons of mass destruction. A few months later Washington made its threats official. The *National Security Strategy* (2002), released in September 2002, outlined in detail how pre-emptive strikes are legitimate and would be employed as a way to 'stop rogue states and their terrorist clients before they are able to threaten or use weapons of mass destruction against the United States'.

FIGURE 26.8
The heavily mined demilitarized zone between North and South Korea seen from a South Korean military observation post. The zone has become a haven for wildlife.
Photo: Seokyong Lee for the *New York Times*

BOX 26.4 THE WAR ON TERROR

Terrorism is as old as politics. But over the last decade or so the phenomenon has gained renewed political significance. The terrorist attacks of 11 September 2001 marked a key turning point in international politics. The death toll alone would not necessarily render the event so central, for many other recent conflicts, from Bosnia to Rwanda, produced far more casualties. September 11 is significant because it fundamentally questioned the prevailing sense of security in the West. The terrorist attack of September 11 represents a type of threat that cannot easily be anticipated, nor prevented, through prevailing state-based structures of security. The danger stemmed not from another state, but from a non-state organization, and one that cannot be precisely defined and located. The conflict was not launched with conventional military equipment, but with simple means. The attack itself took place in surprise, revealing a fundamental weakness in the state's intelligence apparatus. The attack neither involved opposing forces nor was it directed at a battlefield or a military target. It struck at the very heart of political, economic and civilian life.

The response by the US and its allies, most notably the UK, was swift and determined. The ensuing so-called war on terror was meant to punish those responsible for the attacks of September 11 and prevent a similar future attack from occurring. An invasion of Afghanistan in 2001 targeted terrorist cells directly. But soon the war on terror was expanded to include so-called rogue states: states that were said to be sympathetic to terrorism or have the ambition to develop nuclear arms and other weapons of mass destruction. The US identified Iraq, Iran and North Korea as rogue states and termed them the axis of evil. In 2003, the US and its allies invaded Iraq with the objective of preventing the regime from further developing and using weapons of mass destruction. But no such weapons were ever discovered, nor was there any evidence that could connect the country to the perpetrators of the terrorist attacks of September 11.

Although heralded as a new form of conducting international politics, the war on terror was characterized by a striking similarity with thinking patterns that dominated foreign policy during the Cold War. Once again the world was divided into 'good' and 'evil', and once again military means occupied the key, if not the only role in protecting the former against the latter. Since the election of Barack Obama as US president in 2008, the term 'war on terror' has dropped from official usage, but arguably the way of thinking remains much the same.

FIGURE 26.9
'Maybe you should reconsider those place cards.' Artist: Dave Carpenter. CartoonStock ref.: dcr0435h www.CartoonStock.com

The confrontational and militaristic attitude to security does not necessarily exclude negotiations. Diplomacy and dialogue are seen as continuously important, but they occupy only a supporting role. On numerous occasions President Bush publicly declared a willingness to engage Pyongyang in diplomatic negotiations. At the same time, though, the projection of threats towards North Korea was carefully maintained, even intensified. Ever since the latest nuclear crisis emerged in Korea, officials in Washington have kept stressing that military power is always an option.

Prevailing approaches to security, based on deterrence and the projection of military threats, have failed to deal successfully with the key security challenges in Korea. There are various reasons why the confrontational approach has not worked. Four of them stand out particularly.

First, the use of military power as an instrument of deterrence and pressure has proven to be relatively ineffective with regard to North Korea. The US has, of course, threatened and used military power quite frequently to achieve political goals, most recently in Afghanistan, Iraq and Libya. Such actions were aimed at either pressuring a regime to change its behaviour or at actually removing it from power altogether. But strategic experts largely agree that a military solution to the nuclear crisis in Korea is highly problematic. One of the world's biggest cities, Seoul, is only 50 kilometres away from the heavily militarized Demilitarized Zone. Even if pre-emptive strikes were to neutralize North Korea's growing nuclear arsenal, they would not be able to destroy all its conventional weapons. The latter alone could easily trigger a second Korean war with disastrous consequences on all sides. Intensifying threats against North Korea would also provide its regime with a welcome source of legitimacy. The result might be a population rallying around its threatened government, no matter how despotic it is.

The second element of the confrontational approach is economic sanctions. Such sanctions were pronounced against North Korea by the UN Security Council in a unanimously accepted resolution on 14 October 2006. Taken in direct response to Pyongyang's nuclear test, these sanctions were the most far-reaching ones imposed against North Korea since the end of the Korean War in 1953. They included not only any material that could be used to produce nuclear, biological and chemical weapons, but also bans on international travel and a freeze of assets held by people associated with Pyongyang's contentious weapons programmes. The problem with sanctions is that they have historically been of very limited use. Miroslav Nincic (2005) stresses that failure is the norm, as in the cases of Iran, Iraq, Yugoslavia, Afghanistan and North Korea. In fact, Nincic goes as far as believing that comprehensive economic sanctions often had a counter-productive effect, leading to a modification of a regime's ideology and economy that actually ended up strengthening its grip on power.

Third, despite paying lip service to the idea of negotiations, a confrontational approach forecloses most options other than those based on military means and economic sanctions. 'The opposition between good and evil is not negotiable', Allan Bloom (1987: 142) already noted at the time of Ronald Reagan's presidency. It is a question of principles, and thus 'a cause of war'. Expressed in other words, the rhetoric of evil moves the phenomena of rogue states into the realm of irrationality. Evil is in essence a term of condemnation for a phenomenon that can neither be fully comprehended nor addressed, except through militaristic forms of power politics. This is why various commentators believe that the rhetoric of evil prevents rather than encourages understanding. They go as far as arguing that it evades accountability, for it leads to policy positions that 'deny negotiations and compromise' (Klusmeyer and Suhrke 2002: 27–9, 35–7; Euben 2002: 4). How is it, indeed, possible to negotiate with evil without being implicated in it?

See **Chapter 2** for a discussion of the importance of language and rhetoric in another case, that of torture.

Fourth, the confrontational approach fails to take into account the interactive nature of conflicts. Very few policy makers, security analysts and journalists ever make the effort to imagine how threats are perceived from the North Korean perspective, and how these perceptions are part of an interactive security dilemma in which the West is implicated too. North Korea does not exist in a vacuum. It cannot be understood outside the insecurities and fear left by four decades of Japanese colonialism, followed by the Korean War and half a century of national division and Cold War tension (Cumings 2004: ix, 151). Particularly significant is the current policy of pre-emptive strikes against rogue states, for it reinforces half a century of American nuclear threats towards North Korea.

For a detailed examination of how colonialism works and what its legacies can be see **Chapter 16**.

Engagement

There are alternatives to confrontation. A second, opposing approach holds that engaging North Korea and integrating it into the world community is the best opportunity to prevent a military escalation and create a more peaceful political environment. Several humanitarian organizations, for instance, stayed behind in North Korea, believing that the possibility of providing humanitarian assistance and development co-operation was essential, even if the conditions were far from ideal. Withdrawing aid, they feared, would only heighten the danger of a confrontation and worsen the situation of the population but not necessarily bring about change for the better. Underlying

People who advocate engagement with apparently hostile regimes are sometimes accused of being too 'soft'. This can translate into an accusation of not being 'masculine' enough.

FIGURE 26.10 Demilitarized Zone opens for train passage, Paju, South Korea, 17 May 2007. Photo: Chung Sung-Jun/Getty Images

the logic of this position was the recognition that there are very few cases where famines have brought down an authoritarian regime (Savage 2002: 155).

South Korea has become the strongest proponent of a policy of engagement with the North. Starting with his inaugural speech in February 1998, South Korea's president, Kim Dae-jung, called for a new approach towards the North. Kim's initiative revolved around moving from a deeply entrenched politics of confrontation towards an attitude that promotes reconciliation and co-operation (Kihl 1998: 23; Moon and Steinberg 1999). Kim's successor, Roh Moo-hyun, supported and continued this approach.

The engagement policy is driven by a key emphasis on dialogue. The notion of dialogue goes substantially further than the diplomatic positioning advocated by the confrontational approach. The attempt, rather, consists of engaging the parties to the conflict in genuine negotiations. The most spectacular result of this policy was an unprecedented summit meeting between the two Korean heads of state in June 2000. The most recent success of engagement is an agreement reached in February 2007 between North Korea, South Korea, the US, China, Russia and Japan. The agreement ended, at least temporarily, the tense standoff that culminated four months earlier with North Korea's first nuclear test. Resembling the agreement reached in 1994, the 2007 deal foresees North Korea abandoning its nuclear weapons programme in exchange for fuel oil, food aid and other economic assistance. The agreement, which was strongly critiqued by conservative policy analysts in Washington, also constitutes an implicit acknowledgment by the Bush administration that confrontation did not work: that engagement offers the most promising approach to solving the security crisis on the Korean peninsula. Half a year after this agreement, in October 2007, there was a second historic summit meeting between the two Korean heads of state, Kim Jong-il and Roh Moo-hyun.

Perhaps even more important than high level diplomatic negotiations is the fact that Kim and Roh's engagement policy generated various forms of low-level cross-border exchanges, from tourist visits, cultural and sports engagements to family reunions. Central here was a substantial increase in cross-border economic activities, which had been all but non-existent until recently. The 2007 Agreement foresees further cross-border economic activities, such as cooperative shipbuilding complexes, common fishing zones and the opening of a cargo rail service. By international standards these economic activities may be insignificant. But they are spectacular in the context of the hermetically sealed Korean peninsula.

The engagement policy is based on the traditional liberal assumption that increased economic interactions will eventually engender common interest and understanding. In a context where commercial activities are at stake, the key actors have a strong interest in reducing the likelihood of conflict since it would jeopardize profit and investment (Moon 2001: 188–89). But there is more to cross-border activities than mere interdependence. The ensuing contacts may also help to reduce the deeply entrenched stereotypical perceptions that Koreans have of their compatriots across the dividing line (Chung 1999: 125). They may also bring North Koreans in contact with the outside world. There is, in fact, evidence that North Korea's tightly sealed borders are becoming more porous. As a result of North Korea's desperate economic situation, starving refugees go to China in search for food. They bring back information about the outside world. Videos, DVDs and tuneable radios are smuggled in. Alternative news sources, such as 'Open Radio for North Korea', also bring in information that allows the population to compare its situation with the outside world (Lankov 2008).

BROADER ISSUES
DEALING WITH ANTAGONISM

Engagement and dialogue offer viable alternatives to confrontation. But they are not without problems either. The Sunshine Policy of South Korean presidents Kim Dae-jung and Roh Moo-hyun might have been more effective in bringing North Korea to the negotiating table, but there are major ethical dilemmas in negotiating with and delivering aid to an authoritarian regime that commits widespread human rights violations. Not surprisingly, North Korea frequently 'cheated', pursing nuclear programmes in secret while negotiating in seeming good faith with the international community. This is one of the reasons why after a decade of engagement South Korea reversed course. The latest president, Lee Myung Bak, was inaugurated in 2008 and opted for a much more confrontational approach to the North. He did so even though the new US president, Barack Obama, pursued a more conciliatory diplomacy.

Both confrontation and engagement leave unaddressed larger questions about how to develop the type of tolerance necessary to live with deep seated antagonisms that inevitably exist after major traumas. Wars, genocides or terrorist attacks shape people and societies for decades to come. They not only become an essential component of individual and collective identities, but also risk re-igniting new forms of tension and violence.

When facing seemingly intractable conflicts, one of the most difficult challenges consists of accepting the existence of deep seated wounds and grievances without letting them degenerate into violence. The promotion of dialogue is important in this process, but not enough. Just as crucial is a certain level of tolerance: an acceptance that there are – and for the foreseeable future will be – major differences between the conflicting parties and their attitudes.

Collective memory after the world wars in Europe is contentious and contested too: see **Chapter 22**.

In Korea this challenge largely revolves around coming to terms with the traumatic past, most notably with the legacy of the Korean War. The memory of pain and death is far too present for a single unified understanding of history to emerge. Each side does, in essence, blame the other for causing the war. And each side has rehearsed and institutionalized its particular understanding of the past while making every effort to shield their respective populations from the diametrically opposed position promoted by the other side. Little does it matter that some of the respective historical perspectives, such as North Korea's hero worship of its first leader, Kim Il Sung, are based far more on fiction than on fact. The different understandings of history and society are so deeply entrenched that they cannot easily be overcome, at least not in the near future.

Recognizing the existence of historical differences is a crucial element in moving beyond conflict. The French philosopher Paul Ricoeur (1999: 13) stresses that by 'acknowledging that the history of an event involves a conflict of several interpretations and memories, we in turn open up the future'. Susan Dwyer (1999: 89) takes this idea further and offers a useful way of conceptualizing what is at stake in the process of reconciliation. Three steps, she argues, are necessary. The first consists of an effort to find agreement on 'the barest of facts'. The second stage involves an effort to identify a range of different interpretations of the respective events. And the third stage would entail narrowing things down to a limited set of interpretations that the two sides can tolerate. While such a goal of agreeing to disagree seems modest, the path towards it is littered with seemingly insurmountable obstacles. The first hurdle alone is already very difficult, for Dwyer defines agreeing on 'the barest of facts' as finding a clear view on 'who did what to whom and when'. In Korea, these 'bare facts' are, of course, precisely the major point of contention – and the source of trauma and hatred.

Moving beyond conflict requires a compromise between a search for justice and the ability to forgive – a compromise that is all too often neglected by prevailing confrontational approaches. Holding people accountable for past wrongdoings is essential. But so is a willingness to 'forget' some aspects of the traumatic past that continuously fuel conflict. The German philosopher Friedrich Nietzsche (1981: 118) stresses that the past suffocates the present unless we forget it. He calls upon people to have the courage to 'break with the past in order to live'. Forgetting, in this sense, does not mean ignoring what happened. Forgetting, after all, is a natural process, an inevitable aspect of remembering; we all do it, whether we want to or not. We cannot possibly remember everything. We cannot give every event the same weight. Our memory of the past is the result of a process through which certain events and interpretations are remembered and prioritized, while others are relegated to secondary importance or forgotten altogether. This is particularly the case with a major event like the Korean War, which is far too complex to be remembered in its totality. The task of historians is to select the few facts, perspectives and interpretations that ought to be remembered. The combination of forgetting and remembering is as inevitable as it is political. Being aware of this inevitability is to explore possibilities for reshaping the past and using this process in the service of creating a better future (Nietzsche 1981: 100). Nietzsche is particularly critical of periods when historical understandings lack critical awareness of this process –

It has been pointed out that we forget much more than we remember: most of what happens is in this sense 'forgotten'.

BOX 26.5 FRIEDRICH NIETZSCHE

Friedrich Nietzsche is a German philosopher (1844–1900) whose work has shaped a range of contemporary thinkers. Nietzsche's influence has less to do with the particular political views he held than with the manner in which he approached more fundamental questions of knowledge. In particular, he challenged the deeply entrenched modern search for universal forms of truth, whether they be based in Christian morals or scientific foundations. Nietzsche believed that the search for truth always contained a will to power. Seen from such a vantage point, a critical investigation into a political issue would need to pay attention to processes of inclusion and exclusion, to how knowledge and power are always intertwined.

FIGURE 26.11
Friedrich Nietzsche

situations, say, when illegitimate rulers misappropriate historical events and mythologies to justify their form of dominance (Nietzsche 1981: 106–7, 111). Such is undoubtedly the case in contemporary Korea, where history has been geared far more towards supporting particular regimes than towards actually representing what happened in the past.

Politics in Korea also displays signs of what Nietzsche calls 'critical histories': attempts to challenge the notion of a single historical reality and create the political space in which diverging understandings of the past can co-exist in an atmosphere of tolerance. A recent example of a breakthrough in this direction, timid as it may well be, can be found in revisions of history school textbooks in South Korea. The composition and use of school textbooks has always been very tightly controlled by the government. These texts, in turn, were then used to legitimize and spread an ideologically driven perspective on history, society and politics. Several generations of history texts have, for instance, studiously avoided even mentioning the role that northern communist guerrillas played in the fight against the Japanese colonial occupiers. Doing so would have been seen as sympathizing with the communist North, even if the presented facts are historically accurate. One of six new secondary school history textbooks, released in 2003, for the first time mentions the existence of communist resistance. It does so in a passage dealing with a 1937 clash between Japanese colonial forces and resistance fighters allegedly led by Kim Il Sung, the future leader of North Korea. In addition to these textbook revisions there is an increasing willingness by school administrators, teachers and students to open up a cross border-dialogue about the past. Some government officials have suggested that the North and South could exchange 'narrative memories' by making available, on both sides, a range of commonly agreed upon historical documents and teaching materials, which could then be used in addition to the official textbooks that each side employs. Young teachers in particular appear willing to move beyond existing patterns of hatred. They often supplement the use of the prescribed textbooks with alternative methods, such as historical simulation, television documentaries, cartoons and newspapers (Hoang 2002).

This is a small example that demonstrates how South and North Korea may be able to open up political spaces in which it becomes possible to contemplate the other's memory of the past, even if this memory appears distorted and inherently wrong. But this small example highlights two very important points.

First: an effort to accept deep seated differences is an important addition to dialogue. But it too is not enough. Accepting difference must go beyond acknowledging that people or societies in conflict have diverging understandings of the past. Leaving it at that would only entrench existing antagonisms, and thus legitimize or even intensify the existing conflict. Keith Krause and Michael Williams (1997: xv) draw attention to this danger, pointing out that in places like Bosnia and Rwanda an awareness of difference led 'not to celebration but destruction'. The objective, much rather, would be a political attitude that is based on tolerance but that can also generate the type of understanding and respect needed for a commonly acceptable and non-violent relationship between former arch-enemies.

Second: the greatest push forward towards reconciliation often comes not from politicians, diplomats or generals, but from the realm of the everyday: from normal citizens, grassroots organizations or popular culture. There have been an increasing number of South Korean films that defy the deeply entrenched tendency to vilify the North. Early and influential examples of this trend include *Heuk Su Seon* ('Last Witness', 2001), *Swiri* (1999) and *Joint Security Area* (or '*JSA*', 2000). The domestic and international success of the latter is particularly important, for the film is one of the rare public features that clearly resists perpetuating the entrenched stereotypical image of cold and evil North Koreans. Instead, *JSA* narrates how a small group of soldiers from both sides develop a friendship, secretly and against all odds. In the end conflict becomes inevitable and the respective soldiers must choose country over friendship. But the film is nevertheless a milestone, for it portrays soldiers on both sides as normal Koreans, with a variety of similar emotions, concerns and interests. This contrasts quite sharply with the confrontational approach that prevails among security experts in Korea.

Novels that resist stereotypes of national identity and that deal with stories of exile and the complicated sense of allegiance and estrangement that many people have in relation to a national community are explored in **Chapter 13**.

Poets and novelists from both sides of the dividing line have embarked on a similarly innovative grassroots attempt at healing the wounds of national division and war. In 2005 a group of North and South Korean writers issued a joint declaration, aiming to promote reconciliation on the peninsula. Numerous activities followed, such as a visit to the North by ninety-eight South Korean writers – a first in more than 60 years. The delegation was led by one of the country's most famous poets, Ko Un. Projects that have already emerged from these efforts include plans for a joint magazine, a literary prize, and the first unified Korean dictionary.

There are many cases where poets have influenced global politics. The war poets in England after the First World War are one example; dissident writers in the Soviet Union are another. Can you think of more? Other forms of cultural output are also important – not only 'high culture' but things like rock music or reggae for example.

Ko Un has not only played a leading role in bringing together writers from both South and North Korea, but also expressed a vision of moving beyond conflict in his own poetry. Having experienced the trauma of war and national division, Ko Un (2002: 20) writes of 'birds that all flew away at the sound of a gun'. He recalls the senseless violence he witnessed as a young man (Ko Un 1996):

Every morning heaven and earth
are piled with dead things.
Our job is to bury them all day long.

BOX 26.6 KOREAN POET KO UN

FIGURE 26.12
Ko Un

Ko Un is one of South Korea's best known poets. Born in 1933, he was shortlisted for the Nobel Prize several times. As a young man, Ko Un directly experienced the atrocities of the Korean War, including the death of several relatives and friends. He then spent 10 years as a Buddhist monk, eventually holding several high ranks in monastic life. In 1966 he rejoined the secular world to set up a charity on the Korean island of Jejudo. A few years later he moved to Seoul in the context of struggling with alcoholism and making several suicide attempts. During the 1970s and 1980s Ko Un was active in the democracy movement, gaining prominence as an outspoken nationalist poet. As a result he spent two years in prison under the regime of general Chun Doo-Hwan. Released in 1982 as part of a general pardon, Ko Un devoted himself to a life of poetry. Most recently he used his reputation to advance the cause of reconciliation with North Korea. Ko Un's literary output comprises over a hundred volumes of poetry, novels, autobiography, dramas, essays, travel books and translations. His is particularly known for a style that brings everyday language to poetry.

In an attempt to show a way out of the ensuing cycle of violence, Ko Un believes in a vision for peace, a vision that views security not only in terms of a military-based defence of the state apparatus, but also as a comprehensive endeavour that promotes the rights and well-being of people. In the same vein as his accessibly written poems, Ko Un implies that the key impetus of genuine transformation often stems from the mass of people and not from their leaders. But he also knows that this process is inevitably slow and littered with obstacles. Deeply entrenched hatred and mistrust cannot disappear overnight. But a policy of engagement, combined with a respect for difference, can offer a way forward. Or so suggests one of Ko Un's (2002: 7) poems:

> Peace is waves.
> Waves breaking, alive
> and beneath those waves
> swim fish of every kind, alive.

CONCLUSION

This chapter has sought to address a political problem that is as old as it is of contemporary relevance: how is it possible to deal with and perhaps even overcome conflicts that are so deeply entrenched that they seem intractable? There are no easy answers to the problems at stake, nor is there a general theory that can offer a comprehensive explanation of conflict and its possible resolution. Each conflict is rooted in particular historical circumstances. Understanding and dealing with these circumstances is essential if conflict is to give way to a more peaceful environment.

The chapter has illustrated the issues at stake by focusing on the seemingly intractable conflict on the divided Korean peninsula, where mutual hatred and constant tensions have dominated politics for over half a century now. One of the most difficult questions today is how to approach a North Korean regime that clearly violates the human rights of its citizens and poses a threat to regional and even global peace. Should one engage in a dialogue with North Korea? Should one try to reach a compromise in order to avoid a dangerous escalation of tension or even a possible war on the peninsula? Or is such an approach merely a policy of appeasement that prolongs the suffering of people and renders the situation in the long run more dangerous? The prevailing approach certainly believes that the latter is the case: it advocates a confrontational stance which relies on military threats and economic sanctions to coerce North Korea into compliant behaviour. Dialogue and negotiations play a role in this policy only to the extent that they reinforce the underlying political and strategic objectives.

The prevailing confrontational approach, which is exemplified by US policy during the administration of President George W. Bush, has not been able to solve the conflict in Korea. Instead, it has rendered the situation in Korea more volatile than it already was, triggering a new nuclear crisis. The two key instruments of the confrontational approach, namely the threat of a military intervention and the use of economic sanctions, have been ineffective policy instruments. Given North Korea's predictable foreign policy behaviour, no amount of threat will convince Pyongyang to abandon its nuclear programme. To the contrary, American projection of military might, including the explicit threat of pre-emptive nuclear strikes against North Korea, only fuelled Pyongyang's perceived need for a nuclear based defence.

A policy of engagement, as practised by the South Korean government between 1998 and 2008, offers a viable alternative to the US-sponsored confrontational approach. The engagement policy advocates genuine negotiations with the North in an attempt to integrate the isolated country into the world community. Essential to this process is the promotion of cultural and economic exchanges across the hermetically sealed dividing line. The ensuing face-to-face encounters between average Koreans have the potential to dismantle at least some of the deeply entrenched antagonistic attitudes that have fuelled conflict in Korea for decades.

Dialogue is crucial in the process of moving beyond conflict. But it is not enough. Just as important is the development of a certain level of tolerance: a willingness to accept that after years of conflict the former enemies will have developed deep seated differences that cannot easily be removed. Key here is an attempt to come to terms with the influence of traumatic past events: an effort to find a compromise between remembering past atrocities and moving beyond them in a spirit of reconciliation. This can only work if all parties concerned engage questions of tolerance and forgiveness in an attempt to establish a political climate in which former enemies can interact in a respectful, or at least non-violent manner.

Sustained engagement and a genuine acceptance of difference cannot, of course, not offer ready-made solutions to deeply entrenched conflicts. No conflict is alike. Each has different causes and thus requires different solutions. Not all lessons learned from Korea can automatically be applied to other situations. But at least some aspects of the

Korean experience can provide important insights that are of a general nature. This applies as well to the following limits to engagement.

First, there will always be suspicion and mistrust in a political situation that has been dominated by conflict. There is deep and very justified suspicion that North Korea may simply misuse offers of engagement, that it may, for instance, 'cheat' and pursue a nuclear programme in secret, independently of the assurances it gives in public. Dealing with an authoritarian regime also poses a range of difficult moral dilemmas. This is particularly the case when humanitarian aid is involved. But no matter how problematic and porous a policy of dialogue may be, it still offers more opportunity to diffuse conflict than the situation engendered by the confrontational approach, which sees North Korea openly pursuing a nuclear weapons programme that destabilizes the entire region.

Second, promoting a policy of engagement and reconciliation inevitably takes time. Entrenched antagonisms cannot be uprooted over night. But the lessons learned from Korea show that it is crucial to think about the values and implications of different approaches to security and conflict. Based on historical evidence, the engagement policy has the best track record of diffusing tension on the peninsula. The fact that it has only been partially successful cannot be held against it, for the confrontational approach has always played an important and all too often a dominant role. Be it in a realist, neo-conservative or communist version, confrontational attitudes are so deeply entrenched that they have come to fulfil their own promises of doom and gloom.

Third and finally: no amount of engagement and tolerance can absolve decision makers, commentators and individuals from making choices, from separating right from wrong. For instance, engaging North Korea in negotiations and accepting that several decades of conflict have deeply divided the peninsula, is not the same as agreeing with or supporting the authoritarian regime in Pyongyang. Even an ethics of difference must, at times, decide about the type of values that are to play a central role in political projects. But the process of articulating and defending these values is likely to be more successful, and less violent, if it is done with the knowledge of and sensitivity towards the complex factors that cause and fuel seemingly intractable conflicts.

FURTHER READING

Bell, Duncan S. A. (ed.) (2006) *Memory, Trauma and World Politics: Reflections on the Relationship between Past and Present*, New York: Palgrave.

A collection of scholarly investigations that illuminate how traumatic events shape political dynamics and how the ensuing conflicts may be understood and overcome.

Cha, Victor D. and David C. Kang (2003) *Nuclear North Korea: A Debate on Engagement Strategies*, New York: Columbia University Press.

An accessibly written exchange between two scholars and policy advisors.

Cumings, Bruce (1997) *Korea's Place in the Sun: A Modern History*, New York: W. W. Norton.

A brief and engagingly presented history of modern Korea, written by one of the most authoritative historians. Cumings' positions are controversial, particularly for challenging the prevailing black-and-white understandings of the Korean War, but they offer very insightful background information about the ongoing conflict in Korea.

Hassig, Ralph and Kongdan, Oh (2009) *The Hidden People of North Korea: Everyday Life in the Hermit Kingdom*, Baltimore, MD: Rowman and Littlefield.

An account of life in North Korea, based on numerous sources, including interviews with hundreds of defectors.

Kim, Samuel S. (2006) *The Two Koreas and the Great Powers*, Cambridge: Cambridge University Press.
An analysis by a leading scholar of how the conflict in Korea is intertwined with regional and global political patterns. Focuses in particular on questions of identity.

Lankov, Andrei (2010) 'How to Stop the Next Korean War', *Foreign Policy*, December 16.
A concise essay by one of the most innovative scholars on the topic, advocating the need to open up North Korea to the outside world.

Moon, Chung-in (2001) 'The Kim Dae Jung Government's Peace Policy towards North Korea', *Asian Perspective* 25, 2: 177–98.
A concise summary of the engagement policy towards North Korea, articulated by one of the most influential South Korean scholars and policy advisors.

WEBSITES

The *Korea Herald*, http://www.koreaherald.co.kr/
This is South Korea's most popular English language newspaper.

KCNA, or the Korean Central News Agency, http://www.kcna.co.jp/index-e.htm
This is North Korea's news agency. It publishes a bulletin of news reflecting North Korea's position.

The Korea Web-Weekly, http://www.kimsoft.com/korea.htm
A site that aims to be independent and non-partisan, offering a range of useful information and links about Korea, including the political situation.

Ko Un, http://www.koun.co.kr/
The website of the Korean poet Ko Un, offering a portrayal of him and his work.

REFERENCES

Bloom, Allan (1987) *The Closing of the American Mind*, New York: Simon and Schuster.

Campbell, David (1998) *National Deconstruction: Violence, Identity, and Justice in Bosnia*, Minneapolis: University of Minnesota Press.

Cha, Victor D. (2002) 'Korea's Place in the Axis', *Foreign Affairs* 81, 3: 79–92.

Chung, Oknim (1999) 'The US-ROK Private Sector Role in Peace and Security on the Korean Peninsula', *The Korean Journal of Defense Analysis* 11, 1: 101–26.

Cumings, Bruce (1997) *Korea's Place in the Sun: A Modern History*, New York: W. W. Norton.

——(2004) *North Korea: Another Country*, New York: The New Press.

Demick, Barbara (2009) *Nothing to Envy: Ordinary Lives in North Korea*, New York: Spiegel and Grau.

Dujarric, Robert (2001) 'North Korea: Risks and Rewards of Engagement', *Journal of International Affairs* 54, 2: 465–87.

Dwyer, Susan (1999) 'Reconciliation for Realists', *Ethics and International Affairs* 13: 81–98.

Eberstadt, Nicholas (1997) 'Hastening Korean Unification', *Foreign Affairs* 76, 2: 77–92.

Euben, Roxanne L. (2002) 'Killing (for) Politics: Jihad, Martyrdom, and Political Action', *Political Theory* 30, 1: 4–35.

Grinker, Roy Richard (1998) *Korea and Its Futures: Unification and the Unfinished War*, London: Macmillan.

Harrison, Selig S. (1997) 'Promoting a Soft Landing in Korea', *Foreign Policy* 106: 56–75.

Hart, Dennis (1999) 'Creating the National Other: Opposing Images of Nationalism in South and North Korean Education', *Korean Studies* 23: 68–93.

Hassig, Ralph and Kongdan, Oh (2009) *The Hidden People of North Korea: Everyday Life in the Hermit Kingdom*, Baltimore, MD: Rowman and Littlefield.

Hoang, Young-ju (2002) Interviews with administrators and history teachers at Haeundae Girls' High School and Keumjeon High School, South Korea, March and April.

Kaplan, Robert D. (2005) *Balkan Ghosts: A Journey Through History*, London: Picador.
Kihl, Young Whan (1998) 'Seoul's Engagement Policy and US–DPRK Relations', *The Korean Journal of Defense Analysis* 10, 1: 21–48.
Kim, Dae-jung (2000) 'Presidential Inaugural Address, February 1998', in Yong-ho Ch'oe, Peter H. Lee and William de Bary (eds) *Sources of Korean Tradition: Volume II: From the Sixteenth to the Twentieth Centuries*, New York: Columbia University Press.
Klusmeyer, Douglas and Astri Suhrke (2002) 'Comprehending "Evil": Challenges for Law and Policy', *Ethics and International Affairs* 16, 1: 27–42.
Ko Un (1996) 'Destruction of Life', in *The Sound of My Waves*, translated by Brother Anthony of Taize and Young-Moo Kim, Ithaca, NY: Cornell University East Asia Program.
——(2002) 'Song of Peace from Jeju Island', in Keun-Min Woo (ed.) *Building Peace and Prosperity in Northeast Asia*, Seoul: Yonsei University Press.
Krause, Keith and Michael C. Williams (1997) 'Preface', in Keith Krause and Michael C. Williams (eds) *Critical Security Studies*, Minneapolis: University of Minnesota Press.
Lankov, Andrei (2008) 'Staying Alive', *Foreign Affairs* 87, 2; 9–16.
——(2010) 'How to Stop the Next Korean War', *Foreign Policy*, December 16.
Luttwak, Edward (2010) 'The Guns of December: It's About Time South Korea Started Shooting Back', *Foreign Policy*, December 21.
Moon, Chung-in (2001) 'The Kim Dae Jung Government's Peace Policy towards North Korea', *Asian Perspective* 25, 2: 177–98.
Moon, Chung-in and David I. Steinberg (eds) (1999) *Kim Dae-jung Government and Sunshine Policy*, Seoul: Yonsei University Press.
Myers, B. R. (2010) *The Cleanest Race: How North Koreans See Themselves – And Why It Matters*, Brooklyn, NY: Melville House.
Naimark, Norman M. (2002) *Fires of Hatred: Ethnic Cleansing in Twentieth-Century Europe*, Cambridge, MA: Harvard University Press.
The National Security Strategy of the United States of America (2002) http://www.whitehouse.gov/nsc/nss.html.
Nietzsche, Friedrich (1981) 'Vom Nutzen und Nachteil der Historie für das Leben', in *Unzeitgemässe Betrachtungen*, Frankfurt a.m.: Insel Taschenbuch. Translated by R. J. Hollingdale (1983) as *Untimely Meditations*, Cambridge: Cambridge University Press.
Nincic, Miroslav (2005) *Renegade Regimes: Confronting Deviant Behavior in World Politics*, New York: Columbia University Press.
Noland, Marcus (2000) *Avoiding the Apocalypse: The Future of the Two Koreas*. Washington, DC: Institute for International Economics.
Perry, William J. (1999) *Review of United States Policy Toward North Korea: Findings and Recommendations*. Washington, DC: US Department of State, http://www.state.gov/www/regions/eap/991012_northkorea_rpt.html (accessed 18 May 2006).
——(2000) 'The United States and the Future of East Asian Security: Korea – Quo Vadis?', in Woo Keun-Min (ed.) *Building Common Peace and Prosperity in Northeast Asia*, Seoul: Yonsei University Press.
Rice, Condoleezza (2000) 'Promoting the National Interest', *Foreign Affairs* 79, 1: 45–62.
Ricoeur, Paul (1999) 'Imagination, Testimony and Trust', in Richard Kearney and Mark Dooley (eds) *Questioning Ethics: Contemporary Debates in Philosophy*, London: Routledge.
Savage, Timothy and Nautilus Team (2002) 'NGO Engagement with North Korea: Dilemmas and Lessons Learned', *Asian Perspective* 26, 1: 151–67.

For a range of further resources supporting this chapter, please visit the companion website for *Global Politics, 2nd Edition* at www.routledge.com/cw/edkins/

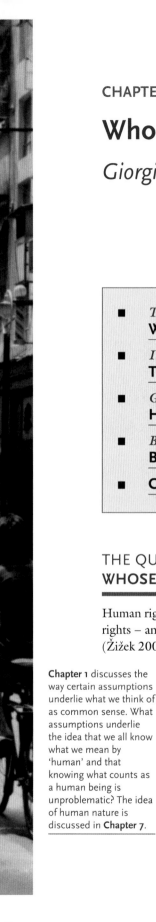

CHAPTER 27

Who has rights?

Giorgio Shani

THE QUESTION
WHOSE RIGHTS?

Human rights are part of the common sense of our modern world; to be against human rights – and the associated values of freedom and equality – is to be against humanity (Žižek 2005). The United Nations Universal Declaration of Human Rights (UNDHR) has been ratified by the vast majority of states, irrespective of culture or ideology, and human rights are enshrined in the constitutions of most. Protection of human rights has recently been made an international obligation for all states, and violations are subject to prosecution by the International Criminal Court and various international tribunals convened to investigate crimes against humanity, most notably in the former Federal Republic of Yugoslavia and Rwanda. The notion that all human beings have rights by virtue of their common humanity is, however, a recent development.

Chapter 1 discusses the way certain assumptions underlie what we think of as common sense. What assumptions underlie the idea that we all know what we mean by 'human' and that knowing what counts as a human being is unproblematic? The idea of human nature is discussed in **Chapter 7**.

The first institutionalization of rights was in post-Enlightenment revolutionary France and the United States of America. In the French

BOX 27.1 THE UNITED NATIONS UNIVERSAL DECLARATION OF HUMAN RIGHTS

Unanimously adopted by the General Assembly in December 1948, the United Nations Universal Declaration of Human Rights (UNDHR) has come to symbolize, more that any other legal document, the international community's commitment to protecting human rights. Arising out of the experiences of the Second World War, the Declaration was the first systematic attempt to extend the concept of legal rights beyond the nation-state.

Following the adoption of the UNDHR, the fundamental rights spelled out in the Declaration have subsequently been elaborated in the International Covenant of Civil and Political Rights and International Covenant on Economic, Social and Cultural Rights, both adopted by the General Assembly in 1966 and institutionalized within the UN system respectively through the Human Rights Committee and Economic and Social Council (United Nations 1948).

FIGURE 27.1
Eleanor Roosevelt regarded the Universal Declaration as her greatest accomplishment. http://www.udhr.org/history/images/hr18.GIF; http://www.udhr.org/history/Biographies/bioer.htm

Declaration of the Rights of Man and the Citizen (1789), all men – regardless of nationality – were seen as endowed with natural rights. However, in practice, rights are not always given to all human beings but only to citizens. The contradiction of rights discourse is that, despite its proclamations of universality, rights are enjoyed only within the context of a particular community. The classical, early modern answer to the question of who has rights was connected to thinking that brought the modern state into existence. Thomas Hobbes's *Leviathan* guaranteed rights through a framework of law. Obedience to the *Leviathan* would be binding since its origins lie in a mythical social contract between governors and the governed. The alternative to the order of the *Leviathan* was anarchy: a war of everyman against everyman (Hobbes [1651] 2006). John Locke later argued that it would be irrational of men *as* citizens to surrender their natural rights to life, liberty and estate unless they received guarantees from the state (Locke [1689] 1988). Thus, legal rights were substituted for natural rights. In order to ensure that the state fulfilled its contractual obligations to those it governed, the state's power was limited by a constitution that guaranteed a separation of powers and, much later, by representative democracy.

Who counts as a citizen and what rights they have is something that is also considered in **Chapter 10**.

Chapter 7 discusses Hobbes' notion of the social contract; **Chapter 13** also comments on the mythical social contract.

Questions, however, remain: is the state the best guarantor of human rights given its violent history? More fundamentally, who has rights? I will suggest in the course of this chapter that human rights cannot be assumed *a priori* as something we should all be entitled to by virtue of a common humanity but, rather, ideas of human rights help define what it is to be human. The answer to the question of who has rights therefore depends on what we consider to be worthy of protection. In order to answer this question, I look at the ban on the display of external religious symbols in public places

What Agamben means by bare life is explained in the final section and in **Chapter 20**.

in France before examining general responses to the ban and broader issues relating to the purported universality of human rights. Contemporary conceptions of human rights are based on a particular vision of humanity as bare life (Agamben 1998). The origins of human rights discourse stretch beyond the Enlightenment and are rooted in the Judaeo-Christian tradition. This makes their extension to different cultures problematic.

ILLUSTRATIVE EXAMPLE
THE FRENCH HEADSCARF BAN

Immigration by Muslims from former French colonies has posed a challenge to the principle of *laïcité* or secularism enshrined in the French constitution. The presence of Muslim headscarves, *hijabs*, in public places has given rise to a controversial debate. On the one hand are those who consider the *hijab* to constitute a threat to the secularity of the public sphere and the egalitarianism of the 1789 *Declaration of the Rights of Man and the Citizen*, which states that all citizens are equal in the eyes of the law. On the other hand are people who believe wearing the *hijab* is a fundamental human right guaranteed by the *Declaration* and the UNDHR. In French, this debate is termed *L'Affaire du foulard*.

L' Affaire du foulard, a series of long and drawn-out public confrontations between students and school authorities, first arose in 1989 as a result of the exclusion of three students from a school in Creil, a Parisian *banlieue* (suburb), for wearing a headscarf (*foulard*). It continued to the mass exclusion of twenty-three Muslim girls from their schools in November 1996 upon the decision of the highest legislative body in France, the Conseil d'etat (Benhabib 2002: 95). Until then, public schools had mostly tolerated the wearing of the veil by students but not by teachers. Although wearing the *hijab* is an integral part of many women's lives in the Islamic world, it is mainly viewed as a cultural practice and not a religious stipulation. Few Muslim women seeking to assimilate into French society initially chose to wear a veil, since it carried a stigma of backwardness. However, the increasing assertiveness of Muslims globally following the rise of political Islam resulted in a shift in the public perception of the *hijab*: from being a symbol of conservatism it became one of rebellion. For Seyla Benhabib, the initial decision to wear a headscarf by the three schoolgirls in Creil was a 'conscious political gesture on their part, a complex act of identification and defiance' (Benhabib 2002: 96). Wearing the veil in a public place came to be invested with political significance.

The rise of political Islam and the politics of secularism are discussed in **Chapter 6**.

The events of 11 September 2001, and the purported threat of terrorism from radical Islamic groups, led the French state to attempt decisive action to protect the public sphere from what they considered manifestations of an Islamic fundamentalist identity. An Act passed in 2004 outlawed the wearing in state schools of signs or dress by which pupils 'overtly' manifest a religious affiliation. The term 'overt' (*ostensible* in French) was preferred to *visible,* since 'overt' implies that the wearer wants to be seen whereas 'visible' was deemed to be in conformity with the European Convention of Human Rights which guarantees the right to freely manifest one's religion (Joppke 2009: 51). This Act was followed in 2010 with the passing of a law banning face-covering garments – the *niqab* and *burqa* – in public spaces such as restaurants, schools and public

Islam, and fundamentalism in all religions, is discussed in **Chapter 6**.

BOX 27.2 THE VEIL

The term 'the Islamic veil' refers to a variety of forms of female clothing of which the most commonly worn by Muslims in Western Europe are the *hijab*, *niqab* and *burqa*.

Derived from the Arabic for veil, the *hijab* is a scarf which covers the head and neck but leaves the face clear. Frenchwomen are allowed to wear the *hijab* in public places but not in schools.

The *niqab* is a veil for the face that leaves the area around the eyes clear. In September 2011, two Frenchwomen were fined for wearing the *niqab* in public.

The *burka* (*burqa*) is the most restrictive, covering the entire face, leaving just a mesh screen to see through. It is illegal to publicly wear it in France (BBC 2011).

FIGURE 27.2
Hijab, image from: http://www.bbc.co.uk/news/world-europe-15013383

FIGURE 27.3
Niqab, image from: http://www.bbc.co.uk/news/world-europe-15013383

FIGURE 27.4
Burka, image from: http://www.bbc.co.uk/news/world-europe-15013383

transportation. Under the bill's provisions, women wearing a face-covering veil in public spaces could be fined 150 euros or asked to take classes on the values of French citizenship. More recently still, a law was passed banning praying in the street, a directive clearly aimed at Muslims. The French state evidently believes the 'overt' manifestation of the Islamic faith *publicly* to be incompatible with the core values of the Republic.

According to official republican discourse, the ban on Muslim headscarves in schools helps further five central values of *laïcité*: the preservation of a shared, non-sectarian public sphere; the distinction between the private and the public identities of individuals; equality before the law and non-discrimination; universal civic education in common schools; and the guarantee of equal religious rights for all. In the first place, Muslim headscarves are deemed to introduce signs of private difference and religious divisiveness in the public sphere. They constitute an 'ostensible' intrusion of religious identities into public schools, which should be protected from their destabilizing effects. As a religious obligation, they symbolize the primacy of the believer over the citizen. Muslims, it is argued, should make more effort to reconcile their faith with the demands of national integration. Furthermore, headscarves and other clearly visible religious symbols infringe upon difference-blind equality in two ways: by introducing ostensible distinctions in public schools which threaten the neutrality of the public sphere; and by creating an unjustified exemption from a general requirement of religious restraint on the part of

BOX 27.3 *LAÏCITÉ*

In France, *laïcité* is an ideological form of secularism that has developed on two levels and encompasses both legal and philosophical implications. In the first place, it involves a very strict separation of church and state, a legacy of the political conflict between the state and the Catholic Church that resulted in the 1905 Law on the Separation of Churches and the State regulating the presence of religion in public life. The guiding principles of the law are contained in the first two articles. Under Article 1 the Republic 'ensures freedom of conscience', whereas under Article 2 the Republic 'does not recognize, fund or subsidize any religion'.

Second, *laïcité* claims to provide all citizens with an ideological and philosophical value system by effectively privatizing religion and excluding it from the public sphere. *Laïcité* defines 'national cohesion by asserting a purely political identity that confines to the private sphere any specific religious or cultural identities' and protects the neutrality of the public sphere (Roy 2007: xiii). Article 1 of the 1946 Constitution defines France as an 'indivisible, *laïque*, democratic and social republic'. Between 1946 and 1980 the main challenge to *laicism* came from the demand from private schools, which were mainly Catholic, for public subsidies. It was only later, with increased Muslim immigration, that manifestations of the Islamic faith came to be seen as problematic.

believers. Moreover, they undermine the civic mission of schools based on a national curriculum that is universal in scope and, more generally, undermine the overall scheme of religious freedoms (Laborde 2008: 53–5).

However, there are problems with these arguments. First, the difference-blind egalitarianism of the French state's position belies an inequality of treatment between the religion of the majority and those of migrant communities. In the first place, although Article 2 of the 1905 Law stipulates that the state shall not 'recognize or subsidize' any specific religion, it provides public funds for the maintenance of the public buildings owned by Catholic churches and Jewish synagogues. It does not, however,

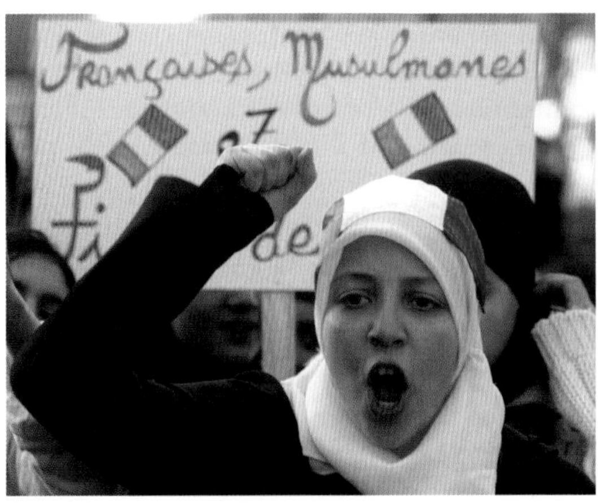

FIGURE 27.5
Women protesting against the headscarf ban in France. http://4.bp.blogspot.com/_ab8YFYIB-5U/SWO7sbThwSI/AAAAAAAAAJ4/Dwh8-Y-PQGo/s400/040202_france_headscarves_hmed1p.h2.jpg

BOX 27.4 MUSLIMS IN FRANCE

It is estimated that France has the highest percentage of Muslims in the EU, although no accurate figures are available since the census does not include a separate category for religion. Muslims account for between 5 and 10 per cent of the French population, with the latest estimates being approximately 5 million out of a total of 60 million (Pew Forum 2011).

Most Muslim migrants came to France in the aftermath of the Second World War and the war of independence in Algeria. France recruited immigrant workers from their former colonies in Muslim countries such as Algeria, Morocco and Tunisia, as well as Turkey. The first generation of Muslim immigrants, who arrived in the 1960s and early 1970s, did not bring their families with them and confined their religious practices to makeshift facilities. Islam only became more visible in the 1970s when this first generation decided to stay and bring their families to join them. From then on the French government shifted from simply policing immigration flows to a policy of assimilation (Fetzer and Soper 2005). In order to be considered French, immigrants were (and still are) expected to assimilate to secular culture, confining their differences to the private sphere. In the assimilationist view, cohesion is attained when the nation lives under the Republic as one and indivisible, in other words, when differences are not visible and everybody is equal and the same in the public sphere.

make these funds available for the 1,600 Muslim mosques and prayer halls, arguing that Islam was not covered in the 1905 Law (McGoldrick 2006: 37).

Second, not all religious communities are equally affected by the 2004 ban. Although the law does not explicitly target any one religious community, the implementation of the law left no doubt that it was intended to target the Muslim community since *hijabs*, unlike crucifixes, were deemed 'overt' religious symbols by most school authorities. In the first year of the ban, some forty-four students were expelled for wearing the *hijab*. A much larger number agreed to take the *hijab* off to attend school after being summoned for a talk with the head teacher (McGoldrick 2006: 92). However, the tiny Sikh community was most affected by the ban since Sikh religio-cultural identity is an embodied entity. Orthodox or *Khalsa* (usually male) Sikhs wear a turban and maintain five 'signs' or symbols of Sikh identity. The wearing of these symbols is seen as an integral part of *Khalsa* Sikh identity, which means that members of the 7,000-strong French Sikh community have been faced with a stark dilemma: either to cease wearing the religious symbols which are the very embodiment of their faith, or to face exclusion from state schools and the public sphere in general. The ban on religious symbols in the classroom has already resulted in the expulsion of six Sikh schoolboys. Furthermore, two adult French Sikh citizens were unable to renew important documents because they declined to remove their turbans for the ID photo; they subsequently lost their appeal in the *Conseil d'Etat* (Shani 2007, 2010).

The French headscarf ban, and its unintended effects upon Sikh communities living in France, clearly illustrates the contentious nature of human rights. On the one hand, the French authorities have argued that displaying religious symbols compromises the integrity and secularity of the public sphere. By wearing a headscarf or a turban, female

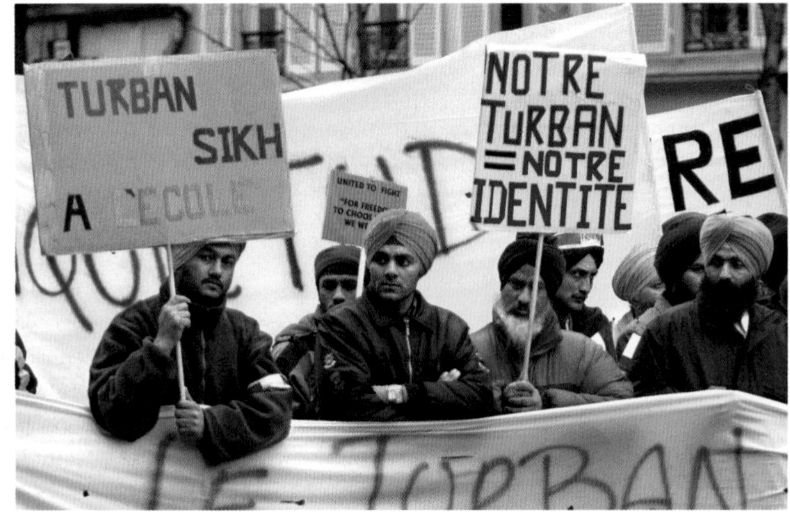

FIGURE 27.6
Sikhs in France protesting against the ban on wearing turbans in schools. http://www.sikhnet.com/files/news/2009/February/France.jpg

Secularism is discussed in **Chapter 6**.

Muslims and male Sikhs are perceived by the state to be making a statement: that they are Muslim or Sikh first and French second. The French authorities place emphasis on the ideals of the French Revolution, which gave rise to modern human rights discourse, and see the expression of religious beliefs in the public sphere as undermining the egalitarianism on which revolutionary France is based. The public expression of religious difference introduces distinctions into the French body politic and compromises the French state's ability to secure due recognition and respect for the rights and freedoms of others in accordance with Article 29 of the UNDHR.

Opponents of the ban, including leading international human rights groups such as Amnesty International, Human Rights Watch, the Minority Rights Group, and the International Helsinki Federation for Human Rights, argue that it severely curtails the rights of citizens to express their own religious beliefs. This is explicitly guaranteed by Article 18 of the UNDHR which unequivocally states:

> Everyone has the right to freedom of thought, conscience and religion; this right includes freedom to change his religion or belief, and freedom, either alone or in community with others and in public or private, to manifest his religion or belief in teaching, practice, worship and observance.
>
> (UN 1948)

However, Article 18 of the International Convention on Civil and Political Rights (ICCPR) is more ambiguous, providing ammunition for both supporters and opponents of the ban. Whereas Paragraph 1 guarantees the same rights to 'thought, conscience and religion' as stated in the UNDHR, it is qualified by Paragraph 3:

> Freedom to manifest one's religion or beliefs may be subject only to such limitations as prescribed by law and are necessary to protect public safety, order, health or morals or the fundamental rights and freedoms of others.
>
> (ICCPR 1966)

Furthermore, French authorities may justify the ban on human rights grounds by citing Paragraph 2 which states that:

> No one shall be subject to coercion which would impair his freedom to have or to adopt a religion or belief of his choice.
>
> (ICCPR 1966)

The argument presumably would be that many Muslim girls, and presumably Sikh boys, are forced to manifest the external symbols of their faith by their elders and are not in a position to be free to choose their religion. This is a position advocated by many liberals and some feminists, who would agree with Christian Joppke (2009: ix) that 'the Islamic headscarf is a challenge to liberalism' because it inevitably and incontestably signals the subordination of women. It needs to be pointed out that the French Muslim Council (Le Conseil Français du Culte Musulman) supported the 2004 ban, declaring itself against the veil and stating that many French Muslim women regard the *hijab* and especially *burqa* as a symbol of patriarchal oppression within Islam. Indeed, Patrick Weil, who was on the Stasi Commission which first proposed the ban, argues that in the schools the commission visited 'a strong majority of Muslim girls who did not wear the headscarf called for the protection of the law and asked for the commission to ban all exterior religious signs' (Weil 2009: 2707). Even critics of the ban, such as Fadela Amara, founder of a women's group representing the interests of predominately Islamic women, Ni Putes Ni Soumises (Neither *Whores* Nor *Submissives*), regard the veil as a 'tool of oppression, of alienation, of discrimination, an instrument of the power of men over women' (quoted in Joppke 2009: 14).

Questions of identity are discussed in relation to feminist politics in **Chapter 5**, the role of women in democratic politics in Argentina in **Chapter 14** and questions of gender in the global political economy in **Chapter 17**.

However, many Muslim women consciously decide to wear the veil and regard it as symbol of their faith and, consequently, their identity. Indeed, Hind Ahmas, who was arrested for wearing a face-covering garment in public, is an educated single mother from a 'secular' background who freely chose to wear the *niqab*. She has vowed to challenge the ban in the European Court of Human Rights (BBC 2011).

FIGURE 27.7
Hind Ahmas, one of two French women facing a fine for wearing the niqab in a town near Paris. Photograph: Magali Delporte for the *Guardian* http://www.guardian.co.uk/world/2011/sep/19/battle-for-the-burqa

GENERAL RESPONSES
HUMAN RIGHTS AND UNIVERSALITY

Revolutionary France is known as the birthplace of human rights as an institution. The 1789 Declaration of the Rights of Man and the Citizen (La Déclaration des droits de l'homme et du citoyen) was the first modern, secular articulation of human rights. Unlike the American Declaration of Independence in 1776, the French declaration grounds rights in human nature rather than divine authority. However, in contrast with the American Bill of Rights (1789), which concerns itself primarily with the rights of the European settlers of the newly independent state, it is unclear who the subjects of the rights espoused by the French declaration are. Are they men in general or citizens? The authors of the Declaration considered the rights to be universal: that is applicable to all human beings irrespective of location or even the time when they lived. This can clearly be seen in Article 1, which claimed that 'Men are born and remain free and equal in rights'. However, Article 3 declares that 'the principle of all sovereignty resides essentially in the nation' and that '[No] body nor individual may exercise any authority which does not proceed directly from the nation' (National Assembly 1789). Whereas the French state was assigned the responsibility of protecting the rights of its citizens, it was not (and is still not) clear at all who was responsible for the protection of the rights of man in general.

Note that at the time these discussions were taking place, no one even noticed that women were not included. It was so obvious that they didn't count politically. Demands that women be given the vote are discussed in **Chapter 5**.

This gave rise to the view first expressed by Edmund Burke that the only real rights were those of citizens, not man in general (Waldron 1987: 96–118). As another conservative critic of the revolution, Joseph de Maistre put it, 'I have met Italians, Russians, Spaniards, Englishmen, Frenchmen, but I do not know man in general' (cited in

FIGURE 27.8
Opening of the National Assembly at Versailles of 5 May 1979, where on 26 August 1789, the Deputies publish *La Déclaration des droits de l'homme et du citoyen*. http://www.pyepimanla.com/mars-2009-2/politique/Leonce-lebrun/image/etats_generaux.jpg

BOX 27.5
EDMUND BURKE (1729–97)

Edmund Burke is regarded as one of the founders of the British conservative tradition. While he supported the American Revolution, calling for a pragmatic approach that accepted the need for change whilst affirming traditional values, he was notable for his opposition to the French Revolution. In his 'Reflections on the Revolution in France', published in 1790, he emphasized the dangers of mob rule; the Revolution was, as he saw it, destroying French society.

FIGURE 27.9
Edmund Burke. http://www.bbc.co.uk/history/historic_figures/burke_edmund.shtml

Douzinas 2007: 93). The subject of the Rights of Man appeared as an abstract entity: an individual without gender or nationality 'unencumbered' (Hopgood 2000) by attachments to culture, class, family, tradition or religion. Subsequently, more radical critics concurred. Marx wrote that the individual who enjoyed these abstract entitlements was 'an egoistic man, man separated from other men and community' (Marx [1844] 1977: 54). He shared the secular world-view brought into being by the French Revolution and believed that man's self-realization could only come about through emancipation from religious belief, which he famously regarded as the 'opium of the people' in that its intoxicating effects concealed real social relations.

One of the objectives of the French Revolution (1789–95) was to contest the political, social and cultural hegemony of the Roman Catholic Church. To this end, the Constituent Assembly nationalized Church property and the Constitution of 1795 replaced divine right with popular sovereignty as the source of state legitimacy. The Vatican objected to these changes and resisted attempts by the Revolutionaries to export their republican ideals to neighbouring countries in Europe. The 1801 Concordat between Napoleon Bonaparte and Pope Pius VII brought an uneasy truce between Church and state; Catholicism was recognized as the religion of the great majority of the French people yet the Church itself was brought under the tutelage of the state which appointed bishops, paid the salaries of the clergy and, in turn, required them to swear an oath of allegiance to the French state. This truce was to last over a century, until the Law of 1905.

The authority of the Roman Catholic Church was challenged during the Reformation in Europe, which took place from the late fifteenth to early eighteenth century: see **Chapters 6 and 7**.

There are two standard responses to the question of whether 'rights' are universal. The first asserts the universality of human rights on the basis of a purported universal human nature. Human beings everywhere, it is argued, are the same, so each human being should be equally deserving of the same rights, guaranteed by the protection of the state. This is the position of most liberals and of the French state as outlined above. The assumption that we all share a common human nature *a priori*, however, is problematic in that it ignores the culturally contested nature of human identities.

There are many different attributes and implications of being 'human'. Consequently, a common human nature cannot be considered a given but can only be discerned by seriously engaging with different culturally defined notions of what it is to be human.

The second position, however, may be seen as equally problematic. It asserts the radically incompatible nature of human values and identities (Huntington 1996). For Anthony Pagden (2003), human rights are based on an essentially Western European understanding of the human that evolved in the context of the European struggle to legitimate its overseas empires through the notion of the 'civilizing mission'. Human rights are tied not only to a specific ethico-legal code but also implicitly to a particular kind of political system – liberal democracy – both of inescapably European origin. For Pagden, the principles which underpin the UNDHR are based 'squarely on "Western" notions of human agency', that is, of persons as beings able to conduct their relations with one another through reasoned argument. Their implementation, Pagden argues, can only be realized in a specific political order – liberal democracy – which is also of 'Western' origin (Pagden 2003: 193). This is a position held by many non-Western critics of human rights discourse. At the Vienna Conference on Human Rights (1993) an attempt was made to contrast implicitly Western human rights with so-called Asian values. Asians, it was argued, value order, community and social harmony over individual freedom and democracy. Consequently, emphasis was placed on sovereignty, self-determination and non-intervention – all constitutive features of the Westphalian international order – at the expense of individual human rights.

The Peace of Westphalia is discussed in **Chapter 11**.

Notwithstanding the fact that Asia itself, as well as the values espoused by the Asian leaders, are Western constructs, such a view mistakes the content for the institution of rights. Although the institution of rights may have had its origins in Western Europe, the content of rights – freedom and equality – has deep roots in many non-Western cultures. Indeed, both Buddhist and Hindu religious philosophies have had as their ultimate goal the liberation of the individual from the endless cycle of suffering and rebirth (*karma*) millennia before the Enlightenment discovery of freedom. Freedom and equality are equally at heart of Muslim notions of the *umma* as a universal community of believers and the Sikh concept of the *Khalsa Panth*. In both collectivities, the individual experiences freedom and dignity as an equal member of a community (Shani 2008). To argue that the West values freedom and equality and Asians order and stability is to reproduce an Orientalist stereotype that served to legitimize imperial expansion in the first place. Furthermore, it essentializes the different cultures of Europe and Asia and ignores the role which the non-Western world played in the co-constitution of modernity.

The *umma* is discussed in **Chapter 6**, as is Edward Said's concept of Orientalism and his work more broadly.

Islamic conceptions of modernity are discussed in **Chapter 20**.

Human rights are the global language of modernity and the human is supposed to be a universal category which cannot be appropriated exclusively by any one specific culture. If Pagden is right and the institution of human rights is based on a Western European concept of the human, then instead of rejecting human rights as the authoritarian advocates of the Asian values discourse suggest, an alternative strategy would be to reconceptualize them in order to take into account other culturally informed notions of the human. As our example of the headscarf ban illustrates, the headscarf or turban is central to the humanity of many Islamic women and Sikh men. Why, therefore, should the Western secular concept of the human be privileged? Do not other cultures also have values they consider to be universal?

BOX 27.6 RELIGIOUS PHILOSOPHIES

Philosophy	Community	Entitlements	Reasons
Secularism	Humanity	Everyone	Birth/Rationality
Christianity	Christendom	Everyone/Christians	*Imago Dei*
Islam	*Umma*	Muslims/Everyone	*Shari'a/Jizya*
Hinduism	Different communities	Caste-based Hindus	Karma
Buddhism	*Sangha*	All sentient beings	Karma
Sikhism	*Khalsa Panth*	Everyone	*Ek O-aankar*

FIGURE 27.10
Tabulated comparison of religious philosophies

Different secular and religious philosophies understand the notion of community and entitlements differently. Whereas secular notions of human rights consider rights to be entitlements which derive from the mere fact of birth or our capacity to think (which are thought to distinguish us from other sentient beings), other religious philosophies have differing views on the origins of these entitlements. For most Christians, all human beings have rights because we are created in the image of God (*Imago Dei* in Latin). This is the position of the Catholic Church after the Second Vatican Council in 1962, which discussed the place of the Church in the modern world. However, Catholicism and other forms of Christianity were previously hostile to the notion of rights and in particular to the 'right' to one's own religious beliefs which was denied to religious minorities in Europe and the colonial subjects of European empires until the time of the French Revolution. In contrast, religious minorities in Islamic societies and empires were allowed to keep their religions upon payment of a tax (*jizya*). This was levied on those whom Muslims considered to be 'people of the book' (i.e. Christians and Jews) but not on all religious minorities. Muslims were supposed to follow *Shari'a* law which regulated relations between members of the universal community of believers, the *umma*, and prescribed rights and duties. Women within Islamic societies are widely seen as not having the same rights as men but, even if this is the case, it may have little to do with Islam itself. Hinduism, which was the religion of the majority of the population of South Asia during the time of the Islamic Mughal Empire, is traditionally seen as more tolerant of religious diversity. However, different castes are seen as having different rights and duties as a result of what they have done in their previous lives (*karma*). Brahmans and other 'twice-born' castes have more 'rights' than those of other castes as they are nearer to achieving *moksha* (liberation from suffering). Finally, both Buddhism and Sikhism regard all human beings as equally able to achieve liberation from suffering and, although they don't explicitly use the language of rights, are firmly committed to human equality. Gender equality is particularly emphasized in Sikhism, whereas Buddhism extends the principle of equality to all sentient beings while questioning the uniqueness of individual identity through the doctrine of *anatman* (no self).

BOX 27.7 STRATEGIES FOR INCORPORATING MIGRANTS

The UNDP estimates that approximately 200 million people – 2 per cent of the world's population – are international migrants, that is to say they live outside the state of their birth (UNDP 2009: 5). During the colonial period a majority of these international migrants came from Europe to settle in the New World and Australasia, but following decolonization, migration was encouraged into Europe from former colonial territories. In recent years, there has been a marked increase in migration from South to North, from the developing to the developed world. In many cases, migrants have no historical connection to their place of settlement and may not speak the language, participate in the political process or understand local laws or customs. Three main strategies are used to incorporate migrants: *exclusion*, *assimilation*, and *multiculturalism* (Modood 2005).

Exclusion refers to the incorporation of migrants into selected and marked-off sectors of the host society, such as the *Gastarbeiter* (guest workers) in Germany or migrant labour in Japan. The assumption is that migrants are temporary residents of host societies and will eventually return to their place of origin once their contract is over. Therefore, no attempt is made to *integrate* migrants into their host societies. Although exclusion is still practised in many states – particularly in the Middle East – changes in the laws governing citizenship in the EU have conferred rights to many migrants and their families. Consequently, many migrants are now citizens and are expected to take part in social or political life.

Assimilation refers to the process whereby migrants are expected to assimilate to the dominant culture if they are to be accepted as citizens. They are expected to familiarize themselves with the dominant language, the local customs and laws and, importantly, to participate in national and local institutions as equal citizens. In return, migrants can expect to enjoy the same rights as their fellow citizens and protection from discrimination on ethnic or racial grounds through the law. The assumption is that the national community is a 'melting pot' (Glazer and Moynihan 1970) where cultural and ethnic differences will dissolve over time. Barack Obama's election as president of the US is seen by some as a vindication of the success of the 'melting pot' in creating equality of opportunity. Laicism, as in France, is a distinctive form of assimilation where migrants are expected assimilate to a *secular* national culture and to confine their religious or cultural identities to the private sphere.

Multiculturalism is where processes of integration are seen both as two-way and as working differently for different groups. It differs from assimilation because it recognizes the social reality of ethno-cultural groups, not just of individuals and organizations. As Tariq Modood points out, this reality can be of different kinds; for example, a sense of solidarity with people of similar origins or faith or mother tongue. It might be an act of imagination but may also be rooted in lived experience and embodied in formal organizations dedicated to fostering group identity and keeping it alive (Modood 2005). Politically, a commitment to multiculturalism tends to involve active state policies designed to accommodate immigrants through equal opportunities legislation, granting full access to social service, education and housing and, finally, access to citizenship whilst not requiring immigrants to give up or privatize their pre-existing ethno-cultural identities.

In the post-9/11 world, many states have watered down or abandoned multicultural approaches to immigration and sought to promote policies which would lead to greater integration of immigrants into the host culture through the privatization of cultural identities. This is particularly true of the Netherlands, which may be considered a pioneer of multiculturalism in the EU through its Ethnic Minorities Policy, and of the UK after the terrorist attacks on London of 7 July 2005. The London suicide bombers were British citizens from Muslim backgrounds. They were seen as home-grown children of Britain's multicultural society (Modood 2007: 10–14). This view, however, overstates the extent to which Britain was indeed a multicultural society, particularly in light of the hostile reaction to the publication of the Parekh Report, which called for a rethinking of Britain's national identity as a multi-ethnic 'community of communities' (Commission on the Future of Multi-Ethnic Britain 2000).

BROADER ISSUES
BARE LIFE, HUMAN RIGHTS AND SOVEREIGN POWER

Returning to our question, it seems that the ambiguity of institutionalized human rights makes them very difficult to deal with. For what is at stake in our example are two fundamentally different conceptions of human subjectivity. On the one hand, the French state considers the subject of human rights to be a citizen endowed with equal rights, unencumbered by primordial attachments to religion or culture. On the other hand, many opponents of the ban consider religion, culture and tradition to be integral to the *bios* of Muslim and Sikh immigrants.

The notion of something being primordial also comes up in connection with ideas about nationalism in **Chapter 12**.

The term *bios* in Ancient Greece denoted a qualified life: a life with dignity, endowed with meaning, in contrast to *zoē* which expresses the simple fact of living. In recent years, this Aristotelian distinction has been elaborated by Giorgio Agamben to critique the concept of human rights. For Agamben, the subject of institutionalized human rights is *zoē*, which he considers as 'bare life': a life which can be killed but yet not sacrificed. In the classical world, *zoē* was excluded from the *polis*, the political community or public sphere, and confined to the sphere of the *oikos*, the home. Indeed, the concept of *zoē* made politics possible: 'There is politics because man is the living being who, in language, separates and opposes himself to his own bare life and, at the same time, maintains himself in relation to that bare life in an *inclusive exclusion*' (Agamben 1998: 8, emphasis added). Agamben contends that it is 'the entry of *zoē* into the sphere of the *polis* – the politicization of bare life as such' which 'constitutes the decisive event of modernity' (Agamben 1998: 4).

What Agamben calls *homo sacer*, or, roughly translated, sacred man, is a life taken out of the ordinary rule of law, where killing counts as murder, but not taken into the divine or sacred realm, where killing could be regarded as a sacrifice. *Homo sacer* and 'bare life' or *zoē* are arguably not quite the same but are often equated, as here.

Agamben's work is also discussed in **Chapter 20**.

This entry of bare life into politics can be seen in La Déclaration des droits de l'homme et du citoyen (1789), where Agamben contends that 'it is precisely bare natural life – which is to say, the pure fact of birth – that appears here as the source and bearer of rights' (Agamben 1998: 81):

> 'Men', the first article declares, 'are born and remain free and equal in rights' . . . At the same time, however, the very natural life that, inaugurating the biopolitics of modernity, is placed at the foundation of the order vanishes into the figure of the citizen, in whom rights are 'preserved' (according to the second article: 'The goal of every political association is the preservation of the natural and indefeasible rights of man'). And the Declaration can attribute sovereignty to the 'nation' (according to the third article: 'The principle of all sovereignty resides essentially in the nation') precisely because it has already inscribed this element of birth in the

> very heart of the political community. The nation – the term derives etymologically from nascere (to be born) – thus closes the open circle of man's birth.
>
> (Agamben 1998: 127–28)

So, the first article of the Declaration gives 'men' rights by virtue of the 'pure fact of birth'. However, according to the second article, these rights can only be exercised by citizens. And the third article defines citizens as citizens of a sovereign 'nation'. But the nation, Agamben points out, is already defined by the notion of birth, thus closing the circle: 'bare natural life', is the main criterion for entry into the 'nation' and, therefore, citizenship. So birth is equated with citizenship.

Equating birth with citizenship has profound consequences for immigrant communities. It makes them 'bare life' subject to the power of the state. The state can decide whether to include them or exclude them from the nation and, even in a modern democracy, can invoke a 'state of exception' to deprive them of their 'natural' human rights. Thus, there is no contradiction between the power of the state and the Rights of Man for it is precisely the Rights of Man which legitimizes the power of the state over 'bare life' and it is the state in turn which produces the 'bare life' which is the subject of the Rights of Man.

This means that human rights can't be used as a defence against the state or any abuse of its power, because the state itself is produced by and responsible for defining and defending those rights.

For Agamben, modern democracy has more in common with the totalitarianism of the Nazi regime than classical democracy, as it shares a similar conception of human subjectivity. Whereas classical democracy seeks to exclude *zoē* from the *polis*, 'modern democracy presents itself from the beginning as a vindication and liberation of *zoē*, and . . . is constantly trying to transform its own bare life into a way of life and to find, so to speak, the *bios* of *zoē*' (Agamben 1998: 9).

Seen in this light, rather than being considered a restriction of individual freedom, the banning of the veil in public spaces may be seen as an attempt by the state to 'liberate' *zoe*, to produce 'a *bios* of *zoē*'. In the words of one of its leading intellectual defenders in France, the ban 'is not an attack upon liberty but, on the contrary, a subtle art not only of proclaiming it, but of permitting its concrete practice' (Weil 2009: 2714). The state must not only protect but also empower its citizens if they are to really exercise their right to freedom of thought and conscience.

A constitutive outside is something that, whilst it is outside the concept or institution or practice, is necessary to produce or enable the concept. For example, if we talk of memory, we need to have an idea of forgetting for the term memory to be meaningful. 'Forgetting' is the constitutive outside of memory – forgetting constitutes memory, although it is outside memory.

The Republic, founded on the purportedly universal values of *Liberté, Égalité, Fraternité*, needs, following Agamben, a constitutive outside in order to permit its particularization as a bounded, political community. After all, if everybody everywhere were free, then there would be no rationale for the establishment of the Republic as a territorialized, sovereign state. In order to be a sovereign community, the Republic needs to locate sources of unfreedom within, for it is only through the emancipation and empowerment of those enslaved by patriarchal customs and traditions that the Republic can embody the ideals upon which it is founded. Since covering one's head on the grounds of religion is an affront to the dignity of all women in the Republic as citizens, the *bios* of the pious Muslim woman needs to be sacrificed in order for the *zoē* of all French to be liberated. Thus, saving 'brown women from brown men' (Spivak 1999) helps produce a Republican *bios*, a secularized body, empowered yet rendered docile (Foucault 1991) and compliant with the wishes of the state.

Indeed, the very constitution of the secular Republic and its protection from religious fanaticism and the patriarchal values of unassimilated communities in a post

Café
"Zis unifurm durz nurt allow urz to see ze personne be'ind ze stereotarp, non?"

FIGURE 27.11
'Zis unifurm durz nurt allow . . . ' Artist: Wilbur. CartoonStock ref.: wda2189. www.CartoonStock.com

BOX 27.8 GAYATRI CHAKRAVORTY SPIVAK

A professor at Columbia University in New York, Gayatri Spivak's most famous work, her first article, which was called 'Can the Subaltern Speak?' (Spivak 1999), discussed the practice of sati in India – the tradition, not regularly observed, where a widow would immolate herself on the pyre of her husband. She described the attempts of the English colonizers to halt this practice as white men 'saving brown women from brown men'. She is considered as a pioneer of post-colonial feminism.

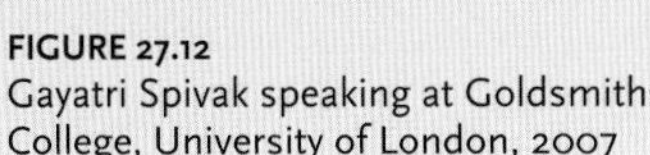

FIGURE 27.12
Gayatri Spivak speaking at Goldsmiths College, University of London, 2007

9/11 world can only be achieved through the securitization of the bodies of 'brown' women from the body politic. The French state's decision to prohibit the display of religious symbols in the classroom and ban the *niqab* and *burqa* from the public sphere simultaneously politicizes and depoliticizes the wearing of the veil. In the first place, it politicizes the veil in that the wearing of the veil in a public place is invested with political significance. Women who wear the veil are seen as directly challenging the main principle upon which the Republic is based: *laïcité*. Consequently, the veil must be de-politicized by expelling it from the public sphere. This de-politicization can only be achieved by extending the regulatory power of the state over mainly female bodies in the name of national security.

Patriarchy is a structure of male domination, a system where control and authority is vested in men; it is a system where the assignment of rights – such as political rights – to men alone can go unquestioned. See also **Chapter 5**.

BOX 27.9 SECURITIZATION AND POLITICIZATION

Securitization may be understood as an extreme form of politicization, whereby an issue comes to be either politicized or placed above politics. Following Buzan *et al.*, 'security' denotes the move which takes politics beyond 'the established rules of the game and frames the issue either as a special kind of politics or as above politics' (Buzan *et al.* 1998: 23).

A securitized issue is something which is of vital importance to the national interest as defined by the state and which, therefore, cannot be subject to the same critical scrutiny by the media, politicians and citizens as other issues deemed less important. It is treated as an *existential threat* requiring emergency measures and justifying 'exceptional' responses by the state. In this sense, a securitized issue can be seen as *de-politicized* in that it is no longer seen as part of public discourse but is articulated in technical terms (Edkins 1999: 10).

How then should one's rights to freely manifest one's religious or cultural identity or identities be protected? What unites both the advocates and opponents of the ban is the logic of making the state primarily responsible for the protection of its subjects, even in cases where the state itself is the principal source of insecurity for its citizens. As the experience of the last century teaches us, the modern state – through its monopoly of the use of violence – has a historically unprecedented capacity to inflict harm on a massive scale on those who live within its borders. Is the state really best suited to protect the rights of its citizens? Moreover, are rights themselves an adequate safeguard to protect the individual from the power of the state? Do they not serve instead to legitimize the state's monopoly of the use of violence against its citizens? Indeed, do they not make the sovereign power of the state possible? As Agamben has argued,

> The spaces, the liberties and the rights won by individuals in their conflicts with certain powers always simultaneously prepared a tacit but increasing inscription of individual's lives within the state order, thus offering a new and more dreadful foundation for the very sovereign power from which they wanted to liberate themselves.
>
> (Agamben 1998: 121)

Seen from this perspective, the extension of rights from a minority of white, Christian, property (and in some cases slave) owning men to subaltern groups such as the working classes, women and so-called people of colour have not brought freedom but strengthened the hegemony of the state over the populations it controls. The best way to protect human rights, therefore, may be to liberate the content of rights, a demand to equal freedom, from its specific form – institutionalized human rights – which has been instituted to legitimize the power of the state. Human rights, therefore, may need to be protected from their own institutionalization in order for everyone to enjoy the equal freedom and dignity that ought to come from being human.

CONCLUSION

This chapter has attempted to examine the question: who has rights? It has showed how the ambiguity or contradictory nature of a human rights discourse, which claims to be universal yet makes human beings subjects of a particular political community, makes thinking about human rights difficult and contentious. As an illustrative example, it took the French state's decision to prohibit the display of religious symbols in public as a case study. Arguments were made for and against the ban being in compliance with domestic and international human rights legislation. It was suggested that both arguments were based upon different views of human subjectivity. For the French state, the subject of rights discourse is the citizen, endowed with equal rights and unencumbered by prior identification with a religious or cultural community that may inhibit her or his participation in the public affairs of the Republic. The objective of the ban, therefore, was to liberate women from the veil – a symbol of patriarchal culture – and safeguard the democratic, public sphere. For many opponents of the ban, including many French citizens from non-minority backgrounds, one's religious or cultural identity is precisely *what permits one to be human*. By banning the veil, the French state literally and metaphorically strips its citizens of their *bios* and reduces them to what Agamben refers to as bare life. In conclusion, it is not clear *who* has rights. However, if rights are to be considered universal, there needs to be an acceptance that there is more than one way to be 'human'. Culture remains an important attribute of human identity and cannot be removed like a veil in order to promote greater integration without *dehumanizing* the individual.

FURTHER READING

Each year a series of internationally reputed scholars are invited to deliver a lecture on an aspect of human rights at Oxford University, with the proceeds going to Amnesty International. The resulting lectures are subsequently published as the *Oxford Amnesty Lectures*. Some of the most interesting volumes have been:

Shute, Stephen and Susan Hurley (ed.) (1994) *On Human Rights: Oxford Amnesty Lectures, 1993*, New York: Basic Books.

The second volume examines the philosophical basis of human rights including contributions by John Rawls, Richard Rorty, Stephen Lukes and Jean- François Lyotard.

Tunstall, Kate E. (ed.) (2006) *Displacement, Asylum, Migration: Oxford Amnesty Lectures*, Oxford: Oxford University Press.

This volume contains a fascinating exchange between Slavoj Žižek and Michael Ignatieff.

Other suggestions for further reading include two articles critical of contemporary human rights discourse:

Rancière, Jacques (2004) 'Who is the Subject of the Rights of Man?', *South Atlantic Quarterly* 103, 2–3: 307–9.

Žižek, Slavoj (2005) 'Against Human Rights', *New Left Review* 34, July–August: 115–133.

Finally, the following two books contain chapters examining the relationship between biopolitics, human rights and international relations:

Douzinas, Costas (2007) *Human Rights and Empire: The Political Philosophy of Cosmopolitanism*, Abingdon and New York: RoutledgeCavendish.

Shani, Giorgio, Makoto Sato and Mustapha Kamal Pasha (eds) (2007) *Protecting Human Security in a Post 9/11 World: Critical and Global Insights*, Basingstoke: Palgrave.

WEBSITES

Declaration of Independence, http://www.constitution.org/usdeclar.htm
Text of the American Declaration of Independence (1776) which introduced the concept of 'inalienable rights'.

Declaration of the Rights of Man and the Citizen, http://www.hrcr.org/docs/frenchdec.html
English translation of the original 1789 declaration.

Oxford Amnesty Lectures, http://www.oxford-amnesty-lectures.org/
See further reading for details.

The United Nations Universal Declaration of Human Rights, http://www.un.org/en/documents/udhr/index.shtml
Full text of the original 1948 declaration of human rights.

REFERENCES

Agamben, Giorgio (1998) *Homo Sacer: Sovereign Power and Bare Life*, trans. Daniel Heller-Roazen, Stanford CA: Stanford University Press.

BBC (2011) 'France Imposes First Niqab Fines', http://www.bbc.co.uk/news/world-europe-15013383.

Benhabib, Seyla (2002) *The Claims of Culture: Equality and Diversity in the Global Era*, Princeton, NJ and Oxford: Princeton University Press.

Buzan, Barry, Ole Waever and Jaap de Wilde (1998) *Security: A New Framework of Analysis*, Boulder, CO: Lynne Rienner.

Commission on the Future of Multi-Ethnic Britain (2000) *The Future of Multi-Ethnic Britain*, London: Profile Books.

Douzinas, Costas (2007) *Human Rights and Empire: The Political Philosophy of Cosmopolitanism*, Abingdon and New York: RoutledgeCavendish.

Edkins, Jenny (1999) *Poststructuralism and International Relations: Bringing the Political Back In*, Boulder, CO and London: Lynne Rienner.

Fetzer, Joel. S. and Christopher J. Soper (2005) *Muslims and the State in Britain, France, and Germany*, Cambridge: Cambridge University Press.

Foucault, Michel (1991) 'Governmentality', in Graham Burchell, Colin Gordon and Peter Miller (eds) *The Foucault Effect: Studies in Governmentality*, Chicago: University of Chicago Press.

Glazer, Nathan and Patrick Moynihan (1970) *Beyond the Melting Pot, Second Edition: The Negroes, Puerto Ricans, Jews, Italians, and Irish of New York City*, Cambridge, MA: Harvard–MIT Joint Center for Urban Studies Series.

Hobbes, Thomas [1651] (2006) *The Leviathan*, new edn, Mineola, NY: Dover Publications.

Hopgood, Stephen (2000) 'Reading the Small Print in Global Civil Society: The Inexorable Hegemony of the Liberal Self', *Millennium: Journal of International Studies* 29, 1: 1–25.

Huntington, Samuel P. (1996) *The Clash of Civilizations and the Remaking of the World Order*, New York: Simon and Schuster.

ICCPR (1966) International Covenant on Civil and Political Rights, http://www2.ohchr.org/english/law/ccpr.htm.

Joppke, Christian (2009) *Veil: Mirror of Identity*, Cambridge: Polity Press.

Laborde, Cécile (2008) *Critical Republicanism. The Hijab Controversy and Political Philosophy*, Oxford: Oxford University Press.

Locke, John [1689] (1988) *Two Treatises of Government*, Student edition, Cambridge Texts in the History of Political Thought, ed. Peter Laslett, 3rd edn, Cambridge: Cambridge University Press.

McGoldrick, Dominic (2006) *Human Rights and Religion: The Islamic Headscarf Debate in Europe*, Oxford and Portland, OR: Hart Publishing.

Marx, Karl [1844] (1977) *On the Jewish Question*, in David McLellan (ed.) *Karl Marx: Selected Writings*, Oxford: Oxford University Press.

Modood, Tariq (2005) *Multicultural Politics: Racism, Ethnicity and Muslims in Britain*, Minneapolis: University of Minnesota Press.

——(2007) *Multiculturalism*, Cambridge: Polity Press.

National Assembly (1789) *The Declaration of the Rights of Man and the Citizen*, http://www.hrcr.org/docs/frenchdec.html.

Pagden, Anthony (2003) 'Human Rights, Natural Rights, and Europe's Imperial Legacy', *Political Theory* 31: 171–99.

Pew Forum (2011) *The Future of the Global Muslim Population*, http://www.pewforum.org/The-Future-of-the-Global-Muslim-Population.aspx.

Roy, Olivier (2007) *Secularism Confronts Islam*, New York: Columbia University Press.

Shani, Giorgio (2007) *Sikh Nationalism and Identity in a Global Age*, London: Routledge.

——(2008) 'Toward a Post-Western IR: The Umma, Khalsa Panth, and Critical International Relations Theory', *International Studies Review* 10: 722–34.

——(2010) 'Securitizing "Bare Life": Critical Perspectives on Human Security Discourse', in David Chandler and Niklas Hynek (eds) *Critical Perspectives on Human Security: Discourses of Emancipation and Regimes of Power*, Abingdon: Routledge.

Spivak, Gayatri Chakravorty (1999) *A Critique of Postcolonial Reason: Toward a History of the Vanishing Present*, Cambridge, MA: Harvard University Press.

United Nations (1948) *Universal Declaration of Human Rights*, http://www.un.org/en/documents/udhr/index.shtml.

UNDP (United Nations Development Programme) (2009) *Human Development Report 2009: Overcoming Barriers: Human Mobility and Development*, Oxford: Oxford University Press.

Waldron, Jeremy (ed.) (1987) *Nonsense Upon Stilts: Bentham, Burke and Marx on the Rights of Man*, London and New York: Methuen.

Weil, Patrick (2009) 'Why the French Laicite is Liberal', *Cardoso Law Review* 30, 6: 2699–714.

Žižek, Slavoj (2005) 'Against Human Rights', *New Left Review* 34, July–August: 115–33.

For a range of further resources supporting this chapter, please visit the companion website for *Global Politics, 2nd Edition* at www.routledge.com/cw/edkins/

CHAPTER **28**

Conclusion

What can we do to change the world?

Maja Zehfuss

THE QUESTION
CHANGING WHAT'S WRONG WITH THE WORLD

Not everyone wants to find out about global politics in order to change things; some people in fact treat the world as something we should seek to understand, rather than change, as they consider it beyond our control.

Many of the questions we have about global politics are borne of a sense of dissatisfaction with the state of the world. We want to know why some people are better off than others because the unequal distribution of wealth seems to us unfair. More than that, many of us will be appalled at widespread poverty and its very serious implications for people's lives. Similarly, we want to know why politics turns to violence because it would be better, we think intuitively, if it did not. We are unsettled by the thought that so many should die, and often at a young age, due to such violence. If we ask whether we can move beyond conflict, we do so because we can think of many cases where this has not happened, often despite people trying very hard. So one question that seems to really vex many of us and that motivates us to study global politics is how to change what's wrong with the world. Put differently, we would like to know how to respond – and respond effectively – to the sorts of things that we object to: poverty, war, slavery, environmental degradation and so on.

These are extraordinarily important questions. Yet, at the same time, our desire to change the world – to make it a better place – raises all sorts of difficult questions and some of them are often overlooked. After all, how do we decide what is wrong? And why do we think we can – or should – change the world? The question of what we can do to change the world makes some huge assumptions about the world and our role in it. In this conclusion, I want to examine what might be wrong with the idea of changing what's wrong with the world.

Most of us are pretty good at identifying problems with the world. Global politics is certainly replete with states of affairs that we object to: child labour; war; vastly differential access to resources; people having to live in conditions of poverty and violence that many of us find difficult to even imagine; famine; disease; and so on. Thinking about this can be quite frustrating. This is not just because the list of wrongs in the world seems to be very long, but also because it can be difficult to figure out what to do about them. Some of these things seem to be happening in far away places and it is not clear how, if at all, we could do anything about it. Many of us try, however. Across the world people occupied public spaces in order to protest against the way in which the global financial system benefits the few at the expense of the many. But even those of us who do not set up camp somewhere to make our views known often work towards change. We attempt to reduce our 'carbon footprint' in order to make a contribution to fighting climate change. We give money to charities supporting people suffering from poverty in order to help, in a small way, to alleviate the effects of the unequal distribution of resources. At times, we may participate in demonstrations to express our dissatisfaction, for example to protest against war. Often this feels quite unsatisfactory: our contribution appears too small. The world does not change in the way we have envisaged, and we may therefore lose courage. We may begin to think that thinking about the problems of global politics is quite futile: what is the use of identifying wrongs if we cannot rectify them?

Often the Occupy movement or other groups take over private space too. Is the point that all space could be claimed as public, as the commons? That space isn't a commodity, to be bought and sold?

This sense of frustration reveals some really interesting underlying assumptions about the world and our role in it. The expectation that we must be able to rectify wrongs, that this is what in a sense justifies our thinking about them, reveals a very particular attitude towards the world. In this vision of the world, we are at its centre and very much in charge. The world is there for us to do with as we please. This seems to go back all the way to the Old Testament: God created man and woman and charged them to 'subdue it: and have dominion over the fish of the sea, and over the fowl of the air, and over every living thing that moveth upon the earth' (Genesis 1: 27–28). Chapter 3 asked what it would mean to think in terms of the anthropocene: there might be more to this world than just us.

But we approach the world from our point of view. For many of us, the centrality of the human is firmly lodged at the heart of our thought. This attitude is, if anything, underlined by the way in which God has been displaced from the political universe. As Chapter 7 explained, authority or sovereignty now derives from within our world rather than from a God who is transcendent, somehow beyond our human world. The centrality of the human is therefore reinforced through the Reformation. The Enlightenment, with its ideas of human reason and liberty, further translated this shift

The Enlightenment is discussed in **Chapter 6**.

into the political sphere. The idea of sovereign 'man' as somehow independent of the world and yet in control of it has proved to be extremely powerful. 'Man' is no longer just central as God's creation, but because 'he' can use reason to decide what to do. 'He' has an impact on the world.

It is important to ask who we think we are when we think that we want to change the world. Put differently, the idea of changing what's wrong with the world seems to imply that we humans are doing the changing and therefore that we have some kind of control over the world. It implies an idea of sovereign 'man' and with it a rather simplistic idea of power. We can fix things. Chapter 7 discussed the limitations of such a way of conceptualising power and showed that the problem of power in fact raises complex questions about who influences whom and in what way, and indeed about how we would know. It is not just about the ability to make others do what we want them to do or, in terms of our current question, about whether we have the ability to change the world. Power is not something that we 'have' and that we can then use to achieve change. Rather power is something that happens in all social relations, and that happens precisely because we never have full control. Power relations are productive, not just repressive. This makes the world interesting, but also messy. It's not easy to see how 'we' can simply change the world with others bringing their own views and resources to the world, creating a complicated set of ever-changing power relations.

Chapter 7 discusses Michel Foucault's work on power which develops these ideas further.

FIGURE 28.1
Occupy Wall Street protesters in Los Angeles. Photo: Reuters. http://www.ibtimes.com/articles/228298/20111010/occupy-wall-street-jobs-banks-financial-crisis-protest-protesters-activists-unemployment-unemploymen.htm

The idea that we need to change what's wrong with the world of course also implies that we are able to identify how the world should be in order for it to be better. This, again, is not easy. We may think that it is obvious that war is a pretty bad idea because of all its negative effects, but there are of course those who believe that some wars are just (Chapter 21). Often the devil is in the detail. We might spontaneously subscribe to the idea that fighting a war against the Third Reich was right, but does that mean that we approve of civilians being burned to death as their cities were bombed (Chapter 1)? Chapter 2 talks about the very fundamental questions about who we are and what politics is about that arise and are resolved in some way when we make claims about what it is right to do.

Despite these profound questions and difficulties, many of us do have deeply held convictions about what we should do. There may well be some who endorse war, but that does not mean that you cannot be passionately opposed to it. Because we are not alone in the world, having a clear idea about the right way forward almost always involves having ideas about what others should do and what is good for them. It is altogether likely, for example, that you are opposed to war (if you are), not merely because of what it might be doing to you (you wouldn't have the opportunity to read this book, probably, if you lived in a war zone or were fighting a war, though you may well know and love people who do), but also – and perhaps even primarily – because of what it is doing to others: the families whose lives are disrupted, the women who are raped, the children who go hungry, miss out on education and might even be killed, the soldiers who have horrifying experiences, might be seriously injured and, again, might be killed, to name just a few examples. So you might think war has to be avoided or overcome because it would be better for these others if war did not exist. This line of thinking, of course, involves us in the kinds of problems that have been discussed in Chapter 21. Why is it actually that we think we know what is good for others? You may think that it is obvious that people would prefer not to live in a war zone (or that developing countries ought not to be crippled by debt or that we should make real efforts to reduce carbon emissions, for example) but as we propose our solution we need to be mindful of whether we are not making assumptions about others' needs and our knowledge that are more problematic than we would like to admit.

ILLUSTRATIVE EXAMPLE
THE IRAQ WAR

In March 2003 a coalition of approximately forty countries led by the United States supported an invasion of Iraq. Most of the troops actually involved in the operation came from the United States, the United Kingdom and Australia. The war was initially declared to be over on 1 May 2003 but fighting very much continued. Now the war is considered to have ended in December 2011 with the withdrawal of the remaining US troops, but violence within the country continues to lead to fatalities. The invasion was of course seen by its supporters to promote change of a sort we should support. In their view, it was about changing what was wrong with the world. But at the same time many people passionately opposed the war. I want to look at this particular example in a little more detail.

Chapter 8 says more about war and the media.

In Chapter 1, we briefly looked into the question of why there are wars and we examined in particular the problem that people get killed, often in gruesome ways. You may recall the story of a survivor of the bombing of Dresden that we recounted: he tells of discovering the bodies of the many people from his street, including his immediate family, who had been killed – asphyxiated – in the air raid shelter during the bombing of Dresden. Having heard this story and perhaps media reports about the impact of contemporary military operations, you may well decide that war is not a very good idea. Many people are opposed to war, and they often express their anger at wars being fought by their countries. Protest against the war in Vietnam was widespread in the 1960s and 1970s, especially amongst students in the United States. In May 1965 a group of students publicly burnt their draft cards (the documents that informed them that they were being conscripted into the US armed forces) and it was subsequently made a crime to do so. There were also mass demonstrations against the 1991 Gulf War. 'No blood for oil' was one of the protestors' common slogans. Even though the Federal Republic of Germany, for example, did not deploy its military to the war, many young men there registered as conscientious objectors at the time, to ensure that they could not be compelled to fight. The proposed US-led invasion of Iraq in 2003 met with fierce opposition across the globe. Protests were often coordinated such that

FIGURE 28.2
London, 15 February 2003. Photo: Jenny Edkins

demonstrations would occur simultaneously in different places. On 15 February 2003 millions of people in over 600 cities across the world went on marches in order to make their profound opposition to this war heard. Groups continued to campaign and demonstrate against the war all over the world long after it had started.

Many of these campaigns have sought to get us to acknowledge and remember the human cost of war. They have employed different strategies to do so. Sometimes campaigners have been relatives of soldiers killed on duty in Iraq and their actions have drawn attention to the troops' deaths. Military Families Against the War (www.mfaw.org.uk), for example, was founded by Rose Gentle and Reg Keys. Both have sons who were killed in Iraq. The group campaigned to end the involvement of UK troops in the war in Iraq which they considered to be 'based on lies'; they reminded us of their loved ones killed – or at risk to be killed or injured – in Iraq. Both the militaries of the UK (Ministry of Defence 2008) and the US (www.defendamerica.mil/fallen.html) have maintained websites to memorialise individual fallen soldiers, often giving some details about their lives. We learn, for example, that Corporal Paul Joszko, who died in Basra on 28 June 2007, 'always looked scruffy, had a cheeky smile and a cigarette in his hand, but he never failed to deliver the goods' (Ministry of Defence 2007).

In contrast, those killed by these militaries have not been remembered in the same way. Neither the US nor the UK military make any count available of the fatalities that they have caused. The failure to provide the public with information about the death toll has been seized upon by critics of the war. Judith Butler (2004), for example, has drawn attention to how Western lives are construed as 'grievable', whilst those of the civilians they kill are not. Through this idea of grievability she wants to pursue larger questions: 'Who counts as human? Whose lives count as lives?' (Butler 2004: 20). She points out that the failure to grieve some lives – those of Iraqi civilians – suggests that other lives are regarded as more valuable.

Various groups have attempted to make up for the militaries' failure to tell us how many people they have killed in Iraq. Iraq Body Count (www.iraqbodycount.org) maintains a database of violent civilian deaths both during the 2003 invasion (the official war which lasted from 20 March until 1 May 2003) and since. Their count covers non-combatants killed by military or paramilitary action and as a consequence of the breakdown of law and order in the aftermath of the invasion. The count continues, despite attempts to declare the war to have ended. If you go to their website, you will see their current estimate. As I write this, it is 105,721–115,476. In other words, it is not a precise figure. So the first thing we notice, even looking at only this one count, is that it is difficult to come up with a reliable figure. In fact, this is what the US and the UK say: it's really difficult to know how many civilians you've killed in a military operation. Our troops can't be expected to go around counting the dead when they are busy protecting themselves against attack.

Indeed often they may not even know that they have killed someone: if you blow up a building from a distance, how are you to know how many people were in it and whether they were combatants? So, how do groups such as Iraq Body Count figure out how many have been killed? Iraq Body Count relies on media reports (which are cross-checked), figures from hospitals, mortuaries and NGOs and any official figures that are available. Their website does more than count, though: it is an attempt to memorialise the forgotten civilians killed by the war (Zehfuss 2007). This has also been attempted

Even over 60 years after the fact it is not clear how many people were killed by the bombing of German cities during the Second World War: see **Chapter 1**.

FIGURE 28.3
Boots for 'Eyes Wide Open: The Human Cost of War' exhibition. The exhibition comprised a pair of boots for each of the US military personnel killed in Iraq, and pairs of shoes symbolising the estimated civilian deaths, and was organised by the American Friends Service Committee.
See http://www.afsc.org/eyes/.
Photo: Terry Foss, AFSC/Photographer

by the 'Eyes Wide Open' exhibition which showed a pair of boots for each of the US military personnel killed in the current war in Iraq and pairs of shoes symbolising civilian deaths.

War has a very serious effect on people, both on combatants and on civilians. Those opposed to war have often drawn attention to this human cost of war. Yet this does not mean that supporters of war deny the death and destruction caused by war or that they callously disregard it. They may well agree that this is one of the wrongs in the world that we would like to change. In the next section I examine some of the problems that arise in trying to respond to such wrongs.

GENERAL RESPONSES
NO RIGHT WAY FORWARD

In Chapter 1 we observed that being confronted with the fate of individual people in war – the gruesomeness of their deaths, for example – may produce in you a strong emotional reaction and therefore a desire to do something about it, to respond in some way. But how precisely you will react depends on the circumstances of the particular case. You might disapprove of the UK's role in the Iraq War and approve of its contribution to the Second World War. You might approve of a particular war, but feel profoundly unsettled by a particular incident within it. Your reaction might also depend on an assessment of what your chances are of making a difference. As a rule, there will be a lot of things that you don't actually know. And, worst of all, there is unlikely to be a solution that will be unambiguously good. These things are messy. They don't usually fit in with general rules. Even if you don't think we should kill people, you might struggle with what this means when people are already being killed by others.

There are therefore at least two underlying problems in thinking through the dilemma of war, and it is useful to make them explicit. The first concerns the problem that in any given situation we will have responsibilities towards a range of people and we cannot fulfil them all simultaneously. The second is to do with the impossibility of knowing everything before making a decision.

All sorts of claims have been made about the necessity of the war in Iraq by the countries that were part of the invasion. On the one hand it was claimed that Iraq was in illegal possession of weapons of mass destruction and was therefore a threat to the security of Western countries. On the other hand it was argued that the Iraqi leader Saddam Hussein was a cruel dictator and that the Iraqi people had to be liberated from his oppressive rule. US secretary of state Colin Powell explained in September 2002 that the administration 'would hope that [. . .] rather than [the war] being seen as an assault, it would be seen as a liberation and it would be seen as the beginning of a new era in that part of the world' ('US Policy Towards Iraq' 2002: 17). His colleague US secretary of defense Donald Rumsfeld claimed that the 'goal is to free those people' (United States Department of Defense 2002). And indeed Saddam Hussein was toppled by the invasion, tried for particular crimes against his own population and sentenced to death. However, the country was plunged into a state of war, endangering people and their livelihoods.

The argument that the overthrow of Saddam Hussein following the military intervention in Iraq constitutes a liberation of the Iraqi people is also made in the Euston Manifesto: see **Chapter 21**.

I don't want to examine here what the reasons for going to Iraq actually were or whether they made any sense. But I would like to draw attention to one aspect of both of the arguments mentioned above. Both propose, in one way or another, to sacrifice some lives in order to achieve, or so it is claimed, the protection of others. Soldiers of the US-led coalition as well as Iraqi soldiers were put into harm's way. So were Iraqi civilians. The first argument suggests that this will protect Western civilians, the second that it will protect Iraqi civilians from a different sort of harm, that inflicted by Saddam Hussein and his supporters. This is of course what makes the question of war so difficult: people die. Many of us don't like this idea. But supporters of wars often claim that people will also die if there is no war, in this case Iraqi civilians killed by their own regime and Western civilians at risk from weapons of mass destruction allegedly in Iraq's possession. So there is no obvious way forward that does not involve some wrongs, that is, in this case, people getting killed. To overcome this impasse, some claims to life are privileged over others. If we grant for a moment that the war in Iraq serves to protect Western civilians (which is of course an enormously problematic claim, not least because it is difficult to see what evidence would be used to prove this either way), then we have a situation where Western civilians' lives are apparently valued more highly than the lives of those who, for one reason of another, find themselves in the war zone. The war is to protect their lives by sacrificing other lives. As I noted earlier, this privileging of some lives over others can to an extent be seen in the way in which some deaths are grieved whilst others appear not to be grievable in the same way, as Butler (2004) puts it. Yet arguably things are complicated: some of the lives that are officially grieved – those of the US-led coalition's soldiers – are treated as more expendable than other lives – those of the Western civilians that are to be protected (Zehfuss 2009a).

This apparent need to sacrifice some lives to protect others makes for a tricky moral dilemma. People often try to resolve these sorts of dilemmas by arguing for a general rule that will settle the matter. One could argue, for example, that we have duties towards members of our own community that we do not have towards others (Chapter 2). So if a choice has to be made between protecting US civilians and Iraqi civilians (and, remember, this is what is *claimed* by some, but that does not necessarily make it true), the US government is right to opt for the former. I do not think that this sort of argument works.

Another way of deciding whether the human cost of war is justified involves applying the criteria of just war thinking, explained in **Chapter 21**.

The dilemma we seem to confront when contemplating the possibility of war seems based on something that Jacques Derrida calls an aporia: there is no way forward, the path is blocked (2006: 63). There is no course of action that would resolve or escape the dilemma. In such a situation, anything you might do involves you in committing some wrong. Put differently, if you take responsibility towards one person or group of people – say Iraqi civilians who will be liberated from an oppressive regime – this involves you in not taking responsibility towards others – the combatants and Iraqi civilians killed in the process. More generally speaking, if you expend your resources on this conflict, you might not be able to intervene in another, say in Darfur, and thereby you fail your responsibility towards those others affected by the other conflict. This is a problem we constantly face: To whose call do we respond? And whom do we end up ignoring? It is not possible to act responsibly towards everyone at the same time. We simply do not have the capacity. In Derrida's words, 'I cannot respond to the call, the request, the obligation, or even the love of another without sacrificing the other other, the other others' (Derrida 1995: 68). Whilst we give our support to one person, for example, another may be in need of our attention, too, but we are already occupied. So there is a paradox at the heart of responsibility:

The idea of taking responsibility for others also raises a host of further tricky questions: see **Chapter 21**.

> As soon as I enter into a relation with the other, with the gaze, look, request, love, command, or call of the other, I know that I can respond only by sacrificing ethics, that is, by sacrificing whatever obliges me also to respond, in the same way, in the same instant, to all the others.
>
> (Derrida 1995: 68)

Acting responsibly therefore does not mean doing good rather than evil. It means negotiating a difficult situation in which no purely good way forward is possible.

This is why you have to make a decision: there are many demands on you, and you cannot respond to them all simultaneously. Some of them may contradict each other. Moreover, you often have to respond under less than ideal circumstances because the matter is urgent (Derrida 2002: 296). Urgency means not least that you will be unable to gather all the knowledge that you might want before making your decision. Whilst you are gathering more information about the precise circumstances of a conflict, for example, people could already be dying. At some point, you need to make your choice,

BOX 28.1 JACQUES DERRIDA

Jacques Derrida (1930–2004) is one of the most important contemporary philosophers. His work is a radical critique of the inescapable tensions within Western thought (Derrida 1998). His strategy of 'deconstruction' involves showing how arguments rely on assumptions that at the same time undermine them. This has profound political implications. Derrida shows that accepted institutions such as the state monopoly of power are logically unfounded and that it is impossible to arrive at justice through applying rules (1992). Rather justice or responsibility becomes necessary when knowledge does not provide an answer. It requires a leap, what he calls the madness of decision (Zehfuss 2009b).

FIGURE 28.4
Jacques Derrida. Photo: Joel Robine, AFP/Getty Images

even if you do not know everything that could be useful in helping you make your decision. Derrida also points out that it is anyway a mistake to think that there is some piece of knowledge that will somehow settle the matter and tell us the right way forward. For him knowledge is one thing, but an ethico-political decision is quite another. We should certainly try to know as much as possible, but knowledge is not enough. An ethico-political decision involves a leap of faith (Derrida 2003: 118). Although we may be under pressure to make a decision, at times it actually feels like the decision has already taken place. So the idea of a decision is tricky and Derrida has quite a bit to say about it. What is important here is that the decision that we may make in response to others' demands is not under our control. I have already mentioned that it involves a leap of faith. Derrida also talks of a decision being 'the Other's decision in me, or through me' (2006: 103). That is, even when we make a decision, we are not somehow separate from the world that we respond to. I will say more about our inextricable involvement in the world and what that means in the next section.

A decision involves committing to one way, despite not knowing the right way forward. It is not possible to keep all the options open. The invasion of Iraq on 20 March 2003 closed down the possibility of non-intervention. Waiting and not intervening often looks like it keeps more options open, and in some ways it does. But if you wait you cannot go back. You may choose what looks like the same option later, but by then the situation will already have changed. Whatever you do, you will have made a choice. Nevertheless, making a choice, under these circumstances, is not for the faint-hearted. You know that it is impossible to act responsibly towards everyone. On top of that, whatever you may know about the situation is actually not enough to lead to the right decision. So you cannot get this entirely right. You need some courage to make a decision despite knowing this, though you cannot actually avoid a decision altogether either. After all, you are involved. You need some courage to admit that your position – where you stand – is not determined by secure knowledge. Whilst you might be prepared to passionately stand up for your views, you know that you don't know

This is similar to the situation in **Chapter 21** where the 'stretch' inherent in thinking about 'exclusive knowledge' is explored.

whether you are right. You could be wrong. No: you *are* wrong, at least in part, because there is no option that makes everything all right. More generally, there is no way forward that you could take that would rectify all that is wrong with the world and change it for the better.

BROADER ISSUES
CHANGE AND COMPLICITY

I want now to turn to different and broader issues the idea of change entails. When we ask how to change what's wrong with the world we make a number of assumptions about the world and our role in it, and I want to use this section to draw some of them out more explicitly. We seem not only to think that we can identify what is wrong with the world, but we also seem to expect that we should be able to rectify what is wrong. So there is an assumption here about what we know, but also about what we are in control of, the sort of power that we might have in relation to the world. These are assumptions about how the world works and about our role within that world. In some way, the question seems to suggest that we are separate from this world – able to step back and diagnose the problem. But at the same time we seem to expect to be able to act upon the world – able to act on the diagnosis and solve the problem. These are assumptions about knowledge and power, about thought and action. They are also assumptions about identity: who is the 'we' that we assume has the ability to change the world?

In Chapter 1 we talked about Robert Cox's ideas about different sorts of theories, which he calls problem-solving theory and critical theory. Problem-solving theory assumes that the world is as it is, with particular power and social relationships that frame the possibility for action; it is 'a guide to solve the problems posed within the terms of the particular perspective which was the point of departure' (Cox 1981: 128). Critical theory, in contrast, calls the prevailing institutions and power relationships into question; it is 'directed towards an appraisal of the very framework for action' (Cox 1981: 128). Problem-solving theory seems to be just the thing we need when we want to fix what's wrong with the world. This sort of theory should be able to tell us how the global economy works and what we therefore need to do if we want to reduce inequality, for example. Or it should tell us what causes wars and what we need therefore do to avoid them. This is what many scholars studying global politics have in fact tried to do, but they don't seem to have succeeded. Cox thinks that this way of thinking is based on a false premise. It involves looking at particular problems in isolation and fails to appreciate the larger picture. It assumes that the social order is fixed and that we must solve problems within this fixed order.

Cox argues that the social and political order changes, at least in the longer term (1981: 129). Chapter 7 examined some very fundamental changes in the political order in Europe that were related to changes in the way people conceived of their own being in the world. How we think and how we act within the world are deeply connected. After the Enlightenment, the legitimacy of the political order could no longer be derived from God and therefore had to come from somewhere within our world. This makes a very big difference and historically we therefore saw a shift towards democracy. Problem-solving theory seems to be unable to cope with such change. Cox argues that such theory is conservative. By acting as a guide to action within the prevailing order it implicitly accepts this order and therefore reinforces the status quo. Measures such as debt relief or development aid may alleviate global inequality in a small way. They may appear to rectify what's wrong with the world, but they achieve only very limited change. Such 'solutions' seem to assume that the system of global capitalism is malfunctioning in a particular way and that this can be fixed. They make the global economy run more smoothly. But what if the global economy as we know it is the cause of global inequality in the first place? Then this is not a very good solution. If we want to reduce global inequality and if global capitalism produces such inequality not when it is malfunctioning but when it is working perfectly, then we need to do something other than propose measures that take the system of global capitalism as given. This is what the Occupy movement is suggesting, and it is what makes their cause so challenging. Similarly, the idea that there are some bad states that are violent towards their own citizens and others – sometimes called 'rogue states' – and that this is in some way against the values of the international community which must therefore intervene to bring such states back into the fold, makes out that the system is just fine. Saddam Hussein's Iraq was a problem that needed to be fixed. But what if the existence of such regimes is an inevitable outcome of the system of state sovereignty? Then we would need to change something far more fundamental to get away from politics turning to violence. This is where critical theory is important.

The idea of an 'international community' that shares values is often used to support claims in favour of intervention, but this is quite problematic. For more on this see **Chapter 25**.

Critical theory is concerned with possible alternative orders. As Cox puts it, 'critical theory can be a guide to strategic action for bringing about an alternative order, whereas problem-solving theory is a guide to tactical actions which, intended or unintended, sustain the existing order' (1981: 130). So critical theory is interested in how we might actually get out of the system that is causing the problems that we then need to fix. Cox works this through in one particular way, and you might wish to follow up these arguments by reading his article. What is important here is that how we think about the world and how we act within it are not two separate issues. They are inextricably linked. Sometimes we cannot see an alternative, but that does not mean that there can never be one. What is conceivable has changed over time and therefore there is no reason to assume that the world as we know it now will or must remain as it is. One of our problems is that we are caught up in the world as it is. We cannot step back from the world and identify its problems objectively: what appears to us to be a problem is already related to who we are and where we are situated in the world. We are in a sense part of the problem that we are trying to respond to.

Nevertheless we do, of course, respond. Acting is not an optional extra, a choice we make after identifying a problem and figuring out a solution. Often we do not quite know what to do. As I noted earlier, we might not have all the information that we might wish to have before acting. And we might be quite unable to identify a right way forward. But we are involved, whether we like it or not. In fact, this is what makes us so frustrated at times. You may have been against the war in Iraq and yet, if you paid tax in one of the countries that were part of the US-led coalition, you were in some way contributing to the war effort. Or you might feel passionately that the conditions under which people have to work in some parts of the developing world are appalling, but it is altogether likely that you have bought products made by them. The issue is not that you have control over war or exploitation. But you are involved.

Chapter 7 discusses different ways of thinking about power; this is also relevant to the issues of involvement and control raised here.

BOX 28.2 THE OCCUPY MOVEMENT

In September 2011 Occupy Wall Street set up in Zuccotti Park, in New York's financial district, in order to protest against economic inequality, greed and the influence of corporations on government, in particular by the financial services industry. Instigated by individuals associated with the Canadian-based Adbusters Media Foundation, the protest was inspired by the student protests in the UK in 2010, the anti-austerity protests in Greece and Spain and the protests and revolutions across the Middle East that have come to be known as the Arab Spring. Occupy protests later spread across all continents (though there are more of them in North America and Europe than elsewhere) and their slogan 'We are the 99%' – designed to highlight the income inequality between the wealthiest 1 per cent and the rest of the people in the United States – came to be used well beyond the Occupy movement itself. It is seen as one of the most successful protest slogans ever.

The movement is notable not only because it spread across the world, but also for its distinctive style. The protest in Manhattan formed the New York General Assembly which meets regularly. Although the meetings are facilitated, no leaders were appointed or elected and anyone can speak. The outdoors location with large numbers of people in attendance also required the development of distinctive communication mechanisms, with short phrases being passed on relay-style from the speaker to the back and people waggling their hands in agreement rather than applauding.

What perhaps led to most comment from outside the movement is that Occupy did not formulate concrete lists of demands, leading to the suggestion that without a strategy or clear plans for the future the movement might be unable to accomplish change and indeed fizzle out. Others, however, see Occupy and other similar recent demonstrations and protests as reflecting changes in society that amount to something new (Mason 2012).

Judith Butler took up the issue of the lack of demands directly when she spoke at Occupy Wall Street in October 2011:

> People have asked, so what are the demands? What are the demands all of these people are making? Either they say there are no demands and that leaves your critics confused, or they say that the demands for social equality and economic justice are impossible demands. And the impossible demands, they say, are just not practical. If hope is an impossible demand, then we demand the impossible — that the right to shelter, food and employment are impossible demands, then we demand the impossible. If it is impossible to demand that those who profit from the recession redistribute their wealth and cease their greed, then yes, we demand the impossible.
>
> (cited in Elliott 2011)

Elsewhere Butler thinks through in more detail what broader issues arise around the question 'So, what are the demands?' She points out not least that formulating demands that are capable of being satisfied necessitates attributing legitimacy to the institutions the demands would be directed at, a profoundly problematic move if these same institutions are complicit in producing the system that generates the inequality that the protests are directed against (Butler, 2012: 10). In other words, the demand that there should be demands implies that the protestors should operate within the existing system.

The Occupy movement is seen by some as uninterested in or even opposed to theory (Mason 2012). Nevertheless, academics and intellectuals have sought to make a positive contribution not only by participating in protests but also, for example, through offering 'theory and strategy as a means of empowering occupiers' (Tidal 2012; see also Coombs *et al.* 2012).

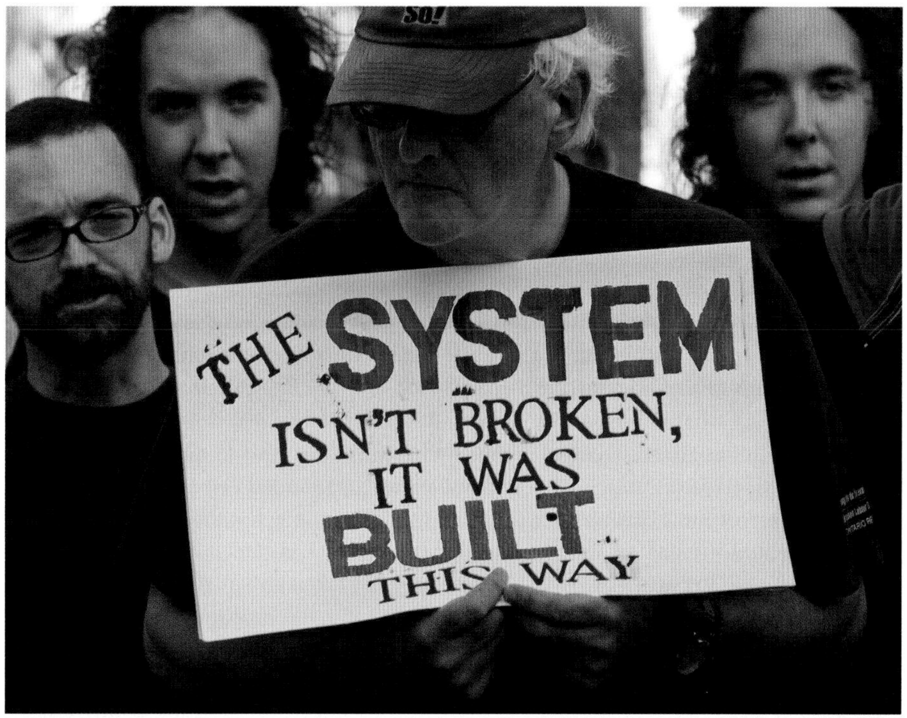

FIGURE 28.5.
Occupy Halifax protest sign, October 2011. http://images.ctv.ca/archives/CTVNews/img2/20111015/800_occupy_halifax_cp_111015.jpg; http://chewychunks.wordpress.com/2011/10/17/occupy-wallstreet-protest-signs/

Thinking through what it means to respond from this position of being *involved* but not *in control* helps us to understand more about what Cox means when he talks of critical theory. We observed in Chapter 1 that there seem to be two ways in which one might think of responding to a question: by thinking it through or by taking some form of action in response to it. We noted then that different chapters seemed to emphasise one or other way of conceptualising response but that these two are by no means quite as different or separate as might appear to be the case. Thinking about something in a different way can already be an intervention, part of changing the world. Chapter 5 showed, for example, how the ways in which feminists rethought the world had significant political implications. That is not to say that you can just think differently about something and expect that the world will suddenly be different: after all, it took a committed feminist movement – the efforts of many women and indeed men – in order to bring about changes. Change is difficult precisely because we are already involved. We are always already part of a social context and our critique, our attempt at change, is part of it too. We, as people, or subjects, who think and speak, confront language as a system that already exists (Edkins 1999). When we speak we draw on this system: the system is what allows us to communicate. Therefore language also limits what may be said. If we try to say something that is not envisaged in the system, something for which there is literally no language, this is very difficult and we risk

This way in which language or discourse always already exists is also discussed in **Chapter 5**.

becoming unintelligible. Over time, of course, language and its rules may and do change. This happens, for example, when language users persist in doing something new, say, in using a new word, such as 'blog'. The new word or rule becomes part of the system and can then be used by others. But you can't just change the language on your own, by thinking about the language differently. Language can change if others are involved. Your new use of language only works if it is understood by others. In fact, all social action is like this. We, as social beings, are always already part of a context that both enables action and circumscribes what we may do. It is possible to move things, to change work patterns such that they allow for people having family commitments at the same time, for example, but it takes effort. Such change is often actively resisted and sometimes people are stuck in their ways and cannot see how what they are doing is creating difficult conditions for others.

So changing what is wrong with the world is difficult, but that is not because change is impossible. Significant change involves changing the prevailing order. Problem solving as defined by Cox may appear to be easier and indeed more effective because it seems that you can know what can be done within the prevailing order. When we start talking about really changing the world, then things can be quite uncertain. What exactly would be put in the place of global capitalism? Would any alternative not have its own problems? Even if it was possible to have a different system, would it end global inequality? You can see how someone proposing a shift to the whole system could be in a difficult position. Such a shift would only be possible if others agreed to it, and how do you persuade someone to contribute to an outcome that you can't be quite certain is better in any respect than what we already have?

No doubt being able to convince people that you are certain about something is a powerful political move. There are those, for example, who have undermined environmental policy for years with the argument that there isn't really enough scientific evidence that climate change is happening. But the debate about climate change, discussed in Chapter 3, is very interesting in this context, because of course many people argue that we need to do something even if we might not be entirely sure. Certainty about the precise mechanisms underpinning climate change really is neither here nor there for them, as the consequences of not doing anything might just be devastating.

Chapter 24 explores the issue of certainty and uncertainty in the context of thinking about security.

Certainty can even be dangerous. When people are very certain about something we do not agree with, we often see them as fanatics. More pragmatically, if you are completely convinced that you are right, then you might see no need to talk to and listen to others. But this can seriously damage your chances of implementing your policy. In politics you typically need to get people to cooperate with you and, whilst you may persuade some with the strength of your convictions (your certainty that you are right), those who disagree with you will be likely to feel disrespected and have little desire to cooperate.

Sometimes people have come together, fought for change to the prevailing order, and accomplished something. I have mentioned the feminist movement already. The Black power movement would be another such example (Chapter 5). You may also think of the waves of protest that have collectively come to be known as the Arab Spring (Chapter 9). Successfully promoting change often involves many people doing things in some way together. If great numbers of people were to decide to avoid behaviours and products that are damaging to the environment, this would have some impact, not least because companies want to sell us their products and services and so they'll play to our preferences. Sometimes the actions of ordinary people dramatically alter the expected course of events. This effect is often called 'people power'.

Chapter 7 examined one such example, the fall of the Berlin Wall in 1989. This was something that was considered quite unthinkable at the time. So it's really unlikely that this is what all the people who went to checkpoints between East and West Berlin on the evening of 9 November 1989 had in mind. They took considerable risks to go into the border area, and yet from the stories that Chapter 7 examines it seems that people just wanted to find out whether it really was possible to travel to the other part of the city as the press release earlier that day had seemed to suggest. They were not planning on changing the world, or at any rate not all of them were. A number of them had left their children asleep in their beds (Hertle and Elsner, n.d.: 145): they clearly intended to be back to the routine of their lives later in the night. Some just wanted to see for a couple of hours what 'the West' was really like. Some only turned up because there were so many people already and they went to figure out what the fuss was about. They challenged the authorities at no small risk to themselves, but they did not expect to set off German unification or the end of the Cold War. Yet if so many people had not turned up at the checkpoints on that one night in November 1989, it is possible that the authorities in the GDR might have been able to persist with their plan to issue visas to a limited number of people who would have had to apply for them in an orderly fashion with the correct government authority (Hertle and Elsner, n.d.). Things could have turned out differently.

On 9 November 1989 no one had the outcome under their control, neither the authorities nor the people. But as it turned out life happened and significant change ensued. This is important because we have still been talking here of change and response as though we are at the centre of the universe and somehow in control of it. This view of the world is rather limited – we have seen that social action and power are much more complex – and it also makes it easy for us to slide into a conceptualisation of the world where 'we' are responsible for 'them'. We have to be really careful so that this does not end up as just another way of suggesting that we know what is good for them. The problem that we face is that we are so used to thinking of us as separate from the world that surrounds us that we find it really difficult to absorb the insight that it makes really no sense to imagine ourselves as separate from the social world. We are always already within it, subject to demands from others, but also to what they offer. It is difficult to see ourselves as always already tied into the social world because we have no fully-developed language for it. In contrast, we do have a language for being in charge. The subject that we outlined at the beginning of the chapter is at the heart of English and other Western languages: it acts. But who is this subject? Who is this 'we' that is to change the world? I have observed that the question seems to assume a 'we' that can know what is wrong and know how to put it right, a 'we' that is separate from the world and able to act upon it. But when we thought this through we found something quite different. We found that our knowledge of the wrongs is imperfect as is our ability to identify a right way forward. We found that we are not in control but that we are always already implicated in the social and political order that produces the wrongs that we want to rectify. We found that we cannot respond to the wrongs in the world in a way that would allow us to know that we have done the right thing.

The idea of 'saving the planet' would be like that, as discussed in **Chapter 4**.

So there is actually something wrong with the idea of changing what's wrong with the world. It is a question that envisages us at the centre of the universe, able to make things all right. It imagines us as potential heroes, and if we lived up to this idea of ourselves we would be able to feel really good. But of course we realise that this is not how things are, and so at times we get frustrated at our apparent inability to change what's wrong with the world. Yet what we may experience as an incapacity is in many ways no bad thing. Being heroes who change what's wrong with the world would mean imposing our views on others, disregarding them. So when we find that we cannot be such heroes, that instead we are involved in creating the problems in the first place – that we are complicit – this is no reason to despair. For if you accept that this is the deal, you can stop throwing your energies at the futile attempt to escape this situation. Then you can use your creativity, your intelligence and your passion to figure out how to be in this world – how to live despite not being able to bring about or even know 'the good'.

CONCLUSION

We are, all of us, already involved in global politics. We often treat the question of how to respond as a really big issue that causes us considerable anxiety. Yet whenever we look closely at issues – in particular those that involve the sort of wrongs that we might want to fix – we find that people are already there, responding, every day. People drop water in the US–Mexico border region to save those trying to cross without authorisation from dying of dehydration. They set up alternative banking schemes to provide opportunities to those who traditionally find it difficult to get credit (Chapter 20). They try to move beyond conflict (Chapter 26). And just occasionally something happens that is totally unexpected and at the same time quite wonderful – such as the peaceful

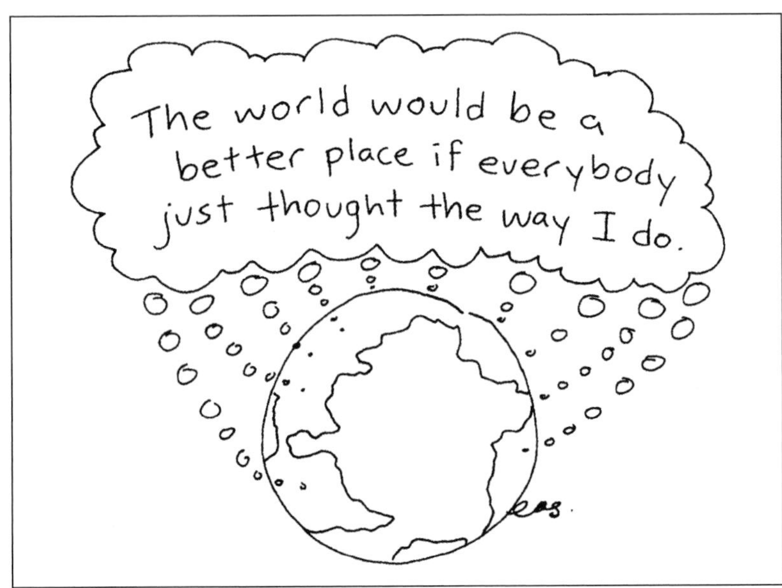

FIGURE 28.6
'The world would be a better place.'
Artist: Betsy Streeter. CartoonStock ref.: bstn29h. www.CartoonStock.com

opening of the Berlin Wall – to remind us that things may happen without a mastermind planning it and indeed that it is our being with others that makes life exciting and worthwhile in the first place.

Many of us have a passionate interest in global politics precisely because we think there are things wrong with the world. Even though it is often difficult to know what to do, it is good that we care. What we have tried to show is that in responding to global politics we have to tackle many large and fascinating questions. Many of them remain unresolved. Over some we may disagree in the strongest possible terms. The problem is, of course, that the world is full of other people and they do not always agree with us. So one really difficult question that we often face in global politics is how we know the right way forward when things are contested. Often other people think quite differently from us. But at the same time this is what makes global politics endlessly fascinating. Other people are, after all, also the best bit about our world. Learning about different ways of thinking about and tackling a problem can be quite an experience. Being able to do that requires remembering that others' views are important, even if we may disagree with them or if they appear to be strange. Our 'solutions' will not work if we cannot get others to join in and cooperate. Learning from and about global politics requires therefore a certain generosity or hospitality, if you will. Sometimes we find that hard because we cannot see what assumptions we are making in our own views, whilst it is apparent to us that others do make assumptions, at times ones we might wish to contest. The answers to larger questions flow from the answers we give to the question of 'life, the universe and everything'. In the end, this is what makes politics, and in particular global politics, so important: it is an arena in which hugely important questions are raised, on which people disagree.

REFERENCES

Butler, Judith (2004) *Precarious Life: The Powers of Mourning and Violence*, London: Verso.

——(2012) 'So What Are the Demands? And Where Do They Go From Here?', *Tidal: Occupy Theory, Occupy Strategy*, issue 2: 8–11.

Coombs, Nathan, Amin Samman and Pepijn van Houwelingen (eds) (2012) 'Imperialism, Finance, #Occupy', *Journal of Critical Globalisation Studies*, issue 5.

Cox, Robert W. (1981) 'Social Forces, States and World Orders', *Millennium: Journal of International Studies* 10, 2: 126–55.

Derrida, Jacques (1992) 'Force of Law: The "Mystical Foundation of Authority"', in David Gray Carlson, Drucilla Cornell and Michel Rosenfeld (eds), *Deconstruction and the Possibility of Justice*, London: Routledge.

——(1995) *The Gift of Death*, trans. David Wills, Chicago: University of Chicago Press.

——(1998) *Of Grammatology*, trans. Gayatri Chakravorty Spivak, corrected edn, Baltimore, MD: Johns Hopkins University Press.

——(2002) *Negotiations: Interventions and Interviews 1971–2001*, ed. and trans. Elizabeth Rottenberg, Stanford, CA: Stanford University Press.

——(2003) 'Autoimmunity: Real and Symbolic Suicides', in Giovanna Borradori, *Philosophy in a Time of Terror: Dialogues with Jürgen Habermas and Jacques Derrida*, Chicago: University of Chicago Press.

——(2006) *Deconstruction Engaged: The Sydney Seminars*, ed. Paul Patton and Terry Smith, Sydney: Power Publications.

Edkins, Jenny (1999) *Poststructualism and International Relations: Bringing the Political Back In*, Boulder, CO: Lynne Rienner.

Elliott, Justin (2011) 'Judith Butler at Occupy Wall Street', *salon.com*, 24 October (http://www.salon.com/2011/10/24/judith_butler_at_occupy_wall_street/).

Hertle, Hans-Hermann and Kathrin Elsner (n.d.) *Mein 9. November: Der Tag an dem die Mauer fiel*, Berlin: Nicolai.

Mason, Paul (2012) *Why It's Kicking Off Everywhere: The New Global Revolutions*, London: Verso.

Ministry of Defence (2007) 'Corporal Paul Joszko and Privates Scott Kennedy and James Kerr killed in Basra roadside bomb attack on 28 June 2007', http://www.mod.uk/DefenceInternet/DefenceNews/MilitaryOperations/CorporalPaulJoszkoAndPrivatesScottKennedyAndJamesKerrKilledInBasraRoadsideBombAttackOn28June2007.htm.

——(2008) 'Operations in Iraq: British Fatalities', http://www.mod.uk/DefenceInternet/FactSheets/OperationsFactsheets/OperationsInIraqBritishFatalities.htm.

Tidal (2012) mission statement (http://occupytheory.org/).

United States Department of Defense (2002) *News Transcript: Secretary Rumsfeld Interview with Fox Affiliate – WGA Channel 5, Atlanta, Ga.*, 27 September.

'US Policy Towards Iraq: Administration Views' (2002) Hearing before the Committee on International Relations, House of Representatives, 107th Congress, 2nd session, 19 September, Serial no. 107–117.

Zehfuss, Maja (2007) 'Subjectivity and Vulnerability: On the War with Iraq', *International Politics* 44, 1: 58–71.

——(2009a) 'Hierarchies of Grief and the Possibility of War: Remembering UK Fatalities in Iraq', *Millennium: Journal of International Studies* 38, 2: 419–40.

——(2009b) 'Jacques Derrida', in Jenny Edkins and Nick Vaughan-Williams (eds), *Critical Theorists and International Relations*, Abingdon: Routledge.

For a range of further resources supporting this chapter, please visit the companion website for *Global Politics, 2nd Edition* at www.routledge.com/cw/edkins/

Figures

Boxes

Acknowledgements and permissions

DISCLAIMER

The publishers have made every effort to contact authors/copyright holders of works reprinted in *Global Politics, 2nd edition* and to obtain permission to publish extracts This has not been possible in every case, however, and we would welcome correspondence from those individuals/companies whom we have been unable to trace. Any omissions brought to our attention will be remedied in future editions.

Figure 0.1 Calvin and Hobbes © 1989 Watterson. Dist. by Universal Uclick. Reprinted with permission. All rights reserved. Image ID: 16449.

Figure 0.2 Magnum Photos for permission to reprint Figure 0.2 *FRANCE. Ile de France region. Paris. FRANCE. Paris. 5th arrondissement. The Sorbonne University occupied by students. May 14th, 1968.* PAR8977. BAB1968027 W00001/04 – Bruno Barbey.

Figure 0.3 Calvin and Hobbes © 1991 Watterson. Dist. by Universal Uclick. Reprinted with permission. All rights reserved. Image ID: 8643.

Figure 0.4 Carlos A. Furuti for kind permission to reprint Map of the world http://www.progonos.com/furuti/HIDDEN/Routledge/mp_Winkel3-s450_Routledge120723A.png.

Figure 1.1 The Ronald Grant Archive for permission to reprint Martin Freeman as Arthur Dent and Mos Def as Ford Prefect in Touchstone Pictures' *The Hitchhiker's Guide to the Galaxy.* © Touchstone Pictures/Spyglass Entertainment/RGA.

Figure 1.2 'Like all of us, he asked many different questions throughout his life.' Artist: Richard Jolley. CartoonStock Ref: rjo0698. www.CartoonStock.com.

Figure 1.3 Tahrir Square, Cairo, during 8 February 2011, at the height of the protests in Egypt. Source: Wikipedia commons: http://en.wikipedia.org/wiki/File:Tahrir_Square_during_8_February_2011.jpg.

Figure 1.5 Library of Congress for permission to reprint Dresden, 1945: Cremation on Altmarkt. Photo: Library of Congress. Digital Ref: 3b40632. Hahn, Walter (d. 1969) published in Dresdener Verlagsgesellschaft Kg, 1950, from photographs taken in 1945.

Figure 1.6 Antonio Gramsci 152189417 (RM) Antonio Gramsci, Universal Images Group.

Figure 2.1 Reuters for permission to reprint Iraqi man sits against mural based on the scandal of prisoners' abuse in the suburb of Sadr City. Photo: Ali Jasim/Reuters. File name: RTRKG2C.jpg.

Figure 2.2 A detainee is escorted to interrogation by US military guards at Camp X-Ray at Guantánamo Bay US Naval Base. The government is holding about 550 terrorist suspects at the US Navy base in Cuba. An additional 214 have been released since the facility opened in January 2002 some into the custody of their home governments, others freed outright. Picture by: Andres Leighton/AP/Press Association Images.

Figure 2.3 'I found out what makes him tick . . .' Artist: Mike Baldwin. CartoonStock Ref: mba0459. www.CartoonStock.com.

Figure 2.4 John Rawls. Photo: Jane Reed, University of Harvard. http://www.news.harvard.edu/gazette/2002/12.05/03-rawls.html.

Figure 2.6 Ludwig Wittgenstein and Estate of Knut Erik Tranøy, Bent Sofus Tranøy/The von Wright and Wittgenstein Archives, University of Helsinki for kind permission to reprint Wittgenstein, © Knut Erik Tranøy. Getty for permission to reprint 2673420 (RM) Wittgenstein, Hulton Archive.

Figure 2.7 Veronique Pin-Fat as executor for Olivier Pin-Fat for permission to reprint Samrong Military Hospital, Cambodia. Photo: Olivier Pin-Fat.

Figure 3.1 'Human Watch: Conference'. Artist: Patrick Hickey. CartoonStock Ref: phin28. www.CartoonStock.com.

Figure 3.2 CO_2 concentrations from the Mauna Loa Observatory, Hawaii. Global Monitoring Division, Earth System Research Laboratory, National Oceanic and Atmospheric Administration. Permission granted.

Figure 3.3 Getty images for permission to reprint 89195341 (RM) Traffic jam on the M25 Motorway near London, England, UK. © John Miller/Robert Harding.

Figure 3.4 Image of smokestacks producing hurricanes from INCONVENIENT TRUTH, AN. Year: 2006 Dir: Guggenheim, Davis, Ref: INC027AL Credit: Lawrence Bender Prods./The Kobal Collection.

Figure 3.5 Greenpeace for permission to reprint Demonstration on climate change, London November 2006. Photo: Dave Walsh, Greenpeace.

Figure 3.6 Getty for permission to reprint #: 94946104/148869592 (RM). Petroleum plant between Elizabeth and Perth Amboy. Collection: Lonely Planet Images. Photographer: Ionas Kaltenbach.

Figure 3.7 'There is nobody else'. Artist: Stan Eales. CartoonStock Ref: sea0186. www.CartoonStock.com.

Figure 3.8 *The Economist* for permission to reprint 'Welcome to the Anthropocene'. The cover illustration of *The Economist Magazine* on 26 May 2011. Source: http://www.economist.com/node/18744401.

Figure 4.1 Green Party MP Caroline Lucas was elected to Brighton Pavilion in the 2010 UK general election. © ANDY RAIN/epa/Corbis/

Figure 4.2 International Institute for Sustainable Development (IISD) for kind permission to reprint South African President Thabo Mbeki signing the Political Declaration at the end of the summit negotiations, 4 September 2002. Photograph courtesy of IISD/Earth Negotiations Bulletin.

Figure 4.3 Greenpeace for permission to reprint photograph of Greenpeace activists who scaled the Koeberg Nuclear Power Plant near Cape Town, during the World Summit on Sustainable Development in August 2002. © Daniel Beltra/Greenpeace.

Figure 4.4 International Institute for Sustainable Development (IISD) for kind permission to reprint Social movement protestors march from Alexandra township to the World Summit on Sustainable Development to protest against unsustainable development. 31 August 2002. Photograph courtesy of IISD/Earth Negotiations Bulletin.

Figure 4.5 South Africa under apartheid. source: http://finalproject2009ec.wikispaces.com/file/view/HMOF7–27-c.gif/75456821/508x409/HMOF7–27-c.gif.

Figure 4.6 Corbis for permission to reprint South African President Nelson Mandela (R) and Second Deputy President F. W. de Klerk hold their hands high as they address the people after the Inauguration ceremony in front of Union Building, Pretoria, May 10, 1994. File photo. 42–16917586 © JUDA NGWENYA/X00201/Reuters/Corbis.

Figure 4.7 Victor Cox for permission to reprint image of Garrett Hardin. © Vic Cox.

Figure 4.8 The German Green Party unveiling a campaigning slogan in 2009. Thomas Grabka's photo no. 0171768. © Thomas Grabka/laif/Redux.

Figure 4.9 'Environment Policy'. Cartoonstock ref. Forn 880. www.cartoonstock.com.

Figure 5.2 Women's lib[eration] march from Farrugut Square to Layfette Park. Reproduction Number: LC-DIG-ppmsca-03425 (digital file from original). Library of Congress Prints and Photographs Division Washington, D.C. 20540 USA. Creator(s): Leffler, Warren K., photographer.

Figure 5.3 'I heard they spent all day arguing.' Artist John Morris. CartoonStock Ref: jmo1622. www.CartoonStock.com.

Figure 5.4 Nancy Palmieri for permission to reprint image of Carol Gilligan.

Figure 5.5 Corbis for permission to reprint Betty Friedan Sophie Bassouls/Corbis Sygma. Stock Photo ID: 0000311371–001. Photographer: Sophie Bassouls. Credit: © Sophie Bassouls/Sygma/Corbis.

Figure 5.6 bell hooks, for kind permission to reprint her photo. © Pinderhughes Photography, Inc.

Figure 5.7 *This Bridge Called My Back: Writings by Radical Women of Color*, eds Cherríe Moraga and Gloria Anzaldúa, published by Persephone Press, Inc. 1981. Book cover design by Maria von Brincken.

Figure 5.8 The depiction of supposed essences, as imagined in natural history. From S. Wells, *New Physiognomy or Signs of Character*. . ., New York, 1871 OOC.

Figure 5.9 Jacques Lacan. Photo Fair use is claimed because there is no free-license equivalent, the image is widely available and has no commercial value, and is being used for educational purposes to illustrate an article about the subject.

Figure 5.10 Judith Butler for kind permission to reprint her photograph. Photo: Berkeley University. Judith Butler at European Graduate School. Copyright: Hendrik Speck.

Figure 5.11 The Black Power salute in the 1968 Summer Olympics: Tommie Smith (centre) and John Carlos (right) salute while Silver medallist Peter Norman (left) wears an Olympic Project for Human Rights badge to show his support for the two Americans. Photo: AP/PA Photos.

Figure 5.12 Patricia Hill Collins, University of Maryland, College Park, for kind permission to reprint her photograph.

Figure 6.1 'Do you believe in God?' Artist: Bryan Bartholomew. CartoonStock Ref: bbrn51 www.CartoonStock.com.

Figure 6.2 Distribution of Muslim population by country and territory (only countries with more than 1 million Muslims are shown). Source: Pew Research Center's Forum on Religion & Public Life, 'Mapping the Global Muslim Population', © 2009, Pew Research Center, http://www.pewforum.org

Figure 6.3 The late Ayatollah Ruhollah Khomeini, centre, is greeted by supporters after arriving at the airport in Tehran Iran in this Feb. 1, 1979 photo. Monday Feb. 1, 1999 is the 20th anniversary of Khomeini's return from exile to lead the Islamic revolution in his country. Picture by: AP/AP/Press Association Images. Copyright: AP/Press Association Images.

Figure 6.4 Richard A. Johnson and Ingeborg Moa for permission to reprint Women demonstrate: At Ramallah's Al Manara plaza, two schoolgirls take part in a solidarity demonstration of Palestinian women – the wives, mothers, and sisters of many killed in the first days of the uprising. Photo: Ingeborg Moa.

Figure 6.5 Reuters for permission to reprint A general view for the first Egyptian parliament session after the revolution that ousted former President Hosni Mubarak in Cairo, Jan. 23, 2012. Asmaa Waguih/Reuters. File name: RTR2WPXS.jpg

Figure 6.6 Bridgeman Art for permission to reprint An example of 'Orientalist' art in Edward Said's sense: *The Snake Charmer*, Jean-Léon Gérôme, 1870. © Sterling and Francine Clark Art Institute, Williamstown, Massachusetts, USA/The Bridgeman Art Library.

Figure 6.7 President Bush dressed as Bin Laden on the cover of Tariq Ali's *The Clash of Fundamentalisms*. Verso.

Figure 7.1 'I am going to close my eyes'. Artist: Aaron Bacall. CartoonStock. Ref: aba0400. www.CartoonStock.com.

Figure 7.2 Magnum Photos for permission to reprint *CHINA. Beijing. Tianamen Square. Revolution. CHINA. Beijing. Tiananmen Square 'the tank man' 4th June 1989.* FRS1989009T079 – Stuart Franklin. LON2651.

Figure 7.4 German Federal Archive for permission to reprint Berlin, Bornholmer Straße. – Grenzöffnung, Menschenmenge mit Transparenten u.a. 'Test the West!', Pkw 'Trabant' auf Böse-Brücke, 10 November 1989.

Photographer: Lochmann, Hans Peter. Allgemeiner Deutscher Nachrichtendienst – Zentralbild (Bild 183). Accession number, Bild 183–1989–1118–028.

Figure 7.5 British Library for permission to reprint the title page from Thomas Hobbes' *Leviathan* (London, Andrew Crooke, 1651), shelfmark: 522.k.6. © The British Library Board.

Figure 7.6 The hole in the Romanian Flag, 1989. Source: Andrei Codrescu, *The Hole in the Flag: A Romanian exile's story of return and revolution* (Avon Books, a division of The Hearst Corporation, 1991. Cover photo: Gamma Liason published by arrangement with the author.

Figure 8.1 Contact Press Images for permission to reprint Portrait of a shell-shocked marine, Hue, Vietnam, 1968. Photo © Don McCullin.

Figure 8.2 South Vietnamese forces follow terrified children fleeing down Route 1, near Trang Bang, South Vietnam, June 8 1972, after an accidental aerial napalm strike. Girl at center had ripped off her burning clothes (AP Photo/Huynh Cong Nick Ut). Picture by: Huynh Cong/AP/Press Association Images. Copyright: AP/Press Association Images.

Figure 8.3 Cox & Forkum http://www.CoxAndForkum.com for permission to reprint ATWAR: Rumsfeld and Liberal Media Bias. Cox & Forkum © 2004.

Figure 8.4 Micah Wright for permission to reprint You write what you're told. Micah Wright poster from the Propaganda Re-Mix Project. Poster © Micah Ian Wright, courtesy of *PropagandaRemix.com.*

Figure 8.5 Stuart Hall for kind permission to reprint his photo.

Figure 8.6 A simple formulation of Hall's model of encoding/decoding. © Stuart Hall.

Figure 8.7 Ronald Grant Archive for permission to reprint Tom Hanks, Matt Damon and Ed Burns in *Saving Private Ryan* (1998). © Dreamworks SKG, RGA.

Figure 9.1 Subcommandante Marcos on twitter. Source: http://a0.twimg.com/profile_images/552229340/000_sub.jpg.

Figure 9.2 TeleGeography's Global Traffic Map 2010: The world's international telephone traffic, presented as a route-flow diagram. www.telegeography.com.

Figure 9.3 Reuters for permission to reprint Arab Spring – Yemen: A girl raises her hand with her fingers painted with flags of Yemen, Egypt, Syria, Tunisia and Libya as she marches during a demonstration to demand the ousting of Yemen's President Ali Abdullah Saleh in the southern city of Taiz, June 22, 2011. Photo: Khaled Abdullah/Reuters. Ref RTR2SF5A.jpg

Figure 9.4 Map of Middle East and North Africa © Adrian Morgan: Family Security Matters. http://familysecuritymatters.org/imgLib/20110220_MidEastMap6.jpg.

Figure 9.5 Getty Images for permission to reprint Protestors use mobile phones in Tunisia. Photo: Fred Dufour/AFP/Getty Images.

Figure 9.6 From poster for *Cet obscur objet du désir*, Luis Buñuel. © 1977 Greenwich Film Productions, Fr.

Figure 9.7 Globecartoon.com for permission to reprint Chappatte: http://www.globecartoon.com.

Figure 9.8 Donna Haraway with Cayenne, 2006; photograph by Rusten Hogness. Source: Wikipedia commons: en.wikipedia.org/wiki/File:Donna_Haraway_and_Cayenne.jpg.

Figure 9.9 Selçuk for permission to reprint *Le Monde diplomatique* (2010). © Selçuk Demirel.

Figure 10.2 The USGS U.S.–Mexico Border Environmental Health Initiative (BEHI) provides maps of the border; this one displays the BEHI regions and shaded relief. http://borderhealth.cr.usgs.gov/Projectdescription.html.

Figure 10.4 Marc Campos for permission to reprint Martin Margas Posadas, 18, from Puebla, Mexico, right, and another man wait in the US Border Patrol holding cell in Campo near California's border with Mexico. Photo: Marc Campos.

Figure 10.5 People partake in a mass separated at the Mexico/U.S. border during Day of the Dead celebrations, Tuesday, Nov. 2, 2004, in Anapra, State of Chihuahua, Mexico. The Mass is a six-year tradition and is the culmination of a week-long trek along the border for missionaries and migrant-rights activists (AP Photo/Eduardo Verdugo). Picture by: Eduardo Verdugo/AP/Press Association Images. Copyright: AP/Press Association Images.

Figure 10.6 Los Angeles Immigration Demonstration, 25 March 2006; Photo: Lucas Jackson, Reuters.

Figure 10.7 John Ditchburn, INKCINCT Cartoons for permission to reprint Australian citizenship test. Artist: John Ditchburn 1/05 2006–240 © John Ditchburn.

Figure 11.1 Map of Central Europe in 1360. From *Atlas to Freeman's Historical Geography*, edited by J. B. Bury, Longmans Green and Co. Third Edition 1903.

Figure 11.2 Map of Africa in 1892. From *A School Atlas of English History*, edited by Samuel Rawson Gardiner, London: Longmans, Green, and Co., 1892.

Figure 11.4 Max Weber, Deutsches Historisches Museum, Berlin. Ref: F52/2693. Reprinted with permission.

Figure 11.5 National Gallery for permission to reprint *The Swearing of the Oath of Ratification of the Treaty of Westphalia at Munster, 24th October 1648* by Gerard Ter Borch (1648). © The National Gallery, London.

Figure 11.6 Map of Ethnic distribution of the Habsburg Empire, 1914. Source: http://www.historyonmaps.com/BWSamples/HabsburgEthnic.html.

Figure 11.7 Magnum Photos for permission to reprint FRANCE. Paris. 1973. Demonstration in support of immigrant workers. In the foreground: the French philosopher Michel FOUCAULT. PAR100135. PEG1973004 W00004/07A8 – Gilles Peress.

Figure 12.1 Imperial China: Ming and Manchu Dynasties. Source: http://warandgame.files.wordpress.com/2010/03/chin2.jpg.

Figure 12.2 Bettmann/Corbis for permission to reprint Sun Yatsen on the balcony of his house in Guangzhou, China, 1923. © Bettmann/Corbis Photograph.

Figure 12.3 Chinese Civil War: South Park philosophy. http://fc04.deviantart.net/fs42/i/2010/290/d/b/south_park_chinese_civil_war_by_southpark philosopher-d1yynjd.jpg.

Figure 12.4 Former Chinese Chairman *Mao Zedong* announcing the founding of the *People's Republic of China* on *October 1, 1949.* http://en.wikipedia.org/wiki/File:China_Mao_%282%29.jpg.

Figure 12.5 Ethnolinguistic map of China 1983. Courtesy of the University of Texas Libraries, The University of Texas at Austin. http://upload.wikimedia.org/wikipedia/commons/thumb/9/95/Ethnolinguistic_map_of_China_1983.png/640px-Ethnolinguistic_map_of_China_1983.png.

Figure 12.6 Getty images for permission to reprint Olympic Games in Beijing on August 8, 2008. The three-hour show at Beijing's iconic 'Bird's Nest' national stadium is set to see more than 15,000 performers showcase the nation's ancient history and its rise as a modern power. AFP Photo/Pedro Ugarte. Editorial image #: 82215095.

Figure 12.7 'We can't stay here, and your father has connections in China.' www.cartoonstock.com.

Figure 12.9 Dow Jones And Company, Inc. for permission to reprint Chinese Diaspora map, from *Wall Street Journal* article Strangers at Home; Chinese living abroad have played a huge role in the country's economic miracle. But back in China, they are both welcome and vulnerable, 19 July 2010.

Figure 12.10 Chinese Root-Seeking Tour. Corbis Stock Photo ID: 42–35523106. July 20, 2012, *Hangzhou, Zhejiang Province, China.* © Li Zhong/Xinhua Press/Corbis.

Figure 12.11 Chinese American contestant Lou Jing, center, stands with host Cao Kefan and hostess Chen Rong during a session of the reality TV show, Go! Oriental Angel, in Shanghai, China, 4 September 2009. Credit: Bi yueping/Imaginechina.

Figure 12.12 Homi Bhabha for permission to reprint his photo. © Stephanie Mitchell, Harvard University.

Figure 13.1 The Art Archive/Kobal Collection for permission to reprint *Congress adopting the Declaration of Independence* by John Trumbull (1756–1843). US Engraving after John Trumbull's 1816 version painted for the US Capitol Building Rotunda. © The Art Archive. Ref: AA401943.

Figure 13.2 Rainer Ganahl for permission to reprint Seminar/Lecture, Pierre Bourdieu, Recherches récentes, Collège de France, Paris, 1/12/2000.

Figure 13.3 Michelle Cliff, photo from *Everything Is Now,* reprinted with kind permission.

Figure 13.4 Sherman Alexie, photo © Jérôme de Perlinghi/Corbis.

Figure 13.5 Toni Morrison. Photo Kate Kunz from cover of *Paradise*, Publisher Alfred A. Knopf, New York, 1998.

Figure 13.6 Artifice, Inc. for permission to reprint cid_2896783 Paris Opera, © Laurence A. Martin/Artifice Images.

Figure 13.7 Shakespeare's Globe Theatre in London. Photo: © Laura Porter (2007) licensed to About.com, Inc.

Figure 13.8 Youths look at cars burning in Paris suburb, Le Blanc Mesnil, early Thursday, Nov. 3, 2005. For a seventh straight night, groups of youths set fire to cars and shops in at least nine towns northeast of the capital. (AP Photo/Christophe Ena.) Picture by: Christophe Ena/AP/Press Association Images. Copyright: AP/Press Association Images.

Figure 13.9 Gilles Deleuze and Felix Guattari. Photo courtesy of Charles J. Stivale.

Figure 13.10 National Portrait Gallery for permission to reprint *David Hume*, by and published by David Martin, after Allan Ramsay, mezzotint, 1767 (1766). Given by Sir Herbert Henry Raphael, 1st Bt, 1916. NPG D19565.

Figure 14.1 Pro-democracy leader Suu Kyi and US Secretary of State Clinton hold hands as they speak after meeting in Yangon at Suu Kyi's house December 2, 2011. Reuters/Soe Zeya Tun.

Figure 14.2 Latin America. http://ec.europa.eu/europeaid/images/maps/latin-america_continent_en.png.

Figure 14.3 In this Oct. 17, 1950 file photo, Argentina's first lady Maria Eva Duarte de Peron, known as 'Evita', waves next to her husband, President Juan Peron, from the balcony of Casa Rosada, the government house, during an event marking Loyalty Day in Buenos Aires, Argentina. Argentina commemorates the 60th anniversary of the death of Argentina's most famous first lady on Thursday, July 26, 2012. Evita died of cancer on July 26, 1952 at the age of 33. © AP/Press Association Images.

Figure 14.4 Corbis for permission to reprint Mothers of Plaza de Mayo demonstration in Buenos Aires 42–29302562 © Steve Raymer/Corbis.

Figure 14.5 Children pass a community centre painted with images of Eva and Juan Domingo Perón, in Buenos Aires. The community centre was built by a large political social movement called the Popular Front and National Cross. Several new political movements, mostly populated by youth activists, have been gaining positions in the government and some of their leaders are candidates for the legislature in Sunday's general election. Oct. 5, 2011 Victor R. Caivano/AP.

Figure 14.6 Anil Mundra for permission to reprint Afro-Cultural Movement protesters march to the beats of candombé drumming, a quintessential Afro-Argentine musical form. Many supporters of Afro-Argentine culture these days appear to be white, although some of them self-identify as Afro-descendants. © Anil Mundra/GlobalPost.

Figure 14.7 Press Association for permission GREECE PROTESTS Backdropped by the ancient Parthenon, protesters can be seen after they placed giant banners off the Acropolis hill, in Athens, Wednesday Dec. 17, 2008. Protesters in Greece have hung the two banners over the ancient monument's walls with slogans calling for mass demonstrations and 'resistance' after days of violent protest sparked by the fatal police shooting of a teenager in Athens. Ref #: PA.6661597 Picture by: Lefteris Pitarakis/AP/Press Association Images.

Figure 14.8 Agencia Efe, S.A. for permission to reprint The President of Bolivia, Evo Morales, with indigenous priests during a ritual at the pyramid of Akapana – Efe Agencia.

Figure 15.2 Getty Images for permission to reprint Children in a police vehicle after being apprehended at the border on their way out of Nigeria to the Republic of Benin. Photograph: STR/AFP/Getty Images.

Figure 15.4 Felix Houphouet-Boigny. Courtesy of Célestin Mbenti Nkoudou.

Figure 15.5 US Commodity Price Index adjusted for Consumer Price Inflation. Source: Mineweb.com. With permission. http://bigpicture.typepad.com/comments/2005/09/are_real_commod.html.

Figure 15.6 General structure of the global coffee-marketing chain. Stefano Ponte (2002) 'The "Latte Revolution"? Regulation, Markets and Consumption in the Global Coffee Chain', *World Development*, 30, 7: 1099–1122.

Figure 15.7 Corbis for permission to reprint portrait of Kwame Nkrumah, F9577 © Bettmann/Corbis.

Figure 15.8 Andre Gunder Frank. Photo: Permission from http://wsarch.ucr.edu/archive/gunder97cd.html.

Figure 16.1 Getty Images for permission to reprint Joseph Conrad. Photograph: Alvin Langdon Coburn/George Eastman House/Getty Images. ARP:3206992 A Man Of Mark Photographer/Artist: Alvin Langdon Coburn.

Figure 16.2 Sopan Joshi for permission to reprint image of Ashis Nandy. Source: http://westheavens.net/en/ashis-nandy/.

Figure 16.3 Painting. Court. Jahangir investing a courtier with a robe of honour watched by Sir Thomas Roe, English ambassador to the court of Jahangir at Agra from 1615–18, and others. On paper. Colophon on verso gives calligrapher's name, As`af `Ibadallah al-Rahim and date 23 Ramadan 985/4 December 1577. © The Trustees of the British Museum. AN0006660001 Mughal dynasty.

Figure 16.4 Special Collections Department, Toronto Reference Library, T.P.L. for kind permission to reprint East India House, Leadenhall from the magazine *British History Illustrated*, August 1974.

Figure 16.5 British Library for permission to reprint Map of India in 1937. Produced in 1937 before the constitutional reform took place in India and Burma. ORW.1986.a.2501, Map of India in 1937 © The British Library Board.

Figure 16.6 Lin Zexu supervising the destruction of 2.6 million tons of Opium in 1839 over 26 days (June 3 – June 29, 1839) in the sea off Humen town. Source: Destroy_opium_2.jpg_ (400 _ 239 pixels, file size: 17 KB, MIME type: image/jpeg.

Figure 16.7 Villagers in Rajputana in 1899. Fig 5.9 from the book by Mike Davies, *Late Victorian Holocausts*/Verso.

Figure 16.8 The British Cartoon Archive, University of Kent, www.cartoons.ac.uk, and Solo Syndication for permission to reprint 'Free India', published on May 20, 1947, *Daily Mail*, Leslie Gilbert Illingworth. Gandhi, and a group of protesters, including a US sympathiser, are holding placards demanding that the British get out of India. All around them are the bodies of those who have died of hunger or civil war.

Figure 16.9 Map of the Colonial Empres 1907. Reprinted with permission of Probert Encyclopaedia.

Figure 16.10 Corbis for permission to reprint English writer George Orwell was the author of such books as *Animal Farm* and *1984*, London. BE065637. Credit: © Bettmann/Corbis.

Figure 17.1 Getty Images for permission to reprint Textile Mill in Lancashire, England. Photo: Getty Images, HGE:2665429 Winding Room. Photographer/Artist: James Valentine.

Figure 17.2 Baker Library | Bloomberg Center 123B, Harvard Business School for permission to reprint Portrait of Adam Smith. Kress Collection, olvwork389444.

Figure 17.3 Gender segmentation of the informal economy, from *Mainstreaming Informal Employment and Gender in Poverty Reduction: A Handbook for Policy-makers and other Stakeholders*, by Martha Alter Chen, Joann Vanek, and Marilyn Carr, Commonwealth Secretariat/IDRC 2004. Source: http://web.idrc.ca/es/ev-83646–201–1-DO_TOPIC.html.

Figure 17.4 Cagle Cartoons, Inc. for permission to reprint *Injusticia Global.* Artist: Sergio Langer, *El Clarin*, Argentina.

Figure 17.5 Average size of informal economy around the world measured as a percentage of GDP. Source: http://www.atmmarketplace.com/article/129691/Another-100-years-of-cash *also at* http://www.greensheet.com/emagazine.php?story_id=745.

Figure 17.6 Barry Deutsch for permission to reprint Don't stop believing cartoon.

Figure 17.7 Getty for permission to reprint Karl Marx. Editorial image #: 2638388. Henry Guttmann/Hulton Archive.

Figure 17.8 Wiego for permisson to reprint Informal economic activity. Source: http://wiego.org/wiego/core-programmes/urban-policies.

Figure 17.9 The wider informal economy. www.cartoonstock.com.

Figure 18.1 Corbis Images for permission to reprint Writer Henri Lefebvre Reading Newspaper. Photo ID: 0000214897–001, January 23, 1978. © Sophie Bassouls/Sygma/Corbis.

Figure 18.2 Do we want to apply for a credit card . . . www.cartoonstock.com.

Figure 18.3 Godfrey Mwampembwa/Gado for kind permission to reprint his cartoon, Crisis? What Crisis?

Figure 18.4 Jacques Rancière. Jacques Rancière at a conference held in the *Universidad Internacional de Andalucía*, in Seville (Spain) in 2006. Source: http://en.wikipedia.org/wiki/Jacques_Ranci%C3%A8re http://en.wikipedia.org/wiki/File:Jacques_Ranciere.jpg.

Figure 18.5 Lehman Brothers Bankruptcy: Women carrying boxes leave the Lehman Brothers headquarters, Monday, Sept. 15, 2008, in New York. Lehman Brothers, a 158-year-old investment bank choked by the credit crisis and falling real estate values, filed for Chapter 11 bankruptcy protection from its creditors on Monday and said it was trying to sell off key business units. Picture by: Louis Lanzano/AP/Press Association Images.

Figure 18.6 Icelanders voting in a referendum in Reykjavik, Iceland, Saturday, March 6, 2010. Icelanders are voting in a nationwide referendum on approving the use of taxpayers' money to repay international debts. Opinion polls suggest that a majority of Icelanders will vote 'no' on Saturday to the $5.3 billion deal to compensate Britain and the Netherlands for deposits lost in a collapsed Icelandic bank. That is expected to complicate Iceland's effort to recover from a deep recession and a banking collapse. (AP Photo/Brynjar Gauti). Picture by: Brynjar Gauti/AP/Press Association Images. Copyright: AP/Press Association Images ref. 8473313.

Figure 18.7 A woman shouts while taking part in an anti-austerity rally in Athens' Syntagma Square, 18 October 2011. Photo: *Reuters/Yorgos Karahalis*, ref. RTR2SUBX.jpg.

Figure 18.8 Getty Images for permission to reprint A man brushes his teeth as he camps near St Paul's Cathedral in London, on October 17, 2011, as protesters awoke in London's financial district on Monday for a third day of demonstrations against corporate greed and state spending cutbacks. The London encampment began on Saturday following a demonstration by about 2,000–3,000 people, as part of Europe-wide anti-capitalist protests inspired by the Occupy Wall Street movement born in New York in September. AFP Photo/Carl Court. Editorial image #: 129436891.

Figure 18.9 Jarvis Group LLC, and Jonathan Jarvis for permission to reprint clip from YouTube 'Crisis of Credit'. Source: http://youtube/Q0zEXdDO5JU.

Figure 18.10 Reprinted courtesy of the RSA and Cognitive Media, David Harvey clip from YouTube. Source: http://youtube/qOP2V_np2c0.

Figure 19.1 Emmanuel Saez for permission to reprint Average Incomes table. Source: Emmanuel Saez, Updated Tables and GPs.

Figure 19.2 American Economic Association for permission to reprint Top 0.1 per cent income shares across countries. Source: Thomas Piketty and Emmanuel Saez (2006) 'The Evolution of Top Incomes: A Historical and International Perspective', *American Economic Review, Papers and Proceedings*, 96, 2: Figure 3, p. 203.

Figure 19.5 Chinese workers labor on the construction of the Shanghai World Financial Center still under construction in Shanghai, eastern China, Monday, Dec. 4, 2006. China wants to start direct negotiations with OPEC to ensure a stable oil supply, a top official said Monday, in comments that underline the Chinese economy's rapidly growing energy needs (AP Photo). Picture by: AP/Press Association Images Copyright: AP/Press Association Images.

Figure 19.6 Corbis for permission to reprint Zuccotti Park November 4, 2011 – Manhattan, NY : A general view of the Occupy Wall Street encampment in Zuccotti Park on the morning of Thursday, Nov. 4, 2011. Credit: Karsten Moran 42–31195354 © Karsten Moran/Aurora Photos/Corbis.

Figure 19.7 Protestors on a San Francisco beach Human Banner 'Tax the 1%'. © Aerial Photo by John Montgomery, 2011.

Figure 19.8 ADAGP and DACS for permission to reprint Alberto Korda's famous photograph of Che Guevara, Korda, Alberto Diaz Gutierrez, Guerrillero heroico, 1960. © ADAGP, Banque d'images, Paris 2012.

Figure 19.9 'We Are the 99%' – image widely circulated on the internet. Source: http://www.quickmeme.com/meme/356ml1/, 25 January 2012.

Figure 20.1 A visualization of global income distribution. Photomontage by Dr Kurt Källblad, Malmö, Sweden. Source: The Challenge of Inequality, *Poverty in Focus*, International Poverty Centre, June 2007, cover, www.undp.org/povertycentre.

Figure 20.2 Kirk Anderson for permission to reprint Structural Adjustment. Artist: Kirk Anderson.

Figure 20.3 Map of South Asia (India, Pakistan, Bangladesh, Sri Lanka, the Maldives, Bengal, Bhutan, and Nepal) and neighbouring regions.

Figure 20.4 Yunus Centre for kind permission to reprint Muhammad Yunus visits Grameen Bank Centres and loan holders, who are mostly women. Copyright © Grameen Bank Audio Visual Unit, 2006.

Figure 20.5 Make Poverty History wristbands. Photo: Global Call to Action Against Poverty (GCAP).

Figure 20.6 Price of poverty: Pakistani farmers who sold their kidneys, show scars Oct. 17, 2006 in Jandala near Multan, Pakistan. Debt and poverty is driving hundreds of Pakistanis to sell their own kidneys for cash, turning this South Asian nation into a regional hub for unregulated, cut-price transplant operations (AP Photo/Khalid Tanveer). Picture by: Khalid Tanveer/AP/Press Association Images. Copyright: AP/Press Association Images.

Figure 20.7 Giorgio Agamben. Copyright: *European Graduate School/License Image.*

Figure 20.8 A passenger waits for bus in front of the Malaysian Islamic Bank billboard at a bus stop in down town Kuala Lumpur Wednesday, July 28, 2004. All conventional banks will be issued full-fledged Islamic banking licenses eventually by the Government in a move to not only grow Islamic banking in Malaysia but also encourage local banks to expand such services offshore (AP Photo/Teh Eng Koon). Picture by: TEH ENG KOON/AP/Press Association Images. Copyright: AP/Press Association Images.

Figure 20.9 Activists of Workers Women's Association chant slogans during a rally to mark International Women's Day, Thursday, March 8, 2007 in Lahore, Pakistan. Thousands of women demonstrated in nation-wide rallies on International Women's Day, demanding freedom, equal rights and an end to discriminatory laws in this Muslim nation (AP Photo/K. M. Chaudary). Picture by: K. M. Chaudary/AP/Press Association Images. Copyright: AP/Press Association Images.

Figure 21.1 Francisco de Vitoria. Source: http://en.wikipedia.org/wiki/File:Francisco_vitoria.jpg.

Figure 21.2 Library of Congress for permission to reprint The Mexica (Aztec) peoples, followers of Moctezuma, face a powerful Spanish force under Hernando Cortés in the 1519–1521 campaigns. Source: Fray Diego Durán. *La Historia antigua de la Nueva España*. 1585. Manuscript facsimile, Peter Force Collection, Library of Congress.

Figure 21.3 Viv Quillin for permission to reprint 'Oh let them go' cartoon. © Viv Quillin.

Figure 21.4 Innocentivs IIII PP Ianvensis. C 1910. Photomechanical print. Source: Library of Congress. Reproduction Number: LC-USZ62–98463.

Figure 21.5 Archivio Segreto Vaticano, Rome for permission to reprint Letter of Güyük Khan to Pope Innocent IV.

Figure 21.6 Map of colonial powers, 1914. Source: Peter Mandaville, *Global Political Islam* (Routledge 2007).

Figure 22.1 Carl von Clausewitz. Lithograph by Franz Michaelis after a missing painting by Karl Wilhelm Wach. Source: Bildarchiv Preußischer Kulturbesitz.

Figure 22.2 Matthew White for kind permission to reprint Wars, Massacres and Atrocities of the Twentieth Century: Year by Year Death Toll. Graphic and data: Matthew White, 1998.

Figure 22.3 Colour photograph showing damage in Hiroshima in March of 1946 (US National Archives).

Figure 22.4 Imperial War Museum for permission to reprint Supporting infantry walk forward up the slope into the bombardment during the First World War, The Battle of Ginchy, 9 September 1916, the Somme. Photo: (Lt) Ernest Brooks; Source: Imperial War Museum IWM Q1306.

Figure 22.5 Milgram Experiment. From the film *Obedience*, © 1968 by Stanley Milgram, © renewed 1993 by Alexandra Milgram and distributed by Alexander Street Press.

Figure 22.6 US Army trainees practice hand-to-hand combat using pugil sticks during basic combat training at Fort Jackson, South Carolina. Photo by Air Force Staff Sgt. Stacy Pearsall. Courtesy of US Army.

Figure 22.7 May 1945 file photo shows Soviet soldiers hoisting the red flag over the Reichstag in Berlin. The photo was made by Yevgeny Khaldei, a veteran photographer whose pictures of Soviet soldiers hoisting the red flag over the Reichstag in Berlin are among the best-known images of World War II. Khaldei has died at 80. He began his career in 1935 as the reporter for the official Soviet news agency TASS (AP Photo/Yevgeny Khaldei, ITAR-TASS). Picture by: Yevgeny Khaldei/AP/Press Association Images. Copyright: AP/Press Association Images.

Figure 22.8 Getty for permission to reprint AFP:77397232 (FILES) Flowers and candles decorate the Bronze Solder, a Soviet soldier inscribed 'To the fallen of the Second World War' in Tallinn Estonia., Photographer/Artist: AFP.

Figure 23.1 Afghanistan–Pakistan borderlands: A US Government map from the 1980s now in the public domain showing the Afghanistan–Pakistan frontier (Durand Line area) and seeming to indicate Pashtun areas. Source: http://independentindian.com/category/afghanistan/; http://drsubrotoroy.files.wordpress.com/2009/10/afghan1.jpg?w=780.

Figure 23.2 Corbis for permission to reprint MQ-1 Predator in flight. Stock photo image 42–22609454. © DoD/Corbis.

Figure 23.3 THE BOONDOCKS © 2001 Aaron McGruder. Dist. By Universal Uclick. Reprinted with permission. All rights reserved.

Figure 23.4 Areas affected by 2010 floods in Pakistan.

Figure 23.5 Reuters for permission to reprint Residents carry their belongings through a flooded road in Risalpur in Pakistan's Northwest Frontier Province. Photographer: © Adrees Latif. Reuters image no. RTR2GVZW.

Figure 23.6 German-born American political thinker, teacher, and writer Hannah Arendt (1906–1975) smokes a cigarette in her Manhattan apartment, New York, April 21, 1972 (Photo by Tyrone Dukes/New York Times Co./Getty Images). Editorial image #: 51088708.

Figure 23.7 Zeitgeist Films Ltd and the ICA for kind permission to reprint Slavoj Žižek: Still from the documentary *ZIZEK!* directed by Astra Taylor, 71 mins, USA 2005. http://www.zeitgeistfilms.com.

Figure 24.1 A reflective view of the Blue Force Tracker (BFT) networking tool. Northrop Grumman Corp.

Figure 24.2 Airmen with the 67th Network Warfare Wing monitor internet activity to maintain security of Air Force computer networks at Lackland Air Force Base, Texas. Photo: Master Sgt. Jack Braden. Reprinted Courtesy of US Air Force.

Figure 24.3 Admiral Arthur Cebrowski.

Figure 24.4 Joint Vision 2020 from http://www.dtic.mil/futurejointwarfare/. Public domain.

Figure 24.5 Professor S. Shankar Sastry for kind permission to reprint Critical Infrastructures. From 'Information Technology Research for Critical Infrastructure Protection', Shankar Sastry *et al.*, Summary of NSF/OSTP workshop 19–20 September 2002.

Figure 24.6 Press Association for permission to reprint US IRAQ Defense Secretary Donald H. Rumsfeld gestures during a news conference at the Pentagon, Wednesday, Oct. 11, 2006 (AP Photo/Evan Vucci). Ref# PA.4048282.

Figure 24.7 Still from Steven Spielberg's science fiction film *Minority Report.* Pers: Von Sydow, Max. Year: 2002. Dir: Spielberg, Steven Ref: MIN021AK Credit: 20th Century Fox/Dreamworks/The Kobal Collection.

Figure 24.8 Well . . . at least we don't have to worry about anarchy any more. Artist: Ron Cobb, 1968.

Figure 25.1 United Nations for permission to reprint The UN Security Council United Nations, New York. A wide-view of the Security Council voting on the situation in Bosnia and Herzegovina. © UN Photo/Eskinder Debebe.

Figure 25.3 David Dare Parker for permission to reprint Australian troops, members of Interfet, disarm and arrest members of the Aitarak Militia. Dili, East Timor, 21 September 1999. Photo: David Dare Parker.

Figure 25.5 José Ramos Horta. Photo: Glenn Campbell.

Figure 25.6 East Timor Gas, Bush Oil. Cartoon by Nicholson from *The Australian* www.nicholson.com.au. Reprinted with permission.

Figure 25.7 Lenin disguised as 'Vilén', wearing a wig and with his beard shaved off. Finland, 11 August 1917. Source: http://en.wikipedia.org/wiki/File: Lenin_05d.jpg.

Figure 25.8 Ullstein Bild for permission to reprint Carl Schmitt Image No. 00006548.

Figure 25.9 Jürgen Habermas. Source: http://commons.wikimedia.org/wiki/File: JuergenHabermas.jpg.

Figure 25.10 The UN for kind permission to reprint a photograph which appears on many UN and national government websites. The image is of members of the United Nations Transitional Administration in East Timor (UNTAET) Portuguese contingent accompanied by a group of local children as they conduct a security patrol in the Becora district of Dili. © UN Photo/Eskinder Debebe.

Figure 25.11 Magnum Photos for permission to reprint YUGOSLAVIA. Kosovo. Djakovica. 1999. Ethnic Albanians on a horse-drawn cart at a crossroads in downtown Djakovica after the Serbian withdrawal in June. PEG1999005W00381/04 – Gilles Peress. NYC22608.

Figure 26.3 John F. Kennedy Presidential Library for permission to reprint KN-C29210, President Kennedy views the Berlin Wall from an elevated platform, 26 June 1963. Accompanying him are German Chancellor Konrad Adenauer, Secretary of State Dean Rusk, Chief of White House Secret Service Detail Jerry Behn, an interpreter, and others. Photograph by Robert Knudsen in the John F. Kennedy Presidential Library and Museum, Boston.

Figure 26.4 Getty Images for permission to reprint A North Korean soldier looks through a pair of binoculars as a South Korean solider stands guard in the demilitarized zone dividing the two Koreas, in the village of Panmunjom, on the North–South border, 2007. Photo: Jung Yeon-Je/AFP/Getty Images.

Figure 26.5 Nuclear, chemical and biological weapons proliferation status in 2005. © Carnegie Endowment for International Peace. Reprinted by permission of the publisher from *Deadly Arsenals: Nuclear, Biological, and Chemical Threats*, Second Editon, Joseph Cirincione, Jon B. Wolfsthal and Miriam Rajkumar (Washington DC: Carnegie Endowment for International Peace, 2005). www.CarnegieEndowment.org.

Figure 26.6 AP Photo for permission to reprint Non-proliferation Treaty signing ceremony, July 1968, Moscow. US Ambassador Llewellyn E. Thompson, left, signs the treaty in Moscow with Soviet Foreign Minister Andrei A. Gromyko. Among US embassy and Soviet government officials witnessing the ceremony is Soviet Premier Alexei N. Kosygin, standing third from right. Photo: AP Wide World Photos. PA. 8684188.

Figure 26.7 The National Archives Image Library for permission to reprint The British nuclear test code-named Hurricane. Photo: The National Archives, Kew, Richmond, Surrey. Ref: ADM280/966.

Figure 26.8 The heavily mined demilitarized zone between North and South Korea seen from a South Korean military observation post. The zone has become a haven for wildlife. Photo: Seokyong Lee for *The New York Times.*

Figure 26.9 Cartoonstock for permission to reprint Maybe you should reconsider those place cards. Artist: Dave Carpenter. CartoonStock. Ref: dcr0435h. www.CartoonStock.com.

Figure 26.10 Demilitarized Zone opens for train passage, Paju, South Korea, 17 May 2007. Photo: Chung Sung-Jun/Getty Images.

Figure 26.11 Getty for permission to reprint Portrait of Friedrich Nietzsche. Editorial #3093290, Hulton Archive. 141555162 (RM) Collection: Mondadori.

Figure 26.12 Ko Un, reprinted with kind permission.

Figure 27.1 Getty for permission to reprint Eleanor Roosevelt regarded the Universal Declaration as her greatest accomplishment. Fotosearch Archive Photos #96813261.

Figure 27.2 Hijab: Maria Mawla, 27, wears a hijab in this Aug. 4, 1999 photo at an unknown Danish location. Jens Dresling/AP/Press Association Images.

Figure 27.3 Niqab: A supporter of Pakistani religious party Jamaat-i-Islami attends a rally to condemn the ban imposed on the burqa or veil in France, on Tuesday, April 19, 2011 in Karachi, Pakistan. Shakil Adil/AP/Press Association Images.

Figure 27.4 Burka: A protester wearing a burka marches during a demonstration in Barcelona, Spain, Saturday March 15, 2008 marking the fifth anniversary of US-led war in Iraq. Carmelo Esteban/AP/Press Association Images.

Figure 27.5 Reuters for permission to reprint Young Muslim woman with a French flag on her headscarf protests during protest in Lille, against the passage of a new law banning the display of religious signs at schools in Lille last month. Photographer: © Pascal Rossignol. Reuters image no. RTRAGWM.

Figure 27.6 Reuters News Agency for permission to reprint street protest of Sikhs against French ban on religious symbols in state schools in Paris. © Charles Platiau. Reuters image number RTRRKTY.

Figure 27.7 Magali Delporte for permission to reprint One of two French women facing a fine for wearing the *niqab* in a town near Paris. Photograph © Magali Delporte for the *Guardian*. Source: http://www.guardian.co.uk/world/2011/sep/19/battle-for-the-burqa.

Figure 27.8 The Image Works, Inc. for permission to reprint The Declaration of the Rights of Man and of the Citizen was approved by the National Constiuent Assembly of France, 26 August 1789.

Figure 27.9 Edmund Burke, Studio of Sir Joshua Reynolds. 655 © National Portrait Gallery, London.

Figure 27.11 Stereotypes. www.cartoonstock.com

Figure 27.12 Gayatri Chakravorty Spivak at Goldsmiths College, University of London, 2007. Photo by Shih-Lun Chang. Source: http://en.wikipedia.org/wiki/File:Gayatri_Chakravorty_Spivak_at_Goldsmiths_College.jpg.

Figure 28.1 Reuters for permission to reprint Thousands of demonstrators march through streets of downtown Los Angeles. Photographer: © Lucas Jackson. Reuters no. RTR1CZPR.

Figure 28.2 London, 15 February 2003. Photo: Jenny Edkins.

Figure 28.3 Boots for 'Eyes wide open: the human cost of war' exhibit, 2 July 2004, Philadelphia, PA. The exhibition comprised a pair of boots for each of the US military personnel killed in Iraq, and pairs of shoes symbolizing the estimated civilian deaths and was organized by the American Friends Service Committee, see http://www.afsc.org/eyes/. Photo: Terry Foss, AFSC/Photographer.

Figure 28.4 Getty Images for permission to reprint Jacques Derrida. Photo: Joel Robine, AFP/Getty Images.

Figure 28.5 The Canadian Press for permission to reprint Occupy Halifax protest sign, October 2011.

Figure 28.6 The world would be a better place. Artist: Betsy Streeter. CartoonStock. Ref: bstn29h www.CartoonStock.com.

Index of names

Page numbers in *italics* refer to figures.

General index

Page numbers in *italics* refer to figures.